D1032884

The Poems of T. S. Eliot

Volume I

Collected Poems 1909–1962
Uncollected Poems
The Waste Land: An Editorial Composite

Commentary

Volume II

Old Possum's Book of Practical Cats
Anabasis
Other Verses
Noctes Binanianæ
Improper Rhymes

Commentary
Textual History

The Poems of
T. S. ELIOT

Volume I
Collected and Uncollected Poems

Edited by
Christopher Ricks and Jim McCue

Johns Hopkins University Press
Baltimore

First published in 2015
by Faber & Faber Ltd, Bloomsbury House,
74–77 Great Russell Street, London WC1B 3DA

Text design by Paul Luna
Typeset by Donald Sommerville
Printed in England by T. J. International Ltd,
Padstow, Cornwall

Johns Hopkins University Press
2715 N. Charles Street
Baltimore, MD 21218
www.press.jhu.edu

Library of Congress Control Number: 2015950322

A CIP record for this book is available from the
British Library

ISBN 978-1-4214-2017-2

2 4 6 8 10 9 7 5 3 1

Contents · Volume I

This Edition

1. Arrangement of the Present Edition   2. *The Waste Land*: A Composite
3. Titles   4. Text of the Poems   5. Spacing and Punctuation
6. TSE on Treatments of his Poems

1. ARRANGEMENT OF THE PRESENT EDITION

This first volume opens with *Collected Poems 1909–1962* as issued by T. S. Eliot shortly before his death. There follow the "Uncollected Poems", which include those published in *Poems Written in Early Youth* and *Inventions of the March Hare*, as well as some poems from the manuscript *Valerie's Own Book* (for which, see headnote to the Textual History, in Volume II). Also within this first volume is an editorial composite of the drafts of *The Waste Land.* The Commentary for all these poems then follows.

The second volume contains the children's book *Old Possum's Book of Practical Cats* and Eliot's only sustained translation, *Anabasis*, each followed by a Commentary. The second volume also includes, within contextual notes, three categories of private verses: "Other Verses", *Noctes Binanianæ* and "Improper Rhymes". The Textual History covers the *Collected Poems 1909–1962*, the Uncollected Poems, Old *Possum's Book of Practical Cats* and *Anabasis.* Textual details of the Other Verses and Improper Rhymes are incorporated within those sections, and textual details of *Noctes Binanianæ* appear at the end of that section.

2. *THE WASTE LAND*: A COMPOSITE

The editorial composite of the drafts of *The Waste Land* (*WLComposite*) includes passages excised by Eliot, such as the description of a night on the town at the beginning of Part I, as well as others that were excised by Ezra Pound, such as Fresca's waking at the beginning of Part III and the original long version of Part IV. Running to 678 lines, as opposed to the 433 of the published poem, the editorial composite has independent line-numbering given in **bold**, with equivalent line numbers from the published poem running alongside. Where appropriate, the numbering in the Commentary and Textual History appears in the form [III] 246 = 404.

References to the facsimile edition of the drafts of *The Waste Land* give the page numbers of both the facsimile and its facing-page transcription: "Admonished by the sun's inclining ray", *WLFacs* 38/39.

3. TITLES

Many of Eliot's poems originated as parts which had been published in other contexts, perhaps separately or in different combinations. What began as autonomous poems became sections and vice versa. Although a distinction has in the past been made between titles of short poems within a collection, given within quotation marks ("The Hollow Men"), and those published as volumes (*Ash-Wednesday*), this cannot hold firm in Eliot's case. The first of the *Four Quartets*, for instance, was originally published within a volume, before appearing as a pamphlet; the others were published in *New English Weekly* and then as pamphlets before the four were collected. To distinguish one of these manifestations from another implies a change that is more than bibliographical, yet the great majority of references to *Burnt Norton* or *Little Gidding* are not specifically to any one manifestation. Nor is it always the case that a poem published separately is more substantial than one that is part of a collection: *The Cultivation of Christmas Trees* is not a more substantial poem than *Gerontion*.

Placing a title within quotation marks rather than italicising it offers a certain kind of information (or makes a ruling), but in the vicinity of compacted quotations, that distinction is less useful to the reader than an immediate visual distinction between the words quoted and the identification of their source by title.

When Valerie Eliot inaugurated the editing of Eliot in 1971 with the facsimile edition of *The Waste Land*, she used italics for titles whether of a short poem or a whole book, throughout her Introduction and Editorial Notes. The present edition follows this example and many other scholarly editions in italicising titles. Poems without authorial titles are referred to by italicising the first line (without additional capitals or quotation marks): *The wind sprang up at four o'clock*. The four poems entitled *Song* and the two entitled *Ode* are distinguished by supplying their opening words in brackets after the title.

Other titles, by any author, are likewise italicised (with the exceptions of the Bible and its constituent books, Johnson's Dictionary and The Oxford English Dictionary).

4. TEXT OF THE POEMS

The number of printings of Eliot's poems is so large that first editions, editions published during Eliot's lifetime and Faber editions necessarily take priority over reprints, posthumous editions and printings overseas or by other houses.

Although Eliot was reluctant to revise after publication, examination has shown that even repeated impressions of the same edition diverge to an unexpected extent. He wrote to Djuna Barnes, 15 Oct 1936: "I have never succeeded in getting a first edition of one of my own books printed without some errors in it, and I sometimes find that when those are corrected new errors appear." Printers did not always use authoritative texts—a reprint of the cheapest available, *The Waste Land and Other Poems*, was used by Giovanni Mardersteig to set the limited edition of the poem which sold at ten guineas—and the competence of typesetters varied considerably. So did Eliot's vigilance as a proofreader. Once errors had been overlooked, they could be perpetuated, the most striking being the absence, from all editions, of the last line of part II of *The Hollow Men*. Sometimes a new reading was born, apparently because Eliot emended an error without reference to his previous text. Sometimes the *Collected Poems* was emended but not the *Selected Poems* (which was handled by different printers). Sometimes Eliot acknowledged that a text was inaccurate and said he would ask for it to be emended but failed to effect the change. In other cases, where accidental changes did not injure the sense, it is impossible to know whether he overlooked or acquiesced in them. Many date from the beginning of his career, and were never subsequently emended. A conservative approach has been adopted towards poems that were reprinted in his lifetime, with the present edition usually following *1963* (some exceptions are discussed in *McCue 2012*). On the same principle of preferring the final authorised text, the "Uncollected Poems" are given in their last known (or last decipherable) form.

Apart from the addition of new items to *Selected Essays*, more changes were made in *Anabasis* after publication than in any other book of Eliot's, in verse or prose. Published in 1930, it was revised, with St.-John Perse's encouragement, in 1938, 1949 and 1959. The last of these revisions is given in the present edition, with the earlier texts being recorded in the Textual History in Volume II.

At different times Eliot proposed several batches of emendations to *Old Possum's Book of Practical Cats*, some of them contradictory. The last authorially supervised text appears to be that of the second edition of the paperback, *1964 pbk.*

A striking editorial dilemma is what to do about an error in the dedication to Jean Verdenal which stands at the head of *Prufrock and Other Observations*, where the date of birth of Eliot's friend appears as 1889 rather than the historically correct 1890. The dedication has stood for almost a century and it has been thought best not to alter it.

5. SPACING AND PUNCTUATION

In verse that is not in regular stanzas, a line-space that falls between pages may become invisible. If the text is then reset, this can lead to the loss of a space that was intended or the introduction of one that was not. Eliot wrote to Robert Beare, 10 Mar 1953, about such discrepancies in editions of his own work: "Occasionally a strophe has occurred in one edition at the end of the page with nothing to show on the next page that there is meant to be a break at that point. This has been overcome in the Penguin edition of my *Selected Poems* by an ingenious typographer who has indented the first line of every new strophe. I hope eventually to have my *Collected Poems* reset with this device." (Such indents are not general in the Penguin series and appear to have been contrived especially to meet Eliot's case.)

The Penguin edition of 1948—Eliot's first British *Selected Poems*, in the year of his Nobel Prize—indents the opening line of the second and subsequent "paragraphs" of each section of each poem, including single lines (excepting only *The Waste Land* [III] 311, "Burning"). When *Selected Poems* was retrieved by Faber and reissued, as a hardback, in 1954, these indents were inherited from the Penguin, which was followed page for page. They also appeared in Faber's first paperback of the *Selected Poems* in 1961. The "device" was not completely successful, however, because it was not obvious whether it should be applied, for instance, to an isolated couplet such as

> In the room the women come and go
> Talking of Michelangelo.

In addition, Eliot had used indents for other purposes. At the end of *Ash-Wednesday* V, for instance, the solitary line "O my people" was already indented. Here, in a different form, was the original problem once more: how could the author's deliberate spacing be distinguished from the contingencies of book production?

Faber adopted Penguin's procedure in the first paperback edition of *Four Quartets* in 1959 but handled it badly, causing distortions for instance of the shape of the lyrical sections numbered IV in both *Burnt Norton* and *Little Gidding*. In *1963*, the inconsistencies among the indents continued to proliferate. If the first line of each subsection in *Portrait of a Lady* required an indent, for instance, there is no reason why this did not also apply to *Rhapsody on a Windy Night* or *Conversation Galante*. Nor is there a reason why the first lines of *East Coker* and *The Dry Salvages* should be indented, but not those of *Burnt Norton* and *Little Gidding*. Many of the lines indented in the Faber edition were not indented in Harcourt, Brace's equivalent, *US 1963*. The American edition also failed to insert new line spaces before the final line of *Landscapes* V. *Cape Ann* and that of *Lines for an Old Man*, and these have continued to be absent from American printings.

In the event, attempts to solve the problem of line-spacing by indenting caused more difficulties than they overcame. There are so many exceptions that satisfactory rules cannot be derived from the practice of either the Penguin or *1963*. Consequently, despite the wish Eliot expressed to Robert Beare, the present edition reverts to an arrangement of the poems closer to their appearance in the original *Collected Poems* (1936), which was used in the planning of *1963* as late as the bound-proof stage. Line spaces which have appeared in or disappeared from different printings are recorded in the Textual History. Variant indentings are usually not recorded. Where they are mentioned, single lines are described as "indented", whereas passages are described as "inset" (within which individual lines may be further indented).

Where, in the present edition, a line space is intended at the foot of a page, it is signalled on the page by a marginal chevron (<), the mark Eliot himself sometimes used to indicate line spaces. (Eliot showed his care for the arrangement of his lines in corrections he made on the *1933 proof* of *Ash-Wednesday* III: "I should prefer it if p. 18 could be spaced so as to bring the first "Lord, I am not worthy" onto the top of p. 19.")

Double quotation marks cannot be confused with apostrophes, whether as abbreviations, elisions or possessives. They are standard in many British newspapers and in publications such as the *Times Literary Supplement* as well as throughout American publishing, and are not uncommon in British publishing. They are used here throughout the editorial material and the composite of the drafts of *The Waste Land*. Within the Commentary their clarity is particularly advantageous. Avoiding the momentary elusiveness of

> 1 **The golden foot I may not kiss or clutch**: Kipling: 'a-wastin' Christian kisses on an 'eathen idol's foot', *Mandalay* 14.

the pointing is immediately clear:

> 1 **The golden foot I may not kiss or clutch**: Kipling: "a-wastin' Christian kisses on an 'eathen idol's foot", *Mandalay* 14.

The Textual History likewise records Eliot's preference for double quotation marks, as manifest in manuscript and typescript.

The poems themselves are printed with single quotation marks, by the wish of the T. S. Eliot Estate and the publishers.

Ellipses that are raised · · · indicate an omission editorially introduced in the present edition. Those printed in the ordinary way are from the immediate source. These ellipses may have been in the original wording (Eliot's "I grow old . . . I grow old . . ."), or may have been introduced subsequently ("the sense of rhythm and the sense of structure . . . The use of recurrent themes is as natural to poetry as to music": from Eliot, but the ellipsis being John Hayward's). Occasional occurrences of a fourth stop in ellipses (intended to indicate a completed sentence) have not been retained or collated. Ellipses are rendered as three stops throughout, except when reproduced from OED, where its editorial ellipses have two stops. In quotations within the Commentary, paragraph breaks have not always been noted.

Because it is significant that, for instance, "Lady, three white leopards sat under a juniper-tree" is a new beginning, the line numbering begins again with each new part of a poem (making this II 1). The exception is *The Waste Land*, where the present edition follows the original continuous numbering introduced in the American first edition by Boni & Liveright, along with the Notes. In this case the part number is provided in square brackets: "Dry bones can harm no one", [V] 390.

6. TSE ON TREATMENTS OF HIS POEMS

> Peter du Sautoy of Faber to D. A. F. Sutherland of Collins, 16 Dec 1965, declining to grant permission for an annotated edition of TSE: "We may well be doing annotated editions of the poems ourselves."

Eliot: "Our only complaint against both editors [H. Harvey Wood and G. B. Harrison] is that they have conscientiously limited themselves, in their notes, to what is verifiable, and have deprived themselves and their readers of that delight in aside and conjecture which the born annotator exploits", *John Marston* (1934). "I pray that during my lifetime someone may bring out an edition, as bulky as Frazer's *Pausanius*, which shall give the natural history of the Questing Beast, and the etymology of the names of all the knights and kings. I accept Sir La Cote Male Taile, but what about Sir Marhaus, and Sir Suppinabiles, and King Bagdemagus, and Sir Meliagrance, Sir Lamorak and Sir Persant of Inde?" *Le Morte Darthur* (1934).

To Wolf Mankowitz, 20 Oct 1947: "I am averse to the publication of any of my poems with explanatory notes. I should not raise objection to the inclusion of my poems alone in any reputable anthology for the purposes you have in mind, but I cannot give my consent to their publication in an annotated edition."

"Good commentaries can be very helpful but to study even the best commentary on a work of literary art is likely to be a waste of time unless we have first read and been excited by the text commented upon even without understanding it", *In Parenthesis* (1961), A Note of Introduction.

To Nancy Cannon, 27 May 1943: "As for the publication of any of my poems in an illustrated edition, this is something to which I have always objected strongly, and although it has once or twice been somewhat embarrassing to refuse friends, I have never made any exception." (The Ariel Poems, however, were illustrated in their original pamphlet publications. For Gerald Wilde's lithograph illustrations to *Rhapsody on a Windy Night*, see headnote to the poem.) To Catherine McCarthy of Harcourt, Brace, 8 July 1947: "I have always been strongly averse to illustrated editions of any of my poems. I can have no objection, of course, to anyone publishing a separate volume or portfolio of illustrations, but I don't want to give the kind of authorization to anyone's illustrations which implies my allowing them the text."

To Dulcie Bowie, English Verse Speaking Association, 12 Feb 1935: "I have no objection to your using Part 5 of *Ash Wednesday* for the purpose indicated, if you think fit. As you know, my opinion is that for choral speaking one should have verse written for the purpose, and that to orchestrate a poem like this for a chorus is like setting a piano piece for a full symphony orchestra. I admit, however, that the amount of choral verse to choose from is very limited, and in any case I should not dream of allowing my own views to be an obstacle to your using my verse for any sized choirs that you like." (For Eliot's reaction to a semi-dramatised version of *The Waste*

Land, with music, broadcast in 1938, see headnote to the poem, 8. ANTHOLOGIES, TRANSLATIONS, ADAPTATIONS.)

To Martin Shaw, 18 Oct 1940: "I have your letter of the 15th. You were quite right to have set my piece to music first and asked my permission afterward because I should like you to feel sure that I have no hesitation in giving my consent. On the contrary I am highly pleased. But if you want to publish the music setting with the words, that is a matter of asking permission officially from Faber and Faber." (When Graham Whettam's *The Wounded Surgeon Plies the Steel*, a setting of words from *East Coker* "Printed by permission of T. S. Eliot and Faber & Faber", turned out to have changed lines of the poem, Eliot protested to the publishers, Boosey & Hawkes, and wrote a memo to Peter du Sautoy, 22 Dec 1960, saying "I am furious about this.")

To Eleanor Follansbee von Erffa, 10 July 1944: "As you ask me, I should definitely prefer that you should call the ballet *The Fisher King* (a good title, too). I feel that I ought not to obstruct anyone who is inspired by any of my poetry to make a ballet (and am a great lover of the Ballet anyway). I am anxious always that it should be clear that I do not associate myself with any *particular interpretation* of the poem, and that I took no part in the transformation. The question is the more serious, as there is someone here also who wishes to make a ballet: and if I authorise one, I must authorise both on the same terms. I take the same view about *illustrations* to my poems: while I consider any artist free to interpret the poems into his visual art, and to publish the illustrations if he can, I will not allow any illustrated edition of the text, or express particular approval of one interpretation rather than another."

To Dale E. Fern, 20 Mar 1947: "But as for a sort of ballet, which I imagine is what you mean by a choreographic setting of the *Dry Salvages*, it simply makes my stomach turn over. There are two things to which I have a strong dislike. One is the publication of any of my poems as a picture book with illustrations, and the other is ballets inspired by anything I have written. I cannot possibly conceive any such ballet having any relation to the poem except the title. Please do anything else you like but don't do this."

To Joseph Vogel, 31 Mar 1947: "while I appreciate the interest in my poetry which prompts you to make a short film of *The Love Song of J. Alfred Prufrock*, I am obliged to tell you that I am strongly averse to having any of my non-dramatic writing adapted for the screen or used as a basis for any screen work."

To the Master of Magdalene College, Cambridge, and Francis Turner, 9 Nov 1962:

> From time to time I have been approached by composers who have set to music poems or sections of poems of mine which I do not wish to have set to music and who have done so before making enquiries of me or of Faber and Faber ··· My permission in the past has always been given for more lyrical passages such as Section four of each of my *Four Quartets*, short lyrical passages such as those which are entitled *Landscapes* and an occasional chorus from *The Rock* for use on some religious occasion. For instance, Stravinsky, with my full permission and encouragement, has set Section four of my poem *Little Gidding* to music, but *Ash Wednesday* is a different matter altogether; it does not seem at all suitable for the purpose. I hope you will see that my firmness on this point is not wholly unreasonable. If I gave permission even once for publication of my text with a musical setting, I should find it almost impossible to resist leaving the whole of my verse to the disposal of composers.
>
> With the publication of my own verse I have always been firm on three points. First, I will not allow any artist to illustrate my poems. Second, I will not allow any academic

critic (and there are plenty of these in America only too willing) to provide notes of explanation to be published with ~~any of~~ my poems. Third, I will not allow any of my poems to be set to music unless they seem to me to be lyrics in the proper sense of being suitable for singing. My objection to all three of these methods of employing my works is the same, that I should be allowing interpretation of the poem to be interposed between me and my readers. An artist is providing the illustrations which should be left to the imagination of the reader, the commentator is providing information which stands between the reader and any immediate response ~~in~~ of his sensibility, and the music also is a particular interpretation which is ~~also~~ interposed between the reader and the author. I want my readers to get their impressions from the words alone and from nothing else.

Acknowledgements

This edition has been made possible by those who recognised Eliot's genius and treasured and preserved his writings, particularly his mother, Charlotte; his brother, Henry; Ezra Pound; John Hayward; and Valerie Eliot. We have been very fortunate to have been preparing this edition with the blessing of Valerie Eliot (who died in 2012) and of the T. S. Eliot Estate.

The editors are grateful to a number of individuals and estates for use of their material. Though it has not, due to the number and diversity of the sources, been possible to treat each citation individually, thanks are due to Dr Henry Oakeley and Auriol Chisholm for permission to include published and unpublished material by John Hayward; and to Faber & Faber and the Faber Archive, for material by Geoffrey Faber, Stephen Spender and Charles Williams.

Also reproduced is previously unpublished material, including letters and manuscript annotations, by Ezra Pound: copyright © 2015 by Mary de Rachewiltz and the Estate of Omar S. Pound; published letters by Ezra Pound, from *Selected Letters 1907–1941 Of Ezra Pound,* copyright © 1950 by Ezra Pound; excerpts by Ezra Pound published in journals, literary magazines, etc., copyright © 1991 by the Trustees of the Ezra Pound Literary Property Trust; excerpts from from *Literary Essays of Ezra Pound*, copyright © 1935 by Ezra Pound and from *Pavannes & Divagations* copyright © 1958 by New Directions Publishing Corp. All of these are reprinted by permission of New Directions Publishing Corp.

The drawing by David Jones from *The Cultivation of Christmas Trees* is reproduced by permission of Nicholas Elkin; the "Bolo" drawing by T. S. Eliot from a letter to Bonamy Dobrée is reproduced with the permission of Special Collections, Leeds University Library (BC ms 20c Dobrée); the drawings illustrating *Five-Finger Exercises* IV and V are reproduced by permission of the Beinecke Rare Book and Manuscript Library, Yale University; the drawing by Margaret Wolpe is reproduced by permission of Deborah Wolpe.

The editors are also grateful for the support of the Mellon Foundation; the Arts and Humanities Research Council; the Master and Fellows of Magdalene College, Cambridge; the Institute of English Studies, University of London; and Boston University, particularly the Editorial Institute.

The bibliography of Eliot by Donald Gallup remains indispensable, eighty years after he began work on its first embodiment as *A Catalogue of English and American First Editions of Writings by T. S. Eliot* for an exhibition at Yale in 1937. The bibliography is being updated by Archie Henderson.

We are especially indebted to Jennifer Formichelli, Ben Mazer and Allison Vanouse, who helped to check the Commentary and Textual History, and to Shawn Worthington, who undertook much research and compiled the index to the edition. Our copy editor, Donald Sommerville, has saved us from many errors, added to our knowledge and been exceptional for his pertinacity and patience. This book was designed by Paul Luna in the Department of Typography & Graphic Communication,

University of Reading. It was set in types designed by Fred Smeijers: a special version of Arnhem Fine for Eliot's poetry and Arnhem Pro for the remainder of the text.

Thanks partly to the widespread love of Eliot, not only colleagues and friends but many who were previously unknown to us have also been most generous with their time and knowledge. With apologies to anyone we have inadvertently omitted, we should like to thank:

David Addyman, Catherine Ahearn, Michael Alexander, William Arrowsmith, Alp Atabay, Rowley Atterbury, Joseph Baillargeon, Elena Baranes, John Barnard, Marvin Bensman, Matthew Bevis, Chelsea Bingham, Ann Bird, W. H. Bizley, John Bodley, Andrew Boxer, Owen Boynton, David Bradshaw, Laurence Breiner, Charlotte Brewer, Catherine Brown, Ian Brunskill, Archie Burnett, Ronald Bush, Mark Byron, Katherine Calver, Brian and Genie Casey, Peter Chasseaud, Ted Cheers, Carol Clark, Keith Clements, David Coleman, Constantine Contogenis, Connie Contogenis and Clio Contogenis, Eleanor Cook, Bonnie Costello, David Crystal, Robert Dagg, Roy Davids, Ben de la Mare, Giles de la Mare, James Dempsey, Christie Dennis, Rodney Dennis, Frances Dickey, Jeremy Dibble, Martin Dodsworth, Robert Douglas-Fairhurst, Peter Doyle, Trevor Dunmore, Lauren Eckenroth, Paul Edwards, Michael Elliott, Pat Fenteman, Anne Ferry, David Ferry, Philip Finkelpearl, Carol Fitzgerald, Stephen and Mary Jo Foley, Christopher H. Freeble, Arthur Freeman, Donald Gallup, Matthew Geary, Henry Gott, Warwick Gould, James Griffin, Eric Griffiths, John Gross, Jeffrey Gutierrez, John Haffenden, R. F. Hall, Vanessa Hall-Smith, Paul Hartle, Kenneth Haynes, Thomas Healey, Archie Henderson, Anne Holmes, Philip Horne, Rob House, Mark Hruby, Richard Humphreys, Bruce Hunt, Clare Hutton, Christoph Irmscher, Steven Isenberg, Manju Jaidka, Iman Javadi, Roger Johnson, Marcia Karp, Richard Kaye, Charlotte King, Stephen Krishnan, Jonas Kurlberg, Barbara Lauriat, Stephen Layton, Philip and Sally Le Brocq, Hermione Lee, Ronald Levao, Eliot Levin, A. Walton Litz, Peter Lockley, William Logan, James Longenbach, James Loucks, Richard Luckett, Oliver Lyne, John Lyon, Ann McCue, Betty McCue, Kenneth Mcnab, Jane Mansbridge, Jérôme Martin, Dave Mason, David Matthews, Jeremy Maule, Ben Mazer, Edward Mendelson, Silke Mentchen, Elizabeth Micakovic, Tim Miller, Stephanie Nelson, Christopher Ohge, Lee Oser, Graham Parker, Ian Patterson, April Pierce, Adrian Poole, Michael Prince, Lawrence Rainey, Claude Rawson, Cal Revely-Calder, Jonathan Ribner, David Ricks, Angelo Righetti, John Paul Riquelme, Paul Robert, Wallace Robson, Lisa Rodensky, Peter Sacks, Cliff Saxton, Ronald Schuchard, Sanford Schwartz, Roger Shattuck, Susan Shaw, Abner Shimony, Alyn Shipton, Eric Sigg, John R. Silber, George Simmers, Abby Love Smith, Grover Smith, Oliver Soden, Richard Sorabji, Natasha Spender, Robert Spoo, Jon Stallworthy, Jayme Stayer, Anne Stillman, Christopher Stray, Kendon Stubbs, Michael F. Suarez, Peter Swaab, Eleanor Talbot, Nigel Tattersfield, Mark Thompson, Roger E. Thompson, Jeanne Tift, Kit Toda, Angela Todd, Gail Trimble, Mike Truax, Ana Urrutia-Jordana, William L. Vance, Julian Walker, Philip Warner, William Waters, Louise Watts, E. S. C. Weiner, Jon Westling, Clive Westwood-Dunkley, Frances Whistler, Kieron Winn, Susan Wolfson, Henry Woudhuysen, William Zachs.

The librarians and staff of the BBC Written Archive Centre (Rachel Bowles); the Beinecke Library, Yale University (Patricia C. Willis, Nancy Kuhl, Melissa Barton and Diane Ducharme); the Berg Collection, New York Public Library (Francis O. Mattson,

Rodney Phillips and Isaac Gewirtz); Bloomsbury Auctions (Dido Arthur); the Bodleian Library (Andrew Honey, Judith Priestman, Colin Harris and Eva Oledzka); Museum Boijmans Van Beuningen, Rotterdam (Friso Lammertse); the Borthwick Institute, York (Philippa Hoskin); Bristol University Library and the Penguin Archive (Hannah Lowery and George Donaldson); the British Library; British Postal Museum & Archive (Barry Attoe); the Brotherton Library, Leeds University (Christopher Sheppard and Stephen Clatworthy); the University of Buffalo Library; Bryn Mawr College Library (Eric Pumroy); Cambridge University Library (Margaret Jones); Cheltenham College archive (Jill Barlow); Christie's, London (Meg Ford); the Library of Congress; Daley Library, University of Illinois at Chicago; University of Delaware Library (Lora J. Davis); Denison Library, Scripps College (Judy Sahak); the Institute of Education Library, University of London; the James Joyce Library, University College Dublin (Eugene Roche); Eton College Library (Michael Meredith and Rachel Bond); Faber & Faber, especially Robert Brown, Ron Costley, Vic Gray, Matthew Hollis, Paul Keegan, Stephen Page and John Porter; the Firestone Library, Princeton (Margaret M. Sherry, AnnaLee Pauls and Gabriel Swift); the Guildhall Library (Isabelle Chevallot); Hamilton College Library (Christian Goodwillie); the Harry Ransom Center, University of Texas at Austin (Cathy Henderson, Richard Workman and Jean Cannon); Haverford College Library; the Hornbake Library, University of Maryland (Beth Alvarez and Ann L. Hudak); the Houghton Library, Harvard University (Leslie A. Morris, Susan Halpert and Betty Falsey); the Hunterian Museum, Glasgow; the Huntington Library, Los Angeles; University of Iowa Special Collections (Stephen Sturgeon); the Archive Centre at King's College, Cambridge (Patricia McGuire, Peter Monteith and Jacqueline Cox); the Lindley Library of the Royal Horticultural Society, Wisley; London Fire Brigade Museum (Jane Rugg); Magdalene College Library, Cambridge (Jane Hughes); the Mary Institute and St. Louis County Day School archive (Anne McAlpine); the University of Memphis Library (Christopher Ratliff); Merton College Library (Julia Walworth); the Vincent Voice Library, Michigan State University (John D. Shaw); the Missouri History Museum Library (Jason D. Stratman and Dennis Northcott); the Mitchell Library, Glasgow (Susan Taylor); the National Library of Scotland Manuscripts Division (Iain G. Brown); the New York Public Library (Thomas Lannon); Newberry Library, Chicago (Jill Gage); the Oxford English Dictionary (John Simpson and Margot Charlton); the Van Pelt-Dietrich Library, University of Pennsylvania; the Pierpont Morgan Library (Clara Drummond); the Regenstein Library, University of Chicago (Julia Gardner and Christine Colburn); St. Louis Public Library (Jean M. Gosebrink); the Signet Club, Harvard (Katharine Urbati); Sotheby's, London (Philip Errington); University of Sussex Special Collections (Karen Watson); Templeman Library, University of Kent (Jane Gallagher); University College London Library, Special Collections (Laurie McNamee); the Albert and Shirley Small Special Collections Library, University of Virginia (Molly Schwartzburg, Margaret D. Hrabe, Regina Rush and Sharon Defibaugh); Washington University in St. Louis, Special Collections (John Hodge and Erin Davis); the Wilson Library, University of North Carolina at Chapel Hill; the David Wilson Library, University of Leicester (Caroline Sampson); the Worcester Museum of Art; the Working Class Movement Library, Salford (Lynette Cawthra).

The British and American book trade, including Allen and Patricia Ahearn (Quill & Brush); Adam Blakeney (Peter Harrington); Ron Chapman and James Tindley (Tindley & Chapman); Ann Gate (Waterfield's); Rick Gekoski and Peter Grogan

(Gekoski); Ted Hoffman (Bernard Quaritch); Larry Hutchison; Sabrina Izzard (Halls); James Jaffé; Ed Maggs and Joe McCann (Maggs Brothers); Jeanette Murch (Greenwich Book Place); Anthony Payne; Gary Oleson and Francine Ness (Waiting for Godot Books); Mary Phillips (September Books), Anthony Sillem; Veronica Watts; Terry Westcott; Joy Young, and many others who have tracked down and supplied materials or willingly answered queries about books that would otherwise have been inaccessible to us.

Glossary

blind-ruled	impressed with rules but without ink
braced	with added brackets or square brackets not in themselves intended as punctuation (often for further consideration)
cognate	ribbon and carbon copies from the same act of typing and therefore textually identical unless annotated or edited (see *reciprocal*)
draft	preliminary manuscript or typescript
excised leaves	leaves removed, for instance from the *March Hare* Notebook, and not accompanying the original
eye-skip	omission caused by eye of copyist or compositor jumping to a later repetition of words (such as "The nymphs are departed", *The Waste Land* [III] 175, 179)
indented	(of an individual line) set to the right of the left-hand margin of the poem
inset	(of a group of lines) set to the right of the left-hand margin of the poem
laid in	of extraneous leaves introduced into a manuscript volume such as the *March Hare* Notebook but not bound as part of it
orphan	the first line of a paragraph set as the last line of a page or column
overtyped	typed in the same position so as to supersede what originally appeared
part	a division of a poem marked by the author with a numeral
quad-ruled	printed with vertical and horizontal lines forming rectangles
reciprocal	of typescripts in which the two or more pages are a mixture of cognate ribbon copies and carbons, and which together would constitute the complete ribbon copy and the complete carbon
scored	marked with a vertical line in the margin
section	a division of the text of a book ("The section of 'Occasional Poems' was introduced in *1963*")
separately	constituting an entire book, pamphlet or broadsheet
stepped	arranged on more than one line; unless specified, each step beginning where the previous ends
variant	difference in the text; within TSE's poems, unless otherwise specified, variants are differences from the main text of the present edition (see Textual History)
widow	a last word or short last line of a paragraph falling at the top of a page or column

Abbreviations and Symbols

ANQ	*American Notes and Queries*
AraVP	*Ara Vos Prec* (Ovid Press, 1920)
Ariel	Faber Ariel Poem pamphlets (standard editions)
Ash-Wed	*Ash-Wednesday* (Faber, 1930)
Beinecke	Beinecke Library, Yale University
BL	British Library
BN	*Burnt Norton* pamphlet (1941)
Composition FQ	Helen Gardner, *The Composition of "Four Quartets"* (Faber, 1978)
del.	delete, deleted
DS	*The Dry Salvages* pamphlet (1941)
EC	*East Coker* pamphlet (1940)
ed.	edition, editor, edited (by)
EinC	*Essays in Criticism*
ELH	*English Literary History*
ELN	*English Language Notes*
Fr.	French
Ger.	German
Houghton	Houghton Library, Harvard University
Inf.	*Inferno* (Dante)
King's	Modern Archive Centre, King's College, Cambridge
L.	Latin
LG	*Little Gidding* pamphlet (1942)
Magdalene	Library of Magdalene College, Cambridge
March Hare	*Inventions of the March Hare*
MLN	*Modern Language Notes*
MLR	*Modern Language Review*
ms	manuscript
N&Q	*Notes and Queries*
NEW	*New English Weekly*
NY	New York
NYPL	New York Public Library
OED	The Oxford English Dictionary (2nd ed., 1989, with online updates)
Oxf Bk of English Verse	*The Oxford Book of English Verse* ed. A. T. Quiller-Couch (1900)
PMLA	*Publications of the Modern Language Association of America*
Purg.	*Purgatory* (Dante)
repr.	reprint, reprinted

RES — *Review of English Studies*
rev. — revised
Sw. Ag. — *Sweeney Agonistes* (Faber, 1932)
Texas — Harry Ransom Center, University of Texas at Austin
TLS — *Times Literary Supplement*
tr. — translation, translated (by)
ts — typescript
U. — University, University of
VE — Valerie Eliot
WLComposite — composite text of the drafts of *The Waste Land* (present edition)
WLFacs — *The Waste Land: A Facsimile and Transcript of the Original Drafts including the Annotations of Ezra Pound* ed. Valerie Eliot (1971)

Abbreviated titles are detailed in the Index of Identifying Titles for Prose by T. S. Eliot. Abbreviated titles for TSE's poetic works are detailed in Volume II, within the Textual History headnote, 3. KEY TO EDITIONS.

Abbreviated titles for works by other authors are detailed in the Bibliography.

Quotations from OED retain its abbreviations.

SYMBOLS

| — line break, used in quotations from verse
| | — stanza break, used in quotations from verse
& — informal ampersand, used in quotations from manuscript
+ — "and in derived text" (of a reading within a poem, or a poem within editions)
¶ — new paragraph
> or < — line space (used at the foot of a page in the poems)
[ ] — enclosing a date not specified by the author or publisher
^ — insertion, used to indicate where additional material was to be placed
· · · — ellipsis (raised), used to indicate omissions made by the editors of the present edition
. . . — ellipsis (baseline), used in quotation where the ellipsis is present in the original
. . — ellipsis in entries quoted from OED
‖ — used to separate different readings within textual history collations; see Volume II, Textual History headnote, 2. NOTATION
~ — to indicate a range of instances most of which, but not necessarily all, have a certain feature; see Volume II, Textual History headnote, 2. NOTATION

Collected Poems 1909–1962
(1963)

Prufrock

and Other Observations

1917

For Jean Verdenal, 1889–1915
mort aux Dardanelles

Or puoi la quantitate
comprender dell'amor ch'a te mi scalda,
quando dismento nostra vanitate,
trattando l'ombre come cosa salda.

The Love Song of J. Alfred Prufrock

S'io credessi che mia risposta fosse
a persona che mai tornasse al mondo,
questa fiamma staria senza più scosse.
Ma per ciò che giammai di questo fondo
non tornò vivo alcun, s'i' odo il vero, [5]
senza tema d'infamia ti rispondo.

Let us go then, you and I,
When the evening is spread out against the sky
Like a patient etherised upon a table;
Let us go, through certain half-deserted streets,
The muttering retreats 5
Of restless nights in one-night cheap hotels
And sawdust restaurants with oyster-shells:
Streets that follow like a tedious argument
Of insidious intent
To lead you to an overwhelming question . . . 10

Oh, do not ask, 'What is it?'
Let us go and make our visit.

In the room the women come and go
Talking of Michelangelo.

The yellow fog that rubs its back upon the window-panes, 15
The yellow smoke that rubs its muzzle on the window-panes,
Licked its tongue into the corners of the evening,
Lingered upon the pools that stand in drains,
Let fall upon its back the soot that falls from chimneys,
Slipped by the terrace, made a sudden leap, 20
And seeing that it was a soft October night,
Curled once about the house, and fell asleep.

<

And indeed there will be time
For the yellow smoke that slides along the street
25 Rubbing its back upon the window-panes;
There will be time, there will be time
To prepare a face to meet the faces that you meet;
There will be time to murder and create,
And time for all the works and days of hands
30 That lift and drop a question on your plate;
Time for you and time for me,
And time yet for a hundred indecisions,
And for a hundred visions and revisions,
Before the taking of a toast and tea.

35 In the room the women come and go
Talking of Michelangelo.

And indeed there will be time
To wonder, 'Do I dare?' and, 'Do I dare?'
Time to turn back and descend the stair,
40 With a bald spot in the middle of my hair—
(They will say: 'How his hair is growing thin!')
My morning coat, my collar mounting firmly to the chin,
My necktie rich and modest, but asserted by a simple pin—
(They will say: 'But how his arms and legs are thin!')
45 Do I dare
Disturb the universe?
In a minute there is time
For decisions and revisions which a minute will reverse.

For I have known them all already, known them all—
50 Have known the evenings, mornings, afternoons,
I have measured out my life with coffee spoons;
I know the voices dying with a dying fall
Beneath the music from a farther room.
    So how should I presume?

>

And I have known the eyes already, known them all— 55
The eyes that fix you in a formulated phrase,
And when I am formulated, sprawling on a pin,
When I am pinned and wriggling on the wall,
Then how should I begin
To spit out all the butt-ends of my days and ways? 60
    And how should I presume?

And I have known the arms already, known them all—
Arms that are braceleted and white and bare
(But in the lamplight, downed with light brown hair!)
Is it perfume from a dress 65
That makes me so digress?
Arms that lie along a table, or wrap about a shawl.
    And should I then presume?
    And how should I begin?

. . . . .

Shall I say, I have gone at dusk through narrow streets 70
And watched the smoke that rises from the pipes
Of lonely men in shirt-sleeves, leaning out of windows? . . .

I should have been a pair of ragged claws
Scuttling across the floors of silent seas.

. . . . .

And the afternoon, the evening, sleeps so peacefully! 75
Smoothed by long fingers,
Asleep . . . tired . . . or it malingers,
Stretched on the floor, here beside you and me.
Should I, after tea and cakes and ices,
Have the strength to force the moment to its crisis? 80
But though I have wept and fasted, wept and prayed,

Though I have seen my head (grown slightly bald) brought in
upon a platter,
I am no prophet—and here's no great matter;
I have seen the moment of my greatness flicker,
85 And I have seen the eternal Footman hold my coat, and snicker,
And in short, I was afraid.

And would it have been worth it, after all,
After the cups, the marmalade, the tea,
Among the porcelain, among some talk of you and me,
90 Would it have been worth while,
To have bitten off the matter with a smile,
To have squeezed the universe into a ball
To roll it towards some overwhelming question,
To say: 'I am Lazarus, come from the dead,
95 Come back to tell you all, I shall tell you all'—
If one, settling a pillow by her head,
Should say: 'That is not what I meant at all.
That is not it, at all.'

And would it have been worth it, after all,
100 Would it have been worth while,
After the sunsets and the dooryards and the sprinkled streets,
After the novels, after the teacups, after the skirts that trail along
the floor—
And this, and so much more?—
It is impossible to say just what I mean!
105 But as if a magic lantern threw the nerves in patterns on a screen:
Would it have been worth while
If one, settling a pillow or throwing off a shawl,
And turning toward the window, should say:
'That is not it at all,
110 That is not what I meant, at all.'

. . . . .

No! I am not Prince Hamlet, nor was meant to be;
Am an attendant lord, one that will do
To swell a progress, start a scene or two,
Advise the prince; no doubt, an easy tool,
Deferential, glad to be of use, 115
Politic, cautious, and meticulous;
Full of high sentence, but a bit obtuse;
At times, indeed, almost ridiculous—
Almost, at times, the Fool.

I grow old . . . I grow old . . . 120
I shall wear the bottoms of my trousers rolled.

Shall I part my hair behind? Do I dare to eat a peach?
I shall wear white flannel trousers, and walk upon the beach.
I have heard the mermaids singing, each to each.

I do not think that they will sing to me. 125

I have seen them riding seaward on the waves
Combing the white hair of the waves blown back
When the wind blows the water white and black.

We have lingered in the chambers of the sea
By sea-girls wreathed with seaweed red and brown 130
Till human voices wake us, and we drown.

Portrait of a Lady

Thou hast committed—
Fornication: but that was in another country,
And besides, the wench is dead.
The Jew of Malta

I

Among the smoke and fog of a December afternoon
You have the scene arrange itself—as it will seem to do—
With 'I have saved this afternoon for you';
And four wax candles in the darkened room,
5 Four rings of light upon the ceiling overhead,
An atmosphere of Juliet's tomb
Prepared for all the things to be said, or left unsaid.
We have been, let us say, to hear the latest Pole
Transmit the Preludes, through his hair and finger-tips.
10 'So intimate, this Chopin, that I think his soul
Should be resurrected only among friends
Some two or three, who will not touch the bloom
That is rubbed and questioned in the concert room.'
—And so the conversation slips
15 Among velleities and carefully caught regrets
Through attenuated tones of violins
Mingled with remote cornets
And begins.
'You do not know how much they mean to me, my friends,
20 And how, how rare and strange it is, to find
In a life composed so much, so much of odds and ends,
(For indeed I do not love it . . . you knew? you are not blind!
How keen you are!)
To find a friend who has these qualities,
25 Who has, and gives
Those qualities upon which friendship lives.

Commentary I 400–405 · Textual History II 319–321

How much it means that I say this to you—
Without these friendships—life, what *cauchemar!*'

Among the windings of the violins
And the ariettes 30
Of cracked cornets
Inside my brain a dull tom-tom begins
Absurdly hammering a prelude of its own,
Capricious monotone
That is at least one definite 'false note.' 35
—Let us take the air, in a tobacco trance,
Admire the monuments,
Discuss the late events,
Correct our watches by the public clocks.
Then sit for half an hour and drink our bocks. 40

II

Now that lilacs are in bloom
She has a bowl of lilacs in her room
And twists one in her fingers while she talks.
'Ah, my friend, you do not know, you do not know
What life is, you who hold it in your hands'; 5
(Slowly twisting the lilac stalks)
'You let it flow from you, you let it flow,
And youth is cruel, and has no remorse
And smiles at situations which it cannot see.'
I smile, of course, 10
And go on drinking tea.
'Yet with these April sunsets, that somehow recall
My buried life, and Paris in the Spring,
I feel immeasurably at peace, and find the world
To be wonderful and youthful, after all.' 15
<

The voice returns like the insistent out-of-tune
Of a broken violin on an August afternoon:
'I am always sure that you understand
My feelings, always sure that you feel,
20 Sure that across the gulf you reach your hand.

You are invulnerable, you have no Achilles' heel.
You will go on, and when you have prevailed
You can say: at this point many a one has failed.
But what have I, but what have I, my friend,
25 To give you, what can you receive from me?
Only the friendship and the sympathy
Of one about to reach her journey's end.

I shall sit here, serving tea to friends . . .'

I take my hat: how can I make a cowardly amends
30 For what she has said to me?

You will see me any morning in the park
Reading the comics and the sporting page.
Particularly I remark
An English countess goes upon the stage.
35 A Greek was murdered at a Polish dance,
Another bank defaulter has confessed.
I keep my countenance,
I remain self-possessed
Except when a street piano, mechanical and tired
40 Reiterates some worn-out common song
With the smell of hyacinths across the garden
Recalling things that other people have desired.
Are these ideas right or wrong?

III

The October night comes down; returning as before
Except for a slight sensation of being ill at ease
I mount the stairs and turn the handle of the door
And feel as if I had mounted on my hands and knees.
'And so you are going abroad; and when do you return? 5
But that's a useless question.
You hardly know when you are coming back,
You will find so much to learn.'
My smile falls heavily among the bric-à-brac.

'Perhaps you can write to me.' 10
My self-possession flares up for a second;
This is as I had reckoned.
'I have been wondering frequently of late
(But our beginnings never know our ends!)
Why we have not developed into friends.' 15
I feel like one who smiles, and turning shall remark
Suddenly, his expression in a glass.
My self-possession gutters; we are really in the dark.

'For everybody said so, all our friends,
They all were sure our feelings would relate 20
So closely! I myself can hardly understand.
We must leave it now to fate.
You will write, at any rate.
Perhaps it is not too late.
I shall sit here, serving tea to friends.' 25

And I must borrow every changing shape
To find expression . . . dance, dance
Like a dancing bear,
Cry like a parrot, chatter like an ape.
Let us take the air, in a tobacco trance— 30
<

Well! and what if she should die some afternoon,
Afternoon grey and smoky, evening yellow and rose;
Should die and leave me sitting pen in hand
With the smoke coming down above the housetops;
35 Doubtful, for a while
Not knowing what to feel or if I understand
Or whether wise or foolish, tardy or too soon . . .
Would she not have the advantage, after all?
This music is successful with a 'dying fall'
40 Now that we talk of dying—
And should I have the right to smile?

Preludes

I

The winter evening settles down
With smell of steaks in passageways.
Six o'clock.
The burnt-out ends of smoky days.
And now a gusty shower wraps 5
The grimy scraps
Of withered leaves about your feet
And newspapers from vacant lots;
The showers beat
On broken blinds and chimney-pots, 10
And at the corner of the street
A lonely cab-horse steams and stamps.

And then the lighting of the lamps.

II

The morning comes to consciousness
Of faint stale smells of beer
From the sawdust-trampled street
With all its muddy feet that press
To early coffee-stands. 5

With the other masquerades
That time resumes,
One thinks of all the hands
That are raising dingy shades
In a thousand furnished rooms. 10

III

You tossed a blanket from the bed,
You lay upon your back, and waited;
You dozed, and watched the night revealing
The thousand sordid images
Of which your soul was constituted; 5
They flickered against the ceiling.
And when all the world came back
And the light crept up between the shutters,
And you heard the sparrows in the gutters,
You had such a vision of the street 10
As the street hardly understands;
Sitting along the bed's edge, where
You curled the papers from your hair,
Or clasped the yellow soles of feet
In the palms of both soiled hands. 15

IV

His soul stretched tight across the skies
That fade behind a city block,
Or trampled by insistent feet
At four and five and six o'clock;
And short square fingers stuffing pipes, 5
And evening newspapers, and eyes
Assured of certain certainties,
The conscience of a blackened street
Impatient to assume the world.

I am moved by fancies that are curled 10
Around these images, and cling:
The notion of some infinitely gentle
Infinitely suffering thing.

>

Wipe your hand across your mouth, and laugh;
The worlds revolve like ancient women 15
Gathering fuel in vacant lots.

Rhapsody on a Windy Night

Twelve o'clock.
Along the reaches of the street
Held in a lunar synthesis,
Whispering lunar incantations
5 Dissolve the floors of memory
And all its clear relations,
Its divisions and precisions.
Every street lamp that I pass
Beats like a fatalistic drum,
10 And through the spaces of the dark
Midnight shakes the memory
As a madman shakes a dead geranium.

Half-past one,
The street-lamp sputtered,
15 The street-lamp muttered,
The street-lamp said, 'Regard that woman
Who hesitates toward you in the light of the door
Which opens on her like a grin.
You see the border of her dress
20 Is torn and stained with sand,
And you see the corner of her eye
Twists like a crooked pin.'

The memory throws up high and dry
A crowd of twisted things;
25 A twisted branch upon the beach
Eaten smooth, and polished
As if the world gave up
The secret of its skeleton,
Stiff and white.

A broken spring in a factory yard, 30
Rust that clings to the form that the strength has left
Hard and curled and ready to snap.

Half-past two,
The street-lamp said,
'Remark the cat which flattens itself in the gutter, 35
Slips out its tongue
And devours a morsel of rancid butter.'
So the hand of the child, automatic,
Slipped out and pocketed a toy that was running along the quay.
I could see nothing behind that child's eye. 40
I have seen eyes in the street
Trying to peer through lighted shutters,
And a crab one afternoon in a pool,
An old crab with barnacles on his back,
Gripped the end of a stick which I held him. 45

Half-past three,
The lamp sputtered,
The lamp muttered in the dark.
The lamp hummed:
'Regard the moon, 50
La lune ne garde aucune rancune,
She winks a feeble eye,
She smiles into corners.
She smooths the hair of the grass.
The moon has lost her memory. 55
A washed-out smallpox cracks her face,
Her hand twists a paper rose,
That smells of dust and eau de Cologne,
She is alone
With all the old nocturnal smells 60
That cross and cross across her brain.'

The reminiscence comes
Of sunless dry geraniums
And dust in crevices,
65 Smells of chestnuts in the streets,
And female smells in shuttered rooms,
And cigarettes in corridors
And cocktail smells in bars.

The lamp said,
70 'Four o'clock,
Here is the number on the door.
Memory!
You have the key,
The little lamp spreads a ring on the stair.
75 Mount.
The bed is open; the tooth-brush hangs on the wall,
Put your shoes at the door, sleep, prepare for life.'

The last twist of the knife.

Morning at the Window

They are rattling breakfast plates in basement kitchens,
And along the trampled edges of the street
I am aware of the damp souls of housemaids
Sprouting despondently at area gates.

The brown waves of fog toss up to me 5
Twisted faces from the bottom of the street,
And tear from a passer-by with muddy skirts
An aimless smile that hovers in the air
And vanishes along the level of the roofs.

The 'Boston Evening Transcript'

The readers of the *Boston Evening Transcript*
Sway in the wind like a field of ripe corn.

When evening quickens faintly in the street,
Wakening the appetites of life in some
5 And to others bringing the *Boston Evening Transcript*,
I mount the steps and ring the bell, turning
Wearily, as one would turn to nod good-bye to La Rochefoucauld,
If the street were time and he at the end of the street,
And I say, 'Cousin Harriet, here is the *Boston Evening Transcript*.'

Aunt Helen

Miss Helen Slingsby was my maiden aunt,
And lived in a small house near a fashionable square
Cared for by servants to the number of four.
Now when she died there was silence in heaven
And silence at her end of the street. 5
The shutters were drawn and the undertaker wiped his feet—
He was aware that this sort of thing had occurred before.
The dogs were handsomely provided for,
But shortly afterwards the parrot died too.
The Dresden clock continued ticking on the mantelpiece, 10
And the footman sat upon the dining-table
Holding the second housemaid on his knees—
Who had always been so careful while her mistress lived.

Cousin Nancy

Miss Nancy Ellicott
Strode across the hills and broke them,
Rode across the hills and broke them—
The barren New England hills—
5 Riding to hounds
Over the cow-pasture.

Miss Nancy Ellicott smoked
And danced all the modern dances;
And her aunts were not quite sure how they felt about it,
10 But they knew that it was modern.

Upon the glazen shelves kept watch
Matthew and Waldo, guardians of the faith,
The army of unalterable law.

Mr. Apollinax

Ω τῆς καινότητος. Ἡράκλεις, τῆς παραδοξολογίας.
εὐμήχανος ἄνθρωπος.

LUCIAN

When Mr. Apollinax visited the United States
His laughter tinkled among the teacups.
I thought of Fragilion, that shy figure among the birch-trees,
And of Priapus in the shrubbery
Gaping at the lady in the swing. 5
In the palace of Mrs. Phlaccus, at Professor Channing-Cheetah's
He laughed like an irresponsible fœtus.
His laughter was submarine and profound
Like the old man of the sea's
Hidden under coral islands 10
Where worried bodies of drowned men drift down in the green
silence,
Dropping from fingers of surf.

I looked for the head of Mr. Apollinax rolling under a chair
Or grinning over a screen
With seaweed in its hair. 15
I heard the beat of centaurs' hoofs over the hard turf
As his dry and passionate talk devoured the afternoon.
'He is a charming man'—'But after all what did he mean?'—
'His pointed ears . . . He must be unbalanced.'—
'There was something he said that I might have challenged.' 20
Of dowager Mrs. Phlaccus, and Professor and Mrs. Cheetah
I remember a slice of lemon, and a bitten macaroon.

Hysteria

As she laughed I was aware of becoming involved in her laughter and being part of it, until her teeth were only accidental stars with a talent for squad-drill. I was drawn in by short gasps, inhaled at each momentary recovery, lost finally in the dark caverns of her throat, bruised by the ripple of unseen muscles. An elderly waiter with trembling hands was hurriedly spreading a pink and white checked cloth over the rusty green iron table, saying: 'If the lady and gentleman wish to take their tea in the garden, if the lady and gentleman wish to take their tea in the garden . . .' I decided that if the shaking of her breasts could be stopped, some of the fragments of the afternoon might be collected, and I concentrated my attention with careful subtlety to this end.

Conversation Galante

I observe: 'Our sentimental friend the moon!
Or possibly (fantastic, I confess)
It may be Prester John's balloon
Or an old battered lantern hung aloft
To light poor travellers to their distress.' 5
She then: 'How you digress!'

And I then: 'Someone frames upon the keys
That exquisite nocturne, with which we explain
The night and moonshine; music which we seize
To body forth our own vacuity.' 10
She then: 'Does this refer to me?'
'Oh no, it is I who am inane.'

'You, madam, are the eternal humorist,
The eternal enemy of the absolute,
Giving our vagrant moods the slightest twist! 15
With your air indifferent and imperious
At a stroke our mad poetics to confute—'
And—'Are we then so serious?'

La Figlia Che Piange

O quam te memorem virgo . . .

Stand on the highest pavement of the stair—
Lean on a garden urn—
Weave, weave the sunlight in your hair—
Clasp your flowers to you with a pained surprise—
5 Fling them to the ground and turn
With a fugitive resentment in your eyes:
But weave, weave the sunlight in your hair.

So I would have had him leave,
So I would have had her stand and grieve,
10 So he would have left
As the soul leaves the body torn and bruised,
As the mind deserts the body it has used.
I should find
Some way incomparably light and deft,
15 Some way we both should understand,
Simple and faithless as a smile and shake of the hand.

She turned away, but with the autumn weather
Compelled my imagination many days,
Many days and many hours:
20 Her hair over her arms and her arms full of flowers.
And I wonder how they should have been together!
I should have lost a gesture and a pose.
Sometimes these cogitations still amaze
The troubled midnight and the noon's repose.

Poems

1920

Gerontion

Thou hast nor youth nor age
But as it were an after dinner sleep
Dreaming of both.

Here I am, an old man in a dry month,
Being read to by a boy, waiting for rain.
I was neither at the hot gates
Nor fought in the warm rain
Nor knee deep in the salt marsh, heaving a cutlass, 5
Bitten by flies, fought.
My house is a decayed house,
And the Jew squats on the window-sill, the owner,
Spawned in some estaminet of Antwerp,
Blistered in Brussels, patched and peeled in London. 10
The goat coughs at night in the field overhead;
Rocks, moss, stonecrop, iron, merds.
The woman keeps the kitchen, makes tea,
Sneezes at evening, poking the peevish gutter.

I an old man, 15
A dull head among windy spaces.

Signs are taken for wonders. 'We would see a sign!'
The word within a word, unable to speak a word,
Swaddled with darkness. In the juvescence of the year
Came Christ the tiger 20

In depraved May, dogwood and chestnut, flowering judas,
To be eaten, to be divided, to be drunk
Among whispers; by Mr. Silvero
With caressing hands, at Limoges
Who walked all night in the next room; 25

By Hakagawa, bowing among the Titians;
By Madame de Tornquist, in the dark room
Shifting the candles; Fräulein von Kulp
Who turned in the hall, one hand on the door. Vacant shuttles
30 Weave the wind. I have no ghosts,
An old man in a draughty house
Under a windy knob.

After such knowledge, what forgiveness? Think now
History has many cunning passages, contrived corridors
35 And issues, deceives with whispering ambitions,
Guides us by vanities. Think now
She gives when our attention is distracted
And what she gives, gives with such supple confusions
That the giving famishes the craving. Gives too late
40 What's not believed in, or if still believed,
In memory only, reconsidered passion. Gives too soon
Into weak hands, what's thought can be dispensed with
Till the refusal propagates a fear. Think
Neither fear nor courage saves us. Unnatural vices
45 Are fathered by our heroism. Virtues
Are forced upon us by our impudent crimes.
These tears are shaken from the wrath-bearing tree.

The tiger springs in the new year. Us he devours. Think at last
We have not reached conclusion, when I
50 Stiffen in a rented house. Think at last
I have not made this show purposelessly
And it is not by any concitation
Of the backward devils.
I would meet you upon this honestly.
55 I that was near your heart was removed therefrom
To lose beauty in terror, terror in inquisition.
I have lost my passion: why should I need to keep it

Since what is kept must be adulterated?
I have lost my sight, smell, hearing, taste and touch:
How should I use them for your closer contact? 60

These with a thousand small deliberations
Protract the profit of their chilled delirium,
Excite the membrane, when the sense has cooled,
With pungent sauces, multiply variety
In a wilderness of mirrors. What will the spider do, 65
Suspend its operations, will the weevil
Delay? De Bailhache, Fresca, Mrs. Cammel, whirled
Beyond the circuit of the shuddering Bear
In fractured atoms. Gull against the wind, in the windy straits
Of Belle Isle, or running on the Horn. 70
White feathers in the snow, the Gulf claims,
And an old man driven by the Trades
To a sleepy corner.

Tenants of the house,
Thoughts of a dry brain in a dry season. 75

Burbank with a Baedeker: Bleistein with a Cigar

Tra-la-la-la-la-la-laire—nil nisi divinum stabile est; caetera fumus—the gondola stopped, the old palace was there, how charming its grey and pink—goats and monkeys, with such hair too!—so the countess passed on until she came through the little park, where Niobe presented her with a cabinet, and so departed.

Burbank crossed a little bridge
Descending at a small hotel;
Princess Volupine arrived,
They were together, and he fell.

Defunctive music under sea (5)
Passed seaward with the passing bell
Slowly: the God Hercules
Had left him, that had loved him well.

The horses, under the axletree
Beat up the dawn from Istria (10)
With even feet. Her shuttered barge
Burned on the water all the day.

But this or such was Bleistein's way:
A saggy bending of the knees
And elbows, with the palms turned out, (15)
Chicago Semite Viennese.

A lustreless protrusive eye
Stares from the protozoic slime
At a perspective of Canaletto.
The smoky candle end of time (20)

>

Declines. On the Rialto once.
   The rats are underneath the piles.
The Jew is underneath the lot.
   Money in furs. The boatman smiles,

Princess Volupine extends 25
   A meagre, blue-nailed, phthisic hand
To climb the waterstair. Lights, lights,
   She entertains Sir Ferdinand

Klein. Who clipped the lion's wings
   And flea'd his rump and pared his claws? 30
Thought Burbank, meditating on
   Time's ruins, and the seven laws.

Sweeney Erect

And the trees about me,
Let them be dry and leafless; let the rocks
Groan with continual surges; and behind me
Make all a desolation. Look, look, wenches!

Paint me a cavernous waste shore
  Cast in the unstilled Cyclades,
Paint me the bold anfractuous rocks
  Faced by the snarled and yelping seas.

5 Display me Aeolus above
  Reviewing the insurgent gales
Which tangle Ariadne's hair
  And swell with haste the perjured sails.

Morning stirs the feet and hands
10 (Nausicaa and Polypheme).
Gesture of orang-outang
  Rises from the sheets in steam.

This withered root of knots of hair
  Slitted below and gashed with eyes,
15 This oval O cropped out with teeth:
  The sickle motion from the thighs

Jackknifes upward at the knees
  Then straightens out from heel to hip
Pushing the framework of the bed
20 And clawing at the pillow slip.

Sweeney addressed full length to shave
  Broadbottomed, pink from nape to base,

Knows the female temperament
    And wipes the suds around his face.

(The lengthened shadow of a man 25
    Is history, said Emerson
Who had not seen the silhouette
    Of Sweeney straddled in the sun.)

Tests the razor on his leg
    Waiting until the shriek subsides. 30
The epileptic on the bed
    Curves backward, clutching at her sides.

The ladies of the corridor
    Find themselves involved, disgraced,
Call witness to their principles 35
    And deprecate the lack of taste

Observing that hysteria
    Might easily be misunderstood;
Mrs. Turner intimates
    It does the house no sort of good. 40

But Doris, towelled from the bath,
    Enters padding on broad feet,
Bringing sal volatile
    And a glass of brandy neat.

A Cooking Egg

En l'an trentiesme de mon aage
Que toutes mes hontes j'ay beues . . .

Pipit sate upright in her chair
    Some distance from where I was sitting;
Views of the Oxford Colleges
    Lay on the table, with the knitting.

5 Daguerreotypes and silhouettes,
    Her grandfather and great great aunts,
Supported on the mantelpiece
    An *Invitation to the Dance*.

. . . . .

I shall not want Honour in Heaven
10   For I shall meet Sir Philip Sidney
And have talk with Coriolanus
    And other heroes of that kidney.

I shall not want Capital in Heaven
    For I shall meet Sir Alfred Mond.
15 We two shall lie together, lapt
    In a five per cent. Exchequer Bond.

I shall not want Society in Heaven,
    Lucretia Borgia shall be my Bride;
Her anecdotes will be more amusing
20   Than Pipit's experience could provide.

I shall not want Pipit in Heaven:
    Madame Blavatsky will instruct me

In the Seven Sacred Trances;
   Piccarda de Donati will conduct me.

.   .   .   .   .

But where is the penny world I bought   25
   To eat with Pipit behind the screen?
The red-eyed scavengers are creeping
   From Kentish Town and Golder's Green;

Where are the eagles and the trumpets?

   Buried beneath some snow-deep Alps.   30
Over buttered scones and crumpets
   Weeping, weeping multitudes
Droop in a hundred A.B.C.'s.

Le Directeur

Malheur à la malheureuse Tamise
Qui coule si près du Spectateur.
Le directeur
Conservateur
Du Spectateur (5)
Empeste la brise.
Les actionnaires
Réactionnaires
Du Spectateur
Conservateur (10)
Bras dessus bras dessous
Font des tours
A pas de loup.
Dans un égout
Une petite fille (15)
En guenilles
Camarde
Regarde
Le directeur
Du Spectateur (20)
Conservateur
Et crève d'amour.

Mélange Adultère de Tout

En Amérique, professeur;
En Angleterre, journaliste;
C'est à grands pas et en sueur
Que vous suivrez à peine ma piste.
En Yorkshire, conférencier; 5
A Londres, un peu banquier,
Vous me paierez bien la tête.
C'est à Paris que je me coiffe
Casque noir de jemenfoutiste.
En Allemagne, philosophe 10
Surexcité par Emporheben
Au grand air de Bergsteigleben;
J'erre toujours de-ci de-là
A divers coups de tra là là
De Damas jusqu' à Omaha. 15
Je célébrai mon jour de fête
Dans une oasis d'Afrique
Vêtu d'une peau de girafe.

On montrera mon cénotaphe
Aux côtes brûlantes de Mozambique. 20

Lune de Miel

Ils ont vu les Pays-Bas, ils rentrent à Terre Haute;
Mais une nuit d'été, les voici à Ravenne,
A l'aise entre deux draps, chez deux centaines de punaises;
La sueur aestivale, et une forte odeur de chienne.
5 Ils restent sur le dos écartant les genoux
De quatre jambes molles tout gonflées de morsures.
On relève le drap pour mieux égratigner.
Moins d'une lieue d'ici est Saint Apollinaire
En Classe, basilique connue des amateurs
10 De chapitaux d'acanthe que tournoie le vent.

Ils vont prendre le train de huit heures
Prolonger leurs misères de Padoue à Milan
Où se trouve la Cène, et un restaurant pas cher.
Lui pense aux pourboires, et rédige son bilan.
15 Ils auront vu la Suisse et traversé la France.
Et Saint Apollinaire, raide et ascétique,
Vieille usine désaffectée de Dieu, tient encore
Dans ses pierres écroulantes la forme précise de Byzance.

The Hippopotamus

And when this epistle is read among you, cause that it be read also in the church of the Laodiceans.

The broad-backed hippopotamus
Rests on his belly in the mud;
Although he seems so firm to us
He is merely flesh and blood.

Flesh and blood is weak and frail, 5
Susceptible to nervous shock;
While the True Church can never fail
For it is based upon a rock.

The hippo's feeble steps may err
In compassing material ends, 10
While the True Church need never stir
To gather in its dividends.

The 'potamus can never reach
The mango on the mango-tree;
But fruits of pomegranate and peach 15
Refresh the Church from over sea.

At mating time the hippo's voice
Betrays inflexions hoarse and odd,
But every week we hear rejoice
The Church, at being one with God. 20

The hippopotamus's day
Is passed in sleep; at night he hunts;
God works in a mysterious way—
The Church can sleep and feed at once.

<

25 I saw the 'potamus take wing
Ascending from the damp savannas,
And quiring angels round him sing
The praise of God, in loud hosannas.

Blood of the Lamb shall wash him clean
30 And him shall heavenly arms enfold,
Among the saints he shall be seen
Performing on a harp of gold.

He shall be washed as white as snow,
By all the martyr'd virgins kist,
35 While the True Church remains below
Wrapt in the old miasmal mist.

Dans le Restaurant

Le garçon délabré qui n'a rien à faire
Que de se gratter les doigts et se pencher sur mon épaule:
  'Dans mon pays il fera temps pluvieux,
  Du vent, du grand soleil, et de la pluie;
  C'est ce qu'on appelle le jour de lessive des gueux.' 5
(Bavard, baveux, à la croupe arrondie,
Je te prie, au moins, ne bave pas dans la soupe).
  'Les saules trempés, et des bourgeons sur les ronces—
  C'est là, dans une averse, qu'on s'abrite.
  J'avais sept ans, elle était plus petite. 10
  Elle était toute mouillée, je lui ai donné des primevères.'
Les taches de son gilet montent au chiffre de trente-huit.
  'Je la chatouillais, pour la faire rire.
  J'éprouvais un instant de puissance et de délire.'

Mais alors, vieux lubrique, à cet âge . . . 15
  'Monsieur, le fait est dur.
  Il est venu, nous peloter, un gros chien;
  Moi j'avais peur, je l'ai quittée à mi-chemin.
  C'est dommage.'

Mais alors, tu as ton vautour! 20
Va t'en te décrotter les rides du visage;
Tiens, ma fourchette, décrasse-toi le crâne.
De quel droit payes-tu des expériences comme moi?
Tiens, voilà dix sous, pour la salle-de-bains.

Phlébas, le Phénicien, pendant quinze jours noyé, 25
Oubliait les cris des mouettes et la houle de Cornouaille,
Et les profits et les pertes, et la cargaison d'étain:
Un courant de sous-mer l'emporta très loin,

Le repassant aux étapes de sa vie antérieure.
30 Figurez-vous donc, c'était un sort pénible;
Cependant, ce fut jadis un bel homme, de haute taille.

Whispers of Immortality

Webster was much possessed by death
And saw the skull beneath the skin;
And breastless creatures under ground
Leaned backward with a lipless grin.

Daffodil bulbs instead of balls 5
Stared from the sockets of the eyes!
He knew that thought clings round dead limbs
Tightening its lusts and luxuries.

Donne, I suppose, was such another
Who found no substitute for sense, 10
To seize and clutch and penetrate;
Expert beyond experience,

He knew the anguish of the marrow
The ague of the skeleton;
No contact possible to flesh 15
Allayed the fever of the bone.

. . . . .

Grishkin is nice: her Russian eye
Is underlined for emphasis;
Uncorseted, her friendly bust
Gives promise of pneumatic bliss. 20

The couched Brazilian jaguar
Compels the scampering marmoset
With subtle effluence of cat;
Grishkin has a maisonnette;

<

25 The sleek Brazilian jaguar
Does not in its arboreal gloom
Distil so rank a feline smell
As Grishkin in a drawing-room.

And even the Abstract Entities
30 Circumambulate her charm;
But our lot crawls between dry ribs
To keep our metaphysics warm.

Mr. Eliot's Sunday Morning Service

Look, look, master, here comes two religious caterpillars.
The Jew of Malta

Polyphiloprogenitive
The sapient sutlers of the Lord
Drift across the window-panes.
In the beginning was the Word.

In the beginning was the Word, 5
Superfetation of *τὸ ἕν*,
And at the mensual turn of time
Produced enervate Origen.

A painter of the Umbrian school
Designed upon a gesso ground 10
The nimbus of the Baptized God.
The wilderness is cracked and browned

But through the water pale and thin
Still shine the unoffending feet
And there above the painter set 15
The Father and the Paraclete.

. . . . .

The sable presbyters approach
The avenue of penitence;
The young are red and pustular
Clutching piaculative pence. 20

Under the penitential gates
Sustained by staring Seraphim

Where the souls of the devout
Burn invisible and dim.

25 Along the garden-wall the bees
With hairy bellies pass between
The staminate and pistillate,
Blest office of the epicene.

Sweeney shifts from ham to ham
30 Stirring the water in his bath.
The masters of the subtle schools
Are controversial, polymath.

Sweeney Among the Nightingales

ὤμοι, πέπληγμαι καιρίαν πληγὴν ἔσω.

Apeneck Sweeney spreads his knees
Letting his arms hang down to laugh,
The zebra stripes along his jaw
Swelling to maculate giraffe.

The circles of the stormy moon 5
Slide westward toward the River Plate,
Death and the Raven drift above
And Sweeney guards the hornèd gate.

Gloomy Orion and the Dog
Are veiled; and hushed the shrunken seas; 10
The person in the Spanish cape
Tries to sit on Sweeney's knees

Slips and pulls the table cloth
Overturns a coffee-cup,
Reorganised upon the floor 15
She yawns and draws a stocking up;

The silent man in mocha brown
Sprawls at the window-sill and gapes;
The waiter brings in oranges
Bananas figs and hothouse grapes; 20

The silent vertebrate in brown
Contracts and concentrates, withdraws;
Rachel *née* Rabinovitch
Tears at the grapes with murderous paws;

<

25 She and the lady in the cape
Are suspect, thought to be in league;
Therefore the man with heavy eyes
Declines the gambit, shows fatigue,

Leaves the room and reappears
30 Outside the window, leaning in,
Branches of wistaria
Circumscribe a golden grin;

The host with someone indistinct
Converses at the door apart,
35 The nightingales are singing near
The Convent of the Sacred Heart,

And sang within the bloody wood
When Agamemnon cried aloud
And let their liquid siftings fall
40 To stain the stiff dishonoured shroud.

The Waste Land

1922

'Nam Sibyllam quidem Cumis ego ipse oculis meis vidi in ampulla pendere, et cum illi pueri dicerent: *Σίβυλλα τί θέλεις*; respondebat illa: *ἀποθανεῖν θέλω*.'

For Ezra Pound
il miglior fabbro.

I. *The Burial of the Dead*

April is the cruellest month, breeding
Lilacs out of the dead land, mixing
Memory and desire, stirring
Dull roots with spring rain.
Winter kept us warm, covering 5
Earth in forgetful snow, feeding
A little life with dried tubers.
Summer surprised us, coming over the Starnbergersee
With a shower of rain; we stopped in the colonnade,
And went on in sunlight, into the Hofgarten, 10
And drank coffee, and talked for an hour.
Bin gar keine Russin, stamm' aus Litauen, echt deutsch.
And when we were children, staying at the archduke's,
My cousin's, he took me out on a sled,
And I was frightened. He said, Marie, 15
Marie, hold on tight. And down we went.
In the mountains, there you feel free.
I read, much of the night, and go south in the winter.

What are the roots that clutch, what branches grow
Out of this stony rubbish? Son of man, 20
You cannot say, or guess, for you know only
A heap of broken images, where the sun beats,
And the dead tree gives no shelter, the cricket no relief,
And the dry stone no sound of water. Only
There is shadow under this red rock, 25
(Come in under the shadow of this red rock),
And I will show you something different from either
Your shadow at morning striding behind you
Or your shadow at evening rising to meet you;
I will show you fear in a handful of dust. 30

<

Frisch weht der Wind
Der Heimat zu,
Mein Irisch Kind,
Wo weilest du?

35 'You gave me hyacinths first a year ago;
'They called me the hyacinth girl.'
—Yet when we came back, late, from the hyacinth garden,
Your arms full, and your hair wet, I could not
Speak, and my eyes failed, I was neither
40 Living nor dead, and I knew nothing,
Looking into the heart of light, the silence.

Oed' und leer das Meer.

Madame Sosostris, famous clairvoyante,
Had a bad cold, nevertheless
45 Is known to be the wisest woman in Europe,
With a wicked pack of cards. Here, said she,
Is your card, the drowned Phoenician Sailor,
(Those are pearls that were his eyes. Look!)
Here is Belladonna, the Lady of the Rocks,
50 The lady of situations.
Here is the man with three staves, and here the Wheel,
And here is the one-eyed merchant, and this card,
Which is blank, is something he carries on his back,
Which I am forbidden to see. I do not find
55 The Hanged Man. Fear death by water.
I see crowds of people, walking round in a ring.
Thank you. If you see dear Mrs. Equitone,
Tell her I bring the horoscope myself:
One must be so careful these days.

60 Unreal City,
Under the brown fog of a winter dawn,

A crowd flowed over London Bridge, so many,
I had not thought death had undone so many.
Sighs, short and infrequent, were exhaled,
And each man fixed his eyes before his feet. 65
Flowed up the hill and down King William Street,
To where Saint Mary Woolnoth kept the hours
With a dead sound on the final stroke of nine.
There I saw one I knew, and stopped him, crying: 'Stetson!
'You who were with me in the ships at Mylae! 70
'That corpse you planted last year in your garden,
'Has it begun to sprout? Will it bloom this year?
'Or has the sudden frost disturbed its bed?
'O keep the Dog far hence, that's friend to men,
'Or with his nails he'll dig it up again! 75
'You! hypocrite lecteur!—mon semblable,—mon frère!'

II. *A Game of Chess*

The Chair she sat in, like a burnished throne,
Glowed on the marble, where the glass
Held up by standards wrought with fruited vines
80 From which a golden Cupidon peeped out
(Another hid his eyes behind his wing)
Doubled the flames of sevenbranched candelabra
Reflecting light upon the table as
The glitter of her jewels rose to meet it,
85 From satin cases poured in rich profusion.
In vials of ivory and coloured glass
Unstoppered, lurked her strange synthetic perfumes,
Unguent, powdered, or liquid—troubled, confused
And drowned the sense in odours; stirred by the air
90 That freshened from the window, these ascended
In fattening the prolonged candle-flames,
Flung their smoke into the laquearia,
Stirring the pattern on the coffered ceiling.
Huge sea-wood fed with copper
95 Burned green and orange, framed by the coloured stone,
In which sad light a carvèd dolphin swam.
Above the antique mantel was displayed
As though a window gave upon the sylvan scene
The change of Philomel, by the barbarous king
100 So rudely forced; yet there the nightingale
Filled all the desert with inviolable voice
And still she cried, and still the world pursues,
'Jug Jug' to dirty ears.
And other withered stumps of time
105 Were told upon the walls; staring forms
Leaned out, leaning, hushing the room enclosed.

Footsteps shuffled on the stair.
Under the firelight, under the brush, her hair
Spread out in fiery points
Glowed into words, then would be savagely still. 110

'My nerves are bad to-night. Yes, bad. Stay with me.
'Speak to me. Why do you never speak. Speak.
'What are you thinking of? What thinking? What?
'I never know what you are thinking. Think.'

I think we are in rats' alley 115
Where the dead men lost their bones.

'What is that noise?'
The wind under the door.
'What is that noise now? What is the wind doing?'
Nothing again nothing. 120
'Do
'You know nothing? Do you see nothing? Do you remember
'Nothing?'
I remember
Those are pearls that were his eyes. 125
'Are you alive, or not? Is there nothing in your head?'
But
O O O O that Shakespeherian Rag—
It's so elegant
So intelligent 130

'What shall I do now? What shall I do?
'I shall rush out as I am, and walk the street
'With my hair down, so. What shall we do tomorrow?
'What shall we ever do?'
The hot water at ten. 135
And if it rains, a closed car at four.
And we shall play a game of chess,

137a (The ivory men make company between us)
Pressing lidless eyes and waiting for a knock upon the door.

When Lil's husband got demobbed, I said—
140 I didn't mince my words, I said to her myself,
HURRY UP PLEASE ITS TIME
Now Albert's coming back, make yourself a bit smart.
He'll want to know what you done with that money he gave you
To get yourself some teeth. He did, I was there.
145 You have them all out, Lil, and get a nice set,
He said, I swear, I can't bear to look at you.
And no more can't I, I said, and think of poor Albert,
He's been in the army four years, he wants a good time,
And if you don't give it him, there's others will, I said.
150 Oh is there, she said. Something o' that, I said.
Then I'll know who to thank, she said, and give me a straight look.
HURRY UP PLEASE ITS TIME
If you don't like it you can get on with it, I said.
Others can pick and choose if you can't.
155 But if Albert makes off, it won't be for lack of telling.
You ought to be ashamed, I said, to look so antique.
(And her only thirty-one.)
I can't help it, she said, pulling a long face,
It's them pills I took, to bring it off, she said.
160 (She's had five already, and nearly died of young George.)
The chemist said it would be all right, but I've never been the
same.
You *are* a proper fool, I said.
Well, if Albert won't leave you alone, there it is, I said,
What you get married for if you don't want children?
165 HURRY UP PLEASE ITS TIME
Well, that Sunday Albert was home, they had a hot gammon,
And they asked me in to dinner, to get the beauty of it hot—

HURRY UP PLEASE ITS TIME
HURRY UP PLEASE ITS TIME
Goonight Bill. Goonight Lou. Goonight May. Goonight. 170
Ta ta. Goonight. Goonight.
Good night, ladies, good night, sweet ladies, good night,
good night.

III. *The Fire Sermon*

The river's tent is broken; the last fingers of leaf
Clutch and sink into the wet bank. The wind
175 Crosses the brown land, unheard. The nymphs are departed.
Sweet Thames, run softly, till I end my song.
The river bears no empty bottles, sandwich papers,
Silk handkerchiefs, cardboard boxes, cigarette ends
Or other testimony of summer nights. The nymphs are departed.
180 And their friends, the loitering heirs of City directors;
Departed, have left no addresses.
By the waters of Leman I sat down and wept . . .
Sweet Thames, run softly till I end my song,
Sweet Thames, run softly, for I speak not loud or long.
185 But at my back in a cold blast I hear
The rattle of the bones, and chuckle spread from ear to ear.

A rat crept softly through the vegetation
Dragging its slimy belly on the bank
While I was fishing in the dull canal
190 On a winter evening round behind the gashouse
Musing upon the king my brother's wreck
And on the king my father's death before him.
White bodies naked on the low damp ground
And bones cast in a little low dry garret,
195 Rattled by the rat's foot only, year to year.
But at my back from time to time I hear
The sound of horns and motors, which shall bring
Sweeney to Mrs. Porter in the spring.
O the moon shone bright on Mrs. Porter
200 And on her daughter
They wash their feet in soda water
Et O ces voix d'enfants, chantant dans la coupole!

Twit twit twit
Jug jug jug jug jug jug
So rudely forc'd. 205
Tereu

Unreal City
Under the brown fog of a winter noon
Mr. Eugenides, the Smyrna merchant
Unshaven, with a pocket full of currants 210
C.i.f. London: documents at sight,
Asked me in demotic French
To luncheon at the Cannon Street Hotel
Followed by a weekend at the Metropole.

At the violet hour, when the eyes and back 215
Turn upward from the desk, when the human engine waits
Like a taxi throbbing waiting,
I Tiresias, though blind, throbbing between two lives,
Old man with wrinkled female breasts, can see
At the violet hour, the evening hour that strives 220
Homeward, and brings the sailor home from sea,
The typist home at teatime, clears her breakfast, lights
Her stove, and lays out food in tins.
Out of the window perilously spread
Her drying combinations touched by the sun's last rays, 225
On the divan are piled (at night her bed)
Stockings, slippers, camisoles, and stays.
I Tiresias, old man with wrinkled dugs
Perceived the scene, and foretold the rest—
I too awaited the expected guest. 230
He, the young man carbuncular, arrives,
A small house agent's clerk, with one bold stare,
One of the low on whom assurance sits
As a silk hat on a Bradford millionaire.

235 The time is now propitious, as he guesses,
The meal is ended, she is bored and tired,
Endeavours to engage her in caresses
Which still are unreproved, if undesired.
Flushed and decided, he assaults at once;
240 Exploring hands encounter no defence;
His vanity requires no response,
And makes a welcome of indifference.
(And I Tiresias have foresuffered all
Enacted on this same divan or bed;
245 I who have sat by Thebes below the wall
And walked among the lowest of the dead.)
Bestows one final patronising kiss,
And gropes his way, finding the stairs unlit . . .

She turns and looks a moment in the glass,
250 Hardly aware of her departed lover;
Her brain allows one half-formed thought to pass:
'Well now that's done: and I'm glad it's over.'
When lovely woman stoops to folly and
Paces about her room again, alone,
255 She smoothes her hair with automatic hand,
And puts a record on the gramophone.

'This music crept by me upon the waters'
And along the Strand, up Queen Victoria Street.
O City city, I can sometimes hear
260 Beside a public bar in Lower Thames Street,
The pleasant whining of a mandoline
And a clatter and a chatter from within
Where fishmen lounge at noon: where the walls
Of Magnus Martyr hold
265 Inexplicable splendour of Ionian white and gold.

>

The river sweats
Oil and tar
The barges drift
With the turning tide
Red sails 270
Wide
To leeward, swing on the heavy spar.
The barges wash
Drifting logs
Down Greenwich reach 275
Past the Isle of Dogs.
Weialala leia
Wallala leialala

Elizabeth and Leicester
Beating oars 280
The stern was formed
A gilded shell
Red and gold
The brisk swell
Rippled both shores 285
Southwest wind
Carried down stream
The peal of bells
White towers
Weialala leia 290
Wallala leialala

'Trams and dusty trees.
Highbury bore me. Richmond and Kew
Undid me. By Richmond I raised my knees
Supine on the floor of a narrow canoe.' 295

<

'My feet are at Moorgate, and my heart
Under my feet. After the event
He wept. He promised "a new start."
I made no comment. What should I resent?'

300 'On Margate Sands.
I can connect
Nothing with nothing.
The broken fingernails of dirty hands.
My people humble people who expect
305 Nothing.'
la la

To Carthage then I came

Burning burning burning burning
O Lord Thou pluckest me out
310 O Lord Thou pluckest

burning

IV. *Death by Water*

Phlebas the Phoenician, a fortnight dead,
Forgot the cry of gulls, and the deep sea swell
And the profit and loss.
                    A current under sea   315
Picked his bones in whispers. As he rose and fell
He passed the stages of his age and youth
Entering the whirlpool.
                    Gentile or Jew
O you who turn the wheel and look to windward,   320
Consider Phlebas, who was once handsome and tall as you.

V. *What the Thunder said*

After the torchlight red on sweaty faces
After the frosty silence in the gardens
After the agony in stony places
325 The shouting and the crying
Prison and palace and reverberation
Of thunder of spring over distant mountains
He who was living is now dead
We who were living are now dying
330 With a little patience

Here is no water but only rock
Rock and no water and the sandy road
The road winding above among the mountains
Which are mountains of rock without water
335 If there were water we should stop and drink
Amongst the rock one cannot stop or think
Sweat is dry and feet are in the sand
If there were only water amongst the rock
Dead mountain mouth of carious teeth that cannot spit
340 Here one can neither stand nor lie nor sit
There is not even silence in the mountains
But dry sterile thunder without rain
There is not even solitude in the mountains
But red sullen faces sneer and snarl
From doors of mudcracked houses
345 If there were water
And no rock
If there were rock
And also water
And water
350 A spring

A pool among the rock
If there were the sound of water only
Not the cicada
And dry grass singing
But sound of water over a rock 355
Where the hermit-thrush sings in the pine trees
Drip drop drip drop drop drop drop
But there is no water

Who is the third who walks always beside you?
When I count, there are only you and I together 360
But when I look ahead up the white road
There is always another one walking beside you
Gliding wrapt in a brown mantle, hooded
I do not know whether a man or a woman
—But who is that on the other side of you? 365

What is that sound high in the air
Murmur of maternal lamentation
Who are those hooded hordes swarming
Over endless plains, stumbling in cracked earth
Ringed by the flat horizon only 370
What is the city over the mountains
Cracks and reforms and bursts in the violet air
Falling towers
Jerusalem Athens Alexandria
Vienna London 375
Unreal

A woman drew her long black hair out tight
And fiddled whisper music on those strings
And bats with baby faces in the violet light
Whistled, and beat their wings 380
And crawled head downward down a blackened wall
And upside down in air were towers

Tolling reminiscent bells, that kept the hours
And voices singing out of empty cisterns and exhausted wells.

385 In this decayed hole among the mountains
In the faint moonlight, the grass is singing
Over the tumbled graves, about the chapel
There is the empty chapel, only the wind's home.
It has no windows, and the door swings,
390 Dry bones can harm no one.
Only a cock stood on the rooftree
Co co   rico   co co   rico
In a flash of lightning. Then a damp gust
Bringing rain

395 Ganga was sunken, and the limp leaves
Waited for rain, while the black clouds
Gathered far distant, over Himavant.
The jungle crouched, humped in silence.
Then spoke the thunder
400 DA
Datta: what have we given?
My friend, blood shaking my heart
The awful daring of a moment's surrender
Which an age of prudence can never retract
405 By this, and this only, we have existed
Which is not to be found in our obituaries
Or in memories draped by the beneficent spider
Or under seals broken by the lean solicitor
In our empty rooms
410 DA
Dayadhvam: I have heard the key
Turn in the door once and turn once only
We think of the key, each in his prison
Thinking of the key, each confirms a prison

Only at nightfall, aethereal rumours 415
Revive for a moment a broken Coriolanus
DA
Damyata: The boat responded
Gaily, to the hand expert with sail and oar
The sea was calm, your heart would have responded 420
Gaily, when invited, beating obedient
To controlling hands

I sat upon the shore
Fishing, with the arid plain behind me
Shall I at least set my lands in order? 425

London Bridge is falling down falling down falling down

Poi s'ascose nel foco che gli affina
Quando fiam uti chelidon—O swallow swallow
Le Prince d'Aquitaine à la tour abolie
These fragments I have shored against my ruins 430
Why then Ile fit you. Hieronymo's mad againe.
Datta. Dayadhvam. Damyata.

Shantih shantih shantih

Notes on the Waste Land

Not only the title, but the plan and a good deal of the incidental symbolism of the poem were suggested by Miss Jessie L. Weston's book on the Grail legend: *From Ritual to Romance* (Cambridge). Indeed, so deeply am I indebted, Miss Weston's book will elucidate the difficulties of the poem much better than my notes can do; and I recommend it (apart from the great interest of the book itself) to any who think such elucidation of the poem worth the trouble. To another work of anthropology I am indebted in general, one which has influenced our generation profoundly; I mean *The Golden Bough*; I have used especially the two volumes *Adonis, Attis, Osiris*. Anyone who is acquainted with these works will immediately recognise in the poem certain references to vegetation ceremonies.

I. THE BURIAL OF THE DEAD

Line 20. Cf. Ezekiel II, i.

23. Cf. Ecclesiastes XII, v.

31. V. *Tristan und Isolde*, I, verses 5–8.

42. Id. III, verse 24.

46. I am not familiar with the exact constitution of the Tarot pack of cards, from which I have obviously departed to suit my own convenience. The Hanged Man, a member of the traditional pack, fits my purpose in two ways: because he is associated in my mind with the Hanged God of Frazer, and because I associate him with the hooded figure in the passage of the disciples to Emmaus in Part V. The Phoenician Sailor and the Merchant appear later; also the 'crowds of people', and Death by Water is executed in Part IV. The Man with Three Staves (an authentic member of the Tarot pack) I associate, quite arbitrarily, with the Fisher King himself.

60. Cf. Baudelaire:

'Fourmillante cité, cité pleine de rêves,
'Où le spectre en plein jour raccroche le passant.'

63. Cf. *Inferno*, III, 55-57:

sì lunga tratta
di gente, ch'io non avrei mai creduto,
che morte tanta n'avesse disfatta.

64. Cf. *Inferno*, IV, 25-27:

Quivi, secondo che per ascoltare,
non avea pianto, ma' che di sospiri,
che l'aura eterna facevan tremare.

68. A phenomenon which I have often noticed.

74. Cf. the Dirge in Webster's *White Devil*.

76. V. Baudelaire, Preface to *Fleurs du Mal*.

II. A GAME OF CHESS

77. Cf. *Antony and Cleopatra*, II, ii, 190.

92. Laquearia. V. *Aeneid*, I, 726:

dependent lychni laquearibus aureis
incensi, et noctem flammis funalia vincunt.

98. Sylvan scene. V. Milton, *Paradise Lost*, IV, 140.

99. V. Ovid, *Metamorphoses*, VI, Philomela.

100. Cf. Part III, 204.

115. Cf. Part III, 195.

118. Cf. Webster: 'Is the wind in that door still?'

125. Cf. Part I, 39, 48.

137. Cf. the game of chess in Middleton's *Women beware Women*.

III. THE FIRE SERMON

176. V. Spenser, *Prothalamion*.

192. Cf. *The Tempest*, I, ii.

196. Cf. Marvell, *To His Coy Mistress*.

197. Cf. Day, *Parliament of Bees*:

'When of the sudden, listening, you shall hear,
'A noise of horns and hunting, which shall bring
'Actaeon to Diana in the spring,
'Where all shall see her naked skin . . .'

199. I do not know the origin of the ballad from which these lines are taken: it was reported to me from Sydney, Australia.

202. V. Verlaine, *Parsifal.*

210. The currants were quoted at a price 'cost insurance and freight to London'; and the Bill of Lading, etc., were to be handed to the buyer upon payment of the sight draft.

218. Tiresias, although a mere spectator and not indeed a 'character', is yet the most important personage in the poem, uniting all the rest. Just as the one-eyed merchant, seller of currants, melts into the Phoenician Sailor, and the latter is not wholly distinct from Ferdinand Prince of Naples, so all the women are one woman, and the two sexes meet in Tiresias. What Tiresias *sees*, in fact, is the substance of the poem. The whole passage from Ovid is of great anthropological interest:

. . . Cum Iunone iocos et 'maior vestra profecto est
Quam quae contingit maribus', dixisse, 'voluptas.'
Illa negat; placuit quae sit sententia docti
Quaerere Tiresiae: venus huic erat utraque nota.
Nam duo magnorum viridi coeuntia silva
Corpora serpentum baculi violaverat ictu
Deque viro factus, mirabile, femina septem
Egerat autumnos; octavo rursus eosdem
Vidit et 'est vestrae si tanta potentia plagae',
Dixit 'ut auctoris sortem in contraria mutet,
Nunc quoque vos feriam!' percussis anguibus isdem
Forma prior rediit genetivaque venit imago.
Arbiter hic igitur sumptus de lite iocosa
Dicta Iovis firmat; gravius Saturnia iusto
Nec pro materia fertur doluisse suique
Iudicis aeterna damnavit lumina nocte,

At pater omnipotens (neque enim licet inrita cuiquam
Facta dei fecisse deo) pro lumine adempto
Scire futura dedit poenamque levavit honore.

221. This may not appear as exact as Sappho's lines, but I had in mind the 'longshore' or 'dory' fisherman, who returns at nightfall.

253. V. Goldsmith, the song in *The Vicar of Wakefield.*

257. V. *The Tempest*, as above.

264. The interior of St. Magnus Martyr is to my mind one of the finest among Wren's interiors. See *The Proposed Demolition of Nineteen City Churches* (P. S. King & Son, Ltd.).

266. The Song of the (three) Thames-daughters begins here. From line 292 to 305 inclusive they speak in turn. V. *Götterdämmerung*, III, i: the Rhine-daughters.

279. V. Froude, *Elizabeth*, Vol. I, ch. iv, letter of De Quadra to Philip of Spain:

'In the afternoon we were in a barge, watching the games on the river. (The Queen) was alone with Lord Robert and myself on the poop, when they began to talk nonsense, and went so far that Lord Robert at last said, as I was on the spot there was no reason why they should not be married if the queen pleased.'

293. Cf. *Purgatorio*, V, 133:

'Ricorditi di me, che son la Pia;
'Siena mi fe', disfecemi Maremma.'

307. V. St. Augustine's *Confessions*: 'to Carthage then I came, where a cauldron of unholy loves sang all about mine ears.'

308. The complete text of the Buddha's Fire Sermon (which corresponds in importance to the Sermon on the Mount) from which these words are taken, will be found translated in the late Henry Clarke Warren's *Buddhism in Translations* (Harvard Oriental Series). Mr. Warren was one of the great pioneers of Buddhist studies in the Occident.

309. From St. Augustine's *Confessions* again. The collocation of these two representatives of eastern and western asceticism, as the culmination of this part of the poem, is not an accident.

V. WHAT THE THUNDER SAID

In the first part of Part V three themes are employed: the journey to Emmaus, the approach to the Chapel Perilous (see Miss Weston's book) and the present decay of eastern Europe.

356. This is *Turdus aonalaschkae pallasii*, the hermit-thrush which I have heard in Quebec Province. Chapman says (*Handbook of Birds of Eastern North America*) 'it is most at home in secluded woodland and thickety retreats . . . Its notes are not remarkable for variety or volume, but in purity and sweetness of tone and exquisite modulation they are unequalled.' Its 'water-dripping song' is justly celebrated.

359. The following lines were stimulated by the account of one of the Antarctic expeditions (I forget which, but I think one of Shackleton's): it was recorded that the party of explorers, at the extremity of their strength, had the constant delusion that there was *one more member* than could actually be counted.

366–76. Cf. Hermann Hesse, *Blick ins Chaos*: 'Schon ist halb Europa, schon ist zumindest der halbe Osten Europas auf dem Wege zum Chaos, fährt betrunken im heiligen Wahn am Abgrund entlang und singt dazu, singt betrunken und hymnisch wie Dmitri Karamasoff sang. Ueber diese Lieder lacht der Bürger beleidigt, der Heilige und Seher hört sie mit Tränen.'

401. 'Datta, dayadhvam, damyata' (Give, sympathise, control). The fable of the meaning of the Thunder is found in the *Brihadaranyaka–Upanishad*, 5, 2. A translation is found in Deussen's *Sechzig Upanishads des Veda*, p. 489.

407. Cf. Webster, *The White Devil*, V, vi:

'. . . they'll remarry
Ere the worm pierce your winding-sheet, ere the spider
Make a thin curtain for your epitaphs.'

411. Cf. *Inferno*, XXXIII, 46:

'ed io sentii chiavar l'uscio di sotto
all'orribile torre.'

Also F. H. Bradley, *Appearance and Reality*, p. 306.

'My external sensations are no less private to myself than are my thoughts or my feelings. In either case my experience falls within my own circle, a circle closed on the outside; and, with all its elements alike, every sphere is opaque to the others which surround it . . . In brief, regarded as an existence which appears in a soul, the whole world for each is peculiar and private to that soul.'

424. V. Weston: *From Ritual to Romance*; chapter on the Fisher King.

427. V. *Purgatorio*, XXVI, 148.

> 'Ara vos prec, per aquella valor
> 'que vos guida al som de l'escalina,
> 'sovegna vos a temps de ma dolor.'
> Poi s'ascose nel foco che gli affina.

428. V. *Pervigilium Veneris*. Cf. Philomela in Parts II and III.

429. V. Gérard de Nerval, Sonnet *El Desdichado*.

431. V. Kyd's *Spanish Tragedy*.

433. Shantih. Repeated as here, a formal ending to an Upanishad. 'The Peace which passeth understanding' is our equivalent to this word.

The Hollow Men

1925

Mistah Kurtz — he dead.

The Hollow Men

A penny for the Old Guy

I

We are the hollow men
We are the stuffed men
Leaning together
Headpiece filled with straw. Alas!
Our dried voices, when 5
We whisper together
Are quiet and meaningless
As wind in dry grass
Or rats' feet over broken glass
In our dry cellar 10

Shape without form, shade without colour,
Paralysed force, gesture without motion;

Those who have crossed
With direct eyes, to death's other Kingdom
Remember us—if at all—not as lost 15
Violent souls, but only
As the hollow men
The stuffed men.

II

Eyes I dare not meet in dreams
In death's dream kingdom
These do not appear:
There, the eyes are
Sunlight on a broken column 5
There, is a tree swinging

And voices are
In the wind's singing
More distant and more solemn
10 Than a fading star.

Let me be no nearer
In death's dream kingdom
Let me also wear
Such deliberate disguises
15 Rat's coat, crowskin, crossed staves
In a field
Behaving as the wind behaves
No nearer—

Not that final meeting
20 In the twilight kingdom
With eyes I dare not meet in dreams.

III

This is the dead land
This is cactus land
Here the stone images
Are raised, here they receive
5 The supplication of a dead man's hand
Under the twinkle of a fading star.

Is it like this
In death's other kingdom
Waking alone
10 At the hour when we are
Trembling with tenderness
Lips that would kiss
Form prayers to broken stone.

IV

The eyes are not here
There are no eyes here
In this valley of dying stars
In this hollow valley
This broken jaw of our lost kingdoms   5

In this last of meeting places
We grope together
And avoid speech
Gathered on this beach of the tumid river

Sightless, unless   10
The eyes reappear
As the perpetual star
Multifoliate rose
Of death's twilight kingdom

The hope only   15
Of empty men.

V

Here we go round the prickly pear
Prickly pear prickly pear
Here we go round the prickly pear
At five o'clock in the morning.

Between the idea   5
And the reality
Between the motion
And the act
Falls the Shadow
For Thine is the Kingdom   10

<

Between the conception
And the creation
Between the emotion
And the response
15 Falls the Shadow
Life is very long

Between the desire
And the spasm
Between the potency
20 And the existence
Between the essence
And the descent
Falls the Shadow
For Thine is the Kingdom

25 For Thine is
Life is
For Thine is the

This is the way the world ends
This is the way the world ends
30 *This is the way the world ends*
Not with a bang but a whimper.

Ash-Wednesday

1930

I

Because I do not hope to turn again
Because I do not hope
Because I do not hope to turn
Desiring this man's gift and that man's scope
I no longer strive to strive towards such things 5
(Why should the agèd eagle stretch its wings?)
Why should I mourn
The vanished power of the usual reign?

Because I do not hope to know again
The infirm glory of the positive hour 10
Because I do not think
Because I know I shall not know
The one veritable transitory power
Because I cannot drink
There, where trees flower, and springs flow, for there is
nothing again 15

Because I know that time is always time
And place is always and only place
And what is actual is actual only for one time
And only for one place
I rejoice that things are as they are and 20
I renounce the blessèd face
And renounce the voice
Because I cannot hope to turn again
Consequently I rejoice, having to construct something
Upon which to rejoice 25

And pray to God to have mercy upon us
And I pray that I may forget
These matters that with myself I too much discuss

Too much explain
30 Because I do not hope to turn again
Let these words answer
For what is done, not to be done again
May the judgement not be too heavy upon us

Because these wings are no longer wings to fly
35 But merely vans to beat the air
The air which is now thoroughly small and dry
Smaller and dryer than the will
Teach us to care and not to care
Teach us to sit still.

40 Pray for us sinners now and at the hour of our death
Pray for us now and at the hour of our death.

II

Lady, three white leopards sat under a juniper-tree
In the cool of the day, having fed to satiety
On my legs my heart my liver and that which had been contained
In the hollow round of my skull. And God said
Shall these bones live? shall these 5
Bones live? And that which had been contained
In the bones (which were already dry) said chirping:
Because of the goodness of this Lady
And because of her loveliness, and because
She honours the Virgin in meditation, 10
We shine with brightness. And I who am here dissembled
Proffer my deeds to oblivion, and my love
To the posterity of the desert and the fruit of the gourd.
It is this which recovers
My guts the strings of my eyes and the indigestible portions 15
Which the leopards reject. The Lady is withdrawn
In a white gown, to contemplation, in a white gown.
Let the whiteness of bones atone to forgetfulness.
There is no life in them. As I am forgotten
And would be forgotten, so I would forget 20
Thus devoted, concentrated in purpose. And God said
Prophesy to the wind, to the wind only for only
The wind will listen. And the bones sang chirping
With the burden of the grasshopper, saying

Lady of silences 25
Calm and distressed
Torn and most whole
Rose of memory
Rose of forgetfulness

30 Exhausted and life-giving
Worried reposeful
The single Rose
Is now the Garden
Where all loves end
35 Terminate torment
Of love unsatisfied
The greater torment
Of love satisfied
End of the endless
40 Journey to no end
Conclusion of all that
Is inconclusible
Speech without word and
Word of no speech
45 Grace to the Mother
For the Garden
Where all love ends.

Under a juniper-tree the bones sang, scattered and shining
We are glad to be scattered, we did little good to each other,
50 Under a tree in the cool of the day, with the blessing of sand,
Forgetting themselves and each other, united
In the quiet of the desert. This is the land which ye
Shall divide by lot. And neither division nor unity
Matters. This is the land. We have our inheritance.

III

At the first turning of the second stair
I turned and saw below
The same shape twisted on the banister
Under the vapour in the fetid air
Struggling with the devil of the stairs who wears 5
The deceitful face of hope and of despair.

At the second turning of the second stair
I left them twisting, turning below;
There were no more faces and the stair was dark,
Damp, jaggèd, like an old man's mouth drivelling, beyond repair, 10
Or the toothed gullet of an agèd shark.

At the first turning of the third stair
Was a slotted window bellied like the fig's fruit
And beyond the hawthorn blossom and a pasture scene
The broadbacked figure drest in blue and green 15
Enchanted the maytime with an antique flute.
Blown hair is sweet, brown hair over the mouth blown,
Lilac and brown hair;
Distraction, music of the flute, stops and steps of the mind over
the third stair,
Fading, fading; strength beyond hope and despair 20
Climbing the third stair.

Lord, I am not worthy
Lord, I am not worthy

but speak the word only.

IV

Who walked between the violet and the violet
Who walked between
The various ranks of varied green
Going in white and blue, in Mary's colour,
5 Talking of trivial things
In ignorance and in knowledge of eternal dolour
Who moved among the others as they walked,
Who then made strong the fountains and made fresh
the springs

Made cool the dry rock and made firm the sand
10 In blue of larkspur, blue of Mary's colour,
Sovegna vos

Here are the years that walk between, bearing
Away the fiddles and the flutes, restoring
One who moves in the time between sleep and waking,
wearing

15 White light folded, sheathed about her, folded.
The new years walk, restoring
Through a bright cloud of tears, the years, restoring
With a new verse the ancient rhyme. Redeem
The time. Redeem
20 The unread vision in the higher dream
While jewelled unicorns draw by the gilded hearse.

The silent sister veiled in white and blue
Between the yews, behind the garden god,
Whose flute is breathless, bent her head and signed but
spoke no word

>

But the fountain sprang up and the bird sang down 25
Redeem the time, redeem the dream
The token of the word unheard, unspoken

Till the wind shake a thousand whispers from the yew

And after this our exile

V

If the lost word is lost, if the spent word is spent
If the unheard, unspoken
Word is unspoken, unheard;
Still is the unspoken word, the Word unheard,
5 The Word without a word, the Word within
The world and for the world;
And the light shone in darkness and
Against the Word the unstilled world still whirled
About the centre of the silent Word.

10 O my people, what have I done unto thee.

Where shall the word be found, where will the word
Resound? Not here, there is not enough silence
Not on the sea or on the islands, not
On the mainland, in the desert or the rain land,
15 For those who walk in darkness
Both in the day time and in the night time
The right time and the right place are not here
No place of grace for those who avoid the face
No time to rejoice for those who walk among noise and deny
the voice

20 Will the veiled sister pray for
Those who walk in darkness, who chose thee and oppose thee,
Those who are torn on the horn between season and season,
time and time, between
Hour and hour, word and word, power and power, those
who wait
In darkness? Will the veiled sister pray
25 For children at the gate

Who will not go away and cannot pray:
Pray for those who chose and oppose

O my people, what have I done unto thee.

Will the veiled sister between the slender
Yew trees pray for those who offend her 30
And are terrified and cannot surrender
And affirm before the world and deny between the rocks
In the last desert between the last blue rocks
The desert in the garden the garden in the desert
Of drouth, spitting from the mouth the withered apple-seed. 35

O my people.

VI

Although I do not hope to turn again
Although I do not hope
Although I do not hope to turn

Wavering between the profit and the loss
5 In this brief transit where the dreams cross
The dreamcrossed twilight between birth and dying
(Bless me father) though I do not wish to wish these things
From the wide window towards the granite shore
The white sails still fly seaward, seaward flying
10 Unbroken wings

And the lost heart stiffens and rejoices
In the lost lilac and the lost sea voices
And the weak spirit quickens to rebel
For the bent golden-rod and the lost sea smell
15 Quickens to recover
The cry of quail and the whirling plover
And the blind eye creates
The empty forms between the ivory gates
And smell renews the salt savour of the sandy earth

20 This is the time of tension between dying and birth
The place of solitude where three dreams cross
Between blue rocks

But when the voices shaken from the yew-tree drift away
Let the other yew be shaken and reply.

Blessèd sister, holy mother, spirit of the fountain, spirit of
25 the garden,
Suffer us not to mock ourselves with falsehood

Teach us to care and not to care
Teach us to sit still
Even among these rocks,
Our peace in His will 30
And even among these rocks
Sister, mother
And spirit of the river, spirit of the sea,
Suffer me not to be separated

And let my cry come unto Thee. 35

Ariel Poems

Journey of the Magi

'A cold coming we had of it,
Just the worst time of the year
For a journey, and such a long journey:
The ways deep and the weather sharp,
The very dead of winter.' 5
And the camels galled, sore-footed, refractory,
Lying down in the melting snow.
There were times we regretted
The summer palaces on slopes, the terraces,
And the silken girls bringing sherbet. 10
Then the camel men cursing and grumbling
And running away, and wanting their liquor and women,
And the night-fires going out, and the lack of shelters,
And the cities hostile and the towns unfriendly
And the villages dirty and charging high prices: 15
A hard time we had of it.
At the end we preferred to travel all night,
Sleeping in snatches,
With the voices singing in our ears, saying
That this was all folly. 20

Then at dawn we came down to a temperate valley,
Wet, below the snow line, smelling of vegetation,
With a running stream and a water-mill beating the darkness,
And three trees on the low sky.
And an old white horse galloped away in the meadow. 25
Then we came to a tavern with vine-leaves over the lintel,
Six hands at an open door dicing for pieces of silver,
And feet kicking the empty wine-skins.
But there was no information, and so we continued

30 And arrived at evening, not a moment too soon
Finding the place; it was (you may say) satisfactory.

All this was a long time ago, I remember,
And I would do it again, but set down
This set down
35 This: were we led all that way for
Birth or Death? There was a Birth, certainly,
We had evidence and no doubt. I had seen birth and death,
But had thought they were different; this Birth was
Hard and bitter agony for us, like Death, our death.
40 We returned to our places, these Kingdoms,
But no longer at ease here, in the old dispensation,
With an alien people clutching their gods.
I should be glad of another death.

A Song for Simeon

Lord, the Roman hyacinths are blooming in bowls and
The winter sun creeps by the snow hills;
The stubborn season has made stand.
My life is light, waiting for the death wind,
Like a feather on the back of my hand. 5
Dust in sunlight and memory in corners
Wait for the wind that chills towards the dead land.

Grant us thy peace.
I have walked many years in this city,
Kept faith and fast, provided for the poor, 10
Have given and taken honour and ease.
There went never any rejected from my door.
Who shall remember my house, where shall live my children's
children
When the time of sorrow is come?
They will take to the goat's path, and the fox's home, 15
Fleeing from the foreign faces and the foreign swords.

Before the time of cords and scourges and lamentation
Grant us thy peace.
Before the stations of the mountain of desolation,
Before the certain hour of maternal sorrow, 20
Now at this birth season of decease,
Let the Infant, the still unspeaking and unspoken Word,
Grant Israel's consolation
To one who has eighty years and no to-morrow.

According to thy word. 25
They shall praise Thee and suffer in every generation
With glory and derision,
Light upon light, mounting the saints' stair.

Not for me the martyrdom, the ecstasy of thought and prayer,
30 Not for me the ultimate vision.
Grant me thy peace.
(And a sword shall pierce thy heart,
Thine also.)
I am tired with my own life and the lives of those after me,
35 I am dying in my own death and the deaths of those after me.
Let thy servant depart,
Having seen thy salvation.

Animula

'Issues from the hand of God, the simple soul'
To a flat world of changing lights and noise,
To light, dark, dry or damp, chilly or warm;
Moving between the legs of tables and of chairs,
Rising or falling, grasping at kisses and toys, 5
Advancing boldly, sudden to take alarm,
Retreating to the corner of arm and knee,
Eager to be reassured, taking pleasure
In the fragrant brilliance of the Christmas tree,
Pleasure in the wind, the sunlight and the sea; 10
Studies the sunlit pattern on the floor
And running stags around a silver tray;
Confounds the actual and the fanciful,
Content with playing-cards and kings and queens,
What the fairies do and what the servants say. 15
The heavy burden of the growing soul
Perplexes and offends more, day by day;
Week by week, offends and perplexes more
With the imperatives of 'is and seems'
And may and may not, desire and control. 20
The pain of living and the drug of dreams
Curl up the small soul in the window seat
Behind the *Encyclopaedia Britannica*.
Issues from the hand of time the simple soul
Irresolute and selfish, misshapen, lame, 25
Unable to fare forward or retreat,
Fearing the warm reality, the offered good,
Denying the importunity of the blood,
Shadow of its own shadows, spectre in its own gloom,
Leaving disordered papers in a dusty room; 30
Living first in the silence after the viaticum.

<

Pray for Guiterriez, avid of speed and power,
For Boudin, blown to pieces,
For this one who made a great fortune,
35 And that one who went his own way.
Pray for Floret, by the boarhound slain between the yew trees,
Pray for us now and at the hour of our birth.

Marina

Quis hic locus, quae regio, quae mundi plaga?

What seas what shores what grey rocks and what islands
What water lapping the bow
And scent of pine and the woodthrush singing through the fog
What images return
O my daughter. 5

Those who sharpen the tooth of the dog, meaning
Death
Those who glitter with the glory of the hummingbird, meaning
Death
Those who sit in the sty of contentment, meaning 10
Death
Those who suffer the ecstasy of the animals, meaning
Death

Are become unsubstantial, reduced by a wind,
A breath of pine, and the woodsong fog 15
By this grace dissolved in place

What is this face, less clear and clearer
The pulse in the arm, less strong and stronger—
Given or lent? more distant than stars and nearer than the eye

Whispers and small laughter between leaves and hurrying feet 20
Under sleep, where all the waters meet.

Bowsprit cracked with ice and paint cracked with heat.
I made this, I have forgotten
And remember.
The rigging weak and the canvas rotten 25

Between one June and another September.
Made this unknowing, half conscious, unknown, my own.
The garboard strake leaks, the seams need caulking.
This form, this face, this life
30 Living to live in a world of time beyond me; let me
Resign my life for this life, my speech for that unspoken,
The awakened, lips parted, the hope, the new ships.

What seas what shores what granite islands towards my timbers
And woodthrush calling through the fog
35 My daughter.

The Cultivation of Christmas Trees

There are several attitudes towards Christmas,
Some of which we may disregard:
The social, the torpid, the patently commercial,
The rowdy (the pubs being open till midnight),
And the childish—which is not that of the child 5
For whom the candle is a star, and the gilded angel
Spreading its wings at the summit of the tree
Is not only a decoration, but an angel.
The child wonders at the Christmas Tree:
Let him continue in the spirit of wonder 10
At the Feast as an event not accepted as a pretext;
So that the glittering rapture, the amazement
Of the first-remembered Christmas Tree,
So that the surprises, delight in new possessions
(Each one with its peculiar and exciting smell), 15
The expectation of the goose or turkey
And the expected awe on its appearance,
So that the reverence and the gaiety
May not be forgotten in later experience,
In the bored habituation, the fatigue, the tedium, 20
The awareness of death, the consciousness of failure,
Or in the piety of the convert
Which may be tainted with a self-conceit
Displeasing to God and disrespectful to the children
(And here I remember also with gratitude 25
St. Lucy, her carol, and her crown of fire):

So that before the end, the eightieth Christmas
(By 'eightieth' meaning whichever is the last)
The accumulated memories of annual emotion
May be concentrated into a great joy 30

Which shall be also a great fear, as on the occasion
When fear came upon every soul:
Because the beginning shall remind us of the end
And the first coming of the second coming.

Unfinished Poems

Sweeney Agonistes
Fragments of an Aristophanic Melodrama

Orestes: *You don't see them, you don't—but* I *see them: they are hunting me down, I must move on.*
Choephoroi.

Hence the soul cannot be possessed of the divine union, until it has divested itself of the love of created beings.
St. John of the Cross.

Fragment of a Prologue

DUSTY. DORIS.

DUSTY: How about Pereira?
DORIS: What about Pereira?
I don't care.
DUSTY: You don't care!
Who pays the rent?
DORIS: Yes he pays the rent
DUSTY: Well some men don't and some men do
Some men don't and you know who 5
DORIS: You can have Pereira
DUSTY: What about Pereira?
DORIS: He's no gentleman, Pereira:
You can't trust him!
DUSTY: Well that's true.
He's no gentleman if you can't trust him
And *if* you can't trust him— 10
Then you never know what he's going to do.
DORIS: No it wouldn't do to be too nice to Pereira.
DUSTY: Now Sam's a gentleman through and through.
DORIS: I like Sam
DUSTY: *I* like Sam
Yes and Sam's a nice boy too. 15
He's a funny fellow
DORIS: He *is* a funny fellow
He's like a fellow once I knew.
He could make you laugh.
DUSTY: Sam can make you laugh:
Sam's all right
DORIS: But Pereira won't do.
We can't have Pereira
DUSTY: Well what you going to do? 20

TELEPHONE: Ting a ling ling
Ting a ling ling
DUSTY: That's Pereira
DORIS: Yes that's Pereira
DUSTY: Well what you going to do?
TELEPHONE: Ting a ling ling
Ting a ling ling
25 DUSTY: That's Pereira
DORIS: Well can't you stop that horrible noise?
Pick up the receiver
DUSTY: What'll I say?
DORIS: Say what you like: say I'm ill,
Say I broke my leg on the stairs
Say we've had a fire
30 DUSTY: Hello Hello are you there?
Yes this is Miss Dorrance's *flat*—
Oh Mr. Pereira is that you? how do you do!
Oh I'm *so* sorry. I *am* so sorry
But Doris came home with a terrible chill
35 No, just a chill
Oh I *think* it's only a chill
Yes indeed I hope so too—
Well I *hope* we shan't have to call a doctor
Doris just hates having a doctor
40 She says will you ring up on Monday
She hopes to be all right on Monday
I say do you mind if I ring off now
She's got her feet in mustard and water
I said I'm giving her mustard and water
45 All right, Monday you'll phone through.
Yes I'll tell her. Good bye. Goooood bye.
I'm sure, that's very kind of *you*.
Ah-h-h
DORIS: Now I'm going to cut the cards for to-night.

Oh guess what the first is

DUSTY: First is. What is? 50

DORIS: The King of Clubs

DUSTY: That's Pereira

DORIS: It might be Sweeney

DUSTY: It's Pereira

DORIS: It might *just* as well be Sweeney

DUSTY: Well anyway it's very queer.

DORIS: Here's the four of diamonds, what's that mean? 55

DUSTY: (*reading*) 'A small sum of money, or a present
Of wearing apparel, or a party'.
That's queer too.

DORIS: Here's the three. What's that mean?

DUSTY: 'News of an absent friend'.—Pereira! 60

DORIS: The Queen of Hearts!—Mrs. Porter!

DUSTY: Or it might be you

DORIS: Or it might be you
We're all hearts. You can't be sure.
It just depends on what comes next.
You've got to *think* when you read the cards, 65
It's not a thing that anyone can do.

DUSTY: Yes I know you've a touch with the cards
What comes next?

DORIS: What comes next. It's the six.

DUSTY: 'A quarrel. An estrangement. Separation of friends'.

DORIS: Here's the two of spades.

DUSTY: The *two* of *spades*! 70
THAT'S THE COFFIN!!

DORIS: THAT'S THE COFFIN?
Oh good heavens what'll I do?
Just before a party too!

DUSTY: Well it needn't be yours, it may mean a friend.

DORIS: No it's mine. I'm sure it's mine. 75
I dreamt of weddings all last night.

Yes it's mine. I know it's mine.
Oh good heavens what'll I do.
Well I'm not going to draw any more,
80 You cut for luck. You cut for luck.
It might break the spell. You cut for luck.
DUSTY: The Knave of Spades.
DORIS: That'll be Snow
DUSTY: Or it might be Swarts
DORIS: Or it might be Snow
DUSTY: It's a funny thing how I draw court cards—
85 DORIS: There's a lot in the way you pick them up
DUSTY: There's an awful lot in the way you feel
DORIS: Sometimes they'll tell you nothing at all
DUSTY: You've got to know what you want to ask them
DORIS: You've got to know what you want to know
90 DUSTY: It's no use asking them too much
DORIS: It's no use asking more than once
DUSTY: Sometimes they're no use at all.
DORIS: I'd like to know about that coffin.
DUSTY: Well I never! What did I tell you?
95 Wasn't I saying I always draw court cards?
The Knave of Hearts!
(*Whistle outside of the window.*)
Well I *never*
What a coincidence! Cards are queer!
(*Whistle again.*)
DORIS: Is that Sam?
DUSTY: Of course it's Sam!
100 DORIS: Of course, the Knave of Hearts is Sam!
DUSTY (*leaning out of the window*): Hello Sam!
WAUCHOPE: Hello dear
How many's up there?
DUSTY: Nobody's up here
How many's down there?

WAUCHOPE: Four of us here.
Wait till I put the car round the corner
We'll be right up 105
DUSTY: All right, come up.
WAUCHOPE: We'll be right up.
DUSTY (*to* DORIS): Cards are queer.
DORIS: I'd like to know about that coffin.
KNOCK KNOCK KNOCK 110
KNOCK KNOCK KNOCK
KNOCK
KNOCK
KNOCK

DORIS. DUSTY. WAUCHOPE. HORSFALL.
KLIPSTEIN. KRUMPACKER.

WAUCHOPE: Hello Doris! Hello Dusty! How do you do! 115
How come? how come? will you permit me—
I think you girls both know Captain Horsfall—
We want you to meet two friends of ours,
American gentlemen here on business.
Meet Mr. Klipstein. Meet Mr. Krumpacker. 120
KLIPSTEIN: How do you do
KRUMPACKER: How do you do
KLIPSTEIN: I'm very pleased to make your acquaintance
KRUMPACKER: Extremely pleased to become acquainted
KLIPSTEIN: Sam—I should say Loot Sam Wauchope
KRUMPACKER: Of the Canadian Expeditionary Force— 125
KLIPSTEIN: The Loot has told us a lot about you.
KRUMPACKER: We were all in the war together
Klip and me and the Cap and Sam.
KLIPSTEIN: Yes we did our bit, as you folks say,
I'll tell the world we got the Hun on the run 130
KRUMPACKER: What about that poker game? eh what Sam?
What about that poker game in Bordeaux?

Yes Miss Dorrance you get Sam
To tell about that poker game in Bordeaux.
135 DUSTY: Do you know London well, Mr. Krumpacker?
KLIPSTEIN: No we never been here before
KRUMPACKER: We hit this town last night for the first time
KLIPSTEIN: And I certainly hope it won't be the last time.
DORIS: You like London, Mr. Klipstein?
140 KRUMPACKER: Do we like London? do we like London!
Do we like London!! Eh what Klip?
KLIPSTEIN: Say, Miss—er—uh—London's swell.
We like London fine.
KRUMPACKER: Perfectly slick.
DUSTY: Why don't you come and live here then?
145 KLIPSTEIN: Well, no, Miss—er—you haven't quite got it
(I'm afraid I didn't quite catch your name—
But I'm very pleased to meet you all the same)—
London's a little too gay for us
Yes I'll say a little too gay.
150 KRUMPACKER: Yes London's a little too gay for us
Don't think I mean anything *coarse*—
But I'm afraid we couldn't stand the pace.
What about it Klip?
KLIPSTEIN: You said it, Krum.
London's a slick place, London's a swell place,
155 London's a fine place to come on a visit—
KRUMPACKER: Specially when you got a real live Britisher
A guy like Sam to show you around.
Sam of course is at *home* in London,
And he's promised to show us around.

Fragment of an Agon

SWEENEY. WAUCHOPE. HORSFALL. KLIPSTEIN.
KRUMPACKER. SWARTS. SNOW. DORIS. DUSTY.

SWEENEY: I'll carry you off
To a cannibal isle.
DORIS: You'll be the cannibal!
SWEENEY: You'll be the missionary!
You'll be my little seven stone missionary! 5
I'll gobble you up. I'll be the cannibal.
DORIS: You'll carry me off? To a cannibal isle?
SWEENEY: I'll be the cannibal.
DORIS: I'll be the missionary.
I'll convert you!
SWEENEY: I'll convert *you*!
Into a stew. 10
A nice little, white little, missionary stew.
DORIS: You wouldn't eat me!
SWEENEY: Yes I'd eat you!
In a nice little, white little, soft little, tender little,
Juicy little, right little, missionary stew.
You see this egg 15
You see this egg
Well that's life on a crocodile isle.
There's no telephones
There's no gramophones
There's no motor cars 20
No two-seaters, no six-seaters,
No Citroën, no Rolls-Royce.
Nothing to eat but the fruit as it grows.
Nothing to see but the palmtrees one way
And the sea the other way, 25
Nothing to hear but the sound of the surf.

Nothing at all but three things

DORIS: What things?

SWEENEY: Birth, and copulation, and death.
That's all, that's all, that's all, that's all,
30 Birth, and copulation, and death.

DORIS: I'd be bored.

SWEENEY: You'd be bored.
Birth, and copulation, and death.

DORIS: I'd be bored.

SWEENEY: You'd be bored.
Birth, and copulation, and death.
35 That's all the facts when you come to brass tacks:
Birth, and copulation, and death.
I've been born, and once is enough.
You don't remember, but I remember,
Once is enough.

SONG BY WAUCHOPE AND HORSFALL
SWARTS AS TAMBO. SNOW AS BONES

40 *Under the bamboo*
Bamboo bamboo
Under the bamboo tree
Two live as one
One live as two
45 *Two live as three*
Under the bam
Under the boo
Under the bamboo tree.

Where the breadfruit fall
50 *And the penguin call*
And the sound is the sound of the sea
Under the bam

Under the boo
Under the bamboo tree.

Where the Gauguin maids 55
In the banyan shades
Wear palmleaf drapery
Under the bam
Under the boo
Under the bamboo tree. 60

Tell me in what part of the wood
Do you want to flirt with me?
Under the breadfruit, banyan, palmleaf
Or under the bamboo tree?
Any old tree will do for me 65
Any old wood is just as good
Any old isle is just my style
Any fresh egg
Any fresh egg
And the sound of the coral sea. 70

DORIS: I don't like eggs; I never liked eggs;
And I don't like life on your crocodile isle.

SONG BY KLIPSTEIN AND KRUMPACKER.
SNOW AND SWARTS AS BEFORE

My little island girl
My little island girl
I'm going to stay with you 75
And we won't worry what to do
We won't have to catch any trains
And we won't go home when it rains
We'll gather hibiscus flowers
For it won't be minutes but hours 80
For it won't be hours but years

diminuendo
And the morning
And the evening
And noontime
85 *And night*
Morning
Evening
Noontime
Night

90 DORIS: That's not life, that's no life
Why I'd just as soon be dead.
SWEENEY: That's what life is. Just is
DORIS: What is?
What's that life is?
SWEENEY: Life is death.
I knew a man once did a girl in—
95 DORIS: Oh Mr. Sweeney, please don't talk,
I cut the cards before you came
And I drew the coffin
SWARTS: *You* drew the coffin?
DORIS: I drew the COFFIN very last card.
I don't care for such conversation
100 A woman runs a terrible risk.
SNOW: Let Mr. Sweeney continue his story.
I assure you, Sir, we are very interested.
SWEENEY: I knew a man once did a girl in
Any man might do a girl in
105 Any man has to, needs to, wants to
Once in a lifetime, do a girl in.
Well he kept her there in a bath
With a gallon of lysol in a bath
SWARTS: These fellows always get pinched in the end.
110 SNOW: Excuse me, they don't all get pinched in the end.
What about them bones on Epsom Heath?
I seen that in the papers

You seen it in the papers
They *don't* all get pinched in the end.
DORIS: A woman runs a terrible risk. 115
SNOW: Let Mr. Sweeney continue his story.
SWEENEY: This one didn't get pinched in the end
But that's another story too.
This went on for a couple of months
Nobody came 120
And nobody went
But he took in the milk and he paid the rent.
SWARTS: What did he do?
All that time, what did he do?
SWEENEY: What did he do! what did he do? 125
That don't apply.
Talk to live men about what they do.
He used to come and see me sometimes
I'd give him a drink and cheer him up.
DORIS: Cheer him up?
DUSTY: Cheer him up? 130
SWEENEY: Well here again that don't apply
But I've gotta use words when I talk to you.
But here's what I was going to say.
He didn't know if he was alive
and the girl was dead
He didn't know if the girl was alive
and he was dead 135
He didn't know if they both were alive
or both were dead
If he was alive then the milkman wasn't
and the rent-collector wasn't
And if they were alive then he was dead.
There wasn't any joint
There wasn't any joint 140
For when you're alone

When you're alone like he was alone
You're either or neither
I tell you again it don't apply
145 Death or life or life or death
Death is life and life is death
I gotta use words when I talk to you
But if you understand or if you don't
That's nothing to me and nothing to you
150 We all gotta do what we gotta do
We're gona sit here and drink this booze
We're gona sit here and have a tune
We're gona stay and we're gona go
And somebody's gotta pay the rent

DORIS: I know who

155 SWEENEY: But that's nothing to me and nothing to you.

FULL CHORUS: WAUCHOPE, HORSFALL, KLIPSTEIN, KRUMPACKER

When you're alone in the middle of the night and
you wake in a sweat and a hell of a fright
When you're alone in the middle of the bed and
you wake like someone hit you on the head
You've had a cream of a nightmare dream and
you've got the hoo-ha's coming to you.
Hoo hoo hoo
You dreamt you waked up at seven o'clock and it's
160 foggy and it's damp and it's dawn and it's dark
And you wait for a knock and the turning of a lock
for you know the hangman's waiting for you.
And perhaps you're alive
And perhaps you're dead
Hoo ha ha
165 Hoo ha ha
Hoo

Hoo
Hoo
Knock Knock Knock
Knock Knock Knock 170
Knock
Knock
Knock

Coriolan

I. *Triumphal March*

Stone, bronze, stone, steel, stone, oakleaves, horses' heels
Over the paving.
And the flags. And the trumpets. And so many eagles.
How many? Count them. And such a press of people.
We hardly knew ourselves that day, or knew the City. 5
This is the way to the temple, and we so many crowding the way.
So many waiting, how many waiting? what did it matter, on such
a day?
Are they coming? No, not yet. You can see some eagles. And hear
the trumpets.
Here they come. Is he coming?
The natural wakeful life of our Ego is a perceiving. 10
We can wait with our stools and our sausages.
What comes first? Can you see? Tell us. It is

5,800,000 rifles and carbines,
102,000 machine guns,
28,000 trench mortars, 15
53,000 field and heavy guns,
I cannot tell how many projectiles, mines and fuses,
13,000 aeroplanes,
24,000 aeroplane engines,
50,000 ammunition waggons, 20
now 55,000 army waggons,
11,000 field kitchens,
1,150 field bakeries.

What a time that took. Will it be he now? No,
Those are the golf club Captains, these the Scouts, 25
And now the *société gymnastique de Poissy*
And now come the Mayor and the Liverymen. Look
There he is now, look:
There is no interrogation in his eyes

30 Or in the hands, quiet over the horse's neck,
And the eyes watchful, waiting, perceiving, indifferent.
O hidden under the dove's wing, hidden in the turtle's breast,
Under the palmtree at noon, under the running water
At the still point of the turning world. O hidden.

35 Now they go up to the temple. Then the sacrifice.
Now come the virgins bearing urns, urns containing
Dust
Dust
Dust of dust, and now
40 Stone, bronze, stone, steel, stone, oakleaves, horses' heels
Over the paving.

That is all we could see. But how many eagles! and how many
trumpets!
(And Easter Day, we didn't get to the country,
So we took young Cyril to church. And they rang a bell
45 And he said right out loud, *crumpets*.)
Don't throw away that sausage,
It'll come in handy. He's artful. Please, will you
Give us a light?
Light
50 Light
Et les soldats faisaient la haie? ILS LA FAISAIENT.

II. *Difficulties of a Statesman*

CRY what shall I cry?
All flesh is grass: comprehending
The Companions of the Bath, the Knights of the British Empire,
    the Cavaliers,
O Cavaliers! of the Legion of Honour,
The Order of the Black Eagle (1st and 2nd class), 5
And the Order of the Rising Sun.
Cry cry what shall I cry?
The first thing to do is to form the committees:
The consultative councils, the standing committees, select
    committees and sub-committees.
One secretary will do for several committees. 10
What shall I cry?
Arthur Edward Cyril Parker is appointed telephone operator
At a salary of one pound ten a week rising by annual increments of
    five shillings
To two pounds ten a week; with a bonus of thirty shillings at
    Christmas
And one week's leave a year. 15
A committee has been appointed to nominate a commission of
    engineers
To consider the Water Supply.
A commission is appointed
For Public Works, chiefly the question of rebuilding the
    fortifications.
A commission is appointed 20
To confer with a Volscian commission
About perpetual peace: the fletchers and javelin-makers and
    smiths
Have appointed a joint committee to protest against the reduction
    of orders.

Meanwhile the guards shake dice on the marches
25 And the frogs (O Mantuan) croak in the marshes.
Fireflies flare against the faint sheet lightning
What shall I cry?
Mother mother
Here is the row of family portraits, dingy busts, all looking
    remarkably Roman,
30 Remarkably like each other, lit up successively by the flare
Of a sweaty torchbearer, yawning.
O hidden under the . . . Hidden under the . . . Where the dove's
    foot rested and locked for a moment,
A still moment, repose of noon, set under the upper branches
    of noon's widest tree
Under the breast feather stirred by the small wind after noon
There the cyclamen spreads its wings, there the clematis
35   droops over the lintel
O mother (not among these busts, all correctly inscribed)
I a tired head among these heads
Necks strong to bear them
Noses strong to break the wind
40 Mother
May we not be some time, almost now, together,
If the mactations, immolations, oblations, impetrations,
Are now observed
May we not be
45 O hidden
Hidden in the stillness of noon, in the silent croaking night.
Come with the sweep of the little bat's wing, with the small
    flare of the firefly or lightning bug,
'Rising and falling, crowned with dust', the small creatures,
The small creatures chirp thinly through the dust, through the
    night.
50 O mother
What shall I cry?

We demand a committee, a representative committee, a committee
of investigation

RESIGN RESIGN RESIGN

Minor Poems

Eyes that last I saw in tears

Eyes that last I saw in tears
Through division
Here in death's dream kingdom
The golden vision reappears
I see the eyes but not the tears 5
This is my affliction

This is my affliction
Eyes I shall not see again
Eyes of decision
Eyes I shall not see unless 10
At the door of death's other kingdom
Where, as in this,
The eyes outlast a little while
A little while outlast the tears
And hold us in derision. 15

The wind sprang up at four o'clock

The wind sprang up at four o'clock
The wind sprang up and broke the bells
Swinging between life and death
Here, in death's dream kingdom
5 The waking echo of confusing strife
Is it a dream or something else
When the surface of the blackened river
Is a face that sweats with tears?
I saw across the blackened river
10 The camp fire shake with alien spears.
Here, across death's other river
The Tartar horsemen shake their spears.

Five-Finger Exercises

I. *Lines to a Persian Cat*

The songsters of the air repair
To the green fields of Russell Square.
Beneath the trees there is no ease
For the dull brain, the sharp desires
And the quick eyes of Woolly Bear. 5
There is no relief but in grief.
O when will the creaking heart cease?
When will the broken chair give ease?
Why will the summer day delay?
When will Time flow away? 10

II. *Lines to a Yorkshire Terrier*

In a brown field stood a tree
And the tree was crookt and dry.
In a black sky, from a green cloud
Natural forces shriek'd aloud,
Screamed, rattled, muttered endlessly. 5
Little dog was safe and warm
Under a cretonne eiderdown,
Yet the field was cracked and brown
And the tree was cramped and dry.
Pollicle dogs and cats all must 10
Jellicle cats and dogs all must
Like undertakers, come to dust.
Here a little dog I pause
Heaving up my prior paws,
Pause, and sleep endlessly. 15

III. *Lines to a Duck in the Park*

The long light shakes across the lake,
The forces of the morning quake,
The dawn is slant across the lawn,
Here is no eft or mortal snake
5 But only sluggish duck and drake.
I have seen the morning shine,
I have had the Bread and Wine,
Let the feathered mortals take
That which is their mortal due,
10 Pinching bread and finger too,
Easier had than squirming worm;
For I know, and so should you
That soon the enquiring worm shall try
Our well-preserved complacency.

IV. *Lines to Ralph Hodgson Esqre.*

How delightful to meet Mr. Hodgson!
(Everyone wants to know *him*)
With his musical sound
And his Baskerville Hound
5 Which, just at a word from his master
Will follow you faster and faster
And tear you limb from limb.
How delightful to meet Mr. Hodgson!
Who is worshipped by all waitresses
10 (They regard him as something apart)
While on his palate fine he presses
The juice of the gooseberry tart.
How delightful to meet Mr. Hodgson!
(Everyone wants to know *him*.)
15 He has 999 canaries

And round his head finches and fairies
In jubilant rapture skim.
How delightful to meet Mr. Hodgson!
    (Everyone wants to meet *him*.)

V. *Lines for Cuscuscaraway and Mirza Murad Ali Beg*

How unpleasant to meet Mr. Eliot!
With his features of clerical cut,
And his brow so grim
And his mouth so prim
And his conversation, so nicely 5
Restricted to What Precisely
And If and Perhaps and But.
How unpleasant to meet Mr. Eliot!
With a bobtail cur
In a coat of fur 10
And a porpentine cat
And a wopsical hat:
How unpleasant to meet Mr. Eliot!
    (Whether his mouth be open or shut.)

Landscapes

*

I. *New Hampshire*

Children's voices in the orchard
Between the blossom- and the fruit-time:
Golden head, crimson head,
Between the green tip and the root.
Black wing, brown wing, hover over; 5
Twenty years and the spring is over;
To-day grieves, to-morrow grieves,
Cover me over, light-in-leaves;
Golden head, black wing,
Cling, swing, 10
Spring, sing,
Swing up into the apple-tree.

II. *Virginia*

Red river, red river,
Slow flow heat is silence
No will is still as a river
Still. Will heat move
Only through the mocking-bird 5
Heard once? Still hills
Wait. Gates wait. Purple trees,
White trees, wait, wait,
Delay, decay. Living, living,
Never moving. Ever moving 10
Iron thoughts came with me
And go with me:
Red river, river, river.

III. *Usk*

Do not suddenly break the branch, or
Hope to find
The white hart behind the white well.
Glance aside, not for lance, do not spell
Old enchantments. Let them sleep. 5
'Gently dip, but not too deep',
Lift your eyes
Where the roads dip and where the roads rise
Seek only there
Where the grey light meets the green air 10
The hermit's chapel, the pilgrim's prayer.

IV. *Rannoch, by Glencoe*

Here the crow starves, here the patient stag
Breeds for the rifle. Between the soft moor
And the soft sky, scarcely room
To leap or soar. Substance crumbles, in the thin air
Moon cold or moon hot. The road winds in 5
Listlessness of ancient war,
Languor of broken steel,
Clamour of confused wrong, apt
In silence. Memory is strong
Beyond the bone. Pride snapped, 10
Shadow of pride is long, in the long pass
No concurrence of bone.

V. *Cape Ann*

O quick quick quick, quick hear the song-sparrow,
Swamp-sparrow, fox-sparrow, vesper-sparrow
At dawn and dusk. Follow the dance
Of the goldfinch at noon. Leave to chance
5 The Blackburnian warbler, the shy one. Hail
With shrill whistle the note of the quail, the bob-white
Dodging by bay-bush. Follow the feet
Of the walker, the water-thrush. Follow the flight
Of the dancing arrow, the purple martin. Greet
10 In silence the bullbat. All are delectable. Sweet sweet sweet
But resign this land at the end, resign it
To its true owner, the tough one, the sea-gull.

The palaver is finished.

Lines for an Old Man

The tiger in the tiger-pit
Is not more irritable than I.
The whipping tail is not more still
Than when I smell the enemy
Writhing in the essential blood 5
Or dangling from the friendly tree.
When I lay bare the tooth of wit
The hissing over the archèd tongue
Is more affectionate than hate,
More bitter than the love of youth, 10
And inaccessible by the young.
Reflected from my golden eye
The dullard knows that he is mad.

Tell me if I am not glad!

Choruses from 'The Rock'

I

The Eagle soars in the summit of Heaven,
The Hunter with his dogs pursues his circuit.
O perpetual revolution of configured stars,
O perpetual recurrence of determined seasons,
O world of spring and autumn, birth and dying! 5
The endless cycle of idea and action,
Endless invention, endless experiment,
Brings knowledge of motion, but not of stillness;
Knowledge of speech, but not of silence;
Knowledge of words, and ignorance of the Word. 10
All our knowledge brings us nearer to our ignorance,
All our ignorance brings us nearer to death,
But nearness to death no nearer to GOD.
Where is the Life we have lost in living?
Where is the wisdom we have lost in knowledge? 15
Where is the knowledge we have lost in information?
The cycles of Heaven in twenty centuries
Bring us farther from GOD and nearer to the Dust.

I journeyed to London, to the timekept City,
Where the River flows, with foreign flotations. 20
There I was told: we have too many churches,
And too few chop-houses. There I was told:
Let the vicars retire. Men do not need the Church
In the place where they work, but where they spend their Sundays.
In the City, we need no bells: 25
Let them waken the suburbs.
I journeyed to the suburbs, and there I was told:
We toil for six days, on the seventh we must motor
To Hindhead, or Maidenhead.
If the weather is foul we stay at home and read the papers. 30

In industrial districts, there I was told
Of economic laws.
In the pleasant countryside, there it seemed
That the country now is only fit for picnics.
35 And the Church does not seem to be wanted
In country or in suburb; and in the town
Only for important weddings.

CHORUS LEADER:

Silence! and preserve respectful distance.
For I perceive approaching
40 The Rock. Who will perhaps answer our doubtings.
The Rock. The Watcher. The Stranger.
He who has seen what has happened
And who sees what is to happen.
The Witness. The Critic. The Stranger.
45 The God-shaken, in whom is the truth inborn.

Enter the ROCK, *led by a* BOY:

THE ROCK:

The lot of man is ceaseless labour,
Or ceaseless idleness, which is still harder,
Or irregular labour, which is not pleasant.
I have trodden the winepress alone, and I know
50 That it is hard to be really useful, resigning
The things that men count for happiness, seeking
The good deeds that lead to obscurity, accepting
With equal face those that bring ignominy,
The applause of all or the love of none.
55 All men are ready to invest their money
But most expect dividends.
I say to you: *Make perfect your will.*
I say: take no thought of the harvest,
But only of proper sowing.

>

The world turns and the world changes, 60
But one thing does not change.
In all of my years, one thing does not change.
However you disguise it, this thing does not change:
The perpetual struggle of Good and Evil.
Forgetful, you neglect your shrines and churches; 65
The men you are in these times deride
What has been done of good, you find explanations
To satisfy the rational and enlightened mind.
Second, you neglect and belittle the desert.
The desert is not remote in southern tropics, 70
The desert is not only around the corner,
The desert is squeezed in the tube-train next to you,
The desert is in the heart of your brother.
The good man is the builder, if he build what is good.
I will show you the things that are now being done, 75
And some of the things that were long ago done,
That you may take heart. Make perfect your will.
Let me show you the work of the humble. Listen.

The lights fade; in the semi-darkness the voices of WORKMEN *are heard chanting.*

In the vacant places
We will build with new bricks 80
There are hands and machines
And clay for new brick
And lime for new mortar
Where the bricks are fallen
We will build with new stone 85
Where the beams are rotten
We will build with new timbers
Where the word is unspoken
We will build with new speech
There is work together 90

A Church for all
And a job for each
Every man to his work.

Now a group of WORKMEN *is silhouetted against the dim sky. From farther away, they are answered by voices of the* UNEMPLOYED.

No man has hired us
95 *With pocketed hands*
And lowered faces
We stand about in open places
And shiver in unlit rooms.
Only the wind moves
100 *Over empty fields, untilled*
Where the plough rests, at an angle
To the furrow. In this land
There shall be one cigarette to two men,
To two women one half pint of bitter
105 *Ale. In this land*
No man has hired us.
Our life is unwelcome, our death
Unmentioned in 'The Times'.

Chant of WORKMEN *again.*
The river flows, the seasons turn
110 *The sparrow and starling have no time to waste.*
If men do not build
How shall they live?
When the field is tilled
And the wheat is bread
115 *They shall not die in a shortened bed*
And a narrow sheet. In this street
There is no beginning, no movement, no peace and no end
But noise without speech, food without taste.

Without delay, without haste
We would build the beginning and the end of this street. 120
We build the meaning:
A Church for all
And a job for each
Each man to his work.

II

Thus your fathers were made
Fellow citizens of the saints, of the household of GOD, being built upon the foundation
Of apostles and prophets, Christ Jesus Himself the chief cornerstone.
But you, have you built well, that you now sit helpless in a ruined house?
Where many are born to idleness, to frittered lives and squalid deaths, embittered scorn in honeyless hives, 5
And those who would build and restore turn out the palms of their hands, or look in vain towards foreign lands for alms to be more or the urn to be filled.
Your building not fitly framed together, you sit ashamed and wonder whether and how you may be builded together for a habitation of GOD in the Spirit, the Spirit which moved on the face of the waters like a lantern set on the back of a tortoise.
And some say: 'How can we love our neighbour? For love must be made real in act, as desire unites with desired; we have only our labour to give and our labour is not required.
We wait on corners, with nothing to bring but the songs we can sing which nobody wants to hear sung;
10 Waiting to be flung in the end, on a heap less useful than dung.'

You, have you built well, have you forgotten the cornerstone?
Talking of right relations of men, but not of relations of men to GOD.
'Our citizenship is in Heaven'; yes, but that is the model and type for your citizenship upon earth.

>

When your fathers fixed the place of God,
And settled all the inconvenient saints, 15
Apostles, martyrs, in a kind of Whipsnade,
Then they could set about imperial expansion
Accompanied by industrial development.
Exporting iron, coal and cotton goods
And intellectual enlightenment 20
And everything, including capital
And several versions of the Word of God:
The British race assured of a mission
Performed it, but left much at home unsure.

Of all that was done in the past, you eat the fruit, either rotten
or ripe. 25
And the Church must be forever building, and always decaying,
and always being restored.
For every ill deed in the past we suffer the consequence:
For sloth, for avarice, gluttony, neglect of the Word of God,
For pride, for lechery, treachery, for every act of sin.
And of all that was done that was good, you have the inheritance. 30
For good and ill deeds belong to a man alone, when he stands
alone on the other side of death,
But here upon earth you have the reward of the good and ill that
was done by those who have gone before you.
And all that is ill you may repair if you walk together in humble
repentance, expiating the sins of your fathers;
And all that was good you must fight to keep with hearts as
devoted as those of your fathers who fought to gain it.
The Church must be forever building, for it is forever decaying
within and attacked from without; 35
For this is the law of life; and you must remember that while there
is time of prosperity
The people will neglect the Temple, and in time of adversity they
will decry it.

<

What life have you if you have not life together?
There is no life that is not in community,
40 And no community not lived in praise of GOD.
Even the anchorite who meditates alone,
For whom the days and nights repeat the praise of GOD,
Prays for the Church, the Body of Christ incarnate.
And now you live dispersed on ribbon roads,
45 And no man knows or cares who is his neighbour
Unless his neighbour makes too much disturbance,
But all dash to and fro in motor cars,
Familiar with the roads and settled nowhere.
Nor does the family even move about together,
50 But every son would have his motor cycle,
And daughters ride away on casual pillions.

Much to cast down, much to build, much to restore;
Let the work not delay, time and the arm not waste;
Let the clay be dug from the pit, let the saw cut the stone,
55 Let the fire not be quenched in the forge.

III

The Word of the LORD came unto me, saying:
O miserable cities of designing men,
O wretched generation of enlightened men,
Betrayed in the mazes of your ingenuities,
Sold by the proceeds of your proper inventions: 5
I have given you hands which you turn from worship,
I have given you speech, for endless palaver,
I have given you my Law, and you set up commissions,
I have given you lips, to express friendly sentiments,
I have given you hearts, for reciprocal distrust. 10
I have given you power of choice, and you only alternate
Between futile speculation and unconsidered action.
Many are engaged in writing books and printing them,
Many desire to see their names in print,
Many read nothing but the race reports. 15
Much is your reading, but not the Word of GOD,
Much is your building, but not the House of GOD.
Will you build me a house of plaster, with corrugated roofing,
To be filled with a litter of Sunday newspapers?

1ST MALE VOICE:

A Cry from the East: 20
What shall be done to the shore of smoky ships?
Will you leave my people forgetful and forgotten
To idleness, labour, and delirious stupor?
There shall be left the broken chimney,
The peeled hull, a pile of rusty iron, 25
In a street of scattered brick where the goat climbs,
Where My Word is unspoken.

2ND MALE VOICE:

A Cry from the North, from the West and from the South
Whence thousands travel daily to the timekept City;
30 Where My Word is unspoken,
In the land of lobelias and tennis flannels
The rabbit shall burrow and the thorn revisit,
The nettle shall flourish on the gravel court,
And the wind shall say: 'Here were decent godless people:
35 Their only monument the asphalt road
And a thousand lost golf balls.'

CHORUS:

We build in vain unless the LORD build with us.
Can you keep the City that the LORD keeps not with you?
A thousand policemen directing the traffic
40 Cannot tell you why you come or where you go.
A colony of cavies or a horde of active marmots
Build better than they that build without the LORD.
Shall we lift up our feet among perpetual ruins?
I have loved the beauty of Thy House, the peace of Thy
sanctuary,
45 I have swept the floors and garnished the altars.
Where there is no temple there shall be no homes,
Though you have shelters and institutions,
Precarious lodgings while the rent is paid,
Subsiding basements where the rat breeds
50 Or sanitary dwellings with numbered doors
Or a house a little better than your neighbour's;
When the Stranger says: 'What is the meaning of this city?
Do you huddle close together because you love each other?'
What will you answer? 'We all dwell together
55 To make money from each other'? or 'This is a community'?
And the Stranger will depart and return to the desert.

O my soul, be prepared for the coming of the Stranger,
Be prepared for him who knows how to ask questions.

O weariness of men who turn from GOD
To the grandeur of your mind and the glory of your action, 60
To arts and inventions and daring enterprises,
To schemes of human greatness thoroughly discredited,
Binding the earth and the water to your service,
Exploiting the seas and developing the mountains,
Dividing the stars into common and preferred, 65
Engaged in devising the perfect refrigerator,
Engaged in working out a rational morality,
Engaged in printing as many books as possible,
Plotting of happiness and flinging empty bottles,
Turning from your vacancy to fevered enthusiasm 70
For nation or race or what you call humanity;
Though you forget the way to the Temple,
There is one who remembers the way to your door:
Life you may evade, but Death you shall not.
You shall not deny the Stranger. 75

IV

There are those who would build the Temple,
And those who prefer that the Temple should not be built.
In the days of Nehemiah the Prophet
There was no exception to the general rule.
5 In Shushan the palace, in the month Nisan,
He served the wine to the king Artaxerxes,
And he grieved for the broken city, Jerusalem;
And the King gave him leave to depart
That he might rebuild the city.
10 So he went, with a few, to Jerusalem,
And there, by the dragon's well, by the dung gate,
By the fountain gate, by the king's pool,
Jerusalem lay waste, consumed with fire;
No place for a beast to pass.
15 There were enemies without to destroy him,
And spies and self-seekers within,
When he and his men laid their hands to rebuilding the wall.
So they built as men must build
With the sword in one hand and the trowel in the other.

V

O Lord, deliver me from the man of excellent intention and
impure heart: for the heart is deceitful above all things, and
desperately wicked.
Sanballat the Horonite and Tobiah the Ammonite and Geshem the
Arabian: were doubtless men of public spirit and zeal.
Preserve me from the enemy who has something to gain: and from
the friend who has something to lose.
Remembering the words of Nehemiah the Prophet: 'The trowel in
hand, and the gun rather loose in the holster.'
Those who sit in a house of which the use is forgotten: are like
snakes that lie on mouldering stairs, content in the sunlight. 5
And the others run about like dogs, full of enterprise, sniffing and
barking: they say, 'This house is a nest of serpents, let us
destroy it,
And have done with these abominations, the turpitudes of the
Christians.' And these are not justified, nor the others.
And they write innumerable books; being too vain and distracted
for silence: seeking every one after his own elevation, and
dodging his emptiness.
If humility and purity be not in the heart, they are not in the home:
and if they are not in the home, they are not in the City.
The man who has builded during the day would return to his
hearth at nightfall: to be blessed with the gift of silence, and
doze before he sleeps. 10
But we are encompassed with snakes and dogs: therefore some
must labour, and others must hold the spears.

VI

It is hard for those who have never known persecution,
And who have never known a Christian,
To believe these tales of Christian persecution.
It is hard for those who live near a Bank
5 To doubt the security of their money.
It is hard for those who live near a Police Station
To believe in the triumph of violence.
Do you think that the Faith has conquered the World
And that lions no longer need keepers?
10 Do you need to be told that whatever has been, can still be?
Do you need to be told that even such modest attainments
As you can boast in the way of polite society
Will hardly survive the Faith to which they owe their significance?
Men! polish your teeth on rising and retiring;
15 Women! polish your fingernails:
You polish the tooth of the dog and the talon of the cat.
Why should men love the Church? Why should they love her
laws?
She tells them of Life and Death, and of all that they would forget.
She is tender where they would be hard, and hard where they like
to be soft.
20 She tells them of Evil and Sin, and other unpleasant facts.
They constantly try to escape
From the darkness outside and within
By dreaming of systems so perfect that no one will need to be
good.
But the man that is will shadow
25 The man that pretends to be.
And the Son of Man was not crucified once for all,
The blood of the Martyrs not shed once for all,
The lives of the Saints not given once for all:

But the Son of Man is crucified always
And there shall be Martyrs and Saints. 30
And if blood of Martyrs is to flow on the steps
We must first build the steps;
And if the Temple is to be cast down
We must first build the Temple.

VII

In the beginning GOD created the world. Waste and void. Waste and void. And darkness was upon the face of the deep.
And when there were men, in their various ways, they struggled in torment towards GOD
Blindly and vainly, for man is a vain thing, and man without GOD is a seed upon the wind: driven this way and that, and finding no place of lodgement and germination.
They followed the light and the shadow, and the light led them forward to light and the shadow led them to darkness,
Worshipping snakes or trees, worshipping devils rather than nothing: crying for life beyond life, for ecstasy not of the flesh. 5
Waste and void. Waste and void. And darkness on the face of the deep.

And the Spirit moved upon the face of the water.
And men who turned towards the light and were known of the light
Invented the Higher Religions; and the Higher Religions were good
10 And led men from light to light, to knowledge of Good and Evil.
But their light was ever surrounded and shot with darkness
As the air of temperate seas is pierced by the still dead breath of the Arctic Current;
And they came to an end, a dead end stirred with a flicker of life,
And they came to the withered ancient look of a child that has died of starvation.
Prayer wheels, worship of the dead, denial of this world, affirmation of rites with forgotten meanings 15

In the restless wind-whipped sand, or the hills where the wind
will not let the snow rest.
Waste and void. Waste and void. And darkness on the face of the
deep.

Then came, at a predetermined moment, a moment in time and
of time,
A moment not out of time, but in time, in what we call history:
transecting, bisecting the world of time, a moment in time
but not like a moment of time,
A moment in time but time was made through that moment: for
without the meaning there is no time, and that moment of
time gave the meaning. 20
Then it seemed as if men must proceed from light to light, in the
light of the Word,
Through the Passion and Sacrifice saved in spite of their negative
being;
Bestial as always before, carnal, self-seeking as always before,
selfish and purblind as ever before,
Yet always struggling, always reaffirming, always resuming their
march on the way that was lit by the light;
Often halting, loitering, straying, delaying, returning, yet
following no other way. 25

But it seems that something has happened that has never
happened before: though we know not just when, or why,
or how, or where.
Men have left GOD not for other gods, they say, but for no god;
and this has never happened before
That men both deny gods and worship gods, professing first
Reason,
And then Money, and Power, and what they call Life, or Race, or
Dialectic.

The Church disowned, the tower overthrown, the bells
upturned, what have we to do
But stand with empty hands and palms turned upwards
In an age which advances progressively backwards?

VOICE OF THE UNEMPLOYED (*afar off*):
In this land
There shall be one cigarette to two men,
To two women one half pint of bitter
Ale . . .
CHORUS:
What does the world say, does the whole world stray in
high-powered cars on a by-pass way?
VOICE OF THE UNEMPLOYED (*more faintly*):
In this land
No man has hired us . . .

CHORUS:
Waste and void. Waste and void. And darkness on the face
of the deep.
Has the Church failed mankind, or has mankind failed the
Church?
When the Church is no longer regarded, not even
opposed, and men have forgotten
All gods except Usury, Lust and Power.

VIII

O Father we welcome your words,
And we will take heart for the future,
Remembering the past.

The heathen are come into thine inheritance,
And thy temple have they defiled. 5

Who is this that cometh from Edom?

He has trodden the wine-press alone.

There came one who spoke of the shame of Jerusalem
And the holy places defiled;
Peter the Hermit, scourging with words. 10
And among his hearers were a few good men,
Many who were evil,
And most who were neither.
Like all men in all places,

Some went from love of glory, 15
Some went who were restless and curious,
Some were rapacious and lustful.
Many left their bodies to the kites of Syria
Or sea-strewn along the routes;
Many left their souls in Syria, 20
Living on, sunken in moral corruption;
Many came back well broken,
Diseased and beggared, finding
A stranger at the door in possession:
Came home cracked by the sun of the East 25
And the seven deadly sins in Syria.

<

But our King did well at Acre.
And in spite of all the dishonour,
The broken standards, the broken lives,
30 The broken faith in one place or another,
There was something left that was more than the tales
Of old men on winter evenings.
Only the faith could have done what was good of it;
Whole faith of a few,
35 Part faith of many.
Not avarice, lechery, treachery,
Envy, sloth, gluttony, jealousy, pride:
It was not these that made the Crusades,
But these that unmade them.

40 Remember the faith that took men from home
At the call of a wandering preacher.
Our age is an age of moderate virtue
And of moderate vice
When men will not lay down the Cross
45 Because they will never assume it.
Yet nothing is impossible, nothing,
To men of faith and conviction.
Let us therefore make perfect our will.
O God, help us.

IX

Son of Man, behold with thine eyes, and hear with thine ears
And set thine heart upon all that I show thee.
Who is this that has said: the House of GOD is a House of Sorrow;
We must walk in black and go sadly, with longdrawn faces,
We must go between empty walls, quavering lowly, whispering
    faintly, 5
Among a few flickering scattered lights?
They would put upon GOD their own sorrow, the grief they should
    feel
For their sins and faults as they go about their daily occasions.
Yet they walk in the street proudnecked, like thoroughbreds ready
    for races,
Adorning themselves, and busy in the market, the forum, 10
And all other secular meetings.
Thinking good of themselves, ready for any festivity,
Doing themselves very well.
Let us mourn in a private chamber, learning the way of penitence,
And then let us learn the joyful communion of saints. 15

The soul of Man must quicken to creation.
Out of the formless stone, when the artist unites himself with
    stone,
Spring always new forms of life, from the soul of man that is joined
    to the soul of stone;
Out of the meaningless practical shapes of all that is living or
    lifeless
Joined with the artist's eye, new life, new form, new colour. 20
Out of the sea of sound the life of music,
Out of the slimy mud of words, out of the sleet and hail of verbal
    imprecisions,

Approximate thoughts and feelings, words that have taken
the place of thoughts and feelings,
There spring the perfect order of speech, and the beauty of
incantation.

25 LORD, shall we not bring these gifts to Your service?
Shall we not bring to Your service all our powers
For life, for dignity, grace and order,
And intellectual pleasures of the senses?
The LORD who created must wish us to create
30 And employ our creation again in His service
Which is already His service in creating.
For Man is joined spirit and body,
And therefore must serve as spirit and body.
Visible and invisible, two worlds meet in Man;
35 Visible and invisible must meet in His Temple;
You must not deny the body.

Now you shall see the Temple completed:
After much striving, after many obstacles;
For the work of creation is never without travail;
40 The formed stone, the visible crucifix,
The dressed altar, the lifting light,

Light

Light

The visible reminder of Invisible Light.

X

You have seen the house built, you have seen it adorned
By one who came in the night, it is now dedicated to GOD.
It is now a visible church, one more light set on a hill
In a world confused and dark and disturbed by portents of fear.
And what shall we say of the future? Is one church all we can
build? 5
Or shall the Visible Church go on to conquer the World?

The great snake lies ever half awake, at the bottom of the pit of
the world, curled
In folds of himself until he awakens in hunger and moving his
head to right and to left prepares for his hour to devour.
But the Mystery of Iniquity is a pit too deep for mortal eyes to
plumb. Come
Ye out from among those who prize the serpent's golden eyes, 10
The worshippers, self-given sacrifice of the snake. Take
Your way and be ye separate.
Be not too curious of Good and Evil;
Seek not to count the future waves of Time;
But be ye satisfied that you have light 15
Enough to take your step and find your foothold.

O Light Invisible, we praise Thee!
Too bright for mortal vision.
O Greater Light, we praise Thee for the less;
The eastern light our spires touch at morning, 20
The light that slants upon our western doors at evening,
The twilight over stagnant pools at batflight,
Moon light and star light, owl and moth light,
Glow-worm glowlight on a grassblade.
O Light Invisible, we worship Thee! 25
<

We thank Thee for the lights that we have kindled,
The light of altar and of sanctuary;
Small lights of those who meditate at midnight
And lights directed through the coloured panes of windows
30 And light reflected from the polished stone,
The gilded carven wood, the coloured fresco.
Our gaze is submarine, our eyes look upward
And see the light that fractures through unquiet water.
We see the light but see not whence it comes.
35 O Light Invisible, we glorify Thee!

In our rhythm of earthly life we tire of light. We are glad when the day ends, when the play ends; and ecstasy is too much pain.
We are children quickly tired: children who are up in the night and fall asleep as the rocket is fired; and the day is long for work or play.
We tire of distraction or concentration, we sleep and are glad to sleep,
Controlled by the rhythm of blood and the day and the night and the seasons.
And we must extinguish the candle, put out the light and
40 relight it;
Forever must quench, forever relight the flame.
Therefore we thank Thee for our little light, that is dappled with shadow.
We thank Thee who hast moved us to building, to finding, to forming at the ends of our fingers and beams of our eyes.
And when we have built an altar to the Invisible Light, we may set thereon the little lights for which our bodily vision is made.
45 And we thank Thee that darkness reminds us of light.
O Light Invisible, we give Thee thanks for Thy great glory!

Four Quartets

τοῦ λόγου δ'ἐόντος ξυνοῦ ζώουσιν οἱ πολλοί
ὡς ἰδίαν ἔχοντες φρόνησιν.

I. p. 77. Fr. 2.

ὁδὸς ἄνω κάτω μία καὶ ὡυτή.

I. p. 89. Fr. 60.

Diels: *Die Fragmente der Vorsokratiker* (Herakleitos).

Burnt Norton

I

Time present and time past
Are both perhaps present in time future,
And time future contained in time past.
If all time is eternally present
All time is unredeemable. 5
What might have been is an abstraction
Remaining a perpetual possibility
Only in a world of speculation.
What might have been and what has been
Point to one end, which is always present. 10
Footfalls echo in the memory
Down the passage which we did not take
Towards the door we never opened
Into the rose-garden. My words echo
Thus, in your mind.
                                    But to what purpose 15
Disturbing the dust on a bowl of rose-leaves
I do not know.
                              Other echoes
Inhabit the garden. Shall we follow?
Quick, said the bird, find them, find them,
Round the corner. Through the first gate, 20
Into our first world, shall we follow
The deception of the thrush? Into our first world.
There they were, dignified, invisible,
Moving without pressure, over the dead leaves,
In the autumn heat, through the vibrant air, 25
And the bird called, in response to
The unheard music hidden in the shrubbery,

And the unseen eyebeam crossed, for the roses
Had the look of flowers that are looked at.
30 There they were as our guests, accepted and accepting.
So we moved, and they, in a formal pattern,
Along the empty alley, into the box circle,
To look down into the drained pool.
Dry the pool, dry concrete, brown edged,
35 And the pool was filled with water out of sunlight,
And the lotos rose, quietly, quietly,
The surface glittered out of heart of light,
And they were behind us, reflected in the pool.
Then a cloud passed, and the pool was empty.
40 Go, said the bird, for the leaves were full of children,
Hidden excitedly, containing laughter.
Go, go, go, said the bird: human kind
Cannot bear very much reality.
Time past and time future
45 What might have been and what has been
Point to one end, which is always present.

II

Garlic and sapphires in the mud
Clot the bedded axle-tree.
The trilling wire in the blood
Sings below inveterate scars
5 Appeasing long forgotten wars.
The dance along the artery
The circulation of the lymph
Are figured in the drift of stars
Ascend to summer in the tree
10 We move above the moving tree
In light upon the figured leaf
And hear upon the sodden floor

Below, the boarhound and the boar
Pursue their pattern as before
But reconciled among the stars. 15

At the still point of the turning world. Neither flesh nor fleshless;
Neither from nor towards; at the still point, there the dance is,
But neither arrest nor movement. And do not call it fixity,
Where past and future are gathered. Neither movement from nor
towards,
Neither ascent nor decline. Except for the point, the still point, 20
There would be no dance, and there is only the dance.
I can only say, *there* we have been: but I cannot say where.
And I cannot say, how long, for that is to place it in time.

The inner freedom from the practical desire,
The release from action and suffering, release from the inner 25
And the outer compulsion, yet surrounded
By a grace of sense, a white light still and moving,
Erhebung without motion, concentration
Without elimination, both a new world
And the old made explicit, understood 30
In the completion of its partial ecstasy,
The resolution of its partial horror.
Yet the enchainment of past and future
Woven in the weakness of the changing body,
Protects mankind from heaven and damnation 35
Which flesh cannot endure.
Time past and time future
Allow but a little consciousness.
To be conscious is not to be in time
But only in time can the moment in the rose-garden,
The moment in the arbour where the rain beat, 40
The moment in the draughty church at smokefall
Be remembered; involved with past and future.
Only through time time is conquered.

III

Here is a place of disaffection
Time before and time after
In a dim light: neither daylight
Investing form with lucid stillness
5 Turning shadow into transient beauty
With slow rotation suggesting permanence
Nor darkness to purify the soul
Emptying the sensual with deprivation
Cleansing affection from the temporal.
10 Neither plenitude nor vacancy. Only a flicker
Over the strained time-ridden faces
Distracted from distraction by distraction
Filled with fancies and empty of meaning
Tumid apathy with no concentration
15 Men and bits of paper, whirled by the cold wind
That blows before and after time,
Wind in and out of unwholesome lungs
Time before and time after.
Eructation of unhealthy souls
20 Into the faded air, the torpid
Driven on the wind that sweeps the gloomy hills of London,
Hampstead and Clerkenwell, Campden and Putney,
Highgate, Primrose and Ludgate. Not here
Not here the darkness, in this twittering world.

25 Descend lower, descend only
Into the world of perpetual solitude,
World not world, but that which is not world,
Internal darkness, deprivation
And destitution of all property,
30 Desiccation of the world of sense,
Evacuation of the world of fancy,

Inoperancy of the world of spirit;
This is the one way, and the other
Is the same, not in movement
But abstention from movement; while the world moves 35
In appetency, on its metalled ways
Of time past and time future.

IV

Time and the bell have buried the day,
The black cloud carries the sun away.
Will the sunflower turn to us, will the clematis
Stray down, bend to us; tendril and spray
Clutch and cling? 5
Chill
Fingers of yew be curled
Down on us? After the kingfisher's wing
Has answered light to light, and is silent, the light is still
At the still point of the turning world. 10

V

Words move, music moves
Only in time; but that which is only living
Can only die. Words, after speech, reach
Into the silence. Only by the form, the pattern,
Can words or music reach 5
The stillness, as a Chinese jar still
Moves perpetually in its stillness.
Not the stillness of the violin, while the note lasts,
Not that only, but the co-existence,
Or say that the end precedes the beginning, 10
And the end and the beginning were always there
Before the beginning and after the end.
And all is always now. Words strain,

Crack and sometimes break, under the burden,
15 Under the tension, slip, slide, perish,
Decay with imprecision, will not stay in place,
Will not stay still. Shrieking voices
Scolding, mocking, or merely chattering,
Always assail them. The Word in the desert
20 Is most attacked by voices of temptation,
The crying shadow in the funeral dance,
The loud lament of the disconsolate chimera.

The detail of the pattern is movement,
As in the figure of the ten stairs.
25 Desire itself is movement
Not in itself desirable;
Love is itself unmoving,
Only the cause and end of movement,
Timeless, and undesiring
30 Except in the aspect of time
Caught in the form of limitation
Between un-being and being.
Sudden in a shaft of sunlight
Even while the dust moves
35 There rises the hidden laughter
Of children in the foliage
Quick now, here, now, always—
Ridiculous the waste sad time
Stretching before and after.

East Coker

I

In my beginning is my end. In succession
Houses rise and fall, crumble, are extended,
Are removed, destroyed, restored, or in their place
Is an open field, or a factory, or a by-pass.
Old stone to new building, old timber to new fires, 5
Old fires to ashes, and ashes to the earth
Which is already flesh, fur and faeces,
Bone of man and beast, cornstalk and leaf.
Houses live and die: there is a time for building
And a time for living and for generation 10
And a time for the wind to break the loosened pane
And to shake the wainscot where the field-mouse trots
And to shake the tattered arras woven with a silent motto.

In my beginning is my end. Now the light falls
Across the open field, leaving the deep lane 15
Shuttered with branches, dark in the afternoon,
Where you lean against a bank while a van passes,
And the deep lane insists on the direction
Into the village, in the electric heat
Hypnotised. In a warm haze the sultry light 20
Is absorbed, not refracted, by grey stone.
The dahlias sleep in the empty silence.
Wait for the early owl.

In that open field
If you do not come too close, if you do not come too close,
On a summer midnight, you can hear the music 25
Of the weak pipe and the little drum
And see them dancing around the bonfire

The association of man and woman
In daunsinge, signifying matrimonie—
30 A dignified and commodious sacrament.
Two and two, necessarye coniunction,
Holding eche other by the hand or the arm
Whiche betokeneth concorde. Round and round the fire
Leaping through the flames, or joined in circles,
35 Rustically solemn or in rustic laughter
Lifting heavy feet in clumsy shoes,
Earth feet, loam feet, lifted in country mirth
Mirth of those long since under earth
Nourishing the corn. Keeping time,
40 Keeping the rhythm in their dancing
As in their living in the living seasons
The time of the seasons and the constellations
The time of milking and the time of harvest
The time of the coupling of man and woman
45 And that of beasts. Feet rising and falling.
Eating and drinking. Dung and death.

Dawn points, and another day
Prepares for heat and silence. Out at sea the dawn wind
Wrinkles and slides. I am here
50 Or there, or elsewhere. In my beginning.

II

What is the late November doing
With the disturbance of the spring
And creatures of the summer heat,
And snowdrops writhing under feet
5 And hollyhocks that aim too high
Red into grey and tumble down
Late roses filled with early snow?

Thunder rolled by the rolling stars
Simulates triumphal cars
Deployed in constellated wars 10
Scorpion fights against the Sun
Until the Sun and Moon go down
Comets weep and Leonids fly
Hunt the heavens and the plains
Whirled in a vortex that shall bring 15
The world to that destructive fire
Which burns before the ice-cap reigns.

That was a way of putting it—not very satisfactory:
A periphrastic study in a worn-out poetical fashion,
Leaving one still with the intolerable wrestle 20
With words and meanings. The poetry does not matter.
It was not (to start again) what one had expected.
What was to be the value of the long looked forward to,
Long hoped for calm, the autumnal serenity
And the wisdom of age? Had they deceived us, 25
Or deceived themselves, the quiet-voiced elders,
Bequeathing us merely a receipt for deceit?
The serenity only a deliberate hebetude,
The wisdom only the knowledge of dead secrets
Useless in the darkness into which they peered 30
Or from which they turned their eyes. There is, it seems to us,
At best, only a limited value
In the knowledge derived from experience.
The knowledge imposes a pattern, and falsifies,
For the pattern is new in every moment 35
And every moment is a new and shocking
Valuation of all we have been. We are only undeceived
Of that which, deceiving, could no longer harm.
In the middle, not only in the middle of the way
But all the way, in a dark wood, in a bramble, 40

On the edge of a grimpen, where is no secure foothold,
And menaced by monsters, fancy lights,
Risking enchantment. Do not let me hear
Of the wisdom of old men, but rather of their folly,
45 Their fear of fear and frenzy, their fear of possession,
Of belonging to another, or to others, or to God.
The only wisdom we can hope to acquire
Is the wisdom of humility: humility is endless.

The houses are all gone under the sea.

50 The dancers are all gone under the hill.

III

O dark dark dark. They all go into the dark,
The vacant interstellar spaces, the vacant into the vacant,
The captains, merchant bankers, eminent men of letters,
The generous patrons of art, the statesmen and the rulers,
5 Distinguished civil servants, chairmen of many committees,
Industrial lords and petty contractors, all go into the dark,
And dark the Sun and Moon, and the Almanach de Gotha
And the Stock Exchange Gazette, the Directory of Directors,
And cold the sense and lost the motive of action.
10 And we all go with them, into the silent funeral,
Nobody's funeral, for there is no one to bury.
I said to my soul, be still, and let the dark come upon you
Which shall be the darkness of God. As, in a theatre,
The lights are extinguished, for the scene to be changed
With a hollow rumble of wings, with a movement of darkness
15 on darkness,
And we know that the hills and the trees, the distant panorama
And the bold imposing façade are all being rolled away—
Or as, when an underground train, in the tube, stops too long
between stations

And the conversation rises and slowly fades into silence
And you see behind every face the mental emptiness deepen 20
Leaving only the growing terror of nothing to think about;
Or when, under ether, the mind is conscious but conscious
of nothing—
I said to my soul, be still, and wait without hope
For hope would be hope for the wrong thing; wait without love
For love would be love of the wrong thing; there is yet faith 25
But the faith and the love and the hope are all in the waiting.
Wait without thought, for you are not ready for thought:
So the darkness shall be the light, and the stillness the dancing.

Whisper of running streams, and winter lightning,
The wild thyme unseen and the wild strawberry, 30
The laughter in the garden, echoed ecstasy
Not lost, but requiring, pointing to the agony
Of death and birth.

You say I am repeating
Something I have said before. I shall say it again.
Shall I say it again? In order to arrive there, 35
To arrive where you are, to get from where you are not,
You must go by a way wherein there is no ecstasy.
In order to arrive at what you do not know
You must go by a way which is the way of ignorance.
In order to possess what you do not possess 40
You must go by the way of dispossession.
In order to arrive at what you are not
You must go through the way in which you are not.
And what you do not know is the only thing you know
And what you own is what you do not own 45
And where you are is where you are not.

IV

The wounded surgeon plies the steel
That questions the distempered part;
Beneath the bleeding hands we feel
The sharp compassion of the healer's art
5 Resolving the enigma of the fever chart.

Our only health is the disease
If we obey the dying nurse
Whose constant care is not to please
But to remind of our, and Adam's curse,
10 And that, to be restored, our sickness must grow worse.

The whole earth is our hospital
Endowed by the ruined millionaire,
Wherein, if we do well, we shall
Die of the absolute paternal care
15 That will not leave us, but prevents us everywhere.

The chill ascends from feet to knees,
The fever sings in mental wires.
If to be warmed, then I must freeze
And quake in frigid purgatorial fires
20 Of which the flame is roses, and the smoke is briars.

The dripping blood our only drink,
The bloody flesh our only food:
In spite of which we like to think
That we are sound, substantial flesh and blood—
25 Again, in spite of that, we call this Friday good.

V

So here I am, in the middle way, having had twenty years—
Twenty years largely wasted, the years of *l'entre deux guerres*—
Trying to learn to use words, and every attempt
Is a wholly new start, and a different kind of failure
Because one has only learnt to get the better of words 5
For the thing one no longer has to say, or the way in which
One is no longer disposed to say it. And so each venture
Is a new beginning, a raid on the inarticulate
With shabby equipment always deteriorating
In the general mess of imprecision of feeling, 10
Undisciplined squads of emotion. And what there is to conquer
By strength and submission, has already been discovered
Once or twice, or several times, by men whom one cannot hope
To emulate—but there is no competition—
There is only the fight to recover what has been lost 15
And found and lost again and again: and now, under conditions
That seem unpropitious. But perhaps neither gain nor loss.
For us, there is only the trying. The rest is not our business.

Home is where one starts from. As we grow older
The world becomes stranger, the pattern more complicated 20
Of dead and living. Not the intense moment
Isolated, with no before and after,
But a lifetime burning in every moment
And not the lifetime of one man only
But of old stones that cannot be deciphered. 25
There is a time for the evening under starlight,
A time for the evening under lamplight
(The evening with the photograph album).
Love is most nearly itself
When here and now cease to matter. 30
Old men ought to be explorers

Here or there does not matter
We must be still and still moving
Into another intensity
35 For a further union, a deeper communion
Through the dark cold and the empty desolation,
The wave cry, the wind cry, the vast waters
Of the petrel and the porpoise. In my end is my beginning.

The Dry Salvages

(The Dry Salvages—presumably *les trois sauvages*—is a small group of rocks, with a beacon, off the N.E. coast of Cape Ann, Massachusetts. *Salvages* is pronounced to rhyme with *assuages*. *Groaner*: a whistling buoy.)

I

I do not know much about gods; but I think that the river
Is a strong brown god—sullen, untamed and intractable,
Patient to some degree, at first recognised as a frontier;
Useful, untrustworthy, as a conveyor of commerce;
Then only a problem confronting the builder of bridges. 5
The problem once solved, the brown god is almost forgotten
By the dwellers in cities—ever, however, implacable,
Keeping his seasons and rages, destroyer, reminder
Of what men choose to forget. Unhonoured, unpropitiated
By worshippers of the machine, but waiting, watching and
waiting. 10
His rhythm was present in the nursery bedroom,
In the rank ailanthus of the April dooryard,
In the smell of grapes on the autumn table,
And the evening circle in the winter gaslight.

The river is within us, the sea is all about us; 15
The sea is the land's edge also, the granite
Into which it reaches, the beaches where it tosses
Its hints of earlier and other creation:
The starfish, the horseshoe crab, the whale's backbone;
The pools where it offers to our curiosity 20
The more delicate algae and the sea anemone.
It tosses up our losses, the torn seine,
The shattered lobsterpot, the broken oar
And the gear of foreign dead men. The sea has many voices,

Many gods and many voices.
The salt is on the briar rose, 25
The fog is in the fir trees.
The sea howl
And the sea yelp, are different voices
Often together heard: the whine in the rigging,
The menace and caress of wave that breaks on water,
30 The distant rote in the granite teeth,
And the wailing warning from the approaching headland
Are all sea voices, and the heaving groaner
Rounded homewards, and the seagull:
And under the oppression of the silent fog
35 The tolling bell
Measures time not our time, rung by the unhurried
Ground swell, a time
Older than the time of chronometers, older
Than time counted by anxious worried women
40 Lying awake, calculating the future,
Trying to unweave, unwind, unravel
And piece together the past and the future,
Between midnight and dawn, when the past is all deception,
The future futureless, before the morning watch
45 When time stops and time is never ending;
And the ground swell, that is and was from the beginning,
Clangs
The bell.

II

Where is there an end of it, the soundless wailing,
The silent withering of autumn flowers
Dropping their petals and remaining motionless;
Where is there an end to the drifting wreckage,
5 The prayer of the bone on the beach, the unprayable
Prayer at the calamitous annunciation?

>

There is no end, but addition: the trailing
Consequence of further days and hours,
While emotion takes to itself the emotionless
Years of living among the breakage 10
Of what was believed in as the most reliable—
And therefore the fittest for renunciation.

There is the final addition, the failing
Pride or resentment at failing powers,
The unattached devotion which might pass for devotionless, 15
In a drifting boat with a slow leakage,
The silent listening to the undeniable
Clamour of the bell of the last annunciation.

Where is the end of them, the fishermen sailing
Into the wind's tail, where the fog cowers? 20
We cannot think of a time that is oceanless
Or of an ocean not littered with wastage
Or of a future that is not liable
Like the past, to have no destination.

We have to think of them as forever bailing, 25
Setting and hauling, while the North East lowers
Over shallow banks unchanging and erosionless
Or drawing their money, drying sails at dockage;
Not as making a trip that will be unpayable
For a haul that will not bear examination. 30

There is no end of it, the voiceless wailing,
No end to the withering of withered flowers,
To the movement of pain that is painless and motionless,
To the drift of the sea and the drifting wreckage,
The bone's prayer to Death its God. Only the hardly, barely
        prayable 35
Prayer of the one Annunciation.

<<

It seems, as one becomes older,
That the past has another pattern, and ceases to be a mere
sequence—
Or even development: the latter a partial fallacy
40 Encouraged by superficial notions of evolution,
Which becomes, in the popular mind, a means of disowning the
past.
The moments of happiness—not the sense of well-being,
Fruition, fulfilment, security or affection,
Or even a very good dinner, but the sudden illumination—
45 We had the experience but missed the meaning,
And approach to the meaning restores the experience
In a different form, beyond any meaning
We can assign to happiness. I have said before
That the past experience revived in the meaning
50 Is not the experience of one life only
But of many generations—not forgetting
Something that is probably quite ineffable:
The backward look behind the assurance
Of recorded history, the backward half-look
55 Over the shoulder, towards the primitive terror.
Now, we come to discover that the moments of agony
(Whether, or not, due to misunderstanding,
Having hoped for the wrong things or dreaded the wrong things,
Is not in question) are likewise permanent
60 With such permanence as time has. We appreciate this better
In the agony of others, nearly experienced,
Involving ourselves, than in our own.
For our own past is covered by the currents of action,
But the torment of others remains an experience
65 Unqualified, unworn by subsequent attrition.
People change, and smile: but the agony abides.
Time the destroyer is time the preserver,

Like the river with its cargo of dead negroes, cows and chicken
coops,
The bitter apple and the bite in the apple.
And the ragged rock in the restless waters, 70
Waves wash over it, fogs conceal it;
On a halcyon day it is merely a monument,
In navigable weather it is always a seamark
To lay a course by: but in the sombre season
Or the sudden fury, is what it always was. 75

III

I sometimes wonder if that is what Krishna meant—
Among other things—or one way of putting the same thing:
That the future is a faded song, a Royal Rose or a lavender spray
Of wistful regret for those who are not yet here to regret,
Pressed between yellow leaves of a book that has never been 5
opened.
And the way up is the way down, the way forward is the way back.
You cannot face it steadily, but this thing is sure,
That time is no healer: the patient is no longer here.
When the train starts, and the passengers are settled
To fruit, periodicals and business letters 10
(And those who saw them off have left the platform)
Their faces relax from grief into relief,
To the sleepy rhythm of a hundred hours.
Fare forward, travellers! not escaping from the past
Into different lives, or into any future; 15
You are not the same people who left that station
Or who will arrive at any terminus,
While the narrowing rails slide together behind you;
And on the deck of the drumming liner
Watching the furrow that widens behind you, 20
You shall not think 'the past is finished'

Or 'the future is before us'.
At nightfall, in the rigging and the aerial,
Is a voice descanting (though not to the ear,
25 The murmuring shell of time, and not in any language)
'Fare forward, you who think that you are voyaging;
You are not those who saw the harbour
Receding, or those who will disembark.
Here between the hither and the farther shore
30 While time is withdrawn, consider the future
And the past with an equal mind.
At the moment which is not of action or inaction
You can receive this: "on whatever sphere of being
The mind of a man may be intent
35 At the time of death"—that is the one action
(And the time of death is every moment)
Which shall fructify in the lives of others:
And do not think of the fruit of action.
Fare forward.
O voyagers, O seamen,
40 You who come to port, and you whose bodies
Will suffer the trial and judgement of the sea,
Or whatever event, this is your real destination.'
So Krishna, as when he admonished Arjuna
On the field of battle.
Not fare well,
45 But fare forward, voyagers.

IV

Lady, whose shrine stands on the promontory,
Pray for all those who are in ships, those
Whose business has to do with fish, and
Those concerned with every lawful traffic
5 And those who conduct them.
>

Repeat a prayer also on behalf of
Women who have seen their sons or husbands
Setting forth, and not returning:
Figlia del tuo figlio,
Queen of Heaven. 10

Also pray for those who were in ships, and
Ended their voyage on the sand, in the sea's lips
Or in the dark throat which will not reject them
Or wherever cannot reach them the sound of the sea bell's
Perpetual angelus. 15

V

To communicate with Mars, converse with spirits,
To report the behaviour of the sea monster,
Describe the horoscope, haruspicate or scry,
Observe disease in signatures, evoke
Biography from the wrinkles of the palm 5
And tragedy from fingers; release omens
By sortilege, or tea leaves, riddle the inevitable
With playing cards, fiddle with pentagrams
Or barbituric acids, or dissect
The recurrent image into pre-conscious terrors— 10
To explore the womb, or tomb, or dreams; all these are usual
Pastimes and drugs, and features of the press:
And always will be, some of them especially
When there is distress of nations and perplexity
Whether on the shores of Asia, or in the Edgware Road. 15
Men's curiosity searches past and future
And clings to that dimension. But to apprehend
The point of intersection of the timeless
With time, is an occupation for the saint—
No occupation either, but something given 20

And taken, in a lifetime's death in love,
Ardour and selflessness and self-surrender.
For most of us, there is only the unattended
Moment, the moment in and out of time,
25 The distraction fit, lost in a shaft of sunlight,
The wild thyme unseen, or the winter lightning
Or the waterfall, or music heard so deeply
That it is not heard at all, but you are the music
While the music lasts. These are only hints and guesses,
30 Hints followed by guesses; and the rest
Is prayer, observance, discipline, thought and action.
The hint half guessed, the gift half understood, is Incarnation.
Here the impossible union
Of spheres of existence is actual,
35 Here the past and future
Are conquered, and reconciled,
Where action were otherwise movement
Of that which is only moved
And has in it no source of movement—
40 Driven by dæmonic, chthonic
Powers. And right action is freedom
From past and future also.
For most of us, this is the aim
Never here to be realised;
45 Who are only undefeated
Because we have gone on trying;
We, content at the last
If our temporal reversion nourish
(Not too far from the yew-tree)
50 The life of significant soil.

Little Gidding

I

Midwinter spring is its own season
Sempiternal though sodden towards sundown,
Suspended in time, between pole and tropic.
When the short day is brightest, with frost and fire,
The brief sun flames the ice, on pond and ditches, 5
In windless cold that is the heart's heat,
Reflecting in a watery mirror
A glare that is blindness in the early afternoon.
And glow more intense than blaze of branch, or brazier,
Stirs the dumb spirit: no wind, but pentecostal fire 10
In the dark time of the year. Between melting and freezing
The soul's sap quivers. There is no earth smell
Or smell of living thing. This is the spring time
But not in time's covenant. Now the hedgerow
Is blanched for an hour with transitory blossom 15
Of snow, a bloom more sudden
Than that of summer, neither budding nor fading,
Not in the scheme of generation.
Where is the summer, the unimaginable
Zero summer?

If you came this way, 20
Taking the route you would be likely to take
From the place you would be likely to come from,
If you came this way in may time, you would find the hedges
White again, in May, with voluptuary sweetness.
It would be the same at the end of the journey, 25
If you came at night like a broken king,
If you came by day not knowing what you came for,

It would be the same, when you leave the rough road
And turn behind the pig-sty to the dull façade
30 And the tombstone. And what you thought you came for
Is only a shell, a husk of meaning
From which the purpose breaks only when it is fulfilled
If at all. Either you had no purpose
Or the purpose is beyond the end you figured
35 And is altered in fulfilment. There are other places
Which also are the world's end, some at the sea jaws,
Or over a dark lake, in a desert or a city—
But this is the nearest, in place and time,
Now and in England.

If you came this way,
40 Taking any route, starting from anywhere,
At any time or at any season,
It would always be the same: you would have to put off
Sense and notion. You are not here to verify,
Instruct yourself, or inform curiosity
45 Or carry report. You are here to kneel
Where prayer has been valid. And prayer is more
Than an order of words, the conscious occupation
Of the praying mind, or the sound of the voice praying.
And what the dead had no speech for, when living,
50 They can tell you, being dead: the communication
Of the dead is tongued with fire beyond the language of the living.
Here, the intersection of the timeless moment
Is England and nowhere. Never and always.

II

Ash on an old man's sleeve
Is all the ash the burnt roses leave.
Dust in the air suspended
Marks the place where a story ended.

Dust inbreathed was a house— 5
The wall, the wainscot and the mouse.
The death of hope and despair,
    This is the death of air.

There are flood and drouth
Over the eyes and in the mouth, 10
Dead water and dead sand
Contending for the upper hand.
The parched eviscerate soil
Gapes at the vanity of toil,
Laughs without mirth. 15
    This is the death of earth.

Water and fire succeed
The town, the pasture and the weed.
Water and fire deride
The sacrifice that we denied. 20
Water and fire shall rot
The marred foundations we forgot,
Of sanctuary and choir.
    This is the death of water and fire.

In the uncertain hour before the morning 25
  Near the ending of interminable night
  At the recurrent end of the unending
After the dark dove with the flickering tongue
  Had passed below the horizon of his homing
  While the dead leaves still rattled on like tin 30
Over the asphalt where no other sound was
  Between three districts whence the smoke arose
  I met one walking, loitering and hurried
As if blown towards me like the metal leaves
  Before the urban dawn wind unresisting. 35
  And as I fixed upon the down-turned face

That pointed scrutiny with which we challenge
The first-met stranger in the waning dusk
I caught the sudden look of some dead master
40 Whom I had known, forgotten, half recalled
Both one and many; in the brown baked features
The eyes of a familiar compound ghost
Both intimate and unidentifiable.
So I assumed a double part, and cried
45 And heard another's voice cry: 'What! are *you* here?'
Although we were not. I was still the same,
Knowing myself yet being someone other—
And he a face still forming; yet the words sufficed
To compel the recognition they preceded.
50 And so, compliant to the common wind,
Too strange to each other for misunderstanding,
In concord at this intersection time
Of meeting nowhere, no before and after,
We trod the pavement in a dead patrol.
55 I said: 'The wonder that I feel is easy,
Yet ease is cause of wonder. Therefore speak:
I may not comprehend, may not remember.'
And he: 'I am not eager to rehearse
My thought and theory which you have forgotten.
60 These things have served their purpose: let them be.
So with your own, and pray they be forgiven
By others, as I pray you to forgive
Both bad and good. Last season's fruit is eaten
And the fullfed beast shall kick the empty pail.
65 For last year's words belong to last year's language
And next year's words await another voice.
But, as the passage now presents no hindrance
To the spirit unappeased and peregrine
Between two worlds become much like each other,
70 So I find words I never thought to speak

In streets I never thought I should revisit
When I left my body on a distant shore.
Since our concern was speech, and speech impelled us
To purify the dialect of the tribe
And urge the mind to aftersight and foresight, 75
Let me disclose the gifts reserved for age
To set a crown upon your lifetime's effort.
First, the cold friction of expiring sense
Without enchantment, offering no promise
But bitter tastelessness of shadow fruit 80
As body and soul begin to fall asunder.
Second, the conscious impotence of rage
At human folly, and the laceration
Of laughter at what ceases to amuse.
And last, the rending pain of re-enactment 85
Of all that you have done, and been; the shame
Of motives late revealed, and the awareness
Of things ill done and done to others' harm
Which once you took for exercise of virtue.
Then fools' approval stings, and honour stains. 90
From wrong to wrong the exasperated spirit
Proceeds, unless restored by that refining fire
Where you must move in measure, like a dancer.'
The day was breaking. In the disfigured street
He left me, with a kind of valediction, 95
And faded on the blowing of the horn.

III

There are three conditions which often look alike
Yet differ completely, flourish in the same hedgerow:
Attachment to self and to things and to persons, detachment
From self and from things and from persons; and, growing
between them, indifference

5 Which resembles the others as death resembles life,
Being between two lives—unflowering, between
The live and the dead nettle. This is the use of memory:
For liberation—not less of love but expanding
Of love beyond desire, and so liberation
10 From the future as well as the past. Thus, love of a country
Begins as attachment to our own field of action
And comes to find that action of little importance
Though never indifferent. History may be servitude,
History may be freedom. See, now they vanish,
15 The faces and places, with the self which, as it could, loved them,
To become renewed, transfigured, in another pattern.

Sin is Behovely, but
All shall be well, and
All manner of thing shall be well.
20 If I think, again, of this place,
And of people, not wholly commendable,
Of no immediate kin or kindness,
But some of peculiar genius,
All touched by a common genius,
25 United in the strife which divided them;
If I think of a king at nightfall,
Of three men, and more, on the scaffold
And a few who died forgotten
In other places, here and abroad,
30 And of one who died blind and quiet,
Why should we celebrate
These dead men more than the dying?
It is not to ring the bell backward
Nor is it an incantation
35 To summon the spectre of a Rose.
We cannot revive old factions
We cannot restore old policies

Or follow an antique drum.
These men, and those who opposed them
And those whom they opposed 40
Accept the constitution of silence
And are folded in a single party.
Whatever we inherit from the fortunate
We have taken from the defeated
What they had to leave us—a symbol: 45
A symbol perfected in death.
And all shall be well and
All manner of thing shall be well
By the purification of the motive
In the ground of our beseeching. 50

IV

The dove descending breaks the air
With flame of incandescent terror
Of which the tongues declare
The one discharge from sin and error.
The only hope, or else despair 5
    Lies in the choice of pyre or pyre—
    To be redeemed from fire by fire.

Who then devised the torment? Love.
Love is the unfamiliar Name
Behind the hands that wove 10
The intolerable shirt of flame
Which human power cannot remove.
    We only live, only suspire
    Consumed by either fire or fire.

V

What we call the beginning is often the end
And to make an end is to make a beginning.
The end is where we start from. And every phrase
And sentence that is right (where every word is at home,
5 Taking its place to support the others,
The word neither diffident nor ostentatious,
An easy commerce of the old and the new,
The common word exact without vulgarity,
The formal word precise but not pedantic,
10 The complete consort dancing together)
Every phrase and every sentence is an end and a beginning,
Every poem an epitaph. And any action
Is a step to the block, to the fire, down the sea's throat
Or to an illegible stone: and that is where we start.
15 We die with the dying:
See, they depart, and we go with them.
We are born with the dead:
See, they return, and bring us with them.
The moment of the rose and the moment of the yew-tree
20 Are of equal duration. A people without history
Is not redeemed from time, for history is a pattern
Of timeless moments. So, while the light fails
On a winter's afternoon, in a secluded chapel
History is now and England.

25 With the drawing of this Love and the voice of this Calling

We shall not cease from exploration
And the end of all our exploring
Will be to arrive where we started
And know the place for the first time.
30 Through the unknown, remembered gate

When the last of earth left to discover
Is that which was the beginning;
At the source of the longest river
The voice of the hidden waterfall
And the children in the apple-tree 35
Not known, because not looked for
But heard, half-heard, in the stillness
Between two waves of the sea.
Quick now, here, now, always—
A condition of complete simplicity 40
(Costing not less than everything)
And all shall be well and
All manner of thing shall be well
When the tongues of flame are in-folded
Into the crowned knot of fire 45
And the fire and the rose are one.

Occasional Verses

Defence of the Islands

Defence of the Islands cannot pretend to be verse, but its date—just after the evacuation from Dunkirk—and occasion have for me a significance which makes me wish to preserve it. McKnight Kauffer was then working for the Ministry of Information. At his request I wrote these lines to accompany an exhibition in New York of photographs illustrating the war effort of Britain. They were subsequently published in *Britain At War* (the Museum of Modern Art, New York, 1941). I now dedicate them to the memory of Edward McKnight Kauffer.

Let these memorials of built stone—music's
enduring instrument, of many centuries of
patient cultivation of the earth, of English
verse

be joined with the memory of this defence of [5]
the islands

and the memory of those appointed to the grey
ships—battleship, merchantman, trawler—
contributing their share to the ages' pavement
of British bone on the sea floor [10]

and of those who, in man's newest form of gamble
with death, fight the power of darkness in air
and fire

and of those who have followed their forebears
to Flanders and France, those undefeated in de- [15]
feat, unalterable in triumph, changing nothing
of their ancestors' ways but the weapons

and those again for whom the paths of glory are
the lanes and the streets of Britain:

<

[20] to say, to the past and the future generations
of our kin and of our speech, that we took up
our positions, in obedience to instructions.

A Note on War Poetry

A Note on War Poetry was written at the request of Miss Storm Jameson, to be included in a book entitled *London Calling* (Harper Brothers, New York, 1942).

Not the expression of collective emotion
Imperfectly reflected in the daily papers.
Where is the point at which the merely individual
Explosion breaks

In the path of an action merely typical 5
To create the universal, originate a symbol
Out of the impact? This is a meeting
On which we attend

Of forces beyond control by experiment—
Of Nature and the Spirit. Mostly the individual 10
Experience is too large, or too small. Our emotions
Are only 'incidents'

In the effort to keep day and night together.
It seems just possible that a poem might happen
To a very young man: but a poem is not poetry— 15
That is a life.

War is not a life: it is a situation,
One which may neither be ignored nor accepted,
A problem to be met with ambush and stratagem,
Enveloped or scattered. 20

The enduring is not a substitute for the transient,
Neither one for the other. But the abstract conception
Of private experience at its greatest intensity
Becoming universal, which we call 'poetry',
May be affirmed in verse. 25

To the Indians who Died in Africa

To the Indians who Died in Africa was written at the request of Miss Cornelia Sorabji for *Queen Mary's Book for India* (Harrap & Co. Ltd., 1943). I dedicate it now to Bonamy Dobrée, because he liked it and urged me to preserve it.

A man's destination is his own village,
His own fire, and his wife's cooking;
To sit in front of his own door at sunset
And see his grandson, and his neighbour's grandson
5 Playing in the dust together.

Scarred but secure, he has many memories
Which return at the hour of conversation,
(The warm or the cool hour, according to the climate)
Of foreign men, who fought in foreign places,
10 Foreign to each other.

A man's destination is not his destiny,
Every country is home to one man
And exile to another. Where a man dies bravely
At one with his destiny, that soil is his.
15 Let his village remember.

This was not your land, or ours: but a village in the Midlands,
And one in the Five Rivers, may have the same graveyard.
Let those who go home tell the same story of you:
Of action with a common purpose, action
20 None the less fruitful if neither you nor we
Know, until the judgment after death,
What is the fruit of action.

To Walter de la Mare

To Walter de la Mare was written for inclusion in *Tribute to Walter de la Mare* (Faber & Faber Ltd., 1948), a book presented to him on his seventy-fifth birthday.

The children who explored the brook and found
A desert island with a sandy cove
(A hiding place, but very dangerous ground,

For here the water buffalo may rove,
The kinkajou, the mangabey, abound 5
In the dark jungle of a mango grove,

And shadowy lemurs glide from tree to tree—
The guardians of some long-lost treasure-trove)
Recount their exploits at the nursery tea

And when the lamps are lit and curtains drawn 10
Demand some poetry, please. Whose shall it be,
At not quite time for bed? . . .

Or when the lawn
Is pressed by unseen feet, and ghosts return
Gently at twilight, gently go at dawn,
The sad intangible who grieve and yearn; 15

When the familiar scene is suddenly strange
Or the well known is what we have yet to learn,
And two worlds meet, and intersect, and change;

When cats are maddened in the moonlight dance,
Dogs cower, flitter bats, and owls range 20
At the witches' sabbath of the maiden aunts;

<

When the nocturnal traveller can arouse
No sleeper by his call; or when by chance
An empty face peers from an empty house;

25 By whom, and by what means, was this designed?
The whispered incantation which allows
Free passage to the phantoms of the mind?

By you; by those deceptive cadences
Wherewith the common measure is refined;
30 By conscious art practised with natural ease;

By the delicate, invisible web you wove—
The inexplicable mystery of sound.

A Dedication to my Wife

To whom I owe the leaping delight
That quickens my senses in our wakingtime
And the rhythm that governs the repose of our sleepingtime,
  The breathing in unison

Of lovers whose bodies smell of each other 5
Who think the same thoughts without need of speech
And babble the same speech without need of meaning.

No peevish winter wind shall chill
No sullen tropic sun shall wither
The roses in the rose-garden which is ours and ours only 10

But this dedication is for others to read:
These are private words addressed to you in public.

Uncollected Poems

A Lyric

If Time and Space, as Sages say,
  Are things which cannot be,
The sun which does not feel decay
  No greater is than we.
So why, Love, should we ever pray 5
  To live a century?
The butterfly that lives a day
  Has lived eternity.

The flowers I gave thee when the dew
  Was trembling on the vine, 10
Were withered ere the wild bee flew
  To suck the eglantine.
So let us haste to pluck anew
  Nor mourn to see them pine,
And though our days of love be few 15
  Yet let them be divine.

Song

If space and time, as sages say,
  Are things that cannot be,
The fly that lives a single day
  Has lived as long as we.
But let us live while yet we may, 5
  While love and life are free,
For time is time, and runs away,
  Though sages disagree.

<

The flowers I sent thee when the dew
Was trembling on the vine
Were withered ere the wild bee flew
To suck the eglantine.
But let us haste to pluck anew
Nor mourn to see them pine,
And though the flowers of life be few
Yet let them be divine.

A Fable for Feasters

In England, long before that royal Mormon
King Henry VIII found out that monks were quacks,
And took their lands and money from the poor men,
And brought their abbeys tumbling at their backs,
There was a village founded by some Norman
Who levied on all travelers his tax;
Nearby this hamlet was a monastery
Inhabited by a band of friars merry.

They were possessors of rich lands and wide,
An orchard, and a vineyard, and a dairy;
Whenever some old villainous baron died,
He added to their hoards—a deed which ne'er he
Had done before—their fortune multiplied,
As if they had been kept by a kind fairy.
Alas! no fairy visited their host,
Oh, no; much worse than that, they had a ghost.

Some wicked and heretical old sinner
Perhaps, who had been walled up for his crimes;
At any rate, he sometimes came to dinner,
Whene'er the monks were having merry times.

He stole the fatter cows and left the thinner
  To furnish all the milk—upset the chimes,
    And once he sat the prior on the steeple,
    To the astonishment of all the people.

When Christmas time was near the Abbot vowed 25
  They'd eat their meal from ghosts and phantoms free,
The fiend must stay at home—no ghosts allowed
  At this exclusive feast. From over sea
He purchased at his own expense a crowd
  Of relics from a Spanish saint—said he: 30
    'If ghosts come uninvited, then, of course,
    I'll be compelled to keep them off by force.'

He drencht the gown he wore with holy water,
  The turkeys, capons, boars, they were to eat,
He even soakt the uncomplaining porter 35
  Who stood outside the door from head to feet.
To make a rather lengthy story shorter,
  He left no wise precaution incomplete;
    He doused the room in which they were to dine,
    And watered everything except the wine. 40

So when all preparations had been made,
  The jovial epicures sat down to table.
The menus of that time I am afraid
  I don't know much about—as well's I'm able
I'll go through the account: They made a raid 45
  On every bird and beast in Æsop's fable
    To fill out their repast, and pies and puddings,
    And jellies, pasties, cakes among the good things.

A mighty peacock standing on both legs
  With difficulty kept from toppling over, 50
Next came a viand made of turtle eggs,

And after that a great pie made of plover,
And flagons which perhaps held several kegs
Of ale, and cheese which they kept under cover.
55 Last, a boar's head, which to bring in took four pages,
His mouth an apple held, his skull held sausages.

Over their Christmas wassail the monks dozed,
A fine old drink, though now gone out of use—
His feet upon the table superposed
60 Each wisht he had not eaten so much goose.
The Abbot with proposing every toast
Had drank more than he ought t' have of grape juice.
The lights began to burn distinctly blue,
As in ghost stories lights most always do.

65 The doors, though barred and bolted most securely,
Gave way—my statement nobody can doubt,
Who knows the well known fact, as you do surely—
That ghosts are fellows whom you *can't* keep out;
It is a thing to be lamented sorely
70 Such slippery folk should be allowed about,
For often they drop in at awkward moments,
As everybody'll know who reads this romance.

The Abbot sat as pasted to his chair,
His eye became the size of any dollar,
75 The ghost then took him roughly by the hair
And bade him come with him, in accents hollow.
The friars could do nought but gape and stare,
The spirit pulled him rudely by the collar,
And before any one could say 'O jiminy!'
80 The pair had vanisht swiftly up the chimney.

Naturally every one searcht everywhere,
But not a shred of Bishop could be found,

The monks, when anyone questioned, would declare
St. Peter'd snatcht to heaven their lord renowned,
Though the wicked said (such rascals are not rare) 85
That the Abbot's course lay nearer underground;
But the church straightway put to his name the handle
Of Saint, thereby rebuking all such scandal.

But after this the monks grew most devout,
And lived on milk and breakfast food entirely; 90
Each morn from four to five one took a knout
And flogged his mates 'till they grew good and friarly.
Spirits from that time forth they did without,
And lived the admiration of the shire. We
Got the veracious record of these doings 95
From an old manuscript found in the ruins.

To the Class of 1905

I

Standing upon the shore of all we know
We linger for a moment doubtfully,
Then with a song upon our lips, sail we
Across the harbor bar—no chart to show,
No light to warn of rocks which lie below, 5
But let us yet put forth courageously.

II

As colonists embarking from the strand
To seek their fortunes on some foreign shore
Well know they lose what time shall not restore,
And when they leave they fully understand 10
That though again they see their fatherland
They there shall be as citizens no more.

III

We go; as lightning-winged clouds that fly
After a summer tempest, when some haste
15 North, South, and Eastward o'er the water's waste,
Some to the western limits of the sky
Which the sun stains with many a splendid dye,
Until their passing may no more be traced.

IV

Although the path be tortuous and slow,
20 Although it bristle with a thousand fears,
To hopeful eye of youth it still appears
A lane by which the rose and hawthorn grow.
We hope it may be; would that we might know!
Would we might look into the future years.

V

25 Great duties call—the twentieth century
More grandly dowered than those which came before,
Summons—who knows what time may hold in store,
Or what great deeds the distant years may see,
What conquest over pain and misery,
30 What heroes greater than were e'er of yore!

VI

But if this century is to be more great
Than those before, her sons must make her so,
And we are of her sons, and we must go
With eager hearts to help mold well her fate,
35 And see that she shall gain such proud estate
As shall on future centuries bestow

VII

A legacy of benefits—may we
In future years be found with those who try
To labor for the good until they die,
And ask no other guerdon than to know 40
That they have helpt the cause to victory,
That with their aid the flag is raised on high.

VIII

Sometime in distant years when we are grown
Gray-haired and old, whatever be our lot,
We shall desire to see again the spot 45
Which, whatsoever we have been or done
Or to what distant lands we may have gone,
Through all the years will ne'er have been forgot.

IX

For in the sanctuaries of the soul 50
Incense of altar-smoke shall rise to thee
From spotless fanes of lucid purity,
O school of ours! The passing years that roll
Between, as we press onward to the goal,
Shall not have power to quench the memory.

X

We shall return; and it will be to find 55
A different school from that which now we know;
But only in appearance t'will be so.
That which has made it great, not left behind,
The same school in the future shall we find
As this from which as pupils now we go. 60

XI

We go; like flitting faces in a dream;
Out of thy care and tutelage we pass
Into the unknown world—class after class,
O queen of schools—a momentary gleam,
65 A bubble on the surface of the stream,
A drop of dew upon the morning grass;

XII

Thou dost not die—for each succeeding year
Thy honor and thy fame shall but increase
Forever, and may stronger words than these
70 Proclaim thy glory so that all may hear;
May worthier sons be thine, from far and near
To spread thy name o'er distant lands and seas!

XIII

As thou to thy departing sons hast been
To those that follow may'st thou be no less;
75 A guide to warn them, and a friend to bless
Before they leave thy care for lands unseen;
And let thy motto be, proud and serene,
Still as the years pass by, the word 'Progress!'

XIV

So we are done; we may no more delay;
80 Thus is the end of every tale: 'Farewell',
A word that echoes like a funeral bell
And one that we are ever loth to say.
But 'tis a call we cannot disobey,
Exeunt omnes, with a last 'farewell'.

Song

When we came home across the hill
  No leaves were fallen from the trees;
  The gentle fingers of the breeze
Had torn no quivering cobweb down.

The hedgerow bloomed with flowers still, 5
  No withered petals lay beneath;
  But the wild roses in your wreath
Were faded, and the leaves were brown.

Before Morning

While all the East was weaving red with gray,
The flowers at the window turned toward dawn,
Petal on petal, waiting for the day,
Fresh flowers, withered flowers, flowers of dawn.

This morning's flowers and flowers of yesterday 5
Their fragrance drifts across the room at dawn,
Fragrance of bloom and fragrance of decay,
Fresh flowers, withered flowers, flowers of dawn.

Circe's Palace

Around her fountain which flows
With the voice of men in pain,
Are flowers that no man knows.
Their petals are fanged and red
With hideous streak and stain; 5

They sprang from the limbs of the dead.—
We shall not come here again.

Panthers rise from their lairs
In the forest which thickens below,
10 Along the garden stairs
The sluggish python lies;
The peacocks walk, stately and slow,
And they look at us with the eyes
Of men whom we knew long ago.

On a Portrait

Among a crowd of tenuous dreams, unknown
To us of restless brain and weary feet,
Forever hurrying, up and down the street,
She stands at evening in the room alone.

5 Not like a tranquil goddess carved of stone
But evanescent, as if one should meet
A pensive lamia in some wood-retreat,
An immaterial fancy of one's own.

No meditations glad or ominous
10 Disturb her lips, or move the slender hands;
Her dark eyes keep their secrets hid from us,
Beyond the circle of our thought she stands.

The parrot on his bar, a silent spy,
Regards her with a patient curious eye.

Song

The moonflower opens to the moth,
  The mist crawls in from sea;
A great white bird, a snowy owl,
  Slips from the alder tree.

Whiter the flowers, Love, you hold, 5
  Than the white mist on the sea;
Have you no brighter tropic flowers
  With scarlet lips, for me?

Ballade of the Fox Dinner

May 15, 1909

Muse of the rye and ginger ale,
Muse of the Cocktail and the Bar,
Open a bottle ere you hail
The members met from near and far.
A host of loyal graduates 5
Oblivious of bonds and stocks,
Your genial influence awaits
Here at a dinner of the Fox.

When Cordon Rouge like water flows
And cheers for Yale affright the air 10
And Leland through a window goes
While summersaulting on his chair,
We then consign us to your care;
Save us from self inflicted knocks!
And see us safely down the stair 15
After a dinner at the Fox.

<

Our faithful hearts will be the same
When twenty years have passed between us.
When Nick still runs his gambling game,
20 McNeil his partnership with Venus,
When Short is advertising booze
And Talbot selling vests and socks
I'm sure then will the loyal muse
Attend the dinners of the Fox.

25 So temporize with demon Rum!
To all who're here a toast bestow,
And all of those who could not come
And those from college soon to go
And those who now here first we see;
30 To everyone the muse unlocks
The gates of hospitality
Here at a dinner of the Fox.

Envoi.

O Muse, I pray, do something for us
Unless the scene your virtue shocks
35 While Bowen leads the cocktail chorus
Here at a dinner of the Fox.

Nocturne

Romeo, *grand sérieux*, to importune
Guitar and hat in hand, beside the gate
With Juliet, in the usual debate
Of love, beneath a bored but courteous moon;
5 The conversation failing, strikes some tune
Banal, and out of pity for their fate
Behind the wall I have some servant wait,
Stab, and the lady sinks into a swoon.

>

Blood looks effective on the moonlit ground—
The hero smiles; in my best mode oblique 10
Rolls toward the moon a frenzied eye profound,
(No need of 'Love forever?'—'Love next week?')
While female readers all in tears are drowned:—
'The perfect climax all true lovers seek!'

First Caprice in North Cambridge

A street-piano, garrulous and frail;
The yellow evening flung against the panes
Of dirty windows: and the distant strains
Of children's voices, ended in a wail.

Bottles and broken glass, 5
Trampled mud and grass;
A heap of broken barrows;
And a crowd of tattered sparrows
Delve in the gutter with sordid patience.
Oh, these minor considerations! 10

Second Caprice in North Cambridge

This charm of vacant lots!
The helpless fields that lie
Sinister, sterile and blind—
Entreat the eye and rack the mind,
Demand your pity. 5
With ashes and tins in piles,
Shattered bricks and tiles
And the débris of a city.

<

Far from our definitions
10 And our aesthetic laws
Let us pause
With these fields that hold and rack the brain
(What: again?)
With an unexpected charm
15 And an unexplained repose
On an evening in December
Under a sunset yellow and rose.

Opera

Tristan and Isolde
And the fatalistic horns
The passionate violins
And ominous clarinet;
5 And love torturing itself
To emotion for all there is in it,
Writhing in and out
Contorted in paroxysms,
Flinging itself at the last
10 Limits of self-expression.

We have the tragic? oh no!
Life departs with a feeble smile
Into the indifferent.
These emotional experiences
15 Do not hold good at all,
And I feel like the ghost of youth
At the undertakers' ball.

Humouresque

(AFTER J. LAFORGUE)

One of my marionettes is dead,
Though not yet tired of the game—
But weak in body as in head,
(A jumping-jack has such a frame).

But this deceasèd marionette 5
I rather liked: a common face,
(The kind of face that we forget)
Pinched in a comic, dull grimace;

Half bullying, half imploring air,
Mouth twisted to the latest tune; 10
His who-the-devil-are-you stare;
Translated, maybe, to the moon.

With Limbo's other useless things
Haranguing spectres, set him there;
'The snappiest fashion since last spring's, 15
'The newest style, on Earth, I swear.

'Why don't you people get some class?
(Feebly contemptuous of nose),
'Your damned thin moonlight, worse than gas—
'Now in New York—' and so it goes. 20

Logic a marionette's, all wrong
Of premises; yet in some star
A hero!—Where would he belong?
But, even at that, what mask *bizarre!*

Convictions (Curtain Raiser)

Among my marionettes I find
The enthusiasm is intense!
They see the outlines of their stage
Conceived upon a scale immense
5 And even in this later age
Await an audience open-mouthed
At climax and suspense.

Two, in a garden scene
Go picking tissue paper roses;
10 Hero and heroine, alone,
The monotone
Of promises and compliments
And guesses and supposes.

And over there my Paladins
15 Are talking of effect and cause,
With 'learn to live by nature's laws!'
And 'strive for social happiness
And contact with your fellow-men
In Reason: nothing to excess!'
20 As one leaves off the next begins.

And one, a lady with a fan
Cries to her waiting-maid discreet
'Where shall I ever find the man!
One who appreciates my soul;
25 I'd throw my heart beneath his feet.
I'd give my life to his control.'
(With more that I shall not repeat.)

My marionettes (or so they say)
Have these keen moments every day.

Spleen

Sunday: this satisfied procession
Of definite Sunday faces;
Bonnets, silk hats, and conscious graces
In repetition that displaces
Your mental self-possession 5
By this unwarranted digression.

Evening, lights, and tea!
Children and cats in the alley;
Dejection unable to rally
Against this dull conspiracy. 10

And Life, a little bald and gray,
Languid, fastidious, and bland,
Waits, hat and gloves in hand,
Punctilious of tie and suit
(Somewhat impatient of delay) 15
    On the doorstep of the Absolute.

First Debate between the Body and Soul

The August wind is shambling down the street

A blind old man who coughs and spits sputters
Stumbling among the alleys and the gutters.

He pokes and prods
With senile patience 5
The withered leaves
Of our sensations—

And yet devoted to the pure idea
One sits delaying in the vacant square
10 Forced to endure the blind inconscient stare
Of twenty leering houses that exude
The odour of their turpitude
And a street piano through the dusty trees
Insisting: 'Make the best of your position'—
15 The pure Idea dies of inanition
The street pianos through the trees
Whine and wheeze

Imaginations
Masturbations
20 The withered leaves
Of our sensations

The eye retains the images,
The sluggish brain will not react
Nor distils
25 The dull precipitates of fact
The emphatic mud of physical sense
The cosmic smudge of an enormous thumb
Posting bills
On the soul. And always come
30 The whine and wheeze
Of street pianos through the trees

Imagination's
Poor Relations
The withered leaves
35 Of our sensations.

Absolute! complete idealist
A supersubtle peasant
(Conception most unpleasant)

A supersubtle peasant in a shabby square
Assist me to the pure idea— 40
Regarding nature without love or fear
For a little while, a little while
Standing our ground—
Till life evaporates into a smile
Simple and profound. 45

Street pianos through the trees
Whine and wheeze

Imagination's
Defecations
The withered leaves 50
Of our sensations—

Easter: Sensations of April

[I]

The little negro girl who lives across the alley
Brings back a red geranium from church;
She repeats her little formulae of God.

Geraniums, geraniums
On a third-floor window sill. 5
Their perfume comes
With the smell of heat
From the asphalt street.
Geraniums geraniums
Withered and dry 10
Long laid by
In the sweepings of the memory.

The little negro girl across the alley
Brings a geranium from Sunday school

II

Daffodils
Long yellow sunlight fills
The cool secluded room
Swept and set in order—
5 Smelling of earth and rain.
And again
The insistent sweet perfume
And the impressions it preserves
Irritate the imagination
10 Or the nerves.

Ode

THOMAS STEARNS ELIOT

For the hour that is left us Fair Harvard, with thee,
Ere we face the importunate years,
In thy shadow we wait, while thy presence dispels
Our vain hesitations and fears.
5 And we turn as thy sons ever turn, in the strength
Of the hopes that thy blessings bestow,
From the hopes and ambitions that sprang at thy feet
To the thoughts of the past as we go.

Yet for all of these years that to-morrow has lost
10 We are still the less able to grieve,
With so much that of Harvard we carry away
In the place of the life that we leave.
And only the years that efface and destroy
Give us also the vision to see
15 What we owe for the future, the present, and past,
Fair Harvard, to thine and to thee.

Silence

Along the city streets
It is still high tide,
Yet the garrulous waves of life
Shrink and divide
With a thousand incidents 5
Vexed and debated:—
This is the hour for which we waited—

This is the ultimate hour
When life is justified.
The seas of experience 10
That were so broad and deep,
So immediate and steep,
Are suddenly still.
You may say what you will,
At such peace I am terrified. 15
There is nothing else beside.

Mandarins

1

Stands there, complete,
Stiffly addressed with sword and fan:
What of the crowds that ran,
Pushed, stared, and huddled, at his feet,
Keen to appropriate the man? 5

Indifferent to all these baits
Of popular benignity
He merely stands and waits
Upon his own intrepid dignity;

With fixed regardless eyes— (10)
Looking neither out nor in—
The centre of formalities.

A hero! and how much it means;
How much—
The rest is merely shifting scenes. (15)

2

Two ladies of uncertain age
Sit by a window drinking tea
(No persiflage!)
With assured tranquillity
                    Regard (5)
A distant prospect of the sea.
The outlines delicate and hard
Of gowns that fall from neck and knee;
Grey and yellow patterns move
From the shoulder to the floor. (10)

    By attitude
It would seem that they approve
The abstract sunset (rich, not crude).

And while one lifts her hand to pour
You have the other raise (15)
A thin translucent porcelain,
Murmurs a word of praise.

3

The eldest of the mandarins,
A stoic in obese repose,
With intellectual double chins,
Regards the corner of his nose;

>

The cranes that fly across a screen 5
Pert, alert,
Observe him with a frivolous mien—
Indifferent idealist,
  World in fist,
    Screen and cranes. 10

And what of all that one has missed!
And how life goes on different planes!

4

Still one more thought for pen and ink!
  (Though not indicative of spleen):
How very few there are, I think
Who see their outlines on the screen.
And so, I say, I find it good 5
(Even if misunderstood)
That demoiselles and gentlemen
Walk out beneath the cherry trees,
The goldwire dragons on their gowns
Expanded by the breeze. 10
The conversation dignified
Nor intellectual nor mean,
And graceful, not too gay . . .

          And so I say
How life goes well in pink and green! 15

Goldfish
(Essence of Summer Magazines)

I

Always the August evenings come
With preparation for the waltz
The hot verandah making room
For all the reminiscent tunes
5 —The *Merry Widow* and the rest—

That call, recall
So many nights and afternoons—
August, with all its faults!

And the waltzes turn, return;
10 The *Chocolate Soldier* assaults
The tired Sphinx of the physical.
What answer? We cannot discern.

And the waltzes turn, return,
Float and fall,
15 Like the cigarettes
Of our marionettes
Inconsequent, intolerable.

II

Embarquement pour Cythère

Ladies, the moon is on its way!
Is everybody here?
And the sandwiches and ginger beer?
If so, let us embark—
5 The night is anything but dark,
Almost as clear as day.

>

It's utterly illogical
Our making such a start, indeed
And thinking that we must return.

Oh no! why should we not proceed 10
(As long as a cigarette will burn
When you light it at the evening star)
To porcelain land, what avatar
Where blue-delft-romance is the law.

Philosophy through a paper straw! 15

III

On every sultry afternoon
Verandah customs have the call
White flannel ceremonial
With cakes and tea
And guesses at eternal truths 5
Sounding the depths with a silver spoon
And dusty roses, crickets, sunlight on the sea
  And all.

And should you ever hesitate
Among such charming scenes— 10
Essence of summer magazines—
Hesitate, and estimate
How much is simple accident
How much one knows
How much one means 15
Well! among many apophthegms
Here's one that goes—
Play to your conscience, through the maze
Of means and ways
And wear the crown of your ideal 20
  Bays
  And rose.

IV

Among the débris of the year
Of which the autumn takes its toll:—
Old letters, programmes, unpaid bills
Photographs, tennis shoes, and more,
5 Ties, postal cards, the mass that fills
The limbo of a bureau drawer—
Of which October takes its toll
Among the débris of the year
I find this headed 'Barcarolle'.

10 'Along the wet paths of the sea
A crowd of barking waves pursue
Bearing what consequence to you
And me.
The neuropathic winds renew
15 Like marionettes who leave their graves
Walking the waves
Bringing the news from either Pole
Or knowledge of the fourth dimension:
'We beg to call to your attention
20 'Some minor problems of the soul.'

—Your seamanship is very neat
You scan the clouds, as if you knew,
Your language nautical, complete;
There's nothing left for me to do.
25 And while you give the wheel a twist
I gladly leave the rest to fate
And contemplate
The aged sybil in your eyes
At the four crossroads of the world
30 Whose oracle replies:—

'These problems seem importunate
But after all do not exist.'

Between the theoretic seas
And your assuring certainties
I have my fears: 35
—I am off for some Hesperides
Of street pianos and small beers!

Suite Clownesque

I

Across the painted colonnades
Among the terra cotta fawns
Among the potted palms, the lawns,
The cigarettes and serenades

Here's the comedian again 5
With broad dogmatic vest, and nose
Nose that interrogates the stars,
Impressive, sceptic, scarlet nose;
The most expressive, real of men,
A jellyfish impertinent, 10
A jellyfish without repose.

Leaning across the orchestra
Just while he ponders, legs apart,
His belly sparkling and immense:
It's all philosophy and art. 15
Nose that interrogates the stars
Interrogates the audience
Who still continue in suspense

<

Who are so many entities
20 Inside a ring of lights!
Here's one who has the world at rights
Here's one who gets away with it
By simple spreading of the toes,
A self-embodied rôle, his soul
25 Concentred in his vest and nose.

II

Each with a skirt just down to the ancle
Everybody is under age
Three on a side and one in the centre
(Who would venture to be a dissenter)
5 Hello people!
People, hello!
Just while they linger shaking a finger
Perched on stools in the middle of the stage:—

'We've started out to take a walk
10 Each in a simple hat and gown,
Seven little girls run away from school
Now for a peek about the town.
Here's a street car—let's jump in
Oh see the soldiers—let's descend.
15 When you're out for an afternoon
Find somebody with money to spend.

But we're perplexed.
Hello people!
Yes indeed we're fearfully vexed;
20 People, hello!
In trying to construe this text:
"Where shall we go to next?"'

III

If you're walking down the avenue,
Five o'clock in the afternoon,
I may meet you
Very likely greet you
Show you that I know you 5

If you're walking up Broadway
Under the light of the silvery moon,
You may find me
All the girls behind me,
Euphorion of the modern time 10
Improved and up to date—sublime
Quite at home in the universe
Shaking cocktails on a hearse.
It's Broadway after dark!
Here let a clownesque be sounded
on the sandboard and bones.

If you're walking on the beach 15
When the girls are ready for a swim
You hear everyone remark
Look at him!
You will find me looking them over
Just out of reach 20
First born child of the absolute
Neat, complete,
In the quintessential flannel suit.
I guess there's nothing the matter with us!
—But say, just be serious, 25
Do you think that I'm all right?

IV

In the last contortions of the dance
The milkmaids and the village girls incline
To the smiling boys with rattan canes
Withdraw, advance;
5 The hero captures the Columbine
The audience rises hat in hand
And disdains
To watch the final saraband
The discovered masquerades
10 And the cigarettes and compliments

But through the painted colonnades
There falls a shadow dense, immense

It's the comedian again
Explodes in laughter, spreads his toes
15 (The most expressive, real of men)
Concentred into vest and nose.

The Triumph of Bullshit

Ladies, on whom my attentions have waited
If you consider my merits are small
Etiolated, alembicated,
Orotund, tasteless, fantastical,
5 Monotonous, crotchety, constipated,
Impotent galamatias
Affected, possibly imitated,
For Christ's sake stick it up your ass.

Ladies, who find my intentions ridiculous
10 Awkward insipid and horridly gauche

Pompous, pretentious, ineptly meticulous
Dull as the heart of an unbaked *brioche*
Floundering versicles feebly versiculous
Often attenuate, frequently crass
Attempts at emotions that turn out *isiculous*, 15
For Christs sake stick it up your ass.

Ladies who think me unduely vociferous
Amiable cabotin making a noise
That people may cry out 'this stuff is too stiff for us'—
Ingenuous child with a box of new toys 20
Toy lions carnivorous, cannons fumiferous
Engines vaporous—all this will pass;
Quite innocent—'he only wants to make shiver us.'
For Christs sake stick it up your ass.

And when thyself with silver foot shalt pass 25
Among the Theories scattered on the grass
Take up my good intentions with the rest
And then for Christs sake stick them up your ass.

Fourth Caprice in Montparnasse

We turn the corner of the street
    And again
Here is a landscape grey with rain
On black umbrellas, waterproofs,
And dashing from the slated roofs 5
Into a mass of mud and sand.
Behind a row of blackened trees
The dripping plastered houses stand
Like mendicants without regrets
For unpaid debts 10

Hand in pocket, undecided,
Indifferent if derided.

Among such scattered thoughts as these
We turn the corner of the street;
15 But why are we so hard to please?

Inside the gloom

1
Inside the gloom
Of a garret room

2
The constellations
Took up their stations

3
5 Menagerie
Of the August sky

4
The Scorpion
All alone

5
With his tail on fire
10 Danced on a wire

6
And Cassiopea
Explained the Pure Idea

7

The Major Bear
Balanced a chair

8

To show the direction 15
Of intellection

9

And Pegasus the winged horse
Explained the scheme of Vital Force

10

And Cetus too, by way of a satire
Explained the relation of life to matter 20

11

And the Pole Star while the debate was rife
Explained the use of a Place in Life

12

Then Bootes, unsettled
And visibly nettled

13

Said Are not all these questions 25
Brought up by indigestions?

14

So they cried and chattered
As if it mattered.

Entretien dans un parc

[Was it a morning or an afternoon
That has such things to answer for!]
We walked along, under the April trees,
With their uncertainties
5 Struggling intention that becomes intense.
I wonder if it is too late or soon
For the resolution that our lives demand.
With a sudden vision of incompetence
I seize her hand
10 In silence and we walk on as before.

And apparently the world has not been changed;
Nothing has happened that demands revision.
She smiles, as if, perhaps, surprised to see
So little her composure disarranged:
15 It is not that life has taken a new decision—
It has simply happened so to her and me.

And yet this while we have not spoken a word
It becomes at last a bit ridiculous
And irritating. All the scene's absurd!
20 She and myself and what has come to us
And what we feel, or not;
And my exasperation. Round and round, as in
    a bubbling pot
That will not cool
Simmering upon the fire, piping hot
25 Upon the fire of ridicule.

—Up a blind alley, stopped with broken walls
Papered with posters, chalked with childish scrawls!—

>

But if we could have given ourselves the slip
What explanations might have been escaped—
No stumbling over ends unshaped. 30
We are helpless. Still . . . it was unaccountable . . . odd . . .
Could not one keep ahead, like ants or moles?
Some day, if God—
But then, what opening out of dusty souls!

Interlude: in a Bar

Across the room the shifting smoke
Settles around the forms that pass
Pass through or clog the brain;
Across the floors that soak
The dregs from broken glass 5

The walls fling back the scattered streams
Of life that seems
Visionary, and yet hard;
Immediate, and far;
But hard . . . 10
Broken and scarred
Like dirty broken fingernails
Tapping the bar.

Bacchus and Ariadne: 2nd Debate between the Body and Soul

I saw their lives curl upward like a wave
And break. And after all it had not broken—
It might have broken even across the grave
Of tendencies unknown and questions never spoken.

5 The drums of life were beating on their skulls
The floods of life were swaying in their brains

A ring of silence closes round me and annuls
These sudden insights that have marched across
Like railway-engines over desert plains.

10 The world of contact sprang up like a blow
The wind beyond the world had passed without a trace
I saw that Time began again its slow
Attrition on a hard resistant face.

Yet to burst out at last, ingenuous and pure
15 Surprised, but knowing—it is triumph unendurable to miss!
Not to set free the purity that clings
To the cautious midnight of its chrysalis
Lies in its cell and meditates its wings
Nourished in earth and stimulated by manure.
20 —I am sure it is like this
I am sure it is this
I am sure.

The smoke that gathers blue and sinks

The smoke that gathers blue and sinks
The torpid smoke of rich cigars
The torpid after-dinner drinks
The overpowering immense
5 After dinner insolence
Of matter 'going by itself'
Existence just about to die
Stifled with glutinous liqueurs
Till hardly a sensation stirs
10 The overoiled machinery . . .
>

What, you want action?
Some attraction?
Now begins
The piano and the flute and two violins
Someone sings 15
A lady of almost any age
But chiefly breast and rings
'Throw your arms around me—Aint you glad you found me'
Still that's hardly strong enough—
Here's a negro (teeth and smile) 20
Has a dance that's quite worth while
That's the stuff!
(Here's your gin
Now begin!)

He said: this universe is very clever

He said: this universe is very clever
The scientists have laid it out on paper
Each atom goes on working out its law, and never
Can cut an unintentioned caper.

He said: it is a geometric net 5
And in the middle, like a syphilitic spider
The Absolute sits waiting, till we get
All tangled up and end ourselves inside her.

He said: 'this crucifixion was dramatic
He had not passed his life on officechairs 10
They did not crucify him in an attic
Up six abysmal flights of broken stairs.'

<

He said I am put together with a pot and scissors
Out of old clippings
15 No one took the trouble to make an article.

Interlude in London

We hibernate among the bricks
And live across the window panes
With marmalade and tea at six
Indifferent to what the wind does
5 Indifferent to sudden rains
Softening last year's garden plots

And apathetic, with cigars
Careless, while down the street the spring goes
Inspiring mouldy flowerpots,
10 And broken flutes at garret windows.

Ballade pour la grosse Lulu

I

The Outlook gives an interview
By Lyman Abbot kindly sent
Entitled 'What it means to You
That God is in his Firmament.'
5 The papers say '300 Boers
On Roosevelt have paid a call,'
But, My Lulu, 'Put on your rough red drawers
And come to the Whore House Ball!'

II

The Outlook gives an interview
An interview from Booker T. 10
Entitled 'Up from Possum Stew!'
Or 'How I set the nigger free!'
The papers say 'the learned horse
Jim Key, was murdered in his stall.'
But My Lulu 'Put on your rough red drawers 15
And come to the Whore House Ball!'

III

The Outlook gives an interview
From Rockefellar, fresh & frank,
Entitled 'How my Money grew'
Or 'Jesus as a Savings Bank.' 20
The papers say 'South Boston scores
On Roxbury at basket ball'
But, My Lulu, 'Put on your Rough Red Drawers
And come to the Whore House Ball.'

IV

The Outlook gives an interview 25
From Harvard's great ex-president
Called 'Oh if only people knew
That Virtue doesn't cost a cent!'
The papers say 'For hard wood floors
TURPTINO WAX is best of all'. 30
But My Lulu 'Put on your rough red drawers
And come to the Whore House Ball!'

The Little Passion

From 'An Agony in the Garret'

Upon those stifling August nights
I know he used to walk the streets
Now following the lines of lights
Or diving into dark retreats

Or following the lines of lights
And knowing well to what they lead:
To one inevitable cross
Whereon our souls are pinned, and bleed.

The Burnt Dancer

sotta la pioggia dell' aspro martiro

Within the yellow ring of flame
A black moth through the night
Caught in the circle of desire
Expiates his heedless flight
With beat of wings that do not tire
Distracted from more vital values
To golden values of the flame
What is the virtue that he shall use
In a world too strange for pride or shame?
A world too strange for praise or blame
Too strange for good or evil:
How drawn here from a distant star
For mirthless dance and silent revel

O danse mon papillon noir!

The tropic odours of your name 15
From Mozambique or Nicobar
Fall on the ragged teeth of flame
Like perfumed oil upon the waters
What is the secret you have brought us
Children's voices in little corners 20
Whimper whimper through the night
Of what disaster do you warn us
Agony nearest to delight?
Dance fast dance faster
There is no mortal disaster 25
The destiny that may be leaning
Toward us from your hidden star
Is grave, but not with human meaning

O danse mon papillon noir!

Within the circle of my brain 30
The twisted dance continues.
The patient acolyte of pain,
The strong beyond our human sinews,
The singèd reveller of the fire,
Caught on those horns that toss and toss, 35
Losing the end of his desire
Desires completion of his loss.
O strayed from whiter flames that burn not
O vagrant from a distant star
O broken guest that may return not 40

O danse danse mon papillon noir!

Oh little voices of the throats of men

Oh little voices of the throats of men
That come between the singer and the song;
Oh twisted little hands of men held up
To rend the beautiful and curse the strong.
5 Impatient tireless undirected feet!
So confident on wrinkled ways of wrong.
On what remote frontier of heaven and hell
Shall time allow our divers paths to meet?

Yet you do well to run the roads you run,
10 Yes you do well to keep the ways you keep;
And we who seek to balance pleasure and pain
We blow against the wind and spit against the rain:
For what could be more real than sweat and dust and sun?
And what more sure than night and death and sleep?

15 Appearances appearances he said,
I have searched the world through dialectic ways;
I have questioned restless nights and torpid days,
And followed every by-way where it led;
And always find the same unvaried
20 Intolerable interminable maze.
Contradiction is the debt you would collect
And still with contradiction are you paid,
And while you do not know what else you seek
You shall have nothing other to expect.
25 Appearances, appearances, he said,
And nowise real; unreal, and yet true;
Untrue, yet real;—of what are you afraid?
Hopeful of what? whether you keep thanksgiving,

Or pray for earth on tired body and head,
This word is true on all the paths you tread 30
As true as truth need be, when all is said:
That if you find no truth among the living
You will not find much truth among the dead.
No other time but now, no other place than here, he said.

He drew the shawl about him as he spoke 35
And dozed in his arm-chair till the morning broke.

Across the window panes the plumes of lilac swept
Stirred by the morning air.
Across the floor the shadows crawled and crept
And as the thin light shivered through the trees 40
Around the muffled form they danced and leapt.
They crawled about his shoulders and his knees;
They rested for a moment on his hair
Until the morning drove them to their lair.
And then sprang up a little damp dead breeze 45
That rattled at the window while he slept,
And had those been human voices in the chimneys
And at the shutters, and along the stair,
You had not known whether they laughed or wept.

The Love Song of St. Sebastian

I would come in a shirt of hair
I would come with a lamp in the night
And sit at the foot of your stair;
I would flog myself until I bled,
And after hour on hour of prayer 5
And torture and delight
Until my blood should ring the lamp
And glisten in the light;

I should arise your neophyte
10 And then put out the light
To follow where you led,
To follow where your feet are white
In the darkness toward your bed
And where your gown is white
15 And against your gown your braided hair.
Then you would take me in
Because I was hideous in your sight
You would take me in without shame
Because I should be dead
20 And when the morning came
Between your breasts should lie my head.

I would come with a towel in my hand
And bend your head beneath my knees;
Your ears curl back in a certain way
25 Like no one's else in all the world.
When all the world shall melt in the sun,
Melt or freeze,
I shall remember how your ears were curled.
I should for a moment linger
30 And follow the curve with my finger
And your head beneath my knees—
I think that at last you would understand.
There would be nothing more to say.
You would love me because I should have strangled you
35 And because of my infamy;
And I should love you the more because I had mangled you
And because you were no longer beautiful
To anyone but me.

Paysage Triste

The girl who mounted in the omnibus
The rainy day, and paid a penny fare
Who answered my appreciative stare
With that averted look without surprise
Which only the experienced can wear 5
A girl with reddish hair and faint blue eyes

An almost denizen of Leicester Square.
We could not have had her in the box with us
She would not have known how to sit, or what to wear
Yet if I close my eyes I see her moving 10
With loosened hair about her chamber
With naked feet passing across the skies

She would have been most crudely ill at ease
She would not have known how to sit, or what to wear
Nor, when the lights went out and the horn began 15
Have leaned as you did, your elbow on my knees
To prod impetuously with your fan
The smiling stripling with the pink soaped face
Who had your opera-glasses in his care.

Afternoon

The ladies who are interested in Assyrian art
Gather in the hall of the British Museum.
The faint perfume of last year's tailor suits
And the steam from drying rubber overshoes
And the green and purple feathers on their hats 5
Vanish in the sombre Sunday afternoon

<

As they fade beyond the Roman statuary
Like amateur comedians across a lawn
Towards the unconscious, the ineffable, the absolute

Suppressed Complex

She lay very still in bed with stubborn eyes
Holding her breath lest she begin to think.
I was a shadow upright in the corner
Dancing joyously in the firelight.

5 She stirred in her sleep and clutched the blanket with her fingers
She was very pale and breathed hard.
When morning shook the long nasturtium creeper in the tawny
bowl
I passed joyously out through the window.

In the Department Store

The lady of the porcelain department
Smiles at the world through a set of false teeth.
She is business-like and keeps a pencil in her hair

But behind her sharpened eyes take flight
5 The summer evenings in the park
And heated nights in second story dance halls.

Man's life is powerless and brief and dark
It is not possible for me to make her happy.

Do I know how I feel? Do I know what I think?

Do I know how I feel? Do I know what I think?
Let me take ink and paper, let me take pen and ink . . .
Or with my hat and gloves, as if to take the air
Walk softly down the hall, stop at the foot of the stair
Take my letters from the porter—ask him for a drink 5
If I questioned him with care, would he tell me what I think and feel
—Or only 'You are the gentleman who has lived on the second floor
For a year or more'—
Yet I dread what a flash of madness might reveal
If he said 'Sir we have seen so much beauty spilled on the open
street 10
Or wasted in stately marriages or stained in railway carriages
Or left untasted in villages or stifled in darkened chambers
That if we are restless on winter nights, who can blame us?'

Do I know how I feel? Do I know how I think?
There is something which should be firm but slips, just at my
finger tips. 15
There will be a smell of creolin and the sound of something
that drips
A black bag with a pointed beard and tobacco on his breath
With chemicals and a knife
Will investigate the cause of death that was also the cause of
the life—
Would there be a little whisper in the brain 20
A new assertion of the ancient pain
Or would this other touch the secret which I cannot find?

My brain is twisted in a tangled skein
There will be a blinding light and a little laughter
And the sinking blackness of ether 25
I do not know what, after, and I do not care either

The Death of Saint Narcissus

Come under the shadow of this gray rock—
Come in under the shadow of this gray rock,
And I will show you something different from either
Your shadow sprawling over the sand at daybreak, or
5 Your shadow leaping behind the fire against the red rock:
I will show you his bloody cloth and limbs
And the gray shadow on his lips.

He walked once between the sea and the high cliffs
When the wind made him aware of his limbs smoothly passing
    each other
10 And of his arms crossed over his breast.
When he walked over the meadows
He was stifled and soothed by his own rhythm.
By the river
His eyes were aware of the pointed corners of his eyes
15 And his hands aware of the pointed tips of his fingers.
Struck down by such knowledge
He could not live men's ways, but became a dancer before God.
If he walked in city streets
He seemed to tread on faces, convulsive thighs and knees.
20 So he came out under the rock.

First he was sure that he had been a tree,
Twisting its branches among each other
And tangling its roots among each other.

Then he knew that he had been a fish
25 With slippery white belly held tight in his own fingers,
Writhing in his own clutch, his ancient beauty
Caught fast in the pink tips of his new beauty.

>

Then he had been a young girl
Caught in the woods by a drunken old man
Knowing at the end the taste of his own whiteness 30
The horror of his own smoothness,
And he felt drunken and old.

So he became a dancer to God.
Because his flesh was in love with the burning arrows
He danced on the hot sand 35
Until the arrows came.
As he embraced them his white skin surrendered itself to
the redness of blood, and satisfied him.
Now he is green, dry and stained
With the shadow in his mouth.

To Helen

While you were absent in the lavatory
There came a negro with broad flat eyes
Bringing a dish with oranges and bananas,
And another brought coffee and cigars.
I was impatient, my dear, and a little unhappy 5
Needing your large mouth opposite me.
I hung suspended on the finger bowl
Till a white rabbit hopped around the corner
And twitched his nose toward the crumbs.

After the turning of the inspired days

After the turning of the inspired days
After the praying and the silence and the crying
And the inevitable ending of a thousand ways
And frosty vigil kept in withered gardens

After the life and death of lonely places
After the judges and the advocates and wardens
And the torchlight red on sweaty faces
After the turning of inspired nights
And the shaking spears and flickering lights—
After the living and the dying—

After the ending of this inspiration
And the torches and the faces and the shouting
The world seemed futile—like a Sunday outing.

I am the Resurrection and the Life

I am the Resurrection and the Life
I am the things that stop, and those that flow.
I am the husband and the wife
And the victim and the sacrificial knife
I am the fire, and the butter also.

So through the evening, through the violet air

So through the evening, through the violet air
One tortured meditation dragged me on
Concatenated words from which the sense seemed gone—
—When comes, to the sleeping or the wake
The This-do-ye-for-my-sake
When to the sullen sunbaked houses and the trees
The one essential word that frees
The inspiration that delivers and expresses
This wrinkled road which twists and winds and guesses:
Oh, through the violet sky, through the evening air
A chain of reasoning whereof the thread was gone
Gathered strange images through which we walked alone:

A woman drew her long black hair out tight
And fiddled whisper-music on those strings
The shrill bats quivered through the violet air 15
Whining, and beating wings.
A man, distorted by some mental blight
Yet of abnormal powers
I saw him creep head downward down a wall
And upside down in air were towers 20
Tolling reminiscent bells.
And there were chanting voices out of cisterns and of wells.

My feverish impulsions gathered head
A man lay flat upon his back, and cried
'It seems that I have been a long time dead: 25
Do not report me to the established world
It has seen strange revolutions since I died'.

As a deaf mute swimming deep below the surface
Knowing neither up nor down, swims down and down
In the calm deep water where no stir nor surf is 30
Swims down and down;
And about his hair the seaweed purple and brown.

So in our fixed confusion we persisted, out from town.

Introspection

The mind was six feet deep in a
cistern and a brown snake with a tri-
angular head having swallowed his
tail was struggling like two fists
interlocked. His head slipped along
the brick wall, scraping at the
cracks.

The Engine

I

The engine hammered and hummed. Flat faces of American business men lay along the tiers of chairs in one plane, broken only by the salient of a brown cigar and the red angle of a six-penny magazine. The machine was hard, deliberate, and alert; having chosen with motives and ends unknown to cut through the fog it pursued its course; the life of the deck stirred and was silent like a restless scale on the smooth surface. The machine was certain and sufficient as a rose bush, indifferently justifying the aimless parasite.

II

After the engine stopped, I lay in bed listening while the wash subsided and the scuffle of feet died out. The music ceased, but a mouth organ from the steerage picked up the tune. I switched on the light, only to see on the wall a spider taut as a drumhead, the life of endless geological periods concentrated into a small spot of intense apathy at my feet. 'And if the ship goes down' I thought drowsily 'he is prepared and will somehow persist, for he is very old. But the flat faces . . .' I tried to assemble these nebulae into one pattern. Failing, I roused myself to hear the machine recommence, and then the music, and the feet upon the deck.

Hidden under the heron's wing

Hidden under the heron's wing
Or the song before daybreak that the lotos-birds sing
Evening whisper of stars together
Oh my beloved what do you bring—

With evening feet walking across the grass 5
And fragile arms dividing the evening mist.

I lie on the floor a bottle's broken glass
To be swept away by the housemaid's crimson fist.

O lord, have patience

Justitia mosse il mio alto fattore

Mi fece la divina potestate

La somma sapienza e il primo amore
O lord, have patience
Pardon these derelictions—
I shall convince these romantic irritations
By my classical convictions.

In silent corridors of death

In silent corridors of death
Short sighs and stifled breath,
Short breath and silent sighing;
Somewhere the soul crying.
And I wander alone 5

Without haste without hope without fear
Without pressure or touch—
There is no moan
Of Souls dying
10 Nothing here
But the warm
Dry airless sweet scent
Of the alleys of death
Of the corridors of death

Airs of Palestine, No. 2

God from a Cloud to Spender spoke
And breathed command: 'Take thou this Rod,
And smite therewith the living Rock';
And Spender hearkened unto God.

5 God shook the Cloud from East to West,
Riding the swart tempestuous blast;
And Spender, like a man possess'd,
Stood quaking, tremulous, aghast.

And Spender struck the living Rock,
10 And lo! the living Rock was wet,
From which henceforth at twelve o'clock
Issues the Westminster Gazette.

Swift at the stroke of Spender's pen
The viscid torrents crawl and writhe
15 Down the long lanes of dogs and men
To Canning Town and Rotherhithe,

To Bermondsey and Wapping Stair,
To Clapham Junction and to Sheen,

To Leicester and to Grosvenor Square
Bubble those floods of bilious green. 20

To Old Bond Street, the street of gems,
To Hammersmith and Stamford's rill;
Troubling the sources of the Thames
Mounting the crest of Highgate Hill.

And higher still the torrent flows 25
And circles Zion's pearly wall,
Wherein, by Mary's garden close,
There sit Saint Peter and Saint Paul.

For there the risen souls flock in
And there they innocently strip, 30
And purge themselves of all their sin
Up to the navel or the hip.

And such as have the skill to swim
Attain at length the farther shore
Cleansed and rejoiced in every limb, 35
And hate the Germans more and more.

They are redeemed from heresies
And all their frowardness forget;
The scales are fallen from their eyes
Thanks to the Westminster Gazette. 40

Petit Epître

Ce n'est pas pour qu'on se dégoute
Ou gout d'égout de mon Ego
Qu'ai fait des vers de faits divers
Qui sentent un peu trop la choucroute.
Mais qu'est-ce que j'ai fait, nom d'un nom, 5

Pour faire ressortir les chacals?
J'ai dit qu'il y a une odeur mâle
Et aussi une odeur fémelle
Et que ces deux sont pas la même.
10 (L'autre jour, à mi-carême,
Je l'ai constaté, chez une telle).
Ce que dit autrement le prêtre.
Surtout à la saison de rut.
Alors, on a fait chahue
15 Et enfoncé mes deux fenêtres.

Qu'est-ce que j'ai fait, nom d'un nom,
Pour agiter les morpions?
Ce que j'ai fait, je te le dis,
Je conçevais un Paradis
20 Ou l'on partagerait ses biens;
(J'aurais également les tiens).
Monsieur le préfet de police
Il en a assez, de ses vices,
Il marmotte, lunettes sur le nez:
25 'C'est de la promiscuité.'
Alors, il faut que je lui rende
Cinq cents balles, qui sert d'amende.

Messieurs les rédacteurs
Et tous les autres maîtres-chanteurs
30 Et tous les gens étiquetés
M'ont dressé tous, leur questionnaires.
'Il se moque de l'égalité?'
—'Mais c'est un vrai réactionnaire'.
'Il dit du mal de nos ministres?'
35 —'Mais c'est un saboteur, le cuistre'.
'Ici il cite un allemand?'
—'Mais c'est un suppôt de Satan!'

'Est-ce qu'il doute la vie future?'
—'Certes, c'est un homme de moeurs impures'.
'Ne nie pas l'existence de Dieu?' 40
—'Comme il est superstitueux!'
'Est-ce qu'il n'a pas d'enfants?'
—'Il est eunuque, ça s'entend'.
'Pour les dames
Ne réclame 45
pas la vote? Pédéraste, sans doute'.

'Quant à son livre, qu'on s'en foute!'
Ces baragouins
De sagouins
Je les entends le long de la route. 50

Tristan Corbière

'Il devint pour un instant parisien'

Marin! je te connais, rentier du cinquième
Qui veillait dans la nuit comme un vieil hibou;
Râclant sa gorge, toi qu'on nomme *an Ankou*,
Sur un grabat accroupi, barbe pointue, gueule blême.

Dans la chambre voisine s'entretiennent des scandales 5
Un commis portugais et une dame à cent sous:
Entre les chuchotements à travers quelques trous
—Bat sur les côtes brétonnes la mer en rafales.

Des rayons de soleil, par une chaude après-midi
Nous montrent, au Luxembourg, des messieurs barbus gris 10
Redingotés, clignant des dames à la poudre de riz.

Et Lieutenant Loti, très bien dans sa tenue,
Se promène dans les pages des complaisantes Revues
Comme au coin du boulevard une vielle ancienne grue.

Ode

> *To you particularly, and to all the Volscians*
> *Great hurt and mischief.*

Tired.
Subterrene laughter synchronous
With silence from the sacred wood
And bubbling of the uninspired
Mephitic river.

5 Misunderstood
The accents of the now retired
Profession of the calamus.

Tortured.
When the bridegroom smoothed his hair
10 There was blood upon the bed.
Morning was already late.
Children singing in the orchard
(Io Hymen, Hymenæe)
Succuba eviscerate.

15 Tortuous.
By arrangement with Perseus
The fooled resentment of the dragon
Sailing before the wind at dawn.
Golden apocalypse. Indignant
20 At the cheap extinction of his taking-off.
Now lies he there
Tip to tip washed beneath Charles' Wagon.

The Death of the Duchess

I

The inhabitants of Hampstead have silk hats
On Sunday afternoon go out to tea
On Saturday have tennis on the lawn, and tea
On Monday to the city, and then tea.
They know what they are to feel and what to think, 5
They know it with the morning printer's ink
They have another Sunday when the last is gone
They know what to think and what to feel
The inhabitants of Hampstead are bound forever on the wheel.

But what is there for you and me 10
For me and you
What is there for us to do
Where the leaves meet in leafy Marylebone?

In Hampstead there is nothing new
And in the evening, through lace curtains, the aspidistra grieves. 15

II

In the evening people hang upon the bridge rail
Like onions under the eaves.
In the square they lean against each other, like sheaves
Or walk like fingers on a table
Dogs' eyes reaching over the table 5
Are in their heads when they stare
Supposing that they have the heads of birds
Beaks and no words,

What words have we?

<

10 I should like to be in a crowd of beaks without words
But it is terrible to be alone with another person.

We should have marble floors
And firelight on your hair
There will be no footsteps up and down the stair

15 The people leaning against another in the square
Discuss the evening's news, and other bird things.

My thoughts tonight have tails, but no wings.
They hang in clusters on the chandelier
Or drop one by one upon the floor.
20 Under the brush her hair
Spread out in little fiery points of will
Glowed into words, then was suddenly still.

'You have cause to love me, I did enter you in my heart
Before ever you vouchsafed to ask for the key'.

25 With her back turned, her arms were bare
Fixed for a question, her hands behind her hair
And the firelight shining where the muscle drew.

My thoughts in a tangled bunch of heads and tails —
One suddenly released, fell to the floor
30 One that I knew:
'Time to regain the door'.
It crossed the carpet and expired on the floor.

And if I said 'I love you' should we breathe
Hear music, go a-hunting, as before?
35 The hands relax, and the brush proceed?
Tomorrow when we open to the chambermaid
When we open the door

Could we address her or should we be afraid?
If it is terrible alone, it is sordid with one more.

If I said 'I do not love you' we should breathe 40
The hands relax, and the brush proceed?
How terrible that it should be the same!
In the morning, when they knock upon the door
We should say: This and this is what we need
And if it rains, the closed carriage at four. 45
We should play a game of chess
The ivory men make company between us
We should play a game of chess
Pressing lidless eyes and waiting for a knock upon the door.

Time to regain the door. 50

'*When I grow old I shall have all the court*
Powder their hair with arras, to be like me.
But I know you love me, it must be that you love me'.

Then I suppose they found her
As she turned 55
To interrogate the silence fixed behind her.

I am steward of her revenue
But I know, and I know she knew . . .

Song

The golden foot I may not kiss or clutch
Glowed in the shadow of the bed
This thought this ghost this pendulum in the head
Swinging from life to death
5 Bleeding between two lives

Waiting a touch a breath

The wind sprang up and broke the bells
Is it a dream or something else
When the surface of the blackened river
10 Is a face that sweats with tears?
I saw across an alien river
The campfire shake the spears

Elegy

Our prayers dismiss the parting shade
And breathe a hypocrite's amen!
The wrong'd Aspatia returned
Wreathed in the wingèd cyclamen.

5 How steadfastly I should have mourned
The sinking of so dear a head!
Were't not for dreams: a dream restores
The always inconvenient dead.

The sweat transpirèd from my pores!
10 I saw sepulchral gates, flung wide
Reveal (as in a tale by Poe)
The features of the injured bride!

>

That hand, prophetical and slow
(Once warm, once lovely, often kissed)
Tore the disordered cerements, 15
Around that head the scorpions hissed!

Remorse unbounded, grief intense
Had striven to expiate the fault—
But poison not my present bliss!
And keep within thy charnel vault! 20

God, in a rolling ball of fire
Pursues by day my errant feet.
His flames of anger and desire
Approach me with consuming heat.

Dirge

Full fathom five your Bleistein lies
Under the flatfish and the squids.
Graves' Disease in a dead jew's eyes!
When the crabs have eat the lids.
Lower than the wharf rats dive 5
Though he suffer a sea-change
Still expensive rich and strange

That is lace that was his nose
See upon his back he lies
(Bones peep through the ragged toes) 10
With a stare of dull surprise
Flood tide and ebb tide
Roll him gently side to side
See the lips unfold unfold
From the teeth, gold in gold 15
Lobsters hourly keep close watch
Hark! now I hear them scratch scratch scratch

Those are pearls that were his eyes. See!

Those are pearls that were his eyes. See!
And the crab clambers through his stomach, the eel grows big
And the torn algae drift above him,
And the sea colander.
5 Still and quiet brother are you still and quiet

Exequy

Persistent lovers will repair
(In time) to my suburban tomb,
A pilgrimage, when I become
A local deity of love,
5 And pious vows and votive prayer
Shall hover in my sacred grove
Sustained on that Italian air.

When my athletic marble form
Forever lithe, forever young,
10 With grateful garlands shall be hung
And flowers of deflowered maids;
The cordial flame shall keep me warm,
A bloodless shade among the shades
Doing no good, but not much harm.

15 While the melodious fountain falls
(Carved by the cunning Bolognese)
The Adepts twine beneath the trees
The sacrificial exercise.
They terminate the festivals
20 With some invariable surprise
Of fireworks, or an Austrian waltz.

>

But if, more violent, more profound,
One soul, disdainful or disdained,
Shall come, his shadowed beauty stained
The colour of the withered year, 25
   Self-immolating on the Mound
Just at the crisis, he shall hear
   A breathless chuckle underground.
SOVEGNA VOS A TEMPS DE MON DOLOR.

The Builders

Song for Unison Singing from 'The Rock'

Ill done and undone
London so fair.
We will build London
Bright in dark air,
With new bricks and mortar 5
Beside the Thames bord
Queen of Island and Water
A House of our Lord.
A Church for us all and work for us all
And God's world for us all even unto this last. 10

Dwellings for all men
Churches for all
Shall the fruit fall, then
By the waste wall?
And shall the fruit fall then 15
The harvest be waste
When the Saviour of all men
Our sowing has graced?
A Church for us all and work for us all
And God's world for us all even unto this last. 20

<

Shall arms be useless
Fingers unbent
Effort be fruitless
Money misspent?
25 We build the new towers
And raise the new shrine
In this London of ours
Of yours and of mine.
A Church for us all and work for us all
30 And God's world for us all even unto this last.

Mr. Pugstyles: The Elegant Pig

There are plenty of folk with fantastical notions
Of foreign bred pigs which our village disdains;
With their hairy wild Irish, their little French cochons,
Their bloated Westphalians, and burly blond Danes.
5 I says of all such, pitch 'em into the ocean,
For if you touch pitch, why it only defiles:
There is only one pig what deserves our devotion—
Our Worcestershire heavyweight, Mr. Pugstyles.
Mr. Pugstyles, Mr. Pugstyles,
10 What a wonderful pig is our Mr. Pugstyles.

From the tips of his ears to the ends of his pedals
He's enough to make all other champions despair.
He takes the blue ribbons, he takes the gold medals
At all the stock shows and our grand county fair.
15 Other counties have schemers, contrivers and plotters;
Their underbred swine only merit our smiles:
For the curve of his chaps and the trim of his trotters
Proclaim the perfections of Mr. Pugstyles.
Mr. Pugstyles, Mr. Pugstyles,
20 Our Worcestershire heavyweight, Mr. Pugstyles.
>

Not at Highbury Barn, or in sweet Maida Vale,
Or at shady Nine Elms can such porkers be seen;
Not at rural Chalk Farm, or remote Notting Dale,
Or where the cows graze along Camberwell Green.
No not in the Minories, not in Old Jewry, 25
Not where the swine along Lothbury glide;
Not in the sweet-smelling stys of Old Drury
Or where the hogs roll down the lanes of Cheapside
Can you find such a pig
No not such a pig 30
As our Worcestershire heavyweight, Mr. Pugstyles.

We had an election down our way last week,
Which seems an unreasonable thing for to do;
And some gentlemen come down from London to speak
And they talked and they talked and they talked their selves blue. 35
They talked their selves hoarse till they hardly could croak.
So we rushed to the Wheatsheaf, we rushed to the Boar,
We rushed to the Angel, we rushed to the Oak,
And we all had a pint, and a pint or two more,
Until suddenly somebody started to roar: 40
'Mr. Pugstyles, Mr. Pugstyles,
What a wonderful pig is our Mr. Pugstyles'.

Then we laughed and we laughed till we thought we should choke,
And we rushed from the Wheatsheaf, we rushed from the Boar,
We rushed from the Angel, we rushed from the Oak, 45
Some come through the window and some through the door;
We rushed down the street till we reached the town hall,
All cheering until you could hear us for miles,
And together we bust out to bellow and bawl:
'The man for our money is Mr. Pugstyles. 50
Mr. Pugstyles, we want Pugstyles,
We won't have any member but Mr. Pugstyles'.

<

So Mr. Pugstyles he received every vote
And we chaired him, and give him a gallon of milk,
55 And a tall shiny hat, and a long taily coat
And a shilling cigar and a necktie of silk.
So now we live quiet, and leave well alone
And ignore all those Parliament folk and their wiles.
Let 'em mind their own business, we'll manage our own,
60 While we're represented by Mr. Pugstyles.
Mr. Pugstyles, Mr. Pugstyles,
Our Worcestershire heavyweight, Mr. Pugstyles.

Bellegarde

Leaping pleasure passes tunefully,
Is medecined mournfully,
Follows futility, greedily grasped;
Pleasure, not only, not of lushness:
5 Pleasure of vanity, imagination
Self-conceitfulness, greedily grasped,
Lust were more real, some thing apprehensible,
Held in the hand, matchless a moment,
Fades fast, perishes in impotence. Light lives
10 Slip from fingers slip
When freely fingered.

What strange apparition presents itself.
All men have their ghosts from the past.
And some are more unwelcome than this
15 Which has a silken smell of jollity.

The Anniversary

It is not right for likes of me
To speak upon a jubilee
Occasion of solemnity.
I have no skill of noble phrase,
Nor am I practised in the ways 5
Of poetry, like Mr. Mase-
field. When he writes about the King,
His classic measures rock and swing
And bump along like anything.
So having asked your pardon all, 10
My present subject I'll recall.
I'd gladly drink a pt. of beer
In honour of the Dr. here
Or drain a glass of apple juice
Or anything you might produce: 15
There's nothing that I would refuse
For wishing him the best of health
And peace of mind, and moderate wealth.
So take your pipkins, panikins or firkins
While I propose the Toast of DOCTOR PERKINS. 20

A Valedictory

Forbidding Mourning: to the Lady of the House.

In springtime, when the year was new,
The morning grass was fresh with dew;
In autumn's season of regret
The morning flowers are moister yet
5 When now the tardy rose appears,
It sparkles, not with dew, but tears;
Its head is bent with patient grief;
There runs a shudder through the leaf.
The violas and hollyhocks
10 Have now put off their coloured frocks.
The zinnia and marigold
Shall go to join beneath the mould
The tulip and the daffodil.
But on the wall there quivers still
15 A tear within the lonely eye
Of Clematis Jackmanii.
The myosotis blue proclaim
With colour shrill, their English name;
And still the robin tries to sing
20 And cheat the winter into spring.

—

O long procession, happy flowers,
That passed through spring and summer hours,
Eager to blossom, and to try
To win approval, and to die,
25 With grateful knowledge, that they grew
To greet the eyes of one who knew
Their ways and needs in every kind,
And when to prune, and when to bind

And when to cut and when to move,
With tender skill inspired by love. 30

—

O happy flowers, that have gone
Quietly, to oblivion,
And with your beauty have repaid
The hand that trimmed, and trained, and sprayed.
O happy stems, that not resent 35
The winter's long imprisonment;
O happy roots, that live beneath
The calm impertinence of death.
When the revolving year shall bring
The sweet deception of the spring, 40
Dare you put on your gaudy jerkins,
Unsupervised by Mrs. Perkins?

—

We often think that man alone
Remembers in the singing bone.
'Green earth forgets': but I surmise 45
That gardens have long memories;
Like houses, have familiar ghosts
Of dear and hospitable hosts.
Laughter and happiness and grief
Revive within the budding leaf. 50
Houses remember: since you came,
Nothing in Campden is the same.
Objects inanimate will yearn
Inaudibly, for your return,
And human wishes shall be full 55
Of aspirations audible,
Which, ratified from hour to hour,
Possess, we hope, magnetic power.

Pollicle Dogs and Jellicle Cats

I was lunching one day at The Princess Louise,
When I passed some remark to a man in white spats
Who had ordered a plate of fried gammon and peas,
So we soon fell to talking of thisses and thats—
5 Such as Pollicle Dogs and Jellicle Cats.

I have been, he confided, a jack of all trades,
A true rolling stone that has gathered no moss,
I have seen much of life, in its various shades,
And the fat and the lean, and the profit and loss;
10 I have done everything and I've been everywhere,
(I'm at present an agent for small furnished flats)—
But the one thing that's made life worth while, I declare,
Is Pollicle Dogs and Jellicle Cats.

I have been, he continued, involved with the Turf
15 In the work of Accountant, in quite a small way,
I invented an excellent specific for scurf,
I bought second-hand goods, and I once wrote a play;
I have acted as guide, on a Levantine Tour,
And at one time I travelled (from Luton) in hats:
20 And for all my misfortunes I've found but one cure—
And that's Pollicle Dogs and Jellicle Cats.

Now my sister, for instance, who lives in the hills
That lie on the border of Shropshire and Wales,
In a comfortable house where her husband fulfils
25 His vocation of retail purveyor of ales,
She says, and for me I've no reason to doubt
Her opinion, repeated in dozens of chats—
She says there is one thing she can't do without
And that's Pollicle Dogs and Jellicle Cats.

>

And my brother, for instance, who lives in the plains 30
That lie on the border of Surrey and Kent,
In a house newly built and with adequate drains,
You would be quite surprised to know how much he spent
On that house—he has actually had to employ
Two men snaring rabbits and two catching rats— 35
He says, there is nothing that he can enjoy
Like Pollicle Dogs and Jellicle Cats.

Now my sister, of whom I have told you before,
Is musically gifted, can sing like a bird,
She can learn any tune and can read any score, 40
She can sing any song that you ever have heard.
I have never known anyone had such an ear,
And she never goes wrong on the sharps or the flats:
She says, there are no voices so pleasant to hear
As of Pollicle Dogs and Jellicle Cats. 45

And my brother, of whom you have just heard me speak,
Is a talented artist, I mean amateur;
He only has time at the end of the week,
But his portraits have made a considerable stir.
He can sketch you, in no time, almost anybody, 50
From Lady Godiva to Ingoldsby Oddie—
He can draw like Italians, or Frenchmen, or Dutch,
But prefers to draw people with whiskers and hats:
And *he* says, there's no subject that suits him so much
As Pollicle Dogs and Jellicle Cats. 55

Well, I said very quickly, that's quite understood,
So now let me order a small glass of port—
It will set your tongue wagging, and do your heart good,
(Any port in a storm, as a final resort):
Besides, there's a question I now wish to put, 60
Though I know what is what, and I know that is that.

What you've said is exceedingly curious. But
What's a Pollicle Dog? and a Jellicle Cat?

Well at that he turned round with a look of surprise,
65 As much as to say, Well now what about that?
Do I actually see with my own very eyes
A man who's not heard of a Jellicle Cat?
And a man who's not heard of a Pollicle Dog
Can't know enough even to fall off a log—
70 Well, he said, at the worst there is hope for you yet;
It's exceedingly lucky for you that we met.
If you do not object to my talking in verse—
Not at all, I replied, I enjoy it of all things,
It's a good way to put either large things or small things;
75 There is nothing like poetry for real monologues—
So with that he began

ABOUT POLLICLE DOGS.

The Country Walk

An Epistle, to John Hayward Esqre., suggested by certain experiences of the Author, in the Countryside of the West of England, and set down after parting from Canon Tissington Tatlow, at the corner of Lime Street and Fenchurch Street.

Of all the beasts that God allows
In England's green and pleasant land
I most of all dislike the Cows.
Their ways I do not understand.
5 It puzzles me why they should stare
At me, who am so innocent;
Their stupid gaze is hard to bear—
It's positively truculent.

I'm very inconspicuous
And scarlet ties I never wear; 10
I'm not a London Transport Bus
And yet at me they always stare.
You may reply, to fear a Cow
Is Cowardice the rustic scorns:
But still your reason must allow 15
That I am weak, and she has horns.
But most I'm terrified when walking
With country dames in brogues and tweeds,
Who will persist in hearty talking
And stopping to discuss the breeds. 20
To country people Cows are mild
And flee from any stone they throw,
But I'm a timid City Child,
As all the cattle seem to know.
But when in lanes alone I stroll, 25
O then in vain their horns are tossed,
In vain their bloodshot eyes they roll,
Of me they shall not make their boast.
Beyond the wall, or five-barred gate,
My sober wishes never stray; 30
For me their deadly prongs may wait,
But I can always run away!
Or I could take sanctuary
In any oak or apple tree.

T. S. Eliot

6. xii. 36

I am asked by my friend, the Man in White Spats

I am asked by my friend, the Man in White Spats—
  Who, to my way of thinking, has nothing to do
But attend to the horrible sharps and the flats
  Of his Budgerigars and his prize Cockatoo,
5 But who still has one feature we may call redeeming
  (I've observed him quite closely and know it is true),
And which briefly and shortly is this: to all seeming
  He has a most touching devotion to YOU—
I am asked by my friend, as I started to say,
10 And I may say he said it quite off his own bat—
I am asked by the Man in White Spats to convey
  This informative poem on a Curious Cat.

[*The Rum Tum Tugger*]

Now that's what my friend, the Man in White Spats,
Has asked me to convey, in the matter of Cats.

A Proclamation

Fair stood the wind for France
  When the Jellicle Cat jumped out;
But O for the touch of a vanished hand,
  And sixpenny-worth of stout.

5 The farmer gave his daughter the ring,
  And the Jellicle Cat stood by,
The face that launched a thousand ships
  Had a knowing look in its eye.

The toadstool on the mossy bank
10 Muttered aloud in its sleep;

Jellicle Cats are Jellicle Cats.
　　They sow and they also reap.

Once more unto the breach, dear friend
　　The Jellicle hosts proclaim;
Make wing at once to the rooky wood, 15
　　It's all a part of the game.

Ring out the old, ring in the new,
　　Jellicle Cats have got the vote;
Helen of Troy set out to sea
　　In a beautiful pea-green boat. 20

Jellicles all, come blow up your horn,
　　The year's at the spring, too-wit too-woo;
Cassia buds and Venetian blinds,
　　And never a spray of rue.

Let Jellicle joy be unconfined, 25
　　And Jellicle love bring down the sky;
For Cats may come since Cats must go
　　For an annual holiday.

Cetera desunt......

Roger Roughton

A Practical Possum

A Practical Possum once lived in a Pye,
Surrounded by Gravy and Sweet Pertaters,
And he always walked out with a Glass in his Eye
And a Clerical Hat and an apron and gaiters.
For a Possum who dresses in Style 5
　Is certain to be observed;

And everyone said: 'What a Charming Smile!
    And isn't he Well Preserved!'

Now a Possum who lives in a Pye
10   Is Doing Himself very well.
There was only one thing that was wrong with the Pye
    And that one thing was the Smell.
There was nothing exactly precisely wrong—
It wasn't too mild and it wasn't too strong,
15   There was nothing you'd wish to subtract—
    Only something or other it lacked.

No one could say, in such a Pye,
    That the Possum was in the Soup.
Still less was he high & dry;
20   It was better by far than a cage or a coop,
    It was better than having the measles or croup,
But once again, let me tell
You, something was wrong with the Smell.

So the Possum went to the Grocer,
25 And he said to the Grocer: 'O! Sir!
    Can you give me a Smell for my Pye?'
    Said the Grocer: 'That can I.
Some Condy's Fluid, some Keating's Powder,
Some Onions from Spain, and a Cheese from Gouda
30 And a cake of Life Buoy Soap', said the Grocer,
    'Will give the right Smell to your Pye.'
But the Possum answered: 'No! Sir!'
    And he shut his Other Eye.

Then the Possum lighted a large Cheroot
35 And he went to the Chemist (whose name was Boot)
    And he asked for a Smell for his Pye.
And the Chemist said: 'I am willing to try.

I suggest some cod liver oil and malt,
With some syrup of figs and Eno's Salt
And a pinch of iodoform as a Spice, 40
All for a small inclusive price.
The Smell', said the Chemist, 'will be very nice.'
  So the Possum heaved a Sigh
  And shut his Other Eye.
And the Chemist went on talking, but 45
The Possum by now had Both Eyes shut.

But while the Possum was fast asleep
  The Lavender Fairy was wide awake.
She flew to the Pye and took a peep
  And gave her Magical Bag a shake 50
      Right into the Possum's Pye.
      And darted away in the sky.
Then the Possum awoke and composed this song:
'I must be right and I can't be wrong;
It isn't too mild and it isn't too strong. 55
      The Perfect Pye for a Possum
      Must be flavoured with Lavender Blossom.
Asleep or awake, there is no mistake:
A Lavender Pye, we must now suppose,
Is the best for a Practical Possum's Nose 60
And the tips of his ears and his tail and his toes.'

The Practical Cat

The Practical Cat goes up the flues,
The Practical Cat goes down the drains;
He keeps in order the boots and shoes,
He tidies the pillows and counterpanes.
The Practical Cat arranges flowers, 5

He loves to polish a shiny hat;
He sweeps and scrubs and scrapes and scours:
Oopsa! The Practical Cat.

The Practical Cat is the Family Friend,
10 The Practical Cat objects to waste;
He knows when the jam has come to an end,
And whether the soup has the proper taste.
If there's anything spilt in the kitchen his pride is
To clear up the mess on table or mat;
15 He's always ready for fish on Fridays:
OOPSA! The Practical Cat.

The Practical Cat can straighten pictures,
He always knows what game is in season;
He keeps an eye on the bathroom-fixtures,
20 If there's anything wrong he knows the reason.
He sets his hair with a brush and comb—
And isn't he neat in his best cravat!
INDISPENSABLE in the Home!
O O P S A ! ! ! The Practical Cat.

The Jim Jum Bears

The Jim Jum Bears are at their Tricks,
The Jim Jum Bears have been at it again;
They've broken a clock and scattered the bricks
And one went right through a window pane.
5 And when there's a noise when we ought to be quiet,
And we're in bed and the lights are out,
Then Nurse declares:
'It's those Jim Jum Bears,
Those Jim Jum Bears!
10 Was ever a Nurse so put about!'
>

The Jim Jum Bears are sharp as mustard,
They splash right into the mutton broth;
They get their faces all covered with custard,
They leave Dirty Marks on the table cloth.
They drop the toys all down the stairs, 15
They track muddy feet all over the hall;
And Nurse declares:
'The Jim Jum Bears,
The Jim Jum Bears,
I can't a-bear those Bears at all!' 20

The Marching Song of the Pollicle Dogs

There are dogs out of every nation,
 The Irish, the Welsh and the Dane;
The Russian, the Dutch, the Dalmatian,
 And even from China and Spain;
The Poodle, the Pom, the Alsatian 5
 And the mastiff who walks on a chain.
And to those that are frisky and frollical
 Let my meaning be perfectly plain:
That my name it is Little Tom Pollicle—
 And you'd better not do it again. 10

There are dogs that are sniffy and curious,
 There are dogs that are drowsy and dumb;
There are dogs that are sleeky and spurious,
 There are dogs that are mimsy and mum.
There are dogs that are frantic and furious— 15
 And I say of such: let 'em all come.
And to those that are rowdy and rollical
 Let my meaning be perfectly plain:

That my name it is Little Tom Pollicle—
20 And you'd better not do it again.

There are dogs that are frowsy and frumpious,
There are dogs that are freaky and frail;
There are dogs that are growly and grumpious,
There are dogs that are puny and pale.
25 But I say, if you're surly and scrumpious,
Just you tread on the tip of my tail!
For my meaning is not amphibolical
And I'd like it to be very plain
That my name it is Little Tom Pollicle—
30 And you'd better not do it again.

For our motto is still *cave canem*—
That's the cry of the Pollicle Clan,
And our words we'll not stop to explain 'em,
But bark 'em as loud as we can.
35 For the way to show how you disdain 'em
Is to bark at dog, devil and man.
And be ye the most diabolical
Of what diabolic may be—
Yet my name it is Little Tom Pollicle,
40 And WHA MAUN MEDDLE WI' ME?

Billy M'Caw: The Remarkable Parrot

Oh, how well I remember the old Bull and Bush,
Where we used to go down of a Sattaday night —
Where, when anythink happened, it come with a rush,
For the boss, Mr. Clark, he was very polite;
5 And he wouldn't have anythink what wasn't right.
And what with the Station it being so near,

And what with the water got into the beer
    (There was two kinds of beer, the thick and the clear)
A very nice House it was. Oh dear!
I'll never forget it. From basement to garret 10
A very nice House. Ah, but it was the parret—
The parret, the parret named Billy M'Caw,
    That brought all those folk to the bar.
    Ah! he was the Life of the bar.
Of a Sattaday night, we was all feeling bright, 15
And Lily La Rose—the Barmaid that was—
She'd say: 'Billy!
                Billy M'Caw!
Come give us a dance on the bar!'
    And Billy would dance on the bar.

Lily, she was a girl what had brains in her head; 20
She wouldn't have nothink, no not that much said.
If it come to an argument, or a dispute,
She'd settle it offhand with the toe of her boot
    Or as likely as not put her fist through your eye.
But when we was thirsty, and just a bit sad, 25
Or when we was happy, and just a bit dry,
She would rap on the bar with that corkscrew she had
And say: 'Billy!
                Billy M'Caw!
Come give us a tune on your pastoral flute!'
    And Billy'd strike up on his pastoral flute. 30

And then we'd feel balmy, in each eye a tear,
And emotion would make us all order more beer—
For the way that Bird played, with his Robin Adairs,
And his All in the Downs, and his Wapping Old Stairs,
Would bring tears to the eyes of a donkey, it would. 35
There was no use of saying that Bird wasn't good.

And when we was feeling exceedingly tearful,
Then Lily would say: 'Now, let's have somethink cheerful!
Billy!
        Billy M'Caw!
40 Come give us a tune on your moley guitar!'
    And Billy'd strike up on his moley guitar.

Oh, how well I remember the old Bull and Bush
    Where the folk came from near and from far.
A very nice House. From basement to garret
45 A very nice House. Ah but it was the parret,
    The parret, the parret named Billy M'Caw,
Who brought all those folk to the bar.
    Ah, he was the Life of the bar.

Grizabella: The Glamour Cat

. . . She haunted many a low resort
    Near the grimy road of Tottenham Court;
    She flitted about the No Man's Land
    From *The Rising Sun* to *The Friend at Hand.*
5 And the postman sighed, as he scratched his head:
    'You'd really ha' thought she'd ought to be dead—
    And who would ever suppose that THAT
    Was Grizabella, the Glamour Cat!"

In Respect of Felines

Dear Madam,
Thank you for your letter. I am grieved to find
That in respect of felines you are so confused in mind.

You would be qualified to criticise me if you had
Perceived the truth that no one Cat is wholly good or bad.

At least, of all the Cats between Mousehole and John o'Groats, 5
You can't say, some of them are sheep and other Cats are goats.

For even the nicest tabby that was ever born and weaned
Is capable of acting, on occasion, like a fiend.

And even my toughest characters, who gloat in doing harm,
Are not entirely destitute (admit it, please) of Charm. 10

And all my Cats with one accord disclaim the title 'pets',
Which is only suitable to parrots, Pekes and marmosets.

I trust that on consideration you may come to see
The strength of my contention.
Yours truly,
T. S. E.

LINES

Addressed to Geoffrey Faber Esquire, on his Return from a Voyage to the Bahamas, and the Parts about New Spain

ULYSSES, in his age, had tales to tell
Of battle, shipwreck, and descents to hell;
Of foreign people, with peculiar names,
Of feasts and frolicks and funereal games,
5 Of sirens' quiring, and enchantress' art:
His patient consort knew them all by heart.
He told of polyphemes, and clashing rocks:
She went on darning and un-darning socks.
At Circe or Calypso (which was which?)
10 She sighed, and only dropped another stitch,
And, regist'ring th' expected smiles and tears,
Murmur'd, 'a lot can happen in ten years'.
FABRICIUS, an we credit what he speaks,
Compressed as much experience into weeks . . .
15 Let both Ulysses and his Bard avow,
Which of the three could draw the longest bow.

Morgan Tries Again

It's our Mr. Eliot what started me writin';
'E says to me, 'Morgan, you'd easily do worse
Now you're too fat for mousin' and too old for fightin'
Than set down your life; jist you put it in verse'.

5 Well it wasn't no use jist to tell 'im I couldn't,
So I got it all down, and in rhyme more or less.
And I done pretty good, though I says it as shouldn't;
And everyone says that I got a good press.

>

'Well, Morgan' 'e says, 'now you made a good start,
And you got what I call quite a natural style; 10
Now you jist try your paw—let it come from the 'art—
At a birthday oration to honour Miss 'Ile.

'What!' says I, 'that Miss 'Ile what's a friend of Miss Swan?
If you mean that Miss 'Ile, I can't 'ardly decline'.
'Right!' 'e says, 'that's the lady; and now you git on: 15
And what's more, I'll pay you a kipper a line'.

'Coo!' I says, 'that's a bargain. I'll do you a nice prime 'un,
For she 'as a kind way and she 'as a nice smile'.
So with that I set straight down to work at my rhymin'
This birthday oration to honour Miss 'Ile. 20

She's one that old Morgan would most like to see,
Be it winter or summer, in snow-boots or slippers,
At breakfast or luncheon, at dinner or tea:
'And now,' I says, 'jist you 'and over them kippers.'

Montpelier Row

DE LA MARE delicate
China tea and porcelain
Matter-of-fact initiate
Leans against the window pane

Vista of Hanoverian trees 5
His right décor (take care!) which yet
The old enchanter, if he please
May change to haunt of marmoset

Amphisbaena, or ichneumon;
Dissolve the real, make real the dream: 10

Domestic, alien, kind, aloof—
One moment! and we have the proof
As down the far, invisible stream
There drifts, there drifts the visible swan.

NOTES

Line 1. The omission of punctuation makes it possible for the adjective to refer both backwards and forwards. V. Empson: *Seven Types of Ambiguity.* No mention of this type of ambiguity will be found in the work mentioned.

Line 5. *Hanoverian.* It is not assumed that all the trees were planted before the death of William IV, still less that the identical vista could be seen from this window in the eighteenth century. The trees represent, by a sort of metonymy, the effect of the total scene, both indoors and out of doors.

Line 9. For the habits of the amphisbaena, see a poem on this subject by A. E. Housman, published in a periodical of London University.

For the habits of the ichneumon, and its behaviour at windows, see *The Crooked Man* (in *The Memoirs of Sherlock Holmes*).

The possible content of a single sonnet is so restricted, by the limitation to fourteen lines, that a series of sonnets may ensue.

Line 13. *Stream* is weak, but what can you do with *Thames*? It has no rhyme, for, if I mistake not, an A is too long and an E is too short. The only comparable vowel is the A in Pall Mall, which does not rhyme, and could not have been introduced into this sonnet anyway. The nearest rhyme is the name of the German town *Ems*, and if that is pronounced correctly, it is not the same vowel either. And Ems would have been still more remote from the subject than Pall Mall.

Let quacks, empirics, dolts debate

Let quacks, empirics, dolts debate
The quandaries of Church and State.
Let intellectuals address
The latest Cultural Congress.
Here is the true Contemplative, 5
Content to live—perhaps let live—
The Sage, disposed to sit and stare
With a vacant mind in a vacant square.

Inscriptions to Sir Geoffrey Faber on the occasion of his knighthood

AMAZ'D astronomers did late descry

AMAZ'D astronomers did late descry
A new great luminary in the sky.
Straight to the Queen the prompt petition came:
Would She be pleased to give this Star a Name?
5 'Sir Geoffrey let it be'. Her word benign
The Heav'ns approved, and all the Muses Nine.

VERSES

To Honour and Magnify Sir Geoffrey Faber Kt.;

Preſented by Several
of his faithful Henchmen, Satellites & Feodaries
to mark the Occaſion of his *Safe Return*
together with his Good Lady
from the *Antipodes* & the more *Tropick Parts* of Africa.
For which *Safe Return*, and Delivery from all *Perils*
by Land, Sea & Air
We deſire to return *Thanks* to Divine Providence.

÷÷÷÷÷÷÷÷÷÷

A Man ſo various that he ſeem'd to be
A ſcore of Crichtons in epitome;
Practiſ'd in field of War and field of Sport,
Cunning to tame a Bull, or charm a Court;*
A Man of Letters whom we all Admire 5
As Chairman, and reſpect as Country Squire,
And, in the Space of one revolving Moon,
As ſcholar, poet, burſar and patroon,
Eximious in Adminiſtrative Skill,
Or ſkies to ſcan, or Compoſt-land to till. 10
The wondering World exclaim'd, in mild affright:
'Should ſuch a noble Man be leſs than Knight?'
The ſwelling rumour thus to Windſor came,
And Lo! At laſt Sir Geoffrey is his Name.

÷÷÷÷÷÷÷÷÷÷

* *'Court' Reference here is both to the St. Jameſ's and to the Old Bailey.*

Long may this Glass endure, and brim with wine

Long may this Glass endure, and brim with wine
To chant the honours of the Faber line
Sev'rally charactered amidst its quaint design

ANN, in whom bounteous Nature has conjoined
5 Genial creative with calm critic mind

RICHARD, whose subtile diplomatic arts
Uphold the Queen's estate in foreign parts

THOMAS, whose penetrative eyes explore
The darkest secrets of hermetic lore

The gourmet cat was of course Cumberleylaude

The gourmet cat was of course Cumberleylaude,
Who did very little to earn his dinner and board,
Indeed, he was always out and about,
Patronising the haunts where he would find,
People are generous and nice and kind, 5
Serving good food to this culinary lout!

With care he chooses his place to dine,
And dresses accordingly, if he has time,
Tasting all that Neville Road offers,
With never a thought for anyone's coffers! 10
The best is only fit for the best he opines,
When he wants salmon, or duck, or expensive French wines.

Until one day when he will find,
All of the doors closed and the windows blind.
Then monocle and cane he will have to discard 15
And realise that hunting isn't so hard,
That mouse is tasty and starling sweet,
And that Neville Road is a bounteous street!

How the Tall Girl and I Play Together

I love a tall girl. When we stand face to face
She with nothing on and I with nothing on;
She in high heels and I in bare feet,
We can just touch nipple to nipple
5 Tingling and burning. Because she is a tall girl.

I love a tall girl. When she sits on my knee
She with nothing on, and I with nothing on,
I can just take her nipple in my lips
And stroke it with my tongue. Because she is a tall girl.

10 I love a tall girl. When we lie in bed
She on her back and I stretched upon her,
And our middle parts are busy with each other,
My toes play with her toes and my tongue with her tongue,
And all the parts are happy. Because she is a tall girl.

15 When my tall girl sits astraddle on my lap,
She with nothing on and I with nothing on
And our middle parts are about their business,
I can stroke her back and her long white legs
And both of us are happy. Because she is a tall girl.

20 I love a tall girl.
I have a tall girl.
I am glad she is not a small girl.

Sleeping Together

Sleeping together includes a little waking,
Waking for the joy of watching over the beloved,
Listening for the deep and regular breathing
    That tells me she is sleeping.

My arm is round her naked body, 5
My hand is cupping her breast; her nipple
Pushes into the very centre of my palm
    Which quivers with tenderness.

My fingers move softly below, to her navel
And touch the delicate down beneath her navel, 10
Coming to rest on the hair between her thighs.

The miracle of sleeping together is: Confidence
Why should my hand wake her? Even in her sleep
Unconscious but aware, she knows the hand that holds her,
    Knows the fingers that caress her 15

How the Tall Girl's Breasts Are

When my beloved stands tall and naked
Proud and rejoicing, not in her own beauty
But in the knowledge of the power of her beauty
To quicken my desire (as I stand erect before her
5 And quiver with the swelling of my concupiscence)
Her breasts look ripe and full
    In their summer of perfection.

But when my beloved lies upon her back,
Her breasts wide apart look small and firm
10 And high, not ripe but as if still ripening
As they must have looked
    When she was fifteen.

And when my beloved lies upon her side
Her breasts are close together, one lying on the other,
15 So that when I squeeze my hand between them
It is caught and held
    A happy prisoner.

And when my beloved stands beside our bed
Leaning over me and I lie and look up at her,
20 Then her breasts are like ripe pears that dangle
Above my mouth
    Which reaches up to take them.

Dedication II

No peevish winter wind shall chill
No sullen tropic sun shall wither
The love of two minds which are clear to each other
The adoration of two souls which revere each other
The desire of two bodies which adhere to each other. 5

To you I offer this dedication
In three words which for us are at one with each other:
Love adoration desire

Love seeketh not Itself to please

'Love seeketh not Itself to please,
But feareth it give no delight
Dreadeth another's loss of ease
And builds a Hell in Heaven's despite.'

So sang a Pebble of the brook 5
Trodden with the Cattle's feet.
But a little Clod of Clay
Warbled out these metres meet:

'Love that seeketh not to please
And for the other has no care 10
But joys in taking its own ease
Builds a Heaven in Hell's despair.'

The Waste Land: An Editorial Composite

For the genesis of *The Waste Land*, see Commentary headnote to the poem, 1. COMPOSITION.

This editorial composite is a 678-line reading text of the earliest available drafts of the various parts and passages of the poem. By showing TSE's earliest surviving thoughts as a contrast to the published poem, it aims to illustrate how radically it changed during composition. The earliest surviving drafts are not all of the same stage of development (nor all compatible in a reading text), so this composite does not represent the poem at any particular moment.

In places, TSE's sketches are so tentative that the earliest decipherable readings do not make continuous coherent sense and other readings have been preferred. Where an emendation has been made at the time of writing (such as an immediate deletion replaced on the same line rather than above or below), the emendation is followed and the deleted matter is recorded among the variants as *1st reading*. Where a passage has been deleted and immediately redrafted on the same leaf, it is deemed preferable for the reading text to give only the redrafting rather than giving both versions one after the other or to give priority to the deleted draft and treat redrafting as a variant (this applies to the drafts of "Highbury bore me" *WLFacs* 50/51). Where the surrounding text exists only in a later continuous draft, to use the earliest possible sketch of the lines would mean alternating between different archaeological layers of text, so the continuous draft has been preferred (as in the case of "London, the swarming life you kill and breed", 334–47, which has been taken from the continuous typescript *ts3* rather than the earlier *ms1*).

All readings not given in *WLComposite* appear in the Textual History of the poem, along with readings of the three pre-publication typescripts not made by TSE, published texts, and two late manuscripts made by TSE.

Some of the earliest material in "the original manuscript" of *The Waste Land*, sent by TSE to John Quinn on 21 September 1922 had been drafted within autonomous poems or sketches. In her facsimile edition of the drafts (*WLFacs*), Valerie Eliot printed these after the five parts of *The Waste Land* and in the present edition they are printed among the "Uncollected Poems". The likely positions of four of them as "Interludes" between the Parts of *The Waste Land* as TSE conceived it in 1921 are indicated within this editorial composite. It would, however, be impracticable to collate all of the miscellaneous materials as part of the textual history of *The Waste Land* on the grounds that TSE considered them to be part of "the original manuscript". The interludes and the contributory drafts therefore all appear in the chronological sequence of "Uncollected Poems". In common with the rest of that section, but unlike the text of *WLComposite*, they are given in their final form.

Line numbering for *WLComposite* is given in bold, with that of the published poem's equivalent passages appearing in ordinary roman type. Throughout the Commentary and Textual History, references to this editorial composite text use the bold line numbers (**1–678**).

THE WASTE LAND.

By

T. S. Eliot.

"Did he live his life again in every detail of desire, temptation, and surrender during that supreme moment of complete knowledge? He cried in a whisper at some image, at some vision,—he cried out twice, a cry that was no more than a breath—

'The horror! the horror!'"

CONRAD.

HE DO THE POLICE IN DIFFERENT VOICES: Part I.

THE BURIAL OF THE DEAD.

First we had a couple of feelers down at Tom's place,
There was old Tom, boiled to the eyes, blind,
(Don't you remember that time after a dance,
Top hats and all, we and Silk Hat Harry,
5 And old Tom took us behind, brought out a bottle of fizz,
With old Jane, Tom's wife; and we got Joe to sing
"I'm proud of all the Irish blood that's in me,
"There's not a man can say a word agin me").
Then we had dinner in good form, and a couple of Bengal lights.
10 When we got into the show, up in Row A,
I tried to put my foot in the drum, and didn't the girl squeal,
She never did take to me, a nice guy—but rough;
The next thing we were out in the street, Oh was it cold!
When will you be good? Blew in to the Opera Exchange,
15 Sopped up some gin, sat in to the cork game,
Mr. Fay was there, singing "The Maid of the Mill";
Then we thought we'd breeze along and take a walk.
Then we lost Steve.
("I turned up an hour later down at Myrtle's place.
20 What d'y' mean, she says, at two o'clock in the morning,
I'm not in business here for guys like you;
We've only had a raid last week, I've been warned twice.
Sergeant, I said, I've kept a decent house for twenty years,
There's three gents from the Buckingham Club upstairs now,
25 I'm going to retire and live on a farm, she says,
There's no money in it now, what with the damage done,
And the reputation the place gets, on account of a few bar-flies,
I've kept a clean house for twenty years, she says,

And the gents from the Buckingham Club know they're safe here;
You was well introduced, but this is the last of you. 30
Get me a woman, I said; you're too drunk, she said,
But she gave me a bed, and a bath, and ham and eggs,
And now you go get a shave, she said; I had a good laugh,
Myrtle was always a good sport").
We'd just gone up the alley, a fly cop came along, 35
Looking for trouble; committing a nuisance, he said,
You come on to the station. I'm sorry, I said,
It's no use being sorry, he said; let me get my hat, I said.
Well by a stroke of luck who came by but Mr. Donavan.
What's this, officer. You're new on this beat, aint you? 40
I thought so. You know who I am? Yes, I do,
Said the fresh cop, very peevish. Then let it alone,
These gents are particular friends of mine.
—Wasn't it luck? Then we went to the German Club,
We and Mr. Donavan and his friend Joe Leahy, 45
Found it shut. I want to get home, said the cabman,
We all go the same way home, said Mr. Donavan,
Cheer up, Trixie and Stella; and put his foot through the window.
The next I know the old cab was hauled up on the avenue,
And the cabman and little Ben Levin the tailor, 50
The one who read George Meredith,
Were running a hundred yards on a bet,
And Mr. Donavan holding the watch.
So I got out to see the sunrise, and walked home. *[end of leaf]*

* * * *

[I] 1 April is the cruellest month, breeding 55
Lilacs out of the dead land, mixing
Memory and desire, stirring
Dull roots with spring rain.
[I] 5 Winter kept us warm, covering

60 Earth in forgetful snow, feeding
A little life with dried tubers.
Summer surprised us, coming over the Königssee
With a shower of rain; we stopped in the colonnade,
And went on in sunlight, into the Hofgarten, [I] 10
65 And drank coffee, talking an hour.
Bin gar keine Russin, stamm' aus Litauen, echt deutsch.
And when we were children, staying at the archduke's,
My cousin's, he took me out on a sled,
And I was frightened. He said, Marie, [I] 15
70 Marie, hold on tight. And down we went.
In the mountains, there you feel free.
I read, much of the night, and go south in the winter.

* * * *

What are the roots that clutch, what branches grow
Out of this stony rubbish? Son of man, [I] 20
75 You cannot say, or guess, for you know only
A heap of broken images, where the sun beats,
And the dead tree gives no shelter, the cricket no relief,
And the dry stone no sound of water. Only
There is shadow under this red rock, [I] 25
80 (Come in under the shadow of this red rock),
And I will show you something different from either
Your shadow at morning striding behind you
Or your shadow at evening rising to meet you;
I will show you fear in a handful of dust. [I] 30

* * * *

85 Frisch schwebt der Wind
Der Heimat zu,
Mein Irisch' Kind,
Wo weilest du?

[I] 35 "You gave me hyacinths first a year ago;
"They called me the hyacinth girl". 90
—Yet when we came back, late, from the hyacinth garden,
Your arms full, and your hair wet, I could not
Speak, and my eyes failed, I was neither
[I] 40 Living nor dead, and I knew nothing,
Looking into the heart of light, the silence. 95

Madame Sosostris, famous clairvoyant,
Had a bad cold, nevertheless
[I] 45 Is known to be the wisest woman in Europe,
With a wicked pack of cards. Here, said she,
Is your card, the drowned Phoenician Sailor, 100
(Those are pearls that were his eyes. Look!)
Here is Belladonna, the Lady of the Rocks,
[I] 50 The lady of situations, *[end of leaf]*
Here is the man with three staves, and here the Wheel,
And here is the one-eyed merchant, and this card, 105
Which is blank, is something he carries on his back,
Which I am forbidden to see. I look in vain
[I] 55 For the Hanged Man. Fear death by water.
I see crowds of people, walking round in a ring.
(I John saw these things, and heard them). 110
Thank you. If you see dear Mrs. Equitone,
Tell her I bring the horoscope myself,
One must be so careful these days.

[I] 60 Terrible city, I have sometimes seen and see
Under the brown fog of your winter dawn 115
A crowd flow over London Bridge, so many,
I had not thought death had undone so many.
Sighs, short and infrequent, were expired,
[I] 65 And each one kept his eyes before his feet.
Flowed up the hill and down King William Street, 120

To where Saint Mary Woolnoth kept the time,
With a dead sound on the final stroke of nine.
There I saw one I knew, and stopped him, crying: "Stetson!
"You who were with me in the ships at Mylae! [I] 70
125 "That corpse you planted last year in your garden,
"Has it begun to sprout? Will it bloom this year?
"Or has the sudden frost disturbed its bed?
"Oh keep the Dog far hence, that's foe to men,
"Or with his nails he'll dig it up again! [I] 75
130 "You! *hypocrite lecteur,—mon semblable,—mon frère!"* [*end of leaf*]

[Interlude: *Exequy*. See "Uncollected Poems".]

HE DO THE POLICE IN DIFFERENT VOICES: Part II.

IN THE CAGE.

The Chair she sat in, like a burnished throne
Glowed on the marble, where the swinging glass
Held up by standards wrought with golden vines
From which one tender Cupidon peeped out [II] 80
135 (Another hid his eyes behind his wing)
Doubled the flames of seven-branched candelabra
Reflecting light upon the table as
The glitter of her jewels rose to meet it,
From satin cases poured in rich profusion; [II] 85
140 In vials of ivory and coloured glass
Unstoppered, lurked her strange synthetic perfumes
Unguent, powdered, or liquid—troubled, confused
And drowned the sense in odours; stirred by the air
That freshened from the window, these ascended, [II] 90
145 Fattening the candle flames, which were prolonged,

And flung their smoke into the laquenaria,
Stirring the pattern on the coffered ceiling.
Upon the hearth huge sea-wood fed with copper
[II] 95 Burned green and orange, framed by the coloured stone,
In which sad light a carved dolphin swam; 150
Above the antique mantel was displayed
In pigment, but so lively, you had thought
A window gave upon the sylvan scene,
The change of Philomel, by the barbarous king
[II] 100 So rudely forced, yet there the nightingale 155
Filled all the desert with inviolable voice,
And still she cried (and still the world pursues)
Jug Jug, into the dirty ear of death;
And other tales, from the old stumps and bloody ends of time
[II] 105 Were told upon the walls, where staring forms 160
Leaned out, and hushed the room and closed it in.
There were footsteps on the stair,
Under the firelight, under the brush, her hair
Spread out in little fiery points of will,
[II] 110 Glowed into words, then would be savagely still. 165

"My nerves are bad tonight. Yes, bad. Stay with me.
"Speak to me. Why do you never speak. Speak.
"What are you thinking of? What thinking? What?
"I never know what you are thinking. Think".

[II] 115 I think we met first in rats' alley, 170
Where the dead men lost their bones.

"What is that noise?"

The wind under the door.

"What is that noise now? What is the wind doing?" *[end of leaf]*

<

175 Carrying
Away the little light dead people.

"Do you know nothing? Do you see nothing? Do you remember
"Nothing?"

I remember
180 The hyacinth garden. Those are pearls that were his eyes, yes! [II] 12

"Are you alive, or not? Is there nothing in your head?"

But
O O O O that Shakespeherian Rag—
It's so elegant—
185 So intelligent— [II] 13

"What shall I do now? What shall I do?
"I shall rush out as I am, and walk the street
"With my hair down, so. What shall we do tomorrow?
"What shall we ever do?"

190 The hot water at ten. [II] 13
And if it rains, the closed carriage at four.
And we shall play a game of chess:
The ivory men make company between us
Pressing lidless eyes and waiting for a knock upon the door.

[*5-line space*]

195 When Lil's husband was coming back out of the Transport Corps
I didn't mince my words, I said to her myself, [II] 14
HURRY UP PLEASE IT'S TIME.
"Now Albert's coming back, make yourself a bit smart.
"He'll want to know what you did with that money he gave you
200 "To get yourself some teeth". He did, I was there.
"You have them all out, Lil, and get a nice set", [II] 14
He said, "I swear, I can't bear to look at you".
"And no more can I", I said, "and think of poor Albert,

"He's been in the army four years, he wants a good time,
"And if you don't give it him, there's many another will". 205
[II] 150 "Other women", she said. "Something of that", I said.
"Then I'll know who to thank", she said, and gave me a straight
look.
HURRY UP PLEASE IT'S TIME.
"No, ma'am, you needn't look old-fashioned at me", I said,
"Others can pick and choose if you can't. 210
[II] 155 "But if Albert makes off, it won't be for lack of telling.
"You ought to be ashamed," I said, "to look so antique".
—(And her only thirty-one).
"I can't help it", she said, putting on a long face,
"It's that medicine I took, in order to bring it off". 215
[II] 160 (She's had five already, and nearly died of young George).
"The chemist said it would be allright, but I've never been the
same".
"You *are* a proper fool", I said.
"Well if Albert won't leave you alone, there it is", I said. *[end of leaf]*
"You want to keep him at home, I suppose". 220
[II] 165 HURRY UP PLEASE IT'S TIME.
Well that Sunday Albert was home, they had a hot gammon,
And they asked me in to dinner, to get the beauty of it hot—
HURRY UP PLEASE IT'S TIME.
HURRY UP PLEASE IT'S TIME. 225
[II] 170 Good night, Bill. Good night, Lou. Good night, George. Good
night.
Ta ta. Good night. Good night.
Good night, ladies, good night, sweet ladies, good night, good
night. *[end of leaf]*

[Interlude: *Song*. See "Uncollected Poems".]

THE FIRE SERMON.

Admonished by the sun's inclining ray,
230 And swift approaches of the thievish day,
The white-armed Fresca blinks, and yawns, and gapes,
Aroused from dreams of love and pleasant rapes.
Electric summons of the busy bell
Brings brisk Amanda to destroy the spell;
235 With coarsened hand, and hard plebeian tread,
Who draws the curtain round the lacquered bed,
Depositing thereby a polished tray
Of soothing chocolate, or stimulating tea.

Leaving the bubbling beverage to cool,
240 Fresca slips softly to the needful stool,
Where the pathetic tale of Richardson
Eases her labour till the deed is done.
Then slipping back between the conscious sheets,
Explores a page of Gibbon as she eats.
245 Her hands caress the egg's well-rounded dome,
She sinks in revery, till the letters come.
Their scribbled contents at a glance devours,
Then to reply devotes her practic'd powers.

"My dear, how are you? I'm unwell today,
250 And have been, since I saw you at the play.
I hope that nothing mars your gaity,
And things go better with you, than with me.
I went last night—more out of dull despair —
To Lady Kleinwurm's party—who was there?
255 Oh, Lady Kleinwurm's monde— no one that mattered—
Somebody sang, and Lady Kleinwurm chattered.
What are you reading? anything that's new?
I have a clever book by Giraudoux.

Clever, I think, is all. I've much to say—
But cannot say it—that is just my way— 260
When shall we meet—tell me all your manoeuvers;
And all about yourself and your new lovers—
And when to Paris? I must make an end,
My dear, believe me, your devoted
friend". 265

This ended, to the steaming bath she moves,
Her tresses fanned by little flutt'ring Loves;
Odours, confected by the cunning French,
Disguise the good old hearty female stench. [*end of leaf*]
Fresca! in other time or place had been 270
A meek and lowly weeping Magdalene;
More sinned against than sinning, bruised and marred,
The lazy laughing Jenny of the bard.
(The same eternal and consuming itch
Can make a martyr, or plain simple bitch); 275
Or prudent sly domestic puss puss cat,
Or autumn's favourite in a furnished flat,
Or strolling slattern in a tawdry gown,
A doorstep dunged by every dog in town.
For varying forms, one definition's right: 280
Unreal emotions, and real appetite.
Women grown intellectual grow dull,
And lose the mother wit of natural trull.
Fresca was baptised in a soapy sea
Of Symonds—Walter Pater—Vernon Lee. 285
The Scandinavians bemused her wits,
The Russians thrilled her to hysteric fits.
From such chaotic misch-masch potpourri
What are we to expect but poetry?
When restless nights distract her brain from sleep 290
She may as well write poetry, as count sheep.

And on those nights when Fresca lies alone,
She scribbles verse of such a gloomy tone
That cautious critics say, her style is quite her own.
295 Not quite an adult, and still less a child,
By fate misbred, by flattering friends beguiled,
Fresca's arrived (the Muses Nine declare)
To be a sort of can-can salonnière.
But at my back from time to time I hear [III] 1
300 The rattle of the bones, and chuckle spread from ear to ear.

A rat crept softly through the vegetation
Dragging its slimy belly on the bank
While I was fishing in the dull canal
On a winter evening round behind the gashouse, [III] 1
305 Musing upon the king my brother's wreck
And on the king my father's death before him.
White bodies naked on the low damp ground,
And bones cast in a little low dry garret,
Rattled by the rat's foot only, year to year. [III] 1
310 But at my back from time to time I hear
The sound of horns and motors, which shall bring
Sweeney to Mrs. Porter in the spring.
O the moon shone bright on Mrs. Porter
And on her daughter [III] 2
315 They wash their feet in soda water
Et O ces voix d'enfants, chantant dans la coupole! *[end of leaf]*

Twit twit twit twit twit twit twit
Tereu tereu
So rudely forc'd. [III] 2
320 Ter

Unreal City, I have seen and see
Under the brown fog of your winter noon
Mr. Eugenides, the Smyrna merchant,

II] 210 Unshaven, with a pocket full of currants
(C.i.f. London: documents at sight), 325
Who asked me, in abominable French,
To luncheon at the Cannon Street Hotel,
And perhaps a weekend at the Metropole.

Twit twit twit
Jug jug jug jug jug jug 330
Tereu
O swallow swallow
Ter

London, the swarming life you kill and breed,
Huddled between the concrete and the sky, 335
Responsive to the momentary need,
Vibrates unconscious to its formal destiny,

Knowing neither how to think, nor how to feel,
But lives in the awareness of the observing eye.
~~London, your people is bound upon the wheel!~~ 340
Phantasmal gnomes, burrowing in brick and stone and steel!
Some minds, aberrant from the normal equipoise
(London, your people is bound upon the wheel!)
Record the motions of these pavement toys
And trace the cryptogram that may be curled 345
Within these faint perceptions of the noise
Of the movement, and the lights!

Not here, O Ademantus, but in another world.

I] 215 At the violet hour, the hour when eyes and back and hand
Turn upward from the desk, the human engine waits— 350
Like a taxi throbbing waiting at a stand—
To spring to pleasure through the horn or ivory gates,

I Tiresias, though blind, throbbing between two lives,
Old man with wrinkled female breasts, can see

355 At the violet hour, the evening hour that strives [III] 22
Homeward, and brings the sailor home from sea, *[end of leaf]*

The typist home at teatime, who begins
To clear away her broken breakfast, lights
Her stove, and lays out squalid food in tins,
360 Prepares the room and sets the room to rights.

Out of the window perilously spread
Her drying combinations meet the sun's last rays, [III] 2
And on the divan piled, (at night her bed),
Are stockings, dirty camisoles, and stays.

365 A bright kimono wraps her as she sprawls
In nerveless torpor on the window seat;
A touch of art is given by the false
Japanese print, purchased in Oxford Street.

I Tiresias, old man with wrinkled dugs,
370 Perceived the scene, and foretold the rest,
Knowing the manner of these crawling bugs,
I too awaited the expected guest. [III] 2

A youth of twentyone, spotted about the face,
One of those simple loiterers whom we say
375 We may have seen in any public place
At almost any hour of night or day.

Pride has not fired him with ambitious rage,
His hair is thick with grease, and thick with scurf,
Perhaps his inclinations touch the stage—
380 Not sharp enough to associate with the turf.

He, the young man carbuncular, will stare
Boldly about, in "London's one cafe",
And he will tell her, with a casual air,
Grandly, "I have been with Nevinson today".

>

Perhaps a cheap house agent's clerk, who flits 385
Daily, from flat to flat, with one bold stare;
One of the low on whom assurance sits
As a silk hat on a Bradford millionaire.

He munches with the same persistent stare,
He knows his way with women and that's that! 390
Impertinently tilting back his chair
And dropping cigarette ash on the mat.

II] 235 The time is now propitious, as he guesses,
The meal is ended, she is bored and tired;
Endeavours to engage her in caresses, 395
Which still are unreproved, if undesired. *[end of leaf]*

Flushed and decided, he assaults at once,
II] 240 Exploring hands encounter no defence;
His vanity requires no response,
And makes a welcome of indifference. 400

(And I Tiresias have foresuffered all
Enacted on this same divan or bed,
II] 245 I who have sat by Thebes beneath the wall
And walked among the lowest of the dead.)

—Bestows one final patronising kiss, 405
And gropes his way, finding the stairs unlit;
And at the corner where the stable is,
Delays only to urinate, and spit.

She turns and looks a moment in the glass,
II] 250 Hardly aware of her departed lover; 410
Across her brain one half-formed thought may pass:
"Well now that's done, and I am glad it's over".

When lovely woman stoops to folly and
She moves about her room again, alone,

415 She smoothes her hair with automatic hand, [III] 2
And puts a record on the gramophone.

[*9-line space*]

"This music crept by me upon the waters"
And along the Strand, and up the ghastly hill of Cannon Street,
Fading at last, behind by flying feet,
420 There where the tower was traced against the night
Of Michael Paternoster Royal, red and white. [*end of leaf*]

O City, City, I have heard & hear
The pleasant whining of a mandoline
Outside a public bar in lower Thames Street [III] 2
425 And a clatter & a chatter in the bar
Where fishmen lounge at noon time, there the walls
Of Magnus Martyr stood, & stand, & hold
Their joyful splendour of Corinthian white & gold [*end of leaf*] [III] 2

The river sweats
430 Oil & tar
The barges drift
With the turning tide
Red sails swing wide [III] 2
to leeward
435 On the heavy spar.
The barges wash,
Like drifting logs,
Past Greenwich reach [III] 2
Past the Isle of Dogs.
440 Weialala leia
Wallala leialala

Elizabeth & Leicester.
Beating oars. [III] 2

The barge was formed
Of gilded shells, 445
Red and gold.
The slow swell
I] 285 Rippled both shores
South west wind
Carried down stream 450
The peal of bells.
There are still white towers.

I] 290 Weialala lalalala
Weialala. [*end of leaf*]

"Trams and dusty trees. 455
Highbury bore me. Richmond & Kew
Undid me. Beyond Richmond I raised my knees
I] 295 Stretched on the floor of a perilous canoe".

"My feet were at Moorgate, and my heart
Under my feet. After the event 460
He wept. He promised 'a new start.'
I made no outcry: what shd *I* resent?" [*end of leaf*]

I] 300 "On Margate Sands.
I can connect
Nothing with nothing. 465
The broken finger nails of dirty hands.
My people are plain people, who expect
II] 305 nothing".

la la

To Carthage then I came. 470

Burning burning burning burning
O Lord thou pluckest me out
II] 310 O Lord thou pluckest

burning [*end of leaf*]

[Interlude: *Dirge*. See "Uncollected Poems".]

Part IV. Death by Water.

475 The sailor, attentive to the chart or to the sheets,
A concentrated will against the tempest and the tide,
Retains, even ashore, in public bars or streets
Something inhuman, clean and dignified.

Even the drunken ruffian who descends
480 Illicit backstreet stairs, to reappear,
For the derision of his sober friends,
Staggering, or limping with a comic gonorrhea,

From his trade with wind and sea and snow, as they
Are, he is, with "much seen and much endured,"
485 Foolish, impersonal, innocent or gay,
Liking to be shaved, combed, scented, manucured.

* * * *

"Kingfisher weather, with a light fair breeze,
Full canvas, and the eight sails drawing well.
We beat around the cape and laid our course
490 From the Dry Salvages to the eastern banks.
A porpoise snored upon the phosphorescent swell,
A triton rang the final warning bell
Astern, and the sea rolled, asleep.
Three knots, four knots, at dawn; at eight o'clock
495 And through the forenoon watch, the wind declined; [*end of leaf*]
Thereafter everything went wrong.
A water cask was opened, smelt of oil,
Another brackish. Then the main gaffjaws
Jammed. A spar split for nothing, bought
500 And paid for as good Norwegian pine. Fished.

And then the garboard-strake began to leak.
The canned baked beans were only a putrid stench.
Two men came down with gleet; one cut his hand.
The crew began to murmur; when one watch
Was over time at dinner, justified 505
Extenuated thus: "Eat!" they said,
"It aint the eating what there is to eat—
"For when you got through digging out the weevils
"From every biscuit, there's no time to eat".
So this injurious race was sullen, and kicked; 510
Complained too of the ship. "*Her* sail to windward,"
Said one of influence among the rest,
"I'll see a dead man in an iron coffin,
"With a crowbar row from here to Hell, before
"This vessel sail to windward." 515
So the crew moaned; the sea with many voices
Moaned all about us, under a rainy moon,
While the suspended winter heaved and tugged,
Stirring foul weather under the Hyades.
Then came the fish at last. The northern banks 520
Had never known the codfish run so well. [*end of leaf*]
So the men pulled the nets, and laughed, and thought
Of home, and dollars, and the pleasant violin
At Marm Brown's joint, and the girls and gin.
I laughed not. 525
For an unfamiliar gust
Laid us down. And freshened to a gale.
We lost two dories. And another night
Observed us scudding, with the trysail gone,
Northward, leaping beneath invisible stars 530
And when the lookout could no longer hear
Above the roar of waves upon the sea
The sharper note of breakers on a reef,
We knew we had passed the farthest northern islands

535 So no one spoke again. We ate slept drank
Hot coffee, and kept watch, and no one dared
To look into anothers face, or speak
In the horror of the illimitable scream
Of a whole world about us. One night
540 On watch, I thought I saw in the fore cross-trees
Three women leaning forward, with white hair
Streaming behind, who sang above the wind
A song that charmed my senses, while I was
Frightened beyond fear, horrified past horror, calm,
545 (Nothing was real) for, I thought, now, when
I like, I can wake up and end the dream. [*end of leaf*]
—Something which we knew must be a dawn—
A different darkness, flowed above the clouds,
And dead ahead we saw, where sky and sea should meet,
550 A line, a white line, a long white line,
A wall, a barrier, towards which we drove.
My God man there's bears on it.
Not a chance. Home and mother.
Where's a cocktail shaker, Ben, here's plenty of cracked ice.
555 Remember me.

And if *Another* knows, I know I know not,
Who only know that there is no more noise now.

* * * * *

Phlebas, the Phoenician, a fortnight dead, [IV] 31
Forgot the cry of gulls, and the deep-sea swell
560 And the profit and loss.
A current under sea [IV] 31
Picked his bones in whispers. As he rose and fell
He passed the stages of his age and youth
Entering the whirlpool.
565 Gentile or Jew,

IV] 320 O you who turn the wheel and look to windward,
Consider Phlebas, who was once handsome and tall as you.

[end of leaf]

[Interlude: "I am the Resurrection and the Life". See "Uncollected Poems".]

[V. *What the Thunder said*]

After the torchlight red on sweaty faces
After the frosty silence in the gardens
After the agony in stony places 570
[V] 325 The shouting & the crying
Gardens and palaces and reverberation
Of thunder of spring over the mountains
He who was living is now dead,
We who were living are now dying 575
[V] 330 With a little patience

Here is no water but only rock
Rock and no water and the sandy road
The road winding ahead among the mountains
Which are mountains of rock without water 580
[V] 335 If there were water we should stop and drink
Among the rock one cannot stop or think
The sweat is dry and the feet cannot stop
If there were only water among the rock
Dead mountain mouth with carious teeth that cannot spit 585
[V] 340 Here one can neither stand nor lie nor sit
There is not even silence in the mountains
But dry sterile thunder and no rain
There is not even solitude in these mountains
But red sullen faces sneer and snarl 590
[V] 345 From doors of mudcracked houses *[end of leaf]*

If there were water

And no rock
If there were rock
595 And also water
And water
A spring [V] 350
A pool among the rock
If there were the sound of water only
600 Not the cicada, and
The dry grass singing
But sound of water over rock [V] 355
Where the hermit thrush sings in the pines
Drip-drop drop drop drop
605 But here is no water

Who is the third that walks beside you?
When I count, there is only you and I together [V] 360
But when I look ahead up the white road
There is always another walking beside you
610 Gliding wrapt in a brown mantle, hooded
I do not know whether a man or woman
—But who is that on the other side of you? [V] 365

What is that sound high in the air
Murmur of maternal lamentation
615 Who are those hooded hordes swarming
Over Polish plains, stumbling in cracked earth
Ringed with a flat horizon, only. [V] 370
What is the city over the mountains
Cracks and reforms and breaks in the violet air
620 Tumbling towers
Jerusalem, Athens, Alexandria
Vienna, London. Unreal [V] 375

A woman drew her long black hair out tight
And fiddled whisper music on those strings

And bats with baby faces, in the violet light, 625
[V] 380 Whistled, and beat their wings
A man crawled downward down a blackened wall
And upside down in air were towers
Tolling reminiscent bells, that kept the hours.
And voices singing out of empty cisterns and exhausted wells. 630

[*end of leaf*]

[V] 385 In this decayed hole among the mountains
In the faint moonlight, the grass is singing
Over the tumbled graves, about the chapel,
There is the empty chapel, only the wind's home,
There are no windows, and the door's swing; 635
[V] 390 Dry bones can harm no one.
Only a black cock stood on the rooftree
Co co rico Co co rico
In a flash of lightning, then a damp gust
Bringing rain . . . 640

[V] 395 Ganga was sunken, and the limp leaves
Writhed for the rain, while the black clouds
Gathered far distant, over Himavant.
The jungle crouched, humped in silence.
Then spoke the thunder
DA 645
[V] 400 DATTA. well then, what have we given?
My friend, my friend, beating in my heart,
The awful daring of a moment's surrender
Which an age of prudence cannot retract—
By this, and this only, we have existed, 650
[V] 405 Which is not to be found in our obituaries.
Nor in that which will busy beneficent spiders
Nor in documents eaten by the lean solicitor
In our empty rooms. [*end of leaf*] 655

DA. [V] 41[illegible]
Dayadhvam. friend, my friend I have heard the key
Turn in the door, once and once only.
We think of the key, each in his prison,
660 Thinking of the key, each has built a prison.
Only at nightfall, aetherial murmurs [V] 41[illegible]
Repair for a moment a broken Coriolanus,
DA
Damyata. the wind was fair, and the boat responded
665 Gaily, to the hand expert with sail and wheel.
The sea was calm, and your heart responded [V] 42[illegible]
Gaily, when invited, beating responsive
To controlling hands. I left without you
Clasping empty hands I sit upon the shore
670 Fishing, with the desolate sunset behind me
Shall I at least set the kingdom in order? [*end of leaf*] [V] 42[illegible]

London Bridge is falling down falling down falling down

Poi s'ascose nel fuoco che gli affina.
Why then Ile fit you. Hieronimo's mad againe.
675 Le prince d'Aquitaine de la tour abolie
These fragments I have spelt into my ruins. [V] 43[illegible]
Datta, dayadhvam, damyata

Shantih shantih shantih.

Commentary

Commentary: Introduction

1. SCOPE

From the beginning, commentators on TSE have found precedents of all kinds, and the resources of the internet now enable editors to search non-literary materials beyond the scope of the reference shelf or even the Oxford English Dictionary (for which, see "Where Every Word is at Home").

An effort has been made not to use the Commentary for *critical* elucidation. The frontiers are uncertain, but the principle has been to provide only notes which constitute or proceed from a point of information. Parallels with other writers will sometimes not only suggest a source but amount to an allusion. Conversely, it may not be a source but an analogue that brings back what was in the air. Notes of this kind try to put down only the parallels themselves (though in the awareness that annotation is inseparable from interpretation, selection and judgement), leaving the reader to decide what to make of what the poet may have made of this. As often in literary matters, the case is altered incrementally. Percy Allen, TSE wrote, had mustered "many other parallels, each slight in itself, but having a cumulative plausibility", *Poets' Borrowings* (1928). Similarly, "Miss Jeffery has not quite as clear a case as Dr. Schoell had in tracing the borrowings of Chapman, but her accumulation of probabilities, powerful and concurrent, leads to conviction", *The Early Novel* (1929).

Parallels between different passages from within the couple of hundred pages of the *Collected Poems* have been given only when part of a larger collocation.

Scholars who have discovered pertinent information are credited, not least to indicate what was available at different stages in the appreciation of the poems. But in the face of a vast secondary bibliography, we cite interpretative articles and books only when they contain informative findings.

The Commentary to each section, such as "*Poems* (1920)" or "Uncollected Poems", has a headnote, as does each individual poem. The headnote to *Four Quartets* is supplemented by a headnote to each individual Quartet.

The annotation by John Hayward for French editions of *The Waste Land* and *Four Quartets*, and by Valerie Eliot to the drafts of *The Waste Land*, are included in the Commentary to those poems. *Inventions of the March Hare* has been drawn upon for all parts of the edition, but some notes have been entirely or partly omitted.

TSE was recorded reading many of his poems. "It's always worthwhile to hear a poet read his own poetry", *The Daily Illini* 5 June 1953, reported him as saying at a reading at the University of Illinois the previous day. "It's always interesting, once." In the Preface to *Anabasis* he wrote that the "*declamation*, the system of stresses and pauses, which is partially exhibited by the punctuation and spacing, is that of poetry and not of prose". Recordings of some poems more than once indicate that his sense of their stresses and pauses scarcely varied over the years. An exception is

Shantih shantih shantih

at the end of *The Waste Land* in 1933 as against 1946.

Pronunciations have been selectively noted when they involve any of the following: American English as against British English; foreign languages; names; unusual words; disputed or idiosyncratic pronunciation; changes over time, or differences between one recording and another. Not all recordings can be securely dated or have been available to the editors, so a note that TSE pronounced a word in a particular way in, say, 1947, does not mean that he did or did not do so at other times.

Information about the writing of the poems and their appearances in print appears in the Textual History.

2. REFERENCES

Unattributed quotations are from TSE. Poems and the corresponding pages of Commentary can be located using the Index of Titles and First Lines. (The rejected draft addition to *The Love Song of J. Alfred Prufrock* headed *Prufrock's Pervigilium* is referred to simply by that title and is printed in Vol. II, within the Textual History to the published poem, after line 69.)

TSE's prose appeared in many places and has been widely reprinted. The present edition provides information about the most important of these printings, without insisting upon the use of particular editions. References to the prose writings are standardised by the use of Identifying Titles, which consist of the item's title in italics, followed by the year of first publication: *Ben Jonson* (1919). The Index of Identifying Titles in this volume gives exact details of first publication, along with the title of the first collection of TSE's (if any) in which the item was collected, as well as indicating if it appeared in the final lifetime edition of *Selected Essays* (1951). Unless specified, the text used is that of its final authorised appearance. The Identifying Title of an item published by TSE under more than one title is that of the item's final appearance, with earlier titles listed in the Index in brackets and alphabetically as cross-references. The date, however, is always that of the first appearance (under which the item will be found listed in Donald Gallup's Bibliography).

When items appeared in two or more parts, the numerals "I", "II" etc. are adopted as part of the titles, without square brackets irrespective of the original appearance. "Separately" indicates that an item was issued independently as well as previously or subsequently in a periodical, collection or anthology. Items listed as appearing within *Selected Essays* were in the book from the first edition (1932) unless otherwise specified. Later printings of essays from *Selected Essays* or TSE's other collections are not noted.

Identifying Titles have also been assigned to a small number of documents often referred to in the Commentary, such as the typed inventory *TSE's books: Bodleian list* (*c.* 1933) and Henry Eliot's record of TSE's year in America, *Excerpts from Lectures 1932–1933*. In the case of unpublished prose items (other than letters), locations of manuscripts and typescripts are given when known. TSE's plays and full-length books are referred to without dates (which can be found in the Index of Identifying Titles).

Letters quoted are from TSE unless otherwise specified:

> To Lytton Strachey, 6 Aug 1919: "Besides, my dear Lytton, I am a very ill-read person."

Notation of letters is as economical as possible in the particular context, with the year and the correspondents' names often not repeated in the course of exchanges. References to "*Letters*" are to the original edition (1988) of the first volume of T. S.

Eliot's letters. The revised edition is referred to as "*Letters 1*", corresponding to the abbreviations for subsequent volumes ("*Letters 2*" etc). Letters by other people are mostly to be found within standard collections listed in the Bibliography, although some texts have been corrected from originals.

Many books and articles not by TSE are keyed to the Bibliography by the use of italics for the names of the author or editor: *Fowler* or *Litz ed.* If more than one title by an author is listed, the italicised name without date signifies the most important in this context, which is listed first; references to other titles are then given with name and date. So *Gallup* signifies his *T. S. Eliot: A Bibliography* (1952, rev. ed. 1969), while *Gallup 1970* signifies his *T. S. Eliot & Ezra Pound: Collaborators in Letters* (1970). If more than one title from a single year is listed, then the abbreviation is expanded, as for instance *Harmon 1976a*, *Harmon 1976b.* For economy's sake, similarly, other references in the Commentary to articles not by TSE have been pared to the author's name, journal and date.

In references to primary materials by other writers, the Commentary generally gives preference to editions that were or might have been known by TSE, and to British rather than American editions. When annotations from TSE's own copy of a book are quoted, the current whereabouts of that copy is given in the Bibliography. Because many of the books used by TSE and quoted in the present edition are a century old or more, an attempt has been made to avoid page references which depend upon the exigencies of particular editions. Authorial divisions such as chapter or section numbers have been preferred to page numbers (although exceptions are made for books never likely to be reprinted). This has disadvantages, but does offer a consistent and widely applicable means of reference without encumbering the Commentary with bibliographical detail.

Within quoted material, titles have been standardised, unless the exact form is of interest and to change it would be misleading, as when TSE referred to "THE HIPPOPOTOMOS" or Arnold Bennett asked "Were the notes to *Wastelands* a lark or serious?" Other references within quoted material are likewise brought into conformity with the reference system of the present edition. (For inconsistencies in TSE's "Notes on the Waste Land" and his misnumbering of his own lines, see Textual History headnote to those Notes.)

The Bodleian Library manuscript classmarks "MS Eng. misc c." and "MS Eng. misc d." are abbreviated to "c." and "d." in references such as "c. 624 fols 107–108".

"A Beginner in 1908"

1. A Break with Tradition   2. Symons and Laforgue   3. *Vers Libre*

1. A BREAK WITH TRADITION

> One usually expects to find with a young man of poetic genius that he expresses in his verse a more mature aspect of himself than that which appears in his life and personal relations. (To E. Graham Howe, 11 Aug 1939)

"Whatever may have been the literary scene in America between the beginning of the century and the year 1914, it remains in my mind a complete blank. I cannot remember the name of a single poet of that period whose work I read: it was only in 1915, after I came to England, that I heard the name of Robert Frost. Undergraduates at Harvard in my time read the English poets of the '90s who were dead: that was as near as we could get to any living tradition. Certainly I cannot remember any English poet then alive who contributed to my own education. Yeats was well-known, of course; but to me, at least, Yeats did not appear, until after 1917, to be anything but a minor survivor of the '90s · · · There were in the early years of the century, a few good poets writing in England, but I did not know of their existence until later; and it was often Pound (whose appreciation was much more comprehensive than most people realise) who directed my attention to them. But I do not think it is too sweeping to say, that there was no poet, in either country, who could have been of use to a beginner in 1908. The only recourse was to poetry of another age and to poetry of another language. Browning was more of a hindrance than a help, for he had gone some way, but not far enough, in discovering a contemporary idiom. And at that stage, Poe and Whitman had to be seen through French eyes. The question was still: where do we go from Swinburne? and the answer appeared to be, nowhere", *Ezra Pound* (1946).

To Pound, 22 Dec 1924: "Probably the fact that Swinburne and the poets of the nineties were entirely missed out of my personal history counts for a great deal. I never read any of these people until it was too late for me to get anything out of them, and until after I had assimilated other influences which must have made it impossible for me to accept the Swinburnians at all. The only exception to the above is Rossetti. I am as blind to the merits of these people as I am to Thomas Hardy."

"The kind of verse which began to be written about 1910 or so made the same break with tradition that we find in that of Wordsworth and Coleridge. But it had its origins in the sources to which the younger men of that time went for inspiration. Some of these sources are to be found in the earlier symbolist poets of France, or to be precise, in Baudelaire and his immediate followers, Laforgue, Corbière, Rimbaud and Mallarmé. Some are to be found in English poetry, both dramatic and lyric, of the sixteenth and seventeenth centuries · · · The young American poets, who came to London about that time, had left a country in which the status of poetry had fallen still lower than in England: there was not one older poet writing in America whose writing a younger man could take seriously", *The Last Twenty-Five Years of English Poetry* (1940).

To A. Benedict Crannigan, 12 Dec 1945: "All I can say is that I began to write differently after my first acquaintance with the work of Laforgue and that it seemed to me to suggest the possible medium for the sort of thing I wanted to say, only I was not quite sure what it was that I wanted to say until coming across a poet who showed me how to say it · · · The best of the poems published in 1917 were written between 1909 and 1911. Some of the others were written again in 1915, and again, some in 1917. There are no poems in my published works written prior to my contact with the Symbolists but I should point out that I had no knowledge of the so-called Imagists until 1915, and Imagism made very little impression upon me. That is to say, the Imagist poetry had no influence upon me. I gained a great deal at that time from the critical writing and conversation of Ezra Pound."

"The innovator of a new period will be the man who begins a contemporary idiom. What makes an idiom contemporary is never easy to state. It is not so much a matter of using new words, and is still more superficially a matter of mentioning new objects such as aeroplanes and machine-guns. Nor is it essentially a matter of new metres, for the abstract possibilities of metric are limited: it may be a change of cadence and inflexion or vocabulary in the same metres. It is the difference between the blank verse of Wordsworth and that of Mallet, between the lyric of Blake and that of Collins. A poet is likely to begin by using the speech of his immediate predecessors, and to be urged on rather by a sense of its inadequacy for his purposes, than by a clear provision of what he wants. Simplicity and naturalness of speech are not necessarily his gift at the beginning; he is more likely to arrive at them in his maturity by years of hard work", *The Development of Shakespeare's Verse* (1937). (David Mallet, orig. Malloch, 1705?–65. Johnson's *Lives*: "his blank verse seems to my ear the echo of Thomson".)

"Some of my strongest impulse to original development, in early years, has come from thinking: 'here is a man who has said something, long ago or in another language, which somehow corresponds to what I want to say now; let me see if I can't do what he has done, in my own language—in the language of my own place and time'", *American Literature and the American Language* (1953) 19. In his copy of William Henry Schofield's *English Literature from the Norman Conquest to Chaucer* ch. I, TSE underlined the sentence "Originality of matter was deplored as a fault." (To Anne Ridler, 15 Dec 1956: "The difference between saying something new, and saying something old in a new way, in poetry, seems to me often negligible, if it exists at all.")

TSE to Egon Vietta, 23 Feb 1947: "I do not know about other writers of verse, but I find myself that my interest in poetry is very much directed by the question: has this man discovered or invented anything that I could make use of in my own work? So I have learned nothing from Rilke, and know only a little of his poetry; I have I think got something from Hofmannsthal, and perhaps something from Morgenstern! I have always inclined to the belief that while poets are the most authoritative critics of poetry, *within their limits*, we must always weigh what any poet says about poetry or about the work of other poets, in relation to what he writes or wants to write in the way of poetry himself." (TSE's misspellings of Hugo von Hofmannsthal here and elsewhere are corrected. The German poet Christian Morgenstern, 1871–1914, drew inspiration from English nonsense verse.)

To Mrs. Branford, 1 June 1934: "I cannot but feel that it is impossible to do much to forward the recognition of another man's poetry unless one is in sympathy with the form, as well as the content and message. I have a different, and partly un-English, tradition behind me, and my habits in metric and vocabulary are different. I do not pretend to understand, still less to judge, any of my contemporaries: I can only really understand what I try to do myself."

Modern Tendencies in Poetry (1920):

> The one Victorian poet whom our contemporary can study with much profit is Browning · · · When I discovered Jules Laforgue, ten years ago, he gave me the same revelation which I imagine he has given to other people before and since: that is, he showed how much more use poetry could make of contemporary ideas and feelings, of the emotional quality of contemporary ideas, than one had supposed. Browning, at his best, for example in *Bishop Blougram's Apology*, had done as much; and Browning's poetry is much greater poetry. But the development of Browning had been such as to conceal from us some of the implications of his work. He had begun as a disciple of Shelley, and emerged from this into a developed mature impersonal stage: his *adolescence* had not been so important as Laforgue's. It is easier for a young poet to understand and to profit by the work of another young poet, when it is good, than from the work of a mature poet. I am no longer of the opinion that Laforgue, at the stage which he had reached at his death, was a great poet; I can see sentimentalism, absorption in himself, lack of balance. But in Laforgue there was a young man who was generally intelligent, critical, interested in art, science and philosophy, and always himself: that is, every mental occupation had its own precise emotional state, which Laforgue was quick to discover and curious to analyse. So Laforgue has been more *important*, as a laboratory study for the young poet, than either Rimbaud or Corbière. For their work, though always personal in the right sense, is either indifferent or mature. At their best, they present much more solid achievement than Laforgue.

Virginia Woolf: "on or about December 1910 human character changed" and "the men and women who began writing novels in 1910 or thereabouts had this great difficulty to face—that there was no English novelist living from whom they could learn their business", *Mr. Bennett and Mrs. Brown*, a talk printed as *Character in Fiction* in *Criterion,* July 1924, and reviewed there in Jan 1925 by "F. M." (for whom, see headnote to Index of Identifying Titles). TSE to Woolf, 22 May 1924: "It also expresses for me what I have always been very sensible of, the absence of any masters in the previous generation whose work one could carry on, and the amount of waste that goes on in one's own work in the necessity, so to speak, of building one's own house before one can start the business of living. I feel myself that everything I have done consists simply of tentative sketches and rough experiments. Will the next generation profit by our labours?" For Woolf on TSE's "inclination—to develop in the manner of Henry James", see headnote to "*Poems* (1920)", 6. PUBLICATION OF *POEMS* (1919).

"At different periods, of course, there may be greater or less sympathy between the older writers and the younger. What the help and encouragement of men of an older generation may be like, what it feels like, what useful stimulus or perhaps misdirection it may give, I do not know. At a time which may be symbolised by the figures 1910, there was literally no one to whom one would have dreamt of applying. One learnt something, no doubt, from Henry James, and might have learnt more. But Henry James was a novelist, and one who gave the most formidable appearance of exclusive concentration on his own kind of work", *Views and Reviews*, 12 Sept 1935.

To Herbert Read, 18 Jan 1927: "I only feel that H. J. is especially difficult because to me he seems *not wholly conscious*. There is something bigger there, of which he is hardly aware, than 'civilisation' & its 'complexities'. In some ways he seems to me, as a conscious person, a child: which is perhaps why I like some of his poorer stuff better than his best; in his poorer stuff something bigger appears without his knowing it—e.g. I like specially *The Altar of the Dead* & *The Friends of the Friends*."

2. SYMONS AND LAFORGUE

> I have written about Baudelaire, but nothing about Jules Laforgue, to whom I owe more than to any one poet in any language. (*To Criticize the Critic* 22)

"But if we can recall the time when we were ignorant of the French symbolists, and met with *The Symbolist Movement in Literature* [1899, 2nd ed. 1908], we remember that book as an introduction to wholly new feelings, as a revelation. After we have read Verlaine and Laforgue and Rimbaud and return to Mr. Symons' book, we may find that our own impressions dissent from his. The book has not, perhaps, a permanent value for the one reader, but it has led to results of permanent importance for him", *The Perfect Critic* (1920).

To Symons, 14 Nov 1923: "I hope you will not mind if I take this opportunity—as it is the first occasion on which I have written to you—of expressing my warm admiration both for your prose and for your verse. I have a peculiar debt of gratitude to your *Symbolist Movement* for that was my introduction, for [which] I have never ceased to be grateful to you, to a poetry which has been one of the strongest influences on my life." To Desmond MacCarthy, 23 Dec 1924: "The book was my first introduction to modern French verse and in this way had the most immeasurable influence on my own poetical evolution."

Reviewing a later study of the Symbolists: "Mr. Quennell has done for his generation what Arthur Symons did many years ago with his *Symbolist Movement in Literature*. I am not disposed to disparage Mr. Symons's book; it was a very good book for its time; it did make the reader want to read the poets Mr. Symons wrote about. I myself owe Mr. Symons a great debt: but for having read his book, I should not, in the year 1908, have heard of Laforgue or Rimbaud: I should probably not have begun to read Verlaine; and but for reading Verlaine, I should not have heard of Corbière. So the Symons book is one of those which have affected the course of my life · · · I look back to the dead year 1908; and I observe with satisfaction that it is now taken for granted that the current of French poetry which sprang from Baudelaire is one which has, in these twenty-one years, affected all English poetry that matters", *Baudelaire and the Symbolists* (1930).

Again, in 1933: "when I first came across these French poets, some twenty-three years ago, it was a personal enlightenment such as I can hardly communicate. I felt for the first time in contact with a tradition, for the first time, that I had, so to speak, some backing by the dead, and at the same time that I had something to say that might be new and relevant. I doubt whether, without the men I have mentioned—Baudelaire, Corbière, Verlaine, Laforgue, Mallarmé, Rimbaud; I should have been able to write poetry at all", *The Varieties of Metaphysical Poetry* 287 (Turnbull Lecture III).

Three years later:

> I cannot help wondering how my own verse would have developed, or whether it would have been written at all, supposing that the poets of the generation of the 'nineties had survived to my own time and had gone on developing and increasing in power ··· I certainly had much more in common with them than with the English poets who survived to my own day—there were no American poets at all. Had they survived, they might have spoken in an idiom sufficiently like my own to have made anything I had to say superfluous. They were in contact with France, and they might have exhausted the possibilities of cross-fertilisation from Symbolist Poetry (as they called it) before I had a chance. What happened was that they made it possible for me to discover these poets: Arthur Symons' book on the French Symbolists was of more importance for my development than any other book. I must be grateful to him for putting me in touch with the work of the French poets, and for not having got out of them, for his own poetry, what I was to find there myself. When one reviews one's own writing, as when one reviews one's own life, how much there is that bears the appearance of mere chance! One has been dependent upon one's predecessors for what they did not do, as much as for what they did! The one poet of that period, the youngest and the greatest, who survived, was of course Yeats; and it happened that in my own formative period Yeats was in his most superficially local phase, in which I failed to appreciate him.
>
> *Tradition and the Practice of Poetry* (1936)

"Symons did perform the function of bringing important poets to the attention of English readers; and for that reason his book will remain a landmark. As criticism I cannot say that Symons's book stands the test of time. He omitted one or two poets of the first importance—notably Tristan Corbière; he included one or two writers—Maeterlinck and Villiers de l'Isle Adam—whose reputation is now somewhat diminished; and even when he admired the right authors, one cannot say that it was always for the right reason ··· Symons could treat certain poets as forming, between them, the outline of a period, so that he had no need to refer to a number of admirable poets much of whose work has permanent value (I mention in passing only the names of Verhaeren, Jammes, Samain, Tailhade, Kahn, Regnier, Vielé-Griffin)", *Contemporary French Poetry* (1952).

Interviewed by Donald Hall in *Paris Review* (1959), TSE referred to "Arthur Symons's book on French poetry, which I came across in the Harvard Union". In his own copy, in the chapter on Laforgue, he marked the sentence, "The old cadences, the old eloquence, the ingenuous seriousness of poetry, are all banished, on a theory as self-denying as that which permitted Degas to dispense with recognisable beauty in his figures."

Edward J. H. Greene: "Il m'a dit aussi qu'il croit être le premier en Amérique à avoir possédé les oeuvres complètes de Laforgue" [TSE has also told me that he believes he was the first person in America to own the complete works of Laforgue], *Greene* 20. It was with Laforgue in mind that TSE wrote *Reflections on Contemporary Poetry* IV (1919):

> It is not true that the development of a writer is a function of his development as a man, but it is possible to say that there is a close analogy between the sort of experience which develops a man and the sort of experience which develops a writer. Experience in living may leave the literary embryo still dormant, and the progress of

> literary development may to a considerable extent take place in a soul left immature in living. But similar types of experience form the nourishment of both. There is a kind of stimulus for a writer which is more important than the stimulus of admiring another writer. Admiration leads most often to imitation; we can seldom remain long unconscious of our imitating another, and the awareness of our debt naturally leads us to hatred of the object imitated. If we stand toward a writer in this other relation of which I speak we do not imitate him, and though we are quite as likely to be accused of it, we are quite unperturbed by the charge. This relation is a feeling of profound kinship, or rather of a peculiar personal intimacy, with another, probably a dead author. It may overcome us suddenly, on first or after long acquaintance; it is certainly a crisis; and when a young writer is seized with his first passion of this sort he may be changed, metamorphosed almost, within a few weeks even, from a bundle of second-hand sentiments into a person. The imperative intimacy arouses for the first time a real, an unshakeable confidence. That you possess this secret knowledge, this intimacy, with the dead man, that after few or many years or centuries you should have appeared, with this indubitable claim to distinction; who can penetrate at once the thick and dusty circumlocutions about his reputation, can call yourself alone his friend: it is something more than *encouragement* to you. It is a cause of development, like personal relations in life. Like personal intimacies in life, it may and probably will pass, but it will be ineffaceable.
>
> The usefulness of such a passion is various. For one thing it secures us against forced admiration, from attending to writers simply because they are great. We are never at ease with people who, to us, are merely great. We are not ourselves great enough for that: probably not one man in each generation is great enough to be intimate with Shakespeare. Admiration for the great is only a sort of discipline to keep us in order, a necessary snobbism to make us mind our places. We may not be great lovers; but if we had a genuine affair with a real poet of any degree we have acquired a monitor to avert us when we are not in love. Indirectly, there are other acquisitions: our friendship gives us an introduction to the society in which our friend moved; we learn its origins and its endings; we are broadened. We do not imitate, we are changed; and our work is the work of the changed man; we have not borrowed, we have been quickened, and we become bearers of a tradition.
>
> I feel that the traces of this sort of experience are conspicuously lacking from contemporary poetry, and that contemporary poetry is deficient in tradition. We can raise no objection to "experiments" if the experimenters are qualified; but we can object that almost none of the experimenters hold fast to anything permanent under the varied phenomena of experiment. Shakespeare was one of the slowest, if one of the most persistent, of experimenters; even Rimbaud shows process. And one never has the tremendous satisfaction of meeting a writer who is more original, more independent, than he himself knows. No dead voices speak through the living voice; no reincarnation, no re-creation. Not even the *saturation* which sometimes combusts spontaneously into originality.

TSE told Greene that he first read Baudelaire in 1907 or 1908, "with great impact" (*Greene* 18). "I had discovered the French poets in question in 1909 when I was an undergraduate. Baudelaire was not a symboliste, but the fore-runner of the symbolistes. My *Prufrock* was written in 1911 and there was no 'stream of new American poetry' at the time when it was written. I was not aware of any in 1915 either. I met Ezra Pound in 1914", *Northrop Frye corrigenda* (1963). To Greene, 30 June 1947:

> My present impression is that I read a good deal of Rimbaud within the same year in which I made the acquaintance of Laforgue. At that time, however, from perhaps

> 1908 until 1912 I was so much under the influence of Laforgue that Rimbaud could have made only a slighter impression. In subsequent years however I have certainly reread Rimbaud as well as Mallarmé a number of times. Whereas Laforgue is a poet to whom I have felt no need to return. Apart from that period when I was first reading these poets, that is to say before I went to Paris in 1910 I also possessed myself of the two volumes edition of *Van Bever et Léautaud* [*Poètes d'aujourd'hui*] and was struck by the poems included of Tailhade. It was not for many years after that that I acquired a volume of Tailhade's poems. His work still gives me much pleasure. Before I went to France in 1910 I was acquainted with Corbière only in the *Van Bever* anthology, but I bought a copy of his poems in Paris during that year. I should say that it was Corbière rather than Rimbaud who succeeded Laforgue in my affections.

The anthology, which was frequently reprinted, also contained work by Remy de Gourmont, Francis Jammes, Jean Lorrain, Maeterlinck, Stuart Merrill, Valéry and Verlaine.

To Robert Nichols, 8 Aug 1917: "I remember getting hold of Laforgue years ago at Harvard, purely through reading Symons, and then sending to Paris for the texts. I puzzled it out as best I could, not finding half the words in my dictionary, and it was several years later before I came across anyone who had read him or could be persuaded to read him. I do feel more grateful to him than to anyone else, and I do not think that I have come across any other writer since who has meant so much to me as he did at that particular moment, or that particular year."

To René Taupin, 12 Apr 1928: "I came across the work of Jules Laforgue in 1908, and from that time on for several years was very much under the influence of that poet. I was already familiar with the work of Baudelaire. I did not think that my friend Pound became aware of Laforgue until some years later ··· I cannot say to what causes was due the influence of this type of French poetry in America ··· As for Rimbaud ··· I cannot say that that poet ever has very much more influence on myself. I have indeed been much more affected by Tristan Corbière ··· I can only speak for myself ··· I am ignorant of the influences on contemporary American poetry."

3. *VERS LIBRE*

> Charlotte C. Eliot to Bertrand Russell, 23 May 1916, on her son's prospects: "I have absolute faith in his Philosophy but not in the *vers libres*." (TSE, *Letters 1*)

"The *vers libre* of Jules Laforgue, who, if not quite the greatest French poet after Baudelaire, was certainly the most important technical innovator, is free verse in much the way that the later verse of Shakespeare, Webster, Tourneur, is free verse ··· My own verse is, so far as I can judge, nearer to the original meaning of *vers libre* than is any of the other types: at least, the form in which I began to write, in 1908 or 1909, was directly drawn from the study of Laforgue together with the later Elizabethan drama; and I do not know anyone who started from exactly that point", *Selected Poems of Ezra Pound* (1928), Introduction.

> People often wonder why poets do not remain content with the vocabulary and the verse forms inherited from older poets who have done well with them, and why poets insist on devising new forms which seem at first uglier or more disorderly. No good poet wants novelty or eccentricity for its own sake: the element of surprise in good

> poetry is something which remains forever, and is not only valid for its own time. But something is constantly happening to any living language; the changes in the world about us and in the lives we live are reflected in our speech; so that a verse form which once was natural, which once was a development of the way men talked in ordinary intercourse, can become artificial. I think that this superannuation has happened to blank verse; that the way in which we talk nowadays does not fit naturally into that frame. I find that blank verse is what I tend to write when I have been working too long, when I am tired or inattentive, and that when I am at my best I avoid any line which must be scanned as regular blank verse, and admit only a line here or there which *can* be scanned in that way.
>
> *A New Tradition of Poetic Drama* (1940)

"There are two kinds of free verse (or rather two things which pass under that name): one, verse in which regular and established metres are broken up almost—not quite—out of recognition. The pleasure one gets out of the irregularity of such verse is due to the shadow or suggestion of regular metre behind. Another kind of free verse—rarer and more difficult (in fact, hardly possible, unless one is born to it)—is the verse which has a particular rhythm for that author, with no suggestion of a familiar metre behind it. Whitman's is of this type · · · D. H. Lawrence wrote a kind of free verse, but his poems are more notes for poems than poems themselves. Lawrence did not have the necessity to write in this manner, and so there is no excuse for his having written these poems", *Walt Whitman and Modern Poetry* (1944).

To Kay Dick, 10 June 1943, rejecting her poems: "The effect is rather of notes for poems or notes for something, rather than of poems, and I find them lacking in form. It is all the more important in free verse to attend to something analogous to musical structure and to attain original and patterned rhythms when rejecting a regular beat and the restrictions of rhyme. I don't know from what I have seen whether you are really a poet or a prose writer." TSE used the expression "notes for poems" (rather than poems) in similar letters in 1944, 1945 and 1946. To Miss A. Pratt Barlow, 19 Jan 1943: "If one is adopting a recognised form, then I think the variety is given within its rules and not by simply breaking them. What is needed is rather a more subtle variation of tempo." The same day, to Miss D. N. Dalglish: "The trouble with free verse is that in giving up the pattern of more formal verse one must find another musical pattern instead."

To Jill Hillyer, 11 Dec 1946: "All free verse that is good has a certain regularity about it because it always suggests versification from which it is a departure. Conversely the greatest masters of regular verse have always found how to introduce subtle irregularities to give variety. From this point of view, the great master of free verse in English is Milton."

Offering reassurance to Alexander Langridge Ford, 5 Oct 1934: "I should not expect anybody to accept my 'philosophy' at 19; neither did I; at 19 one is still a conservative, and thinks in 19th century terms · · · It is equally undesirable to think oneself a poet and to think that one is not a poet. That is something that we never find out."

Prufrock and Other Observations

1. Contents in Order of First Publication 2. Composition and Shaping
3. Pound's Advocacy 4. Title, Dedication and Epigraph to the Volume

1. CONTENTS IN ORDER OF FIRST PUBLICATION

The Love Song of J. Alfred Prufrock	*Poetry*	June 1915
Preludes	*Blast 2*	July 1915
Rhapsody on a Windy Night	*Blast 2*	July 1915
Portrait of a Lady	*Others*	Sept 1915
The "Boston Evening Transcript"	*Poetry*	Oct 1915
Aunt Helen	*Poetry*	Oct 1915
Cousin Nancy	*Poetry*	Oct 1915
Hysteria	*Catholic Anthology*	Nov 1915
Conversation Galante	*Poetry*	Sept 1916
La Figlia Che Piange	*Poetry*	Sept 1916
Mr. Apollinax	*Poetry*	Sept 1916
Morning at the Window	*Poetry*	Sept 1916

These twelve poems were gathered to form TSE's first book, "PRUFROCK | AND | OTHER OBSERVATIONS | BY | T. S. ELIOT | THE EGOIST LTD | OAKLEY HOUSE, BLOOMSBURY STREET | LONDON | 1917". (The title page verso read "PRINTED AT THE COMPLETE PRESS | WEST NORWOOD | LONDON".) The book was advertised in *Egoist* June 1917 as "now ready". Ezra Pound to Margaret Anderson, 11 June: "*Prufrock* advance copy just came yesterday."

In May 1917, thanks to a recommendation (and subsidy) from Pound, TSE had become assistant editor of the journal the *Egoist* (formerly *Freewoman*, 1911–12, then *New Freewoman*, 1913–14). His first contribution, in July 1917, was a review of Pound's selection of *Passages from the Letters of John Butler Yeats*; his last, in the final issue, [Nov/]Dec 1919, was *Tradition and the Individual Talent* II and III. A sheet entitled *The Egoist Press Publications* (*c.* 1920) announced *The Art of Poetry* by TSE as "in preparation". The book did not appear (see *Gallup* E60). The Egoist Press closed in 1924 (*Publishers' Circular and Booksellers' Record* 16 Aug 1924).

2. COMPOSITION AND SHAPING

TSE to Eudo C. Mason, 21 Feb 1936: "*J. Alfred Prufrock* was written in 1911, but parts of it date from the preceding year. Most of it was written in the summer of 1911 when I was in Munich. The text of 1917, which remains unchanged, does not differ from the original in any way [see Textual History]. I did at one time write a good bit more of it, but these additions I destroyed without their ever being printed [see *Prufrock's Pervigilium* in Textual History]. It is by no means true that all of the other poems in the 1917 volume were written after *Prufrock*. *Conversation Galante*, for instance, was written in 1909, and all of the more important poems in that volume are earlier than *Prufrock*, except *La Figlia Che Piange*, 1912, and two or three short pieces written in 1914 or '15." To Edward J. H. Greene, 18 Oct 1939, of *Conversation Galante*, *Portrait of a Lady*, *The Love Song of J. Alfred Prufrock* and *La Figlia Che Piange*: "You are correct ··· in assembling these four poems under the sign of Laforgue." Reporting this, *Greene* 23 claimed this had been the order of composition of the four. (*Portrait of a Lady* appears to have been written concurrently with *The Love Song of J. Alfred Prufrock* but completed earlier.)

The earliest of the dates TSE gave for any of the poems is 1909, the year of Swinburne's death and of TSE's starting to write in the Notebook that he purchased and entitled *Inventions of the March Hare* (see the beginning of the Textual History for a description). The date became part of the title of *Poems 1909–1925* and its successor volumes, although dates of composition were assigned and none of the poems had been published until 1915. The first section of *1925* and its successors was "PRUFROCK | AND OTHER OBSERVATIONS", bearing the date 1917. When Ethel Stephenson enquired about these dates, TSE replied, 29 Mar 1944: "The date 1917 applied to *Prufrock* refers not to the particular poem but to my first collected volume which was entitled *Prufrock and Other Observations* and which did appear in 1917. I have not so far followed the practice in any edition of dating individual poems."

TSE's Harvard friend Conrad Aiken was among the first to appreciate his poetry, and wrote to Babette Deutsch, 28 Feb 1921: "I made Prufrock's acquaintance in 1911—long before its publication (in which I was instrumental, indirectly)." He wrote to TSE [23 Feb 1913]: "What have you been writing—futurist poems? If you have a superfluous copy of *The Love-Song of J. Alfred Prufrock*, any time, here is one who hath an appetite for it. Or anything new." After publication Aiken wrote to Harriet Monroe, editor of the Chicago magazine *Poetry*, 4 Sept 1915, saying "I had a copy of it from the first" and claiming that "as Eliot himself was heartlessly indifferent to its fate, it was I who sought publication for it". Later he recalled taking to London "the typescript of *Prufrock*, typed by its author with meticulous care on a Blickensderfer which produced only italics, and *La Figlia Che Piange*, neither of which was I able to sell ··· But Pound, serving tea not so exquisitely among his beautiful Gaudiers [works by Henri Gaudier-Brzeska], recognized *Prufrock* instantly, and this was the beginning", *March & Tambimuttu eds.* 22. No such typescript of *La Figlia Che Piange* is now known. Aiken suspected that his uncle, Alfred Potter, who worked at Harvard as a librarian, "provided one model for Alfred Prufrock", *Selected Letters of Conrad Aiken*, ed. Joseph Killorin (1978) 25.

Aiken again: "it was I who brought the typescript of *Prufrock* to London in 1914, in an endeavour to find a publisher for it—it was offered to Harold Monro, at the Poetry Bookshop [publisher of *Poetry and Drama*, Mar 1913 to Dec 1914], and to Austin Harrison, of *The English Review*, among others—and it was I who, after it had been summarily rejected by everyone, gave it to Ezra Pound for *Poetry*, of Chicago. The poem had been written during the previous year, was given to me in Cambridge, Massachusetts, and I believe was written there ··· Let me add for the record, while I am about it, that Mr. Eliot maintains to this day that on my suggestion a certain passage—now presumably lost—had been dropped from the poem. I can only say that I have no recollection of this, but if so, what a pity!" *TLS* 3 June 1960. TSE replied, *TLS* 8 July: "It is quite true that Mr. Aiken tried in vain to place *Prufrock* for me with a London periodical and it is quite true that it was Mr. Aiken who sent me to Ezra Pound, through whose efforts the poem finally appeared in *Poetry*, Chicago. Mr. Aiken is wrong only on one point. *Prufrock* was not written in 1913 but over a period of time in 1910–11, that is to say all that survives in the printed version. I did,

I think, in 1912, make some additions to the poem and I am grateful to Mr. Aiken for having perceived at once that the additions were of inferior quality. The suppressed parts, however, have not disappeared from view like the script of *The Waste Land*; I am pretty sure that I destroyed them at the time, and I have enough recollection of the suppressed verses to remain grateful to Mr. Aiken for advising me to suppress them", *Mr. Eliot's Progress* (1960). By this time, TSE had forgotten that the lines of *Prufrock's Pervigilium* were in the *March Hare* Notebook, which he had last seen in 1922 (for *Prufrock's Pervigilium*, see Textual History, *The Love Song of J. Alfred Prufrock*, after 69).

3. POUND'S ADVOCACY

TSE to A. H. Cooke, 18 Sept 1929: "At nineteen, I wrote some verse worth publishing, but I did not get anyone to publish it until I was twenty-eight."

In 1958, on Pound: "It was owing to his efforts that poems of mine were first published and but for his encouragement I might at an early period have abandoned the writing of poetry altogether" (Introduction to the translation of Pound's *Selected Poems* into the Indian language Oriya).

"I had kept my early poems (including *Prufrock* and others eventually published) in my desk from 1911 to 1915—with the exception of a period when Conrad Aiken endeavoured, without success, to peddle them for me in London. In 1915 (and through Aiken) I met Pound. The result was that *Prufrock* appeared in *Poetry* in the summer of that year; and through Pound's efforts, my first volume was published by the Egoist Press in 1917", *Ezra Pound* (1946). TSE toast to Robert Frost, *Books across the Sea*, June 1957: "Mr. Frost, I'd never heard your name until I came to this country, and I heard it first from Ezra Pound, of all people ··· In time I gathered that your work—or what had appeared at that time—was not in Ezra Pound's opinion required reading for *me* ···" [Frost:] "It was interesting that both of us come out of the same ... the same *room*, you might say. Wasn't it in Church Walk that you first saw Ezra Pound? Had he moved then?" [TSE:] "He'd moved to Holland Place Chambers by then." [Frost:] "··· I took it one way—and Mr. Eliot took it another way. He took Ezra in charge, and still has him in charge" (transcript by Beatrice Warde, Faber archive).

TSE's first meeting with Pound actually took place in 1914. Acting as a scout for the Chicago magazine *Poetry* (begun Oct 1912), Pound wrote to its editor, Harriet Monroe, 22 Sept 1914: "An American called Eliot called this P.M. I think he has some sense tho' he has not yet sent me any verse." (Pound's letters to Monroe were retrospectively dated, many to the day, which suggests reference to postmarked envelopes not now in the *Poetry* archive. For Pound's letters on *The Love Song of J. Alfred Prufrock* in particular, see headnote to the poem.)

Pound wrote again to Monroe, 30 Sept 1914: "I was jolly well right about Eliot. He has sent in the best poem I have yet had or seen from an American. PRAY GOD IT BE NOT A SINGLE AND UNIQUE SUCCESS. He has taken it back to get it ready for the press and you shall have it in a few days. He is the only American I know of who has made what I can call adequate preparation for writing. He has actually trained himself AND modernized himself ON HIS OWN ··· It is such a comfort to meet a man and not have to tell him to wash his face, wipe his feet, and remember the date (1914) on the calender." On the same day, Eliot wrote to Aiken: "Pound has been *on n'est pas plus aimable*, and is going to print *Prufrock* in *Poetry* and pay me for it. He wants me to bring out a Vol. after the war." Pound to Monroe [Oct 1914], enclosing *ts2*: "Here is the Eliot poem. The most interesting contribution I've yet had from an american. Yrs E.P. Hope you will get it *in* soon."

Of a visit to Chicago in Dec 1914, John Gould Fletcher wrote: "Miss Monroe seemed frankly disconcerted and bewildered by the explosions of modernistic literary frankness her magazine was already provoking. Especially she seemed to be in awe of Pound. And I recall that she showed me, either now or on my later visit of a week in February, a poem that Pound had just sent in from London, written, as he said, by a young American who was the most intelligent American he had ever met in London, T. S. Eliot. She did not know what to make of the poem ··· and so she asked me for my frank opinion. I read it, and advised her to print it", *Life Is My Song* (1937) 191.

Monroe, however, procrastinated for eight months in all. Pound wrote again to her on 31 Jan 1915: "Now as to Eliot: 'Mr. Prufrock' does not 'go off at the end.' It is a portrait of failure, or of a character which fails, and it would be false art to make it end on a note of triumph. I dislike the paragraph about Hamlet, but it is an early and cherished bit and T. E. won't give it up, and as it is the only portion of the poem that most readers will like at first reading, I don't see that it will do much harm. For the rest a portrait satire on futility cant end by turning that quintessence of futility Mr P. into a reformed character breathing out fire and ozone." 10 Apr: "*Do* get on with that Eliot." Then, 20 June: "In being the first American magazine to print Eliot you have scored again though you may not yet think so. He has intelligence and wont get stuck in one hole." TSE to the New York lawyer and patron John Quinn, 4 Mar 1918: "Personally, I cannot forget the length of time that elapsed before Pound succeeded in persuading Miss Monroe to print *Prufrock* for me, nor do I forget that she expunged, in another poem, a whole line containing the word 'foetus' without asking my permission." (See note to *Mr. Apollinax* 7.)

Despite his role as "Foreign Correspondent" of *Poetry*, Pound let Monroe know on 28 June [1915] that he had submitted poems of his own along with TSE's *Portrait of a Lady* to Alfred Kreymborg's *Others* in Grantwood, New Jersey. He also mentioned TSE's scabrous mock-epic (in the present edition, *The Columbiad*):

> I have also sent a longish poem of Eliot's to Kreymborg, partly because you dont like him and partly because I want his next batch of stuff in *Poetry* to be made up exclusively of his newest work. You mark my blossoming word, that young chap will go quite a long way. He and Masters are the best of the b'ilin'. If you think he lacks vigour merely because he happens to have portrayed Mr Prufrock the unvigorous, vous vous trompez. His poem of Christopher Columbus is vigorous, and male, not to say coarse. I think however he may produce something both modest and virile before the end of the chapter.

In a survey of the artistic scene sent to Quinn, 11 Aug 1915, Pound wrote: "The only live wires among the U.S.A. writers that have come to my notice are Orrick Johns and Edgar Lee Masters ··· A young chap named Eliot has gone back to America for a bit. I have more or less discovered him."

A month after publication in *Poetry* of *The Love Song of J. Alfred Prufrock*, Pound wrote to Monroe again, mentioning the *Catholic Anthology* that he was planning (OED "Catholic" 3b: "Having sympathies with, or embracing, all"). July 1915: "I want you to hold two or three pages open for Eliot in either Sept. or Oct. First because I want the stuff out in time for my anthology. Second because he has just married precipitately and cant afford not to be paid for his best things. He has done three small (half page) jems and will have enough for three pages I should think." Pound fulfilled this promise in a letter ascribed to Aug 1915: "I send also the three jems of Eliot for 'September' and a fourth thing *Cousin Nancy* which may do to fill the second page."

Pound to Monroe, 2 Oct 1915, on the prizes offered by *Poetry*: "I have cabled my vote for Eliot. As you might have known." Then: "No, if your committee dont make the award to Eliot, God only knows what slough of ignominy they will fall into, reaction, death, silliness!!!!!! ··· Eliot's poem is the only [*added*: eligible] thing in the year that has any distinction ··· If you dont give the £40 to Eliot for god's *sake* award it to *yourself*." Prizes, however, were awarded to Vachel Lindsay, Constance Lindsay Skinner and H. D., with *The Love Song of J. Alfred Prufrock* given honourable mention, along with twenty other poems (including work by Padraic Colum, D. H. Lawrence, Amy Lowell, Wallace Stevens and William Carlos Williams). Pound to Monroe, 1 Dec 1915: "As to T. S. E. the *Prufrock* IS more individual and unusual than the *Portrait of a Lady*. I chose it of the two as I wanted his first poem to be published to be a poem that would at once differentiate him from everyone else, in the public mind. I am sending on some more of his stuff in a few days, I want to see him and talk it over first ··· The *Cat. Anth.* is out." Dispatch of the third submission, however, was long delayed. Pound to Monroe, 21 Apr 1916: "Eliot has been worried with schools etc. (i.e. teaching not schools of verse or porpoises). He is to come in next week to plan a book, and I will then send you a group of his things."

As well as publication of the individual poems, Pound advised TSE on how to shape the volume. Hugh Kenner: "In 1913 Pound compared the epic to a temple, the *Commedia* to a cathedral, and collected short poems to picture galleries [*New Age* 9 Oct 1913] ··· It was Pound who took pains, Eliot recalled 40 years later, over the arrangement of *Prufrock and Other Observations*", *Kenner 1972* 355 ("*viva voce*, 1964"). Pound to Marianne Moore, 16 Dec 1918: "I am inclined to think you would 'go' better in bundles about the size of Eliot's *Prufrock and Other Observations.* For what it is worth, my ten or more years of practice, failure, success, etc. in arranging tables of contents, is à votre service. Or at any rate unless you have a definite scheme for a sequence, I would warn you of the very great importance of the actual order of poems in a booklet." (For TSE's non-chronological arrangement of Moore's poems in her *Selected Poems* (1935), see Andrew J. Kappel, *Journal of Modern Literature* Summer 1994.)

On the arrangement of volumes. TSE wrote to Herbert Read, 20 June 1920, about the first sequence within *Naked Warriors* (1919): "they support each other and produce a cumulative effect, as such still life pieces should do". To Louis MacNeice, 17 Jan 1934: "I think that a first volume ought, if possible, to be able to start off with one or two longish poems which will arrest the attention of the reader at once, and these, if possible, should be among the poet's most recent work." (To MacNeice again, 2 Dec 1943: "it isn't good for any book, and especially for poetry, to be stored too long.") To Henry Treece, 21 June 1941: "It is a mistake to make a first book too long: even when everything is good—readers must not be allowed to feel surfeited."

Pound to the assistant editor of *Poetry*, Alice Corbin Henderson, 3 May 1916, of a new publisher, John Marshall: "I believe Marshall in N.Y. is to publish a large prose work of mine, on *This Generation* ··· Marshall may also do Joyce's novel [*A Portrait of the Artist as a Young Man*] in America, and I hope a book by Eliot." Pound to his mother, 25 May: "Marshall ··· is to bring out Joyce's novel as well as my prose book. I shall send him mss. of Eliot's poems in a few days." Pound to Harriet Monroe, 29 May:

"Here are five poems by Eliot. I am sending off the mss. of his book to the publisher by the same post so there wont be unlimited time for printing these. (I should think three months.)" Marshall had helped to finance Kreymborg's magazine *Others*, but his business was not sound and he disappeared in Canada. On 19 Aug, Pound told Quinn that he had asked Kreymborg to "go steal the mss", but this appears to refer only to his own book, as when he wrote to Henderson, 26 Aug 1916: "no one seems able to find the mss. (unique mss.) of *This Generation*, which Marshall promised to publish". (*Reid* 273 claims that the same fate befell TSE's putative volume, "the manuscript of which had also disappeared with John Marshall into the Canadian wilds", but offers no evidence.)

Pound then sent to his own London publisher, Elkin Mathews, a typescript of TSE's book. Valerie Eliot in 1971 (*WLFacs* xii, quoting a letter of 11 Apr 1917):

> Since the previous April, when he had helped Eliot to select the poems for his first volume, Pound had been urging a reluctant Elkin Mathews to undertake publication. Finally, because the latter was "fussing about cost of paper, etc., and risk, and wanting part expenses paid", Pound explained to Quinn . . . "I told him if he wouldn't publish . . . without fuss, someone else would. *The Egoist* is doing it. That is *officially* The Egoist. As a matter of fact I have borrowed the cost of the printing bill (very little) and am being the Egoist. But Eliot don't know it, nor does anyone else save my wife, and Miss Weaver of The Egoist [*VE*: the two lenders] & it is not for public knowledge." Quinn offered to stand the charge, but Pound was confident that the book would pay its way.

Pound told his father of the book on 27 Mar 1917: "The Egoist is going to publish Eliot's poems," adding on 27 Apr: "Eliot's poems are in proof." The *Publisher's Circular* announced the appearance on 9 June of "*Pinfrock and other Observations*". The Egoist Press account book for the book *Prufrock* (BL) shows that 36 review copies were sent out the day before publication. At a party at Garsington Manor, Clive Bell distributed copies to the Morrells, Mary Hutchinson, Middleton Murry and Katherine Mansfield, who read *The Love Song of J. Alfred Prufrock* aloud. The printer's bill, paid on July 24, was for £13 4s 6d, of which Pound paid more than £5. He was to distribute more than fifty of the copies, sending twelve to America on 28 June. Joyce took a copy—without paying for it—on 7 October. Other customers included Herbert Read, John Quinn (more than a dozen copies), Richard Garnett and Wyndham Lewis (at least seven). The Poetry Bookshop bought batches regularly, as did Hatchard's. By 4 January 1918, 112 had been paid for, and a year later this had risen to 188. On 28 Oct 1919 only one copy was sold "at Mr Eliot's lecture", but this for an inflated 3s. A single copy, probably signed, was sold for 10s 6d on 28 Sept 1920, and the account was closed on 20 Feb 1922 with the entry "last copy Shakespeare & Co 10s 6d". In all 357 had been sold. Pound was repaid the balance of his loan, TSE's total royalty was calculated at £6, and the Egoist was left with "commission on edition 18s 8d".

Gallup records that on 12 June 1917 Pound had "proposed to Alfred Knopf that he should bring out an American edition". Quinn to Knopf, 7 July, forwarding a letter from Pound: "I, of course, should like to have you bring out Elliot's book of poems, including his late ones." Knopf to Quinn, 17 July: "With regard to Eliot's Poems, it is impossible for me to say much until I see them. Let him send me a copy and also anything new that he would want to include in my edition. I might say frankly, however, that I do not want to over-burden my list with free verse" (NYPL, Quinn Papers, box 36). Quinn reported to Knopf on 6 Aug that since seeing him he had read Eliot's volume: "They are very fine poems indeed. The book in paper covers, published by The Egoist, is, I should say, rather too slender a volume for an American publisher, but it is a corker. The poems are the real things · · · I have read these poems, most of them out loud, and they are great." Knopf to Quinn, 8 Aug: "What you say about Eliot's poems makes me exceedingly anxious to see them. I feared that what you say about the slenderness of the volume would be true, but I suppose Eliot will go on writing, and before very long there will be enough to justify independent publication over here." Quinn sent Knopf a copy of *Prufrock and Other Observations* on 10 Aug, commenting "I don't like the title · · · The poems are really splendid things." Knopf to Quinn, 17 Aug: "I have read Eliot's little book of poems with immense enjoyment. I do not know whether it is great poetry or not. I do know that it is great fun and I like it. I surely hope that he writes some more of it so that we can make a book of him over here. You see the present volume consists of only 32 pages of poetry, and it would be quite impossible to do anything with such a thing over here, except to give it away as an advertisement. And even that would be difficult."

Pound's review of the Egoist volume in *Egoist* June 1917, *Drunken Helots and Mr. Eliot*, picked up a jibe by Arthur Waugh from Oct 1916, and included what purports to be a comment by TSE: "'I have tried to write of a few things that really have moved me' is so far as I know, the sum of Mr. Eliot's 'poetic theory.'"

After publication, the *Egoist* Mar 1918 ran an advertisement for "PRUFROCK | By T. S. Eliot" (1/- net; postage 1d.), quoting the press response:

> *Westminster Gazette*: "A poet who finds even poetry laughable, who views life with a dry, cool derision and comments on it with the true disengagement of wit. He is not like any other poet, not even the Imagists whom he seems at first sight to follow . . . He writes in an apparent *vers libre* which has a decidedly rhythmical effect; his handling of language is pointed and often brilliant."
>
> *New Statesman*: "Mr. Eliot may possibly give us the quintessence of twenty-first century poetry. Much of what he writes is unrecognizable as poetry at present, but it is all decidedly amusing . . . He has a keen eye as well as a sharp pen and draws wittily whatever his capricious glance descends upon."
>
> *Daily News*: "A witty and dissatisfying book of verse . . . which flourishes many images that are quite startling in their originality."
>
> *Southport Guardian*: "One of the moderns; an imagist; an impressionist . . . Inevitably as impressions these poems are very unequal. Some are strangely vivid."
>
> *Literary World*: "The subjects of the poems, the imagery, the rhythms, have the wilful outlandishness of the young revolutionary idea . . . With him it seems to be a case of missing the effort by too much cleverness . . . the strangeness overbalances the beauty."

Reviewing *Passages from the Letters of John Butler Yeats, Selected by Ezra Pound*, TSE quoted a letter that describes how a poet "does not seek to be original, *but the truth*; and to his dismay and consternation, it may be, he finds the original, thereby to incur hostility and misunderstanding". TSE called this "a thought which takes very deep roots; it strikes through the tangle of literature direct to the subsoil of the greatest—to Shakespeare and Dante and Aeschylus", *The Letters of J. B. Yeats* (1917).

Orwell: "If I were asked for the starting-point of modern literature—and the fact that we still call it 'modern' shows that this particular period isn't finished yet—I should put it at 1917, the year in which T. S. Eliot published · · · *Prufrock*", *The Rediscovery of Europe* in *Listener* 19 Mar 1942.

4. TITLE, DEDICATION AND EPIGRAPH TO THE VOLUME

The plain buff wrapper of the book stated only "PRUFROCK | T. S. ELIOT", the full title appearing on the title page. The single word was from the beginning used both for *The Love Song of J. Alfred Prufrock* and for *Prufrock and Other Observations*. An advertisement in the *Egoist* May 1917 read: "Prufrock | THE EGOIST, LTD., is publishing in May a small book of Poems | Prufrock and other Observations". In the same month in the *Little Review*, Pound reported publication of TSE's poems "under the title *Mr. Prufrock and Observations*". TSE himself continued to use word *Prufrock* alone to mean the volume for the rest of his life, as in the Contents pages of *1925*, *1936* and *1963*. For the name itself, see note on the poem's title. This first book consisted of twelve poems, of which four had a person's name in the title, and three had a name in the first line; plus *Portrait of a Lady*. Of the twelve new poems in *Poems* (1920), four were again to have a person's name in the title, and four were to have a name in the first line; plus *Gerontion* (Portrait of a Little Old Man).

When *Conversation Galante*, *La Figlia Che Piange*, *Mr. Apollinax* and *Morning at the Window* were published in *Poetry* Sept 1916, Harriet Monroe gave them the general title *Observations* (for both the remarkings and the remarks). TSE wrote to her on 7 Sept 1916: "The title you have given will do excellently." Although "and Other Poems" and "and Other Stories" were common in book titles, and H. G. Wells had published *The Stolen Bacillus and Other Incidents* in 1895, there is apparently no precise precedent for "and Other Observations". In a footnote of F. H. Bradley's in *Appearance and Reality* ch. XIX, TSE underlined "In this connection I may remark that to observe a feeling is, to some extent, always to alter it", commenting "Cf. Neo-Realism on introspection". To Marianne Moore, 20 June 1934, on the contents of her planned *Selected Poems* and referring to her volume of 1924: "I take it that the order which you give them, which is the same as in *Observations* (a title, by the way, to which you have better claim than I) is the order of composition."

In 1917, *Prufrock and Other Observations* bore the dedication "TO | JEAN VERDENAL | 1889–1915". Verdenal, to whom the *March Hare* Notebook was also dedicated, was born on 11 May 1890, some twenty months after TSE. The dedication made him a still closer contemporary by giving his year of birth as 1889. Although his true date of birth was established by *Watson* in 1976 and confirmed by Valerie Eliot, *Letters* (1988) 20, it has not been corrected in editions of the poems. Verdenal had befriended TSE in Paris in 1910–11, and his surviving letters to TSE appear in *Letters 1*. To his mother, 22 Jan 1921: "If I had not met such a number of new people there Paris would be desolate for me with prewar memories of Jean Verdenal and the others."

Watson translates Verdenal's service record: "'Killed by the enemy on the 2nd May 1915 in the Dardanelles,' and then follows, in another hand, a citation dated 30 April 1915: 'Scarcely recovered from pleurisy, he did not hesitate to spend much of the night in the water up to his waist helping to evacuate the wounded by sea, thus giving a notable example of self-sacrifice.'" TSE: "I am willing to admit that my own retrospect is touched by a sentimental sunset, the memory of a friend coming across the Luxembourg Gardens in the late afternoon, waving a branch of lilac, a friend who was later (so far as I could find out) to be mixed with the mud of Gallipoli", *A Commentary* in *Criterion* Apr 1934. That memory can perhaps be dated to May 1911, when TSE mentioned a visit to the Musée du Luxembourg in a letter to Edward Forbes. The volume epigraph from Dante (see below) was reprinted in

AraVP without Verdenal's name, and when Valerie Eliot bought a copy for TSE late in his life he wrote in it: "This quotation is pointless without Verdenal's name. This was the dedication to Jean Verdenal, a medical student from Pau who lodged in the same boarding house as I in Paris in 1910–11, with whom I became very friendly and who, as I learned much later, was killed in the trenches at the beginning of the 1914 war. It was an American woman, a Miss Crotty, who had been another lodger at the Casaubon's at 151 bis Rue St. Jaques, who told me some years later. Two other friends killed in action: Carl [Karl] Culpin, Alain Fournier" (Valerie Eliot collection; copy previously owned by A. C. Benson, then Stephen Gaselee). The addition to the dedication "mort aux Dardanelles" (on the section title page for *Prufrock and Other Observations* within *1925+*) resembles the wording "Died before the Dardanelles, April, 1915", which had been printed immediately below the title of Arthur Davison Ficke's *To Rupert Brooke* when it appeared in the same issue of *Poetry* as *The Love Song of J. Alfred Prufrock.*

The dedication in *The Sacred Wood* was "FOR | H.W.E. | 'TACUIT ET FECIT'". Since this is not the imperative form of the family motto *Tace et fac*, but the past tense, it refers not to TSE's brother, as stated in *Letters 1*, but to their father, who had died in 1919. (For "the silent motto", see note to *East Coker* I 13.) In *1925*, the preposition in the Verdenal dedication on the *Prufrock* section title page was changed from "TO" to "For", because the book as a whole was dedicated "TO HENRY WARE ELIOT | 1843–1919". When every other element of *1925* was taken up into the extended *Collected Poems 1909–1935* (1936), this dedication to TSE's father was not preserved.

TSE dropped other dedications when individual publications were superseded. *Selected Essays*, for instance, did not preserve the dedication "To George Saintsbury" from *Homage to John Dryden* or that "For Charles Maurras" from *Dante* (1929). In both the limited first edition and the trade edition of *Ash-Wednesday* (1930), when the poem constituted a whole book, a dedication leaf opposite the printer's imprint read "TO | MY WIFE", and this was retained in the only other separate edition, the second of 1933 (after TSE's separation from Vivien); but it was not retained when the poem was reprinted as part of *1936+*. Similarly, the acknowledgement at the foot of the contents page of *Four Quartets* to TSE's friends, "and particularly to John Hayward", was not retained when *Four Quartets* first appeared within a larger collection of TSE's poems, *US 1952*, or on their appearance as part of *1963* (see Textual History headnote to *Four Quartets*).

Some of TSE's childhood writings are dedicated "to My Wife" (see headnote to *Fireside*). TSE deprecated the dedication "For J. F. Hendry" in the typescript of Henry Treece's *Towards a Personal Armageddon* (1942): "better omit · · · poems shd. be written for their own sake not for particular people" (Texas). Declining to be dedicatee of Herbert Read's *Collected Poems 1913–1925* (1926), TSE wrote to him, 11 Dec 1925: "About the dedication: for myself, modesty is not proof against such a compliment, and I am candidly immensely flattered and pleased. I know no greater compliment. Dedications are too often used for paying off worldly debts; as there is no debt at all in this case, I am all the more honoured. There is only one point that occurs to me as an objection, which I will put to you: namely: whether the statement of a certain community of interest and point of view implied by such a dedication is, from the point of view of efficacy, good or injurious? For the purpose of implanting the right ideas in the public mind, is an obvious intimacy a good thing or does it raise the spectre of a Gunpowder Plot? I have doubts. As you say, my knowledge of your wish is the main thing: and I hope you will base your decision on your judgment of what is most to the public interest! After all, no harm is done by your *not* dedicating the book!" The published book was dedicated to Read's friend William Prior Read. (For a similar warning to Pound against the appearance of cliquery, see note to *The Waste Land* [V] 430.) To George Barker, 19 Mar 1935, however: "I have received your poem · · · I should, of course, feel honoured by the dedication." The poem was probably *Calamiterror* (1937), although as published this was dedicated to Albert Gordon Barker. To Henry Treece, 29 Jan 1948: "I can't see any reason for my preventing you from dedicating your book of Swinburne to me, if you think that a dedication is suitable on what is a selection from somebody else's poems. But you will never be able to dedicate to me any book that Faber & Faber publish because I should certainly not allow that." TSE continued to dedicate books of his own prose, including *On Poetry and Poets*, which is dedicated "To Valerie". In 1959 *The Elder Statesman* had on a prefatory leaf the poem *To My Wife*, subsequently *A Dedication to My Wife*, the dedicatory verse printed at the close of *1963*.

The volume epigraph to *Prufrock and Other Observations* is from *Purgatorio* XXI 133–36. TSE quoted the lines in 1926 in his second Clark Lecture (*The Varieties of Metaphysical Poetry* 88–89) using the words "Puote veder" which he had adopted in this epigraph in *1925* in place of "comprender". Quoting them again in *Dante* (1929), he reverted to "comprender" (small slips are here corrected):

> The meeting with Sordello *a guisa di leon quando si posa*, like a couchant lion, is no more affecting than that with the poet Statius, in Canto XXI. Statius, when he recognizes his master Virgil, stoops to clasp his feet, but Virgil answers—the lost soul speaking to the saved:
>
> *"Frate,*
> *non far, chè tu se' ombra, ed ombra vedi."*
> *Ed ei surgendo: "Or puoi la quantitate*
> *comprender dell'amor ch'a te mi scalda,*
> *quando dismento nostra vanitate,*
> *trattando l'ombre come cosa salda."*
>
> *"Brother! refrain, for you are but a shadow, and a shadow is but what you see." Then the other, rising: "Now can you understand the quantity of love that warms me towards you, so that I forget our vanity, and treat the shadows like the solid thing."*

TSE's translation differs from the Temple Classics, which reads: "'Brother, do not, for thou art a shade, and a shade thou seest.' And he, rising: 'Now canst thou comprehend the measure of the love which warms me toward thee, when I forget our nothingness, and treat shades as a solid thing.'"

To Sir Herbert Grierson, 21 Sept 1949, enclosing a reprint of *1936*: "you will be able to exercise your ingenuity on a number of misquotations. It is curious that the book should have been reprinted again and again for so many years without anyone commentating on the first misquotation of Dante." This may refer to either the volume epigraph or to that of *The Love Song of J. Alfred Prufrock*, each of which TSE emended repeatedly (see Textual History).

The Love Song of J. Alfred Prufrock

Published in *Poetry* (Chicago) June 1915, where the "Notes" on contributors introduced the new writer: "Mr. T. S. Eliot is a young American poet resident in England, who has published nothing hitherto in this country." Printed next in Nov 1915 in *Catholic Anthology 1914–1915* [ed. Pound] (Elkin Mathews). Collected by TSE in *1917+*, *Sesame* and *Penguin / Sel Poems.* Pound quoted 49–61 (adding a full stop at the end of 50) and 70–72, within *Drunken Helots and Mr. Eliot*, a review of *1917* in *Egoist* June 1917, perhaps slightly before the volume's publication. S. P. B. Mais quoted 99–110 and 120–31 from *Cath Anth*, in his *From Shakespeare to O. Henry* (1917, 104–105).

Recorded 23 May 1947, Washington. Second: 1948, London; released by Harvard Vocarium Records, 1949 (a recording from TSE's Morris Gray Poetry Reading in 1947 had been found "imperfect", *Harvard Crimson* 8 Feb 1949). Third: 26–28 Sept 1955, London; released Caedmon 1955 (US), 1959 (UK). Fourth: Nov 1959, Chicago, part of a celebration of *Poetry* magazine.

Undated in Notebook. Dated "Cambridge, Mass., 1909/10, Paris-Munich 1911" in *Isaacs's US 1920*; "Paris-Munich 1911", with 111–19 bracketed with "Cambridge Mass 1909 or 1910?" by TSE in *Hayward's 1925*; 1910 in *VE's 1951*; "1911 Munich" by TSE in *Morley's US 1920*. To Edward J. H. Greene, 18 Oct 1939: "it was begun at Harvard, and finished in Munich". In reply to Kenneth Allott's conjecture, 20 June 1935, that in the "paragraph in Prufrock 'No I am not Hamlet etc . . .' the rhythm was 'first' and remained unchanged but not the phrasing", TSE wrote, 12 Nov 1935: "The page in question antedates the rest of the poem by some months." (See volume headnote, 3. POUND'S ADVOCACY, for Pound to Harriet Monroe, 31 Jan 1915: "the paragraph about Hamlet · · · is an early and cherished bit".)

TSE to Harriet Monroe, 27 Mar 1916, regarding her request to reprint *The Love Song of J. Alfred Prufrock* in an anthology drawn from *Poetry*: "I am very much pleased that you want to reprint the poem; but as it has already appeared in the *Catholic Anthology* here, and as it will form the ballast of a *very* small volume in the future, I really feel that I should be making a mistake in reprinting it again in an Anthology before it appears in a book." Again to Monroe, 7 June 1916: "It is so much longer and confessedly so much better, than anything else I have done, that I cannot afford (or so I think) to scatter my forces."

John C. Pope proposed in *American Literature* Nov 1945 that TSE had probably read Constance Garnett's 1914 translation of *Crime and Punishment.* TSE wrote to him, 8 Mar 1946:

> The poem of Prufrock was conceived some time in 1910. I think that when I went to Paris in the autumn of that year I had already written several fragments which were ultimately embodied in that poem, but I cannot at this distance remember which. I think that the passage beginning "I am not Prince Hamlet", a passage showing the influence of Laforgue, was one of these fragments which I took with me, but the poem was not completed until the summer of 1911. During the period of my stay in Paris, Dostoievsky was very much a subject of interest among literary people and it

was my friend and tutor, Alain Fournier, who introduced me to this author. Under his instigation, I read *Crime and Punishment*, *The Idiot* and *The Brothers Karamazov* in the French translation during the course of the winter. These three novels made a very profound impression on me and I had read them all before *Prufrock* was completed, so I think you have established very conclusively the essentials of your case, and the only red herring that led you astray was that I could only have read *Crime and Punishment* in Mrs. Garnett's translation!

Conrad Aiken's statement of trying unsuccessfully to place *Prufrock* in London in 1914 is quite correct. This would have been the spring of 1914. I had had the poem by me, therefore, unpublished for three years. Indeed, as I remember it was only with great difficulty that Ezra Pound finally persuaded Miss Harriet Monroe to accept the poem for *Poetry Chicago* in 1915.

This was quoted by Pope, *American Literature* Jan 1947, noting that Aiken's statement had been made in *Harvard Advocate* Dec 1938. *Greene* 42 adds to Pope's account that TSE read *Crime et Châtiment* in the translation by Victor Derély (1901), "sans doute". *TSE's books: Bodleian list* (1934), however, includes the English titles of the three novels (whereas many titles are given in French). TSE to Pope, 13 May 1947: "Your comparison of the French and English translations of the two passages is most interesting and indeed makes it seem very odd that *Prufrock* should have been written before Mrs. Garnett's translation appeared. Professor Richards tells me, however, that there was a much earlier American translation. He believes that the name of the translator is Vizetelly" (pub. NY and London, 1886).

Other than Pound's, perhaps the earliest critical reaction to the publication of TSE's poetry came in a letter from Louis Untermeyer, 13 Aug 1915, to the Editor of *Poetry* (which did not publish it): "I confess that his *Love Song* is the first piece of the English language that utterly stumped me. As a post-impression, the effect was that of the Muse in a psychopathic ward—drinking the stale dregs of revolt. The other Sunday night there was a group at the house—one of those not-too-'arts-&-crafty' mélanges—a few poets, a lawyer, a couple of musicians and one psychoanalyst. I read it to them quite seriously—and no one · · · could keep a straight face. No one, that is, except the psychoanalyst who said, 'An extremely interesting case. I think a lot could be done for him. It's a muddled case of infantile repressions and inhibitions'", *Dear Editor: A History of "Poetry" in Letters*, ed. Joseph Parisi and Stephen Young (2002). Untermeyer published a verse parody of Aiken and Eliot in *Including Horace* (1919).

Chapin, of TSE's reading at the National Gallery, Washington, 23 May 1947: "He almost dissociated himself from this poem by speaking of it as belonging to a time and a person that no longer existed in him."

In 1962 TSE was asked of Prufrock: "Did the person you had in mind represent the age, or is he a character from *The Waste Land?*" He replied: "I could not have answered that question at all when I wrote *Prufrock*. It was partly a dramatic creation of a man of about 40 I should say, and partly an expression of feeling of my own through this dim imaginary figure", *Grantite Review* (1962).

Title **Love Song**: "I once wrote a poem called *The Love Song of J. Alfred Prufrock*: I am convinced that it would never have been called *Love Song* but for a title of Kipling's that stuck obstinately in my head, *The Love Song of Har Dyal*", *The Unfading Genius of Rudyard Kipling* (1959). TSE included Kipling's poem in *A Choice of Kipling's Verse* (1941). TSE: "it is indeed a tribute to the many volumes in which such vast vulgarity, humanity and genius are displayed, that no critic has yet taken the measure of Kipling", *A Commentary* in *Criterion* Apr 1936. For *The Love Song of St. Sebastian* (1914), see "Uncollected Poems". ***J. Alfred Prufrock***: in *Hodgson's 1932*, which TSE inscribed on 5 Apr 1932, Ralph Hodgson wrote beneath the "J" of the title: "(Joseph) so T.S.E. told me, amused by my question—R. H." His wife Aurelia recorded the conversation (Bryn Mawr, box 25, Notebook 7):

> T.S.E. May 22 [1932]—(earlier)—to R. H. *J.* Alfred Prufrock (almost *Proudfoot*)—*Joseph*, tho he would be ashamed and suppress it. Book written 1910–11. Published 1917. Re. writers who contract for advance books: "I would never write another line if I did that".

And again:

> *Prufrock* was written over two years ··· R. H. asked what the "J." stood for. He thought *Joseph*. J. Alfred would have felt rather ashamed of it, and suppressed it. *Proudfoot* was his alternative surname

In *The Confidential Clerk*, B. Kaghan (whose father's name was Alfred) suppresses his name, "Barnabas", because he doesn't want it shortened to "Barney" (121).

During 1915–16 TSE signed himself variously "T. Stearns Eliot", "Thomas S. Eliot" and "Thomas Stearns Eliot". The naming of the poet proved difficult. In a review in Aug 1915 Pound wrote of "J. S. Eliot's newest work". Subsequently *Poetry* published *Observations* in Sept 1916 over the name "T. R. Eliot". In 1910 his first work to be printed beyond school and university magazines, *Ode* ("For the hour that is left us Fair Harvard"), had been ascribed to "Thomas Stearns Elliott" by the *St. Louis Republic* (on such Scottish spelling variants, see headnote to *The Marching Song of the Pollicle Dogs*), and when printing his *Syllabus: Victorian Literature* (1917), Oxford University Press was to call him "T. G. Eliot". In Jan 1925, the group of *Three Poems* in the *Criterion* bore the name "Thomas Eliot".

As to conventions of naming, all five of the correspondents invented by TSE for his spoof letters in *Egoist* Dec 1917 had middle initials or middle names (and *The Love Song of J. Alfred Prufrock* having recently been collected, the first of the invented names is "J. A. D. Spence"). See *Clerihews* I: "Mr Maurice *B.* Reckitt". TSE to the Librarian of the London Library, 3 July 1935: "Your assistant has so long addressed me as 'T. Steoms Eliot' that I hesitate to introduce any change. But this designation does give me pain, as my middle name is STEARNS (or STERNE); and I should be grateful if she would in future address me simply, as I subscribe myself, as | Your obedient servant, | T. S. Eliot." On the need for "three different names", see note to *The Naming of Cats* 2, and on delicacies of address see note to *Five-Finger Exercises* V. *Lines for Cuscuscaraway and Mirza Murad Ali Beg* 1: "Mr. Eliot". ***Prufrock***: "Several correspondents have recently called my attention to the Prufrock-Littau Company, furniture dealers of St. Louis. I did not have, at the time of writing the poem, and have not yet recovered, any recollection of having acquired the name in this way, but I think that it must be assumed that I did, and that the memory has been obliterated" (to Stephen Stepanchev; *MLN* June 1951). The store—correctly "Prufrock-Litton"—placed several advertisements for "Prufrock's" furniture in the *Smith Academy Record* 1899–1900 (*Stayer*). TSE told an audience in Chicago on 6 Nov 1959 that Prufrock was "a name he used to see on the sign of a shop in St. Louis, when he was a boy" (*St. Louis Post-Dispatch*, 29 Nov 1959). "There has been a good deal of nonsense written about the name *Prufrock.* Someone discovered that there had been a shop in St. Louis, Missouri, where I spent my boyhood up to the age of 16, which bore the name Prufrock. Then the question arose whether as a boy I had ever had occasion to pass down the street in which the shop was found. And someone else has discovered symbolism in the name which allied it to *Touchstone*! But I chose the name because it sounded to me very very prosaic. I have taken names often because they sounded to me euphonious—like Sweeney or Rabinovitch", *Grantite Review* (1962).

Unadopted subtitle (***Prufrock among the Women***): Elizabeth Barrett Browning's title *Bianca Among the Nightingales* later gave TSE his title *Sweeney Among the Nightingales.*

Epigraph] *Inf.* XXVII 61–66, Guido da Montefeltro ["If I thought my answer were to one who ever could return to the world, this flame should shake no more; but since none ever did return alive from this depth, if what I hear be true, without fear of infamy I answer thee"]. See note to *The Waste Land* [II] 110. At first, the manuscript of *The Love Song of J. Alfred Prufrock*, in the *March Hare* Notebook, had no epigraph, but TSE supplied the closing lines of *Purg.* XXVI:

"Sovegna vos al temps de mon dolor"—
Poi s'ascose nel foco che gli affina.

["be mindful in due time of my pain". Then he hid him in the fire which refines them.]

These lines about Arnaut Daniel did not appear in this poem in later drafts or in print. For TSE's returns to the passage, see note to title *Ara Vos Prec* in headnote to "*Poems* (1920)", 7. PUBLICATION OF *ARA VOS PREC*.

1 **Let us go then, you and I**: "Let us quickly gather and go", *Circe's Palace* (*variant after* 14). To Kristian Smidt, 5 June 1959: "As for *The Love Song of J. Alfred Prufrock* anything I say now must be somewhat conjectural, as it was written so long ago that my memory may deceive me; but I am prepared to assert that the 'you' in *The Love Song* is merely some friend or companion, presumably of the male sex, whom the speaker is at that moment addressing, and that it has no emotional content whatever. I shall be glad if this simplifies the problem, because I have recently seen some quite astonishing over-interpretation of this poem."

1–2 **Let us go then, you and I, | When the evening is spread out against the sky**: "let us embark— | The night is anything but dark", *Goldfish* II 4.

1–4 **Let us go then ··· streets**: George Eliot: "Let us go now ··· We will get down at the end of the street", *Daniel Deronda* ch. XL, closely following "See the sky, how it is slowly fading".

2 **When the evening is spread out against the sky**: "The yellow evening flung against the panes | Of dirty windows", *First Caprice in North Cambridge* 2–3 ("window-panes", 15). "when the evening ··· spread out", *Prufrock's Pervigilium* [10, 13]. **spread out against the sky**: Job 37: 18: "Hast thou with him spread out the sky." TSE: "His soul stretched tight across the skies", *Preludes* IV 1. **against the sky**: Hardy: "forms there flung | Against the sky", *The Abbey Mason* 204–205 (Archie Burnett, personal communication).

2–3 **evening ··· spread out ··· sky ··· upon a table**: Laforgue: "Le couchant de sang est taché | Comme un tablier de boucher; | Oh! Qui veut m'écorcher!" [The setting sun with blood is stained like a butcher's apron; oh! who wants to skin me!] *Complainte sur certains temps déplacés* [*Complaint on Certain Displaced Times*]. W. E. Henley: "To the theatre, a cockpit | Where they stretch you on a table", *In Hospital* V 3–4 (Hans Borchers, *Yeats-Eliot Review* Spring 1978). Among books owned by TSE in his Harvard years, Henry Eliot listed a copy of Henley's *Poems* (Scribner, 1905). TSE: "We can never, I mean, wholly explain the practical world from a theoretical point of view, because this world is what it is by reason of the practical point of view and the world which we try to explain is a world spread out upon a table—simply *there*!" *Knowledge and Experience* 136. Of John Middleton Murry: "a real pleasure, an exceptional pleasure, to have a patient like Mr. Murry extended on the operating table; we need our sharpest instruments, and steadiest nerves, if we are to do him justice", *The Poetic Drama* (1920) (*Childs* 126). In 1950: "In talking to the matron, you are still the subject, | The centre of reality. But, stretched on the table, | You are a piece of furniture in a repair shop | For those who surround you, the masked actors; | All there is of you is your body | And the 'you' is withdrawn", *The Cocktail Party* I i. (For "'Prufrock's' furniture", see note to poem title.)

3 **Like a patient etherised:** Gautier: "Comme une Aphrodite éthérée" [Like an ethereal Aphrodite], *La Nue* [*The Cloud / The Sky / The Naked Woman*] 7 (*Ricks 1993*). For Gautier's poem, see note to 82. Use of ether for pain relief was pioneered in 1846 at Massachusetts General Hospital, in the operating theatre later called the Ether Dome. This breakthrough in anaesthesia is commemorated by the Ether Monument (1867) in Boston Public Gardens. TSE: "With chemicals and a knife ··· the sinking blackness of ether", *Do I know how I feel? Do I know what I think?* 18, 25. "Or when, under ether, the mind is conscious but conscious of nothing", *East Coker* III 22. *Moody* 32: "*aethereal* may lie just beyond 'etherised'". In his *Harvard index cards* (1914), TSE noted, from William James's *The Varieties of Religious Experience*, that B. P. Blood had shown how ether might stimulate mystical consciousness (*Crawford* 80). To J. H. Oldham, 11 Feb 1943: "The term, 'religious experience' was done a good deal of damage by William James going to the dentist and having laughing gas." Laforgue: "Morte? Se peut-il pas qu'elle dorme | Grise de cosmiques chloroformes?" [Dead? Can't she be sleeping, drunk on cosmic chloroforms?], *Jeux* [*Pastimes*] 3–4 (*Ricks 1993*). **etherised upon a table**: operating tables were formerly known as "anesthetic tables" (Russell S. Fowler, *The Operating Room and the Patient*, 1906).

3–4 **etherised ··· streets:** William James on effects of "haschish": "Objects comparatively near will recede to a vast distance, a short street assume to the eye an immeasurable perspective. Ether and chloroform occasionally produce not wholly dissimilar results ··· etherized" (TSE "etherised"), *The Principles of Psychology* (1890) II 142–3. In TSE's copy of *An Experimental Study of Sensation* by Edwin B. Holt and Robert M. Yerkes [1903] 17, he noted to himself "Reading: James. *Pr. Psy.* Vol II pp. 134–44" (Houghton).

4 **certain ··· streets:** officialese (esp. US), as in payment "To R. D. Bennett, for sprinkling a certain street", *Acts and Resolutions of the 29th General Assembly of Iowa* (1902) 217. Dickens: "he sought out a certain street and number", *Little Dorrit* ch. XX. "certain ··· street", *Preludes* IV 7–8.

4–5 **half-deserted streets, | The muttering retreats:** James Thomson: "along the silent streets · · · countless lanes and close retreats", *The City of Dreadful Night* III 1, 3. TSE: "At sixteen I discovered (by reading a section of our history of English Literature which we were *not* required to read) Thomson's *City of Dreadful Night*, and the poems of Ernest Dowson. Each was a new and vivid experience. But *The City of Dreadful Night* or Dowson's *Impenitentia Ultima* would hardly, even today, be considered suitable for academic study at the age I have in mind", *On Teaching the Appreciation of Poetry* (1960). "streets · · · retreats", *The Little Passion: From "An Agony in the Garret"* 2–4.

4–7 **certain half-deserted streets · · · one-night cheap hotels | And sawdust:** William Acton: "even if some women are to be seen in certain streets in Paris in the early part of the evening, after half-past eleven the streets are quite deserted · · · In London a man has prostitution thrust upon him; in Paris he has to go out of his way to look for it", *Prostitution* (1858, 2nd ed. 1870) 112. In Charles-Louis Philippe's *Bubu de Montparnasse* ch. I, Pierre walks the sordid streets by night:

> Et souvent ses désirs l'avaient mené. Certains soirs, ayant travaillé jusqu'à onze heures, il fermait ses livres et se sentait triste à côté de leur science. Tous les diplômes ne valaient pas le bonheur de vivre. Deux ou trois images des femmes rencontrées lui apparaissaient à l'imagination et ils les suivait, d'abord pour se délasser. Puis tout le feu de ses vingt ans s'animait, tous ses sens sentaient ce que contient une femme qui passe. Alors il se dressait, la gorge sèche et le coeur serré, éteignait sa lampe et descendait dans la rue.
>
> Il marchait. Des prostituées pirouettaient à des coins de rue, avec de pauvres jupes et des yeux questionneurs: il ne les regardait même pas. Il marchait comme marche l'espérance.
>
> [And often his desires swept him away. On certain nights, having studied until eleven, he closed his books and sat crushed with sadness before all their knowledge. All the diplomas in the world were not worth the joy of life. Two or three visions of women he had encountered came to his mind, and he followed them, at first merely to divert himself. Then all the fire of his twenty years flared to life, and his senses sensed the magic contained in a passing woman. He leapt up, his throat parched, his heart contracted. He blew out the lamp and went out into the street. He walked. Prostitutes pirouetted on the street-corners, with their threadbare skirts and their querying eyes. He did not even look at them. He walked as hope walks.]

Again: "Ils passèrent la nuit dans un hôtel meublé de la rue Saint-Sauveur et il lui donna quinze francs" [They spent the night in a cheap hotel in the rue Saint-Saveur and he gave her fifteen francs], *Bubu* ch. VII. (For TSE and Charles-Louis Philippe, see headnote to *Preludes*.) TSE, aged 26, to Aiken, 31 Dec 1914: "I have been going through one of those nervous sexual attacks which I suffer from when alone in a city. Why I had almost none last fall I don't know—this is the worst since Paris · · · I am very dependent upon women (I mean female society); and feel the deprivation at Oxford—one reason why I should not care to remain longer—but there, with the exercise and routine, the deprivation takes the form of numbness only; while in the city it is more lively and acute. One walks about the street with one's desires, and one's refinement rises up like a wall whenever opportunity approaches. I should be better off, I sometimes think, if I had disposed of my virginity and shyness several years ago: and indeed I still think sometimes that it would be well to do so before marriage." (Philippe:

"Un homme qui marche porte toutes les choses de sa vie ··· nos désirs" [A man walks carrying with him all the properties of his life ··· our desires], *Bubu* ch. I. See note to *The Waste Land* [I] 2–3.) **one-night:** OED "one" 35, special combinations *one-night*: "lasting, residing, or used for a single night"; *one-night stand*: "*transf.* and *fig.*, *spec.* a casual sexual encounter", from 1963. W. R. Burnett's *High Sierra* (1940) has "She was ··· a one-night stand type". OED: "orig. *U.S.*, a single performance of a play, show or the like", from 1880; the sense in TSE's letter to John Hayward, 10 Oct 1941, on an invitation to speak in Newcastle and Durham: "These one night stands are very tiring". **cheap hotels:** Edward Winslow Martin: "There are over one hundred houses of assignation in New York, known to the police. Besides these, there are places, used as such ··· cheap hotels, where women hire rooms without meals, and receive visitors, with whom they make appointments on the streets ··· Some really good houses have been ruined in this way ··· Even the first-class hotels are kept busy in purging themselves of the evil", *The Secrets of the Great City* (1868).

4–8 **half-deserted streets ··· restless nights ··· sawdust ··· Streets that follow like a tedious argument:** see note to *Preludes* II 1–4 for John Davidson's *A Woman and her Son*.

6 **Of restless nights in one-night cheap hotels:** "And heated nights in second story dance halls", *In the Department Store* 6. **restless nights:** "restless on winter nights", *Do I know how I feel? Do I know what I think?* 13. "When restless nights distract her brain from sleep", *WLComposite* 290.

6–10 **Of restless nights in one-night cheap hotels ··· Streets that follow like a tedious argument ··· to an overwhelming question:** "I have questioned restless nights and torpid days, | And followed every by-way where it led", *Oh little voices of the throats of men* 17–18. "through the evening air | A chain of reasoning whereof the thread was gone ··· I walked along", *So through the evening, through the violet air* 10–12.

7 **sawdust restaurants:** OED "sawdust" 3b: "With reference to the use of sawdust for strewing the floor of a place of public entertainment" (now quoting this line). **restaurants ··· oyster-shells:** TSE's London *Baedeker*, acquired 14 Oct 1910, indicated the social standing of different establishments: "Restaurants. Dining Rooms. Oyster Shops" (10). **restaurants:** TSE sounds the final *t* in his recordings. OED also gives a pronunciation in which it is not sounded, and the spelling of its first citation, from Fenimore Cooper, 1827, points to the French derivation: "At the most renowned of the Parisian restaurans" (*The Prairie* II ii 28).

10 **lead ··· question:** "every man who thinks and lives by thought must have his own scepticism, that which stops at the question, that which ends in denial, or that which leads to faith", *The "Pensées" of Pascal* (1931). **overwhelming question:** Fenimore Cooper: "The whole company were a good deal astounded with this overwhelming question", *The Pioneers* ch. XXIII. **question:** *Hamlet* III i: "To be, or not to be, that is the question." Perhaps also OED 6: "to pop the question (*slang* or *colloq.*), to propose marriage" (1725).

11–12, 27 **"What is it?" ··· our visit ··· To prepare a face to meet the faces that you meet:** Emerson: "But the unit of the visit, | The encounter of the wise,— | Say, what other metre is it | Than the meeting of the eyes?" *The Visit.* TSE: "There, the eyes are", *The Hollow Men* II 4. For "wearing a mask among people", see note to *Oh little voices of the throats of men* 15, "Appearances appearances".

13 **In the room ... come and go:** James Thomson: "pacing to and fro", *In the Room* 51. Valerie Eliot wrote to Christopher Ricks, 20 Apr 1995, that among Thomson's poems, this was "another favourite". Paul Elmer More had discussed it in *Shelburne Essays* fifth series (1908) (*Crawford* 40). See note to 126–31 and notes to *The Waste Land* [III] 215–18 and *The Little Passion: From "An Agony in the Garret" ms1* **21** *variant.* TSE's extension lectures of 1917 included "Three Poets of Doubt—Matthew Arnold, Edward FitzGerald, James Thomson", *Syllabus: Victorian Literature* (1917). "in the room alone", *On a Portrait* 4.

13–14 **In the room the women come and go | Talking of Michelangelo:** an error in *Southam* has been often repeated: that TSE here is indebted to lines by Laforgue: "Dans la pièce les femmes vont et viennent | En parlant des maîtres de Sienne". But this is the 1947 translation of TSE's own lines by Pierre Leyris. Hugh Kenner inadvertently precipitated the error by quoting TSE's couplet and then saying: "The lines scale down severely in French: 'Dans la pièce . . .'", with an equivocal mention of "the translator" (*Kenner* 6). "The ladies who are interested in Assyrian art", *Afternoon* 1. **women come and go:** Christina G. Rossetti: "Love-music warbling in their throat | Young men and women come and go", *The Convent Threshold* (*Ricks* 19). For TSE on Christina G. Rossetti, see note to *The Hollow Men* I 4–10. David Gascoyne claimed to have heard TSE give a reading of her poems at the Poetry Bookshop in the early 1930s (Gascoyne, *Selected Poems*, 1994, xi). Poe: "Mere puppets they, who come and go", *The Conqueror Worm* 12. **go | Talking of:** "Going ··· Talking of trivial things", *Ash-Wednesday* IV 5. "talking of effect and cause", *Convictions (Curtain Raiser)* 15. "Talking of art and of aesthetic laws", *WLComposite* **229–98** [21]. **Michelangelo:** pronounced "Michael Angelo" in TSE's recordings; see *Ricks* 17–18. (For Napoleon Bonaparte changing the spelling of his name along with his nationality, see TSE to Nelson Landale, 22 June 1938, in headnote to *Four Quartets*, 3. COMPOSITION.) In his copy of *Studies in the History of the Renaissance*, ch. V, TSE scored Pater's comment that Michelangelo "is one of those who incur the judgment of Dante, as having *wilfully lived in sadness*" (a quotation repeated five pages later). According to Oscar Wilde, who cites the same passage of Pater in *De Profundis* (1906) 45, the allusion is to the end of *Inferno* VII. In *A Neglected Aspect of Chapman* (1924), TSE wrote of Pater "whose 'Renaissance' can be fixed nearer to 1890 than to 1500 A.D."

15 **The yellow fog ··· the window-panes:** Conan Doyle: "Stand at the window here. Was ever such a dreary, dismal, unprofitable world? See how the yellow fog swirls down the street and drifts across the dun-coloured houses", *The Sign of Four* ch. 1; itself invoking *Hamlet* I ii: "How weary, stale, flat, and unprofitable | Seem to me all the uses of this world" (Mark Thompson, personal communication). TSE to Mrs. Greacen [Patricia Hutchins], 11 Dec 1956: "As for the fog in *Prufrock*, it certainly came to seem to me also an English fog, but I assure you that when I wrote those lines I had never seen a London, or an English, fog! We used to have something similar in St. Louis in the old days before smoke abatement had been thought of, on winter mornings when a moist East wind blew the smoke [*at the foot*: very soft coal!] from the factories in east St. Louis across the

river." For Baudelaire's "Un brouillard sale et jaune" [a dirty yellow fog], see note to *The Waste Land* [I] 60.

15–22 **fog ··· Slipped by the terrace, made a sudden leap ··· fell asleep**: "It leapt to the floor and made a sudden hiss", *Prufrock's Pervigilium* [21]. Feline again: "the GREAT RUMPUSCAT ··· gave a great yawn ··· looked out through the bars of the area ··· looked at the sky and he gave a great leap", *Of the Awefull Battle of the Pekes and the Pollicles* 50–57.

17–20 **Licked its tongue ··· Slipped**: "the cat which flattens itself ··· Slips out its tongue", *Rhapsody on a Windy Night* 35–36. "She slips down the stairs", *The Old Gumbie Cat* 8. **made a sudden leap**: Carroll: the White Knight (the leaping chess-piece) "made a sudden pause", *Through the Looking-Glass* ch. VIII, "It's My Own Invention". **a sudden leap**: Bergson: "un saut brusque de l'animal à l'homme" [a sudden leap from the animal to man], *L'Evolution créatrice* (1907) ch. II, final paragraph (Mitchell's translation, 1911).

17–22 **corners of the evening ··· Curled once about the house and fell asleep**: Wilde: "shadows crawl into the corners of the room, and crouch there. Outside ··· wind ··· wandering round the silent house, as though it feared to wake the sleepers ··· sleep", *The Picture of Dorian Gray* ch. XI. For the same pages of Wilde, see notes to 49 and *Prufrock's Pervigilium* [25, 28], *Oh little voices of the throats of men* 38–40, and *The Waste Land* [II] 84–87, [II] 87–95. (Richard Shusterman related Wilde's ch. VII to *The Love Song of J. Alfred Prufrock* and to *Rhapsody on a Windy Night* in *T. S. Eliot Annual* I, ed. S. Bagchee, 1990.) TSE: "Dorian Grey has fled to Germany, where a cigarette has been named after him; and the 'Nineties' æsthetic eccentricities may now be ignored", *The Borderline of Prose* (1917). "I am much deceived if *Dorian Gray* be not perfect rubbish, and the best of Wilde be not in *Intentions*", *A Preface to Modern Literature* (1922). Writing to Eric Barton, 19 Mar 1954, TSE declined to officiate at the unveiling of a plaque for Wilde's centenary.

18, 22 **lingered ··· fell asleep**: Van Wyck Brooks: "the genius of romance had lingered here and grown forgetful of itself and fallen asleep", *The Wine of the Puritans: A Study of Present-Day America* (1908) 10. TSE reviewed the book in *Harvard Advocate* 7 May 1909: "Mr. Brooks has handled successfully a difficult form—the dialogue; never allowing it to degenerate into soliloquy, and often rendering a slight difference in the point of view, a shift of personality."

22 **Curled once about the house**: "a wave of excitement curled into the street", *Eeldrop and Appleplex* I (1917). **Curled ··· and fell asleep**: "England puts her Great Writers away securely in a Safe Deposit Vault, and curls to sleep", *Observations* (1918).

23 **And indeed there will be time**: Marvell: "Had we but world enough and time", *To his Coy Mistress* 1. For Marvell's poem, see notes to 92–93 and to *The Waste Land* [III] 196–97 and *Elegy* 9.

24–27 **smoke that slides along the street ··· prepare a face to meet the faces that you meet**: Emerson: "We come to wear one cut of face and figure ··· foolish face ··· the forced smile which we put on in company where we do not feel at ease ··· by-standers look askance on him in the public street or in the friend's parlor ··· faces ··· put on and off as the wind blows and a newspaper directs", *Self-Reliance* in *Essays: First Series* ("gusty ··· newspapers", *Preludes* I 5, 8). Tennyson: "And

I loathe the squares and streets, | And the faces that one meets", *Maud* II [iv] 233–34 (*Wimsatt 1952*). Charles-Louis Philippe: "Louis Buisson, passionné pour deux ou trois principes philosophiques, y trouvait assez de force pour regarder les hommes en face" [Louis Buisson, in his zeal for two or three philosophical principles, derived therefrom strength enough to look men in the face]; "Le bonheur des filles publiques ressemble aux gueules des rues" [The happiness of the prostitute is like those faces of the street]; "l'on met son sourire aux rencontres des rues et où toute chose se passe avec une ironie française" [a smile is worn for the people met in the street, and wherein everything is carried off with the irony of France], *Bubu de Montparnasse* ch. I, VII, IX. See note to *Little Gidding* II 36–47. "the man who in the morning | Has to make up his face before he looks in the mirror", *The Elder Statesman* I. **to meet the faces that you meet:** "to keep the ways you keep", *Oh little voices of the throats of men* 10.

24–39 **there will be time · · · Time to:** Ecclesiastes 3: 1–8 (see *East Coker* I 9–11 and note).

28–29 **murder · · · works and days of hands:** Revelation 9: 20–21: "yet repented not of the works of their hands · · · neither repented they of their murders".

29, 60 **works and days · · · days and ways:** Tennyson, adopting Hesiod's title: "he that sang the Works and Days", *To Virgil* 3. TSE on Tennyson: "for this side of him you should read the two beautiful poems, to Virgil and to Catullus", *"The Voice of His Time"* (1942). Hesiod's title was also adopted for an essay by Emerson (John Clendinning in *Roby ed.*). "the maze | Of means and ways", *Goldfish* III 19.

32–33, 48 **indecisions · · · visions and revisions · · · decisions and revisions which a minute will reverse:** "revision · · · decision", *Entretien dans un parc* 12, 15. "divisions and precisions", *Rhapsody on a Windy Night* 7. In a palm-reader's report on himself, TSE pencilled "The Prufrock Complex" against "when faced with a personal problem, any prolonged contemplation of probabilities merely produces hesitancy and indecision. You must make quick decisions but not the impulsive ones." He wrote "Prufrock complex" again in the matching report on Henry, against "you are inclined to weigh too carefully the pros and cons of your difficulty, with the result that you merely become hesistant and undecided", *Palm Readings—1938* by Noel Jaquin (ts Houghton). (To Henry Eliot, 26 March 1920: "It is almost impossible for any of our family to make up their minds.")

34 **a toast:** OED "toast" *n.*[1] 2: "(without *a* or *pl.*): Bread so browned by fire, electric heat, etc."

38–39, 45–46, 122 **"Do I dare?" and, "Do I dare?" | Time to turn back · · · Do I dare | Disturb the universe? · · · Do I dare to eat a peach?:** Hector Chainaye, tr. Stuart Merrill: "dare not prevent them · · · do not dare to press too hard · · · does not dare to come forth · · · not daring to make a sound · · · And I dare not move. Yet I should leave · · · Ah! why am I human? · · · my presence disturbs them—and yet I do not move, I dare not", *The Guests* in *Pastels in Prose.* Emerson: "Do that which is assigned to you, and you cannot hope too much or dare too much", *Self-Reliance.*

39 **Time to turn back:** "'Time to regain the door'", *The Death of the Duchess* II 31.

40 **with a bald spot in the middle of my hair:** Richard Barham: "a little bald patch on the top of his crown", *The Brothers of Birchington: A Lay of St. Thomas à Becket* 40

in *The Ingoldsby Legends*, for which see headnote to *A Fable for Feasters* (*Crawford 2015* 72).

40–43 **bald ··· morning coat ··· collar ··· necktie rich and modest:** *Symons* 101 on Laforgue: "*D'allures?* says M. Gustave Kahn, *fort correctes, de hauts gibus, des cravates sobres, des vestons anglais, des pardessus clergymans, et de par les nécessités, un parapluie immuablement placé sous le bras.*" [His aspect? firmly correct, tall hats, sober ties, jackets in the English style, overcoats à la clergyman, and by way of being indispensable, an umbrella unalterably tucked under the arm.] TSE: "And Life, a little bald and gray ··· Waits, hat and gloves in hand, | Punctilious of tie and suit", *Spleen* 11–14.

40, 43, 49, 55 **hair— | ··· pin— | ··· all— | ··· all—:** on Arnold's *Memorial Verses*: "The dashes at the end of two lines are a symptom of weakness, like Arnold's irritating use of italicised words", *The Use of Poetry and the Use of Criticism* 107.

44 **(They will say: "But how his arms and legs are thin!"):** Laforgue: "(Oh! comme elle est maigre!)" [Oh! how thin she's got!] *Légende*. In TSE's copy of Coleridge's poems (Houghton), he wrote at the head of *Religious Musings*: "barbarous splendour of exclamation points". For Gautier's "Carmen est maigre", see note to *Whispers of Immortality* 17, 20.

48 **decisions and revisions which a minute will reverse:** "You made a decision. You set in motion | Forces in your life and in the lives of others | Which cannot be reversed ··· it is a serious matter | To bring someone back from the dead", *The Cocktail Party* I iii (here: "Lazarus ··· dead", 94).

49 **known them all already, known them all:** *The Picture of Dorian Gray* ch. XI: "He felt that he had known them all, those strange terrible figures that had passed across the stage of the world". For Wilde's chapter, see note to 17–22.

49–50 **For I have known them all already, known them all— | Have known the evenings, mornings, afternoons:** "evenings ··· all ··· call, recall | So many nights and afternoons ··· all", *Goldfish* I 1–8.

50–51 **mornings . . . I have measured out my life with coffee spoons:** Pope: "morning ··· pass her time ··· Or o'er cold coffee trifle with the spoon, | Count the slow clock", *Epistle To Miss Blount, on her leaving the Town, after the Coronation* 14–18 (Valentine Cunningham, personal communication). **measured out my life with coffee spoons:** Samuel Osgood: "Measuring life by its moral worth", *Mile-Stones in our Life-Journey* (1855). "Time, as an old man, measuring life with an hour-glass", *The Crayon* Sept 1857. Sending F. S. Flint a copy of René Taupin's *L'influence du symbolisme français sur la poésie américaine, 1910–1920* (Paris, 1929; Berg), TSE corrected Taupin's misquotation in this line, "with a coffee spoon" (Patricia Clements, *N&Q* June 1980). TSE: "Sounding the depths with a silver spoon", *Goldfish* III 6. **coffee spoons:** used for stirring, but unlike teaspoons, not usually for measuring.

52 **a dying fall:** *Twelfth Night* I i: "That strain again, it had a dying fall." TSE: "This music is successful with a 'dying fall'", *Portrait of a Lady* III 39.

52–53 **a dying fall | Beneath the music from a farther room:** *2 Henry IV* IV iv, King Henry: "whisper music to my weary spirit." Warwick: "Call for the music in the other room." A moment later the Prince enters, and stays to watch his dying father while the others withdraw "into the other room". TSE: "whisper music", *The Waste Land* [V] 378.

56 **The eyes that fix you:** Emerson: "do right and scorn eyes", *Self-Reliance* in *Essays: First Series*, two pages before "An institution is the lengthened shadow of one man" (for which see note to *Burbank with a Baedeker: Bleistein with a Cigar* 25–26). **fix ··· formulated phrase:** the fixative formaldehyde was in production by this time ("etherised", 3). **formulated phrase:** "We may therefore formulate as follows", *Reflections on "vers libre"* (1917). "formulaic recurrence" and "formulaic iterancy" are terms in *The Higher Criticism applied to a Modern Science* (anon.), *The Living Age*, 13 May 1899.

56, 58 **fix ··· formulated phrase ··· pinned:** William James in *Some Problems of Philosophy* on the inadequacy of concepts to our perceptions: "The concepts themselves are fixed, even though they designate parts that move in the flux ··· our flowing life must be cut into discrete bits and pinned upon a fixed relational scheme", ch. V. And on empiricism: "it stays inside the flux of life expectantly, recording facts, not formulating laws, and never pretending that man's relation to the totality of things as a philosopher is essentially different from his relation to the parts of things as a daily patient or agent in the practical current of events", ch. VI (TSE: "patient", 3). See note to 73–74 and headnote to *I am the Resurrection and the Life*.

58 **pinned and:** "one inevitable cross | Whereon our souls are pinned, and bleed", *The Little Passion: From "An Agony in the Garret" ms1 7–8 variant.*

60 **butt-ends of my days and ways:** Swinburne: "the ending of the days and ways", *Laus Veneris* 139 (see *Prufrock's Pervigilium* [21–22]). TSE quoted *Laus Veneris* in a letter to Aiken, 19 July 1914, and considered it one of the Swinburne poems that "a volume of selections ··· should certainly contain", *Swinburne as Poet* (1920). "a life composed so much of ways and ends", *Portrait of a Lady* I 21, *ms 1st reading.*

60–61, 65, 68 **days and ways ··· presume ··· lamplight ··· perfume ··· presume:** Herbert: "way ··· day ··· light ··· perfume ··· presume", *Easter* 19–26.

60, 71 **butt-ends of my days ··· light ··· smoke:** Kipling: "And the light of Days that have Been, the dark of the Days that Are, | And Love's torch stinking and stale, like the butt of a dead cigar— || The butt of a dead cigar ··· And a woman is only a woman, but a good Cigar is a smoke", *The Betrothed.* OED "camel" 4 quotes "butt-end of your cigar" from 1827. TSE: "burnt-out ends of smoky days", *Preludes* I 4. **butt-ends:** OED 1b: "*fig.* The mere concluding part; the 'fag end'", with *Richard III* II ii: "The butt-end of a mother's blessing".

63–64 **Arms ··· braceleted ··· hair:** Donne: "That subtile wreath of haire, which crowns my arme", *The Funeral* 3 (*Grover Smith 1996* 155). TSE quoted Donne's "A bracelet of bright haire about the bone" (*The Relique* 6) in *The Metaphysical Poets* (1921), and then in the fourth Clark Lecture as "an example of those things said by Donne which could not have been put equally well otherwise, or differently by a poet of any other school. The associations are perfect: those of 'bracelet', the brightness of the hair, after years of dissolution, and the final emphasis of 'bone'", *The Varieties of Metaphysical Poetry* 125–26. **Arms ··· bare | (But in the lamplight, downed with light brown hair!):** "her arms were bare | Fixed for a question, her hands behind her hair | And the firelight shining", *The Death of the Duchess* II 25–27 (relating "Fixed" to "hair", as here "pinned", 58). **light brown hair**: Stephen C. Foster's popular song of 1854: "I dream of Jeanie with the light brown hair, | Borne like a vapor on the summer air" (George Monteiro, *Explicator* Spring 1987).

65–66 **Is it perfume from a dress | That makes me so digress**: "Bonnets, silk hats, and conscious graces | In repetition that displaces | Your mental self-possession | By this unwarranted digression", *Spleen* 3–6. "'How you digress!'" *Conversation Galante* 6. **perfume from a dress**: Judith Gautier, tr. Stuart Merrill: "the wind blows perfumes from their dresses", *By the River* in *Pastels in Prose.*

69 **And how should I begin?**: *Aeneid* IV 284: "quae prima exordia sumat?" [And how should he begin?], tr. Dryden, IV 408 (Joshua Richards, personal communication). Baudelaire: "Pourquoi réussirais-je, puisque je n'ai même pas envie d'essayer?" [How should I succeed, since I have not even the desire to make the attempt?], *Mon Cœur mis à nu* [*My Heart Laid Bare*], *Journaux Intimes* XXXIII.

Prufrock's Pervigilium (*The Love Song of J. Alfred Prufrock*, after 69. Printed in Textual History.)

The indenting of the opening lines of *Prufrock's Pervigilium* is uncertain in ms. The first three lines of *Prufrock's Pervigilium* correspond to 70–72 of the final poem. In *March Hare* it was taken as including also, at the end, 73–74 of the final poem and four further deleted lines, 74^75, making it six lines longer in all. See Textual History, description of *ms1*.

Gordon 65–66: "*Prufrock's Pervigilium* is undated, but it was probably copied into Eliot's Notebook in 1912. The rest of *Prufrock* (i.e. the poem as it was eventually published) was copied into the Notebook, in his spiky hand, in Munich, July–August 1911. But Eliot deliberately left four pages in the middle of the poem blank, which suggests he had a rough draft of the *Pervigilium* which awaited completion."

Title **Pervigilium**: OED "pervigilation": "*Obs.* a watching through the night." The *Pervigilium Veneris*, a poem of 93 lines, later than the second century, is preserved in the Latin Anthology. Set on the eve of the spring festival, it ends with the nightingale: "*illa cantat; nos tacemus; quando ver venit meum?*" [he sings; we are silent; when will my own springtime come?]. For "when will", see note to *Five-Finger Exercises* I. *Lines to a Persian Cat* 7–8, 10.

In *The Spirit of Romance* (1910), Pound printed the poem in translation, after commenting:

> The point is that the *metric* of the *Pervigilium* probably indicated as great a change of sensibility in its day as the change from Viennese waltzes to jazz may indicate in our own.
>
> Cras amet qui nunquam amavit
> Quique amavit cras amet
> Let whoever never loved, love tomorrow,
> Let whoever has loved, love tomorrow

W. H. Porter translated the *Pervigilium* as *The Watch-Night of Venus* in 1909. J. W. Mackail's translation was printed by T. J. Cobden-Sanderson for the Doves Press in 1910, and another edition with translation by Cecil Clementi was published in 1911. TSE refers to the *Pervigilium* in his Note to *The Waste Land* [V] 428 (see Commentary), and in relation to "the native measure of Latin poetry" in *The Music of Poetry* (1942).

In *Marius the Epicurean* (1885) ch. VI–VII, Walter Pater had elaborately fantasised an author for the Latin poem. After catching the plague, "the terrible new disease" brought back from foreign lands, Flavian writes "a kind of nuptial hymn" while dying, and Marius keeps a nightlong vigil. So *Veneris* suggests not only "of Venus" but "of the venereal" (Pater: "depositing various degrees of lifelong infirmity in this member or that"). TSE: "Pater is inclined to emphasize whatever is morbid or associated with physical malady ··· *Marius* itself is incoherent; its method is a number of fresh starts ··· To the end, Marius remains only a half-awakened soul ··· The true importance of the book, I think, is as a document of one moment in the history of thought and sensibility in the nineteenth century", *Arnold and Pater* (1930). (To William Blissett, 12 Aug 1953: "Pater had a much greater influence upon me at one period of my life than any reader would gather from my essay ··· At the age of sixteen or seventeen, I was fascinated ··· and think that I read all of his work—some of his books several times, especially *Studies in the Renaissance*, *Marius the Epicurean* and *Imaginary Portraits*".)

A Parisian pervigilium, Laforgue's sonnet *La Première nuit*, similarly has children, and an old man in a sexual setting, with—below the gas-light—prostitutes soliciting: "Ses filles aux seins froids qui, sous le gaz blafard | Voguent, flairant de l'oeil un mâle de hasard" [Its cold-breasted girls who, under the ashen gas-light, sail along, sniffing out with their eyes a random male]. Laforgue: "je rêve à ma fenêtre" [I dream at my window]. (TSE: "I fumbled to the window to experience the world", [28].) Laforgue twice refers in his sonnet to "mon chat Mürr"; he praised Baudelaire's originality: "Le premier, parla de Paris en damné quotidien de la capitale (les becs de gaz que tourmente le vent de la Prostitution qui s'allument dans les rues ··· et les chats)" [The first who spoke of Paris and the everyday damnation of the capital (the gaslamps lighting up the streets and tormented by the wind of Prostitution ··· and cats)], *Notes sur Baudelaire*. (This, the text of 1903 available to TSE, is corrected by P. Bonnefis in his edition of *Mélanges posthumes*, 1979, 111.) TSE: "It leapt to the floor and made a sudden hiss", *Prufrock's Pervigilium* [21], and see note to *The Love Song of J. Alfred Prufrock* 15–22.

Wilde: "He remembered wandering through dimly-lit streets, past gaunt black-shadowed archways and evil-looking houses. Women with hoarse voices and harsh laughter had called after him. Drunkards had reeled by cursing, and chattering to themselves like monstrous apes. He had seen grotesque children huddled upon doorsteps, and heard shrieks and oaths from gloomy courts", *The Picture of Dorian Gray* ch. VII. Paul Elmer More on James Thomson's *The City of Dreadful Night*: "For this poem of unrelieved pessimism is simply the impressions of an insomniac changed from self-complaining to a phantom evocation of the London as he came to know it from his fierce nocturnal vigils—'the City is of Night, but not of Sleep'", *Shelburne Essays* fifth series (1908) 184.

[5] **the children whimpering in corners**: Charles-Louis Philippe: "parce que

dans nos âmes il y a le bon coin qui, du temps où nous ne faisions pas le mal, était plein de sentiments simples et qui reste toujours à sa place et où des voix parfois descendent et viennent crier commes des enfants abandonnés" [because in the soul is a good corner which, in the days before doing harm, was replete with simple emotions, and there it remains forever, and at times voices descend into it, and come crying like forsaken children], *Bubu de Montparnasse* ch. VIII. TSE: "Children's voices in little corners | Whimper whimper", *The Burnt Dancer* 20–21. **in corners:** "Dust in sunlight and memory in corners", *A Song for Simeon* 6.

[7–15] **Women, spilling out of corsets, stood in entries · · · up stairs · · · at night through narrow streets · · · evil houses:** see TSE to Aiken 31 Dec 1914: "One walks about the street with one's desires", quoted in note to *The Love Song of J. Alfred Prufrock* 4–7. **spilling out of corsets:** Laurent Tailhade: "Vous dont la gorge flotte en amont du corset" [You whose bosom overflows the corset], *Vieilles Actrices* [*Old Actresses*] 34. For Tailhade, see headnote to *Cousin Nancy* and note to *Afternoon* 1–2.

[8–9] **flickered | And the oil cloth curled up stairs:** Keats: "the wide stairs · · · lamp was flickering · · · And the long carpets rose along the gusty floor", *The Eve of St. Agnes* 355–60. **oil cloth:** defined in *Webster's Dictionary* (1828): "cloth oiled or painted for covering floors".

[12] **drifted:** of *Marius the Epicurean* (see headnote): "Marius merely *drifts* towards the Christian Church", *Arnold and Pater* (1930). "The artist is part of him a drifter, at the mercy of impressions", *Eeldrop and Appleplex* II (1917).

[13] **drug store:** OED: "orig. *U.S.* and chiefly *N.Amer.* A pharmacy", from 1810; by the end of the century, established as "often also dealing extensively or mainly in other articles".

[14–16] **I have gone at night through narrow streets, || Where evil houses leaning all together · · · in the darkness:** Proverbs 2: 13–18: "Who leave the paths of uprightness, to walk in the ways of darkness; who rejoice to do evil · · · deliver thee from the strange woman · · · For her house inclineth unto death."

[14–17] **night · · · evil houses · · · me in the darkness:** Job 17: 12–13: "night · · · the grave is mine house: I have made my bed in the darkness."

[15] **evil houses leaning all together:** "staring forms | Leaned out, leaning, hushing the room enclosed", *The Waste Land* [II] 105–106. "We are the stuffed men | Leaning together", *The Hollow Men* 12–13. "And breastless creatures under ground | Leaned backward with a lipless grin", *Whispers of Immortality* 3–4. "Leaves the room and reappears | Outside the window, leaning in", *Sweeney Among the Nightingales* 29–30. "In the square they lean against each other · · · The people leaning against another in the square", *The Death of the Duchess* 18, 30. **evil houses:** including the sense of houses of evil repute, brothels (from 16th century).

[15–17] **evil · · · Whispering all together, chuckled at me:** Psalm 41: 5, 7: "speak evil of me · · · All that hate me whisper together".

[16–17] **in the darkness | Whispering all together:** "Evening whisper of stars together", *Hidden under the heron's wing* 3. "whispers in darkness", *Murder in the Cathedral* I.

[19] **watch the darkness:** *Symons* 25 on the supreme artist: "when he looks into the darkness, he sees".

[19–21, 35] **the darkness | Crawling among the papers on the table | It leapt to the floor ··· the darkness creep along the wall:** "Across the floor the shadows crawled and crept", *Oh little voices of the throats of men* 39. "crawled head downward down a blackened wall", *The Waste Land* [V] 381.

[21–22] **sudden hiss ··· across:** Swinburne: "sudden serpents hiss across her hair", *Laus Veneris* 116.

[23] **Flattened itself:** "the cat which flattens itself in the gutter", *Rhapsody on a Windy Night* 35. Wilde: "the squat misshapen figure that flattened itself into the shadow as he passed", *The Picture of Dorian Gray* ch. XVI, an opium den night-scene with "gas-jets", "an old man" and "chattered" (TSE: "gas-jet", [8]; "A blind old drunken man", [30]; "chatter", [36]).

[24–25] **Stretched out ··· And when the dawn at length:** *Paradise Lost* I 208–209: "and wished morn delays: | So stretcht out huge in length the arch-fiend lay".

[25, 28] **And when the dawn at length had realized itself ··· the world:** in F. H. Bradley: "an idea's general tendency to realize itself"; "Truth is the whole Universe realizing itself in one aspect ··· For it is the whole Universe which, immanent throughout, realizes and seeks itself in truth"; "The Universe is nowhere apart from the lives of the individuals, and, whether as truth or otherwise, the Universe realizes itself not at all except through their differences"; "That which we call our real world ··· It is the Universe realizing itself as truth within finite centres", *Essays on Truth and Reality* (1914) 80, 116, 121, 332 (first pub., respectively, July 1904; Apr 1907, the two; and July 1911). TSE: "a consciousness gradually realising itself by the effort of making itself its own objects; so that the term of the process would be an infinite consciousness contemplating the whole world", *The Ethics of Green and Sidgwick* (1914). "The morning comes to consciousness", *Preludes* II 1. **the dawn ··· the world:** Wilde: "we watch the dawn remaking the world", *The Picture of Dorian Gray* ch. XI (for which see note to 17–22).

[25, 28–29] **realized itself ··· experience ··· singing:** "a poem, or a passage of a poem, may tend to realize itself first as a particular rhythm before it reaches expression in words ··· and I do not believe that this is an experience peculiar to myself", *The Music of Poetry* (1942), which mentions the *Pervigilium Veneris.*

[25, 30] **realized itself ··· blind:** Henry Adams: "society in America was always trying, almost as blindly as an earthworm, to realize and understand itself; to catch up with its own head, and to twist about in search of its tail", *The Education of Henry Adams* ch. XVI (see note to the title *Introspection*).

[28–29] **the world ··· my Madness:** "the real world is quite mad, and it is the self-appointed task of ethics and metaphysics to organise it", *The Ethics of Green and Sidgwick* (1914).

[28, 30–33] **fumbled · · · blind · · · man · · · gutters · · · fall:** Adams: "one fumbled over it as feebly as ever. In such labyrinths, the staff is a force almost more necessary than the legs; the pen becomes a sort of blind-man's dog, to keep him from falling into the gutters", *The Education of Henry Adams* ch. XXV.

[29] **hear my Madness singing:** "heard the mermaids singing", *The Love Song of J. Alfred Prufrock* 124. *King Lear* IV iv: "As mad as the vexed sea, singing aloud" (Lear in his madness, an "old · · · man", in a play with a "blind old · · · man" too: TSE's next line). Caliban on the forms which harass him, *The Tempest* II ii: "sometime like apes that mow and chatter at me · · · Do hiss me into madness" (TSE: "hiss" [21], "my Madness chatter", *The Love Song of J. Alfred Prufrock* 74^75 [2]). *Purg.* XXVI 142–43: "*Ieu sui Arnaut, que plor e vau cantan; | consiros vei la passada folor*" ["I am Arnold, that weep and go a-singing; in thought I see my past madness"]. For the uses to which TSE put this passage, see note to title *Ara Vos Prec* in headnote to "*Poems* (1920)", 7. PUBLICATION OF *ARA VOS PREC*.

[30–31] **A blind old drunken man who sings and mutters, | With broken boot heels stained in many gutters:** Kipling: "When the drunken comrade mutters and the great guard-lantern gutters", *Gentleman-Rankers* 29 (included by TSE in *A Choice of Kipling's Verse*). Baudelaire: "L'âme d'un vieux poëte erre dans la gouttière | Avec la triste voix d'un fantôme frileux" [An old poet's soul is walking the tiles, lifting a voice as miserable as a shivering ghost's] (tr. *Scarfe*, taking *gouttière* as roof gutter), *Le Spleen: Pluviôse* 7–8. In *Madame Bovary*, Emma is haunted by the blind old man, half-mad, who sings. TSE: "A blind old man who coughs and spits and sputters | Stumbling among the alleys and the gutters", *First Debate between the Body and Soul* 2–3. "Sneezes at evening, poking the peevish gutter", *Gerontion* 14. **With broken boot heels stained in many gutters:** Wyatt: "With naked foot stalking in my chamber", *They flee from me that sometime did me seek* 2 (see note to *Paysage Triste* 10–12).

Notes to published poem resume.

70 **Shall I say:** Isaiah 38: 15: "What shall I say?" John 12: 27: "Now is my soul troubled; and what shall I say?"

70, 72 **at dusk through narrow streets · · · lonely men in shirt-sleeves · · · windows:** Henry James: "narrow streets—that vague historic dusk", and "I not only don't curse my wakefulness, but go to my window to listen. Three men · · · or a lonely troubadour in his shirt-sleeves draws such artful love-notes", *Siena Early and Late* I in *Italian Hours* (1909). In *Prufrock's Pervigilium* the line following "Of lonely men in shirtsleeves, leaning out of windows" [3] began "And when the evening woke".

73 **I should have been a pair of ragged claws:** Darwin on the "sexual characters" of crabs: "development of these hook-like processes has probably followed from those females who were the most securely held during the act of reproduction, having left the largest number of offspring", *The Descent of Man* ch. IX, a passage marked by TSE in his copy. TSE: "crabs · · · ragged toes · · · Lobsters", *Dirge* 4, 10, 16. For "crab-louse" and Turgenev's *Smoke*, see *March Hare* 187–88.

73–74, 120 **I should have been a pair of ragged claws | Scuttling · · · I grow old:** *Hamlet* II ii (Folio): "you yourself sir, should be as old as I am, if like a crab you could go backward". For TSE and the submarine world, see note to *Mr. Apollinax* 11–15. **Scuttling:** OED "scuttle" *n.*4 "= cuttle · · · Also *scuttle fish*". **across the floors of silent seas:** Coleridge: "that silent sea", *The Rime of the Ancient Mariner* [II] 106. TSE: "Across the floors that soak", *Interlude: in a Bar* 4.

74^75 [1] **seen · · · darkness creep:** Milton: "They creep, yet see, I dark in light exposed", *Samson Agonistes* 75 (TSE: "blind · · · man", [30]). Writing to Olive Walker, 4 Feb 1946, TSE's brother Henry recalled that at twelve or thirteen TSE "read (much to the family's astonishment) Milton's *Samson Agonistes*". **seen · · · creep along the:** Keats: "See, as they creep along the river side, | How she doth whisper to that aged Dame", *Isabella* 345–46 (TSE: "Whispering", Prufrock's Pervigilium [17]).

74^75 [1–2] **I have seen · · · along the wall · · · I have heard · · · chatter:** Tennyson: "I have led her home · · · Just now the dry-tongued laurels' pattering talk | Seemed her light foot along the garden walk", *Maud* I [xviii] 599, 606–607. TSE: "I have heard · · · I have seen", *The Love Song of J. Alfred Prufrock* 124, 126. "I have seen · · · I have had", *Five-Finger Exercises* III. *Lines to a Duck in the Park* 6–7. **my Madness chatter:** Tennyson: "And then to hear a dead man chatter | Is enough to drive one mad", *Maud* II [v] 257–58. Isaiah 38: 14: "so did I chatter" (for this chapter of Isaiah, see note to *The Love Song of J. Alfred Prufrock* 70).

74^75 [1, 3] **I have seen:** more than thirty biblical occurrences, among them Job 5: 3: "I have seen the foolish taking root: But suddenly I cursed his habitation"; and Psalm 37: 35–36: "I have seen the wicked in great power". Symons: "I have seen love, that was so quick a flame, | Go out in ashes; I have seen desire | Go out in smoke, that was so bright a fire", *Time and Memory* (1906) 5–7. "I have seen · · · I have seen · · · I have seen · · · I have seen", *The Love Song of J. Alfred Prufrock* 82–85, 126. "I have seen eyes in the street", *Rhapsody on a Windy Night* 41. See note to *WLComposite* 321–27, for "Unreal City, I have seen and see".

74^75 [3] **I have seen the world roll up into a ball:** for Marvell's *To his Coy Mistress*, see note to *The Love Song of J. Alfred Prufrock* 92–93. Bergson on Aristotle's treatment of ideas: "Aristote les pressa les unes dans les autres, les ramassa en boule, et plaça au-dessus du monde physique une Forme" [Aristotle pressed them into each other, rolled them up into a ball, and set above the physical world a Form], *L'Evolution créatrice* ch. IV.

74^75 [3–4] **I · · · the world · · · dissolve · · · fall away:** Keats: "That I might drink, and leave the world unseen, | And with thee fade away · · · dissolve, and quite forget", *Ode to a Nightingale* 19–21. **the world roll · · · a ball · · · away:** Blake: "The Senses roll themselves in fear | And the flat Earth becomes a Ball || The Stars Sun Moon all shrink away", *The Mental Traveller* 63–65.

75, 77 **evening · · · malingers:** *Schmidt 1982a* objects that despite "apt associations with both *malign* and *lingers*", the idea of an evening pretending illness (OED) "seems absurd". OED: "To pretend illness, or to produce or protract disease, in order to escape duty", quoting "The question comes to be, whether the patient .. is malingering" and (under "malingering") "Malingering is generally easily detected by one who is accustomed to examine nervous cases", 1899 (TSE: "the evening · · · like a patient etherised", 2–3, and "the nerves" , 105).

76–77 **Smoothed by long fingers, | Asleep . . . tired . . . or it malingers:** "I should for a moment linger | And follow the curve with my finger", *The Love Song of St. Sebastian* 29–30. "Just while they linger shaking a finger", *Suite Clownesque* II 7.

79–80 **tea and cakes and ices · · · crisis:** Symons: "we 'scape, with sweets and ices, | The folly of Love's sacrifices", *From Paul Verlaine: Fêtes Galantes* XII: *Cythère.* TSE: "With cakes and tea", *Goldfish* III 4. "Evening, lights, and tea!" *Spleen* 7. Edmund Husserl: [No one understands the sentence "There are cakes" as he understands the mathematical sentence "There are regular solids". In the first case we do not mean that cakes exist absolutely and in general, but that there are cakes *here* and *now*—for coffee], *Logische Untersuchungen* ch. 3, §27; beside which TSE wrote in his copy: "*es sollte überhaupt Kuchen geben*" [there should always be cake].

80 **the strength to force the moment to its crisis:** TSE after the Abdication of Edward VIII: "I can speak, at least, as one who, from what may be either a judicial or a vacillating temper of mind, failed to make up his mind until some time after the 'crisis' was over · · · one's feelings might vary several times a day · · · my own private opinion fluctuated constantly, so I can hardly be expected to take at their face value the 'instinctive reactions' of the people at such a moment · · · In taking the step he did, or 'forcing the issue,' King Edward is to be commended", *Mr. Reckitt, Mr. Tomlin and the Crisis* (1937). Contrast "a moment's surrender | Which an age of prudence can never retract", *The Waste Land* [V] 403, 405; see note. **crisis:** OED 1: "*Pathol.* The point in the progress of a disease when an important development or change takes place which is decisive of recovery or death." William James: "medicine used to speak of two ways, *lysis* and *crisis*, one gradual, the other abrupt, in which one might recover", *The Varieties of Religious Experience* lecture VIII. TSE: "every generation, every turn of time when the work of four or five men who count have reached middle age, is a *crisis*", *Observations* (1918).

81 **I have wept and fasted, wept and prayed:** 2 Samuel 1: 12: "they mourned, and wept, and fasted"; 2 Samuel 12: 22: "I fasted and wept" (*Hands*). Edwin Diller Starbuck: "I mourned and wept and prayed", *The Psychology of Religion* (1899) 83; title mentioned in *Harvard index cards* (1914) (Joshua Richards, personal communication).

82 **head · · · brought in upon a platter:** the head of John the Baptist "was brought in a charger" to Salome (Matthew 14: 6–11 and Mark 6: 22–28). Laforgue: "Plat veuf du chef de saint Jean-Baptiste!" [the salver widowed of St. John the Baptist's head!], *Jeux* [*Pastimes*]. TSE: "the head of Mr. Apollinax rolling under a chair", *Mr. Apollinax* 13.

82–85 **slightly bald · · · hold my coat:** see note to *Spleen* 11–14.

83 **I am no prophet:** Amos 7: 14: "I was no prophet, neither was I a prophet's son" (*Southam*). Blake: *I am no Homer's Hero* (see note to *Portrait of a Lady* II 28–30). For Blake's Rossetti ms, which has much on "Michael Angelo", see headnote to *Love seeketh not Itself to please* ("Uncollected Poems"). In *Reflections on Contemporary Poetry* II (1917), TSE quoted Jean de Bosschère: "n'est pas un prophète", from *Homere Mare Habite sa Maison de Planches*, pub. with facing tr. by F. S. Flint in *The Closed Door* (1917). "prophets · · · of whom I am not one"; and of Dante, Donne and Laforgue: "They were no prophets", *The Varieties*

of Metaphysical Poetry 159, 224 (Clark Lectures V, VIII). "Jules Laforgue also was among the prophets, who say *Credo*, not among those lost people who say *Dubito*", *The Varieties of Metaphysical Poetry* 279–80 (Turnbull Lecture II). "I would hesitate to make myself a prophet. In any case, you see, the prophetic element in poetry very often is unconscious in the poet himself. He may be prophesying without knowing it", *A Conversation, recorded in 1958, between T. S. Eliot and Leslie Paul* ([1964/]1965). In 1938 R. G. Collingwood sent TSE a copy of *The Principles of Art* which ends with praise of TSE as prophetic "not in the sense that he foretells things to come, but in the sense that he tells his audience, at risk of their displeasure, the secrets of their own hearts ··· The reason why they need him is that no community altogether knows its own heart ··· For the evils which come from that ignorance the poet as prophet suggests no remedy, because he has already given one. The remedy is the poem itself." TSE to Tom Stauffer, 17 Aug 1944: "do you know Collingwood's ··· *Principles of Art* ··· To a plain literary practitioner like myself, who, as F. H. Bradley said of himself, has no capacity for the abstruse, Collingwood seems very good." TSE began his preface to Leone Vivante's *English Poetry* (1950) with a reference to Collingwood's book. **I am no prophet—and here's no great matter:** "he was no prophet ··· his prose is great prose", *Machiavelli* (1927). *Hamlet* V i: "'tis no great matter there" (Shawn Worthington, personal communication).

83, 111 **I am no prophet ··· I am not Prince Hamlet:** Dante on his unworthiness: "Io non Enea, io non Paolo sono" [I am not Æneas, am not Paul], *Inf.* II 32

84 **I have seen the moment of my greatness flicker:** "I have seen the darkness creep along the wall | I have heard my Madness chatter before day", *The Love Song of J. Alfred Prufrock* 74^75 [1–2]. "I have seen the morning shine", *Five-Finger Exercises* III. *Lines to a Duck in the Park* 6.

85 **eternal Footman:** for the Footman in *Alice's Adventures in Wonderland* ch. VI, see note to *Portrait of a Lady* II 28, III 25. Bunyan, *The Heavenly Foot-Man; or, A Description of the Man that Gets to Heaven* (1689) (*Moody* 32). In response to an untraced letter about *Poems 1909–1925*, TSE wrote to Wyndham Lewis, 9 Jan 1926: "Of course I agree with you about the footman and indeed about most [of] the early stuff" (possibly referring to the "footman" of *Aunt Helen*).

88 **the cups, the marmalade, the tea:** "With marmalade and tea at six", *Interlude in London* 3.

89 **Among the porcelain, among some talk:** the preposition is at odds with these nouns. "Among the music", 53 *variant*. (For "along", see note to *Oh little voices of the throats of men* 48, and for "across", see note to *Suite Clownesque* I 1, 12.) **porcelain ··· talk:** "porcelain, | Murmurs a word", *Mandarins* 2 16–17. **some talk of you and me:** FitzGerald: "Some little Talk awhile of ME and THEE | There was—and then no more of ME and THEE", *Rubáiyát of Omar Khayyám*, 4th ed., XXXII (*Unger*). TSE: "But what is there for you and me | For me and you ··· ?" *The Death of the Duchess* I 10–11.

92–93 **To have squeezed the universe into a ball | To roll it:** Marvell: "Let us roll all our strength and all | Our sweetness up into one ball, | And tear our pleasures with rough strife, | Thorough the iron gates of life", *To his Coy Mistress* 41–44; quoted in *Andrew Marvell* (1921). "I have seen the world roll up into a ball", *The Love Song of J. Alfred Prufrock* 74^75 [3]. With "squeezed" in one and "the world" in the other, TSE's two adaptations divide the debt to *Symons* 109: "In Laforgue, sentiment is squeezed out of the world before one begins to play at ball with it" (*Kenner* 134). TSE translating Mauron: "*all* the phenomena of nature are irrational, inasmuch as we have not yet squeezed the world into syllogisms", *Concerning "Intuition"* (1927).

92–102 **To have squeezed the universe into a ball ··· teacups:** Mary Elizabeth Braddon, on women: "If they can't agitate the universe and play ball with hemispheres, they'll make ··· social storms in household teacups"; and "the universe is suddenly narrowed into about half a dozen acres; the mighty scheme of creation is crushed into a bandbox", *Lady Audley's Secret* ch. VI, ch. IX (*Heywood*). For the novel, see notes to 122 and to *The Waste Land* [II] 78–87. TSE: "I should say that the mind of any poet would be magnetised in its own way, to select automatically, in his reading (from picture papers and cheap novels, indeed, as well as serious books, and least likely from works of an abstract nature, though even these are aliment for some poetic minds) the material—an image, a phrase, a word—which may be of use to him later", *The Use of Poetry and the Use of Criticism* 78.

92–93, 120 **To have squeezed the universe into a ball | To roll ··· grow old:** Bergson: "This inner life may be compared to the unrolling of a coil, for there is no living being who does not feel himself coming gradually to the end of his rôle; and to live is to grow old. But it may just as well be compared to a continual rolling up, like that of a thread on a ball, for our past follows us ··· and consciousness means memory", *An Introduction to Metaphysics* (tr. T. E. Hulme, 1912) 11–12. (TSE to David Higham, 11 May 1934: "although I used to attend Bergson's lectures in 1910, and at that time studied all of his works very carefully, I am now wholly incompetent to write about such subjects ··· I might possibly consent to write an essay on Bergson, if you could induce Bergson to write an essay about me.")

93 **to roll it towards:** "Rolls toward the moon a frenzied eye", *Nocturne* 11. **towards:** to Hope Mirrlees, 25 July 1948: "In my absence you will receive a copy of a profound, but brief book called *Notes towards a Definition of Culture* (I am never sure when to write 'towards' and when 'toward')." With the exception of the printing in *Catholic Anthology*, the reading was "toward" until the proof of *1963* (as it remains at 108). "Toward", the more American form, is usual in the *March Hare* poems and appears in *Rhapsody on a Windy Night* and *Sweeney Among the Nightingales*. In *WLComposite* 551, TSE adds -s apparently as a second thought in forming the word (*WLFacs* 60), after which "towards" is usual in his poems, although he sometimes pronounced it *to'rd* (both 1946–47 recordings of *Little Gidding* II 34). *Fowler*: "best pronounced tōr-d(z), but in recent use the influence of spelling is forcing tōōwor'd(z) on the half educated ··· the -s form is the prevailing one, & the other tends to become literary on the one hand & provincial on the other."

94 **Lazarus:** at Luke 16: 19–31, Christ tells the parable of the deaths of Dives, the rich man who went to hell, and Lazarus, the beggar who went to heaven. Dives then besought Abraham to send Lazarus to his five brothers, urging them to repent. Abraham replied: "If they hear not Moses and the prophets, neither will they be persuaded, though one rose from the dead." At John 11: 1–44, Christ raises a different Lazarus, the brother of Mary and Martha, from the

dead (Clifford J. Fish, *Explicator* VIII, 1949–50). Similar dualities include St. Narcissus/Narcissus (*The Death of Saint Narcissus*), Euphorion (*Suite Clownesque* III 10), and St. John (see headnote to *The Love Song of St. Sebastian*). Geographic dualities: "Belle Isle ··· the horn ··· the Gulf" (*Gerontion* 69, 71), and Cairo (see note to *Ash-Wednesday* unadopted part title to I, and headnote to II). TSE's mother wrote a poem entitled *The Raising of Lazarus* (*Hands*). **come from the dead**: Elizabeth Barrett Browning: "a special revelation, shakes the heart | Of all the men and women in the world, | As if one came back from the dead and spoke", *Aurora Leigh* bk. 1 906–908 (TSE: "shaking my heart", *The Waste Land* [V] 402). *Aurora Leigh* bk. 1 178 also mentions Lazarus, but in *What is Minor Poetry?* (1944), TSE said he had not read the poem. **I shall tell you all**: Matthew 18: 26: "I will pay thee all" (see note to *O lord, have patience* 1).

96 **one, settling a pillow by her head**: Donne: "Where, like a pillow on a bed, | A Pregnant banke swel'd up, to rest | The violets reclining head", *The Extasie* 1–3. TSE: "To compare a bank to a pillow (it is surely superfluous to add 'on a bed' since a pillow may be presumed to have much the same shape wherever it be disposed) does neither dignify nor elucidate", *The Varieties of Metaphysical Poetry* 109 (Clark Lecture III); also, for Crashaw's pillow, 172 (Lecture VI). Pope: "As long as *Atalantis* shall be read, | Or the small Pillow grace a Lady's Bed", *The Rape of the Lock* III 165–66. (TSE's schoolboy copy of Pope's *Poetical Works* was catalogued at Milton Academy in the late 1930s.) **one ··· her head**: *Fowler*: "the impersonal *one* always can, & now usually does, provide its own possessive &c.—*one's*, *oneself*, & *one*; thus, *One does not like to have one's word doubted* ··· But ··· in American, in older English, & in a small minority of modern British writers, the above sentences would run *One does not like to have* his *word doubted*; *If one fell,* he *would hurt* himself *badly*." **one ··· her head**: specific: "while one lifts her hand", *Mandarins* 2 14; unspecific: "one who smiles ··· his expression in a glass", *Portrait of a Lady* [III] 16–17.

97–108 **at all ··· not it, at all ··· If one, settling a pillow or throwing off a shawl ··· should say**: "F. M.": "On my replying faintly, painfully aware of all that was involved, that I found Gilbert and Sullivan a bore, the same expression convulsed his features as, at a certain moment in 1919, would have distorted the marble countenance of Dorilant, if one had said, 'settling a pillow or throwing off a shawl': No, I did not care for the *Boutique* at all, not at all", *Letters of the Moment* II (1924). For Gilbert and Sullivan, see note to 122–25.

101 **sprinkled streets**: streets were watered in summer to control dust. Henley: "I can smell the sprinkled pavement", *In Hospital* XXIII 18. TSE: "the sawdust trampled street", "trampled by insistent feet", *Preludes* II 3, IV 3. "the trampled edges of the street ··· Sprouting", *Morning at the Window* 2–4.

101–102 **After the sunsets and the dooryards ··· After the novels, after the teacups, after the skirts**: Charles K. Harris: "After the ball is over, | After the break of morn, | After the dancers' leaving, | After the stars are gone", *After the Ball* (1892); reputedly the sheet music sold more than 5 million copies. Whitman: "After the sea-ship, after the whistling winds, | After the white-gray sails taut to their spars and ropes", *After the Sea-Ship* (*Musgrove* 27). TSE: "After the praying and the silence and the crying ··· After the judges and the advocates and wardens", *After the turning of the inspired days* 2, 6. "After the torchlight ··· After the frosty silence ··· After the agony", *The Waste Land* [V] 322–24.

101–102, 108 **sunsets · · · teacups · · · toward the window**: "by a window drinking tea · · · sunset", *Mandarins* 2 2, 13.

104 **It is impossible to say just what I mean**: to Richard Aldington, 13 Oct 1921: "I really cannot say enough—but it is not merely quantity of expression, but impossibility of saying what I feel."

105 **as if a magic lantern threw the nerves in patterns on a screen**: just such a projection using "the X-Ray with microscopic attachment" was illustrated beside an article on *Seeing the Brain* in *St. Louis Daily Globe-Democrat* 17 Jan 1897 (reproduced *Crawford* 8). Clough: "Severing · · · As by a magic screen, the seer from the sight | (Palsying the nerves · · ·)", *Why should I say* 50–53. (Pound to Joyce, 6 Sept 1915, on literary reviewing: "anything which casts the human psychology on the screen or makes it act visibly from ascertainable motives is of interest".) TSE: "images · · · flickered against the ceiling", *Preludes* III 4–6. **as if a magic lantern**: Henley: "as when you change | Pictures in a magic lantern", *In Hospital* XXIII 5–6. **threw**: the standard verb: "pictures thrown on a screen with the ordinary magic lantern", *Popular Mechanics* Sept 1909. **nerves**: OED "nerve" 8d: "*pl.* A disordered nervous system; nervousness" (a distinct sense since 1890). Symons's *Nerves* (1895) begins: "The modern malady of love is nerves", and the penultimate line has "Nerves, nerves!" *Symons* 108: "It is an art of the nerves, this art of Laforgue, and it is what all art would tend towards if we followed our nerves on all their journeys." TSE: "the imagination | Or the nerves", *Easter: Sensations of April* II 9–10 (see note). On Donne's *Satires*: "this deliberate over-stimulation, *exploitation* of the *nerves*—for such it is—has in it, to me, something unscrupulous", *The Varieties of Metaphysical Poetry* 158 (Clark Lecture V). On Baudelaire: "We cannot be *primarily* interested in any writer's nerves (and remember that 'nerves' used in this way is a very vague and unscientific term)", *Baudelaire in our Time* (1927). See note to *The Waste Land* [II] 111 "nerves".

110 **That is not what I meant**: Kipling: "(And it wasn't the least what the lady meant)", *The Vampire* 16 (in *A Choice of Kipling's Verse*). TSE: "we cannot wholly discriminate *what we mean* from *the meaning of* our words ⁊ deeds. The former is *extension*, the latter *description*. The former gives something which really seems more nearly what we *had in mind* than what we thought we had in mind. The latter is so remote that it is not even thought that we might or should have had it in mind. When you can say 'Oh yes! I beg pardon—*that* is what I meant,' you have *extension*", *The Ethics of Green and Sidgwick* (1914).

111 **No! I am not Prince Hamlet, nor was meant to be**: Pater: "No! Shakespeare's Kings are not, nor are meant to be, great men", *Shakespeare's English Kings* in *Appreciations* (1889) (Robert F. Fleissner, *American Literature* Mar 1966). Byron (quoting *Hamlet* III i): "'To be or not to be! That is the question,' | Says Shakespeare, who just now is much in fashion. | I am neither Alexander nor Hephaestion'", *Don Juan* IX xiv; for the passage, see notes to *Whispers of Immortality* 4 and *The Waste Land* [III] 186. "But I'm not Oedipus · · · *Davus sum*", *Don Juan* XIII xii–xiii (alluding to Terence, *Andria*, where Davus the slave explains he cannot solve the Sphinx's riddle, because "Davus sum, non Oedipus").

112 **Am an attendant lord**: the stage direction heralding the play scene in

Hamlet III ii (Folio) begins: "*Enter King, Queen, Polonius, Ophelia, Rosencrantz, Guildenstern, and other Lords attendant*".

112–13 **one that will do | To swell a progress, start a scene:** Henry Adams: "One felt one's self a supernumerary hired to fill the scene", *The Education of Henry Adams* ch. XIX. **a progress:** a royal procession. *2 Henry VI* I iv: "The King is now in progress towards Saint Albans."

113, 116 **swell a progress, start a scene or two ··· Politic, cautious, and meticulous:** HAMLET (of Polonius): "A certain convocation of politic worms are e'en at him ··· A king may go a progress through the guts of a beggar" (IV iii). POLONIUS (to Ophelia): "And that in way of caution—I must tell you" (I iii). Polonius does "start a scene or two": II i, III iv. **Politic, cautious, and meticulous:** with the letters *Pol-o-n-i-us* spanning the line (Christopher Ricks, *Proceedings of the British Academy* 2003). Blake: "Lawful, cautious and refined", *Love to faults is always blind*. **meticulous:** OED 1: "Fearful, timid. *Obs.*" ("In short, I was afraid", 86.) OED 2: "Over-careful about minute details, over-scrupulous. In present usage: careful, punctilious, scrupulous, precise." This "present usage" was not in OED 1st ed. and was deprecated by *Fowler*: "What is the strange charm that makes this wicked word irresistible to the British journalist?"

116, 118 **Politic, cautious, and meticulous ··· ridiculous:** Verlaine: "Correct, ridicule et charmant", *Nuit de Walpurgis classique* 4 (*Kenner* 15). For "fastidious ··· Punctilious", see note to *Spleen* 11–14. "Ladies, who find my intentions ridiculous ··· Pompous, pretentious, ineptly meticulous", *The Triumph of Bullshit* 11. (Ottoline Morrell to Bertrand Russell, spring 1916, on TSE: "He is obviously very ignorant of England and imagines that it is essential to be highly polite and conventional and decorous, and meticulous.")

117 **Full of high sentence:** Chaucer's Clerk of Oxenford: "Noght o word spak he moore than was neede, | And that was seyd in forme and reverence, | And short and quyk and ful of hy sentence", *The Canterbury Tales*, General Prologue 304–306 (*Grover Smith* 302).

118 **At times ··· ridiculous:** "at last a bit ridiculous", *Entretien dans un parc* 18.

118–19 **ridiculous ··· the Fool:** "It will do you no harm to find yourself ridiculous. | Resign yourself to be the fool you are", *The Cocktail Party* I i.

120 **I grow old . . . I grow old:** *1 Henry IV* II iv, FALSTAFF: "There lives not three good men unhang'd in England; and one of them is fat, and grows old" (*Kenner 1972* 275). *2 Henry IV* II iv, FALSTAFF: "I am old, I am old" (Henry W. Wells, *New Poets from Old*, 1940, 74). TSE to Warner Allen, 25 May 1960: "That line, if I remember rightly, was borrowed from Sir John Falstaff." Yeats: "I grow old among dreams", *Men Improve with the Years* 16 (a poem TSE discussed at Harvard, Mar 1933). TSE: "'*When I grow old, I shall have all the court | Powder their hair with arras, to be like me*'", *The Death of the Duchess* II 51–52, misquoting Webster, *The Duchess of Malfi*; see note. TSE to I. B. Cauthen, 29 Aug 1962: "I also have no doubt that the page from Webster's play was at the back of my mind" (presumably referring to this line). Brigit Patmore: "I remember very clearly one evening before August 1914, when Tom asked me to have dinner with him and talked for many minutes of how old he was ··· 'I am so old that it makes me despair'", *My Friends When Young* 89. TSE: "The young man in *Prufrock* is meant to signify someone young and sportive and a man conscious of growing old", reported *Time* 13 Nov 1950.

"A poet must express his vision at the age at which he is. When he is young he will write of one kind of experience in one way, and when he is older he should be writing of another kind of experience in another way, and that is the difference", *The Development of Shakespeare's Verse* (1950 recording). "Which is worse: a child writing as an adult or an adult writing as a child? Just received enclosed from a fellow poet · · · But as I was born old, I wouldn't know" (undated leaf in the Pierpont Morgan Library, among TSE's letters to McKnight Kauffer).

121 **I shall wear the bottoms of my trousers rolled:** to John Hayward, 31 May 1940, mocking himself in Italian and Romanian:

> Well, as the poet says so aptly
>
> Portero pantelone arrotelati in fondo
>
> or as he has said elsewhere, voicing the same idea but I think a little more aptly
>
> Voiu purta pantalonii suflecati . . .

(TSE had just received *cântecul de lubire a lui J. A. Prufrock*, and wrote to Dragos Luta on the same day: "it is a matter of pride for me to receive this first translation of any of my work into Roumanian".) Trousers are often rolled for paddling ("on the beach", 123). (OED "turn-up" 2. cites *Minister's Rep. of Fashion for Gentlemen* 1925: "Permanent turn-ups are still worn for outdoor wear.")

121 *variant* **trowsers:** changed after the first two printings to "trousers" (*1917+*) although in 1926 *Fowler* recommended that "*trowsers*" be "so spelt". TSE did not abandon his earlier spelling altogether, writing to Bonamy Dobrée, 2 Sept 1927: "When appointing Morley President of the newly founded Bolovian Club I think it will be only fair to warn him that as President he will be expected to wear Top Hat and Morning Coat at Dinners (Trowsers facultative)." In New England, "petticoat trousers" (or trowsers) were "wide baggy trousers". "Trowsers", with nautical associations, occurs under several headwords in OED and in the sailor's ballad *Wapping Old Stairs* (see note to *Billy M'Caw: The Remarkable Parrot* 34). For the spelling "ancle", see note to *Suite Clownesque* II 1.

122 **Shall I part my hair behind:** C. S. Calverley: "Though my scalp is almost hairless · · · Striven to part my backhair straight", *"Hic* Vir, *Hic Est"* 15, 62 ("With a bald spot in the middle of my hair", 40). Mary Elizabeth Braddon: "do you suppose that because people · · · part their hair on the wrong side · · · that they may not be just as sensible of a · · · girl", *Lady Audley's Secret* ch. XVI. Aiken on TSE: "The Tsetse, early inoculated by the subtle creative venoms of Laforgue and Vildrac, looked rather to France than to England: an editor of the Advocate had returned from Paris, after a year, in exotic Left Bank clothing, and with his hair parted behind: it had made a sensation", *Ushant* 143. **Do I dare to eat a peach:** E. C. Gaskell: "we felt very genteel · · · When oranges came in, a curious proceeding was gone through. Miss Jenkyns did not like to cut the fruit; for, as she observed, the juice all ran out nobody knew where; sucking (only I think she used some more recondite word) was in fact the only way of enjoying oranges; but then there was the unpleasant association with a ceremony frequently gone through by little babies; and so, after dessert, in orange season, Miss Jenkyns and Miss Matty used to rise up, possess themselves each of an orange in silence, and withdraw to the privacy of their own rooms, to indulge in sucking oranges", *Cranford* ch. III. TSE: "she is among those English (and American) writers who have known how to make a virtue out of provinciality", *Letters of*

Mrs. Gaskell and Charles Eliot Norton, 1855–1865, review (1933). TSE: "Horace demands an orange. Conversation with Felise about how to eat an orange. Covered in orange pulp ⁊ juice he suddenly turns his back on everybody ⁊ reads a paper" (ms for "F. M.", Maryland folder 2, fols. 1–3). **peach**: Marvell: "The nectarine and curious peach, | Into my hands themselves do reach ··· I fall on grass", *The Garden* 37–40. Like Eve's apple, the peach (*pêche*) tempts to sin (*péché*). Blake: "I asked a thief to steal me a peach: | He turned up his eyes. | I ask'd a lithe lady to lie her down: | Holy & meek she cries."

122–25 **Do I dare to eat a peach? ··· the beach ··· each to each ··· to me**: Gilbert and Sullivan: "Over the ripening peach | Buzzes the bee. | Splash on the billowy beach | Tumbles the sea. | But the peach | And the beach | They are each | Nothing to me!" *Ruddigore* act I.

123 **I shall wear white flannel trousers and walk upon the beach**: following the excision of two leaves from the *March Hare* Notebook, the ms of *The Love Song of J. Alfred Prufrock* begins on a leaf opposite the lines "If you're walking on the beach | You hear everyone remark | Look at him! ··· In the quintessential flannel suit", *Suite Clownesque* III 15–17, 25. "White flannel ceremonial", *Goldfish* III 3. To Eleanor Hinkley, 5 Sept 1916: "I lived most of the time in a shirt and flannel trowsers. The chief occupations bathing, boating, and bicycling."

123–28 **I shall ··· walk upon the beach ··· the white hair of the waves blown back | When the wind blows the water**: Beaumont and Fletcher, *The Maid's Tragedy* II ii, ASPATIA: "Suppose I stand upon the sea-beach now, | Mine arms thus, and mine hair blown with the wind" (see note to *Sweeney Erect* epigraph). "I am forsaken", two lines later in Aspatia's speech, may have prompted thoughts of Arnold's *The Forsaken Merman*.

123–29 **walk upon the beach. | I have heard the mermaids singing ··· I do not think that they will sing to me ··· seaward ··· Combing the white hair ··· in the chambers of the sea**: Arnold: "In the caverns where we lay, | Through the surf and through the swell ··· comb'd its bright hair ··· But, ah, she gave me never a look ··· Singing ··· sweet airs come seaward ··· On the blanch'd sands ··· beaches", *The Forsaken Merman* 32–33, 53, 80, 88, 128, 131–32.

123, 130 **I shall wear white flannel trousers, and walk upon the beach ··· sea-girls**: "walking on the beach ··· the girls ··· flannel suit", *Suite Clownesque* III 15, 19, 23.

124 **I have heard the mermaids singing**: Donne: "Teach me to heare Mermaides singing", *Song: Goe, and catche a falling starre* 5. *A Midsummer Night's Dream* II i: "I ··· heard a mermaid on a dolphin's back | Uttering such dulcet and harmonious breath | That the rude sea grew civil at her song." TSE: "hear my Madness singing", *Prufrock's Pervigilium* [29]. To Pound, 22 Oct 1936, querying a collocation in a draft Canto: "'see weed' etc. To one raised on the shore of the manymermaidcrowded sea, this collocation suggests ALGAE such as a child I dried and classified on the shores of Massachusetts."

124–29 **I have heard the mermaids singing, each to each ··· lingered in the chambers of the sea**: Gérard de Nerval: "J'ai rêvé dans la grotte où nage la sirène ··· tour à tour" [I have dreamed in the cave where the siren swims ··· one by one], *El Desdichado* [*The Disinherited*]. The first of these lines is quoted by *Symons* 35 (*Howarth* 196). *Lemprière* "Sirenes, sea nymphs": "as soon as any persons passed by them without suffering themselves to be charmed by their songs, they should perish."

124–31 **I have heard the mermaids singing · · · white hair | Streaming behind · · · wake us:**

> One night
> On watch, I thought I saw in the fore cross-trees
> Three women leaning forward, with white hair
> Streaming behind, who sang above the wind
> A song that charmed my senses, while I was
> Frightened beyond fear, horrified past horror, calm,
> (Nothing was real) for, I thought, now, when
> I like, I can wake up and end the dream.
>
> *WLComposite* 539–46

126–31 **I have seen ... back ... white and black ... human:** James Thomson: "murmured back . . . Behind me and before is black . . . human . . . I have seen", *In the Room* 25–29 (TSE: "In the room", 13; see note).

127 **hair · · · blown back:** Keats: "With hair blown back", *The Eve of St. Agnes* 36 (for the Keats passage see note *The Waste Land* [II] 96–105). "Blown hair is sweet, brown hair over the mouth blown", *Ash-Wednesday* III 17.

127–29 **the waves · · · the chambers of the sea:** Job 9: 8–9: "the waves of the sea · · · the chambers of the south". **the chambers of the sea:** Wilde: "the chambers of the brain", *The Picture of Dorian Gray* ch. XI (for the passage, see note to 17–22).

127–31 **hair of the waves · · · lingered in the chambers of the sea · · · wreathed with seaweed red and brown | Till human voices wake us, and we drown:** John Davidson: "like seaweed droops | My tangled beard, my tangled hair · · · cavernous · · · As if a still voice fell from heaven | To where sea-whelmed the drowned folk lie | In sepulchres", *A Loafer* (1894) (*Crawford* 55).

128 **When the wind blows the water white and black:** Swinburne: "For ever the dark wind whitens and blackens the hollows and heights of the sea", *The Armada* VI iii 14 (Archie Burnett, personal communication). **When the wind blows the:** "When the wind blows the cradle will rock", nursery rhyme.

129 **We have lingered in the chambers of the sea:** "I have lain on the floor of the sea", *Murder in the Cathedral* II chorus. **lingered in the chambers:** Braddon: "He had lingered · · · found his way to his chambers" *Lady Audley's Secret* 441 (*Heywood*).

130 **sea-girls:** OED first citation. **seaweed red and brown:** "And about his hair the seaweed purple and brown", *So through the evening, through the violet air* 32.

131 **Till human voices wake us, and we drown:** "human voices", *Oh little voices of the throats of men* 47 (and see note for Tennyson). To Adrienne Monnier, 29 Apr 1925, approving the ending of the translation she made with Sylvia Beach (*La Chanson d'amour de J. Alfred Prufrock* in *Le Navire d'Argent* June 1925): "'Coulons à pic' est très bien" [We sink straight to the bottom]. (In the same letter: "Je pense que *Prufrock* se traduit en français mieux que *The Waste Land*, à cause du fait que l'influence de Laforgue y est pour beaucoup" [I think *Prufrock* goes into French better than *The Waste Land*, because Laforgue's influence counts for a good deal].) For TSE and the submarine world, see note to *Mr. Apollinax* 11–15.

Portrait of a Lady

Published in *Others* (New Jersey) Sept 1915; then *Catholic Anthology* (Nov 1915) and *Others: An Anthology of the New Verse*, ed. Alfred Kreymborg (1916), *1917+* and *Penguin / Sel Poems.*

Recorded 26 Sept 1955, London; released Caedmon 1955 (US), 1959 (UK).

Dated "Cambridge, Mass., Feb 1910" (II), "Nov 1910" (I) and "Nov 1911" (III) in *ms1*. Dated "Cambridge (Mass.), 1910" (I & II), "Paris, 1910" (III) and "Cambridge (Mass.), 1911" in *Poèmes.* Dated "Cambridge Mass 1910" by TSE in *Hayward's 1925*; and "1910–11 Paris" by TSE in *Morley's US 1920*. TSE to Edward J. H. Greene, 18 Oct 1939, dates the poem 1910.

Pound to H. L. Mencken of *The Smart Set*, 3 Oct 1914: "I enclose a poem by the last intelligent man I've found—a young American, T. S. Eliot (you can write to him direct, Merton College, Oxford. I think him worth watching—mind 'not primitive.' His 'Lady' is very nicely drawn." Mencken did not publish the poem.

TSE to Pound, 2 Feb [1915]: "I enclose a copy of the Lady, which seems cruder and awkwarder and more juvenile every time I copy it. The only enhancement which time has brought is the fact that by this time there are two or three other ladies who, if it is ever printed, may vie for the honour of having sat for it. It will please you, I hope, to hear that I had a Christmas card from the lady, bearing the 'ringing greetings of friend to friend at this season of high festival'. It seems like old times." Valerie Eliot noted in *Letters*: "Miss Adeleine Moffatt, the subject of the poem, lived behind the State House in Boston and invited selected Harvard undergraduates to tea. During a visit to London in 1927 she asked the Eliots to dine, offering 'a modest choice of dates to sacrifice yourselves on the altar of New England', but they were away." In 1948, Conrad Aiken recalled Moffatt: "our dear deplorable friend, Miss X, the *précieuse ridicule* to end all preciosity, serving tea so exquisitely among her bric-à-brac", *March & Tambimuttu eds.* 21 (also "Madeleine, the Jamesian lady of ladies", *Ushant* 186).

TSE: "I have some knowledge of old ladies, and I have always been very fond of old ladies, and in the course of my life have collected in my memory some very choice specimens indeed", "*Those Who Need Privacy and Those Whose Need is Company*" (1951).

In a letter to Henry Eliot, 2 July 1915, TSE lists his "assets up to date" as "the poem you have seen" (*The Love Song of J. Alfred Prufrock*) and "another long poem (earlier and inferior) which will be out presently in a small new publication called *Others*". For the second, *Portrait of a Lady*, he also had "the assurance of a dozen pages in an anthology like *Imagistes*, to be out in the autumn".

Pound to Wyndham Lewis (before July 1915): "With regard to future potentialities I think that this thing of Eliot's would probably be more advantageous than anything of Rodker's admitting that it is a bit archaic ··· if you want to use this Portrait you'll have to get his permission." But *Portrait of a Lady* did not appear in Lewis's *Blast.* So Pound, in order to ensure its appearance before his *Catholic Anthology* was published, sent it to *Others* in New Jersey—not to *Poetry*. He wrote to

Harriet Monroe on 25 Sept 1915: "It was a great waste to let *The Portrait of a Lady* go to *Others*, but I was in a hurry for it to come out before the *Anth.*" Kreymborg, editor of *Others*, recalled that Pound insisted he "accept and publish immediately 'the strange poem inclosed.' The expatriate swore in the strongest handwriting that no man on the horizon of English or American letters could compete with this fellow, T. S. Eliot", *Troubadour* (1925) 237.

Despite the similarity of TSE's title to Henry James's *The Portrait of a Lady*, the poem's closest affinities are with Mrs. Luna in *The Bostonians* ch. XXII:

> She had not made him a scene ··· She might have made up her mind that she had lost him as what she had hoped, but that it was better than desolation to try and keep him as a friend ··· rang for some tea ··· a winter's evening ··· (Mrs. Luna's tea was excellent) ··· A silence of a few moments had fallen upon their talk ···

These all from James's first two paragraphs. Then:

> "Olive came home six weeks ago. How long did you expect her to endure it?"
>
> "I am sure I don't know; I have never been there," Ransom replied ··· She answered that she didn't care about ends, she cared about beginnings ··· he didn't in the least long for this arrangement, and was conscious that the most pertinent sequel to her conjecture would be for him to take up his hat and walk away ··· His life, on the whole, had not been rich in episode ··· capricious ··· He did not pick up his hat to go ··· such a distinct place in her mind, especially when she might die twenty deaths before he came near her ··· clock, saw it was not yet late ··· at last he took up his hat in earnest.

TSE: "You cannot effectively 'borrow' an image, unless you borrow also, or have spontaneously, something like the feeling which prompted the original image. An 'image', in itself, is like dream symbolism, is only vigorous in relation to the feelings out of which it issues, in the relation of word to flesh. You are entitled to take it for your own purposes in so far as your fundamental purposes are akin to those of the one who is, for you, the author of the phrase, the inventor of the image; or if you take it for other purposes then your purposes must be consciously and *pointedly* diverse from those of the author, and the contrast is very much to the point; you may not take it merely because it is a good phrase or a lovely image. I confess that I never felt assured that Henry James was justified in naming a novel *The Golden Bowl*, though my scruples may only show that I have not understood the novel", *The Bible as Scripture and as Literature* (1932). On TSE's learning from Henry James, see "A Beginner in 1908", 1. A BREAK WITH TRADITION.

Paul Elmer More's Introduction to *The Great Refusal* (1894) tells of being cordially received, with a third occasion corresponding particularly to TSE's Part III: "It had grown late. I had said what I could, very little perhaps, but words seemed quite ineffectual; and rose to leave. At his urgent request, however, I remained to take tea with him, which he had served in the same room ··· the final impression on me was something akin to sadness, and it was a relief when I left him and passed out into the clear atmosphere of a winter night. I never saw him again, and only learned of his death some months afterwards when these letters were put into my hands to edit ··· The letters are all to one person, the lady who was our friend."

Title] Henry James's *The Portrait of a Lady* had been preceded by Winthrop Mackworth Praed's *Portrait of a Lady | in the exhibition of the Royal Academy* in his series of poems *Every-Day Characters.* Jerome K. Jerome's *Sketches in Lavender Blue and*

Green (1897) also included a *Portrait of a Lady.* Among the paintings ticked in TSE's catalogue of the Isabella Stewart Gardner Museum (*c.* 1910; Houghton) is Antonio Pollajuolo's *Portrait of a Lady* (now reattributed to his brother, Piero del Pollaiuolo). Among TSE's marks in his London *Baedeker* in the list of National Gallery paintings are one against Antonio Pollaiuolo's *Martyrdom of St. Sebastian* and another (176) which may indicate Moroni's *Portrait of a Lady.* Pound's *Ripostes* (1912) included *Portrait d'une Femme.*

Epigraph] Marlowe, *The Jew of Malta* IV i. Punctuated with quotation marks in *Others*, so acknowledging the two speakers, the Second Friar and Barabas.

I

I 1 **Among:** OED *prep.*: "In the mingling or assemblage of", but overwhelmingly of objects or persons.

I 1–14 **smoke · · · light · · · finger-tips · · · the bloom · · · slips:** "to reduce the world to a set of formulae is to let it slip through our fingers in a fine dust; but to · · · retire into a sunlit stupor is to let the world slip through our fingers in a thin smoke", *The Relativity of Moral Judgment* (1915) ("fingers · · · you let it flow · · · the world", II 3, 7, 14).

I 2 **You have the scene arrange itself:** "You have the other raise", *Mandarins* 2 15. "Behind the wall I have some servant wait", *Nocturne* 7. "Arrange and comprehend the scene", *Mandarins* 4 4 *variant*. James: "She had not made him a scene", *The Bostonians* ch. XXII.

I 3–4 **afternoon · · · four wax candles:** to Conrad Aiken, 30 Sept [1914]: "Do you think it possible, if I brought out *Inventions of the March Hare*, and gave a few lectures, at 5 P.M. with wax candles, that I could become a sentimental Tommy?" (*Letters* notes: "Playing on his own name and J. M. Barrie's title, *Sentimental Tommy,* 1896". Aiken to Grayson P. McCouch [spring 1911?]: "Tom and I get along pretty well together · · · he irritates me with his 'sentimental Tommy'.")

I 4–5 **four wax candles · · · Four rings of light:** Exodus 25: 12, 31: "And thou shalt cast four rings of gold · · · a candlestick". **the darkened room:** Dickens: "the dull old house, the yellow light in the darkened room, the faded spectre in the chair by the dressing-table glass · · · as if the stopping of the clocks had stopped Time", *Great Expectations* ch. XVII (TSE: "Correct our watches by the public clocks", I 39). **Four rings of light:** "a ring of lights", *Suite Clownesque* I 20. *Murder in the Cathedral* II, chorus: "I have seen | Rings of light coiling downwards, descending | To the horror of the ape". **upon the ceiling overhead:** "Flattened itself upon the ceiling overhead", *Prufrock's Pervigilium* [23].

I 4–6 **four wax candles · · · Juliet's tomb:** *Romeo and Juliet* V iii: "This is the place. There, where the torch doth burn." Baedeker on Verona: "on the Campo della Fiera · · · is a chapel · · · containing a mediæval sarcophagus called the *Tomba di Giulietta*, or '*Tomb of Juliet*'. The whole scene is prosaic and unattractive", *Northern Italy* (13th ed., 1906). Bulwer Lytton: "Nothing can equal the sadness and gloom of the spot · · · the old tomb · · · is but a broken cistern to the eyes of the brethren of the convent!" *Juliet's Tomb in Verona* in *"The Honey-Moon" by the Countess of Blessington and Other Tales* (1837).

I 7 **things to be said, or left unsaid:** to Lady Rhondda, 7 Oct 1943: "Indeed it is very difficult for anyone I think to come to a conclusion as to what should be said and left unsaid." To Ottoline Morrell, 4 May 1924: "there will be a thousand and one things to be left undone during that time". Of his own reflections: they are not "intended to give any direct guidance as to what we should do, or what we should leave undone", *Responsibility and Power* (1943).

I 8–9 **the latest Pole | Transmit the Preludes, through his hair:** the Polish pianist Artur Rubinstein, known like the earlier Polish virtuoso Ignace Paderewski for his hair, made his American debut aged 19 at Carnegie Hall in 1906, then toured the country, playing a programme at Jordan Hall, Boston, on 16 Mar, which included two Chopin Preludes and other showpieces (Roger Craik, personal communication). Laurent Tailhade: "Elles viennent d'ouïr Ladislas Talapoint, | Pianiste hongrois que le *Figaro* vante" [The women go to hear Ladislas Talapoint, a Hungarian pianist praised by *Figaro*], *Place des Victoires* (*Greene* 65); see note to *Afternoon* 1–2. Where Greene quoted Tailhade's lines for comparison with *Cousin Nancy*, TSE wrote on Greene's typescript: "cf also *Portrait of a Lady*—'latest Pole'?" To John Hayward, 14 Nov 1939, of a reading at the Student Mission House, Gower Street: "What a reading it was. It appeared that there was a large contingent of Polish waifs, which I had not considered, so I felt a little selfconscious when I recited 'we have been, let us say, to hear the latest Pole' etc." TSE: "'her passion for experience has taken her to a Russian pianist in Bayswater'", *Eeldrop and Appleplex* II (1917). **the latest Pole:** TSE: "on se repose des fatigues de la journée en lisant un roman du dernier russe, tchèque, serbe" [one rests from the fatigue of daily life by reading a novel by the latest Russian, Czech, Serbian], *Autour d'une Traduction d'Euripide* (1916). "In the *Karamazoff* ··· the party carouse with a couple of quite irrelevant Poles", *A Neglected Aspect of Chapman* (1924). **the latest:** OED 2a: "most recent. Also *ellipt.* as *n.* in *the latest*: the most recent story, piece of news, fashion, etc.", with *Kansas City Times & Star* 1889, "The latest the dear girls hereabouts are singing .. is, Will he love you as today?", and Arnold Bennett, 1911, "This was Denry's 'latest'". Van Wyck Brooks: "conversation is largely morning paper conversation, the newest developments ··· the latest happenings ··· the latest book ··· the latest play that we have seen", *The Wine of the Puritans* 59. TSE: "the latest tune", *Humouresque* 10. **Preludes:** pronounced *Pree-ludes* in TSE's recordings of *Preludes.*

I 9–10 **Transmit ··· finger-tips ··· intimate:** in his recording, TSE pronounces "intimate" as *intermit.*

I 9, 14 **finger-tips ··· slips:** Arthur Symons's sonnet *The Chopin Player* ends: "Dying delicately at my finger tips?", rhyming with "and drips". TSE: "something which should be firm but slips, just at my finger tips ··· that drips", *Do I know how I feel? Do I know what I think?* 15–16.

I 10 **Chopin:** pronounced *show-pan* in TSE's recording.

I 10, 19, 27; II 18, 26, 29, 38; III 11, 15, 18, 20–21, 36 **intimate ··· how much they mean to me, my friends ··· How much it means ··· sure that you understand ··· the friendship and the sympathy ··· how can I make a cowardly amends? ··· I remain self-possessed ··· My self-possession flares up for a second ··· we have not developed into friends ··· My self-possession gutters; we are really ···**

relate | So closely! · · · Not knowing what to feel or if I understand: Van Wyck Brooks: "an old friend's misfortune · · · sympathy · · · We are really regretful of all our former thoughtlessness · · · sympathy · · · two not particularly intimate friends · · · our own self-respect is quite needlessly injured by our mortification · · · poor, dazed creature who only wanted five minutes of moderate attention from week to week · · · really to understand what it all means", *The Wine of the Puritans* 60–62. TSE to Herbert Read, 18 Jan 1927: "I imagine it is impossible for a person in my position to be any more detached about H. J. than, from an opposite point of view, is Van Wyck Brooks."

I 11 **resurrected only among friends · · · two or three:** Matthew 18: 20: "For where two or three are gathered together in my name, there am I in the midst of them."

I 12–13 **touch the bloom | That is rubbed and questioned:** W. D. Howells: "vulgarized or coarsened · · · forgetting that modern invention has found a way of fixing the chalks, I have felt, in going over these little pieces, that the slightest rudeness of touch might shake the bloom, the color, from them", "The Prose Poem": Introduction to *Pastels in Prose* tr. Stuart Merrill (see headnote to *Hysteria*).

I 13 **questioned in the concert room:** "It is in the concert room, rather than in the opera house, that the germ of a poem may be quickened", *The Music of Poetry* (1942).

I 14 **And so the conversation slips:** James: "A silence of a few moments had fallen upon their talk", *The Bostonians* ch. XXII. TSE: "And the conversation rises and slowly fades into silence", *East Coker* III 19.

I 15 **Among velleities and carefully caught regrets:** "regrets · · · Among such scattered thoughts", *Fourth Caprice in Montparnasse* 9, 13. **velleities:** OED "velleity" 2: "A mere wish, desire, or inclination without accompanying action or effort. Very common in the 17th c.; now somewhat rare." Pronounced *vel-ee-ities* in TSE's recording (as OED).

I 15–19 **regrets · · · tones of violins · · · You do not know how much they mean to me:** Kipling: "tunes that mean so much to you alone— | Common tunes · · · rip your very heartstrings", *The Song of the Banjo* 61–64 (in *A Choice of Kipling's Verse*); see notes to *The Waste Land* [III] 261–77, and *Landscapes* II. *Virginia* 2, 4, 11.

I 16–18 **violins · · · And begins:** Symons: "When a sighing begins | In the violins", *From Poèmes Saturniens* I. *Soleils Couchants* [*Saturnian Poems* I. *Setting Suns*]. TSE: "Now begins | The piano and the flute and two violins", *The smoke that gathers blue and sinks* 13–14.

I 17, 31 **cornets:** given the draft spelling "cornetts" (31), Derek Roper asks whether this is the early wooden "cornetto" or the modern instrument associated with jazz and ragtime (*N&Q* June 2007); "Almost certainly these are the brass *cornets à piston* · · · The 'cracked' note in line 31 may be caused by overblowing" (*Roper 2007*). John Marston's *Entertainment of Alice, Dowager-Countess of Derby*, quoted in the epigraph to *Burbank with a Baedeker: Bleistein with a Cigar*, begins with "a full noise of cornets winded". Pronounced *cor-nètts* in TSE's recording, although OED stresses the first syllable.

I 19–21 **how much they mean · · · And how, how rare · · · In a life composed so much, so much of odds and ends:** "how much it means; | How much", *Mandarins*

I 13–14. "How much ··· How much ··· How much one means", *Goldfish* III 13–15.

I 21 **a life composed so much, so much of odds and ends:** James: "His life, on the whole, had not been rich in episode", *The Bostonians* ch. XXII.

I 24 **who has these qualities:** in his recording, TSE says "who has those qualities", reverting to the manuscript reading (perhaps an eye-skip to 26).

I 28 **what *cauchemar!*:** Laforgue: "Quels cauchemars pleins de talent!" [What nightmares full of genius!], *Locutions des Pierrots* [*The Things that Pierrots Say*] III 2. The form of dialogue in TSE's poem, with one side silent, derives from Laforgue's *Autre Complainte de Lord Pierrot.* TSE: "what mask *bizarre!*" *Humouresque* 24. ***cauchemar*:** OED "mare" (*Obs.*): "The Teut. word is the source of Old French *mare*, appearing also in the compound *cauchemar* nightmare, f. *caucher*, to trample". Pronounced as French (*co-sh'marre*) in TSE's recording. *Fowler* "French Words": "To use French words that your reader or hearer does not know or does not fully understand, to pronounce them as if you were one of the select few to whom French is second nature when he is not of those few ··· is inconsiderate & rude."

I 29 **Among the windings:** Hawthorne: "among the windings of the wood-path", *The Blithedale Romance* ch. XI. **windings of the violins:** Whitman: "sweet flutes and violins ··· the different voices winding in and out", *That Music Always Round Me* 6–8 (*Musgrove* 62). TSE: "The pleasant whining of a mandoline", *The Waste Land* [III] 261. **windings:** OED *vbl. n.*[1] 2b: "A melodic alternation or variation" (obs., citing musical guides 1667–1706 and now this line).

I 30 **ariettes:** *Oxford Companion to Music* "ariette": "(Fr.) A shorter and simpler aria ··· occasionally applied to instrumental music."

I 30–31 **ariettes | Of cracked cornets:** Braddon: "listening to a dreary band with a cornet that was a note and a half flat. Again he heard the old operatic airs", *Lady Audley's Secret* 56 (*Heywood*). TSE: "a cracked violin", II 17 *variant.*

I 32 **Inside my brain a dull tom-tom begins:** Kipling: "There is a tomtom outside, isn't there? I thought it was my head at first", *At the End of the Passage* (1890). "The drums of life were beating on their skulls | The floods of life were swaying in their brains", *Bacchus and Ariadne* 5–6 (and note). "Beats like a fatalistic drum", *Rhapsody on a Windy Night* 9. Second Clark Lecture: "Instead of ideas as meanings, as references to an outside world, you have suddenly a new world coming into existence, inside your own mind and therefore by the usual implication inside your own head. Mankind suddenly retires inside its several skulls, until you hear Nietzsche—pretty well tormented in *his* cranial lodging—declaring that 'nothing is inside, nothing is outside'", *The Varieties of Metaphysical Poetry* 80–81. Goethe, rather: "Nichts ist drinnen, nichts is draussen; | Denn was innen, das ist aussen" [Nothing is within, nothing is without; that which was within is without], *Epirrhema* (Jennifer Formichelli, personal communication). Hermann Hesse often quoted or adapted this, notably as the motto to the first essay in *Blick ins Chaos* (1920); see note to *The Waste Land* [V] 366–76. TSE: "Within the circle of my brain | The twisted dance", *The Burnt Dancer* 30. **tom-tom:** for "sentimental Tommy", see note to I 3–4. Corbière: "—Va donc balancier soûl affolé dans ma tête! |Bats en branle ce bon tam-tam, chaudron fêlé | Qui rend la voix de femme ainsi qu'une sonnette"

[Go then, pendulum, distracted in my head, boozed! | Beat with a swing this fine tom-tom, a tinny piano so flat], *Rapsodie du sourd* [*Deaf Man's Rhapsody*] 47–48 (*Grover Smith*, 301). (TSE to Ruth Harrison, 1 Apr 1935: "Corbière ··· seems to me much the greatest French poet after Baudelaire". To Edward J. H. Greene, 30 June 1947: "it was Corbière rather than Laforgue who succeeded Baudelaire in my affections.")

I 32–34 **a dull tom-tom begins ··· monotone**: Geoffrey Faber to TSE, 15 Sept 1927: "You spoke once to me of the influence which the drum-taps had on your rhythmic preferences. It tends to monotony?" (For reading in a monotone and accentuation by "drum-beats", see headnote to *Sweeney Agonistes*, 4. JAZZ and 5. ARNOLD BENNETT'S ADVICE.)

I 32–36 **Inside my brain ··· "false note" ··· take the air**: James: "the poor Assinghams ··· were the only approach to a false note in the concert, the stir of the air was such, for going, in a degree, to one's head", *The Golden Bowl* bk. III vii. **"false note"**: James: "these last words struck him as a false note", *The Portrait of a Lady* ch. X (Eleanor Cook, *N&Q* Dec 1980); as often in James.

I 33–34 **prelude of its own, | Capricious monotone**: J. R. Lowell: "Singing, in dreary monotone, | A Christmas carol of its own", *The Vision of Sir Launfal*, Prelude to Part Second (*Grover Smith* 301). At Christmas in 1904, TSE read aloud an essay, now untraced, *"The Vision of Sir Launfal," A Christmas Study* (programme at Washington U.; Jayme Stayer, personal communication). "There is a prose arbitrariness and a verse arbitrariness ··· there is a verse monotone and a prose monotone ··· we never allow this ground-monotone to become entirely inaudible", *The Borderline of Prose* (1917).

I 33, 36, 40 **prelude ··· tobacco ··· drink our bocks**: Laforgue: "Vous fumez dans vos bocks" [You smoke over your beer glasses], *Complainte de l'oubli des Morts* [*Complaint for the Forgetting of the Dead*] 9. The American Beer Company produced a "St. Louis Bock Beer". TSE: "street pianos and small beers!" *Goldfish* IV 36–37.

I 34–36 **Capricious monotone ··· take the air**: Whitman: "some wild trumpeter, some strange musician, | Hovering unseen in air, vibrates capricious tunes to-night", *The Mystic Trumpeter* 1–2, with "cornet", 10 (TSE: "cornets", 17, 31) (*Musgrove* 62). **monotone ··· let us take the air, in a tobacco trance**: Laforgue: "—Allons, fumons une pipette de tabac" [Come, let us smoke a little pipe of tobacco], *Complainte de l'automne monotone* [*Complaint of Monotonous Autumn*] 45 (*Greene* 37). I 36 **tobacco trance**: Dickens: "fell into a kind of tobacco-trance", *Barnaby Rudge* ch. XXX.

II

II 1 **Now that lilacs are in bloom ··· in her room**: Whitman on the death of Lincoln (15 Apr 1865): "When lilacs last in the dooryard bloom'd, | And the great star early droop'd in the western sky in the night, | I mourn'd, and yet shall mourn with ever-returning spring", *When Lilacs Last in the Dooryard Bloom'd* 1–3 (*Musgrove* 33). TSE: "When Whitman speaks of the lilacs or of the mocking-bird, his theories and beliefs drop away like a needless pretext", *Whitman and Tennyson* (1926). "I never read Whitman properly until I was of an age where I could no longer be influenced by him", *Walt Whitman and Modern Poetry*

(1944). Rupert Brooke: "Just now the lilac is in bloom | All before my little room", *The Old Vicarage, Grantchester* (pub. *Poetry Review* Nov 1912), quoted by TSE, after Brooke's death, in *Reflections on Contemporary Poetry* I (1917). To Geoffrey Faber, 25 Mar 1941: "I don't think you are on very secure ground with Rupert Brooke. I still believe that he was never anything but a poetaster, not in the same class with De la Mare, Hodgson, Davies or Binyon at their best."

II 3 **twists one in her fingers:** Symons: "one who twists a kerchief's lace | Between her well-gloved finger-tips", *From Paul Verlaine. Fêtes Galantes* VIII (*Cortège*). *Murder in the Cathedral* II, chorus: "more horror | Than when twisting in the fingers".

II 4–5 **"Ah ··· you do not know ··· who hold it in your hands":** Austin Dobson: "I plunge my hand among the leaves ··· 'If youth but knew!' Ah! 'if,'" *Pot-Pourri* 1, 7, with epigraph "'*Si jeunesse savait?*—'" (TSE: "youthful", II 15) (*Ricks 1998*); see note to *Burnt Norton* I 16. Dobson's poems are listed among TSE's books, to be sent to him, *c.*Aug 1920 (*Letters 1* 486).

II 8 **cruel:** two syllables in TSE's recording.

II 9 **situations which it cannot see:** "a situation is for Stendhal something deliberately constructed ··· definitely visual. Hawthorne and James have a kind of sense ··· which is not of sight. Not that they fail to make you *see* ··· The point is that Hawthorne was acutely sensitive to the situation; that he did grasp character through the relation of two or more persons to each other", *The Hawthorne Aspect* (1918), with "situation" nine times in all. To Eleanor Hinkley, 1 Apr 1918, on Henry James: "he has about the keenest sense of Situation of any novelist, and his always alert intelligence is a perpetual delight." See note on *Entretien dans un parc* variant title, *Situation*.

II 9, 29, III 33, 41 **And smiles ··· I take my hat ··· pen in hand ··· the right to smile:** *Symons* 109, on Laforgue: "an inflexible politeness towards man, woman, and destiny. He composes love-poems hat in hand, and smiles with an exasperating tolerance before all the transformations of the eternal feminine."

II 11, 28 **drinking tea ··· sit here, serving tea:** "ladies of uncertain age | Sit by a window drinking tea", *Mandarins* 2 1–2. "out to tea ··· and tea ··· and then tea", *The Death of the Duchess* I 2, 3, 4. James: "rang for some tea ··· (Mrs. Luna's tea was excellent)", *The Bostonians* ch. XXII.

II 12–13 **April ··· buried life:** Tennyson: "regret for buried time | That keenlier in sweet April wakes", *In Memoriam* CXVI 1–2. Arnold's *The Buried Life* (1852) gave the phrase general currency (*Southam*); see note to III 36, 41. **recall | My buried life ··· Paris in the Spring:** for Paris see note to III 5–7. For "recall the moments of our lives which were passed there ··· a life that is buried", see *Inoubliable France* in note to *The Dry Salvages* II 56–66, III 3–15. James: "Buried for long years in dark corners at any rate these few germs had sprouted again under forty-eight hours of Paris", *The Ambassadors* bk. II ii (*Grover Smith* 12). TSE later recommended James's novel to Mary Hutchinson (*Crawford 2015* 269).

II 15^16 [1–6] *variant* **Tinctured attar of rose ··· Will pardon this digression:** "Is it perfume from a dress | That makes me so digress?" *The Love Song of J. Alfred Prufrock* 65–66. (See Textual History for this six-line interpolation.)

II 16 **returns like the insistent:** "again | The insistent", *Easter: Sensations of April*

II 6–7. **out-of-tune**: quoted by OED "out" III, as an elliptical use of the adjectival phrase as though a noun.

II 18 **"I am always sure that you understand**: Bradley: "What ··· we are convinced of, is briefly this, that we understand and, again, are ourselves understood", *Appearance and Reality* ch. XXIII; scored by TSE.

II 21 **Achilles' heel**: Achilles' body was invulnerable except the heel by which his mother held him as she plunged him in the Styx. He died of an arrow in his heel. OED "heel" records the colloquial phrase back to Coleridge (1810).

II 26–27 **the friendship and the sympathy | Of one**: Van Wyck Brooks (on reasons for visiting Europe): "the sympathy and co-operation one meets", *The Wine of the Puritans* 121.

II 28–30 **friends ··· how can I make a cowardly amends | For what she has said to me?**: Blake: "My Generosity is to my Friends, | That for their Friendship I may make amends", *I am no Homer's Hero* (*Roper 2007*). **a cowardly amends**: OED: "The sing., common in Fr., is very rare in Eng., in which *amends* has been used as a collective sing. from the first".

II 28, III 25 **I shall sit here ··· I shall sit here**: likewise repeated in *Alice's Adventures in Wonderland* ch. VI: "'I shall sit here,' the Footman remarked, 'till to-morrow—' ··· '—or next day, maybe,' the Footman continued in the same tone, exactly as if nothing had happened ··· 'I shall sit here,' he said, 'on and off, for days and days'" (*Sewell*).

II 29 **take my hat ··· amends**: James: "he didn't in the least long for this arrangement, and was conscious that the most pertinent sequel to her conjecture would be for him to take up his hat and walk away ··· He did not pick up his hat to go ··· at last he took up his hat in earnest", *The Bostonians* ch. XXII. "I'm sorry, I said, | It's no use being sorry, he said; let me get my hat, I said", *WLComposite* 37–38.

II 31 **any morning in the park**: "The summer evenings in the park", *In the Department Store* 5.

II 32 **comics**: OED 2a: "the comic strips in a newspaper" (from 1889 and citing this line).

II 39 **a street-piano, mechanical and tired**: *Oxford Companion to Music* "Mechanical Reproduction": "a barrel-and-pin-operated pianoforte, with no proper claim to the name, however, since no 'piano' ··· is in any way possible." Carlyle, Tennyson, Holman Hunt and Millais supported a Bill proposed by the brewer Michael T. Bass MP to restrain street music. Charles Babbage considered that "one-fourth of his entire working power had been destroyed by audible nuisances, to which his highly strung nerves rendered him peculiarly sensitive". TSE: "A street-piano, garrulous and frail'", *First Caprice in North Cambridge* 1. "And a street piano through the dusty trees", *First Debate between the Body and Soul* 13. **piano**: pronounced with long *a* in TSE's recording (as the adverb), although OED gives only a short *a* for the instrument.

II 39–40 **tired | Reiterates**: in *Morley's US 1920*, TSE added the comma after "tired" that sense appears to require, but he never emended the text in print. John Quinn to TSE, 24 Sept 1920: "Your avoidance of punctuation marks is obviously studied, but it occurred to me that in some cases the sense, in others the grammar and in others the rhythm required a certain pause that might be indicated by a comma." TSE to Quinn, 9 May 1921: "I see reason in your objection to my punctuation; but I hold that the line itself punctuates, and the addition of a comma, in many places, seems to me to over-emphasise the arrest. That is because I always pause at the end of a line in reading verse, which perhaps you do not." For "the end of a line is a kind of punctuation in itself", see headnote to *The Waste Land* V (letter to Montgomery Belgion, 19 July 1940). For punctuation "which includes the *absence* of punctuation marks", see the Author's Note on the recording of *Four Quartets* (headnote, 9. TSE ON *FOUR QUARTETS*). For omission of "all punctuation at the end of lines", see letter to Laurence Whistler, 28 Sept 1955, quoted in headnote to *Long may this Glass endure* ("Uncollected Poems").

II 43 **Are these ideas right or wrong**: to A. L. Rowse, 2 Mar 1931: "I dare say Mosley *is* a 'careerist', but the point is are his ideas right or wrong?" To John Hayward, 27 Jan 1937: "Am I Right or am I Wrong?" (see headnote to *A Proclamation*). To Bonamy Dobrée, 9 Jan 1938, on dramatic verse: "*Hamlet* isn't poetry while it's going on: it's poetry after it's over. Are these ideas right or wrong?"

III

III 1 **The October night comes down**: John Davidson: "The London fog comes down", *Yuletide*; "The day wears; twilight ends; the night comes down", *The Crystal Palace* (1909). Both poems are in *John Davidson: A Selection* (1961), with Preface by TSE. (TSE had confessed to Maurice Lindsay, 20 Dec 1946, that after re-reading Davidson he was "rather disappointed", and unable to recommend that Faber print his work.) TSE: "a soft October night", *The Love Song of J. Alfred Prufrock* 21. "The winter evening settles down", *Preludes* I 1.

III 2–4 **Except for a slight sensation of being ill at ease | I mount the stairs ··· as if I had mounted on my hands and knees**: "mounted ··· stare ··· ill at ease ··· on my knees", *Paysage Triste* 1, 3, 13, 16. **I mount the stairs and turn the handle of the door**: "I mount the steps and ring the bell", *The "Boston Evening Transcript"* 6. "F. M.": "it is not necessary for Camille and Victorine to descend one staircase and mount another", *Diary of the Rive Gauche* I (1925). **stairs ··· mounted on my hands and knees**: Davidson: "I came, a penitent; and on my knees | I climbed their stairs", *The Testament of a Man Forbid* (1901), included in *John Davidson: A Selection* (1961).

III 5–7 **and when do you return? | But that's a useless question. | You hardly know when you are coming back**: James, on a return from Europe: "'Olive came home six weeks ago. How long did you expect her to endure it?' ¶ 'I am sure I don't know; I have never been there,' Ransom replied", *The Bostonians* ch. XXII. TSE: "'And when to Paris?'", *WLComposite* 263. To Virginia Woolf, 5 Sept 1925: "So *when do you return*? I want to come to see you as soon as you are here."

III 9 **among the bric-à-brac**: "among the bricks", *Interlude in London* 1 (see Hawthorne's "to vegetate among the bricks of an enclosed court", quoted in note to *Morning at the Window* 3–4). For "among the" and then "bric-à-brac", see note to *Mr. Apollinax* 2–5. "Among the débris", *Goldfish* IV 1.

III 12 ***This* is as I had reckoned**: to Bonamy Dobrée [Tues after 9th Sunday after Trinity] 1927: "Italics are bad in poetry. Abused by M. Arnold" (Brotherton Library). See note to *The Love Song of J. Alfred Prufrock* 40, 43, 49, 55.

III 14 **(But our beginnings never know our ends!)**: Corbière: "Sauf les amoureux commençants ou finis qui peuvent commencer par la fin il y a tant de choses qui finissent par le commencement que le commencement commence à finir par être la fin . . ." [Apart from lovers who are starting or who have finished who want to begin at the finish, there are so many things that finish at the start, that the start begins to finish by being the finish], prefatory (mis)quotation from *Sagesse des Nations* [*Wisdom of the Nations*] in *Les Amours jaunes* (*Grover Smith 1950* 420). TSE bought a copy of *Les Amours jaunes* during his year in Paris (*Greene* 62). James: "She answered that she didn't care about ends, she cared about beginnings", *The Bostonians* ch. XXII (Matthew Peters, *N&Q* Dec 2008). *A Midsummer Night's Dream* V i: "That is the true beginning of our end." TSE: "I take this period to have persisted until my nineteenth or twentieth year. Being a period of rapid assimilation, the end may not know the beginning", *The Use of Poetry and the Use of Criticism* 33 (TSE was 22–23 when he wrote *Portrait of a Lady*). "In my beginning is my end", *East Coker* I 1.

III 14–15 **(But our beginnings never know our ends!) | Why we have not developed into friends**: Hawthorne: "Our beginnings might readily be adapted to his great end · · · he held out both his hands to me · · · But I stood aloof · · · 'be my friend of friends forever'", *The Blithedale Romance* ch. XV (TSE: "Sure that across the gulf you reach your hand", II 20). **our ends!) | Why we have not developed into friends**: James: "She might have made up her mind that she had lost him as what she had hoped, but that it was better than desolation to try and keep him as a friend", *The Bostonians* ch. XXII. James again:

> "we might, you and I, have been friends · · · I've wanted you too."
> "Ah, but you've *had* me!" he declared, at the door with an emphasis that made an end.
>
> *The Ambassadors*, end of bk. XII II (*Grover Smith* 301)

III 16–17 **shall remark | Suddenly, his expression in a glass**: General Epistle of James 1: 23–24: "a man beholding his natural face in a glass · · · straightway forgetteth what manner of man he was." For TSE's "the sight of one's face in the glass" in a draft of *Letters of the Moment* I (1924) by "F. M.", see *McCue 2016.*

III 18 **self-possession gutters**: "repetition that displaces | Your mental self-possession | By this unwarranted digression", *Spleen* 4–6. **gutters; we are really in the dark**: *King Lear* I iv: "So out went the candle, and we were left darkling." TSE: "'Just now you saw that bright flame burning itself out,' said Appleplex, 'now you see it guttering thickly'", *Eeldrop and Appleplex* II (1917). ("street-lamp sputtered", *Rhapsody on a Windy Night* 14.)

III 19–20 **everybody said so · · · They were all sure our feelings would relate**: Edward explains why he thought he was in love, *The Cocktail Party* I iii: "Everybody told me that I was; | And they told me how well suited we were."

III 23 **You will write**: to Henry Eliot, 2 July 1915, of Isabella Stewart Gardner, "I shall write to her at once about my affairs". He was to send back to Boston full reports on London's artistic scene, 4 Apr and 7 Nov 1915. See notes to *The Engine* I and *Mr. Apollinax* 21.

III 27 **To find expression . . . dance, dance**: Rimbaud: "Faim, soif, cris, danse, danse, danse, danse!" [Hunger, thirst, shouts, dance, dance, dance, dance!], *Mauvais Sang* [*Bad Blood*].

III 27–28 **To find expression · · · Like a dancing bear**: Flaubert: "la parole humaine est comme un chaudron fêlé où nous battons des mélodies à faire danser les ours, quand on voudrait attendrir les étoiles" [human speech is like a cracked kettle on which we tap crude rhythms for bears to dance to, while we long to make music that will melt the stars], *Madame Bovary* II xii (Mark Thompson, personal communication).

III 28 **Like a dancing bear · · · chatter**: "The dancing bear · · · chattered", *Inside the gloom* 13, 27 *1st reading*. To judge by Gino Severini's painting *La danse de l'ours au Moulin Rouge* (1913; Pompidou Centre), dancing bears were exhibited in Edwardian Paris. For Symons, "Chained by enchantment to my stall · · · Dance to amuse a music-hall", see note to *Little Gidding* I 79–82, 84. **chatter like an ape**: *The Tempest* II ii: "apes, that mow and chatter at me". Shelley: "chattering like restless apes", *The Triumph of Life* 493.

III 31 **Well! and what if she should die some afternoon**: Laforgue: "Mais voici qu'un beau soir, infortunée à point, | Elle meurt!—Oh! là, là; bon, changement de thème!" [But now one fine evening, with perfectly timed ill-luck, she dies!—Oh goodness, let's change the subject!] *Pierrots* (*On a des principes*) [*Pierrots: One has Principles*] 9–10 (*Rees* 80).

> Enfin, si, par un soir, elle meurt dans mes livres,
> Douce; feignant de n'en pas croire encore mes yeux,
> J'aurai un: "Ah çà, mais, nous avions De Quoi vivre!
> "C'était donc sérieux?"
>
> [At last, if one evening she dies among my books, quietly; pretending not to believe my eyes, I'll react with a "Drat it, we had the wherewithal to live on! Was it serious after all?"]
>
> *Autre Complainte de Lord Pierrot* [*Another Complaint from Lord Pierrot*]

Symons 110 quoted the whole poem. James: "she might die twenty deaths before he came near her", *The Bostonians* ch. XXII.

III 31, 41 **if she should die · · · Not knowing what to feel · · · should I have the right to smile**: to Middleton Murry [mid-April? 1925]: "I have done it deliberately · · · *but it has killed* V [Vivien] · · · What will happen if I live again? 'I am I' but with what feelings, with what results to *others*—Have I the right to be I · · · ?"

III 32 **Afternoon grey and smoky, evening yellow and rose**: "'I shall pay my call on Mrs. Howexden,' murmured Appleplex · · · The suburban evening was grey and yellow on Sunday", *Eeldrop and Appleplex* (1917) I, then opening of II. **evening yellow and rose**: Baudelaire: "Vous êtes un beau ciel d'automne, clair et rose!" [You are a fine autumn sky, clear and rosy], *Causerie* [*Monologue*] 1; see note to *The Waste Land* [II] 74–75. TSE: "yellow evening", *First Caprice in North Cambridge* 2. "evening in December | Under a sunset yellow and rose", *Second Caprice in North Cambridge* 17.

III 34 **above the housetops**: Isaiah 22: 1: 'What aileth thee now, that thou art wholly gone up to the housetops?" Jeremiah 48: 38: "lamentations generally upon all the housetops."

III 36 **Not knowing what to feel**: *Do I know how I feel? Do I know what I think?* (see note on its opening line). **what to feel**: "intelligence, of which an important function is the discernment of exactly what, and how much, we feel in any given situation", *Reflections on Contemporary Poetry* III (1917).

III 36–37 **Not knowing · · · if I understand | Or whether wise or foolish, tardy or too soon**: "I wonder if it is too late or soon", *Entretien dans un parc* 6.

III 36, 41 **Not knowing what to feel · · · should I have the right to smile?**: Arnold: "We know, we know that we can smile! · · · powerless to reveal | To one another what indeed they feel", *The Buried Life* 5, 14–15 (see note to II 12–13).

Preludes

Published in *Blast* 2 (July 1915), then *Others: An Anthology of the New Verse (1917)*, ed. Alfred Kreymborg (1917, not in *Gallup*), and collected in *1917+*, *Sesame* and *Penguin / Sel Poems*. A letter from Wyndham Lewis to TSE [Nov 1923?], makes clear that TSE gave this poem and *Rhapsody on a Windy Night* to *Blast* without fee.

Recorded 13 May 1947, Harvard, as part of the Morris Gray Poetry Reading, introduced by Theodore Spencer. (TSE started by saying that he liked to read poems "strictly in chronological order, in the order in which you find them in the book, trying to choose a few representative poems from each period of my work and varying the choice as much as is possible with such a meagre output · · · I should like to begin by reading all four of my *Preludes* for the reason that they were written here in Cambridge.") Second: 12 Nov 1950, for U. Chicago Round Table, broadcast by NBC. Third: 26 Sept 1955, London; released Caedmon 1955 (US), 1959 (UK).

Dated "Oct. 1910" (I & II), "July 1911" (III) in Notebook. Dated "1909–1910" (I & II) and "1911 (later part)" (III & IV) in *VE's 1951*. Dated Cambridge, Mass., 1910 (I & II), Paris, 1910 (III) and Cambridge, Mass., 1911 (IV) in *Poèmes*. Dated Cambridge, Mass., 1910 (I & II), Paris, 1910 (III); Cambridge, Mass., 1911 (IV) in *Isaacs US 1920* and by TSE in *Morley's US 1920*. TSE wrote these dates and places also in a third copy, *Hayward's 1925*, except "Cambridge Mass 1911 or 1912?" (IV). Dated 1909–11, "so far as I can remember", to Norman Foerster, 15 June 1932. To Edward J. H. Greene, 18 Oct 1939: "*Preludes* are 1909–10; the first two having been written at Harvard, and the latter two in Paris." To Greene, 28 Nov 1947: "it is still my impression that the first two *Preludes* were written at Harvard in 1908 or 1910 and the last two at Harvard in 1912. I am certain about the fourth but doubtful about the third."

Scripps College, California, possesses a rough ms translation into French of Part III in the hand of Vivien Eliot. For TSE's revision of this see III 5.

The variant epigraph to III, "'son âme de petite putain': Bubu" [her little whore's soul], apparently mingles phrases from Charles-Louis Philippe's *Bubu de Montparnasse*: "Elle avait un sourire de pauvre petite putain" [She smiled like the poor little whore she was], ch. III; "ses histoires de pauvre petite putain" [stories of the poor little trot-about whore], ch. VIII; and "son âme" throughout, including "où l'on vend son âme pendant que l'on vend sa chair" [wherein you sell your soul at the same time you sell your flesh], ch. VII. TSE's Preface of 1932 to *Bubu of Montparnasse* recalled reading the novel when he arrived in Paris in 1910: "*Bubu* stood for Paris as some of Dickens' novels stand for London." To Jacques Porel, 6 Jan 1931: "I should be quite glad to write a short preface to *Bubu*, to the best of my ability; but · · · I have not read the book, or had a copy in my hands, since 1910; so you will see that I am rather behind." To Violet Schiff (Hudson), 22 Sept 1949, thanking her for her translation of *Marie Donadieu*: "It will be a very interesting experience to read this book again, because I have not read it since 1911, at a period when the works of Philippe made a very deep impression upon me. It is extraordinary that such a book should have waited so many years for translation, and I congratulate you upon having done it."

TSE: "While they are probably not those of my early poems which showed the most promise, I think they are still the most satisfactory to myself", *Chicago Round Table* (1950).

Title] Pronounced *Pree-ludes* by TSE in his recordings. OED gives both short and long *e*, with "The first pronunciation prevails in Great Britain." *Fowler* recommends "short e". Laforgue, *Préludes Autobiographiques* (*Les Complaintes*). "Transmit the Preludes, through his hair and finger-tips", *Portrait of a Lady* I 9. Of the Nineties: "Gautier had written the *Symphonie en blanc majeur*, and Whistler had painted symphonies in various colours · · · critics took alarm at the confusion of genres", *The Borderline of Prose* (1917); see note to *Burnt Norton* V 4–7. From 1895 Arthur Symons also used many musical titles for poems (including *Caprice*, *Intermezzo*, *Madrigal* and *Air de Ballet*), and TSE's titles too were often from musical forms. Among the poems he did not publish are *First Caprice in North Cambridge*, *Opera*, *Suite Clownesque*, *Interlude: in a Bar*, *Interlude in London*, *Airs of Palestine, No. 2* and *Dirge*; and among those he did publish are *Nocturne*, *Rhapsody on a Windy Night*, *Five-Finger Exercises* and *Four Quartets.* Other titles are suggestive of music, such as *Inventions of the March Hare*, *Ballade of the Fox Dinner*, *The Love Song of J. Alfred Prufrock* and *A Song for Simeon*. Three early poems were entitled *Song.* To L. A. G. Strong, 30 June 1925, *The Hollow Men*: "I am still in doubt as to how I wish this suite to be arranged". To Vernon Watkins, 22 Apr 1941: "The committee don't like a title with 'Music' in it, and the department who have to sell a book know best."

Part titles] In *ms1*, *Preludes* I was *Prelude in Roxbury* (*Houses*), emended from *Prelude in Dorchester* (*Houses*), and *Preludes* II and III were each *Prelude in Roxbury*. Roxbury and Dorchester are neighbourhoods in south Boston. (Concerning recordings, TSE wrote to Lloyd Frankenberg, 29 Mar 1949: "For a record the *Four Preludes* presents the advantage of unity".)

I

I 4 **burnt-out ends of smoky days:** *Romeo and Juliet* III v: "Night's candles are burnt out, and jocund day". TSE: "the butt-ends of my days", *The Love Song of J. Alfred Prufrock* 60 (with "smoke", 71). "The smoky candle-end of time", *Burbank with a Baedeker: Bleistein with a Cigar* 20.

I 7–8 **withered leaves · · · vacant lots:** "withered leaves · · · vacant square", *First Debate between the Body and Soul* 6, 9.

I 9–10 **beat | On broken blinds:** "The sunlight beating in through broken blinds, and broken blinds keeping out the sun", *Eeldrop and Appleplex* II (Anne Stillman, personal communication).

I 11 **And at the corner of the street:** "We turn the corner of the street", *Fourth Caprice in Montparnasse* 1.

I 13 **the lighting of the lamps:** gas streetlamps were lit by means of a wick on a long pole. William Allingham, of London: "We were just in time to see the effect of the lighting of the lamps. The dusky mass awoke", *Diary* 18 Aug 1849. TSE, outdoors and indoors: "They are lighting up the lamps, and it begins to rain", *Portrait of a Lady*, *variant after* I 40. "And when the lamps are lit and curtains drawn · · · twilight", *To Walter de la Mare*. "And the evening circle in the winter gaslight", *The Dry Salvages* I 14. Laforgue's *Hamlet*, tr. Symons: "They, too, were the little people of History · · · lighting the dirty lamp every evening", *Symons* 105 (for Laforgue's *Hamlet* see notes to *Rhapsody on a Windy Night* 57–59, *The Waste Land* [II] 172 and *Animula* 5).

II

II 1 **The morning comes to consciousness:** "the evening fought itself awake · · · when the dawn at length had realized itself", *Prufrock's Pervigilium* [10, 25].

II 1–2 **morning · · · stale smells:** "waking up in the morning · · · stale tobacco", *Eeldrop and Appleplex* II (1917). "the stale smell of morning!" *Anabasis* V xi (where "stale" was "sick" prior to *1959*). (Perse: "*l'odeur fade du matin!*")

II 1–4 **The morning comes to consciousness · · · beer · · · the sawdust-trampled street · · · muddy:** John Davidson: "On muddy beer | The melancholy mean suburban street | Grew maudlin for an hour; pianos waked", *A Woman and her Son* (for which see note to *The Waste Land* [III] 220–23). TSE on Davidson's *Thirty Bob a Week*: "I am sure that I found inspiration in the content of the poem, and in the complete fitness of content and idiom: for I also had a good many dingy urban images to reveal", *John Davidson* (1961). See note to *Coriolan* II. *Difficulties of a Statesman* 14.

III

Epigraph] See headnote. *Grover Smith* 20 points to Charles-Louis Philippe:

> Dans la chambre d'hôtel, rue Chanoinesse, à midi, la fenêtre donnant sur la cour, avec ses rideaux gris et ses carreaux sales, envoyait un jour sale et gris · · · il y avait le lit défait où les deux corps marquèrent leur place de sueur brune sur les draps usés, ce lit des chambres d'hôtels, où les corps sont sales et les âmes aussi. Berthe, en chemise, venait de se lever. Ses épaules étroites, sa chemise grise et ses pieds malpropres, mince et jaune, elle semblait sans lumière non plus. Par ses yeux bouffis et ses cheveux écartés, au milieu du désordre de la chambre elle était en désordre et ses idées étaient couchées en tas dans sa tête. Les réveils de midi sont lourds et poisseux comme la vie de la veille avec l'amour, l'alcool et le sommeil · · · Elle ressentit encore ce poids d'angoisse qui, depuis hier, l'empêchait de respirer. Elle se rappela tout, et cela s'appuyait à deux genoux sur sa poitrine comme un monstre en colère.
>
> [At noon, in the hotel room of the rue Chanoinesse, a grey and dirty light filtered through the grey curtains and dirty panes of the window · · · there was the unmade bed where the two bodies had left the impress of brownish sweat upon the worn sheets—this bed of hotel rooms, where the bodies are dirty and the souls are as well. Berthe, in her chemise, had just got up. With her narrow shoulders, her grey

shirt and her unclean feet, she too seemed, in her pale yellow slimness, to have no light. With her puffy eyes and scraggly hair, in the disorder of this room, she too was in disorder and her thoughts lay heaped confusedly in her head. These awakenings at mid-day are heavy and sticky like the life of the night before with its love-making, its alcohol, and its torpid sleep ··· She remembered everything, and it all pressed its two knees upon her chest, like a raging monster.]

Bubu de Montparnasse ch. IV

III 1–3 **You tossed a blanket from the bed, | You lay upon your back ··· and watched the night:** "I tossed the blankets back, to watch the darkness", *Prufrock's Pervigilium* [19].

III 3–9 **watched the night revealing ··· sordid images ··· flickered against the ceiling ··· shutters ··· gutters:** Kipling: "When the drunken comrade mutters and the great guard-lantern gutters | And the horror of our fall is written plain, | Every secret, self-revealing on the aching whitewashed ceiling, | Do you wonder that we drug ourselves from pain?" *Gentlemen-Rankers* (in *A Choice of Kipling's Verse*).

III 4 **sordid images:** "from Baudelaire I learned first, a precedent for the poetical possibilities, never developed by any poet writing in my own language, of the more sordid aspects of the modern metropolis, of the possibility of fusion between the sordidly realistic and the phantasmagoric, the possibility of the juxtaposition of the matter-of-fact and the fantastic", *What Dante Means to Me* (1950).

III 4, 9 **The thousand sordid images ··· And you heard the sparrows in the gutters:** "sparrows | Delve in the gutter with sordid patience", *First Caprice in North Cambridge* 8–9.

III 5 **Of which your soul was constituted:** in her French translation, Vivien wrote "Desquelles votre âme était constituée", which TSE revised to "Desquelles fut constitué votre âme".

III 6–7 **flickered against the ceiling. | And when all the world came back:** "darted stealthily across the wall | Flattened itself upon the ceiling ··· And when the dawn ··· world", *Prufrock's Pervigilium* [22–23, 25, 32].

III 8–9 **And the light crept up between the shutters | And you heard the sparrows in the gutters:** "A blind old drunken man who sings and mutters, | With broken boot heels stained in many gutters", *Prufrock's Pervigilium* [30–31].

III 10–11 **such a vision of the street | As the street hardly understands:** Conrad: "between the tall houses of a street as still and decorous as a well-kept alley in a cemetery, I had a vision of him on the stretcher", *Heart of Darkness* pt. 3.

III 10, 14 **vision of the street ··· feet:** Paul Elmer More: "a wonderfully radiant lady ··· that vision of the street", *The Great Refusal* 18, introducing a poem (of his own) which begins with the rhyme "feet ··· street" and uses it again three times in seventeen pages. TSE: "a sudden vision of incompetence ··· we walk on", *Entretien dans un parc* 8–10. For Hulme, "visions, alien to long streets", see note to *Morning at the Window* 2–9.

III 10, IV 1, 3 **a vision of the street ··· across the skies ··· trampled by insistent feet:** W. G. Tinckom-Fernandez: "newly burnished skies ··· the vision in my wintry eye ··· And a thousand feet are stamping on familiar trails again!" *Song of the*

Sap 10, 14, 16 in *The Argonaut* 11 June 1910 (TSE: "winter" I 1). For the poem, see note to *Cousin Nancy* 2.

III 10–11, IV 8–9 **such a vision of the street | As the street hardly understands ··· The conscience of a blackened street | Impatient to assume the world:** William James, on a graduate student: "he had always taken for granted that when you entered a philosophic classroom you had to open relations with a universe entirely distinct from the one you left behind you in the street. The two were supposed to have so little to do with each other, that you could not possibly occupy your mind with them at the same time. The world of concrete personal experiences to which the street belongs is multitudinous beyond imagination, tangled, muddy, painful and perplexed. The world to which your philosophy-professor introduces you is simple, clean and noble", *Pragmatism* (1907) Lecture I. TSE later wrote that an antithesis "seems to belong to the year 1910, with the pleasant essays of William James (as popular a writer for his time as are Eddington and Jeans in ours) and with the epidemic of Bergsonism", *A Commentary* in *Criterion* Oct 1932. "I fumbled to the window to experience the world", *Prufrock's Pervigilium* [28]. Symons on Henley: "the humanity of streets, if we have but the vision", *Studies in Two Literatures* (1897) 188.

III 12–15 **Sitting along the bed's edge ··· hair, | Or clasped the yellow soles of feet | In the palms of both soiled hands:** Swinburne: "She, sitting edgewise on her bed, | Holding her feet ··· I sit still and hold | In two cold palms her cold two feet. | Her hair, half grey half ruined gold", *The Leper* 42–43, 101–103, one of the Swinburne poems that a volume of selections "should certainly contain", *Swinburne as Poet* (1920).

III 13–14 **clasped the yellow soles of feet | In the palms of both soiled hands:** against the quotation of these lines in *G. Jones* (225), TSE wrote "Marie Donadieu", perhaps a mistake for *Bubu de Montparnasse* ch. IV (see first note to *Preludes* III).

IV

IV 1, 13 **His soul stretched tight ··· Infinitely suffering thing:** to A. L. Rowse, 3 Mar 1941 on the "metaphysicality" of William Empson: "it springs from a peculiarly twisted and tormented, but very painfully suffering soul" (recalling also the next poem, *Rhapsody on a Windy Night* 24–32: "twisted things ··· twisted ··· broken spring ··· curled and ready to snap").

IV 3, 8 **insistent feet:** "insistent sweet", *Easter: Sensations of April* II 7.

IV 5 **short square fingers stuffing pipes:** Dickens: "the speaker's square forefinger", "squarely pointing with his square forefinger", "the square finger", *Hard Times* ch. I, II (Archie Burnett, personal communication).

IV 5–7 **fingers stuffing pipes ··· Assured:** Charles-Louis Philippe: "fumant sa pipe ··· tassait la cendre du bout de son doigt ··· avec l'assurance" [smoking his pipe ··· tapped off the ash with his fingertip ··· with assurance], *Marie Donadieu* (1904) II i (*Grover Smith* 21). **stuffing pipes, | And evening newspapers:** "reading evening papers | And boys were smoking cigarettes", *Prufrock's Pervigilium* [11–12].

IV 6–7 **and eyes | Assured of certain certainties:** "eyes ··· And your assuring certainties", *Goldfish* IV 28, 34. "certain uncertainties", *Entretien dans un parc*

4 *variant.* **certain**: OED I 1: "Determined, fixed, settled". II 7a: "Used to define things which the mind definitely individualizes or particularizes from the general mass, but which may be left without further identification in description; thus often used to indicate that the speaker does not choose further to identify or specify them. Different as this seems to be from sense 1, it is hardly separable from it in a large number of examples: thus, in the first which follows, the hour was quite 'certain' or 'fixed', but it is not communicated to the reader; to him it remains, so far as his knowledge is concerned, quite indefinite; it may have been, as far as he knows, at any hour; though, as a fact, it was at a particular hour."

In his copy of Mallarmé's *Vers et Prose*, TSE marked the word "certain" in the description of when Jules Laforgue "nous initia au charme certain du vers faux" [initiated us into the certain charm that artificial verses have], and wrote "indubitable". In his copy of I. A. Richards's *Principles of Literary Criticism*, TSE underlined "certain" in the phrase "certain individuals" (177) and wrote "Which?" (for a similar concern, see note to *Little Gidding* II 39–45, "some dead master"). For "uncertain age", see note to *Mandarins* 2 1.

IV 8 **a blackened street**: Henry Blackburn: "for landscape a damp, dreary, muddy, blackened street, with a vista of areas and lamp-posts", *Artists and Arabs* (1878) ch. III. "blackened trees", *Fourth Caprice in Montparnasse* 7 (with "street" 1, 14). "a blackened wall", *The Waste Land* [V] 381 (see note to [V] 379–81).

IV 8–16 **street ··· assume the world ··· moved by fancies ··· and laugh; | The worlds revolve like ancient women | Gathering fuel in vacant lots**: "We have ··· Gathered wood against the winter ··· Talked at the corners of streets ··· had laughter and gossip ··· In a void apart ··· the doom of the world", *Murder in the Cathedral* I second chorus. "The old without fire ··· Gathering faggots at nightfall", third chorus.

IV 9 **assume**: OED I: "To take unto (oneself), receive, accept, adopt ··· b. *esp.* To receive up into heaven" (this sense *arch.* or *obs.*); III: "To take as being one's own, to arrogate, pretend to"; 11: "*Logic.* To add the minor premise to a syllogism", quoting "The antecedent is assumed, when the words of it are barely repeated in the second proposition, or assumption."

IV 10 **moved by fancies**: Geraldine Stewart: "One should never allow one's self to be moved by fancies, as if they were realities", *The Laird's Return* (1861) 79–80.

IV 12–13 **The notion of some infinitely gentle | Infinitely suffering thing**: according to Valerie Eliot, these lines were written "with his brother in mind", *Letters* (1988) 54.

IV 12–14 **some infinitely gentle | Infinitely suffering thing. | Wipe your hand across your mouth, and laugh**: *Symons* 53 (on Villiers de l'Isle-Adam): "Contempt, noble as it may be, anger, righteous though it may be, cannot be indulged in without a certain lack of sympathy ··· It is certain that the destiny of the greater part of the human race is either infinitely pathetic or infinitely ridiculous" (TSE: "certain certainties", IV 7 and note).

IV 14–15 **Wipe ··· mouth ··· women**: Proverbs 30: 20: "an adulterous woman ··· wipeth her mouth, and saith, I have done no wickedness."

IV 16 **fuel**: pronounced as two syllables in TSE's three recordings. **vacant lots**: Whitman: "out on the vacant lot at sundown after work", *I sing the body electric*

21. Laforgue has "terrains vagues" in *Complainte sur certains ennuis*, *Cythère* and *Pierrots* I. TSE: "This charm of vacant lots!" *Second Caprice in North Cambridge* 1 (and see note to 1, 7). "Perpetual crackling of insects in this quarter of vacant lots and rubbish", *Anabasis* IV x. (Perse: "· · · *ce quartier aux détritus!*") In the 1933 revised (though unadopted) ending to *Sweeney Agonistes*: *Fragment of an Agon*, "The old gentleman" who appears like the choric Time in *The Winter's Tale* introduces himself: "Good evening. My name is Time. I come from the vacant lot in front of the Grand Union Depot."

Rhapsody on a Windy Night

Published in *Blast* 2, then *Others: An Anthology of the New Verse (1917)*, *1917+* and *Penguin / Sel Poems.* Excerpts were printed with lithographs by Gerald Wilde in *Poetry London* Dec 1944. TSE to Anthony Sylvestre, 30 June 1944: "I have seen some of Mr. Wilde's illustrations of *Rhapsody on a Windy Night,* and have found them very interesting. Indeed, I should hardly call them illustrations, as their value is independent of the value of the poem. But I fear that material considerations prevent us, at present, from entertaining any suggestion, however interesting, for illustrated editions: the practical difficulties, both of materials and of expert labour, are too great."

No recording has been traced. However, TSE read this poem at Columbia University on 28 Apr 1958 and a recording was broadcast on 30 Apr and again on 5 May by the university's radio station WKCR. A transcript of the occasion appeared in *Columbia University Forum* Fall 1958. The poems read that day were *The Love Song of J. Alfred Prufrock*, *Rhapsody on a Windy Night*, *The Hippopotamus*, *The Waste Land* II and V, *Growltiger's Last Stand*, *Sweeney Agonistes* II. *Fragment of an Agon*, *Ash-Wednesday* V, *The Cultivation of Christmas Trees*, *Lines for an Old Man*, a chorus from *Murder in the Cathedral* act II and *East Coker*.

Dated Mar 1911, *ms1*; Paris, 1911 in *Isaacs's US 1920* and by TSE in both *Morley's US 1920* and *Hayward's 1925*. Dated "1910, Paris" by TSE to Edward J. H. Greene, 18 Oct 1939. Before reading the poem at Columbia, 28 Apr 1958: "This was written in Paris in 1910 or '11. I don't know very much about it now. If it needs an explanation I must leave it to others to explain it."

"My early *vers libre*, of course, was started under the endeavour to practise the same form as Laforgue. This meant merely rhyming lines of irregular length, with the rhymes coming in irregular places. It wasn't quite so *libre* as much *vers*, especially the sort which Ezra called 'Amygism' [after Amy Lowell]. Then, of course, there were things in the next phase which were freer, like *Rhapsody on a Windy Night.* I don't know whether I had any sort of model or practice in mind when I did that. It just came that way", *Paris Review* (1959).

To John Collier, 4 Oct 1923, on a poem submitted to the *Criterion*: "it reminds me somewhat of the work of Mr. Conrad Aiken, which you probably have not read; it reminds me certainly of my own earlier verse. This is something which I have outgrown, and which I think you will outgrow also: I think that there is a great deal of sentimentality to be purged out of it. This particular type of fragmentary conversation ··· was invented by Jules Laforgue and done to death by Aldous Huxley ··· I have been a sinner myself in the use of broken conversations punctuated by three dots."

Title **Rhapsody**: OED 3b: "A literary work consisting of miscellaneous or disconnected pieces, etc.; a written composition having no fixed form or plan. *Obs.*" Also: 4. "An exalted or exaggeratedly enthusiastic expression of sentiment or feeling; an effusion (e.g. a speech, letter, poem) marked by extravagance of idea or expression, but without connected thought or sound argument", and 5. "*Mus.* An instrumental composition enthusiastic in character but indefinite in form." **Windy Night**: Shakespeare: "Give not a windy night a rainy morrow", Sonnet 90.

3–4 **lunar ··· lunar**: *Symons* 107 on Laforgue: "He has constructed his own world, lunar and actual."

4, 6 **incantations ··· clear relations**: "Imagination's | Poor Relations", *First Debate between the Body and Soul* 32–33.

5 **Dissolve the floors of memory**: Henry M. Lyman: "The residual strata which, so to speak, have been deposited from the sea of events upon the *floor of memory*, have become broken and 'faulted.' The line of rupture marks the division between the two fields of consciousness", *Insomnia, and other Disorders of Sleep* (1885) 205. Oliver Wendell Holmes: "pegs to hang facts upon which would otherwise have strewed the floor of memory", *Medical Essays* (1891) 373. Holmes: "The area of consciousness is covered by layers of habitual thoughts, as a sea-beach is covered with wave-worn, rounded pebbles, shaped, smoothed, and polished by long attrition against each other ··· The tides of wakening consciousness roll in upon them daily as we unclose our eyelids, and keep up the gentle movement and murmur of ordinary mental respiration until we close them again in slumber. When we think we are thinking, we are for the most part only listening to the sound of attrition between these inert elements of intelligence. They shift their places a little, they change their relations to each other, they roll over and turn up new surfaces. Now and then a new fragment is cast in among them, to be worn and rounded and take its place with the others, but the pebbled floor of consciousness is almost as stationary as the pavement of a city thoroughfare", *Over the Teacups* (1891) 11. William Fleming on G. H. Lewes: he "proposes to apply the word *subconscious* to perceptions which do not appear above the 'floor of consciousness'", *The Vocabulary of Philosophy* (4th ed. rev. Henry Calderwood, 1890), "Perceptions (Obscure)". The phrase "floor of consciousness" became current and in 1920 H. Wildon Carr translated Bergson's "au-dessous de la scène illuminée par la conscience" as "below the floor of consciousness", *Mind-Energy* ch. IV "Dreams" (*Jain 1992* 55). Bradley: "which quietly, or it may be longingly, remains below the 'floor of consciousness'", *Ethical Studies* Essay I. In Bradley's *Appearance and Reality* ch. XXI, TSE underlined "Memory is plainly a construction from the ground of the present." **Dissolve ··· memory**: On Coleridge's definition of imagination: "it is not enough to say that the one 'dissolves, diffuses and dissipates' the memories in order to re-create", *The Use of Poetry and the Use of Criticism* 79.

7 **precisions**: OED 1b: "An instance of precision; a nicety; in *pl.* exact minutiæ.

Obs. rare", with Locke the only example: "I have left out the utmost Precisions of Fractions in these Computations."

8–9 **street lamp · · · Beats:** *réverbère* (Fr.) gas street lamp with reflector, from Latin *verbere*, to beat (*Hands*). "torchlight · · · reverberation", *The Waste Land* [V] 321, 325. To John Hayward, 9 Sept 1942, concerning the proposed use of "lantern" in *Little Gidding* II: "On the other hand, any reference to the reverberes wd. take the mind directly to *pre-war* London".

8–11 **street · · · Midnight:** Blake: "But most through midnight streets I hear | How the youthful harlot's curse | Blasts the new-born infant's tear, | And blights with plagues the marriage hearse", *London* 13–16, quoted by TSE in *William Blake* (1920).

9 **Beats like a fatalistic drum:** Charles-Louis Philippe: "Le grand mot sortit, qu'il promenait à grands pas, et, comme un tonnerre, éclata, pendant qu'il marchait, et puis roula, battant sa marche comme un noir tambour" [it broke like thunder as he walked, and then rolled in time to his step like the beating of a black drum], *Bubu de Montparnasse* ch. IV. Henry King, *An Exequy To his Matchless never to be forgotten Friend* 111–14:

> But heark! My Pulse, like a soft Drum
> Beats my approach, tells Thee I come;
> And slow howere my marches be,
> I shall at last sit down by Thee.

In *The Metaphysical Poets* (1921), TSE quotes 99–114, commenting: "In the last few lines there is that effect of terror which is several times attained by one of Bishop King's admirers, Edgar Poe." For the impression made upon TSE as a child by King's poem, see headnote to *Elegy*. **fatalistic drum:** "fatalistic horns", *Opera* 2.

9, 12 **Beats · · · drum · · · madman:** Thomas Heywood: "Astonishment, | Fear, and amazement play against my heart, | Even as a madman beats upon a drum", *A Woman Killed with Kindness* IV v (*Grover Smith* 302). Scene number from Mermaid; editions vary. In the copy of René Taupin's *L'influence du symbolisme français sur la poésie américaine* which he gave to F. S. Flint, TSE wrote against the quotation of his own lines "Dekker!" (probably an error for Heywood). Two undated pages of notes by TSE on characters and plots in Heywood and Shirley are at Harvard. Wilde: "But each man's heart beat thick and quick, | Like a madman on a drum!" *The Ballad of Reading Gaol* III xxxiv (*Grover Smith* 24).

11 **Midnight shakes the memory:** Wilde: "The troubled plumes of midnight shook | The plumes upon a hearse", *The Ballad of Reading Gaol* III xviii.

12 **madman shakes a dead geranium:** "morning shook the long nasturtium", *Suppressed Complex* 7.

12, 63 **geranium · · · geraniums:** after reading the poem at Columbia, 28 Apr 1958: "I can't explain that now. I recognize the geraniums as Jules Laforgue's geraniums, not mine, I'm afraid, originally. Adopted them." Laforgue: "La bouche clownesque ensorcèle | Comme un singulier géranium" [The clownish mouth casts a spell like a singular geranium], *Pierrots* I 7–8 (TSE's title: *Suite Clownesque*). Again: "Dans un album, | Mourait fossile | Un géranium | Cueilli aux Iles" [In an album, there was dying, fossilized, a geranium plucked from the islands], *Rigueurs à nulle autre pareilles* [*Unparalleled Severities*] 1–4. TSE quoted the first ten lines of Laforgue's *Derniers Vers* x ("O géraniums diaphanes . . .") in *The Metaphysical Poets* (1921). Laforgue "is at once the sentimentalist day-dreaming over the *jeune fille* at the piano with her geraniums, and the behaviourist inspecting her reflexes", *The Varieties of Metaphysical Poetry* 216 (and again, rephrased, 285). To John Collier, 4 Oct 1923: "Incidentally, Laforgue has made it impossible for anyone else to talk about geraniums."

14 **street-lamp sputtered:** "gas-jet flickered", *Prufrock's Pervigilium* [8].

16–21 **Regard that woman | Who hesitates toward you in the light of the door | Which opens on her like a grin · · · border of her dress | Is torn · · · the corner of her eye:** "in corners | Where women took the air, standing in entries— | Women, spilling out of corsets, stood in entries", *Prufrock's Pervigilium* [5–7].

16, 50 **Regard · · · Regard:** "Regarde", *Le Directeur* 18. "Regard", *Mandarins* 2 5 (see note).

17 **hesitates towards:** OED "hesitate" 1e (not in 1st ed.): "To move in an indecisive, faltering manner", citing only this line and H. G. Wells "He hesitated towards the door of the cabin", *The War in the Air* (1908) ch. V.

23, 25 **high and dry · · · beach:** OED: "said of a vessel cast or drawn up on the shore out of the water", from 1822: "Another surf sent Ensign George True high and dry on the beach."

23–32 **memory · · · twisted things · · · broken spring · · · clings · · · ready to snap:** "twisted · · · snappiest · · · spring's", *Humouresque* 10, 15. To Middleton Murry [12 Apr 1925], on Vivien's illness: "I don't know what is the spring that is snapped, the formula of her mind, her temperament, personality · · · she dwells · · · on the past".

25 **twisted branch:** "Twisting its branches", *The Death of Saint Narcissus* 22.

35 **the cat which flattens itself in the gutter:** "Flattened itself upon the ceiling", *Prufrock's Pervigilium* [23]. "flickered against the ceiling · · · the sparrows in the gutters", *Preludes* III 6–9.

35–38 **the gutter · · · the child:** "children's voices · · · Delve in the gutter", *First Caprice in North Cambridge* 4–9.

38 **hand · · · automatic:** see note to *The Waste Land* [III] 255, "She smoothes her hair with automatic hand".

38–39, 41, 45 **hand of the child, automatic | Slipped out and pocketed a toy · · · street · · · Gripped:** Baudelaire recommends carrying a stock of penny toys when going for a stroll: "you must give your gifts to the unknown children and to the poor people whom you meet on the way · · · their hands suddenly grip the gift, and they take to their heels", *Le Joujou du Pauvre* [*The Poor Boy's Toy*] (tr. Symons) (*Grover Smith 1983* 8). TSE: "Record the motions of these pavement toys", *WLComposite* 344. Arnold: "the humming street, and the child with its toy!" *The Forsaken Merman* 90.

39 *variant* **quai:** *Bubu de Montparnasse* has "le Quai aux Fleurs", "le Quai de l'Horloge", etc.

40 **nothing behind that child's eye:** Laforgue: "ces yeux! mais rien n'existe | Derrière!" [Your eyes · · · but what exists | Behind them? What's there?], *Pierrots*

(*Scène courte mais typique*) loosely tr. Pound, under the pseudonym John Hall, *Little Review* May 1917, the issue that printed TSE's *Eeldrop and Appleplex* I.

43–44 **a crab one afternoon in a pool, | An old crab**: Lewis Carroll: "One ancient crab, that was forever shuffling frantically from side to side of the pool, had particularly fascinated me", *Sylvie and Bruno* ch. VIII. TSE knew Carroll's book by 1899: see headnote to his *Fireside* verses. See note to *The Dry Salvages* I 20–1.

44–45 **An old crab ··· Gripped the end of a stick which I held him**: "a fish ··· held tight in his own fingers, | Writhing in his own clutch ··· ancient", *The Death of Saint Narcissus* 24–26.

51 **La lune ne garde aucune rancune**: [The moon never holds any grudge]. Laforgue: "—Là, voyons, mam'zell' la Lune, | Ne gardons pas ainsi rancune" ["Come now, Miss Moon, don't cherish a grudge like that"], *Complainte de cette bonne lune* [*Ballad of the Dear Old Moon*] 7–8 (*Grover Smith* 302).

54 **smooths the hair of the grass**: Whitman: "What is the grass? ··· And now it seems to me the beautiful uncut hair of graves", *Song of Myself* 99, 110. Swinburne: "soft hair of the grass", *Hertha* 9 (in *Oxf Bk of English Verse*). Pound: "very often a Romance or Latin word stands between two English words, or includes them: thus in the Pervigilium Veneris, 'nemus resolvit comam' can scarcely be translated 'the grove unbinds its hair'; yet the Latin phrase is more picturesque than 'puts forth its foliage'; as the word *coma* is used for hair, foliage, standing corn or grass, indifferently", *The Spirit of Romance* (1910) ch. 2.

55, 62–63 **memory ··· The reminiscence comes | Of sunless dry geraniums**: "Geraniums geraniums | Withered and dry | Long laid by | In the sweepings of the memory", *Easter: Sensations of April* I 9–12. See note to 12, 63 on Laforgue's geraniums.

56 **washed-out ··· face**: "face ··· washed-out", *The Little Passion: From "An Agony in the Garret" ms1* 19–21.

57–59 **Her hand twists a paper rose ··· alone**: Laforgue has his Hamlet tell Kate to wait a moment, "le temps cueillir une fleur, une simple fleur en papier" [time to gather a flower, a simple paper-flower]. Remy de Gourmont: "Rose en papier de soie, simulacre adorable des grâces incréées, rose en papier de soie, n'es-tu pas la vraie rose, fleur hypocrite, fleur du silence?" [Tissue-paper rose, adorable representation of increate graces, tissue-paper rose, are you not the true rose, the hypocritical rose, the rose of silence?], *Litanies de la rose* (1892): this prose poem appeared in *Poètes d'aujourd'hui* (see headnote to "*Poems* (1920)", 4. WHAT FRANCE MEANT TO TSE). De Gourmont again: "ce que l'on peut recomposer avec les produits de la distillation d'un style ressemble au style comme une rose en papier parfumé ressemble à la rose" [what one can reconstitute thanks to the quintessence of a style resembles a style as a perfumed paper rose resembles a rose], *Du Style ou de l'écriture* in *La Culture des idées* (1900). TSE: "picking tissue paper roses ··· alone", *Convictions* 9–10. "lilacs ··· twists one in her fingers ··· hands", *Portrait of a Lady* II 2, 3, 5.

58 **eau de Cologne**: against a suggestion that the change from the original reading "old cologne" was a compositor's error, TSE wrote: "It was the author, this time" (ts of *Beare*, U. Maryland). Two lines later: "old nocturnal smells".

61 **That cross and cross across her brain:** Byron: "that such a thought should cross | Her brain", *Don Juan* I lxxxiv.

65 **Smells of chestnuts in the streets:** "smell of heat | From the asphalt street", *Easter: Sensations of April* I 7–8.

65–66 **Smells of chestnuts in the streets | And female smells in shuttered rooms:** Charles-Louis Philippe: "des odeurs de filles publiques mêlées à des odeurs de nourriture" [streetwalkers' smells mixed with the smells of food], *Marie Donadieu* II ii (tr. eds) (*Grover Smith* 24). TSE: "so rank a feline smell | As Grishkin in a drawing-room", *Whispers of Immortality* 27–28. Corbière's story *L'Américaine* has "Ce poison, l'odeur de femme, m'emplissait les narines" [This poison, the smell of woman, filled my nostrils]; and his *Bonne Fortune et fortune* has as its epigraph "*Odor della feminita*". Charles-Louis Philippe: "Ces chambres · · · une odeur de prostitution", *Bubu de Montparnasse* ch. I. "les deux femmes et leur odeur s'étiraient, se secouaient et sautaient du lit vers midi · · · Connaissez-vous l'odeur du vice qu'une fois on respira? · · · Il y a l'atmosphère des prostituées, qui sent d'abord la liberté de vivre, puis qui descend et qui pue comme mille sexes tout un jour" [the two women in their odour, stretched, shook themselves, and towards noon, got out of bed · · · Do you know the odour of vice once it has entered the lungs? · · · There is the air of prostitution which at first smells of liberty, and which then sinks and stinks like a thousand sexes all the day], ch. VII. TSE: "Odours, confected by the cunning French, | Disguise the good old hearty female stench", *WLComposite* **268–69**. "un odeur fémelle", *Petit Epître* 8. "Elle avait une odeur fraîche qui m'était inconnue", *Dans le Restaurant* 14 *variant*. "une forte odeur de chienne", *Lune de Miel* 4. "Improper Rhymes": "I'm *Sure* that I Smell Bitches!" *America Discover'd.* "*I* Smell Whore!" (both sent to Bonamy Dobrée).

65–66 *variant* **on the streets · · · in darkened rooms:** "on the open street · · · darkened chambers", *Do I know how I feel? Do I know what I think?* 10–12. "darkened room", *Portrait of a Lady* I 4; see note.

70, 77–78 **"Four o'clock · · · sleep, prepare for life." || The last twist of the knife:** *Measure for Measure* III i, DUKE (*as Friar*): "Reason thus with life · · · Thy best of rest is sleep"; "therefore prepare yourself to death." IV ii, PROVOST: "Provide your block and your axe tomorrow at four o'clock"; "Well, go, prepare yourself." DUKE (*reading the warrant*): "Let Claudio be executed by four of the clock". See epigraph to *Gerontion*, "*an after dinner sleep*", from *Measure for Measure* III i.

74 **The little lamp spreads a ring on the stair:** "at the foot of your stair · · · ring the lamp", *The Love Song of St. Sebastian* 3–7. "a little lamp", *The Love Song of St. Sebastian* 2 *variant*.

76 **The bed is open:** an 1871 Boston advertisement for Berry's Patent Folding Spring Bed-Lounge illustrated it both "Closed" and "Open". TSE: "On the divan · · · (at night her bed)", *The Waste Land* [III] 226; see note. Vivien Eliot to Mary Hutchinson, 9 Oct [1917]: "Huxley quoted a saying of Gertler's · · · that the Mallesons might be said to keep '*open bed*'".

77–78 **life · · · last twist of the knife:** Ford: "in my fists I bear the twists of life", *'Tis Pity She's a Whore* V vi (Giovanni speaks, dagger in hand, having revealed his incest). TSE: "this revelation | Drives the knife deeper and twists it in the wound", *The Confidential Clerk* III.

Morning at the Window

Published as the last of four *Observations* in *Poetry* Sept 1916, then *1917+*.

Recorded 13 May 1947 at Harvard, as part of the Morris Gray Poetry Reading, following *Preludes*. "I'll read next a short poem belonging to the following period, written that is to say, four years later, for comparison."

Undated in Notebook. Dated "1915 ~~Oxford~~ London" by TSE in *Morley's US 1920*; Oxford, 1915 by TSE in *Hayward's 1925* and by *Poèmes*. Dated 1914, "so far as I can remember", to Norman Foerster, 15 June 1932. To Edward J. H. Greene, 30 June 1947: "*Morning at the Window* belongs with the 1915 poems. It is inferior to the earlier preludes." *Grover Smith* 30: "Inspired by the neighborhood of Russell Square, where Eliot stayed in the autumn of 1914 ··· at 28 Bedford Place". Assigned to Sept 1914 by *Rainey* 198; "1915 when Eliot was lodging in Bedford Square" by *Gardner 1969*; and "Early September? [1914]" in *Letters* Chronology (1988).

The whole poem draws upon Hawthorne's *The Blithedale Romance* ch. XVII:

> thick, foggy, stifled element of cities ··· sordid ··· loud voices ··· steps echoing on the staircase ··· feet of chambermaids scudding along the passages ··· From the street came the tumult of the pavements ··· foot-tramp ··· rattle ··· Eliot's pulpit ··· I felt a hesitation about plunging into this muddy tide ··· It suited me better to ··· hover in the air above it ··· out of the window ··· an apology for a garden ··· this area ··· high above the roof of the houses ··· the area ··· a cat ··· creeping along the low, flat roofs ··· all looked into the same area ··· housemaids ··· I cast my eyes downward to the lower regions ··· the kitchen-range ··· an Irish man-servant ··· threw away the fragments of a china dish which, unquestionably, he had just broken ··· All at once, this dove ··· launching herself in the air ··· flew upward, and vanished.

Title, 1, 3–4, 9 ***Morning at the Window* ··· rattling ··· damp souls ··· Sprouting ··· along the level of the roofs:** "morning air ··· then sprang up a little damp dead breeze | That rattled at the window ··· and along the stair", *Oh little voices of the throats of men* 38, 45–46, 48.

Title, 2–4, 7 ***at the Window* ··· trampled edges of the street ··· housemaids ··· area gates ··· the street ··· muddy skirts:** to Henry Eliot, 7 Sept [1914], also anticipating other poems in the volume: "The noise hereabouts is like hell turned upside down ··· pianos, street piano accordions, singers, hummers, whistlers ··· Ten o'clock in the evening ··· men with late editions ··· windows ··· a dreadful old woman, her skirt trailing on the street ··· windows ··· the housemaid resumes her conversation at the area gate."

Title, 2, 7, 9 ***at the Window* ··· the street ··· a passer-by ··· And vanishes:** Irving Babbitt: "The absolute in this sense is a metaphysical illusion. The attempt of the mind to set up a theory of itself is equally illusory. It is as though a man should look out of a window in order to see himself pass by in the street", *The Masters of Modern French Criticism* (1912) 195. (See note to *Preludes* III 10–11,

IV 8–9.) TSE gave Babbitt as a referee when applying in Oct 1916 to join the local lecturing staff of Cambridge University, offering courses on "*Contemporary France* ··· French and English Literature and on Philosophy".

1–9 **breakfast plates ··· area gates ··· in the air ··· vanishes:** Dickens: "'fond of spoons I find, and silver-plate in general, whenever area-gates is left open' ··· vanished long ago, and these remarks had been bestowed on empty air", *Barnaby Rudge* ch. XXXV, concluding lines.

2, 5 **And along the trampled edges of the street ··· The brown waves of fog:** "Along the city streets ··· the garrulous waves of life", *Silence* 1, 3.

2–9 **along the trampled edges of the street ··· housemaids ··· the bottom of the street ··· a passer-by with muddy skirts | An aimless smile that hovers in the air | And vanishes along the level of the roofs:** T. E. Hulme: "at the end of westward streets ··· visions, alien to long streets ··· heaven's jocund maid | flaunting a trailed red robe | along the fretted city roofs ··· a vain maid, lingering", *A City Sunset* (1909). TSE of T. E. Hulme's *The Embankment*: "in the world of 1910 or so, this and a dozen poems one might choose from the work at that time of Pound, Richard Aldington, H.D., F. S. Flint, were evidence of a radical change in the whole practice of verse", *The Last Twenty-Five Years of English Poetry* (1940). For Hulme see note to *Conversation Galante* 1–5.

3–4 **damp souls of housemaids | Sprouting:** Pound to Marianne Moore, 16 Dec 1918: "T.S.E. first had his housemaids drooping like the boas in my 'Millwins', and it was only after inquisition of this sort, that he decided, to the improvement of his line, to have them sprout." ("The mauve and greenish souls of the little Millwins | Were seen lying along the upper seats | Like so many unused boas", *Lustra* II in *Poetry* Nov 1913.) The word both in TSE's drafts and in *Poetry* was "Hanging", so Pound may be confusing this line with "Droop in a hundred A.B.C.'s", *A Cooking Egg* 33 (wr. 1917). "'That corpse ··· 'Has it begun to sprout?'" *The Waste Land* [I] 71–72. TSE to Aiken, 30 Sept [1914]: "it's interesting to cut yourself to pieces once in a while, and wait to see if the fragments will sprout." **housemaids ··· area gates:** *Courtship and Matrimony* (a volume in *The Fun Library*, ed. J. A. Hammerton, 1890) shows a housemaid at the area gate, "Engaged" (the one-word heading) in conversation with the delivery boy: "A Study from the Parlour Window: Susan taking in what she not unaptly calls the 'area-ated bread'" (TSE's title: *at the Window*). **area:** OED 2a: "An enclosed court, *spec.* a sunken court, shut off from the pavement by railings, and approached by a flight of steps, which gives access to the basement of dwelling-houses". (TSE: "the bars of the area", *Of the Awefull Battle of the Pekes and the Pollicles* 34.)

3–8 **souls ··· despondently ··· a passer-by with muddy skirts ··· in the air:** Clough: "prophet-soul ··· despair ··· soul ··· on the dusky air | His Skirts, as passed He by", *The New Sinai* 71–79. TSE's passer-by may be male. OED "skirt" 2a: "The lower part of a man's gown or robe", as in 1797: "I saw the skirts of his garments ascending up those steps". But this is "Now chiefly *Hist.* or with reference to Eastern countries", so TSE's line suggests also 1a: "The lower part of a woman's dress or gown". ("the skirts that trail along the floor", *The Love Song of J. Alfred Prufrock* 102.) **housemaids ··· at area gates ··· aimless smile ··· air:** C. S. Calverley: "None of those engaging smiles is | Unreciprocated there. || Often, ere yet thou hast hammered | Through thy four delicious airs, | Coins are flung thee by enamoured | Housemaids upon area stairs", *Lines on Hearing the Organ* 43–48.

6 **from the bottom of the street:** commonplace, but with "Twisted", perhaps Henry James: "I approached with a vain tortuosity poor Limbert's door. A smart victoria waited before it in which from the bottom of the street I saw that a lady who had apparently just issued from the house was settling herself", *The Next Time* (1895). If distinct from "end of the street" (*The "Boston Evening Transcript"* 8, *Aunt Helen* 5; likewise ends of lines), perhaps because "bottom of the" suggests the sea ("waves", 5). "Seen from the depths of a New York street", *Suite Clownesque* III 12^13. A music-hall favourite of TSE's ran: "My name is Tough | And I live in Tough Alley | And the further down you go | The tougher it gets, | And I live in the last house, | I am so tough my spit bounces!" (Valerie Eliot, *Observer* 20 Feb 1972).

8–9 **smile that hovers in the air | And vanishes:** Carroll's Cheshire Cat repeatedly vanishes from tree level, as shown in John Tenniel's two engravings in *Alice's Adventures in Wonderland* ch. VI. On Carroll and TSE, see introduction to *March Hare* 6–8. TSE: "Life evaporates into a smile", *First Debate between the Body and Soul* 44.

9 **along the level of the roofs:** "no longer aloof, | But some from the balcony, some from the roof", *Of the Awefull Battle of the Pekes and the Pollicles* 38–39. **along:** often taking an unusual turn: "Along the garden stairs", *Circe's Palace* 10; "Along the wet paths of the sea", *Goldfish* IV 10; "Flat faces of American business men lay along the tiers of chairs", *The Engine* I; "Arms that lie along a table", *The Love Song of J. Alfred Prufrock* 67; "Sitting along the bed's edge", *Preludes* III 12.

The "Boston Evening Transcript"

Published in *Poetry* Oct 1915 and *Catholic Anthology*, then *1917+*.

No recording known.

Dated Oxford, 1915 in *Poèmes*, and by TSE in both *Morley's US 1920* and *Hayward's 1925*.

In a letter to his father shortly after 31 May 1915, Pound reported "Eliot has done a few amusing poems". In a letter ascribed to Aug 1915 (and mentioning the recent appearance of the second issue of *Blast*, in July), Pound sent Harriet Monroe "the three jems of Eliot for 'September' and a fourth thing *Cousin Nancy* which may do to fill the second page." *Poetry* printed *The "Boston Evening Transcript"*, *Aunt Helen* and *Cousin Nancy* in Oct 1915. The first two were reprinted in *Catholic Anthology*.

The *Boston Evening Transcript* (1830–1941) had printed TSE's *Ode* ("For the hour that is left us Fair Harvard") on 24 June 1910, as had the *Boston Evening Herald*. Pound's *Provença* was reviewed unfavourably by the *Transcript* later that year (*Ezra Pound: The Critical Heritage* ed. Eric Homberger, 1972, 75–76). The literary editor was William

Stanley Braithwaite, who from 1905 wrote an annual survey of magazine verse, and who compiled anthologies of each year's verse, 1913–29 (*Williams* 7–8). Pound, contending that Braithwaite had neglected to appreciate his role in Robert Frost's career, wrote a letter to the paper which appeared on 14 July 1915 (misdated "August" in his *Letters*). "From the first", Harriet Monroe wrote, *Poetry* took exception to Braithwaite's "autocratic tone and criticized his somewhat provincial opinions", which had assumed "an authority quite out of proportion to their value" (*Sir Oracle* in *Poetry* Jan 1917). Yet the "Bawston Transcript", as Pound referred to it (to John Quinn, 8 Apr 1916), was too influential to ignore, and a copy of *Catholic Anthology* was sent for review (Elkin Mathews to Pound, 21 Feb 1916, printed in *Letters of Ezra Pound to Alice Corbin Henderson*). Braithwaite's review, *The Creed of a New Poetic Catholicism*, appeared on 18 Mar. Then, on 28 Oct 1916, Braithwaite's annual poetry round-up claimed that Pound's "collected poems" had "so little interested the American public that they find it difficult to find an American publisher". A hostile review of TSE's *US 1920* by Braithwaite followed on 14 Apr 1920. The jacket of the American edition of *Murder in the Cathedral* carried a quotation from the *Boston Evening Transcript*: "The author makes himself much clearer in this work than he has in the past" (*Kenner* 68). For other newspapers, see *Airs of Palestine, No. 2* and *Le Directeur.*

TSE: "It is true that the common newspaper reader no longer consciously asks his paper to provide his opinions for him; but that would be a superior state of consciousness to what actually exists. What the reader allows his paper to do for him is to select what is important and to suppress what is unimportant, to divert his mind with shallow discussions of serious topics, to destroy his wits with murders and weddings and curates' confessions, and to reduce him to a condition in which he is less capable of voting with any discrimination at the smallest municipal election, than if he could neither read nor write", *A Commentary* in *Criterion* Jan 1930. "the inarticulate folk is almost always mumbling the speech, become jargon, of its ancestors or of its newspaper editors", *The Varieties of Metaphysical Poetry* 289 (Turnbull Lecture III). "To be filled with a litter of Sunday newspapers?" *Choruses from "The Rock"* III 19. On the readers of a daily or Sunday newspaper: "It helps, surely, to affirm them as a complacent, prejudiced and unthinking mass, suggestible to head-lines and photographs, ready to be inflamed to enthusiasm or soothed to passivity, perhaps more easily bamboozled than any previous generation upon earth", *A Commentary* in *Criterion* July 1938. "Pastimes and drugs, and features of the press", *The Dry Salvages* V 12. "Not the expression of collective emotion | Imperfectly reflected in the daily papers", *A Note on War Poetry.* To Hayward, 19 June 1940: "I never see a news sheet or hear the news in the morning: that is a point of principle with me, a punctilio." See *Ricks* 270–73.

2 **like a field of ripe corn:** Shelley: "The ripe corn under the undulating air | Undulates like an ocean", *Letter to Maria Gisborne* 119–20. Dante Gabriel Rossetti: "hair that lay along her back | Was yellow like ripe corn", *The Blessed Damozel* 11–12 (see note to *La Figlia Che Piange* 1).

7 **La Rochefoucauld:** François, Duc de La Rochefoucauld (1613–80). *TSE's books: Bodleian list* (1934) includes the *Maximes*. TSE used the single-word "Rochefoucauld" here prior to *1963* (see Textual History), as in other early writings: "Rochefoucauld is hard, but there is not in him even the germ of cynicism: he is an implacable moralist. With the rest of the seventeenth

century, he persists in measuring men by an invisible standard, fundamentally a Christian standard", *Marivaux* (1919); also *The Perfect Critic* II (1920). He used the correct form, "La Rochefoucauld", in *The "Pensées" of Pascal* (1931) and *The Use of Poetry and the Use of Criticism* (1933), and in 1964 inserted "La" in this line in his copy of *G. Jones* (149). To Theodore Spencer, 10 Nov 1936, on John Hayward: "John H. is as usual in the vortex of society and having Musical Evenings, and last week he asked me in to meet the Duchesse de La Rochefoucauld. It would not surprise me to meet Madame de Guermantes there." (For Proust, see next note.)

7–8 **as one would turn to nod good-bye to La Rochefoucauld, | If the street were time and he at the end of the street:** Irving Babbitt, quoting Sainte-Beuve: "'If you live in a subject a short time,' he says, 'you are, as it were, in a city filled with friends. You can scarcely take a step in the main street without being instantly accosted'"; "This theory of the essential vice ··· Sainte-Beuve probably took from La Rochefoucauld", *The Masters of Modern French Criticism* (1912) 153, 156. Sainte-Beuve's own essay on La Rochefoucauld is repeatedly quoted in Babbitt's pages ("his cult for La Rochefoucauld", 110). Virginia Woolf recorded in her *Diary* for 15 Nov 1918 that Desmond MacCarthy asked TSE "how on earth he came to add that remark at the end of a poem on his Aunt & the Boston Evening Transcript, that phrase about an infinitely long street, & 'I like La Rochefoucauld saying good bye' (or words to that effect). Eliot replied that they were a recollection of Dante's Purgatorio!" Perhaps Virgil's taking leave of Dante (*Purg.* XXVII 124–42) or Virgil's final departure, when Dante turns to Beatrice (*Purg.* XXX 43–45). Maxim 104: "There is a particular point at which men and things are in proper perspective: some must be seen close up to be well judged, but others can never be so well appreciated as from a distance" (tr. Leonard Tancock). Proust, *À la recherche du temps perdu: Du côté de chez Swann* (1913): "l'air de vous apercevoir comme au bout d'une route interminable et à une si grande distance qu'elles se contentent de vous adresser un signe de tête minuscule pour le proportionner à vos dimensions de marionnette" [seem to have caught sight of you at the far end of an interminably straight road, and at so great a distance that they content themselves with directing towards you an almost imperceptible movement of the head, in proportion to your doll-like proportions], Scott Moncrieff tr. i 162 (*Hands*). Without naming the questioner, William Empson recorded that in an after-breakfast session during TSE's Clark Lectures, Hayward asked what TSE thought of Proust. "'I have not read Proust' was the deliberate reply." Yet when asked about the Scott Moncrieff translation the following week, TSE "delivered a very weighty, and rather long, tribute to that work" (*March & Tambimuttu eds.* 36–37). *The Death of Albertine*, an extract from *À la recherche du temps perdu: Albertine disparue*, appeared in *Criterion* July 1924. TSE to William Matchett, 19 Jan 1949: "I am almost completely ignorant of the work of Marcel Proust with the exception of a few essays. Of course I have dipped into his first volume but never more than enough merely to get the movement of his prose style."

9 **Cousin:** see note on the title *Cousin Nancy*. **Harriet:** perhaps owing something to Shelley (see note to 2) and newspaper scandal: E. A. Freeman, during Oxford's debates on the place of English studies: "A saying which fell from myself in one of the debates ··· has been quoted ··· 'chatter about Shelley'

··· I mentioned that I had lately read a review of a book about Shelley in which the critic ··· praised or blamed the author ··· for his 'treatment of the Harriet problem'" (1887); *Oxford Dictionary of Quotations* notes: "often telescoped as "chatter about Harriet". (After an entanglement with his cousin, Harriet Grove, Shelley eloped with 16-year-old Harriet Westbrook.)

Aunt Helen

Published in *Poetry* Oct 1915, then *Catholic Anthology*, then *1917+*.

No recording known.

Dated Oxford, 1915 in *Poèmes* and *Isaacs's US 1920*, and by TSE in *Morley's US 1920* and *Hayward's 1925*.

A female relation, house and street, servants, ceremonious funeral and dead pet bird, all feature in an untitled prose sketch by TSE of *c.* 1924 (ms, U. Maryland):

> There was once a young girl who was very poor but she was very beautiful. ~~A young man who was very rich~~ She had a passion for everything yellow. She had everything in their house yellow. A young man who was very rich and ~~very~~ titled came and married her and took her away and they lived in a great house and the world was at their feet. They had a wonderful wedding and the carriages were decorated with red and yellow roses.
>
> A year later ~~they~~ another carriage came through the streets, but this was draped in black and had black roses. They were both dead.
>
> And several years later a great carriage was often seen, with coachman and footmen, driving from the great house to the humble house where the young girl had lived. In it was a little pale shrivelled twisted boy, very delicate & fragile, going to see his grandmother. The coachman was sorrier for him than anyone. He used to visit his grandmother. She thought he came because he loved her. But once he said at last "Grannie, you know I LOVE everything yellow." He looked at the stuffed canary.

1 **Slingsby**: one of the "four little people" in Edward Lear, *The Story of the Four Little Children Who Went round the World* (*Grover Smith* 31). TSE to his sister Marion, 18 Dec 1948, recounting the celebrations at the Nobel Prize ceremony: "I explained to Professor Tiselius the importance of Edward Lear and promised to send him Lear's Complete Poetical works".

2–10 **house ··· servants ··· there was silence | And silence ··· clock**: Revelation 8: 1: "there was silence in heaven about the space of half an hour" (*Moody* 57). Job 4: 16–19: "there was silence ··· he put no trust in his servants ··· houses of clay."

6 **wiped his feet**: Pound to Harriet Monroe, 30 Sept 1914, on first impressions of TSE: "such a comfort to meet a man and not have to tell him to wash his face, wipe his feet, and remember the date (1914) on the calender."

10 **Dresden clock**: rococco porcelain from the Meissen factory, where 18th-century taste continued to be imitated. C. H. Ross and A. Clarke: "Mademoiselle Coraline took possession of a Dresden clock 'as a souvenir of madame;' and then ··· practical steps were taken by sending for a doctor, a lawyer, and an

undertaker", *Little France: A London Story* ch. II, printed in *Under the Crown* Jan–June 1869 (TSE: "undertaker", 6).

11–12 **the footman ··· Holding the second housemaid on his knees:** "young Bistwick, who three months ago married his mother's housemaid and now is aware of the fact", *Eeldrop and Appleplex* I (1917). Aunts and servants are prominent in Jerome K. Jerome's *Fanny and the Servant Problem*: "His lordship, I take it, would hardly welcome the discovery that he had married his butler's niece" (act I). TSE to Leonard Lyons of a performance at Harvard: "In the play in which e. e. cummings was the second footman, I played a charming young man, of the peerage. I was merely Lord Bantock, and a Jerome K. Jerome peer at that", *Lyons Den* in *San Mateo Times* 7 June 1969.

Cousin Nancy

Published in *Poetry* Oct 1915; then (within an editorial disparaging *vers libre*) *New York Times Book Review* 17 Oct 1915; then *1917+*.

No recording known.

Dated Oxford, 1915 by TSE in both *Morley's 1920* and *Hayward's 1925*, and dated "??Oxford, 1915" in *Isaacs's US 1920*. See note to 12. For Pound's reference in a letter ascribed to Aug 1915 to "a fourth thing *Cousin Nancy*", apparently newly composed, see headnote to *The "Boston Evening Transcript".*

Where Greene compares Tailhade's sonnet "Les femmes laides qui déchiffrent des sonates", TSE wrote "Good" on Greene's typescript. TSE's copy of Tailhade was printed in 1915 (see note to *Afternoon* 1–2). TSE included him among "a number of admirable poets much of whose work has permanent value", *Contemporary French Poetry* (1952); see headnote to "*Poems* (1920)", 4. WHAT FRANCE MEANT TO TSE.

One of the earliest reviews of TSE's verse commented on this poem's "dull data concerning one Miss Nancy Ellicott", and accused *Poetry* of publishing "Imagism and plagiarism": "The old-fashioned reader to whom poetry is something more than capitalized lines of irregular length, if he finds sufficient entertainment in following this society item to the end, will be struck at once by the closing line,—a phrase whose genuine poetic quality stands out in vivid contrast with the prose wish-wash that precedes it. 'The army of unalterable law,'—there is a familiar ring to that; and the old-fashioned reader will probably not be long in identifying it as the closing line, also, of Meredith's fine sonnet, *Lucifer in Starlight*. It would be edifying to have Meredith's own comment on this incident, and his opinion of the company into which his fastidious muse had been forcibly introduced", unsigned *Casual Comment* in *Dial* 25 Nov 1915. (Meredith had died in 1909.) The poet Arthur Davison Ficke wrote to the editor: "Plagiarism is the corrupt attempt to pass off as one's own the work of another writer; there is no possible relation between it and Mr. Eliot's employment of a great and world-famous phrase in a position where the reader's recognition of it *as* a quotation is precisely the effect aimed at", *Dial* 9 Dec 1915. An editor's note was appended, stating that "quotations must be enclosed in quotation marks or otherwise plainly acknowledged", and that the phrase could not be regarded as common currency because not included in *Bartlett's Dictionary of Quotations* (although Meredith's poem was in *Oxf Bk of English Verse*). In his essays, it was characteristic of TSE not to attribute quotations. To William Jeffrey, 7 May 1937, on classical references: "The trouble with these is that when they are well known, like most of yours, they appear trite and hackneyed, and when they are fresh they are obscure."

Clive Bell noted TSE's "disconcerting habit of omitting inverted commas ··· The other day a rather intemperate admirer quoted at me the line, 'The army of unalterable law,' and declared that no modern could match it. You know it is by Meredith", *Nation & Athenæum* 22 Sept 1923. TSE: "In one of my early poems I used, without quotation marks, the line 'the army of unalterable law . . .' from a poem by George Meredith, and this critic accused me of having shamelessly plagiarised, pinched, pilfered, that line. Whereas, of course, the whole point was that the reader should recognise where it came from and contrast it with the spirit and meaning of my own poem", *Talking Freely*, interview (1961). "our education indeed is so chaotic that no two persons in the same company can be assumed to have their minds stocked with the same furniture; you cannot make a quotation or an allusion to which the whole of any company can respond", *Views and Reviews* in *NEW* 20 June 1935. For failure to appreciate allusiveness in TSE, see headnote to *Macavity: The Mystery Cat*. For the distinction between borrowings that are and are not allusive, see letter to Warner Allen in note to *Ash-Wednesday* I 1. TSE quoted Meredith again, within quotation marks, in *A Valedictory Forbidding Mourning: to the Lady of the House* (see note to 45; also notes to *Goldfish* III 7, *Entretien dans un parc* 34 and *WLComposite* 50–51).

In Baker's *The Development of Shakespeare as a Dramatist* (1907), the observation that in the 1590s "what was re-presented, if skilfully done, was as good as new" (12–13) is scored in TSE's copy. TSE: "One of the surest of tests is the way in which a poet borrows. Immature poets imitate; mature poets steal; bad poets deface what they take, and good poets make it into something better, or at least something different. The good poet welds his theft into a whole of feeling which is unique, utterly different from that from which it was torn; the bad poet throws it into something which has no cohesion. A good poet will usually borrow from authors remote in time, or alien in language, or diverse in interest", *Philip Massinger* (1920).

To Robert Gathorne-Hardy, 12 Dec 1929: "'Veteris vestigia flammae' is the same, and yet utterly different from the segni etc.—partly the difference between veteris and antica: the context does it for both Dante and Virgil, and they both emerge triumphant from the borrowing. The moral seems to be that one test of a man's originality is the success of his borrowing; for to borrow a phrase and make a right use of it in a context utterly different from the original, is as original as originality." (Dante's words to Virgil "conosco i segni dell' antica fiamma" [I recognise the tokens of the ancient flame], *Purg.* XXX 48, recall *Aeneid* IV 23, "agnosco veteris vestigia flammae" [I recognise the traces of the olden flame]. See note in *Letters 4*.) TSE in his Preface to *A Choice of Kipling's Verse*: "There were, however, literary influences in the background." TSE included Kipling's *When 'Omer Smote 'Is Blooming Lyre*:

When 'Omer smote 'is bloomin' lyre,
He'd 'eard men sing by land an' sea;
An' what 'e thought 'e might require,
'E went an' took—the same as me!

For TSE's hesitation over attributing a phrase from Vaughan, see Textual History, *Mr. Eliot's Sunday Morning Service* 24.

TSE to L. W. Payne, 7 Nov 1927, concerning Payne's *Selections from Later American Writers* (1927): "I must express a slight regret that you have thought fit to select as representative of my work a rather insignificant poem like *Cousin Nancy*. In this connection I can correct you on one point. The niece was not called 'Cousin Nancy' by her aunts; indeed in New England it is uncommon for an aunt to address a niece as 'Cousin'. My reference was to the extensive consanguinity in New England where everybody, if not nearly related, is at least a cousin of everybody else. 'Cousin Nancy' is therefore an imaginary cousin of the author of the lines; but I must add emphatically that you must understand that the lady in the verses is an entirely imaginary character and in no way a portrait of any of my female relations."

1 **Ellicott**: "Hawthorne had even the minor token of literary genius, the genius for titles, as *Endicott and the Red Cross*", *American Literature* (1919). After reading a proof of Herbert Read's *Selected Writings*, TSE wrote to him on 1 Aug 1963, pointing out the error "Cousin Nancy Ellicot" in the Foreword by Allen Tate: "The only thing wrong that I can find is that Ellicott is spelt with only one t (the name is a conflation of Eliot and Endicott)." On forms of TSE's own name see headnotes to *Prufrock and Other Observations* and *The Marching Song of the Pollicle Dogs*.

2 **Strode across the hills**: W. G. Tinckom-Fernandez: "Across the hills I see her stride with offerings in her hand", *Song of the Sap* 8 in *The Argonaut* 11 June 1910. TSE described Tinckom-Fernandez as "a crony of mine", *Paris Review* (1959).

2–3 **Strode across the hills and broke them, | Rode across the hills and broke them**: Kipling: "You've done something that Kings and Knights and Scholars in old days would have given their crowns and spurs and books to find out ··· You've broken the Hills—you've broken the Hills! It hasn't happened in a thousand years", *Weland's Sword* in *Puck of Pook's Hill.* OED "break" 14: "To ··· tame, train (horses or other animals, also human beings)".

5 **Riding to hounds**: on George Wyndham: "We can criticize his writings only as the expression of this peculiar English type, the aristocrat, the Imperialist, the Romantic, riding to hounds across his prose, looking with wonder upon the world as upon a fairyland", *A Romantic Aristocrat* (1919) (*Bush* 23).

8–10 **danced all the modern dances ··· modern**: to John W. Nance, 19 Dec 1929: "I must record my disgust with the foul word *modernist.* It is, unhappily, necessary in theology; but it could easily be avoided in poetry. It implies a desire to be 'modern'; and no poet should care whether his work is 'modern' or not."

10, 12 **But they knew that it was modern ··· Matthew and Waldo**: although dead since 1888 and 1882 respectively, Arnold and Emerson had been listed as "Modern Writers" (as opposed to "Standard English Classics"), as recently as an advertisement for the Eversley Series from Macmillan, *Athenæum* 30 Aug 1913.

11 **glazen shelves kept watch**: OED "glassen, glazen": "*Obs.* exc. *dial.* and *arch.* 1. Made of glass ··· 2. Resembling glass. Of eyes: Glassy, glazed", with 1605 Jonson: "Old glazen-eyes", *Volpone* V i (Mermaid ed.; commonly V iii), wearing glasses to read.

11–12 **kept watch ··· guardians of the faith**: Carlyle on Novalis: "observe how these

Common-sense Philosophers, men who brag chiefly of their irrefragable logic, and keep watch and ward ··· against 'Mysticism' and 'Visionary Theories,' are themselves obliged to base their whole system on ··· Faith", *Novalis* (1829).

12 **Matthew and Waldo, guardians of the faith**: TSE: "Arnold's prose writings fall into two parts ··· and the books about Christianity seem only to say again and again ··· that the Christian faith is of course impossible to the man of culture", *Arnold and Pater* (1930). To A. L. Rowse, 18 Apr 1931: "I have the greatest respect for *Culture and Anarchy*—at one time I could almost repeat passages by heart; but the weakness of his political or rather social views, I have come to believe, is due to the flimsiness of his religious views." (In another letter to Rowse, 17 Mar 1945, TSE wrote of "Matthew", to distinguish him from his father, Dr. Thomas Arnold.) To John Hayward, 29 May 1943: "In my youth I was a fervent admirer of *Culture and Anarchy*, and latterly I have come to regard Matt as one of the Enemies: there is a smug superiority in all he writes which marks him as a plebeian." For Arnold, religion and poetry, see note to *Whispers of Immortality* 10–12. "When Emerson as a young man stood in his pulpit and made clear to his congregation that he could no longer administer the Communion, he impressed upon them that he had no prejudice and passed no judgment upon those who continued in the practice, but that he could take no part himself—because (in his own words) it did not interest him. That is an instance of the point of view of several thousands of well-bred people in a provincial American town", *A Sceptical Patrician* (1919). For TSE on Emerson (who was known as Waldo rather than Ralph), see note to *Sweeney Erect* 25–26. "there is a 'something' there, a dignity, about Emerson ··· which persists after we have perceived the taint of commonness about some English contemporary, as for instance, the more intelligent, better educated, more alert Matthew Arnold", *The Hawthorne Aspect* (1918). The Harvard course on Florentine painting taken by TSE in 1910 was given by Emerson's grandson, Edward Waldo Forbes. **Matthew and Waldo**: Edgar Lee Masters: "friend of the great, and lover of letters, | And host to Matthew Arnold and to Emerson", *John Horace Burleson* in *Spoon River Anthology*. Masters's volume was in Pound's hands by 16 May 1915, when he wrote to his father: "Be sure and get Edgar Masters' *Spoon River Anthology*, it is the best home grown product America has seen for SOME time." TSE probably read the book shortly afterwards, and he mentioned it in *Mr. Lee Masters* (1916).

13 **The army of unalterable law**: Meredith, *Lucifer in Starlight*, concluding the sonnet:

> With memory of the old revolt from Awe,
> He reached a middle height, and at the stars,
> Which are the brain of heaven, he looked, and sank.
> Around the ancient track marched, rank on rank,
> The army of unalterable law.

For the controversy over TSE's appropriation, and for Meredith, see headnote. Temple Classics Dante: "'Wherewithal a man sinneth, by the same shall he be punished' ··· is the unalterable law which Dante sees written", *Inf.* XXXIII, Argument. TSE: "whether in Argos or England | There are certain inflexible laws | Unalterable", *The Family Reunion* II i chorus.

Mr. Apollinax

Published as the third of four *Observations* in *Poetry* Sept 1916, then *1917+*.

No recording known.

Undated in drafts. Dated Oxford, 1915 by TSE in *Hayward's 1925*; and in *Poèmes* and *Isaacs's US 1920*. Dated "1915 S.S. St. Paul" by TSE in *Morley's US 1920*. TSE to Edward J. H. Greene, 18 Oct 1939: "*Mr Apollinax* is late 1915." *Gordon 1974* claimed the poem must have been written by Jan 1915, but see headnote to *The Death of Saint Narcissus*. Assigned to Apr 1915 by *Rainey* 198.

Following his sudden marriage to Vivien Haigh-Wood on 26 June 1915, TSE wrote to his father on 23 July, "the night before I sail". To Conrad Aiken, 5 Aug, from Gloucester, Massachusetts: "I hear you have plunged into the *Atlantic*" (by publishing a poem in *Atlantic Monthly*). To Scofield Thayer, 4 Sept: "I have just returned to England ··· My address (anyhow till Christmas) will be care of Bertie Russell, 34 Russell Chambers, Bury Street, W.C. He is lending us his flat for a time." Vivien had declined to accompany TSE to the US, for fear of submarines (Russell, *Autobiography* II 54). The *Lusitania* had been sunk by a German submarine in May, and the danger continued throughout the war. TSE to his father, 14 Jan 1916: "There are some signs of war even in this remote western country—a torpedo boat from time to time, and a naval officer at the hotel who goes out in a motor boat, looking for submarines." TSE's mother to Bertrand Russell, 23 May 1916, eight weeks after a cross-Channel steamer was torpedoed: "It was natural you should feel as you did with the awful tragedy of the *Sussex* ··· I am sure your influence in every way will confirm my son in his choice of Philosophy as a life work ··· I have absolute faith in his Philosophy but not in the *vers libres*. Tom is very grateful to you for your sympathy and kindness." TSE to J. H. Woods, 23 Mar 1917, concerning his doctoral dissertation: "I do not quite like to trust the fruit of so much labour to the submarines in the Channel, but perhaps I can offer it as an inducement to you to come and fetch it, until I can transcribe it." To his father, 13 June 1917: "I like to think of you at Gloucester soon. The submarines won't go there!" The only typescript of Pound's *Arnaut* was sent in January 1918 to a printer in Ohio but never arrived and was presumed "submarined" (*Pound 2010* 411–12).

TSE's dating note in *Morley's US 1920* suggests that he wrote this poem aboard the SS *St. Paul*. His crossings in 1915 were, however, on the USMS *St. Louis* (Liverpool to NY, 24 July–1 Aug) and on the *New York* (NY to Liverpool, arr. 29 Aug). The *St. Paul* plied the same route for the US Shipping Board in 1917–18, but capsized in the North River, NY, in Apr 1918. On his outward voyage TSE drafted *The Engine* (see headnote), which he did not publish (although another prose poem of 1915, *Hysteria*, has followed *Mr. Apollinax* since *1917*). A further crossing, to complete his doctorate at Harvard, was booked for 1 Apr 1916 but cancelled at the last minute (*Reid* 253). His next crossing was not until his visit to Harvard for nine months in 1932–33. To John Hayward, [29 Sept] 1932, thanking him for a telegram found aboard: "it was the only missive of the sort which I received, and helped to raise my already sinking spirits".

Vivien Eliot died in January 1947, and later that year TSE made a trip to the US during which his brother Henry also died. A letter to Frank Morley, 5 July 1947, recalls TSE's state of mind at the time of his marriage and of *Mr. Apollinax*: "It has all been very strange. I don't think that I have been through such a bad patch since 1915."

In 1967 Russell recalled his year as a professor of philosophy at Harvard: "I had a post-graduate class of twelve, who used to come to tea with me once a week. One of them was T. S. Eliot, who subsequently wrote a poem about it, called *Mr Appolinax*" (*Autobiography* I 212). Russell to Ottoline Morrell, 27 Mar 1914, about TSE and another Harvard pupil: "I found they were not nearly so well grounded as I had thought. They were absolutely candid and quite intelligent, but obviously had not been taught with the minute thoroughness that we practise in England".

In May 1914 Russell described to Morrell a visit to the Massachusetts house of Prof. B. A. G. Fuller, author of *The Problem of Evil in Plotinus*: "I have been spending the week-end in the country at the house of Fuller (of Plotinus). It was beautiful there, weather like mid-summer and the trees like early spring. He has a lake and woods and various agreeable things and by all the rules he ought to be agreeable himself, being good-natured and cultivated, but for some reason I am always saying to myself, 'After all, you are an ass' ··· My pupil Eliot was there—the only one who is civilized, and he is ultra-civilized, knows his classics very well, is familiar with all French literature from Villon to Vildrach, and is altogether impeccable in his taste but has no vigour or life—or enthusiasm. He is going to Oxford where I expect he will be very happy" (*Morrell 1963* 257, with her comment: "I imagine it was during this week-end visit or in consequence of it that T. S. Eliot wrote *Mr. Apollinax*"). Charles Vildrac's prose poems, *Découvertes* [*Discoveries*] had appeared in 1912 and TSE mentioned him among the "more important men" in a letter to Aiken, 14 Feb 1920; see *March Hare* 297. For Russell, Villon and Morrell, see headnote to *A Cooking Egg*. TSE's *Before Morning* had been criticised by Fuller in the *Harvard Crimson*, 20 Nov 1908. Presumably TSE gave Fuller an introduction to the *pension* near the Sorbonne where he had stayed, for Jean Verdenal reported on 22 Apr 1912 that Fuller was there. For Fuller's book on Plotinus, see notes to *A Cooking Egg* 24 and *Mr. Eliot's Sunday Morning Service* 6.

TSE took notes on Russell's courses in Advanced Logic and Theory of Knowledge (Houghton). Russell's *Mysticism and Logic, and other Essays* occasioned TSE's only review for the *Nation* before it merged with the *Athenæum*: "literary standards help us to perceive just those moments when a writer is scrupulously and sincerely attending to his vision; help us to dissociate the social and the histrionic from the unique", *Style and Thought* (1918).

Herbert Read, in notes for what became his essay *The Nature of Metaphysical Poetry* (*Criterion* Apr 1923): "A particular sphere for which a sustained metaphysical poetry is appropriate: the summary of the discrete phenomena of science and assimilation of them into an emotional unity." Below this TSE wrote: "Philosophical poetry can be digestion of one or more sciences, but of all? Some philosophies in themselves incoherent & emotional (e.g. B. Russell) and therefore useless for poetry. Bradley more useful than Russell. Influence e.g. Frazer, Fabré, Freud, Einstein, Poincaré" (Herbert Read papers, U. Victoria).

Russell had become an opponent of Bradley ("For some years I was a disciple of Mr. Bradley, but about 1898 I changed my views", *Logical Atomism*, 1924). Bradley: "No abstraction ··· is in the end defensible ··· the amount of possible error must remain unknown ··· The truth asserted is not, and cannot be, taken as real by itself", *Appearance and Reality* ch. XXVII; alongside this TSE wrote: "This does for Mr. Russell." Even readers beyond this circle soon identified Russell with the poem; Louis Untermeyer, for instance, wrote in *Freeman* 30 June 1920 that Mr. Apollinax "sounds suspiciously like Bertrand Russell".

TSE's friendship with Russell ended in the 1920s (he wrote to Henry Treece, 8 Feb 1946, "I have not been in touch with Bertrand Russell for something over twenty years"). To Ottoline Morrell, from Harvard, 14 Mar 1933: "Bertie, because at first I admired him so much, is one of my lost illusions. He has done Evil, without being big enough or conscious enough to Be evil. I owe him this, that the spectacle of Bertie was one contributing influence to my conversion. Of course he had no good influence on Vivienne. He excited her mentally, made her read books and become a kind of pacifist, and no doubt was flattered because he thought he was influencing her. (I have tried to subdue the desire to influence anyone). Unfortunately, she found him unattractive."

Organised pacifism in Britain began when Fenner Brockway, editor of the *Labour Leader*, published an appeal on 12 Nov 1914 asking men of military age to join him in forming the No-Conscription Fellowship. Russell was among the most famous, writing *The Ethics of War* (*International Journal of Ethics* Jan 1915), *War and Non-Resistance* (*Atlantic Monthly* Aug 1915) and many other papers and letters to editors. He was fined, deprived of his Cambridge lectureship and prevented by the confiscation of his passport from taking up a post at Harvard. For the "Order of the White Feather", see note to *Gerontion* 71.

Title **Apollinax**: *Apollonis arx*, a place at the entrance of the Sibyl's cave where the Sibyl left her prophecies, written on leaves (*Aeneid* VI 9). *Arx* = stronghold. TSE's original spelling of the name, used twice in *ms1*, was "Apollonax" (see Textual History). *Grover Smith* 303: "Eliot's title may have originated in Ford Madox Hueffer's *Mr. Apollo* (London, 1908), with some admixture with the name of M. Aronnax in Jules Verne's *Twenty Thousand Leagues under the Sea.*" On a secretarial letter to Floyd Watkins, 9 Apr 1963, TSE wrote: "Say I have never read Jules Verne's romance".

Gautier's *Apollonie* invokes the Pythia, the sibyl at Delphi who was priestess of Apollo:

J'aime ton nom d'Apollonie,
Echo grec du sacré vallon,
Qui, dans sa robuste harmonie,
Te baptise sœur d'Apollon.

Sur la lyre au plectre d'ivoire,
Ce nom splendide et souverain,
Beau comme l'amour et la gloire,
Prend des résonances d'airain.

Classique, il fait plonger les Elfes
Au fond de leur lac allemand,
Et seule la Pythie à Delphes
Pourrait le porter dignement,

Quand relevant sa robe antique
Elle s'assoit au trépied d'or,

> Et dans sa pose fatidique
> Attend le dieu qui tarde encor.

> [I love your name of Apollonie, a Greek echo from the sacred vale, which in its strong harmony baptizes you the sister of Apollo. To the lyre with its ivory plectrum, this splendid sovereign name, beautiful as love and glory, takes on the resonance of brass. Classical, it makes the Elves dive to the bottom of their German lake, and the Pythian sibyl at Delphi alone could bear the name with dignity, when exalting her ancient robe, she takes her seat on the golden tripod and in her fateful pose awaits the god who still delays.]

OED "Apollonian" 1: "Pertaining to, resembling or having the characteristics of Apollo, the sun-god of the Greeks and Romans, the patron of music and poetry." 2: "Of Apollonius of Perga, a famous Greek geometer and investigator of conic sections." Bertrand Russell had published his *Principles of Mathematics* in 1903. The three volumes of *Principia Mathematica*, written with Alfred North Whitehead, followed in 1910, 1912 and 1913; TSE owned the first volume. Both Apollo and Apollonius were bringers of light (for dualities of name, see note to *The Love Song of J. Alfred Prufrock* 94, "Lazarus"). OED "Apollonian" B: "having the characteristics of Apollo (opp. Dionysian)." Nietzsche: "We shall have gained much for the science of aesthetics, when once we have perceived ··· that the continuous development of art is bound up with the duplexity of the *Apollonian* and the *Dionysian* : in like manner as procreation is dependent on the duality of the sexes", opening words of *The Birth of Tragedy.*

Epigraph] Not printed until *AraVP*, then not again until *1932*. The attribution to Lucian was not added until *1936*, although TSE added it by hand in *Thayer's AraVP*. **Ω τῆς καινότητος. Ἡράκλεις, τῆς παραδοξολογίας. εὐμήχανος ἄνθρωπος**: [What novelty! What marvellous paradoxes! How inventive he is!], Lucian, *Zeuxis or Antiochus* (Loeb VI, tr. K. Kilburn, 1959). The Greek is quoted in a footnote to Charles Whibley's *Lucian* II in *Studies in Frankness* (1896) 217, with the comment "The shouts of the people were as fatuous then as to-day" (*Worthington* 4). On the letter to Floyd Watkins (see note to title), TSE wrote that he "had read in Greek a small selection of Lucian's work, from which I took the epigraph". The phrases are those of Lucian's audience, admiring a lecture of his for its "freshness of thought". Finding that "this praise caused me considerable annoyance", he reflects that he was not commended for "good vocabulary, conformity to the ancient canon, penetration of intellect, power of perception, Attic grace ··· their approval is little different from that which they would give a conjuror." He compares the acclamation with that afforded to the painter Zeuxis for a picture of a mother Centaur nursing infant Centaur twins: "The Centaur herself is depicted lying on fresh young grass with all the horse part of her on the ground ··· The human part is slightly raised up on her elbows ··· Towards the top of the picture ··· is a Hippocentaur, clearly the husband of her who is feeding her children ··· He is leaning down and laughing ··· and his glance, although he is laughing, is altogether savage, wild, and of the hills." John Hayward wrote in *Hayward's 1936 proof*: "'What a ~~wonder~~ novelty! O Hercules, what a wonder! Man is a crafty creature of many wiles'". TSE in *Second Thoughts about Humanism* (1929): "the teaching of Plato and Aristotle to youths who know no Greek, and are completely ignorant of ancient history, is one of the tragic farces of American education ··· Incidentally, it is a public misfortune that Mr. Bertrand Russell did not have a classical education." TSE, the year after writing *Mr. Apollinax*: "Dans nos lycées, dans nos universités, la déchéance de la langue grecque est un crime contre la civilisation" [The decline of Greek in our schools and in our universities is a crime against civilisation], *Autour d'une Traduction d'Euripide* (1916). To Sir Richard Livingstone, 31 Mar 1941, on being invited to become President of the Classical Association: "In my younger days I found it paid me to pretend discreetly to more learning than I possessed (so long as I could keep a line of retreat open) but when one is past middle age I think it is wiser to be honest. It is the imperfection of my own classical education that has made me such a strong defender of the classics." To Helen Gardner, 4 June 1959: "The study of Latin ··· is essential, if people are to understand and speak and write correctly the English language. Besides, some knowledge of Latin literature, if not of Greek literature, is essential for appreciation of so much in English poetry also." **[What paradoxes!]**: for the sciences in addition to the arts, see "Apollonian" in note to title; for the Dionysiac in addition to the Apollonian, see note to 6. **LUCIAN**: among the itinerant orator's best known works is *A True Story*, involving a voyage to the moon. In opening he writes: "as I had nothing to tell, not having had any adventures of significance, I took to lying ··· though I tell the truth in nothing else, I shall at least be truthful in saying that I am a liar" (Loeb I, tr. A. M. Harmon, 1913).

Epigraph, 2, 4, 7 **LUCIAN ··· laughter ··· Priapus ··· laughed**: Lucian, *Dialogues of the Gods* XXIII (discussing Eros, Hermaphroditus and Priapus), DIONYSUS: "as for Priapus ··· the other day ··· he invited me home with him and put me up for the night. Now we'd gone to sleep in his dining-room after and were pretty well soaked, when about midnight up gets our bold lad—but I'm ashamed to tell you. APOLLO: And made an attempt on you, Dionysus? DIONYSUS: Something like that. APOLLO: How did you deal with the situation? DIONYSUS: What could I do but laugh?" (Loeb VII, tr. M. D. Macleod, 1967) (Paul Hartle, personal communication).

2 *variant* **across the teacups**: "across the floors of silent seas", *The Love Song of J. Alfred Prufrock* 74 ("submarine ··· sea's ··· silence", *Mr. Apollinax* 8–11, and variant "Without sound"). "Across the floors that soak", *Interlude: in a Bar* 4. For Oliver Wendell Holmes's *Over the Teacups*, see note to *Rhapsody on a Windy Night* 5.

2–3 **tinkled among the teacups ··· that shy figure:** *Alice's Adventures in Wonderland* ch. VII:

> "*Up above the world you fly,*
> *Like a teatray in the sky.*
> *Twinkle, twinkle*——"
>
> Here the Dormouse shook itself, and began singing in its sleep "*Twinkle, twinkle, twinkle, twinkle*—" ···
>
> A bright idea came into Alice's head. "Is that the reason so many tea-things are put out here?" she asked.
>
> "Yes, that's it," said the Hatter with a sigh: "it's always tea-time."

2–5 **among the teacups ··· Fragilion ··· swing:** "among the bric-à-brac", *Portrait of a Lady* III 9. In his London *Baedeker*, TSE ticked three paragraphs of the description of the Wallace Collection, including descriptions of rooms devoted to the French 18th century, where "the sumptuous contemporary furniture and bric-à-brac are admirably in harmony with the decorative character of the paintings." He underlined the numeral in "Room XVIII", which contained "a charming series of fêtes champêtres, conversations galantes, pastoral and romantic scenes" (TSE's title: *Conversation Galante*). Room XIX contained Fragonard's *The Swing*, in which a swain points up the petticoats of the elegant lady as she throws off a shoe. The cupids of a formal garden are surrounded by dark trees in which contorted figures are suggested. Nearby were displays of Sèvres porcelain. To Eleanor Hinkley, 26 Apr [1911]: "note that I have seen / National Gallery / Brit Mus / Wallace Collection (made notes!!)" See note to 4 *variant.*

2, 4, 5, 16, 17 **laughter ··· Priapus in the shrubbery ··· the lady ··· turf ··· afternoon:** "The ladies ··· Sunday afternoon ··· fade beyond the Roman statuary ··· comedians across a lawn", *Afternoon* 1, 6–8 (for "week-end" see Russell to Ottoline Morrell in headnote above).

3 **Fragilion**: the pronunciation may be with soft or hard *g*, but "fragile" and "fragility" are the only entries beginning "fragi-" in OED. "fragile" 1b: "Of persons, etc. Of weak or tender frame or constitution, delicate", quoting Ouida, "so pretty and so fragile". 2: "Liable to err or fall into sin: frail. *Obs.*" with 1548: "Suche is the blyndnes of our fraile and fragile nature, euer giuen to carnal concupiscence."

3–4 **Fragilion ··· shy ··· Priapus**: *Megalobulimus fragilion* is a species of air-breathing land snail. OED "fragility" cites Tate on the brown snail: "The shell of this species is .. characterized by its extreme thinness and fragility", *A Plain and Easy Account of the Land and Fresh-Water Molluscks of Great Britain* (1866) 131. OED "priapus" 5: "A kind of holothurian [F. *priape de mer*]", *obs.*", a sea-slug. **shy**: Russell to Ottoline Morrell, 19 Mar 1914, of his first lecture at the Lowell Institute: "There were 500 people, I was seized with shyness." **Priapus**: *Lemprière*: "Priapus was deformed in all his limbs, particularly the genitals ··· and he received the name of Priapus, *propter deformitatem & membri virilis magnitudinem.* He soon became a favourite of the people of Lampsacus, but he was expelled by the inhabitants on account of the freedom he took with their wives. This violence was punished by the son of Venus, and when the Lympsacenians had been afflicted with a disease in the genitals, Priapus was recalled, and temples erected to his honour ··· and the people ··· gave themselves up to every lasciviousness and impurity ··· the Romans revered him more as a god of orchards and gardens than as the patron of licentiousness ··· He is generally represented with a human face and the ears of a goat ··· often represented by the epithet of *phallus*". ("His pointed ears", 19.) OED 1: "The Greek and Roman god of procreation; hence, also, of gardens, vineyards, etc. (in which his statues were placed)." **Priapus in the shrubbery**: "Pudibund, in the clinging vine", *Exequy* 15–21 *variant.*

4 *variant* **terra cotta in the shrubbery**: "the terra cotta fawns | Among the potted palms, the lawns", *Suite Clownesque* I 2–3. Among the terra cotta items in the Wallace Collection listed by *Baedeker* (282) is a "head of John the Baptist (Ital. 16th cent.)" (TSE: "I looked for the head", 13).

6 **palace of Mrs. Phlaccus**: combining "flaccid" (*Fowler*: "pronounce -ks-") with "phallus". OED "phallus" 1a: "An image of the male generative organ ··· *spec.*

that carried in · · · Dionysiac festivals". For "official disapproval" of Dionysus, see note to *The Dry Salvages* V 10. **Mrs. Phlaccus**: see note to 21. **Professor Channing-Cheetah's**: in his copy of *English Literature from the Norman Conquest to Chaucer*, TSE later wrote: "I had to use this book at Harvard when I took Professor Schofield's course in this subject, in 1907–08. (Schofield, I do not quite know why, was in my mind in inventing Professor Channing-Cheetah)". As well as attending William Henry Schofield's courses on "The Literary History of England and its relations to that of the Continent" at Harvard, TSE may have heard him lecture at the Sorbonne in 1911. In a letter received by Donald J. Childs on 4 Apr 1984, Charles Monteith recalled a conversation with TSE: "I said to him—as a piece of lunch-table conversation—that everybody knew that Mr. Apollinax was Bertrand Russell—from which he didn't dissent, but that I'd often wondered who Professor and Mrs. Channing-Cheetah were. He reflected for a moment and then said, 'They were in fact a Professor and Mrs. Schofield'" (quoted by Childs, *Journal of Modern Literature* Mar 1986). Russell: "Schofield, the professor of Fine Arts, considered Alfred Noyes a very good poet", *Autobiography* I 211.

William Ellery Channing (1780–1842) was a preacher at King's Chapel, Boston, whose "1819 sermon on 'Unitarian Christianity' gave the classic definition of the Unitarian faith in America" (*Oser* 45). His philosophy was discussed in Josiah Royce's seminar of 1913, which TSE attended (*Costello* 67–68). TSE on his mother's play: "This Savonarola is a disciple of Schleiermacher, Emerson, Channing and Herbert Spencer", *Savonarola* (1926). Edward Channing taught history at Harvard in or just before Eliot's time (*Copey* 99). On 7 May 1936 TSE sent John Hayward a press cutting, which he headed "Thought for the Day: Art in Boston", underlining the name of the artist "Mrs. Channing Frothingham" (King's).

6–7 **Channing-Cheetah's | He laughed like an irresponsible fœtus**: Tailhade: "innommables fœtus" [unnamable fœtuses], rhyming with "Rictus" [grin], *Candidats à l'immortalité*. Richard Aldington quoted from elsewhere in the poem in his introduction to Tailhade, *Egoist* 1 Oct 1915. (For Tailhade, see headnote to *Cousin Nancy* and note to *Afternoon* 1–2.) Laforgue's *Complainte du fœtus de poète* [*The Dirge of the Poet's Fœtus*] (*Mordell* 31). Against Robert L. Beare's suggestion that the omission of TSE's line in *Poetry* was editorial, TSE wrote "Yes, Harriet Monroe, I think" (ts of *Beare*). Yet the ts sent to *Poetry* shows the editors doing no more than change the spelling to "fetus", so it may have been the printers who refused to countenance the line (and possible prosecution). Pound to Harriet Monroe, 16 Sept 1916: "I have this a.m. written you what I think of the alterations in the text. The editorial office ought at least to have the courage of its own prudery. If you are going to knuckle under to the super-degenerate now reigning in the place of the dead decayed dung-minded Comstock of putrid memory, at least you ought to leave dots (in my case and Eliot's), indicating that the author has written something which the editors blush to reproduce." (Anthony Comstock had died in 1915, but his New York Society for the Suppression of Vice remained active until 1950.) For censorship in 1932, see headnote to *Animula*. **irresponsible**: OED 1: "not answerable · · · incapable of legal responsibility". TSE: "exercise of the irresponsible activity of a legal mind", *A Neglected Aspect of Chapman* (1924).

8 **His laughter was submarine and profound:** on submarines, see headnote. "Subterrene laughter", *Ode* ("Tired. | Subterrene") 2. "A breathless chuckle underground", *Exequy* 28. "under ground | Leaned backward with a lipless grin", *Whispers of Immortality* 3–4. "laughter · · · where all the waters meet", *Marina* 20–21. "Our gaze is submarine", *Choruses from "The Rock"* X 32. "a smile | Simple and profound", *First Debate between the Body and Soul* 44–45. A revision of OED after the 2nd ed. differentiates a new sense of "submarine", with this line as the first citation: "*fig.* That possesses a quality, colour, atmosphere, etc. associated with or suggestive of that found beneath the surface of the sea" (with second citation from Aldous Huxley: "With a kind of submarine laughter below the surface of his voice", *Those Barren Leaves*, 1925). **submarine and profound:** if a submarine in 1915 was deep down, it was not in attack mode (Kevin Barents, personal communication). **profound:** OED 1a: "Having great or considerable downward (or inward) measurement; of great depth", with *The Winter's Tale* IV iv: "for all the · · · profound sea hides in unknown fathoms". 1c: "deeply drawn, deep-fetched (as a sigh)". 2a: "Of a person: Characterized by intellectual depth · · · Deep or subtle in contrivance, crafty, cunning. (The earliest sense in English)" with "profound geometers" (1734) and "profoundest of metaphysicians" (1869). 3a: "Difficult to 'fathom' · · · having a meaning that does not lie on the surface". 3b: "concealed or involving concealment". B 1b: "*spec.* · · · the deep sea, 'the deep'. *poetical.*"

10–12 **under coral islands · · · drift down in the green silence · · · fingers of surf:** Rimbaud: "Dévorant les azurs verts; où, flottaison blême | Et ravie, un noyé pensif parfois descend" [Devouring the green azures; where, entranced and pallid flotsam, a dreaming drowned man sometimes goes down]; "Et je voguais, lorsqu'à travers mes liens frêles | Des noyés descendaient dormir, à reculons!" [And I was scudding along when across my frayed cordage drowned men sank backwards into sleep!], *Le Bateau ivre* [*The Drunken Boat*] 23–24, 67–68 (*Greene* 63–64; in the margin of Greene's ts, TSE wrote "Good. I was unaware of this"). **worried bodies of drowned men:** Dickens, on a visit to America, wrote to Mrs. J. T. Fields, 19 Mar 1868, describing how his train became flooded, and how he helped release "sheep that had been in the water I don't know how long · · · leaping wildly · · · over the worried body of a deceased companion".

11–15 **drowned men drift down · · · I looked for the head · · · With seaweed in its hair:** John Davidson: "About my face like seaweed droops | My tangled beard, my tangled hair", *A Loafer.* (An extract from Davidson's poem of 1894 appeared in *John Davidson: A Selection* (1961), with Preface by TSE; see note to *The Love Song of J. Alfred Prufrock* 127–31.) The submarine world is imagined with both (i) fear of death by water, heightened perhaps by TSE's own transatlantic crossing; and (ii) longing, as here, for its passivity.

(i) "the drowned Phoenician Sailor · · · Fear death by water", *The Waste Land* [I] 47–55, with its quotation from Ariel's song, *The Tempest* I ii; see notes to *Dirge*, which also influenced *The Waste Land* IV. *Death by Water*. With its mention of the Dry Salvages, *WLComposite* **490** anticipates the third Quartet. *Richard III* I iv, CLARENCE: "Methought what pain it was to drown · · · dead men's skulls, and · · · holes | Where eyes did once inhabit." See also *Lycidas* in note to *Ode to a Roman Coot* 43.

(ii) to Conrad Aiken, 25 Feb 1915: "The idea of a submarine world of clear green light—one would be attached to a rock and swayed in two directions—would one be happiest or most wretched at the turn of the tide?" TSE: "Flood tide and ebb tide | Roll him gently side to side", *Dirge* 12–13 (see note). Swinburne: "Ah God, that I were as all souls that be ··· As bones of men under the deep sharp sea", *Laus Veneris* 77–80. For William Morris's *Hylas*, "Forgetting the rough world, and every care; | Not dead, nor living, among faces fair, | White limbs, and wonders of the watery world", see note to *The Waste Land* [IV] 312. TSE: "I should have been a pair of ragged claws | Scuttling across the floors of silent seas", *The Love Song of J. Alfred Prufrock* 73–74. "Still ⁊ quiet brother are you still and quiet", *Those are pearls that were his eyes. See!* 5. "he knew that he had been a fish", *The Death of Saint Narcissus* 24. See note to *The Dry Salvages* I 20–21.

11–12, 15 **drift down ··· surf ··· seaweed in its hair**: "surf ··· Swims down and down; | And about his hair the seaweed purple and brown", *So through the evening, through the violet air* 30–32. "torn algae drift above", *Those are pearls that were his eyes. See!* 3.

12^13] at different times the poem has been a single paragraph, or else two, with the break after twelve, thirteen or fifteen lines. The present spacing dates from *1963*. See Textual History and *McCue 2012* Proposal 12.

13, 19 **I looked for the head of Mr. Apollinax rolling under a chair ··· "··· He must be unbalanced"**: *Alice's Adventures in Wonderland* ch. VII, "A Mad Tea-Party", is followed by the Queen screaming for heads to roll ("'Off with their heads!'"), by croquet with hedgehogs as balls, and by the appearance of the head of the Cheshire Cat. OED has "heads will roll" only from 1930, but Bourrienne's *Memoirs of Napoleon Bonaparte* has "'I only wait the decree ··· and soon shall their heads roll in the kennels!'" (1830, I 72). OED has from before 1845 "off one's head": "Out of mind or wits"; and from 1855 "to talk (*etc.*) a person's head off", with—apt to a philosopher—"the standing danger of having one's head talked off one's shoulders" (1897). Mark Twain: "it was enough to make a person laugh his head off", *Autobiography* (1871). TSE: "I have seen my head (grown slightly bald) brought in upon a platter", *The Love Song of J. Alfred Prufrock* 82.

16 **I heard the beat of centaurs' hoofs over the hard turf**: see centaur twins in note to epigraph. Meredith: "Hears the heart of wildness beat | Like a centaur's hoof on sward", *The Woods of Westermain* III. Although in *ms1* TSE had used the singular possessive, which returned in *US 1920* and subsequent printings, he emended it in typescript to the plural possessive, which became the reading of the first three printings. "horses' heels | Over the paving", *Coriolan* I. *Triumphal March* 1–2. Harold Joachim: "A 'significant whole' is such that all its constituent elements reciprocally involve one another ··· in this sense a Centaur is inconceivable", *The Nature of Truth* (1906) 66 (*Crawford 2015* 216).

18 **"He is a charming man"**: Jean Verdenal to TSE, 5 Feb 1912 (in *Letters 1*): "votre philosophe Fuller. C'est un homme charmant" (*Crawford 2015* 156). For "charming", see note to 2–5.

19 **His pointed ears**: see note to epigraph. Hawthorne: "The pointed and furry ears, therefore, are the sole indications of his wild, forest nature"; "how delightful, if it really includes the pointed ears!" and "if Hilda and you and I—if I, at least,—had pointed ears! For I suppose the Faun had no conscience, no remorse, no

burthen on the heart, no troublesome recollections of any sort; no dark future either", *The Marble Faun* ch. I, II. Vivien Eliot to Bertrand Russell, anticipating the birth of his son, 1 Nov 1921: "Tom says he is quite sure the baby *will* have pointed ears, so you need not be anxious. Even if not pointed at birth, they will sharpen in time." **He must be unbalanced:** TSE wrote to Eleanor Hinkley, 21 Mar 1915, that Russell had "a sensitive, but hardly a cultivated mind, and I begin to realise how unbalanced he is".

21 **dowager Mrs. Phlaccus:** below this in a copy of *1936* 13th imp. (1949), Valerie Eliot wrote "Mrs Jack Gardner", and in a footnote to TSE's letter to Mrs. Gardner, 4 Apr [1915], she records: "Isabella Stewart Gardner (1840–1924), prominent Boston hostess and art collector, who bequeathed her Venetian-style house, Fenway Court, with its contents, to the city. Her guest book records two visits by TSE in 1912, on 16 September and between 31 October and 3 November." (For "Mrs. Phlaccus", see note to 6.) The Society column of the *Pittsburgh Press* 22 Nov 1910 announced "Mrs. Flaccus Names Aids for Smart Tea: Prettily Appointed Event to Be Given Next Friday Afternoon at Her Home · · · Mrs. Charles L. Flaccus, who has cards out for a tea to be given next Friday afternoon, has chosen as her aids for the affair, Mrs. H. Fred Mercer, Mrs. Newton Chapin, Mrs. George Bliss, Mrs. Raymond D. Jenks, Miss Kathryn E. Rea and Miss Miriam and Miss Madeline Stemmeyer. The hours are from 4 to 6 o'clock, and the appointments will be handsome and artistic. There is no special guest." Russell, the grandson of a prime minister and heir to an earldom, was a catch. The full name of the Roman poet Horace was Quintus Horatius Flaccus, and the cognomen "Flaccus" was an illustrious one. **dowager:** OED a: "A woman whose husband is dead and who is in the enjoyment of some title or some property that has come to her from him. Often added to the title so enjoyed, as princess-dowager, queen-dowager, dowager-duchess, dowager-queen, dowager-lady, etc." c: "*famil.* An elderly lady of dignified demeanour." For "*Alice, Countess Dowager of Derby*", see headnote to *Burbank with a Baedeker: Bleistein with a Cigar.*

22 **lemon:** OED b: "(*slang*) · · · a loser; a person easily deluded or taken advantage of", with 1908, Sullivan, *Criminal Slang*: "*Sucker* or *lemon*". Van Wyck Brooks: "True poetry is quite as likely to come from young men as from old · · · and it is absurd to insist that the most appropriate poetry college men can produce is college poetry; as if 'goodies' [college servants] and 'exams' and 'lemons' after all were the chief emotions of which sensible men of twenty are capable", *Varied Outlooks* II in *Harvard Advocate* 5 Apr 1907. **bitten:** OED 6b: "To take or be caught by any bait." **macaroon:** OED 3: "dolt · · · *Obs.*" Donne: "To hear this *macaroon* talk on in vain", *Satire* IV 115–17. OED 1: "A small sweet cake or biscuit". S. Baring-Gould: "Mr Cheek set down a macaroon he was eating, which was bitten in half · · · then he laughed insultingly", *Court-Royal* (1887) ch. LIV (TSE: "laughter", 8). **a slice of lemon and a bitten macaroon:** "They squeezed lemon-juice on their pancakes · · · 'Curse them,' he said bitterly", *On the Eve* (1925); TSE's authorship uncertain, see Index of Identifying Titles. "To have bitten off the matter with a smile · · · squeezed", *The Love Song of J. Alfred Prufrock* 91–92. "The bitter apple and the bite in the apple", *The Dry Salvages* II 69, with *variant*: "The [*added*: bitten/bitter] fruit and the bite in the fruit". "But bitter tastelessness of shadow fruit", *Little Gidding* II 80. "influenza · · · which leaves extreme dryness and a bitter taste in the mouth", *London Letter* in *Dial* Aug 1921. ("As his dry and passionate talk devoured the afternoon", 17.)

Hysteria

Published in *Catholic Anthology* (Nov 1915), *1917*, *US 1920* (not *AraVP*), *1925+*.

No recording known.

Dated Oxford, 1915 by TSE in both *Morley's US 1920* and *Hayward's 1925*. Probably submitted to *Poetry*, but not used, before publication in *Catholic Anthology* (see headnote to *The Death of Saint Narcissus*).

"Is this prose or verse? or prose *and* verse? It is whatever is most exciting", TSE's jacket copy for David Jones's *The Anathemata* (1952). For TSE's other prose poems, see *The Engine* and *Introspection*, as well as *Anabasis*.

Baudelaire: "Sois toujours poète, même en prose" [Always be a poet, even in prose], *Mon Cœur mis à nu* (*Journaux Intimes* CIII). TSE: "in the long forgotten 'Nineties when sins were scarlet, there appeared a little book called *Pastels in Prose*. It was mostly, if not altogether, translations from the French—from Ephraim Mikhaël, Judith Gautier, Mallarmé, and many less-remembered names. This book introduced to the English reader the Prose-Poem · · · I have remarked recently a recrudescence of the poem in prose · · · Rimbaud, who I suspect is responsible for everything that is good in Verlaine, wrote his prose poems between 1872 and 1875. They are short prose pieces, as obscure as *Kubla Khan* or *Christabel* and of a similar inspiration. They are amazingly convincing, and their prose is good French prose · · · The *Illuminations* · · · find their proper expression in prose because they seem to have come to their author already clothed in that form · · · Mr. Aldington's prose poems, delicately handled, yet seem to hesitate between two media · · · There could be no prose equivalent for *The Rape of the Lock*. There could be no verse equivalent for *Madame Bovary* or *Bubu de Montparnasse* · · · Both verse and prose still conceal unexplored possibilities, but whatever one writes must be definitely and by inner necessity either one or the other", *The Borderline of Prose* (1917). Pasted into TSE's copy of Stuart Merrill's *Pastels in Prose* (1890) is a five-paragraph parody of the prose-poem, headed "The Latest Form of Literary Hysterics". Having first appeared in the *Chicago Tribune*, this was syndicated from coast to coast throughout 1893 and reprinted in *Good Humour for Reading and Recitation* ed. Henry Firth Wood (1893). TSE was interested in Merrill as an American who had become a French symbolist poet, to the point of inclusion among the *Poètes d'aujourd'hui* (see headnote to "*Poems* (1920)", 4. WHAT FRANCE MEANT TO TSE). On Aldous Huxley: "In his prose poems, he has made the mistake of going for a model to Laforgue instead of to Rimbaud. The prose poem is an aberration which is only justified by absolute success", *The Post-Georgians* (1919).

"I have not yet been given any definition of the prose poem which appears to be more than a tautology or a contradiction. Mr. Aldington, for example, has provided me with the following: 'The prose poem is poetic content expressed in prose form.' Poetic content must be either the sort of thing that *is usually*, or the sort of thing that *ought to be*, expressed in verse. But if you say the latter, the prose poem is ruled out; if you say the former, you have said only that certain things can be said in either prose or verse, or that anything can be said either in prose or verse. I am not disposed to contest either of these conclusions, as they stand, but they do not appear to bring us any nearer to a definition of the prose poem", *Prose and Verse* (1921). In Grierson's Introduction to *Metaphysical Lyrics and Poems of the Seventeenth Century* (1921) xxxi, TSE scored the sentence "The metaphysicals are the masters of the 'neutral style', of a diction equally appropriate, according as it may be used, to prose and verse." (TSE had had the same cadence, in verse, in *Mr. Eliot's Sunday Morning Service* 31: "The masters of the subtle schools". For writing in the "*plain* style", see note to *Little Gidding* II 38.)

"The greatest possible mistake would be to label the poetry of Dryden and his successors *prosaic.* The infusion of the prosaic into verse is an accomplishment of the greatest masters of verse ··· if there is a reproach to be levelled against the poetry of the age ··· it is that this poetry is not prosaic enough; it is from our point of view often much too poetical. But so was much of their prose; and the prose and verse of a period should be considered in relation to each other", *The Minor Metaphysicals* (1930). "Prose which has nothing in common with verse is dead; verse which has nothing in common with prose is probably artificial, false, diffuse, and syntactically weak", *Dryden the Dramatist* (1931). On North: "your reviewer ··· quotes the well-known passage from North's Plutarch (Coriolanus's speech to Aufidius), and follows it with the equally famous version of Shakespeare, which he prints as prose. He observes that the version of Shakespeare is 'a far better piece of prose than the original.' I make precisely the opposite observation. The prose of North is fine prose, the verse of Shakespeare is great poetry. And printed as prose, the verse of Shakespeare seems to me to be bad prose. As prose, it is difficult to grasp; as prose, it is badly constructed. North's I find much superior—as prose. What I think your reviewer ··· has overlooked is this: that verse, whatever else it may or may not be, is itself a system of *punctuation*; the usual marks of punctuation themselves are differently employed. If your reviewer were right, the method ought to be reversible; so that some passages of great prose could be converted into fine verse; and I do not believe he can find an example", *Questions of Prose* (1928). Returning to the same example: "I admire ··· the consummate skill of the man who could, by altering *so little*, turn a piece of fine prose into great poetry ··· The fact that Shakespeare altered so little, is the best possible testimonial to the beauty of North's prose; and his alterations are a comment on its limitations ··· Every change made by Shakespeare is not merely the change from prose to verse, but an absolute improvement in force, concision, and ease of syntax", *The Tudor Translators* (1929). On *Antony and Cleopatra*: "The verse speech is so perfectly conversational that it can, on occasion, be interpolated with prose without any disturbance. In Act I sc. ii, Enobarbus speaks in prose, Antony in what might be either, and the short dialogue in which Antony announces the death of his wife is either verse or prose", *The Development of Shakespeare's Verse* (1950 text).

On St.-John Perse's *Anabase*: "I refer to this poem as a poem. It would be convenient if poetry were always verse—either accented, alliterative, or quantitative; but that is not true. Poetry may occur, within a definite limit on one side, at any point along a line of which the formal limits are 'verse' and 'prose'. Without offering any generalized theory about 'poetry', 'verse' and 'prose', I may suggest that a writer, by using, as does Mr. Perse, certain exclusively poetic methods, is sometimes able to write poetry in what is called prose", Preface to *Anabasis*. To Hugh Chisholm, 3 Sept 1942: "I have read your prose poems. While I respect the imagination and craftsmanship which I find in them I cannot find anything that I want to say about them in public, because this form of writing always seems to me a mistake. Years ago

I did a little of the sort myself but was never able to persuade myself that the result was more than just a note for a poem to be written. Your prologue reminds me of St.-J. Perse though I am glad to see that that influence is not evident later. I admire Perse's work but I think there is much more to be said for the prose poem in the French language than in English." To Edward J. H. Greene, 25 Feb 1948: "I have never read any of Lautréamont's work and have never been an enthusiast for prose poetry."

To A. J. Matthews, 27 Dec 1934, about *Hysteria*: "I regard the 'prose poem' as a minor form of a past era, and of less importance for English literature than for French. As to the only one which I have committed myself, I regard it as a kind of note for a poem, but not as a poem." To Roberto Sanesi, 10 Dec 1959, responding to a list of 29 poems Sanesi proposed to translate into Italian: "On reviewing your list it seems to me comprehensive enough to be representative. I should say that the short piece in prose called *Hysteria* was too slight to be worth translating."

Title **Hysteria**: OED: "Cf. Fr. *hystérie.* Women being much more liable than men to this disorder, it was originally thought to be due to a disturbance of the uterus and its functions" (entry pub. 1897–99). Resident in Paris in 1910–11, TSE read Pierre Janet (whom he recalled as "the great psychologist", *A Commentary* in *Criterion* Apr 1934). *Grover Smith 1998*: Janet "gave a series of fifteen lectures at the Harvard Medical School in 1906 and issued them in the following year as *The Major Symptoms of Hysteria.* These lectures, founded on decades of clinical observation, gave a preview substantially of *Les Névroses*, Janet's 1909 cumulative account of his work. Janet always focussed on hysterical disorders, to which he attributed several types of dissociated personality · · · The symptoms may range from sleepwalking (for Janet always hysterical) or momentary trance and confusion to gross physical afflictions such as hysterical paralysis, blindness, and alimentary or erotic breakdowns. Janet considered the idée fixe to be moral—that is, social in origin. It was always created by a trauma the details of which eluded conscious memory. The hysteric confronts anew an image precipitating turmoil but does not know why it does so." Houghton has several pages of notes by TSE on cases from Janet's *Névroses et idées fixes* (1898) (*Childs* 96–97).

teeth: Edwin B. Holt: "while the teeth serve as a symbol of repugnance, their associated context in the dreamer's mind shows clearly how they come to have such a meaning. [*Footnote*: In hysteria, vomiting is regularly a symptom of repugnance]", *The Freudian Wish and Its Place in Ethics* (1915), which TSE mentioned in *New Philosophers* (1918) (*Crawford 2015* 293). **short gasps, inhaled**: see Commentary on *The Waste Land* [I] 63–68 for "Sighs, short · · · exhaled". **aware of**: often discomfiting in TSE. "I am aware of the damp souls of housemaids", *Morning at the Window* 3. "aware of his limbs smoothly passing each other · · · And his hands aware of the pointed tips of his fingers", *The Death of Saint Narcissus* 9, 15. "lives in the awareness of the observing eye", *WLComposite* 339. "She was aware of her small square room: alone, alone in a glass coffin", ms story for Vivien Eliot (beginning "Fanny lying in bed late"), *c.* 1924–25 (U. Maryland). **she laughed · · · the dark caverns of her throat**: "the one great line that leaps out so surprisingly towards the end of *Love's Labour's Lost*: 'To move wild laughter in the throat of death'", *The Development of Shakespeare's Verse* (1937), quoting V ii. **I decided that if the shaking of**

her breasts could be stopped, some of the fragments of the afternoon might be collected, and I concentrated my attention with careful subtlety to this end: "I tried to assemble these nebulae into one pattern", *The Engine* II. "These fragments I have shored against my ruins", *The Waste Land* [V] 430.

Conversation Galante

Published as the first of four *Observations* in *Poetry* Sept 1916, then *1917+*. Quoted in full by Pound in *Drunken Helots and Mr. Eliot* (*Egoist* June 1917), a review of *1917* perhaps slightly preceding its publication. No recording known. Faber & Faber letter to Allen Lane of Penguin, 13 May 1947, on the selection previously made for *Guild* ed.: "omitted ··· two short passages, *Hysteria* (which is prose) and *Conversation Galante* (which I think he regarded as not up to the level of the others)."

Dated Nov 1909 in Notebook. Dated Cambridge, Mass., 1909 in *Isaacs's US 1920*, and by TSE in both *Morley's US 1920* and *Hayward's 1925*. TSE to Edward J. H. Greene, 18 Oct 1939: "*Conversation Galante* is very early. It should be dated, I think, 1909."

Pound to Harriet Monroe, 16 Sept 1916: "I vote that the lyric prize be given to T. S. Eliot for *Conversation Galante* ··· (If anyone votes for a different poem by Eliot please transfer my vote to it.)" The prize of $100 for a lyric poem offered by Mrs. Julius Rosenwald was awarded to Muna Lee of Oklahoma City, for *Foot-notes*, with *Conversation Galante* being one of twenty poems to receive honourable mention (*Poetry* Nov 1916).

Modelled, as the *Westminster Gazette* reviewer noted on 28 July 1917, on Laforgue's *Autre Complainte de Lord Pierrot*, which *Symons* 110 had quoted in full. In *Thayer's AraVP*, TSE wrote beside the title: "Laforgue".

Title **Conversation Galante**: not in OED. For its appearance in *Baedeker*, see *Mr. Apollinax* 2–5 note. ***Galante***: Watteau was received into the French Academy in 1717 "pour un tableau qui représentait une fête galante", his *Embarquement pour l'Île de Cythère* (see note to *Goldfish* II). Verlaine's title *Fêtes galantes* was adopted by "F. M." for *Fête Galante* (1925).

1 **sentimental friend the moon:** Gautier: *Variations sur le carnaval de Venise* IV. *Clair de lune sentimental*. For "a sentimental sunset" in Paris, see volume headnote on the dedication to Verdenal (in 4. TITLE, DEDICATION AND EPIGRAPH TO THE VOLUME).

1–3 **moon ··· balloon:** Laforgue's prose: "oui, une lune naïve en son énormité comme un ballon lâché!" [Yes, a moon whose innocent enormity is like a liberated balloon!], *Lohengrin, fils de Parsifal* (*Greene* 27).

1–5 **the moon! ··· balloon | Or an old battered lantern hung aloft | To light poor travellers to their distress:** T. E. Hulme's *Above the Dock* (published by Pound, 1912):

> Above the quiet dock in mid night,
> Tangled in the tall mast's corded height,

Hangs the moon. What seemed so far away
Is but a child's balloon, forgotten after play.

To Mary Hutchinson, [9 July? 1919]: "I am not sure whether you thought that Hulme is a really great poet, as I do, or not. I can't think of anything as good as two of his poems since Blake." To Emily Hale, 6 Oct 1930, on Hulme's *Speculations* ed. Herbert Read (1924):

> You may wonder particularly why I sent a big book of prose by Hulme with only five little poems at the end. The reason is that these little poems have been a kind of symbol of the whole of the first phase of modern poetry in England: say from about 1909. Hulme was an extraordinary man, who has had a great *stimulating* influence on many of us (his views on Humanism and Original Sin are the starting point for Herbert Read and myself, and Ivor Richards and Ramon Fernandez know his work etc.) He wrote the poems as a tour de force, among a group of friends, Monro, Flint, Pound and others, as a kind of illustration of 'Imagism' and they should be read in connexion with what he says about modern poetry in the prose text. I think *Conversation Piece* is very beautiful, though I do not understand it.

To F. O. Matthiessen, 18 Oct 1934: "I didn't know T. E. Hulme personally although I had heard much about him. I never read anything he wrote until *Speculations* came out. Herbert Read didn't know him personally either: only people living in London before the War knew him." **the moon · · · To light poor travellers:** Dryden: "Moon and Stars | To lonely, weary, wandering Travellers", *Religio Laici* 1–3 (Richard Luckett, personal communication).

3 **Prester John's balloon**: in R. E. Raspe's *The Surprising Adventures of Baron Munchausen* (1785) ch. XXXI, Prester John, the legendary medieval Christian monarch of an exotic realm, sends a "Wauwau" bird to London from Africa by balloon (Barbara Lauriat, personal communication). Writing to Bonamy Dobrée in Egypt in 1927, TSE repeatedly joked about Dobrée being an envoy to "the University of Ethiopia and Nubia and the land of Prester John" (see "Improper Rhymes"). **balloon**: on the meaning of a name: "it disappears like a gas-balloon into the sky: the person who let the toy escape, and who continues to fix his eye upon it, can still see it long after it has become impossible for a random eye to find · · · The extension of meaning (on the one hand extension of the meaning of names, and on the other hand extension of the being of facts) is, it must be insisted, not a falsification; it is imprudent, but so is a balloon ascension; though our balloon finally collapse, we have taken a certain number of observations while in the air; and it will be only to the eyes of the vulgar that our descent appear a disaster", *The Validity of Artificial Distinctions* (1914).

5 **To light poor travellers to their distress:** OED "ignis fatuus": "A phosphorescent light seen hovering or flitting over marshy ground, and supposed to be due to the spontaneous combustion of an inflammable gas · · · When approached, the *ignis fatuus* appeared to recede, and finally to vanish · · · This led to the notion that it was the work of a mischievous sprite, intentionally leading benighted travellers astray. Hence the term is commonly used allusively or fig. for any delusive guiding principle, hope, aim, etc." See note to *East Coker* II 42, "fancy lights". Edward Young: "to light revellers from shame to shame", *Night Thoughts* IX 680. See note to *The Burnt Dancer* 34, and for Young's volume see headnote to *Whispers of Immortality*. **to their distress**: Gautier (at the line-ending):

"Dans ce regard, à ma détresse" [In this regard, to my distress], *Tristesse en mer* [*Sadness at Sea*] 9.

13 **humorist**: OED 3: "One given to humouring or indulging. *Obs.*", last citation 1686: "Man is the greatest Humorist and Flatterer of himself."

14 **the absolute**: of Laforgue: "It is noticeable how often the words 'inconscient', 'néant', and 'L'absolu' and such philosophical terms ··· recur", *The Varieties of Metaphysical Poetry* 215 (Clark Lecture VIII). Laforgue often stationed the word at the line-ending: "Me laisser éponger mon Moi par l'Absolu?" [allow my Self to be rubbed out by the Absolute?], *Préludes autobiographiques* 106 [*Autobiographical Preamble*]. "Nul Absolu; | Des compromis; | Tout est pas plus; | Tout est permis" [No Absolute. | Some compromise. | The whole is not more. | All is allowed], verse within the prose tale *Lohengrin* II (tr. Frances Newman). TSE, similarly: "On the doorstep of the Absolute", *Spleen* 16. "Just out of reach | First born child of the absolute", *Suite Clownesque* III 21. "Towards the unconscious, the ineffable, the absolute", *Afternoon* 9 (see note).

Much debated in Harvard philosophy circles in TSE's youth. *Jain 1991* 15–16: "The chief exponent of Kantian idealism in America was Josiah Royce. It was predominantly his thought that shaped the emphases of twentieth-century American philosophy until the First World War. Eliot paid tribute to him as the '*doyen* of American philosophers' [*Knowledge and Experience* 10]. In his attempts at resolving the dispute between evolution and religion, Royce posited an absolute, a world soul that reconciled the antithesis between the finite and the infinite." (On what the Absolute meant to Royce, Bradley and William James see *Jain 1992* passim; for Bergson's Absolute, see note to *He said: this universe is very clever* 6–7, "like a syphilitic spider | The Absolute sits waiting".) *Jain 1991* 19–20: "Bradley's metaphysical system is constructed on the basis of the immediately given, or immediate experience ··· Bradley's Absolute is a perfect, harmonious, all-inclusive system that contains in itself all experience. When viewed from the standpoint of the Absolute the parts—time, space, the self, thought, truth, God—are finite, incomplete, and contradictory. They are therefore appearances in relation to the Reality into which they are ultimately absorbed. These appearances, however, are true or false, real or unreal, in degree—relative to the Absolute." TSE to Norbert Weiner, 6 Jan 1915: "it is all one if one call the Absolute, Reality or Value. It does not exist for me, but I cannot say that it does not exist for Mr. Bradley. And Mr. Bradley may say that the Absolute is implied *for* me *in* my thought—and who is to be the referee?"

Bradley's Absolute, wrote TSE, "represents in fact only the pathetic primitive human *Credo* in ultimate explanations and ultimate reality which haunts us like the prayers of childhood", *Report on the Relation of Kant's Criticism to Agnosticism* (1913). "The crudest experience and the abstrusest theory end in identity, and this identity I call the absolute. If you choose to call it nothing, I will not dispute the point. But whichever it is, it is both beginning and end", *Degrees of Reality* (1913). "The Absolute, we find, does not fall within any of the classes of objects: it is neither real nor unreal nor imaginary", *Knowledge and Experience* 169. "Professor Bosanquet is the prophet who has put off his shoes and talks with the Absolute in a burning bush", *The Relationship between Politics and Metaphysics* (1913). (For Bosanquet, see note to *Do I know how I feel? Do I know what I think?* 1.) Jean Verdenal to TSE, 22 Apr 1912: "Voici sans doute le prélude de quelque nouvelle course après l'absolu, et comme les autres fois on se laissera tromper" [This is no doubt the prelude to some new pursuit of the absolute and, as on previous occasions, I shall be taken in]. TSE: "It is to the immense credit of Hulme that he found out for himself that there is an *absolute* to which Man can *never* attain", *Second Thoughts about Humanism* (1929).

In 1923 TSE commissioned a *Criterion* article on "the attempt to conceive the Absolute as a spirtual life" from his former Oxford tutor, Harold Joachim, but it was eventually printed elsewhere (TSE's letters 24 Jan 1924, 21 Jan 1927). TSE returns often to the Absolute in his Clark Lectures, 1926: "You know how the Absolute of Bergson is arrived at: by a turning back on the path of thought, by divesting one's mind of the apparatus of distinction and analysis, by plunging into the flow of immediate experience"; "whether you seek the Absolute in marriage, adultery or debauchery, it is all one—you are seeking in the wrong place"; "In these lines of Donne there is a great deal of the modern *recherche de l'absolu* [the search after the absolute], the disappointed romanticism, the vexation of resignation at finding the world other than one wanted it to be", *The Varieties of Metaphysical Poetry* 99, 115, 128.

15 **slightest:** on W. J. Turner's *Ecstasy*: "Mr. Turner is not very happy in his adjectives. He weakens one of them by a superlative ('frieze on whitest marble')", *Verse Pleasant and Unpleasant* (1918).

18 **Are we then so serious?:** Laforgue: "'C'était donc sérieux?'" ["Was it serious after all?"], *Autre Complainte de Lord Pierrot* [*Another Complaint from Lord Pierrot*] 20. TSE: "Romeo, *grand sérieux*", *Nocturne* 1 ("nocturne", 8).

La Figlia Che Piange

Published as the second of four *Observations* in *Poetry* Sept 1916, then *1917+*. Included in full and with no variants in Pound's *Drunken Helots and Mr. Eliot* (see headnote to *Conversation Galante*). Reprinted in *An Anthology of Modern Verse*, ed. A. Methuen (1921) with epigraph reading "*O quam te memorem virgo . . . O dea certe!*" (see note to epigraph).

Dated Cambridge, Mass., 1911 by *Poèmes*; "1911 (near the end)" in *VE's 1951*; 1912 by TSE to Edward J. H. Greene, 18 Oct 1939; and Cambridge, 1912, by TSE in both *Morley's US 1920* and *Hayward's 1925*. For Aiken's claim to have offered this poem "at a party" to Harold Monro, who rejected it, see volume headnote, 2. COMPOSITION AND SHAPING.

Recorded May 1942 in Stockholm for the Swedish Broadcasting System. Second: 23 May 1947, National Gallery of Art, Washington. Third: 12 Nov 1950, for U. Chicago Round Table, broadcast by NBC.

Vassar Miscellany News 10 May 1933, on a reading by TSE at the college three days earlier: "he read his poem, *La Figlia Che Piange*, a poem, he said, which other people liked, and for which he did not care a great deal. People might think, he remarked, that this poem had been suggested by an incident, the sight of a deserted girl. But not at all. Some one had advised him to see a stone stele of Egyptian origin in an Italian museum. The figure was of a woman, and the Italians called it *La Figlia Che Piange*. He never saw the stele, but the title stuck in his head, so that in the end the poem gave his impression of what that piece of sculpture ought to be. Here the picture and the verbal image were the starting point, and the subject of the poem was the last thing to arrive. 'About such things one can only say that different poets' minds work differently and one poet's mind works differently at different times,' Mr. Eliot explained." In 1907–1908, TSE took George Henry Chase's History of Ancient Art course at Harvard on "Architecture, sculpture, and painting in Egypt, Assyria, and Greece, with some account of the lesser arts".

In *Wellesley College News* 8 May 1947, Judy Wolpert reported TSE's reading at Wellesley three days earlier, which included this poem, "inspired by an Egyptian carving in Italy which the poet never saw. This is one of Mr. Eliot's most oft requested readings, and he noted that 'people are often disappointed if they don't get what they expect, even if they don't want it'." On the BBC Third Programme 4 Aug 1948, John Hayward mentioned "faint reminiscences" of Rossetti's *The Blessed Damozel* (see note to 1), adding that many readers had supposed "that 'The Weeping Girl' must have been a real girl with whom the poet had been in love ··· The poem in fact is one of speculation and regret, about a statue which Mr. Eliot had looked for in a museum in Italy but had failed to find", ts of Hayward's *"Prufrock and Other Observations"* (King's HB/M/9). Louis Bertrand, tr. Stuart Merrill: "'Ah, Signora, you are as a statue in a garden!'" *Evening on the Water* in *Pastels in Prose.* TSE: "Not like a tranquil goddess carved of stone | But evanescent, as if one should meet | A pensive lamia in some wood-retreat, | An immaterial fancy of one's own", *On a Portrait* 5–8. On poems and paintings (such as Rossetti's sonnets *For a Venetian Pastoral by Giorgione* and *Rend, rend thine hair, Cassandra*, and Swinburne's *Hermaphroditus* and *Before the Mirror*), see *Roper 2002*.

The Daily Illini 5 June 1953, reporting TSE's reading the previous day: "Eliot commented people had often asked him to tell them about the emotional experience behind his work *La Figlia Che Piange*, the Weeping Girl. He said he wouldn't talk about his emotion behind a poem. It is unimportant. Besides, he added, there wasn't any emotion. The poem, Eliot said, was suggested by an Italian painting which his friends had told him about. He never got to see the painting."

To Sir Algernon Methuen, 2 Nov 1920, responding to his request for a poem for an anthology for schools and general readers: "The only poem that strikes me as possible is one called *La figlia che piange*." But the following year TSE wrote to Richard Aldington, 8 Sept 1921, of "Messrs. Methuen, against whom I have no grievance except that they chose *La figlia che piange* to print in an anthology because it is the mildest of my productions". TSE referred to this poem as having "a certain low popularity", *Excerpts from Lectures 1932–1933*. *Chapin*, of TSE's reading at the National Gallery, Washington, 23 May 1947: "Of *La Figlia Che Piange* he said, whimsically, he read it because people expected it and that, as it was his first to be put in any respectable anthology, it must be completely inoffensive." When reading it for broadcast: "in its time the most popular, I suppose, because it seemed to many people to be more like poetry than my other work", *Chicago Round Table* (1950).

Title] [The Girl Who Weeps]. *Purg.* XVI 87–88: "che piangendo e ridendo pargoleggia, | l'anima semplicetta" [like a little child that plays, with weeping and laughter, the simple soul], tr. TSE (see headnote to *Animula*). Dante's tercet ends "volentier torna a ciò che la trastulla" [willingly she turneth to that which delights her] (TSE: "she turned away", 17). "Figlia del tuo figlio", *The Dry Salvages* IV 9.

Epigraph] Against this TSE wrote in *Thayer's AraVP*: "Aenaeid", changed to "Aeneid" and "O dea certe". Aeneas to his mother, Venus, who is disguised as a huntress (I 327–28):

> O—quam te memorem, virgo? namque haud tibi voltus
> mortalis, nec vox hominem sonat; o dea certe!

> [by what name should I call thee, O maiden? for thy face is not mortal nor has thy voice a human ring; O goddess surely!]

1 **Stand on the highest pavement of the stair**: Rossetti: "It was the rampart of God's house | That she was standing on", *The Blessed Damozel* 25–26 (*Praz*). The poem is in *Oxf Bk of English Verse.* TSE: "Rossetti's *Blessed Damozel*, first by my rapture and next by my revolt, held up my appreciation of Beatrice by many years", *Dante* (1929).

2–7 **Lean on a garden urn— | Weave, weave the sunlight in your hair · · · But weave, weave the sunlight in your hair**: Laforgue: "Penche, penche ta chère tête, va, | Regarde les grappes des premiers lilas" [Bend, bend your darling head – come, look at the bunches of the first lilacs], *Dimanches* [*Sundays*] IV 61–62 (*Greene* 48).

3 **Weave, weave the sunlight in your hair**: Tennyson: "with her sunny hair · · · She meant to weave me a snare", *Maud* I [vi] 212–14 (*Musgrove* 88). Swinburne: "Always the shuttle cleaves clean through, and he | Weaves with the hair of many a ruined head", *Laus Veneris* 43–44. Symons: "With what flounces and what curls | To weave the painted web of light?" *Bal Masqué.*

3–4 **weave the sunlight · · · Clasp your flowers**: "While all the East was weaving red with gray, | The flowers at the window turned toward dawn", *Before Morning* 1–2.

4–5 **flowers · · · Fling**: Ernest Dowson: "We fling up flowers and laugh", *The Carthusians* 29 ("and laugh", *Preludes* IV 14). TSE described Methuen's *An Anthology of Modern Verse* (in which *La Figlia Che Piange* appeared) as "not so bad as meaningless", but added that Dowson's poem, though "not one of his best · · · is distinguished from the verse of our contemporaries, which surrounds it, precisely by an intellectual dignity", *A Preface to Modern Literature: Being a Conspectus Chiefly of English Poetry, Addressed to an Intelligent and Inquiring Foreigner* (1923).

6–7 **your eyes · · · weave · · · your hair**: Coleridge: "His flashing eyes, his floating hair! | Weave a circle round him thrice, | And close your eyes", *Kubla Khan* 50–52.

8–15 **So I would · · · So I would · · · So I would have had her stand and grieve · · · I should find · · · Some way we both should understand**: "I would come · · · I should for a moment linger · · · at last you would understand · · · You would love me", *The Love Song of St. Sebastian* 22–34. "How steadfastly I should have mourned | The sinking of so dear a head!" *Elegy* 5–6.

8, 10, 22 **I would have had him leave · · · he would have left · · · I should have lost**: (i) "You have the scene arrange itself", *Portrait of a Lady* I 2. "You have the other raise", *Mandarins* 2 15. (ii) "Your heart would have responded", *The Waste Land* [V] 420. "you would have to put off", *Little Gidding* I 42.

11 **As the soul leaves the body**: in his *Oxford notes on Aristotle* (1914–15), TSE

recorded R. G. Collingwood on *De Anima*: "If the soul moves in space, it might move out of the body and back again", adding the title of Frazer's *Golden Bough*, where such beliefs are described (*Crawford 2015* 215).

14–22 **Some way incomparably light and deft ··· we both should understand ··· a smile and shake of the hand. || She turned away ··· gesture**: in Hawthorne's *The Blithedale Romance* ch. XVIII, Coverdale, from his hotel, spies Zenobia and Westervelt through a window: "she broke away, and vanished beyond my ken. Westervelt approached the window ··· smile ··· smile ··· endowed with a cat-like circumspection ··· He now proved it, considerably to my discomfiture, by detecting and recognising me, at my post of observation ··· Immediately afterwards, Zenobia appeared ··· She signified her recognition of me by a gesture with her head and hand, comprising at once a salutation and dismissal." **Simple and faithless as a smile and shake of the hand**: Laforgue: "l'Amour | S'échange par le temps qui court. | Simple et sans foi comme un bonjour" [that Love is exchanged the way it is these days. Simple and faithless as a "hello"], *La vie qu'elles me font mener* [*The Life They Make Me Lead*] 11–13. In his prose tale *Hamlet,* Laforgue has these lines of verse. TSE began a translation of Laforgue's *Hamlet* (to Conrad Aiken, 21 Aug 1916). "a smile | Simple and profound", *First Debate between the Body and Soul* 44–45. **a smile and shake of the hand. | She turned away**: "He turned away, and with his motion of dismissal", *Little Gidding* II 67–96, *first venture in verse* [22] *variant.*

17–18, 20 **She turned away ··· Compelled my imagination ··· Her hair over her arms and her arms full of flowers**: Hawthorne: "long after ··· her daily flower affected my imagination" and "She had, as usual, a flower in her hair ··· she turned away, exemplifying ··· that noble and beautiful motion which characterised her", *The Blithedale Romance* ch. VI, XVIII.

17–24 **She ··· many days, | Many days and many hours ··· troubled**: Isaiah 32: 10: "Many days and years shall ye be troubled, ye careless women." **turned away ··· they ··· troubled midnight**: Job 34: 20: "In a moment shall they die, and the people shall be troubled at midnight and pass away."

18 **Compelled my imagination**: reviewing Herbert Read's *Reason and Romanticism*, TSE quoted his remark that the scientific equivalents of Christianity's unconscious symbols "no longer compel the imagination", *Mr. Read and M. Fernandez* (1926).

18, 24 **imagination ··· troubled midnight and the noon's repose**: Wilde: "He saw them at night, and they troubled his imagination in the day", *The Picture of Dorian Gray* ch. XI.

20, 22–23 **flowers ··· pose ··· these cogitations**: "Oh, spare these reminiscences! | How you prolong the pose! ··· attar of rose", *Portrait of a Lady* II 15^16 *variant.*

22 **pose**: "With Byron, if you like, everything was pose, but the existence of a pose implies the possibility of a reality to which the pose pretends", *The Varieties of Metaphysical Poetry* 209 (Clark Lecture VIII).

22, 24 **lost ··· repose**: "It is the mark of the man who has no core, no individual moral existence, to be possessed with moral notions, to be goaded by the necessity of continual moral formulations. In this he finds repose", *London Letter* May 1922. "Baudelaire was man enough for damnation ··· we are not prevented from praying for his repose", *Baudelaire* (1930). Irving Babbitt writes of "vital respose" as against "inert repose"; of "the romanticists" as seeing "in repose only lifelessness and stagnation"; and of what is "suggestive of repose, of something that without being in the least inert and soulless is nevertheless raised above the region of motion and change", *The New Laokoon* (1910) 229–30. "A stoic in obese repose", *Mandarins* 3 2. For "repose" as a verb in Blake, see note to *A Cooking Egg* 25–32.

24 **The troubled midnight and the noon's repose**: Shelley: "The cloud-shadows of midnight possess their own repose", *Stanzas.—April, 1814*, with "autumn woods" (TSE: "autumn weather", 17). TSE's schoolboy copy of *The Poetical Works* of Shelley, ed. Dowden (A. L. Burt, NY, n.d.) is recorded in a Milton Academy catalogue from the late 1930s. **midnight · · · noon's repose**: "the Jellicle Moon appears · · · repose · · · To dance by the light of the Jellicle Moon", *The Song of the Jellicles* 17–18, 28. "by day or night · · · enjoy well-earned repose", *He who in ceaseless labours took delight* 2, 4. **noon's repose**: "repose of noon, set under the upper branches of noon's widest tree | Under the breast feather stirred by the small wind after noon", *Coriolan* II. *Difficulties of a Statesman* 33–34.

Poems (1920)

1. Contents in Order of First Publication 2. A New Start 3. The Dramatists 4. What France Meant to TSE 5. TSE's Proficiency in French 6. Publication of *Poems* (1919) 7. Publication of *Ara Vos Prec* 8. Publication of *Poems* (1920) 9. TSE on the 1920 Poems

1. CONTENTS IN ORDER OF FIRST PUBLICATION

Le Directeur	*Little Review*	July 1917
Mélange Adultère de Tout	*Little Review*	July 1917
Lune de Miel	*Little Review*	July 1917
The Hippopotamus	*Little Review*	July 1917
Sweeney Among the Nightingales	*Little Review*	Sept 1918
Whispers of Immortality	*Little Review*	Sept 1918
Dans le Restaurant	*Little Review*	Sept 1918
Mr. Eliot's Sunday Morning Service	*Little Review*	Sept 1918
A Cooking Egg	*Coterie*	May Day 1919
Burbank with a Baedeker: Bleistein with a Cigar	*Art & Letters*	Summer 1919
Sweeney Erect	*Art & Letters*	Summer 1919
Gerontion	*Ara Vos Prec*	Feb 1920
[*Ode* ("Tired. | Subterrene")	*Ara Vos Prec*	Feb 1920]

These poems formed the first half of two books published in 1920: *Ara Vos Prec* (early Feb) and TSE's first American volume, *Poems* (late Feb), respectively *AraVP* and *US 1920*. In practice, each was a collected poems, with the *Prufrock* poems as the second half. *Ode* ("Tired. | Subterrene"), for which see "Uncollected Poems", was printed in *AraVP*, which omitted *Hysteria* from the second half of the volume. *US 1920* omitted *Ode* but included *Hysteria*. For TSE's fears about his mother's reaction to *Ode*, see headnote. Seven of the "*Poems* (1920)" had appeared the previous year in the Hogarth Press *Poems* (*1919*). None of the French poems was to appear in *Penguin* / *Sel Poems*.

TSE may have known that the US Copyright Office would grant US copyright on a foreign book only if it received two copies of the foreign edition by publication day *and* if an edition was typeset in the US within two months. Although he fulfilled the second condition, he did not fulfil the first. However, change of title and substitution of a poem might have been sufficient to make *US 1920* legally a different book, which could be copyrighted. The copyright status of the *Prufrock* poems in the US was highly uncertain. See *Spoo* 60–61, 94–107.

2. A NEW START

Around the time that proofs were received of *Prufrock and Other Observations*, Pound wrote to the editor of the *Little Review*, Margaret Anderson, 22 Apr 1917: "Eliot has turned in a good bunch of poems, for July. Three french and one english, announce simply 'a group of poems by T. S. Eliot will appear in the July number'. S.V.P. I dare say there'll be one or two more by then. Getting his book into print seems to have set him off again." Vivien Eliot to Charlotte Eliot, 30 Apr [1917]: "Only when he began to be more bright and happy and boyish than I've known him to be for nearly two years, did *I* feel convinced—and only when he has written *five*, most *excellent* poems in the course of one week, did Ezra Pound and many others, believe it possible."

In July four new poems appeared in the *Little Review*: *Le Directeur*, *Mélange Adultère de Tout*, *Lune de Miel* and *The Hippopotamus.* Aldous Huxley to Ottoline Morrell, 6 Feb 1917: "I dined with Eliot in his flat—Mrs. E happily being out we had a very good talk, Eliot in good form all considered and showed me his latest verses—very odd indeed: he is experimenting in a new genre. Philosophical obscenity rather like Laforgue and dimly like a great series of poems which I once planned to be called 'Vomic Songs.' Eliot's are very good: some in English, some in the most astonishingly erudite French." After this, new poems came slowly, although Pound assured Anderson that more were on the way. On 16 July 1917, Pound wrote: "for Oct. Eliot should have finished revising a poem"; 3 Aug: "Poem by Eliot (IF he gets it in. It's writ, but he is still revising)"; 17 Aug: "Eliot is coming tomorrow. I hope with a poem"; 24 May 1918: "Four T.S.E. poems in hand, one or two questions I want to ask T. before sending them"; 10 June: "Here are Eliot's cameos. for Sept." Pound to Quinn, 4 June 1918: "Eliot has emitted a few new and diverting verses. Sending 'em for Sept." Finally, under the heading "Four Poems", the *Little Review* published *Sweeney Among the Nightingales*, *Whispers of Immortality*, *Dans le Restaurant* and *Mr. Eliot's Sunday Morning Service.* (Immediately preceding them in the issue was an extract of a review by Edgar Jepson of American poetry, extolling *Prufrock and Other Observations.*)

3. THE DRAMATISTS

> "My own verse is, so far as I can judge, nearer to the original meaning of *vers libre* than is any of the other types: at least, the form in which I began to write, in 1908 or 1909, was directly drawn from the study of Laforgue together with the later Elizabethan drama; and I do not know anyone who started from exactly that point." (*Ezra Pound's "Selected Poems"* (1928), Introduction)

For TSE, the "Elizabethan" could stretch beyond the Queen's death in 1603, as in the contents of his *Elizabethan Essays* (1934). "The Elizabethan Age had, even in its smallest writers, the sense of tragedy and of comedy, the attitude of a kind of inspired recklessness. The Jacobean–Caroline period has a more civilised grace", *The Minor Metaphysicals* (1930). Beginning in 1916, TSE gave a three-year tutorial class in English literature, in Southall, Middlesex, as part of Oxford University's Committee for the Promotion of Higher Education for Working People (*Schuchard* 26–51). The third year, from autumn 1918 to May 1919, was devoted to Elizabethan and Jacobean literature. To his mother, 10 May 1918: "My Southall people want to do Elizabethan Literature next year which would interest me more than what we have done before, and would be of some use to me too, as I want to write some essays on the dramatists, who have never been properly criticized." In *Studies in Contemporary Criticism* II (1918), TSE listed—slightly inaccurately—some of the books he had read "lately": Swinburne's *The Age of Shakespeare* (1908), John Addington Symonds's *Shakespere's Predecessors in the English Drama* (1884), Frederick S. Boas's *Shakespeare and his Predecessors* (1896) and Felix E. Schelling's *Elizabethan Drama* (1908). Concurrently in "*Poems* (1920)", he drew upon Beaumont & Fletcher, Chapman, Jonson, Marlowe, Marston, Middleton, Tourneur and Webster.

> It was from these minor dramatists that I, in my own poetic formation, had learned my lessons; it was by them, and not by Shakespeare, that my imagination had been stimulated, my sense of rhythm trained, and my emotions fed. I had read them at the age at which they were best suited to my temperament and stage of development, and had read them with passionate delight long before I had any thought, or any opportunity of writing about them. At the period in which the stirrings of desire to write verse were becoming insistent, these were the men whom I took as my tutors. Just as the modern poet who influenced me was not Baudelaire but Jules Laforgue, so the dramatic poets were Marlowe and Webster and Tourneur and Middleton and Ford, not Shakespeare. A poet of the supreme greatness of Shakespeare can hardly influence, he can only be imitated: and the difference between influence and imitation is that influence can fecundate, whereas imitation—especially unconscious imitation—can only sterilize.
>
> *To Criticize the Critic* 18

To Helen Gardner, 13 May 1964: "I am content that I have drawn attention to some of the old dramatists. That is the only value of my criticism, that it should lead people to read works that they have never read, or to re-read them with fresh eyes. As I have said, I don't think that anything I have written about Shakespeare is worth preserving, and my criticism of the others has its only value in its enthusiasm and the introduction of the writers to a new public."

4. WHAT FRANCE MEANT TO TSE

From Oct 1910 to July 1911, TSE lived in Paris. "ce n'est pas un accident qui m'avait conduit à Paris. Depuis plusieurs années, la France représentait surtout, à mes yeux, la *poésie*" [It wasn't an accident that took me to Paris. For many years, France had represented above all, to my eyes, *poetry*], *What France Means to You* (1944).

"The taste of an adolescent writer is intense, but narrow: it is determined by personal needs. The kind of poetry that I needed, to teach me the use of my own voice, did not exist in English at all; it was only to be found in French", *Yeats* (1940). In the Thirties: "Younger generations can hardly realize the intellectual desert of England and America during the first decade and more of this century · · · The predominance of Paris was incontestable. Poetry, it is true, was somewhat in eclipse; but there was a most exciting variety of ideas. Anatole France and Remy de Gourmont still exhibited their learning, and provided types of scepticism for younger men to be attracted by and to repudiate; Barrès was at the height of his influence, and of his rather transient reputation. Péguy, more or less Bergsonian *and* Catholic *and* Socialist, had just become important, and the young were further distracted by Gide and Claudel. Vildrac, Romains, Duhamel, experimented with verse which seemed hopeful, though it was always, I think, disappointing; something was expected of Henri Franck, the early deceased author of *La Danse devant l'arche.* At the Sorbonne, Faguet was an authority to be attacked violently; the sociologists, Durkheim, Lévy-Bruhl, held new doctrines; Janet was the great psychologist; at the Collège de France, Loisy enjoyed his somewhat scandalous distinction; and over all swung the spider-like figure of Bergson", *A Commentary* in *Criterion* Apr 1934.

Pound to Harriet Monroe [May?] 1917: "The only thing I can see for strengthening the prose section of *Poetry* is a series of essays on French poets unknown to the *Atlantic Monthly* and the Great Generation of Pimps ··· *Poetry* could quite well do with essays on LaForgue, Corbiere, Tailhade, possibly Rimbaud, Jammes, possibly Elskamp, possibly a reminder of Mallarmé, Samain, Heredia. I would suggest that a series of this sort by me, Eliot and DeBosschere, would at least keep out a certain amount of slop." A later letter, 26 Aug 1917, shows such an article had been commissioned from TSE: "Here is the first of the French articles [Pound's own, on satirists]. Eliot is uncertain about his copy, undependable for anything at a given date. The work at the bank which at first seemed to leave him freer than teaching, now seems to use a great deal of his energy. It is a great waste."

TSE on Gautier and his influence: "In the best of the slight verse of Gautier there is a satisfaction, a balance of inwards and form, which we do not find in Baudelaire", *Baudelaire* (1930). "At a certain moment, my debt to him [Pound] was for his advice to read Gautier's *Emaux et Camées* [*Enamels and Cameos*], to which I had not before paid any close attention", *Ezra Pound* (1946). "These poems were largely influenced by Ezra Pound's suggestion that one should study Théophile Gautier and take a rest from *vers libre* in regular quatrains", *T. S. Eliot Talks about His Poetry* (1958). "the suggestion of writing quatrains was his. He put me on to *Emaux et Camées* ··· We studied Gautier's poems and then we thought, 'Have I anything to say in which this form will be useful?' And we experimented. The form gave the impetus to the content", *Paris Review* (1959). When TSE gave F. S. Flint a copy of René Taupin's *L'Influence du symbolisme français sur la poésie américaine* (Paris, 1929; Berg), he corrected misquotations from Gautier: changing "visible" to "invisible" (217), "guerroyens" to "guerroyers" (218) and "douches o" to "douches à" (218).

Pound: "at a particular date in a particular room, two authors, neither engaged in picking the other's pocket, decided that the dilutation of *vers libre*, Amygism, Lee Masterism, general floppiness had gone too far and that some counter-current must be set going ··· Remedy prescribed *Emaux et Camées* (or the Bay State Hymn Book). Rhyme and regular strophes. Results: Poems in Mr. Eliot's *second* volume, not contained in his first ··· also *H. S. Mauberley*", *Harold Monro* in *Criterion* July 1932 (collected in *Polite Essays*, 1937). Pound to William Carlos Williams, 12 Sept 1920: "Eliot is perfectly conscious of having imitated Laforgue, has worked to get away from it, and there is very little Laforgue in his Sweeney, or his Bleistein Burbank, or his *Gerontion*, or his Bay State hymn book" (*The Whole Book of Psalms faithfully translated into English Metre*, Cambridge, Mass., 1640).

TSE: "I think that the attention drawn to these French poets has been a very good thing for English verse. I think that the best of the younger poets to-day realise that it is impossible to ignore the discoveries of foreign poets, just as it is impossible for a good scientist to ignore what is going on abroad. So far as I can see, there is no poetry being written in France at present which is making any contribution whatever to the development of poetry; almost none of it is even readable. An infatuation with the French, therefore, would be as fatal as our natural insularity", *Modern Tendencies in Poetry* (1920). See "A Beginner in 1908", 1. A BREAK WITH TRADITION.

5. TSE'S PROFICIENCY IN FRENCH

To Edward J. H. Greene, 28 Nov 1947: "I took private lessons in French from Alain-Fournier in the course of which he also directed my reading in several directions." To Jeanie McPherrin, 3 Oct 1935, recalling Highgate Junior School in 1916: "I found teaching French to children more difficult than any other subject. For instance, although I could usually get any irregular verb right when I was using it in a sentence, I had never got them by heart in paradigms, or whatever they are called, and I think my pupils sometimes thought that I was an imposter."

Irving Babbitt to Dean Briggs of Harvard, recommending TSE for a Sheldon Fellowship, 27 Feb 1914: "He did unusually good work for me a few years ago in French 17" (Harvard Archives, UAIII 10.60).

Ottoline Morrell wrote in spring 1916 of TSE's visiting Garsington with Bertrand Russell: "He is obviously very ignorant of England and imagines that it is essential to be highly polite and conventional and decorous, and meticulous. I tried to get him to talk more freely by talking French to him, as I thought he might feel freer doing so, but I don't think it was a great success, although better than English. He speaks French very perfectly, slowly and correctly", *Morrell 1974* 101–102. Thirty years later, Françoise de Castro recorded: "Il parle le français rapidement, avec un accent chantant qui abaisse les finales et roule doucement les 'R', ce qui me rappelle beaucoup plus l'accent des Orientaux que celui des Britanniques" [He speaks French rapidly, with a singing accent which sinks at the end, and softly rolls his "r"s which calls to my mind the accent rather of an Oriental than a Briton], *Entretien avec T. S. Eliot*, 23 Aug 1948 (ts, King's).

Dora Mussey, Ilkley, Yorkshire, to Dr. D. H. S. Cranage, Cambridge University local lecture syndicate, 26 Oct 1916: "Mr. Eliot has only given us two lectures so far. His manner is not good. His delivery is very monotonous. His voice would not be strong enough for a large hall. But he is inexperienced, & even the second lecture showed improvement. He lectures from a ms., but he rarely looks at it. His matter is excellent, & he uses it in a very interesting way. He gives the impression of wide & thorough knowledge of his subject (Contemporary France). He is very fair-minded. He is friendly & easy in the class. There is nothing of the popular lecturer about him. But at the same time, I find people who know nothing of our present subject, follow him with interest. He has no Americanisms or accent ··· Mr. Eliot's French is delightful" (Cambridge UL, BEMS 55/12; Iman Javadi, personal communication). TSE is not known to have recorded any of his poems in French. To the secretary of the British Institute in Paris, 3 Aug 1939: "As for lecturing in French, I have no experience of public speaking in that language, and should be obliged to have my lecture fully prepared and the style criticized by some French friend, and confine myself to reading the text." Robert Halsband records TSE, over tea with John Hayward, on 10 Oct 1954: "French writers who knew English seldom bothered to speak it. I mentioned Voltaire; he said that in all his meetings with Gide, G had never spoken any English, though he had undoubtedly read a good deal in the language" (ts "Memorandum", Columbia U.). Brigid Donovan, TSE's secretary 1934–36, recalled: "His most remarkable physical characteristic was his extraordinarily flat voice. He had acquired a perfect educated English accent—I don't think any Englishman, nor an American either, could have guessed he was American by birth and childhood education, but he had overlooked the rise and fall that is particularly typical of English English speech. It may have been that he was confused by speaking French before changing over to an English accent" (*Donovan*).

Pound to Joyce, 19 Apr 1917, of *Prufrock and Other Observations* and the three French poems which appeared in the *Little Review* July 1917: "I hope to send you Eliot's poems in a few weeks. He has burst out into scurrilous french during the past few weeks, too late for his book, which is in the press, but the gallicism should enrich the review. He is 'just as bad' as if he had been to Clongowes [Clongowes Wood College, Joyce's school]. But it is perilous trying to manipulate a foreign language." On 6 Nov 1923 TSE wrote to Paul Valéry that French spared him some of the embarrassment he felt writing English: "Quoique je n'ai jamais, hélas! bien parlé ou bien écrit en langue français je préfère l'employer en causant avec les personnes qui me sont sympathiques, parce que votre langue me donne une certaine liberté d'esprit et de sentiments que la langue anglaise me réfuse. En tout cas je me trouve moins gêné." [Although I have never, alas! spoken the French language well or written it well, I prefer to use it in talking to people with whom I am in sympathy, because your language gives me a certain freedom of mind and feeling that the English language denies me. In any case, I find myself less awkward.]

To Kay Dick, 10 June 1943: "I have set a bad example in the way of publishing verse in French and I can only say in excuse that I did not publish very much of it and that I had submitted it to French criticism beforehand." *Lehmann* records TSE's answers to questions after a reading at Bryn Mawr in 1948: Q. "Do you think that the poet may resort to a foreign language if his own language fails him?" A. "The better he knows how to use his own language, the less he will have to use a foreign tongue, though it may happen. But then it is always a second help."

On 3 Dec 1945, TSE wrote to Pierre Leyris, who was preparing a volume of French translations of TSE's earlier poems: "I think the best title would probably be *La Terre Gaste*, précédé de quelques poèmes anciens [*The Waste Land* preceded by some old poems]. Only if you put in the French poem that John Hayward had [*Vers pour la Foulque* from *Noctes Binanianæ*], that dates from 1938 and therefore *ancient* hardly applies. But that is I think, the only one of the French poems which I would like to have included. I do not think that the others [from "*Poems* (1920)"] are good enough to take their place in such a small selection as this. You are quite at liberty to use that poem only I cannot provide you with a copy of it at the moment as the only copy I have is buried somewhere in a box of books, but I daresay Hayward would be very glad to type out a copy for you. It would need a few notes for which I could supply the material."

In his interview published in *Paris Review* (1959), Donald Hall asked whether TSE had written any poems in French since those in his *Collected Poems*:

> ELIOT: No, and I never shall. That was a very curious thing which I can't altogether explain. At that period I thought I'd dried up completely. I hadn't written anything for some time and was rather desperate. I started writing a few things in French and found I *could*, at that period. I think it was that when I was writing in French I didn't take the poems so seriously, and that, not taking them seriously, I wasn't so worried about not being able to write. I did these things as a sort of *tour de force* to see what I could do. That went on for some months. The best of them have been printed. I must say that Ezra Pound went through them, and Edmond Dulac, a Frenchman we knew in London, helped with them a bit. We left out some, and I suppose they disappeared completely. Then I suddenly began writing in English again and lost all desire to go on with French. I think it was just something that helped me get started again.
> INTERVIEWER: Did you think at all about becoming a French symbolist poet like the two Americans of the last century?
> ELIOT: Stuart Merrill and Vielé-Griffin. I only did that during the romantic year I spent in Paris after Harvard. I had at that time the idea of giving up English and trying to

> settle down and scrape along in Paris and gradually write French. But it would have been a foolish idea even if I'd been much more bilingual than I ever was, because, for one thing, I don't think that one can be a bilingual poet. I don't know of any case in which a man wrote great or even fine poems equally well in two languages. I think one language must be the one you express yourself in in poetry, and you've got to give up the other for that purpose. And I think that the English language really has more resources in some respects than the French. I think, in other words, I've probably done better in English than I ever would have in French even if I'd become as proficient in French as the poets you mentioned.

Edmund Dulac had designed the masks for Yeats's Noh play *At the Hawk's Well*, which TSE and Pound saw performed in Lady Cunard's drawing-room on 2 Apr 1916. TSE repeated his acknowledgement to Dulac when inscribing Cyril Connolly's copy of *1919*, writing in it, probably in the 1960s: "This is an opportunity to record the fact that the French verses were vetted by Edmond Dulac" (U. Tulsa). In a testimonial dated 22 Aug 1918 (King's), Dulac had praised TSE's command of colloquial and literary French:

> Connaissant M. T. S. Eliot depuis quelques années, j'ai eu plusieurs fois le plaisir de causer avec lui et de lire les nombreux poèmes qu'il a écrit en français. Je n'ai aucune hésitation à déclarer qu'il possède fort bien cette langue, et que, tout dans les tours de la conversation que dans les finesses de l'écriture il en connaît les subtilités à un rare degré.
>
> [Knowing Mr. T. S. Eliot for some years, I have often had the pleasure of talking with him and of reading the many poems that he has written in French. I have no hesitation in declaring that he has a strong command of the language, and that in conversation as much as in the delicacies of writing, he knows its subtleties to a rare degree.]

Dulac was added as a "Further Appointment" to teach illustration in Pound's prospectus for a College of Arts, Nov 1914. (For a slip in one of TSE's French poems, see note to *Lune de Miel* 13.)

TSE to Amar Bhattacharyya, 22 June 1964: "I was moved to write in French after a period of drought during which I felt that I could not write at all. It was something to me to be able to be released in another language and after these few poems in French I found myself again beginning to write verse in English." ("I suppose, | If you learn to speak a foreign language fluently, | So you can think in it—you feel yourself to be | Rather a different person when you're talking it", *The Confidential Clerk* I.)

"It is possible that to be completely bi-lingual would be a handicap to a man of letters: for to know two languages equally well makes complete intimacy with either more difficult", *A Commentary* in *Criterion* Oct 1937. To H. F. G. Morris, 28 June 1945: "The question in my mind is whether it is possible to be a poet in two languages. What a man writes in a second language will always have something of the character of a *tour de force*. Furthermore, if a man is deliberately to choose a language not his own for writing poetry, he must, I think, like Jean Moreas, live where the language of his adoption is the vernacular. Any poet needs to keep in continual contact with the spoken language which is the language in which he writes. If therefore Senhor [Aurelio] Valls were to be domiciled in any English-speaking country he might be safe in adopting English as the medium for his verse, but if he is to be domiciled in a country where any other language is the vernacular, he would probably be better advised to stick to Spanish which, after all, is a magnificent tongue in which great poetry has been and can still be written."

To I. A. Richards, 9 Aug 1930:

> I shall be very much interested in any results of your study of Chinese abstractions. I dare say it is likely to be more profitable than my attempt, so many years ago, at studying Indian metaphysics in Sanskrit. The conclusion I came to then (after it is true only a couple of years' struggle with the language) was that it seemed impossible to be on both sides of the looking-glass at once. That is, it made me think how much more dependent one was than one had suspected, upon a *particular* tradition of thought from Thales down, so that I came to wonder how much *understanding* anything (a term, a system, etc.) meant merely *being used* to it. (Similarly I have observed with anything new in art, that when people say either that they cannot understand it or that they have come to understand it, that seems to mean largely either that they are not habituated to it or that they are). And it seemed to me that all I was trying to do, and all that any of the pundits had succeeded in doing, was to attempt to translate one terminology with a long tradition into another; and that however cleverly one did it, one would never produce anything better than an ingenious difformation (just as Deussen, who I suppose to be the very best interpreter of the Upanishads, has merely transformed Indian thought into Schopenhauerian—and the orientalism of Schopenhauer is as superficial as superficial can be). In other words, I thought that the only way I could ever come to understand Indian thought would be to erase not only my own education in European philosophy, but the traditions and mental habits of Europe for two thousand years—and if one did that, one would be no better off for 'translating', and even if such a feat could be accomplished, it didn't seem worth the trouble. However, some such study (as far as one can see) is I believe profitable, as getting outside of one's own skin, or jumping down one's own throat.

He applied similar principles to other things. "I believe that for a poet to be also a philosopher he would have to be virtually two men; I cannot think of any example of this thorough schizophrenia, nor can I see anything to be gained by it: the work is better performed inside two skulls than one", *The Use of Poetry and the Use of Criticism* 98–99. To Rayner Heppenstall, 29 May 1936: "If you really hope to become a professional novelist I think the out-look is rather unfavourable for the future of your poetry. I mean that while an exception is always possible I think that the verse of a professional novelist must always be a bye-product. I don't think that a single individual can divide himself so successfully as to make a major art of two occupations requiring very different attitudes."

For the present edition, the French poems have been newly translated by Paul Keegan into plain prose.

6. PUBLICATION OF *POEMS* (1919)

Leonard Woolf to TSE, 19 Oct 1918: "My wife and I have started a small private Printing Press, and we print and publish privately short works which would not otherwise find a publisher easily. We have been told by Roger Fry that you have some poems which you wish to find a publisher for. We both very much liked your book, *Prufrock*; and I wonder whether you would care to let us look at the poems with a view to printing them." Virginia Woolf, *Diary* 15 Nov 1918: "He produced 3 or 4 poems for us to look at—the fruit of two years." In advance of book publication, TSE was to offer some poems to Pound for a projected magazine, as Pound reported to his father, 10 Jan 1919: "Several poems by Eliot for Quarterly." Virginia Woolf,

Diary 19 Mar: "Today we finished the printing of Eliot's poems." TSE to Rodker, 17 May: "Leonard Woolf's edition of a few of my poems is now on the market." *Poems* by T. S. Eliot, "Printed & published by L. & V. Woolf at THE HOGARTH PRESS, Hogarth House, Richmond", contained (in order) *Sweeney Among the Nightingales*, *The Hippopotamus*, *Mr. Eliot's Sunday Morning Service*, *Whispers of Immortality*, *Le Directeur* (as *Le Spectateur*), *Mélange Adultère de Tout* and *Lune de Miel.*

Leonard Woolf in 1964: "I bought a copy of *Prufrock* when it was published ··· Tom showed us some of the poems which he had just written and we printed seven of them and published them in the slim paper covered book", *Beginning Again* 242. Virginia Woolf, *Diary* 20 Sept 1920: "I taxed him with wilfully concealing his transitions. He said that explanation is unnecessary. If you put it in, you dilute the facts. You should feel these without explanation ··· A personal upheaval of some kind came after *Prufrock*, & turned him aside from his inclination—to develop in the manner of Henry James. Now he wants to describe externals." Victoria Glendinning records that "By the beginning of November 1919, 140 copies of *Poems* had been sold, and Eliot received a cheque for £1.13.10d", *Leonard Woolf* (2006).

After this second slender volume, TSE never again published a book consisting entirely of discrete new poems, other than *Old Possum's Book of Practical Cats.*

7. PUBLICATION OF *ARA VOS PREC*

In spring 1919, John Rodker took over from Pound as London editor of the *Little Review* and began the Ovid Press, which lasted about a year. TSE to Rodker, 17 May 1919: "Leonard Woolf's edition of a few of my poems is now on the market, and I understand that yours would not be ready before August, so that is all right. I accordingly authorise, or give you permission, or whatever is the legal phrase, to print your special edition of 250 copies of a book to contain the poems in the Egoist *Prufrock*, the poems in Woolf's small book, and any others that I may send you in a reasonable time. I enclose three new ones [presumably *Burbank with a Baedeker: Bleistein with a Cigar*, *Sweeney Erect* and *Ode*]. I should like to know when you want to start on this book, as I want to think over such questions as the order of the poems, dedication; also I have two more quotations, a Latin and a Greek one, to go in as headings. Will you be able to do Greek type? There are two other short Greek quotations ··· I will send you a copy of Woolf's." 1 June: "If you haven't a *Prufrock* I will get Weaver to send you one. I am sending you Virginia Woolf's book which seems to me very well done. There is one other French poem, which is in one of the later *Little Reviews* [*Dans le Restaurant*], along with some others—you have that have you not? These and the three I sent you and one half-finished one [*Gerontion*] are all I have up to date. Oh, also the thing in *Coterie* [*A Cooking Egg*]." 9 July: "I have the new poem I spoke of—about 75 lines—which will not have appeared anywhere—but I am withholding it until I know you want it, as I may make alterations. It is also quite possible that I may have another about the same length by August 1. So I hope that the book may be more nearly what you had in mind. I think you have all the newer poems: beside the Woolf volume there is a French poem in *L. Review* (*Dans le Restaurant*), *Bleistein* and *Sweeney Erect*, *Cooking Egg*—of which I enclose revised version *with* quotations—and this new one, *Gerontion*."

Unlike all later gatherings by TSE of his poems, both *Ara Vos Prec* and *US 1920* printed the newer poems, beginning with *Gerontion*, in a section before those from *Prufrock and Other Observations.* (On Tues 12 Nov [?1935], TSE wrote to Virginia Woolf about a reader who was "not only an admirer but I believe admires your works in the right order—I mean, I always prefer people to like best what I have written most recently, ⁊ in that order backwards.") Within the first half of *AraVP*, the order was different from that of *US 1920* (which became definitive). *AraVP* had the four French poems together, with *Ode* the only new poem following them. The careless contents list in *AraVP* reads: *Gerontion*, *Burbank*, *Sweeny among the Nightingales*, *Sweeny erect*, *Mr. Eliot's Sunday Morning Service*, *Whispers of Immortality*, *The Hippopotamus*, *A Cooking Egg*, *Lune de Miel*, *Dans le Restaurant*, *Le Spectateur*, *Mélange Adultère de Tout*, *Ode*, *Prufrock*, *Portrait of a Lady*, *Preludes*, *Rhapsody of a Windy Night*, *The Boston Evening Transcript*, *Aunt Helen*, *Cousin Nancy*, *Mr. Apollinax*, *Conversation Galante*, *La Figlia Che Piange*.

To Rodker, 3 Oct 1919: "It has just occurred to me that the title *ARA VUS PREC* would do. For it is non-committal about the newness of the contents, and unintelligible to most people." (For source, see note on volume title.) *Gallup*: "The error 'Vus' for 'Vos' in the title was discovered after all the sheets had been printed and was corrected only on the label. Concerning the title, Mr Eliot wrote me on 21 February 1936: 'The correct title of the book is *Ara Vos Prec.* It only happened to be *Vus* on the title page because I don't know Provençal, and I was quoting from an Italian edition of Dante the editor of which apparently did not know Provençal either. It would seem that there is no such word as *Vus* in that language.'" The edition of Dante has not been identified. TSE: "As for the Provençal poets, I have not the knowledge to read them at first hand. That mysterious people had a religion of their own which was thoroughly and painfully extinguished by the Inquisition; so that we hardly know more about them than about the Sumerians", *Dante* (1929) III. Pound had translated much Provençal poetry, including Arnaut Daniel. The title of Pound's first book, *A Lume Spento* (1908), is from *Purg.* III.

Alongside Beare's opinion that *AraVP* was "an elaborate and, let us be honest, rather tasteless and badly printed volume", TSE wrote "Hear hear!" (*Beare* ts).

Volume title **Ara Vos Prec**: [And so I pray you], *Purg.* XXVI 142–48. The passage from which this is drawn recurs in TSE. *Dante* (1929) II:

> In this canto the Lustful are purged in flame, yet we see clearly how the flame of purgatory differs from that of hell. In hell, the torment issues from the very nature of the damned themselves, expresses their essence; they writhe in the torment of their own perpetually perverted nature. In purgatory the torment of flame is deliberately and consciously accepted by the penitent ··· The souls in purgatory suffer because they *wish to suffer*, for purgation ··· The canto ends with the superb verses of Arnaut Daniel in his Provençal tongue:
>
> "*Ieu sui Arnaut, que plor e vau cantan;*
> *consiros vei la passada folor,*
> *e vei jausen lo jorn, qu' esper, denan.*
> *Ara vos prec, per aquella valor* [145]
> *que vos guida al som de l'escalina,*
> *sovegna vos a temps de mon dolor.*"
> POI S'ASCOSE NEL FOCO CHE GLI AFFINA.
>
> ["I am Arnold, who weeps and goes singing. I see in thought all the past folly. And I see with joy the day for which I hope, before me. And so I pray you, by that virtue which leads you to the topmost of the stair—be mindful in due time of my pain". Then dived he back into that fire which refines them.]

TSE inscribed the first two lines of this Dante passage in Mary Trevelyan's copy of *Ara Vos Prec*, and in Mary Hutchinson's he inscribed the first line and the preceding two (140–42): "'*Tan m'abelis vostre cortes deman, | qu' ieu no-m puesc, ni-m vueil a vos cobrire | Ieu sui Arnaut, que plor e vau cantan*'" ["So doth your courteous request please me that I cannot, nor will I, hide from you. I am Arnold, who weeps and goes singing"]. He inscribed the single line "*Tan m'abelis vostre cortes deman*" (140) in a copy of *US 1920* "For Ezra Pound · · · with the respects of the author. T. S. Eliot 10.iv.20", and it provided a suggested title for *Ash-Wednesday* II. The third line (144) provided another such for *Ash-Wednesday* II: *Jausen lo jorn*. The fifth line (146) provided an unadopted title for *Ash-Wednesday* III: *Som de l'escalina*. The sixth and seventh lines (147, 148) were TSE's first idea for an epigraph for *The Love Song of J. Alfred Prufrock*. The sixth line appears as the last line of *Exequy* (TSE replaced it with the second line, 143, but then deleted that). The first two words of the sixth line became *Ash-Wednesday* IV 11, "Sovegna vos", with TSE's "dolour", five lines earlier, deriving from the last word of Dante's line. The seventh line (148) concludes Dante's canto. TSE marked it in his earliest copy of the *Purgatorio*, and inscribed it with the date "30.vii.26" on the half-title page of John Rodker's copy of *Ara Vos Prec* (correcting the printed "Vus"). The line stands as *The Waste Land* [V] 427 (where it is followed by a line from *Pervigilium Veneris*), it also appears in *ts2* of *Ash-Wednesday* IV (16–29 [7]), and is alluded to in *Little Gidding* II 92. In his Notes on the Waste Land, TSE quotes Dante's final four lines (145–48) in his Note to 427.

Pound: "Arnaut speaks not in Italian, but in his own tongue; an honour paid to no one else in the *Commedia*", *The Spirit of Romance* 16. Pound translated Arnaut Daniel's *Canzoni* in 1911–12, but a proposed edition foundered. F. S. Flint: "Ezra used to sit on the bed and recite Arnaut Daniel, which sounded like Bantu clicks", quoted (from conversation) by Patricia Hutchins, *Ezra Pound's Kensington* (1965) 56. TSE to Mario Praz, 22 May 1936: "I certainly owe a good deal to Ezra Pound in connection with my slight knowledge of the early Italian poets. I don't think that I ever corresponded with him on the subject, because my chief association with him was during the period when he lived in London. I owed a good deal to the essay on Dante in his early book *The Spirit of Romance* · · · I had read a smattering of some of the others, especially the two Guidos and Cino before I knew Pound, but he certainly sharpened my interest in these people, and you must understand that my knowledge has never been more than what everyone would call smattering."

8. PUBLICATION OF *POEMS* (1920)

To John Quinn, 8 Sept 1918: "I have a book ready for Knopf, not a very big one, but I think big enough—miscellany of prose (mostly critical) and verse including *Prufrock* and everything of any merit since *Prufrock*, the manuscript of which is almost ready to go over. It is not the book I should have liked. I should prefer to keep the prose and verse apart; and the former, I fear, bears marks of haste in the writing in many places. But it is time I had a volume in America, and this is the only way to do it; and Pound's book [*Pavannes and Divisions* (1918)] will provide a precedent. I hope you will not find the book a wholly journalistic compilation."

Valerie Eliot detailed the negotiations (*WLFacs* xiv, xvi–xvii):

> It was Pound who made the final adjustments to the manuscript before sending it to the publisher.

> At the end of January [1919] Knopf informed Pound that he was rejecting both his and Eliot's manuscripts, and when they were received by Quinn a fortnight later, he sent them to Boni & Liveright. On 29 April Quinn told Eliot · · · that Knopf "would like to publish your poems alone but not the poems with the prose". Eliot wrote on 25 May that he wished to alter the manuscript if it were possible, as he had two or three essays and a very few poems (including *Gerontion*) to add · · · Quinn cabled him to send what he had and on the same day, 30 June, expressed his anger with Liveright who, he believed, had delayed his answer because he knew the lawyer was about to go on holiday, and hoped to force him to accept his terms at the last minute: ". . . Liveright expected me to put up a guaranty of $100 or $150 in connection with your book. If he had been decent about it, I should have been willing to do so." Having retrieved the manuscript, Quinn arranged for it to be offered (with a $150 advance) to John Lane; apologizing for the delay, they replied early in August: "Mr. Eliot's work is no doubt brilliant, but it is not exactly the kind of material we care to add to our list." Then Quinn contacted Knopf, who "was willing and anxious to publish the poems in a volume by themselves" now that their number had increased. Both men disliked the name *Prufrock*—which they believed would damage the sales—and decided that the title should be *Poems by T. S. Eliot*.

The title proposed by TSE for a volume of poems and prose is unknown, but Quinn's letter of 26 Aug 1919 is clear: "I dislike, apparently as much as Knopf dislikes, the name *Prufrock* in the title. He thinks that title would hurt the sale. I agree with him." (TSE to F. T. Prince, 20 Jan 1938, on accepting his poems for publication: "I should like you to consider whether you wish to call the book *Poems*, or give it some particular title. For my part, I think that *Poems* is quite satisfactory for a first book." To Vernon Watkins, 28 Mar 1941: "I agree with you that *Poems* is the last resource when nothing else can be found.")

US 1920 jacket front panel:

> T. S. Eliot, an American for some years a resident of London, is better known in the English and French worlds of letters than in the United States. And yet, a thinker of keen perceptions and deep understanding, he is certainly one of the most remarkable of the younger poets and critics of today. The occasional appearance of his poems in the magazines has led to an insistent demand for them in book form and here in this slender volume are gathered the very best of them. They are conspicuous for their subtlety of humor and rhythm, the freshness of the author's vision and the keenness of his observation, the originality and fineness of his style.

9. TSE ON THE 1920 POEMS

To Edgar Jepson, 22 Sept 1919, comparing *Burbank with a Baedeker: Bleistein with a Cigar* and *Sweeney Erect*: "I am inclined to agree with you about the poems, though I think the first is much better than the second." To Mary Hutchinson [9 July? 1919]: "'Bleistein' (like 'S among the Nightingales') is meant to be *very serious*! and 'Hippopotamus' and Webster [*Whispers of Immortality*] aren't." "But these w[e]re really serious men" *Whispers of Immortality* 12 *variant* (see Textual History). To Henry Eliot, 15 Feb 1920: "Some of the new poems, the Sweeney ones, especially 'Among the Nightingales' and 'Burbank' are intensely serious, and I think these two are among the best that I have ever done. But even here I am considered by the ordinary

Newspaper critic as a Wit or satirist, and in America I suppose I shall be thought merely disgusting." To Henry Eliot, 8 Dec 1922: "I consider my Sweeney poems as serious as anything I have ever written, in fact much more serious as well as more mature than the early poems but I do not know anybody who agrees with me on this point except Vivien and William Butler Yeats." To John Preston, 30 Sept 1943, about *Murder in the Cathedral*: "The speeches to which you refer are intended to be satirical and should therefore be spoken with complete seriousness." (For satire, see headnote to *A Cooking Egg.* For TSE on writing a political satire, see headnote to *Coriolan*, 2. AFTER PUBLICATION.) On Corbière: "there is the same yoking together of the dissimilar, which Johnson long ago noted in Donne and Cowley—with the effect of irony instead of wit. For the metaphysical poets of the seventeenth century were witty but not ironic—not ironic in so serious a way as this. Real irony is an expression of suffering, and the greatest ironist was the one who suffered the most—Swift", *The Varieties of Metaphysical Poetry* 219 (Clark Lecture VIII). "So · · · we may even come to see Molière in some lights as a more serious dramatist than Corneille or Racine; Wycherley as equally serious (in this sense) with Marlowe", *Shakespearian Criticism I: From Dryden to Coleridge* (1934). For the serious intention of *The Waste Land* and its Notes, see headnote, 6. A HOAX? (William Force Stead's account of a reading) and 7. THE AUTHOR'S NOTES (Arnold Bennett's question).

Gerontion

Published in *AraVP*, *US 1920+*, *Sesame* and *Penguin / Sel Poems.*

Recorded 1933, for the Harvard Poetry Room; released Mar 1934 by Harvard Vocarium Records. Unusually, TSE read the epigraph.

Undated in tss, but dated "July 1919" in the ms copy made by Nancy Cunard. Dated 1917 by TSE in *Hayward's 1925*, but 1919 by TSE in *Morley's US 1920*. Dated London, 1919 in *Poèmes*, and assigned to 1919 by *Rainey* 198.

Having told John Rodker of some poems and "one half-finished one" on 1 June 1919, TSE sent *Gerontion* to Rodker on 9 July. Seven days later he thanked Sydney Schiff "for your great kindness in analysing my poem so carefully", repeating on 25 July that he was "appreciative of your careful study of *Gerontion*". After apparently sending the poem to Mary Hutchinson on 9 July, he wrote again on 6 Aug: "*Please* send *Gerontion* back to me at once. I leave Saturday night, and I must revise it in France, so *just* put it in an envelope and send it by return." Wyndham Lewis wrote to John Quinn, 3 Sept, that he was planning a third issue of *Blast* (which never appeared), to include "a long, new poem by Eliot". Quinn wrote to TSE, 29 Sept, that he had had a letter "a few days ago in which Lewis spoke of your having written a new long poem · · · if that new long poem is finished you might send a copy of it to Knopf at once and tell him where it should appear in the volume" (*US 1920*). TSE had sent *Gerontion* to Quinn the previous day: "I had several articles promised that I had to write, and so did not have time to alter the poem which I enclose." (It is not clear whether this means that he had only just found time to revise it, or still had not done so.) For Pound's trenchant pencilled suggestions on *ts2*, see Textual History.

Vassar Miscellany News 10 May 1933, reporting TSE's reading at the college three days previously: "With *Gerontion*, a poem of old age, Mr. Eliot began to use, in his spoken comments, the method which he employed for the notes in *The Waste Land*. Notes are needed because of the allusiveness and the borrowings of the poem. He specified quotations from A. C. Benson, from Lancelot Andrewes's sermons, from *The Education of Henry Adams*. Then there were references to specific people whose biographies would only confuse the issue, were the reader to know those biographies."

To Seán Ó'Faoláin, 21 Feb 1944: "The poem was written a good many years ago, and in a way in which I do not think I write now. Any attempt to explain a poem like that ··· is inevitably an ex post facto rationalisation. It may certainly be what the poem 'means', so long as that is not identified with what the author is supposed to have consciously meant when he wrote it. So far as that goes, it can only be said to have been the expression of a mood, its variations and associated or evoked memories; and in the construction of the poem (the mental operation of writing it) no intellectual generalisation appears. 'Old age' may of course be taken as 'the symbol of a declining civilisation'; but I wasn't thinking about declining civilisations when I wrote it. And critics sometimes assume that one composes a poem by exactly the same process at every period of one's life. It seems to me that there is a considerable change in my own methods, as a result of the exercise I got in experimenting for the stage."

To Diana Captain, 3 Jan 1945, replying to a request for information for her university entrance paper: "The only thing I can say is that it is an attempt to build up an impression of old age, but the old age of a particular man about whom nothing further is known, looking back on his past. If the examiners think that is not enough you can tell them that it is all I can say, so I don't see why you should say any more."

Lehmann on a reading at Bryn Mawr in Oct 1948: "He defined *Gerontion* as a kind of preliminary stage to *The Waste Land*, from which he read out the fifth part *What the Thunder Said*."

To Grover Smith, 4 July 1949, about the names (in reply to speculations in *Explicator* Feb 1949 and in a letter of 1 June 1949): "As for the etymologies you drive me to dispair. Anybody nowadays has the right to attribute anything he likes to anyone else's unconscious and if you choose to think that I knew all these etymologies you are at liberty to do so. All I can say is that these names came to me spontaneously as suitable for certain persons whom I had known. And that I don't bother myself in the least about etymology. Certainly the lady Fresca had nothing whatever in common that I can discern with Francesca da Rimini."

Symons 155–56, translating Maeterlinck:

> "I have come to believe," he writes, in *Le Tragique Quotidien*, "that an old man seated in his armchair, waiting quietly under the lamplight, listening without knowing it to all the eternal laws which reign about his house, interpreting without understanding it all that there is in the silence of doors and windows, and in the little voice of light, enduring the presence of his soul and of his destiny ··· I have come to believe that this motionless old man lived really a more profound, human, and universal life than the lover who strangles his mistress, the captain who gains a victory, or the husband who 'avenges his honour'."

Title] "The title means 'little old man', a diminutive of *γέρων*", *Excerpts from Lectures 1932–1933*. (Immediately following "T. S. E." at the foot of *American Literature*

(1919), in *Athenæum* 25 Apr 1919, is "PORTRAIT OF A LITTLE LADY", a review of *My War Experiences in Two Continents* by S. Macnaughtan; see note to 3–4.) Pronounced with a hard *g* in TSE's recording, as recommended by *Fowler* "Greek G": "There is something to be said for retaining the hard sound of g even before e, i, & y, in such Greek-derived works as are not in popular but only in learned, technical or literary use. To those who know some Greek the sound of ··· jĕrontŏ'krasĭ (*gerontocracy*) ··· either obscures the meaning ··· or ··· is still repulsive." *Grover Smith 1996* 102: "Named for the Roman general Gerontius, Gerontion shares with his prototype the knowledge of past inaction. Just as Gerontius (in AD 396) failed to mount a proper defense with his army against the onrushing Goths, led by Alaric, at Thermopylae ··· so Eliot's Gerontion did not fight at the 'hot gates' of his own generation's war." See note to 71. Newman's *The Dream of Gerontius* begins "JESU MARIA—I am near to death, | And Thou art calling me; I know it now." (See notes to 59 and to *East Coker* II 16–17.) Newman's poem was the basis of Elgar's choral work of 1900, of which the Angels' Chorus was performed in the Unitarian Church of the Messiah, St. Louis, in 1904 (*Crawford 2015* 68).

Unadopted title ***Gerousia***: "at Sparta, the council of elders composed of the two kings and twenty-eight other members over 60 years of age, elected for life ··· as a judicial body they heard cases involving death, exile, or disenfranchisement and could even put the kings on trial", *The Oxford Companion to Classical Literature.*

Epigraph] TSE in *Thayer's AraVP*: "*Measure for Measure*". The speech (III i) of the Duke, disguised as a Friar, is also echoed at 59 (see note):

Friend hast thou none.
For thine own bowels which do call thee sire,
The mere effusion of thy proper loins,
Do curse the gout, serpigo, and the rheum
For ending thee no sooner. Thou hast nor youth, nor age
But as it were an after-dinner's sleep
Dreaming on both; for all thy blessed youth
Becomes as aged, and doth beg the alms
Of palsied eld: and when thou art old and rich,
Thou hast neither heat, affection, limb, nor beauty
To make thy riches pleasant.

The epigraph as printed by TSE is not quite accurate ("after dinner" for "after-dinner's", "of" for "on"). (TSE to G. K. Chesterton, 6 July 1928: "The last time that I ventured to quote from memory in print, a correspondent ··· pointed out that I had made twelve distinct mistakes in well-known passages of Shakespeare." To John Hayward, 14 Feb 1941: "The something, gout, serpigo and the rheum | Shall call thee something or other." Stress: *ser-pì-go.*) *Measure for Measure* was the "mature play" that TSE asked participants in his 1918 extension lectures to read (*Schuchard 1974*). On an Old Vic production: "The opportunity to see a play—and a very great play—of Shakespeare which is so rarely produced should be enough of an attraction; but it has been also an opportunity to see some very fine acting ··· even those whose principles prevent them from approving either the subject-matter or the profoundly Christian spirit of the play might profit by seeing it so very well performed", letter to the Editor, *The Times*, 14 Dec 1933. The epigraph to Tennyson's poem about the occupant of a decayed house,

Mariana, adapts a line from the same play (*Musgrove* 41–42). ***nor youth nor age · · · an after dinner sleep | Dreaming***: Edgar Lee Masters: "nor youth's delight, nor manhood's power", "the chair · · · the accustomed sleep", *O Glorious France* (*McCue 2014a*). ***Dreaming***: Spenser: "As one then in a dreame, whose dryer braine | Is tost with troubled sights and fancies weake", *The Faerie Queene* I i 42 (TSE: "dry brain", 75) (John M. Major, *MLN* Jan 1959).

Unadopted second epigraph ***Come il mi[o] corpo stea | Nel mondo su, nulla scienza porto***: [How my body stands in the world above, I have no knowledge], *Inf.* XXXIII 121–22 (Friar Alberigo tells how, because he betrayed his guests, his soul was taken while he lived).

1–5] TSE in *Thayer's AraVP*: "cf. Ezra Pound's *The Wayfarer*". This was a slip for *The Seafarer* (see note to 71–73), conflating it with *The Wanderer*, another of the Old English poems in the Exeter Book. To Mary Hutchinson, [9 July? 1919]: "of course you are unjust to Pound. One must learn to appreciate his 'literary-appreciative' style as a medium for expressing something of his own. And I think the *Cathay* and the *Seafarer* in *Ripostes* are wonderfully good."

1 **Here I am**: to Eleanor Hinkley, 26 July 1914, two days before the outbreak of war: "Mit freundlichem Gruss aus Deutschland! [With friendly greetings from Germany!] Here I am, safely out of harm's way", opening of the letter.

1–2 **Here I am · · · in a dry month, | Being read to by a boy, waiting for rain**: "The line quoted from *Gerontion* was lifted bodily from a Life of Edward FitzGerald—I think the one in the 'English Men of Letters' series", *On a Recent Piece of Criticism* (1938). A. C. Benson: "Here he sits, in a dry month, old and blind, being read to by a country boy, longing for rain: 'Last night when Miss Tox was just coming, like a good Soul, to ask about the ruined Dombey, we heard a Splash of Rain, and I had the Book shut up, and sat listening to the Shower by myself—till it blew over, I am sorry to say, and no more of the sort all night. But we are thankful for that small mercy'", *Edward FitzGerald* (1905) 142, quoting FitzGerald to W. Aldis Wright [25 May 1880] (Morton Zabel, *Matthiessen* 73–74). Having strained his eyes, FitzGerald "employed his disability like the ancient blind philosopher, *puero ut uno esset comitatior.* His protégé, Alfred Smith, the son of a farmer at the Hall farm, was now a big boy, and FitzGerald engaged him to come up in the evenings and read to him", *Benson* 33 (quoting Cicero's *Tusculan Disputations* V on Asclepiades, who was asked about the frustrations of blindness and answered "the expense of another servant"). See note to 12–15. The Supplementary Reading list for TSE's extension lectures included W. A. Wright's *Letters of Edward FitzGerald* and recommended the English Men of Letters as "the best series of biography", *Syllabus: Modern English Literature* (1916). To John Hayward, 3 Apr 1940, of a dinner guest: "There was also a small dry prematurely old young man, whose name I didn't catch."

1, 7, 17, 59 **an old man in a · · · decayed house · · · a sign · · · smell**: "An old man in a house is a good sign", "That house is happy which smells of an old man", *Oxford Dictionary of English Proverbs*. TSE: "I am the old house | With the noxious smell and the sorrow before morning, | In which all past is present, all degradation | Is unredeemable. As for what happens— | Of the past you can only see what is past, | Not what is always present. That is what matters", *The Family Reunion* I i.

1, 15, 31, 72 **an old man · · · an old man · · · an old man · · · an old man**: Wilfred

Owen's *The Parable of the Old Man and the Young* (wr. 1918, pub. 1920) expressed the widespread belief that old men safe at home had sacrificed a generation in the Great War.

1, 59, 73 **dry month · · · I have lost my sight, smell, hearing, taste and touch · · · To a sleepy corner**: Laforgue: "O monde de satisfaits, vous êtes dans la béatitude aveugle et silencieuse, et nous, nous desséchons de fringales supra-terrestres. Et pourquoi les antennes de nos sens, à nous, ne sont-elles pas bornées par l'Aveugle, et l'Opaque et le Silence, et flairent-elles au-delà de ce qui est de chez nous? Et que ne savons-nous aussi nous incruster dans notre petit coin pour y cuver l'ivre-mort de notre petit Moi?" [O world of the satisfied, you live in blind and silent blessedness, and we only dry up in super-terrestrial pangs of hunger. Why aren't the antennae of our senses bounded by Blindness, Opacity, and Silence? Why must our senses go hunting about outside of us? Why can't we incrust ourselves in our little corners to sleep off the drunken deaths of our own little Egos?], *Salomé* II (Roberta Morgan and Albert Wohlstetter, *Harvard Advocate* Dec 1938).

3 **the hot gates**: "Thermopylae", TSE in *Thayer's AraVP* (pointing out that his phrase is a literal translation; it derives from the local hot springs, supposed entrances to Hades). At the battle in 480 BC, a small Greek force held back the Persians for three days. TSE, responding to a call for Christians to oppose unemployment in the spirit of "Holy War": "we are not mustered for a mere Thermopylae, but for an active and aggressive campaign with no end", *Full Employment and the Responsibility of Christians* (1945). On imaginative re-creation: "A similar method might be used by an historian, so steeped in Greek history as to see Thermopylæ as he has seen events in his own life, in order to make his readers realise those events", *Thinking in Verse* (1930). To Hayward [11 June 1940] on *Defence of the Islands*: "Is it too much like the epitaph of the Lacedemonians after ~~Marathon?~~ Thermopylae? I thought that if the resemblance seeped in to the minds of the better educated American readers, they might draw for themselves the analogy of these people in the pictures keeping the gates for *them*." For another battle from the classical world, see *The Waste Land* [I] 70, "'You who were with me in the ships at Mylae!'"

3–4 **the hot gates | Nor fought**: Marvell: "rough strife, | Thorough the iron gates of life", *To His Coy Mistress* 43–44. ("the war unlocked the gates of Life · · · the war came to her, locking the gates of life", review of Miss Macnaughtan's war memoir: see note to title.)

3–5 **I was neither · · · Nor · · · Nor**: "neither stand nor lie nor sit", *The Waste Land* [V] 340. To E. M. Forster, 10 Aug 1929: "The War crippled me as it did everyone else; but me chiefly because it was something I was neither honestly in nor honestly out of." ("I was neither | Living nor dead", *The Waste Land* [I] 39–40.)

4–6 **Nor fought in the warm rain | Nor knee deep in the salt marsh, heaving a cutlass, | Bitten by flies, fought**: Tennyson: "from heat to heat, | On stony drought and steaming salt · · · knee-deep in mountain grass", *Mariana in the South* 39–42 (*Musgrove* 42). James Thomson: "I fret 'neath gnat-stings, an ignoble prey, | While others with a sword-hilt in their grasp | Have warm rich blood to feed their latest gasp", *Twenty-third Birthday* 78–80 (*Crawford* 50–51). **knee deep**

in the salt marsh, heaving a cutlass: Sidney Lanier: "marsh-grass, waist-high, broad in the blade", *The Marshes of Glynn* 57.

7 **My house is a decayed house**: Hawthorne: "she saw again her native village, in Old England, and her paternal home; a decayed house of gray stone, with a poverty-stricken aspect, but retaining a half-obliterated shield of arms over the portal, in token of antique gentility", *The Scarlet Letter* ch. 2. TSE to Geoffrey Curtis, 20 Oct 1943: "Hawthorne is, I think, about the best prose writer America produced. In my own opinion, *The House of the Seven Gables* is a greater book than *The Scarlet Letter* and I think the best that he ever wrote. Perhaps I am not a fair judge. It must mean more to me for traditional reasons than it would to an English reader. Hawthorne's background is so much the same as mine both in physical and theological environment. As a matter of fact, his first ancestor in America and mine both engaged in the pursuit of hanging witches in Salem." TSE's ancestor Andrew Eliott (1627–1703/4), who had emigrated from East Coker to escape persecution (see note to *Little Gidding* III 26), became a juror in the Salem witch trials, 1692, and was a signatory to the *Declaration of Regret for Part Taken in Salem Witchcraft, Circulated and Signed by the Jurors*: "we confess that we ourselves were not capable to understand, nor able to withstand the mysterious delusions of the powers of darkness and Prince of the air". (See note to *The Waste Land* [III] 310–11, and Walter Graeme Eliot's *A Sketch of the Eliot Family* [1887] 19–20.)

Joyce: "Houses of decay, mine, his and all", *Ulysses* episode III (Proteus) in *Little Review* May 1918 (Stephen Romer, personal communication). TSE to Marguerite Caetani, 21 Jan 1930: "We have not found moving into a flat beneficial either in health or in any other way, and are on the point of taking another house—a 'decayed house' but I believe a good one." "Houses rise and fall", *East Coker* I 2.

8 **the Jew squats** [jew *until 1963*]: Pope: "ev'ry child hates Shylock, tho' his soul | Still sits at squat, and peeps not from its hole", *Moral Essays: Epistle I. To Richard Temple, Viscount Cobham* 114–15 (*Julius* 29). For the use of "the Jew" to disparage all Jews while permitting the defence that only a particular Jew is meant, see Ricks, *T. S. Eliot and Prejudice* (1988) ch. II, "Anti-Semitism".

8–9 **squats ··· Spawned**: see Beddoes, "Squats ··· A bodiless childfull of life", in note to *Animula* 1.

8–10 **the Jew ··· estaminet of Antwerp, | Blistered in Brussels, patched and peeled in London**: Marlowe: "In Florence, Venice, Antwerp, London, Seville, | Frankfort, Lubeck, Moscow, and where not, | Have I debts owing", *The Jew of Malta* IV i. Apollinaire: "Elle se mettait sur la paille | Pour un maquereau roux et rose | C'était un juif il sentait l'ail | Et l'avait venant de Formose | Tirée d'un bordel de Changai" [She lay down on the straw for a redhaired rosy pimp, it was a Jew, he smelt of garlic, he had her coming from Formosa plucked from a Shanghai brothel], *Marizibill* 8–10, in *Alcools* (1913). TSE: "the metic, like the Jew, can only thoroughly naturalize himself in cities", *Why Rural Verse* (1925). (OED "metic": "A resident alien in a Greek city, having some of the privileges of citizenship.") **estaminet of Antwerp**: André Salmon: "C'est à l'*Estaminet de l'Etoile Polaire*" [It's at the Estaminet of the Pole Star], *Anvers* [Antwerp] in *Le Calumet* (1910). Salmon had influenced TSE's *Embarquement pour Cythère* (1910) and *Interlude in London* (1911); writing of poets in France, TSE praised him to Scofield Thayer, 14 Feb 1920, as among "the most important men there". In *Contemporary French Poetry* (1952), he named Salmon among the "significant figures of the twenties". **Antwerp:** thanks to its port and efficient banking, the centre of world trade in the 16th century, when policies of toleration attracted a large foreign and Jewish populations. The city was held by various powers, but declined over succeeding centuries. As a Belgian fortress in 1914, it was regarded as impenetrable, but was overwhelmed after a short siege and occupied by the Germans until the end of the war. For Ford Madox Ford's war poem *Antwerp*, see note to *Burnt Norton* II 3–5, 12–13. **Brussels ··· London:** Salmon: "Les Belges ··· les Anglais", *Anvers* 17. As TSE has an international *mélange,* Salmon's poem had un Français de Paris, deux chauffeurs de Hambourg, les Russes, Sébastopol, Nagazaki, les Antilles, Singapoor, Chine, Perou.

8–15 **squats ··· iron, merds ··· an old man:** Edward John Waring: "Pill Aloes and Iron ··· Sulphate of Iron ··· In Habitual Constipation ··· whether this be the result of fever and debilitating diseases, old age, or sedentary habits", *A Manual of Practical Therapeutics* (3rd ed. 1871).

9 **estaminet:** pronounced *estaminée* in TSE's recording, as recommended by *Fowler*. OED: "A café in which smoking is allowed. Now, any small establishment selling alcoholic liquor." Frederic Manning, of the Great War: "quite a bon place, two decent estaminets an' some mad'moiselles", *The Middle Parts of Fortune* (1929) ch. 4.

10 **patched and peeled:** Pope: "Peel'd, patch'd, and pyebald, linsey-wolsey brothers", *The Dunciad* (1742) III 115 (Henry Woudhuysen, personal communication). Isaiah 18: 2–7: "a nation scattered and peeled ··· a people scattered and peeled".

10–12 **patched and peeled in London. | The goat coughs ··· in the field ··· iron:** "The peeled hull, a pile of rusty iron, | In a street of scattered brick where the goat climbs", *Choruses from "The Rock"* III 25–26 (see note for TSE's annotation "Shadwell", the London district).

11 **The goat coughs:** TSE in *Thayer's AraVP*: "Cf. Wyndham Lewis: *The Enemy of the Stars*", referring to Lewis's "coughing like a goat". Lewis's play appeared in *Blast* 1 (July 1914).

12 **moss, stonecrop:** Meredith: "Yellow with stonecrop; the moss-mounds are yellow", *Love in the Valley* 115. Mary Elizabeth Braddon: "wall ··· ivy, yellow stonecrop, and dark moss", *Lady Audley's Secret* ch. I (for which see note to *The Waste Land* [II] 78–87). **iron, merds:** Jonson: "merds, and clay, | Powder of bones, scalings of iron", *The Alchemist* II i (Mermaid ed.; commonly II iii) (*Grover Smith* 305). OED "merd, merde": "Now usu. treated as unnaturalized. a. Dung, excrement; a piece of excrement, a turd." Pronounced *murds* in TSE's recording (OED also gives the French pronunciation).

12–15 **iron, merds. | The woman keeps the kitchen, makes tea, | Sneezes at evening, poking the peevish gutter. | I an old man:** FitzGerald to Frederick Tennyson, 8 Dec 1844: "I really do like to sit in this doleful place with a good fire, a cat and dog on the rug, and an old woman in the kitchen ··· the great event of this winter is my putting up a trough round the eaves to carry off the wet. There was discussion whether the trough should be of iron or zinc; iron dear and lasting; zinc the reverse. It was decided for iron; and accordingly iron is put up", quoted *Benson* 29 (John Abbot Clark, *South Atlantic Quarterly* Apr 1949). TSE to John Hayward [16 Apr 1937]: "two days with the plumbers camping in the bathroom both days—no hot water—part of the time no gas—didnt wash—could only rear in the evening ··· depended upon odd unknown parochial females who poked cups of bovril and tea at me". TSE repeated the scene to Geoffrey Faber four days later, but with "women" for "females". **Sneezes at:** OED 2. *colloq.* With *at*: "To regard as of little value, worth, or consideration; to despise, disregard, underrate", from 1806. **at evening, poking the peevish gutter:** "evening ··· sparrows | Delve in the gutter with sordid patience", *First Caprice in North Cambridge* 2, 9–10. **poking the peevish gutter. | I an old man:** "old man who coughs and spits sputters | Stumbling among the alleys and the gutters. || He pokes", *First Debate between the Body and Soul* 2–4. **peevish:** used twice of FitzGerald in *Benson* (70, 86). OED 3: "An epithet of dislike, hostility, disparagement, contempt, execration, etc., expressing the speaker's feeling rather than any quality of the object referred to" (*obs.* with 16th-century citations only). 5: "Morose, querulous, irritable, ill-tempered, childishly fretful".

15–16] indented and isolated by line spaces in *AraVP*, as though a refrain. **I an old man, | A dull head among windy spaces:** "I a tired head among these heads", *Coriolan* II. *Difficulties of a Statesman* 37 (which in draft had been "I a head among these weary heads").

16–17 **A dull head among windy spaces. || Signs are taken for wonders:** to Hope Mirrlees, 16 Sept 1953: "Astronomy bores me—it seems to me a study that interests chiefly people with no precise Christian faith: they like to wander about in the vast interstellar spaces. I have always noticed among non-Christians a hankering for natural wonders, bizarre phenomena, thaumata and odd theories about the origin of the world."

17–19 **Signs are taken for wonders. "We would see a sign!" | The word within a word, unable to speak a word, | Swaddled with darkness:** Matthew 12: 38–39: "Master, we would see a sign from thee. But he answered and said unto them, An evil and adulterous generation seeketh after a sign; and there shall be no sign given." Acts 2: 43: "many wonders and signs were done by the apostles" (see note to *The Cultivation of Christmas Trees* 32). TSE in *Thayer's AraVP*: "Bishop Andrewes: Sermon on the Nativity", referring to Lancelot Andrewes:

> Signs are taken for wonders. "Master, we would fain see a sign," (Matthew 12: 38), that is a miracle. And in this sense it is a sign to wonder at. Indeed, every word here is a wonder. *Τὸ βρέφος*, an infant; *Verbum infans*, the Word without a word; the eternal Word not able to speak a word; 1. a wonder sure. 2. And the *σπαργανισμὸς*, swaddled; and that a wonder too ··· swaddling bands of darkness (Job 38: 9) ··· 3. But yet, all is well.
>
> Christmas Sermon 1618

(The paradox occurs also in the Christmas Sermon 1611. For Andrewes see headnote to *Journey of the Magi.*) Augustine: "with that same end of perverted knowledge magical arts be enquired by ··· signs and wonders are demanded of Him", *Confessions* bk. X 35. North's Plutarch: "Before this war as it is reported, many signs and wonders fell out", Life of Mark Antony (ed. W. H. D. Rouse, Temple Classics, 1898–99) IX 83 (for this volume see note to *Burbank with a Baedeker: Bleistein with a Cigar* 5–8). **wonders ··· a word, unable to speak**

a word: Donne: "The Word but lately could not speake, and loe | It sodenly speakes wonders", *Holy Sonnets* IV 5–6. **Signs ··· unable to speak a word**: FitzGerald: "Who shall interpret us the speechless sign ... ?" *Agamemnon* chorus XI, quoted *Benson* 122 (*Clark* 260). **Swaddled with darkness**: John Mackay Wilson: "Religion, without knowledge, and still swaddled in darkness, fostered the idle fear", *The Doom of Soulis* in *Tales of the Borders* (1835).

18, 20 **The word within a word, unable to speak a word ··· Christ the tiger**: Andrewes on procrastination and the twelve days of Christmas: "We love to make no very great haste ··· Why should we? Christ is no wild-cat. What talk ye of twelve days?" Christmas Sermon 1622; in *The New Elizabethans and the Old* (1919), TSE quoted: "Christ is no wild-cat". In *Thayer's AraVP*, alongside 20, TSE wrote "Andrewes: 'Christ is no tiger'", so associating his own with Andrewes's wording. In *Lancelot Andrewes* (1926), he quoted:

> Phrases such as "Christ is no wild-cat. What talk ye of twelve days?" or "the word within a word, unable to speak a word", do not desert us.

The first of these is now correct, but the second again attributes TSE's words to Andrewes. For the Infant was "without a word", whereas "within a word" is from *Gerontion*. TSE: "the unspoken word, the Word unheard, | The Word without a word, the Word within | The world ··· in darkness ··· the silent Word", *Ash-Wednesday* V 4–9. "the Infant, the still unspeaking and unspoken Word", *A Song for Simeon* 22. To Pound, 10 Apr 1928: "WOT the WORD unable to Speak a Word? Infans Natus? Wot about it?" **unable to**: of the newborn: "Unable to fare forward", *Animula* 26.

19–20 **darkness. In the ··· Christ the tiger**: Blake: "Tyger, Tyger, burning bright, | In the forests of the night", *The Tyger* 1–2. **In the juvescence of the year | Came Christ**: Philip Acton: "And in the juvenescence of the morn, | With feathered choristers on every thorn, | All Earth proclaims 'The Lord is risen indeed'", *Easter* in *Sonnets* (1875) (TSE: "feathers", 71). **juvescence**: not in OED 1st ed., but later added as "*rare*", noting its irregular etymology and defining it as "The state of becoming young, juvenescence", with TSE as first citation. ("Juvenescence" is recorded from 1800, "senescence" from 1695.) The entry for "Old Age restored to Youth" in E. Cobham Brewer, *The Reader's Handbook* (rev. ed. 1911) includes "The *fontaine de jouvence* ··· the river of juvescence at the foot of Olympus." In Robert Wever's *Interlude* (1565), "Lusty Juventus" personifies Youth. (TSE: "Senectus", *Anabasis* III iii *variant*.) Given the epigraph's "nor youth nor age", TSE's word may be a compacting of youth and age. "its source of strength and rejuvenescence", *The Man of Letters and the Future of Europe* (1944).

To R. W. Chapman, 24 May 1949: "I can hardly believe that I was so temeritous as to invent the word 'juvescence' and there doesn't seem to be any other word which in my illiteracy I might have intended. I have a very strong impression that together with certain other phrases in that poem I found the word *juvescence* in a sermon of Lancelot Andrewes's; it is most likely to have been one of his Christmastide sermons before James I, but it might have stuck in my head from a quotation in some other book and so be almost impossible to trace. The word is certainly not a vestige of my Sanskrit studies." To Lynette Roberts, 11 May 1949: "It is all right to invent words for yourself, but when one invents a word the meaning ought to be immediately evident to the reader who ought to be made to feel that the invention was a happy thought." **Christ the tiger**: Richard

Aldington to TSE, 7 Apr 1926: "if I could join the Church I think I would, but my temperament and what little ability to think I have are both violently opposed to it. Moreover, I don't really like the gospels, and I don't much like Christ." TSE, 9 Apr: "I agree with you about Christ and I do not disagree with anything else."

19, 22, 39 **juvescence · · · To be eaten · · · famishes the craving:** Corbière: "Fontaine de Jouvence et Borne de l'envie! | —Toi qui viens assouvir la faim inassouvie!" [Fountain of Youth and Boundary of desire!—You who come to satisfy the hunger that is unsatisfied!], *Litanie du sommeil* [*The Litany of Sleep*] 54–55.

21 **depraved May, dogwood and chestnut:** "Cf. Henry Adams's autobiography", TSE in *Thayer's AraVP.* Henry Eliot noted in his account of TSE in America: "Then two phrases from *The Education of Henry Adams*", *Excerpts from Lectures 1932–33*. Adams: "Here and there a negro log cabin disturbed the dogwood and the judas-tree, the azalea and the laurel. The tulip and the chestnut gave no sense of struggle against a stingy nature · · · The brooding heat of the profligate vegetation; the cool charm of the running water; the terrific splendor of the June thunder-gust in the deep and solitary woods, were all sensual, animal, elemental. No European spring had shown him the same intermixture of delicate grace and passionate depravity that marked the Maryland May", *The Education of Henry Adams* (1918) ch. XVIII (Robert G. Davis, *Matthiessen* 73). **depraved May:** traditionally the merry month. *Love's Labour's Lost* IV iii: "Love whose month is ever May." See notes to *The Waste Land* [I] 1–2, "April is the cruellest month, breeding | Lilacs". **dogwood:** Pound: "a dog-wood tree some syne", *La Fraise* 15 (a reminiscing monologue by a "grave councillor · · · wise, and very old"; *Personae*, 1909).

22 **To be eaten, to be divided, to be drunk:** Luke 22: 17–18: "And he took the cup, and gave thanks, and said 'Take this, and divide it among yourselves: for I say unto you, I will not drink of the fruit of the vine, until the kingdom of God shall come.'" Tourneur: HIPPOLITO: "you vowed once | To give me share to every tragic thought." VENDICE: "By the mass, I think I did too; | Then I'll divide it to thee", *The Revenger's Tragedy* III iv (Mermaid ed., commonly III v). Writing to Henry Dugdale Sykes on 17 Feb 1922, TSE compared *The Revenger's Tragedy* with Tourneur's undisputed work *The Atheist's Tragedy*, and in *Cyril Tourneur* (1930) and *Tourneur and "The Revenger's Tragedy"* (1931) he rejected the case for Middleton's authorship. For the same scene see notes to 65–66, *Dans le Restaurant* 14 and *Burnt Norton* I 11. TSE to Polly Tandy, 23 Dec 1941: "the enclosed, to be divided among the chillun according to their various needs and desires".

23 **Mr Silvero:** TSE drew a swooping line here in *Thayer's AraVP*, with a comment now illegibly erased. Pronounced *Sil-vairo* in TSE's recording.

24 **caressing · · · Limoges:** "Her hands caress the egg's well-rounded dome", *WLComposite* 245. OED "Limoges": "The name of a city in central France used (freq. *attrib.*) to designate painted enamels, porcelain, etc., made there", and quoting Disraeli: "a collection of Limoges ware that is the despair of the dilettanti". Pronounced *Limm-òzj* in TSE's recording. To his mother, 3 Sept 1919: "At 4 we reached Limoges, where I waited an hour for my train." For TSE's intention to revise the poem while in France, see headnote.

24, 29 **caressing hands · · · one hand on the door**: Symons on the actress Eleonora Duse: "her open hand upon a door, certain blind caresses", *Plays, Acting, and Music* (1903) 62. **hand on the door**: Henry James: "hand on the door", "hand on the door", "hand on the door-knob", *Washington Square* ch. XII, XVIII, XXIX (TSE: "knob", 32).

26 **Hakagawa**: pronounced *Harkagawa* in TSE's recording. For Pound on the name, see Textual History.

26–28 **Hakagawa · · · Tornquist · · · Kulp**: TSE drew a line from each name in *Thayer's AraVP* to comments now illegibly erased.

26, 34, 54 **among the Titians · · · History · · · honestly**: Henry James: "stream of history · · · among the Titians and the Turners; she had been honestly nursing the hours", *The Wings of the Dove* bk. V vii (*Ricks* 124–25).

27 **Tornquist**: Carlos Alfredo Tornquist and Ernesto Tornquist each published on Argentina's economy and balance of payments in 1918–19 (*D'Ambrosio* 166). Pronounced *Tornkwist* in TSE's recording.

28 **Shifting the candles**: Crashaw: "Nor by alternate shreds of light, | Sordidly shifting hands with shades and Night", *In the Glorious Epiphany of Our Lord God* 34–35. TSE scored these lines in his Crashaw. Against the description of this as a "Black Mass" ritual in *G. Jones* (197), TSE wrote "!!" underlining Jones's phrase. **von Kulp**: pronounced *Coolp* by TSE in his recording (L. *culpa*: guilt).

29–30 **Vacant shuttles | Weave the wind**: underlined by TSE in *Thayer's AraVP*, with a line to a comment now illegibly erased. Job 7: 6–7: "My days are swifter than a weaver's shuttle, and are spent without hope. O remember that my life is wind: mine eye shall no more see good." Sacheverell Sitwell: "On the never-ceasing shuttles of the wind", *Trumpets* 2, in *The People's Palace*, a book TSE praised in *Contemporanea* (1918). **Weave the wind**: Webster: "To leave a living name behind, | And weave but nets to catch the wind", *The Devil's Law Case* V iv (the play is not in the Mermaid volume of Webster and Tourneur). *Vassar Miscellany News* 10 May 1933 on TSE's reading three days previously: "He mentioned the phrase 'Weave the wind,' which he had anticipated James Joyce in coining." (Joyce: "Words Mulligan had spoken a moment since in mockery to the stranger. Idle mockery. The void awaits surely all them that weave the wind" and "'For them too history was a tale like any other too often told · · · Weave, weaver of the wind'", *Ulysses* episode I (Telemachus) in *Little Review* Mar 1918.) TSE: "weave, weave the sunlight", *La Figlia Che Piange* 7.

32 **Under a windy knob**: OED 2: "A prominent isolated rounded mound or hill; a knoll; a hill in general; esp. in *US.*" TSE: "The dancers are all gone under the hill", *East Coker* II 50.

33 **After such knowledge**: Psalm 139: 1–6: "O Lord, thou hast searched me, and known me. Thou knowest my downsitting and mine uprising · · · For there is not a word in my tongue, but, lo, O Lord, thou knowest it altogether · · · Such knowledge is too wonderful for me." TSE: "by such knowledge", *The Death of Saint Narcissus* 16 (*Grover Smith* 64). "except such knowledge", *Notes on the Way* (12 Jan 1935); see note to *Choruses from "The Rock"* VIII 38. Often in legal contexts with "condone": "To condone means to forgive, and this forgiveness, to be effectual, must be freely given, with a full knowledge of all the surrounding

circumstances ··· Condonation must be with knowledge; such knowledge as will satisfy a prudent man that a crime has been committed", Shackleton *v.* Shackleton, New Jersey, 19 May 1891 (*Central Law Journal* vol. 33).

33–36] Braced by TSE in *Thayer's AraVP* with "Duchess of Malfy" (the brace subsequently extended to 41 or so). No specific reference is apparent, but TSE reviewed a performance by the Phœnix Society in *Art & Letters* Winter [1919/]1920.

33, 39 **knowledge ··· famishes**: Isaiah 5: 13: "they have no knowledge: and their honourable men are famished."

33–42 **knowledge ··· History ··· can be dispensed with**: "A large part of any poet's 'inspiration' must come from reading and from his knowledge of history. I mean history widely taken; any cultivation of the historical sense, of perception of our position relative to the past, and in particular of the poet's relation to poets of the past", *A Note on Ezra Pound* (1918). "Tradition ··· involves, in the first place, the historical sense, which we may call nearly indispensable to anyone who would continue to be a poet beyond his twenty-fifth year; and the historical sense involves a perception, not only of the pastness of the past, but of its presence; the historical sense compels a man to write not merely with his own generation in his bones, but with a feeling that the whole of the literature of Europe from Homer and within it the whole of the literature of his own country has a simultaneous existence and composes a simultaneous order. This historical sense, which is a sense of the timeless as well as of the temporal and of the timeless and of the temporal together, is what makes a writer traditional. And it is at the same time what makes a writer most acutely conscious of his place in time, of his own contemporaneity", *Tradition and the Individual Talent* I (1919).

34 **cunning passages**: *cuniculus*, underground passage (L.). George Chapman: "I am suspicious, my most honour'd father, | By some of Monsieur's cunning passages, | That his still ranging and contentious nostrils, | To scent the haunts of mischief have so used | The vicious virtue of his busy sense", *Bussy d'Ambois* IV i (Mermaid ed.; commonly IV ii). "F. M.": "Proust himself cunningly leads them into every by-way", *"Mr. Bennett and Mrs. Brown"* (1925), review of Virginia Woolf. For "cunning axletree" and the debt to Chapman, see notes to 67–71 and to *Burbank with a Baedeker: Bleistein with a Cigar* 7–12. Sir John Davies: "Now after, now afore, the flattering Dame | With divers cunning passages doth erre", *Orchestra* st. 38. **cunning**: OED 2b: *transf.* "skilfully contrived or executed; skilful, ingenious". Frequent in Webster's plays. **contrived corridors**: "corridors of death ··· alleys of death", *In silent corridors of death*; and, for the Trenches, see headnote to that poem. "The Polish Corridor along the Vistula to the sea" (*The Times* 21 Mar 1919) was a strip of land taken from Germany by the Versailles Treaty (*Bergonzi* 54). For TSE and "the Economic Clauses of the Peace Treaty", see note to *The Waste Land* [III] 277–78, 290–91.

35 **issues**: OED *n.* 1a: "The action of going ··· outgoing, outflow." 6a: "Offspring, progeny ··· Now chiefly in legal use" (TSE: "propagates ··· fathered", 43, 45). 10a: "The outcome of an action". 11c: "A matter or point which remains to be decided". *v.* 5a: "To turn out (in a specified way); to have a certain issue or result; to end or result *in.*"

38–39 **what she gives, gives with such supple confusions | That the giving famishes the craving:** Chapman: "drowning their eternal parts in sense | And sensual affections: while we live | Our good parts take away, the more they give", *The Conspiracy of Charles, Duke of Byron* III i, with "my confusions" later in the scene. (*The Waste Land* [II] 89: "drowned the sense in odours".) Chapman's long scene of losses, cunning and constellations has "neither hot nor cold" ("neither at the hot gates", 3), "infected houses" ("decayed house", 7), "my weak brain" ("dry brain", 75), and "crave" ("craving", 39); it also shares with *Gerontion* "fought", "knee", "passion", "fear", "profit" and, punning on a name, "Gulf/gulfs". For Chapman's scene see note to 62–64. **supple ··· the giving famishes the craving:** *Coriolanus* IV ii, VOLUMNIA: "I sup upon myself, | And so shall starve with feeding." **the giving famishes the craving:** *Antony and Cleopatra* II ii: "other women cloy | The appetites they feed, but she makes hungry | Where most she satisfies" (*Grover Smith* 305). *Hamlet* I ii: "As if increase of appetite had grown | By what it fed on." Chapman: "envy, fed with others' famishment", *The Shadow of Night.* TSE commended "Chapman's long, obscure and very beautiful poems *Ovid's Banquet of Sense* and *The Shadow of Night*", in *Wanley and Chapman* (1925). **confusions:** OED 3: "Mental perturbation or agitation such as prevents the full command of the faculties; embarrassment, perplexity, fluttered condition", with 1611: "What Monarch wrapt in my confusions | Can tell what patience meanes?" 6c: "*pl.* Disorders, commotions", with *Romeo and Juliet* IV v: "Peace ho for shame, confusions' | Cure lies not in these confusions." 39–41 **Gives too late ··· Gives too soon:** "I wonder if it is too late or soon", *Entretien dans un parc* 6. "tardy or too soon", *Portrait of a Lady* III 37.

41–42 **too soon | Into weak hands:** Shelley: "Too soon, and with weak hands", *Adonais* 237 (*Grover Smith 1983* 30).

42–44 **weak hands ··· fear ··· saves us:** Isaiah 35: 3–4: "Strengthen ye the weak hands ··· fear not ··· he will come and save you". **a fear:** Jeremiah 49: 5: "I will bring a fear upon thee."

44 **Neither fear nor courage saves us:** Denham, of the stag: "All safety in despair of safety plac'd, | Courage he thence resumes ··· since 'tis in vain to fear ··· and more | Repents his courage, than his fear before; | Finds that uncertain waies unsafest are", *Cooper's Hill* 290–92, 297–99. TSE: "The description of the stag pursued by hounds has still a mild excitement", *Sir John Denham* (1928). George Pierce Baker: "the weakness or the strength, the courage or the vacillation of a particular king ··· If the dramatist sees these facts, tragedy will be born, for the discovery will correlate his illustrative tragic incidents", *The Development of Shakespeare as a Dramatist* (1907) 179. TSE scored the passage in his copy. (TSE in *Hamlet* (1919): "The only way of expressing emotion in the form of art is by finding an 'objective correlative'; in other words, a set of objects, a situation, a chain of events which shall be the formula of that *particular* emotion ··· Shakespeare's more successful tragedies".)

47 **tears are shaken from the wrath-bearing tree:** Blake: "I was angry with my friend: | I told my wrath, my wrath did end ··· tears ··· beneath the tree", *A Poison Tree* (Wolf Mankowitz in *Rajan ed.* 136). TSE: "Till the wind shake a thousand whispers from the yew"; "voices shaken from the yew-tree ··· Let the other yew be shaken", *Ash-Wednesday* III 28, VI 23–24. "a shudder from afar of space shaking an iron tree", *Anabasis* VI vi.

48 **The tiger springs in the new year**: Tennyson, *In Memoriam* CVI: "ring in the new ··· year ··· Ring in the Christ that is to be" (TSE: "Christ the tiger", 20) (Shawn Worthington, personal communication). **Us he devours**: Chapman: "to devour | Him that devour'd what else had swallowed him", *The Conspiracy of Charles, Duke of Byron* III i (see note to 62–64).

49 **reached conclusion**: without an article (as also with), coming to an end or to a judgment. Thomas Gaspey: "The vagabondizings ··· were not to reach conclusion till near six o'clock", *The Witch-Finder* (1824) I 279. John Esten Cooke: "I have detailed the process by which I reached conclusion", *The Heir of Gaymount* (1870) ch. XLI.

51–54 **I have not made this show purposelessly ··· honestly**: *The Revenger's Tragedy* III iv: "I have not fashioned this only for show". Henry Eliot to TSE, 12 Sept 1935, on the Church: "Unlike a certain character in one of your poems, you cannot declare 'I have not made this show purposelessly'. I believe that you have an irresistible, instinctive, more or less unconscious talent for publicity, but your exercise of it is purposeless." TSE, 1 Jan 1936: "the words of mine that you quote seem to me simple honest words. Their publicity value was not in my mind when I wrote them, nor is it now."

52–53 **concitation | Of the backward devils**: OED "concitation": "*arch.* Stirring up, rousing, or exciting; agitation, excitement; *esp.* of the mind", with no instances quoted between 1656 and TSE's line. TSE to his Italian translator, Roberto Sanesi, 28 Oct 1960: "I think that by 'concitation' I meant co-operative cajolery, or a mixture of cajolery and coercion on the part of the devils. But why were the devils 'backward'? I should like to find an explanation of that because no poet likes to admit that he did not know what he was saying or that his words are meaningless. I suppose I meant taking one back to the past, or holding one's thought in the past. I think you will have to use your own fancy freely and if necessary explain that after a great many years the poet does not know what he meant and is not sure that he meant anything that could be put into other words. It is only in more recent years that I have formed the habit of looking up in the dictionary every important word that appears in my verse!" *The Merchant of Venice* I iii: "The devil can cite scripture for his purpose." Of concitation of scripture: "If for any reason you should wish to call up the Devil, you must say the Lord's Prayer backwards", Angelina Parker, *Collectanea* in *Folk-lore* Mar 1913. Sir Thomas Browne: "the revelations of Heaven are conveyed by new impressions ··· whereas the deceiving spirit, by concitation of humours, produceth his conceited phantasms", with gloss: "How the Devil works his pretended revelations or predictions", *Pseudodoxia Epidemica* (*Vulgar Errors*, 1646) I x. (TSE: "in the prose of Sir Thomas Browne only a commonplace sententiousness is decorated by reverberating language", *Prose and Verse* (1921). For "Damn Sir T. Browne", see note to *Little Gidding* III 35–36.) **backward devils**: augurers in *Inf.* XX, condemned to walk backwards, with heads reversed on their shoulders, for presuming to tell the future. Stephen Gardiner, preaching in 1541: "The devil tempteth the world, and biddeth them to cast themselves backward. There is no 'forward' in the new teaching, but all backward. Now the devil teacheth, come back from fasting, come back from praying, come back from confession, come back from weeping for thy sins; and all is backward", Foxe's *Acts and Monuments* bk. VIII.

54–56 **I would meet you upon this honestly. | I that was near your heart was removed therefrom | To lose beauty in terror, terror in inquisition**: braced by TSE in *Thayer's AraVP* with "v. Middleton: the Changeling", referring to "I that am of your blood was taken from you · · · regardlessly" (V iii). The play is now regarded as a collaboration with Rowley, but in *Thomas Middleton* (1927), TSE wrote with assurance:

> Middleton in the end—after criticism has subtracted all that Rowley, all that Dekker, all that others contributed—is a great example of great English drama · · ·
>
> I that am of your blood was taken from you
> For your better health; look no more upon't,
> But cast it to the ground regardlessly,
> Let the common sewer take it from distinction.
> Beneath the stars, upon yon meteor
> Ever hung my fate, 'mongst things corruptible;
> I ne'er could pluck it from him; my loathing
> Was prophet to the rest, but ne'er believed.
>
> The man who wrote these lines remains inscrutable, solitary, unadmired; welcoming collaboration, indifferent to fame; dying no one knows when and no one knows how; attracting, in three hundred years, no personal admiration.

The 17th-century reading was "I am that of your blood" (a metaphor from blood-letting), but this was emended in the Mermaid edition, ed. Havelock Ellis (2 vols, 1887–90). *Gerontion* has its relations also to two of TSE's other favourite passages from 17th-century drama which turned out to be defective in the Mermaid editions: 65–66 relate to Tourneur's *The Revenger's Tragedy* (see note to *The Waste Land* [V] 403, 405 for the textual crux *bewildering/bewitching*); and 67–71 relate to Chapman's *Bussy d'Ambois* (see note to *Burbank with a Baedeker: Bleistein with a Cigar* 7–12 for the textual crux *burning/cunning*). To Masuru Otaké, 6 Apr 1934: "The Mermaid Series are extremely useful because of the form and size but the establishment of the texts leaves something to seek." For misquotation from *Measure for Measure*, see note to epigraph, and from Lancelot Andrewes, see note to 18–20. For misquotation from Webster's *The Duchess of Malfi*, see note to *The Death of the Duchess* II 23–24, 51–53.

58 **adulterated**: see note on second epigraph to *Sweeney Among the Nightingales*.

59 **I have lost my sight, smell, hearing, taste and touch**: for *Measure for Measure* III i: "Thou hast neither heat, affection, limb, nor beauty", see note to epigraph. *As You Like It* II vii: "Sans teeth, sans eyes, sans taste, sans everything". Newman: Soul: "how comes it then | That I have hearing still, and taste, and touch, | Yet not a glimmer of that princely sense | Which binds ideas in one, and makes them live?" Angel: "Nor touch, nor taste, nor hearing hast thou now", *The Dream of Gerontius* §4 133–37. Newman: "Let us beg and pray Him day by day to reveal Himself to our souls more fully, to quicken our senses, to give us sight and hearing, taste and touch of the world to come", Sermon on Divine Calls (1839). TSE, annotating his Greek text of Aristotle's *De Anima* II ch. 1: "A. says that taste is a kind of touch. If so, touch can not be separated from *all* the other senses. But here he is speaking vaguely and generally." (*De Anima* II ch. 9: "our sense of taste is · · · a modification of touch".)

60–66 **contact · · · a wilderness of mirrors · · · spider · · · Suspend**: Conrad Aiken to

TSE [23 Nov 1913], on Bergson: "It seemed to me that he was not in contact with life: or if he was, in his first premises, he soon lost it in images of light and sound. And I always was impatient with these withered little spiders who spin endless subtleties out of their own consciousness, mainly using the external world as attacking-points, or points of suspension." Bacon: "This kind of degenerate learning did chiefly reign amongst the Schoolmen: who having sharp and strong wits ··· shut up in the cells of a few authors ··· did out of no great quantity of matter and infinite agitation of wit spin out unto those laborious webs of learning ··· as the spider worketh his web ··· admirable for the fineness of thread and work, but of no substance or profit ··· unprofitable subtility", *The Advancement of Learning* bk. I iv 5 (Grover Smith, personal communication). TSE on Paris in the first decade of the century: "over it all swung the spider-like figure of Bergson", *A Commentary* in *Criterion* Apr 1934. ("like a syphilitic spider | The Absolute sits waiting", *He said: this universe is very clever* 6–7.)

62 **delirium**: pronounced in TSE's recording as though to rhyme with *bacterium*.

62–64 **profit of their chilled delirium, | Excite the membrane, when the sense has cooled, | With pungent sauces**: Chapman: "High coolisses, and potions to excite | The lust of their ambition", *The Conspiracy of Charles, Duke of Byron* III i, "coolisses" being "strong broths" (Mermaid footnote). For this scene see notes to 38–39 and 48, and to *The Waste Land* [I] 71–76. TSE mentioned the scene in the last of his Clark Lectures (*The Varieties of Metaphysical Poetry* 220). **chilled delirium | excite**: James Huneker, comparing Baudelaire with Poe, De Quincey, Hoffmann, James Thomson and Coleridge: "Existence for such natures is a sort of muffled delirium", *The Baudelaire Legend in Egoists: A Book of Supermen* (1909), reviewed by TSE in *Harvard Advocate* 5 Oct 1909. Huneker's essay was reprinted as the preface to *The Poems and Prose Poems of Charles Baudelaire* (NY, 1919). **when the sense has cooled**: *Macbeth* V v: "The time has been, my senses would have cool'd" (Jennifer Formichelli, personal communication).

62, 64–65 **delirium ··· multiply variety | In a wilderness of mirrors**: Poe: "Who does not remember that, at such a time as this, the eye, like a shattered mirror, multiplies the images of its sorrow", *The Assignation*. TSE read this Venetian story in childhood (see headnote to *Burbank with a Baedeker: Bleistein with a Cigar*). "I suppose that the *Murders in the Rue Morgue* would be called prose, *Shadow* prose poetry, and *The Assignation* perhaps something between the two", *Prose and Verse* (1921). TSE in *Thayer's AraVP*: "Jonson: The Alchemist", referring to "my glasses | Cut in more subtle angles, to disperse | And multiply the figures, as I walk", *The Alchemist* II i (Mermaid ed.; commonly II ii). TSE quoted these lines and the previous four in *Ben Jonson* (1919), after describing a scene in *Catiline* as "a wilderness of oratory". Pound: "And all the rest of her a shifting change, | A broken bundle of mirrors ··· !" *Near Perigord* III, final lines (TSE: "Shifting", 28) (*Jain 1991*). TSE quoted the last 17 lines of Pound's poem in *Ezra Pound: His Metric and Poetry*. **a wilderness of mirrors**: Poe: "Along that wilderness of glass", *The City in the Sea* 37. *The Merchant of Venice* III i: "I would not have given it for a wilderness of monkeys" (*Grover Smith* 305). TSE: "Levy a wilderness of mirrors on the boneyard of streams", *Anabasis* VII ix. The Versailles Treaty was signed in the Hall of Mirrors, 28 June 1919 (*Bergonzi* 54), where the new German Reich had been proclaimed in 1871. Although contemporary British newspapers made little of this symbolism, the humiliating terms imposed by the Allies were a reflection of the humiliation imposed by Germany on France half a century earlier (see notes to *The Waste Land* [I] 8–17 and [III] 277–78, 290–91). *The Times* 1 July 1919: "The Royalist *Action Française*, which has always refused its benediction to the Treaty, observes:—'German unity, which was formerly made by the error of France, is cemented by the error of the Allies. They will regret it one day.'" TSE: "It is not particularly the Treaty of Versailles that has separated nation from nation; nationalism was born long before; and the process of disintegration which for our generation culminates in that treaty began soon after Dante's time", *Dante* (1929) I.

65 **spider**: "spider ··· he is very old", *The Engine* II (*Gerontion* = little old man).

65–66 **What will the spider do | Suspend its operations**: Remy de Gourmont: "elle fuit, se laisse ··· glisser le long d'un fil ··· On dit même qu'elle n'attend pas toujours la fin de l'opération" [she flees; she lets herself ··· slide down a thread ··· she does not always wait for the end of the operation], *Physique de l'amour: essai sur l'instinct sexuel* (1903) ch. XIII (of the epirus spider); this translation, by Pound, dates from 1922. In *Tradition and the Individual Talent* II (1919), TSE quoted eleven lines of Tourneur's *The Revenger's Tragedy* III iv (giving neither title nor author), including "Does the silkworm expend her yellow labours | For thee? For thee does she undo herself?" **What will the spider do ··· weevil**: *Ricks* 254: "the weevil joins forces with the spider, for the weevil has its etymological filaments back to the web and to weaving, as well as to the root, 'to move about briskly'."

67 **De Bailhache, Fresca, Mrs. Cammel**: TSE drew lines in *Thayer's AraVP* from each of the three names to notes now illegibly erased. **Bailhache**: pronounced *By-ash* in TSE's recording. **Fresca**: "The white-armed Fresca blinks", *WLComposite* **231** (see notes to *WLComposite* **229–98**).

67–71 **whirled ··· Bear ··· snow**: Cicero: "The furthest tip of either axle-end is called the pole. Round the pole circle the two Bears, which never set" (Ursa Major and Ursa Minor), *De natura deorum* II xli 105. *Measure for Measure* III i, Claudio: "thick-ribbed ice; | To be imprison'd in the viewless winds | And blown with restless violence round about | The pendent world" (*Braybrooke ed.* introduction). TSE: "Whirled in a vortex that shall bring | The world to that destructive fire | Which burns before the ice-cap reigns", *East Coker* II 15–17. Sir John Davies: "As the two Beares whom the first mover flings | With a short turne about heavens Axeltree, | In a round daunce for ever wheeling bee", *Orchestra* st. 64 (for Davies's poem see notes to 34 and to *East Coker* I 25–45; for Chapman's "axletree", see note to *Burbank with a Baedeker: Bleistein with a Cigar* 7–12).

67–72 **whirled ··· the wind ··· windy ··· running ··· feathers**: Harriet Monroe: "blow like a feather ··· the winds of fate", *Night in State Street* in *You and I* (1914), followed, two poems later, by "ships that outrun the gale ··· a feather of steam ··· whirling", *The Ocean Liner.* **the wind ··· windy ··· feathers ··· driven**: "a feather on the wind: | Driven", *Choruses from "The Rock"* VII 3 *variant.*

68 **Beyond the circuit of the shuddering Bear**: *glacialis ursæ*, shivering with cold ("chilled", 62); TSE quotes the Latin term within Seneca in *Reflections on Contemporary Poetry* IV (1919). See note to *Ode* ("Tired. | Subterrene") 22,

"Charles' Wagon". **circuit of the ··· Bear:** OED "circuit": "the compass, circumference". OED "arctic": "L. *articus*, *arctic-us*, Gr. *ἀρκτικ-ός* of the Bear, northern, f. *ἄρκτος* bear, the constellation *Ursa Major*." Hence, Arctic Circle. ("The Hunter with his dogs pursues his circuit", *Choruses from "The Rock"* I 2.)

69 **fractured atoms:** Rutherford's splitting of the nitrogen atom was reported by *The Times* on 7 June 1919, some 15 years after he began speculating on potential uses for its vast stores of energy. TSE: "ghosts, influences, strange elements with terrifying properties ('the destruction of the atom' will probably flourish for several years in bad detective stories) are all in the same category", *Homage to Wilkie Collins* (1927). On Henry Adams: "Wherever this man stepped, the ground did not simply give way, it flew into particles", *A Sceptical Patrician* (1919). In Grierson's Introduction to *Metaphysical Lyrics and Poems of the Seventeenth Century* (1921) xxvi, TSE underlined the words "disintegrating collision in a sensitive mind of the old tradition and the new learning". TSE on Gertrude Stein: "I am inclined to wonder ··· whether the mechanical complication of life does not bring about ··· simplification of sensibility ··· In this Hogarth essay ··· the atom is dissociated", *Charleston, Hey! Hey!* (1927).

Describing the "profound melancholy" of Lucretius II 139–74 (in terms similar to *Gerontion*, "fatigue of the will, lassitude in pleasure, corruption and disintegration in society"), George Santayana wrote of "the final dissipation of the atoms of his soul, escaping from a relaxed body, to mingle and lose themselves in the universal flow", *Three Philosophical Poets: Lucretius, Dante, and Goethe* (1910) 44–45 (*Gray* 219). TSE called this "one of the most brilliant of Mr. Santayana's works" (*The Varieties of Metaphysical Poetry* 48). TSE had taken Santayana's course "The Philosophy of History: Ideals of Society, Religion, Art and Science in their Historical Development" at Harvard in 1909. See note to *The Hollow Men* V 31. **Gull against the wind:** "The gull comes against the rain", *Oxford Dictionary of English Proverbs*, citing "The Gull cometh not, but against a tempest" (*against* = in anticipation of).

69–73 *variant* **a shilling against oblivion:** *Troilus and Cressida* III iii: "alms for oblivion".

70–71 **Belle Isle, or running on the Horn ··· the Gulf:** alongside "Belle Isle" in *Thayer's AraVP*, TSE wrote "near Labrador (*not* Belle Isle *France*)", with a line from "Horn" to a note now illegibly erased. Belle Isle is off the coast of Labrador, north of Newfoundland which partly encloses the Gulf of St. Lawrence. Liners en route from Europe to Montreal pass through the straits of Belle Isle, as TSE did in 1932. Many ships have run aground on Cape Horn (as though impaled? see note to *Ash-Wednesday* V 22, VI 4), but many run on round it. The Horn could also refer to the zodiacal signs Aries and Taurus, and to the constellation Ursa Minor (see note to 67–71 and OED "horn" *n.* 1c). **Belle Isle ··· the Gulf:** Tennyson: 'It may be that the gulfs will wash us down: | It may be we shall touch the Happy Isles", *Ulysses* 62–63 (*Jain 1991*). **running:** OED "run" 10a: "To sail swiftly or easily", citing "With a fair wind we ran past the Bird rocks". 10b: "To sail or be driven on or upon the shore, rocks, etc." **the Gulf claims:** OED "gulf" 3: "An absorbing eddy; a whirlpool. In later use chiefly *fig.*, that which devours or swallows up anything." TSE: "Entering the whirlpool", *The Waste Land* [IV] 318. In *Seneca in Elizabethan Translation* (1927), TSE quotes John Studley: "O Lethes Lake of woful Soules the joy that therein swimme, | And *eake* ye *glummy* Gulphes destroy, destroy me wicked wight" (xxx). **claims:** *The Ladies' Companion* May 1837: "The Pestilence which walketh in darkness ··· claimed a victim." *The Times* 1 Aug 1908: "the town of Winchelsea was claimed by the sea".

70–72 **Horn ··· an old man:** Edward Lear: "There was an Old Man of Cape Horn, | Who wished he had never been born; | So he sat on a chair, | till he died of despair, | That dolorous Man of Cape Horn". Also "There was an Old Man of Thermopylæ" (TSE: "an old man ··· the hot gates" 1, 3); "There was an Old Man in a Marsh" (TSE: "an old man ··· marsh ··· an old man", 1, 5, 15). For Lear, see *Five-Finger Exercises* headnote to IV and V.

71 **White feathers in the snow:** A. E. W. Mason: "Three white feathers fluttered out of the box ··· They lay like flakes of snow", *The Four Feathers* (1902), a bestseller about Gordon at Khartoum, ch. IV. "A white feather could mean nothing but an accusation of cowardice", ch. XXI. From Aug 1914, the "Order of the White Feather" shamed men into uniform. TSE's efforts to obtain a commission in Intelligence culminated in a telegram (Missouri History Museum) to his brother in Chicago, 2 Aug 1918:

> ELIOT
> ENQUIRE CHANCE TRAINING COMMISSION MILITARY OR NAVAL IF RETURN AMERICA BANKING JOURNALISM LANGUAGES YACHTING MARRIED THIRTY REPLY IMMEDIATELY MARLOW
> ELIOT

Vivien Eliot's letters to Mary Hutchinson that month show that she was desperate to save him from active service. The couple remained friends of Ottoline Morrell and Bertrand Russell, who were at the centre of the pacifist movement. In his Temple edition of Dante, TSE underlined "che fece per viltate il gran rifiuto" [him who from cowardice made the great refusal], *Inf.* III 60. Hayward compared the phrase to *The Waste Land* [I] 69 (see note). Dante's line may colour "the refusal propagates a fear. Think | Neither fear nor courage saves us ··· our heroism" (43–45). For Paul Elmer More's first book, *The Great Refusal* (1894), see notes to *The Waste Land* [IV] 314 and *Little Gidding* II 67–71.

71–73 **White feathers in the snow ··· An old man driven by the Trades | To a sleepy corner:** Pound: "Storms, on the stone-cliffs beaten, fell on the stern | In icy feathers", *The Seafarer* 23–24 (see note to 1–5). TSE: "waiting for the death wind, | Like a feather ··· memory in corners", *A Song for Simeon* 4–6 (*Kenner* 216). See notes to *Choruses from "The Rock"* VII 3 *variant* and 16 *variant.* **driven by the Trades | To a sleepy corner:** OED "doldrum" (usually in pl. *doldrums*) 3: "A region in which ships are specially liable to be becalmed ··· where the trade winds meet and neutralize each other". (Also 1: "a dull, drowsy or sluggish fellow. *Obs.* citing 1812: "a long sleeper".) Henry Adams: "Adams would rather, as choice, have gone back to the east, if it were only to sleep forever in the trade-winds under the southern stars", *The Education of Henry Adams*, ch. XXI. *Thayer's AraVP* has a line drawn by TSE from "Trades" to a note now illegibly erased.

73, 75 **corner ··· brain:** "some close corner of my brain", *Present in Absence* attributed to Donne in *The Golden Treasury* but probably by John Hoskins.

74–75 **Tenants of the house, | Thoughts:** Tennyson: "Life and Thought have gone away · · · Careless tenants they!" *The Deserted House* 1–4 (*Musgrove* 42).

75 **Thoughts of a dry brain in a dry season:** Austin Dobson: "Thought gets dry in the brain", in two successive stanzas of *In Town*, which in Carolyn Wells's *A Vers de Société Anthology* (1907) is immediately preceded by Dobson's *A Song within the Four Seasons* (*Ricks 1998*). For Dobson see notes to *A Cooking Egg* 1 and 26, and *Burnt Norton* I 16. **dry brain:** Tennyson: "dry brain", *Fatima* 26 (*Musgrove* 42). Bacon: "The Ape is also a witty Beast, and hath a dry Brain", *Sylva Sylvarum* (9th ed., 1670) Century X, 978. Thomas Willis: "those that have a hot and dry Brain are found more prone to a Frenzy", *The London Practice of Physick* (1685) 454–55. Samuel Crook: "if the brain be too hot and dry, it receives no impression · · · the dry brain of age", *Divine Characters* (1658) 615.

Burbank with a Baedeker: Bleistein with a Cigar

Published in *Art & Letters* (edited by Frank Rutter and Osbert Sitwell) Summer 1919, where this and *Sweeney Erect* were editorially numbered I and II. Then *AraVP*, *US 1920+* and *Penguin / Sel Poems.*

No recording known.

Undated in tss. Dated "? London 1918" in *Isaacs US 1920*; and 1918 by TSE in both *Morley's US 1920* and *Hayward's 1925*. *Profile: Ezra Pound: An Anthology Collected in MCMXXXI* (Milan, 1932) gives "about 1915 or 1916". TSE showed the poem to Sacheverell Sitwell on 1 Mar 1919 along with *The Death of the Duchess* (see its headnote). Soon afterwards Sitwell published a series of poems imitating (or parodying) TSE's quatrain poems. TSE sent *Burbank with a Baedeker: Bleistein with a Cigar* to John Rodker 17 May 1919.

TSE on discovering a Venetian tale: "When I was eleven or twelve years old, and once a week or so I had, like many children, to visit a dentist to have my teeth straightened. In this dentist's waiting room · · · was a complete set of Edgar Poe's Works; and while waiting for my appointments I read the whole of Poe's prose and verse writing. One story—and a highly romantic story too, is called *The Assignation.* As the epigraph to this story I found the lines 'Stay for me there! I shall not fail | To meet thee in that hollow vale.' Followed by the attribution to Bishop King", *Personal Choice* (1957). King's poem is *An Exequy To his Matchless never to be forgotten Friend.* (For Poe's tale, see notes to *Gerontion* 64–65 and *The Waste Land* [I] 36–38, [II] 83–88, 85–95.)

Wilkie Collins's novella *The Haunted Hotel: A Mystery of Modern Venice*, was praised by TSE in *Wilkie Collins and Dickens* (1927). *Ricks* 34–35:

> Collins's anguished *femme fatale* is the Countess Narona (kin to "the countess" of Eliot's epigraph and to the poem's Princess Volupine; a cigar is bizarrely important to Collins's plot; so is the Countess's concealment as "Mrs James" (the poem is a Jamesian story); and the central blackmail in the story is the threat by the Countess's brother to sell himself: "'The woman who will buy me', he says, 'is in the next room to us at this moment. She is the wealthy widow of a Jewish usurer.'"

Matthiessen 9 on James's *The Aspern Papers*: "Eliot has said that the method in this story—'to make a place real not descriptively but by something happening there'—was what stimulated him to try to compress so many memories of past moments of Venice into his dramatic poem, superficially so different from James." (Matthiessen's acknowledgements, 1935, thank TSE "for the great benefit of conversation during his recent year at Harvard".)

Title ***Burbank***: Luther Burbank (1849–1926), American horticulturalist known for cross-breeding, whose works appeared in 12 vols in New York and London in 1914. *Crawford* 65–66: "Luther Burbank was a plant breeder over whom there was considerable controversy ··· hailed by the *Nation* as 'the most ingenious and successful of all hybridizers' [13 July 1911] ··· Burbank's ideas did not stop at plant life ··· but went on to deal with 'improving the human plant'." *Grover Smith 1983* 9: "*Burbank* is all about *breeding.*" ("Thus art ennobles even wealth and birth, | And breeding raises prostrate art from earth", *WLComposite* **285^286** [16–17]; from a fragment with affinities to the activities of Princess Volupine.) Pound: "Even Bose with his plant experiments seems intent on the plant's capacity to feel ··· a persistent notion of pattern from which only a cataclysm or a Burbank can shake it", *Cavalcanti* (1934) in *Literary Essays* ed. TSE (1954). ***Burbank with a***: "Burbank Steps Forward with a Super-Wheat", headline in *Popular Science* (US) Jan 1919. ***Baedeker***: for Karl Baedeker's Handbook for Travellers, *London and its Environs*, see notes to *Mr. Apollinax* 2–5 and 4, 13. *TSE's books: Bodleian list* (1934) includes "Five Baedekers". Arthur Symons on Gautier: "It is not everyone who can write poetry like the *Emaux et Camées* ··· to say nothing of such inspired Baedekers as the *Voyage en Espagne*", *Studies in Two Literatures* (1897) 259. Pound: "This essay on Henry James is a dull grind of an affair, a Baedeker to a continent", opening paragraph of his *Henry James* in *Little Review* Aug 1918 (*Literary Essays*). ***Bleistein***: "Bleistein and Company, fur and skin merchants, were established first in St. James Place, Garlick Hill, and then just around the corner in Upper Thames Street ··· the founder, Mr. S. Bleistein, had been engaged in the fur trade in London since the eighteen nineties ··· He used to smoke Coronas, and frequently lunched at the Cannon Street Grill" (B. K. Martin, *N&Q* July 1967). Commenting upon *Dirge*, Valerie Eliot emphatically pronounced the name "*Blest-in*", BBC broadcast 2 Nov 1971. TSE to Pound, 15 July 1939, of Canto LII: "if you remain keen on jew-baiting, that is your affair, but that name of Rothschild should be omitted. Obvious to me from start, but you cant expect all minds to work as fast as mine. Alternative blank or fancy name, and if you care to have it will present you with Bleistein which is almost of equal value METRICALLY." ***with a Cigar***: Kipling: "The butt of a dead cigar ··· And a woman is only a woman, but a good Cigar is a smoke", *The Betrothed* (epigraph: "'*You must choose between me and your cigar.*' BREACH OF PROMISE CASE, CIRCA 1885"). Kipling has "the Moor", and TSE's epigraph quotes *Othello, the Moor of Venice.* For Kipling's poem, see note to *The Love Song of J. Alfred Prufrock* 60, 71. TSE: "with cigars", *Interlude in London* 7.

Epigraph] E. V. Lucas's *A Wanderer in Venice* (1914) follows the convention of giving chapter summaries as short phrases between dashes, a practice TSE followed for this poem alone. F. W. Bateson characterised the epigraph as a literary conundrum or puzzle, to which the answer is "Venice" (*Criticism's Lost Leader* in *Newton-De Molina ed.*). ***Tra-la-la-la-la-laire***: Gautier: "Tra la, tra la, la, la, la laire!", cry of the gondolier, *Variations sur le carnaval de Venise* II: *Sur les lagunes* 1. ***nil nisi divinum stabile est; caetera fumus***: "nothing is permanent unless divine; the rest is smoke", motto on an emblematic candle in a St. Sebastian by Mantegna which TSE saw in Venice in 1911. ("Nil" is a common contraction of the more correct "nihil". Which of these Mantegna wrote is disputed, but guidebooks that TSE may have used give "nil".) TSE in *Thayer's AraVP*: "Lines on Mantegna's great *St. Sebastian* in the Ca d'Oro Venice". To Conrad Aiken, 19 July 1914: "There are *three* great *St. Sebastians* (so far as I know): 1) Mantegna (ca d'Oro) 2) Antonello of Messina (Bergamo) 3) Memling (Brussels)." Less than a week later, on 25 July, he sent Aiken a ts of *The Love Song of St. Sebastian.* To Sydney Schiff, 24 Mar 1920: "Mantegna is a painter for whom I have a particular admiration—there is none who appeals to me more strongly. Do you know the St. Sebastian in the Franchetti's house on the Grand Canal?" In the summer of 1911, TSE had visited the Ca d'Oro—"Mantegna. First quality"—and Bergamo, noting: "*Ant. da Messina: St. Sebastian*" (notes on Italy, Houghton). ***the gondola stopped, the old palace was there, how charming its grey and pink***: Henry James: "the gondola stopped, the old palace was there; it was a house of the class which in Venice carries even in extreme dilapidation the dignified name. 'How charming! It's grey and pink!' my companion exclaimed", *The Aspern Papers* I. The quotation had been contracted to the words that TSE used (though with different punctuation) in Ford Madox Hueffer's *Henry James: A Critical Study* (1913) 141 (John J. Espey, *American Literature* Jan 1958). TSE began both *The Hawthorne Aspect* (1918) and *Observations* (1918) with the book by Hueffer (later Ford). To Eleanor Hinkley, 1 Apr 1918: "I believe that the *Aspern Papers*, the *American Scene*, and the *Middle Years* are very good · · · I am reading *R. Hudson* now in preparation for an article for the James number of the *Little Review.*" ***goats and monkeys***: "Goats and monkeys!" *Othello, the Moor of Venice* IV i. Hueffer also quoted (140, 143) the words "Cats and monkeys, monkeys and cats—all human life is there", from James's *The Madonna of the Future* (Espey). ***with such hair too!***: Browning: "Dear dead women, with such hair, too—what's become of all the gold | Used to hang and brush their bosoms? I feel chilly and grown old", final lines of *A Toccata of Galuppi's* (see note to 12). The Venetian composer Galuppi Baldessare (1706–85) was *maestro di capella* at St. Mark's. ***so the countess passed on · · · and so departed***: concluding words of John Marston's masque *The Hon. Lord and Lady of Huntingdon's Entertainment of their right Noble Mother Alice, Countess Dowager of Derby, the first night of her honour's arrival at the house of Ashby* (1607?). Marston, like all the other components of the epigraph, has a Venetian link: *Antonio and Mellida* and *Antonio's Revenge*—both discussed by TSE in *John Marston* (1934)—are Venetian (see note to 9–11). All six quotations were identified by I. A. Richards, *New Statesman* 20 Feb 1926. TSE summarised them in *Thayer's AraVP*: "Gautier | Lines on Mantegna's great *St. Sebastian* in the Ca d'Oro, Venice. | the Aspern Papers | Othello | Browning: Toccata of Galuppi's. | from a masque by Marston".

1–2 **little · · · small**: on Georgian poetry: "it is not unworthy of notice how often the word 'little' occurs; and how this word is used, not merely as a necessary piece of information, but with a caress, a conscious delight", *Reflections on Contemporary Poetry* I (1917). See note to *WLComposite* **175–76.**

2 **Descending at a small hotel**: reviewing *The Education of Henry Adams*, TSE remarked how Adams in 1858 and Henry James in 1870 "land at Liverpool and descend at the same hotel", *A Sceptical Patrician* (1922) (F. W. Bateson, *The Review* Nov 1962). **Descending**: OED 1c: "To disembark, land from a vessel; to alight from a horse, carriage, etc." Described as *obs.*, with last (maritime) citation 1600. Archaic for water transport such as that in Venice, but in later use for vehicles (such as the street car taken by the "little girls" in *Suite Clownesque* II 14: "Oh see the soldiers—let's descend"). Lewis Carroll: "He thought he saw a Banker's Clerk | Descending from the bus" (see note to TSE's *I thought I saw a elephant* and *I thought I saw a banker's clerk*). Marston's masque has Ariadne pronouncing an invocation "at which they descended", including "Descend" at the head of a line: "Devotely chaste you vow Pasithea, | Descend". TSE to Lord Halifax, 3 Oct 1927: "I will take the same train ··· descending at Doncaster." To Polly Tandy, 5 July 1947: "I descended at Heath Row Airport". **hotel**: *Fowler*: "The old-fashioned pronunciation with the *h* silent ··· is certainly doomed, & is not worth fighting for."

3, 24, 25 **Princess Volupine ··· Money in furs ··· Princess Volupine**: Jonson's *Volpone* (or "The Fox") is set in Venice. OED "voluptuous" 1: "Of or pertaining to ··· gratification of the senses ··· luxuriously sensuous." 1c: "Of modes of life or conduct", with 1432–50: "The luffe of the cuntre and elegancy voluptuous deceyvide his grevous labors." 1d: "Of fare or feasting." 1e: "Of places." 3b: "Suggestive of sensuous pleasure by fulness and beauty of form." *Venus im Pelz* (1870), by Leopold Sacher-Masoch, the Austrian who gave his name to "masochism", was translated as *Venus in Furs* by C. Carrington (Paris, 1902). Baudelaire: "la torture ··· est née de la partie infâme du cœur de l'homme, assoiffé de voluptés" [torture ··· has been devised by the evil half of man's nature, which is thirsty for voluptuous pleasures], *Mon Cœur mis à nu* [*My Heart Laid Bare*], *Journaux Intimes* XLIII.

4 **They were together and he fell**: TSE in *Thayer's AraVP*: "Tennyson The Two Sisters", referring to "They were together, and she fell", *The Sisters* (1832) 4. **fell**: OED "fall" 22: "To yield to temptation, to sin; *esp.* of a woman: To surrender her chastity", citing *Othello, the Moor of Venice* IV iii: "it is their husbands' faults | If wives do fall."

5 **Defunctive music**: TSE in *Thayer's AraVP*: "Phoenix & Turtle", referring to Shakespeare: "Let the priest in surplice white, | That defunctive music can, | Be the death-divining swan, | Lest the requiem lack his rite", *The Phoenix and Turtle* 13–16 (I. A. Richards, *New Statesman* 20 Feb 1926). TSE: "the *Phoenix and Turtle* is a great poem, far finer than *Venus and Adonis*", *A Romantic Aristocrat* (1919). OED: "Of or pertaining to defunction or dying" (originally "*obs. rare*", citing only Shakespeare, but this designation was dropped in the 2nd ed. when TSE and three subsequent citations were added).

5–6 **under sea ··· passing bell**: for Ariel's song from *The Tempest* I ii, see notes to *Dirge* 1–7 and *The Waste Land* [I] 48.

5–8 **music under ··· passing ··· the God Hercules | Had left him, that had loved him well**: *Antony and Cleopatra* IV iii, *Music of the hautboys is under the stage.*

SOLDIER 1: "Music i'th'air." | SOLDIER 3: "Under the earth." · · · SOLDIER 2: "'Tis the god Hercules, whom Antony loved, | Now leaves him" (I. A. Richards, *New Statesman* 20 Feb 1926, and mentioned by TSE in US lectures in 1932–33). TSE in *Thayer's AraVP*: "v. Antony & Cleopatra also North's Plutarch Hercules the god of sensual virility". North:

> within little of midnight, when all the city was quiet · · · suddenly they heard a marvellous sweet harmony of sundry sorts of instruments of musick, with the cry of a multitude of people, as they had been dancing · · · and it seemed that this daunce went through the city unto the gate that opened to the enemies, and that all the troop that made this noise they heard, went out of the city at that gate. Now, such as in reason sought the depth of the interpretation of this wonder, thought that it was the god unto whom Antonius bare singular devotion to counterfeit and resemble him, that did forsake them.
>
> Life of Mark Antony (ed. W. H. D. Rouse, Temple Classics, 1898–99) IX 103–104

6–10 **Passed seaward with the passing bell · · · Beat:** Ruskin, *The Stones of Venice* I 1: "the fast-gaining waves, that beat, like passing bells, against the STONES OF VENICE." TSE's *Syllabus: Modern English Literature* (1916) included Ruskin's book. See note to 32. **passing bell:** OED (adopting Johnson's definition): "The bell which rings at the hour of departure, to obtain prayers for the passing soul: often used for the bell which rings immediately after death."

7–12 **Hercules · · · axletree · · · Burned:** OED "axletree": "being in earlier use than the simple *axle*, formerly included the sense of that word, and of *axis* · · · The fixed bar or beam of wood, etc. on the rounded ends of which the opposite wheels of a carriage revolve." 4. "The imaginary or geometrical line which forms the axis of revolution of any body, e.g. the earth, a planet, the heavens. *Obs.*" The expression "burning axletree", for Phoebus' chariot, the sun, led to OED 5: "*poetically* · · · the heaven, the sky. *Obs.*" Seneca: *Hercules Furens* 129–36 (first chorus):

> signum celsi glaciale poli
> septem stellis Arcados ursae
> lucem verso temone vocat.
> Iam caeruleis evectus equis . . .
> Phoebique fugit reditura soror.

> [The ycye signe of haughtye poale agayne, | With seven starres markt, the Beares of Arcadye, | Do call the light with overturned wayne. | With marble horse now drawne, hys waye to hye · · · And to returne doth Phœbus syster flee]

(Tr. Jasper Heywood (1561), in *Seneca: His Tenne Tragedies*, with Introduction by TSE (1927) I 13.) *Hercules Furens* 1138–42 (start of act V), HERCULES:

> Quis hic locus, quae regio, quae mundi plaga?
> ubi sum? sub ortu solis, an sub cardine
> glacialis ursae? numquid Hesperii maris
> extrema tellus hunc dat Oceano modum?

> [What place is this? what region? or of the world what coast? | Where am I? under ryse of sunne or bond els uttermost | Of th' ycy beare or els doth here of sea of Hespery | The fardest ground appoynt a bond for th' ocean sea to lye?], *Tenne Tragedies* I 46.

TSE used the first of these lines (1138), in Latin, as the epigraph to *Marina.* In

Seneca, *Hercules Œteus* 1521–27, the Chorus sends word of Hercules' death to all parts of the world:

> dic sub Aurora positis Sabaeis,
> dic sub occasu positis Hiberis,
> quique sub plaustro patiuntur ursae
> quique ferventi quatiuntur axe,
> dic sub aeternos properare manes
> Herculem et regnum canis inquieti,
> unde non umquam remeabit ille.

> [Declare to th' Easterlinges whereas the ruddy morne doth ryse, | Declare unto the Irishmen aloofe at western Skies: | Make knowne unto the Moores annoyed by flaming axentree, | Those that with the ysy Wayne of Archas pestred bee. | Display to these that Hercules to th' eternall ghostes is gone]
>
> *Tenne Tragedies* II 243.

Chapman's Bussy d'Ambois, in his death throes: "flie where men feele | The burning axletree: and those that suffer | Beneath the chariot of the Snowy Beare", *Bussy d'Ambois* V i (Mermaid ed.; commonly V iii); the burning and freezing places beneath the sky: the tropics and the poles. (Milton: "He saw a greater Sun appear | Than · · · burning Axletree could bear", *On the Morning of Christ's Nativity* 83–84.)

R. H. Shepherd's edition of Chapman (1873) had contained the misprint "curning axletree", which the Mermaid ed. (1895) erroneously emended to "cunning axletree" (*Grover Smith*; see also *Gerontion* 34: "cunning passages"). TSE quoted the Mermaid text in *Reflections on Contemporary Poetry* IV (1919):

> No dead voices speak through the living voice; no reincarnation, no re-creation. Not even the *saturation* which sometimes combusts spontaneously into originality.
>
> fly where men feel
> The cunning axletree: and those that suffer
> Beneath the chariot of the snowy Bear
>
> is beautiful; and the beauty only appears more substantial if we conjecture that Chapman may have absorbed the recurring phrase of Seneca [quotes *Hercules Furens* 129–31 and 1139–40], a union, at a point at least, of the Tudor and the Greek through the Senecan phrase.

He quoted the defective Mermaid text again in *The Varieties of Metaphysical Poetry* 152, *Seneca in Elizabethan Translation* (1927), *Thinking in Verse* (1930) and *Dryden the Dramatist* (1931). In 1933 he quoted Chapman from F. S. Boas's ed. of 1905:

> I am glad of the opportunity to use it again, as on the previous occasion I had an inaccurate text. It is from Chapman's *Bussy D'Ambois*:
>
> "Fly where the evening from the Iberian vales
> Takes on her swarthy shoulders Hecate
> Crowned with a grove of oaks: fly where men feel
> The burning axletree, and those that suffer
> Beneath the chariot of the snowy Bear . . ."
>
> Chapman borrowed this, as Dr. Boas points out, from Seneca's *Hercules Œteus* [quotes 1521–24] and probably also from the same author's *Hercules Furens* [quotes 1139–40]. There is first the probability that this imagery had some personal saturation value, so to speak, for Seneca; another for Chapman, and

> another for myself, who have borrowed it twice from Chapman. I suggest that what gives it such intensity as it has in each case is its saturation · · · with feelings too obscure for the authors even to know quite what they were.
>
> *The Use of Poetry and the Use of Criticism* 147–48

(The two borrowings referred to are the present lines, 7–12, and *Gerontion* 67–71.)

Comparing Hamlet's soliloquies with Chapman's scene, TSE described them as "full of some stuff that the writer could not drag to light, contemplate, or manipulate into art", *Hamlet* (1919). *Bussy d'Ambois* ends: "may both points of heaven's straight axle-tree | Conjoin in one, before thyself and me" (V i). Sir John Davies: "As the two Beares whom the first mover flings | With a short turne about heavens Axeltree, | In a round daunce for ever wheeling bee", *Orchestra* st. 64. See also note to *Burnt Norton* II 1–2, 8–10, and *McCue 2014a*.

On saturation: "We cannot, as a matter of fact, understand the *Vita Nuova* without some saturation in the poetry of Dante's Italian contemporaries, or even in the poetry of his Provençal predecessors. Literary parallels are most important, but we must be on guard not to take them in a purely literary and literal way."

9 **The horses, under the axletree:** Marlowe's Ovid: "Now o'er the sea from her old love comes she | That drawes the day from heaven's cold axle-tree · · · Hold in thy rosy horses that they move not", *Amores* I, elegy 13, quoted by Pound, *Elizabethan Classicists* in *Egoist* Sept 1917 (*Literary Essays*).

9–11 **The horses · · · Beat up the dawn · · · With even feet:** TSE in *Thayer's AraVP*: "Marston", referring to "For see, the dapple grey coursers of the morn | Beat up the light with their bright silver hooves, | And chase it through the sky", *Antonio's Revenge* I i (*Jones* 297). "aequo pulsat pede" [with an impartial foot], Horace, *Odes* I iv 13; TSE quoted the Latin in *Andrew Marvell* (1921). Kipling: "their hoofs drum up the dawn", *The Ballad of East and West* 37 (in *A Choice of Kipling's Verse*) (*Grover Smith* 53). **Beat up the dawn · · · With even feet:** Beaumont and Fletcher: "Pace out, you watery powers below; | Let your feet, | Like the galleys when they row, | Even beat", *The Maid's Tragedy* I ii, the masque. Neptune leads "Music to lay a storm" and "*descends*" (TSE: "Descending", 2); NIGHT: "I hope to see | Another wild-fire in his axle-tree" (TSE: "the axletree · · · Burned", 9, 12); CYNTHIA: "whip up thy team: | The day breaks here". For this masque, see note to *Sweeney Erect* 5. *The Maid's Tragedy* appears in TSE's *Syllabus: Elizabethan Literature* (1918). **Beat up:** OED "beat" *v.*[1] 19: "(*Naut.*) To strive against contrary winds or currents at sea". **even feet:** "Lady Equistep", *Eeldrop and Appleplex* II (1917).

10–12 **Istria · · · day:** the peninsula, sixty miles from Venice in the direction of the rising sun, provided the piles on which the city is built ("piles", 22). Pope too took liberties in rhyming on names: "Breathing Revenge, in Arms they take their Way | From Chalcis' Walls, and strong Eretria", *Iliad* II 643–44.

11–12 **Her shuttered barge | Burned on the water all the day:** TSE in *Thayer's AraVP*: "Ant. & Cleo.", referring to II ii, ENOBARBUS: "The barge she sat in, like a burnished throne | Burned on the water", lines quoted in *"Rhetoric" and Poetic Drama* (1919). Coleridge: "The water, like a witch's oils, | Burnt green, and blue, and white", *The Rime of the Ancient Mariner* II 47–48 (see note to *The Waste Land*

[II] 94–95). TSE: "flame | Like perfumed oil upon the waters", *The Burnt Dancer* 17–18. "The Chair she sat in, like a burnished throne, | Glowed on the marble", *The Waste Land* [II] 77–78. In the Palazzo Labia on the Grand Canal, TSE may have seen Tiepolo's frescoes of the lives of Antony and Cleopatra (*Drew* 63).

12 **Burned on the water**: John Gould Fletcher: "Lights burn upon the water", *The Red Gates* in *New Paths*, ed. C. W. Beaumont and M. T. H. Sadler (1918). **Burned ··· all the day**: Browning: "Balls and masks begun at midnight, burning ever to mid-day", *A Toccata of Galuppi's* 11 (*Grover Smith* 53). **all the day**: Donne: "All day, the same our postures were, | And wee said nothing, all the day", *The Extasie* 16. On which, TSE: "the 'All day' beginning the third line, echoed by 'all the day' at the end of the fourth, is a real *trouvaille* or euphony which goes to make one of the most perfect quatrains in this form that I have ever met", *The Varieties of Metaphysical Poetry* 110 (Clark Lecture III).

13 **But this or such was Bleistein's way**: Browning: "And this, or something like it, was his way", *How It Strikes a Contemporary* 2 (*Loucks 1976a*).

14–15, 17 **A saggy bending of the knees | And elbows, with the palms turned out ··· eye**: Thomas Wilkes: "Respect and submission may be expressed by the eyes mildly beholding the personage that enforces it, the body bent, and the hands either hanging down not close to the body, the fingers closed, and the palms turned outward; or else by the eye cast down", *A General View of the Stage* (1759) ch. V. **bending of the knees ··· turned out ··· protrusive**: "The usual error ··· is a turning in of the toes, a bending of the knees, and a protrusion of the lower abdomen", *The Water-Cure Journal* July 1856. **with the palms turned out**: Frances Trollope: "joining her hands together on her breast, and then separating them widely, with the palms turned outward, which gesture she repeated at every clause of her discourse: 'Don't tell me of fond indulgence'", *Mabel's Progress* bk. II XI (*All the Year Round* 8 June 1867). TSE: "those who would build and restore turn out the palms of their hands", *Choruses from "The Rock"* II 6; "palms turned upwards", *Chorus* VII 31 (*Hands*).

16 **Chicago Semite Viennese**: "For a number of generations there was some friction between the German Jew and the East European Jews [in Chicago] ··· and each had their own institutions ··· From the 1880s to the 1920s the Jewish population grew from 10,000 to 225,000, or from 2 percent to 8 percent of the general population. In 1900 about 65 percent of Chicago's Jews were of East European origin; in 1920 about 80 per cent", *Encyclopaedia Judaica* (2nd ed., 2006) 4,607–12. Kipling: "But the real reason of my wish to return is because I have met a lump of Chicago Jews and am afraid that I shall meet many more. The ship is full of Americans, but the American-German-Jew boy is the most awful of all", *From Sea to Sea* VI ("Shows how one Chicago Jew and an American Child can Poison the Purest Mind"). Kipling again: "Wait till the Anglo-American-German-Jew—the Man of the Future—is properly equipped ··· He'll be the finest writer, poet, and dramatist, 'specially dramatist, that the world as it recollects itself has ever seen", *From Sea to Sea* XXXIII. TSE to Clive Bell, 25 July 1930: "Your son is a sturdy sprout and I have read his verse with warm approval. He seems to be almost the only one at Cambridge who has escaped the Chicago Semite taint and who is uncontaminated by either Joyce, Lewis, Pound, Léger [St.-John Perse] or myself." (For "the Jew" and cities, see note to *Gerontion* 8–10.) "Jerusalem Athens Alexandria | Vienna London", *The Waste Land* [V] 374–75.

17 **lustreless protrusive eye**: Poe: "the eye-balls protruded", and later "To look at a star by ··· turning toward it the exterior portions of the *retina* ··· is to behold the star distinctly—is to have the best appreciation of its lustre—a lustre which grows dim just in proportion as we turn our vision *fully* upon it. A greater number of rays actually fall upon the eye", *The Murders in the Rue Morgue.* TSE: "And yet one cannot be sure that one's own writing has *not* been influenced by Poe. I can name positively certain poets whose work has influenced me, I can name others whose work, I am sure, has not; there may be still others of whose influence I am unaware, but whose influence I might be brought to acknowledge; but about Poe I shall never be sure", *From Poe to Valéry* (1948). Dickens: "a lustreless eye", *David Copperfield* ch. XVI. Henry James: "'Well, I admire Miss Evers—I don't mind admitting that; but I ain't dangerous,' said Captain Lovelock, with a lustreless eye", *Confidence* ch. XV. James: "every protrusive item almost", *The Middle Years* ch. I; quoted by TSE in *A Sceptical Patrician* (1919) (*Ricks* 70). Rupert Brooke: "behind the eyes ··· sightless ··· Lustreless", *The Fish* (32–35), a poem praised by TSE for its "amazing felicity and command of language", *Reflections on Contemporary Poetry* I (1917). *Arrowsmith 1981* counts Bleistein among "Eliot's whole gallery of one-eyed men" including Polyphemus (*Sweeney Erect* 10), the "one-eyed merchant" (*The Waste Land* [I] 52) and "one-eyed Riley" (Sir Henry Harcourt-Reilly in *The Cocktail Party*).

18 **protozoic slime**: OED cites *Webster's Dictionary* (1864): "*Protozoic*, of, or pertaining to, the protozoa", and T. H. Huxley: "A similar process takes place in sundry Protozoa and gives rise to a protozoic aggregate." Coleridge: "The lowest class of animals or *protozoa* ··· have neither brain nor nerves", *Aids to Reflection* XV.

18–19 **from the protozoic slime | At a perspective of Canaletto**: Luigi Lanzi: "For the greater correctness of his perspectives, Canaletto made use of the optic camera", *The History of Painting in Italy* tr. Thomas Roscoe (1828) III 387. *The Art-Union* 15 Mar 1841: "If buildings, vanishing to a well-defined perspective point, appear (for example, a picture of Canaletto), a few inches below the eye's level would, indeed, be as incorrect as a few inches above it ··· although the perspective of the buildings were evidently correct ··· water will seem not to have been *painted* flat, but ··· incline ··· towards the bottom of the picture." Canaletto's Venice is often a combination of elements from different perspectives.

20 **candle end of time**: "the old stumps and bloody ends of time", *WLComposite* 159.

20, 24 **candle end ··· Money**: Donne: "this covetous man can date his happinesse by an *Almanack* ··· and though all his joy be in his bonds, yet denies himself a candles end to look upon them", *Sermons* ed. Pearsall Smith (1919) 187.

21–22 **On the Rialto once. | The rats**: TSE in *Thayer's AraVP*: "Mcht of Venice", referring to I iii, SHYLOCK: "upon the Rialto ··· there be land-rats, and water-rats". TSE: "it's a play I've never been able to enjoy myself, because it was a text for me at school, and I very much disliked what was called elocution and I was forced to declaim before a class 'The quality of mercy is not strained'—I hated it", *The Development of Shakespeare's Verse* (recording, 1950).

21–24, 29 **On the Rialto ··· the piles ··· smiles ··· lion's wings**: Byron: "I stood in Venice, | On the Bridge of Sighs ··· smiles ··· Look'd to the winged Lion's marble piles", *Childe Harold's Pilgrimage* IV i.

22 **The rats are underneath the piles**: "Lower than the wharf rats dive", *Dirge* 5. "Subsiding basements where the rat breeds", *Choruses from "The Rock"* III 49. "rats' feet ··· In our dry cellar", *The Hollow Men* I 9–10.

22–24 **The rats ··· Money in furs**: J. G. Wood: "Brown Rats ··· are marvellous exterminators of other 'vermin,' and permit none but themselves to be in possession of the domain which they have chosen ··· the brown Rat is not without its value in commerce, as the prepared skin is said to furnish the most delicate leather for the manufacture of the thumbs of the best kid gloves", *Natural History Picture Book: Mammalia* (1869). TSE informed Father Martingale, 30 Jan 1930, that he had been "nourished in my childhood on the Natural History of the Revd. Mr. Wood", but which of Wood's many books he owned is unknown. **piles. | The Jew ··· Money**: William Carson Corsan: "They made piles of money. They're as rich as Jews", *Two Months in the Confederate States* (1863) 133. **The Jew ··· Money in furs**: to the Rev. Agnellus Andrew, 25 Feb 1949: "A young Austrian Jew, aged 27, came to me to ask whether I could find him a position ··· he contrived to leave Vienna in 1939 and came to this country ··· after his discharge in 1945 he was employed in the fur trade. In November last he paid a visit to Rome, which confirmed him in a desire to be received into the Catholic Church ··· He asserts, what seems to me likely, that his present situation renders him unacceptable to Jewish employers; that employment in the fur trade is therefore closed to him." **Money in furs**: beginning as a fur-trading post, St. Louis was long dominated by the Missouri Fur Company, and in TSE's childhood it had the world's largest trade in raw furs. Arthur J. Ray: "high levels of employment in wartime industries served to increase the demand ··· Fur prices surged ··· During the inflationary period the auction business became ever more lucrative ··· Just before the market crashed in late 1920, the February sale in St Louis disposed of more than $27 million worth of fur ··· In the scramble for furs between 1914 and 1920, buying became highly speculative and was financed largely by the lavish use of credit", *The Canadian Fur Trade in the Industrial Age* (1990) 98–102.

23 **Jew**: the lower-case "j" used in all printings until *1963* was marked for capitalisation by Valerie Eliot in *VE's 1951*. Oscar Williams's printing of this poem in his American revision of *The Golden Treasury* in 1953 was perhaps the first to use a capital here, but as an editor Williams took many liberties. Joyce uses "jew" 66 times in *Ulysses* (*Sloane* 64).

25–28 Gautier: "L'esquif aborde et me dépose, | Jetant son amarre au pilier, | Devant une façade rose, | Sur le marbre d'un escalier" [The skiff lands and deposits me, throwing its rope around a pillar, in front of a rose-red façade, upon the marble stairs], *Variations sur le carnaval de Venise* II: *Sur les lagunes* 21–24 (*Grover Smith* 53); see also note to epigraph, above. Gautier's stanza is quoted in *The Picture of Dorian Gray* ch. XIV, Wilde writing of 23–24: "The whole of Venice was in those two lines."

26–27 **phthisic ··· Lights, lights**: OED "phthisic" (pronounced *tisic*) cites 1587 "the disease of the lights, which is, to bee pursie and ptisike" (*lights* = lungs). Laforgue: "Tout à la chère morte phtisique" [devoted to my darling, dead of TB], *Complainte de l'Organiste de Notre-Dame de Nice* [*Lament of the Organist of Notre-Dame de Nice*]. For Laforgue on Baudelaire, "le spleen et la maladie (non la Phtisie poétique mais la névrose)", see note on the title *Spleen*.

Troilus and Cressida V iii, PANDARUS: "a whoreson tisic, a whoreson rascally tisic". **hand ··· waterstair. Lights, lights:** Poe: "the convulsive pressure of that trembling hand ··· hand ··· hand ··· the lights had died away within the palace ··· the water-gate", two paragraphs of *The Assignation*, a story of Byronic and aristocratic adultery (see headnote). **waterstair:** OED "water" VII 24m: "Situated or built on or beside water", including 1608: "orators' wives shortly will be known like images on water stairs." **Lights, lights:** TSE in *Thayer's AraVP*: "Shakespeare". Instances include "Light, I say! Light!" *Othello* I i, and "Lights, lights, lights" in both *Hamlet* III ii and *Romeo and Juliet* I v. Also Marston: "Lights! Lights!" *What You Will* V i (*Jones* 298); and see note to *Coriolan* I. *Triumphal March* 48–50.

28 **entertains:** on *The Relique* by John Donne: "the notion of the violation of the grave for 'entertaining' a 'second guest', and still more the analogy of the fickleness of graves with the fickleness of women, are of very doubtful value in this place", *The Varieties of Metaphysical Poetry* 125 (Clark Lecture IV). See note on additional draft stanzas at the end of *Whispers of Immortality ts2* for this and other terms shared here.

28–29 **Sir Ferdinand || Klein:** *Thayer's AraVP* has a line drawn by TSE to a note now erased, but possibly consisting of four names including (second) "Sir Henry [*illegible*] Bart". ("Lady Kleinwurm's party", *WLComposite* 254.) Jonson breaks his own name across a stanza break: "Such truths as we expect for happy men; | And there he lives with memory—and *Ben* || *Jonson*: who sung this of him, ere he went | Himself to rest", *To the Immortal Memory and Friendship of that Noble Pair, Sir Lucius Cary and Sir H. Morison* 84–87 (in *Oxf Bk of English Verse*). Kipling: "Surely my Kith and Kin will not refuse || Pay—and I promise ···", *The Rupaiyat of Omar Kal'vin* 8–9. ("Kal'vin", as Kipling's headnote made clear, was Sir Auckland Colvin.) **Klein:** (= little, Ger.), in this position (and after the final *d* of "Ferdinand"), a clipped diminutive of "Decline" (21). Klipstein is abbreviated to "Klip" by his friend Krumpacker in *Sweeney Agonistes: Fragment of a Prologue*.

29–30 **Who clipped the lion's wings ··· and pared his claws?:** Ariosto: "And so you par'd the Lyons teeth and pawes | That since that time to feare we had no cause. [*Footnote*: The Lyons teeth and pawes meaning the Venecians, called Lyons of the sea]", *Orlando Furioso*, tr. Sir John Harington, XL 3 (Roy J. Booth, *N&Q* Oct 1981). Swift: "the writers of and for *Grub Street* have in these latter ages so nobly triumphed over Time; have clipped his wings, pared his nails, filed his teeth, turned back his hour-glass", *The Tale of a Tub* I. Byron: "St Mark yet sees his lion where he stood, | Stand, but in mockery of his wither'd power", *Childe Harold's Pilgrimage* IV ix. (The winged lion is the symbol of both St. Mark and Venice.) Charles Lamb on *The Jew of Malta*: "The idea of a Jew, which our pious ancestors contemplated with so much horror, has nothing in it now revolting. We have tamed the claws of the beast, and pared its nails", *Characters of Dramatic Writers, Contemporary with Shakespeare* (*Sloane* 186). TSE to Theodore Spencer, 10 Nov 1936: "I understand that there is a boy on the Haverford team who recently CLIPPED THE TIGER'S CLAWS." For Browning's "clipped her wings", see note to *The Death of the Duchess* II 7–10, 16–17.

29–31 **wings ··· meditating:** "meditates its wings", *Bacchus and Ariadne* 18.

29–32 **Who clipped ··· seven laws:** TSE in *Thayer's AraVP*: "Ruskin". See note to 32.

31–32 **meditating on | Time's ruins:** Byron: "To meditate amongst decay, and stand | A ruin amidst ruins", *Childe Harold's Pilgrimage* IV xxv (*Bush* 27). Edmund Spenser, *The Ruins of Time* (title) in *Complaints* (F. W. Bateson, *the Review* Nov 1962). TSE to Virginia Woolf, 12 Oct [1939]: "In the ruins of time, it may be that posterity—or the posterity of some foreign race—will make various conjectures as to the identity of the T. S. Eliot whose name is associated with the works of Old Possum."

32 **seven laws:** Ruskin's *Seven Lamps of Architecture* offered seven guiding moral and architectural principles, developed in *The Stones of Venice*. On the "incrusted architecture" of St. Mark's: "LAW I. *That the plinths and cornices used for binding the armour are to be light and delicate* ··· LAW VII. *That the impression of the architecture is not to be dependent on size*", *The Stones of Venice* II iv (*Arrowsmith 1981* 25).

Sweeney Erect

Published in *Art & Letters* Summer 1919, then *AraVP, US 1920+* and *Penguin / Sel Poems.*

No recording known.

Undated in tss. Dated "London ? 1917" in *Isaacs US 1920* and 1917 by TSE in *Hayward's 1925*, but 1918 by TSE in *Morley's US 1920*. Assigned to 1918–19 *Rainey* 198. Sent to John Rodker 17 May 1919.

Title] OED "Sweeney" 1: "from the name of Sweeney Todd, a barber who murdered his customers, the central character of a play by George Dibdin Pitt", *Sweeney Todd, the Barber* (for OED 2, see note to 21–24). Asked at his trial in 1910 about patients for whom he might have required the poison hyoscin, the murderer "Dr." Crippen replied: "it is extremely difficult to remember names. I think I can remember one. Sweeney—no, M'Sweeney", Filson Young, *The Trial of Hawley Harvey Crippen* (1920) 90 (*Arrowsmith 1981*). For TSE's association of Sweeney and Crippen, see headnote to *Sweeney Agonistes*, 11. BRITISH PERFORMANCES.

TSE's childhood family newspaper contained a home-drawn advertisement: "When Others | ~ Fail ~ | Come to Me | Dr. Sweany, M.D. | cures INSOMNIA" (with a picture of the doctor), *Fireside* No. 4. *Crawford* 28: "Doctor F. L. Sweaney ··· advertised daily in the *St. Louis Globe-Democrat.* His speciality ··· was 'Nervous Debility' ··· Eliot was so impressed as a child with this advertisement that he drew his own copy in the *Fireside*, reproducing the doctor's name, face, and rubric with its warning to seek consultation 'when others fail'." (TSE suffered from a hernia which needed treatment in childhood.) James Johnson Sweeney to TSE, 27 May 1958: "*Gould's St. Louis Directory* ran an advertisement every year from 1896 to 1950: 'Dr. F. L. Sweaney leading specialist of St. Louis for nervous, chronic and private diseases, located at the Northwest corner of Broadway and Market Street, 1 North Broadway'." TSE replied: "I think the grounds for regarding this Dr. Sweaney, whose name evidently attracted me at the age of ten, as the original of my hero [*added to carbon in unknown hand*: are insufficient]. The fact, however, that the name 'Sweeney' had such a fascination for me at an early age is perhaps one of great significance for subsequent analysts of my work."

Discussing *Sweeney Among the Nightingales* and this poem, *Matthiessen* 105 referred to "'apeneck Sweeney,' whose prototype Eliot has said he first saw in a bar in South Boston" (perhaps quoting TSE in conversation). When TSE read *Sweeney Among the Nightingales* at Harvard on 13 May 1947 (following *Preludes* and *Morning at the Window*), he said he chose it "because it also has a certain local sentimental association. My figure of Sweeney is of course like many other characters of fiction, an amalgam from metals of very different sources and kinds, with, I hope, something in it that I have added myself. But amongst the chief ingredients were three friends of my youth, all now dead, all citizens of South Boston, and none of them was named Sweeney. I should add that two at least of these friends were men of much more loveable disposition than the use which I have made of them might suggest." In the *Criterion*, the review *"Mr. Bennett and Mrs. Brown"* (1925) by "F. M." took issue with Virginia Woolf's idea of character, asking "did Mr. Eliot ··· deduce Sweeney from observations in a New York bar-room?" TSE: "I think of him as a man who in younger days was perhaps a professional pugilist, mildly successful; who then grew older and retired to keep a pub". (For Conrad Aiken on TSE's boxing lessons, see headnote to *Sweeney Agonistes*: 9. AFTER PUBLICATION.) Francis Sweeney described a conversation he had in 1961:

> I asked Eliot about the prototype of the rough-and-ready Sweeney image in his poems—for example, in *Sweeney Erect* and *Sweeney Agonistes*. He had commented once, "It happens that I know many Sweeneys, some of them among friends of mine. I happen to like the name. It has a pleasant sound." Among his friends named Sweeney was John Lincoln Sweeney, a humanities preceptor at Harvard. At the River Club, I said, "Your classmate, Conrad Aiken, traces Sweeney to your boxing instructor in the South End of Boston." "There were others," Eliot said—among them the bartender at the Opera Exchange, also in Boston, where he had gathered with friends in his Harvard student days, circling Champagne corks on the table in a fortune-telling game. Eliot lifted his forefinger and waved it in a circle.
>
> *Boston College Magazine* Winter 2001

For the game with corks, see *WLComposite* **14–15**. *Harvard College Class of 1910: Secretary's Fourth Report* (1921) lists both an Albert and an Arthur Sweeney. ***Erect***: when discovered in 1891, *Homo erectus* was named *Pithecanthropus erectus* (upright ape-man). *Paradise Lost* IV 288–90: "Two of far nobler shape, erect and tall, | Godlike erect, with native Honour clad | In naked majesty". (TSE: "naked ··· I stand erect before her", *How the Tall Girl's Breasts Are* 1, 4.) Emerson: "He who knows that power is inborn, that he is weak because he has looked for good out of him and elsewhere, and, so perceiving, throws himself unhesitatingly on his thought, instantly rights himself, stands in the erect position, commands his limbs, works miracles; just as a man who stands on his feet is stronger than a man who stands on his head", *Self-Reliance* (*Southam*). The essay has an epigraph from "Beaumont and Fletcher's *Honest Man's Fortune*" (the play is now attributed to Field, Fletcher and Massinger);

see note to epigraph, below. Irving Babbitt: "discredit all the higher values of human nature and the words that describe them, until nothing is left erect but a brutal positivism", *The New Laokoon* (1910) 228, citing Emerson in the next paragraph. TSE: "it *is* a great strain for the erect animal to persist in being erect, a physical and still more a moral strain. With or without mechanical aids of movement and noise, most people spend a good deal of their time avoiding the human responsibility", *Literature and the Modern World* (1935).

Epigraph ***And the trees about me ··· wenches!***: TSE in *Thayer's AraVP*: "Beaumont & Fletcher in *The Maid's Tragedy*" (II ii). In a scene that TSE often remembered, Aspatia, who has been deserted by her betrothed, casts herself in the role of Ariadne, forsaken by Theseus on the island of Naxos in the wild Cyclades (see note to 7–8). Aspatia asks to see a picture of Ariadne which her maid Antiphilia has done in needlework, and bids her rework it:

> Fie, you have missed it here, Antiphilia;
> You are much mistaken, wench:
> These colours are not dull and pale enough
> To show a soul so full of misery
> As this sad lady's was. Do it by me,
> Do it again by me, the lost Aspatia;
> And you shall find all true but the wild island.
> Suppose I stand upon the sea-beach now,
> Mine arms thus, and mine hair blown with the wind,
> Wild as that desert; and let all about me
> Tell that I am forsaken. Do my face
> (If thou had'st ever feeling of a sorrow)
> Thus, thus, Antiphilia: strive to make me look
> Like Sorrow's monument: and the trees about me,
> Let them be dry and leafless; let the rocks
> Groan with continual surges; and behind me,
> Make all a desolation. See, see, wenches,
> A miserable life of this poor picture!

(For phrasing, see *The Love Song of J. Alfred Prufrock* 123–28, and *The Waste Land* [II] 132–33. For Aspatia, see *Elegy* 3–4.) **Look, look, wenches!**: Second Quarto text; the reading "See, see, wenches" in the Mermaid text (above), follows the First Quarto. "'Look, look, master'", *Mr. Eliot's Sunday Morning Service*, epigraph. The first line of TSE's five-line *Those are pearls that were his eyes. See!* likewise became "(Those are pearls that were his eyes. Look!)" in *The Waste Land* [I] 48.

Unadopted epigraph ***Voici ton cierge, | C'est deux livres qu'il a coute . . .***: [Here's your candle. It cost two francs], Corbière, *La Rapsode foraine et le Pardon de Sainte-Anne* [*The Strolling Singer and the Festival of Saint Anne*] 145–46 in *Les Amours jaunes* (1873), printed with "(C'est deux livres qu'il a coûté)" in the first ed. and in the anthology *Poètes d'aujourd'hui*, but quoted without brackets by André Barre in *Le Symbolisme* (1911). See note to 13–16 below. Pound praised Corbière's poem highly, and printed it over more than six pages in *A Study of Modern French Poets* in *Little Review* Feb 1918.

1–5 **Paint me ··· Paint me ··· Display me**: resembling, as well as Aspatia's instructions to Antiphilia, the self-addressed creative injunctions of the "Instructions" genre begun by Waller's *Instructions to a Painter* (see note to

The Last Instructions to a Painter in *The Poems and Letters of Andrew Marvell* ed. H. M. Margoliouth, 1927, 3rd ed. 1971).

2 **Cyclades:** *Lemprière*: "a name given to certain islands of the Aegean Sea, those particularly that surround Delos as with a circle; whence the name." Pronounced with short *i* as in *sickle*; three syllables.

2, 3, 9 **Cast · · · rocks · · · feet and hands:** Emerson: "Cast the bantling on the rocks · · · Power and speed be hands and feet", quatrain epigraph to *Self-Reliance* (Anne Stillman, personal communication).

3 **anfractuous:** TSE in *Thayer's AraVP*: "a favourite word of Dr Johnson's". To Johnson's definition, "Winding; mazy; full of turnings and winding passages", OED adds 2: "[After F. *anfractueux* craggy.] Rugged, craggy", with TSE as first citation. Johnson: "Sir, among the anfractuosities of the human mind, I know not if it may not be one, that there is a superstitious reluctance to sit for a picture", *Boswell* IV 4. Laforgue: "elle alla, dégringolant de roc en roc, râler, dans une pittoresque anfractuosité qui lavait le flot" [she toppled from rock to rock, with death rattling in her throat, and in a picturesque anfractuosity which was washed by the waves], *Salomé*, a dozen lines from the end (*Hands*). See note to 7–8.

3–4 **rocks | Faced by the snarled and yelping seas:** T. E. Brown: "the clamour of the yelping seas!" *Old John* 35 in *Collected Poems* (1900). Swinburne: "In the teeth of the hard glad weather, | In the blown wet face of the sea", *A Song in Time of Order* 53–54. TSE: "the sea | A crowd of barking waves", *Goldfish* IV 10–11 (with "winds", 14; here: "gales", 6). "faces sneer and snarl · · · If there were water | And no rock", *The Waste Land* [V] 344–47. "The sea howl | And the sea yelp, are different voices", *The Dry Salvages* I 26–27.

5 **Display:** Seneca, tr. Jasper Heywood: "Display to these that Hercules to th' eternall ghostes is gone", *Hercules Œteus* (see note to *Burbank with a Baedeker: Bleistein with a Cigar* 7–12). **Display me Aeolus:** winds from particular directions, such as Auster or Zepher, often appeared on maps, cheeks puffed out and with their names (Anthony Payne, personal communication). **Aeolus:** pronounced *Ee-olus. Lemprière*: "The king of storms and winds · · · because he was the inventor of sails, and a great astronomer, the poets call him the god of the wind." The personage of Æolus appears in the masque in *The Maid's Tragedy* I ii.

7–8 **Ariadne · · · perjured sails:** daughter of Minos, King of Crete. She gave Theseus the thread by which he found his way out of the Labyrinth after killing the Minotaur. Abandoning her, Theseus sailed back to Athens, but forgot to change his black sail for a white one. His father, Aegeus, concluded that Theseus had perished, and threw himself from a cliff. (Recounted in Ovid's *Heroides* X.)

9 **Morning stirs the feet and hands:** "dawn · · · to see what it had stirred; | The eyes and feet of men", *Prufrock's Pervigilium* [25–27]. "The morning comes to consciousness · · · feet · · · hands", *Preludes* I 1, 4, 8. "When morning stirred the long nasturtium creeper", *Suppressed Complex* 7 *variant*. "Stirred by the morning air", *Oh little voices of the throats of men* 38.

9–37 **Morning · · · Polypheme · · · root of knots of hair | Slitted below and gashed · · · the bed · · · hysteria:** "When the bridegroom smoothed his hair | There was blood upon the bed. Morning · · · (Io Hymen, Hymenæe) | Succuba eviscerate",

Ode ("Tired. | Subterrene") 9–14 (*Arrowsmith 1981*). For Ruskin, "rooted knots of herbage", see note to *Lune de Miel* 10.

10 **Nausicaa:** Pope, *Odyssey* VI, THE ARGUMENT: "Pallas appearing in a dream to Nausicaa ··· commands her to descend to the river, and wash the robes of State, in preparation to her nuptials. Nausicaa goes with her Handmaids to the river; where, while the garments are spread on the bank, they divert themselves in sports. Their Voices awake Ulysses" (Odysseus). Pronounced *Nor-sic-ay-ah*. **Polypheme:** Polyphemus, a Cyclops—the monster with one eye—who held captive Odysseus and his crew (*Odyssey* IX). In Ovid's *Metamorphoses* XIII, Polyphemus lusted after Galatea and "when he saw her surrender herself to the pleasures of Acis, he crushed his rival with a piece of broken rock" (*Lemprière*); see 14–15. TSE: "He told of polyphemes, and clashing rocks", *Lines Addressed to Geoffrey Faber Esquire, on his Return from a Voyage from the Bahamas, and the Parts about New Spain* 7.

10, 13, 21 **Polypheme ··· knots of hair ··· to shave:** Ovid, tr. Golding: "Polypheme ··· His staur stiff hair he kembeth ··· his bristled beard", *Metamorphoses* XIII 901–904. See note to 41.

11 **Gesture of orang-outang:** Poe: "the ape, razor still in hand, occasionally stopping to look back and gesticulate", *The Murders in the Rue Morgue* (*Grover Smith* 47). "Apeneck Sweeney", *Sweeney Among the Nightingales* 1 (here: "from nape to base", 22). **orang-outang:** OED: "'man of the woods' or 'wild man' ··· An anthropoid ape ··· of arboreal habits". Pronounced *our*-ang-*oot*-ang (OED mentions differences of stress). Poe: "Caught—*In the Bois de Boulogne, early in the morning of the — inst.* (the morning of the murder), *a very large, tawny ourang-outang*", *The Murders in the Rue Morgue*. Poe paraphrases Georges Cuvier: "It was a minute anatomical and generally descriptive account of the large fulvous ourang-outang of the East Indian Islands. The gigantic stature, the prodigious strength and activity, the wild ferocity, and the imitative propensities of these mammalia are sufficiently well known to all. I understood the full horrors of the murder at once." Kipling's *Bertran and Bimi* (1891) has a conversation on a "steamer":

> He haf found him when he was a child—der orang-outang—und he was child und brother und opera comique all round to Bertran. He had his room in dot house—not a cage, but a room—mit a bed und sheets, and he would go to bed und get up in der morning und smoke his cigar und eat his dinner mit Bertran, und walk mit him hand in hand, which was most horrible. Herr Gott! I haf seen dot beast throw himself back in his chair und laugh when Bertran haf made fun of me. He was *not* a beast; he was a man.

(TSE: "Morning ··· hands", 9; "sheets", 12.) Kipling's orang-outang tears Bertran's wife to pieces. TSE jotted down the title of the story for comparison with Conrad, in *Lecture Notes as Norton Professor* (1933). For *Bertran and Bimi* see headnote to *The Engine*.

In the 18th century, Lord Monboddo had proposed that the orang-outang be seen as a form of human, prompting Thomas Love Peacock's novel *Melincourt* (1817), about the adventures in polite society of Sir Oran Haut-Ton. When Queen Victoria saw the orang-outang at London Zoo in 1842, she commented: "he is frightfully, and disagreeably human" (see note to 11, 21–29). TSE quoted Disraeli (Lord Beaconsfield) in his third Turnbull Lecture: "'The question is,' as the late Lord Beaconsfield observed, 'is man an ape or an angel?' I think that Lawrence was on the side of the angels; some reformers are certainly on the side of the Apes", *The Varieties of Metaphysical Poetry* 293–94. On 13 Oct 1939, TSE sent to Bruce Richmond the *Selected Shelburne Essays* of Paul Elmer More, for Richmond's anthology *The Pattern of Freedom* (1940): "the last paragraph of the essay on Huxley is good eternal verity in a light and readable form". It describes how Disraeli addressed a Diocesan Conference at Oxford in 1864, "And then, turning to the presiding officer, the same Bishop Wilberforce whom four years earlier [T. H.] Huxley had so crushingly rebuked, he uttered one of his enigmatic and unforgettable epigrams: 'What is the question now placed before society with a glibness the most astounding? The question is this: Is man an ape or an angel? I, my lord, am on the side of the angels' ··· these words contain a truth that shall some day break to pieces the new philosophy which Huxley spent his life so devotedly to establish." TSE on Wyndham Lewis: "*Tarr* is a commentary upon a part of modern civilization: now it is like our civilization criticized, our acrobatics animadverted upon adversely, by an orang-outang of genius, Tarzan of the Apes", *Contemporanea* (1918) (*Arrowsmith 1981*). Of Shelley's note to *Queen Mab* VIII 211–12: "from a poet who tells us, in a note on vegetarianism, that 'the orang-outang perfectly resembles man both in the order and the number of his teeth', we shall not know what not to expect", *The Use of Poetry and the Use of Criticism* 88 (Shelley reads "the order and number").

11, 21–29 **orang-outang ··· addressed full length to shave ··· nape to base, | Knows the female temperament | And wipes the suds around his face ··· the razor**: W. S. Gilbert: "He shaved his bristles, and he docked his tail ··· And he paid a guinea to a toilet club ··· the Ape, despite his razor keen, | Was the apiest Ape that was ever seen! ··· the Maiden fair, whom the Monkey craved, | Was a radiant Being ··· While a Man, however well-behaved, | At best is only a monkey shaved!" Song: *The Ape and the Lady* in *Princess Ida* (1884) act II. The last two lines are given in the World's Classics edition as "While Darwinian man, though well-behaved ···"

13 **withered root**: *The Tempest* I ii: "wither'd roots, and husks" (*Grover Smith* 1996, 161). **root of knots of hair**: Poe: "On the hearth were thick tresses—very thick tresses—of grey human hair. These had been torn out by the roots ··· Their roots (a hideous sight!) were clotted with fragments of the flesh of the scalp", *The Murders in the Rue Morgue*. **root of knots**: Emerson: "A man is a bundle of relations, a knot of roots", *History* (*Peake*). Irving Babbitt: "Man, according to Emerson, is a bundle of roots, and a knot of relations", *The Masters of Modern French Criticism* (1912) 150.

13–14 **root of knots of hair ··· eyes**: Shelley on Rousseau:

> Struck to the heart by this sad pageantry,
> Half to myself I said—"And what is this?
> Whose shape is that within the car? And why—"
>
> I would have added—"is all here amiss?—"
> But a voice answered—"Life!"—I turned, and knew
> (O Heaven, have mercy on such wretchedness!)

<

> That what I thought was an old root which grew
> To strange distortion out of the hill side,
> Was indeed one of those deluded crew,
>
> And that the grass, which methought hung so wide
> And white, was but his thin discoloured hair,
> And that the holes he vainly sought to hide,
>
> Were or had been eyes
>
> *The Triumph of Life* 176–88

TSE quoted from memory the last seven of these lines in *The Use of Poetry and the Use of Criticism* 90, and quoted 176–205 in *What Dante Means to Me* (1950), commenting: "Well, this is better than I could do." (To J. M. Robertson, 23 Aug 1927: "I dislike Shelley as you will have perceived, and only reproach you for not disliking him enough.")

13–15 **This withered root ··· teeth**: to C. A. Bodelsen, 19 Dec 1958, responding to his book *T. S. Eliot's "Four Quartets": A Commentary* (1958): "you take three lines as a description of Sweeney's morning face. What I had in mind, however, as the face described, was the face of the paralytic on the bed."

13–16 **This withered root ··· thighs**: TSE in *Thayer's AraVP*: "Cf. Tristan Corbière: Rhapsode Foraine" (see note to unadopted epigraph, above). TSE quoted 169–70 from Corbière's poem in his last Clark Lecture:

> From his greatest poem, *La Rapsode foraine*, the assemblage of crippled and diseased at a religious festival in Brittany—
>
> Là, ce tronc d'homme où croît l'ulcère,
> Contre un tronc d'arbre où croît le gui . . .
>
> "This trunk of a man on which the ulcer grows, (leaning) against this trunk of a tree on which grows the mistletoe": this sudden and surprising collocation of the animal and vegetable, with the added horror thrown back upon the human disease, is worthy of Dante.
>
> *The Varieties of Metaphysical Poetry* 218

Praising Corbière's description of "the procession of mendicants and cripples to the shrine of the Virgin", TSE had previously written of these two lines: "the phrase burns itself in like the *cotto aspetto* of Dante's Brunetto Latini", *Modern Tendencies in Poetry* (1920); see note to *Little Gidding* II 39–45.

13–14, 20 **root of knots of hair ··· eyes ··· clawing**: Beddoes: "twisting root-like hair up to his eyes ··· hands, | Like roots, with pointed nails", *Fragments of "The Last Man"* IV.

14–15 **eyes, | This oval O**: Ovid, tr. Golding, of Polypheme: "The roundeyd devill", *Metamorphoses* XIII 1035.

15 **cropped**: OED "crop" 6a: "*trans.* To cause to bear a crop; to sow or plant with a crop ··· Chiefly *U.S.*" 10a: "*Min.* and *Geol.* Of a stratum, vein, etc.: To come up to the surface", with 1792: "Where the different strata ··· crop out" (as in *outcrop*). 10c: "*fig.* crop out ··· to come out, appear, or disclose itself incidentally." **cropped out with teeth**: OED "dragon" 21: "dragon's teeth: the teeth of the dragon fabled to have been sown by Cadmus, from which sprang armed men".

16–17 **sickle motion from the thighs || Jackknifes upward at the knees**: OED "jack-knife" *v.*: "(a) *trans.* to cut with a jack-knife; (b) *intr.* to double up like a jack-knife", with 1806: "A sailor..Jacknifed (as he termed it) the poor creature [*sc.* a cat] in several places about the head"; and 1897: "One of their amusements in camp..was to throw stones and chips past one another's heads, and raise a laugh at the active dodging and bending the body low or 'jack-knifing' as the men called it." TSE: "convulsive thighs and knees", *The Death of Saint Narcissus* 19. "A saggy bending of the knees", *Burbank with a Baedeker: Bleistein with a Cigar* 14. "Apeneck Sweeney spreads his knees", *Sweeney Among the Nightingales* 1. "By Richmond I raised my knees", *The Waste Land* [III] 294. For a boxer "doubled up like a jack-knife", see note to *Whispers of Immortality* 32.

19–20 **Pushing the framework of the bed | And clawing**: Poe: "the unwieldy bedstead which is thrust close up against it" (by the orang-outang with its "talons"), *The Murders in the Rue Morgue.*

21 **Sweeney addressed full length to shave**: Shelley: "And the rose like a nymph to the bath addressed", *The Sensitive Plant* I 29. OED "address" 1: "To raise oneself, to stand erect, *lit.* and *fig. Obs.*", quoting Caxton's *Golden Legend* (1483): "The first day that he was wasshen and bayned he addressid hym right up in the bassyn." Last citation 1620.

21–22 **to shave ··· pink from nape to base**: shaving soap was often pink. Pound to John Quinn, 19 Apr 1917, of the portrait painter Giovanni Boldoni: "To think that I should have lived to see another Boldoni hung upon a wall, a pink-shaving-lather-and-safety-razor Boldoni." TSE: "Mike got up early and bathed returning very pink and pleased", jotting for a story by "F. M." (c. 624 fol. 64).

21–24 **Sweeney addressed full length to shave ··· the suds around his face**: Poe of his orang-outang: "Razor in hand, and fully lathered, it was sitting before a looking-glass, attempting the operation of shaving", *The Murders in the Rue Morgue*. OED "Sweeney" 2: "A (nickname for a) barber"; see note to title.

22–24 **pink from nape to base ··· wipes the suds around his face**: "knees ··· The smiling stripling with the pink soaped face", *Paysage Triste* 16, 18 ("knees", 17).

22 **Broadbottomed**: J. W. Croker: "There are some vile, vulgar words adopted in modern politics ··· *Broad-bottomed* administration is a vile phrase, it is meant to express an admiration of weight, *pondere fixa suo*, but it may be turned to denote one that shews its a——", *The Amazoniad* (1806) 52 (with "Fragrant the tepid steam arose" on the same page; TSE: "Rises from the sheets in steam", 12). The Fox–North Coalition had boasted of being a "broadbottomed administration of all the talents". TSE: "broadbacked hippopotamus", *The Hippopotamus* 1. "The broadbacked figure", *Ash-Wednesday* III 15.

23 **the female temperament**: Aristotle: "woman is more compassionate than man, more easily moved to tears, at the same time more jealous, more querulous, more apt to scold and to strike. She is, furthermore, more prone to despondency and less hopeful than the man, more void of shame or self-respect, more false of speech, more deceptive and of more retentive memory", *Historia Animalum* 608b (*Works* IV). Benito Jerónimo Feijoo: "the female temperament being more moist than that of men, women must be the more intelligent of the two", *On the Learning, Genius and Abilities, of the Fair Sex* (1774) 122.

25–26 **The lengthened shadow of a man | Is history, said Emerson**: "An institution is the lengthened shadow of one man; as Monarchism, of the Hermit Antony;

the Reformation, of Luther; Quakerism, of Fox; Methodism, of Wesley; Abolition, of Clarkson ··· all history resolves itself very easily into the biography of a few stout and earnest persons", *Self-Reliance.* (See note to *Erect* in title.) Emerson again: "If the whole of history is in one man, it is all to be explained from individual experience", *History* (*Peake*). TSE on the Transcendentalists: "Neither Emerson nor any of the others was a real observer of the moral life ··· The essays of Emerson are already an encumbrance", *American Literature* (1919). To Herbert Read, 27 Feb 1926, on a projected series of biographies: "Emerson might well be included much as I dislike him." On his significance: "Emerson is himself a 'Representative Man', of a deplorable variety, representative of much modern American 'spirituality'", *Report on a dissertation entitled "Emerson and the Romantic Revival"* (1927). To Janet Adam Smith, 24 Apr 1934: "I am not a very good person to talk about Emerson, as I dislike him and his works." See also note to *Cousin Nancy* 12.

Hegel: "A World-historical individual is not so unwise as to indulge a variety of wishes to divide his regards. He is devoted to the One Aim, regardless of all else. It is even possible that such men may treat other great, even sacred interests, inconsiderately", *Lectures on the Philosophy of History* 34, scored by TSE in his copy. TSE: "no honest man can be a hero to himself; for he must be aware how many causes in world history, outside of abilities and genius, have been responsible for greatness", *The Varieties of Metaphysical Poetry* 289 (Turnbull Lecture III).

29 **Tests the razor on his leg**: *Mandarins* 1 1 also has a present tense verb opening a sentence: "Stands there, complete".

31 **epileptic**: *Arrowsmith 1981* quotes Owsei Temkin on the history of epilepsy: "The epileptic attack was compared to the sexual act, and both Hippocrates and Democritus were credited with the saying that 'coitus is a slight epileptic attack'", *The Falling Sickness* (1945) 30.

33, 38 **The ladies ··· misunderstood**: Emerson: "Ah, then, exclaim the aged ladies, you shall be sure to be misunderstood! Misunderstood! It is a right fool's word. Is it so bad then to be misunderstood? Pythagoras was misunderstood, and Socrates, and Jesus, and Luther, and Copernicus, and Galileo, and Newton, and every pure and wise spirit that ever took flesh. To be great is to be misunderstood", *Self-Reliance* (*Peake*).

37 **hysteria**: see note to *Hysteria* title.

39 **Mrs. Turner**: against the name in *Thayer's AraVP*, TSE wrote a three-line note now illegibly erased. The name may have been prompted by a patron recalled by Wyndham Lewis: "Amongst the people I came across immediately before the War ··· was a very attractive American, of the name of Mrs. Turner. Since then she has become the wife of General Spears, and is best known as [the novelist] Mary Borden, which was her maiden name", *Blasting and Bombardiering* (1937) 60. Lewis's first letter mentioning TSE, to Pound [Jan 1915], describes how "The excellent Mrs. Turner is going to take a large studio or hall near Park Lane and there house my squadron of paintings." *Arrowsmith 1981* cites Shakespearean puns, suggesting that the name "*declares* her a bawd" (see next note for "Mrs. Walker").

40 **It does the house no sort of good**: "There's no money in it now, what with the

damage done, | And the reputation the place gets, on account of a few bar-flies, | I've kept a clean house for twenty years, she says", *WLComposite* 26–28. For "some really good houses have been ruined in this way", see note to *The Love Song of J. Alfred Prufrock* 6, "cheap hotels". Goldsmith: "Were you not told to drink freely, and call for what you thought fit, for the good of the house?", *She Stoops to Conquer* act IV. TSE: "A very nice House it was", *Billy M'Caw: The Remarkable Parrot* 9. In a letter to John Hayward, 11 Apr 1938, TSE annotated both sides of a newspaper cutting, heading it: SPOTLIGHT ON 22, BINA GARDENS: THROWN BY JOHN FOSTER—

	Mr. Foster said that	
Will the	the club was the resort of	**Things**
	undesirables, habitual disorder	
Goblin	and drunkenness occurred there,	**don't**
	and the police had frequently been	
Nuisance	called in to quell disturbances.	**look too**
	"The premises are badly	
be put	conducted, and the police regard	**good for**
	them as one of the worst	
an End to?	in the district," the inspector	**Mrs. Walker**
	added.	

41 **Doris:** *Grover Smith 1998*: "Doris's name comes in oddly. [But] Sweeney has been likened to Polyphemus, who (in Ovid) vainly wooed Galatea, daughter of the sea-nymph Doris." (See note to 10, "Polypheme".) **towelled:** OED's earliest citation for 3. "*ppl. a.*, wrapped in a towel".

41–42 **towelled from the bath, | Enters:** "I would come with a towel in my hand | And bend your head beneath my knees", *The Love Song of St. Sebastian* 22–23. ("Jackknifes upward at the knees", 17.)

43 **sal volatile:** smelling salts, to treat fainting. Pronounced *sal vol-lattily.* "F. M." on a play by William Archer: "I betook myself with a queasy stomach to *The Green Goddess* and found it as settling as a nice dose of bicarbonate of soda with sal volatile as handed to one over the counter by any chemist for fourpence", *Letters of the Moment* II (1924).

43–44 **sal ··· a glass of brandy neat:** Wilkie Collins: "'Let me prescribe for you. A glass of brandy neat. So,' he went into the *salle à manger* and returned with his medicine", *Blind Love* ch. LII. (If taken medicinally, brandy did not breach America's Prohibition, 1919–33, for which see note to *WLComposite* 2.) Joyce: "Toss off a glass of brandy neat while you'd say knife", *Ulysses* episode VIII (Lestrygonians) in *Little Review* Jan 1919. Joyce sent this episode to Pound on 25 Oct 1918.

A Cooking Egg

Published in *Coterie* May Day 1919, then *AraVP, US 1920+* and *Penguin / Sel Poems.* (Six issues of *Coterie,* one a double number, were published by the Bomb Shop, of which this was the first. TSE was on its editorial committee, along with Richard Aldington, T. W. Earp, Aldous Huxley and Wyndham Lewis.) Read by TSE at the house of Sibyl Colefax 12 Dec 1917.

No recording known.

Undated in tss. Dated "? London 1917" in *Isaacs US 1920* and 1917 by TSE in both *Morley's US 1920* and *Hayward's 1925.* Assigned to 1917 by *Rainey* 198. TSE apparently sent a typescript to John Rodker on 17 May 1919.

To Norman Furlong, 4 Feb 1946, on selections for his *English Satire: An Anthology* (1946): "I agree with the choice you have made from among my poems with the exception of *A Cooking Egg* which does not seem to me satirical but sentimental. I have no objection in principle to your using the others. Incidentally, I think that the poem called *Burbank with a Baedeker* might more truly be described as satirical verse than *A Cooking Egg.*" (To Sherard Vines, 22 Dec 1931: "I do not know whether I have ever written anything that could be called verse satire or not. What do you think?")

Title **Cooking Egg**: not in OED. Fannie Merritt Farmer: "It is surprising how many intelligent women ··· are satisfied to use what are termed 'cooking eggs' ··· Strictly fresh eggs should always be used if obtainable. An egg after the first twenty four hours steadily deteriorates", *The Boston Cooking-School Cookbook* (1896, rev. ed. 1918) 92 (Barbara Lauriat, personal communication).

Epigraph ***En l'an trentiesme de mon aage | Que toutes mes hontes j'ay beues . . .*** : [In the thirtieth year of my life, when I drank up all my shame], Villon, *Le Grand Testament* 1–2. *TSE's books: Bodleian list* (1934) includes "Villon: Poesies, Oeuvres". On the politician and man of letters George Wyndham:

> There is no conclusive evidence that he realized all the difference, the gulf of difference between lines like:
>
> En l'an trentiesme de mon age
> Que toutes mes hontes j'ay beues;
>
> and even the very best of Ronsard or Bellay.
>
> *A Romantic Aristocrat* (1919)

In the same year (when TSE was 30): "We are a little wearied, in fact, by the solemnity with which Mr. Osborn accepts the youthful mind and the youthful point of view. 'Youth knows more about the young,' he says, 'than old age or middle age.' If this were so, civilization would be impossible, experience worthless. *Hommes de la trentaine, de la quarantaine*, assert yourselves", *The New Elizabethans and the Old* (1919). Bertrand Russell on TSE at Harvard in 1914: "He was extraordinarily silent, and only once made a remark which struck me. I was praising Heraclitus, and he observed: 'Yes, he always reminds me of Villon.' I thought this remark so good that I always wished he would make another", *Autobiography* (I, 1967) 212. Ottoline Morrell explained the remark in her memoirs (*Morrell 1963* 258) as a comparison between Heraclitus' "If you do not expect the unexpected, you will not find it" and Villon's Ballade, "Je meurs de soif auprès de la fontaine":

> Rien ne m'est sûr que la chose incertaine:
> Obscur, fors ce qui est tout évident;
> Doute ne fais, fors en chose certaine;
> Science tiens à soudain accident

> [Nothing is sure to me but the uncertain, nothing obscure except the obvious. I have no doubts except for the certain, and I hold knowledge to be a random accident]

The Heraclitus, frag. 18, was given in Burnet's *Early Greek Philosophers* (147), and was used in 1913 by Ernest Jones as one of the epigraphs to *Papers on Psycho-analysis*.

1 **Pipit**: Austin Dobson: "men wore stocks ··· And maids short waists and tippets, | When this old-fashioned screen was planned | From hoarded scraps and snippets", *The Screen in the Lumber Room* 34–36; see note to "behind the screen", 26 (*Ricks 1998*). The name of the pipit bird is thought to derive from its "short and feeble note" (OED). I. A. Richards told Elizabeth Drew that TSE "had corrected him about the interpretation of Pipit as an old nurse, and had said that the clue was in *Dans le Restaurant*". Drew suggested that this clue as to her being a young girl was a childhood memory of "un instant de puissance et de délire" (14), *EinC* June 1953. TSE may rather have had in mind the variant line from the poem as published in *Little Review* and *AraVP*: "Elle avait une odeur fraîche qui m'était inconnue". To Helen Gardner, 20 Oct 1956, after a critical dispute about Pipit in three issues of *EinC*, 1953–54: "it seemed to me that the nadir of critical futility had been touched (so far as my own work is concerned) by the dispute as to whether the personage in *A Cooking Egg* was a little girl, an inamorata, a female relative, or an old nurse." See note to 9–24. **sate**: Dryden: "Philip's warlike son | —Aloft in awful state | The godlike hero sate", *Alexander's Feast* (in *The Golden Treasury*), with "Honour but an empty bubble" (TSE: "Honour", 9; "Sir Philip Sidney", 10). Responding to a query about the spelling "sat" in the first-line index to *1969*, Valerie Eliot wrote: "Sate is correct and must be corrected in the index" (8 Oct 1969, Faber archive). This archaic spelling occurs three times in Arnold's *The Forsaken Merman*, was favoured by Edward Lear (*Southam*) and is pronounced to rhyme with "fate" in TSE's 1957 recording of *Growltiger's Last Stand* (29). For the convention, see note to 15–16.

3 ***Views of the Oxford Colleges***: no book of precisely this title existed, with or without the definite article (see variant), but Elsie M. Lang's *The Oxford Colleges* (1910), with twenty-four illustrations, was published in London and Philadelphia, and a concertina of twelve *Views of Oxford* had been published *c.* 1873.

5 **Daguerrotypes**: the earliest photographic process, invented *c.* 1837, had proliferated in the US in the 1840s but was superseded in the 1850s. OED gives stress on the first syllable not the second. *Fowler*: "The OED pronounces -gĕr*o*-."

8 **An *Invitation to the Dance***: italics suggest a title (as of several songs and piano pieces, or of a picture such as E. M. W. Tillyard imagined, *EinC* June 1953), yet "supported on the mantelpiece" evokes a printed invitation card. (To John

Hayward, 29 Nov 1939: "You speak of receiving 'absurd little invitation cards' to various College functions. Let me impress upon you—as a Newcomer to Cambridge—the importance of not ignoring these invitations.") Weber's piano piece *L'Invitation à la Valse* was orchestrated by Berlioz, whose version was used by the Ballets Russes for *Le Spectre de la Rose* in its Paris season, 1911 (*Hargrove*). TSE: "With preparation for the waltz", *Goldfish* I 2.

8^9 *draft stanzas* [2, 4] **repose · · · toes:** "take their repose · · · Jellicles dry between their toes", *The Song of the Jellicles* 18, 20.

8^9 *draft stanzas* [3] **My self-esteem was somewhat strained:** Pound's annotation "used before" may refer to "My self-possession flares up for a second", *Portrait of a Lady* III 11.

9–21 **I shall not want Honour · · · Capital · · · Society · · · Pipit:** Psalm 34: 10: "they that seek the Lord shall not want any good thing." Psalm 23: 1: "The Lord is my shepherd; I shall not want" (*Williamson*). The "shall" repeatedly anticipating conditions in Heaven also echoes through *Exequy*: "Shall hover in my sacred grove · · · The cordial flame shall keep me warm", 6, 12.

9–24 **I shall not want Honour in Heaven · · · I shall not want Pipit in Heaven · · · Piccarda de Donati will conduct me:** Ruskin to Susan Beever, 25 June 1874, about the loss of Rose La Touche: "But, Susie, *you* expect to see your Margaret again, and you will be happy with her in heaven. I wanted my Rosie *here*. In heaven I mean to go and talk to Pythagoras and Socrates and Valerius Publicola. I shan't care a bit for Rosie there, she needn't think it. What will gray eyes and red cheeks be good for *there*?" (*Matthiessen* 92 on "the little girl with whom he fell in love when himself in middle life". TSE to Matthiessen, 22 Oct 1935: "By the way, that is a good point about Rose La Touche. Was that pure inspiration, or did we ever mention the subject in conversation?") In Edward Tyas Cook's *Life of John Ruskin* (1911), the letter is quoted immediately after Ruskin's opinion that Dante's *Vita Nuova* was "the record of the poet's real love for a real person, and not a mere allegory" (II 264–65), an opinion TSE was strongly to endorse. Pipit appeared again in an additional draft stanza in the earliest typescript of *Whispers of Immortality*: "As long as Pipit is alive | One can be mischievous and brave; | But where there is no more misbehaviour | I would like my bones flung into her grave" (see Textual History).

10, 12 **Sir Philip Sidney:** died, according to popular legend, heroically at the battle of Zutphen, 1586. **Sidney · · · kidney:** recurrent in 17th-century verse: "each Ladies Kidney | Twitter'd to heare but of the Name of *Sydney*", Samuel Sheppard, *Epigrams* 70; "And thou, swain, shall sing as sweet as Sidney · · · To make Jack Sprat a man of kidney", *A Catch* in *Pills to Purge Melancholy* ed. Thomas d'Urfey (Henry Woudhuysen, personal communication). Thomas Hood: "Bold Sidney, and his kidney", *A Lament for the Decline of Chivalry* (1828) (James Loucks, *N&Q* July 1976). Walter Savage Landor: "Cursing Milton, Hampden, Sidney, | And all others of their Kidney", *Excommunication, Denounced on January 30, 1850* (Daniel Clay, *N&Q* Sept 1994).

11 **have talk with:** "He seemeth to have talk with one afar off", *A True and Faithful Relation of What passed · · · Between Dr. John Dee · · · and Some Spirits* (1659) 242. OED "talk" 1. cites "We had *talk* enough, but no *conversation*", *Boswell* IV 186.

14 **Sir Alfred Mond:** industrialist and Liberal MP of German Jewish extraction

(1868–1930). Commissioner of Works in Lloyd George's Coalition Government of 1916–21. During the Great War his family business (Brunner, Mond: a forerunner of ICI) made munitions at Silvertown, East London, where fifty tons of TNT exploded on 19 Jan 1917, killing 73 people. Pound to TSE, 14 March 1922: "When Hueffer sold the old *English Review* to Mond [in 1910], it was with the understanding that he was to remain Editor ··· Mond turned him out at the end of four months." (The replacement was Austin Harrison, who declined *The Love Song of J. Alfred Prufrock* when it was offered by Conrad Aiken.) TSE: "Lord Melchett is the independent and intelligent Alfred Mond", *A Commentary* in *Criterion* Apr 1929. (Mond: essence of the worldly. Charles Cotton: "one that's banish'd the Grand Mond", *Epistle to John Bradshaw, Esq.* II 49.)

When TSE read these stanzas at Sibyl Colefax's house on 12 Dec 1917, "there was a rumpus in the audience, and Lady Mond sailed indignantly out of the room", Richard Aldington, *Life for Life's Sake* (1968) 204. In July 1914, *Blast* had asked "MAY WE HOPE FOR ART FROM LADY MOND?" See headnote to *The Hippopotamus*, and, for TSE's suggestion that he might read something even more outrageous, see letter to Pound, 31 Oct 1917, in "Improper Rhymes". ("Lady Kleinwurm's monde", *WLComposite* 255.)

14, 17 *variant* **I shall meet ··· Company**: Webster on defiance of death: DUCHESS: "Who would be afraid on't, | Knowing to meet such excellent company | In the other world?" *The Duchess of Malfi* IV ii (for the scene, see notes to 24 and to *The Waste Land* [II] 117–23).

15 **We two shall lie**: Rossetti: "'We two will lie i' the shadow of | That living mystic tree'", *The Blessed Damozel* 85–86 (*Grover Smith* 50).

15–16 **lapt | In a five per cent. Exchequer Bond**: "plenty of money, | Wrapped up in a five pound note", Edward Lear, *The Owl and the Pussycat* 3–4. Tennyson: "There the common sense of most shall hold a fretful realm in awe, | And the kindly earth shall slumber, lapt in universal law", *Locksley Hall* 129–30. "*Poems* (1920)" has several clipped past tenses: "kist" and "wrapt" (*The Hippopotamus* 34, 36; also "past" for "passed" in early editions at 22), "Blest" (*Mr. Eliot's Sunday Morning Service* 28), "drest" (*A Cooking Egg* 24^25 *variant*). The practice goes back to TSE's earliest poetry ("drencht ··· soakt", *A Fable for Feasters* 33, 35) and continued in a draft for *The Waste Land* ("pact", *ms1* [13] *variant*), *Ash-Wednesday* ("drest", III 15) and *Five-Finger Exercises* II. *Lines to a Yorkshire Terrier* ("crookt", 2). Commenting on lines by Bonamy Dobrée, "The wind shivered the cropt grass, and the small bright clouds | Passed evenly over the sky", TSE wrote in a letter [?1927]: "Passed: why not print 'past'?" **a five per cent. Exchequer Bond**: the outbreak of war in Aug 1914 immediately forced the pound off the gold standard, enabling the government to print money to prosecute the war. War loans were then issued, the first paying 3½ per cent, the third, of Jan 1917, paying 5 per cent. *Glasgow Herald* 27 May 1916: "people have come to regard the giving of money for the prosecution of the War ··· as a profit-making medium". *Nation*, June 1917: "when the War is over ··· the propertied men in this country will be several thousand million pounds the wealthier". In June 1919, the so-called "Joy Bond" promised interest of 5% until 1960, which the *Manchester Guardian* of 13 June 1919 described as "a gift of thousands of millions of pounds unearned increment to the investor out of the taxpayer's pocket". (Thomas Johnson, *The Financiers and the Nation*, 1934, ch. VI, "Usury on the Great War".)

Pope: "While with the silent growth of ten per Cent, | In Dirt and darkness, hundreds stink content", *The First Epistle of the First Book of Horace Imitated* 132–33. Kipling: "The widow and the orphan | That pray for ten per cent", *The Broken Men* (acknowledged by TSE as influencing the title *The Hollow Men*). TSE's mother had substantial holdings in bonds as well as commercial property (see her correspondence with TSE's brother Henry, Houghton).

18 **Lucretia Borgia · · · Bride**: as illegitimate daughter of the Spanish cardinal who became Pope Alexander VI, three-times married Lucretia Borgia (1480–1519) was notorious for the kinds of excess depicted in Webster's plays. William Bodham Donne reported to Fanny Kemble on 20 Jan 1857 that Edward FitzGerald had taken new rooms, less than three months after his doomed marriage: "and he says that 'his contemporary'—which, being interpreted, means his wife! looks in this chamber of horrors like Lucrezia Borgia", quoted *William Bodham Donne and His Friends*, ed. Catharine B. Johnson (1905) 217.

18–24 *Pound's annotation* (*ts1a*): "le preux Bayard mirrour of Chivalry ⁊ Coriolanus. Cola da Rienzi". Pierre Terrail, the "doughty" Chevalier de Bayard (1473–1524). Byron: "So much for chivalry · · · Before the days of Bayard", *Childe Harold's Pilgrimage* Preface. Cola di Rienzi, 14th-century senator. Byron: "hope of Italy— | Rienzi! last of Romans!" *Childe Harold's Pilgrimage* IV st. 114.

20 **experience**: various senses; OED 7a: "Knowledge resulting from actual observation or from what one has undergone". 8: "The state of having been occupied in any department of study or practice, in affairs generally, or in the intercourse of life; the extent to which, or the length of time during which, one has been so occupied; the aptitudes, skill, judgement, etc. thereby acquired". 4b: "A state of mind or feeling forming part of the inner religious life; the mental history (of a person) with regard to religious emotion". Locke: "Let us then suppose the mind to be · · · without any ideas · · · Whence has it all the materials of reason and knowledge? To this I answer, in one word, from EXPERIENCE. In that all our knowledge is founded; and from that it ultimately derives itself", *Essay Concerning Human Understanding* bk. II ch. 1 §2. The nature and significance of experience were of much concern to the philosophers TSE studied, including Josiah Royce (whose seminars he attended). Bradley: "Sentient experience, in short, is reality, and what is not this is not real", *Appearance and Reality* ch. XIV; underlined by TSE. Bradley: "Everything is experience, and also experience is one", ch. XXVI; TSE, alongside: "But experience is only experience *internally*. The complex, looked at from the outside, is not experience. So there is no experience *as such*, and no truth *as such*." Alongside a paragraph beginning "The total unity of experience", ch. XXVII, TSE: "Has not 'experience' here become as meaningless as 'personality'?" Recommending a study of Shaw, Gide, Freud and Russell: "he finds · · · they all approve three cults: that of 'personality', that of 'experience', and that of 'irresponsibility'", *"Our Present Philosophy of Life"* by Montgomery Belgion, reader's report (1929).

Inf. XXVI 94–99, Ulysses speaks: "neither fondness for my son, nor reverence for my aged father, nor the due love that should have cheered Penelope, could conquer in me the ardour that I had to gain experience of the world, and of human vice and worth." Pater on Aristippus: "The persuasion that all is vanity · · · became the stimulus towards every kind of activity, and prompted a perpetual, inextinguishable thirst after experience", *Marius the*

Epicurean ch. VIII, "Animula Vagula" (see note to *Do I know how I feel? Do I know what I think?* 1). TSE: "that averted look without surprise | Which only the experienced can wear", *Paysage Triste* 4–5. [Eeldrop:] "What curiosity and passion for experience!" [Appleplex:] "· · · her passion for experience has taken her to a Russian pianist in Bayswater · · · the passion for experience—have you remained so impregnably Pre-Raphaelite as to believe in that? What real person, with the genuine resources of instinct, has ever believed in the passion for experience? The passion for experience is a criticism of the sincere, a creed only of the histrionic", *Eeldrop and Appleplex* II (1917). TSE, outlining a story for "F. M.": "*Mrs. Molden*—the ex-midwife. Had brought 3 corpses into the world & therefore person of experience · · · Mrs. M and her experiences fill Fanny with a kind of horror" (verso of draft leaf of *Letters of the Moment* II (1924), U. Maryland). "des expériences", *Dans le Restaurant* 23.

On Shakespeare: "experience, for the poet, is a very different thing from experience for the stockbroker. A love affair, successful or fatal, might cause a successful or bad investment; it cannot, without a great many other and alien experiences of which the ordinary man is incapable, cause good poetry. Nowhere is the public, in general, more at fault than in its decipherings of the meaning of poems according to some 'experience.' A fine poem which appears to be the record of a particular experience may be the work of a man who has never had that experience; a poem which *is* the record of a particular experience may bear no trace of that or of any experience. About good poetry, the public (including often critics and experts) is usually quite wrong: the experience it sees behind the poem is its own, not the poet's. I do not say that poetry is not 'autobiographical': but this autobiography is written by a foreign man in a foreign tongue, which can never be translated", *The Problems of the Shakespeare Sonnets* (1927). "And finally · · · many people act upon the assumption that the mere accumulation of 'experiences', including literary and intellectual experiences, as well as amorous and picaresque ones, is—like the accumulation of money—valuable in itself", *After Strange Gods* 34. On modern literature: "its tendency is to encourage its readers to get what they can out of life while it lasts, to miss no 'experience' that presents itself", *Religion and Literature* (1935). See also note to epigraph for quotation from *The New Elizabethans and the Old* (1919) on valuable experience brought by age; and headnote to *Marina* for letter to Hayward, 29 Nov 1939, on "lack of experience".

21–23 **in Heaven: | Madame Blavatsky will instruct me | In the Seven Sacred Trances:** Psalm 32: 8: "I will instruct thee in the way which thou shalt go." Deuteronomy 4: 36: "Out of heaven he made thee to hear his voice, that he might instruct thee." Song of Solomon 8: 2: "bring thee into my mother's house, who would instruct me." **Heaven · · · Seven Sacred Trances:** Emerson: "And pine in vain the sacred Seven · · · Find me, and turn thy back on heaven", *Brahma* 14–16. For Emerson see note to *Sweeney Erect* 25–26. **Madame Blavatsky · · · Seven Sacred Trances:** the Russian mystic Helena Blavatsky (1831–91) lived in America, India and then England. Yeats joined her Theosophical Society in 1888. Her *magnum opus* explains how super-sensuous states "can be perceived by the SEER or the Adept during the hours of trance, under the *Sushumna ray*—the first of the Seven *Mystic* rays of the Sun. [*Footnote*: The names of the Seven Rays · · · are all mystical, and each has its distinct application in a distinct state of consciousness, for occult purposes]", *The Secret Doctrine: The Synthesis of Science, Religion and Philosophy* (1888, repr. 1993) I 515 (*Childs* 94).

24 **Piccarda de Donati**: a nun, whose brother, Forese Donati, tells Dante (*Purg.* XXIV 10–15) that she is already in heaven. For her reply to Dante's question in *Paradiso* (and TSE's opinion "it is great poetry, and there is a great philosophy behind it"), see note to *Ash-Wednesday* VI 30–33, "Our peace in His will". TSE, quoting *The Duchess of Malfi* IV ii: "If the duchess had insisted on being 'Duchess of Malfi still,' she would not have been admitted to Dante's heaven at all. Piccarda had been a great lady herself, but when she got to Heaven she did not talk like that", *John Webster* (1928). (TSE saw the Phœnix Society's production of Webster's play in Nov 1919 and a letter from him in support of the society appeared in the *Athenæum* 27 Feb 1920. Harold Child lists 24 Phœnix Society revivals of 16th–18th-century dramas excluding Shakespeare, and some three dozen by other companies, 1919–25, in *RES* Apr 1926.)   **conduct**: OED 2: "To guide or direct to a certain course of action. 1557: 'Thy good spirite shall conduite me into the lande of rightfulness.'"

25 **penny world**: Stevenson on his discovery of Skelt's juvenile dramas: "The world was plain before I knew him, a poor penny world; but soon it was all coloured with romance", *Memories and Portraits* ch. 13, "A Penny Plain and Twopence Coloured" (R. G. Howarth, *N&Q* 23 Nov 1940). Dickens: "a penny bun is a penny bun, always the same size at the same shop, whether prices be high or low", *Dainty Bread* in *All the Year Round* 10 Sept 1870 (TSE: "scones and crumpets", 31).

25, 29 **where is · · · Where are**: *Ubi sunt* [Where are] was a turn common in mediaeval Latin poetry. Villon, tr. Rossetti: "Mais où sont les neiges d'antan?" [But where are the snows of yester-year?], *Ballade des dames du temps jadis* [*Ballade of the Ladies of Former Times*]. And "Où sont les gracieux gallans | Que je suivoye au temps jadis" [Where are the gracious gallants whom I followed in former times], *Le Grand Testament* XXIX.

Péguy: "Où sont vos martyrs? Où sont vos héros? Où sont seulement vos victimes?" [Where are your martyrs? Where are your heroes? Where are your victims, even?], *À nos amis, à nos abonnés* [*To Our Friends, To Our Subscribers*] (20 June 1909). For this passage of Péguy, see note to *Burnt Norton* II 1–2. TSE: "Charles Péguy · · · was one of the most illustrious of the dead who have fallen in this war · · · There may be passages in his verse which are pure poetry; there are certainly passages in his prose which are of the best prose · · · in Paris which had seen the termination of an epoch · · · Paris given up to radical and reactionary movements which were largely movements for the sake of moving, Péguy · · · stood for a real re-creation, a return to the sources · · · a witness to the eternal fertility of the French soil · · · Péguy on the Marne is an essential part of this Péguy", *Charles Péguy* (1916); for this review of *Avec Charles Péguy de la Lorraine à la Marne* (*août–septembre, 1914*), a memoir by Victor Boudon, his commanding officer, see note to *Animula* 32, 33, 36. "Péguy had the ability to combine a variety of doctrines by a force of imagination which sometimes concealed and usually atoned for incoherence", *A Commentary* in *Criterion* Apr 1934. *TSE's books: Bodleian list* (1934) includes "Peguy: Oeuv. Choisies". To Robert Waller, 1 Sept 1945: "Péguy was a very great writer, I think perhaps the greatest of my time, or a little before. I know some of his prose a good deal better than I know his 'poetry', though I admire the latter too. I believe that if I had his complete works, which were voluminous, I should read them all."

25–32 **penny world ··· creeping | From Kentish Town and Golder's Green ··· Where are the eagles and the trumpets? ··· Weeping, weeping**: TSE in the margin of *Thayer's AraVP*: "Blake. *What are the golden builders doing | In melancholy, ever weeping Paddington?*", referring to Blake's *To the Jews*:

> The fields from Islington to Marylebone,
> To Primrose Hill and Saint John's Wood,
> Were builded over with pillars of gold,
> And there Jerusalem's pillars stood.
> ...
> Pancras & Kentish Town repose
> Among her golden pillars high ···
> ...
> What are those golden builders doing
> Near mournful ever-weeping Paddington,
> Standing above that mighty ruin
> Where Satan the first victory won
>
> Quatrain section of *Jerusalem* I, Plate 27

TSE referred to the same lines in his Clark Lecture VII:

> Blake is I think in one aspect like Chapman, and rather like Mr. Yeats, in being a poet of juxtaposition of two worlds, rather than a metaphysical.
>
> What are these golden builders doing
> In melancholy, ever-weeping Paddington?
>
> *The Varieties of Metaphysical Poetry* 205

26 **behind the screen**: Austin Dobson's *The Screen in the Lumber Room* ends "I kissed you first behind it". Dobson has "aunt" three times and his volume is *Vers de Société* (TSE: "great great aunts", 6; "Society", 17) (*Ricks 1998*). Charlie Chaplin, *Behind the Screen* (1916) (Ben Mazer, personal communication).

27 **The red-eyed scavengers**: Dickens: "The last few red-eyed stragglers", *Barnaby Rudge* ch. LV. **scavengers**: OED 2a: "A person whose employment is to clean streets, by scraping or sweeping together and removing dirt."

27, 28 **scavengers ··· Kentish Town**: Jonson, *A Tale of a Tub* III i, *Kentish Town*. TURFE: "I had rather be mark'd out Tom Scavinger, | And with a shovel make clean the highways."

27, 29 **scavengers ··· eagles**: Charles Allston Collins: "These wrinkly-necked and scavenger vultures proclaim, as most things do, their nature by their foul outside. How different are these from the eagles! The vulture is as large as the eagle", *Our Eye-Witness and a Salamander* in Dickens's *All the Year Round* 19 May 1860. TSE's first printed story concerned vultures: "The dead lay scattered about in great heaps, which were already black with the countless scavengers who had scented them from afar", *The Birds of Prey* (1905). To Emily Hale, 27 Nov 1956: "I had assumed that the letters of mine which you are giving to Princeton University would be sealed up at once ··· My God! does this mean that a complete stranger, a professional librarian, is already reading letters which were composed for your eye alone? I seem to have heard of dying travellers in a desert, with the vultures starting to dismember them before the end. I feel somewhat like that." See TSE to Geoffrey Faber, 21 Jan 1941, quoted in headnote to *The Dry Salvages*, 3. COMPOSITION.

28 **Golder's Green:** often "Golders", but TSE generally used the apostrophe, as for instance in the Bolo lines sent to Aiken, 10 Jan 1916 (see "Improper Rhymes") and in writing to Virginia Woolf (26 Jan 1940). To James Joyce, 21 May 1921, on the publication of *Ulysses* as a book:

> I am delighted to hear that even a limited and very expensive edition is to appear. Has it been properly circularised in England? If not, I might supply a few names. I wish that Miss Beach would bring out a limited edition of my epic ballad on the life of Christopher Columbus and his friend King Bolo, but
>
> Bolo's big black bastard queen
> Was *so* obscene
> She shocked the folk of Golder's Green.

29–30 **eagles · · · snow-deep Alps:** OED "eagle" 2: "an ensign in the Roman army, and . . . an ensign and badge in the French army under the empire". Hannibal and his Carthaginian army crossed the Alps into Italy in Oct 218 BC through deep snow. Napoleon's army crossed the Alps in spring 1800.

29–31 **the eagles · · · buttered scones and crumpets:** Psalm 103: 5: "who satisfieth thy mouth with good things; so that thy youth is renewed like the eagle's". **eagles · · · trumpets · · · Alps · · · scones · · · crumpets:** Job 39: 24–27: "He swalloweth the ground · · · the trumpets · · · Doth the eagle mount up · · · and make her nest on high?" TSE: "But how many eagles! and how many trumpets! · · · *crumpets*", *Coriolan* I. *Triumphal March* 42–45.

30 **snow-deep Alps:** Hannibal and his Carthaginian army crossed the Alps into Italy in Oct 218 BC through deep snow.

31–32 **Over buttered scones and crumpets | Weeping:** Psalm 102: 9: "eaten ashes like bread and mingled my drink with weeping".

32 **Weeping, weeping:** Blake: "I laid me down upon a bank | Where love lay sleeping. | I heard among the rushes dank | Weeping, weeping", *I laid me down upon a bank.*

32–33 **Weeping, weeping multitudes · · · A.B.C.'s:** Kipling imagined an Aerial Board of Control in his story *As Easy as A.B.C.* (1912):

> Oh, cruel lamps of London,
> If tears your light could drown,
> Your victims' eyes would weep them,
> Oh, lights of London Town!
>
> Then they weep · · · The old world always weeped when it saw crowds together. It did not know why, but it weeped. We know why, but we do not weep, except when we pay to be made to.

The last page of the story: "We shall go on preaching in London", and the very end: "Then some began to weep aloud, shamelessly—always without shame."

33 **A.B.C.'s:** *US 1920* had an asterisk with a footnote: "i.e. an endemic teashop, found in all parts of London. The Initials signify: Aerated Bread Company, Limited." (OED "endemic" a: "Constantly or regularly found among a (specified) people, or in a (specified) country · · · opposed to *exotic*." b: "Of diseases: Habitually prevalent in a certain country.") Wyndham Lewis listed who and what to BLESS

and BLAST in both issues of *Blast* (imitated in TSE to Conrad Aiken, 19 July 1914); the second issue (July 1915) blasted "Lyons' shops (without exception)" and blessed "All A.B.C. shops (without exception)", as well as "The War Loan" (TSE: "five per cent. Exchequer Bond", 16). (Tennyson: "O you, the Press! ··· What power is yours to blast a cause or bless!" *Suggested by Reading an Article in a Newspaper* 7–8.) In these years the contributors' meetings of A. R. Orage's *The New Age* were held in the basement of the A.B.C. in Rolls Passage, Chancery Lane (Patricia Hutchins, *Twentieth Century* Oct 1958). Aldous Huxley to Ottoline Morrell, 21 June 1917: "I lunch now frequently with Evan [Morgan] at the Savoy and with Murry at the A.B.C." (the letter also reported meeting Vivien Eliot for the first time). TSE to Virginia Woolf, 5 Mar 1933: "In Los Angeles ··· they have a restaurant called the Brown Derby which is built of concrete to look like a Brown Bowler Hat, and you go there and eat Buckwheat Cakes & Maple Syrup and Coffee at Midnight, and it seems just as normal as an A.B.C."

Le Directeur

Published in *Little Review* July 1917 (with this title), then *1919* and *Ara VP* (both titled *Le Spectateur*), then *1920+*. Pound to Margaret Anderson, 10 May 1917: "Eliot's poems for July I will send soon." 15 May: "His *Hippopotamus* must be in full size type, the french can be packed rather close, if necessary."

No recording known.

No drafts known. Dated 1916 by TSE in *Hayward's 1925* but 1918 by TSE in *Morley's US 1920.*

[*The Editor*]

[Woe betide the hapless Thames, that flows so close to *The Spectator*. The conservative editor of *The Spectator* befouls the breeze. The reactionary shareholders of the conservative *Spectator* go arm in arm, round and round, stealthily. In the gutter a small girl in rags, snub-nosed, gazes at the editor of the conservative *Spectator* and starves for love.]

Title **Le Directeur**: editor-in-chief, as opposed to *rédacteur*, a working editor (*Arrowsmith 1989*). For Baudelaire on "Les directeurs de journaux", see note to *Sweeney Agonistes: Fragment of an Agon* 108–12. Lytton Strachey's cousin John St. Loe Strachey had been Proprietor and Editor-in-Chief of *The Spectator* since 1898. Pound to his father [3 June 1913]: "'Strachey' is actually the edtr. of *The Spectator* but I use him as the type of male prude". Pound's *Salutation the Second* adjured: "Rejuvenate even *The Spectator* ··· Dance the dance of the phallus ··· Speak of the indecorous conduct of the Gods! | (Tell it to Mr. Strachey)". When TSE included this in Pound's *Selected Poems*, the last of these lines appeared in smaller type. TSE to Amar Bhattacharyya, 22 June 1964: "*Le Directeur* was a mere *jeu d'esprit*, and I had no particular grievance against Mr. Strachey (that was his name) or against *The Spectator*—'directeur' and 'spectateur' happen to rhyme, that is about all there is in it." The offices of *The Spectator* were at

1 Wellington St, The Strand, 100 yards from Waterloo Bridge. It was printed in Fetter Lane, adjoining Fleet St.

Title (*1919 and AraVP*) ***Le Spectateur***: the magazine *The Spectator*, published from 1828, had been preceded by the papers issued daily by Addison and Steele, 1711–12. Their first issue explained the detachment of Mr. Spectator and the nature of his Observations: "I live in the World, rather as a Spectator of Mankind, than as one of the Species; by which means I have made myself a Speculative Statesman, Soldier, Merchant, and Artizan, without ever medling with any Practical Part in Life ··· In short, I have acted in all the parts of my Life as a Looker-on", 1 Mar 1711 (*Arrowsmith 1989*); see the next poem, *Mélange Adultère de Tout*, for a similar list of roles. For the press, see *Airs of Palestine, No. 2* (with its conjunction with the Thames) and *The "Boston Evening Transcript"*.

6 **Empeste**: particularly, infecting with pox or syphilis.

7–8 **Les actionnaires | Réactionnaires**: Diderot: "La vie, une suite d'actions et de réactions ··· Vivant, j'agis et je réagis en masse ··· mort, j'agis et je réagis en molécules" [Life is a succession of actions and reactions ··· Living, I act and react *en masse* ··· dead, I act and react in molecules], *Le rêve de d'Alembert* [*The Dream of d'Alembert*] (*Arrowsmith 1989*). TSE's *Diderot* (1917) is a review of the early philosophical works. TSE: "The readers of the *Boston Evening Transcript* | Sway in the wind like a field of ripe corn", *The "Boston Evening Transcript"* 1–2. To Conrad Aiken 25 Feb [1915]: "one would be attached to a rock and swayed in two directions" (*Arrowsmith 1989*).

7–8, 12 **Les actionnaires | Réactionnaires ··· Font des tours**: see Anatole France, "Les petites marionnettes | Font, font, font | Trois petits tours" in note to *Convictions* 1.

12–13 **Font des tours | A pas de loup**: "*Here we go round the prickly pear*", *The Hollow Men* V 1; "I see crowds of people, walking round in a ring", *The Waste Land* [I] 56; "the ring of ghosts with joined hands", *The Family Reunion* II iii (*Arrowsmith 1989*).

17 **Camarde**: "snubnose", signifying death's head or Death, is frequent in Gautier and Corbière (*Arrowsmith 1989*). "the skull beneath the skin", *Whispers of Immortality* 2. The bridge of the nose can be deformed or destroyed by syphilis ("Empeste", 6).

17–18 **Camarde | Regarde**: Rostand: "Je crois qu'elle regarde ... Qu'elle ose regarder mon nez, cette Camarde!" [I think she's looking ... Let her dare to look at my nose, that snubnose!], *Cyrano de Bergerac* V vi. See note to *A Practical Possum* 60, "Possum's Nose".

Mélange Adultère de Tout

Published in *Little Review* July 1917, then *1919+*.

No recording known.

Undated in *ts1*. Dated 1916 by TSE in *Hayward's 1925* but 1918 by TSE in *Morley's US 1920*. Assigned to 1917 *Rainey* 198.

[*Adulterous Mixture of Everything*]

[In America, a professor; in England, a journalist; you must stride and sweat merely to keep track of me. In Yorkshire, a lecturer; in London, something of a banker; you will mock me, no doubt. When in Paris I sport the black beret of one who could-not-care-less. In Germany I am a philosopher, overcome by Exaltation, in the pose of a mountaineer. Still I wander here and there, with various breaks for tra la la, from Damascus to Omaha. I shall celebrate my day of festivity in an African oasis, clad in giraffe-skin. They will display my cenotaph—empty—on the burning coasts of Mozambique.]

Wyndham Lewis: "'I am a hundred different things; I am as many people as the different types of people I have lived amongst. I am a "Boulevardier" ··· I am a "Rapin"; I am also a "Korps-student"'", *Tarr* ch. II in *Egoist* June 1917 (immediately above an advertisement for *Prufrock and Other Observations*). Jean de Bosschère: "Pendant quatre saisons Homère voyage | Et dans chaque ville il est un autre personnage; | Bleu sous le ciel bleu, gris à Londres | Recueilli à Paris; perverti à Rome | Parmi l'ordre de tombe des tombes. | Byron dans les îles, et Shakespeare encore | Dans la poussière d'homme de Rome | Mais jamais il n'est Mare ··· n'est pas un prophète ni un critique" [For four seasons Homer travels, | And in each town he is another person: | Blue beneath a blue sky, grey in London, | Composed in Paris, corrupt in Rome | Amid the order of the tomb of tombs; | Byron in the Aegean, and Shakespeare again | In Rome's dust of men. | But never is he Marsh ··· is neither a prophet nor a critic], *Homère Mare habite sa Maison de Planches* [*Homer Marsh Dwells in his House of Planks*]. Bosschère's poem was sent to *Poetry* by Pound on 22 June 1916, but before it could appear there, it was published, with this translation by F. S. Flint facing, in *The Closed Door* (1917) (*Williams* 182). TSE quoted fourteen lines of the French poem in *Reflections on Contemporary Poetry* II (1917).

Title **Mélange Adultère de Tout**: Corbière, *Épitaphe* 7. Byron: "But yet is merely innocent flirtation, | Not quite adultery but adulteration", *Don Juan* XII lxiii. Second epigraph to *Sweeney Among the Nightingales*: "The nightingale sings of adulterate wrong." In *Thayer's AraVP*, TSE wrote: "cf. Tristan Corbière", pointing to the poem which gave him not only the title but a run of roles:

> Poète, en dépit de ses vers;
> Artiste sans art,—à l'envers,
> Philosophe,—à tort à travers.
>
> Un drôle sérieux,—pas drôle.
> Acteur, il ne suit pas son rôle;
> Peintre; il jouait de la musette;
> Et musicien: de la palette.

[Poet,—in spite of his verses. Artist without art,—rather the reverse. Philosopher,—in the wrong, cross-wise. Comic character,—not comical. Actor,—doesn't follow his part. Painter—he played a kind of oboe. And musician—but of the painter's palette.] (tr. eds)

For Corbière's poem see note to *Petit Epître* 1–2. Juvenal: "Grammaticus, Rhetor, Geometres, Pictor, Aliptes, | Augur, Schoenobates, Medicus, Magus, omnia novit", *Satires* III 76–77 (*Oser*, adding that the lines are quoted by Newman in the Preface to *The Idea of a University*). Dryden's translation describes "a nation in a single man": "A Cook, a Conjurer, a Rhetorician, | A Painter, Pedant, a Geometrician, | A Dancer on the Ropes, and a Physician". Dryden again: "But, in the course of one revolving Moon, | Was Chymist, Fidler, States-Man, and Buffoon", *Absalom and Achitophel* 549–50 (see note to *Verses To Honour and Magnify Sir Geoffrey Faber Kt.* 7–8).

1–2 **En Amérique, professeur; | En Angleterre, journaliste**: "The world is full of journalists, | And full of universities", *Fourth Caprice in Montparnasse* 15^16 *variant*.

1–6 **professeur · · · journaliste · · · banquier**: to his sister Charlotte, 21 Mar 1917: "I am at present combining the activities of a journalist, lecturer, and financier." In a spoof letter addressed to "Miss Eleanor Gellielax" (sent to John Hayward, 24 Sept 1935), TSE quotes a series of telegrams from a private detective on the trail of "the person you name, who shall be nameless". Among these, one reports on "JEAN JACQUES AILLEVARD LEDIT AILLEVARD RESORTISSANT SUISSE ORIGINE LEVANTINE STOP CARRIERE MEDIOCRE COMME BOXEUR PROFESSEUR GYMNASTIQUE ANCIENNEMENT MARCHAND DE STUPEFIANTS".

5 **En Yorkshire, conférencier**: *Schuchard* 26: "Eliot's lectures and classes on modern French literature were held in the afternoons from 3 October to 12 December 1916 at Ilkley, in Yorkshire." See headnote to "*Poems* (1920)", 5. TSE'S PROFICIENCY IN FRENCH.

6 **A Londres, un peu banquier**: *Andrew Marvell* (1921) ends with a cryptic flourish: "*C'était une belle âme, comme on ne fait plus à Londres*". This modifies Laforgue's "Ils virent qu'c'était un belle ame, | Comme on n'en fait plus aujourd'hui" [They countered that he was a fine spirit, such as they don't make nowadays], *Complainte de pauvre jeune homme* [*Complaint of the poor young man*] (tr. eds). *Mélange Adultère de Tout* is in Marvell's measure, rhymed octosyllabics.

9 **Casque noir**: Fr. *casque* a protruberance on the head of a bird: given *noir*, pointing to crow, raven—*corbeau*, *corbin*—and so to Corbière.

10 **philosophe**: in a tribute printed originally in French: "Valéry has been called a philosopher. But a philosopher, in the ordinary sense, is a man who constructs or supports a philosophical system; and in this sense, we can say that Valéry was too intelligent to be a philosopher", *"Leçon de Valéry"* (1947).

11 **Emporheben**: (= lifting-up, Ger.) Hegelian terminology.

14 **tra là là**: Rimbaud: "tu sais bien, Monsieur, nous chantions tra la la" [Sire, as you yourself know, we would sing tra la la], *La Forgeron* [*The Blacksmith*]. TSE: "*Tra-la-la-la-la-laire*", *Burbank with a Baedeker: Bleistein with a Cigar* epigraph. "la la", *The Waste Land* [III] 306.

15 **Damas**: Damascus, but also a village in Lorraine, north-eastern France. ("Damas jusqu-" perhaps tilts the balance.) **Omaha**: in Nebraska.

20 **Aux côtes brûlantes de Mozambique**: "The tropic odours · · · from Mozambique · · · flame", *The Burnt Dancer* 15–17.

Lune de Miel

Published in *Little Review* July 1917, then *1919+*. Included, along with *Dans le Restaurant*, in *Poèmes*.

No recording known.

Undated in *ts1*. Dated 1916 by TSE in *Hayward's 1925* but 1918 by TSE in *Morley's US 1920*. Dated London, 1917 in *Poèmes*, and assigned to 1917 by *Rainey* 198.

[*Honeymoon*]

[They have seen the Low Countries, now they return to Terre Haute, but a summer night finds them in Ravenna, at rest between two sheets, the home to two hundred bugs. Seasonal sweat, and a strong smell of bitch. They lie on their backs and stretch out four fleshy legs, all swollen with bites. They lift the sheet to scratch more freely. Less than a league from here is Sant'Apollinaire in Classe, the basilica known to enthusiasts for its acanthus capitals twisted by the wind. They will take the eight o'clock train, prolonging their miseries from Padua to Milan, where they will find The Last Supper, and an inexpensive restaurant. He thinks about tips and calculates the bill. They will have seen Switzerland and crossed France. And Sant'Apollinaire, stiff and ascetic, old decommissioned mill of God, still keeps in its worn stones the precise form of Byzantium.]

1 **Terre Haute**: the name of the city in Indiana derives from the French for "high ground". To Virginia Woolf, 5 Mar 1933: "I have learnt how to pronounce Los Angeles and Albuquerque, but Terre Haute is beyond me."

3–4 **entre deux draps · · · La sueur aestivale**: Charles-Louis Philippe: "le lit défait où les deux corps marquèrent leur place de sueur brune sur les draps usés, ce lit des chambres d'hôtels" [the unmade bed where the two bodies had left the impress of brownish sweat upon the worn sheets—this bed of hotel rooms], *Bubu de Montparnasse* ch. IV.

4–6 **une forte odeur de chienne · · · de morsures**: "(The same eternal and consuming itch | Can make a martyr, or plain simple bitch)", *WLComposite* 274–75 (*Arrowsmith 1982*).

6 **tout gonflées de morsures**: Augustine: "To Carthage I came, where there sang all around me in my ears a cauldron of unholy loves · · · my soul was sickly and full of sores", *Confessions* V, first paragraph; see note to *The Waste Land* [III] 307 (*Arrowsmith 1982*).

8–9 **Saint Apollinaire | En Classe**: 6th-century basilica dedicated to St. Apollinaris, first bishop of nearby Ravenna, Italy.

10 **chapitaux d'acanthe que tournoie le vent**: the acanthus leaves at the top of the columns in the nave are twisted as though buffeted by the wind. Ruskin on St. Mark's: "their capitals rich with interwoven tracery, rooted knots of herbage, and drifting leaves of acanthus and vine"; "the leaves drifted, as it were, by a whirlwind round the capital by which they rise", *The Stones of Venice* IV xiv, V xx.

TSE: "Four fine capitals, Romanesque, of foliage, one leaves blown to the right by the aura", travel notebook, 1911, entry on Verona (Houghton; *Arrowsmith 1982*).

13 **la Cène**: Leonardo's *Last Supper* in Milan. Anne Ridler on visiting TSE's office while a secretary at Faber: "The pretext was a query raised by the proof reader on his *Collected Poems 1909–1935*, and concerned the gender of a noun in *Lune de Miel*, which he had given wrongly, writing 'le Cène'. 'Well, that depends of course on Italian', he said, and I was puzzled, informing him of what I was sure he must know, that the Italian was *cena*, feminine. But it occurred to me afterwards that he was probably thinking of the masculine *cenacolo*, as the allusion is to Leonardo's fresco of the Last Supper" (*Ridler* 5–6); to which she later added: "We didn't have any further conversation, and I went away and corrected it" (interview with Kieron Winn, 9 Feb 2000). **la Cène, et un restaurant pas cher**: "cheap hotels | And sawdust restaurants ··· Talking of Michelangelo", *The Love Song of J. Alfred Prufrock* 6–7, 14.

17 **Vielle usine désaffectée de Dieu**: "Some men can understand the architecture of the cathedral of Albi, for instance, by seeing it as a biscuit factory", *Selected Poems of Ezra Pound* (1928), Introduction (Allison Vanouse, personal communication).

18 **la forme précise de Byzance**: to Mary Hutchinson [11? July 1919]: "What I feel about much contemporary taste is that people have merely assimilated other people's personal tastes without making them personal ··· One could make a short list: Byzantine (a little out of date) ··· Laforgue (really inferior to Corbière at his best)."

The Hippopotamus

Published in *Little Review* July 1917, then *1919+* and *Penguin / Sel Poems*.

No recording known.

Undated in *ts1*. Dated 1917 in *Isaacs US 1920* and by TSE in *Hayward's 1925*, but dated London, 1918 in *Poèmes*. Dated 1917, "as far as I can remember", to Norman Foerster, 15 June 1932, but 1918 by TSE in *Morley's US 1920*. Read by TSE at the house of Sibyl Colefax 12 Dec 1917 (letter to his mother, 22 Dec). *Profile: Ezra Pound: An Anthology Collected in MCMXXXI* (Milan, 1932) gives the date as "1916 or 1917".

TSE, reading at Columbia, 28 Apr 1958: "This is a poem which I originally read, I remember, at a poetry reading for the benefit of some Red Cross affair with Sir Edmund Gosse in the chair, and he was profoundly shocked. On the other hand, the late Arnold Bennett liked it better than anything I'd written up to the time of his death, and kept asking me to write 'another *Hippopotamus*.' ··· it's the only poem of mine which I've any reason to suppose that James Joyce ever read. Once when I saw him in Paris he told me that he'd been to the Jardin des Plantes and had paid his respects to my friend The Hippopotamus. I imagine that he may have read this poem. However, it doesn't seem as shocking to anybody now, I think, as it did all those years ago; I think very few things do remain as shocking", *Columbia U. Forum*

Fall 1958. For the Red Cross reading, see note to *A Cooking Egg* 14 and letter to Pound, 31 Oct 1917, in "Improper Rhymes".

Title In the second number of *Fireside: A Weekly Magazine*, when he was ten, TSE wrote a version of Lewis Carroll's "He thought he saw a Banker's Clerk | Descending from the bus: | He looked again, and found it was | A Hippopotamus" (*Sylvie and Bruno* ch. V). "Descending from the", TSE: "Ascending from the", 26.

Rupert Brooke's *On the Death of Smet-Smet, the Hippopotamus-Goddess* appeared in his *Poems* (1911). TSE's principal source, however, was Théophile Gautier:

L'hippopotame au large ventre
Habite aux Jungles de Java,
Où grondent, au fond de chaque antre,
Plus de monstres qu'on n'en rêva.

Le boa se déroule et siffle,
Le tigre fait son hurlement,
Le buffle en colère renifle,
Lui dort ou paît tranquillement.

Il ne craint ni kriss ni zagaies,
Il regarde l'homme sans fuir,
Et rit des balles de cipayes
Qui rebondissent sur son cuir.

Je suis comme l'hippopotame:
De ma conviction couvert,
Forte armure que rien n'entame,
Je vais sans peur par le désert.

[The big-bellied hippopotamus lives in the Jungles of Java, where in the depths of each cavern snarl more monsters than are dreamt of: the boa uncoils and hisses, the tiger makes his roar, the buffalo snorts in fury—whereas he sleeps or grazes tranquilly. He fears neither kris nor assegai, looks at a man and stands his ground, smiles at the Sepoy's shots that bounce off his hide. I am like this hippopotamus: clothed in conviction, strong armour-plate that none can breach, I wander fearless through the desert.]

Pound: "'The Nineties' never got even so far as *Emaux et Camées*, they stopped with *Elegies* and *Albertus.* I doubt if they ever took pleasure in *L'Hippopotame.* At any rate, a good deal of Seine water has flowed seaward since the days of The Rhymers' Club and France has not remained the France of Dowson and Arthur Symons", *New Freewoman* 15 Sept 1913. (The Rhymers' Club anthologies were published in 1892 and 1894.)

TSE followed the ABAB rhyme-scheme of Gautier's quatrains only in this poem and *Airs of Palestine, No 2.* Gautier's poem and TSE's were printed side by side in 1929 by *Taupin* (238–39).

"US" epigraph **Similiter et omnes revereantur Diaconos, ut mandatum Jesu Christi; et Episcopum, ut Jesum Christum, existentem filium Patris; Presbyteros autem, ut concilium Dei et conjunctionem Apostolorum. Sine his Ecclesia non vocatur; de quibus suadeo vos sic habeo:** "In like manner let all men respect the deacons as Jesus Christ, even as they should respect the bishop as being a type of the Father and the presbyters as the council of God and as the college

of Apostles. Apart from these there is not even the name of a church. And I am persuaded that ye are so minded as touching these matters", St. Ignatius to the Trallians 3: 1–2, tr. J. B. Lightfoot, *The Apostolic Fathers* (1891). Ignatius wrote in Greek. The Latin quoted by TSE is Bishop Ussher's 17th-century translation (with *his* for Ussher's *iis*, and the final six words added apparently by TSE).

"British" epigraph St. Paul, Colossians 4: 16. **Laodicean**: OED A, b: "Having the fault for which the Church of Laodicea is reproached in Revelation 3: 15, 16; hence 'lukewarm, neither cold nor hot', indifferent in religion, politics etc." Harvard's Laodicean Club, *c.* 1890, elected George Santayana its "Pope" but expired after two meetings.

1–2, 10 **hippopotamus | Rests on his belly in the mud ··· compassing**: of the Biblical behemoth: "his strength is in his loins and his force is in the navel of his belly ··· He is the chief of the ways of God ··· He lieth under the shady trees, in the covert of the reed, and fens ··· the willows of the brook compass him about", Job 40: 16–22. OED "behemoth": "An animal mentioned in the book of Job; probably the hippopotamus".

1–4 **hippopotamus ··· belly in the mud ··· blood**: from one of TSE's contributions to *Noctes Binanianæ*: "A Monster who escap'd the *Flood*, | With watery *diluted* Blood, | And, sacrificing *hoof* to *fin*, | Perpetuates pre-diluvial Sin. | Yet ah! might *Whales* perhaps repent? | And leave their fluid Element? | Prepare the higher life to meet, | And stand at last on *legs* and *feet?" The Whale and the Elephant* 19–26. (After the description of behemoth in Job 40, the next chapter describes leviathan, the whale.)

2 **Rests on his belly in the mud**: Cowper: "He plants his footsteps in the Sea", *Light Shining out of Darkness* 3. For Cowper's quatrain poem see notes to 9 and 23. *Paradise Lost* I 195–96: Satan "Prone on the flood, extended long and large". **Rests on**: 2 Kings 2: 15: "The spirit of Elijah doth rest on Elisha." 2 Chronicles 14: 11: "O Lord our God; for we rest on thee."

5 **Flesh and blood is weak and frail**: Matthew 26: 41: "the spirit indeed is willing, but the flesh is weak".

5–8 **Flesh and blood ··· based upon a rock**: Matthew 16: 17–18: "flesh and blood hath not revealed it unto thee, but my Father which is in heaven. And I say also unto thee, That thou art Peter, and upon this rock I will build my church" (with "flesh and blood" being singular, as in TSE). **Flesh ··· weak and frail ··· based upon a rock**: Isaac Watts: "Call'd him the Rock of their abode, | Their high Redeemer and their God ··· He saw their flesh was weak and frail, | He saw temptations still prevail", Psalm 78 (4th part).

6 **Susceptible to nervous shock**: medical diction: "susceptibility to the nervous shock", *Dublin Journal* 1838.

7 **the True Church**: Roman Catholics and Protestants each laid claim to this title during the 16th- and 17th-century religious persecutions. Samuel Butler: "he was of that stubborn crew | Of errant saints, whom all men grant | To be the true Church Militant", *Hudibras* First Part, I 190–92, quoted in Pound's *ABC of Reading*. For "The True Church and the Nineteen Churches" in TSE's *London Letter* in *Dial* May 1921, see note to *The Waste Land* [III] 264. *The Daily Illini* 5 June 1953, reporting TSE's reading the previous day: "'It is about the Church of England,' he said drily 'no one else need be offended.'"

7–8 **the True Church can never fail | For it is based upon a rock:** John Bramhall: "though the rain descend, and the floods come, and the winds blow and beat upon it, yet it shall never fall to ruin or desolation, because it is builded upon a Rock ··· The Catholic Church can never fail; any Patriarchal Church may apostate and fail", *Answer to the Epistle of M. de la Milletière* in *Works* (1842) I 42–43 (*Grover Smith* 40). *John Bramhall* (1927) appears in *Selected Essays.* TSE: "A good many years later I became a churchwarden, and I often thought of those lines ··· when we were wondering how to keep the church going on the collections, which weren't quite so good as one would have liked. So one lives and learns", *T. S. Eliot Talks about His Poetry* (1958).

8, 12 **upon a rock ··· To gather in its dividends:** Thomas Hood, on the charge of two shillings to see Poets' Corner at Westminster Abbey: "The profitable Abbey is | A sacred 'Change for stony stock, | Not that a speculation 'tis— | The profit's founded on a rock", *An Address to the Very Reverend John Ireland D.D.* 25–28.

9 **hippo:** the close of *The Waste Land* III quotes St. Augustine, Bishop of Hippo (now Annaba, Algeria). In 393, the Synod of Hippo approved a Christian biblical canon. **feeble steps may err:** "Thy staff supports my feeble steps, | Thy rod directs my doubtful way", Psalm 23 in *Psalms Carefully Suited to the Christian Worship in the United States of America* (1831). Cowper: "Judge not the Lord by feeble sense ··· Blind unbelief is sure to err", *Light Shining out of Darkness* 13, 21 (see note to 23). Pope: "To Err is *Humane*; to Forgive, *Divine*", *An Essay on Criticism* I 525 (*Sloane* 313).

11–12 **Church ··· dividends:** "Seeing that you destroy the thing you should preserve, | That you ignore the thing you should destroy | As building and destruction find their only | Justification in the dividends | On which the whole creation seems to move", draft ts of *The Rock* (Bodleian). (Tennyson: "One God, one law, one element, | And one far-off divine event, | To which the whole creation moves", *In Memoriam* final lines.)

12 **gather in its dividends***:* Leviticus 25: 20: "gather in our increase."

13 **'potamus:** *The Birth of the Hippopotamus*, Sung with great applause by La Mère Hippopotama in the Zoological Gardens, Regent's Park: "Dat it am born in London and not Paris I am grateful, | Ob little sucking 'potamus dey'd soon ha' made a plateful", *Punch* 4 Mar 1871. OED cites the abbreviation "hippo" from the following year. Archibald Bower: "Hilarius Bishop of Poitiers supposes the Sirmian Confession of Faith to have been drawn up by Osius and Potamus ··· Potamus was Bishop of Lisbone, and a most fanatical stickler for the Orthodox Party", *The History of the Popes* (1749) I 152.

13–15 **reach ··· peach:** Marvell: "The nectarine, and curious peach, | Into my hands themselves do reach", *The Garden* 37–38 (TSE: "the True Church need never stir | To gather", 11–12).

15 **pomegranate:** revered in itself and in representation, throughout the Old Testament; "fruits of" because *pomegranate* = apple of many seeds.

16 **Refresh ··· from over sea:** "At this exclusive feast. From over sea", *A Fable for Feasters* 28 (Rick DeVilliers, personal communication).

18, 22 **inflexions hoarse and odd ··· at night he hunts:** J. G. Wood's *Illustrated Natural History* described the hippopotamus making "a loud and very peculiar snorting noise" and quoted a description of it emerging "to graze by the serene light of the moon".

19, 29 **But every week we hear rejoice ··· Blood of the Lamb shall wash him clean:** Revelation 12: 11: "And they overcame him by the blood of the Lamb." TSE: "Cleansed and rejoiced", *Airs of Palestine, No. 2* 35, similarly hymnal.

21–24 **hippopotamus ··· sleep ··· God works ··· sleep:** Macaulay: "I have seen the hippopotamus, both asleep and awake; and I can assure you that, awake or asleep, he is the ugliest of the works of God", *Life and Letters of Lord Macaulay* by G. O. Trevelyan (1876) I 254–55.

23 **God works in a mysterious way:** Cowper: "God moves in a mysterious way, | His wonders to perform", *Light Shining out of Darkness* 1–2.

24 **The Church can sleep and feed at once:** *Hamlet* IV iv: "What is a man | If his chief good and market of his time | Be but to sleep and feed? A beast, no more" (Shawn Worthington, personal communication). Tennyson: "Battening upon huge seaworms in his sleep", *The Kraken* 12 (TSE in *1919*: "feed and sleep").

26 **savannas:** OED "savannah" 3: "*U.S.* A tract of low-lying damp or marshy ground."

27–28 **And quiring angels round him sing | The praise of God, in loud hosannas:** *The Merchant of Venice* V i: "Still quiring to the young-eyed cherubins". Rowland Hill: "with ceaseless praise | To him their loud hosannas raise", included in *The American Hymn and Tune Book* (1860) (Christine Meyer, *MLN* Apr 1951).

29–32 **the Lamb ··· saints ··· harp of gold:** Revelation 5: 8: "The four beasts ··· fell down before the Lamb, having every one of them harps, and golden vials ··· which are the prayers of saints" (Jeffrey Gutierrez, personal communication).

29, 33 **Blood of the Lamb shall wash him clean ··· He shall be washed as white as snow:** Revelation 7: 14: "These are they which ··· washed their robes, and made them white in the blood of the Lamb." Psalm 51: 7: "Purge me with hyssop, and I shall be clean: wash me, and I shall be whiter than snow." TSE to Richard Aldington, 23 Apr 1928: "the Anglican translation was PURGE whereas the Papists say SPRINKLE (with hyssop)." The latter is the Douay-Rheims version. **white as snow:** Isaiah 1: 18: "though your sins be as scarlet, they shall be as white as snow".

34 **By all the martyr'd virgins kist:** Song of Solomon 1: 2–3: "Let him kiss me with the kisses of his mouth ··· therefore do the virgins love thee."

36 **Wrapt in the old miasmal mist:** Harriet Monroe on the death of Rupert Brooke (*Poetry* June 1915): "Homeric heroes whom some god wrapped in golden mist" ("gold", 32). Edward Lear: "plenty of money, | Wrapped up in a five pound note", *The Owl and the Pussycat* 3–4 (see note to *A Cooking Egg* 15–16). **miasmal:** OED: "Containing miasmatic effluvia or germs", quoting Elizabeth Barrett Browning "We respond with our miasmal fog" (*Aurora Leigh* VII 300) and TSE's line.

Dans le Restaurant

Published in *Little Review* Sept 1918, then *AraVP, US 1920+.*

No recording known.

Undated in *ts1.* Dated 1916 by TSE in *Hayward's 1925* but 1918 by TSE in *Morley's US 1920.* Dated London, 1917 in *Poèmes*, and assigned to 1917 by *Rainey* 198.

The close of the poem was translated by TSE as the close of the original draft of Part IV of *The Waste Land*, before Pound reduced Part IV to the ten lines about Phlebas. Against 25–31 in *Thayer's AraVP,* TSE wrote, "See Waste Land Part IV".

[*In the Restaurant*]

[The ravaged-looking waiter, with nothing to do but rub his hands and lean over my shoulder, says: "In my country now it will be the rainy season. Wind, hot sun—and rain: what we call beggars' washday." (Garrulous, slobbery, big-bottomed—I pray you desist from blathering into my soup.) "The wet willow trees, and the buds on the brambles—it's there in a downpour that one takes shelter. I was seven years old, she younger. She was all wet, I gave her some primroses." The stains on his waistcoat now number thirty-eight. "I was tickling her, to make her laugh. I felt a moment of power and frenzy." An old lecher, then, even at that age . . . "But Monsieur, it was in vain. There comes this big dog, touching us up. I was scared, I left her midway. It's a pity." Enough! I say—you old goat! Go scrub the wrinkles off your face; take my fork and give your scalp a good scrape. How dare you presume to have had experiences like mine. Here's ten sous, take them—for the washroom. Phlebas the Phoenician, this fortnight drowned, forgot the cry of gulls and the Cornish sea swell, and the profits and losses, and the cargo of tin: a current under sea carried him far out, back through the stages of his former life. It is a hard fate, you will agree. And yet he was once handsome, and very tall.]

Translation by Pound. ts (Beinecke): green carbon on two leaves, in Pound's eccentric typing, emended in pencil (*c.* 1917). Published by Gallup in *Yale Lib Gazette* Jan 1976, then by A. Walton Litz in *Essays for Richard Ellmann: Omnium Gatherum* ed. Susan Dick et al. (1989), where dashes are substituted for many of Pound's floating commas. Misattributed to TSE, *Seymour-Jones* 34. Probable turned lines in Pound's ts are here individually numbered.

The waiter idle and dilapidated
With nothing to do but scratch and lean over my shoulder
Says:
        In my country the rain is colder
And the sun hotter and the ground more desicated   5
                and desacrated

Voluminous and spuminous with a leguminous
and cannimaculated vest-front and pantfront

and a graveyperpulchafied yesterdays napkin in a loop
over his elbow 10
(I hope he will not sputter into the soup)

Down in a ditch under the willow trees
Where you go to get out of the rain
I tried in vain,
I mean I was interrupted 15
She was all wet with the deluge and her calico skirt
stuck to her buttocks and belley,
I put my hand up and she giggled,

You old cut-up,
"At the age of eight, sir, what can one do?" 20
she was younger
Besides I'd no sooner got started than a big
poodle
Came sniffing about and scared me pealess,

Your head is not flealess 25
now at any rate, go scrape the cheese off your pate
and dig the slush out of your crowsfeet
take sixpence and get washed, God damn
what a fate
You crapulous vapulous relic, you ambulating offence 30
To have had an experience
so nearly parallel, with, . . .

Go away!
I was about to say mine,
I shall dine 35
elsewhere in future,
to clense this suture

Phlebas the Phenicien, fairest of men,
Straight and tall, having been born in a caul
Lost luck at forty, and lay drowned 40
Two long weeks in sea water, toosed of the
streams under sea, carried of currents
Forgetful of the gains
forgetful of the long days of sea fare
Forgetful of mew's crying and the foam swept coast 45
of Cornwall,
Born back at last, after days
to the ~~ports and stays of his young life,~~
~~A fair man, ports of his former~~ seafare
~~thither at last~~ 50

20] "What can one do at the age of eight, *ts 1st reading*

32 **with, . . .**] with, well, . . . *ts 1st reading*

37^38] *new leaf ts* (*so line space is indeterminate*)

TSE to John Hayward, 27 Dec 1939: "my own infancy, by comparison with yours, seems to have been remarkably protected from, at least, such sexual precocity. True,

I had my first love affair at (as nearly as I can compute from confirmatory evidence) the age of five, with a young lady of three, at a seaside hotel. Her name was Dorothy: that is all I know. My feeling towards her was expressed entirely by bullying, teasing, and making her fetch and carry: yet I remember clearly that I pined for a bit after we were separated in the autumn. That was my preparation for reading (some years later) the *Vita Nuova*. My relations with later inamoratae (?) were more and more distant and respectful: a young lady with ringlets (name unknown) who took the part of the angel child who died, in a performance called *The Birds' Christmas Carol* at another seaside resort—later ladies who have names: Jane Jones, Margaret Lionberger with freckles, Effie Bagnall whose family were considered distinctly *nouveaux riches*, and the reigning beauty of the dancing school: Edwine Thornburgh herself, who subsequently became Lady Peek of Peek Frean & Co Ltd."

Title ***Dans le Restaurant***: A two-word note against this in *Thayer's AraVP* is now illegibly erased.

1, 5 **Le garçon ··· des gueux**: to Amar Bhattacharyya, 22 June 1964: "I never thought of the 'garçon' in *Dans le Restaurant* as being anything in particular. The phrase 'le jour de lessive des gueux' was pure invention on my part and gives no clue to the identity of the waiter."

7 **Je te prie, au moins, ne bave pas dans la soupe**: Rimbaud: "Mon triste cœur bave à la poupe ··· Ils y lancent des jets de soupe" [My poor heart dribbles at the stern ··· They squirt upon it jets of soup], *Le Cœur volé* [*The Cheated Heart*] 1, 3 (*Grover Smith* 37).

14 **un instant de puissance et de délire**: Tourneur: "For the poor benefit of a bewildering minute", *The Revenger's Tragedy* III iv (see note to *The Waste Land* [V] 403, 405).

15 **vieux lubrique**: Laforgue: "le soir, doux au vieillard lubrique" [evening, sweet to the old lecher], *La Première Nuit* [*The First Night*] 1 (*Grover Smith* 37).

20 **Mais alors, tu as ton vautour**: TSE's secretary to E. M. Stephenson, 23 Oct 1942: "Mr. Eliot ··· tells me that this line was suggested by a phrase in a book by André Gide called *Prométhée Mal Enchaîné.* In this particular passage, Prometheus is giving a lecture which is interrupted from time to time by his friend the eagle having to gnaw at Prometheus' liver. Prometheus' lecture is generally on the text: it is necessary to have an eagle." TSE: "As André Gide's Prometheus said, in the lecture which he gave before a large audience in Paris: *Il faut avoir un aigle*", *The Use of Poetry and the Use of Criticism* 69. To Geoffrey Faber, 7 July 1936, concerning a comic accusation signed by their colleague C. W. Stewart: "it would be doing Stewart too much honour to refer to him as a vulture. Morley's friend André Gide once said *il faut avoir un aigle.* He never said *il faut avoir un Stewart.*" See note to *A Cooking Egg* 27, 29.

21 **les rides**: *Grover Smith* 36: "not merely smears or wrinkles but the ripples of waves stripping clean the sailor's bones".

26 **les cris des mouettes**: Laforgue on Corbière: "Mais jamais d'ordures, d'obscénités voyantes de commis. Strident comme le cri des mouettes et comme elles jamais las ··· satyr libidineux" [But never any filth or the manifest obscenities of the travelling salesman. As strident as the cry of gulls, and like

them untiring ··· lubricious satyr], *Littérature* in *Mélanges Posthumes* (1903) 119. See note to 15, "vieux lubrique".

29 **sa vie antérieure:** Baudelaire sonnet *La Vie antérieure* [*The Previous Life*].

Whispers of Immortality

Published in *Little Review* Sept 1918, then *1919*+ and *Penguin / Sel Poems.*

Recorded 13 May 1947, Harvard, as part of the Morris Gray Poetry Reading.

Undated in any of the five typings. Dated "? London 1917" in *Isaacs US 1920* and 1917 by TSE in *Hayward's 1925* but 1918 by TSE in *Morley's US 1920.* Assigned to 1917–18 by *Rainey* 198. See note to 1–6 for Joyce in May 1918.

For Pound's extensive comments on the drafts, see Textual History.

In reply to Kenneth Allott's conjecture, 20 June 1935, that *Whispers of Immortality* "irritates you for coming to pieces in your hand with sharp edges in too many directions", TSE wrote, 12 Nov 1935: "What you say seems to be correct."

Title ***Whispers of Immortality***: common 19th-century diction. Whitman called a sequence of poems *Whispers of Heavenly Death.* ***of Immortality***: TSE on the *Ode: Intimations of Immortality from Recollections of Early Childhood*: "Wordsworth's Ode is a superb piece of verbiage", *The Silurist* (1927). Charlotte Eliot to Bertrand Russell, 18 Jan 1916: "In Bergson's emphasis on *life*, its power and indestructibility, I think some persons found an intimation of immortality." Among the titles suggested for the poem by Pound was *Night Thoughts on immorality* (see Textual History), invoking *Night Thoughts on Life, Death, and Immortality* by Edward Young. *TSE's books: Bodleian list* (1934) includes "Young's Night Thoughts (T. Stearns)".

Unadopted title ***Try this on Your Piano***: sheet music was advertised in the US under this headline during the 1880s and 1890s.

1 **Webster:** "The greatest of Shakespeare's followers is undoubtedly John Webster. His skill in dealing with horror; the beauty of his verse", lecture XVIII on *Syllabus: Elizabethan Literature* (1918). See note to 2–5. **possessed:** OED "possess" 1d: "To take up the attention or thoughts of; to occupy, engross. *Obs.*", with last citation 1719. "possessed" 2a. "Inhabited and controlled by a demon or spirit".

1–6 **death | And saw the skull beneath the skin ··· bulbs instead of balls | Stared from the sockets of the eyes:** *Richard III* I iv, Clarence's dreamscape:

> Inestimable stones, unvalu'd jewels,
> All scatter'd in the bottom of the sea.
> Some lay in dead men's skulls, and in the holes
> Where eyes did once inhabit, there were crept—
> As 'twere in scorn of eyes—reflecting gems,
> That woo'd the slimy bottom of the deep.

For TSE and drowning, see note to *Mr. Apollinax* 11–15. (Ever since *US 1920*, the account of drowned Phlebas which ends *Dans le Restaurant* has immediately preceded *Whispers of Immortality*, the French poem having been detached from the other three with which it had been grouped in *AraVP*.) **death ··· breastless creatures ··· lipless grin ··· eyes:** Joyce: "death ··· his eyes ··· His lips lipped and mouthed fleshless lips of air", *Ulysses* episode III (Proteus) in *Little Review* May 1918 (see dating in headnote). For the episode, see note to *Dirge* 1–7.

1–9 **Webster ··· death ··· skull ··· Donne:** in his copy of Lucas's edition of Webster (1927), 36, TSE wrote "!" beside a paragraph which ends: "In Donne, in Webster, in Burton, in Browne, in Hamlet appears this figure of the subtle humanity of the later Renaissance gazing in fascination on the skull of that more childish world which has suffered and gone down to death before it." TSE reviewed the edition, which is dedicated to John Maynard Keynes, in *John Webster* (1928).

2 **the skull beneath the skin:** *Grover Smith* 40 points to Gautier:

> La squelette était invisible
> Au temps heureux de l'Art païen;
> L'homme, sous la forme sensible,
> Content du beau, ne cherchait rien.

[The skeleton was invisible in the good old time of pagan art; satisfied with beauty, man searched for nothing beneath the tangible.]

Bûchers et tombeaux [*Pyres and Tombs*] 1–4

TSE quoted Gautier's first two lines in both *The Post-Georgians* (1919) and *Andrew Marvell* (1921). Report of TSE's lecture to the Poetry Society of Maryland, 2 Feb 1933: "'Suppose you went into a drawing room where the people were all without their skins,' he suggested. 'At first it would be hard to get used to seeing people like that ··· It would be so entirely new, seeing anyone without human skin ··· Then conceive that you found them more comfortable without their skins. You would then adjust yourself to the sight ··· Afterward you would find them, possibly, more interesting. Their eyes would be more expressive. The play of their muscles would be fascinating'", *The Sun* (Baltimore) 3 Feb 1933. Turgenev: "A sumptuous, brilliantly lighted hall; a number of ladies and gentlemen ··· and suddenly ··· from every head and from every face, slipped off the delicate covering of skin, and instantaneously exposed the deadly whiteness of skulls ··· those lumpy bony balls, and the rolling in them of other smaller balls, the balls of meaningless eyes", *The Skulls* in *Poems in Prose*, tr. Constance Garnett (1897). TSE reviewed Edward Garnett's *Turgenev* in *Egoist* Dec 1917, and *A Sportsman's Sketches* (2 vols.) is given in *TSE's books: Bodleian list* (1934). For poetry compared to "a body stripped of its skin", see headnote to *The Waste Land*, 6. A HOAX?

2–4 **skull ··· under ground ··· grin:** D. H. Lawrence: "My love lies underground | With her face upturned to mine, | And her mouth unclosed in a last long kiss | That ended her life and mine ··· How is it I grin then, and chuckle", *Constancy of a Sort* 1–4, 55 (*English Review* Sept 1917; later retitled *Hymn to Priapus*).

2–5 **skull beneath ··· Daffodil bulbs:** *The White Devil* V iv, *Enter* BRACHIANO'S *ghost, in his leather cassock and breeches, boots and cowl; in his hand a pot of lily-flowers, with a skull in it ···* FLAMINEO: "A dead man's skull beneath the roots of flowers!—" (For the scene, see note to *The Waste Land* [I] 71–75.) *The Golden Treasury* includes Wordsworth's *Ode: Intimations of Immortality from Recollections of Early Childhood* (see note on the title *Whispers of Immortality*) and "I wandered lonely as a cloud" (as *The Daffodils*).

2, 9 **skull beneath the skin ··· Donne**: for TSE on *The Relique*, see note to *The Love Song of J. Alfred Prufrock* 63–64.

3 **breastless creatures**: Ralph Hodgson: "Blind sires and breastless mothers of his fate", *The Journeyman* in *Poems* (1916).

3–4 **under ground ··· grin**: "Subterrene laughter", *Ode* ("Tired. | Subterrene") 2. "His laughter was submarine and profound ··· under a chair | Or grinning", *Mr. Apollinax* 8, 13–14.

4 **lipless grin**: Thomas Lovell Beddoes: "And, when the world is old and dead, the thin wit shall find the angel's record of man's works and deeds, and write with a lipless grin on the innocent first page for a title, 'Here begins Death's Jest-Book'", *Death's Jest-Book* II iii (R. G. Howarth, *N&Q* 24 June 1939). *TSE's library: Bodleian list* (1934) includes the Muses' Library Beddoes (ed. Ramsay Colles). To John Lehmann, 10 Apr 1945: "Beddoes, of course, I know very well". (For Beddoes's father, also Thomas, see note to 20.) Byron: "Mark how its lipless mouth grins without breath!" *Don Juan* IX xi.

5–6 **Daffodil bulbs ··· the eyes:** Harold Monro: "the surface of the land | Budded into head and hand ··· blossomed into eyes. || A flower is looking through the ground", *Strange Meetings* VIII–IX in *Poetry* Sept 1916 (near TSE's four poems headed *Observations*) and, revised, in the volume *Strange Meetings*, which TSE praised in *Reflections on Contemporary Poetry* I (1917). TSE wrote the obituary of Monro in *The Times*, 17 Mar 1932, and a critical note to his *Collected Poems* (1933). OED "blind" 12: "Of plants: Without buds or eyes, or without a terminal flower" (Betty McCue, personal communication).

9 **Donne, I suppose, was such another**: "Coleridge was one of those unhappy persons—Donne, I suspect, was such another—of whom one might say, that if they had not been poets, they might have made something of their lives", *The Use of Poetry and the Use of Criticism* 68. **Donne**: pronounced *Don* in TSE's recording of 1947, despite the pun in *A Hymne to God the Father*: "Thou hast done". To Carlton F. Wells, 12 Dec 1934: "I cannot speak on this subject with personal authority, but I believe that it is pretty well agreed amongst scholars that the correct pronunciation at his period was certainly Dun. The date at which the pronunciation became changed does not appear to be definitely known." H. J. C. Grierson: "the name was pronounced so as to rime with 'done' and was frequently spelt 'Dun' or 'Dunne'", *The Cambridge History of English and American Literature* IV (1909) ch. XI.

9, 12, 15, 18 **Donne ··· experience ··· flesh ··· emphasis**: "A thought to Donne was an experience; it modified his sensibility", *The Metaphysical Poets* (1921). "He is a little of the religious spellbinder ··· the flesh-creeper, the sorcerer of emotional orgy. We emphasize this aspect to the point of the grotesque. Donne had a trained mind; but without belittling the intensity or the profundity of his experience, we can suggest that this experience was not perfectly controlled", *Lancelot Andrewes* (1926).

10–12 **found no substitute for sense ··· penetrate ··· beyond experience**: Bradley:

"From mere pleasure and pain we may pass on to feeling ··· in either of these senses, is it possible to consider feeling as real ··· finite content is necessarily determined from the outside; its external relations ··· penetrate its essence", *Appearance and Reality* ch. XXVI; TSE underlined "external" and wrote: "is this not merely a spatial metaphor? For how cd 'external relations' '*penetrate its essence*'?" **found no substitute for sense ··· Expert beyond experience**: "expression ··· Explosion ··· experiment ··· Experience ··· not a substitute for ··· experience", *A Note on War Poetry* 1–23 (*variant*: "no substitute for"). To Hayward, 2 Feb 1931: "faith is not a *substitute* for anything" (see note to *The Dry Salvages* II 47–48). "For Arnold the best poetry supersedes both religion and philosophy. I have tried to indicate the results of this conjuring trick elsewhere. The most generalised form of my own view is simply this: that nothing in this world or the next is a substitute for anything else; and if you find that you must do without something, such as religious faith or philosophic belief, then you must just do without it", *The Use of Poetry and the Use of Criticism* 113. (Van Wyck Brooks: "we have ··· ingenious devices for manufacturing music and pictures, which are, as we say, 'just about as good' as the true things ··· most of us are quite content with the substitute", *The Wine of the Puritans* 43.) In *ts1* (where the lines are differently disposed), TSE had "He found no substitute for death". **Expert beyond experience**: Pound: "she also will believe it, | Being expert from experience", *Homage to Sextus Propertius* (1919) viii 32–33 (R. G. Howarth, *N&Q* 24 June 1939).

11, 21–22 *variants* **Our sighs pursue th' elusive shade ··· Our sighs pursue the vanishd shade | And breathe a sanctified amen**: Lancelot Andrewes: "So be it, to have our fast conclude with the hypocrite's Amen;—no more fearful punishment in the world", Ash-Wednesday Sermon 1622 (on Matthew 6: 16: "be not, as the hypocrites, of a sad countenance"). TSE: "Our prayers dismiss the parting shade | And breathe a hypocrite's amen!" *Elegy* 1–2.

13 **He knew the anguish of the marrow**: Genesis 42: 21: "We saw the anguish of his soul."

17 **Grishkin**: described as "the flamboyant whore" in *G. Jones* (213), but in his copy TSE underlined "whore" and wrote "not necessarily". Pound to H. B. Parkes, 16 Dec [1931?], on influencing a fellow writer's subject matter: "Only case where I tried it, it was a success. I led Eliot up to her wot posterity now knows as 'Grishkin' with the firm intuito that a poem wd. result, & intention that it should" (*Gallup 1970* 11). Pound in 1960: "I took Parson Elyot to see the Prima Ballerina [Serafima Astafieva], and it evoked 'Grushkin'", *Pavannes & Divagations* 161.

17–20 **Grishkin is nice: her Russian eye ··· bliss**: braced by TSE in *Thayer's AraVP* with "cf. Gautier 'Carmen est maigre'". Théophile Gautier in *Emaux et Camées*: "Carmen est maigre,—un trait de bistre | Cerne son œil de gitana" [Carmen is thin,—a line of bistre rings her gypsy eye], *Carmen* 1–2 (*Taupin*); the lines had been quoted in Pound's *To a Friend Writing on Cabaret Dancers* in *Lustra* (1916), later included by TSE in Pound's *Selected Poems* (*Southam*).

19 **Uncorseted, her**: Alan Seeger: "Uncorseted, her clinging dress with every step and turn betrays, | In pretty and provoking ways her adolescent loveliness",

Paris II in *Poems* (1917), reviewed by TSE, *Egoist* Dec 1917. TSE knew Seeger from Harvard.

20 **pneumatic**: OED b: "Applied to things which are inflated ··· esp. to the tyres of the wheels of bicycles, and the like", with "the india-rubber pneumatic tyre ··· so much in favour to-day" (1896) and "Cyclists owe much to the inventor of the pneumatic tyre" (1898). (Pound: "Grishkin's Dunlap tyre boozum", page of comments on *Whispers of Immortality ts3b*: see Textual History.) OED e: "*humorous* ··· Of a woman: having a well-rounded figure, esp. a large bosom; of or pertaining to a woman having such attributes", with this as first citation. 4a: "Belonging or relating to spirit or spiritual existence". 3c: citing Dunglison's *Medical Lexicon* (1842): "*Pneumatic Physicians*, name given to a sect of physicians, at the head of whom was Athenæus, who made health and disease to consist in the different proportions of an element—which they called Pneuma, *πνεῦμα*—to those of the other elementary principles." For Athenæus see note on the Bolo poem *Deipnosophistic* (sent to Dobrée, 29 Sept [1927]). TSE on Benlowes: "His most considerable poem is called *Pneumato-Sarco-Machia*: otherwise *Theophila's Spiritual Warfare*; and, so far as one can make out, has something to do with theology, and the struggles of the human soul", *The Minor Metaphysicals* (1930). Of Guido Cavalcanti: "very likely a heretic, if not a sceptic—as evidenced partly by his possibly having held some pneumatic philosophy and theory of corpuscular action which I am unable to understand", *After Strange Gods* 42. **pneumatic bliss**: experiments with nitrous oxide by Humphry Davy at Thomas Beddoes's Pneumatic Institute in 1798 gave intoxicating pleasure to Coleridge, Southey and others.

21 **The**: omitted in TSE's recording of 1947. **couched Brazilian**: for tropical associations see Textual History and *The Waste Land* [V] 398 ("The jungle crouched"). **couched**: OED "couch" *v.*[1] I: "To lay down flat". c: "Said of animals; almost always *refl.* or *pass. arch.*"

24 **maisonnette**: OED: "part of a residential building which is let separately, usu. distinguished from a flat by not being all on one floor", only from 1912 (with this as the second citation). Douglas Goldring's sexually suggestive *Maisonnettes*, two quatrains, appeared in *Others Anthology* (1916), near *Portrait of a Lady*. TSE to Philippa Strachey, 8 Feb 1929: "We would not consider taking a maisonette over people of whom we know nothing." See *McCue 2016*.

26, 28 **gloom ··· drawing-room**: "Inside the gloom | Of a garret room", *Inside the gloom* 1–2. "in its own gloom ··· in a dusty room", *Animula* 29–30.

29 **Abstract Entities**: John Stuart Mill on Greek philosophical theories: "Empedokles explained all things by the mixture and mutual action of earth, water, air, and fire. These material substances were usually supposed to require the concurrence of certain abstract entities called Wet and Dry, Cold and Hot, Soft and Hard, Heavy and Light, &c, which were the immediate if not ultimate agents in the generation of phenomena", review of Grote's *Plato* (1866). TSE: "It is equally possible to look upon consciousness as the cause or as the effect of a peculiar grouping of entities, though really I suppose that it is neither, but is the group itself", *The Ethics of Green and Sidgwick* (1914). Rejecting Bertrand Russell's conception of "neutral entities", TSE wrote of immediate experience: "It is certainly neutral, but what ground have we for speaking of it as 'entities'?"

On Real, Unreal, Ideal, and Imaginary Objects (1914). "so many entities", *Suite Clownesque* I 19.

30 *variant* **sacerdotal:** OED "of or pertaining to a priest".

31 **our lot:** Pound: "And he said, 'Have you seen any of our lot?' | I'd seen a lot of his lot ···" *The Gipsy* in *Poetry* Mar 1915. Hugh Kenner asked TSE about "our lot": "He said it meant 'kind,' not 'fate,' and conceded that it perhaps violated the diction of that particular poem", *Kenner* xiii. ("whatever be our lot", *To the Class of 1905* 44.)

32 *variant* **their Ethics of the Dust:** Ruskin, *The Ethics of the Dust* (1865), ten lectures given at a girls' school.

Additional draft stanzas ts2 [3–7] **the vanishd shade ··· the Sons of God descend | To entertain the wives of men. || And when the Female Soul departs ··· The Sons of God:** "*departed* ··· Descending ··· the God Hercules | Had left him ··· Declines ··· She entertains", *Burbank with a Baedeker: Bleistein with a Cigar* epigraph, 2, 7–8, 21, 28.

Mr. Eliot's Sunday Morning Service

Published in *Little Review* Sept 1918, then *1919*+ and *Penguin / Sel Poems.*

Recorded 26 Sept 1955, in London; released Caedmon 1955 (US), 1960 (UK).

Undated in *ts1*. Dated "? London 1917" in *Isaacs US 1920* and 1917 by TSE in *Hayward's 1925*, but dated 1918 by TSE in *Morley's US 1920*. Assigned to 1918 by *Rainey* 198.

Title ***Mr. Eliot's Sunday Morning Service*:** Emerson wrote to his wife, Lidian, 31 Dec 1852, about William Greenleaf Eliot (TSE's grandfather): "Mr. Eliot, the Unitarian minister, is the Saint of the West, & has a sumptuous church, & crowds to hear his really good sermons" (*Letters*, ed. Ralph L. Rush, 1939). *Gordon* 110: TSE "resented Sunday morning services conducted by his cousin Frederick May Eliot, who ··· was ordained as a Unitarian minister". Yet where the 1961 ts of *Howarth* suggested that the poem brought Unitarianism "under withering scrutiny", TSE wrote in the margin "nothing to do with Unitarianism" (*Materer*). TSE to Virginia Woolf [2 Apr? 1934, incomplete], apparently comparing clerical forebears: "For the moment, I will post the Revd. Dan'l Greenleaf, the Revd. Dr. Asahel Stearns, the Revd. Obadiah Smith, and (among Moderns) the Revd. Fred. Eliot (author of *Hammered on the Anvil*, a book of parochial talks to Young Men) in charge of skirmishing parties and raiders ··· It is unfortunate that Julius Caesar Eliot never took orders ··· I have just been made a Churchwarden. That ought to count 3 points." To Henry Eliot, 26 May 1934: "Sometime at your leisure I wish you would look up the names of all clerical ancestors, collaterals, and connexions by marriage that we have. The point being that I have a bet of half-a-crown with Virginia Woolf as to which is descended from more parsons. She has been rather boastful on the point. What's the relationship to Richard Sterne, Archbp. of York? I shall count Laurence Sterne, as a collateral." (TSE later accepted that there was no relation between "Stearns" and "Sterne".) 20 June: "I think there are a few omissions—there were two Rev. Andrew Eliots in succession, one during the Revolution—and wasnt Uncle Oliver Stearns, Dean of the Divinity School, a parson? ··· Aunt Susie has produced (unasked) a Revd. John Rogers, admired by Hooker ··· The family came from Cotlands in Devon and that branch settled at Port Eliot in Cornwall ··· Our people, you remember, went to Coker, near Yeovil in Somerset." To Frederick May Eliot on his election as president of the American Unitarian Association, 24 Feb 1937: "news reached me that the smoke had finally risen from the chimney on Beacon Hill, and the announcement made that you were to wear the triple crown. I congratulate the American Unitarian Association on having made the inevitable choice, and am glad to think that the family retain their proud position of being the Borgias of Unitarianism." (The "triple crown" was worn by Popes, beginning in the 14th century.)

Henry to TSE, 12 Sept 1935, accusing him of sensationalising the change in his religious convictions: "how came you to address to the clergy of Boston, a city saturated with associations of your ancestors, immediate and distant, what seems to me in all truth a fanatically intolerant and shocking tirade? ··· even the Roman Church approves the injunction, 'Honor thy father and mother.'" TSE, 1 Jan 1936: "As for the sensation of a person of my antecedents 'going Romish' etc. as you say; please consider that there was no such sensation, not at any rate in England. Most of the churchfolk I know do not even know that I was once a Unitarian, even if they know what a Unitarian is; they don't know what an Eliot is ··· As for my address to the Unitarian clergy of Boston, I did not want to address them at all, and I only acceded to repeated invitation. I gave them exactly what I was asked for, and I did not get fair treatment either. As for my failure on that occasion to honour my father and my mother, I cannot attach any meaning to your words." Declining to promote the Converts' Aid Society, TSE described himself to F. W. Chambers, 25 Mar 1935, as "a member of the Church of England". ***Mr. Eliot's***: see note to *Five-Finger Exercises* V. *Lines for Cuscuscaraway and Mirza Murad Ali Beg* 1, "How unpleasant to meet Mr. Eliot". ***Sunday Morning Service***: "There was once an organization called the Ethical Culture Society, which held Sunday morning services: that seems to be the kind of liberal religion to which Mr. Foerster's Humanism boils down", *Second Thoughts about Humanism* (1929). In 1960: "I was brought up in the orthodoxy of Boston Unitarianism: I use the word 'orthodoxy', because the tendency of American Unitarianism in our day has been to wander further and further from that attachment to the memory of Jesus Christ which gave it its tenuous claim to being Christian ··· My father was brought up in the atmosphere of Unitarian piety and strict Puritanism, and was a zealous upholder of the church which his father had founded ··· Sundays had both obligations and prohibitions for members of his family. But in the summer months the obligations were relaxed, and some of the prohibitions, indeed, slightly relaxed too. As is usual in American society, we had a house—what Americans call a 'cottage'—at the seaside, in Massachusetts ··· there was a Unitarian church: but I do not remember my parents ever attending Sunday service there. Even if they did once or twice, the fact remains that the summer holiday was for my family a holiday from church-going as well as from other serious occupations. This difference came to strike me as remarkable as I approached the age of serious reflection. Religion was associated with one particular church edifice", *All Souls' Club* (1960). "Sunday: this satisfied procession | Of definite Sunday faces", *Spleen* 1–2. For Sunday observance, see note to *Choruses from "The Rock"* I 24–29.

Epigraph Marlowe, *The Jew of Malta* IV i. *Portrait of a Lady* takes its epigraph from the same scene.

1 **Polyphiloprogenitive**: not in OED 1st ed., but later added: "Very prolific, specifically of a person's talent, imagination, inventive powers, etc.", with this as the first citation, adding "perhaps influenced also by PHILOPROGENITIVE *a.* 2." ("*Phrenol.* Loving one's offspring"). Pronounced *polly-fillow-progenitive* in TSE's recording. Byron:

> That's noble! That's romantic! For my part
> I think that philo-progenitiveness is
> (Now here's a word quite after my own heart,
> Though there's a shorter a good deal than this,
> If that politeness set it not apart,
> But I'm resolved to say nought that's amiss.)—
> I say, methinks that philo-progenitiveness
> Might meet from men a little more forgiveness.
>
> *Don Juan* XII xxii

"Philoprogenitive" occurs in Friedrich Strauss's *A New Life of Jesus*, tr. George Eliot (1846) II 41. Matthew Arnold quotes Robert Buchanan: "'If there is one quality which seems God's, and his exclusively, it seems that divine philoprogenitiveness'", commenting that it seems unjust "to attribute to Divinity exclusively this philoprogenitiveness, which the British Philistine, and the poorer classes of Irish, may certainly claim to share", *Culture and Anarchy* ch. VI. "Philoprogenitiveness" appears also in Charlotte Brontë's *Villette* ch. 11 (Eleanor Cook, personal communication). TSE to Sholom J. Kahn, 27 June 1958, rejecting a suggestion relating this word to Whitman: "One does not need to go to any particular author for words which are known to any educated man and are found in dictionaries, and I think that in my verse the prefix to the word is what makes all the difference."

2 **sapient**: OED: "Wise. (A learned synonym, in serious use now only *poet.*)" Pronounced *saypient* in TSE's recording (as OED). **sutlers**: OED: "One who follows an army or lives in a garrison town and sells provisions to soldiers."

3 **across the window-panes**: "Across the window panes", *Oh little voices of the throats of men* 37. "across the window panes", *Interlude in London* 2. Conan Doyle: "at the window · · · the yellow fog swirls down the street and drifts across the dun-coloured houses", *The Sign of Four* ch. 1 (TSE: "The yellow fog that rubs its back upon the window-panes", *The Love Song of J. Alfred Prufrock* 15.)

4–8] TSE note against this stanza in *Thayer's AraVP* now illegibly erased.

4 **In the beginning was the Word**: John 1: 1: "In the beginning was the Word, and the Word was with God, and the Word was God."

6 **Superfetation**: OED 1: "formation of a second foetus in a uterus already pregnant". Coleridge: "I purchased lately Cicero's work, de officiis, which I had always considered as almost worthy of a Christian. To my surprize it had become a most flagrant libel. Nay! but how?—Some one, I know not who, out

of the fruitfulness of his own malignity had filled all the margins and other blank spaces with annotations—a true *superfœtation* of *examples*, that is, of false and slanderous tales!" *The Friend* (1818) Essay VII, epigraph (Coleridge's own translation from Rudolph von Langen, 1438–1519). **τὸ ἕν**: the One. Pronounced *ta-hen* in TSE's recording (although some scholars recommend *toe-hen*). B. A. G. Fuller's *The Problem of Evil in Plotinus* (1912) devotes eight pages to "The One. Its incomprehensible and ineffable character. Pure unity transcending all multiplicity and variety, even the duality of subject and object in thought. Inability of our experience to furnish any predicate or category descriptive of it. Neither quantity, nor quality, nor being, nor good, nor consciousness, nor mind, nor even one in the ordinary use of the term; but above and beyond them all. Describable in negative terms only. Union with it attained only in a super-rational and super-conscious state of ecstasy."

7 **mensual**: originally "menstrual", ringed and emended by Pound in *ts1*. OED "mensual": "Of or relating to a month; occurring or recurring monthly; monthly", from 1794. (*La Nouvelle Revue Française*, which TSE read keenly from 1911 and on which the *Criterion* was modelled, described itself as "Revue Mensuelle de Littérature et de Critique".) OED "mensal": "In the male as in the female, the maturation of the reproductive elements is a continual process, though we may hardly say that it is not influenced by the mensal periodicity" (1888). TSE to Bonamy Dobrée [22 Nov] 1927: "Mr. Eliot humbly suggests that the University of Ethiopia and Nubia and the land of Prester John might in return subscribe to one mensual copy of the *Criterion*." In *The Method of Mr. Pound* (1919), TSE quoted Pound's poem of 1912, *Canzon* (from Arnaut Daniel): "Her love-touch by none other mensurate".

8 **enervate**: pronounced *in-èrvaight* in TSE's recording. OED *a.* 1: "1 Wanting in strength of character; spiritless, unmanly, effeminate", with Dryden: "The Dregs and Droppings of enervate Love." OED *v.* 2: "To emasculate. *Obs. rare*", with Augustine, *City of God*, tr. J. Healey 1610: "If earth were held no goddesse, men would lay their hands upon her and strengthen themselves by her, & not upon themselves, to enervate themselves for her: If she were no goddess, she would bee made so fertaile by others hands, that shee should never make men barren by their own hands ··· the massacre of man-hood is such, the gelded person is left neither man nor woman" (bk. VII ch. 23). **Origen**: (AD 185–254), most learned and prolific of the early church fathers, who committed zealous self-castration in his youth. *Williamson* 95: "ordained and deposed presbyter ··· he adapted Greek philosophy, especially the Logos doctrine, to Christian thought, particularly to the Gospel of St. John; and thus subtilized, made controversial and polymath, the Christian religion."

8–12 **enervate Origen ··· ground ··· cracked and browned**: "parched eviscerate soil", *Little Gidding* II 13, where draft variants included "fruitless / emasculate / ~~sexless~~" (see Textual History). "the field was cracked and brown", *Five-Finger Exercises* II. *Lines to a Yorkshire Terrier* 8 (John Fuller, *the Review* Nov 1962).

9–16 **Umbrian school ··· Baptized God ··· water ··· The Father and the Paraclete**: the Baptism of Christ (Matthew 3: 16). *Southam*: "The usual treatment of this subject shows Christ standing in a stream or shallow pool, John the Baptist beside him, pouring water over his head from a small bowl. Above Christ's head, the Holy Ghost is often represented by a dove, and over the dove, God looks down from a gap in the clouds." Piero della Francesca's *Baptism of Christ*, in the Umbrian School room of London's National Gallery (identified by *Watkins*), is among the many Italian medieval and Renaissance works marked in TSE's London *Baedeker*.

9–19 **A painter ··· nimbus of the Baptized God ··· red and pustular**: Whitman: "Painters have painted their swarming groups and the centre-figure of all, | From the head of the centre-figure spreading a nimbus of gold-color'd light ··· The shaved face, the unsteady eye, the impure complexion", *To You* ("Whoever you are") 18–19, 31 (*Musgrove* 50). See note to 25–27.

10 **gesso**: pronounced *jesso*. "The *gesso* is much like ground chalk. Glue put on panel first, then gesso", notes from Edward Waldo Forbes's Harvard course "Florentine Painting", which TSE took in spring 1910. *Soldo* 63: "A definition of gesso was one of the examination questions Eliot had to prepare." TSE also noted that the "ground for gilding" was called "bolo" (*Crawford* 83); see headnote to "Improper Rhymes".

11 **nimbus of the Baptized God**: Gautier: "Dans son nimbe trilobe | La Vierge et son Jésus" [Within her triple-lobed nimbus the Virgin and her Jesus], *L'Art* 37–38 in *Emaux et Camées* (*Grover Smith* 304). **nimbus**: OED 2: "*Art.* A bright or golden disk surrounding the head, esp. of a saint."

13–14 **pale and thin ··· feet**: Swinburne: "sweet the feet of the dove ··· Thou hast conquered, O pale Galilean", *Hymn to Proserpine* 5, 35. John Gray: "Pale Sebastian's feet", *Saint Sebastian: On a Picture* 51 (see note to *The Love Song of St. Sebastian* title).

16 **Paraclete**: Holy Spirit, represented in painting as a dove. Igor Stravinsky set *Little Gidding* IV, "The dove descending", in 1962. Robert Craft: "In response to some speculations by IS concerning the word 'paraclete,' T.S.E. fetches a well-worn Liddell and Scott from behind his chair but offers a synonym ('the comforter') himself before opening it", *Stravinsky: Chronicle of a Friendship* (rev. ed. 1994).

18 **The avenue of penitence**: "the way of penitence", *Choruses from "The Rock"* IX 14.

20 **Clutching ··· pence**: Meredith: "And now she screws a gouty fist, | And now she counts to clutch her pence", *To Colonel Charles* 19–20. **piaculative**: not in OED 1st ed., but later added with this as sole citation: "= piacular *a.* 1" ("Making expiation or atonement; expiatory"). Pronounced *pea-aculative* in TSE's recording. *TSE's books: Bodleian list* (1934) includes Émile Durkheim's *The Elementary Forms of the Religious Life* (1915), with its chapter title "Piacular Rites and the Ambiguity of the Notion of Sacredness" (*Harmon 1976b*).

22 **Sustained by staring Seraphim**: "A local deity of love, | And pious vows and votive prayer | Shall hover in my sacred grove | Sustained on that Italian air", *Exequy* 4–7. Writing to Pound [26? Jan 1922], TSE proposed to change *The Waste Land* [II] 79–80 to read "Sustained by standards wrought with fruited vines | Wherefrom [a golden Cupidon peeped out]". Again at the head of the line, though in a different sense: "Sustained by juice of juniper and grape", *Three Sonnets* (to Geoffrey Faber) 7. **staring Seraphim**: *Paradiso* XXI 92: "quel Serafin che in Dio più l'occhio ha fisso" [that Seraph who hath his eye most fixed on God] (Ernest Schanzer, *EinC* Apr 1955).

23–24 **the devout | Burn invisible and dim**: "cf. Henry Vaughan", TSE in *Thayer's AraVP*. Vaughan: "O for that Night! where I in him | Might live invisible and dim", *The Night* 53–54 (Allardyce Nicoll, *English Journal* Apr 1934); TSE decided against a footnote wryly acknowledging the debt (see Textual History). TSE: "Vaughan is usually considered as the poet of occasional fine lines, and of no perfect poem", *The Silurist* (1927). For "a dim religious light", see note to *Burnt Norton* III 3.

25 **Along the garden-wall**: "Along the garden stairs", *Circe's Palace* 10. "I have seen the darkness creep along the wall", *The Love Song of J. Alfred Prufrock* 74^75 [1].

25–26 **the bees | With hairy bellies**: Milton: "the bee with honey'd thigh ··· hairy gown", *Il Penseroso* 142, 169.

25–27 **the bees | With hairy bellies pass between | The staminate and pistillate ··· epicene**: *Jain 1991*: "The pollen clings to the hairs on their bodies and legs. The 'staminate' has stamens [male organs containing pollen] but no pistils; the 'pistillate' has pistils [female seed-bearing organs] but no stamens. The bees are thus 'epicene' in that the worker bees are neuter, having imperfectly developed generative organs, and because they are in contact with both sexes." Irving Babbitt on Chateaubriand's *Génie du Christianisme*: "the celibacy of priests is backed up by the virginity of bees. He points out that 'nature has not been as delicate as disbelievers . . . It has bestowed the form of the cross upon a whole family of flowers.' He proves the necessity of the Sabbath", *The Masters of Modern French Criticism* (1912) 72. Whitman: "The hairy wild-bee that murmurs and hankers up and down, that gripes the full-grown lady-flower, curves upon her with amorous firm legs", *Spontaneous Me* 17 (with "bellies", 13) (*Musgrove* 51).

27 **The staminate and pistillate**: Laforgue: "Une chair bêtement, staminifère, | Un cœur illusoirement pistillé" [A flesh which is stupidly stamen-bearing, a heart delusively wearing pistils], *Ballade* 13–14 (*Southam*).

28 **Blest**: Vaughan: "Most blest believer he!" *The Night* 7. **epicene**: OED *adj.* 1: "In Lat. and Gr. grammar, said of nouns which, without changing their grammatical gender, may denote either sex"; 2c. *fig*: "often in the sense of 'effeminate'"; and *n.* "One who partakes of the characteristics of both sexes. 1609 B. Jonson (*title*), *Epicene, or The Silent Woman*." TSE: "One is particularly struck by an almost epicene refinement and certainly by the absence of references to sexual experience", *"The Poet's Progress"* by H. B. Cresswell, reader's report (1929).

29 **Sweeney shifts from ham to ham**: Joseph Husband on "Sweeney the driver": "An oppressive silence followed and Sweeney shifted uneasily in his chair", *The Summons* in *Harvard Advocate* 29 Mar 1907 (TSE's first appearance in the *Advocate* was 24 May). **ham**: OED *n.*[1] b: "The back of the thigh; the thigh and buttock collectively", with 1796: "They sit on their hams, with their legs and arms disposed in the manner of monkeys."

30 **Stirring the water in his bath**: on 2 Aug 1938, TSE wrote to John Hayward that he was gathering *Pseudodoxia Contemporanea*, a modern collection of Vulgar Errors to match that of Sir Thomas Browne in the 17th century. Among them was "A fart, strained through bathwater, loses both odour and inflammability."

30–32 **Stirring the water in his bath ··· controversial, polymath**: asked to rule in a controversy over the volume of gold in a crown, the polymath Archimedes worked out the means in his "Eureka moment", when he observed the level of his bathwater rise as he stepped in (Doolie Sloman, personal communication). He is famous also for the Archimedes Screw, which raises water against (*contra*) the force of gravity by turning (*vertens*) (Peter Lockley, personal communication).

31 **subtle schools:** Socrates refers to the *κομψοὶ* ("elegant thinkers" such as Zeno) in Plato's *Philebus*. Theodor Gomperz on Plato: "To this is joined an ironical expression of thanks to the 'subtle school'", *Greek Thinkers: A History of Ancient Philosophy* tr. G. G. Berry (1905) III 193. In 1913, TSE jotted down: "T. Gomperz: Greek Thinkers" in his notes from the Harvard course "Philosophy 10" (Houghton). J. H. Woods to Dean Briggs of Harvard, recommending TSE for a Sheldon Fellowship, 25 Feb 1914: "He wrote far the best papers in the Plato course; another year he read philosophical Sanskrit effectively" (Harvard Archives).

32 **polymath:** in the typescript Pound isolates the second syllable for scrutiny by marking "| math", with the comment "*μαθαιος* or *μανθανο*?" He has both Greek words wrong, but is pointing out that in Sweeney's case, *μάταιος* [*mathaios*] = foolish is more applicable than the actual root *μανθανω* [*manthano*] = to learn. For a playful Greek derivation by TSE, see headnote to *Old Deuteronomy*.

Sweeney Among the Nightingales

Published in *Little Review* Sept 1918, then *1919+*, *The Faber Book of Modern Verse* ed. Michael Roberts (1936), *Sesame* and *Penguin / Sel Poems*.

Recorded, 21 Apr 1933, Columbia U. Second: 26 July 1946, NBC (NY) for Library of Congress; released Feb 1949. Third: 13 May 1947, Harvard, as part of the Morris Gray Poetry Reading. Fourth: 23 May 1947, National Gallery of Art, Washington.

Undated in tss. Dated "? 1917–18" in *Isaacs 1920* and "~~1917~~ 1918" by TSE in *Hayward's 1925*, but 1918 by TSE in *Morley's US 1920*. Dated London, 1918 in *Poèmes*, and assigned to 1918 by *Rainey* 198.

Horace Gregory recalled TSE's reading at the New School for Social Research in New York on 27 Apr 1933, where Henry Eliot told him that their mother "did not quite approve of some of Tom's more 'dangerous' poems, his Sweeney poems; they made her wonder what kind of company he kept. As for himself, he liked the poems immensely, he even liked the poems written by Tom's strange friend, Pound—what a very strange, extraordinary man! · · · And when Eliot preceded his reading of *Sweeney Among the Nightingales* by saying that the poem was like a modern painting, abstract and impersonal, I felt that he was addressing his remarks to Henry directly—in mock reassurance that he was only half as wicked as his family supposed him to be", *Gregory* 206. Of the same occasion: "Speaking of *Sweeney*, one of his most discussed, he described the poem as a 'still life,' like a picture in which the methods of the painter can be analyzed but not the excitement caused by the painting. Thus, he said, each reader finds in each poem more or less different things from what the writer meant", *NY Herald Trib*, 28 Apr 1933. However, when *G. Jones* 227 proposed that "In the mythical structure of this dark poem, Clytemnestra is probably Rachel of the murderous paws, while the redeemer-Orestes is 'The silent man in mocha brown'", TSE wrote in the margin, "nonsense".

Vassar Miscellany News 10 May 1933, on TSE speaking at the college three days previously: "He went on to discuss *Sweeney Among the Nightingales*, 'not an obscure poem, simply a series of images. I'm not sure it means anything at all,' Mr. Eliot said. For him, the poem as he read it had an atmosphere of suspense and sultriness like the time of the air-raids in London. It is like a piece of still life, the meaning of which one does not formulate; one merely estimates the way the painter has used planes and angles." (As originally printed, the paragraph has no opening inverted commas, so the attributed speech may begin with the next sentence. The report is not wholly accurate.) *Gallup 1985* recorded TSE in 1944: asked whether modern art had been more readily and widely received than modern poetry, he replied, "What we call modern painting started earlier than modern poetry in English did." Pound on *The Waste Land* II: "'The Game of Chess' poem shows the effect of modern abstract art, but vorticism from my angle was a renewal of the sense of construction", interview in *Paris Review* Summer–Fall 1962. Reporting a reading of 5 May 1947 at Wellesley College, Judy Wolpert recorded that TSE read *Sweeney Among the Nightingales*, "which the poet described as a 'picture and a mood for that picture'", *Wellesley College News* 8 May 1947. Reading the poem at Harvard on 13 May 1947, TSE said he chose it for "a certain local sentimental association" (see notes to the titles *Sweeney Erect* and *Sweeney Agonistes*).

Title] Elizabeth Barrett Browning, *Bianca Among the Nightingales* (F. L. Gwynn, *Grover Smith* 304). ***Nightingales***: though it is not mentioned in OED, a slang sense of "prostitute" is given by *Partridge* as *c.* 1840, and *Chambers Slang Dictionary* gives 1. "a prostitute" as 19th century, and 2. "a singer" as late 19th century to 1910s. *Southam*:

> The "Nightingales" of the title are not only the birds of the final stanzas; the word is also a slang term for prostitutes; and Eliot once remarked to the critic Edmund Wilson that the poem takes place in a dive. Regarding the mood of the poem, Eliot said that "All I consciously set out to create · · · was a 'sense of foreboding'."

William Johnson Cory: "Still are thy pleasant voices, thy nightingales, awake; | For Death, he taketh all away, but them he cannot take", *Heraclitus* (in *Oxf Bk of English Verse*). For the legend that Philomela and Procne were turned into nightingales, see note to *The Waste Land* [II] 99–103. *The Love Song of J. Alfred Prufrock* bore in ms the subtitle "(*Prufrock among the Women*)". For nightingales in classical literature, see note to 35–39.

Epigraph] "Agamemnon", TSE in *Thayer's AraVP*. [Alas, I have been struck deep a mortal blow], Aeschylus, *Agamemnon* 1343: the cry of Agamemnon as he is murdered in his bath by Clytemnestra (see 38). The words written on the two typescripts, *ὤμοι πέπληγμαι ἐν πλευροῖς εἴσω* [Alas I have been struck deep in the ribs], deviate from Aeschylus' text and are not metrical. In *Tradition and the Individual Talent* II (1919), TSE moves within a paragraph from "the murder of Agamemnon" to Keats, whose Ode "contains a number of feelings which have nothing particular to do with the nightingale, but which the nightingale, perhaps partly because of its attractive name, and partly because of its reputation, served to bring together." For Pound's suggestion that TSE translate the *Agamemnon*, see footnote to "Aggymemnon" at the end of Pound's *Sage Homme*, in headnote to *The Waste Land*, 1. COMPOSITION.

Second epigraph (*1919 and AraVP*) ***Why should I speak of the nightingale? The nightingale sings of adulterate wrong***: "Edward III", TSE in *Thayer's AraVP*. Spoken by the King in *The Raigne of K. Edward the Third* II i; see *The Shakespeare Apocrypha*, ed. C. F. T. Brooke (1908), recommended in TSE's *Syllabus: Elizabethan Literature* (1918). For the same play, see note to 5–8. ***adulterate***: OED *ppl. a.*: "Defiled, or stained by adultery". TSE (title): *Mélange Adultère de Tout*.

1 **Apeneck Sweeney**: see note to the title *Sweeney Erect*. **spreads his knees**: "legs apart ··· spreading of the toes", *Suite Clownesque* I 13, 23.

1–2 **Apeneck Sweeney spreads his knees | Letting his arms hang down to laugh**: Kipling's "ape-beast" in *Bertran and Bimi* used to "laugh" (see note to *Sweeney Erect* 11). J. G. Wood: "Its arms are of extraordinary length, the hands reaching the ground when it stands erect", *Illustrated Natural History* (1897) 12. TSE: "Gesture of orang-outang", *Sweeney Erect* 11. For "the body bent, and the hands ··· hanging down", see note to *Burbank with a Baedeker: Bleistein with a Cigar* 14–15, 17.

1–4 **Apeneck Sweeney spreads his knees ··· zebra ··· giraffe**: Laurent Tailhade: "Cœur de lapin, ventre de porc, nez de gorille ··· Et le gros Formentin concague ses genoux" [Heart of rabbit, belly of pig, nose of gorilla ··· And fat Formentin knock-knees his knees], *Gendelettres* [*Manofletters*] 1, 8.

1, 4, 10 **Apeneck Sweeney ··· Swelling ··· shrunken**: OED "sweeny": "*U.S.* Atrophy of the shoulder-muscles in the horse. Also *fig.* of the 'stiffness' of pride", with 1887: "The shrinkage of the muscles of the shoulder, and which is commonly called 'sweeny', is due to some lameness of the foot or limb."

1, 11, 20 **Apeneck ··· Spanish ··· grapes**: "If Spanish Apes ate all the grapes | How should we do for sack'a?" *If all the world were paper* (anon) in *Witt's Recreations* (1641).

3 **zebra**: pronounced *zeebra* (first of the two pronunciations in OED) in TSE's recordings of 1947.

4 **maculate**: pronounced as rhyming with *accurate* in TSE's recordings of 1947. OED: "= MACULATED ··· Now chiefly *lit.* and *poet.*, in expressed or implied antithesis to *immaculate*". TSE's line is now quoted under this sense, although a more obvious meaning can be traced, that of either "maculated" 1: "Spotted, stained, defiled, polluted" or 2: "In scientific use: Marked with maculæ." ("macula" 1: "A spot or stain ··· in the skin, now *esp.* one which is permanent.")

5 **circles of the stormy moon | Slide westward toward**: rings around the Moon are said to indicate approaching bad weather. "Rolls toward the moon", *Nocturne* 11.

5–8 **circles of the stormy moon ··· Raven ··· hornèd**: *The Raigne of K. Edward the Third* III i: "the horned circle of the moon ··· this flight of ravens" (Anne Stillman, personal communication).

6–7 **westward ··· the River Plate, | Death and the Raven drift above**: Corvus, constellation of the raven, is in the southern sky, and so visible from the River Plate in South America. For "the drift of stars", see note to *Burnt Norton* II 8.

7 **Death and the Raven drift above**: TSE in *Thayer's AraVP*: "Marlowe", referring to "Thus, like the sad-presaging raven, that tolls | The sick man's passport in her hollow beak, | And in the shadow of the silent night | Doth shake contagion from her sable wings", *The Jew of Malta* II i. **Death and the Raven**: Schubert (title): *Death and the Maiden* quartet (Anne Stillman). **drift above**: "the torn algae drift above him", *Those are pearls that were his eyes. See!* 3.

8 **hornèd gate**: see note *WLComposite* 352, "the horn or ivory gates".

8, 11 **hornèd gate ··· Spanish**: Kyd: "The gates of Horn, | Where dreams have passage in the silent night", *The Spanish Tragedy* I i.

9 **Gloomy Orion**: *Lemprière*: "a celebrated hunter ··· After death, Orion was placed in heaven, where one of the constellations still bears his name ··· generally supposed to be accompanied, at its rising, with great rains and storms" ("stormy moon", 5). Virgil: "nimbosus Orion", *Aeneid* I 535 (*Southam*). TSE in *Thayer's AraVP*: "Marlowe", referring to "Thither made we | When suddenly gloomie *Orion* rose, | And led our ships into the shallow sands", *Dido, Queen of Carthage* I ii (*Collingwood* 311). **the Dog**: "The Hunter with his dogs pursues his circuit", *Choruses from "The Rock"* I 2. The Dog Star, Sirius, the brightest in the sky, is part of the constellation Canis Major, which along with Canis Minor is imagined as following Orion. *Inside the gloom* catalogues several constellations.

10 **shrunken seas**: significant to, for instance, geologists. Raphael Pumpelly: "deserts, relieved only by oases in high valleys and ··· the mouths of streams emerging from the mountains, or where larger rivers died out on the plains or entered the shrunken seas"; "from a study of the ancient shore-lines ··· of now shrunken seas ··· important records bearing on the archaeology as well as physiography of Central Asia are to be drawn"; "the Aral and Caspian—its two shrunken seas", *Explorations in Turkestan* (1908), 13, 245, 291.

11 **Spanish cape**: Alan Seeger: "In corduroys and Spanish capes and locks uncut and flowing ties", *Paris*, quoted by TSE in *Short Reviews* (1917). For Seeger's poem, see note on the "Fresca couplets" [3–4] *variant* in the Commentary on *The Waste Land* (following note to *WLComposite* 298). For Seeger, see note to *Whispers of Immortality* 19. OED "cape" *n.*[2]: "A Spanish cloak (with a hood). *Obs.*" (last citation 1580).

14 **a coffee-cup**: unexpected in a "dive" (see note to title); for Prohibition, see note to *WLComposite* 2.

14, 16–18 **coffee-cup ··· yawns and draws a stocking up ··· mocha brown ··· gapes**: "Fresca stretches, yawns & gapes | Aroused from dreams of love ··· translucent silks ··· foaming chocolate", *The Waste Land* III *ms1* [3–7] (see Textual History). **draws a stocking up**: to Pound, 2 Feb [1915]:

> even so innocent a rhyme as
>
> ... pulled her stockings off
> With a frightful cry of "Hauptbahnhof!!"
>
> is considered decadent.

See note to *The Triumph of Bullshit*. (*Hauptbahnhof* = "central station".) **gapes**: "Priapus in the shrubbery | Gaping at the lady in the swing", *Mr. Apollinax* 4–5.)

17–20 **The silent man in mocha brown | Sprawls at the window-sill and gapes; | The waiter brings in oranges | Bananas figs and hothouse grapes**: "a negro

··· Bringing a dish with oranges and bananas | And another brought coffee and cigars ··· wide mouth", *To Helen* 2–4, 6. To Eleanor Hinkley, 26 Apr 1911: "one looked through the windows, and the waiter brought in eggs and coffee". (To John Betjeman, 25 Nov 1939: "looking at life through the window ··· the shy mulatto servant ··· laying the table".) "window ··· fruit ··· figure drest in blue and green", *Ash-Wednesday* III 13–15. **mocha**: with the American pronunciation *moe-ka* in TSE's recordings of 1947, as recommended by *Fowler.*

18 **Sprawls at the window-sill**: "A bright kimono wraps her as she sprawls | In nerveless torpor on the window seat", *WLComposite* 365–66. *The Family Reunion* I ii, stage direction: "*The curtains part, revealing the Eumenides in the window embrasure.*" **Sprawls**: Marlowe: "We saw Cassandra sprawling in the streets", *Dido, Queen of Carthage* II i; quoted in *Christopher Marlowe* (1919) (Anne Stillman).

18–20 **window-sill ··· oranges | Bananas figs and hothouse grapes**: Alfred Kreymborg: "*An answer comes through the open window* ··· I got oran*ges,* | I got pineap*ples* ··· I got bana*nas*", *Lima Beans* (1918) (Anne Stillman).

21 **vertebrate**: pronounced *vert-abrate* in TSE's recording of 13 May 1947, but *vert-abr't* in another (probably 1946). (OED 3.*fig.* a: "Of persons: having connective mental powers", citing Oliver Wendell Holmes, 1879.) Alongside TSE's first reading, the unindividuated "individual", Pound wrote "economic unit". Previously he had approvingly quoted Robert Bridges's *Flycatchers*, with "A dry biped he was", in *Poetry* Oct 1915 (which also contained TSE's "Three Poems").

21 *variant* **animalcule**: OED: "pl. animalcula is still frequent in scientific use. (By the ignorant the latter is sometimes made a sing. with pl. animalculæ.)" 1. (*Obs.*): "A small or tiny animal; formerly applied to small vertebrates, such as mice, and all invertebrates."

21–22 **silent vertebrate in brown ··· withdraws**: Conrad: "The servant in brown appeared at the door silently ··· and stood aside", *The Secret Agent* (1907) ch. 2.

22 **Contracts and concentrates**: Irving Babbitt: "a concentration that shall not at the same time seem a contraction", *The Masters of Modern French Criticism* (1912) 93.

23 **Rabinovitch**: marked "X" by TSE in *Thayer's AraVP* with a note now illegibly erased, apparently a name, of which the middle element possibly ended "-dorf". Rachel's married surname is withheld (*Ricks* 31).

24 **murderous paws**: "Marlowe: Dido", TSE in *Thayer's AraVP.* "And after him, his band of Myrmidons, | With balls of wild fire in their murdering paws, | Which made the funeral flame that burnt fair Troy", *Dido, Queen of Carthage* II i; quoted by TSE in *Christopher Marlowe* (1919). In *The Murders in the Rue Morgue*, the dead girl's throat shows "the mark of no human hand", but that of the orang-outang.

27–37 **heavy eyes ··· The nightingales are singing near | The Convent of the Sacred Heart, || And sang within the bloody wood**: "In Italy, from behind the nightingale's thicket, | The eyes stared at me, and corrupted that song", *The Family Reunion* I i (*Grover Smith* 203).

28 **declines the gambit**: OED "gambit" (chess): "A method of opening the game, in which by the sacrifice of a pawn or piece the player seeks to obtain some advantage over his opponent." OED has figurative uses from 1855, including

"The Widow's gambit was played" (1860). Gilbert Frankau: "Where older rakes had never cared a damn bit, | He was too young to recognize the gambit", *One of Us* (1912) 107. (*The Waste Land* II, title: *A Game of Chess*.)

29–31 **Leaves ··· Outside the window, leaning in, | Branches:** Ralph Hodgson: "And the leaves stared in at the window | Like the people at a play", *The House across the Way* in *Poems* (1916).

32 **golden grin:** Jack Johnson, the first black heavyweight boxing champion of the world (1908–15), had several gold teeth and was renowned for his smile. *Vancouver Daily World* 11 Mar 1909: "McLagan ··· doubled up like a jack-knife while Johnson displayed his golden grin in an apologetic way and obligingly backed off." *San Francisco Call* 7 Apr 1912: "DAR'S NO MO' WORK FOH PO' OLE JACK! Champ Has No Tale of Woe, Picks up Fiddle an' de Bow; den Gleams de Golden Grin." See note to 17–20.

35 **The nightingales are singing:** "There's a long, long trail a-winding | Into the land of my dreams, | Where the nightingales are singing | And a white moon beams", American troops' song of 1915 (*Moody* 64). **nightingales:** "I have less knowledge of nightingales, except for their literary associations, which are useful; but I am ready to affirm that a fine mocking-bird in his own pure song is at least the nightingale's equal", *Mocking-Birds* (1930).

35–39 **The nightingales are singing ··· Sacred ··· the bloody wood | When Agamemnon cried aloud ··· liquid siftings:** in a letter to the *Sunday Times*: "Ever since I published a poem called *Sweeney Among the Nightingales*—some forty years ago—I have been waiting for someone to question the presence of nightingales at the obsequies of Agamemnon. Mr Robert Graves, in his letter last week, has ended my suspense, by pointing out that Agamemnon was murdered in a bath-house in mid-January, where and when no nightingales could have been singing. I should like to explain that the wood I had in mind was the grove of the Furies at Colonus; I called it 'bloody' because of the blood of Agamemnon in Argos. As for the 'liquid siftings,' I suspect that they were suggested by the rain dripping on the coffin of Fanny Robin in *Far from the Madding Crowd*. It was a simple matter to bring the dead Agamemnon into the open air, and to transfer the nightingales from one place to another. So they might as well continue to sing in January, though I confess to ignorance of the date of Agamemnon's death. But even had I known, it would have made no difference", *The Silver Bough* (1958). Valerie Eliot in a copy of *1936* 14th imp. (1951): "No nightingales present when A was killed, & TSE took the nightingales in question from the *Œdipus at Colonus* of Sophocles." In the opening lines of the play, blind Oedipus asks Antigone to let him sit "On common ground or by some sacred grove" and she replies: "where we stand is surely holy ground; | A wilderness of laurel, olive, vine; | Within a feathered flock of nightingales | Are warbling" (Loeb). In Aeschylus' *Agamemnon* (1146–49), the Chorus sings of the "wild lyric" that grieves "the brown nightingale" and Cassandra replies, "Ah, fate of the tuneful nightingale! The gods clothed her in winged form and gave to her a sweet life without tears. But for me waiteth destruction by the two-edged sword" (Loeb). See note to *Ode* ("Tired. | Subterrene") 3 for "the sacred wood" and *The Sacred Wood*. **The nightingales are singing ··· the bloody wood ··· liquid:** Milton: "O Nightingale, that on yon bloomy spray | Warblest at eve, when all the woods are still · · · Thy liquid notes that close the eye of day", Sonnet 1 (*Southam*).

36 **The Convent of the Sacred Heart**: to Hans Paeschke, 6 Feb 1947, on a misquotation by Hans Egon Holthusen ("In the convent of Our Dear Lady"): "The actual line · · · should place the convent in the contemporary world as was intended rather than in the Middle Ages when I do not think that the cult of the Sacred Heart was practised. I think that the religious order is comparatively modern."

38 **When Agamemnon cried aloud**: "cf. Orestes", TSE in *Thayer's AraVP*. Aeschylus' ORESTES: "You don't see them, you don't—but I see them: they are hunting me down, I must move on", *Choephoroi*; used by TSE as an epigraph to *Sweeney Agonistes.*

39 **siftings**: OED *vbl. n.* 2: "That which is removed or separated by means of a sieve"; but more often the residue rather than the waste. Old French *crappe*, siftings, gives the later, excremental sense of "crap".

39 *variant* **droppings**: *Hamlet* I v, GHOST: "Curd, like eager droppings into milk, | The thin and wholesome blood" (TSE: "bloody", 37). *Gordon* 105:

> "I had 'droppings' at first," Eliot said, "but Pound gave me 'siftings'—his own word. He hadn't then used it in *Mauberley*—it was typical of his generosity." He [TSE] was talking in 1933 to Professor Theodore Spencer at Harvard, who copied the words into *Poems 1909–1925* by Eliot (now in the Matthiessen Room, Eliot House, Harvard).

In the Introduction to Pound's *Selected Poems* (1928), TSE described *Mauberley* as "much the finest poem, I believe, before the *Cantos*". In 1947: "I think perhaps I was wrong about *Mauberley*; there is something rather scrappy about it. Since then, I've revised my opinion of it: I think *Propertius* and *Cathay* (those semi-translations of Pound's) and the early *Cantos* are bigger stuff" (*Mattingly*).

40 **stiff dishonoured shroud**: Whittier: "Nor brand with deeper shame his dim, | Dishonoured brow", *Ichabod* (Edmund Wilson, *New Republic* 13 Nov 1929).

The Waste Land: Headnote

The present edition prints *The Waste Land* in two forms, that of the published editions beginning in 1922, in its usual position among the *Collected Poems*, and an editorial composite text given separately. Both are described and annotated in this Commentary.

The Waste Land was published without the author's Notes in *Criterion* Oct 1922 and *Dial* Nov 1922. Then separately, with the Notes, by Boni & Liveright (New York), 15 Dec 1922 (1,000 numbered copies; see *Gallup* for state and issue variants). The second American impression of 1,000 numbered copies (mis-described in the colophon as "Second Edition": see *Gallup*) was issued early in 1923, preceding the first separate English edition, which likewise included the Notes and was hand-printed by Leonard and Virginia Woolf in an edition of about 460 copies, published 12 Sept 1923. The poem, always followed immediately by the Notes, was collected in *1925+*, *Sesame* and *Penguin* / *Sel Poems*. On 10 Oct 1929, E. McKnight Kauffer proposed "a special edition" of *The Waste Land*, "not illustrated for that would be impossible—but perhaps annotated—perhaps suggestions arising from its sources". The idea was not taken up (*Letters 4* 714). An edition of 300 signed copies, finely printed by Giovanni Mardersteig in Verona, was published by Faber in 1962.

Recorded in full 1933, Columbia U. (often misdated 1935). Second: 26 July 1946, NBC (NY) for the Library of Congress; released Feb 1949. Third: 23 May 1947, National Gallery of Art, Washington. Additionally: Part V only, May 1942 in Stockholm for the Swedish Broadcasting System. Part I only, 13 May 1947, Harvard, as part of the Morris Gray Poetry Reading ("The two best parts of *The Waste Land* ··· for reading aloud are the first and the last, and I'm going to read you the first section, *The Burial of the Dead*"). Part V only, 23 May 1947, Washington. Part IV only, after the lecture *From Poe to Valéry*, 19 Nov 1948, at the Library of Congress. Parts IV and V only, 12 Nov 1950, for U. Chicago Round Table, broadcast by NBC.

1. COMPOSITION

Shortly after TSE's death in 1965, a detailed reconstruction of the composition of *The Waste Land* was made possible by the recovery of the drafts, which TSE had given away in 1922 (see below, 11. THE FATE OF THE DRAFTS).

The drafts are not dated but other writings reveal the chronology, beginning with a letter of 5 Nov 1919, in which TSE thanks the American lawyer John Quinn for arranging publication of *Poems* (1920): "I am now at work on an article ordered by *The Times* [*Ben Jonson*, *TLS* 13 Nov], and when that is off I hope to get started on a poem that I have in mind." He wrote similarly to his mother, 20 Sept 1920: "I have several things I want to do; and I want a period of tranquility to do a poem that I have in mind." In the meantime he may have seen his friend Hope Mirrlees's poem *Paris* (Hogarth Press, 1919), which has disjunctions and typographical experiments anticipating *The Waste Land*; in 1973, however, she was unable to confirm this (Bruce Bailey, *T. S. Eliot Newsletter* Fall 1974). For *Paris*, see notes to [V] 391–92, *The Hollow Men* I 5 and *Ash-Wednesday* I 36; for Mirrlees's *A Fly in Amber* (Faber, 1962), see TSE's letter to her, 7 July 1956 (quoted by Suzanne Henig in *Virginia Woolf Quarterly* Fall 1972).

Urged to contribute to the *Dial* by its editor, his friend Scofield Thayer, TSE wrote on 30 Jan 1921: "It will be several months before I have any verse ready for publication", but on 7 Feb, Wyndham Lewis reported to Sydney Schiff: "Eliot I saw 2 nights ago ··· He also showed me a new long poem (in 4 parts) which I think will be not only very good, but a new departure for him." When Schiff enquired about this, TSE replied on 3 Apr: "My poem has still so much revision to undergo that I do not want to let anyone see it yet, and also I want to get more of it done—it should be much the longest I have ever written. I hope that by June it will be in something like final form. I have not had the freedom of mind." In the same month: "I see no reason why a considerable variety of verse forms may not be employed within the limits of a single poem; or why a prose writer should not vary his cadences almost indefinitely; that is a question for discretion, taste and genius to settle", *Prose and Verse* (1921). By 9 May 1921, TSE was reporting to Quinn that he had "a long poem in mind and partly on paper which I am wishful to finish". The typescripts of Parts I and II were made before 20 Aug 1921 (when TSE's brother Henry substituted his own typewriter for TSE's dilapidated machine; Vivien Eliot to Henry, 23 Aug).

Aiken recalled the winter that followed: TSE "told me one day, and with visible concern, that although every evening he went home to his flat hoping that he could start writing again, and with every confidence that the material was *there* and waiting, night after night the hope proved illusory", *Tate ed.* 195. Suffering from mental exhaustion, TSE was granted three months' leave of absence by Lloyds Bank (TSE to Richard Cobden-Sanderson, 2 Oct), and he and Vivien retreated to Margate on 14 Oct 1921, moving into the Albemarle Hotel, Cliftonville, on 22 Oct. Vivien stayed until the end of the month, writing to Mary Hutchinson, 28 Oct: "I have started Tom well, and he shows great improvement already ··· Margate is rather queer, and we don't dislike it." And to Bertrand Russell, 1 Nov: "Tom is having a bad nervous—or so called—breakdown ··· In a short time I hope he will go to Switzerland, to see Dr. Vittoz" (a specialist in neuroses, recommended by Ottoline Morrell; see TSE to Julian Huxley, 26 Oct 1921).

TSE to Schiff, "Friday night" [4?] Nov 1921: "I have done a rough draft of part of part III, but do not know whether it will do, and must wait for Vivien's opinion as to whether it is printable. I have done this while sitting in a shelter on the front—as I am out all day except when taking rest. But I have written only some 50 lines, and have read nothing, literally—I sketch the people, after a fashion, and practise scales on the mandoline."

TSE presumably destroyed most of the manuscripts he wrote in that seafront shelter when he superseded them by typing up Part III (probably on his return to London from Margate on 12 Nov 1921). A few passages on a kind of paper that he used in Margate (*Rainey* 23–26) were spared because they bear pencilled passages which TSE did not incorporate into the typescript but which were still under consideration: *ms1* (one leaf, *WLFacs* 36/37) and *ms2* (two leaves, the second with manuscript on both recto and verso, *WLFacs* 48–53). In the first of these, *ms1*, TSE mentions a mandoline, having recently been bought one by Vivien, while in the second, *ms2*, he refers specifically to "Margate Sands". The passage on the lower part of *ms1*, beginning "London, the swarming life you kill ⁊ breed", became the only section of Part III to survive in both manuscript and typescript, and although it is a very rough draft, TSE copied its final readings almost precisely when making the typescript.

TSE was probably hurrying to type Part III before leaving London again, and did so before he was able to fit together the passages he had written. On 18 Nov 1921, he and Vivien left for Paris, where she stayed while he went for treatment with Dr. Vittoz. It is likely that at this stage Pound was lent copies of the typescripts of Parts I–III, to allow him a chance to absorb what TSE had done, before editorial discussions began on TSE's return to Paris after his treatment. This would explain why both the ribbon copy of the typescript of Part III and its carbon are annotated by Pound. His comment "vide other copy" on the ribbon copy of Part III (*WLFacs* 32/33), indicates—as Grover Smith pointed out—that Pound had previously marked the carbon of this Part. His marks on the carbon of Part III were very extensive (*WLFacs* 38–47) and similar marks, presumably also made during his first acquaintance with the poem, can be seen on the ribbon copy of Part II (*WLFacs* 10–15). Only the ribbon copy of Part I is extant, and this is not correspondingly annotated, so presumably Pound marked the carbon of Part I.

TSE composed the final two parts of the poem at a sanatorium at Chardonne, near Lausanne on Lake Geneva (Lac Leman). Although he had "strained one hand in rowing in a single shell while he was in the Harvard Graduate School and used a typewriter in preference to handwriting thereafter" (TSE's secretary to Daniel H. Woodward, 9 Sept 1963), he had no typewriter at Lausanne (to Alan Clodd, 15 Sept 1959). He probably also worked on Part III: the line "By the waters of Leman I sat down and wept . . .", he wrote to J. M. Aguirre on 23 Nov 1956, "was probably written at Lausanne".

Around 2 Jan 1922, he rejoined Vivien and Pound in Paris ("Tom has been here ten days", Vivien to Mary Hutchinson, 12 Jan), and showed Pound the whole poem for the first time. TSE may already have decided to delete the opening scene of the poem, describing a night on the town, but he and Pound worked over TSE's copy of the remaining two pages of Part I (*WLFacs* 6–9).

Their revisions concentrated particularly on Part III, with Pound recommending that its first page-and-a-half be deleted. When TSE drafted a new opening, *ms3* (*WLFacs* 24/25), upside down on the verso of the first page of the ribbon copy, he did not need to write it out in full, because he was incorporating some lines already drafted, so he used the shorthand "(Sweet Thames etc)" and "By the waters".

In Paris, Pound introduced TSE to Horace Liveright, who just the previous month had published Pound's *Poems 1918–21*. Liveright made a tentative offer, sight unseen, of $150 for TSE's unfinished poem, against a royalty of 15 per cent. TSE appears to have disclosed the scale of the poem but not the title. Liveright wrote to Pound from London on 11 Jan 1922: "I'm disappointed that Eliot's material is so short. Can't he add anything? And does it *all* appear in *one* issue of the *Dial*—pls let me know" (Bird/Pound papers, Yale). He may have been concerned that it would be neither sufficiently long nor sufficiently new to publish as a book.

After nearly a fortnight in France, TSE travelled back to London over the weekend of 14–15 Jan ("He will be back on Monday", Vivien to Mary Hutchinson, 12 Jan), while Vivien went to Lyons. Discussions with Pound of the drafts then resumed by post, apparently using a new typescript, although no trace of this survives.

From Paris, Pound wrote to TSE in London on [24 Jan], enclosing a commendatory verse:

> MUCH improved. I think your instinct had led you to put the remaining superfluities at the end. I think you had better leave 'em, abolish 'em altogether or for the present.
>
> IF you MUST keep 'em, put em at the beginng before the April cruelest month. The POEM ends with the Shantih, shantih, shantih.
>
> One test is whether anything wd. be lacking if the last three were omitted. I dont think it wd.
>
> The song, has only two lines which you can use in the body of the poem. The other two, at least the first does not advance on earlier stuff. And even the sovegna doesnt hold with the rest; which does hold.
>
> (It also to yr. horror probably, reads aloud very well. (Mouthing out his OOOOOOze.
>
> I doubt if Conrad is weighty enough to stand the citation.
>
> The thing now runs from April . . . to shantih without break. That is 19 pages, and let us say the longest poem in the Englisch langwidge. Dont try to bust all records by prolonging it three pages further.
>
> The bad nerves is O.K. as now led up to.
>
> / / / /
>
> My squibs are now an bloody impertinence. I send 'em as requested; but dont use 'em with Waste land.
>
> You can tack 'em onto a collected edtn, or use 'em somewhere where they wd. be decently hidden and swamped by the bulk of accompaning matter. They'd merely be an extra and wrong note with the 19-page version.
>
> Complimenti, you bitch. I am wracked by the seven jealousies, and cogitating an excuse for always exuding my deformative secretions in my own stuff, and never getting an outline. I go into nacre and objets d'art. Some day I shall lose my temper, blaspheme Flaubert, lie like a shit-arse and say "Art shd. embellish the umbelicus.

---

to yr. horror · · · **Conrad**: for "The horror! the horror!" from *Heart of Darkness*, see note to unadopted epigraph. **Mouthing out his OOOOOOze**: Tennyson on the poet who "Read, mouthing out his hollow oes and aes, | Deep-chested music", *The Epic* 50–51. **19 pages**: after the cuts already made, to judge by the drafts reproduced in *WLFacs*, the poem now ran to 15 or 16 pages, but it may not be a coincidence that the Quinn, Thayer and Watson typescripts each have 19 pages (see Textual History headnote descriptions). **Englisch langwidge**: for the ethnic overtones of the spelling, see Pound to Alice Corbin Henderson, 20 Jan 1913: "foreigners in the U.S. and their langwidge". **The bad nerves is O.K. as now led up to**: sense unclear, since the typescripts show no structural change in the lead-up to "My nerves are bad tonight", *The Waste Land* [II] 111. **impertinence**: TSE: "I don't think the publication of Ezra's *Cantos* in this country needs any word from me or from anybody else. It is rather an impertinence", *The Cantos of Ezra Pound: Some Testimonies* (1933), publicity for an American edition.

Sage Homme

These are the Poems of Eliot
By the Uranian Muse begot;
A Man their Mother was,
A Muse their Sire.

How did the printed Infancies result 5
From Nuptuals thus doubly difficult?

If you must needs enquire
Know diligent Reader
That on each Occasion
Ezra performed the caesarean Operation. 10

E. P.

//////////////

Caul and grave clothes he brings,
Fortune's outrageous stings,
About which odour clings
Of putrifaction,
Bleichstein's dank rotting clothes 15
Affect the dainty nose,
He speaks of common woes
Deploring action.

He writes of A.B.Cs.
And flaxseed poultices, 20
Observing fate's hard decrees
Sans satisfaction;
Breedings of animals,
Humans and canibals,
But above all else of smells 25
Without attraction.

Vates cum fistula

E. P.

E. P. hopeless ans unhelped

Enthroned in the marmorean skies
His verse omits realities, 30

Title ***Sage Homme***: wise man, and a pun on "sage femme", midwife. 2 **Uranian:** OED b: "A distinctive epithet of Venus (or Aphrodite). Heavenly, spiritual"; c: "Homosexual", with John Addington Symonds (1893): "Live image of Uranian Love" and Wilde (1898): "To have altered my life would have been to have admitted that Uranian love is ignoble." 3–4 **A Man their Mother was, | A Muse their Sire**: Swinburne on Villon: "A harlot was thy nurse, a God thy sire", *A Ballad of François Villon, Prince of All Ballad-Makers* 32. 12 **Fortune's outrageous stings:** HAMLET: "The slings and arrows of outrageous fortune" (III i). 15 **Bleichstein:** see *Dirge* 1. 19 **He writes of A.B.Cs:** *A Cooking Egg* 33. 27 ***Vates cum fistula***: "Poet with a fistula (or ulcer)". Pound's *Fistulae* appeared in his *A Lume Spento* (1908). 29 **in the:** in the The *ts.*

Angelic hands with mother of pearl
Retouch the strapping servant girl,

The barman is to blinded him
Silenus bubling at the brim, (or burbling)
The glasses turn to chalices 35
In his fumbling analysis
And holy hosts of hellenists
Have numbed and honied his cervic cysts,
His follows Yeats into the mists
Despite his hebrew eulogists. 40

Balls and balls and balls again
Can not touch his fellow men.
His foaming and abundant cream
~~Has moulded this world~~
Has coated his world ~~with~~ . The coat of a dream;
Or say that the upjut of his sperm 45
Has rendered his senses pachyderm.

Grudge not the oyster his stiff saliva
Envy not the diligent diver. et in aeternitate

It is after all a grrrreat litttterary period
Thanks for the Aggymemnon.

TSE's reply, [26? Jan], responded in detail to some of Pound's advice, and in turn has annotations by Pound (given here in bold):

Cher maitre,
Criticisms accepted so far as understood, with thanks.

Glowed on the marble, where the glass
Sustained by standards wrought with fruited vines
Wherefrom . . . ??? **OK**

Footsteps shuffled on the stair . . . **OK**

---

34 **Silenus:** *Lemprière*: "attendant of the god Bacchus · · · generally represented as a fat and jolly old man". **Aggymemnon:** around the time of TSE's *Euripides and Professor Murray* (1920), Pound "asked Eliot to have a shot at the *Agamemnon* [of Aeschylus]. He didn't. Or rather he sat on it for eight months or some longer period. I then took over · · · I twisted, turned, tried every elipsis and elimination. I made the watchman talk nigger, and by the time you had taken out the remplissage, there was no play left", *Guide to Kulchur* (1938) 92–93. Pound's fragmentary typescript is dated 1919, but his comment to TSE of [28? Jan 1922], "Aeschylus not so good as I had hoped, but haven't had time to improve him, yet", suggests he had returned to the task. Pound had praised the 17th-century Greek and Latin edition by Thomas Stanley in *Egoist* Jan–Feb 1919, and may have asked TSE to send it to him in Paris. Pound's *Opening for an Agamemnon* was published by Donald Gallup in *Paideuma* Fall/Winter 1986. **Glowed on the marble · · · Wherefrom:** [II] 78–80, but not exactly matching the surviving drafts or any printed text. Perhaps a response to Pound's comment on the typescript "*3 lines* Too tum-pum at a stretch" (*WLFacs* 10/11). For "Wherefrom", the reading in the *Criterion*, see Textual History. **Footsteps shuffled on the stair:** [II] 107, first appearance in final form.

> *A* closed car. I cant use taxi more than once. **OK**
> Departed, *have* left no addresses . . . ??? **OK**
>
> What does THENCE mean (To luncheon at the Cannon St. Hotel)???
> Would D's difficulty be solved by inverting to
>
> Drifting logs
> The barges wash . . . ???
>
> 1. Do you advise printing Gerontion as prelude in book or pamphlet form?
> 2. Perhaps better omit Phlebas also???
> 3. Wish to use caesarean operation in italics in front.
> 4. Certainly omit miscellaneous pieces. **Those at end.**
> 5. Do you mean not use Conrad quot. or simply not put Conrad's name to it? It is much the most appropriate I can find, and somewhat elucidative.
>
> Complimenti appreciated, as have been excessively depressed. V. sends you her love and says that if she had realised how bloody England is she would not have returned.
>
> I would have sent Aeschyle before but have been in bed with flu, now out, but miserable.
>
> Would you advise working sweats with tears &c. into nerves monologue; only place where it can go?
>
> Have writ to Thayer asking what he can offer for this.
>
> Trying to read Aristophane.

Neither the problem with "THENCE" nor the point raised by Dorothy Pound had been mentioned in the letter from Pound. What they were and how they had been conveyed to TSE is unknown. It would have been unlike Pound to enclose a systematic list of suggestions, especially since his letter is itself an unsystematic list. On the other hand, if Pound had annotated a new 19-page typescript sent from London and then returned it, one would expect TSE to have kept it along with the other draft material and letters. The obvious way to discuss the poem by post was for TSE to keep the ribbon copy and send a carbon, as he did in other instances, so that there was no need for a packet to go back and forth. Most probably this is what happened, and there is some reason to believe that Pound still had such a copy in July (see below, 3. THE *DIAL* AND THE *CRITERION*).

Echoing the words of the voice from heaven at the baptism of Christ, "Hic est Filius meus dilectus in quo mihi conplacui" [This is my beloved Son, in whom I am well pleased] (Matthew 3: 17), Pound addressed his next letter, probably on 28 Jan, to "Filio dilecto mihi":

---

closed car: [II] 136, first appearance in final form. **A closed car. I cant use taxi more than once:** Pound had written "1880" against the anachronistic "closed carriage" in *ts2a* (*WLFacs* 12/13), but TSE wanted to keep "the human engine waits | Like a taxi throbbing" (*WLFacs* 30/31) while avoiding duplication. **Departed, *have* left no addresses:** [III] 181, first appearance in final form. Drafted in *ms3* (*WLFacs* 24/25), the group of lines written upside down on the verso of the first page of *ts3a*. No typescript of the passage survives, but Pound had presumably objected to the reading as it stood in the manuscript draft, "Departed, and left no addresses". **THENCE . . . Metropole:** see note to *WLComposite* 326–28. On both *ts3a* and *ts3b*, Pound had objected to "perhaps" in the line "And perhaps a weekend at the Metropole" (*WLFacs* 30/31, 42/43). **Drifting logs | The barges wash:** see note to [III] 273–74. **Perhaps better omit Phlebas also???:** referring to the lines remaining of Part IV following Pound's cuts (*WLFacs* 62–69). **Aristophane:** see headnote to *Sweeney Agonistes*, 2. ARISTOPHANES.

I merely queried the dialect of "thence"; dare say it is o.k.

D. was fussing about some natural phenomenon, but I thought I had crossed out her queery. The wake of barges washes &c., and the barges may perfectly well be said to wash.

I shd. leave it as it is, and NOT invert.

I do *not* advise printing Gerontion as preface. One dont miss it AT all as the thing now stands. To be more lucid still, let me say that I advise you NOT to print Gerontion as prelude.

I DO advise keeping Phlebas. In fact I more'n advise. Phlebas is an integral part of the poem; the card pack introduces him, the drowned phoen. sailor, and he is needed ABSoloootly where he is. [*added*: must stay in.]

Do as you like about my obstetric effort.

Ditto re the Conrad; who am I to grudge him his laurel crown.

Aeschylus not so good as I had hoped, but haven't had time to improve him, yet.

I dare say the sweats with tears will wait.

Aristophanes probably depressing, and the native negro phoque melodies of Dixee more calculated to lift the ball-encumbered phallus of man to the proper 8.30, 9.30 or even ten thirty level now counted as the crowning and alarse too often katachrestical summit of human achievement · · ·

May your erection never grow less. I had intended to speak to you seriously on the subject, but you seemed so mountany gay while here in the midst of Paris that the matter slipped my foreskin.

You can forward the Bolo to Joyce if you think it wont unhinge his somewhat sabbatarian mind. On the hole he might be saved the shock, shaved the sock.

Here Pound writes as though "thence" had been TSE's word, not his own. (In the typescript of Part IV he had changed TSE's "descends | Illicit backstreet stairs, to reappear" to "descends | Illicit stairs, thence to reappear" (*WLFacs* 62/63), but the lines were then cut.)

Describing "the manuscript-typescript of *The Waste Land*", Valerie Eliot wrote: "Someone, possibly Eliot, has divided the leaves into two sections: the main text, and the miscellaneous poems which were considered for it; these now contain forty-two leaves and twelve leaves respectively" (*WLFacs* xxx). Five of the twelve leaves have manuscript on the versos, so in all seventeen pages of miscellaneous material were printed in the facsimile after the end of Part V.

The Death of Saint Narcissus, two copies	4 pages
Song	1 page
Exequy, with draft third stanza on verso	2 pages
The Death of the Duchess	2 pages
After the turning of the inspired days	1 page
I am the Resurrection and the Life	1 page
So through the evening, through the violet air	2 pages
Elegy	1 page
Dirge, two copies	2 pages
Those are pearls that were his eyes. See!	1 page

But in what ways had these miscellaneous poems been "considered for" *The Waste Land*? Some of the miscellaneous poems dated back at least as far as 1915, perhaps even to 1912–13. So why did TSE put these seventeen pages, and only these, with "the manuscript of *The Waste Land*" when he sent it to Quinn, rather than with the sheaf of loose leaves that accompanied the *March Hare* Notebook at the same time?

Some of the miscellaneous poems are obviously related to *The Waste Land* because lines from them were adopted by it. *The Death of Saint Narcissus*, *The Death of the Duchess*, *After the turning of the inspired days*, *So through the evening, through the violet air* and *Those are pearls that were his eyes. See!* are all contributory drafts of this kind.

Three other poems might not be seen to relate to *The Waste Land* but for Pound's letter of [24 Jan 1922], in which he had recommended abolishing "the last three" of the "superfluities":

> One test is whether anything wd. be lacking if the last three were omitted. I dont think it wd.
>
> The song has only two lines which you can use in the body of the poem. The other two, at least the first, does not advance on earlier stuff. And even the sovegna doesnt hold with the rest; which does hold.

Valerie Eliot persuasively suggested that the "last three" that Pound had in mind were *Song* ("The golden foot I may not kiss or clutch"), which he referred to simply as "the song"; *Exequy*, which at one time ended "SOVEGNA VOS AL TEMPS DE MON DOLOR"; and *Dirge*, with drowned Bleistein being referred to in Pound's *Sage homme*.

Each of these would have occupied no more than a page ("Dont try to bust all records by prolonging it three pages further"). The facsimile edition did not, however, speculate where these might have fitted into the poem before TSE's instinct led him to put them "at the end", and Pound's urging led finally to their abolition.

TSE was to write to Donald Gallup, 26 Nov 1946 about *Song* ("The golden foot I may not kiss or clutch"), which had been published in *Tyro* in Apr 1921 as *Song to the Opherian*:

> I don't remember which verses I called *Song to the Opherian* but I think it was one of the short poems which were called the *Dream Songs*. It may or may not have been one of those included as interludes in the first draft of *The Waste Land*. It is impossible to settle this point now. I preserved no copies of those *Waste Land* lyrics; the copies that I know of were those with the original manuscript which was in the possession of John Quinn, and it disappeared from sight after Mr. Quinn's death.

Here he identified "those *Waste Land* lyrics" with "short poems" and "those included as interludes in the first draft of *The Waste Land*". Although two of the *March Hare* poems had been entitled *Interlude*, the meaning in this context of "interludes" as lyrics between the Parts is supported by another of TSE's descriptions: "'There were long passages in different metres, with short lyrics sandwiched in between,' he has since recalled" (*Kenner* 126, no source).

A poem in five parts would presumably have had four interludes. So, for instance, *Exequy* might appear as the interlude between Part I and Part II, with "my suburban tomb" in the second line of the interlude repairing to "That corpse you planted last year in your garden", a few lines from the end of Part I (with *The Burial of the Dead* succeeded by an exequy).

If *Song* were the interlude between Part II and Part III, its opening, "The golden foot I may not kiss or clutch | Glowed in the shadow of the bed", would recall the opening of Part II, "The Chair she sat in, like a burnished throne, | Glowed on the marble · · · golden · · · Glowed into words". (TSE had quoted "Glowed on the marble" in his letter to Pound of [26? Jan].) And in prospect, the second stanza of *Song*, asking "Is it a dream or something else | When the surface of the blackened river | Is a face that sweats with tears?", would point towards the life of the Thames and the City in Part III.

As a third interlude, *Dirge* ("Full fathom five your Bleistein lies") would have been grimly appropriate as moving from Lower Thames Street to "The sailor, attentive to the chart and to the sheets", at the start of the full *Death by Water* narrative that TSE had written as Part IV. Pound, however, had reduced the hundred lines of Part IV to its final ten lines, beginning "Phlebas the Phoenician, a fortnight dead". In their correspondence, TSE then had misgivings—"Perhaps better omit Phlebas also???"— because the ten lines are a translation of the second half of a poem he had published two years before, *Dans le Restaurant*. But Pound insisted: "Phlebas is an integral part of the poem". (For the transition from the Phlébas lines of *Dans le Restaurant* to the next poem in *US 1920*, see note to *Whispers of Immortality* 1–6.) As cut by Pound, Part IV of *The Waste Land* had itself become a lyrical interlude, of a kind TSE had not envisaged. So the need for *Dirge* as a lyrical interlude was obviated.

Part III turns to St. Augustine at Carthage; Part IV accommodates "Gentile or Jew" within the pagan world; and Part V begins with suggestions of Christ's Passion and concludes with "a formal ending to an Upanishad". From the other miscellaneous verses in the sheaf of "the manuscript of *The Waste Land*", the five lines beginning "I am the Resurrection and the Life" suggest themselves as a bridge from Part IV to Part V. Alluding to Emerson's poem *Brahma*, they are a collocation of Western religion and Eastern mysticism. (TSE to Egon Vietta, 23 Feb 1947: "some of my poetry is peculiar in a kind of poetic fusion of Eastern and Western currents of feeling"; see headnote to *The Dry Salvages* III.)

What, then, of *Elegy*, the only poem in the sheaf still unaccounted for? It contributed no lines to *The Waste Land* and could not have been envisaged as a lyric interlude. Most probably, it happens to be preserved with "the manuscript of *The Waste Land*" simply because it has the first draft of *Dirge* on the verso.

An inventory of the miscellaneous materials that were printed following the five parts in the facsimile edition shows their likely relations to *The Waste Land* as published.

1) *The Death of Narcissus* (*WLFacs* 90–97). Manuscript and manuscript fair copy. Date uncertain, but 1912–15. In the sheaf with *The Waste Land* because its first six lines, beginning "Come in under the shadow of this grey rock", are adapted by Part I of *The Waste Land*.

2) *Song* ("The golden foot I may not kiss or clutch") (*WLFacs* 98/99). Typescript, probably an interlude between parts II and III. 1921? First published April 1921.

3) *Exequy* (*WLFacs* 100–103). Typescript, probably an interlude between Parts I and II, with rough draft of an alternative third stanza in manuscript on verso ("Pudibund, in the clinging vine"). 1921?

4) *The Death of the Duchess* (*WLFacs* 104–107). Typescript, 1919. In the sheaf with *The Waste Land* because Part II adapts its lines II 20–22, 27 and 45–49 ("Under the brush her hair", "firelight", "And if it rains, the closed carriage at four").

5) *After the turning of the inspired days* (*WLFacs* 108–109). Manuscript, 1913–15? In the sheaf with *The Waste Land* because the opening of Part V adopts the sequencing of lines all beginning "After the", and adapts lines 4, 5, 7.

6) *I am the Resurrection and the Life* (*WLFacs* 110–11). Manuscript, 1913–15? Probably an interlude between Parts IV and V.

7) *So through the evening, through the violet air* (*WLFacs* 112–15). Manuscript, 1913–15? Included in the sheaf with *The Waste Land* because its opening line was adapted in Part III as "the violet hour" (of evening), and Part III adapts lines 13–16, 19–22.

8) *Elegy* (*WLFacs* 116–17). Manuscript quatrains, written in Margate, Oct–Nov 1921. Preserved by TSE probably only because of the draft of *Dirge* on the verso.

9) *Dirge* (*WLFacs* 118–21). Manuscript, probably an interlude between Parts III and IV, written in Margate, Oct-Nov 1921; with fair copy manuscript, written in Lausanne or Paris.

10) *Those are pearls that were his eyes. See!* (*WLFacs* 122–23). Manuscript, perhaps written before TSE's visit to Margate, Oct 1921. Included in the sheaf with *The Waste Land* because the opening line was adapted as [I] 48 and [II] 125, and because of a relation to *Dirge*.

The idea of intercalating lyrics was dropped, but it was significant in the creation of a five-part poem of which Part IV takes short lyrical form. This would later be the form also of each of the *Four Quartets*.

An element of speculation inevitably remains, but in the present edition the possible stationing of interludes is indicated in *WLComposite*:

I. *The Burial of the Dead*
Exequy
II. *A Game of Chess*
Song
III. *The Fire Sermon*
Dirge
IV. *Death by Water*
"I am the Resurrection and the Life"
V. *What the Thunder said*

2. FROM COMPLETION TO PUBLICATION: BONI & LIVERIGHT

After Pound's letter of [28? Jan 1922], no more is heard about final revisions (the next known text is *Q*, the typescript made in Quinn's office in July 1922), and Pound's role now switched to that of advocate for the poem. In March he wrote to numerous friends about TSE. To Harriet Monroe, Mar 1922: "Eliot is going to pieces physically. He had a break down a few months ago, went to Switzerland, recovered, sufficiently to do probably the most important modern poem of its length (19 pages) that there is. Returned to London too soon and is again wearing out; lloyds bank not being the proper place for him." Rather than offering the poem to *Poetry*, however, Pound was trying to find money for TSE, through his Bel Esprit sponsorship scheme (so named by Natalie Barney). Remembering Browning's title *Dîs Aliter Visum; or, Le Byron de Nos Jours*, Pound wrote to Quinn's lover, Jeanne Robert Foster, 12 Mar: "Say simply that Eliot is the one tragic poet de nos jours; and that I think him the best of my contemporaries." And on the same day to Alice Corbin Henderson: "He broke down completely this winter. HAD to have three months off, in which he did very possibly the most interesting 19 page poem in the language. ~~Certainly~~ the most important poem or poem sequence of that length in American, with ~~nothing but~~ Whitman's *Lilacs* as a possible peer." (*When Lilacs Last in the Dooryard Bloom'd* has 206 lines in sixteen sections.)

A leaflet about the "Bel Esprit" appeal was printed by John Rodker "for private circulation only", at least initially: "The facts are that his bank work has diminished his output of poetry, and that his prose has grown tired. Last winter he broke down and was sent off for three months' rest. During that time he wrote 'Waste Land,' a series of poems, possibly the finest that the modern movement in English has produced, at any rate as good as anything that has been done since 1900, and which certainly lose nothing by comparison with the best work of Keats, Browning or Shelley" (Gallup's *Bibliography of Ezra Pound* E2e; Pound *Letters* 241).

Quinn to Pound, 28 Apr: "For Gawd's sake, keep Liveright out of it. He is vulgarity personified. He would advertise it all over the place. I would rather make my guaranty $350 a year, that is, I would rather add $50 to my $300 a year guaranty, than have Liveright in it. I do this out of pride in Eliot's name ··· What was your arrangement with Liveright? What are you going to do for him for the next two years. Don't let him in on the Eliot thing. I would rather be out of it than have his name on a list with mine."

Unfortunately, in the meantime, Pound had gone public, writing that Bel Esprit aimed "(1) to find the man; (2) to guarantee him food and leisure, by a co-operation of subscribers (individuals or groups) pledging themselves to give £10 a year 'for life or for as long as the artist needs it.' ··· It may be of interest to note that in this group of Parisians and Americans the first choice fell on T. S. Eliot ··· some of us consider Eliot's employment in a bank the worst waste in contemporary literature. During his recent three months' absence due to complete physical breakdown he produced a very important sequence of poems: one of the few things in contemporary literature to which one can ascribe permanent value", *New Age* 30 Mar 1922. Bel Esprit was later abandoned, but a receipt dated June 1923 by Pound reads: "Received from Bel Esprit per Ezra Pound Esq. £20 (twenty pounds) [*signed over two postage stamps*:] T. S. Eliot" (Pound papers, Beinecke).

TSE to D. D. Paige, editor of *The Letters of Ezra Pound*, 22 Sept 1949: "that unfortunate enterprise of *Bel Esprit* ··· was launched and in print before I had heard anything about it, and it subsequently caused me considerable embarrassment. In spite of the way in which it was launched, I was slow in making my mind up about it, but finally came to the conclusion that a precarious subsistence from charity, to say nothing of the obligation to produce some work of genius in consequence, was not a way in which I proposed to live. Evidently Ezra's knowledge of both my private affairs and my character and temperament was superficial."

Two American publishers now had reason to expect TSE's next book: Alfred Knopf (who had published *US 1920* and *The Sacred Wood*) and Horace Liveright. TSE, however, felt himself free to approach others. To Maurice Firuski, 26 Feb 1922: "Your name has been given me by Mr. Conrad Aiken ··· My poem is of 435 lines; with certain spacings essential to the sense, 475 book lines; furthermore it consists of five parts, which would increase the space necessary; and with title pages, some notes that I propose to add, etc., I guess that it would run to from twenty-eight to thirty-two pages. I have had a good offer for the publication of it in a periodical. But it is,

I think, much the best poem I have ever written, and I think it would make a much more distinct impression and attract much more attention if published as a book. If you are interested in this, I should be glad to hear from you." Firuski's offer of $100, however, was inadequate. TSE to Pound, 12 Mar: "Liveright wrote to say he wanted it, and I have written asking what he wants to give."

TSE was bound by the contract for *Poems* (1920) at least to offer to Knopf the opportunity of bidding for his two following books, the first of which, *The Sacred Wood*, Knopf had issued in Feb 1921. On 3 Apr 1922, TSE wrote, saying that Liveright had made an unsolicited offer of "$150 down against 15 per cent royalty", and asking Knopf to match this. As Quinn was to explain to TSE, 28 July 1922, Knopf "did not feel like being placed in the position of being made to 'toe the mark', that is, meet Liveright's offer", so on 1 May Knopf wrote to decline, while expressing continued interest in TSE's prose.

On 25 June, TSE wrote to Quinn in New York asking for his help: "I have written, mostly when I was at Lausanne for treatment last winter, a long poem of about 450 words [lines], which, with notes that I am adding, will make a book of 30 or 40 pages. I think it is the best I have ever done, and Pound thinks so too. Pound introduced me to Liveright in Paris, and Liveright made me the offer of 15 per cent royalty and $150 in advance. I thought I ought to give Knopf the option, and did so; but Knopf said that it was too late for his autumn list this year, and Liveright offered to publish it this autumn, so I cabled him to say he could have it. I then received the letter and memoranda of agreement [dated 3 June] which I enclose ··· I think you will agree that the form of agreement is extremely vague and gives all the advantage to the publisher ··· I cannot see any reason why he should not give a proper formal contract, and if he will not make the same terms as Knopf I authorise you to withdraw the poem from him altogether. I am sending you as quickly as possible a copy of the poem merely for your own interest, and I shall send you later the complete typescript with the notes, in the form to be handed to the publisher. Liveright said he would print it for the autumn if he had the poem by the end of July."

At first Quinn was unable to contact Liveright to negotiate an improved contract, but he did so on 14 July. Borrowing from Knopf the contract for *US 1920*, he used it as a model to draw up terms with Liveright for the new book, learning the poem's title at the last minute from a letter of Pound's. Quinn sent TSE full details of the transaction in a 14-page serial letter, 28 July–1 Aug (*Egleston ed.* 264–67). Meanwhile TSE reported to Quinn, 19 July: "I have yesterday a mild letter from Liveright which sounds as if he would come to terms. As it is now so late I am enclosing the typescript to hand to him when the contract is complete, or to hold if he does not complete. I had wished to type it out fair, but I did not wish to delay it any longer. This will do for him to get on with, and I shall rush forward the notes to go at the end. I only hope the printers are not allowed to bitch the punctuation and the spacing, as that is very important for the sense. I am not sure that you will approve of the punctuation, but I very much hope you will like the poem, as it seems to me the best I have ever done, and I am anxious to hear ··· I should like to present you the manuscript of *The Waste Land*, if you would care to have it—when I say manuscript, I mean that it is partly manuscript and partly typescript, with Ezra's and my alterations scrawled all over it." (For Quinn's reservations about TSE's punctuation, see note to *Portrait of a Lady* II 39–40.)

On 29 July, Quinn cabled TSE: "LIVERIGHT EXECUTED CONTRACT PREPARED BY ME TYPESCRIPT RECEIVED TODAY SUGGEST MAIL LIVERIGHT NEW YORK BRIEF DESCRIPTION FOR CATALOGUE."

Within the serial letter Quinn specified, on 31 July, the progress to publication: "I am writing to Mr. Liveright this morning sending him (a) the original typescript of the poems, which was received from you last Friday, and (b) a careful copy of it." Neither this typescript by TSE nor the secretarial copy sent to Liveright survives, but there does remain another secretarial copy made at the same time, which Quinn sent to Jeanne Robert Foster (*Q*, see Textual History). Posted to her in Schenectady, New York on 31 July, as the postmark shows, this, although not typed by TSE, is the earliest record of the poem in its finished form.

Finally, within the serial letter, on 1 Aug, Quinn related that *The Waste Land* was "going by hand this afternoon", adding: "He may be disappointed in the size of the book. Frankly, if you could add four or five more poems to it, even if it meant delaying the publication of it for a month, I should be inclined to recommend that you do so · · · You won't mind my suggestion" (*Egleston ed.* 267). Liveright might well have preferred a longer book, but six weeks later, *The Waste Land* was in proof and TSE wrote to Pound, 15 Sept: "Liveright's proof is excellent."

Probably in order to extend the book (which finally made 64 pages), it had been widely line-spaced and set across a very narrow measure, so that 164 of the 433 lines were turned (compared to eight in *1963*). TSE to John Hayward, 24 Aug 1940: "I dislike poetry books so narrow that long lines have to be folded over—very bad for both sense and metre."

3. THE *DIAL* AND THE *CRITERION*

Scofield Thayer had known TSE since they were together at Milton Academy. In March 1920, shortly after becoming editor of the *Dial*, he drafted and presumably sent a letter to TSE: "Please do send me your own things. There is no-one writing today whose verse and prose I admire more. I don't think there would often if ever be among them any bit that we couldn't use" (draft, Beinecke). TSE replied, 26 Mar: "I shall willingly let you print anything of mine that appears here that seems to me worth reprinting. I have so little time that I shall not often be able to offer entirely fresh material." Later that year he began to contribute, with *The Possibility of a Poetic Drama* (1920) and *The Second-Order Mind* (1920). His *London Letter* appeared four times in 1921 and four times again in 1922. Thayer, however, hoped for some poetry, and TSE wrote to him on 20 Jan 1922: "I shall shortly have ready a poem of about 450 lines, in four parts, and should like to know whether the *Dial* wishes to print it (*not* to appear in any periodical on this side) and if so approximately what the *Dial* would offer. I should like to know quickly as I shall postpone all arrangements for publication until I hear. It could easily divide to go into four issues, if you like, but not more. It will have been three times through the sieve by Pound as well as myself so should be in final form." This indicates that TSE then intended not to print *The Waste Land* in the journal he was already planning with Lady Rothermere, the *Criterion*, but to hold it for book publication.

On 17 Feb 1922 he wrote to Richard Aldington, another of the poem's earliest readers (and one of the founding subscribers to Bel Esprit): "What you say about my poem gave me great pleasure and gratification · · · I have been hesitating over the *Dial*'s offer of $150." Now, however, a misunderstanding caused both TSE and Thayer to take offence. Valerie Eliot's account is not fully accurate: "While completing *The Waste Land* in January Eliot had written to Scofield Thayer to ask what *The Dial* would offer for it, and the answer, $150, sight unseen, did not displease him. But his thoughts were already turning to book publication when he and Pound heard that the magazine had paid George Moore a hundred pounds for his short story, *Peronnik the Fool*; they were so incensed that Eliot cabled Thayer that he could not accept less than £856" (*WLFacs* xxiii–xxiv). As early as 27 Aug 1912, Pound had written to his father that Moore was "regarded mostly as a joke, or 'a stupid old man'", but it was TSE who heard about the payment to Moore and was incensed, and he acted on his own initiative, informing Pound only afterwards, on 12 Mar: "As it is I wired him some days ago that I would take fifty pounds and no less." This would have been about $250. Unfortunately, as received, the cable read: "CANNOT ACCEPT UNDER !8!56 POUNDS = ELIOT +". (There were no separate number keys on the telegraphic keyboards of the period. Instead numbers and various other characters were typed as the equivalent of the upper case. If, at some stage in the transmission, the number setting was accidentally applied to FIFTY this would result in !8!56.) The mistake in the telegram compounded a misapprehension, since the *Dial* was not in fact paying Moore an inflated rate—as TSE was to acknowledge to Watson on 15 Aug, letters between TSE and Thayer crossed in the post, relations broke down, and TSE withdrew the poem on 16 Mar (Thayer to Pound, 30 Apr, in *Pound, Thayer, Watson, & The Dial*). Only thanks to Thayer's colleagues James Sibley Watson (in Paris) and Gilbert Seldes (in New York) did *The Waste Land* eventually appear in the *Dial*. Hearing of the breakdown, Pound wrote again to Jeanne Robert Foster [6 May], asking: "What wd. Vanity Fair pay Eliot for 'Waste Land'. cd. yr. friend there get in touch with T.S.E., address 12 Wigmore St., London W.1." (Houghton).

Negotiations on behalf of the *Dial* were taken up by Watson. Pound saw TSE in Verona on 2 June 1922, and then met Watson in Paris on 19 July, reporting to Dorothy Pound that he was "amiable · · · wants T's poem for *Dial*". Watson then met Thayer in Berlin, where they discussed offering TSE the incentive of the *Dial* prize of $2,000 in addition to their fee of $150.

On 27 July 1922 Watson again met Pound, who wrote to TSE on behalf of the *Dial* (as Watson reported to Thayer, 29 July). TSE replied to Pound immediately, on 28 July: "I will let you have a copy of *The Waste Land* for confidential use as soon as I can make one. Of the two available copies, one has gone to Quinn to present to Liveright on completion of the contract, and the other is the only one I possess. I infer from your remarks that Watson is at present in Paris. I have no objection to either his or Thayer's seeing the manuscript." TSE's term "the manuscript" might refer to the fresh copy he was promising or to an earlier version which would serve to show the *Dial* the nature of the poem. On 12 Aug, Watson wrote to Thayer: "Eliot seems in a conciliatory mood. The poem is [*added*: better than] not so bad." Watson had evidently seen a typescript, but not one he was free to send on to Thayer. Perhaps he had seen a working draft from January that Pound had kept after his exchange of editorial letters with TSE; if so, it has disappeared. On 16 Aug Watson wrote again to Thayer, having now received the fresh typescript that TSE had promised:

> In response to Pound's letter Eliot has assumed a more conciliatory attitude and has sent on a copy of Waste Land for our perusal. I am forwarding it to you. I am sorry that Pound's vagueness in writing caused Eliot to send the copy to Paris instead of to you direct, but I suppose it will do for a starter. Anyway I wrote him more plainly about the prize and await his answer. I found the poem disappointing on first reading but after a third shot I think it is up to his usual.

Typescript copies were made at the Hotel Meurice in Paris for Thayer and Watson, and survive, respectively in the Beinecke and Berg collections. (For the puzzling relation between them, see Textual History headnote, 2. NON-AUTHORIAL TYPESCRIPTS.)

When he wrote to Thayer on 16 Aug, Watson had not yet received a letter TSE had written the previous day: "I have not only given Mr. Liveright the first publication (book) rights, but also have executed the Contract, under which he is to pay me $150 on publication. I suppose that the poem is now going to press ··· Subject to Mr. Liveright's consent, I would let the *Dial* publish the poem for $150, not before November 1st. In this event, I would forego the $150 advance from Mr. Liveright, and he would delay publication as a book ··· on the possibility of the book's getting the prize, which might increase the sales."

A deal looked possible, but there followed a telegram from TSE to Watson on 17 Aug: "PLEASE TAKE NO STEPS AWAIT NEW LETTER ELIOT". The new letter, dated 21 Aug, expressed a change of heart: "now it seems to me that it is far too late and that matters have gone too far for me to change my plans ··· I should not feel justified in troubling Mr. Quinn in any case, and I should not feel justified in troubling Mr. Liveright unless the alteration were to his advantage as well as mine. Furthermore to put the matter frankly, the advantage to me would be nil unless the receipt of the prize were to form the basis of a contract which of course you would not be likely to give. Let us hope that on a future occasion, if I survive to write another poem, no such difficulty will arise." Also on 21 Aug, however, TSE wrote to Quinn: "A few days ago I had an attractive proposal from Mr. Watson of the *Dial* who was very anxious to publish it ··· They suggested getting Liveright to postpone the date of publication as a book, but I have written to them to say that it seemed to me too late to be proper to make any change now." He told Pound, 30 Aug: "I received a letter from your friend Watson most amiable in tone ··· offering $150 ··· and (in the strictest confidence) the award for virtue also. Unfortunately, it seemed considerably too late, as I had the preceding day got the contract, signed by Liveright and Quinn, book to be out by Nov. 1st etc.)"

"Nevertheless", Valerie Eliot explained, "Gilbert Seldes, the Managing Editor of the *Dial*, approached Quinn and Liveright. They met in Quinn's office on 7 September and soon came to an agreement" (*WLFacs* xxiv). B. L. Reid gave the new contractual details: "The *Dial* would publish the poem, without notes, as soon as possible; they would copyright the poem in Eliot's name, and would pay him for the poem at their standard rates for verse; they would announce that Boni & Liveright would soon publish the poem as a volume, with notes; they bound themselves to award the $2,000 prize to Eliot, and to announce it in advance of the book publication; they agreed also to buy 350 copies of the book when published; Liveright in turn agreed to delay his publication but to accomplish it by January 31, and to pay Eliot his $150 on publication and subsequent royalties as originally stipulated" (*Reid* 538; *Egleston ed.* 269–70).

Quinn to TSE, 7 Sept: "The arrangement insures you (a) $150 from Liveright on publication under his contract, (b) the $2,000 award, and (c) the royalties for the publication of the poem in *The Dial*, which ought to be at least $10 a page, or perhaps more. They used to pay $5 a page for prose articles, and $10 a page for poetry, but perhaps they'll pay you more than $10 a page. That ought to be $150 or $200 or more" (*Egleston ed.* 270–71).

Pound to Jeanne Robert Foster [30 Sept 1922]: "I hope the *Dial* thing IS definitely settled. I knew there was a drift in a certain direction. I have not yet had any

OFFICIAL information. There were still several ifs in the way when I last heard. The 2000 wd. supposedly act as two Bel Esprit subscriptions, if T.S.E. banked it; which he presumably wd. do. (Let us hope, will do.) I hope to see him in a few weeks time · · · I shall try to place a whoop for the pome *The Waste Land* as soon as it is in print" (Houghton).

At the same time, TSE had decided to print the poem in the *Criterion* and was vacillating over how to deploy it. On 30 June he wrote to Aldington that the first issue would include only Parts I and II. Two months later, on 31 Aug he wrote to the printer, Richard Cobden-Sanderson, enclosing "the rest of *The Waste Land* again", which suggests that he had originally sent the whole text, then held over III–V. In letters to Cobden-Sanderson (10 Sept) and Antonio Marichalar (16 Sept), he stated that only I and II would appear in the first issue, and on 21 Sept he wrote to Quinn, "I am publishing *The Waste Land* in two sections in the first and second numbers in the hope that it might bring in a few more readers." A further change of mind, resolving to print the entire poem in the first issue, came very late. He corrected the final proof of the poem (and perhaps of the entire issue) on 3 Oct, writing to Cobden-Sanderson: "I am enclosing the corrected proof of the rest of *The Waste Land*." The issue (dated "October") probably appeared a week or so later. Pound to his mother, [Oct]: "Criterion meritorious but a bit dull. (vide enclosure)"; to his father, 30 Oct: "Eliot's new Quarterly very good, in octogenarian way."

Lady Rothermere paid TSE £25 for the publication of *The Waste Land* in the *Criterion*. TSE to Seldes, 20 Mar 1923: "As a matter of fact, she gave me twenty-five pounds, which was outside of the sum guaranteed for the paper, for publishing my poem and I preferred not to take anything for minor obligations."

The "List of Material Accepted" by the *Dial* in October includes *The Waste Land*, making 13pp., paying $130 (£27), and the payment is mentioned in the list of fees for the November issue (*Dial* papers, Yale).

The notes to TSE's recording of the poem from 1946 state: "*The Waste Land* was first published in *The Criterion* (London) October 1922", and this first issue was in circulation by 14 Oct. *Gallup* (C135) states that the November issue of the *Dial* was "Published almost simultaneously (*i.e., ca.* 15 October)", but this is probably too early since an advertisement placed in the *New York Tribune* 15 Oct by the publisher Little, Brown includes a diary of press comment which happens to mention the October issue of the *Dial* under the date 4 Oct. The November issue is unlikely to have appeared just eleven days later. Burton Rascoe, recently appointed literary editor of the *New York Tribune*, was enthusiastic about TSE (writing about him on 2 July and 10 Sept, and on 19 Nov mentioning that he had defended TSE against criticism from Amy Lowell). If the November issue of the *Dial* had appeared in mid-October, Rascoe would have been unlikely to wait until Sunday 29 Oct to print two extracts of the poem ([I] 1–7, 19–30) or to print another ([III] 266–91) as late as 12 Nov. The *New York Times* wrote admiringly of "T. S. Eliot's long-awaited poem" on the first of these Sundays, 29 Oct, so publication probably occurred within a day or two of this. Jeanne Robert Foster's diary for 30 Oct records a day with Quinn during which "We read *The Dial* together with the first published version of *The Waste Land* by T. S. Elliot." TSE did not receive copies of the *Dial* until 12 Nov. A note at the foot of the first page of the *Dial* reads: "Copyright 1922 by T. S. Eliot. An edition of *The Waste Land* with annotations by Mr Eliot will presently be issued by Boni & Liveright.—The Editors."

TSE to Seldes, 12 Nov 1922: "I am sending you a few circulars of *The Criterion*, and

I trust you have received the first number which I had sent to you. Now sold out. So far, no steps have been taken toward acquiring American subscribers. This is owing to the appearance of my poem in the first number; I do not want the first number to be put upon the American market as it would have been unfair in view of the almost simultaneous appearance of the poem in *The Dial*. I am looking forward to receiving the November number; Liveright's proof was on the whole very good indeed and I have no doubt that the appearance in *The Dial* will be equally good", to which is added in manuscript: "Nov. no. just received. Poem admirably printed. I see some remarks by you which I find very flattering—But I find this poem as far behind me as *Prufrock* now: my present ideas are very different." (Seldes was to write one of the earliest reviews of the poem, in the *Nation* 6 Dec.)

A two-and-a-half-page Comment in the December issue of the *Dial* told readers that "The editors have the pleasure of announcing that for the year 1922 THE DIAL's award goes to Mr T. S. Eliot." The piece ended: "Mr Eliot is now editor of *The Criterion*, a quarterly which we (as it were *en passant*) hereby make welcome. The most active and, we are told, the most influential editor-critic in London found nothing to say of one of the contributions to the first number except that it was 'an obscure, but amusing poem' by the editor. We should hate to feel that our readers can judge of the state of criticism in England by turning to the first page of our November issue and reading the same poem there."

Thayer to TSE, 5 Oct 1922: "I have been very glad to learn from New York that the suggestion I made to Mr. Watson while he was with me in Berlin last July has borne fruit and that we are despite your asperity to have the pleasure of recognising publicly your contribution to contemporary Letters." Thayer to Alyse Gregory, 22 Oct: "I feel forced to refrain in future from publishing such matter as the silly cantos of Ezra Pound and as the very disappointing *Waste Land* and I should like to secure for the *Dial* the work of such recognised American authors as Edith Wharton" (*Joost* 111). On 9 Dec Thayer congratulated TSE on the first issue of the *Criterion*: "I find your contributor Mr. Saintsbury goes on writing like a boy of promise and your contributor Mr. Eliot like a man of genius." (TSE visited Thayer in a sanatorium in 1932. In 1948 Alyse Gregory invited TSE to write an introduction to Thayer's poems. After reading them, TSE replied, 24 May 1949, that he was "for several reasons under permanent obligation to Scofield", but feared that "my commendation would certainly betray my lack of sympathy with this poetry.")

As publisher of the book, Horace Liveright was pleased with his literary coup, but struggled financially. He wrote to Pound, 5 Feb 1923: "*The Waste Land* has sold 1000 copies up to date and who knows, it may go up to 2000 or 3000 copies. Just think, Eliot may make almost $500.00 on the book rights of this poem. And Gene Stratton Porter makes $40,000 to $60,000 a year out of her books." Quinn to TSE, 26 Feb 1923: "I daresay you have received press clippings of all the reviews that have been published here of *The Waste Land*, good or enthusiastic or hostile, but for the most part praising it. In fact, confidentially, the success of *The Waste Land* was rather a surprise to Liveright. He almost had cold feet about it before the *Dial* suggestion was made." TSE to Quinn, 12 Mar: "I am interested to hear that Liveright has sold 1250 copies of my book already and am glad that it has exceeded his expectations." Nonetheless, Wyndham Lewis wrote to Pound, 7 May 1925: "Eliot told me last year that Liver. was peculiarly unreliable". TSE to Charles Stewart at Faber & Gwyer, 29 Aug 1927: "I have no particular affection for Boni and Liberight, having had experience of them as publishers."

In 1928, facing bankruptcy, Liveright brought in new investors, who renamed the firm. TSE's contract with Boni & Liveright had been for five years from 1922, but in 1928 and 1930 third and fourth printings of the poem were issued without permission by Horace Liveright Inc. In addition, in 1930 Charles Boni published *Prize Poems 1913–1929*, ed. Charles A. Wagner (introduction by Mark Van Doren), which included *The Waste Land* without authorisation. TSE to Van Doren, 13 May 1930: "The publishers make acknowledgement to me, but I have no cognisance of them, and have never granted permission to anyone to use *The Waste Land* or any part of it · · · Liveright could not have given permission, because his period of publication expired in 1927, and he had no anthology rights anyway. Charles Boni appears simply to have lifted my best poem and my best financial asset; though even without a Boni, the money I have had out of *The Waste Land* is small recompense for the years of sweat, hell and technical study." To Charles Bloch, 27 Dec 1934: "Strictly speaking, *The Waste Land* was not a prize poem, as the *Dial* award was intended as a recognition of the whole work of the authors chosen, and not for any particular piece."

Henry Eliot visited Horace Liveright's offices on TSE's behalf, after which the firm's T. R. Smith wrote to TSE, 13 Oct 1931. He apologised for having, without consultation, granted permission to Charles Boni to reprint the poem in the anthology, and for Liveright's reprints of the poem. An enclosed account shows that 2,458 copies had been sold at $1.50 before 30 June 1930, and that 116 copies were sold in the US in the following six months, and five in Canada. "We have on hand at the present time about 250 copies of the book unbound, and 40 copies bound · · · Of this sheet stock and bound stock on hand we can do either one of two things. We can just go on selling them until the edition has been exhausted, and then end the matter; or we can 'remainder' them for whatever price we can get for them without any royalty payment." Smith added that Liverights would be very happy to publish TSE's collected poems. The accounts of the Liveright printings, in the archive of W. W. Norton, show that sales continued, in small numbers, until 1938 (Elizabeth Micakovic, personal communication).

4. THE HOGARTH PRESS

In March 1922, TSE offered *The Waste Land* as a book to the Hogarth Press. Virginia Woolf recorded: "He has written a poem of 40 pages, which we are to print in the autumn. This is his best work, he says. He is pleased with it; takes heart, I think, from the thought of that safe in his desk" (*Diary* 12 Mar 1922). Virginia Woolf to TSE [14 Apr 1922]: "When are we to see your poem?—and then I can have a fling at you." After he had read the poem at the Woolfs' house, she wrote: "He sang it & chanted it rhythmed it" (*Diary* 23 June). Daniel H. Woodward to TSE, 13 Dec 1962: "Mr. Woolf · · · does not know the source of the text: *The Criterion* and a manuscript of the notes, the Boni and Liveright edition, which includes the notes (my guess), or some other source. Can you clarify this?" TSE, 26 June 1963: "I am not clear what Mr. Leonard Woolf means in saying that he does not know the source of the text and notes. I presume that I gave him a typescript of the text and notes at the time. If he returned them to me after the book was published, I must have lost or destroyed them."

Virginia Woolf to Barbara Bagenal, 8 July [1923]: "I have just finished setting up the whole of Mr Eliots poem with my own hands: You see how my hand trembles."

TSE to Leonard Woolf [3? Sept 1923], on receiving finished copies: "I am delighted with *The Waste Land* which has just arrived. Spacing and paging are beautifully planned to make it the right length, far better than the American edition. I am afraid it gave you a great deal of trouble. You also had to contend against my abominable proofreading: I see one dreadful oversight for which I owe apologies: p. 7, I left *under* London Bridge instead of *over*!" 14 Sept: "There are 3 mistakes I left: 'under' for 'over' London Bridge; 'Coloured' for 'carven' dolphin; and Macmillan for Cambridge University Press for Miss Weston's book. I hope you will forgive me."

TSE acknowledged £7 5s. 7d. from the Hogarth Press in royalties for *The Waste Land* in a letter to Leonard Woolf, 1 May 1924. By 31 Mar, 330 copies had been sold. Total printing, binding, advertising and distribution costs were £25 6s. 3d. TSE received 25 per cent of gross profits.

Virginia Woolf to TSE, 3 Sept [1925], of J. & E. Bumpus the bookshop: "Bumpus says we *must* reprint *Waste Land*. People worry his life out for copies—so think sometimes, among all your glories and horrors, of that rapacious animal the Hogarth Press." There was, however, to be no Hogarth Press reprint, and the Woolfs were disappointed to see *The Waste Land* becoming part of TSE's *Poems 1909–1925*.

5. APROPOS OF PUBLICATION

Although Quinn had cabled as late as 29 July 1922 to suggest that TSE send Liveright a catalogue description of the poem, the $37 printing bill for Boni & Liveright's Fall catalogue was entered into the accounts for the book on 31 July. The catalogue announced:

> *The Wasteland* by T. S. Eliot. Many poets who became prominent during the contemporary American poetic renascence have sunk quietly into forgetfulness. T. S. Eliot, however, is a name which has acquired a leading significance during the same period. The qualities of Mr. Eliot's verse are enduring. They represent in many ways the keenest inquiry into our lives which American poetry can boast since Ezra Pound entered the lyric lists. Subtle, ironic, and molded to the peculiar form of Mr. Eliot's mind, this poet's work, highly individualistic, has run to caricature of genuine realities, set off by flashes of rhythm and color. He knows how to draw people—not always within the knowledge of a poet—and deals largely with the people he sees around him.
>
> *The Wasteland* is the longest poem T. S. Eliot has ever written and is the first poetry that he has written in the last three years. Mr. Eliot writes from London that this volume represents a new phase in his development, being the ripe fruit of his experimentation in all of his previous work.
>
> T. S. Eliot is a man to be reckoned with, now, and hereafter, among the few unique talents of the times.
>
> *The Wasteland* will be one of the most beautifully printed and bound books that has ever borne our imprint.
>
> (*To be published October 1st* . . . $2.00).

The title had been corrected by 15 Oct, when the *New York Tribune* listed it among the "Recommended Books on Fall Lists". The *New York Times Book Review*, 26 Nov 1922, had the title right but made a different mistake when it announced:

> The annual award of *The Dial*, amounting to $2,000, has been given this year to T. S. Eliot, the American poet living in England. This award, which is not presented as a prize, but in recognition of able work, was given last year to Sherwood Anderson, the novelist. Thomas Seymour Eliot, to give him his full name, is a Harvard graduate and

> a writer who may be regarded as the poetical leader of the Younger Generation. His volume, *Poems*, containing such unusual efforts as *The Love Song of J. Alfred Prufrock* and the *Portrait of a Lady*, appeared several seasons ago. A new volume from his pen, *The Waste Land*, a single poem of some length, is shortly to be published by Boni & Liveright. Mr. Eliot's work is marked by an intense cerebral quality and a compact music that has practically established a movement among the younger men.

The delay in book publication enabled Liveright to enhance the jacket. A panel on the front proclaimed: "Winner of The Dial's 1922 Award. This prize of two thousand dollars is given annually to a young American writer in recognition of his service to letters." The front flap read:

> *The Waste Land* by T. S. Eliot (Winner of the Dial's 1922 Award). Burton Rascoe in the *New York Tribune*, characterizes *The Waste Land* as, "A thing of bitterness and beauty, which is a crystallization or a synthesis of all the poems Mr. Eliot has hitherto written." He goes still further, when he says, *The Waste Land*, "Is, perhaps, the finest poem of this generation; at all events it is the most significant in that it gives voice to the universal despair or resignation arising from the spiritual and economic consequences of the war, the cross purposes of modern civilization, the cul-de-sac into which both science and philosophy seem to have got themselves and the break-down of all great directive purposes which give zest and joy to the business of living. It is an erudite despair; Mr. Eliot stems his poem from a recent anthropological study of primitive beliefs, as embodied in the Grail legend and other flaming quests which quickened men in other times; he quotes, or misquotes, lines from the 'Satiricon of Petronius,' 'Tristan und Isolde,' the sacred books of the Hindus, Dante, Baudelaire, Verlaine, nursery rhymes, the Old Testament and modern jazz songs. His method is highly elliptical, based on the curious formula of Tristan Corbière, wherein reverential and blasphemous ideas are juxtaposed in amazing antitheses, and there are mingled all the shining toys, impressions and catch lines of a poet who has read voraciously and who possesses an insatiable curiosity about life. It is analysis and realism, psychology and criticism, anguish, bitterness and disillusion, with passages of great lyrical beauty."

The rear flap read:

> T. S. Eliot was born in 1888 in St. Louis, Missouri; he is a graduate of Harvard and studied at the Sorbonne and at Oxford, has been a lecturer, editor and banker. For the first few years in which his poems appeared he was known to only a small number of readers, but his first book of poems, and his long poem, *The Waste Land*, which has just been published, have established him, in the opinion of critics, as without question the most significant of the younger American writers. Abroad, and especially in France, he is held to be, in addition, the leader of the strictest and most intelligent school of literary criticism. Only one volume of his critical work has been published, under the title of *The Sacred Wood*.

6. A HOAX?

The first issue of *Time*, 3 Mar 1923, reported: "It is rumored that *The Waste Land* was written as a hoax. Several of its supporters explain that that is immaterial, literature being concerned not with intentions but results."

TSE drafted a letter to the Literary Editor of the *New York Globe*, 4 Apr 1923: "I have received a cutting from your issue of the 6th March in which you quote from the *Chicago News* some statements about myself · · · made by Mr. Ben Hecht. According to this cutting, Mr. Hecht says that he met me in London, and knows that I thoroughly hate Americans and everything they write and read, and that he considers me wholly capable of hoaxing the *Dial* and all its friends. In case there may be anyone in America who believes this statement, I wish to inform you that if Mr. Hecht made the statements quoted he is a liar, and I should be glad if you would make this statement public. Mr. Hecht has never met me in London or anywhere else. He has not the slightest ground for the opinions which he attributes to me, and he must be perfectly aware of this fact. I can only presume that Mr. Hecht believes that my being 3000 miles away will protect him from any legal action, as it certainly protects him from any physical action on my part. I do not know whether Mr. Hecht is the author or merely the supporter of the libel which charges me with having perpetrated a hoax upon the *Dial*, but at least he has found it necessary to lie about me in order to give support to this rumour. If Mr. Hecht has succeeded in hoaxing anybody with such a clumsy falsehood as that reported in the *Chicago News*, it would be hardly worth my while to spend two years' labour upon a poem in order to hoax the *Dial*" (*Criterion* files, box 75. For the revised text of the letter, 6 Apr, see *Letters* 2. It was quoted at length in a mischievous column in the *Globe and Commercial Advertiser*, New York, 17 Apr 1923).

William Force Stead, of an occasion on 4 Feb 1928:

> I remember once when I invited him to read a paper to our Literary Society at Worcester College in Oxford, he announced on arriving that he must have lost his notes on the train from London, perhaps a polite way of saying that he had not prepared any; however, he would read us *The Waste Land*. The poem was not widely appreciated at that time and called forth some very foolish remarks. A few remain in my memory; one youth arose at the end and said,
>
> "Mr. Eliot, did you write all that?"
>
> "Yes."
>
> "Well, I thought some of those words about the barge she sat in came from something else."
>
> Eliot responded with a pleasant smile that he was glad the point had been raised, and that as the speaker had recognized the passage, so he was sure others would understand these and some other well known lines as quotations used for the purpose of association. The reply was framed with such tact that the young man's vanity would not be wounded if he was merely an honest dunce, yet if he was trying to be facetious, he would be quietly silenced. A discussion dragged along for some time until a round-faced youth bounced up and said, "Mr. Eliot, may I ask a question?"
>
> "Certainly."
>
> "Er—did you mean that poem seriously?"
>
> Eliot looked non-plussed for a moment, and then said quietly, "Well, if you think I did not mean it seriously, I have failed utterly."
>
> *Some Personal Impressions of T. S. Eliot* in *Alumnae Journal of Trinity College* [Washington], Winter 1965

TSE annotated Stead's recollections in typescript, making no comment here.

Of the same occasion, *Cherwell* reported on 11 Feb 1928: "Mr Eliot compared his poem to a body stripped of its skin: the 'anatomical' interest is at first more puzzling, but is more unusual and more real. He said, further, when speaking of the self-explanatory nature of the poem, that it was not necessary for the reader to recognise the quotations introduced, although he would lose a little; the effect was independent of recognition. The much-discussed notes and references were included, he said, for the benefit of the curious, and to prevent others from pointing out to him that he had borrowed passages from the Elizabethans; it was not necessary for the reader to make himself acquainted with a large body of literature" (see David Bradshaw, *Yeats Annual* 2013; and for "a tissue of allusions intelligible only to ··· scholars", see note to *Ash-Wednesday* V 10, 28, 36).

7. THE AUTHOR'S NOTES

There is no known manuscript or typescript of the Notes.

In Gotham Book Mart's catalogue *We Moderns* (1940), Pound wrote: "The bearing of this poem was not over-estimated, nevertheless the immediate reception of it even by second rate reviewers was due to the purely fortuitous publication of the notes, and not to the text itself. Liveright wanted a longer volume and the notes were the only available unpublished matter." In 1948, Clive Bell claimed that it was Roger Fry who "urged Eliot to elucidate the text of *The Waste Land* with explanatory notes. Eliot met him half way: he supplied notes, but whether they are explanatory is for others to decide", *How Pleasant to know Mr Eliot* in *March & Tambimuttu eds.* 16. To Daniel H. Woodward, 26 June 1963: "It may be as Mr. Clive Bell says that it was Roger Fry who suggested that I should do notes to the poem. I remember reading the poem aloud to Leonard and Virginia Woolf before they ever read it and I know that the notes were added and were of such length as the poem by itself seemed hardly long enough for book form."

Nicholas Joost claims that "Gilbert Seldes refused to print the notes to the poem, although they had arrived as a part of Eliot's typed copy", *The Dial 1912–1920* (1967) 252. Quinn's letter to TSE, 7 Sept 1922, contradicts this: "Seldes said that the prose notes would make a hit and were interesting and amusing, and he even said 'wonderful'", but it was written into the contract with Liveright that the Notes would not appear in the *Dial*. That the Notes were seen by Seldes suggests collaboration between the magazine and the book publisher, as does TSE's remark to Seldes that "Liveright's proof was on the whole very good indeed and I have no doubt that the appearance in *The Dial* will be equally good" (12 Nov 1922). The logistics of these two American printings are unclear—did the *Dial* set from a typescript, and if so which, or from the Liveright proofs?—but friendly relations are also suggested by Edmund Wilson's having been able to send to John Peale Bishop both a gathering of the *Dial* with the poem and proof sheets of the Notes as set for Boni & Liveright.

Fascination with the Notes followed TSE for the rest of his life. Arnold Bennett, 10 Sept 1924: "I said to him: 'I want to ask you a question. It isn't an insult. Were the notes to *Wastelands* a lark or serious? I thought they were a skit.' He said that they were serious, and not more of a skit than some things in the poem itself", *Journals III, 1921–1928* ed. Newman Flower (1933). In 1956, TSE related the Notes to the accusation of having "plagiarised, pinched, pilfered" (see headnote to *Cousin Nancy*): "I must admit that I am, on one conspicuous occasion, not guiltless of having led critics into temptation. The notes to *The Waste Land*! I had at first intended only to put down all the references for my quotations, with a view to spiking the guns of critics of my earlier poems who had accused me of plagiarism. Then, when it came to print *The Waste Land* as a little book—for the poem on its first appearance in *The Dial* and in *The Criterion* had no notes whatever—it was discovered that the poem was inconveniently short, so I set to work to expand the notes, in order to provide a few more pages of printed matter, with the result that they became the remarkable exposition of bogus scholarship that is still on view to-day. I have sometimes thought of getting rid of these notes; but now they can never be unstuck. They have had almost greater popularity than the poem itself—anyone who bought my book of poems, and found that the notes to *The Waste Land* were not in it, would demand his money back", *The Frontiers of Criticism* (1956). To Bonamy Dobrée, 14 Nov 1957: "my own preference would be to abolish the notes to *The Waste Land*". Finally: "author's notes (as is illustrated by *The Waste Land*) are no prophylactic against interpretation and dissection: they merely provide the serious researcher with more material to interpret and dissect", A Note of Introduction (1961) to a new ed. of David Jones's *In Parenthesis* (1937).

Asked by Gorham Munson how he had influenced *The Waste Land*, Pound wrote in a "Communication" to *1924: A Magazine of the Arts* [Sept/Nov] 1924:

> I don't care a damn where which influence crossed what other, etc. But I suggest that the reader of good will should read *The Waste Land* as I read it; i.e. *without* the notes; in which case he will find these terrible obscurities reduced to a few words of sanskrit (four words I think):
>
> *Datta*—Give.
> *Dayadhvam*—Sympathise.
> *Damyata*—Control.
> and *Shantih*—Peace.
>
> and that of these four the first three are so implied in the surrounding text that one can pass them by—graeca non legitur [L. *Graecum est; non legitur* = it is Greek, so it cannot be read]—without losing the general tone or the main emotion of the passage. They are so obviously the words of some ritual or other, and the sense of the passage so repeats their general import.
>
> Let it go that *shantih* means Peace; I think one does need to be told that. For the rest I saw the poem in typescript, and I did not see the notes till six or eight months afterward; and they have not increased my enjoyment of the poem one atom. The poem seems to me an emotional unit, since Mr. Munson asks for an unity. And perhaps intensity or poignancy of expression is as valuable as any of the other more complicated structural functionatings which he finds lacking.
>
> I have not read Miss Weston's *Ritual to Romance* and do not at present intend to. As to the citations, I do not think it matters a damn which is from Day, which from Milton, Middleton, Webster or Augustine. I mean so far as the functioning of the poem is concerned. One's incult pleasure in reading *The Waste Land* would be the same if Webster had written *Women Before Woman* and Marvell the Metamorphoses.
>
> The poem is there for the reader. The notes are for some other species of fauna, perhaps the Times Lit. Sup. reader with whom we (toi et moi, mon ami) have no concern.
>
> Sincerely yours,
> Ezra Pound.
>
> This demand for clarity in every particular of a work, whether essential or not, reminds me of the preraphaelite painter who was doing a twilight scene but rowed across the river in day time to see the shape of the leaves on the further bank, which he then drew in with full detail.

TSE to John Theobald, 16 Aug 1935, on his poem *The Earthquake*: "There is all the difference ··· between notes which may be helpful to the reader, and notes which are indispensable to him. If the notes are indispensable then the poem is not quite written."

To Gregor Ziemer, 10 Feb 1937: "The notes to the *Waste Land* should be taken at their face value."

8. ANTHOLOGIES, TRANSLATIONS, ADAPTATIONS

To Miss J. Colcord, 28 Jan 1924: "In the case of *The Waste Land* I feel very strongly against publication of any parts separately. The poem is intended to be a whole and if I allowed parts of it to be printed separately, it might not only spread the impression that it is merely a collection of unrelated parts, but might also appear to give sanction from myself of this impression. I do not want people to read the poem at all unless they read the whole thing, and it is quite impossible for any part of the poem to give a fair conception of the whole." To Conrad Aiken, 29 Oct 1928: "it would infringe Liveright's rights if I let anybody print the whole of *The Waste Land* in an anthology, as he printed it as a book by itself. Furthermore the reason why I insisted on keeping the anthology rights was that I did not want anybody to read the poem in bits, and I shall always insist on its being published as a whole, if at all." (Liveright's rights had by this time expired; see above, 3. THE *DIAL* AND THE *CRITERION*.)

To Donald Brace, 27 Aug 1933, headed "*Poems 1909–25*: Anthology Permissions": "I think that the most convenient arrangement for both sides would be for me to give a general authority to you—not to your firm generally, but to you personally—to use your discretion. My stipulations are that only a reasonable small amount of my verse should be used in any one anthology; second, that permission should never be granted without a reasonable fee; third, that *The Waste Land* should not be used in this way either whole or part. For other poems, not in this volume, anthologists should of course apply direct to me."

To Michael Roberts, 11 July 1935, on Roberts's selections for *The Faber Book of Modern Verse* (1936): "I have always in the past refused to allow *The Waste Land* to be used either in part or whole in anthologies. To take a part mutilates it and to take the whole means taking what I regret to say is the only one of my poems which most people feel it necessary to read. You may demur to this last statement, but I am sure there is some truth in it. And, furthermore, if I gave *The Waste Land* for your anthology, I should find it difficult to refuse others in future. I should be glad of course if you thought fit to include *Fragment of an Agon* and most people would expect *Gerontion* to turn up, although I have no feelings about that myself." 19 July: "Your letter of the 13th has been thoroughly discussed by my committee. They are a weak-kneed lot of men and your ferocity has had the desired effect; so you are to have the whole of *The Waste Land* without the notes, and my objection to the quantity of Read, Spender and myself is overruled." The poem was included, without the Notes. To Gerald D. Saunders, 25 Sept 1941: "As for the inclusion of *The Waste Land*, I can say that I have now no objection to this appearing in anthologies provided that the whole poem is printed together and not merely a selection from it." In 1947 TSE insisted that the Notes be dropped when the poem appeared in *The Little Treasury of Modern Poetry* ed. Oscar Williams (1947), and in reply to Edith Sitwell's request to print it in her anthology *The American Genius* (John Lehmann, 1951), he wrote, 29 Dec 1949: "I have for a long time hoped that someone would put *The Waste Land* in an anthology without the notes, but John Lehmann might object to this."

On 1 May 1925, TSE reported to Ottoline Morrell that he had received the typescript of Jean de Menasce's translation of *The Waste Land* (published the following May in *L'Esprit*). In it, he pencilled in the omitted [III] 306 ("la la") and numbered every fifth line (Houghton). Between the ends of the translated lines [V] 364 and 365 he first drew an arrow (pointing right) and then braced the lines. He also underlined nearly thirty lines, apparently to indicate that they are quotations or allusions (in English and other European languages) which should not be translated. The cases took various forms:

Translated by Menasce into French but restored to English in *L'Esprit*: [I] 74–75 (Webster); [III] 176 and 183–84 (Spenser), and 257 (Shakespeare); and [V] 426 (nursery rhyme) and 431 (Kyd). As well as underlining, TSE wrote "English ?" against [III] 176 and 257, and put a wedge at the end of [V] 426.

Translated, but with its Shakespearean words restored to English: in ts, [I] 48 read "(Ces perles ont été ses yeux. Voyez!)", but in print it read "(Those are pearls that were his eyes. Regardez!)"

Translated and allowed to stand: in ts, [V] 428 read "Quando fiam ceu chelidon—O hirondelle, hirondelle". In underlining this, TSE stopped after "O hirond", then made a mark through his underlining to endorse Menasce's use of the Latin of the *Pervigilium Veneris* followed by French, which was duly printed.

English not translated by Menasce but underlined by TSE: [II] 77, 125 and 172 (all Shakespearean; see line note for Laforgue's use of the last); [II] 128–30 and [III] 199–201 (songs; Menasce substituted "bathe" for "wash" in the second); and [III] 253 (Goldsmith, except the final word).

German not translated but nonetheless underlined by TSE: [I] 12, 31–34 and 42; as likewise the untranslated [I] 427, from the *Purgatorio*.

French lines within TSE's English poem and in Menasce's ts, nonetheless underlined by TSE: [I] 76 (Baudelaire); [III] 202 (Verlaine); and [V] 429 (Gérard de Nerval).

(See note to [III] 211 for French equivalents of "C.i.f", and for TSE's comment on place names see note to [III] 276, 300.)

To Montgomery Belgion, 27 Aug 1942: "In my experience, translations of one's own works are extremely useful texts for the study of a foreign tongue, especially as they have the advantage of always being interesting. The alternative in my opinion is to obtain a local translation of Sherlock Holmes."

To Menasce, 5 Oct 1929 on a putative French volume: "What I should like, if possible, would be a selection made by you and myself, and all of the translations to be by you, instead of using the few other translations—Adrienne Monnier's Prufrock, [André] Germain's Preludes, and Leger's [Perse's] Hollow Men, which have already been made. Would you be prepared to do this? If so, let us begin making a list. I should rather like to include several of my later poems—the Magi, the Simeon, possibly Animula, which I shall send you shortly, and the set of six [*Ash-Wednesday*] which includes Perch' Io non Spero and the one which Madame de Bassiano will have sent you (I have just given her your new address). This set will appear in English for the first time early next year."

On 11 Jan 1938 the BBC broadcast D. G. Bridson's semi-dramatised version of *The Waste Land* (script, Lilly). Comments by Michael Roberts and others on the production were broadcast afterwards. TSE to Bridson, 13 Jan:

> I must congratulate you at least on having improved the performance of your actors certainly out of all recognition to their behaviour during the rehearsal that I heard. Assuming for the moment that it is suitable to produce *The Waste Land* in this way, I have three criticisms of detail which it might interest you to know. The first is that there were moments when the incidental business and off noises were so much to the foreground that it was a strain to hear the words, and I don't believe that anyone who had never read the poem could have followed the words in these places. This was particularly evident in the last paragraph of Section I.
>
> Secondly, while I did not otherwise object to the bit about the barges being sung, I thought that it led to an unfortunate reversal; I mean it is a pity that the refrain should have been spoken (which makes it sound foolish) instead of being sung to the excellent bit of music which Wagner provided for the purpose. But what shocked me most of all was that the words of the Thames Daughters which follow were also sung, to the accompaniment of an irrelevant and trivial strumming, instead of being spoken as they should be.
>
> The experiment may have been worth making, as an experiment, and I feel sure that you did the best with it that anyone could do with such material. But that confidence in your own accomplishment only confirms my belief that this sort of poetry is quite wrong for dramatising in that sort of way.

To Anthony Clarke, Cape Town, 26 Apr 1949: "As radio experiments with *The Waste Land* have already been attempted, I see no reason why you should not do the same. So long as the entire text is preserved intact and in the same order of words as in the published text, it seems to me that you are at liberty to use any device of partition between voices and musical accompaniment that you think fit."

9. AFTER PUBLICATION

Conrad Aiken to Robert N. Linscott, 8 Nov 1922, on *The Waste Land* and his own books: "Am I a cuckoo in fancying that it cancels the debt I owed him? I seem to detect echoes or parodies of Senlin, House, Forslin: in the evening at the violet hour etc, Madame Sosostris etc, and in general the 'symphonic' nature, the references to music (Wagner, Strawinsky) and the repetition of motifs, and the 'crowd' stuff beginning 'Unreal city.'" TSE had reviewed *Senlin* unfavourably in *Egoist* July 1919. *The Jig of Forslin* had appeared in 1916 and *House of Dust* in 1920. Aiken to Theodore Spencer, 24 Mar 1923, reporting TSE's reaction to the title of Aiken's review of *The Waste Land* (*An Anatomy of Melancholy* in *New Republic* 7 Feb 1923): "'There's nothing melancholy about it—it's nothing but pure calculation of effect'."

Reviewing *The Waste Land* in *Dial* Dec 1922, Edmund Wilson wrote that "sometimes we feel that he is speaking not only for a personal distress, but for the starvation of a whole civilization". TSE to Wilson, 11 Jan 1923: "I think you have understood it remarkably well, perhaps a little over-understood it! I mean read more into it than it contains here and there. I am very sensible of its fundamental weaknesses, and whatever I do next will be, at least, very different; I feel that it [is] merely a kind of consummation of my past work · · · *The Waste Land* does not leave me well satisfied." (At the time of publication he had written to Richard Aldington, 15 Nov 1922: "As for *The Waste Land*, that is a thing of the past so far as I am concerned and I am now feeling toward a new form and style." To Brian Coffey, 5 June 1934, on Coffey's work: "It is difficult to say whether these poems ought to be printed by themselves or not, but on the whole, I think they are quite good enough to justify it. But whether you make a book of them depends on whether they represent something which is, for you, complete—that is to say, if you feel that the phase in your own history, which they represent, is one out of which you have passed; and if you feel that your work will represent a different stage of maturity, then I should say that you had nothing to lose by their publication. If, on the other hand, you are not certain that they belong altogether to the past, then you may regret publication because you will later wish to alter, delete or amplify.")

On 23 Jan 1923, W. B. Yeats wrote to TSE offering the *Criterion* an extract from his autobiographical *The Trembling of the Veil*. In a postscript he added: "I find *The Waste Land* very beautiful, but here and there are passages I do not understand—four or five lines." TSE replied on the same day: "It is a very great satisfaction to me to know that you like *The Waste Land*. When it is brought out in this country in a month or two as a book, with notes, I shall send you a copy and hope to have at some time either in conversation or by letter, a detailed statement of your criticism. It is quite possible that the passages ought to be repaired."

To Wilhelm Lehmann, 14 May 1923: "I shall be glad of your opinion on *The Waste Land* when you see it, because I think it might *translate* better into German than into any other tongue." (To Alfred Sperber, 1 Nov 1926: "So far as I am competent to judge, the translation is admirable and supports my theory that this poem would translate better into German than into any other language.")

Otto Heller: "enthusiasts are quick to read a marvelous temperamental response of its author to the passing tragedy of the period, the reflection of a civilization torn away from its moorings by deep and violent perturbations. They sense in *The Waste Land* a poet's intense suffering", *St. Louis Post-Despatch* 24 Feb 1923 (see *Letters* 2 242). TSE to Heller, 5 Oct 1923: "Some time ago I read (I think in the *Post-Dispatch*) a review of my poem, *The Waste Land* by you. It struck me as the most intelligent review of that poem that I have seen · · · The poem is neither a success nor a failure—simply a struggle. Practically, one crucifies oneself and entertains drawing rooms and lounges. But the reception is irrelevant." ("I wrote *The Waste Land* simply to relieve my own feelings", *On Poetry* (1947) 10.)

When John Middleton Murry wrote that the poem contradicted TSE's self-proclaimed classicism (*The "Classical" Revival* in *Adelphi* Feb–Mar 1926), TSE wrote in the margin of the typescript: "*The Waste Land* makes *no attempt whatever* to be 'classical'" (*Goldie* 157). Murry also wrote that "Once its armour of impenetrability is penetrated the poem is found to be a cry of grinding and empty desolation · · · a voice from the Dark Night of the Soul of a St. John of the Cross—the barren and dry land where no water is." TSE told the audience at his fourth Clark Lecture that "if Mr. Middleton Murry would study carefully the works of St. John of the Cross, he would see that the parallel he draws between St. John and myself is quite illusory; for what St. John means by the 'dark night' and what Mr. Murry means by my 'dark night' are entirely different things", *The Varieties of Metaphysical Poetry* 104.

To Claude Colleer Abbott, 13 Oct 1927: "I am pleased that you like *The Waste Land* and wish that I could tell you more about it. It is not an evasion, but merely the truth, to say that I think in these cases that an explanation by the author is of no more value than one by anybody else. You see, the only legitimate meaning of a poem is the meaning which it has for any reader, not a meaning which it has primarily for the author. The author means all sorts of things which concern nobody else but himself, in that he may be making use of his private experiences. But these private experiences are merely crude material, and as such of no interest whatever to the public. About the best thing that has been written about this poem is an introductory essay by Professor E. R. Curtius in the *Neue Schweizer Rundschau*, but I do not know whether you know German." To Geoffrey Curtis, 20 Oct 1943: "Such an assertion as that which you quote, that in the South India Scheme the episcopate is 'devoid of particular meaning' seems to me an example of just the sort of thing not to say. [*Footnote*: It involves the assumption that 'meaning' means the same thing to both writer and reader: and this assumption is unwarranted.]"

To Cleanth Brooks, 15 Mar 1937, on a commentary about *The Waste Land*: "Reading your essay made me feel, for instance, that I had been a great deal more ingenious than I had been aware of, because the conscious problems with which one is concerned in the actual writing are more those of a quasi musical nature, in the arrangement of metric and pattern, than those of a conscious exposition of ideas".

To Philip Mairet, 31 Oct 1956: "The fact that a poem can mean different things to different persons—something which I think has been stressed by Paul Valéry as well as myself—must, however paradoxically, be reconciled with the assertion that it has an absolute and unalterable meaning. At the same time, the author, it must be remembered, regarding his own work after it is completed, is hardly more than one reader amongst others, and while the poem is being written, he must be too busy to be fully conscious of what the poem means."

Leone Vivante's distinction in *English Poetry* (Faber, 1950) between "poetic thought" and "the thought of the poet" ought, TSE wrote in his Preface, "to deter thoughtful readers from inquiring of a poet (if living) what he *meant* by any particular poem. Those who ask the question assume that a poem is a poetical dressing up, or disguise, of something which can be put equivalently in simple straightforward terms; and, if the poet cannot put it in other terms—the terms in which a student to be examined on a poem thinks that he can satisfy his examiners—conclude, either that is of the nature of poetry to be 'meaningless', or else that the meaning is to be found by probing into the unconscious mind, or the concealed biography of the author. Signor Vivante disposes of the error of supposing that a poem can be explained by the author, and the error of supposing that a poem has no meaning; and he also contradicts the assumption that all poetry can be explained by investigation of the unconscious."

Meaning and obscurity. I. A. Richards: "by effecting a complete severance between his poetry and *all* beliefs, and this without any weakening of the poetry, he has realised what might otherwise have remained largely a speculative possibility, and has shown the way to the only solution of these difficulties", *A Background for Contemporary Poetry* in *Criterion* July 1925 (repr. as *Poetry and Beliefs* in Richards's *Science and Poetry*, 1926). TSE: "Mr. I. A. Richards did me the honour of employing one of my poems as evidence ··· I cannot for the life of me see the 'complete separation' from all belief", *A Note on Poetry and Belief* (1927). "Mr. Richards's statement ··· that a certain writer has effected 'a complete severance between his poetry and *all* beliefs' is to me incomprehensible", *Dante* (1929) Note to II. And 1933: "when Mr. Richards asserts *The Waste Land* effects 'a complete severance between poetry and *all* beliefs' I am no better qualified to say No! than is any other reader. I will admit that I think that either Mr. Richards is wrong, or I do not understand his meaning", *The Use of Poetry and the Use of Criticism* 130. (Richards's notebook "Notes on Belief-Problems for T.S.E." was published by John Constable in *EinC* July 1990.) For "a complete suspension of belief", see note to *The Hollow Men* V 28–33.

To Thomas McGreevy [14 Feb] 1931, concerning his *T. S. Eliot: A Study*: "Your *explication de texte* of *The Waste Land* interested me very much. I can say without irony that it is extremely acute; but I must add that the author was not nearly so acute or learned as the critic. You have told me, in fact, much that I did not know; and I feel that I understand the poem much better after reading your explanation of it. Well! I supposed that I was merely working off a grouch against life while passing the time in a Swiss sanatorium; but apparently I meant something by it." TSE may have had McGreevy in mind in *Thoughts After Lambeth*, published on 5 Mar 1931: "when I wrote a poem called *The Waste Land* some of the more approving critics said that I had expressed 'the disillusion of a generation', which is nonsense. I may have expressed for them their own illusion of being disillusioned, but that did not form part of my intention." To A. L. Rowse, 18 Apr 1931: "Disillusion is balls—the only people who are really disillusioned are good catholics, and very few of them. The great illusion of young people—or rather of the people who in the press express what they think young people think—is the illusion of being 'disillusioned' · · · to be really disillusioned about anything one must believe in something. I should call myself 'disillusioned' in the only sense possible to me, that is, that I have ceased to care about some things, and ceased to respect some things, and ceased to accept some things, and ceased to believe some, and ceased to expect many, merely in the process of acquiring certain of what most people would call 'illusions'—and I don't mean narrowly theological illusions either" (see note to *Ash-Wednesday* I 1, 12, 38, and for "the Catholic philosophy of disillusion", see headnote to *Ash-Wednesday*, 3. AFTER PUBLICATION). On the *Vita Nuova*: "There is also a practical sense of realities behind it, which is antiromantic: not to expect more from *life* than it can give or more from *human* beings than they can give; to look to *death* for what life cannot give. The *Vita Nuova* belongs to 'vision literature'; but its philosophy is the Catholic philosophy of disillusion", *Dante* (1929) III. (Irving Babbitt: "We not only find in Sainte-Beuve the false illusion of decadence, we also find in him · · · its false disilllusion", *The Masters of Modern French Criticism*, 1912, 119.) TSE: "Nor is disillusion possible as an end in itself; for when it becomes an end, it is paraded, and that again is childish and ill bred", *A Commentary* in *Criterion* Apr 1933. To Sean O'Faolain, 21 Feb 1944, of *Gerontion*: "it can only be said to have been the expression of a mood · · · I wasn't thinking about declining civilisations when I wrote it" (see headnote to *Gerontion*). "It happens now and then that a poet by some strange accident expresses the mood of his generation, at the same time that he is expressing a mood of his own which is quite remote from that of his generation. This is not a question of insincerity: there is an amalgam of yielding and opposition below the level of consciousness", *In Memoriam* (1936). For "a generation which has lost faith in lost causes", see note to *East Coker* V 11–17.

In his essay *Mr. Eliot's Return* (1932), Paul Elmer More wrote: "The writer of *The Waste Land* and other poems of that period appeals to us as one struck to the heart by the confusion and purposelessness and wastefulness of the world about him." In More's typescript TSE circled "as", with "You should say *as if*. I may not have been aware of anything but my own private grouse." Where More asked "And what is the young rebel who rejoices in the disillusion of *The Waste Land* to do with the Bishops of the Church · · · ?", TSE circled "disillusion", with "I believe only in particular ⁊ personal disillusion. A self-styled 'disillusioned age' seems to me merely one whose illusion is that it has no illusions—and we are producing plenty. I am sorry to have contributed (unintentionally) to the spread of this illusion" (More papers, Princeton). To More, 20 July 1934: "I think the poem was, at the time, and to some extent still, misjudged. I was not aware, and am not aware now, of having drawn a contrast between a contemporary world of slums, hysterics and riverside promiscuity etc. with any visibly more romantically lovely earlier world. I mean there is no nostalgia for the trappings of the past, so far as I can see, and no illusion about the world ever having been a pleasanter place to live in than it is now. There is no *time sense* there, in that literal way; the glories and the sordors are both aspects of futility."

After E. M. Forster's remark on *The Waste Land*: "It is just a personal comment on the universe" (*Life and Letters* June 1929; see note to unadopted epigraph), TSE spoke in the same terms in America: "Various critics have done me the honour to interpret the poem in terms of criticism of the contemporary world, have considered it, indeed, as an important bit of social criticism. To me it was only the relief of a personal and wholly insignificant grouse against life; it is just a piece of rhythmical grumbling", *Excerpts from Lectures 1932–1933* documented by Henry Eliot, who adds: "(Goes on to say that the poet's own interpretation may not necessarily be the only satisfactory one.)" Three days after a reading by TSE on 7 May 1933, *Vassar Miscellany News* reported the same remarks. *WLFacs* printed them with the subscription "Quoted by the late Professor Theodore Spencer during a lecture at Harvard University, and recorded by the late Henry Ware Eliot, Jr., the poet's brother". Described by the Contents page as "TSE on *The Waste Land*", they constitute page 1 of *WLFacs*. (For TSE's next poem as the expression of "a subjective dissatisfaction with the pettiness of life", see note to *The Hollow Men* V 28–31.)

TSE to Marianne Moore, 31 Oct 1934: "Whenever I am disposed to be vainglorious, I should remind myself of a remark my mother once made to Sally Bruce Kinsolving of Baltimore. 'Mrs. Kinsolving, I like your poetry, because I can understand it and I don't understand my son's'. There is something in that." To Eudo C. Mason, 21 Feb 1936: "It is curious to learn that Professor Schücking considers my work unintelligible." To J. Bramwell, 11 July 1945: "The first question about a poem is not whether it is intelligible but whether it is readable." Asked about obscurity in modern poetry, TSE replied that it was sometimes "a matter of pretence", but at other times it was caused by "the difficulty of expressing something genuinely felt. There is a little of this obscurity in *The Waste Land*. Things had to be said that way or not at all. A poet becomes less obscure as he masters his craft", *T. S. Eliot Answers Questions* (1949). For obscurity "due to the suppression of 'links in the chain'", see TSE's Preface to *Anabasis* (in headnote).

On Charles Whibley's *Musings*: "Critics sometimes comment upon the sudden transitions and juxtapositions of modern poetry: that is, when right and successful, an application of somewhat the same method without method. Whether the transition is cogent or not, is merely a question of whether the mind is *serré* [compact] or *délié* [loose], whether the whole personality is involved", *Charles Whibley* (1931).

"It is not true that the ideas of a great poet are in any sense arbitrary: certainly in the sense in which imagination is capricious, the ideas of a lunatic or an imbecile are more 'imaginative' than those of a poet. In really great imaginative work the connections are felt to be bound by as logical necessity as any connections to be found anywhere; the apparent irrelevance is due to the fact that the terms are used with more or other than their normal meaning, and to those who do not thoroughly penetrate their significance the relation between the aesthetic expansion and the objects expressed is not visible", *Knowledge and Experience* 75. Recalling the reception of *A Choice of Kipling's Verse*, TSE wrote: "it aroused considerable astonishment in the world of letters, that Kipling should be championed not only as a prose writer but as a writer of verse, by a poet whose verse was generally considered to be at the opposite pole from Kipling's. Whereas my poems had appeared too obscure and recondite to win popular approval, Kipling's had long been considered too simple, too crude, too popular, indeed too near the doggerel of the music hall song", *"The Unfading Genius of Rudyard Kipling"* (1959).

Asked about including prose quotations in poems: "if the poet merely puts these things together, a sort of *collage* of bits, without contributing anything himself, which I was accused of doing in some of my early works because of quotations and references, then there is nothing new, there is nothing original. Nothing to hold the thing together", *Talking Freely* (1961).

On New Year's Day 1936, in reply to a long and censorious letter from his brother Henry, TSE described his state of mind in the early 1920s: "I was of course too much engrossed in the horrors of my private life to notice much outside; and I was suffering from (1) a feeling of guilt in having married a woman I detested, and consequently a feeling that I must put up with anything (2) perpetually being told, in the most plausible way, that I was a clodhopper and a dunce. Gradually, through making friends, I came to find that English people of the sort that I found congenial were prepared to take me quite as an ordinary human being, and that I had merely married into a rather common suburban family with a streak of abnormality which in the case of my wife had reached the point of liking to give people pain. I shall always be grateful to a few people like the Woolfs who unconsciously helped me to regain my balance and self-respect."

To Geoffrey Faber, 15 Apr 1936: "As for our literary reputation, remember that people like Joyce and myself may help to keep the temperature level, but we can't send it any higher. There is something an author does *once* (if at all) in his generation that he can't ever do again. We can go on writing stuff that nobody else could write, if you like, but the *Waste Land* and *Ulysses* remain the historic points." Distinguishing himself from Pound: "what is wanted is an ad interim book which will give more attention to what the authors are trying to do now. This does not matter so much with Pound, whose Cantos just go on; but it matters with me and the juniors ··· so far as this book has to deal with me, I might just as well have stopped writing in 1923", *"Skeleton for a book on Contemporary Poetry"* by Martin Gilkes, a report (1938). *Spender* 115: "Eliot—who tended to take a historic view of his work—once said to me that *The Waste Land* could not have been written at any moment except when it was written."

In the course of writing about *The Hollow Men* (see Commentary), A. S. T. Fisher claimed that *The Waste Land* was the first important poem to reflect recent advances in psychology. In his reply, 19 Jan 1943, TSE wrote: "I would not contest your point about the influence of recent advances in psychology but if it is true the connection was unconscious and not deliberate." (On Freud, to the Rev. Father Superior General, Society of St. John the Evangelist, 15 May 1935, of a book by Dr. Jovetz-Tereschchenko: "I speak ··· as one who has read the works of Freud with alarm, and who feels that the Freudian view of sex is wrong and anti-Christian, and who therefore welcomes any book which, like this, controverts that view." To Warner Allen, 13 Mar 1945: "I am little read in the works of these people (because of a fear that too much psychology might be bad for poetry – I have seen it happen to one poet) but I imagine that I should find Jung the most to my taste.")

To Eudo C. Mason, 19 Apr 1945: "It seems to me so far as I am competent to judge that you are justified in your interpretation of *The Waste Land* but I am surprised to think that any indications of Christian tradition were present in *Prufrock.* I was certainly quite ignorant and unconscious of them myself, and at the time, or at least before the poem was finished, was entirely a Bergsonian; but as I always say, an author's knowledge of certain facts has value, whereas his interpretation or understanding of his own poem, and especially many years after writing it, may be no more authoritative and may for special reasons be less reliable than that of anyone else." (To John Lehmann, 5 Feb 1958: "It certainly was not consciously a Christian poem, though it may perhaps be taken as foreshadowing conversion, but I was certainly not conscious of this at the time.")

To Bonamy Dobrée, 9 Mar 1948: "I am quite sure that *The Prelude* is not an epic and that epic does not mean simply a long poem · · · Some Spaniard called *The Waste Land* an *epopeya.*"

Undated draft letter to John Peter [Nov? 1952], in response to his article *A New Interpretation of "The Waste Land"* (*EinC* July 1952):

> had your article been nothing more than absurd I should have ignored it. I am obliged, however, to take notice of an "interpretation" of any poem of mine the purpose of which is to demonstrate that the poem is essentially concerned with homosexual passion. This is not merely wholly mistaken, but highly offensive.
>
> Nor is this the end of the matter. Some readers may infer that the author of a poem on an homosexual theme must himself be a person of homosexual temperament, if not actually of homosexual practices.

Replying to Alice Quinn, a schoolchild, 19 Feb 1952: "*The Waste Land* is my most famous work, and therefore *perhaps* will prove the most important, but it is not my favourite."

10. ELIOT, POUND AND *THE WASTE LAND*

Pound: "It is nearly impossible to make the RIGHT suggestion for emending another man's work. Even if you do, he never quite thinks it remains his own", reviewing *Dante's Inferno translated into English Triple Rhyme* by Laurence Binyon in *Criterion* Apr 1934. TSE to Ronald Bottrall, 12 Feb 1948, on his collection of poems *The Palisades of Fear* (1948): "I believe that marginal comment is the most useful form of criticism of unpublished verse."

On 20 Nov 1952, TSE's Harvard friend W. G. Tinckom-Fernandez wrote to Harford Powel: "I like to recall that I introduced him to the poetry of Ezra Pound in College." TSE's recollection in *On a Recent Piece of Criticism* (1938) confirms that he came across Pound's work at that time:

> Mr. [G. W.] Stonier is mistaken, both about my relations with Pound in the past, and about my valuation of the different periods of Pound's poetry—if, that is, I have understood Mr. Stonier. (I have the impression that Mr. Stonier's knowledge of literary events before 1918 or so is at secondhand, since he speaks of *The Egoist* as having succeeded *Blast.*) I was introduced to *Personae* and *Exultations* in 1910, while still an undergraduate at Harvard. The poems did not then excite me, any more than did the

> poetry of Yeats: I was too much engrossed in working out the implications of Laforgue. I considered them, however, the only interesting poems by a contemporary that I had found. My indebtedness to Pound is of two kinds: first, in my literary criticism (this debt has been pointed out by Mr. [Hugh Gordon] Porteus and Mr. Mario Praz); and second, in his criticism of my poetry in our talk, and his indications of desirable territories to explore. This indebtedness extends from 1915 to 1922, after which period Mr. Pound left England, and our meetings became infrequent. My greatest debt was for his improvement of *The Waste Land*. But as for the poetry of "the early Pound," there are only three or four original pieces that have made any deep impression upon me; and the Pound whom I find congenial is the author of *Mauberley*, *Propertius*, and the *Cantos*.

The extent of Pound's editorial work on *The Waste Land* had been made public when part of a letter from TSE to Ford Madox Ford (1 Dec 1932) appeared in a pamphlet, *The Cantos of Ezra Pound: Some Testimonies*, which Farrar & Rinehart used in 1933 as publicity for their American edition of *A Draft of XXX Cantos*: "I owe too much to Ezra to be a critic. (I wish that the manuscript of THE WASTELAND with Ezra's criticisms and still more important, his excisions, thank God he reduced a mess of some eight hundred lines to about half its size, might some day be exhumed. John Quinn had it. As a masterpiece of critical literature.)" Pound to TSE, 24 Apr [1933]: "Mussur Rinehaprs pamphlepp dun com, and I see it fur deh furs' time TOOday Ah see you done got it off you' ancestral chest, bout my habin gnawed off deh rind// (ob. W. Lnd) Ah dunno, as you had orter done it. Mebbe you right, enny rate you iz at las' relieved you'self. And probably now it is to th'greater glory and not too soon. I mean it dont interfere with much / I know you dun been rarin fer to say so / ever since 1921. At any rate it wdnt. Have done any good, if 'released sooner'."

TSE to Masuru Otaké, 6 Apr 1934: "I had no deliberate intention of dividing the poems according to the divisions of Elizabethan drama. There may, of course, be some analogy but it formed no part of my conscious purpose. What similarity there is between *The Waste Land* and Mr. Pound's *Cantos* lies I think in versification, in the use of allusion and in a similar kind of concentration. There is no similarity in form."

To Miss E. A. Madge, 16 Oct 1943: "I cannot imagine what means of support she [Dorothy Pound] and her husband have; he was a vehement supporter of the fascist regime and is an outcast from his own country; and their situation, whatever it may be, is a cause for great anxiety to all those who were ever their friends. Her husband is an honest though a very silly man; I owe him much gratitude for kindness in the past: I remain as much admiring [of] his poetry and literary criticism, as exasperated by his political opinions."

In tribute: "It was in 1922 that I placed before him in Paris the manuscript of a sprawling chaotic poem called *The Waste Land* which left his hands, reduced to about half its size, in the form in which it appears in print. I should like to think that the manuscript, with the suppressed passages, had disappeared irrecoverably: yet, on the other hand, I should wish the blue pencilling on it to be preserved as irrefutable evidence of Pound's critical genius", *Ezra Pound* (1946).

In Pound's case, TSE made an exception to his principle that "books *about* F. & F. authors should be published by other firms", writing "This book ··· has the advantage of being an introduction to ALL the poetry, and nothing but the poetry. I mean, it does not concern itself with Pound's economic doctrines or political nonsense; though it inevitably (and rightly) concerns itself with his interest in Chinese ideograms, poetry, and Confucius", *"The Poetry of Ezra Pound"* by Hugh

Kenner, reader's report (1949). The book was published by Faber in 1951, but in 1960 Kenner's *The Invisible Poet: T. S. Eliot* was published in the UK by W. H. Allen.

Revisiting Milton Academy, TSE emphasised how dedicated Pound had been: "I think of a friend who, in the early days, was as much concerned with the encouragement and improvement of the work of unknown writers in whom he discerned talent, as with his own creative work; who formulated, for a generation of poets, the principles of good writing most needful for their time; who tried to bring these writers together for their reciprocal benefit; who, in the face of many obstacles, saw that their writings were published; saw that they were reviewed somewhere by critics who could appreciate them; organized or supported little magazines in which their work could appear—and incidentally, liked to give a good dinner to those who he thought could not afford it, and sometimes even supplied the more needy with articles of clothing out of his own meagre store", *Leadership and Letters* (1949).

"I believe that I have in the past made clear enough my personal debt to Ezra Pound during the years 1915–22. I have also expressed in several ways my opinion of his rank as a poet, as a critic, an impresario of other writers, and as pioneer of metric and poetic language. His 70th birthday is not a moment for qualifying one's praise, but merely for recognition of those services to literature for which he will deserve the gratitude of posterity, and for appreciation of those achievements which even his severest critics must acknowledge", *Ezra Pound at Seventy* (1956). "My criticism has this in common with that of Ezra Pound, that its merits and its limitations can be fully appreciated only when it is considered in relation to the poetry I have written myself", *The Frontiers of Criticism* (1956).

When Leslie Paul asked about Pound's revisions of *The Waste Land*, TSE explained: "He cut out a lot of dead matter. I think that the poem as originally written was about twice the length. It contained some stanzas in imitation of Pope, and Ezra said to me: 'Pope's done that so well that you'd better not try to compete with him.' Which was sound advice. And there was also a long passage about a shipwreck which I think was inspired by the Ulysses canto in Dante's *Inferno*. At any rate, he reduced it in length. Well, the fate of that manuscript or typescript with his blue-pencillings on it is one of the permanent—so far as I know—minor mysteries of literature ··· You know, I'm in two minds about that search. I should like it to be found as evidence of what Ezra himself called his maieutic [obstetric] abilities—evidence of what he did for me in criticizing my script. On the other hand, for my own reputation, and for that of *The Waste Land* itself, I'm rather glad that it has disappeared", *A Conversation, recorded in 1958, between T. S. Eliot and Leslie Paul* ([1964/]1965).

To J. M. Aguirre, 23 Nov 1956: "I am afraid that I am unable to answer most of the questions in your letter of November 19th, some of them because they seem to imply a kind of rational structure in the poem which does not exist." Asked by Donald Hall, "Did the excisions change the intellectual structure of the poem?" TSE replied: "No. I think it was just as structureless, only in a more futile way, in the longer version", *Paris Review* (1959). "No doubt my readers would be interested to see the original version, but it is certain that Pound's editing improved the poem and there is no ground for suggesting that it became more enigmatic", *Northrop Frye corrigenda* (1963).

To Daniel H. Woodward, 3 Apr 1964, on *The Waste Land* draft and then the *March Hare* Notebook: "I cannot feel altogether sorry that this and the notebook have disappeared. The unpublished poems in the notebook were not worth publishing, and there was a great deal of superfluous matter in *The Waste Land* which Pound very rightly deleted. Indeed, the poem in the form in which it finally appeared owes more to Pound's surgery than anyone can realise" (*Woodward* 268).

Despite such public and private tributes to him, Pound sent a message from Rapallo on 31 July 1959:

> TSE
> Forgive us our trespasses. Even you will forgive me when you realize the extent of my failure.
>
> Yrs,
>
> E.

On 5 Aug, TSE replied: "I am distressed and alarmed by your laconic note of the 31st July. What on earth is the failure you are talking about, and I don't like the insinuation that I have an unforgiving nature. Please reply quickly."

Further anguished pages arrived from Pound, impossible to print except in facsimile, but including such phrases as "I am trying to repudiate 30 years of injustice to you, from time of Ash Wednesday", "you doing real criticism and me playing a tin penny whistle" and "30 years of impertinence from me". Pound's daughter, Mary de Rachewiltz, also wrote, on 23 Oct 1959, wondering whether TSE might visit, and reporting: "he is so overwhelmed by fragments that he does not even believe in his Poetry any more & that's the worst part of it all". TSE sent a cable from the US, 30 Oct: "TWO LETTERS RECEIVED I NEVER FORGET MY OWN GREAT DEBT TO YOU TO WHOM ALL LIVING POETS ARE INDEBTED STOP YOUR CRITICISM HAS ALWAYS BEEN IMMENSELY HELPFUL STOP YOUR OWN ACHIEVEMENT EPOCH MAKING STOP NOW JUST GOING WEST BUT WILL WRITE AS SOON AS POSSIBLE LOVE POSSUM". Then a letter, 11 Nov: "Damn it, you're still the biggest man in the poetry world, and have had the greatest influence on poetry of anyone in this century."

Once back in London, TSE wrote again, 28 Dec 1959: "I have known well enough states of mind similar to yours. To tell a man what he has achieved in the world, how big his own work is, all he has done for other people and for the world at large, civilisation, society, etc. etc. doesn't reach to the heart of the doubt, disgust, despair, etc. from which the victim is suffering. He knows all that and yet feels himself an utter failure ··· Your achievement in poetry the greatest that has happened in *my* lifetime."

After letters from Pound of 22 and 30 Dec, and 16 Jan 1960, TSE wrote once more: "Still can't understand why you have been so depressed about your work, or your life—trust you will get the right balance soon. Hell, there's so much in my life I can't bear to think about for long at a time. Still think *Waste Land* and three last quartets worth while. A lot of very silly stuff in my prose ··· Affectuous greetings, TP".

11. THE FATE OF THE DRAFTS

To John Quinn 19 July 1922, thanking him for negotiating the contract for publication of the poem in America: "I should like to present you the MSS of *The Waste Land*, if you would care to have it—when I say MSS, I mean that it is partly MSS and partly typescript, with Ezra's and my alterations scrawled all over it." Quinn replied, 28 July–1 Aug 1922: "I shall be glad to have the MS. of *Waste Land* but I shan't let you 'present it to me'. When you finish the whole thing, poetry and prose, if you will send the MS. or MSS. to me, I shall be glad to have it, but you must agree to the condition that I send you a draft for what I think it is worth. I shall feel happier to do it that way." (For more of this long serial letter, see *Egleston ed.* 264–67.) TSE, 21 Aug 1922: "I certainly cannot accept your proposal to purchase the manuscript at your own price, and if you will not accept it in recognition of what you have done for me lately and in the past, it will not be any pleasure to me to sell it to you. I therefore hope that you will accept it. But as I feel that perhaps you like some of my early poems best I should be glad, for example, to send you the manuscript of Prufrocks instead, and I hope you will let me do this." (There was no mention of any material relating to the 1920 poems, although TSE included typescripts of eleven of these with the early poems.) After a meeting on 7 Sept with Gilbert Seldes, managing editor of the *Dial*, settling terms for periodical publication of the poem, Quinn wrote again: "We won't quarrel about the MS. of The Waste Land. I'll accept it from you, not 'for what I have lately done for you and in the past', but as a mark of friendship, but on this condition: That you will let me purchase of you the MS. of the Early Poems that you referred to. If you have the Prufrock only, then I'll purchase that. But if you have the MS. of the whole volume of your poems [*Poems* (1920)], including the Prufrock, I should *greatly value* that, and then I'll have two complete manuscripts of yours. If you leave to me the fixing of what the MS. of those poems would be worth, I would discuss the matter with one or two dealers in rare books and manuscripts and autograph letters and would be guided by their advice. If I had to choose between the MS. of The Waste Land and the Notes and the Prufrock MS. alone, I would choose The Waste Land MS. But I feel sure that you'll agree to my condition that I pay you for the MS. of the Early Poems. That meets your point and it gives me another MS. of yours, and each of us will be happy" (*WLFacs* xxiv).

Grateful to Pound as well as Quinn for helping to secure both publication in the *Dial* and the *Dial* award, TSE wrote to Quinn on 21 Sept saying that Pound had deserved to be recognised first.

> In the manuscript of *The Waste Land* which I am sending you, you will see the evidences of his work, and I think that this manuscript is worth preserving in its present form solely for the reason that it is the only evidence of the difference which his criticism has made to this poem. I am glad that you at least will have the opportunity of judging of this for yourself. Naturally, I hope that the portions which I have suppressed will never appear in print and in sending them to you I am sending the only copies of these parts.
>
> I have gathered together all of the manuscript in existence. The leather bound notebook is one which I started in 1909 and in which I entered all my work of that time as I wrote it, so that it is the only original manuscript barring of course rough scraps and notes, which were destroyed at the time, in existence. You will find a great many sets of verse which have never been printed and which I am sure you will agree never ought to be printed, and in putting them in your hands, I beg you fervently to keep them to yourself and see they never are printed.
>
> I do not think that this manuscript is of any great value, especially as the large part is really typescript for which no manuscript except scattered lines, ever existed. It is understood that in the valuation you speak of *The Waste Land* is not to be included and the rest must be valued at its actual market value and not at any value which it may (or may not) acquire in course of time.

Valerie Eliot: "The packet containing the manuscripts was sent to Quinn by registered post on 23 October 1922, and reached his office at 31 Nassau Street, New York, on 13 January 1923" (*WLFacs* xxix). Quinn explained to TSE, 26 Feb 1923, how its value was calculated: "With the notebook ··· there are some fifty-three pages of manuscript in the book and some five or six pages of loose manuscript, making roughly sixty pages. Then there are the typewritten drafts, which Drake [a bookdealer] did not rank as manuscript and disregarded in his valuation. He thought that a payment of about $2 a page would be 'about right'. But I thought his figures were somewhat conservative and I am sending you London draft to your order for £29 14s 10d, the equivalent at the present rate of exchange of $140, which I think is fair and reasonable" (*WLFacs* xxvi). TSE responded, 12 Mar 1923: "I consider your payment for the manuscript very generous indeed, and feel that you have thwarted me in my attempt to repay you in some way for all that you have done" (*WLFacs* xxvi).

Quinn, 26 Feb 1923: "I have read the manuscript of *The Waste Land* which you sent me with great interest. I have noted the evidence of Pound's criticisms on the poem. Personally I should not have cut out some of the parts that Pound advised you to cut out. Of course the portions which you have scrapped will never appear in print from the copies that I have" (*Egleston ed.* 276).

Six years after Quinn's death in 1924, his sister proposed an edition of letters received by him (all now NYPL). Lennox Robinson, the editor, sent TSE transcripts of those from him, but there appears to have been no mention of the drafts of *The Waste Land* or the *March Hare* Notebook. Unusually, TSE agreed to the request in principle, lightly editing the copies of his letters and returning them to Robinson, but the edition came to nothing. To Robinson, 17 Sept 1930: "I wish most cordially that I could contribute some memories. But I never had the pleasure of meeting Quinn; the letters themselves show I think the kind and extent of my relations with him; though these letters are far from covering the whole of his benefactions to me."

TSE to Jeanne Robert Foster, 11 Jan 1934: "Your name has been given to me as that of the Literary Executor of the late Mr. John Quinn. I am writing to ask if you can tell me anything of the fate of two MSS. of my own which were in Mr. Quinn's collection. I have never heard what became of them after his death, and I am told that they were not included in the sale. One was a medium-sized note book, bound in half leather, which contained the manuscript of all my early poems, and of a good many youthful poems which I never wished to publish. The other was partly typescript and partly manuscript, and consisted of the original *Waste Land* with Ezra Pound's suggestions and some of my own revisions." TSE does not appear to have written again to Mrs. Foster.

On 30 June 1958, Donald Gallup wrote to Donald Hall that he had had confirmation of a rumour that "the typescript of *The Waste Land* had been offered, at $100,000 (but whether with other manuscripts and letters I don't know), to 'a mid-Western university library.' According to my sources, this library refused the offer and suggested that the Morgan Library might be interested. Apparently the offer was then made to the Morgan and also turned down there." TSE to Donald Hall, 20 Aug 1959: "It is very satisfactory to know that rumour has now reduced the price of *The Waste Land* script from 200,000 to 100,000 dollars, and we can only hope that it will eventually be reduced to such a small amount that I may regard the sale with complete indifference; but I shall be glad to hear any further news that reaches you." Gallup to Alan Clodd, 27 Aug 1959: "I think we may be certain that the typescript of *The Waste Land*, at least, showing Ezra Pound's deletions, is still very much in existence and it will probably come out of hiding before very long". TSE to Hall, 1 Oct 1959: "Thank you for your further news, or rather for letting me know that there is no further news about *The Waste Land* MS. I wonder if the whole thing is imaginary. It seems very odd that the rumour should be so persistent and yet so devoid of foundation."

A draft letter from Jeanne Robert Foster to Valerie Eliot (undated but probably 1971) states: "I believe ~~the year 1966~~ Dr. and Mrs Conroy found the MS in 1966. It would have been held in the Quinn materials shippe in [? shipment] approximately 41 years" (NYPL).

In 1971, Valerie Eliot explained that the drafts

> were not mentioned in Quinn's will, but formed part of the estate inherited by his sister, Julia (Mrs. William Anderson). After Mrs. Anderson's death in 1934, her widower and daughter, Mary (Mrs. Thomas F. Conroy) moved to a smaller apartment, and many cases of Quinn's papers were put in storage. It was not until the early 1950s, after a prolonged search, that Mrs. Conroy found the manuscripts.
>
> On 4 April 1958 she sold them to the Berg Collection of the New York Public Library for $18,000. The purchase remained private, neither Eliot nor Pound being told about it. The Curator, the late Dr. John D. Gordan, asked a common friend if she could arrange an appointment for him with Eliot to discuss "a business matter" when he visited London in May that year. Eliot was in America at the time unfortunately, and Dr. Gordan made no further attempt to communicate with him.
>
> I was informed of the acquisitions when Mr. James W. Henderson gave me a microfilm of them, in the summer of 1968, with the request to observe secrecy until the Library issued a public statement on 25 October, the date of the publication of Professor B. L. Reid's biography, *The Man from New York: John Quinn and His Friends.*
>
> Mrs. Conroy has presented twenty-two letters and six cables from Eliot to her uncle to the Manuscript Division of the Library.
>
> *WLFacs* xxix

Valerie Eliot ended her introduction to the facsimile with a summary:

> The manuscript-typescript of *The Waste Land* consists of fifty-four leaves (of which forty-seven are single), together with three receipted bills for the period 22 October to 12 November 1921, from The Albemarle Hotel, Cliftonville, Margate (where Eliot began his convalescence), and the label from the packet. There are no notes. Someone, possibly Eliot, has divided the leaves into two sections: the main text, and the miscellaneous poems [that] were considered for it; these now contain forty-two leaves and twelve leaves respectively. An assortment of paper has been used.
>
> *WLFacs* xxx

The announcement of the discovery of the drafts was followed by an account of them by Donald Gallup, *TLS* 7 Nov 1968, with illustrations of three leaves (*WLFacs* 4, 10 and 58), and quoting the six lines *WLComposite* 552–57. A slightly revised account was published in the *Bulletin of the New York Public Library* Dec 1968.

Valerie Eliot, interviewed by Timothy Wilson, *The Observer* 20 Feb 1972:

> "We were in New York a number of times between 1958 and 1965, and my husband could have seen his manuscript," Mrs Eliot says. "Part of me is angry that he was never told about it, and part of me feels that it was merciful. The years of *The Waste Land* were a terrible nightmare to him, and I did not want him to relive them: if he had seen these drafts, they might have brought back all the horror. In the last months of his life there was a persistent rumour that the University of Texas had acquired the manuscript for a considerable sum. We never thought it would turn up, but Tom told me that if it did I was to publish it. 'It won't do me any good,' he added, 'but I would like people to realise the extent of my debt to Ezra.'" · · · She also visited Pound in Venice,

> but apparently it distresses him to think that he ever criticised Eliot. "He told me," Mrs Eliot says, "that if my husband had waited until he was better, he would have made the cuts and improvements himself." However, during her second visit to New York, Pound turned up unexpectedly and went with her to the library, to see if the actual manuscript would help his memory. But he was so moved by seeing it that he just sat for a long time in front of it, tears in his eyes.

Valerie Eliot to Mary and Conrad Aiken, 17 June 1969: "You may have heard that Ezra turned up unexpectedly in New York, but even the sight of the manuscript recalled nothing." Peter du Sautoy to Gallup, 5 Jan 1970, on Gallup's booklet *T. S. Eliot & Ezra Pound: Collaborators in Letters*: "Of course the sad end of the story is (though naturally you couldn't say so) that Pound remembers nothing of *The Waste Land* manuscript and was unable to give Valerie any help. But he has written for her a charming little preface."

Valerie Eliot: "Although Pound was unable to volunteer information, it seemed to assist his memory if possible interpretations were put forward. There was not only the intervening period to contend with, but also an emotional block caused by his anguish that he had ever criticized Eliot. 'He should have ignored me. Why didn't he restore some of the cancelled passages when Liveright wanted more pages?'" *TLS* 18 May 1973. Pound's final tribute to TSE, and his last appreciation, appeared as the Preface to *The Waste Land: A Facsimile & Transcript of the Original Drafts*.

> PREFACE
>
> The more we know of Eliot, the better. I am thankful that the lost leaves have been unearthed.
>
> The occultation of the *Waste Land* manuscript (years of waste time, exasperating to its author) is pure Henry James.
>
> "The mystery of the missing manuscript" is now solved. Valerie Eliot has done a scholarly job which would have delighted her husband. For this, and for her patience with my attempts to elucidate my own marginal notes, and for the kindness which distinguishes her, I express my thanks.
>
> EZRA POUND
>
> *Venice*
> *30 September 1969*

Ezra Pound died in Venice on 1 November 1972.

The Waste Land: Commentary

This Commentary intercalates notes on (a) the text of *The Waste Land* printed in the present edition; (b) the draft readings shown in the editorial composite (*WLComposite*), with line numbers in bold; (c) variants from printed texts and from the drafts (for which see Textual History); (d) TSE's own "Notes on the Waste Land"; (e) fragments of verse related to *The Waste Land* other than those printed among the "Uncollected Poems". The Commentary covers these in sequence:

Title

Introductory paragraph of TSE's Notes

Unadopted epigraph

Epigraph

Dedication

PART I. THE BURIAL OF THE DEAD

1–54 ("First we had a couple of feelers down at Tom's place")

[I] 1–76

PART II. A GAME OF CHESS

[II] 77–172

PART III. THE FIRE SERMON

229–85 ("Admonished by the sun's inclining ray",
including "We fear'd that we had bitch'd him quite" *in note to* **270–298**)

285^286 *insertion, ms4* ("From which, a Venus Anadyomene")

286–98 ("The Scandinavians bemused her wits")

Fresca couplets, after **298** ("When the rude entrance of the Tarquin, day")

[III] 173–214

334–48 ("London, the swarming life you kill and breed")

[III] 215–311

PART IV. DEATH BY WATER

475–557 ("The sailor, attentive to the chart and to the sheets")

[IV] 312–21

PART V. WHAT THE THUNDER SAID

[V] 322–433

TSE's "Notes on the Waste Land" are given precedence but are not repeated in full. They are accorded a capital where this is sufficient to make the meaning clear ("as he wrote in his Notes"), or designated *TSE's Notes*. When Valerie Eliot's notes from her edition of the drafts are given verbatim, they appear in quotation marks. Other information from them is retained with the attribution "*WLFacs* notes". Ezra Pound's markings of TSE's drafts are all to be found in the Textual History, and are occasionally annotated in the Commentary. Pierre Leyris's French translation, published in *Poèmes 1910–1930* (1947), contained notes by John Hayward, with TSE's imprimatur. Except for matter already included in *TSE's Notes*, these are incorporated, with the attribution "*Hayward*", and are occasionally corrected silently from his typescript (King's).

Hayward begins with a general note, quoting from *Gardner 1942* and from TSE's comparison of poetry and music:

> Subject matter: "The problem of history and the time process is one of the great themes of *The Waste Land*, where it is mingled with the desire for cosmic and personal salvation. No poem has ever shown a greater sense of the pressure of the past upon the present and of its existence in the present" (Helen Gardner).
>
> Basic theme is death-in-life.
>
> Technique: "I believe that the properties in which music concerns the poet most nearly, are the sense of rhythm and the sense of structure . . . The use of recurrent themes is as natural to poetry as to music. There are possibilities for verse which bear some analogy to the development of a theme by different groups of instruments; there are possibilities of transitions in a poem comparable to the different movements of a symphony or a quartet; there are possibilities of contrapuntal arrangement", *The Music of Poetry* (1942).

Title ***The Waste Land***: Jessie L. Weston of the "Wasting of the land": "As a matter of fact, I believe that the 'Waste Land' is really the very heart of our problem; a rightful appreciation of its position and significance will place us in possession of the clue which will lead us safely through the most bewildering mazes of the fully developed tale", *From Ritual to Romance* (1920) ch. V. Her synopsis of ch. II ends: "Importance of Waste Land *motif* for criticism." The chapter concludes that in the Grail romances "the forces of the ruler being weakened · · · the land becomes Waste" and that readers should "concentrate upon the persistent elements" so that eventually "the constituent elements will reveal their significance." Augustine's *Confessions* bk. II ends: "I sank away from Thee, and I wandered, O my God, too much astray from Thee my stay, in these days of my youth, and I became to myself a barren land." Bk. III then begins: "To Carthage I came" (see *The Waste Land* [III] 307).

Malory: "so befelle there grete pestilence, and grete harme to bothe reallmys; for there encresed nother corne, ne grasse, nother well-nye no fruyte, ne in the watir was founde no fyssh. Therefore men calle hit—the londys of the two marchys—the Waste Londe", *Morte d'Arthur* XVII iii (J. Padmanabha, letter, *TLS* 17 Mar 1972). TSE to L. C. Knights, 28 Dec 1933: "I have agreed to review one book for the *Spectator*, but that was only under extreme temptation, as it is my favourite book—that is, Malory's *Morte d'Arthur*, and I could not resist the opportunity of having this new edition." This was the Shakespeare Head Malory, and TSE's review called for three further editions: "(1) a cheap edition of the text; (2) a scholarly edition with a full commentary by some person as learned as

Miss Jane Harrison or Miss Jessie Weston; and (3) a children's edition. Such an edition was in my hands when I was a child of eleven or twelve", *Le Morte Darthur* (1934). TSE's copy of Charles Morris's *King Arthur and the Knights of the Round Table: A Modernized Version of the "Morte Darthur"* is autographed "T. S. Eliot. First Year Class. Smith Academy" (1899–1900). The Everyman (a cheap edition of the text) is given among *TSE's books: Bodleian list* (1934). "For instance, two of my own favourite authors are Sir Thomas Malory and Racine", *After Strange Gods* 27.

The exact title. To Ezra Pound, 30 Aug 1922: "not 'Waste Land', please, but '*The* Waste Land'". To Lucille Goldthwaite, Librarian for the Blind at the New York Public Library, 16 Apr 1931: "I shall be very glad to give you the permission for which you ask in your letter, so long as you will see that not only the text itself, but the title, is correctly transcribed, as I note that it is incorrectly given in your letter." To his Spanish translator Angel Flores, 22 Feb 1928: "The title, by the way, is not 'The Wasteland' but 'The Waste Land'. The only exact translation of the title is one which my French translator, Jean de Menasce, discovered, although alas! too late to use in his version—'La Gaste Lande'. This is absolutely the exact equivalent as it alludes to the same mediaeval fiction." (*Letters 4* 63 claims that Menasce changed his original title of *L'Esprit* May 1926, *La terre mise a nu*, to *La terre gaste* when reprinting in *Philosophies*, but *Philosophies* ran only 1924–25.) To Bonamy Dobrée [28 Oct] 1932: "The New England landscape is very beautiful in autumn · · · but the *paysage* is, after all, not humanised. Vermont: a beautiful and austere desert (*gaste lande*) which human beings seem to have scratched at for three hundred years and then given up in despair."

Mario Praz: "Professor Renato Poggioli, in a private conversation, suggested a possible reminiscence of *Inf.* XIV 94, where Crete is called 'un paese guasto'", *T. S. Eliot and Dante* in *The Flaming Heart* (1958) 359; the Temple tr. is "a waste country".

Earlier than *The Love Song of J. Alfred Prufrock*, *Poetry* had published Madison Cawein's *Waste Land* (Jan 1913) and James Stephens's *The Waste Places* (Aug 1914). For William Morris's *The Hollow Land*, see note on the title *The Hollow Men*.

TSE pronounced the title with the emphasis on the third word, as did Valerie Eliot. Recordings by TSE's contemporaries also emphasise the third word.

TSE's Notes, opening paragraph **Miss Jessie L. Weston:** (1850–1928); scholar and translator of Arthurian texts, who since 1894 had published more than a dozen such books. She was a member, along with J. G. Frazer, of the Folk-Lore Society, which TSE joined on 22 Nov 1922 (*Folk-Lore* Dec 1922); see note to title of Part I, *The Burial of the Dead*. **the Grail legend:** *McRae*: "Although the Grail legends vary, and no definitive version exists, all concern a Christian knight—Gawain, Percival, or Galahad—who finds himself in a mysterious, hidden castle. In the castle, the knight has a vision of a grail, a spear, and a beautiful woman. In some versions he gains information about a king who is debilitated by a wound in his thigh. This king, known as the Fisher King, is impotent, and for that reason his land is barren. The various Celtic and medieval European legends from which the Grail legend is derived are similar in kind to both the classical myths of the dying god and to the Mystery traditions described by writers such as Ovid, so many turn-of-the-century scholars such as James Frazer, whose work inspired

Weston, conflated them." At Harvard in 1907–08 TSE studied with William Henry Schofield (see note to *Mr. Apollinax* 6), and used his *English Literature from the Norman Conquest to Chaucer*, in which ch. V, "Romance", includes sections on "The Cycle of Lancelot", "The Quest for the Holy Grail" and "The Death of Arthur". In 1908–09, TSE took William A. Neilson's course "Studies in the History of Allegory". TSE: "mythology is dangerous literary material. It should either be a mythology in which the author more or less believes or a mythology in which some people once believed. A mythology cannot be created for literary purposes out of whole cloth", *Mr. Doughty's Epic* (1916). ***From Ritual to Romance***: when on 16 Aug 1937 TSE promised to send his brother some of his "most valuable books" for Eliot House, Harvard, this was among the dozen: "My original copy, which I used in preparing *The Waste Land*." Pages 138–39 and 142–43 had not been cut open (*Grover Smith* 70). To Bonamy Dobrée, 14 Nov 1957: "Now as to *From Ritual to Romance*: the Committee feel that it ought to have an introduction by some person whose name matters in the world of folklore and Arthurian legend. The book does no doubt date, but it is difficult to think of anyone capable of the right introduction. C. S. Lewis, when consulted about the matter several years ago, made the appalling suggestion that instead of reprinting the book we should merely add quotations from it to the notes to *The Waste Land*. As my own preference would be to abolish the notes to *The Waste Land*, the idea of enlarging them with chunks of Jessie Weston appalled me, but that was the attitude of a scholar and mediaevalist. Can you suggest anyone who would be a suitable introducer in the academic world? I certainly won't want to do it myself because after all I was not concerned with the validity of her thesis, but with the value of the imagery as a spring-board!" No Faber edition appeared. ***The Golden Bough***: Sir James Frazer (1854–1941) published the first edition in two volumes in 1890; the third edition comprised twelve (1906–15). *Jain 1991* 138: "Frazer's work belongs to the evolutionary school of English anthropologists who used the comparative-historical method to demonstrate that religion was a product of the mind and not something that had been supernaturally revealed ··· By tracing the connection between primitive rites and customs and the 'higher' forms of religion, especially Christianity, the anthropologist could show that religion had evolved from primitive to more civilized forms. Existing religious beliefs, similarly, could be traced back to their primordial roots and explained away as survivals of the older superstitions." TSE at Harvard, on Frazer: "This historical investigation, and the comparative work, are what give us such results as we can be said to get. Of the second sort of labour J. G. Frazer is unquestionably the greatest master. No one has done more to make manifest the similarities and identities underlying the customs of races very remote in every way from each other ··· I have not the smallest competence to criticize Dr. Frazer's erudition, and his ability to manipulate this erudition I can only admire. But I cannot subscribe for instance to the *interpretation* with which he ends his volume on the Dying God", *The Interpretation of Primitive Ritual* (1913). TSE recalled this graduate paper in *Savonarola* (1926), remarking that in it he had attempted to show "that *no* interpretation of a rite could explain its origin. For the meaning of the series of acts is to the performers themselves an interpretation; the same ritual remaining practically unchanged may assume different meanings for different generations of performers; and the rite may have originated before 'meaning' meant anything at all." Reviewing Stravinsky's *The Rite of Spring*: "The Vegetation Rite upon which the ballet is founded remained, in spite of the music, a pageant of primitive culture. It was interesting to any one who had read *The Golden Bough* and similar works, but hardly more than interesting ··· Even *The Golden Bough* can be read in two ways: as a collection of entertaining myths, or as a revelation of that vanished mind of which our mind is a continuation", *London Letter* in *Dial* Oct 1921. In an article for *Vanity Fair*, TSE focused on Henry James, F. H. Bradley and Sir James Frazer: "with every fresh volume of his stupendous compendium of human superstition and folly, Frazer has withdrawn in more and more cautious abstention from the attempt to explain ··· It is a work of no less importance for our time than the complementary work of Freud—throwing its light on the obscurities of the soul from a different angle; and it is a work of perhaps greater permanence, because it is a statement of fact which is not involved in the maintenance or fall of any theory of the author's ··· He has extended the consciousness of the human mind into as dark a backward and abysm of time as has yet been explored", *A Prediction in Regard to Three English Authors* (1924), subheaded "Writers Who, Though Masters of Thought, are Likewise Masters of Art". To Frederic Manning, 24 Jan 1927: "I think that I agree with you about Frazer. It is perhaps premature to say what his influence will be; as you suggest, he can be used in more than one way. But I do not think that there is any doubt that his influence will not have been very great, certainly as great an influence, and perhaps wider and more enduring, as that of Freud." To Derek Phit Clifford, 6 Apr 1934: "As for your aversion to *The Golden Bough* as a source of inspiration for poets, I am inclined to think that that period is over and done with." Henry Eliot to TSE, 12 Sept 1935: "It is a point of interest to me, at just what date your views of religion changed from the attitude taken in your blasphemous poems. (I have some doubts as to whether these poems fairly reflect your actual personal attitude at the time). I feel pretty sure that you were not a convert in 1921, remembering your enthusiasm at that time for *The Golden Bough*. I feel equally sure, for other reasons, that you were a convert in 1926. Between these two dates you wrote *The Waste Land*." TSE: "Frazer's great work is somewhat paradoxically named: Frazer was a rationalist, and therefore comes to no conclusions except those which rationalism expects to find", jacket material for *The White Goddess* by Robert Graves (1948).

Unadopted epigraph **"Did he live ··· 'The horror! the horror!'"** | CONRAD: *Heart of Darkness* pt. 3.

> Pound to TSE [24 Jan 1922]: "I doubt if Conrad is weighty enough to stand the citation." TSE [26? Jan]: "Do you mean not use Conrad quot. or simply not put Conrad's name to it? It is much the most appropriate I can find, and somewhat elucidative." Pound [28? Jan]: "Do as you like about my obstetric effort. Ditto re the Conrad; who am I to grudge him his laurel crown."

Valerie Eliot, BBC broadcast 2 Nov 1971: "Pound left the decision to him, so he omitted the passage, a fact which he later regretted." TSE: "horrified past horror", *WLComposite* **544**.

To Grover Smith, 21 Mar 1949: "The connection of *Heart of Darkness* with *The Waste Land* is simply that I had thought of using as the epigraph the dying words of Mr. Kurtz. Ezra Pound demurred at this as he thought that the quotation was not weighty enough for the occasion, and it was after that that the quotation from Petronius came into my mind as being what I wanted." (Hugh Kenner pointed out that Pound's comment on the Conrad epigraph was not made until his letter of [24 Jan], which "implies that he had not seen it before, one indication that this title-page [*ts title*], and incidentally this title [*The Waste Land*], was not part of what he saw in Paris", *Litz ed.* 44.) See Commentary to *The Hollow Men* for the epigraph taken from Conrad as the epigraph for the section-page title, "*Mistah Kurtz—he dead.*"

TSE: "the language which is more important to us is that which is struggling to digest and express new objects, new groups of objects, new feelings, new aspects, as, for instance, the prose of Mr. James Joyce or the earlier Conrad", *Swinburne as Poet* (1920), concluding words. To Alan M. Hollingsworth, 22 Mar 1955: "It is certainly true that I was very deeply impressed at an undergraduate stage by Joseph Conrad's works, or those of his books which had then been published, and that I was particularly impressed by *Heart of Darkness* and the other two stories in the same volume. I am not, however, conscious of any evidences of this fact in the text of *The Waste Land* ··· Incidentally, you are mistaken in thinking that what Mr. Pound urged me to cut out was any reference to Conrad in my notes to *The Waste Land*. What he advised me to cut out was an epigraph from *Heart of Darkness*, which I replaced by one from Petronius. The tentative use of the epigraph in question is the only association between the poem and Conrad's stories of which I am aware." Conrad's *Youth: A Narrative and Two Other Stories* appeared in 1902, the other stories being *Heart of Darkness* and *The End of the Tether*. Alain-Fournier's letter to TSE of 25 July 1911 (*Letters 1*) makes clear that TSE had recommended the volume, and Stravinsky recorded TSE's later saying that *Youth* and *The End of the Tether* were "the finest stories of their kind I know" (*Themes and Conclusions*, 1972, 71). *TSE's books: Bodleian list* (1934) includes both *Youth* and Conrad's *Chance* (1913).

E. M. Forster recalled his first acquaintance with TSE's work in 1917: "Here was a protest, and a feeble one, and the more congenial for being feeble. For what, in that world of gigantic horror, was tolerable except the slightest gestures of dissent? He who measured himself against the war ··· and said to Armadillo-Armageddon 'Avaunt!' collapsed at once into a pinch of dust", *Life and Letters* June 1929 (repr. in *Abinger Harvest*). Forster then turned to *The Waste Land*: "It is just a personal comment on the universe, as individual and as isolated as Shelley's *Prometheus*." TSE to Forster, 10 Aug 1929: "On account of the flattery implied by being written about by you, my opinion is anything but reliable, but I liked the article very much. You are right about the 'horror'; and may be interested to know that the first quotation I chose for *the Waste Land*, before I hit on the more suitable one from Trimalchio, was a sentence from the end of *Heart of Darkness*, which you may remember, ending with Kurtz's words 'the horror . . . the horror'. I only think that you exaggerate the importance of the War in this context. The War crippled me as it did everyone else; but me chiefly because it was something I was neither honestly in nor honestly out of, but the *Waste Land* might have been just the same without the War." On tragedy: "to those who have experienced the full horror of life, tragedy is still inadequate", *Shakespearian Criticism* I. *From Dryden to Johnson* (1934). Alan Ansen recorded an anecdote about TSE told by W. H. Auden, 15 Jan 1947: "A woman who was seated next to him at table said, 'Isn't the party wonderful?' He said, 'Yes, if you see the essential horror of it all'", *The Table Talk of W. H. Auden* (1990). **'The horror! The horror!'**: Laforgue: "qu'on | Te nourrisse, horreur! horreur! horreur! à la sonde" [that they force-feed you, horror! horror! horror! with a tube], *Complainte des Blackboulés* [*Complaint of the Blackballed*].

Epigraph **"Nam Sibyllam ··· ἀποθανεῖν θέλω"**: Petronius, *Satyricon* §48, the words of Trimalchio: "I saw with my own eyes the Sibyl at Cumae hanging in a cage, and when the boys said to her: 'Sibyl, what do you want?' she answered: 'I want to die'" (tr. Michael Heseltine, Loeb, 1913; *WLFacs* 126 has the misspelling "Sybil"). Kenner wrote that "Cage" is a mistranslation of *ampulla*, "bottle" (*Litz ed.* 38); see note to the unadopted title to Part II, "In the Cage". TSE to E. M. Stephenson, 9 July 1944, about proofs of her book: "I think you should check, not only your quotations from other languages, but your translations of them: e.g. I saw with my own eyes the Sibyl at Cumae, hanging in a bottle" (apart from "a celebrated Sibyl", this is the translation given at *Stephenson* 19, and it is not clear whether TSE meant that "bottle" was wrong or that it was right).

TSE's secretary to Stephenson, 18 June 1944: "Mr. Eliot ··· asks me to tell you that the quotation is from *Petronius*—Satyricon 48.8. The speaker, Trimalchio, is drunk. He does not know himself what the explanation is, and says that so far as his poem is concerned it does not matter." From Dante Gabriel Rossetti's Notebook Fragments:

"I saw the Sibyl at Cumae"
(One said) "with my own eye.
She hung in a cage, and read her rune
To all the passers-by.
Said the boys, 'What wouldst thou, Sibyl?'
She answered, 'I would die'."

This is preceded by a prose translation with "jar" for "cage" (*Grover Smith* 69). TSE to Giovanni Mardersteig, 15 June 1961, on the Officina Bodoni edition (1962): "Certainly, if you wish, put 'Petronius, Satiricon' after it. I think it is quoted somewhere by Dante Gabriel Rossetti, but at the same time I must defend my use of the quotation by saying that I have read the Satiricon, or most of it."

Lemprière "Sibyllæ": "The most famous of the Sibyls is that of Cumæ in Italy ··· It is said that Apollo became enamoured of her, and that, to make her sensible of his passion, he offered to give her whatever she should ask. The Sibyl demanded to live as many years as she had grains of sand in her hand, but unfortunately forgot to ask for the enjoyment of the health, vigour, and bloom, of which she was then in possession." (For the sufferings of the long-lived Tiresias, with his "wrinkled dugs", see note to [III] 218.) TSE: "The aged sybil", *Goldfish* IV 28. Sibylla, perhaps named after the character in Beddoes's *Death's Jest-Book*, recurs—sometimes as "Sybilla"—in the *Criterion* pieces by "F. M." and Vivien Eliot's notebooks of the 1920s (Bodleian); see *McCue 2016*.

In Virgil, the Sibyl prophesies the destruction of Rome: "bella, horrida bella | et Thybrim multo spumantem sanguine cerno" [Wars, grim wars I see, and Tiber foaming with streams of blood], *Aeneid* VI 86–87.

At Harvard in 1908–09, TSE took Clifford H. Moore's Latin Literature course "The Roman Novel: Petronius and Apuleius". On 15 Oct 1963, TSE's secretary replied to an enquiry from J. V. Healy: "Mr. Eliot ··· certainly read the Satyricon of Petronius with Professor E. K. Rand when he was at Harvard." TSE's copy of selections from Petronius' *Saturae et Liber Priapeorum Quartum*, ed. Bücheler (1904), has a presentation to Hayward: "W[d] you care to add to your library my Harvard (undergraduate) Apuleius and Petronius?" TSE wrote in it that Petronius is "awfully colloquial". (The volume also contains *Varronis Menippearvm Reliquiae*, but TSE noted: "The only points of similarity between Petr. + Varro. | 1. General form of work. | 2. Insertion of pieces reproducing the manner of previous or contemporary poets. | 3. Parody of tragic style. | 4. Popular speech | Scepticism and irreverence.") *Grover Smith 1974* 303–304: "The *Satyricon* enjoyed celebrity and notoriety in the Edwardian and Georgian eras ··· Michael Heseltine's cautious rendering [for Loeb] ··· presaged a spate of references including Compton Mackenzie's suggestive comparisons, in *Sinister Street* (1913–14), of Petronius's underworld to that of London." In July 1922 a charge of obscenity was brought against Boni & Liveright after their publication of W. C. Firebaugh's idiomatic translation of the *Satyricon* (Gareth L. Schmeling and David R. Rebmann, *Comparative Literature Studies* Dec 1975). TSE: "we think more highly of Petronius than our grandfathers did", *Euripides and Professor Murray* (1920). In the same year, TSE used a quotation from Petronius as one of the two epigraphs to *The Sacred Wood*.

The incorporation of Greek speech within the Latin narrative was not unusual in the classics. When reading the Greek text of Aristotle's *De Anima* in 1914–15, TSE annotated his copy in Latin, English and occasionally Greek. (His acquaintance with languages at various times and in different degrees included French, Italian, German, Latin, Greek, Pali, Sanskrit and perhaps some Portuguese.)

Dedication ***il miglior fabbro***: *Purg* XXVI 115–19:

> "O frate," disse, "questi ch' io ti scerno
> col dito" (ed additò un spirto innanzi)
> "fu miglior fabbro del parlar materno.
> Versi d' amore e prose di romanzi
> soperchiò tutti, e lascia dir gli stolti ···"

["O brother," said he, "this one whom I distinguish to thee with my finger" (and he pointed to a spirit in front) "was a better craftsman of the mother tongue. In verses of love, and prose tales of romance, all he surpassed, and let fools talk".]

A note in the Temple edition reads: "Arnaut Daniel, a distinguished Provençal poet, flourished *ca.* 1180–1200. Among his patrons was Richard Cœur-de-Lion. He was a master of the so-called *trobar clus*, or obscure style of poetry, which revelled, besides, in difficult rhymes and other complicated devices. As such, he was very naturally 'caviare to the general'." Pound in 1915: "And the 'best craftsman' sings out his friend's song, | Envies its vigour ··· and deplores the technique", *Near Perigord* II (included by TSE in Pound's *Selected Poems*, 1928). Pound: "Arnaut was the best artist among the Provençals, trying the speech in new fashions, and bringing new words into writing ··· and when Dante was older and had well thought the thing over he said simply, 'il miglior fabbro'", *Arnaut Daniel* in *Art & Letters* Spring 1920 (included by TSE in Pound's *Literary Essays*). For Pound and Eliot on Arnaut, see note on volume title *Ara Vos Prec* ("*Poems* (1920)"). TSE, in *A Brief Treatise on the Criticism of Poetry* (1920):

> there is no more useful criticism and no more precious praise for a poet than that of another poet:
>
> "Fu miglior fabbro del parlar materno · · ·
> e lascia dir gli stolti · · ·"

Pound had previously added the article *il* when he used Dante's tribute to Arnaut as the title of a paper at the Poets' Club (letter to his father, 12 Jan 1910) which became ch. II of *The Spirit of Romance* (1910): "It was not in a fit of senseless enthusiasm, nor yet because of lost narrative poems of uncertain existence, that Dante praised 'il miglior fabbro' but for 'maestria'." In his next paragraph Pound translated the phrase as "'the better craftsman'". Pound's copy of the American first edition of *The Waste Land* is inscribed "for E. P. | miglior fabbro | from T. S. E. | Jan. 1923" (Texas). The dedication was first printed in *1925* (by which time "fabbro" may have glanced at the name of TSE's new publisher, employer and friend, Geoffrey Faber). *Alexander*: the addition of the article "changes the meaning of the phrase from 'a better workman' or 'the better workman' to 'the best craftsman'." TSE: "the phrase, not only as used by Dante, but as quoted by myself, had a precise meaning. I did not mean to imply that Pound was only that: but I wished at that moment to honour the technical mastery and critical ability manifest in his own work, which had also done so much to turn *The Waste Land* from a jumble of good and bad passages into a poem", *On a Recent Piece of Criticism* (1938). On Pound: "the craftsman up to this moment has never failed", *Ezra Pound* (1946). On the artist as craftsman: "No artist produces great art by a deliberate attempt to express his personality. He expresses his personality indirectly through concentrating upon a task which is a task in the same sense as the making of an efficient engine or the turning of a jug or a table-leg", *Four Elizabethan Dramatists* (1924).

WLComposite unadopted heading at head of Part I and again at head of Part II ***HE DO THE POLICE IN DIFFERENT VOICES***: Valerie Eliot, *WLFacs* notes:

> *Our Mutual Friend* by Charles Dickens, bk. I, ch. XVI, "Minders and Re-Minders". Sloppy is a foundling adopted by old Betty Higden, a poor widow. "'I do love a newspaper' she says. 'You mightn't think it, but Sloppy is a beautiful reader of a newspaper. He do the Police in different voices'." Eliot drew on the novel again for one of his *Practical Cats*. The Rum Tum Tugger who "will do | As he do do" is a deliberate echo of Podsnap in bk. I, ch. XI.

(After publication of the heading in *Gallup 1968*, its source had been identified by Douglas Hewitt, *TLS* 1 Jan 1969.)

TSE to Anne Ridler, 30 Sept 1952: "If you want to hear a really 'dramatic' *Waste Land*, you should listen to the recent long-play recording of *The Waste Land* by Bobbie Speaight, who, like Sloppy, can 'do the police in different woices'. (Hear him come the four cats in the wheelbarrow: pledge you my word, sir, four distinct cats. Damme sire, that's genius. Who said that? About whom? to whom? where? General Knowledge Question)." (For the answers, see *Pickwick Papers* ch. XLIV.) To Enid Faber, 25 Feb 1939, after sending her a "Pickwick Paper" mock examination on Dickens: "At your stage of Pickwickian development, you may well be excused for confusing Lord Mutanhed with Lord Frederick Verisopht, and thinking that 'taking a grinder' had something to do with the Minders (and he do the Police in different voices) in *Our Mutual Friend*." With the police again: "You may remember that Mrs. Cluppins, in the trial of the case of Bardell *v.* Pickwick, testified that 'the voices was very loud, sir, and forced themselves upon my ear'. 'Well, Mrs. Cluppins,' said Sergeant Buzfuz, 'you were not listening, but you heard the voices'", *The Three Voices of Poetry* (1953). Dialogue with the police is heard within the poem's cancelled opening part (*WLComposite* 35–43).

TSE's Dickens was the New Century ed. (1899[–1916]), which apparently he began to collect in 1904 with *Great Expectations* (vol. 14, signed and dated by him); *Our Mutual Friend* (vol. 15) was published in 1908. Aurelia Hodgson's notes on TSE's library (probably 1932) record: "Thackeray set; Dickens in front and in use constantly" (Bryn Mawr). TSE gave Mary Trevelyan a copy of *Pickwick Papers* for Christmas 1955 (Texas; see *Sackton* F50 for inscription). A model for the writer: "the force of character by which Dickens, having exhausted his first inspiration, was able in middle age to proceed to such a masterpiece, so different from his early work, as *Bleak House*. It is difficult and unwise to generalize about ways of composition—so many men, so many ways—but it is my experience that towards middle age a man has three choices: to stop writing altogether, to repeat himself with perhaps an increasing skill of virtuosity, or by taking thought to adapt himself to middle age and find a different way of working", *Yeats* (1940).

Commentary, beginning with notes on WLComposite **1–54**.

Valerie Eliot, BBC broadcast 2 Nov 1971, on the first part of *He Do the Police in Different Voices*:

> a typescript on three leaves, revised in pencil and in ink. It opens with 54 unpublished lines, recounting a night on the town, which appears to be Boston, and is interspersed with snatches of music-hall songs. Gus Krutzsch, the pseudonym Eliot was to adopt on one occasion, is recorded as a member of the party. This passage, lightly cancelled by Eliot, has parallels with the brothel scene in *Ulysses*, for which, Eliot wrote to Joyce [21 May 1921], "I have nothing but admiration; in fact, I wish for my own sake that I had not read it."

Episode XV (Circe) was never serialised, but was published in the Shakespeare & Co. edition of *Ulysses* in Paris in Feb 1922. Joyce wrote to Harriet Shaw Weaver, 23 Apr 1921, asking her to pass it on to TSE, along with episodes XIV (Oxen of the Sun) and XVI (Eumaeus).

Anthony Cronin claimed that "some six or seven years before his death" TSE recalled meditating a long poem as far back as 1918, and said that the effect of reading episodes of *Ulysses* was, "for the time being, ruinous ··· He abandoned his poem. Eventually Pound told him that 'even if the thing has been done in prose it is necessary to do it in poetry also'", *Irish Times* 16 June 1972. (For comparisons with Joyce, see note to [I] 1–4 and William B. Worthen, *Twentieth Century Literature* Summer 1981.)

On 18 Apr 1933, at Harvard, TSE and Theodore Spencer gave a class on *Ulysses* and *Work in Progress* (later *Finnegans Wake*), as part of their course "Contemporary English Literature (1890 to the Present Time)". TSE: "*The Synchronisation.* (cf. Pound and myself). Several periods of time and several planes of reality at once. Strong historical sense, and of everything happening at once. *Not* in Woolf or Lawrence. Contrast historical novel. Gets away from straight narrative. (Mrs. Woolf to some extent). Intensity by association ··· intensity is gained at the expense of clarity.

The real deeper emotional current of life is continuous, but ordinarily is not in full consciousness. Scenery is not described but is felt", *Lecture Notes as Norton Professor* (1933). For "planes of reality", see note to *WLComposite* 545, 548. (To Jack P. Dalton, 26 Sept 1963: "It is true that I was responsible for the publication of *Finnegans Wake* but I never felt any warm enthusiasm for the work. [*Footnote*: No one admires Joyce more than I do—but all one can say is that after *Ulysses* there was nothing else for him to do.]")

THE BURIAL OF THE DEAD

1–54] opening page of *ts1*, deleted by TSE. (For his return to the fray in *Sweeney Agonistes*, see notes to 3 and 43.)

1 **feelers**: similar to OED "snifter" 4: "A (small) quantity of intoxicating liquor, a drink, a 'nip'. *colloq*. (orig. *U.S.*)." OED "feel" 4: "To test or discover by cautious trial". 7: "To perceive by smell or taste", including "To feele how the ale dost tast" (1575). 16: "Used (like *taste, smell*) in quasi-passive sense · · · to produce a certain impression on the senses".

2 **boiled to the eyes**: OED "boiled" 1c: "Intoxicated. *slang*", from 1886. **to the eyes**: OED 2e: "to the limit"; "eye" 2d: "*colloq*. or *slang*. Referring to drinking or drunkenness", including *Twelfth Night* V i: "O he's drunk · · · his eyes were set at eight i'th morning". **blind**: OED 1g: "Short for *blind drunk*". Under a Massachusetts law of 1881, municipalities had a right to an annual ballot on whether to grant licences for the sale of liquor within their borders. Unlike Boston, Cambridge voted for Prohibition in 1886 and renewed it (partly because of church campaigns) every year until 1918. The following January, the Eighteenth Amendment to the Constitution prohibited the manufacture, sale, or transportation of intoxicating liquors throughout the US. Alcohol continued to be available in private clubs, however, using a ticket system which was not technically sale. Prohibition proved to be of little use except to criminals and to corrupt policemen, and it was abolished in 1933. Charlotte C. Eliot's biography of TSE's grandfather emphasises his moral zeal, and quotes a newspaper report: "Dr. Eliot may not desire to be police commissioner, and the suggestion of his name may be meant as a joke, but we sincerely wish the joke to become a reality. Forty-eight hours after Dr. Eliot assumed the reins of the police department there would be no gambling houses in St. Louis." He had written to the Senate and House of Representatives of Missouri, "asking that prohibition, as a constitutional amendment be submitted to the vote of the people at the next general election". On brothels and whether they should be acknowledged to exist and be regulated, he concluded "that the 'social evil', considered as a sin and crime, should be treated like all other sins and crimes, to be 'prohibited by law and prevented as far as possible by the conjoined action of legal and moral force'", *William Greenleaf Eliot* (1904) ch. XII, "Social Reform". For Prohibition and "religion is like drink", see note to [II] 149.

3 **Don't you remember that time**: "What about that poker game? eh what Sam?" *Sweeney Agonistes: Fragment of a Prologue* 131.

4 **Silk Hat Harry**: cartoon character from 1910, drawn by Tad Dorgan. Conrad Aiken to TSE, 23 Feb 1913: "Write and tell me about yourself, your latest meditations, and how Silk Hat Harry demeans himself." TSE: "One of the low

on whom assurance sits | As a silk hat on a Bradford millionaire", *The Waste Land* [III] 233–34.

7 **I'm proud of all the Irish blood that's in me**: *WLFacs* notes: "'Harrigan' from the musical play *Fifty Miles from Boston* (1907) by George M. Cohan, American composer and comic actor: 'Proud of all the Irish blood that's in me | Divil a man can say a word agin me'."

7–8 *variant* **Meet me in the shadow of the watermelon Vine | Eva Iva Uva Emmaline**: *WLFacs* notes: "Eliot has adapted lines from two songs: 'Meet me pretty Lindy by the watermelon vine' (from *By the Watermelon Vine*, words and music by Thomas S. Allen, 1904), and 'Meet me in the shade of the old apple tree, Ee-vah, I-vah, Oh-vah, Ev-a-line!' (from *My Evaline*, by Mae Anwerda Sloane, 1901)."

9 **Bengal lights**: *WLFacs* notes: "On page 550 of Connorton's *Tobacco Brand Directory of the United States for 1899*, Bengal Lights are listed as both cigarettes and cheroots". For fireworks, see note to [I] 76.

10–11 *variant* **Tease. Squeeze lovin & wooin | Say Kid what're y' doin'**: *WLFacs* notes: "'Tease, squeeze, lovin' and wooin' | Oh babe, what are you doin'?' *The Cubanola Glide* (words by Vincent Bryan, music by Harry von Tilzer, 1909)." TSE: "'*Throw your arms around me—Aint you glad you found me*'", *The smoke that gathers blue and sinks* 18 (and note). TSE to Enid Faber, 21 Feb 1938, while writing *The Family Reunion*: "Your suggestion that the Eumenides should do a strip tease act is novel, and I believe has box-office possibilities." To Ronald Duncan (*c.* 1940?): "It's what you can do behind the audience's back that counts. Remember they have an appetite for strip-tease", quoted by Duncan, *Religion and Drama* in *Guardian* 2 Mar 1960.

11 **drum**: OED 9e: "*slang.* A house, lodging-place, or other building; esp. (*a*) *U.S.* a drinking-place, saloon, night-club; (*b*) a brothel, low dive". The sequence of thought is unclear.

12, 31, 46 **but rough ··· Get me a woman ··· the cabman**: TSE's second epigraph to the Clark Lectures: "I want someone to treat me rough. | Give me a cabman." with "*Popular song*", *The Varieties of Metaphysical Poetry* 40. See notes to *WLComposite* 34 and [II] 128–30.

14–15 **Blew in to the Opera Exchange | Sopped up some gin, sat in to the cork game**: *WLFacs* notes: "When Eliot was an undergraduate at Harvard, he attended melodrama at the Grand Opera House in Washington Street, Boston, and after a performance he would visit the Opera Exchange (as he recalled later in life, although that name cannot be traced in records of the period) for a drink. The bartender, incidentally, was one of the prototypes of Sweeney." For a report of TSE on "the bartender at the Opera Exchange ··· where he had gathered with friends in his Harvard student days, circling Champagne corks on the table in a fortune-telling game", see note to the title *Sweeney Erect*. **Blew in to**: *Chambers Slang Dictionary* "blow in": "to arrive unexpectedly and casually", from late 19th century, *U.S.* L. M. Hastings in *London Mercury* Apr 1920: "blew in here with Willy Braid for lunch".

16 **"The Maid of the Mill"**: *WLFacs* notes: "Words by Hamilton Aïdé, music by Stephen Adams: 'Do not forget me! Do not forget me! | Then sometimes think

of me still, | When the morn breaks, and the throstle awakes, | Remember the maid of the mill!'"

23–28 **kept a decent house ··· what with the damage done ··· reputation ··· a clean house:** OED "house" 11: "house of ill (evil) fame (repute): a disreputable house; *esp*. a brothel". TSE: "Mrs. Turner intimates | It does the house no sort of good", *Sweeney Erect* 39–40 and see note. **And the reputation the place gets, on account of a few bar-flies, | I've kept a clean house for twenty years, she says:** 2 *Henry IV* II iv, Mistress Quickly: "I am in good name, and fame, with the very best: shut the door, there comes no swaggerers here: I have not lived all this while to have swaggering now." (Mistress Quickly calls the Boar's Head her "house".)

24 **Buckingham Club:** Aiken recalled meeting TSE "at Buckingham and Brattle Hall dances" during their Harvard years (*March & Tambimuttu eds*. 20).

27 **bar-flies:** OED: "*slang* (orig. and chiefly *U.S.*) A person who frequents bars; a habitual drinker", from 1906: "Three dull-witted bar-flies—thick, beer-soaked toughs, such as hang about the East Side bar-rooms".

34 *variant* **treated me white:** Wallace Irwin: "Say, will she treat me white, or throw me down", *The Love Sonnets of a Hoodlum* (1902) I. Harry Leon Wilson: "If you treat me white I'll treat you white", *Ruggles of Red Gap* (1915) 28.

35 **fly cop:** OED: "*slang* ··· *U.S.*, a detective, a plain-clothes policeman". TSE contested an in-house report at Faber on a description of underworld activity: "Pringle is wrong again: the U.S.A. bull is often just as described. If Pringle had ever been battered about the bean by a South Boston fly cop he would know better", *"The Rambling Kid"* by Charles Ashleigh, reader's report (1930).

36 **committing a nuisance:** OED "nuisance" 2f: from 1863, "Commit no Nuisance". (Euphemism for urinating or defecating in public.)

37–38 **I'm sorry, I said, | It's no use being sorry, he said; let me get my hat:** "I take my hat: how can I make a cowardly amends | For what she has said to me?" *Portrait of a Lady* II 29–30. **It's no use being sorry, he said:** Arnold Bennett: "It's no use being sorry if you persist in doing it", *The Old Wives' Tale* (1908) bk. II, ch. 4 (Shawn Worthington, personal communication).

43 **particular friends of mine:** "We want you to meet two friends of ours", *Sweeney Agonistes: Fragment of a Prologue* 118.

45 *variant* **Gus Krutzsch:** Valerie Eliot on the publication of *Song* ("The golden foot I may not kiss or clutch") in *Tyro*, Spring 1921, under its other title:

> Eliot may have used a pseudonym when *Song to the Opherian* was published in Wyndham Lewis's magazine because there were two signed articles [of his] in the same number, but his choice of "Gus Krutzsch" is interesting. In *The Sewanee Review* (Special Issue, Winter 1966), Mr. Frances Noel Lees traces the influence of Petronius' *Satyricon* on *The Waste Land*, and observes that "Gus Krutzsch" is "remarkably reminiscent of the English of 'Encolpius', namely 'the Crutch, or Crotch'." Professor J. P. Sullivan writes that the name Encolpius "like most of the other names in the *Satyricon*, has point . . . and a Peacockian translation might be Mr. Encrotch, an appropriate choice for the protagonist of a predominantly sexual story" (*The 'Satyricon' of Petronius*, 1968).
>
> *WLFacs* notes

August Rodney Krutzsch was one year ahead of TSE at school (*Smith Academy Catalogue*, 1899–1900, Washington U.; *Stayer*). Joseph Wood Krutch (1893–1970), who pronounced his name *Krootch*, was a literary friend of Mark Van Doren. TSE: "I have been reading ··· *Was Europe a Success?* by Joseph Wood Krutch ··· a thoughtful *littérateur* of considerable ability ··· to be regarded with the gravest suspicion by anybody with any positive beliefs", *A Commentary* in *Criterion* Apr 1936. For Petronius, see note to epigraph. In *Charles Whibley* (1931), TSE quoted Whibley on the modern Encolpius: "He haunts the bars of the Strand, or hides him in the dismal alleys of Gray's Inn Road" (*Studies in Frankness*, 1912, 38). **Gus**: "crutch portions and gussets respectively being concave", *US Patent Office Official Gazette* 28 June 1927.

47 **We all go the same way home**: the music hall song *We All Go the Same Way Home* by Harry Castling and C. W. Murphy (1911) ends with the police making arrests (Shawn Worthington, personal communication).

50–51 **little Ben Levin the tailor, | The one who read George Meredith**: *WLFacs* notes: "George Meredith (1828–1909) was the grandson of a remarkable Portsmouth tailor whom he depicted in his novel *Evan Harrington*. When Eliot's father died in 1919, he wrote to his mother: 'I wanted you more for my sake than yours—to sing the Little Tailor to me.' Perhaps the childhood memory of the song his father sang to him prompted the reference." *Worthen* 247: a ballad sometimes called *The Three Rogues*: "The miller he stole the corn | And the weaver he stole yarn | And the little tailor he stole broadcloth | For to keep these three rogues warm". The poem on the page facing the opening of *Preludes* in *Others Anthology (1917)* was Jeanne D'Orge's *The Little Tailor Meditates*. TSE: "the fact is that most of Meredith's profundity is profound platitude", *Studies in Contemporary Criticism* I (1918). "And the suspicion is in our breast that Mr. Whibley might admire George Meredith", *The Sacred Wood* 36. Henry Eliot noted from TSE's American lectures: "dislikes Meredith", *Excerpts from Lectures 1932–1933* (additional leaf). For Meredith see note to [I] 40–41, headnote to *Cousin Nancy* and note to *Entretien dans un parc* 34.

54 **So I go out to see the sunrise, and walked home**: "So in our fixed confusion we persisted, out from town", concluding *So through the evening, through the violet air*. "At which I started; and the sun had risen", *Little Gidding* II 67–96, *first venture in verse*, likewise concluding.

Notes to published poem begin.

I. THE BURIAL OF THE DEAD

Title ***The Burial of the Dead***: TSE's library included the liturgical *Service for The Burial of the Dead*, printed and published by Douglas Pepler, 1922 (Valerie Eliot collection). W. H. F. Basevi's *The Burial of the Dead* was reviewed by R. R. Marett in *Folk-Lore* 30 June 1920, immediately preceding Eleanor Hull's review of Jessie Weston's *From Ritual to Romance*. (Marett's *The Threshold of Religion*, 1909, which TSE read at Harvard, appears to have stirred TSE's interest in cave paintings. As founder of Oxford's Department of Social Anthropology in 1914, Marett had been president of the Folk-Lore Society, which TSE joined at its meeting at University College London in Nov 1922.)

The burial of the dead of the Great War was symbolically marked on Armistice Day, 11 November 1920, when "a vast concourse of the nation" lined the route of a casket brought from France and laid in the Tomb of the Unknown Warrior in Westminster Abbey. A similar ceremony was conducted in France. See note to [I] 71 (and for Victory parades in London and Paris in 1919, see headnote to *Coriolan* I: *Triumphal March*).

The opening and closing of *The Burial of the Dead* have affinities with TSE's April poem *Interlude in London*, with its "hibernate · · · sudden rains · · · garden plots · · · spring". For Nathaniel Wanley on "the burial of the dead", see headnote to *Ash-Wednesday* II.

[I] 1–42] Rupert Brooke on a friend's reaction to the Declaration of War in 1914: "A youth ran down to them with a telegram: 'We're at war with Germany. We've joined France and Russia.' My friend ate and drank · · · His mind was full of confused images, and the sense of strain. In answer to the word 'Germany,' a train of vague thoughts dragged across his brain · · · the wide and restful beauty of Munich; the taste of beer; innumerable quiet, glittering *cafés*; the *Ring*; the swish of evening air in the face, as one *skis* down past the pines · · · long nights of drinking and singing and laughter · · · certain friends; some tunes; the quiet length of evening over the Starnberger-See · · · an April morning · · · Children · · · in Munich", *Letters from America* (with a Preface by Henry James, 1916) 173–74 (John Finley, *Matthiessen* 92–93). TSE to Cleanth Brooks, 15 Mar 1947: "it is quite possible that I read this letter, and I cannot say that it was not at the back of my mind, but actually this particular passage [of the poem] approximates more closely to a recollection of a personal experience of my own than anything else, and indeed is as nearly as I could remember a verbatim report." TSE was himself in Germany, in Marburg, at the outbreak of the Great War. On 26 July 1914, in a comic letter from there, he tried to reassure Eleanor Hinkley: "Here I am, safely out of harm's way." His next surviving letter, postmarked 22 Aug, tells her "I have just got to London after being five days on the route. The Germans treated us royally, but we had to stay in Marburg two weeks without any outside communication, and did not feel very much at ease."

[I] 1 **April:** *Hayward*: "April the month of rebirth. Cf. 'This Birth was | Hard and bitter agony for us, like Death, our death · · · I should be glad of another death', *Journey of the Magi* 38–43'. Cf. *ἀποθανεῖν θέλω* [I want to die]—the Sibyl's wish. Sacrificial death may be an awakening to life." Rebirth after the supreme sacrificial death suffered in April or March: the date of the Crucifixion is disputed. In his copy of *The Golden Bough* (one-volume ed., repr. 1925, 360), TSE marked a sentence about the traditional date of 25 Mar: "The inference appears to be inevitable that the passion of Christ must have been arbitrarily referred to that date in order to harmonise with an older festival of the spring equinox." *The Oxford Companion to the Year* records that Scaliger chose 23 Apr; that modern writers generally adopt either 3 or 7 Apr; and that several relate the partial lunar eclipse of 3 Apr AD 33 to the "darkness over the whole land from the sixth to the ninth hour", Mark 15: 33, Luke 23: 44. *Easter: Sensations of April* (see note to the title) recalls Laforgue, *Simple agonie* 17, "se crucifie".

St. Thomas Becket having suffered martyrdom, Chaucer's pilgrims make their way to Canterbury, "The holy blisful martyr for to seke":

Whan that Aprille with his shoures soote
The droghte of March hath perced to the roote,
And bathed every veyne in swich licour
Of which vertu engendred is the flour;
Whan Zephirus eek with his sweete breeth
Inspired hath in every holt and heeth
The tendre croppes, and the yonge sonne
Hath in the Ram his halve cours yronne,
And smale foweles maken melodye,
That slepen al the nyght with open ye
(So priketh hem nature in hir corages);
Thanne longen folk to goon on pilgrimages.
General Prologue to *The Canterbury Tales* 1–12

Vivien Eliot to Charlotte Eliot, 14 Dec 1920: "April is a charming month. I always love Chaucer's 'Whanne that Aprile, with his showres sote'—I expect I've spelt it all wrong!! But you know what I mean." TSE: "These are Spring days in London—feeling of something struggling & pushing underneath", pencil jotting (Bodleian, c. 624 fol. 121). **April is the cruellest month**: TSE to Natalie Clifford Barney, 11 May 1923: "April is indeed the cruellest month, and the fact follows the word." *The Family Reunion* I ii: "Is the spring not an evil time, that excites us with lying voices?" April falls in the "hungry gap", between the end of winter vegetables and the summer crops, when what is left of the old food (such as tubers) must be buried in the earth for next season's feeding. In the 7th century BC, Alcman wrote of "spring ··· When everything flowers | And nobody has enough | To eat", frag. 20, tr. Guy Davenport (Saskia Hamilton, personal communication). For the story of the nightingale in George Gascoigne's *The Complaynt of Phylomene*, which opens "In sweet April", see note to [II] 98–104. Nightingales go south in the winter, returning to Britain in April with their song of the cruel fate of Philomel.

Conundrum: "Why do ladies talk least in February?" Answer: "Because it is the shortest month", *A Choice Collection of Riddles and Conundrums* by Peter Puzzlewell (1835). (F. T. Prince's opening: "February is the shortest month, and good | For this too", *The Inn*, 1954.)

[I] 1–4 **April ··· cruellest ··· dead ··· mixing ··· Memory ··· roots**: Gautier: "mêle ··· souvenue ··· l'avril ··· Sous l'herbe ··· mêlions ··· si cruel ··· mortel", *Clair de Lune Sentimental* 8–24 (*Ricks 1993*). **April ··· breeding ··· dead land ··· stirring ··· spring**: *Murder in the Cathedral* I: "the springtime fancy ··· waking a dead world". **breeding ··· out of the dead land ··· Dull roots**: Joyce: "A barren land, bare waste ··· the dead sea ··· weedless, sunk deep in earth ··· cities of the plain: Sodom, Gomorrah, Edom. All dead names. A dead sea in a dead land ··· The oldest people. Wandered far away over all the earth, multiplying, dying, being born everything ··· Desolation", *Ulysses* episode IV (Calypso) in *Little Review* June 1918 (Shawn Worthington, personal communication). TSE: "This is the dead land", *The Hollow Men* III 1. "Blooming at this season toward the dead land", *A Song for Simeon* 7 *variant*. **stirring | Dull roots with spring rain**: "sudden rains | Softening last year's garden plots", *Interlude in London* 5–6 (see note to [I] 71–73).

[I] 1–6 **breeding | ··· mixing | ··· stirring | ··· covering | ··· feeding**: "bearing | ···

restoring | ··· wearing", *Ash-Wednesday* IV 12–14. "the 'auditory imagination' is the feeling for syllable and rhythm, penetrating far below the conscious levels of thought and feeling, invigorating ··· sinking ··· returning ··· bringing ··· seeking", *The Use of Poetry and the Use of Criticism* 118–19. (I. A. Richards: "This possibility of being enjoyed at many levels is a recognised characteristic of Elizabethan Drama", *Principles of Literary Criticism* ch. XXVII; scored by TSE. See note to *Mandarins* 3 12, "different planes".)

[I] 1–2, 71, 74 **breeding | Lilacs out of the dead land ··· That corpse you planted ··· Dog:** *Hamlet* II ii: "if the sun breed maggots in a dead dog, | Being a good kissing carrion" (famously emended by Warburton to "God, kissing carrion").

[I] 2–3 **Lilacs ··· mixing | Memory and desire**: on Paris in 1910–11: "I am willing to admit that my own retrospect is touched by a sentimental sunset, the memory of a friend coming across the Luxembourg Gardens in the late afternoon, waving a branch of lilac, a friend who was later (so far as I could find out) to be mixed with the mud of Gallipoli", *A Commentary* in *Criterion* Apr 1934 ("rain", 4; "Earth", 6). For the friend, Jean Verdenal, see note on the volume dedication to *Prufrock and Other Observations*. Whitman on the death of Lincoln (on 15 Apr 1865): "When lilacs last in the dooryard bloom'd, | And the great star early droop'd in the western sky in the night, | I mourn'd, and yet shall mourn with ever-returning spring", *When Lilacs Last in the Dooryard Bloom'd* 1–3. TSE to William Turner Levy, 27 Dec 1954: "it takes my mind back to a steel engraving of a portrait of Lincoln, which hung in our front hall when I was a child. My grandfather had known him slightly." See *Preludes* II 1, "Now that lilacs are in bloom", and note. **mixing | Memory and desire**: Swinburne: "Mixed each in other, or as mist with sea | Mixed, or as memory with desire", *To Victor Hugo* 30–31. James Thomson: "thoughts that raged with memory and desire", *Weddah and Om-el-Bonain* II xix (*Crawford* 38). *The Cocktail Party* II: "shuffling memories and desires". Charles-Louis Philippe: "Un homme qui marche porte toutes les choses de sa vie et les remue dans sa tête. Un spectacle les éveille, un autre les excite. Notre chair a gardé tous nos souvenirs, nous les mêlons à nos désirs" [A man walks carrying with him all the properties of his life, and they churn about in his head. Something he sees awakens them, something else excites them. For our flesh has retained all our memories, and we mingle them with our desires] *Bubu de Montparnasse* ch. I (*Grover Smith* 307); see note to *The Love Song of J. Alfred Prufrock* 4–6 and headnote to *Preludes* III.

[I] 2–5 **dead ··· stirring ··· spring ··· Winter:** "F. M.": "One's soul stirs stiffly out of the dead endurance of the winter—but toward what spring?" *Letters of the Moment* I (1924) (with "hyacinths" and "the essential spring—spring in winter, spring in London").

[I] 3–4 **stirring | Dull roots ··· spring:** *The Family Reunion* I ii: "The cold spring now is the time | For the ache in the moving root" (Harold E. McCarthy, *Philosophy East and West* Apr 1952).

[I] 5 **Winter kept us warm:** Webster: "The ant, the field-mouse, and the mole | To rear him hillocks that shall keep him warm", *The White Devil* V iv. See [I] 71–75 and note (*Drew* 100). *Snow* in *Atlantic Monthly* Feb 1862: "The wool on Sheep keeps them warm in the Winter season. So when the back of the Ground is covered with Snow, it keeps it warm ··· tho' it is itself cold, yet it makes the

Earth warm." TSE to Ottoline Morrell, 20 Aug 1936: "the winter is to me a warm and anaesthetic season".

[I] 6–7 **feeding | A little life with dried tubers:** Swinburne: "Draining a little life from the barren breasts of love", *Hymn to Proserpine* 20. James Thomson: "Our Mother feedeth thus our little life, | That we in turn may feed her with our death", *To Our Ladies of Death* st. 29 (*Grover Smith* 72). (OED "tuber": b. "*Anat.* A rounded projecting part"; etymologically from Latin for "swelling". TSE: "wrinkled female breasts · · · wrinkled dugs", [III] 219, 228.)

[I] 8–17] *Hayward*: "The scene is Munich and its environs." TSE to Edward Forbes, 22 May [1911]: "After the middle of June I shall go to Munich for some time, to study German." Valery Larbaud: "Et l'odeur du foin frais coupé, comme en Bavière | Un soir, après la pluie, sur le lac de Starnberg" [And the scent of fresh-cut grass, as in Bavaria, one evening, after a shower, by the lake at Starnberg], *Nevermore* (1913).

[I] 8–17 **the Starnbergersee · · · In the mountains** ([I] 8 *variant*: **Königssee**): the change of location from one lake to the other may have been prompted by the story of Ludwig II of Bavaria. He and his physician were found drowned in the Starnbergersee (Lake Starnberg), in June 1886, the day after he had been deposed and confined to the grounds of Berg Castle (see Anthony Hecht, *Melodies Unheard*, 2003, 122–30). A lifelong devotee of Wagner (for whom, see notes to [I] 31–34, [I] 42), "Mad King Ludwig" had funded the completion of the opera house at Bayreuth, and spent 17 years building the neo-Gothic Schloss Neuschwanstein on a peak in the Alps, where he loved to walk. Much of the rich decoration of this castle shows legendary scenes from Wagner's operas, notably the Grail symbolism of *Parsifal*. For his swan-boat at Linderhof, see note to [III] 281–85. After the Franco-Prussian War of 1870–71, at a ceremony in Versailles' Hall of Mirrors, Wilhelm I of Prussia was proclaimed Kaiser of a newly united German Empire, which absorbed Bavaria. In 1878, at Herrenchiemsee, Ludwig began constructing a replica of Versailles, including the Hall of Mirrors. The terms of Germany's settlement at that time required France to pay an indemnity of five billion francs, which John Maynard Keynes later called "the only precedent of any importance" for reparations after the Great War (memorandum to the Board of Trade by Keynes and W. J. Ashley, 2 Jan 1916; *Collected Writings* XVI (1971) 315). For Keynes on the Versailles Treaty of 1919, see note to [III] 277–78, 290–91, the Rhine-daughters' song. **In the mountains, there you feel free:** translation of "Auf den Bergen wohnt die Freiheit", the first line of the loyalist song *Das König-Ludwig-Lied* (1886), lamenting the death by water of Ludwig II (Eva Hesse, *T. S. Eliot und "Das Waste Land"*, 1973; her letter, *TLS* 21 June 1974). Milton: "The mountain nymph, sweet Liberty", *L'Allegro* 36. Wordsworth: "The freedom of a mountaineer", *To the Highland Girl of Inversneyde* (in *The Golden Treasury*). TSE to Dorothy Pound, 22 May 1921: "In October I shall be ready for a little mountain air, after I have finished a little poem which I am at present engaged upon" (*The Waste Land*).

[I] 9–18 **a shower of rain · · · the arch-duke's, | My cousin's · · · Marie, hold on tight · · · go south in the winter:** Countess Marie Larisch, *My Past* (1913): "we were overtaken by a storm, and in a few moments we were soaked to the skin" (57); "'Now Marie, let me hold your hand tight'" (171); "in summer one's worries fly before the advent of the bright new day, whereas in winter-time they are not so easily banished. 'O for the sunshine and warmth of the South!' I said to myself" (228) (G. L. K. Morris, *Partisan Review* Mar–Apr 1954; *Variety* Mar–Apr 1954). Marie Larisch, a cousin of Ludwig II, was the unwilling confidante of Crown Prince Rudolph of Austria (the archduke, her cousin) and his 17-year-old mistress Marie (Mary) Vetsera, with whom the Crown Prince committed suicide at Mayerling in 1889. No recollection of sledding appears in the memoirs, but similarities between the Countess's book and the poem include Empress Elizabeth's reaction to meeting Queen Victoria: "Ah · · · I'm glad it's over" (100; TSE [III] 252); an incognito visit to a woman who reads cards (109), and Ludwig's love of Wagner and his *Parsifal* (135) (C. J. Ackerley, personal communication). *WLFacs* notes "The assumption was that Eliot must have read the book, but in fact he had met the author (when and where is not known), and his description of the sledding, for example, was taken verbatim from a conversation he had with this niece and confidante of the Austrian Empress Elizabeth."

[I] 10 **the Hofgarten**: in the centre of Munich, constructed 1613–17.

[I] 12 **Bin gar keine Russin, stamm' aus Litauen, echt deutsch**: [Not a Russian, I'm from Lithuania, genuinely German]. *Moody* 357: "A 'real German', from Lithuania, in Munich, would be a stateless person. Lithuania had been for a long period before 1917 subject to Russia; the German claim to it began · · · with the brief occupation of 1917." The feminine "keine" indicates a female speaker.

The Cocktail Party I i, ALEX: "She never misses anything unless she wants to." CELIA: "Especially the Lithuanian accent." JULIA: "Lithuanian? Lady Klootz?" PETER: "I thought she was Belgian." ALEX: "Her father belonged to a Baltic fam— | One of the *oldest* Baltic families | With a branch in Sweden and one in Denmark." TSE to Dr. Alphonse Sesplaukis, 10 Sept 1958: "The mention of Lithuania in *The Waste Land* does refer to a lady who was daughter of a Baltic baron of German origin and Russian nationality. As for the reference to Lithuanian in *The Cocktail Party*, he [Alexander] was merely thinking that there were several distinguished families which had branches in countries on both sides of the Baltic Sea."

To Eleanor Hinkley, 8 Sept [1914], of Ann Van Ness: "she hasn't really a German mind at all, but quite American." To Henry Eliot, 13 Dec 1921, from Lausanne: "I am very much better, and not miserable here—at least there are people of many nationalities, which I always like, and I like talking French better than English · · · I am certainly well enough to be working on a poem!" In a sketch by Vivien, TSE added: "The Cambridge man · · · thought ~~it~~ things were awfully jolly when he found that Mike was really a *German*. He loved the party. It was quaint. It was international" (c. 624 fol. 88). See note to [I] 18.

[I] 12, 14 **echt deutsch · · · My cousin's**: E. M. Forster: "their cousin, Fräulein Mosebach, who remembers all the time that Beethoven is 'echt Deutsch'", *Howards End* (1910) ch. 5. (Rupert Brooke: "wholly English", *Letters from America*, the paragraphs quoted in note to [I] 1–42.) **echt**: "those poets whom we can agree to be *echt metaphysisch*", *The Varieties of Metaphysical Poetry* 48 (Clark Lecture I). Pound three times praises passages as "echt" in annotating TSE's drafts of *The Waste Land* (see note to [III] 187–202).

[I] 13 **archduke's**: stressed on the first syllable in TSE's recordings 1946 and 1947. The assassination of Archduke Franz Ferdinand precipitated the Great War.

[I] 18 **go south in the winter:** *The Family Reunion* I i, Ivy: "I have always told Amy she should go south in the winter. | Were I in Amy's position, I would go south in the winter. | I would follow the sun" ··· Violet: "Well, as for me, | I would never go south, no definitely never, | Even could I do it as well as Amy: | England's bad enough, I would never go south, | Simply to see the vulgarest people." To Sydney Schiff, 12 Jan 1920: "Vivien got run down largely through nursing me, and she is not at all well. I wish she was in the south." To Sydney Waterlow from Lausanne, 19 Dec 1921: "I shall not stay in this *carte-postale colorée* country any longer than necessary—its chief recommendation is that it is full of foreigners—American countesses, Russian princesses, Rumanians, Greeks and Scandinavians, Czecho counts, Belgian punks etc. I am not quite certain whether I shall immediately rejoin Vivien in Paris, or go south first ··· I am trying to finish a poem—about 800 or 1000 lines." (OED "punk" *n.*[1]: *Obs.* or *rare arch.* "A prostitute".)

[I] 19–20 **What are the roots that clutch, what branches grow | Out of this stony rubbish:** Ibsen, tr. William Archer: "What are those trunks and tree-roots | That grow from the ridge's clefts?" *Peer Gynt* II iv (*Smidt* 79).

[I] 20 **Son of man:** *TSE's Notes* refer to Ezekiel 2: 1: "Son of man, stand upon thy feet, and I will speak unto thee." *Grover Smith* 73: "He thinks of Ezekiel, the 'son of man,' chosen to turn the Israelites in their captivity back to God, and hence of Christ, the 'Son of man,' whose temples, like his own, are now in ruins." Also Ezekiel 37: 1–2, quoted in note to *Ash-Wednesday* II (A. D., *N&Q* 19 Aug 1950) and Ezekiel 40: 4 (see note to *Choruses from "The Rock"* IX 1–2). OED "son" 5: "son of man: a. One of the human race ··· b. *spec.* Jesus Christ."

[I] 22 **A heap of broken images:** Ezekiel 6: 4: "And your altars shall be desolate, and your images shall be broken." Pope: "the last image of that troubled heap", *Epistle to Cobham* 45. Hawthorne, on an excavation in Italy: "that heap of forlorn fragments ··· a heap of worthless fragments", *The Marble Faun* ch. XLVI (Andrew Souter, *N&Q* Sept 2009). Edward Carpenter: "heaps of broken glass and old bones and shoes and pots and pans in blind alleys", *Towards Democracy* (1912 ed.) 17 (Tony Brown, *RES* Aug 1983, as also later notes here on Carpenter). TSE: "A heap of broken barrows", *First Caprice in North Cambridge* 7.

[I] 23 **the dead tree gives no shelter, the cricket no relief:** *TSE's Notes* refer to Ecclesiastes 12: 5: "fears shall be in the way, and the almond tree shall flourish, and the grasshopper shall be a burden, and desire shall fail: because man goeth to his long home, and the mourners go about the streets."

[I] 25 **shadow under this red rock:** Isaiah 32: 2: "And a man shall be as an hiding place from the wind, and a covert from the tempest; as rivers of water in a dry place, as the shadow of a great rock in a weary land" (A. D., *N&Q* 19 Aug 1950). **red rock:** to Colin Still, 13 May 1930: "Some of the symbolism I have used was of course intentional; some was unintentional; and some symbolism is used (as of 'red rock') which has been called to my attention by critics, which so far as I know was wholly spontaneous."

[I] 25–30 **There is shadow ··· handful of dust:** derived from *The Death of Saint Narcissus* 1–7.

[I] 26–27 **(Come in ··· red rock) | And I will show you:** "Come in under the shadow of this gray rock, | And I will show you", *The Death of Saint Narcissus* 2–3, where it was without the parentheses, which are at odds with the surrounding syntax

(*Ricks* 152–53). On Harold Joachim: "In working on the text of Aristotle he taught me, incidentally, the importance of punctuation. Some readers of my verse have maintained that this is a subject of which I am profoundly ignorant: so I would assure them that I could not have violated punctuation so outrageously, had I not devoted some attention to its study", *Christ Church, Oxford*, Speech (1948). TSE to Paul Elmer More, 28 Oct 1930: "Why, my dear More, are you so foolish as to discuss seriously with a mere ignoramus like myself questions of philosophy and theology, and then go for me on the one subject on which I know more than almost anyone living. I am quite aware that I am a minor romantic poet of about the stature of Cyril Tourneur, that I have little knowledge and no gift for abstract thought; but if there is one thing I do know, it is how to punctuate poetry." For "the *absence* of punctuation marks", see headnote to *Four Quartets*, 9. TSE ON *FOUR QUARTETS*. **Come in under**: "Come in under the little bat's wing, with the small flare of the firefly", *Coriolan* II. *The Difficulties of a Statesman* 47 *variant*. **under the shadow of this red rock**: *Hayward*: "'And this stone all men call the Grail ··· As children, the Grail doth call them, | 'neath its shadow they wax and grow', *Parzifal*" (referring to Jessie Weston's translation of Wolfram von Eschenbach's "Knightly Epic" bk. IX).

[I] 27 **something different from either**: *The Cocktail Party* I i: "to be with Celia, that was something different | From company or solitude." **either**: pronounced *eye-ther* in TSE's recordings.

[I] 28–29 **Your shadow at morning striding behind you | Or your shadow at evening rising to meet you**: Beaumont and Fletcher: "How all the good you have is but a shadow, | I' the morning with you, and at night behind you | Past and forgotten", *Philaster* III ii (*Grover Smith* 73). **rising to meet you**: *Purg* XXI 133 (the half-line preceding the epigraph to *Prufrock and Other Observations*): "Ed ei surgendo" [And he, rising]. The shade of Statius rises after stooping before the shade of Virgil.

[I] 30 **fear in a handful of dust**: see the Sibyl and her sand in note to epigraph. Conrad: "He was afraid of that penetrating faltering fear that seems, in the very middle of a beat, to turn one's heart into a handful of dust", *The Return* in *Tales of Unrest* (1898) (A. D. in *N&Q* 8 Dec 1951, with other echoes of the story). Conrad: "the heat of life in the handful of dust", *Youth* (1902; title story of the volume containing *Heart of Darkness*); see note to *Little Gidding* II 78. For Conrad, see note on the epigraph on the section-title page for *The Hollow Men*. Donne: "what's become of man's great extent and proportion, when himself shrinkes himself, and consumes himself to a handful of dust?" *Devotions*, Meditation IV (Genesis 3: 19: "dust thou art, and unto dust shalt thou return"). Nicholas Ferrar: "A handful of dust cast among Bees stilleth their greatest tumults", *The Story Books of Little Gidding*: *Being The Religious Dialogues Recited in the Great Room, 1631–32* (1899). Tennyson: "Long dead! | And my heart is a handful of dust", *Maud* II [v] 240–41; "Two handfuls of white dust, shut in an urn of brass!" *The Lotos-Eaters* 113.

[I] 31–34 ***Frisch weht ··· Wo weilest du?***: *TSE's Notes* refer to the song of the Young Sailor which opens *Tristan und Isolde* I: [Fresh blows the wind towards the homeland. My Irish child, where are you lingering?]; see [I] 42 and note. For TSE and performances of *Tristan*, see note to *Opera* 1. In letters to TSE in 1911–12, Verdenal expressed overwhelming enthusiasm for Wagner, and especially for

Tristan (see headnote to *Opera*). The first British publication of *The Waste Land* was immediately preceded in *Criterion* Oct 1922 by T. Sturge Moore's *The Story of Tristram and Isolt in Modern Poetry* I. TSE: "In spite of a taste for Wagner's music, I find myself bored by the various marital shifts and changes of the Liszts the Wagners and their congeners", *"Cosima Wagner"* by Count Richard du Moulin Eckart, reader's report (1930). After tea with TSE on 10 Oct 1954, Robert Halsband recorded his having said he was "glad he doesn't have to sit through the *Ring* again" ("Memorandum", Columbia U). ***Frisch weht der Wind***: Wagner specifies that the sailor's song is "heard from a height, as if from the masthead, or from off-stage".

85 **schwebt:** (= floats, Ger.) transferred from the lines of Donner, the God of Thunder, in *Das Rheingold* sc. IV: "Schwüles Gedünst schwebt in der Luft" [A sultry haze floats in the air] (Oliver Soden, personal communication).

[I] 33 ***Irisch***: pronounced (correctly) *Earish* in TSE's recordings. TSE took courses in German at Harvard in 1906–07 and 1907–08.

[I] 35 **first:** advice to the Swedish translator, Erik Mesterton, 20 Jan 1932: "You are right about the word 'first'. One might have said 'd'abord' in French but certainly 'pour la première fois' would have been more natural, and I understand the impossibility of putting it in one word."

89–90 *Pound's annotation*: "? ? Marianne".] *WLFacs* notes: "Pound is not certain, but thinks he may have been referring to Tennyson's *Mariana*. It is definitely not a reference to Miss Marianne Moore." Identified by Barbara Everett (*RES* Feb 1980) as the heroine of the unfinished *La Vie de Marianne* by Marivaux. TSE: "But it is the novels, *Marianne* and *Le Paysan Parvenue*, that deserve the most attention", *Marivaux* (1919).

[I] 36–38 **hyacinth girl ··· hyacinth garden ··· Your arms full, and your hair wet:** *Lemprière* on Hyacinthus: "greatly beloved by Apollo and Zephyrus. He returned the former's love, and Zephyrus ··· resolved to punish his rival. As Apollo ··· played at quoits with his pupil, Zephyrus blew the quoit ··· upon the head of Hyacinthus, and he was killed with the blow. Apollo was so disconsolate at the death of Hyacinthus that he changed his blood into a flower, which bore his name and placed his body among the constellations." Poe: "Thy hyacinth hair, thy classic face", *To Helen* 7; and in prose, "Her hair ··· in curls like those of the young hyacinth", *The Assignation*. (For this story of Poe's, see notes to [II] 83–88 and [II] 85–95, and headnote to *Burbank with a Baedeker: Bleistein with a Cigar*.) TSE: "the smell of hyacinths across the garden | Recalling", *Portrait of a Lady* II 41–42. "Her hair over her arms and her arms full of flowers", *La Figlia Che Piange* 20.

[I] 38–40 **I could not | Speak, and my eyes failed, I was neither | Living nor dead:** Sappho, bk I: 2: "When I look on you ··· my speech comes short or fails me quite ··· my eyes grow dim ··· and death itself seems not very far away", tr. J. M. Edmonds (*Lyra Graeca* vol. I, Loeb, 1922). TSE on the *Ode to Aphrodite* (bk. I 1): "A poem like the great ode of Sappho, however acute its observation and statements of the feelings of a lover, is not metaphysical", *The Varieties of Metaphysical Poetry* 294 (Turnbull Lecture III).

[I] 39 **my eyes failed:** Webster, *The Duchess of Malfi* IV ii, FERDINAND: "Mine eyes dazzle". For Webster's scene, see note to [II] 117–23.

[I] 39–40 **I was neither | Living nor dead:** *Inf.* XXXIV 25: "Io non morii, e non rimasi vivo" [I did not die, and did not remain alive] (*Grover Smith* 308). Wordsworth: "Such seemed this Man, not all alive nor dead", *Resolution and Independence* 64 (Shawn Worthington, personal communication). TSE: "I was always dead, | And still alive, and always something other", *Little Gidding* II 46–47 *variant*. To Middleton Murry [mid-April? 1925]: "I have deliberately died—in order to go on with the outward form of living—This I did in 1915."

[I] 40–41 **dead · · · the heart of light, the:** Meredith: "Death · · · the heart of light, the", *Hymn to Colour* 43–45.

[I] 41 **the heart of light, the silence:** *Hayward*: "Cf. *Burnt Norton*", referring to "quietly, quietly, | The surface glittered out of heart of light" (I 36–37) and "answered light to light, and is silent" (IV 9). Also, *Burnt Norton* variant after the closing lines of V: "Light of light || Gone" (see Textual History). In the ts of Jean de Menasce's translation, alongside "au coeur la lumière, le silence", TSE wrote: "query—coeur de la lumière du silence ? Is this not permissible (cf. 'Coeur des ténèbres')." **the heart of light:** *Paradiso* XII 28: "del cor dell'una delle luci nuove | si mosse voce" [from out the heart of one of the new lights there moved a voice] (*Grover Smith* 308). Daubeny's preface to Lancelot Andrewes, *Seventeen Sermons* [1887]: "the rays of truth from its heart of light flash from every facet". Conrad (title): *Heart of Darkness*.

[I] 42 ***Oed' und leer das Meer*:** *TSE's Notes* refer to *Tristan und Isolde* III 24: [Empty and waste the sea]. Quoted, without attribution, in Nietzsche's *The Birth of Tragedy* §21 (C. J. Ackerley, personal communication). *Hayward*: "The watchman's words to Tristan reporting that Isolde's ship is nowhere in sight. The lovelessness of the waste land." *Grover Smith* 76: "The desolation in this second quotation used by Eliot contrasts with the fresh breeze, a portent of happy love, in the first" ([I] 31–34). ***leer · · · Meer*:** pronounced (correctly) *layr* and *mayr* in TSE's recordings.

[I] 43–59] This passage about Madame Sosostris, like *Sweeney Agonistes* I. *Fragment of a Prologue*, resembles Mina Loy's description of a "card-teller" in *At the Door of the House*:

> "You see these three cards
> But here is the double Victory
> And there is an elderly lady
> Ill   in whom you are concerned
> This   is the Devil
> And these two skeletons
> Are mortifications · · ·
> And this ace of spades turned upside-down
> 'With respect'
> Means   that some man
> Has   well you know
> Intentions   little honourable · · ·
> And look
> Here are you
>   And here is he
>   In life and thought
> At the door of the house"

Loy's poem appeared in *Others: An Anthology of the New Verse (1917)* ed. Alfred Kreymborg along with Loy's *Human Cylinders* (for which see headnote to *The Hollow Men*) and TSE's *Preludes* and *Rhapsody on a Windy Night*.

The ancestry of Madame Sosostris is uncertain. TSE to Masuru Otaké, 6 Apr 1934: "So far as I know there are no literary sources whatever for Sosostris or Phlebas or Mrs. Equitone. To the best of my knowledge both names and persons were pure inventions but as you are a student of Coleridge, you will know how large a part memory plays in invention" (referring to *The Road to Xanadu*, 1927, John Livingston Lowes's account of the sources of Coleridge's poetry; see note to [I] 48). Frazer on a Hittite carving: "Herodotus thought that the figure represented the Egyptian king and conqueror Sesostris", *The Golden Bough* V (*Adonis Attis Osiris* I) 185 (*Vickery* 254). Beddoes: "Here's wine of Egypt ... to wash Sesostris' throat", *Death's Jest-Book* V iv 126–28. In Aldous Huxley's *Crome Yellow* (1921), Mr. Scrogan dresses as a "Bohemian hag" to play the part of "Sesostris, the Sorceress of Ecbatana" (*Grover Smith* 76). TSE: "*Crome Yellow* was a coherent book; and its characters, being copied from life to the best of the author's ability, were at least simulacra of human beings", *Misogyny over the Weekend* (1930). To Grover Smith, 10 Mar 1952: "Although I was unaware of the identity of name between my fortune-teller and the role assumed by Mr. Scrogan, I did read *Crome Yellow* on its appearance, and I should think it was almost certain that I borrowed the name from Mr. Huxley without being aware of the fact." However, the typescript, *ts1*, was produced on TSE's dilapidated typewriter, for which his brother substituted his own newer one in Aug 1921, and *Crome Yellow* was not published until Nov 1921. *Stead* 361–63 records Helen Gardner's suggestion that TSE had heard the name in conversation or heard Huxley read a chapter. *Grover Smith 1996* 84: "The Sesostris scene in *Crome Yellow* may have antedated the novel itself in some different context, before Huxley, in Italy between the beginning of June and the early part of August 1921, composed his sixty thousand-word work as published that fall. The preceding year two tentative sketches for *Crome Yellow* had been published, *One Sunday Morning* in *Art and Letters* and *A Country Walk* in *Coterie*."

TSE's Notes deny familiarity with "the exact constitution of the Tarot pack". Much later, TSE recalled an occasion on which he and Huxley were speakers: "I have another reason to remember that dinner. One of my neighbours subsequently invited me to dine at her house; and to her I owe my introduction to the Tarot pack, which I turned to account in *The Waste Land*. I pay this tardy tribute of thanks. But I should not like my present reader to draw the inference that this lady was the original of my Madame Sosostris—a wholly fictitious character!" *Aldous Huxley* (1965). To his Aunt Susie (Mrs. Hinkley), 28 Dec 1931, he wrote of an "elderly member of the Lycaeum Club who explained the Tarot cards to me" (believed to have been in 1921). To William Turner Levy, 28 Sept 1956: "I am sorry to hear that *The Waste Land* has caused the rifling of Tarot Packs. Still, the use of such cards for divination is certainly a black art forbidden to the faithful" (for legal sanctions, see note to [I] 58–59). A Faber secretary to Michael Sayers, 19 Mar 1958: "Mr. Eliot has returned from Italy and has seen your letter · · · his only knowledge of the Tarot pack was many years ago through dining at the house of a lady, whose name he has now forgotten, when she showed him the pack and told him something about its use. He has never, since then, examined the Tarot pack or studied any literature on the subject."

See note to [V] 373, "Falling towers". TSE to Herbert Read, 28 Dec 1929: "I shall have to consult Morley on Monday about Wheen's dream. We may have to visit Madame Sosostris to clear it up."

[I] 43 **Madame ··· clairvoyante:** *Fowler*: "As a prefix to a foreign lady's name ··· *Madame* is right", as opposed to appellation, common noun or prefix (citing "*Madam Fortune*"). OED "clairvoyant" B *n.* 2: "Often treated as Fr. with fem. *clairvoyante*." TSE originally typed "clairvoyant". He pronounced it as French in his recordings but apparently without sounding the *-te*.

[I] 43–45 **Madame Sosostris ··· known to be the wisest woman in Europe:** Henry James: "Madame Merle ··· is one of the most brilliant women in Europe", *The Portrait of a Lady* ch. XIX; "'Honestly, my dear boy, she's perhaps the most remarkable woman in Europe.' ··· Hyacinth was preoccupied with the idea of meeting the most remarkable woman in Europe ··· the most remarkable woman in Europe", *The Princess Casamassima* ch. XII ("the hyacinth girl", [I] 36; for "Hyacinth garden" [I] 37, with a capital, see Textual History). Kipling's *Plain Tales from the Hills* is dedicated to "The Wittiest Woman in India". **clairvoyante, | Had a bad cold:** to Eleanor Hinkley, 23 Mar 1917: "Mrs Howells is a spiritualist, and wanted to give me mental treatment for a cold in the head" (*Crawford 2015* 271).

[I] 46 **wicked:** the first citation for OED 3b, "Excellent, splendid; remarkable. *slang* (orig. *U.S.*)", is from F. Scott Fitzgerald, *This Side of Paradise* (1920).

[I] 46 *TSE's Notes* **the Hanged God:** Frazer's chapter "The Hanged God" includes the story of Marsyas, which "may well reflect a ritual practice of flaying the dead god and hanging his skin upon the pine as a means of effecting his resurrection", *The Golden Bough* V (*Adonis Attis Osiris* I) 293.

[I] 47 **Phoenician Sailor:** *Hayward*: "The type of fertility god, cast annually into the sea to symbolize the death of summer. Tarot cards were used to foretell the rising of the waters." See note to [IV] 312.

[I] 48 **(Those are pearls that were his eyes. Look!):** *The Tempest* I ii, Ariel's song. FERDINAND: "The ditty does remember my drowned father." But his father Alonzo is not among the drowned. The brackets were an addition by TSE. He also added three different exclamatory monosyllables, "Look!" (here), "See!", in the opening line of *Those are pearls that were his eyes. See!* ("Uncollected Poems"), and "Yes!" (*WLComposite* **180**). To look closely at "eyes" is to see "yes". (Whereas the imperative "Look!" is presumably addressed to an observer, "See!" might be an entreaty to the pearls that were eyes.) "Think."—also entreating the faculties of another—likewise ends a line, [II] 114.) On Ariel's song, see headnote to *Dirge*, and note to *Burbank with a Baedeker: Bleistein with a Cigar* 5–6. *Richard III* I iv: "fearful wrecks ··· heaps of pearl, | Inestimable stones, unvalu'd jewels, | All scatter'd in the bottom of the sea. | Some lay in dead men's skulls, and in the holes | Where eyes did once inhabit, there were crept— | As 'twere in scorn of eyes—reflecting gems". For TSE and the submarine world, see note to *Mr. Apollinax* 11–15. Shelley: "the holes he vainly sought to hide, || Were or had been eyes", *The Triumph of Life* 187–88, from the passage which TSE said "made an indelible impression upon me", *What Dante Means to Me* (1950); see note to [I] 60–63. On *Kubla Khan*: "The imagery of that fragment, certainly, whatever its origins in Coleridge's reading, sank to the depths of Coleridge's feeling, was saturated, transformed there—'those are pearls that were his eyes'—and brought up into daylight again", *The Use of Poetry and the Use of Criticism* 146 (*Drew* 40); for "saturation", see "A Beginner in 1908", 2. SYMONS AND LAFORGUE, and note to *Burbank with a Baedeker: Bleistein with a Cigar* 7–12. "Daffodil bulbs instead of balls | Stared from the sockets of the eyes!" *Whispers of Immortality* 5–6.

[I] 49 **Belladonna**: [beautiful lady]. *Grover Smith 1949*: "Belladonna is not only deadly poison (*Atropa belladonna*) and one of the three Fates by virtue of her name, but also (what is to the point here) the lily *Amaryllis belladonna*, a symbol of resurrection like Eliot's hyacinths, violets, and roses." **the Lady of the Rocks**: Leonardo da Vinci's altarpiece *Our Lady of the Rocks* is in the Louvre. Pater refers to it as "the *Madonna of the Rocks*" (see note to [V] 338). Pater on Leonardo's *La Gioconda* (the Mona Lisa): "She is older than the rocks among which she sits; like the vampire, she has been dead many times, and learned the secret of the grave; and has been a diver in deep seas, and keeps their fallen day about her; and trafficked for strange webs with Eastern merchants", *Studies in the History of the Renaissance* ch. VI (*Grover Smith 1949*) ("Smyrna merchant", [III] 209). TSE on Pater: "Compare this whole passage about La Gioconda with the last chapter of Ecclesiastes, and see the difference between direct suggestiveness by precise reference, and the meretricious suggestiveness of vague literary association", *Prose and Verse* (1921). **Rocks**: to his Swedish translator Erik Mesterton, 20 Jan 1932: "You can give either the equivalent for 'rock' or for 'cliff'. There is no particular intention of referring to either use of the word 'rock' in the poem. Here it is definitely 'sea-rocks', i.e. a siren."

[I] 50 **The lady of situations**: *Situation*, cancelled title of *Entretien dans un parc* (see note).

[I] 51 **the man with three staves**: the Tarot pack has a "three of wands".

[I] 52 **one-eyed ··· card**: *Hayward*: "i.e. seen only in profile on the playing-card." Pope: "Th'embroider'd *King* who shows but half his Face", *The Rape of the Lock* III 76. On 26 May 1947, replying to an audience question: "the artist must do more than just state the problem, as many modern writers do. Merely stating it often entails a definite and uncompromising ambiguity that is like a playing card; either way you look at it, the face is the same" (*Mattingly*).

[I] 54 **forbidden to see**: Weston on the Grail: "It is so secret a thing that no woman, be she wife or maid, may venture to speak of it", *From Ritual to Romance* ch. X (Ronald Tamplin, *American Literature* Nov 1967).

[I] 55 **death by water**: Frazer: "in the Emmenthal they say, 'This day will have three persons; one must perish in the air, one in the fire, and the third in the water'", *The Golden Bough* XI 27 (*Vickery* 264).

[I] 56 **crowds of people, walking round in a ring**: Gérard de Nerval: "First of all I imagined that the persons collected in the garden (of the madhouse) all had some influence on the stars, and that the one who always walked round and round in a circle regulated the course of the sun ··· My own part seemed to me to be the re-establishment of universal harmony by Kabbalistic art, and I had to seek a solution by evoking the occult forces of various religions", *Le Rêve et la Vie* (*Symons* 28–29). Wilde: "I walked, with other souls in pain, | Within another ring", *The Ballad of Reading Gaol* I iv (Archie Burnett, personal communication).

110 (I John saw these things, and heard them): Revelation 22: 8 (*WLFacs* notes).

[I] 57 **Mrs. Equitone:** Appleplex has on file a letter with "some damaging but entertaining information about Lady Equistep", *Eeldrop and Appleplex* II (1917).

[I] 58–59 **I bring the horoscope myself: | One must be so careful these days:** Brian Diemert: "Astrologers and other 'fortune tellers' (crystal gazers, tarot readers, and the like) were frequently arrested and brought before the courts on charges of fraud ··· In 1921, for instance, the *Times* of London mentions no fewer than five such cases ··· the mails were being used illegally", *Journal of Modern Literature* Autumn 1998. The Witchcraft Act of 1735 made it illegal to claim that a human being had magical powers, the last conviction coming in 1944. TSE: "We are, at least officially, prohibited from consulting the oracles, and from having our horoscopes cast in the Tottenham Court Road", *Charleston, Hey! Hey!* (1927). "converse with spirits, | Describe the horoscope, haruspicate", *The Dry Salvages* V 1–3. In a reader's report: "This book consists entirely of messages received from persons in the Life Beyond ··· There are three types of communicator about which difficulties might arise: 1. The Blessed Virgin ··· 2. King Arthur ··· 3. Christina Rossetti. I am not sure about the legal position of messages from authors whose works are still in copyright", *"A Book of Preparation for the Coming Light"* by R. M. T., reader's report (1949). For "in these days one cannot look far enough ahead", see letter to John Hayward, 23 June 1940, quoted in headnote to *Four Quartets*, 3. COMPOSITION. **One must be so careful these days:** *Hayward*: "A typical bourgeois catch-phrase, expressive of undefined fears and suspicions of her social inferiors." *The Green Book Magazine* (1913): "One must be so careful nowadays. If it isn't a dictagraph, it's a movie camera." TSE: "Who had always been so careful while her mistress lived", *Aunt Helen* 13.

[I] 60 **Unreal City:** *TSE's Notes* quote Baudelaire: "Fourmillante cité, cité pleine de rêves, | Où le spectre en plein jour raccroche le passant" [O swarming city, city full of dreams, where ghosts accost the passers-by in broad daylight!], *Les Sept vieillards* [*The Seven Old Men*] 1–2. In *What Dante Means to Me* (1950), TSE represented Baudelaire as having used the capital "C" that was in fact his own ("O City city", [III] 259 and note):

> His significance for me is summed up in the lines:
>
> *Fourmillante Cité, cité pleine de rêves,*
> *Où le spectre en plein jour raccroche le passant . . .*
>
> I knew what *that* meant, because I had lived it before I knew that I wanted to turn it into verse on my own account.

Baudelaire continues: "Un matin ··· Un brouillard sale et jaune inondait tout l'espace" [One morning ··· a dirty yellow fog flooded the whole of space]. For Baudelaire, see note to [I] 76. Bertrand Russell: "After seeing troop trains departing from Waterloo, I used to have strange visions of London as a place of unreality. I used in imagination to see the bridges collapse and sink, and the whole great city vanish like a morning mist. Its inhabitants began to seem like hallucinations, and I would wonder whether the world in which I thought I had lived was a mere product of my own febrile nightmares. [*Footnote*: I spoke of this to T. S. Eliot, who put it into *The Waste Land*]", *Autobiography* II (1968) 18. TSE to Alan Wood, 28 July 1956: "You say that some of the ideas in *The Waste Land* were possibly suggested by talks I had with Bertrand Russell. I cannot for the life of me imagine what ideas might have been suggested in this way, and am not sure that there is anything in *The Waste Land* that could properly be called an idea." **Unreal:** see note to [V] 376.

[I] 60–63 **Unreal City · · · A crowd flowed · · · I had not thought death had undone so many:** *TSE's Notes* quote *Inf.* III 55–57, [so long a train of people, that I should never have believed death had undone so many]. TSE underlined III 56–57 of the Italian in the copy his mother had given him. TSE: "For in Dante's Hell souls are not deadened, as they mostly are in life", *Dante* (1920). "Readers of my *Waste Land* will perhaps remember that the vision of my city clerks trooping over London Bridge from the railway station to their offices evoked the reflection 'I had not thought death had undone so many'; and that in another place I deliberately modified a line of Dante by altering it—'sighs, short and infrequent, were exhaled.' And I gave the references in my notes, in order to make the reader who recognized the allusion, know that I meant him to recognize it, and know that he would have missed the point if he did not recognize it · · · *The Triumph of Life*, a poem which is Shelley's greatest tribute to Dante, was the last of his great poems. I think it was also the greatest", *What Dante Means to Me* (1950); after quoting Shelley's 176–205, TSE adds "Well, this is better than I could do." (Earlier in the poem Shelley has: "All hastening onward, yet none seemed to know | Whither he went, or whence he came, or why | He made one of the multitude · · · Of their own shadow walked, and called it death", *The Triumph of Life* 47–59.) *Inf.* XV 16–19: "we met a troop of spirits, who were coming alongside the bank; and each looked at us, as in the evening men are wont to look at one another under a new moon". TSE scored XV 16–21 in the Italian. Paul Elmer More: "so numerous · · · this vision was given to me, and the hurrying eager multitude of the street were but shadows of humanity, unreal things seeking an unreal good. Who shall say that the unseen dead do not flock through our cities, leading over again in shadow-wise their former lives? Who shall say that to some they are not visible, jostling against the living amid the crowded streets in the very light of day?" *The Great Refusal* 127. (For More's title, see note to [I] 69; for this description, see note to *Little Gidding* II 37–38.)

Tennyson: "never an end to the stream of passing feet · · · But up and down and to and fro, | Ever about me the dead men go", *Maud* II [v] 249, 255–56. Kipling: "This is a great and terrible world. I never knew there were so many men alive in it", *Kim* ch. III (Alberto Manguel, *A Reading Diary* 49). Joyce: "How many. All these here once walked around Dublin", *Ulysses* episode VI (Hades) in *Little Review* Sept 1918 (probably the reason for Pound's annotation "J.J." in *ts1*; see next note. TSE: "so many · · · such a press of people. | We hardly knew ourselves that day, or knew the City · · · so many crowding the way. | So many", *Coriolan* I. *Triumphal March* 3–7. On D. H. Lawrence: "most people are only very little alive · · · Against the living death of modern material civilisation he spoke again and again, and even if these dead could speak, what he said is unanswerable", *After Strange Gods* 60.

114–22 *Pound's annotation*: "J.J."] Valerie Eliot wrote that "exhaled" in 64 "reminded Pound of Joyce's *Ulysses*, but Eliot's Notes direct the reader to *Inf.* IV 25–27" (*WLFacs* notes); "Evidently the word reminded Pound of Joyce · · · but its use here stems from the days when Eliot was a master at Highgate Junior School and helped to keep order in the gymnasium. He loved to imitate the way in which the boys mimicked the cockney instructor when he told them to 'Inhale' and 'Exhale'", BBC broadcast 2 Nov 1971 (briefly reported *Listener* 18 Nov). However, Joyce's only use of the word in *Ulysses* is very different ("The beagle ··· exhales a putrid carcasefed breath", episode XV, Circe). For a closer correspondence between TSE and Joyce, see previous note.

[I] 61–65 **Under the brown fog of a winter dawn ··· each man fixed his eyes before his feet:** *Inf.* IV 10–12: "Oscura, profonda era, e nebulosa, | tanto che, per ficcar lo viso al fondo, | io non vi discernea alcuna cosa" [It was so dark, profound, and cloudy, that, with fixing my look upon the bottom, I there discerned nothing] (*Friend*). *Inf.* XXXIV 15: "altra, com'arco, il volto a' piedi inverte" [another, like a bow, bends face to feet]. TSE: "under the oppression of the silent fog", *The Dry Salvages* I 34. **brown fog**: Wilde: "Where, if not from the Impressionists, do we get those wonderful brown fogs that come creeping down our streets, blurring the gas-lamps and changing the houses into monstrous shadows?" *The Decay of Lying*. TSE: "brown waves of fog", *Morning at the Window* 5. For "the brown air", in Dante, see note to [III] 220–23. For "Un brouillard sale et jaune" in Baudelaire, see note to [I] 60.

[I] 62 **A crowd flowed over London Bridge**: *Oxford Dictionary of English Proverbs*: "London Bridge was made for wise men to go over, and fools to go under", noting of Old London Bridge that "The danger to light wherries in shooting the bridge was appreciable." The bridge that stood for five and a half centuries until the 1820s was one of the wonders of Europe. On 29 May 1660 it was especially crowded as the newly returned Charles II rode in a parade of thousands into the City (Gordon Home, *Old London Bridge*, 1931, 229–31). Edward Carpenter (of "New" London Bridge): "I see the solid flow of business men northward across London Bridge in the morning, and the ebb at evening", *Towards Democracy* (1912 ed. 56). TSE's *Baedeker* 122–23: "It is estimated that, in spite of the relief afforded by the Tower Bridge, 22,000 vehicles and about 110,000 pedestrians cross London Bridge daily, a fact which may give the stranger some idea of the prodigious traffic carried on in this part of the city. New-comers should pay a visit to London Bridge on a week-day during business hours to see and hear the steady stream of noisy traffic." **flowed over**: to Virginia Woolf [3? Sept 1923], on his proofreading of the Hogarth Press edition: "I see one dreadful oversight for which I owe apologies: p. 7, I left *under* London Bridge instead of *over*!" However, the surviving proof has here two blank pages (Berg), so he may not have seen this line in proof. He corrected it in the Hogarth Press copy he presented to his mother (Houghton). (TSE, writing as Charles Augustus Conybeare: "much water has flowed under many bridges since the days of my dear old Oxford tutor, Thomas Hill Green", *Egoist* letters column Dec 1917. To Hayward, 4 Aug 1940: "Well John many pontoons have flowed over the river since I last saw you." To Richard Jennings, 25 Feb 1941: "A lot of bridges have flowed etc. since.")

[I] 62–65 **London ··· undone ··· man ··· eyes:** Byron: "they had all been undone | But for the maker, Mr Mann, of London", *Don Juan* II xxix. Shelley: "Hell is a city much like London— | A populous and smoky city; | There are all sorts of people undone", *Peter Bell the Third* 147–49 (S. Viswanathan, *Ariel: A Review of International English Literature* 2, 1971). TSE: "Ill done and undone, | London ··· the Thames ··· Water", *The Builders* 1–7. "Richmond and Kew | Undid me",

[III] 293–94. For the rhyme "undone / London", see note to *Ash-Wednesday* I 1, 26, 30. Housman: "London streets ··· many an eye ··· Undone with misery, all they can | Is to hate their fellow man", *A Shropshire Lad* XLI 21–30 (Mark Thompson, personal communication).

[I] 63–68 **I had not thought death had undone so many. | Sighs, short and infrequent, were exhaled ··· down King William Street ··· final stroke of nine:** *TSE's Notes* quote *Inf.* IV 25–27: "Quivi, secondo che per ascoltare, | non avea pianto, ma' che di sospiri, | che l' aura eterna facevan tremare" [Here there was no plaint, that could be heard, except of sighs, which caused the eternal air to tremble]. *Hayward*: "Those who lived without praise or blame, without hope of death, were wretched people who were never alive—The crowd is the morning crowd of commuters coming into the City from the suburbs on the south side of the Thames, business men, clerks, typists, etc. King William Street is the street running from the north side of the bridge into the heart of the City. A typical London scene during the morning 'crush-hours'. City workers are due at their offices by 9am, hence the reference to St. Mary Woolnoth's bell. This church, on the corner of King William and Lombard streets, designed by Nicholas Hawksmoor, a disciple of Wren, survived the Blitz of 1940–41 and is one of the finest of the remaining City churches. T. S. Eliot worked for a time in the City in the Foreign Department of Lloyds Bank." **death ··· Sighs, short and infrequent, were exhaled:** *Paradise Lost* XI 146–48: "yet this will prayer, | Or one short sigh of human breath, upborne | Even to the seat of God." TSE: "death | Short sighs", *In silent corridors of death* 1–2. "short gasps, inhaled at each momentary recovery", *Hysteria.* **had undone so many:** Thomas Heywood: "Pox o' this use, that hath undone so many", *The English Traveller* III ii (*Stephen Matthews* 104). **down King William Street | To where Saint Mary Woolnoth kept the hours:** in his *Baedeker*, TSE ticked a paragraph under the heading "6. London Bridge. The Monument. Lower Thames Street", beginning: "*King William Street*, a wide thoroughfare with handsome buildings, leads S.E. from the Bank to London Bridge. Immediately on the left, at the corner of Lombard Street, is the church of *St. Mary Woolnoth*, erected in 1716, by *Hawksmoor*." Thomas Kyd was baptised in the church in 1558 (*The Works* ed. Frederick S. Boas, 1901, xv; see [V] 431). TSE's office at Lloyds was at "75, Lombard Street, first floor—Information Department—opposite clock of St. Mary Woolnoth" (to Richard Aldington, 4 Jan 1923). **kept the hours:** also [V] 383. OED "keep" 13: "To observe by attendance, presence, residence, performance of duty, or in some prescribed or regular way ··· Also, in weakened sense, to keep regular or proper ··· hours." Mackenzie E. C. Walcott, the Victorian editor of Thomas Plume's *Life and Death of John Hacket* (1675, 1865), explained that the devout "kept the hours, and compiled devotions for them".

121–22 *Pound's annotation*: "*Blake*. Too ~~old~~ often used"] *WLFacs* notes: "This is a general, not a specific reference to Blake, and by starting to write 'old', Pound may have had 'fashioned' in mind." F. T. Prince suggested, *TLS* 11 May 1973, that Pound was referring to "Till into the high dome of Paul's they like Thames' waters flow", *Holy Thursday* 4 (*Songs of Innocence*). Valerie Eliot replied, *TLS* 18 May: "I put before Pound several passages from Blake, including that suggested by Professor Prince, in case he might have had at least one in mind. But he dismissed them."

[I] 68 **dead sound**: "A phenomenon which I have often noticed", according to *TSE's Notes*; his own hours at Lloyds Bank were 9.15 a.m. to 5.30 p.m. and until lunchtime on Saturdays (speech to the London Library, reported *The Times* 2 July 1958). To J. M. Aguirre, 23 Nov 1956: "that is the way the clock of St. Mary Woolnoth sounded to me when I worked for several years in an office on the first floor just across Lombard Street from the Church". North's Plutarch on the Parthians' use of kettle drums: "they all made a noise everywhere together, and it is like a dead sounde ··· The Romans being put in feare with this dead sounde, the Parthians straight threw the clothes and coverings from them that hid their armour", Life of Marcus Crassus (ed. W. H. D. Rouse, Temple Classics, 1898–99) VI. TSE on George Wyndham's Plutarch essay: "He appreciates the battles, the torchlight, the 'dead sound' of drums, the white, worn face of Cicero in his flight peering from his litter", *A Romantic Aristocrat* (1919) (*Grover Smith* 308); "torchlight ··· faces", [V] 322.

[I] 69 **one I knew ··· Stetson**: "One that I knew", *The Death of the Duchess* II 30. *Hayward*: "Cf. *Inf.* III 58–60. 'After I had distinguished some among them, I saw and knew the shade of him who made, through cowardice, the great refusal.' There is no special significance in the name 'Stetson'. It is simply a typical name for a business man." (Hayward's French note adds: "Cf. le chapeau 'Stetson', marque americaine de coiffures à l'usage des hommes d'affaires respectables.") The Temple *Inferno* gives the lines as: "After I had recognised some amongst them, I saw and knew the shadow of him who from cowardice made the great refusal." (Dante may have meant Celestine V, who became Pope in 1294 at the age of 80 but resigned five months later. For Paul Elmer More's book *The Great Refusal*, see notes to [I] 60–63, [IV] 314 and [V] 359.) TSE to E. M. Stephenson, 27 May 1943: "I notice that you are inclined to identify Stetson with Brunetto Latini. This is an association which had not occurred to my own mind." (See note to *Little Gidding* II 33–47.) To Fergus Fitzgerald, 6 June 1940: "Stetson here does not refer to anybody in particular. With some of my names, it is true, I have had a definite person of my acquaintance in the background, though in most cases the identification would not help in the least to further understanding of the passage. But in this case I simply meant any other superior bank clerk: a person in a bowler hat, black jacket and striped trousers. It would never have occurred to me that anyone would think that this referred to Ezra Pound, who does not dress like that, and who would look rather out of place in King William Street." Valerie Eliot quoted this, *TLS* 11 May 1973, adding: "Since my husband's death I have learnt that there was an American banker called Stetson who worked in London and Copenhagen, so it is possible that T. S. E. heard his name in the course of his duties at Lloyds Bank. At a date not yet determined the two men had a friend in common, E. McKnight Kauffer." In 1867, Congressman Thomas Dawes Eliot, brother of TSE's grandfather, acted with T. M. Stetson in the sensational Howland forgery trial concerning an estate of $2 million. The marriage of Stetson and TDE's daughter in 1856 is recorded in Walter Graeme Eliot's *A Sketch of the Eliot Family* [1887], which TSE consulted in the British Museum (see *Letters 4* 110).

[I] 69–76 **"Stetson! | "You ··· | "That ··· | "Has ··· | "Or ··· | "O ··· | "Or ··· | "You ··· frère!"**: TSE used this old-fashioned convention of repeating quotation marks at the start of each line of spoken or quoted words in *WLComposite* 7–8 and at

[II] 132–34, as also when quoting John Day and Baudelaire within his Notes. Here [I] 76 is complicated by incorporating a quotation. In *Revelation* (1937), TSE likewise put opening quotation marks at the head of four successive paragraphs quoted from Irving Babbitt; similarly, in a letter to his solicitor on 29 Apr 1939. The convention continued to be used into the 1940s by *The Times* when quoting prose. Contrast, for instance, [III] 292–305. **"Stetson! | "You who were with me in the ships at Mylae!:** TSE: "Marin! je te connais", *Tristan Corbière* 1.

[I] 70 **in the ships at Mylae:** *Hayward*: "260 BC. The great naval victory of the Romans over the Carthaginians in the First Punic War. A trade war (cf. 1914–18). All wars *one* war." For Carthage and for Keynes on a Carthaginian peace, see note to [III] 306–307. F. W. Bateson: "those who were 'in'—rather than 'on' or 'with'—the ships ··· propelled the triremes", in *Newton-De Molina ed.* **the ships at:** TSE to his Swedish translator Erik Mesterton, 20 Jan 1932: "I see no great loss in omitting the ships if there are metrical difficulties." **Mylae:** pronounced *Mylee* in TSE's recordings.

[I] 71 **"That corpse you planted ··· in your garden:** Clement Wood: "But these war-killed men should sleep | Planted deep, planted deep", *Seedtime* in *Poetry* Jan 1917. The Imperial War Graves Commission was established in 1917. "Garden-Graves on the Western Front", *The Times* 7 May 1921, concluded with three words from Rupert Brooke: "Somewhere in France there is a white garden graveyard of British warriors which stands complete as it will stand through the centuries to come. Its wealth of flowers and wreaths will change and be renewed ··· this garden which is 'for ever England'."

[I] 71–72 **"That corpse you planted ··· "Has it begun to sprout?:** Lancelot Andrewes: "Christ rising was indeed a gardener, and that a strange one, Who made such an herb grow out of the ground of this day as the like was never seen before, a dead body to shoot forth alive out of the grave", Easter Sermon 1620, on John 20: 15, in which Mary Magdalene, "supposing him to be the gardener", says to Jesus "if thou have borne him hence, tell me where thou hast laid him". TSE: "Their petals ··· They sprang from the limbs of the dead", *Circe's Palace* 4–6. To Conrad Aiken, 30 Sept [1914]: "it's interesting to cut yourself to pieces once in a while, and wait to see if the fragments will sprout". ("the damp souls of housemaids | Sprouting", *Morning at the Window* 3–4.) TSE annotating his Greek text of Aristotle's *De Anima* II ch. 1: "A corpse cannot be said to have the potentiality of life." (Aristotle: "By that which has in it the capacity of life is meant not the body which has lost its soul, but that which possesses it. Now the seed in animals, like the fruit in plants, is that which is potentially such and such a body.") TSE on childhood: "we know that it is something to be buried and done with, though the corpse will from time to time find its way up to the surface", *The Silurist* (1927). See note to [I] 1–2, 71, 74.

[I] 71–73 **"That corpse you planted last year in your garden, | "Has it begun to sprout? Will it bloom this year? | "Or has the sudden frost disturbed its bed?:** "sudden rains | Softening last year's garden plots", *Interlude in London* 5–6. 1 Corinthians 15: 36–37: "that which thou sowest is not quickened, except it die: And that which thou sowest, thou sowest not that body that shall be, but bare grain." Frazer: "priests used to bury effigies of Osiris made of earth and corn. When these effigies were taken up again ··· the corn would be found to have sprouted from the body of Osiris, and this sprouting of the grain would be hailed as an omen, or rather as the cause, of the growth of the crops. The corn-god produced the corn from himself: he gave his own body to feed the people: he died that they might live", *The Golden Bough* VI (*Attis Adonis Osiris* II) 90.

[I] 71–75 **"That corpse you planted ··· dig it up again!:** *TSE's Notes* refer to Webster:

> Call for the robin-red-breast and the wren,
> Since o'er shady groves they hover,
> And with leaves and flowers do cover
> The friendless bodies of unburied men.
> Call unto his funeral dole
> The ant, the field-mouse, and the mole,
> To rear him hillocks that shall keep him warm,
> And (when gay tombs are robbed) sustain no harm:
> But keep the wolf far thence, that's foe to men,
> For with his nails he'll dig them up again.
> They would not bury him 'cause he died in a quarrel
>
> *The White Devil* V iv (stage direction: "Cornelia doth this in several forms of distraction")

The Mermaid ed. adds a footnote quoting Lamb: "I never saw anything like this dirge, except the ditty which reminds Ferdinand of his drowned father in the Tempest. As that is of the water, watery; so this is of the earth, earthy. Both have that intenseness of feeling, which seems to resolve itself into the elements which it contemplates.—C. Lamb, *Spec. of Eng. Dram. Poets*." The two dirges appear consecutively under Palgrave's titles *A Sea Dirge* and *A Land Dirge* in *The Golden Treasury*, which also quotes Lamb's remarks (Joan Brain, pub. John Pikoulis, *N&Q* Oct 1981). *The Golden Treasury* was prescribed reading in TSE's sixth-year class at school (Smith Academy yearbook, 1904–05). For Ariel's song ("Full fathom five"), see headnote to *Dirge*. Webster again: "The wolf shall find her grave, and scrape it up, | Not to devour the corpse, but to discover | The horrid murder", *The Duchess of Malfi* IV ii (Francis Noel Lees, *Tate ed.* 352). Mermaid notes: "This was a commonplace superstition of the time." (For Webster's scene, see note to [II] 117–23.) Again: "they imagine | Themselves to be transformed into wolves ··· And dig dead bodies up", *The Duchess of Malfi* V ii. Chapman: "Whence with my nails and feet I'll dig enough | Horror and savage cruelty to build | Temples to massacre", *The Conspiracy of Charles, Duke of Byron* III i (for Chapman's scene, see notes to [II] 89 and to *Gerontion* 38–39). **corpse ··· dig it up again:** FitzGerald: "As, buried once, Men want dug up again", *Rubáiyát of Omar Khayyám* (4th ed) XV (*Crawford* 35). Pound: "Judge ye! | Have I dug him up again?" *Sestina: Altaforte* (1909) epigraph (TSE included the poem in Pound's *Selected Poems*). Also: "He and the dug-up corpse", Canto II (first version, in *Poetry* July 1917). **keep the Dog far hence, that's friend to men:** *Hayward*: "The suburban garden. The Englishman and his dog—his friendly 'familiar'. The substitution of dog for wolf in this allusion is a striking example of Eliot's use of quotation to bring the past into the present. There is also the suggestion that the dog, by digging up the corpse, might prevent the possibility of rebirth." James Huneker: "The legend of Charles Baudelaire is seemingly indestructible. This French poet himself has suffered more from the friendly malignant biographer and Parisian chroniclers than did Poe. Who shall keep the curs out of the cemetery? asked Baudelaire after he had read Griswold on Poe", *Egoists: A Book of Supermen* (1909) 67 (*Grover Smith* 79). In the same essay on Baudelaire, Huneker quoted "*Hypocrite lecteur!—mon semblable,—mon frère!*" (*Hands*); see note to *Gerontion* 62–64. OED "man" 34: "man's best friend ··· the dog". Keats: "a friend to man", *Ode on a Grecian Urn* 48. TSE: "long lanes of dogs and men", *Airs of Palestine, No. 2* 15. To Bonamy Dobrée, 21 Aug 1926: "individual Gods (my God for my dog, my pipe, my golf-tools and my allotment garden, your god for yours)." *Badenhausen* 183: "the metaphor also evokes Sirius, the Dog Star, for [Jessie] Weston points out the importance of Sirius to the fertility rites of the Egyptians". Virginia Woolf, however, had recorded TSE denying any such connection: "Not a bit of it says Tom: I was having a joke about Webster", *Diary* 10 Sept 1933. TSE: "Gloomy Orion and the Dog", *Sweeney Among the Nightingales* 9.

[I] 74 **O**: *Fowler* "O & Oh": "as the sign of the vocative (*O God our help* ···) *O* is invariable, & as an exclamation the word is *O* when no stop immediately follows it, but before any stop *oh* (*Oh, what a lie! O for the wings of a dove!*)" TSE changed the spelling in *Washington copy 1954* (see Textual History), perhaps to conform to [III] 199, [III] 309–10, and [IV] 320 (but see [II] 150). The sense is not as at *The Dry Salvages* III 39. TSE hesitated over "O" or "Oh" again in *The Country Walk* 26.

[I] 75 **again**: pronounced to rhyme with "men" in TSE's recordings at this point; elsewhere he often said *agayne.*

[I] 76 **"You! hypocrite lecteur ··· frère"**: *TSE's Notes* refer to Baudelaire's *Les Fleurs du Mal*, prefatory poem:

> Tu le connais, lecteur, ce monstre délicat,
> —Hypocrite lecteur,—mon semblable,—mon frère!
>
> [Dear Reader, you are well acquainted with that fastidious monster—hypocritical Reader,—my second self—my brother!]
>
> *Au lecteur* [*To the Reader*]

TSE adds "You" to the line, having in an essay departed differently from Baudelaire in the vocative: "the poets who consider themselves most opposed to Georgianism, and who know a little French, are mostly such as could imagine the Last Judgment only as a lavish display of Bengal lights, Roman candles, catherine-wheels, and inflammable fire-balloons. *Vous, hypocrite lecteur . . .*", *The Lesson of Baudelaire* (1921) conclusion (*Scarfe*); Baudelaire has *Tu* not *Vous* (in the preceding line). Both the *Dial* and the *Criterion* italicised the French words "hypocrite ··· frère", with roman "You" at the head of the line. Subsequently the whole line has appeared in roman, with the effect that "You! hypocrite" can be read simply as English at first, before transition to the French "hypocrite lecteur!" TSE to Middleton Murry, 12 Feb [1926]: "You are in some sort of purgatory, I am perhaps thoroughly damned. But that's one reason why I want to see you. And I always feel with you 'mon semblable—mon frère.'" Richard Aldington: "Here, take my pennies | *Mon semblable, mon frère*", end of Interlude, *Images* in *Egoist* 1 Dec 1915. **mon semblable**: Sir Thomas Elyot: "A man in his natural perfection is ··· desirous of knowledge, appetiting by generation to brynge forthe his semblable", *The Governour* bk. I xxi (see *East Coker* I 28–33).

II. A GAME OF CHESS
~~IN THE CAGE~~

Unadopted title **~~IN THE CAGE~~**: *WLFacs* notes: "The cancelled title refers to the passage from the *Satyricon* of Petronius which replaced that from *Heart of Darkness* as the epigraph to *The Waste Land.*" But Grover Smith and Kenner doubted whether TSE yet had in mind "the quotation from Petronius without which an allusion to the decrepit Sibyl would be impenetrable", Kenner in *Litz ed.* 38.

Pound to Scofield Thayer, 25–26 Nov 1920: "I want to get T. S. E. out of that bank ··· If some one wd. murder or elope with his wife it wd. have the same effect as finding a few hundred £ ··· I think you have done extremely well by him, in offering regular monthly opening [with the *Dial*]. One additional job of equal size ought to tempt him out of the cage." Subsequently, "F. M.", *Letters of the Moment* I (1924):

> Now one begins to beat against the bars of the cage: the typewriter and the telephone, and the sight of one's face in the glass. One's soul stirs stiffly out of the dead endurance of the winter—but toward what spring?
>
> Le temps s'en va, le temps s'en va, madame:
> Las! le temps, non, mais nous nous en allons,
> Et tost serons estendus sous la lame.
>
> What happy meetings, what luminous conversations in twilight rooms filled with the scent of hyacinths, await me now?
>
> [Time passes, time passes, Madame; alas! it is not time but we who pass, and are soon stretched below the stone].

(The first two of these lines from Ronsard's *Sonnet à Marie* appear in TSE's hand, c. 624 fol. 24v.) For Henry James's *In the Cage*, see headnote to *In the Department Store*.

Title ***A Game of Chess***: Middleton's *A Game at Chesse*, staged 1624, was a political allegory. It tells of the attempted rape of a White (English) Virgin by a Black (Spanish) Bishop's Pawn. (For England's Virgin Queen of the previous generation and a Spanish bishop, see note to [III] 279.) TSE's review of R. C. Bald's edition of the play appeared in *TLS* 23 Jan 1930 (see headnote to *Sweeney Agonistes*, 2. ARISTOPHANES). Pound, *The Game of Chess* (title, in *Lustra*, 1916).

Title, [II] 82, 95, 108, 109, 137 **A Game of Chess ··· the flames ··· Burned ··· firelight ··· fiery ··· we shall play a game of chess**: Herbert: "When my house burnes, it's not good playing at Chesse"; "To play at Chesse when the house is on fire", *Outlandish Proverbs* nos. 666, 1136.

[II] 77–110] *Hayward*: "Contrast of high life and low life in a meaningless, sterile land. In Middleton's play the game of chess was used as a cover for a seduction and rape. The curse on the land in the myth followed upon the rape of girls at the Court of the Fisher King. (Lust without Love). Cf. also the 'Thames Daughters'." *TSE's Notes* refer to *Antony and Cleopatra* II ii:

> The barge she sat in, like a burnish'd throne,
> Burn'd on the water. The poop was beaten gold;
> Purple the sails, and so perfumed that

> The winds were love-sick with them; the oars were silver,
> Which to the tune of flutes kept stroke, and made
> The water which they beat to follow faster,
> As amorous of their strokes. For her own person,
> It beggar'd all description. She did lie
> In her pavilion, cloth-of-gold, of tissue,
> O'erpicturing that Venus where we see
> The fancy out-work nature. On each side of her
> Stood pretty dimpled boys, like smiling Cupids,
> With divers-colour'd fans, whose wind did seem
> To glow the delicate cheeks which they did cool,
> And what they undid did.

(The speech is still marked by the ribbon in TSE's childhood copy.) "The great speech of Enobarbus in *Antony and Cleopatra* is highly decorated, but the decoration has a purpose beyond its own beauty", *Rudyard Kipling* (1941). TSE had previously refashioned the speech in *The Burnt Dancer* 17–18 ("flame | Like perfumed oil upon the waters") and in *Burbank with a Baedeker: Bleistein with a Cigar* 11–12 ("Her shuttered barge | Burned on the water all the day"). *Antony and Cleopatra* III vi: "Cleopatra and himself in chairs of gold" ("golden", [II] 80).

Cymbeline II iv, after mention of a tapestry of Cleopatra's barge (*Melchiori*):

> The roof o' th' chamber
> With golden cherubins is fretted. Her andirons—
> I had forgot them—were two winking Cupids
> Of silver, each on one foot standing, nicely
> Depending on their brands.

TSE's Note to [II] 92 quotes Virgil's "dependent lychni laquearibus aureis". For *Cymbeline* again, see note to [II] 80–91.

Apuleius, *The Golden Ass*, Pater's version in *Marius the Epicurean* I 30, as quoted by Pound, in *The Spirit of Romance*:

> Golden pillars sustained the roof, arched most curiously in cedar-wood and ivory. The walls were hidden under wrought silver:—all tame and woodland creatures leaping forward to the visitor's gaze. Wonderful indeed was the craftsman, divine or half-divine, who by the subtlety of his art had breathed so wild a soul into the silver! The very pavement was distinct with pictures in goodly stones. In the glow of its precious metal the house is its own daylight, having no need of the sun. Well might it seem a place fashioned for the conversation of gods with men!

(*TSE's books: Bodleian list* (1934) includes the Teubner ed. of Apuleius. To Robert Graves, 30 June 1947: "I read *The Golden Ass* at Harvard with a good deal of enjoyment, but my Professor of Latin failed to point out that the story was intended as parody.")

Keats, *Lamia* II 173–82 (*Melchiori*):

> Of wealthy lustre was the banquet-room,
> Filled with pervading brilliance and perfume:
> Before each lucid panel fuming stood
> A censer fed with myrrh and spicèd wood,
> Each by a sacred tripod held aloft,
> Whose slender feet wide-swerved upon the soft
> Wool-woofèd carpets; fifty wreaths of smoke
> From fifty censers their light voyage took

To the high roof, still mimicked as they rose
Along the mirrored walls by twin-clouds odorous.

Baudelaire, *Les Fleurs du Mal* LXXIX, *Une Martyre* [*A Martyred Woman*]:

Au milieu des flacons, des étoffes lamées
Et des meubles voluptueux,
Des marbres, des tableaux, des robes parfumées
Qui traînent à plis somptueux,

Dans une chambre tiède où, comme en une serre,
L'air est dangereux et fatal,
Où des bouquets mourants dans leurs cercueils de verre
Exhalent leur soupir final

[Surrounded with scent-bottles, sequined draperies, luxurious furniture, marble sculptures, oil-paintings, perfumed dresses scattered around in sumptuous folds; in a close bedchamber like a hothouse with its threatening morbid atmosphere, in which drooping bouquets in their glass coffins sigh their last]

Marlowe, *Hero and Leander* I 136–44 (incl. in Hayward's *Penguin Book of English Verse*):

The wals were of discoloured *Jasper* stone,
Wherein was *Proteus* carv'd, and overhead,
A lively vine of greene sea agget spread;
Where by one hand, light headed *Bacchus* hung,
And with the other, wine from grapes out wrung.
Of Christall shining faire the pavement was,
The towne of *Sestos* calde it *Venus* glasse.
There might you see the gods in sundrie shapes,
Committing headdie ryots, incest, rapes

For TSE's scene and Conrad's *The Return*, see Robert L. Morris, *MLN* June 1950; for Dickens's *Dombey and Son* ch. LIV, see Patrick Diskin, *N&Q* Dec 1984; for Mallarmé's *Hérodiade* I, see Kenner, *Litz ed.* 39 (but TSE to P. M. Mansell Jones, 9 Dec 1936, of Mallarmé's poetry: "I admit to being very fond of it myself, although I cannot trace ever having been much influenced by him").

[II] 77 **The Chair she sat in:** Leigh Hunt: "Jenny kissed me when we met, | Jumping from the chair she sat in", *Rondeau* (Archie Burnett, personal communication).

[II] 77–78 **burnished · · · Glowed on the:** Shelley, echoing *Antony and Cleopatra*: "the sun's image radiantly intense || Burned on the waters of the well that glowed", *The Triumph of Life* 345–46. TSE conflated Shakespeare, *The Waste Land* and perhaps Shelley in characterising "the speech in which Enobarbus describes the first meeting of Antony and Cleopatra, which is very deliberately grandiose—'The barge she sat in, like a golden throne, | Glowed on the waters' . . .—and in which the language is so strikingly out of character as to make us feel that the rough soldier becomes another man when thinking of the fascination and beauty of the queen", *The Development of Shakespeare's Verse* (1950 text). Pope, on a proposed variant: "tho' the difference between *burn* and *glow* may seem not very material to others, to me I confess the latter has an elegance, a *Jenesçay quoy*, which is much easier to be conceiv'd than explain'd", burlesque note to *The Dunciad* (1728) II 175–76 (Valentine Cunningham, personal communication).

[II] 77–89 **sat · · · throne · · · golden · · · vials · · · odours**: Revelation 5: 7–8: "sat upon the throne · · · golden vials full of odours".

[II] 77, 94 **burnished throne · · · copper**: Pound: "By the mirror of burnished copper, | O Queen of Cypress", *The Alchemist* (1920), one of the poems added by TSE to Anne Ridler's *Selection of Poems* by Pound (1940).

[II] 78–80] *WLFacs* notes: "Eliot offered these revised lines: 'Glowed on the marble, where the glass | Sustained by standards wrought with fruited vines | Wherefrom . . .' 'OK' replied Pound. However, Eliot restored 'Held up' to the second line, and 'Wherefrom' appeared in *The Criterion* only, all later printings reverting to 'From which'" (quoting TSE's letter [26? Jan 1922] and Pound's comments upon it: see headnote, 1. COMPOSITION).

[II] 78–87 **marble · · · the glitter of her jewels · · · ivory · · · Unstoppered · · · perfumes**: Mary Elizabeth Braddon: "her glittering toilette apparatus lay about on the marble dressing-table. The atmosphere of the room was almost oppressive from the rich odours of perfumes in bottles whose stoppers had not been replaced · · · Jewellery, ivory-backed hair-brushes, and exquisite china, were scattered here and there about the apartment", *Lady Audley's Secret* ch. VIII (*Heywood*).

[II] 78, 110 **Glowed on the marble · · · Glowed into words, then would be savagely still**: the return of "Glowed" at the head of 110, as though forming a long syntactic arc, had no counterpart when "Glowed into words, then was suddenly still" was used alone in *The Death of the Duchess* II 22 (which had taken up "suddenly still" from *Silence* 13). TSE's only other use of "Glowed" in his poems is likewise at the head of a line: "Glowed in the shadow of the bed", *Song* ("The golden foot I may not kiss or clutch") 2, for which see headnote to *The Waste Land*, 1. COMPOSITION.

[II] 79 **fruited vines**: William Morris: "the fruited vines a-row", *The Earthly Paradise*, *An Apology* st. 5 (see note to *Ash-Wednesday* I 5–6).

[II] 79–118 **vines · · · golden Cupidon · · · flames of sevenbranched candelabra · · · stirred by the air | That freshened from the window · · · candle-flames · · · ceiling · · · window · · · told upon the walls; staring forms · · · her hair · · · "My nerves are bad · · · "What is that noise?" | The wind**: Poe's *Ligeia* is set in a gothick abbey with "carvings of Egypt · · · golden candelabra · · · trellice-work of an aged vine · · · ceiling vaulted · · · a huge censer · · · so contrived that there writhed in and out of them, as if endued with a serpent vitality, a continual succession of parti-colored fires · · · gorgeous volutes of the curtains which partially shaded the window · · · with arabesque figures · · · wrought · · · ghastly forms · · · The phantasmagoric effect was vastly heightened by the artificial introduction of a strong continual current of wind behind the draperies—giving a hideous and uneasy animation · · · figures upon the wall." The tale tells how a wife, without love for her husband and morbidly "hated" by him, suffered recurrent illnesses and "nervous irritation" which caused "excitability by trivial causes of fear": "She spoke again, and now more frequently · · · of the sounds—of the slight sounds—and of the unusual motions among the tapestries." After her death, as he watched her corpse, she "stirred · · · I repeat, stirred" and finally unloosened "her hair". For Poe's story, see notes to *Elegy* and to *East Coker* III 13–17.

[II] 80 **a golden Cupidon peeped out**: Flaubert: "Il y avait sur la pendule un petit Cupidon de bronze, qui minaudait, en arrondissant les bras sous une guirlande dorée" [On the clock there was a little bronze cupid, simpering and curving its arms under a gilded wreath], *Madame Bovary* III v (J. C. Maxwell, *English Studies* Aug 1963). OED has "Cupidon" only as "a 'beau' or 'Adonis'", citing Byron.

134 **one:** *Pound's annotation*: "'one' wee red mouse"] *WLFacs* notes: "*La Nuit Blanche* [22] by Rudyard Kipling. 'Me and one wee Blood Red Mouse'. The poem itself has no relevance to *The Waste Land*; Pound said he was merely teasing Eliot about 'one'."

[II] 80–91 **peeped out ··· hid his eyes ··· flames ··· light ··· perfumes ··· stirred by the air | That freshened from the window ··· fattening the prolonged candle-flames:** *Cymbeline* II ii: "'Tis her breathing that | Perfumes the chamber thus. The flame o' th' taper | Bows toward her, and would under-peep her lids | To see th' enclosed lights." Before falling asleep Imogen had been reading "The tale of Tereus; here the leaf's turn'd down | Where Philomel gave up" (*Melchiori*); see note to [II] 98–104.

[II] 82–83, 91 **sevenbranched candelabra | Reflecting light upon the table ··· the prolonged candle-flames:** Poe: "flames of the seven lamps ··· Uprearing themselves in tall slender lines of light, they thus remained burning all pallid ··· and in the mirror which their lustre formed upon the round table of ebony", *Shadow—A Parable* (*Grover Smith 1983* 123–25).

[II] 83–88 **light ··· glitter ··· profusion ··· ivory ··· liquid:** Poe: "liquid eyes ··· and a profusion of curling, black hair, from which a forehead of unusual breadth gleamed forth at intervals all light and ivory", *The Assignation* (which has "marble" repeatedly; TSE: [II] 78). See note to [II] 85–95.

[II] 83–96 **Reflecting light ··· coloured glass ··· drowned ··· window ··· ascended ··· Stirring ··· sea-wood ··· coloured stone ··· In which sad light a carvèd dolphin swam:**

> And lights directed through the coloured panes of windows
> And light reflected from the polished stone,
> The gilded carven wood, the coloured fresco.
> Our gaze is submarine, our eyes look upward
> And see the light that fractures through unquiet water.
>
> *Choruses from "The Rock"* X 29–33

(For the submarine world, see note to *Mr. Apollinax* 11–15.)

[II] 83–87, 96, 108–109 **Reflecting light upon the table as | The glitter of her jewels ··· vials of ivory ··· her strange synthetic perfumes ··· swam ··· her hair | Spread out in fiery points:** William Morris: "her hair ··· Like ivory in the sea, and the sun gleamed | In the strange jewels ··· swimming", *The Life and Death of Jason* IV 257–60, 266. TSE quoted Morris's poem in *Andrew Marvell* (1921). See notes to [II] 79 and [IV] 312.

[II] 84–87 **The glitter of her jewels ··· satin cases ··· vials of ivory and coloured glass ··· synthetic perfumes:** Pope: "decks the Goddess with the glitt'ring Spoil. | This Casket *India*'s glowing Gems unlocks, | And all *Arabia* breathes from yonder Box", *The Rape of the Lock* I 132–34 (Irène Simon, *English Studies* Apr 1953, giving other parallels). **jewels ··· cases:** *The Picture of Dorian Gray* ch. XI: "he took up the study of jewels ··· resettling in their cases the various stones". Wilde's chapter (for which see notes to [II] 87–95 and to *The Love Song of J. Alfred Prufrock*

17–22) three times mentions the carbuncle (see note to [III] 231). **vials ··· unstoppered:** Pope: "stopt in *Vials*", *The Rape of the Lock* II 126.

[II] 85–95 **poured ··· perfumes ··· troubled, confused | And drowned the sense ··· the window ··· Flung their smoke ··· Burned green and orange:** Poe: "The senses were oppressed by mingling and conflicting perfumes, reeking up from strange convolute censers, together with multitudinous flaring and flickering tongues of emerald and violet fire. The rays of the newly-risen sun poured in upon the whole, through windows", *The Assignation*.

[II] 87–89 **lurked ··· troubled, confused | And drowned ··· stirred:** main verbs or participles: on the "blurring of the grammar" here, see Empson, *Seven Types of Ambiguity* (1930) ch. II. (For TSE on "intentional ambiguity", see note to [V] 398, "crouched, hunched".) "Flattened ··· Stretched ··· prepared", *Prufrock's Pervigilium* [23–24].

[II] 87–95 **perfumes ··· troubled, confused | And drowned the sense in odours; stirred ··· copper | Burned:** *The Picture of Dorian Gray* ch. XI: "And so he would now study perfumes ··· burning odorous gums ··· that stirred one's passions ··· musk that troubled the brain" (with "copper" in the next paragraph).

[II] 88 **Unguent:** pronounced *ungwent* (as OED) in TSE's recordings.

[II] 89 **drowned the sense:** Chapman: "drowning their eternal parts in sense | And sensual affections", *The Conspiracy of Charles, Duke of Byron* III i. See note to *Gerontion* 38–39. **odours:** in Johnson's Dictionary and OED almost entirely positive or neutral, but see note to "une odeur fémelle", *Petit Epître* 8.

[II] 89–90 **stirred by the air | That freshened from the window:** "Across the window panes the plumes of lilac swept | Stirred by the morning air", *Oh little voices of the throats of men* 37–38.

[II] 91 **prolonged candle-flames:** *Purg.* XVIII 28–30: "come il foco movesi in altura, | per la sua forma, ch'è nata a salire | là dove più in sua materia dura" [even as fire moves upward by reason of its form, whose nature is to ascend, there where it endures longest in its material]. (In the copy his mother had given him, TSE scored XVIII 19–40 in the Italian.) Scientifically: "where flame assumes a prolonged or lengthened appearance, as in the case of the candle", C. W. Williams, *The Combustion of Coals and the Prevention of Smoke* (1840) 139.

[II] 92–93 **laquearia ··· coffered ceiling:** *TSE's Notes* quote two lines from Virgil's description of Dido's banquet for Aeneas, *Aeneid* I 723–30:

> Postquam prima quies epulis mensaeque remotae,
> crateras magnos statuunt et vina coronant.
> fit strepitus tectis vocemque per ampla volutant
> atria; dependent lychni laquearibus aureis
> incensi et noctem flammis funalia vincunt.
> hic regina gravem gemmis auroque poposcit
> implevitque mero pateram, quam Belus et omnes
> a Belo soliti; tum facta silentia tectis

[When first there came a lull in the feasting, and the boards were cleared, they set down great bowls and crown the wine. A din arises in the palace and voices roll through the spacious halls; lighted lamps hang down from the fretted roof of gold, and flaming torches drive out the night. Then the queen called for a cup, heavy with jewels and gold, and filled it with wine—one that Belus and all of Belus' line had been wont to use.]

"Laquearia" did not appear in the first edition of OED, but was added in 1976 as TSE's nonce word ("A ceiling, roof"). OED "laquear": *Arch.* 1706. "a Roof of a Chamber embowed, channelled, and done with Fret-work". OED "lacunar" (*pl.* lacunars, lacunaria): "a. The ceiling or under surface of any part, when it consists of sunk or hollowed compartments. b. *pl.* The sunken panels in such a ceiling. 1823. *Lacunariæ*, or *Lacunars*, panels or coffers formed on the ceilings of apartments." TSE's earliest form, "laquenaria", not recognised by OED, appears in the surviving drafts shown to Pound (*WLFacs*) and then in the Quinn, Watson and Thayer tss (*Q* and *T/W*). Whether the *n* was omitted deliberately is unclear.

[II] 94–95 **copper | Burned green and orange**: Coleridge: "a hot and copper sky ··· The water, like a witch's oils, | Burnt green, and blue and white", *The Rime of the Ancient Mariner* II 29, 47–48 (*Melchiori*).

[II] 94–109 **sea-wood ··· Burned green ··· the sylvan scene ··· withered stumps of time ··· firelight ··· fiery**: Cowper:

> So wither'd stumps disgrace the sylvan scene,
> No longer fruitful and no longer green,
> The sapless wood, divested of the bark,
> Grows fungous and takes fire at ev'ry spark.
>
> *Conversation* 51–54

In *Titus Andronicus*, the "stumps" (V ii) of Lavinia's arms prompt the question "what stern ungentle hands | Hath lopp'd and hew'd and made thy body bare | Of her two branches?" (II iv), and her plight is compared to "the tragic tale of Philomel" (IV i) (*Schmidt 1982b*).

[II] 96 **In which sad light a carvèd dolphin swam**: *Antony and Cleopatra* V ii (on Antony): "his delights | Were dolphin-like" (*Melchiori*). Tennyson: "And in the light the white mermaiden swam", *Guinevere* 243 (*James Smith* 132). **a carvèd dolphin**: the mistaken adjective "coloured" in the Hogarth Press edition (*H*) is from "coloured stone" in the previous line (following "coloured glass", [II] 86). TSE emended "coloured" to "carven" in some copies of *H*, including the one he sent to his mother. Alongside the words "un dauphin de couleur" in the ts of Menasce's translation, TSE wrote: "The English text is wrong here—Read 'carvèn stone dolphin'" ("goddess carved of stone", *On a Portrait* 5). To his Swedish translator Erik Mesterton, 20 Jan 1932: "Porphyry will do."

[II] 96–105 **carvèd ··· upon the walls; staring forms**: Keats: "The carvèd angels, ever eager-eyed, | Stared, where upon their heads the cornice rests, | With hair blown back, and wings put cross-wise on their breasts", *The Eve of St. Agnes* 34–36 (*Melchiori*).

[II] 98–104 **sylvan scene ··· by the barbarous king | So rudely forced ··· the nightingale | Filled all the desert with inviolable voice ··· "Jug Jug" ··· stumps**: *TSE's Notes* refer to Ovid, *Metamorphoses* VI 424–674. *Lemprière* on Philomela: "a daughter of Pandion king of Athens, and sister of Procne, who had married Tereus, king of Thrace ··· he offered violence to Philomela, and afterwards cut out her tongue, that she might not be able to discover his barbarity, and the indignities which she had suffered ··· Philomela, during her captivity, described on a piece of tapestry her misfortunes and the brutality of Tereus, and privately conveyed it to Procne ··· Procne and Philomela died through excess of grief and melancholy, and as the nightingale's and swallow's voice is peculiarly plaintive and mournful, the poets have embellished the fable by supposing that the two unfortunate sisters were changed into birds" (see note to [V] 428). Ovid, tr. Golding: "so barbrous and so beastly was his thought ··· by force bicause she was a Maide | And all alone he vanquisht hir ··· barbrous ··· my voyce the verie woods shall fill ··· He tooke her rudely ··· did catch hir by the tung, | And with his sword did cut it off. The stumpe whereon it hung | Did patter still", *Metamorphoses* VI 655–711. The tale is also told in the *Pervigilium Veneris*. *Williamson* 140 points to John Lyly:

> What Bird so sings, yet so dos wayle?
> O t'is the ravish'd Nightingale.
> Iug, Iug, Iug, Iug, tereu, shee cryes,
> And still her woes at Midnight rise.
> Brave prick-song!
>
> *Campaspe* V i, Trico's song

Kenner 133: "Lyly of course is perfectly aware of what she is trying to say: 'tereu' comes very close to 'Tereus'." Richard Barnfield: "Fie, fie, fie, now would she cry; | Tereu, Tereu, by and by", *An Ode* ("As it fell upon a day") 13–14. *The Golden Treasury* prints this as *The Nightingale*. Camelia Elias and Bent Soerensen suggest that the repetition "Tereu, tereu" in TSE's draft (*WLComposite* **318**) makes Barnfield the likely source, and discuss "Tereu" as both the vocative of "Tereus" and as onomatopoeia (*Explicator* Winter 2004). Barnfield's own spelling was "*Teru Teru*", but both the Lyly and the Barnfield are printed in the *Oxf Bk of English Verse* (as *Spring's Welcome* and *Philomel*), with the spelling "*Tereu*". George Gascoigne:

> In sweet April ··· I walked out alone,
> To hear the descant of the Nightingale" ···
> *Orphæus* harpe, was never halfe so sweete,
> *Tereu*, *Tereu*, and thus she gan to plaine ···
> Hir *Iug*, *Iug*, *Iug*, (in griefe) had such a grace ···
> But one strange note, I noted with the rest
> And that saide thus: *Nêmesis*, *Némesis*
>
> *The Complaynt of Phylomene* (1–6, 74–75, 86, 93–94)

sylvan scene: *TSE's Notes* refer to *Paradise Lost* IV 137–42:

> over head up grew
> Insuperable highth of loftiest shade,
> Cedar, and Pine, and Fir, and branching Palm,
> A Silvan Scene, and as the ranks ascend
> Shade above shade, a woody Theatre
> Of stateliest view.

(TSE: "sevenbranched", [II] 82.) Virgil: "silvis scaena coruscis" [a background of shimmering woods], *Aeneid* I 164. Dryden: "a Sylvan Scene | Appears above, and Groves for ever green", *Aeneid* I 233–34; "A Sylvan Scene with various Greens was drawn", *Palamon and Arcite* 619. Both phrases of Dryden's are quoted by Mark Van Doren, *The Poetry of John Dryden* 71–72, reviewed by TSE in *John Dryden* (1921) (*Grover Smith 1983* 127). TSE: "window ··· And beyond ··· a pasture scene", *Ash-Wednesday* III 13–14. For Cowper's "sylvan scene", see note to [II] 94–109. **sylvan · · · nightingale · · · inviolable · · · still · · · pursues · · · ears:** Arnold: "Still clutching the inviolable shade · · · silver'd · · · where none pursue · · · or listen with enchanted ears, | From the dark dingles, to the nightingales", *The Scholar-Gipsy* 211–20.

[II] 98–106 **window · · · staring forms | Leaned out, leaning**: "leaning out of windows · · · evil houses leaning all together", *Prufrock's Pervigilium* [3, 15]. "Outside the window, leaning in", *Sweeney Among the Nightingales* 30. "*leaning out of the window*", stage direction, *Sweeney Agonistes: Fragment of a Prologue* 101.

[II] 100 **nightingale**: *TSE's Notes* refer to "Jug jug jug jug jug jug", [III] 204. For TSE on Keats's *Ode to a Nightingale*, see note to *Sweeney Among the Nightingales* epigraph. For the *Ode on a Grecian Urn*, see note to [II] 102.

[II] 100–102 **nightingale · · · still · · · still · · · pursues**: Arnold: "the nightingale · · · still · · · still · · · Dost thou again peruse · · · thy dumb sister's shame?" *Philomela* 1–21 (with "sweet, tranquil Thames", 10).

[II] 101 **inviolable voice**: Remy de Gourmont, quoting Ernest Hello: "Le style est l'homme même et l'autre formule, de Hello, le style est inviolable, disent · · · le style est aussi personnel que · · · la voix" [Style is the man himself and the other formula, from Hello, style is inviolable, both say · · · style is as personal as · · · the voice], *Du Style ou de l'écriture* in *La Culture des Idées* (1900). Laforgue: "Les Jeunes Filles inviolables et frêles" [the frail inviolable Young Ladies], *Dimanches: C'est l'automne* 9, quoted in *The Varieties of Metaphysical Poetry* 214 (Clark Lecture VIII). For Laforgue's line see note to *First Caprice in North Cambridge* 1.

156 *Pound's annotation*: "too penty"] *WLFacs* notes: "There is too much of the (iambic) pentameter, too regular a measure." Pound: "to break the pentameter, that was the first heave", Canto LXXXI (1949). TSE: "It's very difficult to write blank verse which is both good poetry and sounds like people talking · · · Therefore I felt it was necessary to find a metric which was as far as possible from the iambic pentameter. That's what I hammered out for myself in *The Family Reunion* and have used since. You asked if it was a personal prosody: it may be too personal a prosody · · · it may be that the norm of English versification is iambic pentameter, but that the only way to refresh it from one time to another will be to get away from it in a curve which will gradually return—having freed itself from the stiffness of previous generations. It may mean future verse dramatists will be able to go back to the iambic pentameter as a fresh instrument. And if I have helped in bringing that about I should be very happy, beyond the grave", *A Conversation, recorded in 1958, between T. S. Eliot and Leslie Paul* [1964/]1965.

[II] 102 **still the world pursues**: *Hayward*: "Cf. Keats, *Ode on a Grecian Urn*" (referring to "still unravished · · · Sylvan · · · What men or gods are these? What maidens loth? | What mad pursuit? What struggle to escape?" 1–9). *Lennard* 192 discusses TSE's punctuation variants, brackets or commas (see Textual History).

[II] 103 **Jug**: OED *n.* 1: "applied as a common noun to a homely woman · · · or as a term of disparagement", with *King Lear*: "Whoop Jugge I love thee". 2: "As the second element in local names of various small birds, as *bank-jug* · · · *hedge-jug*." *Partridge*: "female breasts, low Australian: since c. 1920."

158 **ear of death**: *Pericles* III i: "The seaman's whistle | Is as a whisper in the ears of death | Unheard." Quoted by TSE, with "ear", as among "the very best lines of *Pericles*—and the very best lines are very good lines indeed", *Poets' Borrowings* (1928).

[II] 103, 107 **ears ··· on the stair:** Kipling: "before you ever 'ear us on the stair", *Wilful-Missing*, from a quatrain that begins: "Marry again, and we will not say no, | Nor come to barstardise the kids you bear". (TSE: "What you get married for if you don't want children?" [II] 164.)

[II] 106–110 **Leaned ··· Footsteps shuffled on the stair ··· Under the firelight ··· still:** adapted from *The Death of the Duchess* II 13–22.

162 *Pound's annotation* "Il cherchait des sentiments pour les accommoder a son vocabulaire."] *WLFacs* notes: Henry-D. Davray, reviewing *Georgian Poetry 1916–1917*: "ces jeunes gens sont maîtres dans l'art d'écrire avant d'avoir vécu. Aussi cherchent-ils des sentiments pour les accommoder à leur vocabulaire et non des mots pour exprimer leur passion et leurs idées" [these young people are masters of the art of writing before they have lived. Therefore they search for feelings to accommodate to their vocabulary and not for words to express their passion and their ideas], *Mercure de France* 16 Apr 1918.

[II] 108–110 **under the brush, her hair ··· then would be savagely still:** for *The Duchess of Malfi* III ii, see Valerie Eliot's note to *The Death of the Duchess* II 54–58.

[II] 110 **Glowed into words:** *Inf.* XXVI 85–90:

fiamma antica
cominciò a crollarsi mormorando,
pur come quella cui vento affatica.
Indi la cima qua e là menando,
come fosse la lingua che parlasse,
gittò voce di fuori

[the ancient flame began to shake itself, murmuring, just like a flame that struggles with the wind. Then carrying to and fro the top, as if it were the tongue that spake, threw forth a voice].

Again, XXVII 58–60 (immediately preceding the lines that form the epigraph to *The Love Song of J. Alfred Prufrock*):

Poscia che il foco alquanto ebbe rugghiato
al modo suo, l'aguta punta mosse
di qua, di là, e poi diè cotal fiato

[After the flame had roared awhile as usual, it moved the sharp point to and fro, and then gave forth this breath] (*Melchiori*).

[II] 111–38] To E. M. Stephenson, 27 May 1942: "Your first paragraph is quite right about the sex of the speakers and the attribution of the lines, but as for your second paragraph, the intention is rather to leave open the possibility of a variety of literal interpretations suiting the reader's imagination. The reference to *Women beware Women*, however, is no more than a statement of fact and contains no innuendo. It means simply that the general notion of a dialogue over the chessboard is taken from a scene in that play" (see [II] 137). For arrangement of the dialogue on the page, see Textual History note to [II] 117–28.

[II] 111 **nerves:** specifically sexual implication is present in an advertisement for "*The Sexual Question* by [A. H.] Forel ··· Europe's foremost nerve specialist",

Little Review Nov 1915. TSE to his mother, 31 Oct 1920: "I have simply not had the time to do a single piece of work, and when one has in mind a great many things that one wants to do, that irritates the nerves more and more." To Ottoline Morrell, 30 Nov 1921, from Lausanne, where he was under the care of Dr. Vittoz: "I never did believe in 'nerves', at least for *myself*!" Yet on [26? Jan 1922] he wrote to Pound about the "nerves monologue" in *The Waste Land*. To George Bell, 18 July 1932: "We hope that my absence for a time may have the effect of strengthening her nerves (and nerve)." See *The Love Song of J. Alfred Prufrock* 105 and note. Paul von Boeckmann: "The great war has taught us how frail the nervous system is ··· Shell Shock, it was proved, does not injure the nerve fibres in themselves. The effect is entirely mental", *Nerve Exhaustion: How We Become Shell-Shocked in Every-Day Life* in *Popular Science* Nov 1921.

[II] 111–28 **nerves ··· "What is that noise?" ··· "What is that noise now? What is the wind doing?" ··· "Are you alive, or not?" ··· O O O O**: Edward Lear:

> E: ··· Is it neuralgia, headache or remorse? ···
> E: Why did I take the lodgings I have got,
> Where all I don't want is:—all I want not?
> J: Last week I called aloud, O! O! O! O! ···
> Why must I suffer in this wind and gloom! ···
> How can I write with noises such as those?
>
> *Growling Eclogue* 2, 27–29, 60, 71

166–69, 181 *Pound's annotations*: "photography? photo"] *WLFacs* notes: "Implying too realistic a reproduction of an actual conversation." "F. M." reviewing Virginia Woolf in the *Criterion*: "Mr. Bloom is real: he might almost be called ··· 'photographic'—a dreadful word", *"Mr. Bennett and Mrs. Brown"* (1925). TSE: "The more definite the religious and ethical principles, the more freely the drama can move towards what is now called photography. The more fluid, the more chaotic the religious and ethical beliefs, the more the drama must tend in the direction of liturgy", *A Dialogue on Dramatic Poetry* (1928).

[II] 111, 145 **nerves ··· Lil:** to Lilian Donaghy, wife of the Irish poet Lyle Donaghy, 12 Aug 1931: "You will, I hope, excuse me for writing ··· as if I knew you, but it is only because I happen to have more knowledge of this type of nervous illness than most people. Such cases are very difficult to handle, because they rarely want to stay in a sanatorium voluntarily, and no one wants to go so far as certification ··· All the symptoms you describe are known to me. I am quite certain that people in such a state ought not, as much for their own sakes as for that of others, to be with their family and friends. The manifestations of mania are always more pronounced with the persons they know best than with others ··· Professional outsiders are the only people to deal with such cases, and the only people whose nerves can stand the strain of dealing with them." 18 Nov: "While I am very sorry that he connects me in any way with his supposed persecution I know enough about these matters not to be in the least surprised ··· It is true that there was a passage about a woman named Lil in the poem you mention, but apart from that slight coincidence it has not the slightest bearing whatever, and there is not any mention of epilepsy anywhere in the poem. Your husband is of course mistaken in thinking that the text he saw recently is in any way altered from the original, and it could easily be shown that the whole thing was composed long before I knew him or anything about him; but reasoning is merely a waste of time."

[II] 112 **Why do you never speak.** : printed with a question-mark in the *Criterion* and frequently since, but the earliest typings (in *WLFacs*) had a stop, as had the earliest book edition (*B*) and all Faber editions in TSE's lifetime (except *Mardersteig*), as also TSE's transcription in *Valerie's Own Book*. There has never been a question mark in [II] 150, "Oh is there, she said." (For "violated punctuation", see note to [I] 26–27.) Vivien Eliot to Mary Hutchinson, 27 Sept 1928, of TSE: "he never says anything and one cannot get him to speak" (*Seymour-Jones* 300).

[II] 112–113, 126 **Why do you never speak. Speak. | "What are you thinking of? · · · Is there nothing in your head?"**: Conrad: "'Why don't you speak? · · · What does it mean? · · · What's going on in that head of yours? What are you plotting against me there so hard that you can't say a word?'" *The End of the Tether* VIII (see note on *The Hollow Men* section-title epigraph). Huxley: "Heart-rending question of women—never answered: | 'Tell me, tell me, what are you thinking of?'" *Sympathy* 5–6 in *Leda* (1920) (*Hands*). Conrad Aiken: "What are you thinking?" *The Jig of Forslin* (1916) I VII. For TSE's "Have you nothing else to say?", see headnote to *Sweeney Agonistes*, 10. PREMIÈRE IN AMERICA: ENTER AN OLD GENTLEMAN.

[II] 114 **know what you are thinking**: "he sees knows what you are thinking", *Skimbleshanks: The Railway Cat* 25 *variant*. **thinking. Think**: for George MacDonald, "think—think", see note to [V] 335–36, 352.

[II] 115–16 **rats' alley | Where the dead men lost their bones**: *TSE's Notes* refer to "Rattled by the rat's foot only", [III] 195. Rats Alley was a trench in the Somme sector, taken over from the French by the British in 1916 (Peter Chasseaud, personal communication).

[II] 117–20 **"What is that noise?" · · · the door · · · Nothing**: in John Rodker's *Fear*, a dramatic sketch in Pound's *Catholic Anthology*, Pierrot and Columbine play chess but are driven to distraction by footsteps on the stairs beyond the door, then by a tap at the door, but repeatedly when they open the door they find "Nothing!" As they search the house: "Sometimes a third pair of feet seem to be echoing them · · · Two pairs of feet · · · and after them · · · a third" (TSE: part title, *A Game of Chess*; "Who is the third who walks always beside you?" [V] 359) (*Moody 2007* 280).

[II] 117–23 **"What is that noise?" | The wind under the door · · · Nothing again nothing · · · "Do | You know nothing · · · Do you remember | "Nothing?"**: three plays by Webster probably contributed. *TSE's Notes* refer to *The Devil's Law Case* III ii:

> FIRST SURGEON: Did he not groan?
> SECOND SURGEON: Is the wind in that door still?

OED "door" 6b: "*is the wind in (at) that door?* = is the wind in that quarter?, is that the tendency of affairs?" (*The Devil's Law Case* is not in the Mermaid vol. of Webster and Tourneur.) F. L. Lucas's ed. of Webster emphasises that "there is certainly no banshee-like wailing of the wind in any literal door", and in *On a Recent Piece of Criticism* (1938), TSE described his own "adaptation of a phrase of Webster which Webster uses with quite a different meaning".

The Duchess of Malfi IV ii:

> DUCHESS: What hideous noise was that?
> CARIOLA: 'Tis the wild consort
> Of madmen, lady · · ·
> DUCHESS: · · · nothing but noise and folly
> Can keep me in my right wits; whereas reason
> And silence make me stark mad · · ·
> DUCHESS: This is a prison?
> CARIOLA: What think you of, madam?
> DUCHESS: Of nothing · · ·
> DUCHESS: What noise is that?

"The case of John Webster, and in particular *The Duchess of Malfy*, will provide an interesting example of a very great literary and dramatic genius directed toward chaos", *Four Elizabethan Dramatists* (1924).

The White Devil V vi (the exchange having begun "What noise is that?"):

> LODOVICO: What dost think on?
> FLAMINEO: Nothing; of nothing: leave thy idle questions.
> I am i' the way to study a long silence:
> To prate were idle. I remember nothing.
> There's nothing of so infinite vexation
> As man's own thoughts.
> LODOVICO: O thou glorious strumpet!

After I. B. Cauthen Jr discussed the last (*MLN* Nov 1958), TSE replied, 29 Aug 1962, to an enquiry from him: "I also have no doubt that the page from Webster's play was at the back of my mind" (*Yeats Eliot Review* Spring 1978). *Othello* IV iii, DESDEMONA: "Hark! who's that knocks?" | EMILIA: "It is the wind." (See note to *The Death of the Duchess* 20–21, 36.)

Hamlet III ii, OPHELIA: "I think nothing, my lord" (*Grover Smith* 81). III iv, HAMLET: "Do you see nothing there?" QUEEN: "Nothing at all; yet all that is I see." HAMLET: "Nor did you nothing hear?" QUEEN: "No, nothing but ourselves" (Peter Milward in Milward and Tetsue Anzai (eds.), *Poetry and Drama in the Age of Shakespeare*, 1982).

173 *Pound's annotation*: "Beddoes"] *WLFacs* notes:

> Thomas Lovell Beddoes (1803–49). The line recalled *Death's Jest-Book* to Pound, but in his Notes Eliot refers to "Is the wind in that door still?" from *The Devil's Law-Case* by John Webster. Some years later, Eliot admitted that the source was of no significance, as his adaptation of the phrase gave it a different meaning.
>
> Curious, is it not, that Mr. Eliot
> has not given more time to Mr. Beddoes
> (T. L.) prince of morticians
>
> Pound, Canto LXXX

For Beddoes see note to [II] 131, 159–60 and note to *Whispers of Immortality* 4, "lipless grin".

175–76 **Carrying | Away the little light dead people**: *WLFacs* notes:

> An allusion to Paolo and Francesca, who are in the second circle of Hell, which contains the souls of the lustful: "volontieri | parlerei a que'duo, che insieme vanno, | e paion s' al vento esser leggieri" [Willingly would I speak with those two

that go together, and seem so light upon the wind], *Inf.* V 73–75. In his misery, the protagonist of "A Game of Chess" remembers the moment of ecstasy in the hyacinth garden; Francesca recounting her sad story to Dante, says: "Nessun maggior dolore, | che ricordarsi de tempo felice | nella miseria . . ." [There is no greater pain than to recall a happy time in wretchedness], *Inf.* V 121–23.

TSE: "My life is light, waiting for the death wind", *A Song for Simeon* 4. "O light folk blown by a breath of wind out of the memory of these places", *Anabasis* I xv *variant.* (Perse: "*o gens de peu poids dans la mémoire de ces lieux*".) Laforgue's *Hamlet*, tr. Symons: "the little people of History ··· lighting the dirty lamp", *Symons* 105 (see note to *Animula* 5). **little**: when he boxed this word and wrote "Blot on Scutchen", Pound may have been pointing to its repetition from [II] 109, where he had deleted it. For TSE on over-use of "little", see note to *Burbank with a Baedeker: Bleistein with a Cigar* 1–2. Pound's "Blot on Scutchen" was probably a cliché (from heraldry), not a reference to Browning's tragedy *A Blot in the 'Scutcheon* (1843).

[II] 121–23 **"Do | "You know nothing ··· see nothing ··· remember | "Nothing?"**: Hawthorne: "so he saw nothing, heard nothing, knew nothing", *The Scarlet Letter* ch. XXII.

[II] 125 **Those are pearls that were his eyes**: *TSE's Notes* refer to "my eyes failed", [I] 39 and "(Those are pearls that were his eyes. Look!)", [I] 48.

180 **The hyacinth garden. Those are pearls that were his eyes, yes!**: Pound put a box around "yes!" and wrote "Penelope J.J." *WLFacs* notes: "Molly Bloom's soliloquy in the Penelope episode of *Ulysses* begins and ends with 'Yes', described gaily by Joyce as 'the most positive word in the human language'."

[II] 126 **Is there nothing in your head**: *Hayward*: "Cf. 'headpiece filled with straw', *The Hollow Men* I 4."

[II] 128 **O O O O**: *Hamlet* V ii: "The rest is silence. O, o, o, o. *Dyes*", Hamlet's last utterance in the Folio text (*Grover Smith* 82). *King Lear* V iii: "thanke you, sir, O, o, o, o", Lear's last utterance, First Quarto (Archie Burnett, personal communication). See note on "O" and "Oh", [I] 74, and note to [II] 111–28.

[II] 128–30 **that Shakespeherian Rag— | It's so elegant | So intelligent**: "That Shakes-pea-ri-an rag, Most in-tel-li-gent, ve-ry el-e-gant", chorus of *That Shakespearian Rag* (1912), which became a hit in Broadway's *Ziegfeld Follies*: "That Shakespearian rag, | Most intelligent, very elegant, | That old classical drag, | Has the proper stuff, the line 'Lay on Macduff,' | Desdemona was the colored pet, | Romeo loved his Juliet | And they were some lovers, you can bet, and yet, | I know if they were here today, | They'd Grizzly Bear in a diff'rent way, | And you'd hear old Hamlet say, | 'To be or not to be,' | That Shakespearian Rag" (Gene Buck and Herman Ruby, music by David Stamper) (B. R. McElderry, Jr., *American Quarterly* Summer 1957). TSE:

> "A pick-axe and a spade, a spade,
> For and a winding sheet—"
>
> I 'eard that at the Old Vic once. That's Shakespeare, that is. He wrote some good songs, Shakespeare.
>
> ts draft of *The Rock* (Bodleian, MS Don. d. 44 fol. 107)

Shakespeherian: pronounced *Shakespee-heerian* in TSE's recordings. **Rag:**

Hayward: "ragtime. The syncopated 'jazz' post-war world of the 1920s—restless, aimless, jittery, futile, neurotic." St. Louis was a centre of the controversial ragtime music, attracting musicians including Scott Joplin. See headnote to *Sweeney Agonistes*, 4. JAZZ. TSE: "caper to the rhythm known as 'swing,'" *Three Sonnets* (to Geoffrey Faber) 9.

TSE and popular songs:

(i) adaptation, as here and in **10–11**; likewise in *The smoke that gathers blue and sinks* ("What, you want action? | Some attraction?" 11–12) and *Sweeney Agonistes: Fragment of an Agon* ("*Under the bamboo* | *Bamboo bamboo*", 40–41). Of the two epigraphs to the Clark Lectures (*The Varieties of Metaphysical Poetry* 40), one is from Dante; the other reads: "I want someone to treat me rough. | Give me a cabman. | *Popular song*". This appears to adapt the song "What I want is low-brow love— | Heavy, knock-down, cave-man stuff; | I'm no cooing turtle-dove— | Treat me rough, kid, treat me rough!" (1916).

(ii) imagining songs of his own, apparently, as in *Suite Clownesque* ("I may meet you | Very likely greet you", III 3–4) and again in *Fragment of Agon* ("*My little island girl*", 73). See individual notes and *Chinitz*.

For music hall songs, see note to *WLComposite* 47, and notes to the title *Triumphal March*; *The Dry Salvages* I 1–3; *Suite Clownesque* III 15, 16, 23; and *Billy M'Caw: The Remarkable Parrot* 1.

[II] 128–137a **Shakespeherian · · · make company between us**: Vivien Eliot: "We read Shakespeare aloud | And we two were a crowd", final couplet of a draft poem beginning "During May | J. came to stay" (c. 624 fol. 11). After the poem's final line she wrote: "(Meaning we were good companions & not lonely)".

[II] 131, 159–60 **What shall I do? · · · It's them pills I took, to bring it off, she said. | (She's had five already, and nearly died of young George.)**: Beddoes, *Death's Jest-Book* III iii:

> Squats on a toad-stool under a tree
>   A bodiless childfull of life in the gloom,
> Crying with frog voice, "What shall I be?
> Poor unborn ghost, for my mother killed me
>   Scarcely alive in her wicked womb.
> What shall I be?"

TSE quotes the second and third lines in *The Three Voices of Poetry* (1953).

[II] 132–33 **"I shall rush out as I am, and walk the street | "With my hair down so**: Beaumont and Fletcher: "Suppose I stand upon the sea-beach now, | Mine arms thus, and mine hair blown with the wind", *The Maid's Tragedy* II ii (see note to *Sweeney Erect* epigraph). Also Beaumont and Fletcher, *Philaster* III ii: "send me naked, | My hair dishevelled, through the fiery streets" (*Grover Smith* 309). Dante, *Vita Nuova* [XXIII] tr. Rossetti: "Where ladies through the street, like mournful lights, | Ran with loose hair", *The Early Italian Poets* 271 (*Grover Smith* 313). Walter Besant in London, 1854–55: "the silence grew more and more intolerable · · · When my nerves would stand it no longer, I have taken my hat and rushed out into the streets", *Autobiography* (1902) 275 (turning then to the world of prostitution). **walk the street**: OED "street" 3g: "to walk the street(s)": "to go about on foot in a town." Also: "to be on the streets: to be a prostitute".

[II] 134 **"What shall we ever do?"**: "But what is there for you and me | For me and you | What is there for us to do?" *The Death of the Duchess* I 10–12. E. M. Forster: "'Two philosophic youths repining in the British Museum! What have we done? What shall we ever do?'" *The Longest Journey* (1907) ch. XX.

[II] 135–36 **hot water at ten. | And if it rains, a closed car**: *Hayward*: "Getting up late in order to curtail the boredom of an empty morning. And on a wet afternoon an aimless drive around in a limousine to kill time." For awakening by a servant, see headnote to *Sweeney Agonistes*, 6. THE SUPERIOR LANDLORD (conclusion of this draft). Similarly Fresca and her servant Amanda, *WL Composite* 231–39.

191 closed carriage: ringed by Pound with "Why this between 1922 & Lil" (objecting to the anachronism). Valerie Eliot: "'OK' wrote Pound when Eliot suggested as an alternative: 'A closed car. I cant use taxi more than once'" (*WLFacs* notes, quoting letter of [26? Jan 1922]. See headnote, 1. COMPOSITION, and Textual History.) OED "waiting" quotes James Payn, *The Talk of the Town* (1885): "A closed carriage, well appointed, was at the door, in waiting for her". In the early 1920s, cars commonly had retractable not fixed roofs. Advertisement for Dafoe-Eustice Co.: "For over a decade Ford owners have wanted closed-car luxury without the large first cost that goes with it. They have wanted a Ford Top that could instantly be converted into a closed or open car without the disagreeable work of fastening and unfastening curtains ··· This enables the car to be instantly converted from a cozy closed car in winter to an open car for the breezes of summer. Also it enables you to keep out the dust and rain" (*Popular Science* Oct 1919). TSE: "an open car | Is so undignified: you're blown about so, | And you feel so conspicuous, lolling back | And so near the street, and everyone staring", *The Family Reunion* II i. To Middleton Murry, 25 Apr 1923: "Vivien is so dangerously ill that there is a fresh consultation of doctors every day to decide whether she can be moved to London in a closed car." Continuing a ms story by Vivien Eliot, TSE wrote: "an immense closed car standing waiting at the kerb ··· the chauffeur peered round at her. 'And I expect he thinks I am an odd looking party to be leaving this house' she thought. Nevertheless, she lingered for an instant the more fully to drink in every detail of this super car ··· Rolls-Royce—ah" (d. 936/2, fols. 32–33). To John Hayward, 9 Dec 1936, parodying newspaper reports of the Abdication crisis: "3.30 p.m.—Mr. Eliot left hurriedly in a closed car, in the company of an individual who described himself to the reporters as a taxi-driver." ("shuttered barge", *Burbank with a Baedeker: Bleistein with a Cigar* 11; "female smells in shuttered rooms", *Rhapsody on a Windy Night* 66.)

[II] 136–38 **And if it rains ··· upon the door**: adapted from *The Death of the Duchess* II 45–49.

[II] 137 **And we shall play a game of chess**: *TSE's Notes* refer to Middleton's *Women Beware Women* II ii:

MOTHER: 'Tis a great while
Till supper-time; I'll take my leave then now, madam,
And come again i' th' evening, since your ladyship
Will have it so.
LIVIA: I' th' evening! By my troth, wench,
I'll keep you while I have you: you've great business, sure
To sit alone at home; I wonder strangely

What pleasure you take in't; were't to me now,
I should be ever at one neighbour's house
Or other all day long: having no charge,
Or none to chide you, if you go or stay,
Who may live merrier, ay, or more at heart's ease?
Come, we'll to chess, or draughts; there are an hundred tricks
To drive out time till supper, never fear't, wench.

For Middleton's *A Game at Chesse*, see note to title, part II: *A Game of Chess*. For TSE to E. M. Stephenson on "a dialogue over the chessboard", see note to [II] 111–38. Tristan and Isolde play chess in some versions of their tragedy. "Marivaux' people are a small and well-bred company, none of whom engrosses the conversation ··· It is with a surprisingly small company of actors, and apparent monotony of plots, that Marivaux gets his effects. He does not even invent new names; the Dorantes, the Lisettes, the Madame Argantes, turn up again and again, and they might be the same people, come back to play at life as an end-game with the chessmen shifted about. Yet, though each of them is shadowy, a roomful of them is very real; and it is always to the room, to the situation, that Marivaux directs our attention", *Marivaux* (1919).

[II] 137a] *WLFacs* notes: "This line was omitted at Vivien Eliot's request. The author restored it, from memory, when he made a fair copy of the poem for the sale in aid of the London Library in June 1960." He had previously added it in the margin of Geoffrey Curtis's copy of *1936* and also included it later when copying the poem into *Valerie's Own Book*. For cards as "the eternal duologue which they played" (c. 624 fol. 91), see *McCue 2016*. **ivory men**: Van Zo Post: "If she wanted to fight it out with ivory men instead of words, all right—provided the stakes were the same", *Diana Ardway* (1913) 49. Conrad's *Heart of Darkness* is in a different sense a tragedy of ivory men (see Conrad's "that ivory face" in note to the epigraph on the section-title page to *The Hollow Men*). **make company between us**: on the analogy of "make peace between". Thomas Fuller, *Scripture Observations*: "No purgatory condition between hell and heaven, but instantly, when out devil, in angel. Such is the case of every solitary soul. It will make company for itself", *Good Thoughts in Bad Times* (1645). Conrad: "But the anchors ··· inert and powerful, those emblems of hope make company for the look-out man in the night watches", *Emblems of Hope* in *The Mirror of the Sea* (1906). **company**: among other senses is OED 2: "sexual connexion. *Obs.*" TSE: "I shall not want Company in heaven | Lucrezia Borgia shall be my bride", *A Cooking Egg* 17–18 *variant* ("Company" having previously read "Conversation", which also has a sexual connection: OED "crim. con.": "criminal conversation, i.e. adultery").

[II] 138 **lidless eyes**: Shelley: "Dost imagine | We will but laugh into thy lidless eyes?" *Prometheus Unbound* I 478–79 (George Franklin, *ELH* Winter 1994). James Thomson: "Thy lidless eyes tenebriously bright; | Thy wings, thy vesture, thy dishevelled hair", *To Our Ladies of Death* st.15 (*Hands*) (TSE: "with my hair down", [II] 133). Kipling: "Only lidless eyes see clear", *Outsong in the Jungle*. Tourneur: "Let our two other hands tear up his lids, | And make his eyes like comets shine through blood", *The Revenger's Tragedy* III iv. TSE: "Leaned backward with a lipless grin ··· sockets of the eyes!" *Whispers of Immortality* 4–6. **waiting for a knock upon the door**: "they knock upon the door ··· a knock upon the door",

The Death of the Duchess II 43, 49 (see note). In his 1933 recording, TSE says "the knock upon the door", perhaps suggesting eviction. "KNOCK. Mrs. Porter is expected ··· Pereira ··· intimates his intention of evicting the two girls", *The Superior Landlord* I.

[II] 139 **demobbed:** OED: "colloq. abbrev. of *demobilization* and of *demobilize*", with first citation from 1920, then this line. TSE to Herbert Read, 20 June 1920: "I had been waiting, since the appearance of your first book, to see what you would do when you demobilised your talents."

In *WLFacs* the word is printed in red as Pound's, but Helen Gardner records: "Mrs. Eliot tells me she is not absolutely certain it was his suggestion and he has not pencilled over a suggestion of Vivien Eliot's. [*Footnote:* Mrs. Eliot tells me that she thinks the writing is Vivien's, but that Pound believes that he supplied the word]", *Litz ed.* 76–77.

[II] 139–172 **When Lil's husband ··· good night:** *WLFacs* notes: "Eliot said this passage was 'pure Ellen Kellond', a maid employed by the Eliots, who recounted it to them." Valerie Eliot on Vivien: "It could be that she had a better memory than her husband, because the Eliots had been treated to Lil's monologue by their maid, Ellen Kellond, and it was probably Vivien's keen ear that made her cancel the *d* on each 'Good night' exchanged by the cockneys leaving the pub", BBC broadcast 2 Nov 1971. **husband ··· I said ··· He did, I was there ··· He said, I swear ··· I said ··· He's been in the army ··· I said ··· she said ··· I said ··· she said ··· I said ··· (And her only thirty one.) ··· she said ··· The chemist ··· I said ··· get married ··· they had a hot gammon:** *2 Henry IV* II i, Mistress Quickly (keeper of the Boar's Head Tavern): "Thou didst swear to me then (as I was washing thy wound) to marry me ··· my Lady ··· Did not goodwife Keech the butcher's wife come in then, and call me Gossip Quickly? ··· telling us, she had a good dish of prawns ··· whereby I told thee ··· And didst thou not (when she was gone downstairs) ··· And didst thou not ··· deny it if thou canst?"

[II] 141 **Hurry up please its time:** *Hayward*: "The conventional formula of English publicans, bellowed from the bar of public-houses as closing-time (fixed by the Licensing Acts) approaches." TSE to E. M. Stephenson, 27 May 1942: "meant to be taken literally as the cry of the licensee or barman at closing time in a public house. This section of the poem has nothing to do with the game of chess preceding and is merely a shift to a different stratum of society." Licensing hours had been severely curtailed during the Great War, with drinking-up time earlier by three hours, at 9.30 p.m., strictly policed. The rules were relaxed somewhat in 1921. (For Prohibition in America, see note to *WLComposite* 2.) By 2014, OED gave "time" A 21c: "The moment at which a public house . . . ceases to sell drink; closing time", with TSE's line as first citation. OED has removed "One spake unceasing: 'Gentlemen! Time, please!!'" from Gilbert Frankau's *One of Us* (1912) 104, where it is followed by prolonged goodnights while taxis tick. OED (2014) "time" B: "the end of opening hours in a public house", with G. Hill: "The potmen look to the fastenings of doors, lights are lowered, and cries of 'Time, gentlemen, please!' grow more peremptory", *Living London* (1902). TSE: "rowdy (the pubs being open till midnight)", *The Cultivation of Christmas Trees* 4.

[II] 144 **To get yourself some teeth:** *Hayward*: "The incidence of dental decay among the British working class is notorious, and among young men and women especially so. False teeth, because so common and because so badly fitted, are a popular object of vulgar jokes." Irvin Shrewsbury Cobb: "when he was past sixty he went and got himself some teeth from the dentist", *Cobb's Anatomy* (1912) 44. See note to *How to Pick a Possum* 53 (*Noctes Binanianæ*).

[II] 149 **if you don't give it him, there's others will**: *The Rock* I, ALFRED: "religion is like drink. People may not want it drawn very strong, or very much a' the time, most of 'em; but they seems to like to know that it's always there · · · if they don't get it one way, they will another."

[II] 150 **Something o'**: pronounced *Somethink o'* in TSE's 1933 recording, but *Somethin o'* in that of 1946. In *ts2a* Vivien Eliot had proposed spelling with *-k*, but TSE replied "I want to avoid trying to show pronunciation by spelling" (see Textual History and *WLFacs* 12/13). Another pub scene: "anythink what wasn't right", *Billy M'Caw: The Remarkable Parrot* 5 (*variant* "anything").

[II] 153 **If you don't like it you can get on with it**: "perhaps a more robust comment on the situation is, that if you don't like it, you can get on with it", *The Use of Poetry and the Use of Criticism* 107, after quoting Arnold: "And love, if love, of happier men. || Of happier men—for they, at least, | Have *dreamed* two human hearts might blend | In one", *Isolation. To Marguerite* 36–39.

209 **you needn't look old-fashioned at me**: OED "old-fashioned" 4: "disapproving, tart, reproachful: used *spec.* of facial expression. Also as *adv.*, in a disapproving, reproachful or quizzical manner", quoting this line and Storm Jameson's *Three Kingdoms* (1926).

[II] 155 **it won't be**: TSE omits "it" in his 1933 recording.

[II] 156 **so antique**: "Well you are a antique" (Ethelbert's reaction to the agitator), ts drafts of *The Rock* (Bodleian). "gentility · · · makes the Fabians look to-day so antique", *A Commentary* in *Criterion* Apr 1932.

[II] 159 **them pills · · · to bring it off**: before the age of the Pill, dangerous remedies were available under the counter. *Partridge* gives "bring it away" as 20th-century slang for "effect an abortion".

[II] 160–61 **had five already, and nearly died · · · never been the same**: see note to *A Cooking Egg* 20 for "*Mrs. Molden* the ex-midwife."

[II] 161 **all right**: *ts2* had "allright", and both the *Criterion* and the *Dial* printed "alright". All three appear in TSE's letters, with "alright" the least frequent. The *Criterion* printing of *Sweeney Agonistes: Fragment of a Prologue* had "Allright" (45). The contraction to a single word was the subject of half a dozen pages of "Open Court on *Alright*", Society for Pure English, Tract XVIII (1924): "The question surely is whether *alright* has a fair claim to take its place alongside of such words as *already* · · · *altogether*" (opening section by Matthew Barnes). The editor's final note acknowledges that "the preceding articles arrive at no definite judgement". *Fowler* notes that *alright*, "if seldom allowed by the compositors to appear in print, is often seen in MS".

[II] 163–64, 170 **Well, if Albert won't leave you alone · · · What you get married for · · · Goonight Bill. Goonight Lou**: to Polly Tandy, 17 Apr 1940: "I am stepping the other evening into the Refreshment Room for a drop of the usual (Good Evening, Miss Ward: Good Evening, Mr. E.) when I meet a Lady · · · who passes me the rumour that your old man had been in an escapade and ruining a Car

··· Well Polly you do have your share of trouble but if you marry a man like that what do you expect but the lion's share as the saying is."

[II] 169–71 **HURRY UP PLEASE ITS TIME ··· Ta ta**: Kipling: "Calls for a drink, and a mild cigar, | Batters a sovereign down on the bar, | Collars the change and says 'Ta-Ta'", within the story *The Army of a Dream*. TSE: Mrs. Bert: "Well, tar, tar, boys. Don't forget you're goin' to take me to the pictures to-night, Bert", twice in draft of *The Rock* (after the song in Part II, 68 and 69). **Ta ta**: OED: "A nursery expression for 'Good-bye'; now also in gen. colloq. use."

[II] 172 **Good night, ladies, good night, sweet ladies, good night, good night**: *Hayward*: "Cf. *Hamlet* IV v. These are mad Ophelia's pathetic words of farewell to the ladies of the Court of Denmark. Hamlet had accused Ophelia of being a whore and had told her to remove herself to a 'nunnery'—a slang word in Shakespeare's day for a brothel." Though not her very last lines, Ophelia's farewell anticipates her death by water, for which see note to the next lines of the published poem, [III] 173–76. Laforgue: "Il y avait une langue là-dedans; ça grasseyait: '*Good night ladies; good night, sweet ladies! good night, good night!*'" [He had a tongue in this head, and it burred out "Good night, ladies. Good night sweet ladies! good night, good night!"], *Hamlet* (*Grover Smith* 83). Laforgue's Hamlet, speaking not of Ophelia but of Yorick, and continuing: "Ça chantait, et souvent des gravelures" [It also sang, and it very often sang something ribald].

III. THE FIRE SERMON

Title ***The Fire Sermon***: in Henry Clarke Warren's *Buddhism in Translations* (352–53), which TSE used in 1911–12, "The Fire-Sermon" begins with The Blessed One addressing the priests:

> "All things, O priests, are on fire. And what, O priests, are all these things which are on fire?
>
> "The eye, O priests, is on fire; forms are on fire; eye-consciousness is on fire; impressions received by the eye are on fire; and whatever sensation, pleasant, unpleasant, or indifferent, originates in dependence on impressions received by the eye, that also is on fire.
>
> "And with what are these on fire?
>
> "With the fire of passion, say I, with the fire of hatred, with the fire of infatuation; with birth, old age, death, sorrow, lamentation, misery, grief, and despair are they on fire.
>
> "The ear is on fire; sounds are on fire; . . . the nose is on fire; odors are on fire; . . . the tongue is on fire; tastes are on fire; . . . the body is on fire; things tangible are on fire; . . . the mind is on fire; ideas are on fire; . . . mind-consciousness is on fire; impressions received by the mind are on fire; and whatever sensation, pleasant or unpleasant, or indifferent, originates in dependence on impressions received by the mind, that is also on fire.
>
> "And with what are these on fire?
>
> "With the fire of passion, say I, with the fire of hatred, with the fire of infatuation, with birth, old age, death, sorrow, lamentation, misery, grief, and despair are they on fire.
>
> "Perceiving this, O priests, the learned and noble disciple conceives an aversion for the eye, conceives an aversion for forms, conceives an aversion for eye-consciousness, conceives an aversion for impressions received by the

> eye; and whatever sensation, pleasant, unpleasant, or indifferent, originates in dependence on impressions received by the eye, for that also he conceives an aversion. Conceives an aversion for the ear, conceives an aversion for sounds, . . . conceives an aversion for the nose, conceives an aversion for odors, . . . conceives an aversion for tastes, . . . conceives an aversion for the body, conceives an aversion for things tangible, . . . conceives an aversion for the mind, conceives an aversion for ideas, conceives an aversion for mind-consciousness, conceives an aversion for the impressions received by the mind; and whatever sensation, pleasant, unpleasant, or indifferent, originates in dependence on impressions received by the mind, for this also he conceives an aversion. And in conceiving this aversion, he becomes divested of passion, and by the absence of passion he becomes free, and when he is free he becomes aware that he is free; and he knows that rebirth is exhausted, that he has lived the holy life, that he has done what it behooved him to do, and that he is no more for this world."

TSE: "On one side the conceit is merely the development in poetry of an expository device known to preachers from the earliest times, the extended, detailed, interminable simile. The Buddha used it in the Fire Sermon", *The Varieties of Metaphysical Poetry* 130 (Clark Lecture IV). "There was no widespread interest in Oriental philosophy at Harvard that I knew of. My interest began after my year in Paris. Very, very few people studied it", *Northrop Frye corrigenda* (1963). Back at Harvard after spending 1910–11 in Europe, TSE took C. R. Lanman's "Elementary Sanskrit" course in 1911–12, and both Lanman's "Pali" course and James Haughton Woods's "Philosophical Sanskrit" in 1912–13. TSE on Latimer's "Sermon on the Card": "The method—the analogy, and the repetition—is the same as that once used by a greater master of the sermon than either Donne or Andrewes or Latimer: it is the method of the Fire-Sermon preached by the Buddha", *The Preacher as Artist* (1919). For the "Fire Sermon" at St. Magnus Martyr, see note to [III] 264.

229–98] Cut by Pound. The lines begin with Fresca's awakening, written in the style of Pope (**229–48**), followed by Fresca's letter (**249–65**), which is closer to Restoration Comedy. *WLFacs* notes:

> This opening passage was written in imitation of *The Rape of the Lock.* Cf. also the Calypso episode in Joyce's *Ulysses* [*Little Review* June 1918]. Pound "induced me to destroy what I thought an excellent set of couplets;" wrote Eliot of his pastiche, "for, said he, 'Pope has done this so well that you cannot do it better; and if you mean this as a burlesque, you had better suppress it, for you cannot parody Pope unless you can write better verse than Pope—and you can't'" (Introduction to *Selected Poems of Ezra Pound*, 1928). Eliot added, in the *Paris Review* (1959), that Pound had advised him to "'Do something different'."

The first item in the first issue of the *Criterion* Oct 1922, in which *The Waste Land* appeared, was *Dullness* by George Saintsbury, of which the first words were: "There is of course no foolish intention here of vying in prose with Pope in verse." (Pope and the Goddess Dullness: "Dulness o'er all possess'd her ancient right, | Daughter of Chaos and eternal Night ··· Laborious, heavy, busy, bold, and blind, | She rul'd, in native Anarchy, the mind", *The Dunciad* (1742) I 11–16; TSE: "Women grown intellectual grow dull", *WLComposite* **282**.) In 1934: "the fact that a writer can be satisfied to use the exact idiom of a predecessor is very suspicious; you cannot write satire in the line of Pope or the stanza of Byron", *After Strange Gods* 24. To W. H. Auden, 10 Dec 1936, of his *Letter to Lord Byron*:

"I must say that I started with as much prejudice against it as if you had told me that you had done something like the *Rape of the Lock*, only rather better. But actually it seems to me extremely successful, and is very different from a pastiche." (Gilbert Frankau's "novel in verse" *One of Us* is a Byronic pastiche in ottava rima. For Frankau, see note to [III] 173–82. For TSE's own ottava rima, see headnote to *A Fable for Feasters*.) "a deliberate attempt to *return* to the style of any author or of any period, however accomplished, must always produce an effect of insincerity", *Views and Reviews* in *NEW* 20 June 1935. "the writer to-day who was genuinely influenced by Pope would hardly want to use that couplet at all", *The Use of Poetry and the Use of Criticism* 39. To James Smith, 21 June 1926: "The desire to imitate or emulate Pope is itself rare and commendable. To imitate Pope is in itself highly useful for anyone who wishes to write poetry. I have done it myself, not so very long ago either, and with the exception of one or two lines I do not think that my verses were any better than yours, and perhaps not so evenly good. I destroyed mine and recommend you do the same. Nothing in this style of verse is of any value except as an exercise: and this for the reason that it has already been done literally to perfection. You cannot improve on Pope, nor can you get anywhere by burlesquing him or ragging him because there is just sufficient element of burlesque in Pope himself to render him immune." For *The Dunciad*, see note to *Airs of Palestine, No. 2* 15.

229–30 **the sun's inclining ray ··· the ··· day**: Pope: "*Sol* thro' white Curtains shot a tim'rous Ray, | And op'd those Eyes that must eclipse the Day", *The Rape of the Lock* I 13–14.

231 **Fresca**: "De Bailhache, Fresca, Mrs. Cammel, whirled | Beyond the circuit of the shuddering Bear", *Gerontion* 67–68. (For TSE's enquiry as to whether *Gerontion*, from 1920, should appear as a "prelude" to *The Waste Land* and for Pound's reaction, see headnote, 1. COMPOSITION.) **yawns, and gapes**: "She yawns and draws a stocking up; || The silent man ··· gapes", *Sweeney Among the Nightingales* 16–18.

231–32 **gapes ··· rapes**: see note to "Fresca couplets" [3–5] and *variant*, following **298** below.

237–38 **tray ··· tea**: a rhyme in the 18th century. Pope: "Here Thou, great *Anna*! whom three Realms obey, | Dost sometimes Counsel take—and sometimes *Tea*", *The Rape of the Lock* III 7–8 ("Amanda", **234**). See *Possum now wishes to explain his silence* 13–14: "tea ··· Wednesday". TSE's rhyme "ray/day" (**229–30**) corresponds to Pope's "Ray/Day" (III 19–20).

238–39 **soothing chocolate, or stimulating tea. || Leaving the bubbling beverage**: Pope: "Fumes of burning Chocolate shall glow, | And tremble at the Sea that froths below!" *The Rape of the Lock* II 135–36. In *The Custom of the Country* (1913) ch. IV, Edith Wharton describes how Undine Spragg "usually had her chocolate brought to her in bed by Céleste, after the manner described in the articles on 'A Society Woman's Day' which were appearing in *Boudoir Chat*." **the bubbling beverage to cool**: "Round and round, as in a bubbling pot | That will not cool", *Entretien dans un parc* 22–23.

240 **needful stool**: OED "necessary" 3: "*necessary house*, a privy", with 1761 "He appeared to have just come from his necessary-stool."

241 **Richardson**: *WLFacs* notes: "Samuel Richardson (1689–1761). 'The pathetic tale'

may have been his novel *Clarissa Harlow*." Gilbert Frankau: "Sleep sound, my Meg, and wake refreshed, to write | A new 'Priscilla' for the Tatler's numbers!" *One of Us* (1912) 91. (Though there is no 18th-century novel *Priscilla*, Fielding's *Shamela* and *Amelia* followed Richardson's epistolary *Pamela* and *Clarissa*.)

243 **the conscious sheets**: OED "conscious" 2: "*fig.* Attributed to inanimate things as privy to, sharing in, or witnesses of human actions or secrets. Chiefly *poet.*" For "its conscious darts", see "Fresca couplets" [21] *variant* (following **298**) in Textual History.

244 **Gibbon**: *TSE's books: Bodleian list* (1934) includes "Gibbon [*Decline and Fall of the Roman Empire*]: 6 vols (incomplete)", and "Gibbon's Autobiography (signed by Mary Hutchinson)" which is immediately followed by "12 unbound copies Poems of V.H.E." (Vivien Haigh Eliot; no copy traced). TSE changed "Gibbon" to "the Daily Mirror"—the paper founded in 1903 as "a mirror of the feminine life as well on its grave as on its lighter sides" (Hannah Sullivan, *The Work of Revision*, 2013, 133). TSE: "Addison and Johnson were fortunate in not having to compete with the *Daily Mirror*", *Religious Drama: Mediaeval and Modern* (1937). In Jerome K. Jerome's *Fanny and the Servant Problem*, the Younger Miss Wetherell is prescribed "one page Marcus Aurelius before breakfast—*in case of need*" ("needful", **240**). For the play, see note to *Aunt Helen* 11–12.

245 **Her hands caress the egg's well-rounded dome**: Emerson: "The hand that rounded Peter's dome, | And groined", *The Problem* 19–20.

254–56 **Kleinwurm**: "Here's the Pollicle clan stepping out behind M'Crooner of M'Crooner, last of the hereditary Sandy Pipers (by kind permission of Sir Angus Kleinwurm, Bt., Lord of the Isle of Bugg)", caption to a drawing for children sent by TSE to the Tandy family (late 1930s or early 1940s; BL).

255–56 **Oh, Lady Kleinwurm's monde—no one that mattered— | Somebody sang, and Lady Kleinwurm chattered**: "So they cried and chattered | As if it mattered", *Inside the gloom* 27–28.

258 **Giraudoux**: Jean Giraudoux (1882–1944), French diplomat and novelist. Sending a "*prose lyrique*" of Giraudoux's to the *Dial* on 25 June 1920, Pound noted: "It is derived from Laforgue but = Laforgue was satiric to destruction." The *Dial* published Giraudoux's *The Wreck* in July 1921. *Grover Smith 1983* 65: "Giraudoux's breezy novel *Suzanne et le Pacifique* attained wide success in 1921."

263 **And when to Paris**: "'And so you are going abroad; and when do you return?'" *Portrait of a Lady* III 5.

266–69 **to the steaming bath she moves, | Her tresses ··· the cunning French ··· female stench**: Rimbaud: "Comme d'un cercueil vert en fer blanc, une tête | De femme à cheveux bruns fortement pommadés | D'une vieille baignoire émerge ··· le tout sent un goût | Horrible étrangement" [As from a green zinc coffin, a woman's head with brown hair heavily pomaded rises out of an old bath ··· the whole thing has a smell which is strangely disgusting], *Vénus Anadyomène* 1–3, 9–10. (For Rimbaud's poem, see note to **284, 285^286** *ms4*.)

268–69 **Odours, confected by the cunning French, | Disguise the good old hearty female stench**: TSE: "un odeur fémelle", *Petit Epître* 8. (L. *cunni-* and Fr. *con* suggest a submerged pun.) "cunning ··· contrived ··· deceives ··· confusions", *Gerontion* 34–38. "female smells in shuttered rooms", *Rhapsody on a Windy Night*

66. **the cunning French:** "the cunning Bolognese", *Exequy* 16. **hearty female:** "F. M.": "Life is perhaps a coarse-fibred creature—almost a 'hearty female,' and the proper approach is the slap on the back", *A Diary of the Rive Gauche* II (1925) (*Haffenden*).

270–98 **Fresca! ··· salonnière:** Pope still, but now *Epistle* II: *To a Lady. Of the Characters of Women*, with TSE's Fresca akin to Pope's Narcissa, Flavia, and Atossa. Fresca makes a last appearance in eighteen lines written by TSE and preserved among Vivien Eliot's papers (c. 624 fol. 51), about editing the *Criterion* and dealing with contributors. They are scribbled on an invoice from Hamilton's Bakers and Confectioners, 12 Apr 1924, beneath the stray line "A commentary (would be smart!)", for which see the couplets at the end of this note.

We fear'd that we had bitch'd him quite
But when we met, he showed delight
O what an awfle thing to do
To let upstarts who are taboo
Write nasty articles on apes [5]
Or speak of love in curious shapes
The pal of God whose name is John
The one safe bet to gamble on
Is glory hallelujah John
But Fresca looking rather sly [10]
Says Do appeal to Roger Fry—
I know said she he loves to write
And so for you I think he might.
And great Geo Moore (of carpet fame)
Might—at a price—lend you his name. [15]
√ √ √ √ √
Of course we know the reason *why*—
He keeps the stunt press in his eye.

[4] **upstarts who are**] a man who is *1st reading*

[10] **looking**] *uncertain reading* ‖ questioning *very uncertain 1st reading* **rather sly**] *very uncertain reading* ‖ *1st reading illegible*

[11] **Says Do**] Why not *1st reading*

[13] And therefore write for you he might *1st reading*

The first nine lines of this fragment appear on the verso with, at foot, "Boston 13 / Shall we sail June 21 answer immediately"; the remaining eight lines were added on the recto, inverted.

[1] **bitch'd:** OED *v.*² 2: "To spoil, to bungle." *v.*¹ 2: "*trans.* and *intr.* To behave bitchily towards (a person); to be spiteful, malicious, or unfair (to); to deceive (in sexual matters)", but with first citation from Evelyn Waugh, 1934.

[4–6] *variant* **a man who is taboo ··· nasty articles on apes ··· love in curious shapes:** Pound translated Remy de Gourmont's *Physique de l'amour: essai sur l'instinct sexuel* (1903) as *The Natural Philosophy of Love* (1922), ch. IX of which, "The Mechanism of Love", includes apes. For the book, see note to *Entretien dans un parc* 32.

[6] see note to "Fresca couplets" [3–5] *variant*, following **298** below.

[7] **The pal of God whose name is John:** John 1: 6: "There was a man sent from God, whose name was John." Probably John Middleton Murry, author of *To the Unknown God* (1924), and a regular contributor to the *Criterion*.

[11] **Roger Fry:** the Bloomsbury art critic's translations of Mallarmé appeared in the *Criterion* Jan 1923.

[14] **Geo Moore ··· carpet:** the novelist George Moore was from a landed Irish family, unconnected with George Moore's Carpets of Bury.

[14–15] **Geo Moore ··· at a price:** publication of *The Waste Land* almost foundered over the fee supposedly paid to Moore as contributor to the *Dial* (see headnote, 3. THE *DIAL* AND THE *CRITERION*).

[17] **stunt press:** OED "stunt" *n.*² 2a: *attrib.* 1931: "We are on the eve of a reaction from the 'stunt Press', he believes—the Press of competitions and coupons and catchpenny sensations." Orwell: "the press ··· preserving their 'stunt' make-up, with screaming headlines", *Partisan Review* July–Aug 1941. For the programme of a "Stunt Show" in which TSE took part on 17 Feb 1913, see *Letters 1* 40.

Some related couplets in the hands of TSE and Vivien Eliot (c. 624 fol. 45) read:

[*TSE*:] We know the man's ambitious lust
And literature is but a crust
He serves a charming Tinka Bell
And some w^d say he *serves* her well.

[*Vivien Eliot*:] A [*alt*: The] Commentary wd. be smart
Was more a Commination tart
And what a awful thing to do
to let upstarts who are Taboo
Write nasty articles on Apes
or speak of Love in Curious Shapes [*margin*: Whibley]

[*TSE*:] Exploiting Tory mountebanks
Is the most tedious of pranks

[3] **Tinka Bell:** Tinker Bell, the fairy in J. M. Barrie's *Peter Pan*.

271 **Magdalene:** OED also gives the spelling Magdalen. Each can be pronounced either *Mag-dalen* or *Mag-daleen*. However, "lowly weeping" invokes "the vernacular form of the word ··· *Maudlin*" (see note to **286, 291**), the pronunciation used for both Magdalen College, Oxford and Magdalene College, Cambridge. TSE uses the "Oxford" spelling when writing of "the beauty of the Magdalen" in *Dante* (1929) II. Scofield Thayer, who introduced TSE to Vivien Haigh-Wood in Oxford, and took them punting, was host to a lunch party in Magdalen College. (For TSE on "the nymphs ··· the young ladies whom the young gentlemen took out on the river"—a tributary of the Thames—see note to [III] 175–84.) Pope: "In Magdalen's loose hair and lifted eye", *Of the Characters of Women* 12. OED 2: "*transf.* One whose history resembles that of the Magdalen; *esp.* a reformed prostitute." For cheapening of another female saint, see note to **278**.

272 **More sinned against than sinning:** *King Lear* III ii: "I am a man | More sinn'd against than sinning" (*WLFacs* notes).

273 **The lazy laughing Jenny of the bard:** Rossetti: "Lazy laughing languid Jenny |

Fond of a kiss and fond of a guinea", *Jenny* (*WLFacs* notes). See note to *Paysage Triste* 11.

274–75 **The same eternal and consuming itch | Can make a martyr, or plain simple bitch**: Pope: "*Avidien* or his Wife (no matter which, | For him you'll call a dog, and her a bitch)", *Imitations of Horace: Satire II* ii 49–50. TSE: "La sueur aestivale, et une forte odeur de chienne · · · Saint Apollinaire", *Lune de Miel* 4, 8 (*Arrowsmith 1982* 32).

278 **slattern in a tawdry gown**: OED "tawdry" B: "showy or gaudy without real value"; "tawdry lace", *etym.* "St. Audrey died of a tumour in her throat, which she considered to be a just retribution, because in her youth she had for vain show adorned her neck with manifold splendid necklaces".

281 **Unreal emotions, and real appetite**: "Stendhal's scenes, some of them, and some of his phrases, read like cutting one's own throat; they are a terrible humiliation to read, in the understanding of human feelings and human illusions of feeling that they force upon the reader", *Beyle and Balzac* (1919). "real; unreal", *Oh little voices of the throats of men* 26. See note to [V] 376.

284, 285^286 *ms4* [1] **born upon a soapy sea · · · Venus Anadyomene**: *Lemprière*: "the Venus sprung from the froth of the sea". A subject for artists ever since Pliny described a painting by the Greek artist Apelles, now lost. Pound printed Rimbaud's poem *Vénus Anadyomène* within *A Study of Modern French Poets* in *Little Review* Feb 1918. Gautier: "La Vénus Anadyomène | Est en pelisse à capuchon" [Venus Anadyomene in a hooded fur-lined cloak], *Fantasies d'hiver* III (*Grover Smith 1983* 64). Gautier's women are dressed "En martre, hermine et menu-vair" [In sable, ermine and miniver] (TSE: "Minerva", [9]). TSE: "The re-creation of word and image · · · happens almost incessantly with Shakespeare. Again and again, in his use of a word, he will give a new meaning or extract a latent one; again and again the right imagery, saturated while it lay in the depths of Shakespeare's memory, will rise like Anadyomene from the sea", *The Use of Poetry and the Use of Criticism* 146–47 (on saturation, see note to [I] 48). **Anadyomene**: pronounced *Ana-dy-yòm-enee*.

285 **Symonds—Walter Pater—Vernon Lee**: Valerie Eliot: "John Addington Symonds (1840–93). Walter Horatio Pater (1839–94). Vernon Lee, pseudonym of Violet Paget (1856–1935). These critics of the Renaissance, the source of Fresca's 'culture', are satirically linked together as aesthetes" (*WLFacs* notes, as corrected in copy sent to I. A. Richards from the printed "aesthetics"; later printings also corrected). The conclusion of Browning's *Inapprehensiveness* is an exchange about a book; it

"Was not by Ruskin."

I said "Vernon Lee?"

TSE to de la Mare, 20 Nov 1929: "My only qualification for writing about the 80s is that I was, by a fair margin, born in that decade; I am not an authority on Aesthetics, or on Walter Pater, and I am remarkably ignorant of the work of Vernon Lee. I mean, I could write about Pater, but there seems no obvious reason why I should be the man chosen for that task; and I have no all round knowledge of the aesthetic of the period. I used to know Symonds's work pretty well, but that is long ago." **Symonds**: pronounced as if with a long *i*.

285^286 *insertion ms4* (see Textual History)

[1–6] **Venus Anadyomene | She stept ashore ··· Propelled by Lady Katzegg's guiding hand ··· wealth and fashion ··· She passed ··· our little age:** "*the gondola stopped ··· the countess passed on ··· the little park ···* Descending at a small hotel; | Princess Volupine arrived ··· Passed seaward ··· Money in furs", *Burbank with a Baedeker: Bleistein with a Cigar* epigraph, 2, 3, 6, 24.

[6] **the wonder of our little age:** *WLFacs* notes: "An ironic contrast to 'the wonder of our age', Fulke Greville's tribute to Sir Philip Sidney."

[7] **She gave the turf her intellectual patronage:** "Not sharp enough to associate with the turf", *WLComposite* 380.

[9] **boxing peers:** *WLFacs* notes: "The well-known boxing peers were the eighth Marquis of Queensberry (1844–1900), who supervised the drafting of the 'Queensberry rules', and the fifth Earl of Lonsdale (1857–1944), a notable boxer who donated the Lonsdale belt."

[10–15] **Aeneas' mother ··· worships from afar:** *Aeneid* I 314–417 (see epigraph to *La Figlia Che Piange*).

[12] *variant* **goddess by her smooth celestial pace:** *WLFacs* notes: *Aeneid* I 405: "et vera incessu patuit dea" [And by her graceful Walk, the Queen of Love is known], tr. Dryden I 561.

[14] *variant* **Sees on the screen:** "Who see their outlines on the screen", *Mandarins* 4 4.

286 **The Scandinavians:** for Ibsen, see note to [I] 19–20. On Strindberg: "Forty years ago, his work appeared to most of us the ravings of a morbid man of genius: now, they seem less morbid, because they seem to correspond to the world in which we live ··· he was, as a dramatist, essentially a poet in an age of prose: and the poetic vision is that which sees the matter of fact and sordid as strange and fantastic, and the fantastic and strange as matter of fact. And I think that the experience of the sordid and fantastic 35 years that we have lived through, has prepared us for a juster appreciation of his work", *Strindberg* (1949).

286, 291 **bemused her wits ··· She may as well write poetry:** Pope: "Is there a Parson, much be-mus'd in Beer, | A maudlin Poetess, a rhyming Peer", *An Epistle to Dr. Arbuthnot* 15–16 (see note to 271 on "maudlin").

287 **The Russians:** Dostoevski's *Plan of the novel, "The Life of a Great Sinner"* was published in the first issue of the *Criterion* in Oct 1922 along with *The Waste Land*. TSE to Enid Faber, 24 Feb 1938, of *The Family Reunion*: "The tragedy, as with my Master, Tchehov, is as much for the people who have to go on living, as for those who die. And may I urge you ··· to go to see St. Denis' superb production of *Three Sisters* ··· the best production of a great play that I have seen for a long time." *Hodin* reported TSE in conversation: "what Russia has to give to the West is a peculiar—peculiar, that is, to Russia—spiritual point of view, which is something one is very much aware of in the great Russian novelists", *Horizon* Aug 1945.

287–88 **fits ··· misch-masch:** in 1855 Lewis Carroll's childhood periodical *Misch-masch* included the *Stanza of Anglo-Saxon Poetry* which grew into *Jabberwocky*. In 1876 he gave *The Hunting of the Snark* the subtitle *An Agony in Eight Fits*, punning on the ancient "fytte", a part or section of a poem. (TSE to Aurelia

Hodgson, 25 Mar 1934: "I have a Nonsense Book which I have been working on by fits and starts.")

288 **potpourri:** OED "pot-pourri" 3b: "A literary medley, or collection of miscellaneous extracts." 3c: "Any diverse collection or assortment" (with 1921: "We have a houseful of indiscriminate relatives and it has been hard to collect myself for even this potpourri"). TSE: "'I test people', said Eeldrop, 'by the way in which I imagine them as waking up in the morning. I am not drawing upon memory when I imagine Edith waking to a room strewn with clothes, papers, cosmetics, letters and a few books, the smell of Violettes de Parme and stale tobacco ··· I think of her as an artist without the slightest artistic power'", *Eeldrop and Appleplex* II (1917). For *potpourri* in English and French and for Austin Dobson's *Pot-Pourri*, see note to *Burnt Norton* I 16. *Fowler* recommends the pronunciation *poe-poori.*

290 **When restless nights distract her brain from sleep:** "I have questioned restless nights and torpid days", *Oh little voices of the throats of men* 17. "Of restless nights in one-night cheap hotels", *The Love Song of J. Alfred Prufrock* 6. **distract her brain:** *Symons* 142 (on Huysmans): "It fixes, in precise words, all the uncertainties, the contradictions, the absurd unreasonableness and not less absurd logic, which distract man's brain."

298 **can-can salonnière:** *WLFacs* notes: "Probably the vulgar exhibitionism of the dance is implied in 'can-can', with an element of the gossip too; while 'salonnière' suggests a frequenter or holder of salons, someone who moves in fashionable circles." OED "salonnière": "a woman who holds a salon; a society hostess", with this as first citation.

Notes to the "Fresca couplets" (see Textual History, following **298**).

Although previously thought to be an early manuscript, these two leaves were written by TSE in 1924 as part-reconstruction and part-reimagining of the opening of Part III. In *Letters of the Moment* II by "F. M." in the *Criterion* Apr 1924, the couplets, slightly revised, were "flung" as "obsequies" for the "Caroline renovations" by the Phœnix Society, such as the production of Wycherley's *The Country Wife* in Feb that year ("You beg me not to describe *The Country Wife* and *The Way of the World* as all that, you say, is already too Voguish"). See Textual History headnote, 5. THE "FRESCA COUPLETS".

WLFacs notes:

> It probably amused Eliot to print "these few poor verses" knowing that only two other people knew their source. In addition he drafted (pencil holograph in a black exercise book) the two [prose] paragraphs that follow, ending with a parody of *Prufrock*: "if one had said, yawning and settling a shawl, 'O no, I did not like the *Sacre* at all, not at all'."

The description "these few poor verses" is Vivien's own; the third person was Pound.

[1, 4] **rude entrance of the Tarquin, day ··· rapes:** unwelcome dawn characterised as the rapist in Shakespeare's *Lucrece.*

[3–5] **gapes ··· dreams of love & pleasant rapes | Draped in translucent silks** (*variant* **gapes ··· dreams of love in curious shapes**): Marlowe: "There might you see the gods in sundrie shapes, | Committing headdie ryots, incest, rapes", *Hero and Leander* I 143–44 (see note to [II] 77–110). Alan Seeger: "And painters with big, serious eyes go rapt in dreams, fantastic shapes | In corduroys and Spanish capes and locks uncut and flowing ties", *Paris* II, followed a dozen lines later by "dreams of love". TSE quoted Seeger's two lines in *Short Reviews* (1917). See *Sweeney Among the Nightingales* 11, "Spanish cape", and note. **curious shapes:** writing anonymously of "the verse-producing units circulating on the surface of Great Britain", TSE listed "the ageing, including · · · the curious shapes of Mr. Eliot and Mr. Pound", *Murmuring of Innumerable Bees* (1919). **pleasant rapes:** Dryden: "Doubt not, but when he most affects the frown, | Commit a pleasing rape upon the crown", *Absalom and Achitophel* 473–74, following "like women's lechery", 472 (Shawn Worthington, personal communication).

[6] **Chloe:** Pope: "When bold Sir *Plume* had drawn *Clarissa* down, | *Chloe* stept in, and kill'd him with a Frown", *The Rape of the Lock* V 67–68 (*Haffenden*). Cloe figures in Pope's *Of the Characters of Women* (see note to *WLComposite* 270–98).

[15], [20] *variant* **Dorilant · · · sparkish wits:** Dorilant and Sparkish are characters in *The Country Wife*, where "sparkish" is also used adjectivally. TSE to Virginia Woolf, 7 May 1924. "I wish for nothing better than to attract the sparkish wits of undergraduates."

[21–22] **laws · · · little senate · · · applause:** Pope: "Like Cato, give his little Senate laws, | And sit attentive to his own applause", *Epistle to Dr. Arbuthnot* 209–10.

[25] **And the close rabble in the cinema:** "I am, unfortunately, incapable of being convinced by the arts of the cinema", *A Commentary* in *Criterion* Apr 1932. "I think that the spoken word will always be secondary in the film. Film goes too fast", *The Need for Poetic Drama* (broadcast Nov 1936; the last four words were omitted in the *Listener*). "I think that the cinema comes nearer to pure distraction, to 'taking our minds off . . .' the things they ought to be on as well as the things they need at times to be taken off from. The picture of an actor is never so serious a thing as that actor present on the stage: the film may be nearer in detail to superficial reality, but is always at a further remove from some deeper reality; and to see a moving picture is nearer to merely participating in a common and impersonal dream. (As, in passing, a good photograph is never so near to reality as a good painted portrait)", *Religious Drama: Mediaeval and Modern* (1937). "In looking at a film, we are much more passive; as audience, we contribute less · · · And, as the observer is in a more passive state of mind than if he were watching a stage play, so he has to have more explained to him", *The Film of "Murder in the Cathedral"* (1952), Preface. In *A Dialogue on Dramatic Poetry* (1928), TSE wrote: "The suburban drama has today fundamentally the same morality as it had in the days of *Arden of Feversham* and *The Yorkshire Tragedy*"; but in his copy of the American first edition of *Selected Essays* he wrote alongside (probably in the 1950s): "Alas, no more! The animated picture has changed all that." On mass amusements and boredom, see note to *Sweeney Agonistes* II. *Fragment of an Agon* 18–31.

Notes to published poem resume

[III] 173–76 **The river's tent is broken · · · fingers of leaf · · · sink · · · nymphs · · · my song:** after his soliloquy "To be, or not to be" (III i), Hamlet greets Ophelia as "Nymph". In IV v she bids the court farewell (see note to [II] 172). In IV vii the Queen recounts how Ophelia fell from a broken branch: "There is a willow grows aslant a brook ··· dead men's fingers ··· an envious sliver broke ··· snatches of old lauds ··· her melodious lay" (*Collingwood* 353). Conrad: "the leaves of the tree-tops caught the rays of the low sun, and seemed to shine with a golden-green light of their own shimmering around the highest boughs which stood out black against a smooth blue sky that seemed to droop over the bed of the river like the roof of a tent", *The End of the Tether* (pt. X). E. F. Benson: "even the willow by the side of the bridge had no movement in its slim pendulous fingers of leaf, and the reflecting surface of the slow stream was unbroken", *Robin Linnet* (1919) 18. TSE: "Dropping from fingers of surf", *Mr. Apollinax* 12. **The nymphs are departed. | Sweet Thames:** Pope: "Where *Thames* with Pride surveys his rising Tow'rs ··· Hither the Heroes and the Nymphs resort", *The Rape of the Lock* III 2, 9 (TSE: "Falling towers", [V] 373); for Pope's lines see note to *WLComposite* 237–38).

[III] 173–82 **The river's tent ··· leaf | Clutch and sink into the wet bank. The wind ··· nymphs ··· Thames, run softly, till I end my song ··· summer nights ··· loitering ··· waters:** Gilbert Frankau: "Thames ··· the river's bank ··· water's restful panorama, | Lulled by the music ··· The sun sinks ··· she lingers ··· breezes and wavelets sink ··· Softly ··· another Naiad's yielding ··· The coy resisters of a summer's night", *One of Us* (1912) XIII, the four pages 122–25 ("coy": see note to [III] 185, 196–97 for Marvell's *To His Coy Mistress*).

[III] 175–84 **The nymphs are departed ··· Sweet Thames, run softly, for I speak not loud or long:** *TSE's Notes* refer to the refrain in Spenser's *Prothalamion*, where the speaker "Walkt forth to ease my payne | Along the shoare of silver streaming *Themmes*" (10–11). Nature's beauties (16–21)

> crowne their Paramours,
> Against the Brydale day, which is not long:
> Sweete *Themmes* runne softly, till I end my Song.
>
> There, in a Meadow, by the Rivers side,
> A Flocke of *Nymphes* I chaunced to espy,
> All lovely Daughters of the Flood thereby.

Hayward: "The Thames, above London, from Richmond to Maidenhead and Henley, is a favourite resort for the kind of trippers described in lines 179–80—the latter-day 'nymphs' and their paramours in sports-cars, 'good-time Charlies' and their blonde puppets. Spenser's bridal party has become a 'petting party'." TSE to Dr. Absalom Minola, 5 Nov 1958: "I should say that there is a difference between the two aspects of the river, but that it is not to glorify the past in contrast to the present or to give any suggestion of futility. As for the nymphs, this word is used merely to ~~define~~ indicate the young ladies whom the young gentlemen took out in punts on the river." John Upton on Spenser:

> he plan'd a poem, intitled *Epithalamion Thamesis*, in imitation and friendly rivalship of Cambden's *Bridale of the Isis and Tame*; but afterwards, with many alterations, he made it (by way of Episode) a part of the *Fairy Queen* [Canto XI, "*Where Thames doth the Medway wedd*"] ··· In the Xth Eclogue [of *The Shepheards Calendar*], entitled October, there are plain hints given of some scheme of an heroic poem; and the hero was to have been the Earl of Leicester ··· This great man patronized our poet ··· But Spenser fell under his displeasure for a while ··· it seems owing to some kind of officious sedulity in Spenser, who much desired to see his patron married to the Queen of England.
>
> Preface to Upton's edition of *The Faerie Queene* (1758)

See note to [III] 279 "Elizabeth and Leicester". TSE: "The man who brought order out of the innovations and borrowings of the sixteenth century—a great innovator himself, and with a sensitiveness to words almost equal to that of Chaucer—was Edmund Spenser. He was an elaborator, and he elaborated to excess ··· The great poets who underwent and transmitted his teaching, happened to be dramatic poets", *The Spoken Word* (1951). **The river bears no empty bottles, sandwich papers, | Silk handkerchiefs, cardboard boxes, cigarette ends | Or other testimony of summer nights**: Spenser's swans:

> So purely white they were,
> That euen the gentle streame, the which them bare,
> Seem'd foule to them, and bad his billowes spare
> To wet their silken feathers, least they might
> Soyle their fayre plumes. (46–50)

Vivien Eliot: "The water was dirty, & in it lay many cigarette ends, cards, matches, old rags & bits of refuse flung or dropped from windows above"; TSE changed "lay" to "were" and inserted "dead" before "matches" (c. 624 fol. 123). (TSE: "Like the river with its cargo of dead negroes, cows and chicken coops", *The Dry Salvages* II 68. For *The Dunciad* on "filth" and the Thames, see note to *Airs of Palestine, No. 2* 13–20.) **sandwich papers**: *The Bachelor's Bridal*: "Here, among the debris of their miscellaneous repast,—half hid beneath orange-peel, sandwich papers, and empty wine flasks ··· a sketch-book, forgotten by one of the party", *The New-York Mirror* (1829) (Archie Henderson, personal communication). W. E. Heygate: "the Admiral would have been disgraced—and the only vestiges of the expected battle, sandwich papers and corks and cigar ends having been washed away and the air purified", *Sir Henry Appleton* [1857] 388. Not in OED 1st ed., but TSE's line was added later as first citation (followed by "Motorists' sandwich papers and cigarette cartons", *Public Opinion* 12 Sept 1924). **silk handkerchiefs**: reputedly used as contraceptives or condoms (see Textual History *variant*). Eric Partridge, *A Dictionary of Slang and Unconventional English* (8th ed., rev. Paul Beale, 1984): "strained through a silk handkerchief ··· applied to a very undersized child; since ca. 1930". Truman Capote: "the farmer said: 'Sure she's a pretty baby; oughta be, after having been strained through a silk handkerchief'", *Other Voices, Other Rooms* (1948) I 7. **Sweet Thames, run softly, for I speak not loud or long**: Spenser's refrain: "Against the Brydale day, which is not long: | Sweete *Themmes* runne softly, till I end my Song." The drunken singer in Kipling's story *Brugglesmith* (1891) had Spenser's line as part of his cento:

> Here he stood up in the bows and declaimed:—
>
> "Ye Towers o' Julia, London's lasting wrong,
> By mony a foul an' midnight murder fed—
> Sweet Thames run softly till I end my song—
> And yon's the grave as little as my bed.
>
> I'm a poet mysel' an' I can feel for others".

The story also mentions Dickens and Kew, [III] 293. Many appearances of Spenser's refrain before TSE are adduced by *Whitworth* (and see note to [III] 279).

[III] 176–79, 279, 293 **Sweet Thames run softly ··· song ··· nymphs ··· Elizabeth ··· Richmond and Kew**: Edward Carpenter: "The Thames runs down ···

I glide with tub and outrigger past flower-gardens, meadows, parks; parties of laughing girls handle the oars and tiller ropes; Teddington, Twickenham, Richmond, Brentford glide past; I hear the songs, I hear Elizabethan echoes", *Towards Democracy* (1912 ed. 55–56); see note to [I] 62 for the same passage.

[III] 177–79 **The river bears no ··· handkerchiefs ··· The nymphs are departed:** Laforgue: "Elle est partie hier ··· Son mouchoir me flottait sur le Rhin" [She left yesterday ··· Her handkerchief waved to me on the Rhine], *Complainte d'un Certain Dimanche* [*Lament for a Particular Sunday*] 21–24 ("flottait" suggestive of floating). The Song of the Rhine-daughters is heard [III] 277–78, 290–91.

[III] 179 **testimony:** pronounced *testi-moanie* in TSE's recordings.

[III] 181 **have left no addresses:** to Gilbert Seldes, 11 Aug 1924: "Spaniards never write letters in the summer, because they go to the mountains and leave no addresses."

[III] 182 **By the waters of Leman I sat down and wept . . . :** Psalm 137: 1–3: "By the rivers of Babylon, there we sat down, yea, we wept, when we remembered Zion ··· Sing us one of the songs of Zion." TSE: "What is spring without the Opera? Drury Lane and Covent Garden mourn; the singers have flocked, we are told, to New York, where such luxuries can be maintained. They have forgotten thee, O Sion", *London Letter* in *Dial* Aug 1921.

Hayward: "Babylonian Captivity. Part of the poem was written at Lausanne—hence 'Leman'" (Lake Geneva being Lac Léman in French). Rousseau, on Lake Geneva: "Il me faut absolument un verger au bord de ce lac, et non pas d'un autre; il me faut un ami sûr, une femme aimable, une vache et un petit bateau ··· Combien de fois, m'arrêtant pour pleurer à mon aise, assis sur une grosse pierre, je me suis amusé à voir tomber mes larmes dans l'eau!" [I cannot live without an orchard on the shores of that lake, and no other; I must have a constant friend, a charming wife, a cow, and a little boat ··· How often I would stop to weep at my leisure and, sitting on a large stone, would be amused to see my tears fall into the water!] *Confessions* (tr. J. M. Cohen) IV (*Arrowsmith 1981*, noting Rousseau's Narcissus-like water-gazing, his play *Narcisse*, and the relation of *The Death of Saint Narcissus* to *The Waste Land*). **Leman:** pronounced *Leeman* in TSE's recordings. OED "leman" (pronounced *lem'n* or *leem'n*) 1. "A person beloved by one of the opposite sex" (including citation from *The Faerie Queene*, but with last citation 1739). 2. "One who is loved unlawfully; an unlawful lover or mistress" (last citation 1871).

[III] 182–92 **I sat down and wept ··· bones ··· crept ··· on the bank ··· Musing upon the king my brother's wreck ··· my father's death before him:** *The Tempest* I ii, where Ferdinand hears Ariel's song.

FERDINAND: Sitting on a bank,
Weeping again the king my father's wreck,
This music crept by me upon the waters ···
ARIEL: *Song.* Full fathom five thy father lies;
Of his bones are coral made;
Those are pearls that were his eyes.

TSE has already quoted the song's third line at [I] 48, and he names Ferdinand in his Note to [III] 218. See below at [III] 191–92.

[III] 185, 196–97 **But at my back in a cold blast I hear ··· But at my back from time to**

time I hear | The sound of horns and motors: *TSE's Notes* refer to Marvell: "Had we but world enough and time ··· But at my back I always hear | Time's wingèd chariot hurrying near, | And yonder all before us lie | Deserts of vast eternity", *To His Coy Mistress* 1, 21–24. The poem is quoted in *Andrew Marvell* (1921), and see note to *The Love Song of J. Alfred Prufrock* 92–93.

[III] 186 **rattle of the bones:** Dryden: "When rattling bones together fly, | From the four corners of the sky", *To the Pious Memory of ··· Mrs Anne Killigrew* 184–85, alluding to Ezekiel 37: 1–11, for which see headnote to *Ash-Wednesday* II. **bones ··· chuckle spread from ear to ear:** *Alice's Adventures in Wonderland* ch. VI: "a large cat which was ··· grinning from ear to ear". Byron on a skeleton: "Mark how it laughs ··· From ear to ear | It laughs not ··· the dead bones will grin", *Don Juan* IX xii. Baudelaire: "Tous les mécréants de mélodrame, maudits, damnés, fatalement marqués d'un rictus qui court jusqu'aux oreilles" [All the miscreants of melodrama ··· fatally marked with a grin which runs from ear to ear], *De l'essence du rire* [*On the Essence of Laughter*] III (tr. Jonathan Mayne in *The Mirror of Art*, 1955). (TSE to Edward J. H. Greene, 19 Apr 1940: "Baudelaire's critical work, especially his art criticisms, I have always very much admired. I say always, but I cannot remember when I first began to read it. Perhaps not until the early 'twenties.") Laforgue: "elle alla, dégringolant de roc en roc, râler, dans une pittoresque anfractuosité qui lavait le flot" [she toppled from rock to rock. With death rattling in her throat, and in a picturesque anfractuosity which was washed by the waves], *Salomé* IV (*Hands*).

[III] 187 **crept softly:** "It crept so softly | On silent feet, and stood behind my back, | Quietly", *The Elder Statesman* I.

[III] 187–89 **A rat crept softly through the vegetation ··· on the bank | While I was fishing in the dull canal:** Tennyson: "While fishing in the milldam water ··· A water-rat from off the bank | Plunged in the stream", *The Miller's Daughter* (1832 text) (*Mordell* 52). **fishing in the dull canal:** *Hayward*: "The maimed and impotent Fisher King. (His legendary castle was always situated on a river or by the sea.)" **the dull canal:** Byron: "Damm'd like the dull canal", *Ode on Venice* IV (*Sloane* 144).

301–16 *Pound's annotation*: "Echt"] *WLFacs* notes: "Defined by Pound as 'veritable, real'." TSE's word in [I] 12.

[III] 188 **slimy belly:** "slippery white belly", *The Death of Saint Narcissus* 25.

[III] 189–90 **the dull canal ··· gashouse:** Joyce, *Ulysses* episode VI (Hades) in *Little Review*, Sept 1918:

> Mr. Bloom put his head out of the window.
> —The grand canal, he said.
> Gasworks.

From the same episode, *Grover Smith* 84 points to "An obese grey rat toddled along the side of the crypt, moving the pebbles" (TSE: "A rat crept softly through the vegetation", [III] 187).

[III] 191–92 **Musing upon the king my brother's wreck | And on the king my father's death before him:** *TSE's Notes* refer to *The Tempest* I ii: "the king my father's wreck" (see note to [III] 182–92). In the same scene Ferdinand speaks of having "beheld | The king my father wreck'd". Although Ferdinand's phrase speaks only of his father, TSE splices it to apply to a father and a brother. So doing, he brings together the story of Alonso, King of Naples, and his son Ferdinand, with that of Prospero, the rightful Duke of Milan, and his usurping brother Antonio. *Hamlet* too is the story of a usurping brother and a rightful heir. First soliloquy (I ii): "My father's brother—but no more like my father | Than I to Hercules", followed by HORATIO (of the ghost of Hamlet's father): "My lord, the king your father." HAMLET: "The king my father?" TSE's father had died 7 Jan 1919 (so that TSE no longer had both "Henry, my father" and "Henry, my brother").

[III] 193–94 **on the low damp ground ··· low dry garret:** "In our dry cellar", *The Hollow Men* I 10, first read "In our damp cellar", then "In our dark cellar".

[III] 194 **cast:** pronounced with a short *a* in TSE's recordings. **in a little low dry garret:** (title) *The Little Passion: From "An Agony in the Garret"* ("Uncollected Poems").

[III] 194–95 **And bones ··· Rattled by the rat's foot only:** *Grover Smith* 84 cites *Ulysses* episode VI (Hades), "Rattle his bones. Over the stones. Only a pauper. Nobody owns"; but this was absent from the *Little Review* text, Sept 1918.

[III] 197 **sound of horns and motors:** *TSE's Notes* quote four lines of John Day ("When of the sudden ··· naked skin ···") from *The Parliament of Bees* (wr. 1607?, pub. 1641), Character III, in which Polypragmus imagines a palatial hive:

I will have one built
Like Pompey's theatre; the ceiling gilt
And interseamed with pearl ···
My great hall I'll have paved with clouds; which done,
By wondrous skill, an artificial sun
Shall roll about, reflecting golden beams ···
A roof of woods and forests I'll have spread,
Trees growing downwards, full of fallow-deer;
When of the sudden, listening, you shall hear
A noise of horns and hunting, which shall bring
Actæon to Diana in the spring,
Where all shall see her naked skin; and there
Actæon's hounds shall their own master tear,
As emblem of his folly that will keep
Hounds to devour and eat him up asleep.
All this I'll do that men with praise may crown
My fame for turning the world upside-down.

Lemprière on Actæon: "a famous huntsman ··· He saw Diana and her attendants bathing ··· for which he was changed into a stag, and devoured by his own dogs." *The Parliament of Bees* was included in the Mermaid series in *Nero and Other Plays*, with an introduction by Arthur Symons (1888). Gabriel Pearson suggests that Day's imagined ceiling may have led TSE to Verlaine's "*coupole*" [III] 202 (*New Comparison* Autumn 1992). **horns and motors:** TSE: "Whether Strawinsky's music be permanent or ephemeral I do not know; but it did seem to transform the rhythm of the steppes into the scream of the motor horn, the rattle of machinery, the grind of wheels, the beating of iron and steel, the roar of the underground railway, and the other barbaric cries of modern life; and to transform these despairing noises into music", *London Letter* in *Dial* Oct 1921. "Perhaps the conditions of modern life (think how large a part is now played in our sensory life by the internal combustion engine!) have altered our perception of rhythms", *Savonarola* (1926). For "chorus, which ought to have a noise like a street drill", see headnote to Sweeney Agonistes, 10. PREMIÈRE IN AMERICA: ENTER AN OLD GENTLEMAN.

[III] 198 **Sweeney:** *Hayward*: "Cf. *Sweeney Agonistes*." TSE to his Swedish translator Erik Mesterton, 20 Jan 1932: "Refers certainly to the Sweeney poems, but not by intention to the dialogues which I have renamed *Sweeney Agonistes*, because they were not written at the time. A reference to it is suitable, however, although the dialogue is only obtainable in back numbers of *The Criterion*" (prior to collection in *Sweeney Agonistes* in Dec 1932).

[III] 199–201 **O the moon shone bright on Mrs. Porter · · · soda water:** the ballad which *TSE's Notes* claim was "reported to me from Sydney, Australia" was popular among Australian troops during the Great War:

> O the moon shines bright on Mrs. Porter
> And on the daughter
> Of Mrs. Porter.
> They wash their cunts in soda water
> And so they oughter
> To keep them clean.

Grover Smith 86: "C. M. Bowra states that the song was sung by Australian soldiers at Gallipoli in 1915, but he follows a red herring in alleging that Mrs. Porter herself 'seems to have kept a bawdy-house in Cairo'" (Bowra, *The Creative Experiment*, 1949, 182). *The Columbiad* st. 48: "The Kween sat by to rince her Kwunt". Grover Smith gives the bawdy text, but also:

> O the moon shines bright on Mrs. Porter
> And on the daughter,
> For she's a snorter.
> O they wash their feet in soda water,
> And so they oughter,
> To keep them clean.

Clive Bell on a dinner party in "the middle 'twenties maybe": "somebody wondered whether anything was known of Mrs Porter and her daughter beyond the fact that they wash their feet in soda water. 'These characters are known', said the master, 'only from an Ayrian camp-fire song of which one other line has been preserved: *And so they oughter*. Of such pieces, epic or didactic', he continued, 'most have been lost, wholly or in part, in the mists of antiquity; but I recall one that is generally admitted to be complete: *Some say the Dutch ain't no style, ain't no style, | But they have all the while, all the while*'", in *March & Tambimuttu eds.* 16. Faber secretary to James MacAuley (in Sydney), 4 July 1958: "Mr Eliot · · · cannot satisfy your curiosity about the jingle of Mrs Porter. It was first conveyed to him by an American friend who was a seaman and who had visited several Australian ports. It was on his authority that Mr Eliot attributed the lines to Australia, but he has no knowledge of the song beyond this." Given TSE's own improper rhymes, he was presumably well aware of bawdier versions (as also of ribald versions of *One-eyed Riley* when he incorporated two innocent verses into *The Cocktail Party*). *Oh, Mr. Porter!* (by George Le Brunn, addressed to a railway porter) and "Oh, the moon shines bright | On Charlie Chaplin" were both sung by Marie Lloyd. To the Chief Justice of Australia, 3 Nov 1942:

"thank you for your kind letter of the 17th July; and for sending me the score of *The Moon Shone Bright on Pretty Red Wing.* I am much interested to find that the tune is fundamentally the same as that to which the words of *The Moon Shone Bright on Mrs. Porter* were commonly sung. It is curious that both the original song and this version should have come to me from Australia, because the words you send evidently refer to a tragedy of the American Indians. So I suppose that the song was originally of American composition." In Part II of *The Superior Landlord*, Mrs. Porter is a hearty singer; see *Sweeney Agonistes* headnote, 6. *THE SUPERIOR LANDLORD* **Porter**: a kind of beer, OED: "app. because orig. made for or chiefly drunk by porters". TSE: "Take my letters from the porter—ask him for a drink", *Do I know how I feel? Do I know what I think?* 5.

[III] 201–202 **They wash their feet ··· *chantant***: *Hayward*: "The sound of singing at the ceremonial feet-washing, preceding the restoration of Anfortas (Fisher King) by Parzifal (in the Perceval Legend) and the removal of the curse from the Waste Land." In Wagner's opera, the foot-washing occurs in act III before Parsifal can enter the Grail Castle. **wash their feet**: *The Duchess of Malfi* IV ii: "Don clean linen, bathe your feet", Bosola's taunting of the Duchess before her murder (for the scene, see note to [II] 117–23). **soda water**: "Eliot has emphatically denied that the soda water here is anything but water with soda in it—'Not White Rock,'—he has said" (naming an American brand), *Grover Smith* 86. See note to *Sweeney Agonistes* II. *Fragment of a Prologue* 43, 52, 61. ***Et O ces voix d'enfants, chantant dans la coupole!***: *TSE's Notes* refer to Verlaine's sonnet *Parsifal* (first pub. in the *Revue wagnérienne*), ending: "—Et, ô ces voix d'enfants chantant dans la coupole!" [And, oh those children's voices, singing in the dome!] TSE: "Children singing in the orchard", *Ode* ("Tired. | Subterrene") 12. For other "children's voices" (from *First Caprice in North Cambridge* to *Little Gidding*), see notes to *Landscapes* I. *New Hampshire* 1 and 1, 8, 12.

[III] 202–206 ***Et O ces voix d'enfants* ··· Jug jug jug jug jug jug ··· Tereu**: John Lyly: "O t'is the ravish'd Nightingale. | Iug, Iug, Iug, Iug, tereu, shee cryes", Trico's song, *Campaspe* V i (see note to [II] 98–104). The title page of *Campaspe* (1584, Second Quarto) notes that it was "Played beefore the *Queenes Maieftie on* newyears day at night, by her *Maiefties Children, and the Children of Paules*". (For Elizabethan child actors—Hamlet's "little eyases"—see note to *Gus: The Theatre Cat* 45–48.)

[III] 203–206 **Twit ··· Tereu**: OED "twit", *int.* and *n.* 2: "an imitation of the shrill chirp of a small bird", citing these lines.

[III] 204] As "jug-jug, jug-jug, jug-jug" in TSE's 1933 recording, but as "jug-jug-jug-jug-jug-jug" in that of 1946 (Saskia Hamilton, personal communication).

[III] 205 **So rudely forc'd**: *Hayward*: "Example of re-entry of a theme" (from [II] 100, where the spelling is "forced").

[III] 206 **Tereu**: to Roberto Sanesi, 8 Dec 1960: "Tereus was of course the husband of Procne and ravisher of Philomela. Tereus, according to some accounts, was metamorphosed into a hoopoe, as Procne into a swallow and Philomel into a nightingale. From what literary source I got the use of the name here in the vocative I don't know, but I should say that it also had represented to somebody at least, like the previous ejaculation, the notes of the nightingale herself" (see note to [II] 98–104). Accented on the first syllable, *teerr-oo*, in TSE's 1933 recording, but on the second, *tee-rooo*, in that of 1946.

[III] 207 **Unreal City**: see note to [I] 60–63.

321 **I have seen and see**: *Hamlet* III i, OPHELIA: "Oh woe is me, | T'have seen what I have seen, see what I see" (Shawn Worthington, personal communication). TSE has "I have seen" ten times, including *The Love Song of J. Alfred Prufrock* 82, thirty lines before "Prince Hamlet".

321–22 **Unreal City, I have seen and see | Under the brown fog of your winter noon**: Pound put a box around "your" in *ts3b* and asked "vocative?" presumably questioning whether it was addressed to the Unreal City, or whether TSE intended OED's "your" 5b: "Used with no definite meaning, or vaguely implying 'that you know of' ··· often expressing contempt". Likewise, Pound wrote "vocative ??", apparently referring to "your" again in the line "(London, your people is bound upon the wheel!)", which TSE had typed, typed through, then retyped a few lines later, only for Pound to delete it again, *WLComposite* 343. "Unreal City, I have sometimes seen and see", *WLComposite* **114** *variant*.

321–27 **Unreal City, I have seen and see ··· merchant ··· luncheon**: to Eleanor Hinkley, 23 July 1917: "If I have not seen the battlefield, I have seen other strange things, and I have signed a cheque for £200,000 while bombs fell about me. I have dined with a princess and with a man who expected two years hard labour; and it all seems like a dream. The most real thing was a little dance we went to a few days ago." Reviewing the anthology *Others*: "I have seen the forces of death with Mr. Chesterton at their head upon a white horse", *Observations* (1918).

> I was lunching one day at *The Princess Louise* ···
> I have seen much of life, in its various shades,
> And the fat and the lean, and the profit and loss;
> I have done everything and I've been everywhere
>
> *Pollicle Dogs and Jellicle Cats* 1, 8–10

[III] 209–11 **Mr. Eugenides, the Smyrna merchant ··· with a pocket full of currants | C.i.f. London: documents at sight**: *Hayward*: "Syrian merchants were carriers of the old Grail legends and mysteries. Mr. Eugenides, their modern counterpart, is a deplorable end-product." Smyrna was occupied by Greek forces in May 1919 and recaptured by the Turks in 1922 (see Donald J. Childs, *EinC* Apr 1988). **Eugenides**: ("well-born", Gk.) Pronounced with a hard *g* (*U-ghen-idd-ees*) in TSE's recordings of 1933 and 1946 (see note on pronunciation of "*Gerontion*"). **a pocket full of currants**: "A pocket full of rye", *Sing a song of sixpence*, nursery rhyme (with a mercantile touch: "The king was in his counting house | Counting out his money"). This, says *The Oxford Dictionary of Nursery Rhymes*, "might be the specific 'pocket' sack-measurement of that grain." OED "pocket" 1: "A bag or sack. Sometimes used as a measure of quantity ··· a pocket of hops about 168 lbs." ("seller of currants", Notes on the Waste Land, 218.) *Smidt 1973* 21: "A probably less significant memory is that of the Smyrna merchant, whom Eliot, as he told me, encountered in his Lloyds Bank days, and who really had a pocketful of currants" (see note to [III] 211–14). **currants**: as OED notes, dried grapes imported from the Levant.

[III] 209–10, 214 **the Smyrna merchant | Unshaven · · · at the Metropole**: Baedeker's *Great Britain* (7th ed, 1910) on Brighton: "*Baths* · · · *Métropole Turkish Baths*, at the Hôtel Métropole".

[III] 211 *TSE's Notes* **cost insurance and freight**: this explanation of C.i.f. was emended in *1963* from "carriage and insurance free". TSE's secretary to Alan Clodd, 29 June 1959: "Mr. Eliot says that he is quite likely to have been mistaken about the meaning of 'c. i. f.', but if so it was a piece of misinformation which he picked up while working in the Foreign Department of Lloyds Bank." Norman Nathan had pointed out the error previously (*N&Q* June 1958), but this may not have come to TSE's notice. Clodd reminded TSE in 1962, but too late for corrections for the Mardersteig edition. TSE to Clodd, 19 Apr 1962: "the alteration can be made in notes on *The Waste Land* in other editions, as reprinted. I have confirmed from Lloyds Bank that c.i.f. stands for cost, insurance and freight." David Bland to printers (MacLehose), 22 June 1962 (Faber archive):

> Mr. Eliot has asked us to circulate the following correction for notes to *The Waste Land*, line 210. This would apply to *The Collected Poems* of T. S. Eliot which you print. The note should read: "The currants were quoted at a price 'cost, insurance and freight to London'".

TSE on his own banking career: "I was on inward bills, foreign coins and notes, and documentary credits until I was sent to Head Office to take charge of Pre-War Enemy Debts for the bank and its customers", *Harvard College Class of 1910, Seventh Report* (1935). Leyris's French translation has "C.A.F." [Coût, Assurance et Frêt]. But where Menasce's French translation had retained "C.i.f.", TSE emended to "T.a.p." (Total account payable). Kipling: "How he met with his fate and the V.P.P. | At the hand of Harendra Mukerji", with Kipling's note: "Value Payable Post = Collect on Delivery", *The Ballad of Boh Da Thone*. A letter from TSE to J. D. Aylward, 5 Nov 1944, concerning terms offered to Aylward for a book, is headed:

> Private and Confidential.
> Without Prejudice or Responsibility.
> Errors and Omissions Excepted.
> C.I.F.

[III] 211–14 **documents · · · demotic French · · · Metropole**: Francis Jammes: "Tu écrivais: 'La Métropole | n'en a pas de pareille.' Et tu disais: 'Ma vie | m'a rendu comme un vrai créole'" [You wrote "The Métropole has no parallel." And you said: "My life has turned me into a real creole"], *Tu écrivais* 18–20 (1889). **French · · · Metropole**: Baedeker's *Great Britain* has this hotel head the Brighton list, as the most expensive, and on two occasions observes the acute accent. **To luncheon at the Cannon Street Hotel | Followed by a weekend at the Metropole**: Gilbert Frankau: "Friday lunches at the Ritz | Prelude a week-end at the Metropole", *One of Us* (1912) 113. **the Cannon Street Hotel**: *Hayward*: "The Cannon Street Hotel (at Cannon Street Station) was at this period a common and convenient meetingplace for foreign business men and their British colleagues, being in the heart of the City at the terminus of one of the routes to the Continent. Its importance as a railway terminal has declined and it is now largely used for company meetings." **a weekend at the Metropole**: *Hayward*:

> One of the principal hotels-de-grand-luxe on the sea-front at Brighton, much frequented by wealthy business men for pleasure-jaunts. It is not what is called a 'Family Hotel'! (It is desirable not to make any comment which could be construed as libellous.) The Metropole is notorious for its raffish clientèle, cf. the Music-Hall song, made famous by George Robey:—
>
> Now Henry VIII was a wag in his day
> He had several wives and was very gay
> He founded The Metropole, Brighton, they say ···
> Really! Yes, would you believe it!

(TSE to Pierre Leyris, [26 Oct] 1947, on the proofs of *Poèmes*: "I call your attention also to some matter about the Hotel Metropole, which John has deleted: it was never intended for publication but for your own guidance, and I should certainly not wish it to be included.") In St. Louis, the Metropole Hotel, built 1912, was known to cater for prostitutes until 1920 (*St. Louis Post-Dispatch* 26 Nov 1972; Charles T. Dougherty, *Yeats Eliot Review* June 1982).

[III] 212 **demotic**: OED 1a: "Of or belonging to the people: spec. the distinctive epithet of the popular form of the ancient Egyptian written character (as distinguished from the hieratic"). b. "Of or belonging to the popular written or spoken form of modern Greek." 2: "Of, pertaining or proper to, the common people; popular, vulgar" (quoting this line).

[III] 212 *variant* **abominable**: Housman: "For the nameless and abominable colour of his hair", *Oh who is that young sinner*. OED "abominable": "The abhomynable Synne of Sodomye" (1366). Spelt with an *h* from a mistaken etymology—"away from man, inhuman, beastly"—the only spelling in the First Folio of Shakespeare. For intermediate stages of TSE's revision, see Textual History. *Smidt 1973* 21: "Eliot was annoyed that some critics had found a suggestion of perversion in the incident which he had never intended" (see *Peter* and *Miller*).

326–28 **French, | To luncheon at the Cannon Street Hotel, | And perhaps a weekend at the Metropole**: to Pound [26? Jan 1922], presumably in response to a comment now missing, asking whether it was a comment or a proposed reading: "What does THENCE mean (To luncheon at the Cannon St. Hotel)???" Pound replied [28? Jan 1922]: "I merely queried the dialect of 'thence'; dare say it is o.k." The surviving drafts do not have "thence" either in TSE's text or among Pound's comments, and neither do Pound's previous letters. **And perhaps:** *Pound's annotation*: "dam per'apsez". The annotation was initially transcribed as "dam per'apsey" in *WLFacs*, but was corrected when reprinting. Valerie Eliot also corrected the copy of *WLFacs* she sent to I. A. Richards (Magdalene). J. B. Beer proposed "damn perhapses", *TLS* 13 Apr 1973, suggesting that Pound might have read the phrase in a letter from Coleridge to Southey [26 Sept 1794].

Notes to WLComposite 334–48:

338–40 **Knowing neither how to think, nor how to feel ··· London, your people is bound upon the wheel**: "They know what to think and what to feel | The inhabitants of Hampstead are bound forever on the wheel", *The Death of the Duchess* I 8–9. Also (title) *Do I know how I feel? Do I know what I think?*

341 **Phantasmal gnomes**: *WLFacs* notes: "Palmer Cox (1840–1924) worked in

America as an illustrator and author of children's books. His popular 'Brownie' series portrayed in verse and pictures the activities of a group of benevolent elves."

344 **motions of these pavement toys:** "a toy that was running along the quay", *Rhapsody on a Windy Night* 39.

348 **Ademantus** (*variant* **Glaucon**): *WLFacs* notes:

> Adeimantus and Glaucon, brothers of Plato, were two of the interlocutors in *The Republic*. Appalled by his vision of the "Unreal City", Eliot may be alluding to the passage which inspired the idea of the City of God among Stoics and Christians, and found its finest exponent in St. Augustine. [Plato, *The Republic* bk. IX 592 A–B]:
>
> > *Μανθάνω, ἔφη· ἐν ᾗ νῦν διήλθομεν οἰκίζοντες πόλει λέγεις, τῇ ἐν λόγοις κειμένῃ, ἐπεὶ γῆς γε οὐδαμοῦ οἶμαι αὐτὴν εἶναι. Ἀλλ', ἦν δ' ἐγώ, ἐν οὐρανῷ ἴσως παράδειγμα ἀνάκειται τῷ βουλομένῳ ὁρᾶν καὶ ὁρῶντι ἑαυτὸν κατοικίζειν·*
>
> "'I understand,' he [*VE*: Glaucon] said: 'you mean the city whose establishment we have described, the city whose home is in the ideal; for I think that it can be found nowhere on earth.' 'Well,' said I [*VE*: Socrates], 'perhaps there is a pattern of it laid up in heaven for him who wishes to contemplate it and so beholding to constitute himself its citizen'" (tr. Paul Shorey, Loeb, 1935).

Notes to published poem resume

[III] 215–256 *Hayward*: "The sterile 'love' of modern urban civilization exposed. Tiresias is represented here as the expert on sexual relationships." (For Tiresias, see note to [III] 218.) TSE to Geoffrey Faber, 10 May 1936, in a letter on John O'Hara's *Appointment in Samarra*: "What puzzles me especially, however, is your statement that 'when sex becomes charged with something more than physical pleasure, it means all kinds of results I want to avoid'. If I took this into my mind in what would be literalness for me, I should say that I held just the opposite point of view. But this is improbable, for two reasons. One is, that it seems to me unlikely that you and I should hold directly opposite views on such a fundamental matter; and the other is, that in my experience two people seldom agree closely enough on the meaning of words to be able to disagree exactly about the use of them in propositions ··· I should think that when sex meant merely physical pleasure, it ceased to mean any kind of pleasure; that it had become merely a habit, as the confirmed cigarette smoker (as we know) ceases to get any gustatory or olfactory pleasure from smoking, and the drunkard and the glutton also cease to enjoy the sense of taste and smell. The first and perhaps most universal complication of sex is I think the pleasure of vanity, which can enter in even when there is no reasonable justification for being vain. Further, there is the moral element: the heightening of pleasure by the sense of either doing something positively good or something positively evil (the pleasure of consciously doing evil can be a very refined and intense one). I will not admit, to begin with, that the enjoyment of wine is a purely physical pleasure. It is easier to show that, than in the case of sex. To begin with, the enjoyment of wine is an acquired and trained taste (of course I should make the same claim for the pleasures of sex, but that is less easily proved). At one stage, and perhaps always, the enjoyment of wine is complicated by one's self-approval for having a taste in wine; but I have no doubt that those who really enjoy wine to the keenest are enjoying a sense of discrimination which is almost a spiritual good."

[III] 215–18 **At the violet hour ··· the human engine waits ··· throbbing ··· throbbing:** James Thomson: "throughout the twilight hour ··· Life throbbing held its throbs supprest", *In the Room* 17–20 (*Crawford* 51); for the poem, see note to *The Love Song of J. Alfred Prufrock* 13. On the ts of Vernon Watkins's *The Ballad of Mari Lwyd* (1941), TSE wrote: "there's a throb of genuine passion in almost all these poems" (BL).

[III] 215, 220 **the violet hour ··· the violet hour, the evening hour:** Henry James: "It was the evening hour, but daylight was long now and Paris more than ever penetrating. The scent of flowers was in the streets, he had the whiff of violet", *The Ambassadors* bk. VII II. TSE: "Mr Symons has enveloped Baudelaire in the Swinburnian violet-coloured London fog of the 'nineties", *Baudelaire in Our Time* (1927).

[III] 216 **the human engine:** see *The Engine* and notes.

[III] 217 **a taxi throbbing waiting:** John Buchan: "the throbbing of a stationary car", *The Thirty-Nine Steps* (1915) VI. (TSE to Major Coker, 3 May 1945, of Buchan's *Path of the King*: "I enjoyed the book, like most of Buchan's." See note to *Landscapes* IV. *Rannoch, by Glencoe* 6–7.) The first two typescripts of *The Cultivation of Christmas Trees* have at **21** "Still throbbing" and "Still awaiting", respectively. **throbbing:** Whitman: "the infinite separate houses ··· each with its meals and minutia of daily usages, | And the streets how their throbbings throbb'd", *When Lilacs Last in the Dooryard Bloom'd* 115–16. TSE on the sensibility of James, Frazer and Bradley: "throbbing at a higher rate of vibration with the agony of spiritual life", *A Prediction with Regard to Three English Authors* (1924).

352 **To spring to pleasure through the horn or ivory gates:** Homer's Penelope tells Odysseus of the two gates through which dreams pass on their way from the underworld: "one is fashioned of horn and one of ivory. Those dreams that pass through the gate of sawn ivory deceive men ··· But those that come forth through the gate of polished horn bring true issues to pass", *Odyssey* XIX 563–67 (tr. A. T. Murray, Loeb, 1919). TSE to Jackson Knight, 13 Mar 1945: "I am not an Homeric but a Virgilian." Valerie Eliot quotes Virgil in *WLFacs* notes: "Sunt geminae Somni portae; quarum altera fertur | cornea, qua veris facilis datur exitus umbris, | altera candenti perfecta nitens elephanto, | sed falsa ad caelum mittunt insomnia Manes" [Two Gates the silent House of Sleep adorn; | Of polish'd Iv'ry this, that of transparent Horn: | True Visions through transparent Horn arise; | Through polish'd Iv'ry pass deluding Lyes], *Aeneid* VI 893–96; Dryden tr. VI 1235–38. TSE refers in other poems to each kind of sleep (VE): "And Sweeney guards the hornèd gate", *Sweeney Among the Nightingales* 8; "The empty forms between the ivory gates", *Ash-Wednesday* VI 18. The words from Virgil are spoken to Aeneas and the Sibyl during their journey through Hades by Aeneas' father, who then "dismisses them by the ivory gate". Gérard de Nerval: "Je n'ai pu percer sans frémir ces portes d'ivoire ou de corne qui nous séparent du monde invisible" [I have never been able to penetrate without a shudder those ivory or horned gates which separate us from the invisible world], *Aurélia* I. **spring:** because of "taxi throbbing" in the previous line,

Pound wrote in the margin "Taxi spring ??" (meaning its suspension). He also transposed "horn" and "ivory", perhaps because of "taxi · · · horn".

[III] 218 **Tiresias:** said to have lived as many as nine generations. When he saw two serpents copulating, he struck them and was changed into a woman. *Lemprière*: "Seven years after he again found some serpents together in the same manner, and he recovered his original sex, by striking them with his wand. When he was a woman, Tiresias had married, and · · · Jupiter and Juno referred to his decision · · · which of the sexes received greater pleasure from the connubial state. Tiresias · · · decided in favour of Jupiter, and declared, that the pleasure which the female received was ten times greater than that of the male. Juno, who · · · gave the superiority to the male sex, punished Tiresias by depriving him of his eye-sight. But this dreadful loss was in some measure repaired by the humanity of Jupiter, who bestowed on him the gift of prophecy." *Inf.* XX 40–45: "Behold Tiresias who changed his aspect, when of male he was made woman, all his limbs transforming; and afterwards he had again to strike the two involved serpents with his rod, before he could resume his manly plumes." **throbbing between two lives:** Arnold: "Wandering between two worlds, one dead, | The other powerless to be born", *Stanzas from the Grande Chartreuse* 85–86. TSE: "Bleeding between two lives", *Song* ("The golden foot I may not kiss or clutch") 5. "Being between two lives", *Little Gidding* III 6.

[III] 218 *TSE's Notes* **Tiresias · · · the most important personage in the poem, uniting all the rest:** to Jonathan Edwards, 9 May 1939, on a "partition" of *The Waste Land* into different voices for performance: "partly as a result of the broadcast adaptation of the poem, and partly because this broadcast confirmed my expectations, I have a strong dislike of dividing up for voices poems which were conceived in terms of one voice." (For TSE's letter to the director of the broadcast, see headnote, 8. ANTHOLOGIES, TRANSLATIONS, ADAPTATIONS.) **not wholly distinct from:** F. M. Cornford: "The Cook · · · is not, in origin, distinct from the Learned Doctor", *The Origin of Attic Comedy* 189. See note to *Sweeney Agonistes: Fragment of an Agon* 9–10. **Ferdinand Prince of Naples:** see note to [III] 191–92.

[III] 218–19 **I Tiresias, though blind · · · can see:** *TSE's Notes* quote the description of Jove and Juno in Ovid's *Metamorphoses*, where Jove did

> fall a-jesting with his wife, and saide: a greater pleasure
> In *Venus* games ye women have than men beyonde all measure.
> She answerde no. To trie the truth, they both of them agree
> The wise *Tyresias* in this case indifferent judge to bee,
> Who both the man and womans joyes by tryall understood.
> For finding once two mightie Snakes engendring in a Wood,
> He strake them overthwart the backs, by means whereof beholde
> (As straunge a thing to be of truth as ever yet was tolde)
> He being made a woman straight, seven winter lived so.
> The eight he finding them againe did say unto them tho:
> And if to strike ye have such powre as for to turne their shape
> That are the givers of the stripe, before you hence escape,
> One stripe now will I lende you more. He strake them as beforne
> And straight returnd his former shape in which he first was borne.
> *Tyresias* therefore being tane to judge this jesting strife,

Gave sentence on the side of *Jove*. The which the Queene his wife
Did take a great deale more to heart than needed, and in spight
To wreake hir teene upon hir Judge, bereft him of his sight.
But *Jove* (for to the Gods it is unleeful to undoe
The things which other of the Gods by any meanes have doe)
Did give him sight in things to come for losse of sight of eye,
And so his grievous punishment with honour did supplie.

tr. Arthur Golding (1567), III 401–422

In Sophocles' *Oedipus Tyrannos*, King Laius, Oedipus' father, has been murdered, bringing a plague upon Thebes. Tiresias refuses to explain that it was Oedipus himself who killed the king, and that in taking Jocasta as his queen, he has married his mother. TSE had studied Sophocles' play at Harvard in 1907–08 in a Greek Literature course, given by Charles P. Parker and E. Cary. TSE compared tragedy in Malory to Sophocles' Oedipus: "Arthur throughout is a man under doom, at first admonished by the prophetic voice of Merlin, his Tiresias, himself cursed, not by blindness, but by the blind infatuation which ruins him", *Le Morte Darthur* (1934). Swinburne: "I, Tiresias the prophet, seeing in Thebes | Much evil", *Tiresias* I 43–44 (*Friend*). *WLComposite* **110**: "(I John saw these things, and heard them)." **throbbing between two lives, | Old man with wrinkled female breasts:** Apollinaire's *Les Mamelles de Tiresias* caused controversy when first performed in 1919 (C. J. Ackerley, personal communication). On Tiresias, Frazer's ed. of Apollodorus (Loeb, 1921) I 360–67 contained explicit and suggestive notes (Robert M. Adams, *Litz ed.* 145). TSE: "Then he had been a young girl ··· old man", *The Death of Saint Narcissus* 28–29. To Bonamy Dobrée, 12 Nov 1927, on the Bolo world: "Did I tell you that the Male Bolovians were divided equally at Puberty into Modernists and Fundamentalists, but that the Females communicated in both Kinds? But even Ovid pointed out that the Female has the best of it."

[III] 220–23 **the evening hour that strives | Homeward, and brings the sailor home from sea, | The typist home ··· lays out food:** *TSE's Notes* refer to "Sappho's lines": "Evening Star, that brings back all that the shining Dawn has scattered, you bring back the sheep, you bring back the goats, you bring the child home to its mother" (Fragment 149). *Inf.* II 1–3: "Lo giorno se n'andava, e l'aer bruno | toglieva gli animai, che sono in terra, | dalle fatiche loro" [The day was departing, and the brown air taking the animals, that are on earth, from their toils]; TSE marked the Italian in the copy his mother had given him. *Purg.* VIII 1–2: "'Twas now the hour that turns back the desire of those who sail the seas and melts their heart" (*Friend*). *Paradise Lost* XII 629–32: "evening ··· the labourer's heel | Homeward returning" (Saskia Hamilton, personal communication). Thomas Gray: "The plowman homeward plods his weary way, | And leaves the world to darkness and to me", *Elegy Written in a Country Church Yard* 3–4. Whitman: "scenes of life and the workshops, and the workmen homeward returning", *When Lilacs Last in the Dooryard Bloom'd* 88 (*Musgrove*). Stevenson: "let me lie. | Glad did I live and gladly die, | And I laid me down with a will ··· *Here he lies where he longed to be; | Home is the sailor, home from sea, | And the hunter home from the hill*", *Requiem* (TSE: "and I'm glad it's over", [III] 252). Housman: "Home is the sailor, home from sea ··· Home is the hunter from the hill ··· All flesh lies taken at his will", *R.L.S.* 1, 5, 7. John Davidson: "The thin-shod clerks, the shopmen neat and plump | Home from the city came", *A Woman and her Son* (immediately preceding the passage quoted in note to *Preludes* II 1–4).

TSE'S Notes refer to "the 'longshore' or 'dory' fisherman, who returns at nightfall". James B. Connolly: "A banker's dory is built and equipped for two men. When the dory puts out from the vessel one man takes the job of rowing, the other of heaving the trawl", *Fishermen of the Banks* (1928) 18. In his reader's report on Connolly's book, 8 Oct 1927, TSE wrote: "The author does not make it very clear at first what a *dory* is, or what a *banker* is. But the readers will find out in the course of the book."

[III] 222–23 **home at teatime, clears her breakfast ··· food in tins:** *Hayward*: "The early morning rush to the office prevented her from clearing away her breakfast. A slut, as much by force of circumstance as by nature, she has neither time nor inclination to cook proper meals and eats out of tins. Line 226 places her as one of the many thousands of tenants of a single bed-sitting room or 'bed-sitter' in one of the decaying residential quarters of London." **food in tins** (*variant* **squalid food**): TSE, on television: "just as food comes to be something you have got out of a tin, and not something you have grown for yourself, so drama may mean for millions of people something out of a box or thrown onto a screen", *Religious Drama: Mediaeval and Modern* (1937).

357–60 against the four lines in *ts3b* Pound wrote "*verse* not interesting enough as verse to warrant so much of it". He also underlined the repetition in "Prepares the room and sets the room to rights" (360), commenting: "qui dira les gaffers de la rime" [who will speak of rhyme's gaffes]. Verlaine: "O qui dira les torts de la Rime?" [Oh who will speak of rhyme's wrongs?], *Art Poétique* 25 (*WLFacs* notes).

[III] 224 **Out of the window perilously spread:** "F. M.": "Out of the window she thrusts the upper half of her body", *Diary of the Rive Gauche* I (1925), followed by memories of *Morning at the Window*: "the uproar of *déjeuner* begins ··· in the kitchen, but gradually it spreads through the whole hotel ··· the crashing of china—surely broken?—rattle of cutlery".

362 **the sun's last rays:** Pound underlined the last three words in *ts3b*, perhaps because of "the sun's inclining ray", **229**.

[III] 225–26 **rays ··· divan:** *Paradise Lost* X 457: "Raised from their dark Divan".

[III] 226 **divan ··· (at night her bed):** OED "divan" 3: "a long seat ··· furnished with cushions, so as to form a kind of sofa or couch. Now usually, a low bed or couch with no back or ends", with Dickens: "The bed being soft and comfortable, Mr. Quilp determined to use it, both as a sleeping place by night and as a kind of Divan by day", *The Old Curiosity Shop* ch. XI. Vivien Eliot: "He knew she was in his room because the bed settee was ~~th~~ in it, and she had to lie down for an hour before meals. Sometimes he wished the bed-settee could be in another room. It was in his study because, as Ellison said, that made it a kind of bed-sitting room for him, & he could occasionally sleep there" (c. 624 fols. 3–4).

[III] 226, 244 **divan:** pronounced *divv-àn* in TSE's recordings, except in the second of these lines in 1946, *die-vàn.* The draft reading "And on the divan piled, (at night her bed)" had required *dìe-van*, stressed on the first syllable (for Pound's comment, see Textual History).

[III] 227 **camisoles:** OED 2b: "An underbodice", citing 1916: "Cambric and nainsook combinations are . . becoming obsolete, the camisole-knicker or camisole-chemise taking their place." **stays:** OED "stay" *n.*2 3a: "A laced underbodice, stiffened by the insertion of strips of whale-bone (sometimes of metal or wood) worn · · · to give shape and support to the figure: = corset".

365–66 **A bright kimono wraps her as she sprawls | In nerveless torpor on the window seat:** against these lines Pound wrote "mix up of the couplet + gris*h*kin not good". Although Valerie Eliot quotes *Whispers of Immortality* 17–24, "Grishkin is nice: her Russian eye | Is underlined for emphasis · · · Grishkin has a maisonnette" (*WLFacs*), Pound may have been confusing this quatrain poem with another: "The silent man in mocha brown | Sprawls at the window-sill and gapes", *Sweeney Among the Nightingales* 17–18. *WLFacs* notes: "Pound wrote (Canto LXXVII): 'Grishkin's photo refound years after | with the feeling that Mr. Eliot may have | missed something, after all, in composing his vignette | periplum'." ("Periplum": *Cookson* LIX 324: "(Gk.) voyage round a coast-line · · · sometimes used for voyages of the mind.") For "The married girl who lives across the street | Wraps her soul in orange-coloured robes of Chopinese", see TSE to Conrad Aiken, 25 July 1914, in headnote to *The Love Song of St. Sebastian*.

371 **these crawling bugs:** of nations and language: "the forces of deterioration are a large crawling mass", *Observations* (1918). To Lytton Strachey, 1 June 1919: "I am sojourning among the termites" (see *McCue 2014b*).

[III] 230 **the expected guest:** Hawthorne: "I should hardly judge that she was an expected guest", *The Blithedale Romance* ch. IV. See note to "unfamiliar gust", *WLComposite* 526.

[III] 231 **young man carbuncular:** Milton: "that old man eloquent", *To the Lady Margaret Ley* 8. TSE to Alan M. Hollingsworth, 22 Mar 1955, who had drawn a comparison with "the brash young clerk Marlow meets in the city of the dead" in *Heart of Darkness* pt. 1: "'The young man carbuncular' is a conscious derivation from a sonnet of Milton's, but I am not aware of any of the associations that you mention in your letter. Finally, I must say frankly that such points seem to me of very minor interest to anybody." TSE: "The young are red and pustular", *Mr. Eliot's Sunday Morning Service* 19. Turnbull Lecture III: "Jules Laforgue was a young man · · · He was tuberculous", *The Varieties of Metaphysical Poetry* 281. **carbuncular:** Johnson's Dictionary, "carbuncle": "A jewel shining in the dark, like a lighted coal or candle", citing Wilkins on the lighted coal, "from whence it hath its name." Johnson: "a gem supposed to have intrinsic light, and to shine in the dark; any other gem may reflect light, but cannot give it", Notes to Shakespeare, *Henry VIII* II iii. OED's citations for *carbuncular* are all medical, diverging from *carbuncle* 1. (precious stones). Jonson: "See, a carbuncle | May put out both the eyes of our Saint Mark", *Volpone* III vi, quoted in *Ben Jonson* (1919).

[III] 231–55 **the young man · · · bored and tired · · · finding the stairs unlit . . . | She turns and looks a moment in the glass, | Hardly aware of her departed lover · · · smoothes her hair:** Conrad Aiken (drawing upon TSE's earlier poems):

> all the lighted rooms are bare,
> Numberless gas-jets flare
> Thousands of secret lives, with unconcern,
> Yawn and turn.
> Men in their shirtsleeves reading papers,

Women by mirrors combing out their hair,
Women sleeping, old men dying,
The furtive lover half way up the stair ···
The young man drinks and leans across the table,
Through clamor of music and hurrying feet
Desperate to repeat
What she, who lowers her eyes, has heard before;
And across his shoulder, while he has turned away,
She smiles to her lover who smiles beside the door

The Jig of Forslin (1916) V vi

382 **London's one cafe:** *WLFacs* notes: "The Café Royal. A favourite London rendezvous of writers and artists."

384 **Nevinson:** *WLFacs* notes: "C. R. W. Nevinson, A.R.A. (1889–1946). The painter was an habitué of the Café Royal."

[III] 232 **house agent:** OED: "an agent employed ··· in the sale and letting of houses, the collection of rents, etc."

[III] 234 **silk hat ··· Bradford:** "The inhabitants of Hampstead have silk hats", *The Death of the Duchess* I 1. "Top hats and all, we and Silk Hat Harry", *WLComposite* 4 (see note). "Bonnets, silk hats, and conscious graces", *Spleen* 3. "And at one time I travelled (from Luton) in hats", *Pollicle Dogs and Jellicle Cats* 19. **Bradford millionaire:** *Hayward*: "Bradford, centre of the woollen industry in Yorkshire, profited immensely from war-contracts between 1914 and 1918. The 'millionaire' in this line is the type of the 'war-profiteer'." An editorial in *The Times*, 19 Jan 1920, reported that the Central Profiteering Committee had heard that it was being said "up and down the West Riding and in Bradford that the worsted spinners were making thousands per cent. Mr. Webb added that the spinners thought they were perfectly right in continuing to make these profits, and he was promptly confirmed by the authentic voice of Bradford with the argument that everybody would profiteer if he could." *The Times* of 20 Feb 1920 ran a story headlined "A Bradford Profiteer", about a butcher who had been fined £1,000. Valerie Eliot: "my husband told me that his millionaire came from Yorkshire, and did business with Lloyds Bank", *TLS* 18 June 1976. Julia Bolton Holloway proposed the Yorkshire mill owner Sir James Roberts, who lost a fortune in the Russian Revolution: "After World War I he made many a fruitless visit to the Lloyds Bank on Threadneedle Street seeking reparation payments ··· The clerk in charge of reparations in the Colonial and Foreign Department was Thomas Stearns Eliot", *Yeats Eliot Review* Summer 1979. (Valerie Eliot confirmed this identification to Roberts's family; see *Yorkshire Post* 22 Apr 2013.) From 1939, TSE encouraged Hayward to set down his memories in a "*Recherche du temps perdu*", and later, mentioning the "house of the local family of industrial magnates", 3 Nov 1941, he wrote, "the sociology of these local industrial families ought to provide a separate volume of *La Recherche*: it is the same whether in Leeds, Bristol, Hull, etc. and varies slightly according to the particular dissenting background—in Newcastle, as in Bristol, it is Quaker. In Leeds it is Unitarian."

[III] 235 **the time is now propitious:** Remy de Gourmont, of the water spider: "Ensuite, au moment propice, il crève ··· profite de la surprise causée par son entrée brusque" [at a propitious moment he breaks through ··· and profits by the surprise of his sudden entry], *Physique de l'amour: essai sur l'instinct sexuel* ch. XIII "Le méchanisme de l'amour". This translation by Pound, as *The Natural Philosophy of Love*, was published by Boni & Liveright in 1922.

[III] 235–39 **he guesses ··· she is bored and tired ··· he assaults at once**: "The *Chocolate Soldier* assaults | The tired Sphinx of the physical. | What answer? We cannot discern", *Goldfish* I 10–11.

[III] 238, 242 **unreproved if undesired ··· And makes a welcome of indifference**: "Indifferent if derided", *Fourth Caprice in Montparnasse* 12.

[III] 240 **Exploring hands**: Donne: "Licence my roaving hands, and let them go, | Before, behind, between, above, below. | O my America! my new-found-land", *Elegy* XIX: *To His Mistress Going to Bed* 25–27. (See *Sleeping Together* 9–13: "below ··· beneath ··· between ··· my hand".)

[III] 241 **His vanity requires no response**: "But Tarr's vanity was impatient", *Tarr* ch. I in *Egoist* June 1917 (followed by an advertisement for *Prufrock and Other Observations*).

[III] 243 **I Tiresias have foresuffered all**: Swinburne: "And fiery foresight with foresuffering bought", *Tiresias* XXXIII (*Schmidt*).

[III] 244 **Enacted**: to Hayward, [22 Sept] 1942, of "re-enactment" (*Little Gidding* II 85): "I want to preserve the association of 'enact'—to take the part of oneself on a stage for oneself as the audience" (see headnote to *Little Gidding*, 2. COMPOSITION).

[III] 245 **I who have sat by Thebes below the wall**: Dryden, *Oedipus: A Tragedy* I i, TIRESIAS: "Where are we?" | MANTO: "Under covert of a wall; | The most frequented once, and noisy part | Of Thebes"; quoted by Mark Van Doren, *John Dryden* (1920) 133 (see note to [II] 98–104).

[III] 246 **walked among the lowest of the dead**: having rescued his men from Circe (see note to *Circe's Palace*), Odysseus visits Hades to consult Tiresias (*Odyssey* XI).

[III] 250 **Hardly aware**: to Herbert Read, 18 Jan 1927, of Henry James: "he seems *not wholly conscious*. There is something bigger there, of which he is hardly aware, than 'civilisation' & its 'complexities'. In some ways he seems to me, as a conscious person, a child."

[III] 251 **Her brain allows one half-formed thought to pass**: Poe: "a vague and half-formed conception of the meaning of Dupin flitted over my mind", *The Murders in the Rue Morgue*.

411 may pass: deleting "may", Pound commented "make up yr. mind you Tiresias if you know know damm well or else you dont." See note to *WLComposite* **326–28** for Pound's "dam per'apsez".

[III] 252, 255 **"Well now that's done: and I'm glad it's over." ··· She smoothes her hair**: "When the bridegroom smoothed his hair | There was blood upon the bed ··· (Io Hymen, Hymenæe)", *Ode* ("Tired. | Subterrene") 9–10, 13. "She smooths the hair of the grass", *Rhapsody on a Windy Night* 54 *variant* (with "The bed is open", 76). *Fowler*: "*smooth* is recommended in preference to *smoothe*, but the latter still exists".

[III] 253 **When lovely woman stoops to folly and**: *TSE's Notes* refer to Goldsmith: "When lovely woman stoops to folly, | And finds too late that men betray, | What charm can sooth her melancholy, | What art can wash her guilt away?" *The Vicar of Wakefield* ch. XXIV. The novel was set for TSE's second-year class at school (Smith Academy yearbook, 1900–01).

[III] 253–56 **lovely woman stoops ··· gramophone**: Howells: "Wherever the piano-forte penetrates, lovely woman lifts her fingers from the needle, the broom-handle, and the washboard", *Lexington* (in *Longman's* 1882).

[III] 254 **Paces about her room again, alone**: "She stands at evening in the room alone", *On a Portrait* 4.

[III] 254–55 **Paces about her room ··· smoothes her hair**: "I see her moving | With loosened hair about her chamber", *Paysage Triste* 10–11.

[III] 255 **with automatic hand**: (i) William James: "automatic hand-movements, twitching, etc., had occurred, but having no familiarity with automatic phenomena, Mr. P. thought they were mere 'nervousness,' and discouraged them", *A Case of Automatic Drawing* in *Popular Science Monthly* Jan 1904. Bradley: "What are called (by a metaphor, and no more than a metaphor) 'automatic' acts may be produced by compulsion ··· may the deed still be 'automatic', in the sense of not proceeding from the conscious will?" *Ethical Studies* Essay I. And (ii) OED "automatic" 2a: "Applied *esp.* to machinery and its movements, which produce results otherwise done by hand". *Popular Science Monthly* May 1920: "An automatic hand of metal reaches down into the ground and clutches the beets". *Symons* 111 (on Laforgue): "He thinks intensely about life, seeing what is automatic, pathetically ludicrous in it, almost as one might who has no part in the comedy." TSE: "the hand ··· automatic", *Rhapsody on a Windy Night* 38. **the gramophone**: "when every musical instrument has been replaced by 100 gramophones", *Marie Lloyd* (1923), on "dying from pure boredom" ("She is bored and tired" [III] 236). The original printing of the poem in the *Dial* has "gramaphones", the spelling also in *The Superior Landlord* (see headnote to *Sweeney Agonistes*, 6. THE SUPERIOR LANDLORD) and in TSE to Allen Tate, 1 July 1946. OED "gramophone": "app. formed by inversion of phonogram. The spelling *grammo-* (not the inventor's) is an attempt to make the word look more like a correct formation", with 1888: "His [Edison's] original phonograph has received important modifications..in..Mr. Berliner's gramophone." *Fowler*: "A bad formation; but incurable, & established."

416^417 **gramophone. | | "This music ··· upon the waters"**] in the surviving typescript, TSE left a nine-line lacuna (perhaps with music in mind), but the gap was reduced in the printed poem to a single line space.

[III] 257 **"This music crept by me upon the waters"**: *TSE's Notes* refer to *The Tempest* I ii: "This music crept by me upon the waters, | Allaying both their fury and my passion | With its sweet air."

[III] 258 **the Strand ··· Queen Victoria Street**: *Hayward*: "London, past and present, is invoked. The Strand, now a street of shops and offices linking the City to the West End, was formerly, as its name suggests, a thoroughfare skirting the foreshore of the Thames. Along its length were situated the great houses of Elizabeth's noblemen. The Earl of Leicester lived at Durham House in 1566 and Queen Elizabeth dined with him there (cf. line 279 et seq.). Leicester afterwards occupied Essex House and rebuilt it. Queen Victoria Street, a thoroughfare opened up during the 19th century (1863–72), connects the

City with the Victoria Embankment at Blackfriars Bridge. Its office buildings (including that of *The Times* newspaper) are mainly occupied by firms of engineers, wholesalers, and by similar leading mercantile and commercial companies."

420–21 **traced against the night | Of Michael Paternoster Royal**: *WLFacs* notes: "This Wren church by Upper Thames Street was one of those listed in the *Proposed Demolition of Nineteen London Churches* (see *TSE's Note* to [III] 264). He visited them all while working in the City." As a young tourist in London, TSE had been asked about the sights and named St. Helen's, St. Stephen, St. Bartholomew the Great, St. Sepulchre and St. Etheldreda (to Eleanor Hinkley, 26 Apr [1911]). St. Michael Paternoster Royal might appear in silhouette against the Tower of London from Queen Victoria Street or nearby.

[III] 259 **O City city**: neither the capitalisation nor the punctuation within the phrase is that of Baudelaire (see note to [I] 60). The City of London, with its upper-case "C", is the financial centre of the city that is London. TSE corrected "city" to "City" in the phrase "I am extremely busy at my vocation in the City" on the carbon of a letter to Johan Mortensen, 28 Jan 1924. Matthew 23: 37: "O Jerusalem, Jerusalem, thou that killest the prophets, and stonest them which are sent unto thee." TSE to his Swedish translator Erik Mesterton, 20 Jan 1932: "I do not seem to remember any antecedent for 'City, City' in the Old Testament but of Our Lord's prophecy over Jerusalem. There is of course the reference given to Baudelaire."

[III] 259–63 **O City city · · · whining of a mandoline · · · fishmen**: "the City · · · the City · · · the bankers blowing into their keys. And already in the streets a man sang alone · · · the dock-works and princes paid in currency of fish", *Anabasis* IV i, v, x.

[III] 260 **public bar**: OED quotes L. Golding: "The Public Bar, nothing like so grand as the Saloon Bar, nothing like so cosy as the Private Bar", *Magnolia St.* (1932). **Lower Thames Street**: *Hayward*: "Billingsgate Market, the central fishmarket of London, lies between the street and the river Thames, close to London Bridge. The mandoline would be played by one of the 'buskers' who entertain inside or outside London's public-houses." *Baedeker* 124: "LOWER THAMES street runs eastward from London Bridge to the Custom House and the Tower. Chaucer, the 'father of English poetry', is said to have lived here in 1379–85. Close to the bridge, on the right, stands the handsome church of *St. Magnus the Martyr* (open 12–2), with cupola and a low spire, built by Wren in 1676" (TSE: "*coupole*", [III] 202). TSE marked the last sentence in his *Baedeker*.

[III] 261 **pleasant whining of a mandoline**: "the windings of the violins", *Portrait of a Lady* I 29. "the pleasant violin | At Marm Brown's joint", *WLComposite* 523–24. "Gramophone (husky plaintive whine)", ms story for Vivien Eliot (beginning "Fanny lying in bed late"), *c.* 1924–25 (U. Maryland). To Sydney Schiff [4? Nov 1921] from Margate: "I sketch the people, after a fashion, and practise scales on the mandoline." The instrument had been bought by Vivien. The first two decades of the century saw a craze for the mandoline, and "The Mandolin Club" is often photographed in the Smith Academy yearbook during TSE's time there. **mandoline**: pronounced *mandoleen* in TSE's recordings (despite OED's *mandolin*). TSE rhymes it with "seen" in *Ode to a Roman Coot* (*Noctes Binanianæ*).

[III] 261–77 **mandoline ··· The river sweats ··· Weialala leia**: Kipling: "the new-raised tropic city sweats ··· *Hya! Heeya! Heeya! Hullah! Haul!*" in *The Song of the Banjo* 38–45, after invoking "the London Lights". For Kipling's poem, see note to *Portrait of a Lady* I 15–19.

[III] 262 **a clatter and a chatter from within**: Tennyson: "Clamour and rumble, and ringing and clatter ··· And then to hear a dead man chatter", *Maud* II [v] 251–57 (see note to *The Love Song of J. Alfred Prufrock* 74^75 [1–2]). Emily Brontë: "I distinguished a chatter of tongues, and a clatter of culinary utensils, deep within", *Wuthering Heights* ch. 1 (*Harmon 1976a*).

[III] 262–63 **a clatter and a chatter ··· Where fishmen lounge at noon**: Henry James on Venetian fishermen: "At Burano and Chioggia they sit mending their nets, or lounge at the street corners, where conversation is always high-pitched, or clamour", *Venice* in *Italian Hours*. TSE: "From New Brunswick to Florida to-day lounge the coasters ··· the mackerell fleet slants out to the banks", *Gentlemen and Seamen* (1909). On Kipling: "I have heard from the lips of Gloucester longshoremen that *Captains Courageous* is quite incorrect, the product of three weeks lounging about the wharves", *The Defects of Kipling* (1909). By contrast TSE approved James B. Connolly's accounts: "They are true narratives: most of them can—or could a few years ago—be learnt by word of mouth from the men between trips, as they lounged at the corner of Main Street and Duncan Street in Gloucester", *Fishermen of the Banks* (1928). *Baedeker* 124: "Billingsgate ··· the chief fish-market of London, the bad language used at which has become proverbial." Mark Rogers: "Fish is almost the only commodity sold in the Lane [Love Lane], and the savour of it cannot be kept even out of the church itself", *Down Thames Street* (1921) 127. Wren's windows on the north side were reduced to small lights in 1782 to exclude the noise from the cobbled street and the fishmen's chatter. The market opened at 5 a.m., so the fishmen's work was finished by midday, perhaps explaining "A fishman asleep on his panniers" (1801), cit. OED "fish" 7. **fishmen**: OED "fishman" (*b*): "a fish hawker". The erroneous "fishermen" has repeatedly crept into TSE's text. It appeared in *Penguin* 2nd and 3rd impressions (1951, 1952) and again in the 1954 Faber edition derived from *Penguin* (spotted by J. M. Blackwood, whose letter of 8 Sept 1954 is annotated by TSE "Noted ❧ passed to printer". In John Hayward's copy of the 1954 ed., TSE marked the mistake as "a bad coquille" (= misprint / oyster shell, Fr.); later impressions were corrected. The error reappeared in *1974* (later corrected). **at noon**: "empty naves, to receive the solitary visitor at noon from the dust and tumult of Lombard Street", *London Letter* in *Dial* June 1921. See next note.

[III] 264 **Magnus Martyr**: *TSE's Notes*: "one of the finest among Wren's interiors". *Hayward*: "Saint Magnus the Martyr. One of the finest of the City churches, built by Sir Christopher Wren (1676) to replace the earlier church, destroyed in the Great Fire of London (1666). Its interior is notable for the beauty of the slender Ionic columns which divide the nave from the side aisles." St. Magnus stands on the north bank of the Thames, where old London Bridge met Lower Thames Street. Churches have stood beside the bridge since before the Norman Conquest, but the exact location has changed with that of the bridge (as TSE perhaps suggested in his pencil draft: "walls | Of Magnus Martyr stood, ❧ stand, ❧ hold"). The present church was built under Wren's direction. A fire in 1633 destroyed more than forty houses on the bridge but did not reach the church. A bequest of 1640 provided for an annual "Fire Sermon", originally to give thanks for the sparing of the church, and although this tradition is not thought to have continued into the 20th century, a painted board still records the bequest (transcript: David Boddy, *N&Q* Dec 2008).

Charlotte Eliot on her visit to London in 1921 with TSE's brother: "Henry, reading *Oliver Twist*, came across the account of the meeting of Nancy with Mr. Brownlow and Rose Maylie on London Bridge [ch. XLVI], and determined to identify the spot ··· Close to the foot of the steps leading down to the water from the Bridge, is the Church of St. Magnus. It is small but exquisite, having some beautiful Grinling Gibbons carving on the altar piece and doors. There is a memorial tablet to Miles Coverdale, translator of the Bible and at one time Rector of the church. While we were in the church the Rector entered and made his devotions ··· He told us that Saint Magnus was one of the 19 churches selected for demolition, but he thought it would be spared, as it was used on week days by men employed on the waterfront", *Reminiscences of a Trip to London* (1924). Under the heading "The True Church and the Nineteen Churches", TSE had discussed the threat in his *London Letter* June 1921:

> While the poetry lovers have been subscribing to purchase for the nation the Keats house in Hampstead as a museum, the Church of England has apparently persisted in its design to sell for demolition nineteen religious edifices in the City of London. Probably few American visitors, and certainly few natives, ever inspect these disconsolate fanes; but they give to the business quarter of London a beauty which its hideous banks and commercial houses have not quite defaced. Some are by Christopher Wren himself, others by his school; the least precious redeems some vulgar street, like the plain little church of All Hallows at the end of London Wall. Some, like St Michael Paternoster Royal, are of great beauty. As the prosperity of London has increased, the City Churches have fallen into desuetude; for their destruction the lack of congregation is the ecclesiastical excuse, and the need of money the ecclesiastical reason. The fact that the erection of these churches was apparently paid for out of a public coal tax and their decoration probably by the parishioners, does not seem to invalidate the right of the True Church to bring them to the ground. To one who, like the present writer, passes his days in this City of London (*quand'io sentii chiavar l'uscio di sotto*) the loss of these towers, to meet the eye down a grimy lane, and of these empty naves, to receive the solitary visitor at noon from the dust and tumult of Lombard Street, will be irreparable and unforgotten.

(For the quotation from Dante, see note to [V] 411–14.)

The London County Council report considered St. Magnus "one of the most beautiful of all Wren's works" and concluded: "This is certainly one of the churches which should not be demolished without specially good reasons and after a very full consideration." TSE to Richard Aldington [3? Oct 1921]: "I should love to write a book on Wren, or at least on the *églises assassinées* of London." (Proust's *En mémoire des églises assassinées* appeared in *Pastiches et Mélanges*, 1919.) For Wren and the river, see note to [III] 275–76.

During 1922, the tower of St. Magnus was briefly more visible from London Bridge, between the demolition of one building that had obscured it and the erection of another (etching, *The Times* 3 Apr). TSE deplored "renewed rumours of the design to destroy the City Churches" in *A Commentary* in *Criterion* Oct

1926: "Since the first attempt was made, several years ago, the church of St. Magnus Martyr has been concealed, on the side from which its beauty was most conspicuous, by a large industrial structure (not ill-favoured in itself) which reduces the church to the proportions and importance of a museum piece."

[III] 264 *TSE's Notes* **The Proposed Demolition**: the London County Council report was written in reaction to the "drastic proposal" of a commission set up by the Bishop of London, which had reported in Apr 1920. Bonamy Dobrée recalled: "One Saturday afternoon my wife and I accompanied Eliot at the head of a protest procession through the City, at intervals chanting *Onward, Christian Soldiers* and other hymns. The churches were saved", *Tate ed.* 70. TSE used the anonymous authority of the front page of the *TLS*, 23 Sept 1926: "there are those for whom the City churches are as precious as any of the four hundred odd churches in Rome which are in no danger of demolition", *Lancelot Andrewes* (1926). The House of Commons finally voted against the demolitions on 25 Nov that year. "If Christianity disappeared, it would be more sensible to destroy all the churches in England than to preserve them as monuments", *A Commentary* in *Criterion* Oct 1934 (see "If I were a Dean" in headnote to *Choruses from "The Rock"*; the Foreword to the programme for *The Rock* spoke of building parish churches "probably with financial help from demolished churches from central London"). **P. S. King & Son, Ltd**: not publisher but printer and distribution agent for the LCC report.

[III] 265 **Inexplicable splendour**: John Betjeman noted that TSE "must have entered St Magnus not earlier than 1921, the year when the present rector, Fr. Fynes Clinton, was appointed. Before that St Magnus was low church, box-pewed, dead and dusty. The Ionian white and gold must refer to the redecoration under Fr. Fynes Clinton by Martin Travers", *Braybrooke ed.* 194. The redecoration did not occur until 1924–25, but H. J. Fynes-Clinton was so pronouncedly high church as to cause controversy soon after his induction in May 1921. A Consistory Court in 1922 granted a faculty for the removal of "certain illegal ornaments". It heard of services in Latin, a requiem for the Pope and "a gilded throne of wood placed on the head of the tabernacle" (*The Times* 31 July 1922). A further dispute followed (*The Times* 4 Dec 1922). St. Magnus had previously seen doctrinal struggles when Coverdale was rector, 1564–66, and in the mid-17th century. (For Lancelot Andrewes as "the 'ritualist' of his day" and a description of "his altar with its lights and cushions, the canister for the wafers and the basin for the oblations", see introduction to F. E. Brightman's ed. of *Preces Privatæ* xxxiv.) After entering the Church of England in 1927, TSE attended St. Stephen's, Kensington, which was so high church during the 1930s as to attract demonstrations (*Smart* 104). **Inexplicable**: OED 1: "very intricate or complex. *Obs.*", citing Emerson: "There is never a beginning, there is never an end, to the inexplicable continuity of this web of God." 3: "That cannot be explained; inscrutable, unintelligible; (in recent use) that cannot be accounted for, unaccountable", with 1699: "If God has declared this inexplicable thing concerning himself to us, we are bound to believe it." Accented on the second syllable (not the third) in TSE's recordings. **Ionian**: *variant* Corinthian. The LCC report drew attention both to "slender Ionic columns" dividing the nave from the side aisles, and to the altar-piece "treated with the Corinthian order · · · the whole being richly carved." **white and gold**: liturgical colours of Easter.

[III] 265–68 **white and gold · · · barges drift**: Kipling: "Business took him over London Bridge · · · As we passed over the Thames we paused to look at a steamer unloading great slabs of white and brown marble. A barge drifted under the steamer's stern", *The Finest Story in the World* (*Crawford* 133).

[III] 266–67 **The river sweats | Oil and tar**: "When the surface of the blackened river | Is a face that sweats with tears", *Song* ("The golden foot I may not kiss or clutch") 9–10 (see headnote to that poem and headnote to *The Waste Land*, 1. COMPOSITION). "Like perfumed oil upon the waters", *The Burnt Dancer* 18. "a face that sweats with tears", *The wind sprang up at four o'clock* 8. For Coleridge, "The water, like a witch's oils", see note to *Burbank with a Baedeker: Bleistein with a Cigar* 11–12.

[III] 266–72 **river · · · tide · · · Wide · · · swing**: John Gould Fletcher: "The gates swing wide and open on a dim and lonely water, | In between them, swift and silent, the tide runs out to sea", *The Red Gates* in *New Paths*, ed. C. W. Beaumont and M. T. H. Sadler (1918).

[III] 266–91 **The river sweats · · · Wallala leialala**: *TSE's Notes* call this "The Song of the (three) Thames-daughters", after "the Rhine-daughters" in Wagner's *Götterdämmerung* III i (see note to [II] 277–78, 290–91). The Thames-daughters later speak in turn (292–306).

[III] 268–75 **The barges drift · · · tide | Red sails · · · leeward · · · Drifting logs · · · reach**: Amy Lowell, on Venice: "Leaves fall, | Brown leaves, | Yellow leaves streaked with brown · · · Loosen on their branches | And drift slowly downwards", *1777*, II: *The City of Falling Leaves*. TSE wrote that Lowell's poem had "given me great pleasure by its precision of image and its skill in workmanship", *Reflections on Contemporary Poetry* III (1917). Conrad: "the tanned sails of the barges drifting up with the tide seemed to stand still in red clusters of canvas", *Heart of Darkness* pt. 1 (*Drew* 118–19). Conrad: "a solitary log came out from the bend above and went on drifting down the straight reach", *An Outcast of the Islands* V I.

[III] 270 **Red sails**: *Hayward*: "The familiar and imposing red sails of the Thames barges or wherries."

[III] 272 **leeward**: pronounced *loo'rd* in TSE's recordings (see rhyme with "blew hard · · · manured · · · steward", *The Columbiad* st. 41). OED (which gives priority to the pronunciation *lee-w'd*): "away from the wind". See note to [IV] 320 "windward".

[III] 272–73 **spar. | The barges wash**: Pound: "I cling to the spar, | Washed", *Et Faim Sallir le Loup des Boys* 1–2 in *Blast* 2 (July 1915).

436–37 **The barges wash, | Like drifting logs**: to Pound [26? Jan 1922]:

> Would D's difficulty be solved by inverting to
> Drifting logs
> The barges wash . . . ???

The two lines had appeared (in the opposite order) in *ms2* (*WLFacs* 48/49), but any typescript by TSE that included them is now lost, and Dorothy Pound's difficulty is unknown. Pound, [28? Jan]: "D. was fussing about some natural phenomenon, but I thought I had crossed out her queery. The wake of the barges washes &c., and the barges may perfectly well be said to wash. I shd. leave it as it is, and NOT invert." The original order was restored for publication: "The barges wash | Drifting logs" (the two lines appearing as one in *T/W*). For the correspondence, see headnote, 1. COMPOSITION. Writing to his Swedish translator Erik Mesterton, 20 Jan 1932, TSE appeared to discount the transitive sense (OED 15: "to carry away or transport"): "By 'Wash' I mean both to be carried along by the stream and swayed from side to side by the varying gusts of wind in land-locked waters."

[III] 275–76 **Greenwich reach | Past the Isle of Dogs**: *Hayward*: "The Thames at Greenwich Reach, below the Pool of London, makes a deep bend round the Isle of Dogs (Parish of Poplar, a poor dockland district) on its northern bank and washes to the south of the magnificent range of buildings known as Greenwich Hospital, one of the outstanding masterpieces of Sir Christopher Wren. The contrast between the two banks is doubtless intentional. Greenwich was formerly a Royal Palace. Elizabeth entertained Lord Leicester there." **Greenwich**: pronounced *Grennitch*.

[III] 276, 300 **Isle of Dogs ··· Margate Sands**: to his Swedish translator Erik Mesterton, 20 Jan 1932: "It is better to leave these place names in English."

[III] 277–78, 290–91] Wagner's song of the Rhine-daughters, *Götterdämmerung* III i:

Frau Sonne sendet lichte Strahlen; Nacht liegt in der Tiefe: einst war sie hell, da heil und hehr des Vaters Gold noch in ihr glänzte. Rheingold! Klares Gold! Wie hell du einstens strahltest, hehrer Stern der Tiefe!	Dame Sun sends down her rays of light; night lies in the depths: once they were bright, when safe and glorious our father's gold gleamed there Rhinegold! Lustrous gold! How brightly you once shone, majestic star of the deep!
(*Sie schliessen wieder den Schwimmreigen*)	(*They resume their swimming dance*)
Weialala leia, wallala leialala.	Weialala leia, wallala leialala.
(*Ferner Hornruf.— Sie lauschen.— Sie schlagen jauchzend das Wasser*)	(*A horncall in the distance—they listen. —They splash joyful in the water*)
Frau Sonne, sende uns den Helden, der das Gold uns wiedergäbe! Liess' er es uns, dein lichtes Auge neideten dann wir nicht länger. Rheingold! Klares Gold! Wie froh du dann strahltest, freier Stern der Tiefe!	Dame Sun, send us the hero who will give us back the gold! If he let us have it, we would no longer envy your bright eyes. Rhinegold! Lustrous gold! How happily you shone then, free star of the deep!

Laforgue, alluding to *Die Walküre*, the second part of *The Ring* following *Das Rheingold*: "en poussant des clameurs de Walkyrie! | *Hoyotoho!* | *Heiaha!* | *Hahei! Heiaho! Hoyohei!*" [She shouts out the cry of the Valkyries. "Hoyotoho! | Heiaha! | Hahei! Heiaho! Hoyohei!"] *Pan et la Syrinx* [*Pan and the Syrinx*]. Four paragraphs later: "elle clame un dernier *Hoyotoho!* et alors se jette dans le léger rideau des roseaux et se laisse aller dans les eaux! ··· Il voit la belle enfant sauvé qu'ont reçue ··· les naïades silencieuses" [She cries out "Hoyotoho!" once more, then she throws herself through the light curtain of reeds, and she falls into the water ··· he looks down into the water and he sees that Syrinx has been rescued by the silent naiads]. The naiad Syrinx is another river-daughter. TSE to D. G. Bridson, 11 Jan 1938, of a semi-dramatised broadcast of *The Waste Land*: "while I did not otherwise object to the bit about the barges being sung, I thought that it led to an unfortunate reversal; I mean it is a pity that the refrain should have been spoken (which makes it sound foolish) instead of being sung to the excellent bit of music which Wagner provided for the purpose. But what shocked me most of all was that the words of the Thames Daughters which follow were also sung, to the accompaniment of an irrelevant and trivial strumming, instead of being spoken as they should be", see headnote, 8. ANTHOLOGIES, TRANSLATIONS, ADAPTATIONS.

Adam Trexler: "Great symbolic importance was attached to Britain's suspension of the gold standard in 1919: sterling and all the international currencies dependent on it were now unsecured from value. This loss of symbolic value is dramatised in *The Waste Land* by the woes of the Thames daughters and the Rhine daughters, who are charged with guarding the gold that secures the nations of Britain and Germany", *Harding ed.* 278. TSE wrote that "in the present condition" of Germany, it was "improbable that any currency medium other than a convertible gold note would win back public trust", *Foreign Exchanges* in *Lloyds Bank Monthly* Oct 1923. On a German study: "I have found this book very interesting ··· The book deals very thoroughly with finance in Germany before, and chiefly after the war, up to this year ··· I feel a good deal of sympathy with his criticism of finance and financiers ··· shewing exactly how elections in all parliamentary countries are paid for", *"Das Geld in der Politik"* [*Gold in Politics*] by Richard Lewinsohn, reader's report (1931).

After victory over Germany in 1918, the French avenged the punitive treaty forced upon them in 1871 by the Germans at Versailles (see notes to [I] 8–17 and to *Gerontion* 62, 64–65). The 1919 settlement, likewise signed in the Hall of Mirrors, imposed still more punitive terms. John Maynard Keynes wrote that "the Carthaginian peace is not *practically* right or possible" (see note to [III] 306–307, "Carthage"), and warned that it was a threat to German stability:

> There remain the clauses relating to the river system of Germany. These are largely unnecessary ··· Yet they constitute an unprecedented interference with a country's domestic arrangements, and are capable of being so operated as to take from Germany all effective control over her own transport system ··· Most of the principal rivers of Germany have their source or their outlet in non-German territory. The Rhine, rising in Switzerland, is now a frontier river for a part of its course, and finds the sea in Holland ··· The Treaty, however, has made the international character of these rivers a pretext for taking the river system of Germany out of German control ··· It is almost as though the Powers of Continental Europe were to be placed in a majority on the Thames Conservancy or the Port of London.
>
> *The Economic Consequences of the Peace* (1919) ch. III, IV

(For "economic consequences of the war" quoted on front flap of the Boni & Liveright edition of *The Waste Land*, see headnote, 5. APROPOS OF PUBLICATION.)

Keynes again: "the gold · · · seemed to afford one of the few obvious and certain sources for Reparation · · · no sum worth speaking of can be expected in the form of gold or silver", ch. V, "Reparation" (subheading, "Gold"). TSE: "the River flows, with foreign flotations", *Choruses from "The Rock"* I 20. To his mother, 6 Jan 1920: "I wonder if America realises how terrible the condition of central Europe is. I can never ~~forget~~ quite put Vienna out of my mind. And I have seen people who have been in Germany and they are most pessimistic about the future, not only of Germany, but of the world. They say that there is no hope unless the treaty is revised. I believe by the way that J. M. Keynes: *The Economic Consequences of the Peace* is an important book, if you can get hold of it." This, he wrote in an obituary, was "the only one of his books which I have ever read: I was at that time occupied, in a humble capacity, with the application of some of the minor financial clauses of the treaty", *John Maynard Keynes* (1946). In the *Harvard College Class of 1910: Secretary's Fourth Report* (1921), he had given his profession as "Banker, Critic, Poet", and added: "Specializing in the Economic Clauses of the Peace Treaty". To Quinn, 9 May 1921: "Even what I do—I am dealing with all the debts and claims of the bank under the various Peace Treaties—sometimes takes a good deal of thought and strength." For "the post-War world" and "the post-Peace world", see *Coriolan* headnote, 1. COMPOSITION. TSE: "If he walked in the streets, in the streets of Carthage | He seemed to tread on faces, convulsive thighs and knees", *The Death of Saint Narcissus* 18–19 *variant*.

[III] 277–78, 290–91, 306 **Weialala leia | Wallala leialala · · · Weialala leia | Wallala leialala · · · la la**: other forms of iteration in TSE include:

The Waste Land [III] 309–10:

Burning burning burning burning
O Lord Thou pluckest me out
O Lord Thou pluckest

burning

The Hollow Men V 25–27:

For Thine is
Life is
For Thine is the

Ash-Wednesday I 1–3:

Because I do not hope to turn again
Because I do not hope
Because I do not hope to turn

Ash-Wednesday I 40–41

Pray for us sinners now and at the hour of our death
Pray for us now and at the hour of our death

Bacchus and Ariadne 20–22:

I am sure it is like this
I am sure it is this
I am sure

The only poem to be published by "F. M." appeared in *Criterion* Apr 1925 (see *McCue 2016*); *Necesse est Perstare?* [Is it necessary to endure?] ends:

> Is it necessary—
> Is this necessary—
> Tell me, is it *necessary* that we go through this?

TSE to Jane Heap, 6 Oct 1924: "I have been working in a method of repetition and variation lately."

[III] 279 **Elizabeth and Leicester**: the letter of 30 June 1561 that is quoted by J. A. Froude and taken up in *TSE's Notes* describes a party on the Thames staged by Lord Robert Dudley, Earl of Leicester, for the Queen, who was then living at Greenwich. The Spanish Bishop Alvarez de Quadra wrote: "In the afternoon we were in a barge, watching the games on the river. She was alone with the Lord Robert and myself on the poop, when they began to talk nonsense, and went so far that Lord Robert said at last, as I was on the spot there was no reason why they should not be married if the queen pleased · · · I said gravely to them both, that if they would be guided by me they would shake off the tyranny of those men who were oppressing the realm" and "restore religion and good order" (Everyman ed. I 244). TSE: "For the general history of the Tudor reigns, including that of Elizabeth, the various volumes of Froude are of permanent value, and are many of them obtainable in the 'Everyman' edition", *Syllabus: Elizabethan Literature* (1918). *The Reign of Elizabeth* had been extracted in 1911 as five Everyman volumes, from Froude's 12-vol. *History of England from the Fall of Wolsey to the Defeat of the Spanish Armada* (1856–70). TSE to Hayward, 18 July 1939, describing a performance he had seen: "The Kenilworth Pageant was remarkable. Chiefly written by Miss Thomas, English Mistress at Leamington High School, but bits were contributed by C. Marlowe and W. Shakespeare. The latter showed his versatility by taking a minor part (at the age of 11) in the festivities given by Leicester to Elizabeth, and was wildly cheered as he toddled across the green." TSE may have known of a previous attempt to recreate the kind of masque presented before Elizabeth I at Kenilworth Castle, *The Masque at Kenilworth*, with music by Arthur Sullivan and words by Henry Chorley (1864), which drew on descriptions in Walter Scott's *Kenilworth*.

D. H. Lawrence, of Kingston-on-Thames: "Yet it was a place of kings for her—Richard and Henry and Wolsey and Queen Elizabeth · · · Still she must see the stately, gorgeous barge of the Queen float down, the crimson carpet put upon the landing stairs, the gentlemen in their purple-velvet cloaks, bare-headed, standing in the sunshine grouped on either side waiting. 'Sweet Thames run softly till I end my song'", *The Rainbow* (1915) ch. XIII (John Zubizarreta, *ELN* Sept 1993). Lawrence's "stately, gorgeous barge of the Queen" suggests not only Elizabeth and Leicester's, but also Cleopatra's barge (*Whitworth*, who points out that *The Rainbow* was pub. 30 Sept 1915 and suppressed by 5 Nov). For Spenser's "Sweete *Themmes*" see note to [III] 175–84.

[III] 280 **Beating oars:** for "galleys when they row, | Even beat", in *The Maid's Tragedy*, see note to *Burbank with a Baedeker: Bleistein with a Cigar* 9–11.

[III] 281–85 **The stern was formed | A gilded shell · · · Rippled both shores:** Ludwig II liked to be rowed in a golden swan-boat, with shell-shaped stern, across the miniature lake in his artificial Venus Grotto (based on act I of *Tannhäuser*), at Linderhof Palace. For Ludwig, see note to [I] 8–17.

[III] 289 **White towers:** *Hayward*: "The pinnacles of the White Tower, built from white Caen stone (1078) by William the Conqueror as the Keep of the Tower of London. They are a striking landmark on the left bank of the Thames below London Bridge." Elizabeth had been imprisoned in the Tower in her youth (C. J. Ackerley, personal communication). TSE: "The fine weather and the coal strike have turned a blazing glare on London, discovering for the first time towers and steeples of an uncontaminated white", *London Letter* in *Dial* Aug 1921.

[III] 292 **and dusty trees:** "through dusty trees", *First Debate Between the Body and Soul* 13.

[III] 293 **Highbury ··· Richmond and Kew:** *Hayward*: "Highbury (North-East London) in the metropolitan borough of Islington, is a dreary, lower middle class suburb. It has no personal association in this context and was chosen simply to provide a contrast with the superior and salubrious suburbs of Richmond and Kew which lie to the south-west of London at the opposite pole of the NE-SW axis. Richmond, famous for its river picnics, and Kew, famous for its spacious botanical gardens, are favourite Thames-side resorts for London's holiday-makers. At sunny week-ends and on Bank Holidays both places are packed with trippers and inexperienced but determined oarsmen and canoers."

[III] 293–94 **Highbury bore me. Richmond and Kew | Undid me:** Jean de Bosschère: "Recueilli à Paris; perverti à Rome" [Composed in Paris, corrupted in Rome], *Homère Mare habite sa Maison de Planches* [*Homer Marsh Dwells in his House of Planks*]. (OED "pervert" 12b: "*spec.* To turn (any one) aside from a right to a false or erroneous religious belief or system"). TSE quoted in total fourteen lines of the poem in French in *Reflections on Contemporary Poetry* II (1917). See headnote to *Mélange Adultère de Tout*. "Spawned in ··· Antwerp, | Blistered in Brussels, patched and peeled in London", *Gerontion* 9–10 and note. **Richmond and Kew | Undid me:** the lines of Dante quoted in *TSE's Notes* recur in *Dante* (1929) II, where he quotes the last seven lines of *Purg.* V and translates them (departing from the Temple text): "remember me, who am La Pia. Siena made me, Maremma unmade me: this is known to him who after due engagement wedded me with his ring". La Pia, the Lady of Siena, was murdered at Maremma reputedly on her husband's orders. *Siena me Fe', Disfecemi Maremma* is the title of part VII of Pound's *Hugh Selwyn Mauberley* (1920) (C. J. Ackerley, personal communication).

455–62 *ms2 1st draft* [8–10] **Richmond ⅋ Kew | Undid me ··· on the river, at last I raised my knees:** Fenimore Cooper: "'It was the river that made your fortune, Corny, and undid me'", *Satanstoe* ch. XXX. Describing river excursions on "The Thames from London Bridge to Hampton Court", *Baedeker* noted (388): "It was on an 'eyot' between Richmond and Kew that Prince William (William IV) used to meet Perdita Robinson" (his mistress). Middleton: "how soon maids are to their ruins won, | One minute, and eternally undone", *Michaelmas Term* II ii. For Middleton's play, see note to *Choruses from "The Rock"* II 49–51.

[III] 294–95 **I raised my knees | Supine on the floor of a narrow canoe:** to his mother, 19 Sept 1917: "I spent the afternoon on the river with a man in the bank who owns a 'sailing canoe'; they are tiny little boats like toys. You sit on the edge of the cockpit with your knees up to your chin" (C. J. Ackerley, personal communication).

[III] 295 **Supine:** stress as in *repine* in TSE's recordings (this being described by

OED as the pronunciation "formerly"). To E. M. W. Tillyard, 3 Apr 1947: "In my lecture I made a passing reference to Milton's description of Satan as *prone* while lying on the Infernal Lake. I had always pictured his posture as being *supine* and thought that Milton was using *prone* because the associations of this word are more suitable to the situation than the associations of *supine*. I have just been in correspondence with Mr. E. H. W. Meyerstein who is convinced that Milton meant exactly what he said and that Satan is to be imagined in this scene as lying on his belly · · · I should dearly like to know how you picture this scene yourself."

[III] 296 **Moorgate:** *Hayward*: "Moorgate was not one of the original City gates but was erected to replace a postern in the north wall between Bishopsgate and Cripplegate. The gate was demolished in 1762 and the quarter to which it gave its name is now in the heart of the financial district of the City. The 'Thames Maiden' who sings this lament was presumably a typist in one of the great office buildings of the quarter. When T. S. Eliot worked in a bank in the City he used the Moorgate Underground Station."

[III] 296–97 **my heart | Under my feet:** "I'd throw my heart beneath his feet. | I'd give my life to his control", *Convictions* 25–26 ("your heart would have responded | Gaily, when invited, beating obedient | To controlling hands", *The Waste Land* [V] 420–22).

[III] 298 **"a new start":** having written to Pound, 13 Oct 1925, of *The Hollow Men* as "post-*Waste*", TSE wrote to Wyndham Lewis, 9 Jan 1926, of his new volume (*Poems 1909–1925*): "I wanted to collect all my stuff and get rid of it in one volume so as to get it out of my own way and make a fresh start." Of Pater: "*Marius* itself is incoherent; its method is a number of fresh starts", *Arnold and Pater* (1930).

[III] 300 **Margate:** *Hayward*: "a popular seaside resort in the Isle of Thanet, Kent, 74 miles east of London, at the tip of the North Foreland, much frequented by city workers and their 'humble people' for summer holidays." For TSE's work there on *The Waste Land* in Oct–Nov 1921, see headnote, 1. COMPOSITION.

[III] 301–302 **I can connect | Nothing with nothing:** *King Lear* I i: "Nothing will come of nothing." *Murder in the Cathedral* II, chorus: "No colours, no forms to distract, to divert the soul | From seeing itself, foully united forever, nothing with nothing." **connect:** E. M. Forster: "Only connect! That was the whole of her sermon. Only connect the prose and the passion, and both will be exalted, and human love will be seen at its height. Live in fragments no longer", *Howards End* (1910) ch. XXII (TSE: "fragments", [V] 430).

[III] 303 **The broken fingernails of dirty hands:** "dirty broken finger nails | Tapping the bar", *Interlude: In a Bar* 12–13.

[III] 304–305 **My people humble people who expect | Nothing:** Conrad: "'They are simple people—and I want nothing, you know'", *Heart of Darkness* pt. 3 (*Grover Smith* 309–10). Kipling: "*Humble ye, my people*", *A Song of the English* 2. (Alexander Cruden: "To humble a woman, *is to lie with her, to rob her of her honour.* Deut. 21: 14: 'Thou shalt not make merchandise of her because thou hast humbled her'", *Concordance to the Old and New Testaments*, 1824 ed.) *On the Eve* (1925): "squandering everything that the humble people have worked to create—soldiers and generals and diplomats and administrators are humble people, in my opinion" (TSE's authorship uncertain; see Index of Identifying Titles). "the work of the humble", *Choruses from "The Rock"* I 78 (see note).

[III] 306–307 **la la || To Carthage then I came**: on the ts of Menasce's translation, TSE wrote "la la" above "alors à" and suggested "Je m'en fus alors à Carthage". Spenser: "At length they all to mery *London* came", *Prothalamion* 127. **la la**: OED: "la" b: "Repeated (*a*) as a refrain; (*b*) as an expression of derision. *Obs.* (Hence la-la *adj.* = 'so-so', poor.)" Ezra Pound used "Là-là" or "La! La!!" to mean something like "so it goes", as to Dorothy Shakespear [12 Apr 1913], [28 Feb 1914], [7 Mar 1914]. "*Tra-la-la-la-la-la-laire*", epigraph to *Burbank with a Baedeker: Bleistein with a Cigar*.

[III] 307 **To Carthage then I came**: *TSE's Notes* quote Augustine: "To Carthage I came, where there sang all around me in my ears a cauldron of unholy loves. I loved not yet, yet I loved to love, and out of a deep-seated want, I hated myself for wanting not. I sought what I might love, in love with loving, and safety I hated, and a way without snares. For within me was a famine of that inward food, Thyself, my God; yet, through that famine I was not hungered", *Confessions*, opening of bk. III. (TSE's wording, with the addition of "then" after "Carthage", appears to adapt Pusey's 1838 revision of Watts's translation. For Pilkington's translation of the same passage, see note to *Entretien dans un parc* 22–25.) On 26 Mar 1926, TSE wrote to booksellers John Grant in disappointment that a 15-vol. set of Augustine that he had ordered was in English, not Latin. TSE: "If he walked in city streets, in the streets of Carthage | He seemed to tread on faces", *The Death of Saint Narcissus* 18–19 *draft*. **Carthage**: *Lemprière*: "The city and republic flourished for 737 years · · · It maintained three famous wars against Rome, called the Punic wars, in the third of which Carthage was totally destroyed" in 146 B.C. A punitive peace is named "Carthaginian" after the sacking of Carthage, when the ground was sown with salt to make it barren. Augustine and later historians argued that Rome's decline was hastened by the destruction of this Phoenician colony (see note to [I] 70, "Mylae"; and Eleanor Cook, *ELH* Summer 1979). For Keynes and the "Carthaginian peace" of the Versailles Treaties, see note to [III] 277–278, 290–91 on the Rhine-daughters' song.

[III] 308 **Burning burning burning burning**: *TSE's Notes* refer to the Buddha's Fire Sermon. To his Spanish translator Angel Flores, 22 Feb 1928: "On page 13 of your translation you put 'consumiéndome'. Would not simply 'consumiendo' be enough? My original is 'burning', and after all I was merely translating myself quite literally from the Pali original." (*Consumiendo* = "consuming", transitive; *consumiéndome* = "consuming me / myself".) The Monument to the Great Fire of 1666, which destroyed much of the City of London, stands beside London Bridge. Kipling: "burning—burning—burning", *Through the Fire* (one paragraph after the Policeman's declaring: "it's the story of Francesca da Rimini").

[III] 308 *TSE's Notes* **Henry Clarke Warren's *Buddhism in Translations***: see note to part title "III. *The Fire Sermon*".

[III] 309 **O Lord Thou pluckest me out**: *TSE's Notes* refer again to Augustine: "And I, though I speak and see this, entangle my steps with these outward beauties; but Thou pluckest me out, O Lord, Thou pluckest me out; because Thy loving-kindness is before my eyes. For I am taken miserably, and Thou pluckest me out mercifully", bk. X 34.

[III] 309 *TSE's Notes* **is not an accident**: Irving Babbitt: "You come to feel that the age of Louis XIV was not an *accident* (. . . as an acquaintance of mine once said) but rather the result and natural fruit of a continuous culture and development", *The Masters of Modern French Criticism* (1912) 152.

[III] 310–11 **pluckest || burning**: Amos 4: 11: "I have overthrown some of you, as God overthrew Sodom and Gomorrah, and ye were as a firebrand plucked out of the burning: yet have ye not returned to me, saith the Lord" (*Grover Smith* 90). Zechariah 3: 2: "Save me as a brand plucked out of the fire." Cotton Mather's book on the 17th-century witch trials was entitled *A Brand Plucked out of the Burning*. (In *Dial* Nov 1929, Pound wrote of William Carlos Williams that "None of his immediate forebears burnt witches in Salem", to which, in the *Literary Essays of Ezra Pound*, there was added: "Note: We didn't burn them, we hanged them. T.S.E." To Pound, 8/10 Dec 1933: "As for me, I can't help it. My great-grandfather was on same witch jury with Nat Hawthorne's great-grandfather; and I just naturally smell out witches etc." See note to *Gerontion* 7.)

IV. DEATH BY WATER

Title ***Death by Water***: for fear of or longing for the submarine world, see notes to *Mr. Apollinax* 11–15 and to *Dirge*.

Notes to WLComposite 475–557:

TSE, interviewed by Donald Hall: "There was a long section about a shipwreck. I don't know what that had to do with anything else, but it was rather inspired by the Ulysses canto in the *Inferno*, I think", *Paris Review* (1959). *Inf.* XXVI 133–42:

> n'apparve una montagna bruna
> per la distanza, e parvemi alta tanto,
> quanto veduta non n'aveva alcuna.
> Noi ci allegrammo, e tosto tornò in pianto:
> chè dalla nuova terra un turbo nacque,
> e percosse del legno il primo canto.
> Tre volte il fe' girar con tutte l'acque,
> alla quarta levar la poppa in suso,
> e la prora ire in giù, com'altrui piacque,
> infin che il mar fu sopra noi richiuso.

In *Dante* (1929) I, TSE revised the Temple translation: "there appeared a mountain brown in the distance; and it seemed to me the highest that I had ever seen. We rejoiced, but soon our joy was turned to lamentation: for a storm came up from the new land, and caught the stem of our ship. Three times it whirled her round with all the waters; the fourth time it heaved up the stern and drove her down at the head, as pleased Another; until the sea closed over us." (See notes to *The Waste Land* [V] 321, "Consider", and to *WLComposite* 556, "*Another*".)

Valerie Eliot was presumably quoting TSE when she wrote that his eighty-four draft lines were "rather inspired" not only by Dante's Canto but by Tennyson, adding: "In placing his voyage and shipwreck off the New England coast where he had sailed in his youth, Eliot makes the first mention of The Dry Salvages" (**490**). TSE: "The story of Ulysses, as told by Dante, reads like a straightforward piece of romance, a well-told seaman's yarn; Tennyson's Ulysses is primarily a very self-conscious poet · · · We do not need, at first, to know what mountain the mountain was, or what the words mean *as pleased Another*, to feel that Dante's sense has further depths", *Dante* (1929) I. "But for narrative Tennyson had no gift at all. For a static poem, and a moving poem, on the same subject, you have only to compare his *Ulysses* with the condensed and intensely exciting narrative of that hero in the XXVIth Canto of Dante's *Inferno*. Dante is telling a story. Tennyson is only stating an elegiac mood", *In Memoriam* (1936) (expanded from *WLFacs* notes).

479–81 **ruffian · · · stairs · · · friends**: W. E. Henley, of Life and Death: "He's the ruffian on the stair. || You shall see her as a friend", *To W. R.* 4–5.

483 **trade with wind and sea and snow**: "the wind, in the windy straits · · · the snow · · · the Trades", *Gerontion* 69–72. TSE, anonymously: "There is no harder life, no more uncertain livelihood, and few more dangerous occupations", *Fishermen of the Banks* by James B. Connolly (1928), Publishers' Preface.

484 **"much seen and much endured"**: *WLFacs* notes:

> An allusion to the *Odyssey* I 3–4:
>
> *πολλῶν δ᾽ ἀνθρώπων ἴδεν ἄστεα καὶ νόον ἔγνω,*
> *πολλὰ δ᾽ ὅ γ᾽ ἐν πόντῳ πάθεν ἄλγεα ὃν κατὰ θυμόν*
>
> [He saw the cities and knew the thoughts of many men | And suffered many sorrows in his heart upon the sea].
>
> And also to Tennyson's *Ulysses*: "Much have I seen and known" (13), "all times I have enjoyed | Greatly, have suffered greatly" (7–8).

487 **Kingfisher**: OED "halcyon" B. 1: "Of, or pertaining to, the halcyon or kingfisher. *halcyon days*: fourteen days of calm weather." Sir Thomas Browne: "the common opinion concerning the vertue prognostick of these birds; the natural regard they have unto the windes · · · especially remarkable in the time of their nidulation, and bringing forth of their young; for at that time · · · it hath been observed even unto a proverb, that the Sea is calm, and the windes do cease", *Pseudodoxia Epidemica* III X. See note to *The Dry Salvages* II 72, "halcyon day".

491, 497–98 **swell · · · A water cask was opened · · · brackish**: *Shackleton* ch. IX: "The water-casks were towed behind · · · and the swell · · · drove the boat on to the rocks, where one of the casks was slightly stove in · · · some sea-water had entered the cask and the contents were now brackish" (Shawn Worthington, personal communication). For Shackleton, see note to [V] 359–65.

492 **triton rang the final warning bell**: the mythical creature is generally "represented as a bearded man with the hind quarters of a fish, and usually holding a trident and a shell-trumpet" (OED). Wordsworth: "hear old Triton blow his wreathèd horn", *Sonnet* ("The world is too much with us"). TSE: "And Triton blew his wrinkled shell", *Burbank with a Baedeker: Bleistein with a Cigar 2 variant.*

496–502 **everything went wrong. | A water cask · · · gaffjaws | Jammed. A spar split · · · good Norwegian pine · · · canned baked beans**: Kipling, of explorers of North and South Poles: "Then the wood failed—then the food failed—then the last water dried", *The Song of the Dead* 15. **gaffjaws**: U-shape at the end of a gaff boom which enables it to run up and down a mast and to turn on it. OED has no definition, but cites *Westminster Gazette* 25 July 1894: "*Vigilant's* gaff-jaws broke".

501 **the garboard-strake began to leak:** "The garboard strake leaks", *Marina* 28 (*WLFacs* notes). The garboard strake is animated as a character in Kipling's story *The Ship That Found Herself* (1898): "The garboard strake is the lowest plate in the bottom of a ship", and so crucial to seaworthiness (George Simmers, personal communication). "In a drifting boat with a slow leakage", *The Dry Salvages* II 16.

503 **gleet:** OED 3: "A morbid discharge of thin liquid from a wound, ulcer, etc. Now *rare*".

510 **injurious race:** the *Argonautics* (a maritime poem) of Apollonius Rhodius: "whatever place | The Mossynæci hold, injurious race", tr. W. Preston (1811) II 1601–02.

516 **moaned:** OED "moan" 3c gives this line as the earliest citation for the Navy slang given in Fraser & Gibbons' *Soldier and Sailor Words* (1925): "to complain, to grumble, to be a pessimist". *Partridge*: from no later than 1915. *Chambers Slang Dictionary* has "moan *n.*" from 1910: "(*orig. milit.*) a grievance, complaint".

516–17 **the sea with many voices | Moaned all about us:** Valerie Eliot: Tennyson: "the deep | Moans round with many voices", *Ulysses* 55–56. TSE: "The sea has many voices", *The Dry Salvages* I 24–25 (*WLFacs* notes).

518 **the suspended winter:** "Midwinter spring ··· Suspended in time", *Little Gidding* I 1, 3.

519 **Hyades:** *Lemprière*: "five daughters of Atlas ··· who were so disconsolate at the death of their brother Hyas, who had been killed by a wild boar, that they pined away and died. They became stars ··· The antients supposed that the rising and setting of the Hyades was always attended with much rain."

519, 529 **under the Hyades ··· scudding:** Tennyson: "Thro' scudding drifts the rainy Hyades", *Ulysses* 10 (*Thormählen* 163).

520–21 **The northern banks | Had never known the codfish run so well:** TSE, anonymously: "In the summer, the Gloucester fishing schooner, laden with its seines and dories, can reach the south Banks, or 'Georges'; in the winter the Grand Banks of Newfoundland, where the codfish abound", *Fishermen of the Banks* by James B. Connolly (1928), Publishers' Preface. See note to *Gerontion* 69–71.

523–24 **the pleasant violin | At Marm Brown's joint:** "Beside a public bar in Lower Thames Street, | The pleasant whining of a mandoline", *The Waste Land* [III] 260–61. **Marm:** OED: "Var. of *ma'am*, freq. in U.S. writers" (now citing this line). OED "ma'am": "Prefixed to a surname. *Obs. exc. U.S. vulgar.*" **joint:** OED 14: "slang or colloq. (chiefly U.S.) ··· a place of meeting or resort, esp. of persons engaged in some illicit occupation; spec. (in America) a place illegally kept (usually by Chinese) for opium-smoking, an opium-den; also applied to illicit drinking-saloons", citing this by TSE.

525 **I laughed not:** Genesis 18: 15: "Then Sarah denied, saying, I laughed not; for she was afraid."

526 **unfamiliar gust:** "familiar compound ghost", *Little Gidding* II 42 (typed from

TSE's dictation, in a letter to Kristian Smidt, 25 Sept 1961, as "a familiar compound guest").

529 **trysail:** OED: "A small fore-and-aft sail, set with a gaff, and sometimes with a boom, on the fore- or mainmast."

539–46 **One night | On watch, I thought I saw in the fore cross-trees | Three women leaning forward, with white hair | Streaming behind ··· I thought, now, when | I like, I can wake up and end the dream:** De Quincey: "high aloft amongst the shrouds stood the lady of the pinnace. The deeps opened ahead in malice to receive her, the billows were fierce to catch her. But far away she was borne into desert spaces of the sea ··· still I saw her, as at the moment when she ran past us, standing amongst the shrouds, with her white draperies streaming before the wind. There she stood, with hair dishevelled", *The English Mail Coach: Dream-Fugue*. TSE: "The difference between De Quincey's *Dream Fugue* and Browne's *Urn Burial* is that De Quincey aims to express a content of some intensity, and that he is not diverted into verbal suggestiveness", *Prose and Verse* (1921). For Browne, see notes to *WLComposite* 487 and *Little Gidding* III 35–36.

540 **cross-trees:** OED 1: "Two horizontal cross-timbers supported by the cheeks and trestle-trees at the head of the lower and top masts."

541–43 **Three women leaning forward, with white hair ··· who sang above the wind | A song that charmed my senses:** Sirens. "I have heard the mermaids singing, each to each. || I do not think that they will sing to me. || I have seen them riding seaward on the waves | Combing the white hair of the waves blown back", *The Love Song of J. Alfred Prufrock* 124–27 (*WLFacs* notes, now revised).

545, 548 **(Nothing was real) ··· A different darkness:** "a poet, once he has found his way into these strange lands of more than polar darkness and more than equatorial light, may gradually lose his interest in the ordinary planes of reality. His characters may come to be, in the ordinary sense, less real", *The Development of Shakespeare's Verse* (1937).

550–51 **A line, a white line, a long white line, | A wall, a barrier:** Conrad: "The edge of a colossal jungle, so dark-green as to be almost black, fringed with white surf, ran straight, like a ruled line", *Heart of Darkness* pt. 1.

552 **My God man there's bears on it:** Poe: "Upon coming up with the floe, we perceived that it was in the possession of a gigantic creature of the race of the Arctic bear", *The Narrative of Arthur Gordon Pym* ch. XVII.

554 **Where's a cocktail shaker, Ben, here's plenty of cracked ice:** Ben used to be the nickname for a sailor (*WLFacs* notes). The businessman Benjamin Guggenheim died in the *Titanic* disaster. Apocryphally, a card-player on the ship said: "See if any ice has come aboard: I would like some for this" (Graham Nelson, *N&Q* Sept 1997). "Shaking cocktails on a hearse", *Suite Clownesque* III 13. For fear of sinkings, see note to *The Engine* II. **here's plenty of cracked ice:** *Shackleton* ch. IV: "Suddenly the floe on the port side cracked and huge pieces of ice shot up" (Shawn Worthington, personal communication).

555 **Remember me:** the Ghost in *Hamlet* I v.

556 ***Another*:** the name of God cannot be spoken in Hell. Ulysses in Dante: "com'altrui piacque, | infin che il mar fu sopra noi richiuso" [as pleased Another, till the sea

was closed above us], *Inf.* XXVI 141–42 (Edmund Wilson, *The Devils and Canon Barham*, 1973, 117).

Notes to published poem resume

Part IV translates *Dans le Restaurant* 25–31.

[IV] 312–21] *WLFacs* notes: "Depressed by Pound's reaction to the main passage, Eliot wrote: 'Perhaps better omit Phlebas also???' [26? Jan 1922]. 'I DO advise keeping Phlebas' replied Pound. 'In fact I more'n advise. Phlebas is an integral part of the poem; the card pack introduces him, the drowned phoen. sailor, and he is needed ABSOloootly where he is. Must stay in' [28? Jan 1922]." See headnote, 1. COMPOSITION.

[IV] 312 **Phlebas the Phoenician**: pronounced *Flee-bas* and *F'nissian* in TSE's recordings. The French of *Dans le Restaurant* is accented and has a comma: "Phlébas, le Phénicien". *Hayward*: "Phlebas, the drowned god of the fertility cults. And the merchant. Cf. 'Although I do not hope to turn again ··· Wavering between the profit and the loss | In this brief transit where the dreams cross | The dreamcrossed twilight between birth and dying', *Ash-Wednesday* VI 1–10." For TSE's association of Plato's Philebus with the submarine world, see note to *Mr. Apollinax* 11–15. **Phoenician**: William Morris: "The thin bright-eyed Phœnician | Thou drawest to thy waters wan", and then:

> And as for Hylas, never think to see
> His body more, who yet lies happily
> Beneath the green stream where ye were this morn ···
> Forgetting the rough world, and every care;
> Not dead, nor living
>
> *The Life and Death of Jason* bk. IV 119–20, 693–98

For this book of Morris's poem, see Margaret Gent, *N&Q* Feb 1970, and notes to *Airs of Palestine, No. 2* 20 and 27.

[IV] 314 **the profit and loss**: Paul Elmer More, of the sailors "De Gama or Magellan" discovering the southern seas: they "held in contempt the profit and the control of mundane laws. Both of our explorers reached the desired land, one returning to add a new continent to the realm of his sovereign, the other leaving his body in the new ocean he had traversed", *The Great Refusal* 78 (for the passage see note to *Little Gidding* II 69, 72). John Davidson: "One song you hear in every mouth, | 'Profit and loss, profit and loss'", *Scaramouch in Naxos* sc. iii. TSE: "between the profit and the loss", *Ash-Wednesday* VI 4. "the fat and the lean, and the profit and loss", *Pollicle Dogs and Jellicle Cats* 9.

[IV] 314, 319 **profit and loss ··· Gentile or Jew**: 1 Corinthians 10: 32–33: "Give none offence, neither to the Jews nor to the Gentiles, nor to the church of God: even as I please men in all things, not seeking mine own profit, but the profit of many, that they may be saved". Romans 3: 9: "we have before proved both Jews and Gentiles, that they are all under sin ··· they are together become unprofitable". (Garvie's ed. of Romans, which TSE owned, notes: "The Jew has undoubtedly the advantage in his position and function. But inasmuch as greater privilege involves greater responsibility, the Jew's failure may bring on him a severer doom than the failure of the Gentile.") The order in the Bible is repeatedly "Jews" then "Gentiles" (both in the plural). 1 Corinthians 12: 13: "we are all baptized into one body, whether we be Jews or Gentiles". Likewise Joyce: "—A merchant, Stephen said, is one who buys cheap and sells dear, jew or gentile, is he not?" *Ulysses* episode II (Nestor) in *Little Review* Apr 1918 (*Grover Smith* 60). TSE to H. L. Adlerstein, 30 Dec 1949: "In the long run, of course, the decay of religious faith comes to the same thing for both Jew and Gentile."

[IV] 317–18 **passed the stages of his age and youth | Entering the whirlpool:** Shelley: "We have passed Age's icy caves, | And Manhood's dark and tossing waves, | And Youth's smooth ocean", *Prometheus Unbound* II v 98–100.

[IV] 320 **the wheel:** although sometimes associated by critics with the Wheel of Fortune ([I] 51) or the wheel of torture ("London, your people is bound upon the wheel!" *WLComposite* 340, 343), here the ship's wheel. **windward:** pronounced *winderd* in TSE's 1933 recording (see note to [III] 272 for *loo'rd*); but pronounced *wind-w'rd* in his recordings of 1946 and 1950.

[IV] 321 **Consider:** in *Dante* (1929) I, TSE quotes Ulysses' words from *Inf.* XXVI 118–20, departing slightly from the Temple Classics punctuation and translation:

> *Considerate la vostra semenza,*
> *fatti non foste a viver come bruti*
> *ma per seguir virtute e conoscenza.*

> ··· "*Consider your nature, you were made not to live like beasts, but to pursue virtue and knowledge.*"

V. WHAT THE THUNDER SAID

Lehmann records how, after a reading at Bryn Mawr in Oct 1948, TSE described the composition of *The Waste Land*: "The first three parts were laboured, whereas the fifth part was written down in one afternoon, and no corrections have been made. You cannot tell from the result how long the poet worked to write a line." To Bertrand Russell, 15 Oct 1923: "It gives me very great pleasure to know that you like the *Waste Land*, and especially Part V which in my opinion is not only the best part, but the only part that justifies the whole, at all." In reply to Kenneth Allott's conjecture, 20 June 1935, that the passage "about bats and fiddling on hair and violet and twilight ··· came out very quickly, was touched up very little and was exhilarating to write", TSE wrote, 12 Nov 1935: "Not only that page but the whole section was written at one sitting, and never altered." Henry Eliot to Henry B. Harvey, 16 Sept 1944: "I believe Coleridge claimed that his *Kubla Khan* was a bit of automatic writing. TSE also told Theresa [Eliot] (I didn't hear it, but I take her word for it) that parts of *The Waste Land* were automatically written" (U. North Carolina, Chapel Hill). Stephen Spender: "Eliot considered the last part of *The Waste Land* to be the best part of the poem, partly because it was almost automatic writing", *T. S. Eliot: Voices and Visions* (documentary, 1988). Valerie Eliot confirmed in a broadcast on 7 Nov 1971 that TSE had in mind the composition of Part V of *The Waste Land* when he wrote: "it is a commonplace that some forms of illness are extremely favourable, not only to religious illumination, but to artistic and literary composition. A piece of writing meditated, apparently without progress, for months or years, may suddenly take shape and word; and in this state long passages may be produced which require little or no retouch. I have no good word to say for the cultivation of automatic writing as the model of literary composition; I doubt whether these moments *can* be cultivated by the writer; but he to whom this happens assuredly has the sense of being a vehicle rather than a maker ··· You may call it communication with the Divine, or you may call it a temporary crystallization of the mind", *The "Pensées" of Pascal* (1931). "That there is an analogy between mystical experience and some of the ways in which poetry is written I do not deny ··· I know, for instance, that some forms of ill-health ··· may (if other circumstances are favourable) produce an efflux of poetry in a way approaching the condition of automatic writing ··· it gives me the impression ··· of having undergone a long incubation, though we do not know until the shell breaks what kind of egg we have been sitting on", *The Use of Poetry and the Use of Criticism* 144.

To Montgomery Belgion, 19 July 1940:

> I hold (and I am sure that you will consider this doctrine untenable, so I fling it to you to tear to tatters) that punctuation in poetry is rather different from in prose: that in poetry its value is more largely that of musical notation, and the point is to indicate the emphases for the incantation. Perhaps this is a difference of degree or proportion rather than kind. But it is obvious that the end of a line is a kind of punctuation in itself, so that a comma at the end of a line may have the value of a semi-colon in prose. The absence of commas in parts of the last section of the Waste Land is to indicate that the voice is not to be dropped, and that the passage is to be read aloud in a kind of monotone. Of course I should deprecate the development of any exact notation for poetry, indicating the changes of tempo etc. for I think that latitude should be left to different readings just as a musical piece can be interpreted very differently by different conductors. The author's way of reading a poem is only one possible way: certainly a good poem should be capable of being recited differently by different people, just as it should be capable of meaning different things to different people.

(Hamlet to the Players: "tear a passion to tatters", III ii.) See the Author's Note issued with the recording of *Four Quartets* (headnote, 9. TSE ON *FOUR QUARTETS*).

Title ***What the Thunder said***: John 12: 28–29: "Then came a voice from heaven, saying, I have both glorified it, and will glorify it again. The people therefore, that stood by, and heard it, said that it thundered: others said, An angel spake to him." Jane Ellen Harrison, "The Rite of the 'Thunders'", *Themis* (1912) ch. III, "on the association of thunder with the voice of God and with purification in initiation and fertility rites". TSE's capitalisation follows Keats: *What the Thrush said: Lines from a Letter to John Hamilton Reynolds* (Al Benthall, *Newsletter of the T. S. Eliot Society* Spring 2011). Although many later editors use only the first line, "O thou whose face hath felt the winter's wind", this was the title given by Harry Buxton Forman in his five-volume edition of Keats, listed as "Poems and Letters" in *TSE's books: Bodleian list* (1934).

[V] 322–94] *TSE's Notes* include a general note for Part V, uniquely. C. J. Ackerley, of the biblical story: "The 'torchlight red on sweaty faces' pictures the moment of betrayal; 'torches' are mentioned in John 18: 3, but the Gospels do not refer to sweaty faces, and the image may derive from the many paintings of the scene. The 'frosty silence' suggests the cold night Christ spent in prayer, and the 'agony in stony places' that lonely vigil [Luke 22: 44] and the passion at Golgotha, 'the place of a skull'. The 'prison' is that in which Christ spent what was left of the night before being taken to the palace of Caiaphas, the High

Priest [John 18: 15], and led before Pilate; the 'shouting and the crying' is that of the multitude, demanding Christ's crucifixion."

[V] 322–26 **After · · · | After · · · | After**: see note to *The Love Song of J. Alfred Prufrock* 101–102. **the torchlight · · · faces · · · dead**: "He appreciates the battles, the torchlight, the 'dead sound' of drums, the white, worn face of Cicero in his flight peering from his litter", *A Romantic Aristocrat* (1919) (*Ricks* 174). See note to [I] 68. **the torchlight red on sweaty faces · · · silence in the gardens | After the agony**: *Hayward*: "The association of Jesus in the garden of Gethsemane with the older hanged gods of legend." John 18: 1–3: "he went forth with his disciples · · · where was a garden · · · Judas then, having received a band of men and officers · · · cometh thither with lanterns and torches and weapons." Luke 22: 44: "And being in an agony he prayed more earnestly: and his sweat was as it were great drops of blood." Whitman: "countless torches lit, with the silent sea of faces", *When Lilacs Last in the Dooryard Bloom'd* 38. Conrad: "the effect of the torch-light on the face", *Heart of Darkness* pt. 1. TSE (title): *The Little Passion: From "An Agony in the Garret"*. "a face that sweats with tears · · · The campfire", *Song* ("The golden foot I may not kiss or clutch") 10, 12. "family portraits, dingy busts, all looking remarkably Roman · · · lit up successively by the flare | Of a sweaty torchbearer", *Coriolan* II. *Difficulties of a Statesman* 29–31.

[V] 322, 326 **torchlight · · · reverberation**: see "street lamp · · · Beats", *Rhapsody on a Windy Night* 8–9, and for *réverbère* see note.

[V] 322–26 **faces · · · crying · · · Prison and palace**: Blake: "in every face I meet · · · In every cry · · · manacles · · · cry · · · Runs in blood down Palace walls", *London*. See note to [V] 379–81.

[V] 323 **frosty silence**: OED does not record the sense of social chill. James Beresford: "frosty silence · · · with which it is received", *Miseries of Human Life* (1806–07).

[V] 324–25 **in stony places · · · the crying**: Psalm 141: 1, 6: "I cry unto thee · · · When their judges are overthrown in stony places". To Middleton Murry, 15 Dec 1924, apparently quoting him: "do you really consider it a good sign that the 'time of stony places is over'? If so, you are luckier than the Saviour, who found things pretty stony to the last—and would, I believe, have continued to find them so, had he not been removed at an age less ripe than yours or mine. I do not suppose that I share any other characteristic of the Founder of Christianity, but at least I have nothing but stony places to look forward to. This isolates me, of course, from those who can pass in and out of stony places with practised ease." (Christ was crucified at 33; at the time of this letter TSE was 36, Middleton Murry, 35.)

[V] 326, 330 **reverberation · · · patience**: "patience · · · considerations", *First Caprice in North Cambridge* 9–10. "patience · · · sensations", *First Debate between the Body and Soul* 5–7. "patience · · · irritations", *O lord, have patience* 1, 3.

[V] 326–30 **Prison · · · We who were living are now dying | With a little patience**: 2 Corinthians 6: 4–9: "in much patience · · · in imprisonments · · · as dying, and, behold, we live".

[V] 326–34 **Prison · · · distant mountains · · · mountains of rock without water**: to Stephen Spender, 30 May 1931: "you are wise to avoid mountains · · · Mountains are only tolerable if one is not too near, and if there is a bit of water to break the monotony of the imprisonment—Lake Geneva possibly" (see note to [III] 182).

[V] 328 **He who was living is now dead:** Revelation 1: 18: "I am he that liveth, and was dead" (C. J. Ackerley, personal communication).

[V] 329 **We who were living are now dying:** *Hayward*: "Cf. 'Living and partly living', *Murder in the Cathedral* (chorus of the common women of Canterbury)", the end of I.

[V] 329, 333 **dying · · · among the mountains:** Wordsworth: "The thought of death sits easy on the man | Who has been born and dies among the mountains", *The Brothers* 182–83.

[V] 330 **With a little patience:** Tennyson: "A little patience ere I die", *In Memoriam* XXXIV 12 (*Grover Smith 1996* 27). TSE: "With senile patience", *First Debate between the Body and Soul* 5. "with sordid patience", *First Caprice in North Cambridge* 9. To his German translator, E. R. Curtius, 4 Feb 1927: "I note that you have translated 'with a little patience' by the imperative. Is this right? I meant that we were dying patiently but without any great struggle or revolt, and therefore not much patience was necessary. It is intended to convey a state of torpor or exhaustion after a great or overwhelming event; not as an exhortation."

[V] 331–58 **Here is no water · · · no water:** Psalm 63: 1: "my flesh longeth for thee in a dry and thirsty land, where no water is". Mayne Reid: "The grey, rocky bluff that fronted them, looked parched and forbidding · · · 'O brothers! should there be no water!'" *The Boy Hunters* (1853) ch. XXV (*Crawford* 25). TSE to Ford Madox Ford, 14 Aug 1923: "There are *I* think about thirty *good* lines in *The Waste Land*, can you find them? The rest is ephemeral." 4 Oct: "As for the lines I mention, you need not scratch your head over them. They are the twenty-nine lines of the water-dripping song in the last part."

[V] 332–41 **sandy road · · · road · · · silence in the mountains:** *The Cocktail Party* II, REILLY: "Bless the road." ALEX: "Watch over her in the desert. | Watch over her in the mountain · · · Watch over her by the quicksand." JULIA: "Protect her from the Voices · · · Protect her in the silence" ("voices", [III] 384).

[V] 335–36, 352 **If there were water we should stop and drink | Amongst the rock one cannot stop or think · · · If there were the sound of water only:** George MacDonald: "I am weary, and very lonely, | And can but think—think. | If there were some water only | That a spirit might drink—drink", *Hard Times* (1871) 1–4. For thirst and the sound of water, see note to *Five-Finger Exercises* II. *Lines for a Yorkshire Terrier* 7–8.

582 **Among the rock:** emended to "Amongst the rock". *Fowler*: "The survival of both without apparent differentiation may possibly be due to the unconscious desire for euphony or ease · · · It may be said that · · · (1) *among* is the more normal word, (2) *amongst* is more usual before vowels, but (3) before *the* · · · the two forms are used quite indifferently." ("among these rocks", *Ash-Wednesday* VI 31.)

[V] 337, 342, 354 **dry · · · dry · · · dry:** Charlotte Eliot: "When we were in England in 1921, there was a drouth. Not only were the fields in the country parched and dry, but also the City Parks", *Reminiscences of a Trip to London* (1924).

[V] 338 **If there were only water amongst the rock:** Pater on Leonardo: "In him first, appears the taste for what is *bizarre* or *recherché* in landscape; hollow places full of the green shadow of bituminous rocks · · · all solemn effects of moving water;

you may follow it springing from its distant source among the rocks on the heath of the *Madonna of the Balances*, passing as a little fall into the treacherous calm of the *Madonna of the Lake*, next, as a goodly river below the cliffs of the *Madonna of the Rocks*", *Studies in the History of the Renaissance* ch. VI (TSE: "shadow of this red rock", [I] 26).

[V] 339 **mountain mouth of carious teeth:** Browning: "broken hills | Like an old lion's cheek teeth", *An Epistle Containing the Strange Medical Experience of Karshish, the Arab Physician* 291–92 (a poem on the resurrection of Lazarus, with "through the thunder comes a human voice", 306). *Shackleton* ch. X: "A jagged line of peaks with a gap like a broken tooth confronted us." Shackleton, who died on 5 Jan 1922, was known to love Browning. James Thomson: "carious bone", *A Real Vision of Sin* 14—with its landscape of the "foul canal" and "water-rat" (*Crawford* 48). **carious:** pronounced as rhyming with *various* in TSE's recordings. OED 1: "*Pathol.* Of bones, teeth, etc.: Affected with caries, decayed." 2: "*transf.* Decayed; rotten with dry rot." OED records *calcarious* as the etymological form of *calcareous* "composed of or containing lime or lime-stone".

[V] 340 **Here one can neither stand nor lie nor sit:** Lawrence: "Her mind reverted often to the torture cell of a certain Bishop of France, in which the victim could neither stand nor lie stretched out, never", *The Rainbow* (1915) ch. IV (*Hands*) (TSE: "prison", [V] 326, 413, 414).

[V] 340, 365 **Here one can neither stand nor lie nor sit · · · But who is that on the other side of you:** in Indian legend, three saint-poets experienced a strange meeting. "On a rainy day the first one sought shelter in a small house, the pial [verandah] of which offered him enough space to lie on. A little later, the second one came to the same place seeking accommodation and was told, 'Here one alone can *lie*.' The newcomer answered, 'Where one can *lie* two may *sit*' and his request was complied with. It was very dark and the torrential downpour brought the third Alvar also to the same spot. He was told, 'Two of us are already sitting in this narrow space.' Undeterred by this courteous denial, he argued that where two can *sit*, three may *stand*. He was immediately allowed to join the two and all of them, after standing together for some time, felt troubled by the presence of a fourth person. In the dark they could not identify the intruder and kept asking the question, 'who is the fourth one?' Finally each of the three seers became aware of the mysterious presence of Lord Vishnu himself and gave expression to his ecstasy in a song", P. Marudanayagam, *Explicator* Fall 1986. See note to [V] 359–65.

[V] 341–45 **There is not even silence in the mountains | But dry sterile thunder · · · mudcracked houses:** Max Pemberton: "'His armies come and go like the wind and the thunder. To-day we see them, to-morrow there is silence in the mountains. His enemies die, and their houses crumble to the dust'", *The Phantom Army* (1898) ch. VII. TSE: "there is not enough silence | Not on the sea or on the islands, not | On the mainland, in the desert or the rain land", *Ash-Wednesday* V 12–14.

[V] 344–45 **red sullen faces sneer and snarl · · · From doors of mudcracked houses:** *Hayward*: "Asiatic (Tibetan) faces. The scene has shifted from Palestine to Central Asia." TSE: "sullen sunbaked houses", *So through the evening, through* *the violet air* 6. "in the light of the door | Which opens on her like a grin", *Rhapsody on a Windy Night* 17–18.

[V] 353 **cicada:** pronounced *sicayda* in TSE's recordings (first of OED's two pronunciations).

[V] 354 **dry grass singing:** Kipling: "alone with the winds and the grass singing under the wind", *Kim* ch. XIII (*Grover Smith* 310).

[V] 356 *TSE's Notes* ***Turdus aonalaschkae pallasii*, the hermit-thrush** ··· ***Handbook of Birds of Eastern North America*:** on 18 June 1928, TSE inscribed his copy of Frank M. Chapman's book: "A much coveted birthday present on my 14th birthday T. S. Eliot". Vivien Eliot retained it after the couple separated (as TSE wrote to his brother on 16 Aug 1937), but TSE later retrieved it and presented it to Hayward. To Julian Bell, 2 Jan 1930: "I have spent a great deal of time myself in bird study." Since Thomas Nuttall's *Manual of the Ornithology of the United States and Canada* (1833–34), the hermit thrush has often been said to be the sweetest singer of all American birds. Whitman: "Solitary the thrush, | The hermit ··· Sings by himself a song ··· out of the cedars and pines", *When Lilacs Last in the Dooryard Bloom'd* 20–22, 101 (*Musgrove* 67). See note to [V] 359–65. TSE to Ralph Hodgson, 11 May 1935: "The Nightingales HAVE been something extra this year ··· and there are even other birds here that I prize as highly blackbirds etc. and I think the hermit thrush superior on his own habitat." *Burroughs* untangles how, from Alexander Wilson and Audubon, to Thoreau and Emerson, Chapman and beyond, naturalists have confused (a) the different species of North American thrush, (b) their names, (c) their territories, and (d) their songs. Although Chapman gives *Turdus aonalaschkae pallasii* as the ornithological name, the accepted name now, after many changes, is *Catharus guttatus*. That TSE intended a joke on the name *Turdus* in his note is made more probable by *American Literature and the American Language* (1953): "For the first time, apparently, an American robin, well named *Turdus migratorius*, crossed the Atlantic under its own power", and by his verse *Oh dae ye ken the turdie lads*. The barbarous "*aonalaschkae*", as *Burroughs* explains, survives from an 18th-century catalogue of the flora and fauna of "Russia's Wild East, including Alaska", and was an attempt to Latinise the name of the island Umalaska. **Quebec Province:** on a memo dated 11 Aug 1952 from Peter du Sautoy concerning proofs of the American *Collected Poems and Plays* (1952) TSE asked for the correction from "Quebec County". In the front of Hayward's copy of *Sel Poems* (1954), the first British edition to make the correction, TSE wrote: "Quebec has at last been recognised as a Province" (King's). However, Eleanor Cook points out that in TSE's youth there was a Quebec County within Quebec Province, where he may have heard the bird sing in 1904: "Thrush song in the Quebec woods from May to mid-July and even later is so exquisite that it is a reason in itself for a visit", *N&Q* Dec 2008. For the Eliot family camp in Quebec Province, see headnote to the verse letter of 1904, *Hoping you are better* ("Other Verses"). **Its "water-dripping song" is justly celebrated:** neither Chapman's *Handbook* nor other standard works mention a "water-dripping song", but the phrase is found in relation to a different bird in Ernest Seton-Thompson's story (set in Canada), *The Springfield Fox* in *Wild Animals I Have Known* (1898):

> As I waited in the black woods I heard a sweet sound of dripping water: "Tink tank tenk tink, Ta tink tank tenk tonk." I did not know of any spring so near, and in

the hot night it was a glad find. But the sound led me to the bough of an oak-tree, where I found its source. Such a soft, sweet song; full of delightful suggestion on such a night:

Tonk tank tenk tink
Ta tink a tonk a tank a tink a
Ta ta tink tank ta ta tonk tink
Drink a tank a drink a drunk.

It was the "water-dripping" song of the saw-whet owl.

See *McCue 2014c* and Christoph Irmscher, *Partial Answers* June 2014. (Kipling: "With my '*Tinka-tinka-tinka-tinka-tink!*' ··· we ride the iron stallions down the drink", *The Song of the Banjo* 58–60.)

[V] 357 **Drip drop drip drop drop drop drop**: Coleridge: "Drip! drip! drip! drip!—in such a place as this | It has nothing else to do but drip! drip! drip!", *Osorio* opening act IV. Poe: "And, softly dripping, drop by drop", *The Sleeper* 5. W. E. Henley: "Dropping, dripping, drip-drip-dropping, | In the drip-drop of the cistern", *In Hospital* XXVII 15–16 ("cisterns", [V] 384).

[V] 359–65 **Who is the third who walks always beside you? | When I count, there are only you and I together ··· But who is that on the other side of you?**: *TSE's Notes* hesitantly identify Ernest Shackleton's account (though that was three plus a fourth, not two plus a third): "During that long and racking march of thirty-six hours over the unnamed mountains and glaciers of South Georgia it seemed to me often that we were four, not three. I said nothing to my companions on the point, but afterwards Worsley said to me, 'Boss, I had a curious feeling on the march that there was another person with us.' Crean confessed to the same idea", *South: The Story of Shackleton's Last Expedition 1914–1917* (1919) ch. X. (Pound to his mother [June 1909]: "the american who has any suspicion that he may write poetry will walk very much alone, with his eyes on the beauty of the past of the old world, or on the glory of a spiritual kingdom, or on some earthly new Jerusalem, which might as well be upon Mr Shackletons antarctic ice fields". Pound met Shackleton that October. For Shackleton, see notes to [V] 339 and *WLComposite* **491, 497–98**.)

Dostoevski: "'There's no phantom here, but only us two and one other. No doubt he is here, the third, between us.' 'Who is he? Who is here? What third person?' Ivan cried in alarm, looking about him, his eyes hastily searching in every corner. 'The third is God Himself—Providence. He is the third beside us now. Only don't look for Him, you won't find Him'", *The Brothers Karamazov* (tr. Constance Garnett, 1912) XI viii (C. J. Ackerley, personal communication); for Dostoevski's novel, see note to [V] 366–76. Whitman: "Then with the knowledge of death as walking one side of me, | And the thought of death close-walking the other side of me, | And I in the middle as with companions, and as holding the hands of companions, | I fled", *When Lilacs Last in the Dooryard Bloom'd* 120–23 (*Musgrove* 75). Joyce: "Ask yourself who is he now. *The Mystery Man on the Beach* ··· And that fellow today at the graveside in the brown mackintosh ··· Whistle brings rain they say ··· Signs of rain it is ··· And distant hills seem coming nigh", *Ulysses* episode XIII (Nausicaa) in *Little Review* July–Aug 1920 (*Day 1970* 160). The enigmatic figure appears twelve times in *Ulysses*.

TSE: "Who are you? I expected | Three visitors, not four", *Murder in the Cathedral* I. To Hayward, 27 Mar 1944: "Why is it that there was always one other person, whom one has completely forgotten, even sometimes to the sex, at every party? It's like Shackleton in the Waste Land or somewhere" (see note to [V] 364). *Fireside* No. 1 (1899): "I looked again, and found | Alas! 'Twas only us."

[V] 359 *TSE's Notes* **The following lines were stimulated by the account of one of the Antarctic expeditions (I forget which, but I think one of Shackleton's)**: as well as Shackleton's *South*, TSE read Scott of the Antarctic. Janet Adam Smith on TSE in autumn 1941: "We talked of Scott, and particularly of his *Journal*" (in *Olney ed.*). The *Journals* of Scott's last expedition had been published in 1913. Paul Elmer More: "Was it De Gama or Magellan—the latter, I think in his tragic voyage around the world—who was so alarmed by the new aspect of the southern sky as he sailed southward", *The Great Refusal* 77. For this passage see note to [IV] 314, "the profit and loss". **stimulated**: of Leibniz: "The fact that he could receive stimulation from such various sources and remain so independent of the thought of his own time indicates both the robustness and the sensitiveness of genius", *Leibniz's Monads and Bradley's Finite Centres* (1916). The sequence of *TSE's Notes* here records his own stimulation from various sources: Chapman's *Handbook of Birds of Eastern North America*, then Shackleton's *South*, then Hermann Hesse's *Blick ins Chaos*. (To Mary Hutchinson, [9 July? 1919], on Pound: "I daresay he seems to you derivative. But I can show you in the thing I enclose [*Gerontion*] how I have borrowed from half a dozen sources just as boldly as Shakespeare borrowed from North. But I am as traditionalist as a Chinaman, or a Yankee.")

[V] 361–63 **when I look ahead up the white road | There is always another one ··· Gliding wrapt in a brown mantle**: *TSE's Notes* on the Tarot pack, [I] 46, adduce the journey of the disciples to Emmaus; Luke 24: 13–16: "And, behold, two of them went that same day to a village called Emmaus, which was from Jerusalem about threescore furlongs. And they talked together of all these things which had happened. And it came to pass, that, while they communed together and reasoned, Jesus himself drew near, and went with them. But their eyes were holden that they should not know him." *Hayward*: "The return of the god—or perhaps no more than an illusion?"

[V] 364 **I do not know whether a man or a woman**: Henry Clarke Warren recounts the legend of a saint meeting a husband seeking his wife on the road: "Was it a woman, or a man, | That passed this way? I cannot tell. | But this I know, a set of bones | Is traveling on upon this road", *Buddhism in Translations* 298.

[V] 366–72 **high in the air ··· lamentation ··· cracked earth ··· the violet air**: "the violet air ··· meditation ··· sunbaked ··· the violet sky ··· the evening air", *So through the evening, through the violet air* 1–10.

[V] 366–76 **What is that sound ··· Unreal**: *TSE's Notes* quote in German the closing words of *Die Brüder Karamasoff oder der Untergang Europas* [*"The Brothers Karamazov", or the Downfall of Europe*] by Hermann Hesse: [Already half Europe, at all events half Eastern Europe, is on the road to Chaos. In a state of drunken illusion she is reeling into the abyss and, as she reels, she sings a drunken hymn such as Dmitri Karamazoff sang. The insulted citizen laughs that song to scorn, the saint and seer hear it with tears.] (TSE to his mother, 6 Jan 1920: "I wonder if America realises how terrible the condition of central Europe is.") This and two shorter essays make up Hesse's *Blick ins Chaos* (1920), which TSE sent to Sydney Schiff in Jan 1922. As Stephen Hudson, Schiff translated the book as *In Sight of Chaos* (Zurich, 1923). TSE to Scofield Thayer, 27 Mar 1922: "I discovered when in Switzerland a very admirable essay entitled *Blick ins Chaos* by Hermann Hesse. Mr. Stephen Hudson has made a translation of this and is sending it to you. I think that you will find it an interesting work." The *Dial* published a revision of the translation in June and Aug. In a letter of 24 May 1922 from Lugano, TSE invited Hesse to tea. They met on 28 May and Hesse's *Recent German Poetry* appeared together with *The Waste Land* in the first issue of the *Criterion* in Oct. TSE: "Hermann Hesse, for whose book on Dostoevski *Blick ins Chaos* I have a great admiration, though I do not agree with his conclusions, regards Dostoevski as the prophet of a new religion", *A Neglected Aspect of Chapman* (1924). **that sound ··· lamentation ··· swarming | Over endless plains ··· Ringed by the flat horizon**: "an endless drift | Of shrieking forms in a circular desert ··· contagion", *The Family Reunion* II iii. **sound high in the air**: Whitman: "musician | Hovering unseen in air", *The Mystic Trumpeter* 1–2 (*Musgrove* 63). For Whitman's lines see notes to [V] 381–82 and *Portrait of a Lady* I 34–36.

[V] 368–69 **hordes swarming | Over endless plains**: Hesse regarded as prophetic Kaiser Wilhelm's "fear of the Eastern hordes, which ··· might be enrolled against Europe", *In Sight of Chaos* 23. *Across Mongolian Plains: A Naturalist's Account of China's "Great Northwest"* was published in New York in 1921. TSE: "fierce Mongolian horde", *Growltiger's Last Stand* 41. "across death's other river | The Tartar horsemen shake their spears", *The wind sprang up at four o'clock* 11–12. For "conquest of vast spaces in Asiatic wastes", see Preface to *Anabasis* (in headnote). For "the passing of the horde" [le passage des hordes], see *Inoubliable France* in note to *The Dry Salvages* II 56–66, III 3–15.

[V] 369 **Over endless plains**: "over desert plains", *Bacchus and Ariadne* 9.

[V] 369–98 **plains ··· horizon ··· mountains ··· black hair ··· bats with baby ··· beat ··· Tolling ··· bells ··· cisterns ··· hole ··· grass ··· crouched**: Browning: "grey plain all round: | Nothing but plain to the horizon's bound ··· What made those holes and rents ··· As for the grass, it grew as scant as hair | In leprosy ··· Will the night send a howlet or a bat? ··· It may have been a water-rat I speared, | But, ugh! it sounded like a baby's shriek ··· Toads in a poisoned tank ··· A great black bird, Apollyon's bosom-friend, | Sailed past, nor beat his wide wing dragon-penned ··· All round to mountains ··· those two hills on the right, | Crouched ··· it tolled | Increasing like a bell", *Childe Roland to the Dark Tower Came* IX–XXXIII (A. D., *N&Q* 8 Dec 1951).

[V] 371–73 **over the mountains ··· Falling towers**: Isaiah 30: 25: "upon every mountain ··· in the day of the great slaughter, when the towers fall."

[V] 372 **Cracks ··· reforms ··· bursts**: to his Swedish translator Erik Mesterton, 20 Jan 1932: "The three words are intransitive verbs, the city being the subject." **the violet air**: Thomas Middleton: "violet air, curious garden, quaint walks, fantastical arbours, three back doors, and a coach-gate!" *Your Five Gallants* I i. Poetic diction since early 19th century. Dowson: "In the deep violet air", *Chanson sans paroles* 1 (*Crawford* 36). Henry James: "open to the violet air",

The Ambassadors bk. II ii. See note to [III] 215, 220 for "the violet hour" and *The Ambassadors*.

[V] 373 **Falling towers**: "When cards and images were brought together, the dance could be brought to life in all its complexity, the Juggler (who symbolizes the beginning of all things), the Hanged Man, the Falling Tower, the Fool · · · each having its proper part in the measure", TSE's jacket material for *The Greater Trumps* by Charles Williams (1954). Drafts of *The Rock*:

> When the towers that you build are fallen,
> The bricks made earth again, the streets are traceless,
> Your bridges sunken in the bed of Thames
> The spiritual City will survive you
> And men shall speak of London: that great city.
> Bodleian, MS Don. d. 44 fol. 163, *pencil addition, final readings*

620 Tumbling towers: Edward Carpenter: "the lightning flashes on evil raw places. I stretch uneasily in my grave and tumble the towers of great cities", *Towards Democracy* (1912 ed.) 17. Horace: "Towers tumble · · · Thunderbolts strike", *Odes* II x, tr. David Watson (1712, rev. Samuel Patrick, 1747). *To a Gentleman, Who Desired Proper Materials for a Monody* (*Poetical Calendar*, 1763): "Solemn fanes—and cypress bowers— | Thunder-storms—and tumbling towers" (TSE's part title, *What the Thunder said*).

[V] 374 **Jerusalem Athens**: Shelley: "Athens or Jerusalem", *The Triumph of Life* 134 (shortly before the passage which had made "an indelible impression" on TSE: see notes to [I] 48 and 60–63).

622 Vienna, London. Unreal: this single line from the draft becomes two in the published text, leaving "Unreal" on its own line. A word was likewise isolated when TSE quoted from *Pericles* III i and curtailed the last of three lines in *Poets' Borrowings* (1928):

> The seaman's whistle
> Is as a whisper in the ear of death
> Unheard.

See note to *WLComposite* **158**.

[V] 376 **Unreal**: throughout TSE. "The Nature of Reality" was the subject of Harvard's "Seminary in Metaphysics" by Charles Bakewell (1912–13) and by R. F. A. Hoernlé (first half of 1913–14), which prompted TSE's essay *Degrees of Reality* (1913). "we never, I think, dispense with the blunt 'real' and 'unreal' altogether", *Knowledge and Experience* 89. "Appearances, appearances, he said, | And nowise real; unreal, and yet true", *Oh little voices of the throats of men* 25–26. *Murder in the Cathedral* I, THE FOUR TEMPTERS: "All things are unreal, | Unreal or disappointing · · · All things become less real, man passes | From unreality to unreality." ("human kind | Cannot bear very much reality", *Burnt Norton* I 42–43.)

[V] 377–78 **A woman drew her long black hair out tight | And fiddled whisper music on those strings**: *Hayward*: "One of the 'daughters of music' ('and all the daughters of musick shall be brought low', Ecclesiastes 12: 4)." Tennyson: "combing out her long black hair", *The Princess* IV 257 (*Musgrove* 88). *The Princess* was prescribed reading for TSE's fifth-year class at school (Smith Academy yearbook, 1903–04). TSE: "Compare the description of the agony in *In the Same*

Boat ··· 'Suppose you were a violin string—vibrating—and someone put his finger on you' with the image of the 'banjo string drawn tight' for the breaking wave in *The Finest Story in the World*", *Rudyard Kipling* (1941) (*Crawford* 132). "Transmit the Preludes, through his hair", *Portrait of a Lady* I 9. **fiddled:** *Fowler*: "If the word is, as the OED says, 'now only in familiar or contemptuous use', it is matter for regret, & those who defy this canon deserve well of the language ··· Even now *She fiddles divinely* (as compared with *playing the violin* in that manner) surely supplies a felt need." **whisper music:** see note to *The Love Song of J. Alfred Prufrock* 52–53.

[V] 377, 379 **A woman ··· her long black hair ··· baby faces in the violet light:** Browning: "Gorgon on the breast,— | One loves a baby face, with violets there, | Violets instead of laurel in the hair", *Protus* 4–6.

[V] 377–84 **A woman ··· exhausted wells:** adapting *So through the evening, through the violet air* 13–16, 19–22 (see headnote to that poem).

[V] 377–94 **hair ··· crawled ··· down a blackened wall ··· voices ··· out of empty cisterns ··· only the wind's home. | It has no windows, and the door swings ··· Then a damp gust | Bringing rain:** "the window panes ··· Stirred by the morning air ··· shadows crawled and crept ··· crawled ··· on his hair ··· a little damp dead breeze | That rattled at the window ··· human voices in the chimneys", *Oh little voices of the throats of men* 37–47.

[V] 379–81 **bats ··· Whistled ··· downward down a blackened wall:** Tennyson: "the walls | Blackened about us, bats wheeled", *The Princess* Conclusion 109–110 (*Musgrove* 88). Blake: "Every black'ning Church appalls; | And the hapless Soldier's sigh | Runs in blood down Palace walls", *London* (Helen Watson-Williams, *English* Summer 1955). TSE: "the surface of the blackened river", *Song* ("The golden foot I may not kiss or clutch") 9 (see note). "a blackened street", *Preludes* IV 8.

[V] 379–84 **bats with baby faces ··· exhausted wells:** *Hayward*: "Mr. Eliot thinks that the imagery of this passage was in part suggested by a picture of the school of Hieronimo Bosch." (The form "Hieronimo" occurs in several languages; for "Hieronymo's mad againe", see [V] 431 and note.) *Grover Smith* 95 proposed *Hell*, or *The Sinful World* (Boijmans Museum, Rotterdam), a panel which includes a bat-like creature with dull human features crawling down a rock wall, but the history of the panel before 1927 is unknown. **baby faces ··· light ··· wings ··· towers:** Wordsworth: "at dead of night | And the ancient church was filled with light ··· round the sacred places | They guard, with wingèd baby-faces", *The Redbreast* 53–57.

[V] 381 **crawled head downward down a blackened wall:** Bram Stoker: "my very feelings changed to repulsion and terror when I saw the whole man slowly emerge from the window and begin to crawl down the castle over the dread abyss, *face down* with his cloak spreading out around him like great wings", *Dracula*, ch. III; see note to [V] 384, 388 (Lee J. Richmond, *Explicator* Nov 1971). Valerie Eliot wrote of her annotation of the drafts: "What I regret omitting, under the impression that it was known, is a reference linking the man ('bats' in the received text) who crept 'head downward down a wall' ··· with the scene in *Dracula* where the Count crawls in a similar way", *TLS* 18 May 1973. Tennyson: "To drop head-foremost in the jaws | Of vacant darkness", *In Memoriam* XXXIV

15–16 (see note to [V] 330). Poe: "o'er the floor and down the wall, | Like ghosts the shadows rise and fall", *The Sleeper* 29–30 (the poem immediately preceding *The City in the Sea*, for which see next note). Poe again, in a story: "soot · · · in the chimney, and (horrible to relate!) the corpse of the daughter, head downward, was dragged therefrom", *The Murders in the Rue Morgue* (for which, see notes to *Burbank with a Baedeker: Bleistein with a Cigar* 17 and to *Sweeney Erect*).

[V] 381–82 **crawled head downward · · · wall · · · upside down · · · towers:** for John Day, "A roof · · · growing downwards · · · upside-down", see note to [III] 197. **upside down in air were towers:** Tennyson: "And solid turrets topsy-turvy in air", *Gareth and Lynette* 251 (*Musgrove* 85). Whitman: "musician | Hovering unseen in air", *The Mystic Trumpeter* 1–2. Poe: "pendulous in air, | While from a proud tower · · · Death looks gigantically down", *The City in the Sea* 27–28.

[V] 382–83, 387 **upside down in air were towers | Tolling reminiscent bells · · · the chapel:** "The Church disowned, the tower overthrown, the bells upturned", *Choruses from "The Rock"* VII 30. To R. Webb-Odell, 5 Feb 1934, on potential titles for the pageant: "Is *The Church Bells of London* too flat, or too clumsy, or anything else? 'Bells' has a merry sound."

[V] 383 **kept the hours:** see note to *A Song for Simeon* 17–20, "hour of maternal sorrow".

[V] 384 **voices singing out of empty cisterns and exhausted wells:** Verlaine: "*Et ô ces voix d'enfants, chantant dans la coupole!*", *Parsifal*. Conrad Aiken: "his loud voice crying from the cistern", *The Jig of Forslin* IV iii (1916) (Joseph Warren Beach, *PMLA* Sept 1954). **empty cisterns:** Ecclesiastes 12: 6: "Or ever the silver cord be loosed, or the golden bowl be broken, or the pitcher be broken at the fountain, or the wheel be broken at the cistern" (*Hayward*). Jeremiah 2: 13: "For my people have committed two evils; they have forsaken me the fountain of living waters, and hewed them out cisterns, broken cisterns, that can hold no water" (*Grover Smith* 310). Jeremiah 14: 3–4: "they come to the cisterns, they find no water · · · Because of the ground which is dismayed, since there is no rain on the land", *American Standard Version* (1901) (Florence Jones, *American Literature* Nov 1966). **cistern:** OED 3: "Applied to a pond, or a natural reservoir or depression containing water", quoting "Cisterns supposed to be in the earth, especially in the mountains", 1662.

630^631]

The infant hydrocephalous, who sat
By a bridge end, by a dried-up water course
And fiddled (with a knot tied in one string)

We come

hydrocephalous · · · water course: OED "hydrocephalus": "*Path.* A disease of the brain especially incident to young children · · · with failure of the memory and mental faculties; water on the brain." The noun is used of the disease, not the patient (known as a hydrocephalic). **hydrocephalous · · · fiddled · · · string:** "fiddled whisper-music on those strings · · · contorted by some mental blight · · · feverish impulses gathered head", *So through the evening, through the violet air* 14, 17, 23 (the poem of 1913/14 being strongly related to *The Waste Land*). **fiddled · · · knot · · · string:** "drew her hair out tight | And fiddled whisper-music on those strings", [V] 377–78. "knots of hair", *Sweeney Erect* 13. **sat | By a bridge end, by a dried up water course | And**

fiddled (with a knot tied in one string): "I sat ··· Fishing ··· arid ··· Bridge", [V] 423–26.

[V] 384, 388 **voices ··· the empty chapel**: Malory: "Than Sir Galahad com to a mountayne where he founde a chapell passynge olde, and found therein nobody, for all was desolate. And there he ··· harde a voyce", *Morte d'Arthur* XIII xiv. Bram Stoker: "an old, ruined chapel", *Dracula* ch. IV.

[V] 385–89 **decayed hole ··· tumbled graves ··· empty chapel ··· no windows**: *Hayward*: "Vide *From Ritual to Romance*: the Journey to the Chapel Perilous, an 'initiation' ceremony. The macabre décor of the mythical chapel was intended to test the initiate's courage. The cemetery is associated with the Chapel Perilous in some versions of the Grail legend." **hole**: Weston's ch. XIII, "The Perilous Chapel", quotes the romance *Owain Miles* (*or The Purgatory of Saint Patrick*): "Then with his monks the Prior anon, | With Crosses and with Gonfanon | Went to that hole forthright."

[V] 390 **no one**: to Herbert Read, 1 June 1961: "Why *will* secretaries write no-one for no one?" *Fowler* recommends the hyphen, though "printers are attached to *no one*".

[V] 391 **Only a cock stood on the rooftree**: *Hayward*: "The cock as the dispeller of evil spirits. (Cf. 'It faded on the crowing of the cock', *Hamlet* I i and also 'The strain of strutting Chanticleer | Cry, Cock-a-diddle-dow', *The Tempest* I ii)." **rooftree**: OED: "the main beam or ridge-pole of a roof".

[V] 391–92 **Only a cock stood on the rooftree | Co co rico co co rico**: French equivalent of cock-a-doodle-doo. In Edmond Rostand's *Chantecler*, the cockerel Chantecler believes that it is his cries that cause the sun to rise. The play was a hit in Paris in 1910 and was performed in Boston in 1911; TSE recalled it in *Whether Rostand Had Something about Him* (1919) (Timothy Materer, *N&Q* Oct 1977). Hope Mirrlees: "One often hears a cock | *Do do do mi i i*", *Paris* 6. **rico**: pronounced as in *ricochet* in TSE's recordings.

[V] 393–94, 399 **a damp gust | Bringing rain ··· Then spoke the thunder**: Conrad: "the air full of heat, odorous and sickly, was pierced by a sharp gust of wind, bringing with it the fresh, damp feel of the falling rain ··· there was a short period of formidable immobility above and below, during which the voice of the thunder was heard", *An Outcast of the Islands* IV v; with "tree-tops" (TSE: "rooftree", [V] 391) (*Unger 1956* 234–36).

[V] 395 **Ganga**: pronounced with two hard *g*'s in TSE's recordings. *Hayward*: "Reference to the earliest Aryan beliefs in fertility. *Datta*, *Dayadhvam*, *Damyata* are Sanskrit words." TSE of Tristan Tzara: "at times he becomes difficult to follow: 'Bonjour sans cigarette tzantzanza | ganga | bouzdouc zdouc nfounfa mbaah'", *Reflections on Contemporary Poetry* IV (1919).

[V] 397 **Himavant**: *Warren* 8: "The Himalaya mountains. *Himālaya* and *Himavant* are Sanskrit words of almost identical signification. The former means 'snow-abode,' and is a compound of *hima*, 'snow,' and *ālaya*, 'settling-down place,' or 'abode.' *Hima-vant* means 'snow-y'."

[V] 398 **The jungle crouched, humped in silence**: to his French translator Pierre Leyris, 3 Dec 1945 on this "intentional ambiguity": "*Humped* here can be taken either as predicate or adjective and partakes of both." **The jungle crouched**:

James: "Something or other lay in wait for him, amid the twists and the turns of the months and the years, like a crouching beast in the jungle", *The Beast in the Jungle* ch. II (*Grover Smith 1983* 117).

[V] 399–422 **Then spoke the thunder:** *TSE's Notes* refer to the fable of the Thunder in the Upanishads. *Daiches* 80 points to the translation by TSE's Sanskrit teacher, C. R. Lanman, of the end of "the Great Forest Upanishad", 5.2:

> Three kinds of children of Praja-pati, Lord of Children, lived as Brahman-students with Praja-pati their father: the gods, the human beings, the demons [asuras, an order of deities].—Living with him as Brahman-students, the gods spake. "Teach us, Exalted One."—Unto them he spake this one syllable Da. "Have ye understood?"—"We have understood," thus they spake, "it was dámyata, control yourself, that thou saidest unto us." "Yes," spake he, "ye have understood."
>
> Then spake to him human beings, "Teach us, Exalted One."—Unto them he spake that selfsame syllable Da. "Have ye understood?"—"We have understood," thus they spake, "it was dattá, give, that thou saidest unto us."—"Yes," spake he, "ye have understood."
>
> Then spake to him the demons. "Teach us, Exalted One."—Unto them he spake that selfsame syllable Da. "Have ye understood?"—"We have understood," thus they spake, "it was dáyadhvam, be compassionate, that thou saidest unto us." "Yes," spake he, "ye have understood."
>
> This it is which that voice of god repeats, the thunder, when it rolls "Da Da Da," that is, dámyata dattá dáyadhvam. Therefore these three must be learned, self-control, giving, compassion.
>
> *Hindu Law and Custom as to Gifts* in *Anniversary Papers by Colleagues and Pupils of George Lyman Kittredge* (1913)

(These translated paragraphs are prominent as opening not only Lanman's essay, but the entire festschrift of some 45 papers written for the Harvard teacher.) Lanman: "Old as it all is, there is an amusing touch of modernity, and the thunder is still rolling." See note to [V] 432 and headnote to *The Dry Salvages* III.

TSE's Sanskrit copy of *The Twenty-Eight Upanishads* (Bombay, 1906), was given to him by Lanman on 6 May 1912. Into it is tipped a manuscript key by Lanman to "Pages of Paṇaçtkaris ed.", in which item 11 reads "Bṛhadāraṇyaka, 220 (vo 1, 2, 3), Da-da-da = *dāmyata datta dayadhvam*". *Gordon* 85: TSE "acquired a catalogue of books on Vedanta and, in August and October 1913, bought two books by Paul Deussen, *Upanishads des Veda* and *Die Sûtras des Vedânta*." In being transliterated, Sanskrit is distinct from the European languages quoted in *The Waste Land*, including the Greek of the epigraph. *Southam* 132: "Eliot's model for introducing Sanskrit and Pali into *The Waste Land* was Sir Edwin Arnold's *The Light of Asia* (1879)." Of this "long epic poem on the life of Gautama Buddha", TSE recorded: "I must have had a latent sympathy for the subject-matter, for I read it through with gusto, and more than once. I have never had the curiosity to find out anything about the author but to this day it seems to me a good poem", *What is Minor Poetry?* (1944). To Marco Pallis, 28 Nov 1939, regarding Tibet: "At one time I had even conceived the ambition of studying the language in order to be able to read certain Buddhist texts which are not otherwise available."

"I admit that I am always prejudiced by books about Brahmanism, Buddhism etc. by people who are presumably quite ignorant of the original languages ···

The author does not appear to be acquainted with the Proceedings and Texts of the Pali Text Society", *"Studies in the Middle Way"* by Christmas Humphreys, reader's report (1940).

[V] 402 **My friend**: against "Mon ami" in the ts of Menasce's French translation, TSE wrote "ami*e*" (last letter underlined three times). **My friend, blood shaking my heart**: Dante, *Vita Nuova* [XVI] tr. Rossetti: "blood seems as shaken from my heart", *The Early Italian Poets* 252. In *The Varieties of Religious Experience* (1902) lectures XVI and XVII, "Mysticism" (on which TSE took notes while at Harvard), William James quotes: "'Every man,' says the Sufi Gulshan-Râz, 'whose heart is no longer shaken by any doubt, knows with certainty that there is no being save only One.'"

648 **My friend, my friend**: Dryden: "My friend, my friend | What endless treasure hast thou thrown away", *All for Love* IV i (*Crawford 2015* 399).

[V] 402–404 **shaking my heart | The awful daring of a moment's surrender | Which an age of prudence can never retract** (*variant* **cannot retract**): on Heywood's *A Woman Killed with Kindness*:

> His nearest approach to those deeper emotions which shake the veil of Time is in that fine speech of Frankford which surely no men or women past their youth can read without a twinge of personal feeling:
>
> O God! O God! that it were possible
> To undo things done; to call back yesterday . . .
>
> *Thomas Heywood* (1931), quoting IV vi
> (Mermaid text; commonly IV v)

For "the temptation to attempt to retrace one's steps · · · and make a different choice", see headnote to *Burnt Norton*, 2. GENESIS.

William James quotes J. Delbœuf: "whatever may be done, something remains that can never be reversed", *Some Problems of Philosophy* ch. IX. TSE: "decisions and revisions which a minute will reverse", *The Love Song of J. Alfred Prufrock* 48. "for the man the act is eternal · · · something is done which can not be undone", *Eeldrop and Appleplex* I (1917).

To Paul Elmer More, 10 Aug 1930: "The man who disbelieves in any future life whatever is also a believer in Hell. For in this life one makes, now and then, important decisions; or at least allows circumstance to decide; and some of these decisions are such as have consequences for all the rest of our mortal life. Some people find themselves consequently in circumstances such that the whole of their mortal life *must* be a torment to them. And if there is no future life then Hell is, for such people, here and now; and I can see nothing worse in a Hell which endures to eternity and a Hell which endures until mere annihilation; the mere stretch of endless time, which is the only way in which we can ordinarily apprehend 'immortal life', seems to me to make no difference." ("I find it difficult to separate the notion of 'conscience' from · · · the inestimable benefit and terror of eternity", *Letter from T. S. Eliot* 29 July 1944, a paper for The Moot.) In his copy of the *Lambeth Conference Encyclical Letter* (1930), in a passage on fornication, TSE underlined "Things can never be the same again" (93) with marginal "x". Valéry: "les âges · · · cette prudence infinie qui lui permet les plus folles hardiesses" [the ages · · · that infinite prudence which permits the wildest daring], *La Crise de l'esprit* (1919), letter II. See *A Note on "The Tower"* (1963), quoted in headnote to *Sweeney Agonistes*, 11. BRITISH PERFORMANCES.

[V] 403 **a moment's surrender**: "What happens is a continual surrender of himself as he is at the moment to something which is more valuable. The progress of an artist is a continual self-sacrifice, a continual extinction of personality ··· And the poet cannot reach this impersonality without surrendering himself wholly to the work to be done", *Tradition and the Individual Talent* I, III (1919). "selflessness and self-surrender. | For most of us there is only the unattended | Moment, the moment in and out of time", *The Dry Salvages* V 22–24. "un instant de puissance et de délire", *Dans le Restaurant* 14.

[V] 403, 405 **a moment's surrender ··· By this, and this only, we have existed**: "It is in fact in moments of moral and spiritual struggle depending upon spiritual sanctions, rather than in those 'bewildering minutes' in which we are all very much alike, that men and women come nearest to being real", *After Strange Gods* 42. In *Tradition and the Individual Talent* II (1919), TSE quoted eleven lines of Tourneur's *The Revenger's Tragedy* III iv (giving neither title nor author), including

> Are lordships sold to maintain ladyships
> For the poor benefit of a bewildering minute?

Quoting the last of these lines again in his review of Allardyce Nicoll's edition of Tourneur, TSE commented: "(*Bewildering* is the reading of the 'Mermaid' text; both Churton Collins and Mr. Nicoll give *bewitching* without mentioning any alternative reading: it is a pity if they be right, for *bewildering* is much the richer word here)", *Cyril Tourneur* (1930). Swinburne had quoted the speech with the correct word, "bewitching", adding a footnote on the metre (*The Age of Shakespeare*, 1908, 279–80); TSE on Swinburne's book: "contains no information and conveys no clear impression of the dramatists discussed. A few notable quotations", *Studies in Contemporary Criticism* II (1918). For *The Revenger's Tragedy* see note to *Gerontion* 22. For other variations from the texts of 17th-century drama, see notes to *Gerontion* 54–56 and epigraph. To Stephen Spender, 9 May 1935: "you don't really criticise an author to whom you have never surrendered yourself. Even just the bewildering minute counts: you have to give yourself up, and then recover yourself, and the third movement is having something to say, before you have wholly forgotten both surrender and recovery. Of course the self recovered is never the same as the self before it was given." For "writers to whom it is worth while completely to succumb for a time", see *The Hollow Men*, note to epigraph on the section-title page.

[V] 404 **age**: to his Swedish translator Erik Mesterton, 20 Jan 1932: "means any long period of time with the suggestion of bringing one into old age."

[V] 405 **By this, and this only, we have existed**: "We should say: This and this is what we need", *The Death of the Duchess* II 44. **we have existed**: "So far as we are human, what we do must be either evil or good; so far as we do evil or good, we are human; and it is better, in a paradoxical way, to do evil than to do nothing: at least, we exist", *Baudelaire* (1930) (*Ricks* 220). ("Essential moral preoccupation. Evil is rare, bad is common. Evil cannot even be perceived but by a very few ··· Real Evil is to Bad just as Saintliness & Heroism to Decent Behaviour", *Lecture Notes as Norton Professor* (1933) fol. 37.)

[V] 406–407 **obituaries | Or in memories draped by the beneficent spider:** *TSE's Notes* quote from Webster, *The White Devil* V vi:

> O men
> That lie upon your death-beds, and are haunted
> With howling wives, ne'er trust them; they'll re-marry
> Ere the worm pierce your winding sheet: ere the spider
> Make a thin curtain for your epitaphs.—

The verse speech ends as prose: "we lay our souls to pawn to the Devil for a little pleasure, and a woman makes the bill of sale. That ever man should marry!" Webster again: "flattery in the epitaphs, which shows | More sluttish far than all the spiders' webs | Shall ever grow upon it", *The Devil's Law Case* II iii, with "what a small room" ten lines later (TSE: "empty rooms", [V] 409) (*Friend*). *Hayward*: "'What will the spider do, | Suspend its operations · · · ?' *Gerontion* 65–66." **beneficent spider:** Angelo de Gubernatis: "In the *Mahâbhâratam* we find two women that · · · weave upon the loom of the year with black and white threads, *i.e.* they spin the days and the nights. We, therefore, have a beneficent spider and a malignant one", *Zoological Mythology* (1872) II 164. (For Penelope the weaver, day and night, see note to *The Dry Salvages* I 35–41, "unweave, unwind, unravel".)

[V] 407–13 **memories · · · I have heard the key | Turn in the door · · · We think of the key:** Bergson: "ce sont les nécessités de l'action qui ont déterminé les lois du rappel; elles seules détiennent les clefs de la conscience" [it is the needs of action which determine the laws of recall; they alone hold the keys of consciousness], *L'Energie spirituelle* ch. V (Philip Le Brun, *RES* May 1967). "Memory! | You have the key · · · at the door", *Rhapsody on a Windy Night* 72–77.

[V] 408 **under seals broken by the lean solicitor:** in Stevenson's *Dr Jekyll and Mr Hyde*, Jekyll's solicitor, Utterson, of Gaunt Street, is described in the first sentence as "lean", and breaks several seals. "Utterson locked the door of his business room · · · and set before him an envelope addressed by the hand and sealed with the seal of his dead friend", ch. 6 (Sumanya Satpathy, *Papers on Language and Literature* Summer 1995).

[V] 411, 432 **Dayadhvam:** pronounced *Dye-it-vahm* in TSE's recordings.

[V] 411–14 **I have heard the key · · · Thinking of the key:** *TSE's Notes* quote *Inf.* XXXIII 46–47: "ed io sentii chiavar l'uscio di sotto | all' orribile torre" [and below I heard the outlet of the horrible tower locked up]. Temple ed. noted: "When Guido of Montefeltro took command of the Pisan forces in · · · 1289, the keys of the prison were thrown into the river and the captives left to starve." Geoffrey Carter suggests that TSE was misled by this note and supposed that the Italian verb "chiavare" was related to "chiave", key, whereas Ugolino actually hears the door being *nailed* up (*N&Q* Oct 1977). TSE: "Some wicked and heretical old sinner | Perhaps, who had been walled up for his crimes", *A Fable for Feasters* 17–18. Under the heading "The True Church and the Nineteen Churches": "To one who, like the present writer, passes his days in this City of London (*quand'io sentii chiavar l'uscio de sotto*) the loss of these towers · · · will be irreparable", *London Letter* in *Dial* June 1921 ("towers", [V] 382). See both notes to [III] 264, "Magnus Martyr".

[V] 411–14, 420 **the key | Turn in the door once and turn once only · · · the key · · ·**

the key · · · a prison: "*I did enter you in my heart | Before ever you vouchsafed to ask for the key · · ·* her back turned", *The Death of the Duchess* II 23–25 (following the lines that became *The Waste Land* [II] 108–10).

[V] 413 **each in his prison:** *TSE's Notes* quote Bradley, *Appearance and Reality* 346. In his copy TSE scored (and partly underlined) the following passages: "But there is a natural mistake which, perhaps, I should briefly notice. Our inner worlds, I may be told, are divided from each other, but the outer world of experience is common to all; and it is by standing on this basis that we are able to communicate. Such a statement would be incorrect. My external sensations are no less private to myself than are my thoughts or my feelings · · · So much seems clear, but it is not true that our physical experiences have unity, in any sense which is inapplicable to the worlds we call internal · · · In brief, regarded as an existence which appears in a soul, the whole world for each is peculiar and private to that soul. But, if on the other hand, you are considering identity of content, and, on that basis, are transcending such particular existences, then there is at once, in principle, no difference between the inner and the outer." TSE quoted from the passage in *Leibniz's Monads and Bradley's Finite Centres* (1916). *TSE's books: Bodleian list* (1934) includes Bertrand Russell's *Our Knowledge of the External World* (1914). Pater: "Experience · · · is ringed round for each of us by that thick wall of personality through which no real voice has ever pierced · · · each mind keeping as a solitary prisoner in its own dream of a world", *Studies in the History of the Renaissance* Conclusion. Where I. A. Richards wrote "Communication · · · takes place when one mind so acts upon its environment that another mind is influenced, and in that other mind an experience occurs which is like" (*Principles of Literary Criticism* ch. XXI), TSE underlined "like" and asked "proof?" TSE: "Beyond the circle of our thought she stands", *On a Portrait* 12. "Within the circle of my brain", *The Burnt Dancer* 30. "I could not touch the handle. | Why could I not walk out of my prison?" *The Cocktail Party* I iii.

[V] 416 **a broken Coriolanus:** *Coriolanus* IV v: "broke | And scarred". TSE: "Broken and scarred", *Interlude: in a Bar* 11. See note on the title *Coriolan.*

[V] 418–19] *Hayward*: "Cf. '*Frisch weht der Wind*', 31—the happy moment in Tristan and Isolde's life. T. S. Eliot was, in his youth, a keen and practised amateur yachtsman—a biographical fact which has some bearing on his use of, and delight in, sea-imagery." W. G. Tinckom-Fernandez on TSE in the Harvard class of 1910: "I used to descend on him at his summer home in East Gloucester on my way to Maine · · · He used to take me sailing in his catboat, and he could handle a sheet with the best in Gloucester", *Harvard Advocate* Dec 1938.

[V] 419 **expert:** with stress *expèrt* in TSE's recordings. **expert with sail and oar:** *Purg.* XII 5–6: "chè qui è buon con la vela e coi remi, | quantunque può ciascun, pinger sua barca" [for here 'tis well that with sail and with oars, each one urge his bark along with all his might] (*Friend*).

[V] 420 **The sea was calm:** Arnold: "The sea is calm tonight", *Dover Beach* 1. TSE: "The sea is calm, the sea is still", *The Columbiad* st. 26.

[V] 420–22 **your heart would have responded | Gaily, when invited, beating obedient | To controlling hands:** "my heart beneath his feet. | I'd give my life to his control", *Convictions* 25–26 ("my heart | Under my feet", *The Waste*

Land [III] 296–97). Aristotle: "it is not clear whether the soul may not be the actuality of the body as the sailor is of the ship", *De Anima* bk. II ch. 1. TSE wrote in his copy of the Greek: "This comparison holds only in that the sailor directs the ship as the mind directs the body." Nevertheless: "It is better to go to the *De Anima* than to the *Purgatorio* for a theory of the soul", *Reflections on Contemporary Poetry* II (1917).

[V] 422–24 **controlling hands || I sat upon the shore | Fishing**: *TSE's Notes* refer to *From Ritual to Romance* ch. IX. The Fisher King was "a being semi-divine, semi-human, standing between his people and land, and the unseen forces which control their destiny".

[V] 423–25 **I sat upon the shore | Fishing ··· Shall I at least set my lands in order?**: Edward Carpenter: "I, the King, am come to dwell in my own lands ··· Here on this rock in the sun, where the waves obedient wash at my feet, where the fisherman passing spreads his net on the sands, | I the King sit waiting", *Towards Democracy* (1912 ed.) 337 (TSE: "obedient", [V] 421).

[V] 425 **Shall I at least set my lands in order?**: Isaiah 38: 1: "Set thine house in order: for thou shalt die, and not live" (A. D., *N&Q* 19 Aug 1950), as also 2 Kings 20: 1. TSE: "Swept and set in order", *Easter: Sensations of April* II 4. Title-page epigraph to *For Lancelot Andrewes*: "Thou, Lord, Who walkest in the midst of the golden candlesticks, remove not, we pray Thee, our candlestick out of its place; but set in order the things which are wanting among us, and strengthen those which remain, and are ready to die", a slight adaptation from the Sunday Morning Intercession in Andrewes, *Preces Privatæ* 43. Jacopone da Todi: "Ordina quest'Amore, O tu che m'ami" [Set Love in order, thou that lovest Me]. The Italian is printed on the leaf before the first canto of *Purgatorio* in the Temple ed. The translation given here is the first line of Rossetti's *Cantica* in *The Early Italian Poets* (1861), a poem constructed from a speech by St. Francis of Assisi. TSE: "But there are all sorts of ways of setting the world in order; from the relative precision of physics to the relative confusion of theology", *The Relativity of Moral Judgment* (1915). On Pound: "He added his own extensive erudition, and proceeded to a curious syncretism which I do not think he has ever set in order", *Isolated Superiority* (1928). On the discovery of a "found" tribe: "And until we set in order our own crazy economic and financial systems, to say nothing of our philosophy of life, can we be sure that our helping hands to the barbarian and the savage will be any more desirable than the embrace of the leper?" *A Commentary* in *Criterion* Oct 1935.

[V] 426 **London Bridge is falling down falling down falling down**: *Hayward*: "The refrain of one of the best known traditional English nursery rhymes:— 'London Bridge is broken down | Dance o'er my lady lee.'" The element of sing-song is audible in TSE's recordings. TSE to his Swedish translator Erik Mesterton, 20 Jan 1932: "'London Bridge etc.' is a children's game, and my version is probably merely a variant of yours." ("*Here we go round the prickly pear | Prickly pear prickly pear*", *The Hollow Men* V 1–2.)

[V] 427 ***Poi s'ascose nel foco che gli affina***: *TSE's Notes* quote *Purg.* XXVI 145–48, of which this is the final line: ["Now I pray you, by that Goodness which guideth you to the summit of the stairway, be mindful in due time of my pain." Then he hid him in the fire which refines them.] *Hayward*: "Arnaut, before leaping back into the refining fire (cf. *Little Gidding* II 92), says: 'I am Arnaut who weep and go singing; contrite I see my past folly, and joyful I see before me the day I hope for.'" For TSE's returns to this passage, see next note and note on volume title *Ara Vos Prec* ("*Poems* (1920)").

[V] 428 ***Quando fiam uti chelidon***: [when shall I be as the swallow]. *TSE's Notes* refer to *Pervigilium Veneris* XXII:

> illa cantat, nos tacemus: quando ver venit meum?
> quando fiam uti chelidon ut tacere desinam?
> perdidi musam tacendo, nec me Apollo respicit:
> sic Amyclas, cum tacerent, perdidit silentium.
> cras amet qui nunquam amavit quique amavit cras amet.

> [She sings, we are mute: when is my spring coming? when shall I be as the swallow, that I may cease to be voiceless? I have lost the Muse in silence, nor does Apollo regard me: so Amyclae, being mute, perished by silence. To-morrow shall be love for the loveless, and for the lover to-morrow shall be love].

(For TSE's *Prufrock's Pervigilium*, see Textual History of *The Love Song of J. Alfred Prufrock*, after 69.) TSE to E. M. Stephenson, 19 Aug 1943: "'When I become like the swallow'. You will find a good account of the *Pervigilium Veneris* in [J. W.] Mackail's *Latin Literature*."

To George L. Haskins, 14 Feb 1933, in reply to a query about the use of *ceu* in place of *uti* before *1936*: "You are quite right, but I should be very much interested myself if I could find out why I used ceu instead of uti. I knew perfectly well that uti was correct, but I quoted from memory, and seemed to remember a text which had given the other. Even if my memory is correct, the interesting point is to know why I capriciously chose ceu, but that I am afraid will always remain a mystery. Meanwhile I suppose I ought to correct it in another edition." To John J. Slocum, 19 Feb 1957: "I think that my attention was first drawn to this poem by Walter Pater's *Marius the Epicurean* and Mackail's admirable *History of Latin Literature*. I cannot remember just why I made the change in the quotation. I had quoted it originally in *The Waste Land* from memory but somebody queried the 'ceu'. I think that I then looked up the text of the *Pervigilium Veneris* and found 'uti', and accordingly made the change. I should be very glad if you would tell me how the best text reads. The poem made a great impression on me at the age of seventeen or eighteen and I still admire it very much." The reading "ceu", an editorial emendation, had been printed in the textual apparatus to the *Anthologia Latina, sive Poesis Latinae Supplementum* ed. Franz Buecheler and Alexander Riese (2nd ed. 1894) 175 (Kenneth Haynes, personal communication).

TSE, undated: "If I had known that I was, late in life, to have the felicity to have this radiant angel, Valerie, my Valerie, as my wife—when I had long ceased to *quando fiam ceu chelidon*—I should have been myself radiant with joyful hope", TSE on the epigraph page of her copy of *Ara Vos Prec* (Valerie Eliot collection). **O swallow swallow**: *TSE's Notes* cross-refer to the Philomela legend at [II] 98–103 and [III] 203–206. Tennyson: "O Swallow, Swallow, flying, flying South", *The Princess* IV 75 (A. D., *N&Q* 19 Aug 1950). Swinburne: "Swallow, my sister, O sister swallow, | How can thine heart be full of the spring? | A thousand summers are over and dead. | What hast thou found in the spring to follow?" *Itylus* 1–4. TSE to his Swedish translator Erik Mesterton, 20 Jan 1932:

"The reference is not particularly to Swinburne though I had that in mind, but to the whole history of the swallow in literature since the affair of Procne and Philomela. The swallow of course is also a reference to the nightingale."

[V] 429 ***Le Prince d'Aquitaine à la tour abolie***: *TSE's Notes* refer to Gérard de Nerval (1808–55), *El Desdichado* [*The Disinherited*]:

> Je suis le ténébreux,—le veuf,—l'inconsolé,
> Le prince d'Aquitaine à la tour abolie:
> Ma seule étoile est morte,—et mon luth constellé
> Porte le soleil noir de la Mélancholie.

[I am the shadow, the widower, the unconsoled, the Aquitainian prince with the ruined tower: my only star is dead, and my star-strewn lute bears the black sun of Melancholy.]

Jain 1991 193: "The culture of which the troubadours were a part was destroyed by the Albigensian Crusade against heresy in southern France (1208–13). By that destruction de Nerval's persona, the Prince of Aquitaine, felt himself disinherited of the tradition of the troubadours." After TSE's reading at Columbia U. in Apr 1958, Jacques Barzun wrote to him on 12 Aug, "having gone over the recording several times", to enquire about his pronunciation, "princ' dAquitaine", making "eleven syllables instead of the twelve that a verse reading would require." TSE replied, 5 Sept: "I was unaware of my elision of the mute *e* in the line from Nerval and think it could only have been due to unconscious assimilation of the French to the English context. I do think that to sound the mute *e* there would have given a somewhat precious and self-conscious effect and I am not altogether sorry that I missed it, but I must admit that it was unconscious." (He did not sound the final *e* in "prince" in his recordings.) **la tour abolie**: in the Tarot pack *La Maison Dieu* shows a tower toppling as it is struck by lightning (*Grover Smith* 97).

[V] 430 **These fragments I have shored against my ruins**: TSE: "We have saved a shilling against oblivion", *Gerontion* 69–73 *variant*. "We cannot hope for the comparative unity of Virgil's or Dante's Italy or of Chaucer's or Shakespeare's England, but we can preserve the fragments", *Why Rural Verse* (1925). **fragments I have shored**: "some of the fragments of the afternoon might be collected", *Hysteria*. To Pound, "Sunday" [27 May? 1923], on the opening of Canto VIII, "These fragments you have shelved (shored)": "I object strongly on tactical grounds to yr 1st line. People are inclined to think that we write our verses in collaboration as it is, or else that you write mine & I write yours. With your permission we will begin with line 2." Pound's line was omitted in *Criterion* July 1923 but restored in *A Draft of XVI Cantos* (1925). *WLFacs* notes: "On 19 May 1948 Mr. Peter Russell wrote to Eliot about the first line of Pound's Canto VIII: 'These fragments you have shelved (shored).' Eliot replied (27 May): 'I have no idea whether Canto VIII followed or preceded *The Waste Land*. I am under the impression that it followed [*VE*: it did], because of course Mr. Pound saw the manuscript of *The Waste Land* immediately on its completion and my lines certainly occurred in the draft which he saw in, I think, the month of January 1922. While I made some revisions and chiefly a great many excisions as a result of Pound's criticism of this draft, the final section of the poem remained exactly as I first wrote it. I should think also that his putting the word 'shored' in brackets at the end would indicate a deliberate reference to *The Waste Land* which the reader was intended to appreciate'."

TSE: "Metaphysical poetry involves the existence of a background of thought, of a definite system or fragments of definite systems. Behind Dante there was Aquinas, behind Donne the fragments of every philosophical system and every theological system up to his own time; and although the whole was chaos, the fragments were still sharp and identifiable", *The Varieties of Metaphysical Poetry* 203 (Clark Lecture VII). "It seemed as if, at that time, the world was filled with broken fragments of systems, and that a man like Donne merely picked up, like a magpie, various shining fragments of ideas", *Shakespeare and the Stoicism of Seneca* (1927). On Pascal: "He who reads this book will observe at once its fragmentary nature; but only after some study will perceive that the fragmentariness lies in the expression more than in the thought", *The "Pensées" of Pascal* (1931), with a footnote: "An important modern theory of discontinuity, suggested partly by Pascal, is sketched in the collected fragments of *Speculations* by T. E. Hulme." (To Michael Roberts, 11 June 1936, asking him to write a book on Hulme: "I don't believe that his notes on various subjects at various times are perfectly consistent".)

[V] 431 **Why then Ile fit you. Hieronymo's mad againe**: *TSE's Notes* refer to Kyd, *The Spanish Tragedy* IV i:

HIERONIMO: Is this all?
BALTHAZAR: I, this is all.
HIERONIMO: Why then, ile fit you: say no more.
When I was yong, I gaue my minde
And plide my selfe to fruitles Poetrie;
Which though it profite the professor naught,
Yet is it passing pleasing to the world.

TSE to his Swedish translator Erik Mesterton, 20 Jan 1932: "'Hieronymo's mad againe' is not as I remember a quotation though I have not time to verify this, but was either an alternative title sometimes given to the *Spanish Tragedy* or the title of a similar play, I forget which." The words "*Hieronimo is mad againe*" were an addition to the title-page in the posthumous Seventh Quarto (1615), referring to the hero's intermittent bouts of real or feigned insanity. The page is shown in facsimile in Frederick S. Boas's 1901 edition of Kyd, which TSE mentioned in 1927 in *Seneca in Elizabethan Tragedy* (Arthur Freeman, personal communication). *Hayward*: "'Hieronymo's mad againe.' This means, or it is meant to suggest, that to the modern world all this will seem like madness. But it is, as it was in Hieronymo's case in the old play—a precursor of *Hamlet*—a madness with a purpose. (Cf. 'Though this be madness, yet there is method in't', *Hamlet* II ii.)" TSE: "Hieronymo bites off his own tongue. There is nothing like this in Seneca", *Seneca in Elizabethan Tragedy* (1927). By doing so Hieronymo brings on himself a speechlessness akin to Philomela (John Turner, personal communication). TSE: "There is, of course, a long distance separating the furibund fluency of old Hieronimo and the broken words of Lear", *"Rhetoric" and Poetic Drama* (1919). **fit ··· mad**: "hysteric fits ··· distract her brain", *WLComposite* 287, 290. **fit you**: promising to stage for the murderers of his son a dramatic entertainment at court. TSE to his Swedish translator Erik Mesterton, 20 Jan 1932: "You are right. It is 'furnish'."

[V] 432 **Datta. Dayadhvam. Damyata:** for context see note to [V] 399–422. B. Rajan writes that the original Sanskrit sequence—"Damyata. Datta. Dayadhvam" [Control. Give. Sympathise]—has the advantage of "providing us with an orderly descent through the scale of existence as well as with an indication of the main shortcoming of each of the three orders. Eliot begins with man, and it can be argued that he does so · · · because all three imperatives are heard in the poem as addressed to the human condition" (*Moody ed. 1974* 11). On the rear pastedown of Frank Morley's copy of *1920* (once apparently TSE's own), TSE wrote "damyata | datta | dayadhvam | 'hridayam'". Here the last three words of the Bṛhadāraṇyaka Upanishad 5.2 (see note to [V] 399–422), are followed by the first word (meaning "the heart") of the next section, 5.3: "Hridayam, the heart—it is Prajapati; it is brahman, it is the Whole" (tr. Patrick Olivelle, 2009). Sanskrit rhetoric often has a list of three followed by a fourth which encompasses and transcends them. TSE considered invoking the Upanishads at the close of *East Coker*, but instead postponed their use until *The Dry Salvages*, towards which he pointed by ending with the ocean (*East Coker* V 37 and note).

[V] 433 **Shantih shantih shantih:** *TSE's Notes*: "Repeated as here, a formal ending to an Upanishad. 'The Peace which passeth understanding' is our equivalent to this word." Monier-Williams' *Sanskrit–English Dictionary* (2nd ed. 1899) defines *santi* as "tranquillity, peace, quiet, peace or calmness of mind, absence of passion, averting of pain (*santi! santi! santi!* may the three kinds of pain be averted!)" (*Harmon 1976a*). A. N. Dwivedi: "A Vedic (as well as Upanishadic) *mantra* which is recited at the close of all rituals (cremation of the dead being not excluded), especially on auspicious occasions such as weddings, occupation of a new house, offering of prayers and oblations every morning and evening. Its repetition in the proper way with exact accent and intonation (it is meant to be chanted aloud) echoes the unruffled condition of mind · · · Once such a perfect peace is attained, man becomes liberated from all bonds for good", *Explicator* Fall 1984. In TSE's 1933 recording he clips and lifts the second syllable of each "shantih", whereas in those of 1948 and 1950 each trails away. *Valerie's Own Book* concludes with *Dedication II* ("Uncollected Poems"):

> To you I offer this dedication
> In three words which for us are at one with each other:
> Love adoration desire

[V] 433 *TSE's Notes* **"The Peace which passeth understanding" is our equivalent to this word:** TSE's phrasing prior to *1932* was criticised by F. R. Leavis:

> Mr. Eliot's note that "'the Peace which passeth understanding' is a feeble translation of the content of this word" can impart to the word only a feeble ghost of that content for the Western reader.
>
> *New Bearings in English Poetry* (1932), ch. 3

TSE had written to Leavis, 1 July 1930, that the *Criterion* could not accept a submission "which deals at such length and so kindly with my own work"—presumably a version of this chapter (Christopher McVey, personal communication). To Marguerite Caetani, 27 Sept 1926, on translating Perse's *Anabase*: "One must find equivalents—that cannot be done bit by bit, but by finding an English *key* to the combination." In the prefatory Note to the revised translation in 1949, TSE wrote that originally he had been "concerned, here and there, less with rendering the exact sense of a phrase, than with coining some phrase in English which might have equivalent value". See also letter to Jean Mambrino, 24 July 1952, in headnote to *Landscapes*: "probably no French equivalent. All you can do, is to substitute known European song birds for unknown American birds." **"The Peace which passeth understanding"**: Philippians 4: 7: "And the peace of God, which passeth all understanding, shall keep your hearts and minds through Christ Jesus." In *Revelation* (1937), TSE later quoted Babbitt:

> "Religion also looks upon life as a process of adjustment. This process as envisaged by the Christian is summed up once for all in Dante's phrase: 'In his will is our peace'. A reading of works like the Dhammapada suggests that the psychological equivalent of this form of adjustment was not unknown to Buddha."
>
> One might remark, about the last of these quotations, that it is not proved that there can be any "psychological equivalent"; and it leads us further to remark that Babbitt sometimes appears to be unaware of differences as well as of resemblances between Buddhism and Christianity

"Our peace in His will", *Ash-Wednesday* VI 30 (see note to VI 30–33). To Anne Ridler, 28 Sept 1958: "My most recent Bengali, doing the usual thesis on 'The Mystical Element in Modern English Literature' ··· tried very persistently to get me to admit that the Great Truths of religion were found in Christianity and Brahmanism and Buddhism equally."

The play *The Peace That Passeth All Understanding* by TSE's Harvard contemporary John Reed (performed by the Provincetown Players in New York, 1919) was one of many applications of the phrase to the Versailles Treaties. For the "bad peace" of Versailles, see Keynes in note to [III] 277–78, 290–91 and see headnote to *Coriolan* I. *Triumphal March*.

TSE in 1960: "It cannot be only in America that the image of God can be made to serve human ends, or that the peace that passeth understanding can be equated to a 'tranquilliser'", *All Souls' Club* (1960).

Hayward: "Postscript. 'The World is trying the experiment of attempting to form a civilized but non-Christian mentality. The experiment will fail; but we must be very patient in awaiting its collapse; meanwhile redeeming the time: so that the Faith may be preserved alive through the dark ages before us; to renew and rebuild civilization, and save the World from suicide', *Thoughts After Lambeth* 32. The Inferno of The Waste Land, in fact, looks forward to a Purgatory. It is not, as some critics have supposed, a poem of disillusionment."

The Hollow Men

1. Sequence of Publication   2. Composition   3. After Publication

1. SEQUENCE OF PUBLICATION

The five parts of *The Hollow Men* and the two poems *Eyes that last I saw in tears*—which was a revision of *Song* ("The golden foot I may not kiss or clutch")—and *The wind sprang up at four o'clock* were written separately and tried out in various combinations. The title *The Hollow Men* appeared first in *Dial* Mar 1925, above what became I, II and IV. TSE dated the whole poem "1924" in *Hayward's 1925*.

Chronological order of first appearance	*Places of publication*
Part I	*Commerce* (singly); *Dial* (as I)
Eyes that last I saw in tears	*Chapbook* (as I), *Criterion* (as II)
The wind sprang up at four o'clock	*Chapbook* (as II)
Part III	*Chapbook* (as III)
Part II	*Criterion* (as I); *Dial* (as II)
Part IV	*Criterion* (as III); *Dial* (as III)
Part V	*1925*

I: dated "Nov. 1924", *Commerce* (Paris) Winter 1924[/25], with title "POÈME" on preceding recto, and with "Adaptation de St.-John Perse" facing. (TSE to Leonard Woolf, 28 July 1926: "I think their principle of printing verse in the original language with a French translation is a good one.") Reprinted in *Dial* Mar 1925 as first of three parts, under the title *The Hollow Men*. Reprinted singly in *The Best Poems of 1925* ed. L. A. G. Strong, which preceded *1925* by days.

II and IV: *Criterion* Jan 1925, within "*Three Poems* By Thomas Eliot" (as "I" and "III" with *Eyes that last I saw in tears* as "II"). Then reprinted in *Dial* Mar 1925 under the heading *The Hollow Men*, as "II" and "III", following "I" ("We are the hollow men").

III: *Chapbook* [Nov] 1924, within *Doris's Dream Songs* (as "III", with *Eyes that last I saw in tears* as "I" and *The wind sprang up at four o'clock* as "II"). To Harold Monro (editor of *Chapbook*), 13 Oct 1924, of *Doris's Dream Songs*: "The title is not good, but it has a connexion for me, and I can't think of a better." Doris, from *Sweeney Erect*, reappears in *Sweeney Agonistes*. (This sequence was retitled *Three Dream Songs* in *American Poetry 1925* ed. Louis Untermeyer, which preceded *1925* by eleven weeks.) The letter to Monro continued: "I am sorry to make trouble. But, as I *particularly* should *not* be willing to appear on the same page with anyone else, *I will immediately produce another ½ page of verse* if you have any difficulty with the *cul-de-lampe.*" An illustrative tailpiece by McKnight Kauffer filled the second of the two printed pages on which TSE's verses appeared. To Ottoline Morrell, 30 Nov 1924: "I am pleased that you like the poems—they are part of a longer sequence which I am doing—I laid down the principles of it in a paper I read at Cambridge, on Chapman, Dostoevski and Dante—and which is a sort of *a*vocation to a much more revolutionary thing

I am experimenting on" (that is, *Sweeney Agonistes*). The paper he had read became *A Neglected Aspect of George Chapman* (1925).

V: first published in *1925*.

The Hollow Men (I–V) was collected in *1925*+ and *Penguin* / *Sel Poems*, but always with a line missing from the end of II (see note).

For *Eyes that last I saw in tears* and *The wind sprang up at four o'clock* see "Minor Poems". For TSE's rearrangements of all these elements (and their relation to Dante's *Vita Nuova*), see *Bush* 86–100.

Recorded, 1933, Harvard; released Mar 1934 by Harvard Vocarium Records. Second: 13 May 1947, Harvard, as part of the Morris Gray Poetry Reading (following *The Waste Land* I: "Now, to finish off that same period, *The Hollow Men*").

2. COMPOSITION

To Alfred Kreymborg, 6 Feb 1923: "I think it will take me a year or two to throw off *The Waste Land* and settle down and get at something better which is tormenting me by its elusiveness in my brain." To Louis Untermeyer, 4 July 1924: "I have written nothing whatsoever for three years and I do not see any immediate likelihood of my writing ··· it will be utterly impossible for me to write anything by next November." TSE was working at Lloyds Bank, and busy with journals in Britain, America and Europe. James Joyce wrote to Harriet Shaw Weaver, 9 Nov 1924, that "Mr Eliot had to fly over here to see what Shaun calls the proprietoress"—Marguerite Caetani (Princess di Bassiano), who was helping to fund the *Criterion*. Her journal *Commerce* published Part I of *The Hollow Men* in 1924, Parts I and III of *Ash-Wednesday* in 1928 and 1929, and *Difficulties of a Statesman* in 1931. Pound to his father, 21 June 1923: "The Princess Bassiano is one of those agreeable american ex-flappers married to an Eyetalian ··· very well behaved, gave us an excellent lunch in midst of good and very bad literary company ··· She enthused over Eliot for half an hour, was going to do something for Bel Esprit, and has since mislaid the matter (like any other sassiety enthusiast.)" (For "Bel Esprit", see headnote to *The Waste Land*, 2. FROM COMPLETION TO PUBLICATION: BONI & LIVERIGHT.)

TSE to Harold Monro, 5 Oct 1924: "I am sending you the only things that I have. Print them if you like or not, I dare say that they are bad enough to do the *Chapbook* no good and to bring me considerable discredit. If you want them you are welcome, if not, I am very sorry that I have done nothing better that I could give you. They were all written for another purpose and perhaps would not look quite so foolish in their proper context as they probably do by themselves." Next day TSE requested return of the three manuscripts. "I promise that you shall have them back or their verse equivalent by hand in the evening. I know you are in a hurry, and I wont let you down, but I must have them back today." To Jane Heap, 6 Oct 1924: "I have been working in a method of repetition and variation lately." Conrad Aiken to Maurice Firuski, 15 Dec 1924: "Tom says he is now out of humour with *The Waste Land*, *Portrait of a Lady*, *Prufrock*, *Gerontion*, and in short almost everything except the *Preludes*. He has been doing some new things" (Huntington).

TSE to Marguerite Caetani, 5 Dec 1924: "I propose to send you, as soon as work and worry will allow me, MS copies of five new short poems. I.e. I compose on the typewriter, but there will be *no* other copies of these poems in *long hand.*" No such manuscripts are now known. Of the seven elements listed above, *Commerce* had already printed Part I, while Part V seems not yet to have been written, since it was not among those sent to Scofield Thayer on 6 Jan 1925 for the *Dial.* So the "five new short poems" TSE had in mind were probably those that had appeared in the *Chapbook* and *Criterion*: *Eyes that last I saw in tears*, *The wind sprang up at four o'clock* and II–IV.

For TSE's submission to Scofield Thayer on 6 Jan 1925 of five elements for use in the *Dial*, see description of *ts3* in Textual History. To Thayer, 20 Mar 1925, on the appearance there of I, II and IV: "I am glad that you like the poems. I am not altogether satisfied with them myself. If, however, the other one [Part V] is written, I will let you have it." (Apparently he did not.)

To Harold Monro, 25 Apr 1925: "I should like very much to be represented in the next *Chapbook*, but your date is rather hopeless. I simply can't do any writing until I have had a holiday. I don't expect to be able to make any promises until October." 7 July: "I have not a shred of verse or prose which would be of any use to you. If I had time, I should make a great effort to fabricate something." But TSE did not publish again in *Chapbook* after [Nov] 1924.

To L. A. G. Strong, 30 June 1925, concerning *The Best Poems of 1925*: "I am still in doubt as to how I wish this suite to be arranged; as a matter of fact, it is not quite complete. Therefore I should be very glad if you would use only the poem which provides the title, i.e. Part I of the three poems printed in the *Dial.* This is the only one with which I am at present satisfied." (For titles with analogies to musical forms such as suites, see note to the title *Preludes.*)

To Pound, 13 Oct 1925, asking for a reply post-haste, before proceeding with his first Faber collection, *1925*, in which *The Hollow Men* was the only new work:

> Re enclosed, esp. II, III and IV can you tell me *by return*
> (1) Is it too bad to print?
> (2) If not, can anything be done to it? Can it be cleaned up in any way?
> I feel I want something of about this length (I–V) to end the volume as post-*Waste.*

3. AFTER PUBLICATION

To Wyndham Lewis, 9 Jan 1926, on the publication of *1925*, containing, at the end, *The Hollow Men*: "I wanted to collect all my stuff and get rid of it in one volume so as to get it out of my own way and make a fresh start. I observe that no one but yourself has made any comment on the last part of the volume, so I take it that everyone is waiting for everyone else to decide whether any notice need be taken of it or not."

To Aiken, 13 May 1927, on *Modern American Poets* (1927), where Aiken printed the whole of *The Hollow Men*: "I have received from Knopf a cheque for twenty five dollars, being my share of payment for selected rights from the book of poems which they published used by you in your anthology. They say that they received fifty dollars from the Modern Library Inc. for the right to republish in that anthology. Can you tell me if this is O.K.? Don't think I am grumbling about the price because I didn't expect much anyway and I am quite satisfied with this, only I should like to check up on Knopf. Can you illuminate me on another point? With my consent you published in this anthology *The Hollow Men.* I am not worrying about royalty on this, which is nothing to do with Knopf; but I should like to know: one or two sections of *The Hollow Men* were never printed in America before. They were printed in England over a year ago. Does this printing in America in your anthology secure copyright in America for those parts of the poem?" (Actually only Part V had not previously appeared in America.)

To Miss Judith Wogan, 30 Dec 1929: "However much I appreciate the compliment, and with the most sincere good wishes for the start of the Grafton Theatre, I had rather not have *The Hollow Men* staged at the present time."

To Marianne Moore, 31 Jan 1934: "I have not yet 'enough' either to bring out an expanded *Collected Poems* or a second volume. *The Hollow Men* ends a period; and I must wait until the next period has enough weight (not necessarily bulk) to balance the first."

To Henry Eliot, 1 Jan 1936: "Of course motives are mixed; and therefore it behooves the Christian convert to analyse his own motives for conversion, to confess and reject the bad ones, and lay hold on the good. I believe that this consequence was indicated by my previous interests—my interest in Sanskrit and Pali literature for example, and in the philosophy of Bergson; and that my abortive attempt to make myself into a professor of philosophy was due to a religious preoccupation. But I cannot see that desire for notoriety, or for being on the right side, had anything to do with it. I think that the poems which you mistakenly call 'blasphemous'—'Hippopotamus' and 'Morning Service' point to this end (incidentally, I have written one blasphemous poem, *The Hollow Men*: that is blasphemy because it is despair, it stands for the lowest point I ever reached in my sordid domestic affairs)." To Mrs. Yeo, 29 Jan 1936, giving permission for inclusion in an anthology: "I must allow myself to wonder, however, why *The Hollow Men* should appear classified under the heading 'Social Disease'. I think that 'Spiritual Disease' would be the proper heading, but I notice that you have no such category." To Elizabeth Winters, 18 Sept 1944: "I am afraid that if there was ever any original manuscript of the poem it has long since disappeared, and it is not a poem for which I should care to provide notes."

To Joyce Handford, 22 Apr 1953, expressing surprise that *The Hollow Men* had been "a poem, an understanding of which was required for a school leaving examination, for which it seems to me not particularly suitable ··· It does not seem to me, in fact, a poem which can be explained. What is important is not what the author thought he was doing, put in other terms, but simply what you get out of it yourself."

*

Mina Loy: "The human cylinders | Revolving in the enervating dark ··· Among the litter of a sunless afternoon | Having eaten without tasting | Talked without communion ··· Leaning brow to brow ··· Destroy the Universe | With a solution", *Human Cylinders* in *Others: An Anthology of the New Verse (1917)*, which also included *Preludes* and *Rhapsody on a Windy Night*. Compared to Loy's poem *Effectual Marriage*, however, TSE found *Human Cylinders* "not so good", *Observations* (1918). Her poem had itself been influenced by TSE. For her poem *At the Door of the House* in the same anthology, see note to *The Waste Land* [I] 43–59.

TSE on Marston's two "tragical plays": "Marston's minor comic characters ··· are as completely lifeless as the major characters. Whether decent or indecent, their drollery is as far from mirth-provoking as can be: a continuous and tedious rattle of dried peas. And yet something is conveyed, after a time, by the very emptiness and irrelevance of this empty and irrelevant gabble; there is a kind of significant lifelessness in this shadow-show. There is no more unarticulated scarecrow in the whole of Elizabethan drama than Sir Jeffrey Balurdo" (in *Antonio's Revenge*), *John Marston* (1934) (*Ricks* 220–21).

Title **The Hollow Men**: Ernest Dowson was suggested as the source of this title, in a review of Dowson's *Poetical Works*, *TLS* 3 Jan 1935 (shown to be by Geoffrey Tillotson when collected in his *Essays in Criticism and Research*, 1942). TSE replied: "I do not think that I got the title *The Hollow Men* from Dowson. There is a romance of William Morris called *The Hollow Land*. There is also a poem of Mr. Kipling called *The Broken Men*. I combined the two", *Dowson's Poems* (1935); see description of *ts2* in Textual History, and, for more of TSE's letter to the *TLS*, see note to V 9. Again: "I could never have thought of this title but for Kipling's poem *The Broken Men*. One of the broken men has turned up recently in my work, and may be seen at this time on the stage of the Cambridge Theatre", "*The Unfading Genius of Rudyard Kipling*" (1959), referring to Claverton in *The Elder Statesman*, which ran at London's Cambridge Theatre Sept–Nov 1958. TSE had previously combined Morris with Kipling in *Bacchus and Ariadne* 11: "The winds beyond the world", where Morris's title *The Wood Beyond the World* (1894) meets Kipling's phrase "The Wind that blows between the Worlds", which comes three times in *Tomlinson* (1892). *TSE's books: Bodleian list* (1934) includes Morris's book, and TSE included Kipling's poem in *A Choice of Kipling's Verse*. For Kipling's *A Counting-Out Song*, see headnote to V.

Julius Caesar IV ii: "But hollow men, like horses hot at hand, | Make gallant show and promise of their mettle" (see note to V 7–8). *Julius Caesar* had been one of TSE's set texts at school (Smith Academy yearbooks, 1902–03). **Hollow**: Conrad: "he was hollow at the core", *Heart of Darkness* pt. 3 (*Gardner* 110). Hesse: "the decent, highly respectable magistrate and the other representatives of the bourgeois · · · are shabby, hollow, worthless", *In Sight of Chaos* 16 (see note to *The Waste Land* [V] 366–76). TSE to I. A. Richards, 18 May 1934: "Records arrived. One side is *The HALLOW Men*, sic."

On the oddity of two epigraphs to the poem appearing on different pages, see *Ricks* 218.

Epigraph on section-title page (1925+) **Mistah Kurtz—he dead**: the unadopted epigraph for *The Waste Land* (see note) was taken from earlier in the same passage of Conrad's *Heart of Darkness* pt. 3:

> "One evening coming in with a candle I was startled to hear him say a little tremulously, 'I am lying here in the dark waiting for death.' The light was within a foot of his eyes. I forced myself to murmur, 'Oh, nonsense!' and stood over him as if transfixed.
>
> "Anything approaching the change that came over his features I have never seen before, and hope never to see again. Oh, I wasn't touched. I was fascinated. It was as though a veil had been rent. I saw on that ivory face the expression of sombre pride, of ruthless power, of craven terror—of an intense and hopeless despair. Did he live his life again in every detail of desire, temptation, and surrender during

that supreme moment of complete knowledge? He cried in a whisper at some image, at some vision—he cried out twice, a cry that was no more than a breath—

"'The horror! The horror!'

"I blew the candle out and left the cabin. The pilgrims were dining in the mess-room, and I took my place opposite the manager, who lifted his eyes to give me a questioning glance, which I successfully ignored. He leaned back, serene, with that peculiar smile of his sealing the unexpressed depths of his meanness. A continuous shower of small flies streamed upon the lamp, upon the cloth, upon our hands and faces. Suddenly the manager's boy put his insolent black head in the doorway, and said in a tone of scathing contempt—

"'Mistah Kurtz—he dead.'"

Whether or not Conrad knew its author's identity, he had probably read TSE's *Ezra Pound: His Metric and Poetry*, for John Quinn sent him a copy on publication (NYPL: Quinn Papers). Conrad wrote a Foreword to Edward Garnett's *Turgenev* (1917), of which TSE wrote an initialled review in *Egoist* Dec 1917. TSE to Polly Tandy, 12 June 1948: "I don't identify the name of Mr. Otto Kurz: the only Kurz I know died on the Congo."

TSE on Conrad: "He is, for one thing, the antithesis of Empire (as well as of democracy); his characters are the denial of Empire, of Nation, of Race almost, they are fearfully alone with the Wilderness", *Kipling Redivivus* (1919). "No periodical which professes a devotion to literature could neglect to associate itself with the general regret at the death of a writer who was beyond question a great novelist, and who possessed the modesty and the conviction which a great writer should have. Conrad's reputation is as secure as that of any writer of his time", *A Commentary* in *Criterion* Oct 1924. "Importance of Conrad & James is [*added*: consciously] on several levels—that of Kipling or Wells on one only. These are writers to whom it is worth while completely to succumb for a time. No author final enough to succumb to completely ··· Prose more developed than verse during this period. Modern versifiers (Pound & self) more nourished on prose than verse. Verse only beginning to *reprendre son bien* [recover its wellbeing]", *Lecture Notes as Norton Professor* (1933) fol. 38. To John Hayward, 12 July 1943: "I remember in my youth being offered £25 by Secker to write a critical life of Joseph Conrad."

Epigraph **A penny for the Old Guy**: for Guy Fawkes, see notes to I 10 and I 15. Iona and Peter Opie's *The Lore and Language of Schoolchildren* (1959) 280–83 has various versions of this, but none simply giving "the old guy" (*Southam*). TSE declined the dedication of Herbert Read's *Collected Poems 1913–1925* (Faber, 1926), which appeared shortly after his own *Poems 1909–1925*, writing on 11 Dec 1925: "For the purpose of implanting the right ideas in the public mind, is an obvious intimacy a good thing or does it raise the spectre of a Gunpowder Plot?" (Kieron Winn, personal communication).

In a letter of 7 Jan 1943, A. S. T. Fisher suggested that those who were "Gathered on this beach of the tumid river" (IV 9) were the shades unable to pay Charon the ferryman a penny fare for their passage across the Styx. TSE concurred, 19 Jan: "I certainly had the Styx in mind and perhaps with a rather more antique than Dantesque association but it is not intended to be a very precise reference." (When Dante sees "so long a train of people, that I should never have believed death had undone so many", *Inf.* III 55–57, the river across which Charon is carrying them is the Acheron. For these lines of Dante, see note to *The Waste Land* [I] 60–63.) To Fisher's suggestion that "guy" might be slang, TSE replied: "I was certainly using the word 'guy' wholly in the English and not in the American sense. The American meaning of 'guy' is too imprecise to be of much use."

I

I 2 **stuffed men:** to his Italian translator, Roberto Sanesi, 28 Oct 1960: "I was thinking when I said 'stuffed men' rather definitely of scarecrows stuffed with straw, and I think it likely that the image of the Stravinsky ballet of Petrouchka was in my mind. I think, however, that you already hold the right stick to beat the old guy with." (*Pétrouchka*, 1911.)

I 2–4 **stuffed men · · · filled with straw:** Lewis Carroll: "the wisps of straw, that bristled all about him, suggested that he had been originally stuffed with it", *Sylvie and Bruno* ch. V (immediately following the Gardener's Song: see *I thought I saw a elephant* and note). Jessie L. Weston: "in Lausitz, women with mourning veils carry a straw figure, dressed in a man's shirt, to the bounds of the next village, where they tear the effigy to pieces", *From Ritual to Romance* 51. Virginia Woolf: "to me Dr. Watson is a sack stuffed with straw", *Mr. Bennett and Mrs. Brown*, a talk printed as *Character in Fiction* in *Criterion* July 1924 and reviewed there by "F. M." in Jan 1925. **filled with straw:** military: "Bayonet Practice · · · The figure is of stuffed straw", *Popular Mechanics* Aug 1917.

I 3–4 **Leaning together · · · filled with straw:** "they lean against each other, like sheaves · · · The people leaning against another", *The Death of the Duchess* II 3, 15. "evil houses leaning all together", *Prufrock's Pervigilium* [15]. "Three women leaning forward", *WLComposite* 541.

I 4 **Alas!:** pronounced in TSE's recordings as if rhyming with "farce".

I 4, 8 **Headpiece · · · As wind in dry grass:** Corbière: "Les herbes au vent seront tes cheveux" [The wind-blown grass will be your poll], *Petit mort pour rire* [*Little dead one for fun*]. TSE quoted the whole of the poem—one of the *Rondels pour après*—in his final Clark Lecture (*The Varieties of Metaphysical Poetry* 218). TSE: "the speech of the living is wind in dry grass", *Little Gidding* I 51^52 *variant*. "Not the cicada | And dry grass singing", *The Waste Land* [V] 353–54. "the grass is singing", *The Waste Land* [V] 386. See note to *Rhapsody on a Windy Night* 54, "hair of the grass".

I 4–9 **Alas! | Our dried voices · · · dry · · · glass:** Christina G. Rossetti: "tiring-glass · · · dried-up violets and dried lavender · · · Nor need she cry Alas!" *Passing and Glassing* 10–16. TSE on her *Old and New Year Ditties* III ("Passing away, saith the World"): "What emerges triumphantly from the reserved autobiography of her poems is a surrender to the will of God, an inspired passivity, which is perfectly expressed in her best known, and one of her finest poems", *Types of English Religious Verse* (1939).

I 4–16 **Alas! · · · grass · · · broken glass · · · eyes · · · souls:** Swinburne: "the grass · · · eyes blind as glass, | My body broken · · · stricken ere it saith Alas!", *Laus Veneris* 61–64, one of the Swinburne poems that a volume of selections "should certainly contain", *Swinburne as Poet* (1920). Swinburne again: "grass · · · Seeing each our souls in last year's glass, | Félise, alas!" *Félise* 12–15, a later stanza having "hollower ··· dead men's speech", rhyming with "beach" (TSE: "speech | Gathered on this beach of the tumid river", IV 8–9).

I 5 **dried voices:** Hope Mirrlees: "Hark to the small dry voice", *Paris* (Hogarth Press, 1919) 18. For Mirrlees's poem, see headnote to *The Waste Land*, 1. COMPOSITION.

I 5–9 **voices ··· dry grass ··· broken glass:** "children's voices, ended in a wail. || Bottles and broken glass, | Trampled mud and grass", *First Caprice in North Cambridge* 4–6. "the song ··· walking across the grass ··· a bottle's broken glass", *Hidden under the heron's wing* 2–7.

I 5, 14, 16 **our dried voices ··· eyes ··· souls:** Numbers 11: 6: "our soul is dried away: there is nothing at all, beside this manna, before our eyes."

I 9–10 **rats' feet over broken glass | In our dry cellar:** David E. Lantz: "Even old cellars may be made rat-proof at comparatively small expense. Rat holes may be permanently closed with a mixture of cement, sand, and broken glass", *How to Destroy Rats* (1909); see note to II 12–17. "Rattled by the rat's foot only, year by year", *The Waste Land* [III] 195. "The rats are underneath the piles", *Burbank with a Baedeker: Bleistein with a Cigar* 22.

I 10 **dry cellar:** the Roman Catholic conspirators led by Robert Catesby and Guy Fawkes rented a cellar below Parliament and filled it with gunpowder. They were discovered on the night of 4–5 Nov 1605 and executed for treason.

I 11 **Shape without form:** "Aris. conception of real: to be real means to be a self-subsistent stable entity; and this is to be either form without matter (*not abstracted* from matter) or pure actuality", *Oxford notes on Aristotle* (1914–15) fol. 74. Conrad: "a vision of greyness without form filled with physical pain", *Heart of Darkness* pt. 3 (*Drew* 122).

I 11–12 **Shape without form, shade without colour ··· gesture without motion:** in *A Brief Introduction to the Method of Paul Valéry* (1924), TSE quoted "Servantes sans genoux, | Sourires sans figures" [Servants without knees, smiles without faces] from Valéry's *Cantique des Colonnes* [*Canticle of the Pillars*], commenting: "The indefinable difference is the difference between the fluid and the static: between that which is moving toward an end and that which knows its end and has reached it; which can afford to stand, changeless, like a statue" (*Grover Smith* 102). "In 1910, when I had my first introduction to literary Paris ··· Valéry, if known at all, was known only as a minor, late Symbolist poet whose work was represented in the standard anthology of Symbolist verse, *Poètes d'Aujourd'hui* of Van Bever and Léautaud", *Contemporary French Poetry* (1952). A flyer for the *Criterion* edition of Valéry's *Le Serpent* called him "beyond question the most important French poet of our time" (see note to V 7–8). "*no beginning, no movement, no peace and no end | But noise without speech, food without taste*", *Choruses from "The Rock"* I 117–18.

I 11, 14 **Shape without form, shade without colour ··· death's other Kingdom:** *Paradise Lost* II 666–73, of Death: "The other shape, | If shape it might be called that shape had none ··· Or substance might be called that shadow seemed ··· Kingly". TSE: "death's other river", *The wind sprang up at four o'clock* 11. "O ombre vane, fuor che nell'aspetto!" [O shades empty save in outward show!] *Purg.* II 70.

I 12 **Paralysed force:** Corbière: "Des nerfs,—sans nerf. Vigueur sans force" [Of nerves—without nerve. Of vigour without strength], *Épitaphe* 10 (*Grover Smith 1950*). A line of Corbière's poem had given TSE the title *Mélange Adultère de Tout*.

I 14 **Kingdom:** to A. S. T. Fisher's suggestion that the repetitions of this word evoke "the obsession with Nationalism that possessed the world during the years that followed the treaty of Versailles", TSE replied, 19 Jan 1943: "There was certainly nothing in the way of political criticism in my mind at the time of writing the poem but that is no reason why the reader should not make that application."

I 15 **Remember us—if at all:** Ecclesiasticus 44: 8–9: "There be of them, that have left a name behind them, and that their praises might be reported. And some there be, which have no memorial; who are perished as though they had never been; and are become as though they had never been born, and their children after them." (For "And some there are who", see *Anabasis* closing *Song*.) **Remember us:** "Please to remember | The Fifth of November, | Gunpowder, treason and plot", rhyme for Guy Fawkes' Night (*Southam*).

I 15^16 *variant* **Waters of tenderness | Sealed springs of devotion:** Song of Solomon 4: 12–15: "a spring shut up, a fountain sealed ··· a well of living waters".

II

II 1–5 **Eyes I dare not meet in dreams | In death's dream kingdom ··· eyes are | Sunlight:** *Symons* 18, of Gérard de Nerval: "The sun, as he mentions, never appears in dreams; but, with the approach of night, is not every one a little readier to believe in the mystery lurking behind the world? 'Crains, dans le mur aveugle, un regard qui t'épie!' [Dread, in the blind wall, a look that spies upon you!] he writes in one of his great sonnets; and that fear of the invisible watchfulness of nature was never absent from him" (referring to *Vers dorés* [*Golden Verses*] 9). TSE in 1926: "In so baffling a poet as Gérard de Nerval, about whom I have never yet been able to make up my mind, there are passages obviously of the daydream type ··· as well as the line so admired by Arthur Symons ··· which seems to me consciously of the double-world type", *The Varieties of Metaphysical Poetry* 153–54 (Clark Lecture V).

II 2–5 **In death's dream kingdom | These do not appear: | There ··· sunlight:** on 26 May 1947, TSE was asked whether "there" means "In death's dream kingdom" or some other place, and about the colon after "appear". He replied: "I suppose I meant that in 'death's dream kingdom' 'eyes are sunlight on a broken column', but you might be right in interpreting it another way" (*Mattingly*).

II 2, 5–6 **In death's dream kingdom ··· broken ··· swinging:** Daniel 2: 44, divining and interpreting the king's dream kingdom: "the kingdom shall not be left to other people, but it shall break in pieces and consume all these kingdoms" (see note to *Journey of the Magi* 40–42). TSE: "Swinging between life and death | Here, in death's dream kingdom", *The wind sprang up at four o'clock* 3–4.

II 5 **Sunlight on a broken column:** see notes to *Burnt Norton* V 19, 21, 33 and V 32–33.

II 6–8 **a tree swinging | And voices are | In the wind's singing:** W. O. E. Oesterley: "a tree, swayed by the wind, moved; therefore it was alive", *The Sacred Dance: A Study in Comparative Folklore* (1923), reviewed by TSE in *The Beating of a Drum*

(1923) (*Crawford* 152). Conrad: "He had no restraint, no restraint—just like Kurtz—a tree swayed by the wind", *Heart of Darkness* pt. 2 (*Grover Smith* 106).

II 8–9 **More distant and more solemn | Than a fading star**: TSE in 1947: "I can't see why a fading star should be any more solemn or more distant than any other kind of star" (*Mattingly*). For "the star fades" and John Hayward's objection, see note to *East Coker* I 47.

II 12–17] *Southam*: "Frazer discusses dressing in animal skins for ritual purposes and making divine effigies from straw, the origins of the scarecrow and the country custom of hanging up the bodies of vermin or birds that damage the crops in order to scare off any other of the same species" (see *The Golden Bough* VIII ch. XV, "The Propitiation of Vermin by Farmers").

II 19–21 **that final meeting | In the twilight kingdom | With eyes I dare not meet in dreams**: *Purg.* XXX 76–78, on re-encountering Beatrice: "Mine eyes drooped down to the clear fount; but beholding me therein, I drew them back to the grass, so great a shame weighed down my brow" (*Drew* 123). **twilight**: see note to *Little Gidding* II 38, "waning dusk".

II 21 **With eyes I dare not meet in dreams.**: in printings of the full "suite" of *The Hollow Men* in TSE's books from *1925* onwards, this part has ended with II 20,

In the twilight kingdom

making it the only part not to conclude with a full stop. This anomaly confirms that Part II should end as it had done in the *Criterion* and *Dial*:

With eyes I dare not meet in dreams.

The omission of the line from *1925* was probably accidental (see *McCue 2012*, Proposal 6).

III

III 1 **dead land**: see note to *The Waste Land* [I] 1–4.

III 3–5, 13 **stone images ··· receive | The supplication ··· prayers to broken stone**: F. B. Jevons: "The ex-totemist, therefore, who retains nothing of his forefathers' beliefs and rites but the idea that it is possible to appease a supernatural being by offering sacrifices 'to' him, may gravely mislead the historian of 'primitive' religion ··· To imagine that his inherited habit of offering sacrifices to stones and rocks is a primitive practice out of which religion has sprung, while the truth is that the worship of stones is a degradation of a higher form of worship", *An Introduction to the History of Religion* (1896, rev. 1902) 142 (*Southam*). TSE studied the book at Harvard.

III 6 **twinkle of a fading star**: "Twinkle, twinkle, little star", nursery rhyme *The Star* by Jane Taylor (*Crawford* 154).

III 11–13 **Trembling with tenderness | Lips that would kiss | Form prayers to broken stone**: *Romeo and Juliet* I v: "Ay, pilgrim, lips that they must use in prayer" (*Grover Smith* 102). James Thomson: "Singing is sweet; but be sure of this, | Lips only sing when they cannot kiss", *Art* III; TSE quoted the second line in the final paragraph of *The Use of Poetry and the Use of Criticism* (*Grover Smith* 101). *Inf.* V 135–36: "questi, che mai da me non fia diviso, | la bocca mi baciò tutto tremante" [he, who shall never be divided from me, kissed my mouth all trembling]; quoted in *Dante* (1929) I.

IV

IV 5 **broken jaw of our lost kingdoms**: see note to II 2, 5–6.

IV 9 **Gathered on this beach of the tumid river**: see note to epigraph.

IV 13 **Multifoliate rose**: to A. S. T. Fisher, 19 Jan 1943: "I do not think that I can justify 'multifoliate rose' rather than single rose except that the succession of long and short syllables of 'multifoliate' suited my purpose at the moment, but there is, of course, an allusion to the rose mentioned in the Litany of the Blessed Virgin" (for "the recitation of a litany", see note to V). The Temple Classics prefatory note to *Paradiso* XXXI begins: "The redeemed are seen, rank above rank, as the petals of the divine rose" (see notes to *Ash-Wednesday* II 28 and II 32–33).

IV 15 **The hope only**: *Pearce* 54: "There is a clear ambiguity here in the placing of 'only', a word for whose placing there are no adequate rules": *nothing but the hope of / the hope of none but / the only hope of.* In 1926 *Fowler* devoted three columns to the placing of "only".

V

To Michael Redgrave, who had asked advice for a BBC reading, 5 Dec 1930: "Referring to section five of *The Hollow Men*, the first and the last quatrains should be spoken very rapidly, without punctuation in a flat monotonous voice, rather like children chanting a counting-out game. The intermediate part, on the other hand, should be spoken slowly although also without too much expression, but more like the recitation of a litany."

Asked about reading in a monotone: "A great deal of the melodic arrangement is intuitive. As for chanting verse, for me the incantatory element is very important. So far as possible, the reciter should not dramatize. It is the words that matter, not the feeling about them. When I read poetry I put myself into a kind of trance and move in rhythm to the rhythm of the piece in question", *T. S. Eliot Answers Questions* (1949).

Two years before *The Hollow Men* concluded TSE's *Poems 1909–1925*, Kipling concluded *Land and Sea Tales for Scouts and Guides* (1923) with *A Counting-Out Song*:

> What is the song the children sing
> When doorway lilacs bloom in Spring,
> And the Schools are loosed, and the games are played
> That were deadly earnest when Earth was made?
> Hear them chattering, shrill and hard,
> After dinner-time, out in the yard,
> As the sides are chosen and all submit
> To the chance of the lot that shall make them "It".
> (Singing) *"Eenee, Meenee, Mainee, Mo!*
> *Catch a nigger by the toe!*
> *If he hollers let him go!*
> *Eenee, Meenee, Mainee, Mo!*
> *You—are—It!"*

(For a source shared by TSE and Kipling, Whitman's *When Lilacs Last in the Dooryard*

Bloom'd, see note to *Portrait of a Lady* II 1.) Kipling narrates the prehistory and history of the world, and compares the children's game in which "the player who has the task of catching or touching the others" is "It" (OED "it" B. 1f) to the momentum of war and enlistment through the ages.

> Eenee, Meenee, Mainee, and Mo
> Were the First Big Four of the Long Ago · · ·

But the development of "the Tribes" into "the Nations" has made no difference, for the Big Four of the Versailles Treaty in 1919 (Britain, France, America and Germany) had also "watched the mess" and "Pitied Man in his helplessness".

> Thus it happened, but none can tell
> What was the Power behind the spell—
> Fear, or Duty, or Pride, or Faith—
> That sent men shuddering out to death— · · ·
> (*refrain*)
>
> The men went out who would rather not,
> And fought with the Tiger, the Pig and the Ape,
> To hammer the world into decent shape.
> (*refrain*)
>
> Nothing is left of that terrible rune
> But a tag of gibberish tacked to a tune
> That ends the waiting and settles the claims
> Of children arguing over their games;
> For never yet has a boy been found
> To shirk his turn when the turn came round;
> Nor even a girl has been known to say
> "If you laugh at me I shan't play."
> For— "Eenee, Meenee, Mainee, Mo,
> (Don't you let the grown-ups know!)
> You may hate it ever so,
> But if you're chose you're bound to go,
> When Eenee, Meenee, Mainee, Mo
> Make—you—It!"

V 1–4 ***Here we go round the prickly pear · · · At five o'clock in the morning***: nursery rhymes:

> Here we go round the mulberry bush,
> The mulberry bush, the mulberry bush.
> Here we go round the mulberry bush,
> So early in the morning.

and "Here we go gathering nuts in May · · · At five o'clock in the morning". In ch. IX of *The Ebb-Tide* by Robert Louis Stevenson and Lloyd Osbourne (1894), Huish sings "*'Ere we go round the mulberry bush on a cowld and frosty mornin'*". (For the novel—which TSE praised in *The Defects of Kipling* (1909) as "a triumph"—and for its influence on this poem, see *Ricks 2001*.) Frazer: "how often with the decay of old faiths the serious rites and pageants of grown people have degenerated into the sports of children", *The Golden Bough* IV 77. *Crawford* 154–55: "It was ten years since Eliot had been interested in *Ecstasy and Dance Hypnosis among the American Indians*, and had read about the lively 'moonlight dances' of Bushmen" (in Irving King's *The Development of Religion*,

1910). *prickly pear*: a cactus, but with an edible, fleshy fruit. *prickly*: pronounced as two syllables not three in TSE's recordings. *five o'clock in the morning*: hour of the Resurrection (*Jones* 111).

V 1–4, 28–31] The element of sing-song is audible in TSE's recordings.

V 5–6 **Between the idea | And the reality**: Bradley, *Appearance and Reality* ch. XVI: "We must take our stand on the distinction between idea and reality" (TSE scored the margin shortly before and after this, and the whole of the previous paragraph). Closing words of ch. XXIV: "only a view which asserts degrees of reality and truth, and which has a rational meaning for words such as 'higher' and 'lower'—it is only such a view which can do justice alike to the sides of idea and existence" (beneath which TSE wrote: "In Reality idea and existence coincide: each idea is its own existence, each existence its own idea. This means that both idea and existence are falsified").

V 5, 8 **Between the idea ··· And the act**: Bergson: "la conscience ··· c'est ··· la distance de l'acte à l'idée" [consciousness ··· is ··· the distance between the act and the idea], *L'Evolution créatrice* ch. II.

V 7–8 **Between the motion | And the act**: in *A Brief Introduction to the Method of Paul Valéry* (1924), TSE quotes from Valéry's *Le Cimetière marin* [*The Cemetery by the Sea*], writing of the line "Entre le vide et l'événement pur" [Between the void and the pure event] that it "suggests so strongly though accidentally Brutus's 'Between the acting of a dreadful thing | And the first motion, all the interim is | Like a phantasma or a hideous dream'" (*Grover Smith* 102).

V 9 **Falls the shadow**: Ernest Dowson, *Non sum qualis eram bonae sub regno Cynarae* 1–2, 30–31 (title from Horace IV i):

> Last night, ah, yesternight, betwixt her lips and mine
> There fell thy shadow, Cynara! thy breath was shed ···
> ··· But when the feast is finished and the lamps expire,
> Then falls thy shadow, Cynara! the night is thine

TSE quoted from the poem in *The Last Twenty-Five Years of English Poetry* (1939). To the editor of the *TLS*: "In the interesting review of Ernest Dowson's Poems in your last issue, your reviewer suggests that I caught the phrase 'Falls the shadow' from Dowson's *Cynara*. This derivation had not occurred to my mind, but I believe it to be correct, because the lines he quotes have always run in my head, and because I regard Dowson as a poet whose technical innovations have been underestimated", *Dowson's Poems* (1935); see note to the title *The Hollow Men*. *Crawford* 151, quoting half a dozen Dowson poems: "It is a landscape like Dowson's, 'Hollow Lands' where, in 'the twilight of the year', 'dead people with pale hands | Beckon' by a 'weary river', 'where pale stars shine', where, at passion's enactment, 'There fell thy shadow'."

V 9–10 **Shadow |** ***For Thine is the Kingdom***: the Lord's Prayer: "For Thine is the Kingdom, the power and the glory". 1 Chronicles 29: 11–15: "thine is the kingdom ··· our days on earth are as a shadow, and there is none abiding."

V 16 ***Life is very long***: contesting the aphorism *ars longa, vita brevis*. Conrad: "'you are young yet. Life is very long'", *An Outcast of the Islands* I iv (Vilas Sarang, *N&Q* Feb 1968).

V 21–22 **Between the essence | And the descent**: *Jain 1991*: "In Platonic philosophy the essence is the ideal which finds material expression in its descent to the lower, material plane of reality."

V 25–27 **For Thine is | Life is | For Thine is the**: *Lennard* 201: "the speakers make a desperate attempt to incorporate the Prayer into the text proper, moving the sequence of right-justified lines to the left margin, and resetting them in romans. But in the process the lines are truncated, and do not have the power to prevent the return of the spine-chilling parody" (of the nursery rhyme). For various forms of iteration in TSE, see note to *The Waste Land* [III] 277–78, 290–91, 306.

V 28 ***This is the way the world ends***: "As it was in the beginning, is now and ever shall be: world without end. Amen", *Gloria*, Book of Common Prayer.

V 28–31 ***This is the way the ··· whimper***: among many such formulaic rhymes, *The Oxford Dictionary of Nursery Rhymes* has "This is the way the ladies ride ··· This is the way the gentlemen ride ··· This is the way the farmers ride". After the child has been bounced up and down, the song ends with a fall. *Here we go round the mulberry bush* (see V 1–4) incorporates acting-out lines: "This is the way we clap our hands", etc. A sheet of "OBJÊTS TROUVÉS" which TSE sent to John Hayward, 24 May 1937, includes a cutting with the four lines V 28–31 with "ENTRANCE FEE: £1" (King's). "This is the way to the temple, and we so many crowding the way", *Coriolan* I. *Triumphal March* 6. ***the way the world ends | Not with a bang but a whimper***: "children's voices in little corners | Whimper whimper through the night | Of what disaster do you warn us ··· The destiny that may be leaning | Toward us from your hidden star", *The Burnt Dancer* 20–27 ("Leaning", I 3). "children whimpering in corners", *Prufrock's Pervigilium* [5]. On *Danny Deever* in *Rudyard Kipling* (1941):

> when the climax comes—
>
> "What's that that whimpers over'ead?" said Files-on-Parade,
> "It's Danny's soul that's passin' now," the Colour-Sergeant said.
>
> (the word *whimper* being exactly right) the atmosphere has been prepared for a complete suspension of disbelief.

Adapting Coleridge: "that willing suspension of disbelief for the moment, which constitutes poetic faith" (*Biographia Literaria* ch. XIV).

For the Gunpowder Plot, which ended not with a bang, see notes to the epigraph and I 10. To Philip Mairet, 24 Aug 1945, of Victory in Japan Day, ten days previously: "I have been away ··· depression caused by the hollow gaiety of the public celebrating the Japanese Holiday, after the atom bomb ··· (it is curious that fireworks, just because they are not intended to be lethal, are now more immediately jarring to the nerves than the real bombs seemed at the time)". To Mary Trevelyan, 5 May 1946, after a report from the British Council of Churches: "I wonder what you will think of the B.C.C. Report on Atomic Bombs—to my mind it gets you just nowhere." Thanking her for a copy of the letters of Madame de Sévigné on 16 Sept, he wrote: "Nothing could take one farther away from the *Christian News Letter* and the atomic bomb", before parodying his own lines in a postscript:

> This is the way the world ghosh
> This is the way the world ghosh
> Never to droit but always to ghosh

> And not with a bang but incessant letters
> to the Principal of Leicester College, David
> Cecil, and any people I know in American
> universities.

(Fr. *droit* = right; ghosh = Fr. *gauche* = left. Dr. J. C. Ghosh had edited Otway's works in 1932, and when his lectureship at Leeds U. came to an end after the Second World War, TSE wrote dozens of letters to find him a new post. The Principal of University College, Leicester was Frederick L. Attenborough. The biographer Lord David Cecil was a fellow of New College, Oxford.) TSE had commented on a draft of the report by the B.C.C.'s Commission on the Era of Atomic Power (see J. H. Oldham to TSE, 26 Apr 1946, Texas). TSE to Anne Ridler, 10 Aug 1948: "after Hiroshima, when the *Daily Express* pointed out, in a headline, that 'not with a bang but a whimper' was mistaken (but I am not convinced, because nobody in Hiroshima heard any bang—perhaps I am right after all) I say after that, I am not easily shaken". Henry Hewes reports TSE's saying that he no longer liked *The Hollow Men* very much, "because it represents a period of extreme depression about his future work · · · When asked whether he would still write his famous prophecy · · · Mr. Eliot admits he would not. One reason is that while the association of the H-bomb is irrelevant to it, it would today come into everyone's mind. Another is that he is not sure the world will end with either. People whose houses were bombed have told him they don't remember hearing anything. The original meaning, he explains, 'Was a subjective dissatisfaction with the pettiness of life. When one is young, the expression of that mood is simply an effusion of one's individual situation'", *Eliot on Eliot: "I feel younger than I did at 60"* (1958), with Kipling evoked in the next paragraph. (While at the Princeton Institute of Advanced Study, TSE inscribed a copy of *The Cocktail Party* to Oppenheimer, the nuclear weapons scientist: "to J. Robert Oppenheimer from the author: the play incubated at the Institute. T. S. Eliot, 6.iii.50".) Interviewed by T. S. Matthews in 1958: "I don't often read *The Hollow Men* when I give readings; it's not bad but I think its mood is rather too despairing" (*Mademoiselle* May 1965). OED "bang" 2b: "With allusion to T. S. Eliot's line" (also quoting Aldington, Michael Innes, and *The Times*); OED "whimper" 2: "not with a bang but a whimper".

V 31 ***Not with a bang***: Santayana on Dante's *Commedia*: "As in some great symphony, everything is cumulative: the movements conspire, the tension grows, the volume redoubles, the keen melody soars higher and higher; and it all ends, not with a bang, not with some casual incident, but in sustained reflection, in the sense that it has not ended, but remains by us in its totality, a revelation and a resource forever", *Three Philosophical Poets* (1910) 133 (*Sencourt* 94). This was perhaps the "echo" suggested by Edward J. H. Greene, to whom TSE wrote, 19 Apr 1940: "I certainly read his *Three Philosophical Poets*, and indeed I think I listened to the Harvard lectures · · · As I remember, the essay on Lucretius seemed to me much the best of the three. I certainly read the one on Dante, but if there is an echo, it was quite unconscious." To Ants Oras, 27 July 1932: "I think · · · you are quite right about Santayana, although the idea had never struck me before · · · I always rather disliked Santayana personally, quite without justice. I dislike his style of writing which I find very hard to read · · · However he was very much of a figure in my time, and I read some of his books when I was very young and impressionable indeed, and the influence is more than likely." To Daniel Cory, 28 Sept 1934: "I should be delighted to have a contribution from Mr. Santayana" (for the *Criterion*). See note to *Gerontion* 69. ***with a bang***: OED "click" *v.*[1] 1d: "1926 *Amer. Speech* I. 436/2 [Show-business slang]. A turn is said to click when it proves to be successful, or in the vernacular, 'gets across with a bang'." (Earlier: "The program · · · went off with a 'bang'", *The Rotarian* Aug 1916.) See note to *After the turning of the inspired days* 13 *variant*, "The show was ended". TSE to Sally Cobden-Sanderson, 29 Aug 1932: "I should very much like to see a copy of your son's poem. It certainly starts off with a bang." To Laurence Binyon, 28 Apr 1941: "no translation of it can come with such a bang as to satisfy the reader" (see note to *Ash-Wednesday* VI 30–33). ***whimper***: "'Whatever you do,' I wish someone had said to me then, 'don't whimper but take the consequences'", *Address by T. S. Eliot, '06, to the Class of '33* (1933) (*Bush* 4).

Ash-Wednesday

1. Sequence of Publication 2. Composition 3. After Publication

1. SEQUENCE OF PUBLICATION

Like *The Hollow Men*, *Ash-Wednesday* was written in Parts, some of which were first published separately (with what became II appearing earlier than I). All five Parts were completed or in draft by Oct 1928 (see Textual History description of *ts2*).

I: *Commerce* (Paris) Spring 1928, with title "PERCH'IO NON SPERO . . ." on preceding recto, and a facing translation by Jean de Menasce. (Distribution of *Commerce* had been "taken over" by the Hogarth Press: Leonard Woolf to TSE, 24 July 1926.) On 3 Oct 1929, Walter de la Mare requested permission to reprint *Perch'io non spero* in the anthology that became *Desert Islands*. TSE replied, 18 Oct: "This is merely to tell you that the other directors see no more objection than I do to your reprinting the whole of *Perch'io non spero* in *Islands*. I should be glad if you would omit that title, and if possible print it without any title, because I am reprinting the poem later without that title, merely as no. 1 of a sequence of six which I have called provisionally *Six Poems*, but think of calling *Ash Wednesday Music* (but I should like very much to have your frank opinion of that title, about which I feel doubtful)." De la Mare responded, 21 Oct: "In itself I like the title *Ash Wednesday Music.* There is a covert poetic nuance between Ash and music. My only hesitation is its ironical tinge."

II: *Saturday Review of Literature* (NY) 10 Dec 1927 as *Salutation*. (Frank Morley was an editor of the journal, which he had helped to found.) Announced in Faber's list for Autumn 1927 for publication in the *Criterion* "in the near future", and printed there Jan 1928. Reprinted in *Twentieth-Century Poetry* ed. John Drinkwater, Henry Seidel Canby and William Rose Benét (Boston, 1929). TSE to Harold Monro, 4 June 1929, replying to a request for anthology permissions: "Would you care to consider either the *Salutation* which was published only in the *Criterion*, or a better poem called *Perch'io non Spero*, which was published only in Paris? You are welcome to either of these ··· which I intended to keep back for a sequence I am preparing." (Harold Monro had run the Poetry Bookshop, 1913–26. Penelope Fitzgerald to Richard Garnett, 8 May 1978: "T. S. Eliot ··· told me that the Poetry Bookshop staircase made an appearance in *Ash Wednesday*", *So I Have Thought of You: The Letters of Penelope Fitzgerald*, ed. Terence Dooley, 2008.)

III: *Commerce* (Paris) Autumn 1928, with title "SOM DE L'ESCALINA" on preceding recto, and a facing translation by Jean de Menasce. (Contents page reads "T.-S. Eliott", and the name below both the English and the French reads "T. S. Eliott".)

IV, V and VI: within *Ash-Wednesday* (1930), when this title was first used.

The first edition, published by Faber on 24 Apr 1930, was limited to 600 numbered copies printed at the Curwen Press, of which 200 were for Great Britain and 400 for the United States. The Faber trade edition was published on 29 Apr, and the

American trade edition by Putnam on 26 Sept. The poem was reset for a second British edition, *1933*, then appeared in *1936+*, *Sesame* and *Penguin* / *Sel Poems*. Putnam were to prove awkward in 1936, when they were reluctant to allow the poem to appear in Harcourt, Brace's edition of *Collected Poems 1909–1935* because their stock had not sold out (Frank Morley to Geoffrey Faber, 3 Feb 1936, Faber archive; on the American copyright, see TSE to Faber, 23 Aug 1930).

The 1930 volume and its American counterpart contain the dedication "TO | MY WIFE" (see note on dedication to *Prufrock and Other Observations*). The front panel of the jacket of the trade edition describes *Ash-Wednesday* as "Six Poems". The front flap reads: "¶ A new sequence of six poems with certain recurrent themes. They are further developments of a style used by the author in at least one of his recent Ariel Poems" ("new" and "recent" were omitted in *1933*). TSE and Pound had been inconsistent about whether *The Waste Land* was one poem or a "poem sequence" or a "series of poems" (see headnote, 2. POUND'S PART), and similarly TSE never quite decided whether to speak of *Ash-Wednesday* as one poem or several. (In *1963*, the first line of each part was listed in the Index of Titles, as was the title of each part of *The Waste Land.* The parts of *The Hollow Men* were not individually listed.)

TSE referred repeatedly to *Ash-Wednesday* as "the poem" in his correspondence of 1930. In reply to a request to reprint Part I in an anthology, he wrote to Norman Foerster, 15 June 1932: "I had rather not include *Because I do not hope* inasmuch as that is merely the first section of *Ash Wednesday* and I had rather not have it appear again separately." This had become a rule by the time he wrote to R. J. Wilkinson, 8 Oct 1935: "I do not allow parts of either *Ash Wednesday* or *The Waste Land* to be published separately." Yet *The Faber Book of Modern Verse* (1936) printed Parts I and II of *Ash-Wednesday*, and on 24 May 1938 TSE wrote to the Rev. H. Escott: "I should be quite willing to appear in your anthology, but I consider that the whole of *Ash Wednesday* is too much to concede to an anthology at any price. I suggest that you should choose one section, and write to Messrs Faber & Faber again."

Recorded 1933, Columbia U. Second: 26 July 1946, NBC (NY) for the Library of Congress; released Feb 1949. Third: 26, 28 Sept 1955, London; released by Caedmon, 1955 (US), 1960 (UK). Additionally: Part VI, 23 May 1947, National Gallery of Art, Washington.

2. COMPOSITION

"Writing the 'Ariel' pieces released the stream, and led directly to *Ash-Wednesday*", *T. S. Eliot Talks about Himself and the Drive to Create* (1953). *Journey of the Magi* was published in Aug 1927, and the first part of *Ash-Wednesday* to be published appeared on 10 Dec. Thereafter the writing of the Ariel Poems and *Ash-Wednesday* overlapped, with *Marina* appearing five months later than *Ash-Wednesday* (see Textual History). The Ariel Poems appear as a section after *Ash-Wednesday* in TSE's collected editions.

To Marguerite Caetani, 21 Aug 1926, referring probably to Part II of *Ash-Wednesday*: "I have not got on with my Hymn to the Virgin."

To his mother, 2 Sept 1927: "I have just written another small poem, which I shall offer to *Commerce* (Margaret (Chapin) de Bassiano's review) simultaneously [with a Chronicle for *La Nouvelle Revue Française*], when I have polished it up, and will send you a copy."

To I. A. Richards, 28 Sept 1928: "I am now venturing to send you herewith for inspection and return a copy of most of a group of poems I have been working on. I am not sure whether their weakness is a question of detail, or whether they are fundamentally wrong. They seem to get feebler towards the end too. No. 2 was published in the *Criterion*, No. 1 in *Commerce*; the rest are unprinted." Richards to TSE, 1 Oct: "I don't think there is *much* wrong with the poems. Perhaps you have been working at them too closely. They are stronger—to a stranger's eye—than you suggest. May I keep them a little to see how they *wear*. The last thirds of some of them are perhaps a little thin and a little evidently deliberate. I certainly don't think there is anything *fundamentally* at fault."

TSE to Freda Kirchwey of the *Nation*, 7 Feb 1929: "It is not quite certain but I am at present negotiating for a small number of new poems to be published in America." On 6 Sept 1929, Vivien Eliot reported to Mary Hutchinson that TSE had "finished those poems that he read to you—at last. They have gone to America."

TSE to Marguerite Caetani, 3 Oct 1929, on *Som de l'escalina*: "The poem I sent you of my own is one of a set of six (including *Perch'io non spero* from *Commerce*) which is to be brought out in a limited edition by Faber & Faber and the Fountain Press of New York; but I think it extremely unlikely that the book will be printed before the new year, so it should not affect *Commerce.*"

To Jean de Menasce, 5 Oct 1929, on a proposed French selection of TSE's poems: "What I should like, if possible, would be a selection made by you and myself ··· I should rather like to include several of my later poems—the Magi, the Simeon, possibly *Animula*, which I shall send you shortly, and the set of six which includes *Perch'io non spero* and the one which Madame de Bassiano will have sent you (I have just given her your new address). This set will appear in English for the first time early next year."

To Walter de la Mare, 11 Oct 1929: "I rather hope that you may like one or two other of the poems better than that one" (*Perch'io non spero*).

To I. A. Richards, 29 Oct: "I have also revised for publication in the spring those poems which you criticised, and think that I have much improved them; and that the improvements just make all the difference between sincerity and sham."

To the Rev. E. Gordon Selwyn, 20 Jan 1930 on Frank Morison's *Who Moved the Stone?*, which was to be published on Ash-Wednesday (5 Mar): "By the way my firm is publishing early in the spring, on my recommendation, a very remarkable book on the Trial and the Resurrection. The author is a man, unknown to me, who was convinced by an ingenious examination of the records, to believe in the Resurrection. It is amazingly matter of fact, and the way the man works out the events from the moment of Gethsemane according to the *time* that must have elapsed, is very brilliant. I shall see that a copy is sent to you, even an advance proof copy. If I was wrong about this book, I ought not to be publishing in a firm at all! At the same time, we are publishing a small book of verse of my own, entitled *Ash-Wednesday*." On 9 Apr he promised Selwyn an advance copy of *Ash-Wednesday* the following week, adding "It does not appear (to my vexation) till April 29." (For 17th-century harmonies of the events of gospels, see headnote to *Little Gidding*, 1. HISTORY OF LITTLE GIDDING.)

3. AFTER PUBLICATION

To A. L. Rowse, 14 May 1930: "I feel that you are disappointed in *Ash Wednesday*; and I am disappointed too; because I fancy that parts IV and V of it are much better than II (*Salutation*)." To Laurence Binyon, 16 May, commenting on his translation of Dante: "I shall send you my *Ash Wednesday*, which is merely an attempt to do the verse of the *Vita Nuova* in English, so that you may have me at your mercy" (see headnote to *Little Gidding*, 3. DANTE). To Algar Thorold, 23 May: "I hope [René] Hague will not call *Ash-Wednesday* religious or devotional verse—it is merely an attempt to put down in words a certain *stage* of the journey, a journey of which I insist that all my previous verse represents previous stages." To the Rev. M. C. D'Arcy, 24 May: "I leave *Ash-Wednesday* in your hands with confidence, to interpret to Oxford. But *please* dont let the young men call it 'religious' verse. I had a shock on reading *The Granta* to see stated categorically that it was 'the finest religious poem in English since Crashaw'. If it was, it wouldn't be; and anyhow it was I who told them of a poet named Crashaw; and such assertions can only do me harm. I don't consider it any more 'religious' verse than anything else I have written: I mean that it attempts to state a particular phase of the progress of one person. If that progress is in the direction of 'religion', I can't help that; it is I suppose the only direction in which progress is possible." (See letters of 1946 to Dom Sebastian Moore, quoted in note to I 1–3, 5.)

On the *Vita Nuova*: "There is also a practical sense of realities behind it, which is antiromantic: not to expect more from *life* than it can give or more from *human* beings than they can give; to look to *death* for what life cannot give. The *Vita Nuova* belongs to 'vision literature'; but its philosophy is the Catholic philosophy of disillusion", *Dante* (1929) III. To Paul Elmer More, 2 June 1930, thanking him for praise of *Dante*: "My only original contribution is possibly a few hints about the *Vita Nuova*, which seems to me a work of capital importance for the discipline of the emotions; and my last short poem *Ash Wednesday* is really a first attempt at a sketchy application of the philosophy of the *Vita Nuova* to modern life."

To Geoffrey Curtis, 17 June 1930: "I am pleased that you like the verses. As for obscurity, I like to think that there is a good and a bad kind: the bad, which merely puzzles or leads astray; the good, that which is the obscurity of any flower: something simple and to be simply enjoyed, but merely incomprehensible as anything living is incomprehensible. Why should people treat verse as if it were a conundrum with an answer? when you find the answer to a conundrum it is no longer interesting. 'Understanding' poetry seems to me largely to consist of coming to see that it is not necessary to 'understand'."

To the Rt. Rev. George Bell, 20 July 1930: "I am very much pleased by what you say of *Ash-Wednesday*. Most of the people who have written to say that they couldn't understand it seemed to be uncertain at any point whether I was referring to the Old Testament or to the New; and the reviewers took refuge in the comprehensive word 'liturgy'. It appears that almost none of the people who review books in England have ever read any of these things! But you would be shocked yourself to learn how much of the poem I can't explain myself. Certain imagery—the yew trees, the nun, the garden god—come direct out of recurrent dreams, so I shall abandon them to the ghoulish activities of some prowling analyst. The three leopards are deliberately, however, the World, the Flesh and the Devil; and the whole thing aims to be a modern *Vita Nuova*, on the same plane of hallucination, and treating a similar problem of 'sublimation' (horrid word). However pathetically it falls below that amazing book, the comparison is useful, in making clear that this is not 'devotional' verse. That can only be written by men who have gone far ahead of me in spiritual development; I have only tried to express a certain intermediate phase."

The American poet William Force Stead had become Chaplain of Worcester College, Oxford, in 1927, and in the same year had baptised TSE into the Church of England. TSE to Stead, 9 Aug 1930: "between the usual subjects of poetry and 'devotional' verse there is a very important field still very unexplored by modern poets—the experience of man in search of God, and trying to explain to himself his intenser human feelings in terms of the divine goal. I have tried to do something of that in *Ash-Wednesday*."

In November 1933, the month in which Faber issued what the cover announced as the "second edition" of *Ash-Wednesday*, with no substantive revisions, TSE published the text of his lectures as Charles Eliot Norton Professor at Harvard:

> If a poem of mine entitled *Ash-Wednesday* ever goes into a second edition, I have thought of prefixing to it the lines of Byron from *Don Juan*:
>
> "Some have accused me of a strange design
> Against the creed and morals of this land,
> And trace it in this poem, every line.
> I don't pretend that I quite understand
> My own meaning when I would be *very* fine;
> But the fact is that I have nothing planned
> Except perhaps to be a moment merry . . ."
>
> There is some sound critical admonition in these lines.
>
> *The Use of Poetry and the Use of Criticism*, 30–31,
> slightly misquoting *Don Juan* IV v

(For "Some have accused the Reformed Church of England", see note to *Little Gidding* III 17–19.) TSE also quoted 4–7 of Byron's stanza in a letter to Conrad Aiken, 16 Nov (again omitting Byron's clinching line, "A novel word in my vocabulary"). In his third Turnbull Lecture TSE again slightly misquoted the whole stanza, as being "words which I have often been tempted to quote in extenuation of my own writings", adding that Byron is, "at bottom, affirming that the actual social values, whatever they are, are not the same as the poet's" (*The Varieties of Metaphysical Poetry* 288).

Paul Elmer More, in an essay of 1932 entitled *Mr. Eliot's Return*: "a sensitive mind cannot read *Ash-Wednesday* without an uneasy sense of something fundamentally amiss in employing for an experience born of Anglo-Catholic faith a metrical form and a freakishness of punctuation suitable for the presentation of life regarded as without form and void" (Genesis 1: 1–2: "In the beginning God created the heaven and the earth. And the earth was without form and void"). TSE ringed "freakishness", with "I deny this" (More papers, Princeton).

On 10 May 1933, *Vassar Miscellany News* reported TSE's reading at the college three days previously: "He read two sections from *Ash-Wednesday*, the second and the fifth. 'The three white leopards of the first,' he explained, 'are of course, the World, the Flesh and the Devil.' The second borrowed John Donne's pun of 'world' and 'whirled,' and introduced 'word' into it. It was a protest against spiritual blindness, spiritual deafness, and it made use of a refrain from the Mass for Good Friday. *Ash-Wednesday* celebrated Mr. Eliot's conversion to the Anglo-Catholic faith."

To Stephen Spender, 9 May 1935: "'To relate art to the life of moral values'!

Certainly, there you have Corneille and Racine with you, except that they were not aware of any unrelation to be made relation. I haven't myself any awareness of Art, on the one hand, and (my) moral values on the other, with a problem set: how to relate them. My own 'art' (such as it is) has always been at the disposal of my moral values. *Ash Wednesday* for instance, is an exposition of my view of the relation of *eros* and *agape* based on my own experience. I think and hope that I have overcome any desire to write Great Poetry, or to compete with anybody. One has got at the same time to unite oneself with humanity, and to isolate oneself completely; and to be equally indifferent to the 'audience' and to oneself as one's own audience. So that humility and freedom are the same thing." ("I no longer strive to strive towards such things", I 5.)

Smidt 33 records an exchange with TSE on 13 July 1948: "*S.* There's a painting that comes vividly to my mind when I read *Ash-Wednesday.* Were you ever struck by Murillo's picture of the Immaculate Conception with the Virgin standing on a crescent moon? *E.* It is curious you should mention that. There was a steel engraving of it, my mother's, in my father's house. I also remember a statue I saw in a Benedictine monastery in the Rhineland, which I thought very striking. Things have a way of sticking in the memory."

Lehmann on TSE's reading at Bryn Mawr in Oct 1948: "Then the first and sixth parts of *Ash-Wednesday.* He read the first part quickly, expressing a great inner excitement and restlessness. The last part had the same anxiety to it, only on another level or in another direction: while the first part was like a running in circles, the last went forwards, so to speak, on a path that is still—perhaps permanently—endangered. He said he had to refrain from reading the fifth part, which he would have done otherwise had his voice been better. It made too great demands on the breathing technique. He would have also read this fairly quickly, combining long passages in one breath." The reading of this Part in his recordings suggests a liturgical chant.

Title **Ash-Wednesday**: the first day of Lent, the 40 days of fasting before Easter which commemorate Christ's fasting in the wilderness. On Ash-Wednesday the priest ritually marks a cross of ashes on the congregant's forehead while reciting: "Memento homo quia pulvis es, et in pulverem reverteris" [Remember, man, that thou art dust, and unto dust thou shalt return], Genesis 3: 19. For the hyphenation of the title, see Textual History and *Ricks* 211. TSE frequently wrote of the day and the poem without using a hyphen. Louis Untermeyer's anthology *American Poetry 1925* had contained Untermeyer's own *Ash Wednesday*, as well as reprinting three parts of *The Hollow Men.* To Enid Faber, 1 Feb 1948, declining an invitation (and alluding to *1 Henry IV* V iv): "Ash Wednesday is one of the two days a year when my virtue is not in danger and when I try to live cleanly and forswear sack."

I

Unadopted title ***All Aboard for Natchez Cairo and St. Louis***: (pronounced "Natches, Carro and Saint Lewis"); opening line of *The Early Bird Catches the Worm* (1927) by blackface comedy partnership Two Black Crows (Moran & Mack, stars of radio, record and cinema), referring to stops on the paddlesteamers' route up the Mississippi from New Orleans to St. Louis. I. A. Richards noted that the record was a favourite with TSE in the late 1920s (*Tate ed.* 6), and *Levy 1965* states that as a boy TSE had seen the duo perform. TSE to Richards, 29 Oct 1929: "You left England, I believe, in time to escape *The Two Black Crows in Hades*, which is pitiful." *Levy* 107–108 describes TSE's recital of another of their routines: "Tom was uproarious ... not only in repeating the patter, but also because the Negro dialect which he thought he had mastered made him sound more like an Archbishop of Canterbury!" A letter to Polly Tandy, 3 June 1937, included a photograph of two white men which TSE captioned: "Geoffrey Tandy (clean shaven); and T. P. Eliot (bearded): the popular B.B.C. Comedians ('The Two Black Crows') in their Harry Hall lounge suits" (T. P. = Tom Possum). An account of visits to Natchez, Cairo and St. Louis had appeared in John Gould Fletcher's *The River Flows* in *Criterion* Jan 1926. To Allen Tate, 18 May 1933: "I hope to return in 1935 and visit Richmond, Charleston, Savannah, and so on via Tennessee to New Orleans and then up the River to St. Loouss." To Pound, 15 Apr 1936: "I have every sympathy with yr fulmination against the English Church, in fact I thought of it some time before but you know I need a lot of pressure in the boiler before I let the old Creole Belle out for her record run from St. Louis to Natchez, I dont like to blow up until just as I reach the levee." To his sister Theodora, 4 Jan 1937, thanking her for a print of Old St. Louis: "I have a sentiment about St. Louis which the St. Louis of to-day (or even of my childhood) hardly justifies. It is in fact one of the most unpleasant large towns in the world ··· Nevertheless ··· I have a sentimental feeling which is excited to exaltation by *Show Boat* and *Old Man River* and all that sort of thing: and what I do miss on New Year's Eve is the sound of the steamboat whistles (there aren't any steamboats now, apparently)." *Ol' Man River* was composed for the musical *Show Boat* (Broadway, 1927; London, 1928). To Enid Faber, 17 May 1943: "it is a pity that some of the best places one is never sent to: Richmond, Charleston, Savannah and New Orleans. I have never seen them myself, nor have I been down the Mississippi on a paddle wheel steamer". ***Cairo***: For TSE on Nathaniel Wanley and "Gran Cairo", see headnote to II.

Unadopted title ***PERCH'IO NON SPERO***: see note to I 1, VI 1 and note to I 1.

Unadopted epigraph **di tornar piu mai | ballatetta, in Toscana . . .**: TSE misquotes the Italian (see note to I 1).

I 1, VI 1 **Because ··· Although I do not hope to turn again**: R. P. Blackmur: "*Perche* may be rendered either 'because' or 'although,' depending on the context", *The Double Agent* (1935) 193.

I 1 **Because I do not hope to turn again**: Guido Cavalcanti (1255–1300): "Perch'io non spero di tornar già mai", *Ballata. In Exile at Saranza* 1. (John Hayward in his *1936 proof*: "Cavalcanti".) The poem is again recalled at II 8. Rossetti translated Cavalcanti's first stanza: "Because I think not ever to return, | Ballad, to Tuscany,— | Go therefore thou for me | Straight to my lady's face, | Who, of her noble grace, | Shall show thee courtesy", *The Early Italian Poets* 364. Pound (who translated the first line as "Because no hope is left in me") singled out "that matchless and poignant ballad" in the introduction to his translation of *Sonnets and Ballate of Guido Cavalcanti* (1912, rev. 1920), and quoted it again in *The Serious Artist* in *New Freewoman* (later *Egoist*), 15 Nov 1913 (*Literary Essays* 53). In a reader's report in 1927, TSE recommended that Pound's translation be reissued with the Italian text: "Guido Cavalcanti is the most important of the contemporaries of Dante. He is a very important poet indeed." (The book did not appear.)

To Jean de Menasce, 22 May 1928: "I have sent your translation on to Madame de Bassiano without any alterations ··· I trust that you know the beautiful Ballata of Guido which suggested the poem to me." To L. H. Nouveau, 23 Nov 1955:

> I am much interested by your translations and appreciate your scruples over the various nuances of translation of the first line of *Ash-Wednesday*. The first line itself was, of course, suggested by the opening of one of the most famous poems of Guido Cavalcanti. I have not the text to hand, but I think it goes:— "Perch'io non spero di tornar giammai, | Balatetta, in Toscana". The "tornar" in the verse of Cavalcanti is, of course, much more precise than my own use was intended to be. Mine meant "return" in several senses, to place, to time, and to a past state of emotion. It may interest you to compare your own rendering with two previous translations. This section of the poem was translated in 1928 by my friend, Jean de Menasce, and published in *Commerce*. The first line reads:—"Et puisqu'il n'est plus rien qui me soit un retour". The translation made by Pierre Leyris in 1947 for his volume of my poems, reads:—"Parce que je n'espère plus me tourner à nouveau". I think I prefer "tourner" to "retour", but cannot justify that. It may be simply that I like the suggestion of the physical action of turning round.

To Warner Allen, 25 May 1960: "The line ··· is obviously inspired by the first line of Cavalcanti's poem. It has no other relation to the poem, and further is a straight borrowing and not an allusive borrowing. That is an important distinction. That one line of Guido had stuck in my mind for years and I had to get it out that way." **turn again**: repeatedly in the Bible. Psalms 85: 8: "let them not turn again to folly". Lancelot Andrewes: "shall I continually 'fall' and never 'rise'? 'turn away' and not once 'turn again'?" Ash-Wednesday Sermon 1602. Again: "Repentance itself is nothing else, but *redire ad principia*, a kind of circling; to return to Him by repentance, from whom, by sin, we have turned away. And much after a circle is this text: begins with the word *turn*, and *returns* about to the same word again ··· First, a *turn*, wherein we look forward to God, and with our whole heart resolve to *turn* to Him. Then a *turn* again, wherein we look backward to our sins wherein we have turned from God", Ash-Wednesday Sermon 1619. *Othello* IV i: "Sir, she can turn, and turn, and yet go on, | And turn again". Emerson: "I keep, and pass, and turn again", *Brahma* (in *Oxf Bk of English Verse*); for this poem see also headnote to *I am the Resurrection and the Life*. Pound: "Time has seen this, and will not turn again", *Silet* in *Ripostes* (1912). **turn**: OED *v.* 29 *trans.*: "To induce or persuade to adopt a (different) religious faith (usually with implication of its truth or excellence), or a religious or godly (instead of an irreligious or ungodly) life; to convert"; 30 *intr.*: "To adopt a different (esp. the true) religion, or a godly life; to be converted". Tindale, Matthew 18: 3 "Except ye turn and become as children." Andrewes's "An Act of Confession" begins with three Old Testament verses: Ezekiel 33: 11, "that the wicked turn from his way and live: turn ye, turn ye from your evil ways"; Lamentations 5: 21, "Turn thou us unto thee, O Lord, and we shall be turned"; and Ezekiel 18: 30, "Turn us from all our transgressions", *The Private Devotions of Lancelot Andrewes*, Daily Prayers and Meditations. (TSE to his mother, 5 Oct 1927, sending the *Devotions*: "These are the prayers which he wrote for his own use, and which he bequeathed to the man who became Archbishop Laud. I like to turn to them during the night whenever I cannot sleep.") Joseph Brackett's Shaker song of 1848, *Simple Gifts* ("'Tis the gift to be simple") ends "To turn, turn, will be our delight | Till by turning, turning we come round right."

I 1–3 **Because I do not hope to turn again | Because I do not hope | Because I do not hope to turn**: for various forms of iteration in TSE, see note to *The Waste Land* [III] 277–78, 290–91, 306. To his brother, 19 Oct 1929: "I have begun life three times: at 22, at 28, and again at 40; I hope I shall not have to do so again, because I am growing tired" (leaving America; marrying; acceptance into the Church). **Because ··· Because ··· Because**: at the head of these lines, and of eight others in this Part. Also within four consecutive lines in *The Love Song of St. Sebastian* (34–37). **Because**: Bradley: "*If* there is a 'because' to my acts, responsibility seems to go; and yet we have an irresistible impulse to find a 'because' everywhere. But is it not the *sort* of 'because' which gives all the trouble?" *Ethical Studies* Essay I. The same page has a footnote on "change of character": "Often we feel tolerably sure that this or that old reprobate is hopelessly hardened, but we can not say there is *no* chance of his turning again." TSE: "any explanation in terms of 'because' (a term made necessary by the weakness of human conceiving) can be only misleading unless we turn it about the other way as well", *Knowledge and Experience* 144.

I 1–3, 5 **hope ··· strive to strive**: St. John of the Cross:

> For the mortifying and calming of the four natural passions, which are joy, hope, fear and grief, from the concord and pacification whereof come these and other blessings, the counsels here following are of the greatest help ···
> Strive always to prefer, not that which is easiest, but that which is most difficult;
> Not that which is most delectable, but that which is most unpleasing;
> Not that which gives most pleasure, but rather that which gives least;
> Not that which is restful, but that which is wearisome;
> Not that which is a consolation, but rather that which is disconsolateness;
> Not that which is greatest, but that which is least;
> Not that which is loftiest and most precious, but that which is lowest and most despised;
> Not that which is a desire for anything, but that which is a desire for nothing;
> Strive to go about seeking not the best of temporal things, but the worst.
> Strive thus to enter into complete detachment and emptiness and poverty
> *Ascent of Mount Carmel* I XIII 5–6

In his copy, TSE underlined "hope" in the first sentence and wrote: "*Hope* as a passion—distinction from theological hope?" To Dom Sebastian Moore, 24 Apr 1946, in reply to a submitted script: "As for the spiritual experience and the language in which to express it, you know a great deal more than I do. I am only a poet, and only St. John of the Cross can write something in verse which satisfies the requirements of poetry and of mystical statement both perfectly." 3 May: "I think it is rather a question of where the balance of the author's interest lies. He is either making use of verse as a means of conveying the experience or he is making use of the experience for the purpose of writing poetry. The difference in the result may be difficult or even impossible to detect. Occasionally, as I have suggested, a great mystic may incidentally express his experience in a great poem but I think you are more likely to produce a poem if you take the line I suggested than if you set out to write a poem and attempt to adapt the experience to it." For St. John of the Cross, see notes to the second epigraph to *Sweeney Agonistes* and to *Burnt Norton* III 25–32.

I 1, 7 **turn again ··· mourn:** Joel 2: 12–14: "Therefore also now, saith the Lord, turn ye even to me with all your heart, and with fasting, and with weeping, and with mourning ··· Who knoweth if he will return and repent."

I 1, 12, 38 **I do not hope ··· I know I shall not know ··· Teach us to care and not to care:** to A. L. Rowse, 18 Apr 1931: "I have ceased to care about some things, and ceased to respect some things, and ceased to accept some things, and ceased to believe some, and ceased to expect many" (see headnote to *The Waste Land*, 9. AFTER PUBLICATION).

I 1, 26, 30 **turn again ··· turn again ··· turn again:** trad. rhyme:

> Turn again, Dick Whittington,
> Not yet lost or undone,
> Whittington lord-mayor shall be,
> Whittington thrice mayor shall be.
> Thrice lord-mayor of London!

For Whittington, see *Gus: The Theatre Cat* 32 and *The Rock* 81: "*Ballet: The Legend of* DICK WHITTINGTON *and his* CAT".

I 4–6 **Desiring this man's gift and that man's scope ··· (Why should the agèd eagle stretch its wings?):** Shakespeare Sonnet 29: "Desiring this man's art, and that man's scope ··· Haply I think on thee and then my state, | Like to the lark at break of day arising | From sullen earth, sings hymns at heaven's gate." **this man's gift and that man's scope | I no longer strive to strive:** Arnold: "Who fluctuate idly without term or scope. | Of whom each strives, nor knows for what he strives", *The Scholar-Gipsy* 167–68 (*Grover Smith* 140). TSE: "many people have to be unhappy in this world ··· and some learn ··· to gain, or at least to strive towards, a kind of peace", *"Son of Woman: The Story of D. H. Lawrence"* by John Middleton Murry (1930), review. **I no longer strive to strive towards such things | (Why should the agèd eagle stretch its wings?):** William Morris: "Why should I strive to set the crooked straight? ··· my murmuring rhyme | Beats with light wing", *The Earthly Paradise, An Apology* st. 4 (see note to VI 18, and note to *The Waste Land* [II] 79). **I no longer strive to strive towards such things:** "To get *beyond poetry*, as Beethoven, in his later works, strove to get *beyond music.* We never succeed, perhaps, but Lawrence's words mean this to me, that they express to me what I think that the forty or fifty original lines that I have written strive towards", *English Letter Writers* (1933).

I 5, VI 8 **towards:** pronounced *to'rd* in TSE's recordings.

I 6 **(Why should the agèd eagle stretch its wings?):** Psalm 103: 5: "thy youth is renewed like the eagle's"; echoed by Augustine, *Confessions* XI 9 (*Moody* 138). Hayward in his *1936 proof*: "Dante *Purgatorio.* Legend that eagle in old age flies up into a circle of fire, is burned and blinded and falls into a fountain of water with his youth renewed (cf. Bestiaries)." *Smidt 1973* 25: "The eagle and leopards and unicorn belong to the pageantry of the 'high dream' described in Eliot's major essay on *Dante* (1929) II" (see IV 20 and note). *Purg.* IX 19–30: "in a dream methought I saw an eagle poised in the sky, with plumes of gold, with wings outspread, and intent to swoop ··· Then meseemed that, having wheeled awhile, terrible as lightning, he descended and snatched me up far as the fiery sphere." Deuteronomy 31: 11: "an eagle stirreth up her nest, fluttereth over her young, spreadeth abroad her wings", cited in Andrewes's Christmas Sermon 1606 (*Stephen Matthews* 143). TSE to Warner Allen, 25 May 1960: "I am afraid that my mind was very empty of allusions when I used the phrase 'agèd eagle'. It just came that way. I was afterwards upbraided by Edmund Wilson for referring to myself as an agèd eagle at the age of forty or so, but I suppose I was turning myself into a dramatic character. After all, I wrote a poem when I was twenty-two which contains the line 'I grow old . . . I grow old'".

I 6, 14 **the agèd eagle ··· I cannot drink**: Nicholas Udall: "Aquilae senectus, the old age of an eagle is a Latin proverb used to be spoken of old men, or others that live more by drink than by meat", *Flowers* (1533–34), from Pliny; cited *Oxford Dictionary of English Proverbs*.

I 7 **Why should I mourn**: Andrewes: "If weep we cannot, mourn we can: and mourn we must", Ash-Wednesday Sermon 1619.

I 10 **The infirm glory of the positive hour**: *Two Gentlemen of Verona* I iii: "The uncertain glory of an April day" (*Ricks* 224). **infirm glory**: Virginia Woolf: "all the poets, all the novelists, all the beautiful women and distinguished men of her time ··· now either dead or secluded in their infirm glory", *Night and Day* (1919) ch. III (*Southam*).

I 13 **veritable**: *Fowler*: "OED records that by about 1650 the word was dead, but the early 19th c. revived it ··· has the effect of taking down the reader's interest a peg or two ··· as the now familiar herald of a strained top note." **transitory**: pronounced as three syllables in TSE's recording of 1933, but as four full syllables in that of 1955.

I 15 **there is nothing again**: *King Lear* I i: "Nothing will come of nothing. Speak again." TSE: "Nothing again nothing", *The Waste Land* [II] 120.

I 18–19 **what is actual is actual only for one time | And only for one place**: "The objective world is only actual in one or other point of view", *Knowledge and Experience* 90.

I 24–25 **rejoice, having to construct something | Upon which to rejoice**: Shelley: "to hope till Hope creates | From its own wreck the thing it contemplates", *Prometheus Unbound* IV, quoted in *The Use of Poetry and the Use of Criticism* 92.

I 26 **pray to God to have mercy upon us**: repeated throughout the Litany. The final chorus of *Murder in the Cathedral* ends: "Lord, have mercy upon us. | Christ, have mercy upon us. | Lord, have mercy upon us. | Blessed Thomas, pray for us."

I 32 **For what is done, not to be done again**: Donne: "When thou hast done, thou hast not done", *A Hymne to God the Father* 5, 11 (*Southam*).

I 33 **heavy upon us**: frequent in the Bible. 1 Samuel 5: 6: "the hand of the Lord was heavy upon them". Job 33: 7: "neither shall my hand be heavy upon thee".

I 34–35 **no longer wings to fly | But merely vans to beat the air**: Arnold: "Shelley, beautiful and ineffectual angel, beating in the void his luminous wings in vain", *Byron*. TSE, of Sacheverell Sitwell: "He tends in his weaker moments to fly off like a beautiful but ineffectual aeroplane, beating its propeller vainly in a tree", *Verse Pleasant and Unpleasant* (1918). Of Henry Adams: "the wings of a beautiful but ineffectual conscience beating vainly in a vacuum jar", *A Sceptical Patrician* (1919) (*Bush* 137). Dryden on the death of Periclymenos, in the shape of an eagle: "He wheel'd in Air, and stretch'd his Vans in vain; | His Vans no longer cou'd his Flight sustain", *Ovid's Metamorphoses* XII 749–52 (TSE: "stretch his wings", I 6). **van:** OED 3: "a wing. Chiefly *poet.*"

I 36 **The air which is now thoroughly small:** Virgil's "largior aether", *Aeneid* VI 640, as "larger air", Elizabeth Barrett Browning, *Aurora Leigh* VIII 356, and Tennyson, *The Mystic* 44. **small and dry:** William Morris: "they grow gray with time, grow small and dry", *The Blue Closet* 48 (a poem praised by TSE in *The Music of Poetry* as having "an effect somewhat like that of a rune or charm, but runes and charms are very practical formulae designed to produce definite results"). T. E. Hulme: "It is essential to prove that beauty may be in small, dry things", *Romanticism and Classicism* in *Speculations* (1924) 131 (*Grover Smith* 314). Andrewes: "For dry and lean both is our sorrow", Ash-Wednesday Sermon 1619. E. B. Pusey: "my Lord, I am all too cold and dry and hard", *Private Prayers* 27. TSE mentioned Pusey's prayers along with "the Private Prayers of Lancelot Andrewes" in *The Bible as Scripture and as Literature* (1932), and wrote to Frank Morley, 4 Aug 1938: "I recommend strongly Pusey's Private Prayers". Hope Mirrlees: "Hark to the small dry voice", *Paris* (1919) 18 (see headnote to IV, and headnote to *The Waste Land*, 1. COMPOSITION). **dry:** OED 13: "In early use, chiefly: Wanting spiritual emotion or unction."

I 37 **dryer than the will:** St. John of the Cross: "leaving the understanding dark, the will dry", *Dark Night of the Soul* II III 3 (Unger in *Unger ed.* 355–56). For *Dark Night of the Soul* see note to *Burnt Norton* III 25–32. To Geoffrey Curtis, 2 Apr 1936: "I do not approve of extreme mortification of the flesh—taking heaven by negative physical means—but I like to think that men should sometimes be impelled in this direction, and then 'moderated' · · · I should agree that St. John of the Cross illustrates admirably the *via media*". Concerning a list of the world's greatest books, TSE wrote to Daniel Starch, 11 Mar 1937, that he disapproved of the enterprise, but naming some writers who "deserve no place" and then suggesting one additional name, St. John of the Cross.

I 38–39, *as also* VI 27–28 **Teach us to care · · · Teach us to:** "wisdom; something which, certainly, educational institutions cannot teach · · · but which they can teach us to desire", *Catholicism and International Order* (1933).

I 39 **Teach us to sit still:** Psalm 46: 10: "Be still and know that I am God." Coleridge: "For not to think of what I needs must feel, | But to be still and patient, all I can", *Dejection: An Ode* 87–88; TSE scored 87–90 in the *Poetical Works* (1907). In *The Cloud of Unknowing* ch. 8, he scored a paragraph: "a man may not be fully active, except he be contemplative · · · The condition of active life is such, that it is both begun and ended in this life; but not so of the contemplative life. For it is begun in this life, and shall last without end. Because that part that Mary chose *shall never be taken away.* Active life is *troubled and travailed about many things*; but contemplative *sitteth in peace with one thing*" (TSE: "The Lady is withdrawn · · · to contemplation", II 16–17). Although this copy of *The Cloud of Unknowing* is dated 1942 by TSE, he knew the work earlier, writing to Naomi Mitchison, 18 Apr 1939, about *The Family Reunion*: "I don't think that there are any direct—certain no intentional—borrowings from *The Cloud of Unknowing* in the play. It is some time since I read that work, and although I have a keen admiration for the 14th-century mystics, I was not aware of using more than this very beautiful phrase" (II ii, AGATHA: "Accident is design | And design is accident | In a cloud of unknowing"). Emerson: "I see action to be good, when the need is, and sitting still to be also good", *Essays: Spiritual Laws*. Henry Adams: "one of the greatest minds, between Descartes and Newton—Pascal—saw the master-motor of man in *ennui*, which was also scientific: 'I have often said that all the troubles of man come from his not knowing how to sit still'", *The Education of Henry Adams* ch. XXIX, apparently paraphrasing *Pensées* 139: "all the unhappiness of men arises from one single fact, that they cannot stay quietly in their own chamber". TSE: "everybody, at least according to Fleet Street, is on the march; it does not matter what the destination is, the one thing contemptible is to sit still", *Thoughts After Lambeth* (1931). Hugh Ross Williamson: "We are not altogether inclined to join with Mr. Eliot in the prayer: 'Teach us to sit still,' for we feel that we battled through the waste land to find some nobler occupation than that", *The Bookman* Mar 1931. TSE to Williamson, 31 Aug 1931, thanking him for his article: "why should the mention of 'sitting still' suggest a static conception of life, and is the distinction between the static and the dynamic so easily transferable from physics to ethics as everybody seems to think?" For "the still point of the turning world", see *Burnt Norton* II 16–21. "The stillness ··· Moves perpetually in its stillness", *East Coker* V 6–7.

I 39, II 1 **Teach us to sit still ··· sat under a juniper-tree**: "the unprofitable habits of The Blessed One had been extirpated ··· at the time he sat cross-legged under the Bo-tree. Profitable habits, however remained to The Blessed One", *Buddhism in Translations* tr. Henry Clarke Warren (1896) 91 ("The Buddha's Daily Habits", which tells how he would "sit retired" and "sit down, and for a while remain solitary").

I 40–41 **Pray for us sinners now and at the hour of our death ··· our death**: having sent Part I to Marguerite Caetani for *Commerce* on 19 Mar 1928, TSE wrote again on 4 Apr: "At the beginning of each of the last two lines please alter the words 'be with' to 'pray for'. One might as well stick to the exact quotation." (The Hail Mary, the prayer of the angelic salutation: "Holy Mary, Mother of God, pray for us sinners now and at the hour of our death.") "Pray for ··· Pray for us now and at the hour of our birth", *Animula* 36–37. To Frank Morley, 4 Aug 1938: "so may the B. V. M. pray for us sinners now and at the hour of our death, yours etc." **the hour ··· the hour**: "the hour ··· the hour", *Silence* 7–8.

II

Ezekiel 37: 1–11: "The hand of the Lord was upon me, and carried me out in the spirit of the Lord, and set me down in the midst of the valley which was full of bones, And caused me to pass by them round about: and, behold, there were very many in the open valley; and, lo, they were very dry. And he said unto me, Son of man, can these bones live? And I answered, O Lord God, thou knowest. Again he said unto me, Prophesy upon these bones, and say unto them, O ye dry bones, hear the word of the Lord. Thus saith the Lord God unto these bones; Behold, I will cause breath to enter into you, and ye shall live: And I will lay sinews upon you, and will bring up flesh upon you, and cover you with skin, and put breath in you, and ye shall live; and ye shall know that I am the Lord. So I prophesied as I was commanded: and as I prophesied, there was a noise, and behold a shaking, and the bones came together, bone to his bone. And when I beheld, lo, the sinews and the flesh came up upon them, and the skin covered them above: but there was no breath in them. Then said he unto me, Prophesy unto the wind, prophesy, son of man, and say to the wind, Thus saith the Lord God; Come from the four winds, O breath, and breathe upon these slain, that they may live. So I prophesied as he commanded me, and the breath came into them, and they lived, and stood up upon their feet, an exceeding great army. Then he said unto me, Son of man, these bones are the whole house of Israel."

Nathaniel Wanley: "many Christians ··· went from *Cairo* to a little barren Mountain ··· in times past assign'd for the burial of the dead: in this place there meet ordinarily every year an incredible multitude of persons to see the dead bodies there interred, coming out (as it were) of their Grave and Sepulchres ··· There may you see Bodies wrapped in their cloaths after the old fashion: but they see them not either standing or walking, but only the arms or the thighs, or some other part of the body which you may touch; if you go farther off, and presently come forward again, you shall find these arms or limbs appearing more out of the ground", *The Wonders of the Little World* (1678) ch. XXXVIII, "Of the entombed Bodies, how found at the opening of their Monuments; and of the parcel Resurrection near Gran Cairo". Noting in a *TLS* review in 1925 that Wanley, "like some contemporary poets, is very sparing in punctuation", in *Wanley and Chapman* (1925) TSE quoted more than half of his poem *The Resurrection* (see note to II 5–6), observing that Wanley was

> much interested in the problems of resurrection. In a prose book, *The Wonders of the Little World*—a sort of Burtonian collection of odds and ends, there is a note on "Parcel [partial] Resurrection" which is so good that we cannot forbear to quote it ··· This Parcel Resurrection of Legs and Arms Etc. useth to be seen and believed upon Good Friday [i.e., near "Gran Cairo"] and the Eve of that, saith Mr. *Gregory* ··· And he told me moreover that he had ··· touched divers of these rising members. And he was once doing so upon the hairy head of a child, a man of *Cairo* cryed out aloud, *Kali, kali ante materasde*, that is to say, *Hold, hold, you know not what you do*
>
> (glosses in square brackets by TSE)

"It is to be hoped", TSE's review added, "that we may have an edition not only of Mr. Wanley's *Scintillulae Sacrae* and other poems, but of his *Wonders of the Little World*." (L. C. Martin's edition of Wanley's *Poems* (1928) was duly followed in 1931 by J. C. Furnas's edition of this prose work.) See Bush 138; also note to "Cairo" within the unadopted title for *Ash-Wednesday* I; and for ambiguous names, see note to *The Love Song of J. Alfred Prufrock* 94, "Lazarus". TSE to his mother, 7 Feb 1928, on Hardy's funeral: "That was a scandal ··· They put his body in Westminster Abbey, and they buried his heart in Dorchester. Curio hunting I call it. Why not divide him joint from joint, and spot him about the country? I think that if one is buried at all one should decently be buried all in one place."

J. C. Squire had ended his review of TSE's *Poems 1909–1925*: "Why on earth he bothers to write at all is difficult to conceive: why, since he must write, he writes page after page from which no human being could derive any more meaning (much less edification or pleasure) than if they were written in Double-Dutch (which parts of them possibly are) is to me beyond conjecture. Why to the Waste Land add a Valley of peculiarly Dry Bones?" *London Mercury* Mar 1926. *The Waste Land* had "bones" five times; *The Hollow Men*, at the close of *1925*, had "valley" twice but no bones. TSE to Bonamy Dobrée, advising on his poetry [16 Aug 1927] (Brotherton): "Keep away from Bones they are my Patent". Three years later, *Ash-Wednesday* was to have "bones" six times.

Unadopted title ***Salutation***: Dante, *Vita Nuova* [XVIII] tr. Rossetti: "'Ladies, the end and aim of my Love was but the salutation of that lady of whom I conceive that ye are speaking; wherein alone I found that beatitude which is the goal of desire'", *The Early Italian Poets* 253. The Italian furnished one of two epigraphs for TSE's Clark Lectures, in the fourth of which he quoted a longer passage of Rossetti's translation (*The Varieties of Metaphysical Poetry* 40, 116). When editing Pound's *Selected Poems* (1928), TSE included *Salutation* and *Salutation the Second*.

Unadopted title ***Jausen lo jorn***: *Purg.* XXVI 142: "*e vei jausen lo jorn, qu' esper, denan*" ["and I see with joy the day which I await before me"]. For TSE's returns to this passage about Arnaut Daniel, see note to title *Ara Vos Prec* in headnote to "*Poems* (1920)", 7. PUBLICATION OF *ARA VOS PREC*. Pound: "We await, *vei jauzen lo jorn*, the time when the student will be encouraged to say which poems bore him to tears", *Notes on Elizabethan Classicists* III in *Egoist* Nov 1917 (*Literary Essays*).

Unadopted title ***TAN M'ABELIS*** *Purg.* XXVI 140: "'*Tan m'abelis vostre cortes deman*'" ["So doth your courteous request please me"].

Unadopted epigraph **The Hand of the Lord Was Upon Me:—*e vo significando***: Ezekiel 37: 1 (see headnote to II); *Purg.* XXIV 52–54: "'Io mi son un che, quando | amor mi spira, noto, ed a quel modo | che ditta dentro, vo significando'" ["I am one who, when Love inspires me take note, and go setting it forth after the fashion which he dictates within me."] ("vo significando": "setting it forth".) Hayward in his *1936 proof*: "e vo significando (Dante, *Purg.*) 'I am one who when love inspires finds melody and as he dictates to my mind, so do I give utterance.'"

II 1 **Lady, three white leopards sat under a juniper tree**: Pound: "The milk-white girls | Unbend from the holly-trees, | And their snow-white leopard | Watches", *Heather* (1913), included by TSE in Pound's *Selected Poems*. Also: "The black panther lies under his rose tree", *Cantus Planus* (1915). TSE to Philip Parker, 17 May 1930: "Do not worry at being unsure of the meaning, when the author cannot be sure of it either. The *Vita Nuova* might give you some help; but on the other hand it is much more obscure than I have the talent to be. If you call the three leopards the World, the Flesh and the Devil you will get as near as one can, but even that is uncertain." Litany: "Good Lord, deliver us. From fornication, and all other deadly sin; and from all the deceits of the world, the flesh, and the devil"; see letter to George Bell, 20 July 1930, quoted in headnote, 3. AFTER PUBLICATION. St. John of the Cross, *Spiritual Canticle* III II 4–5:

> it behoves him that will go forward not to turn aside and pluck these flowers · · · but it behoves him also to have the courage and the fortitude to say:
>
> · · · nor fear the wild beasts;
> I will pass by the mighty and cross the frontiers.
>
> In these lines the Bride speaks of the three enemies of the soul, which are world, devil and flesh, and these are they that war upon her and make her way difficult. By the "wild beasts" she understands the world; by the "mighty," the devil; and by the "frontiers," the flesh.

TSE to Charles Williams, 22 May 1930: "if the three leopards or the unicorn contain any allusions literary, I don't know what they are. Can't I sometimes invent nonsense, instead of always being supposed to borrow it?" To Gregor Ziemer, 10 Feb 1937: "I do not remember any leopards in the Bible, but I have no Concordance; my leopards represent simply the world, the flesh and the devil. I have been told that there is a similar use of white leopards in certain Sudanese folk lore, but I did not know this at the time." (Jeremiah 13: 23: "Can the Ethiopian change his skin, or the leopard his spots?" Though their skin colour is unusual, white leopards too have spots.) Stephen Spender on a meeting of the Oxford Poetry Club: "an undergraduate asked him: 'Please, sir, what do you mean by the line: *Lady, three white leopards sat under a juniper tree?*' Eliot looked at him and said: 'I mean, *Lady, three white leopards sat under a juniper tree*'", *Spender* 129. **sat under a juniper-tree**: "cf. Isaiah 1", Hayward in *1936 proof* (although this chapter does not mention the juniper). 1 Kings 19: 4–5 of Elijah: "But he himself went a day's journey into the wilderness, and came and sat down under a juniper tree: and he requested for himself that he might die ··· And as he lay and slept under a juniper tree, behold, then an angel touched him, and said unto him, Arise and eat" (this passage is quoted in Donne's sermon *Death's Duel*, as is Ezekiel 37: 1, for which see headnote to II) (*Smidt 1973* 28). "when the juniper tree breaks the tombstone", *Anabasis* VII viii (*1930* text; later revised to "jujuba tree"); Perse: "*quand l'arbre jujubier fait éclater l'assise des tombeaux*" (*asseoir*, to seat).

II 1–2 **leopards ··· fed to satiety**: in the *Encyclopaedia of Religion and Ethics* (ed. Hastings *et al.*, 1908–26) the entry for Animals: Leopard ends "a man who has killed a leopard remains in his hut three days; he practises continence and is fed to satiety" (Unger in *Unger ed.* 360).

II 1–5 **juniper-tree ··· having fed ··· On my legs my heart my liver ··· Shall these bones live?**: Unger in *Unger ed.* 357–58:

> *The Juniper Tree*, one of Jakob Grimm's tales, is an account of a husband and wife who, having no children, but desiring one, finally acquire a boy by supernatural aid. When the wife dies in childbirth the man marries a woman who, having a daughter of her own, Marlinchen, hates the boy. She kills him, makes puddings of his flesh which she gives to her husband for food, and lies about the boy's absence. Marlinchen carries the boy's bones to a juniper tree. Then there are mist and flames, and a bird appears, singing—
>
> My mother she killed me,
> My father he ate me,
> My sister little Marlinchen,
> Gathered together all my bones,
> Tied them in a silken handkerchief
> Laid them beneath the juniper tree,
> Kywitt, kywitt, what a beautiful bird am I!
>
> The bird finally causes the death of the stepmother and becomes a boy again.

II 2 **in the cool of the day**: see note to II 50.

II 4 **In the hollow round of my skull**: "Within the circle of my brain", *The Burnt Dancer* 30.

II 5–6 **Shall these bones live? shall these | Bones live?**: Nathaniel Wanley: "Or shall my tombe restore my scattred dust? | Shall ev'ry haire find out its' proper pore | And crumbled bones be joined as before", *The Resurrection* 2–4. Auden: "No, these bones shall live", *Poems* (1930) XXIII ("Nor was that final").

II 7 **chirping**: to his Italian translator, Roberto Sanesi, 2 June 1960: "I think the right word for 'chirping' in that passage of *Ash-Wednesday* is 'stridere'. We have the word 'stridulate' in English, and the sound in my own ears as I speak the lines is that of crickets or grasshoppers, and you are quite right, we want a dry word for it. 'Cavalletta' [grasshopper] is a charming word. I should not have thought of that myself. I would not say 'locusta', but if my Italian was good enough I should probably have thought of 'grillo' [cricket]."

II 8 **Because of the goodness of this Lady**: Cavalcanti, tr. Pound: "Unto my Lady straightway, | And out of her courtesy | Great honour will she do thee", *Sonnets and Ballate of Guido Cavalcanti* (1912), *Ballata XI* (*Praz* 370); see note to I 1.

II 8–9 **Lady · · · loveliness:** Rossetti: "Lady, I thank thee for thy loveliness", *The House of Life* XXIX 1 (*Grover Smith* 314). Cavalcanti, tr. Pound: "There where this Lady's loveliness appeareth", *Ballata V.*

II 8–10 **this Lady · · · and because | She honours the Virgin in meditation:** to Geoffrey Faber [18 Sept 1927]: "I have found my own love for a woman enhanced, intensified and purified by meditation on the Virgin." On the language of the New English Bible: "It is sufficient for the moment for me to cite Luke 1: 27, where the word *παρθένος* appears as 'girl' instead of the Authorized Version 'virgin' ('a girl . . . and the girl's name was Mary'). This alteration cannot be in correction of a previous mistranslation: both Liddell & Scott and Westcott & Hort give 'virgin' as a correct translation · · · what moved the learned committee to approve the change?" *New English Bible* (28 Apr 1961).

II 11 **dissembled:** OED "dissemble" *v.* 3: "*Obs. rare.* To separate, disperse: = DISASSEMBLE", intransitive only, with one citation, 1591.

II 12 **Proffer my deeds to oblivion:** *Troilus and Cressida* III iii: "Time hath, my lord, a wallet at his back, | Wherein he puts alms for oblivion · · · Those scraps are good deeds past" (*Southam*).

II 13 **gourd:** Jonah 4: 3–11: "Therefore now, O Lord, take, I beseech thee, my life from me; for it is better for me to die than to live · · · And the Lord God prepared a gourd, and made it to come up over Jonah, that it might be a shadow over his head, to deliver him from his grief. So Jonah was exceeding glad of the gourd · · · Then said the Lord, Thou hast had pity on the gourd, for the which thou hast not laboured, neither madest it grow; which came up in a night, and perished in a night: And should not I spare Nineveh, that great city, wherein are more than sixscore thousand persons that cannot discern between their right hand and their left hand; and also much cattle?" OED "gourd" 1, 2b lists the name of the plant "used allusively after Jonah", for something that perishes abruptly. TSE: "he who has his opinions on the use of a gourd", *Anabasis* X vii. OED and *Fowler* recommend the pronunciation *gored*, but TSE says *goourd* in his recordings.

II 15 **My guts the strings of my eyes and the indigestible portions:** "Racine or Donne looked into a good deal more than the heart. One must look into the cerebral cortex, the nervous system, and the digestive tracts", *The Metaphysical Poets* (1921). **strings of my eyes:** OED: "The 'eyestrings' were formerly supposed to break or crack at death or loss of sight." For Donne, "Our eye-beames twisted, and did thred | Our eyes, upon one double string" (*The Extasie* 7–8), see note to *Burnt Norton* I 28, "unseen eyebeam crossed". **indigestible portions:** TSE had quoted with approval Marianne Moore's words "portions of the food it could not eat" (*My Apish Cousins*) in *Marianne Moore* (1923). **portions:**

see note to II 52–54. For Wanley's "Parcel Resurrection" (glossed by TSE as "partial") see headnote to II.

II 16 **reject**: OED 3a: "To refuse (something offered)"; 4a: "To expel from the mouth or stomach", quoting *Paradise Lost* X 567: "Bitter Ashes, which th'offended taste | With spattering noise rejected." Pound to TSE, 12 Apr 1940: "mebbe you is TOUGH. The leopards done tried to ate you and then bent their goddam tin teeth. At least I had the helluva argument as to whether 'reject' meant spit out. I sez trown back; I sez as to food it CAN mean THAT the animal just leaves it on the plate or desert sand and DONT TRY to eat it. No sez the lady [Dorothy Pound], it means spit it out. Waaal, I sez, I will ASK the author. No, she sez, DONT. however . . ." TSE: "the dark throat which will not reject them", *The Dry Salvages* IV 13. For "rejects a proffered morsel", see note to *The Dry Salvages* I 20–21.

II 17 **In a white gown, to contemplation, in a white gown**: Dante, *Vita Nuova* [II] tr. Rossetti: "the same wonderful lady appeared to me dressed all in pure white", *The Early Italian Poets* 225. TSE: "your gown is white | And against your gown your braided hair", *The Love Song of St. Sebastian* 14–15 (*Smith 1985*). **contemplation**: "I do not think that *contemplation* can be correctly defined as 'the attitude of the spectator'. In the theological sense, it is an activity; and I think that in *any* sense it implies activity. We may contemplate taking certain steps: that is a deliberative activity. We may 'contemplate' a sunset; but that that implies some suggestion of slight spiritual activity I think is indicated by the fact that we do not ordinarily 'contemplate' a football match ··· contemplation *is* an encounter", *Letter from T. S. Eliot* 28 Apr 1944, a paper for The Moot.

II 19 **I am forgotten**: Psalm 31: 12: "I am forgotten as a dead man out of mind."

II 23, 48 **the bones sang**: Herbert: "the broken bones may joy, | And tune together in a well-set song, | Full of his praises, | Who dead men raises", *Repentance* 32–35. Yeats: "'O cruel death, give three things back,' | Sang a bone upon the shore", *Three Things* (Ariel Poem, 1929) 1–2.

II 24 **burden of the grasshopper**: Ecclesiastes 12: 5: "and the grasshopper shall be a burden, and desire shall fail: because man goeth to his long home" (*Williamson* 174). For an allusion to the succeeding biblical verse, see note to *The Waste Land* [V] 384. Further, OED "burden" 10: "the refrain or chorus of a song". *Purg.* XXVIII 16–18: "singing, with full gladness they welcomed the first breezes within the leaves, which were murmuring the burden to their songs".

II 25, 28 **Lady of silences ··· Rose of memory**: e. e. cummings: "Lady of Silence | from the winsome cage of | thy body | rose", IX in *XLI Poems* (Dial Press, 1925: the year cummings won the *Dial* prize).

II 26 **Calm and distressed**: to Stephen Spender, 1 July 1935: "As for 'calmness', I often refer to a phrase of Goethe's which you no doubt know. Someone complimented him on his serenity. Yes, he said, but it is a serenity which has to be composed afresh every morning."

II 28 **Rose**: Hayward in his *1936 proof*: "Rosa mystica = Mary—'that Rose in which the Word Divine made itself flesh'—Dante *Paradiso*" (XXIII 73–74). Litany of the Blessed Virgin, to be recited on its own or after praying the rosary, especially during the month of May; see note to *The Hollow Men* IV 13.

II 28–29 **memory ··· forgetfulness**: in Dante's Earthly Paradise, the water pours down the Mount of Purgatory as the rivers Lethe and Eunoë: "On this side it descends with a virtue which takes from men the memory of sin; on the other it restores the memory of every good deed", *Purg.* XXVIII 127–29 (*Jain 1991*).

II 29 **Rose of forgetfulness**: Psalm 88: 12: "land of forgetfulness". TSE: "Waters of tenderness | Sealed springs of devotion", *The Hollow Men* I 15^16 *variant.*

II 31 **reposeful**: OED 2: "Full of repose". 1: "*Obs.* In whom confidence is or may be placed" (last citation 1644, but the idiom "to repose trust" remains).

II 32–33 **The single Rose | Is now the Garden**: Dante sees Heaven as a white rose, a "great flower adorned with so many leaves" forming a whole "garden" (*Paradiso* XXXI 10–11, 97). "Multifoliate rose", *The Hollow Men* IV 13. Evelyn Underhill: "watering of the garden of the soul, is a cultivation of this one flower—this *Rosa Mystica* which has its root in God", *Mysticism* II VI (Joshua Richards, personal communication).

II 32^33 *variant* **With worm-eaten petals**: "pitted as if worm-eaten", *The Varieties of Metaphysical Poetry* 121 (Clark Lecture IV). "a society like ours, worm-eaten with Liberalism", *After Strange Gods* 13 (*Ricks* 228). "It seems to me that all of us, so far as we attach ourselves to created objects and surrender our wills to temporal ends, are eaten by the same worm", *Nightwood* (1937) Introduction.

II 32–38 *variant* **Rose | With worm-eaten petals ··· love ··· love ··· love**: Blake: "O Rose ··· worm ··· love", *The Sick Rose.*

II 34–38 **Where all loves end | Terminate torment | Of love unsatisfied | The greater torment | Of love satisfied**: Corbière: "Borne de l'envie!—Toi qui viens assouvir la faim inassouvie!" [Boundary of desire!— You who come to satisfy the hunger that is unsatisfied], *Litanie du sommeil* [*The Litany of Sleep*] 54–55. TSE on *Inferno* V: "To have lost all recollected delight would have been, for Francesca, either loss of humanity or relief from damnation. The ecstasy, with the present thrill at the remembrance of it, is a part of the torture. Francesca is ··· damned; and it is a part of damnation to experience desires that we can no longer gratify. For in Dante's Hell souls are not deadened ··· they are actually in the greatest torment of which each is capable. 'E il modo ancor m'offende'", *Dante* (1920). (Last phrase of the tercet *Inf.* V 100–102: "Love, which is quickly caught in gentle heart, took him with the fair body of which I was bereft; and the manner still afflicts me.") 1 John 4: 18: "perfect love casteth out fear: because fear hath torment". TSE: "Who then devised the torment? Love", *Little Gidding* IV 8. For "the only love that is wholly satisfactory and final", see letter to Geoffrey Faber, 10 May 1936, in note to the second epigraph to *Sweeney Agonistes.*

II 35 **Terminate**: pronounced as the verb by TSE in his recordings. OED also, *ppl. a.* pron. *termin'et*, "Limited, bounded ··· having a definite limit", with Daniel's paraphrase of Ecclesiasticus 41 (1639): "What if the uncertaine Date of Mortalls in ten years be Terminate".

II 35–36, 39–40] Hayward in his *1936 proof*: "St Bernard's hymn to Virgin, *Paradiso* XXX" (*for* XXXIII).

II 36–38 **love unsatisfied ··· love satisfied**: Hegel: "Belief ··· has in fact become the same as enlightenment ··· the difference is merely that the one is enlightenment satisfied, while belief is enlightenment unsatisfied", *The Phenomenology of*

Mind, tr. J. B. Baillie (1910) (*Donoghue* 181–82). Bradley: "To love unsatisfied the world is a mystery, a mystery which love satisfied seems to comprehend. The latter is wrong only because it cannot be content without thinking itself right", *Appearance and Reality*, Preface. TSE double-scored both margins.

II 39 **End of the endless:** Chapman: "THE END OF ALL THE ENDLESS WORKS OF HOMER", concluding line of "The Hymns of Homer". *TSE's books: Bodleian list* (1934) includes "Chapman's Minor Poems".

II 39–40 **End of the endless | Journey to no end:** St. Bernard to Dante: "'That thou mayest consummate thy journey perfectly'", *Paradiso* XXXI 94. Bradley: "What does endless mean? Not the mere negation of end, because a mere negation is nothing at all and infinite would thus = 0. The endless is something positive; it means a positive quantity which has no end", *Ethical Studies* Essay II. See note to IV 6 on "*infinite* and *eternal*".

II 42 **inconclusible:** OED: *rare.* "Not capable of being concluded; endless", with this and only one previous citation, "That inconclusible Controversie", 1660. Pronounced *inconcluzible* in TSE's recordings.

II 48 **bones ··· scattered:** *Purg.* XXXI 50–52: "membra ··· in terra sparte" [members ··· scattered to dust] (*Praz* 368).

II 50 **Under a tree in the cool of the day:** Genesis 3: 8: "And they heard the voice of the Lord God walking in the garden in the cool of the day: and Adam and his wife hid themselves from the presence of the Lord God amongst the trees of the garden." In his 1933 recording, TSE says "Under the tree".

II 52–54 **This is the land which ye | Shall divide by lot ··· We have our inheritance:** Ezekiel 48: 29: "This is the land which ye shall divide by lot unto the tribes of Israel for inheritance, and these are their portions, saith the Lord God" (TSE: "portions" II 15).

III

The turnings of the stair in this part correspond to the divisions of Dante's hill of Purgatory (*Matthiessen* 66–67). TSE: "mounting the saints' stair", *A Song for Simeon* 28.

Unadopted title **SOM DE L'ESCALINA:** *Purg.* XXVI 145–47: "*Ara vos prec, per aquella valor | que vos guida al som de l'escalina, | sovegna vos a temps de mon dolor*" ["Now I pray you, by that Goodness which guideth you to the summit of the stairway, be mindful in due time of my pain"]. For TSE's returns to this passage about Arnaut Daniel, see note to unadopted title for II and note to title *Ara Vos Prec* in headnote to "*Poems* (1920)", 7. PUBLICATION OF *ARA VOS PREC*.

III 1 **At the first turning of the second stair:** Emerson: "At the first mounting of the giant stairs", *The Adirondacs* 63.

III 1–5 **the second stair | I turned and saw below ··· Under the vapour in the fetid air | Struggling with the devil of the stairs:** Whitman: "My feet strike an apex of the apices of the stairs ··· I mount and mount. || Rise after rise bow the phantoms behind me, | Afar down ··· through the lethargic mist ··· the fetid carbon", *Song of Myself* [44] 1149–55 (*Musgrove* 55–56). **Under the vapour in the fetid air:** *Inf.* VI 10–12: "acqua tinta, e neve | per l'aer tenebroso si riversa; |

pute la terra che questo riceve" [turbid water, and snow, pour down through the darksome air; the ground, on which it falls, emits a putrid smell].

III 1, 3, 6 **stair · · · twisted · · · banister · · · despair:** Herbert Read to TSE, 16 Nov 1929, acknowledging a proof of the projected quarto ed. of *Ash-Wednesday*: "The only detail that worries me is the clash of the false & true rhymes of 'banister', 'stairs' & 'despair' · · · I'm not sure, too, that I like 'twisted' and 'banister' in the same line". TSE replied, 18 Nov: "I am not sure about that line; the point had not struck me. I don't think the poem is really first rate, but I do think that it just does escape insincerity, somehow."

III 5–6 **the devil of the stairs who wears · · · despair:** *Paradise Lost* III 523–24: "The stairs were then let down, whether to dare | The Fiend" (*Ricks* 225). **the devil · · · who wears | The deceitful face of hope:** "the demon of doubt which is inseparable from the spirit of belief", *The "Pensées" of Pascal* (1931). "hope would be hope for the wrong thing", *East Coker* III 24 (see note). To Fred Clarke, Good Friday [11 Apr] 1941: "I have to warn myself against being either optimistic or pessimistic: for in either mood I am probably hoping or despairing about only human schemes: and if there is a brighter future preparing it must almost necessarily be invisible."

III 11 **toothed gullet of an agèd shark:** *Macbeth* IV i: "maw and gulf | Of the ravin'd salt-sea shark" (*Grover Smith* 315). Swinburne: "shark-toothed and serpentine-curled", *Hymn to Proserpine* 53 (see note to *Marina* 6). André Salmon: "les gueules de requins" [sharks' mouths, or gullets], *Anvers* [*Antwerp*] 12.

III 13 **the fig's fruit:** Dante, tr. E. H. Plumptre: "'mid the sour crab's kind | It is not meet the sweet fig's fruit to see", *Hell* XV 65–66, *The Commedia and Canzoniere: A New Translation* (1886).

III 14–16 **pasture scene · · · broadbacked · · · green · · · the maytime · · · flute:** Emerson: "May · · · the broad-backed hills · · · the pipes of the trees · · · green", *May-Day* 212–26. On Mary and the month of May, see note to II 28.

III 17–19 **Blown hair:** Beaumont and Fletcher: "mine hair blown with the wind", *The Maid's Tragedy* (see note on epigraph to *Sweeney Erect*). "the white hair of the waves blown back", *The Love Song of J. Alfred Prufrock* 127. **brown hair over the mouth blown:** Archibald MacLeish: "Front against front, not hair blown | Dark over eyes in a dream and the mouth gone", *Land's End* I in *Criterion* July 1927 (*Crawford* 187). (TSE to MacLeish, 25 May 1927: "we should like to have you on our list · · · Congratulations on the poem I am publishing.")

III 19 **Distraction · · · stops and steps of the mind:** F. E. Brightman, introduction to Lancelot Andrewes's *Preces Privatæ*: "steps and stages of the movement." See note to *Little Gidding* II 92–93 for more of this paragraph as given in *Lancelot Andrewes* (1926), where TSE quotes two of Donne's sermons on distractions from prayer. See notes to *Burnt Norton* III 10–12, 14 and V 13–22.

III 23–24 **Lord, I am not worthy || but speak the word only:** Matthew 8: 8: "The centurion answered and said, Lord, I am not worthy that thou shouldest come under my roof: but speak the word only, and my servant shall be healed."

IV

At the end of this Part in his *1936 proof* Hayward wrote the liturgical colours: "violet—penance; green—hope; white—purity; blue—celestial". See note to IV 1–4. Hope Mirrlees: "The Virgin sits in her garden; | She wears the blue habit ··· Lillies bloom, blue, green, and pink", *Paris* (1919).

Unadopted title ***VESTITA DI COLOR DI FIAMMA***: *Purg.* XXX 31–33: "sopra candido vel, cinta d'oliva, | donna m'apparve, sotto verde manto, | vestita di color di fiamma viva" [olive-crowned over a white veil, a lady appeared to me, clad, under a green mantle, with hue of living flame], Dante's first sight of Beatrice in the *Commedia*. TSE quoted XXX 31–48 in *Dante* (1929) II, giving this phrase as "clad under a green mantle, in colour of living flame."

IV 1–4 **violet ··· green ··· white and blue**: the 274 pages of small type in *English Liturgical Colours* by William St. John Hope and E. G. Cuthbert F. Atchley (1918) demonstrate the complexity of their subject. Atchley's table of "liturgical use of colours in England up to the middle of the 16th century" in *Essays on Ceremonial* ed. Vernon Staley (1904) gives red and secondarily ash-colour for Ash-Wednesday; white for Feasts of our Lady and predominant from Easter to Whitsunday; "blue and white" for Michaelmas. Elsewhere: "according to some, violet and black were to be held identical for liturgical purposes", 104; "green has generally been held to symbolise fruitfulness" 167; "It was with the significance of hope that Dante attired the Angels of Purgatory in green", 173 (citing *Purg.* VIII 28–30).

IV 1–3, 12 **Who walked between the violet and the violet | Who walked between | The various ranks of varied green ··· that walk between**: *Purg.* XXVIII 36, 40–41: "la gran variazion dei freschi mai ··· una donna soletta, che si gia | cantando ed iscegliendo fior da fiore" [the great diversity of the tender blossoms ··· a lady solitary, who went along singing, and culling flower after flower] (*Praz* 368–69). Swinburne: "She walked between the blossom and the grass", *Laus Veneris* 309, one of the Swinburne poems that TSE said a volume of selections "should certainly contain", *Swinburne as Poet* (1920). Writing to Marquis W. Childs, 8 Aug 1930, TSE recalled his nursemaid Annie Dunne taking him "to the little Catholic church ··· when she went to make her devotions; the spring violets", *American Literature and the American Language* 29 (*Bush* 146–47).

IV 3–4 **green | Going in white and blue**: "How life goes well in pink and green!" *Mandarins* 4 15.

IV 4 **in white and blue, in Mary's colour**: see note to *Burnt Norton* IV 3 "clematis" (virgin's bower). J. Wickham Legg: "in all the liturgical books that I have come across, white is invariably given as the colour of Blessed Mary. To this there is no exception; but it appears that by a special licence the Spanish dioceses, and also some churches of Naples, are allowed to wear blue for feasts of the B. V. M.", *Essays Liturgical and Historical* (1917) 162.

IV 6 **eternal dolour**: inscription on the Gate of Hell: "per me si va nell' eterno dolore" [through me the way into the eternal pain], *Inf.* III 2. **eternal** (*variant* **perpetual**): TSE on revisions in the Prayer Book: "The two words to which we would call attention again are *infinite* and *eternal*, where they have been substituted for *incomprehensible* and *everlasting* ··· The word *eternal* evades all difficulties of time ··· when fences are down the cattle will roam, including two vagrant beasts named *infinite* and *eternal*, words which will wander so far, the fence of meaning being down, that they will cease to belong anywhere", *A Commentary* in *Criterion* May 1927. **dolour:** pronounced *doller* in TSE's recordings.

IV 8 **made strong the fountains and made fresh the springs:** Baudelaire, of the goddess Cybele: "Fait couler le rocher et fleurir le désert" [makes the rocks gush water and the desert flower], *Bohémiens en voyage* [*Wandering Gypsies*] 12 (*Southam*).

IV 10 **blue of larkspur:** Edgar Lee Masters: "skies are blue | As larkspur", *The Conversation* in *Songs and Satires* (1916) (*McCue 2014a*). **larkspur:** OED a: "Any plant of the genus *Delphinium*"; b: "The blue colour characteristic of the larkspur". Both citations for b. are from 1927, including "Larkspur, a pastel blue slightly inclining to the mauve" (*Daily Express*). TSE to his mother, 13 June 1926: "Our little garden is doing well, the rosebushes and lupins and larkspur will soon be in flower, and I wish Vivien was here to see them." (When printed as a volume in 1930 and 1933, *Ash-Wednesday* was dedicated "TO | MY WIFE".)

IV 11 **Sovegna vos:** see note to unadopted title for III.

IV 13–14 **restoring ··· between sleep and waking:** "hesitating at the angles of stairs, | And between sleeping and waking", *Murder in the Cathedral* I. **between sleep and waking:** Swinburne: "Between a sleep and a sleep", *Atalanta in Calydon* 361 (see note to *Eyes that last I saw in dreams* 1–15).

IV 15 **White light folded, sheathed about her, folded:** *Paradiso* XXX 49–51: "così mi circonfulse luce viva, | e lasciommi fasciato di tal velo | del suo fulgor, che nulla m'appariva" [so there shone around me a living light, leaving me swathed in such a web of its glow that naught appeared to me].

IV 16–29 *ts2* [1–4] **the flowers rejoice ··· one who has heard the unheard, seen the unseen:** "The unheard music ··· the unseen eyebeam ··· the roses | Had the look of flowers that are looked at", *Burnt Norton* I 27–29.

IV 16–29 *ts2* [2–6] **blessed face ··· the unheard ··· the unseen ··· grace:** "grace dissolved in place || What is this face ··· this face ··· that unspoken", *Marina* 16–17, 29, 31. See note to V 18–19.

IV 16–29 *ts2* [5] **Desire chills:** "chilled delirium ··· when the sense has cooled", *Gerontion* 62–63. **and the hidden thoughts outrace ··· grace:** Carroll: "And the mome raths outgrabe", *Jabberwocky* in *Through the Looking-Glass* ch. I.

IV 16–29 *ts2* [7] **Poi s'ascose nel foco:** *Purg.* XXVI 148; see *The Waste Land* [V] 427 and note, and for TSE's returns to this passage of Dante see note to title *Ara Vos Prec* in headnote to "*Poems* (1920)", 7. PUBLICATION OF *ARA VOS PREC*.

IV 18–19, 26 **Redeem | The time ··· Redeem the time:** Ephesians 5: 15–16: "See then that ye walk circumspectly, not as fools, but as wise, Redeeming the time, because the days are evil." Colossians 4: 5: "Walk in wisdom toward them that are without, redeeming the time." TSE in 1931: "The World is trying the experiment of attempting to form a civilized but non-Christian mentality. The experiment will fail; but we must be very patient in awaiting its collapse; meanwhile redeeming the time: so that the Faith may be preserved", *Thoughts*

After Lambeth (1931) final paragraph (Unger in *Unger ed.* 366). "If · · · All time is unredeemable", *Burnt Norton* I 4–5.

IV 20 **the higher dream**: "We have nothing but dreams, and we have forgotten that seeing visions—a practice now relegated to the aberrant and the uneducated—was once a more significant, interesting, and disciplined kind of dreaming", *Dante* (1929) I. Dante's "'Divine Pageant' · · · belongs to the world of what I call the *high dream*, and the modern world seems capable only of the *low dream*", *Dante* (1929) II.

IV 21 **jewelled unicorns draw by the gilded hearse**: *Purg.* XXIX 106–108: "The space within the four of them contained a car triumphal, upon two wheels, which came drawn at the neck of a grifon" (*Praz* 368). Conrad Aiken: "White unicorns come gravely down to the water · · · white horses drawing a small white hearse · · · The gilded face and jewelled eyes of her", *Senlin: A Biography* (1918) I iii, iv, vi (*Grover Smith* 315, *Schneider* 121–22). **jewelled unicorns**: after Virginia Woolf wrote anonymously "Thus, in spite of dullness, bombast, rhetoric, and confusion, we still read the lesser Elizabethans, still find ourselves adventuring in the land of the jeweller and the unicorn" (*Notes on an Elizabethan Play* in *TLS* 5 Mar 1925), TSE wrote to her, [8? Mar 1925]: "I recognised your imagination in the *Times* à propos of unicorns and jewellers." **jewelled**: pronounced *jew-well'd* in TSE's recordings.

IV 21–22 **unicorns · · · The silent sister**: TSE: "the point about unicorns is that they can only be tamed by a pure virgin · · · If there was a bright light the unicorn would dematerialise", *"Synthetic Unicorn"* by George McTavish, reader's report (1935) ("Virgin", II 10; "White light", IV 15). David Jones's illustration for *The Cultivation of Christmas Trees* incorporates a unicorn.

IV 22 **The silent sister veiled**: Dante's first sight of Beatrice, *Purg.* XXX 31–32: "olive-crowned over a white veil, a lady appeared to me" (see note to unadopted title for IV, *Vestita di color di fiamma*). TSE to Colin Still, 13 May 1930: "although my recently published poem ('Ash Wednesday') is a deliberate modern *Vita Nuova*, I was not fully aware of the significance of the 'veiled lady' until I read your book. My 'veiled lady' was, as a matter of fact, a direct employment of a dream I had, together with the yew trees and the garden god." Still's *Shakespeare's Mystery Play: A Study of "The Tempest"* (1921) compares Shakespeare's Miranda to Dante's veiled Beatrice, and to the personification of Truth and Wisdom in the Jewish Kabbalah. **sister**: Baudelaire: "Mon enfant, mon soeur" [My child, my sister], first line of *L'Invitation au voyage* [*The Invitation to the Voyage*]. TSE, quoting this line and the next two: "The word *soeur* here is not, in my opinion, chosen merely because it rhymes with *douceur*; it is a moment in that sublimation of passion toward which Baudelaire was always striving", *Baudelaire in Our Time* (1927) (*Jain 1991*).

IV 22, 25 **sister · · · sprang up**: Coleridge: "The lady sprang up suddenly", *Christabel* 37 (Richard Eberhart, *Harvard Advocate* Dec 1938). See note to *The wind sprang up at four o'clock* 1.

IV 23, 28, V 30, VI 23] For TSE's remarks to Hayward about the yew, see note to *Animula* 36.

IV 29 **And after this our exile**: *Salve Regina* (prayer following the celebration of Mass): "To thee do we send up our sighs mourning and weeping in this valley of tears;

turn, then, most gracious advocate, thine eyes of mercy towards us; and after this our exile, show unto us the blessed fruit of thy womb, Jesus" (*Matthiessen*).

V

Unadopted title **la sua voluntade**: *Paradiso* III 85. See note to VI 30–33.

V 3–9 **Word ··· Word**: John 1: 1: "In the beginning was the Word".

V 6–7 **for the world ··· light shone in the darkness and**: John 1: 5: "And the light shineth in darkness; and the darkness comprehended it not." John 8: 12: "I am the light of the world: he that followeth me shall not walk in darkness, but shall have the light of life."

V 8 **the Word**: to Donald Brace, 22 May 1936: "The line should read: 'Against the Word the unstilled world still whirled'." For "Word / World" errors, see Textual History (also *After Strange Gods* 59: "wordly shrewdness"). **the unstilled world still whirled**: Sir John Davies: "Behold the *World*, how it is *whirled round*, | And for it is so *whirl'd*, is named so", *Orchestra* st. 34. (For Davies's poem see notes to *Gerontion* 67–71, *Burnt Norton* II 6 and *East Coker* I 25–45.) Despite his judgement in *Sir John Davies* (1926) that "Davies may be said to have little in common with Donne", TSE perhaps confused the two when he wrote to G. Wilson Knight, 25 May 1930: "The line you like so much is not absolutely original. Somewhere or another Donne makes a pun on the world being so called because it is 'whirled'. But I think without modesty that I have improved upon the hint, and any rhythmical value the line has is mine." (In his poem of the Easter season, *Goodfriday, 1613. Riding Westward*, Donne has: "The intelligence that moves, devotion is, | And as the other Spheares ··· our Soules ··· are whirld by it", but with apparently no pun on "world".) TSE again: "The first stanza is a kind of word play used by Donne and Andrewes in sermons, and the pun on 'world' and 'whirled' is Donne's", *Excerpts from Lectures* (1933). *Paradiso* XXXIII 143–45 (the closing lines of the *Commedia*): "ma già volgeva il mio disiro e il *velle*, | sì come rota ch' egualmente è mossa, | l'amor che move il sole e l' altre stelle" [but already my desire and will were rolled—even as a wheel that moveth equally—by the Love that moves the sun and the other stars] (*Southam*). TSE: "Whirled in a vortex that shall bring | The world to that destructive fire", *East Coker* II 15–16.

V 9 **silent Word**: Lancelot Andrewes: "What, *Verbum infans*, the Word an infant? The Word, and not able to speak a word?" Christmas Sermon 1611 (on the text of John 1: 14). See notes to *Gerontion* 17–19 and *East Coker* I 13.

V 10, 28, 36 **O my people, what have I done unto thee**: "The refrain does not come directly from the Bible but from the Reproaches of the Pre-sanctified of Good Friday", *Excerpts from Lectures* (1933). Micah 6: 3: "O my people, what have I done unto thee? and wherein have I wearied thee? testify against me", with the three words "O my people" returning, as in TSE, at 6: 5. TSE on Charles A. Claye's masque:

> The later scenes will have a fuller meaning for those who are familiar with the offices of Holy Week, with *Tenebrae*—the Mattins of Maundy Thursday, Good Friday, and Holy Saturday, with the mournful refrain
>
> Jerusalem, Jerusalem, return unto the Lord thy God.

> with The Reproaches
>
> > O my people, what have I done unto thee, or wherein have I wearied thee? Testify against me.
>
> · · · To make these observations is not to imply that the Masque is merely a tissue of allusions intelligible only to liturgical scholars, though certainly it will have a fuller meaning to those who know the impressive Masses of Holy Week. The Masque · · · should appeal to every one according to his knowledge
>
> *"The Merry Masque of Our Lady in London Town"* (1928)

Grover Smith 153: "Dante is said to have addressed to the citizens of Florence, from his asylum in Verona, a letter beginning with the same phrase, 'Popule mi, quid feci tibi?'"

V 14–16 **On the mainland, in the desert or the rain land · · · day time · · · night time:** "In the may time, the play time", *Little Gidding* 24^25 *variant.*

V 14–21 **mainland · · · rain land | For those who walk in darkness · · · night · · · right · · · right · · · Those who walk in darkness:** Isaiah 9: 2: "The people that walked in darkness have seen a great light; they that dwell in the land of the shadow of darkness".

V 15 **those who walk in darkness:** Byron, *Childe Harold's Pilgrimage* III 627 (Richard Eberhart, *Harvard Advocate* Dec 1938).

V 18–19 **No place of grace for those who avoid the face · · · the voice:** *Paradise Lost* III 140–42: "in his face | Divine compassion visibly appeared, | Love without end, and without measure Grace, | Which uttering thus he to his Father spake" (*Ricks* 226).

V 22–24 **between | Hour and hour · · · In darkness:** Rupert Brooke: "between | Darkness and darkness!" *The Fish*, a poem TSE praised in *Reflections on Contemporary Poetry* I (1917).

V 22, VI 4 **torn on the horn · · · the profit and the loss:** "Caught on those horns that toss and toss · · · Desires completion of his loss", *The Burnt Dancer* 35–37 (*Jain 1992* 187); see note.

V 26 **Who will not go away and cannot pray:** Herbert: "I could not go away, nor persevere", *Affliction* (I) 48 (*Schneider* 123).

V 34 **The desert in the garden the garden in the desert:** Milton: "I who e're while the happy Garden sung · · · Into the Desert", *Paradise Regained* I 1, 9.

V 34–35 **the desert | Of drouth:** Milton: "the Arabian drouth", *Paradise Regained* III 274; see note to *Little Gidding* II 8–9.

V 35 **the withered apple-seed:** the tree upon which Christ was crucified was said to have grown from the seed of the forbidden fruit eaten by Adam and Eve. "The apple-seed, it should hardly be necessary to mention, refers to an incident in the life of our first parents", *Excerpts from Lectures* (1932–33). Joel 1: 12: "the apple tree, even all the trees of the field, are withered" (*Hands*).

VI

VI 3–4 **Although I do not hope to turn || Wavering:** Pound: "The trouble in the pace and the uncertain | Wavering!" *The Return* (1912) 3–4 (*Ricks 2010* 198). TSE quoted the first four lines of the poem in *Ezra Pound: His Metric and Poetry* (1917) and included it in Pound's *Selected Poems*. See *Little Gidding* V 16 and note.

VI 4 **between the profit and the loss:** "Et les profits et les pertes", *Dans le Restaurant* 27. "And the profit and loss", *The Waste Land* [IV] 314. "I have seen much of life, in its various shades, | And the fat and the lean, and the profit and loss", *Pollicle Dogs and Jellicle Cats* 8–9.

VI 4–6, 21 **the loss . . . dreams cross · · · dreamcrossed · · · where three dreams cross:** OED has this as sole citation for "dreamcrossed". *Romeo and Juliet* Prologue 6: "star-crossed lovers". TSE: "Those who have crossed · · · not as lost · · · dreams · · · dream kingdom · · · star · · · dream kingdom · · · crossed · · · dreams", *The Hollow Men* I 13, 15; II 1–2, 10, 12, 15, 21.

VI 7 **Bless me father:** "Bless me, father, for I have sinned", the penitent's first words to the priest during Confession.

VI 8 **From the wide window towards the granite shore:** "what shores what granite islands towards my timbers", *Marina* 33 (*Leavis* 130). "The sea is the land's edge also, the granite | Into which it reaches", *The Dry Salvages* I 16–17. (The Eliots' house at Cape Ann has a picture window looking out to sea, across granite rocks.)

VI 8–10 **shore | The white sails still fly seaward, seaward flying | Unbroken wings:** Tennyson: "And white sails flying on the yellow sea", *The Marriage of Geraint* 829 in *Idylls of the King*. Coleridge: "the Islands and white sails, | Dim coasts, and cloud-like hills, and shoreless Ocean", *Reflections on Having Left a Place of Retirement* 36–37; TSE scored these lines in Coleridge's *Poetical Works* (1907). Harold Monro: "to sail | Seaward on white enormous wings", *Trees* IV (1916).

VI 14 **golden-rod and the lost sea smell:** "in Missouri I missed the fir trees, the bay and goldenrod, the song-sparrows, the red granite and the blue sea of Massachusetts", *This American World* (1928); see headnote to *The Dry Salvages*, 2. "THE RIVER IS WITHIN US, THE SEA IS ALL ABOUT US" (*Williamson* 207–208).

VI 16 **whirling plover:** James Grahame: "the wheeling plover ceas'd | Her plaint", *The Sabbath* 165–66; misquoted by Walter Scott in *Paul's Letters to his Kinsfolk* letter XV as "whirling plover". **plover:** pronounced (correctly) *pluvver* in TSE's recordings.

VI 17 **And the blind eye creates:** "I do not know whether the thought of possible blindness haunts other writers, but I know that it has always haunted me. And this, without any physical premonition: my sight, I am thankful to say, is as reliable as most people's. For a writer, blindness need not be, of course, the end of his activity, as it must be for a painter: but it involves re-adjustments so great as to frighten *me* · · · That is why, if I were suddenly blinded, or if I found the world slowly dimming before my eyes, I should be thankful for the invention of braille", *Some Thoughts on Braille* (1952). (In 1949 TSE had sat for what was probably the final oil painting by Wyndham Lewis before he lost his sight; Magdalene.)

VI 18 **The empty forms between the ivory gates:** William Morris: "Beats with light wing against the ivory gate · · · empty", *The Earthly Paradise, An Apology* st. 4 (for which see note to I 5–6). **ivory gates:** see note to *WLComposite* 352.

VI 19–35 *ts2*] See note to *Marina* 21.

VI 30–33 **Our peace in His will · · · spirit of the sea:** in *Paradiso* III, Dante encounters Piccarda de Donati in the lowest sphere of heaven and asks whether she desires a more lofty place. She replies:

"Frate, la nostra volontà quieta [70]
virtù di carità, che fa volerne
sol quel ch'avemo, e d'altro non ci asseta.
Se disiassimo esser più superne,
foran discordi gli nostri disiri
dal voler di colui che qui ne cerne, [75]
che vedrai noi capere in questi giri,
s'essere in caritate è qui *necesse*,
e se la sua natura ben rimiri.
Anzi è formale ad esto beato *esse*
tenersi dentro alla divina voglia, [80]
per ch'una fansi nostre volgie stesse.
Sì che, come noi sem di soglia in soglia
per questo regno, a tutto il regno piace,
come allo re ch'a suo voler ne invoglia;
e la sua volontate è nostra pace: [85]
ella è quel mare, al qual tutto si move
ciò ch'ella crea e che natura face."

["Brother, the quality of love stilleth our will, and maketh us long only for what we have, and giveth us no other thirst. Did we desire to be more aloft, our longings were discordant from his will who here assorteth us, and for that, thou wilt see, there is no room within these circles, if of necessity we have our being here in love, and if thou think again what is love's nature. Nay, 'tis the essence of this blessed being to hold ourselves within the divine will, whereby our own wills are themselves made one. So that our being thus, from threshold unto threshold throughout the realm, is a joy to all the realm as to the king, who draweth our wills to what he willeth; and his will is our peace; it is that sea to which all moves that it createth and that nature maketh."]

In the copy his mother gave him, TSE scored these lines, with the final tercet scored in both margins.

Arnold twice cited "In la sua volontade è nostra pace" in *The Study of Poetry* (1880). In *Byron* (1881), he wrote of "the great poets who made such verse" as this line, alongside touchstones from the *Iliad* and *King Lear.* In 1913, in the Harvard Festschrift for George Kittredge (see note to *The Waste Land* [V] 399–422), William T. Brewster quoted Arnold's judgement from 1880 that the line was "altogether beyond Chaucer's reach", while Jefferson B. Fletcher took issue with Santayana: "According to him, 'For Piccarda to say that she accepts the will of God means not that she shares it, but that she submits to it' · · · Piccarda fairly sings her joy; Dr. Santayana would have her but sighing her resignation." (For Piccarda de Donati, see note to *A Cooking Egg* 24.) TSE: "Let us therefore make perfect our will", *Choruses to "The Rock"* VIII 48 (see note).

Quoted as "*la sua voluntade e nostra pace*" in *Shakespeare and the Stoicism of Seneca* (1927). The following year TSE used a text beginning "E 'n la sua", translating it "And in His Will is our peace" and commenting "I like this passage because it seems to me to express, better than any other lines of Dante or of any other poet, one of the greatest ideas of the Christian religion", *My Favourite Passage from Dante* (1928). "the statement of Dante seems to me *literally true*. And I confess that it has more beauty for me now, when my own experience has deepened its meaning, than it did when I first read it", *Dante* (1929) Note to II. "*La sua voleuntade è nostra pace* is the last word about free will", *Notes on the Way* in *Time & Tide* 19 Jan 1935 (with a letter from TSE on 2 Feb correcting the spelling to *volontate*). Spellings: Temple Classics "volontate"; Arnold "volontade"; TSE in *Dante* (1929) and the unadopted title to *Ash-Wednesday* V, "voluntade" (misspelling after the Latin noun *voluntas, -atis*); *Dante* in *Selected Essays* (1932) "voluntate" (Jennifer Formichelli, personal communication).

To Laurence Binyon, 28 Apr 1941: "I am flattered that you should want my opinion about Sua Voluntade. I should think it was one of the most difficult things to translate in the whole Commedia: partly because it is one of the few lines that everybody knows, and therefore no translation of it can come with such a bang as to satisfy the reader. By itself, I do prefer just 'in his will is our peace' which is what 99 readers out of 100 will expect and want: but how you are to fill out the line I don't know, unless you can append an extension, or begin the following line. I mean, I don't think you want to carry over the preceding line: the line in the speech comes at just the right point and is just right as a whole line—that is the difficulty. You may have to use the stuffed line: anyway, I shall be most excited to know your final decision." (Binyon: "And in His will is perfected our peace.") For Binyon's Dante, see headnote to *Little Gidding*, 3. DANTE.

"When Dante says *la sua voluntade e nostra pace* it is great poetry, and there is a great philosophy behind it", *Shakespeare and the Stoicism of Seneca* (1927). "Consider what is perhaps the most purely philosophical and scientific of all great poems, Lucretius *On the Nature of Things*. Dante's and Milton's long poems are also philosophical, but mixed with narrative of events happening to human beings and beings conceived similarly. There is no *a priori* reason why Lucretius should not have worked out his own system of philosophy, and then expressed it in verse. But in practice, that would mean doing two men's work: first, to think out the system solely with the aim of finding abstract truth, and second to examine what it feels like to believe that system ··· What Lucretius actually does, is to express what it feels like to believe that particular philosophy, and to have a passionate emotion about it. To believe anything, and to believe it to be of great importance, is necessarily to have an emotion about it. Lucretius, therefore, is giving us some very important information about the atomistic philosophy of his time, by telling us what it feels like to believe it. In the course of doing this, he has to give us a good many details about natural phenomena, such as the causes of hail and snow, which, if taken out of the whole poem, do not strike us as very poetical", *Poetical and Prosaic Use of Words* (1943). (In his copy of *A History of Literary Criticism in the Renaissance* by J. E. Springarn, 1899, TSE scored Castelvetro's convictions that "Prose is not suited to imitative or imaginative subjects, for we expect themes treated in prose to be actual facts" and that science is "not suitable material for poetry, and accordingly such writers as Lucretius and Fracastoro are not poets".) For TSE's judgement that "for a poet to be a philosopher he would have to be virtually two men ··· the work is better performed inside two skulls", see headnote to "*Poems* (1920)", 5. TSE'S PROFICIENCY IN FRENCH.

VI 31 **among these rocks**: see note to *WLComposite* 582 "Among the rock".

VI 32, 34 **Sister, mother · · · Suffer me not to be separated**: TSE's mother died in 1929. Apart from Theodora (who had died in infancy before TSE's birth), the first of his siblings to die, in 1926, had been the sister named Charlotte after their mother.

VI 33 **spirit of the river, spirit of the sea**: see letter to Herbert Read, 15 Sept 1932, quoted in headnote to *The Dry Salvages*, 2. "THE RIVER IS WITHIN US, THE SEA IS ALL ABOUT US". **spirit of the sea**: OED "Stella Maris": "'star of the sea'. A title given to the Virgin Mary · · · used allusively for a protectress or a guiding spirit" (with first citation from George Eliot, 1876). See Textual History for "the waves · · · the seas · · · the waves", VI 19–35 *tsAW* [2–4].

VI 34 **Suffer me not to be separated:** Hayward in his *1936 proof*: "Anima Christi" ("Soul of Christ, sanctify me · · · Suffer me not to be separated from Thee").

VI 35 **And let my cry come unto Thee**: Psalm 102 ("A Prayer of the afflicted, when he is overwhelmed, and poureth out his complaint before the Lord"), 1, 3: "Hear my prayer, O Lord, and let my cry come unto thee · · · For my days are consumed like smoke, and my bones are burned as an hearth." To Henry Eliot, 19 Apr [1924]: "You know what you can do—I only know my own need, and merely cry out to you."

Ariel Poems

Dates of publication:

Journey of the Magi	Aug 1927	
A Song for Simeon	Sept 1928	
Animula	Oct 1929	
Marina	Sept 1930	
[*Triumphal March*	Oct 1931	Subsequently Part I of *Coriolan*; see "Unfinished Poems"]
The Cultivation of Christmas Trees	Oct 1954	

Faber's Autumn Catalogue 1927 announced Ariel Poems 1–8, by various poets: "This series of little booklets consists of single previously unpublished poems each suitably decorated in colours and dressed in the gayest wrappers. It has been designed to take the place of Christmas cards and other similar tokens that one sends for remembrance sake at certain seasons of the year. Some of the poems have Christmas for their subject: but a genuine poem is not a thing appropriate only to one season of the year, and any one of these poems with its attendant decorations would be a joy to read and to see at any time, whatever the season might be · · · For collectors of first editions it is worth remembering that most of these poems have been written specially for the series and that *all* of them appear here separately for the first time and are thus 'first editions'—and first editions that have been printed at the Curwen Press!"

During the late 1920s Faber published occasional poetry anthologies and reprints, as well as volumes by TSE himself, by Pound and by Herbert Read, mainly gathering previously published poems. TSE was sceptical about the availability of good new poetry, as he told Faber's directors in his reader's report of 1926 on William Jeffrey's *The Lamb of Lomond*:

> This book raises a question of policy: how much verse do we wish to publish and with what purpose? There are, I believe, some authors of verse such as John Oxenham and Mrs. [Ella Wheeler] Wilcox who have no literary reputation whatever but whose books do repay their publishers: are we to publish verse of this sort? There are also a few authors of established reputation such as Kipling, Hardy, Yeats, de la Mare, etcetera, whom I suppose we should have no hesitation in publishing if we could get them. No other versifiers can do more than add distinction to our list. I should make exception, I suppose, of young or unknown poets who impress us so tremendously that we are sure that they will eventually add distinction to the list. Practically all of the verse which has been submitted to me for examination falls into none of these categories.

Faber published poetry by John Gould Fletcher in 1926 and 1928, and went ahead, despite TSE's tepid reader's reports, with volumes by Richard Church in 1927 and C. Henry Warren in 1928.

Selwyn & Blount had published Walter de la Mare's *A Ballad of Christmas* (1924) and *The Hostage* in small format pamphlets (illustrated by Alec Buckels) in 1924–25, and the Ariel series was conceived by de la Mare's son Richard, whose letters commissioning the poets mentioned that his father and TSE would be contributing. The other poets for 1927 were all long established: Hardy, Newbolt, Binyon, Chesterton, Wilfrid Gibson and Sassoon. The same was true in succeeding years, and of the 21 poets who contributed to the first series (1927–31), only de la Mare, TSE, Sassoon and Roy Campbell would come to be associated with Faber.

In 1930 Faber published Auden's *Poems*, Joseph Gordon Macleod's *The Ecliptic* and P. P. Graves's *The Pursuit* (announced together on a bookmark), signifying a new initiative. To J. Edward Fisher, 9 Feb 1937: "We began our publication of poetry some years ago with paper-bound volumes at half a crown [2s. 6d.], which we published at a loss, and we only learnt through experience the sad fact that we can sell just as many copies of a volume of new verse by producing it more expensively and pricing it at 6s. or 7s. 6d. as we could by reducing costs and profit."

From series to section title. "*Ariel Poems* was the title of a series of poems which included many other poets as well as myself; these were all new poems which were published during four or five successive years as a kind of Christmas card. Nobody else seemed to want the title afterward, so I kept it for myself simply to designate four of my poems which appeared in this way. *Journey of the Magi* is obviously a subject suitable for the Christmas season", *Chicago Round Table* (1950). Over the years the series included Blunden, de la Mare, Edith Sitwell and Yeats. They were published as small four-page pamphlets with designs by artists including Edward Bawden, Eric Gill, Paul and John Nash, and Eric Ravilious. As a director of Faber, TSE contributed to the series each year: *Journey of the Magi* (no. 8, 1927) and *A Song for Simeon* (no. 16, 1928) both with drawings by E. McKnight Kauffer, *Animula* (no. 23, 1929) with wood-engravings by Gertrude Hermes, and *Marina* (no. 29, 1930) and *Triumphal March* (no. 35, 1931) again both with drawings by Kauffer. To Norman Foerster, 15 June 1932: "The *Ariel* poems were all written in the year of publication." Later Ariel Poems by lesser known writers sold poorly, and on 11 Aug 1932, TSE told George Bell: "the Ariel series has come to an end, or at least is postponed indefinitely". TSE collected his contributions in *1936*, writing to Geoffrey Curtis, 14 Feb 1936: "These little pamphlets are to be scrapped, I am glad to say: all these bits are being gathered together in my *Collected Poems*, now in proof." Creating the section "Ariel Poems", he transferred *Triumphal March* to the section of "Unfinished Poems" as part of *Coriolan*. "*Triumphal March* originally appeared in this form too; but I took it out of the series because I meant it to be the first part of a sequence in the life of the character who appears in this first part as Young Cyril", *Chicago Round Table* (1950).

In both *Collected Poems* and *Selected Poems*, the "Ariel Poems" section follows *Ash-Wednesday*, although *Journey of the Magi* was published earlier than any part of *Ash-Wednesday*.

In 1954 Faber published a second series of Ariel Poems, in larger format, by eight poets (Auden, Roy Campbell, de la Mare, TSE, Day Lewis, MacNeice, Edwin Muir and Spender). Writing to commission a poem from Walter de la Mare as early as 20 Mar 1952, TSE described the terms, beginning by saying that once again "the proposal of a new series of ARIEL POEMS originated in the fertile brain of Dick [de la Mare] · · · According to our estimates it will be possible to issue a new set of Ariel Poems, each to be provided with an illustration by a different artist, at the price of two shillings and sixpence each. Each poem should not be more than sixty and not less than twenty lines long; and must, of course, be a poem not previously published anywhere. As the new series, like the old one, will be aimed at the Christmas market, to serve the purpose of Christmas cards for the discerning public, a subject suitable for the season would be most acceptable: though any poem not obviously inappropriate will, from the right poets, be welcome. For such a poem we offer an outright fee of twenty guineas · · · It is strongly felt that your name, and—alas!—my own, are needed in this series, as senior sponsors." Walter de la Mare and TSE became the only poets to contribute in every year of the Ariel Poems series, including 1954.

To C. W. Dilke, 18 Dec 1948, offering to record for the BBC German service a short commentary explaining the history of the Ariel Poems: "The four poems which appear in my collected works as 'Ariel Poems' represent my contribution to the series during four years. *Journey of the Magi* was the first of these. Like my *Song for Simeon* which followed it a year later, it asks the question: how fully was the Trust revealed to those who were inspired to recognise Our Lord so soon after the Nativity?"

The series of six poems altogether (including *Triumphal March* and *The Cultivation of Christmas Trees*) was published as a separate illustrated volume, *Ariel Poems*, in 2014.

Journey of the Magi

Published separately Aug 1927, with drawings by E. McKnight Kauffer, then *1936+*, *Sesame* and *Penguin / Sel Poems*. A limited edition of the Ariel pamphlet in boards was issued in Nov 1927. To secure American copyright, an edition of 27 copies was printed by William Edwin Rudge, Mount Vernon, New York, in Dec 1927.

Recorded May 1947, for the Harvard Poetry Room; released by Harvard Vocarium Records, 1948. Second: 23 May 1947, National Gallery of Art, Washington. Third: 12 Nov 1950, for U. Chicago Round Table, broadcast by NBC.

The year before TSE's birth, Charlotte C. Eliot published *The Three Kings* in *The Christian Register* Christmas 1887:

"We are three kings who have traveled far,
  O'er desert waste and sandy plain.
Before us moved a radiant star,
  Its light along our path has lain.
Faint and weary, our journey's end
  We seek; but the star moves onward still.
We know not whither our footsteps tend,
  Obedient to a higher will.

"So each of us, omnipotent
  Within his kingdom, holdeth sway · · ·"

The Christmas of 1927, which saw publication of the first group of Ariel Poems, was TSE's first after his reception into the Church of England in June. To Sister Mary J. Power, 6 Dec 1932: "perhaps the simplest account that I can give is to say that I was brought up as a Unitarian of the New England variety; that for many years I was without any definite religious faith, or without any at all; that in 1927 I was baptised and confirmed into the Church of England; and that I am associated with what is called the Catholic movement in that Church, as represented by Viscount Halifax and the English Church Union. I accordingly believe in the Creeds, the invocation of the Blessed Virgin and the Saints, the Sacrament of Penance, etc." To Michael de la Bedoyère, 28 Apr 1936, offering to write for the *Catholic Herald* from his own experience: "assuming that Anglican and Roman Orders and Sacraments are equally valid, on what grounds did a person brought up altogether outside the Christian Faith elect to become a member of the former community rather than the latter?"

To Conrad Aiken, 13 Sept 1927: "Thanks for your compliments about the Christmas poem. I have no illusions about it: I wrote it in three quarters of an hour after church time and before lunch one Sunday morning, with the assistance of half a bottle of Booth's gin."

Horace M. Kallen to TSE, 12 Oct 1927: "There is no way that men travelling with horse and camel can pass from snowline to vegetation over-night and reach Bethlehem. That sink lies in the arid Judean hills, which stick up sharp and nude all around. They slope eastward to the waste lands of the Dead Sea, south to the Desert. There is no snow nearer than Hermon, to the north, several camel journeys away." TSE, 22 Oct: "I am much interested to hear your criticism of my geographical ignorance. Theoretically I believe one ought to make verse as watertight as prose on such points. On the other hand, if I had bothered about the topography and archaeology of Asia Minor, I should have had to omit a good deal of detail which really is meant to be symbolical." To Alan Porter, 13 Dec: "As the whole story of the Magi is not, I believe, an essential matter of Christian doctrine, I felt a certain liberty to treat it according to my own fantasy of realism. I did not intend to put forward, and still do not believe that I did put forward, any view which would either conflict with Christian doctrine or any imagination which would tend to weaken belief. The notion that the three Magi were the three religious leaders whom you mention does not appeal to me because what little I know of their religions makes me unable to accept the imaginative possibility of such a tribute ··· I meant that the Magi were drawn by a power which they did not understand, and I used them as types of a kind of person who may be found at almost any period of history. I meant them to be pathetic as Dante's Virgil is pathetic."

To Harold Monro, 4 June 1929: "had I had a volume of verse ready this year I should probably have included it [*Journey of the Magi*]; but as things are, and as it still sells a little, my co-directors would rather I did not allow it [to] appear in any anthology".

Vassar Miscellany News 10 May 1933 reported TSE's reading at the college three days previously: "There was a comparatively simple piece, *The Christmas Carol of the Magi*, which showed the Three Wise Men, having gone on the quest for the infant Christ, alienated from and lost among their own more materialistic people. Three trees were mentioned which foreshadowed the Crucifixion, and there was a phrase about dicing for silver, which was to recall both Judas and the soldiers casting lots for the garments of the dead Christ, Mr. Eliot explained."

Lancelot Andrewes, Christmas Sermon 1622 (on Matthew 2: 1–2):

> For they sat not still gazing on the star. Their *vidimus* begat *venimus*; their *seeing* made them come, come, a great journey. *Venimus* is soon said, but a short word; but many a wide and weary step they made before they could come to say *Venimus*, Lo, here "we are come;" come, and at our journey's end. To look a little on it. In this their coming we consider, 1. First, the distance of the place they came from. It was not hard by as the shepherds—but a step to Bethlehem over the fields; this was riding many a hundred miles, and cost them many a day's journey. 2. Secondly, we consider the way that they

came, if it be pleasant, or plain and easy; for if it be, it is so much the better. 1. This was nothing pleasant; for through deserts, all the way waste and desolate. 2. Nor secondly, easy either; for over the rocks and crags of both Arabias, specially Petræa, their journey lay. 3. Yet if safe—but it was not, but exceeding dangerous, as lying through the midst of the "black Tents of Kedar," [Cant. 1: 5], a nation of thieves and cut-throats; to pass over the hills of robbers, infamous then, and infamous to this day. No passing without great troop, or convoy. 4. Last we consider the time of their coming, the season of the year. It was no summer progress. A cold coming they had of it at this time of the year, just the worst time of the year to take a journey, and specially a long journey in. The ways deep, the weather sharp, the days short, the sun farthest off, *in solstitio brumali*, "the very dead of winter." *Venimus*, "we are come," if that be one, *venimus*, "we are now come," come at this time, that sure is another.

And these difficulties they overcame, of a wearisome, irksome, troublesome, dangerous, unseasonable journey; and for all this they came. And came it cheerfully and quickly, as appeareth by the speed they made. It was but *vidimus, venimus*, with them; "they saw," and "they came;" no sooner saw, but they set out presently. So as upon the first appearing of the star, as it might be last night, they knew it was Balaam's star; it called them away, they made ready straight to begin their journey this morning. A sign they were highly conceited of His birth, believed some great matter of it, that they took all these pains, made all this haste that they might be there to worship Him with all the possible speed they could. Sorry for nothing so much as that they could not be there soon enough, with the very first, to do it even this day, the day of His birth ··· And we, what should we have done? ··· Our fashion is to see and see again before we stir a foot, specially if it be to the worship of Christ. Come such a journey at such a time? No; but fairly have put it off to the spring of the year, till the days longer, and the ways fairer, and the weather warmer, till better travelling to Christ.

Seventeen Sermons on the Nativity (1887)

In *Lancelot Andrewes* (1926), where he quoted from this passage from "It was no summer progress" to "'the very dead of winter'", TSE used the 1887 edition and recommended it. Andrewes's Christmas Sermon 1620 has a similar passage, again with emphasis on "a new light kindled in Heaven", the star which TSE markedly does not ever mention. For TSE on Andrewes's sermons, see note to *Little Gidding* V 29–37.

To John Hayward, 11 May 1931, thanking him for Peter Hall's ed. of Andrewes (Pickering, 1828): "I feel I did not succeed in expressing my pleasure at your gift of Pickering *Preces Privatae*; I never do appear very appreciative, I fear. I shall truly treasure it; but the next time you come I want you to write my name in it, please." To Mrs. Stuart Moore, 30 Sept 1931: "I hardly feel that I know enough about Lancelot Andrewes to write any more about him. Indeed I fear that the one essay which I have written appears to lay claim to a much more profound knowledge than I possess."

Speech on modern religious drama, after a performance of Charles Williams's *The Seed of Adam* in Brentford, 9 Dec 1936: "Of course what people do today must be very different from the work of the fourteenth and fifteenth centuries. It cannot be so simple, but then our religious faith is not such a simple thing. It has to have a certain surface simplicity, in order to be good drama at all; but when it is sincere it will have under the surface all the complexity of feeling that we experience ourselves ··· And so I think we must see the Nativity story with a consciousness of everything that has happened in the 1900 odd years since. We have to put ourselves there, and we have to see those events here", quoted in John Hayward's *London Letter* in *New York Sun* 23 Jan 1937.

After the war, an ephemeral Cambridge publication, *Oasis* 1, printed *Journey of the Magi* with eight poems by other authors. In Hayward's copy (King's), TSE added alternative titles:

Yeats: *For Anne Gregory* – Or, Gentlemen Prefer Blondes
Auden: *Culture* – Or, Gentlemen Prefer Cricketers [emending the line "May warm each other with their wicked hands" to "wicket hands"].
Spender: *Regnum Ultima Ratio* – Or, Gentlemen Prefer Apprentices
Day Lewis: *Newsreel* – Or, Gentlemen Prefer Jill
MacNeice: *Bagpipe Music* – Or, Old Gentlemen are Tired
Graves: *No More Ghosts* – Or, Ghosts Prefer Ghosts
[Dylan] Thomas: *Among those Killed in the Dawn Raid was a Man Aged a Hundred* – Bards Prefer Centenarians
Henry Reed: *Naming of Parts* – Privates Prefer Parts
Eliot: *Journey of the Magi* – Or, Old Gentlemen Prefer Silken Girls

Title **Journey of the Magi**: Among the paintings in the National Gallery marked by TSE in his *Baedeker* 174 is "*Giorgione*, Adoration of the Magi".

1–5 **"A cold coming ··· winter"**: to his French translator Paul Gilson, 6 Mar 1928: "the first five lines which I have enclosed in inverted commas are taken from a sermon on the Nativity preached by Bishop Andrewes before James Ist of England" (see headnote).

2–3 **Just the worst time of the year ··· journey**: to John Hayward, 9 Dec [1938]: "Why on earth am I going away again for a weekend, and just at the time of year when I am worried to death with the problems of Christmas cards and what not." To E. M. W. Tillyard, 26 Oct 1947: "I have *got* to go to Aix and Marseilles and Rome early in December (just the worst time of the year for a journey and such a long journey): I had to postpone this from June which might have been pleasant."

3–6 **such a long journey ··· sore-footed**: to Paul Elmer More, 3 Aug 1929: "Most critics appear to think that my catholicism is merely an escape or an evasion ··· it [is] rather trying to be supposed to have settled oneself in an easy chair, when one has just begun a long journey afoot." On More: "What is significant to me ··· is not simply the conclusions at which he has arrived but the fact that he *arrived* there from somewhere else; and not simply that he came from somewhere else, but that he took a particular route ··· the stages of the journey ··· analogy with my own journey ··· It was possibly Irving Babbitt himself in 1927 or 1928, in a conversation in London, during which I had occasion to indicate the steps I had recently taken, who first made me clearly cognizant of the situation ··· The English Church was familiar with the backslider, but it knew nothing of the convert—certainly not of the convert who had come such a long way", *Paul Elmer More* (1937).

6 **the camels galled**: Kipling: "the camels shall not gall", *The Man Who Would be King* (W. R. Childe, in Kenneth Muir, *N&Q* Sept 1954). See notes to 12 and 21.

8, 10 **we regretted ··· the silken girls**: Conrad: "He regretted the clink of sabre and spurs on a fine afternoon, the barrack-room witticisms, the girls of garrison towns", *An Outpost of Progress* I (*Unger 1956* 232–33, quoting from Conrad's story two further uses of OED's first sense of "regret": "To remember, think of (something lost), with distress or longing").

9–10 **The summer palaces on slopes, the terraces, | And the silken girls bringing sherbet:** "with our scented girls clad in a breath of silk webs, | we set in high places our springes for happiness ··· a crossing of lights to the corners of terraces", *Anabasis* VI i–iv. Of this passage: "I am aware of being influenced by the *Anabase* of St.-John Perse", *Excerpts from Lectures 1932–1933* (for TSE on Perse's influence on his own subsequent work, see *Anabasis* headnote, 4. *ANABASE* TO *ANABASIS*). *Greene* 136: "Eliot lui-même qui m'a signalé le rapprochement entre son poème et celui de Perse" [Eliot himself indicated to me the parallel between his poem and Perse's]. TSE to Frank Morley, 22 Mar 1946: arranging to visit New York "before the publishing world melts away under the heat and retires to its summer palaces on slopes". **terraces:** OED 4: "The flat roof of a house, resorted to for coolness in warm climates. *Obs.*" (but with quotations from 1572 to 1892). **And the silken girls bringing sherbet:** Pound: "And the vermilioned girls getting drunk about sunset", *Exile's Letter* (1915) 50 (Michael Roberts, *Critique of Poetry*, 1934, 116). As TSE begins five lines with "And the", so Pound begins his line, as likewise his 51 ("And the water"), 45 ("And the girls singing back at each other"), and 56 ("And the wind lifted the song"). TSE included *Exile's Letter* in Pound's *Selected Poems*. **silken girls:** *Grim, The Collier of Croydon* IV i: "These silken girls are all too fine for me", in *A Select Collection of old English Plays* ed. W. Carew Hazlitt (1874).

12 **wanting their liquor and women:** Kipling: Dan and Peachey agree not to "look at any Liquor, nor any Woman", *The Man Who Would be King* (Childe, in Muir, *N&Q* Sept 1954).

14 **cities hostile:** Kipling: "Up along the hostile mountains ··· future cities", *The Explorer* 45, 49.

20, 35 **folly ··· were we led all that way:** Lawrence: "Glad as the Magi were when they saw the brow | Of the hot-born infant bless the folly which had | Led them thither", *Red Moon-Rise* (1912) 19–21.

21 **we came down to a temperate valley:** Kipling: "a big level valley all among the mountains", *The Man Who Would be King* (Childe, in Muir, *N&Q* Sept 1954). For the family camp of TSE's youth, see notes to *Dear Charlotte, Hoping you are better* ("Other Verses").

22 **below the snow line:** Kipling: "Till I camped above the tree-line", *The Explorer* 15.

23–27 **water-mill ··· Six hands at an open door dicing:** "certain images recur ··· six ruffians seen through an open window playing cards at night at a small French railway junction where there was a water-mill: such memories may have symbolic value, but of what we cannot tell", *The Use of Poetry and the Use of Criticism* 148. See *Marina* 3–4 and note. Henry James on a woman novelist: "These opportunities consisted in her having once, in Paris, as she ascended a staircase, passed an open door where, in the household of a *pasteur*, some of the young Protestants were seated at table round a finished meal. The glimpse made a picture; it lasted only a moment, but that moment was experience ··· she converted these ideas into a concrete image", *The Art of Fiction* (1884). TSE: "In some minds certain memories, both from reading and life, become charged with emotional significance", *Lecture Notes as Norton Professor* (1933). For "impressions and emotions", see note to *East Coker* III 33–35. *Tradition and the Individual Talent* II (1919): "Impressions and experiences which are important for the man may take no place in the poetry, and those which become important in the poetry may play quite a negligible part in the man, the personality"; in TSE's copy of the first American edition of *Selected Essays* (Magdalene), he scored the entire paragraph with a jagged line. **darkness · · · sky · · · hands at an open door dicing**: Rupert Brooke: "sky · · · playing cards, or standing in the doorway · · · darkness", *Fragment* 2–5.

24 **three trees on the low sky**: to Paul Gilson, 6 Mar 1928: "When I say 'Three trees on the low sky', I mean that three trees are outlined against the sky on the top of a very low hill." "The three trees are an anticipation of Golgotha", *Excerpts from Lectures 1932–1933*. Conrad Aiken: "Three crosses toss and rise | Black and little against the skies", *The Jig of Forslin* (1916) 95.

25 **an old white horse**: Revelation 19: 11–14: "I saw heaven opened, and behold a white horse; and he that sat upon him was called Faithful and True · · · and his name is called The Word of God. And the armies which were in heaven followed him upon white horses" (*Hands*). Kristian Smidt reported TSE saying the white horse was part of a remembered French landscape with no mythic significance (*Aftenposten*, Oslo, 25 Sept 1963).

27 **Six hands at an open door**: to Gilson, 6 Mar 1928: "you say '*Six mains, près d'une porte ouverte*'. What I mean is that the six hands are around a table inside the door and are seen through the door. Your translation seems to me to suggest that the hands were outside the door." **hands · · · pieces of silver**: Matthew 26: 15, 27: 35 : "And they covenanted with him for thirty pieces of silver · · · And they crucified him, and parted his garments, casting lots."

28 **empty wine-skins**: Matthew 9: 17 (Revised Version): "Neither do men put new wine into old wineskins."

31 **(you may say)**: to Gilson, 6 Mar 1928: "when I say · · · 'you may say', it is more 'perhaps', or '*pour ainsi dire*'. A certain doubt is left." **(you may say) satisfactory**: OED 1: "*Eccl.* and *Theol.* Serving to make satisfaction or atonement for sin." To H. B. Vaisey, 14 Jan 1937: "It is a relief · · · that you should have found my words on the whole satisfactory." After quoting a line of Poe: "We cannot admit that a poem which must have recourse to nonsense to convey its meaning is altogether satisfactory", *Poetical and Prosaic Use of Words* (1943). TSE's secretary to Nancy Pearce, 11 Dec 1958: "He has asked me to say · · · that he does not regard it as unsatisfactory that several people should disagree about the meaning of the word 'satisfactory' in *The Journey of the Magi*."

33–35 **but set down | This set down | This**: Andrewes: "Secondly, set down this; that to find where He is, we must learn of these to ask where He is", Christmas Sermon 1622.

34–35, 37 **set down | This · · · I had seen birth and death**: OTHELLO, about to kill himself: "Nor set down aught in malice · · · Set you down this", V ii (*Grover Smith* 313). "the true mystic is not satisfied merely by feeling, he must pretend at least that he *sees* · · · The poet does not aim to excite · · · but to set something down", *Dante* (1920).

37 **I had seen birth and death**: "We have seen births, deaths and marriages · · · A fear like birth and death, when we see birth and death alone", *Murder in the Cathedral* I. Birth and death in other Ariel Poems: *A Song for Simeon* 37: "this birth season of decease"; *Animula* 37: "Pray for us now and at the hour of our

birth"; *Marina* 7, 29: "Death · · · this life"; *The Cultivation of Christmas Trees* 1, 21: "Christmas · · · the awareness of death".

37–38 **I had seen birth and death, | But had thought they were different**: R. B. Cunninghame Graham: "'Fate has deprived me of the joy of being present at the birth of him the star announced; I can at least be present at his death · · · and birth and death are not so very different, after all'", *The Fourth Magus* in *Hope* (1910) (Neil Taylor, *N&Q* Aug 1982).

38–39 **this Birth was | Hard and bitter agony**: on a contributor to *NEW*: "when he speaks of 'agony and passion' he is transferring to the Incarnation two terms · · · properly applicable to the Atonement", *The Theology of Economics* (1934).

40–41 **We returned to our places, these Kingdoms, | But no longer at ease here**: "That though again they see their fatherland | They there shall be as citizens no more", *To the Class of 1905* 11–12.

40–42 **these Kingdoms · · · alien people · · · their gods**: Daniel 2: 44: "shall the God of heaven set up a kingdom · · · the kingdom shall not be left to other people, but it shall break in pieces and consume all these kingdoms." **Kingdoms · · · an alien people**: "an alien reign", *Ash-Wednesday* I 8 *variant*. **an alien people**: Pound: "among some | Alien people!" *The Plunge* (1912) 19–20 (included by TSE in Pound's *Selected Poems*). TSE: "My alien people", *Little Gidding* II 67–93, *prose synopsis* [6], also *second venture in verse* [14]. "We are certainly a minority, even in what are called Christian countries; we find the minds of the people about us growing more and more alien, so that on vital matters we often find we have no common assumptions", *The Christian in the Modern World* (1935).

41 **dispensation**: frequent in Andrewes's Christmas Sermon for 1623 (on Ephesians 1: 10), which devotes two paragraphs to the word. Also Ephesians 3: 2: "the dispensation of the grace of God which is given me to you-ward."

43 **I should be glad of another death**: to Paul Gilson, 6 Mar 1928: "in the English text I think it is quite clear to the readers that the speaker of the verses means that he would be glad to die himself. As I read your translation I cannot call it incorrect, but it would seem to me, if I did not know the original, that the speaker would be glad if *somebody else* died. The whole point is that in his state of indecision he would be glad if his own death came to settle it." "Birth, and copulation, and death. | I've been born, and once is enough", *Sweeney Agonistes: Fragment of an Agon* 36–37.

A Song for Simeon

Published separately Sept 1928, with a drawing by E. McKnight Kauffer. A signed, limited edition on large paper was issued in Oct 1928; repr. in *The Modern Muse: Poems of To-day British and American* (1934; not in *Gallup*), then *1936+* and *Penguin* / *Sel Poems*.

Recorded, 13 May 1947, Harvard, as part of the Morris Gray Poetry Reading. Second: May 1947, for the Harvard Poetry Room; released by Harvard Vocarium Records, 1948. Third: 28 Sept 1955, London; released by Caedmon 1955 (US), 1960 (UK).

McKnight Kauffer was sent the poem on 30 May 1928.

Title **A Song for Simeon**: Luke 2: 25–34, the presentation of the infant Christ for circumcision in the Temple, at Candlemas, now 2 February:

> And, behold, there was a man in Jerusalem, whose name was Simeon; and the same man was just and devout, waiting for the consolation of Israel · · · And it was revealed unto him by the Holy Ghost, that he should not see death, before he had seen the Lord's Christ. And he came by the Spirit into the temple: and when the parents brought in the child Jesus, to do for him after the custom of the law, Then took he him up in his arms, and blessed God, and said, Lord, now lettest thou thy servant depart in peace, according to thy word: For mine eyes have seen thy salvation · · · A light to lighten the Gentiles, and the glory of thy people Israel. And Joseph and his mother marvelled at those things which were spoken of him. And Simeon blessed them.

A Song *for* Simeon may be one for him to sing or one sung for him (Patrick Comerford, personal communication); see *Tomlin* in headnote to *Lines for an Old Man*. The Song *of* Simeon, or *Nunc Dimittis*, appears in the Prayer Book for use at evening service. (For Andrewes on "bring this to a *Nunc*", see note to *Burnt Norton* I 1.) In 1886, shortly before his death, TSE's grandfather wrote his own two-stanza *Nunc Dimittis*, printed by TSE's mother in her biography *William Greenleaf Eliot* (1904) 351–52 (*Oser* 94–95). Against a speculation in the 1961 ts of *Howarth* that this Ariel poem concerned his grandfather, TSE wrote "This is utter nonsense. I was not thinking of my grandfather" (*Materer*). ***Song***: to the translator Georges Cattaui, 21 July 1932: "I think that *Cantique* is preferable to *chant*".

1–2 **the Roman hyacinths are blooming in bowls and | The winter sun**: "F. M.": "My hyacinths are bursting clumsily out of their pots, as they always do, coming into misshapen bloom before their time. And this is the essential spring—spring in winter", opening words of *Letters of the Moment* I (1924), dated "February 10th" (*Loretta Johnson 1988*). "Midwinter · · · short day · · · brief sun · · · bloom", *Little Gidding* I 1, 4–5, 16. Roman hyacinths bloom in time for Christmas.

3 **The stubborn season:** Beaumont and Fletcher: "the stubborn season, | That yet holds in the fruit", *The Coxcomb* IV ii.

4 **My life is light, waiting for the death wind:** "the wind · · · Carrying | Away the little light dead people", *WLComposite* 174–76.

6 **Dust in sunlight:** "Sudden in a shaft of sunlight | Even while the dust moves", *Burnt Norton* V 33–34 (*Preston* 22). "And dusty roses, crickets, sunlight on the sea", *Goldfish* III 7.

7 **towards:** pronounced *to'rd* in all three of TSE's recordings, as also in *Marina* 33 in the recordings of 1933 and 1955.

7 *variant* **Blooming at this season toward the dead land:** "breeding | Lilacs out of the dead land, mixing", *The Waste Land* [I] 1–2. "This is the dead land", *The Hollow Men* III 1.

8 **Grant us thy peace:** morning and evening prayer: "Grant us thy salvation · · · Give peace in our time, O Lord", Book of Common Prayer.

12 **rejected:** Isaiah 53: 3: "despised and rejected of men" (*Grover Smith* 126).

15 **the fox's home**: Lamentations 5: 18: "Because of the mountain of Zion, which is desolate, the foxes walk upon it" (*Jain 1991*). Matthew 8: 20: "And Jesus saith unto him, The foxes have holes, and the birds of the air have nests; but the Son of man hath not where to lay his head" (*Grover Smith* 126).

15–16 *variant* **into rocky places, | Fleeing from the foreign faces**: "on sweaty faces ··· in stony places", *The Waste Land* [V] 322–24.

16 **the foreign faces and the foreign swords**: Conrad: "the foreign shores, the foreign faces", *Heart of Darkness* pt. 1 (*Grover Smith* 313).

17 **scourges**: Matthew 27: 26: "when he had scourged Jesus, he delivered him to be crucified".

17–20 **Before the ··· Before the ··· mountain of desolation ··· Before the**: "After the ··· After the ··· After the ··· distant mountains", *The Waste Land* [V] 322–27. **lamentation ··· mountain of desolation ··· the certain hour of maternal sorrow**: "murmur of maternal lamentation ··· the city over the mountains ··· the hours", *The Waste Land* [V] 367–71, 383. **stations of the mountain**: the fourteen Stations of the Cross represent the scenes of Christ's suffering and death. **mountain of desolation**: Calvary. Mark 13: 14: "when ye shall see the abomination of desolation ··· then let them that be in Judæa flee to the mountains" (*Jain 1991*). Lamentations 5: 18: "the mountain of Zion, which is desolate". **desolation**: pronounced *dezolation* in TSE's three recordings.

20–21 **maternal sorrow, | Now at this birth season of decease**: John 16: 20–21: "ye shall be sorrowful, but your sorrow shall be turned into joy. A woman when she is in travail hath sorrow, because her hour is come: but as soon as she is delivered of the child, she remembereth no more the anguish, for joy that a man is born into the world." See note to *Journey of the Magi* 37, "I had seen birth and death".

22 **the still unspeaking and unspoken Word**: see *Gerontion* 17–19 and note. "the unspoken word, the Word unheard", *Ash-Wednesday* V 4.

24 **one who has eighty years and no to-morrow**: Donne: "This, no to morrow hath, nor yesterday", *The Anniversary* 8. Herbert: "When a friend askes, there is no to morrow", *Outlandish Proverbs* no. 32. Johnson: "Tho' now his eightieth year was nigh ··· Death broke at once the vital chain", *On the Death of Dr. Robert Levet* 32, 35. TSE: "(By 'eightieth' meaning whichever is the last)", *The Cultivation of Christmas Trees* 28. Also: "the 80th Xmas tree ··· the 80th Festival", *The Cultivation of Christmas Trees, first full draft* 21, 33.

27 **glory and derision**: Milton: "glorious for a while ··· Thy foes' derision", *Samson Agonistes* 363–66.

29 **Not for me the martyrdom**: to Karin Henn, 22 Oct 1958: "Personally I am of the opinion that Archbishop Becket was a real martyr, because I believe that he had overcome the temptation of wishing to become a martyr." Donne: "Oh, to some | Not to be Martyrs, is a martyrdome", *The Litanie* X, "The Martyrs".

31 **Grant me thy peace**: "Graunt us thy peace", Bk. of Common Prayer (1549), *Agnus Dei* (Jamie Callison, *N&Q* Dec 2014).

32–33 **(And a sword shall pierce thy heart, | Thine also)**: Luke 2: 35: "(Yea, a sword shall pierce through thy own soul also)."

36 **Let thy servant depart:** see note to title. Pound had adapted Luke 2: 29 in *Instigations* (1920): "Nunc dimittis, now lettest thou thy servant, | Now lettest thou thy servant | Depart in peace", *Cantico del Sole* 9–11.

Animula

Published separately Oct 1929, with engravings by Gertrude Hermes. A signed, limited edition on large paper was issued later the same month; repr. in *Modern Things* ed. Parker Tyler (1934), the first US publication; then *1936+* and *Penguin / Sel Poems*.

TSE was at first dissatisfied with the engraving for inside the booklet, by Gertrude Hermes (1901–83), whose husband Blair Hughes-Stanton had illustrated Ariel poems by Walter de la Mare in 1927 (*Alone*) and 1928 (*Self to Self*). She was instructed by Richard de la Mare "that if there is to be a figure in it at all, he thinks it should be made to appear very much younger" (19 July 1929, Faber archive). She submitted a second design, but TSE then expressed his preference for the first.

On 28 Oct 1932 United States Customs notified the Intimate Bookshop, Chapel Hill, that a copy of *Animula*, imported from London, had been seized as being "in violation of Section 305 of the Tariff Act of 1930". TSE to Milton Abernethy, 18 Nov 1932: "I have been puzzling over the matter for a week, as not by the maddest imagination could one find anything censorable in this poem. I finally asked a friend to exercise his wits upon it; and he pointed out, what I should never have thought of for myself, that the trouble must be with the illustration. It is a perfectly irrelevant decorative drawing by Gertrude Hermes, somewhat in the manner of Blake, depicting a naked man with normal genitalia. I suppose that this must be the cause of offense, though I should never have thought of it."

Recorded 23 May 1947, National Gallery of Art, Washington.

TSE in *Dante* (1929) II, quoting *Purg.* XVI 85–96 with his own translation:

> In the XVIth Canto of the *Purgatorio* we meet Marco Lombardo, who discourses at some length on the Freedom of the Will, and on the Soul:
>
> *Esce di mano a lui, che la vagheggia*
> *prima che sia, a guisa di fanciulla*
> *che piangendo e ridendo pargoleggia,*
> *l'anima semplicetta, che sa nulla,*
> *salvo che, mossa da lieto fattore,*
> *volentier torna a ciò che la trastulla.*
> *Di picciol bene in pria sente sapore;*
> *quivi s'inganna, e retro ad esso corre,*
> *se guida o fren non torce suo amore.*
> *Onde convenne legge per fren porre;*
> *convenne rege aver, che discernesse*
> *della vera cittade almen la torre.*
>
> *From the hands of Him who loves her before she is, there issues like a little child that plays, with weeping and laughter, the simple soul, that knows nothing except that, come from the hands of a glad creator, she turns willingly to everything that delights her. First she tastes*

> *the flavour of a trifling good; then is beguiled and pursues it, if neither guide nor check withhold her. Therefore laws were needed as a curb; a ruler was needed, who should at least see afar the tower of the true City.*

TSE had previously quoted 85–93 in *Sir John Davies* (1926), adding the Temple tr. when reprinting the essay in *On Poetry and Poets*: "From his hands who fondly loves her ere she is in being, there issues, after the fashion of a little child that sports, now weeping, now laughing, the simple, tender soul, who knoweth naught save that, sprung from a joyous maker, willingly she turneth to that which delights her. First she tastes the savour of a trifling good; there she is beguiled and runneth after it, if guide or curb turn not her love aside."

Two years before *Animula*, TSE criticised Wordsworth's *Ode: Intimations of Immortality from Recollections of Early Childhood* and other such writings about the "imagined radiance" of childhood: "it does not occur to Mr. Blunden that this love of one's own childhood, a passion which he appears to share with Lamb and Vaughan, is anything but a token of greatness. We all know the mood; and we can, if we choose to relax to that extent, indulge in the luxury of reminiscence of childhood; but if we are at all mature and conscious, we refuse to indulge this weakness to the point of writing and poeticizing about it", *The Silurist* (1927).

To John Cournos, 28 Dec 1929, after promising to send a copy of *Dante*: "I will also send a copy of my Christmas verses—though they are rather depressing ones!"

Title ***Animula***: at the head of the translations in Byron's *Hours of Idleness* stands the short poem by the Emperor Hadrian entitled *Adrian's Address* | *To His Soul When Dying*, followed by Byron's translation:

> Animula! vagula, blandula,
> Hospes, comesque, corporis,
> Quæ nunc abibis in loca?
> Pallidula, rigida, nudula,
> Nec, ut soles, dabis jocos.
>
> Ah! gentle, fleeting, wav'ring sprite,
> Friend and associate of this clay!
> To what unknown region borne,
> Wilt thou now wing thy distant flight?
> No more, with wonted humour gay,
> But pallid, cheerless, and forlorn.

Hadrian's first four lines were used by Pater as the epigraph to *Marius the Epicurean* ch. VIII, "Animula Vagula" (*Grover Smith* 129). Like Heraclitus' Greek followers, Pater writes, Marius too "paused at the apprehension of that constant motion of things—the drift of flowers, of little or great souls, of ambitious systems, in the stream around him, the first source, the ultimate issue, of which, in regions out of sight, must count with him as but a dim problem." (For Pater's chapter see notes to *Do I know how I feel? Do I know what I think?* 1 and *A Cooking Egg* 20.) Pound's *"Blandula, Tenulla, Vagula"* appeared first in *Canzoni* (1911); he explained the connection with Pater to his father [28–30 Sept 1911], adding: "gentle, tender, wandering. only the 'ula' is a diminutive—which makes the adjectives all more whimsical, or ironical."

1 **Issues from the hand of God, the simple soul**: *Purg.* XVI 85–90 (see headnote).

TSE marked XVI 85–96 of the Italian in the copy his mother gave him; also XVIII 19–40, beginning "The mind which is created quick to love, is responsive to everything that is pleasing, soon as by pleasure it is awakened into activity." He quoted XVI 88 again in *The Varieties of Metaphysical Poetry* 56 (Clark Lecture I). "the soul crying", *In silent corridors of death* 4. "we may think, in rather mythological language, of a consciousness gradually realising itself by the effort of making itself its own objects", *The Ethics of Green and Sidgwick* (1914). **Issues:** for the abrupt opening syntax and stationing, *Mandarins* 1 1: "Stands there". But whereas the first line of *Animula* could follow on grammatically from the title, the singular verb "Stands there" could not follow on from the plural title *Mandarins*. In Beddoes's *Death's Jest-Book* III iii, Isbrand's Song begins: "Squats on a toad-stool under a tree | A bodiless childfull of life" (III iii 328–29); see note to *Coriolan* I. *Difficulties of a Statesman* 1. (TSE: "squats · · · spawned", *Gerontion* 8–9.) "at twelve o'clock | Issues the Westminster Gazette", *Airs of Palestine, No.* 2 11–12. To Bonamy Dobrée, 16 Oct 1955: "Now, on issuing into the world again, I am reminded that I had engaged myself." **simple soul:** "As a matter of fact, the human soul—*l'anima semplicetta*—is neither good nor bad; but in order to be good, in order to be human, requires *discipline*", *An American Critic* (1916) (*Ricks* 229); for Dante's "laws were needed", see headnote. TSE again: "the choice between Christianity and secularism is not simply presented to the innocent mind, *anima semplicetta*", *Revelation* (1937) 37. "a Dog is, on the whole, | What you would call a simple soul", *The Ad-dressing of Cats* 22–23.

2 **To a flat world:** see *Burnt Norton* I 21–22, "Into our first world · · · Into our first world", and note on Adamson's *The Individual and the Environment* (1921). The bestselling satirical novel *Flatland: A Romance of Many Dimensions* by "A Square" (Edwin Abbott Abbott) was published in 1884.

2, 14 **flat world · · · playing-cards and kings and queens:** see note to *The Waste Land* [I] 52, "the one-eyed merchant · · · this card". Pope: "Th' embroider'd *King* who shows but half his Face, | And his refulgent *Queen*", *The Rape of the Lock* III 76–77.

5 **grasping at kisses:** Laforgue's *Hamlet*, tr. Symons: "the little people of History, learning to read · · · fond of compliments, handshakes, and kisses", *Symons* 105–106 (for Laforgue's *Hamlet* see note to *Preludes* I 13 and related notes).

10 **Pleasure in the wind, the sunlight and the sea:** Swinburne: "Child of my sunlight and the sea", *Thalassius* 483–84 (Archie Burnett, personal communication). TSE: "And dusty roses, crickets, sunlight on the sea", *Goldfish* (*Essence of Summer Magazines*) III 7.

10–11 **the sea; | Studies the sunlit pattern on the floor:** "the sea · · · patterns · · · the floor", *Mandarins* 2 6–10.

14 **Content with playing-cards and kings and queens:** Baudelaire:

> Pour l'enfant, amoureux de cartes et d'estampes,
> L'univers est égal à son vaste appétit.
> Ah, que le monde est grand à la clarté des lampes!
> Aux yeux du souvenir que le monde est petit!

[For the child who adores maps and prints, the universe matches his vast appetite. Ah, how big the world is in the lamplight, but how small when viewed through the eyes of memory!] *Le Voyage* I 1–4, quoted in French in *The Metaphysical Poets* (1921) (*Grover Smith* 313).

14, 23 **playing-cards ··· the *Encyclopaedia Britannica*:** "against card houses ··· or objecting to the insistent advertisements of what he held to be a debased *Encyclopædia Britannica*", *Charles Whibley* (1931).

19 **imperatives of "is and seems":** *Hamlet* I ii: "Seems, madam! Nay it is; I know not seems" (*Jain 1991*).

22 **Curl up the small soul in the window seat:** "In nerveless torpor on the window seat", *WLComposite* 366.

22–23 **the small soul in the window seat | Behind the *Encyclopaedia Britannica*:** H. E. Bates: "The child was perching on a stool and the stool had been set on two volumes of the *Encyclopaedia Britannica*, so that the child could survey the world", *The Child* in *Criterion* Dec 1928 (K. N. Chandran, *English Studies* Aug 2007). Charlotte Brontë: "It contained a bookcase: I soon possessed myself of a volume, taking care that it should be one stored with pictures. I mounted into the window-seat", *Jane Eyre* ch. 1.

26 **fare forward:** see note to *The Dry Salvages* III 44–45.

27 **the warm reality:** "Inanimate objects take on animation of a kind; his old houses are not so much haunted by ghosts as they are ghosts themselves haunting the folk who briefly visit them. Under the influence of this sincere and tormented introspection, the warm reality dissolves: both that for which we hold out our arms, and that at which we strike vain blows", *Harold Monro* (1933) (*Ricks* 229).

29–30 **in its own gloom ··· in a dusty room:** "Inside the gloom | Of a garret room", *Inside the gloom* 1–2. "gloom ··· drawing-room", *Whispers of Immortality* 26, 28.

30 **Leaving disordered papers in a dusty room:** "'I suspect that within there is only the confusion of a dusty garret' ··· 'a room strewn with clothes, papers, cosmetics, letters and a few books'", *Eeldrop and Appleplex* II (1917). "Nor in documents eaten by the lean solicitor | In our empty rooms", *WLComposite* 654–55.

31 **viaticum:** OED 1: "*Eccl.* The Eucharist, as administered to or received by one who is dying"; 2: "A supply of money or other necessaries for a journey ··· travelling expenses."

32, 33, 36 **Guiterriez ··· Boudin, blown to pieces ··· Floret:** to Dudley Fitts, 6 June 1940: "Certainly the name I had in mind was Gutiérrez, and I cannot give any reason for having altered it. Like some other names, it just came into my head that way, and down it went. The figure, of course, is meant to be a type, but I did, as with the man blown to pieces, have a particular person in mind: a writer I used to know who was interested in politics and also had a passion for high-powered racing cars and motor cycles. But in this case, as in some others, identification would only obscure instead of clarifying". To Morris Gilbert, 10 Sept 1942: "if you have identified two persons alluded to in *Animula* you have preceded me in so doing because in neither line did I have any particular person in mind. Floret, I am afraid, is a pure piece of dream imagery not related to any person whom I know. As for Boudin and Guiterriez, they do not [*for* do] represent personal friends of mine, but the identification could neither throw light upon the poem nor add any pleasure to the reading of it. I must explain that at the time of writing the poem I was unaware that *boudin* is the French for black pudding. This is to me a nauseous dish, eaten in Scotland and in parts of France, and I have also observed it eaten in a Swedish restaurant-car with a sauce of stewed fruit. I regret very much that I chose such an unlucky name for a friend who was a very fine person and a gallant non-commissioned officer." (To Grover Smith, 4 July 1949: "You are right in saying that Boudin means black pudding in French. My only comment on this is that I did not know it at the time and if I had known it I would have made up some other name, because the last thing I wished to do was to associate this particular man with a black pudding.") To E. M. Stephenson, 25 May 1945: "As for the references about which you ask · · · I don't believe in inventing answers to satisfy people who ask the wrong questions, nor could any answer I gave really help the readers of that poem. The third of these figures is so entirely imaginary that there is really no identification to be made though perhaps it may suggest not wholly irrelevantly to some minds certain folklore memories. Of the first two, it is only necessary to say that they represent different types of career, the successful person of the machine age and someone who was killed in the last war." Victor Boudon's memoir of Charles Péguy, reviewed by TSE in *Charles Péguy* (1916), described how "At Villeroy, near Meaux, about 25 kilos. from Paris, he was killed; death was supposed to have been instantaneous—a bullet through the head"; see note to *A Cooking Egg* 25, 29.

36 **by the boarhound slain between the yew trees**: to John Hayward, 27 Apr 1930, on *Ash-Wednesday*: "Perhaps the yew does not mean so much as you suppose. It happened to occur in two or three dreams—one was a dream of 'the boarhound between the yewtrees'; and that's all I know about it." ("among the birch-trees", *Mr. Apollinax* 3.) **by the boarhound slain**: Actæon the hunter was torn to pieces by his own hounds after he saw Diana bathing; Adonis was killed by a wild boar.

Marina

Published separately 25 Sept 1930, with drawings by E. McKnight Kauffer. A signed, limited edition on large paper was issued later the same month. Published in the US in *The New Poetry* ed. Harriet Monroe and Alice Corbin Henderson (rev. ed. 1932) and repr. in *An "Objectivists" Anthology*, ed. Louis Zukofsky (1932). Repr. in Britain in *The Modern Muse: Poems of To-day British and American* (1934; not in *Gallup*), then *1936+*, *Sesame* and *Penguin* / *Sel Poems*.

Recorded May 1933, Columbia U. Second: 1946, Levy's Sound Studios, London for the Writers Group of the Society for Cultural Relations between the Peoples of the British Commonwealth and the USSR. Third: 23 May 1947, Washington DC. Fourth: 26 Sept 1955, London; released by Caedmon 1955 (US), 1959 (UK).

In *John Ford* (1932), TSE discusses *The Lover's Melancholy* in relation to "the Recognition Scene, so important in Shakespeare's later plays, to the significance of which as a Shakespeare symbol Mr. Wilson Knight has drawn attention. In Shakespeare's plays, this is primarily the recognition of a long-lost daughter, secondarily of a wife;

and we can hardly read the later plays attentively without admitting that the father-and-daughter theme was one of very deep symbolic value to him in his last productive years: Perdita, Marina and Miranda share some beauty of which his earlier heroines do not possess the secret."

In 1919: "Years of patient labour have so purified, transmogrified, and debased Shakespeare that several of his plays can be produced before audiences of the most civilized householders and shareholders in the world. And, of course, everyone knows that Shakespeare is not responsible for *Pericles*", *"The Duchess of Malfi" at the Lyric: and Poetic Drama* (1919/20). Despite its publication in 1609 as Shakespeare's, *Pericles* was not in the First Folio. It was staged at the Old Vic in 1921.

TSE on Shakespeare's late plays:

> The less popular plays are sometimes produced, and for *Troilus and Cressida*, *Measure for Measure*, and even *Timon*, there has been a small but enthusiastic public. I should say that in these plays there is as good dramatic verse as any Shakespeare ever wrote, and I would make that claim even for *The Winter's Tale* and *Pericles* · · ·
>
> · · · To compare Perdita or Miranda or Imogen or Marina, with, for instance, Juliet, to call them by comparison insipid or unreal, is to use a wholly irrelevant standard. They belong in a world from which some emotions have been purified away, so that others, ordinarily invisible, may be made apparent. To my mind the finest of all the "recognition scenes" is Act V, sc. i of that very great play *Pericles*. It is a perfect example of the "ultra-dramatic", a dramatic action of beings who are more than human. Shakespeare's consummate dramatic skill is as bright as ever; his verse is as much *speech* as ever: only, it is the speech of creatures who are more than human, or rather, seen in a light more than that of day.
>
> I am a maid
> My lord, that ne'er before invited eyes,
> But have been gazed on like a comet: she speaks,
> My lord, that maybe hath endured a grief
> Might equal yours, if both were justly weighed.
>
> The two voices, Pericles and Marina, are perfectly harmonized:
>
> Now, blessing on thee! rise; thou art my child.
> Give me fresh garments. Mine own, Helicanus:
> She is not dead at Tarsus, as she should have been,
> By savage Cleon.
>
> The "Give me fresh garments" emphasised presently by "Give me my robes" has great significance. The scene becomes a ritual; the poetic drama developed to its highest point turns back towards liturgy: and the scene could end in no other way than by the vision of Diana.
>
> *The Development of Shakespeare's Verse* (1937)

G. Wilson Knight's *Myth and Miracle: On the Mystic Symbolism of Shakespeare* (1929; collected in *The Crown of Life*, 1946) compares the works of Dante and Shakespeare to "that mystic truth from which are born the dogmas of the Catholic Church · · · the temptation in the desert, the tragic ministry and death, and the resurrection of the Christ". TSE in the Introduction to Wilson Knight's *The Wheel of Fire* (1930): "I like a definite and dogmatic philosophy, preferably a Christian and Catholic one · · · It happened, fortunately for myself, that when I read some of his papers, I was mulling over some of the later plays, particularly *Pericles*, *Cymbeline*, and *The Winter's Tale*;

and reading the later plays for the first time in my life as a separate group, I was impressed by what seemed to me important and very serious recurrences of mood and theme."

Wilson Knight: "That Eliot's response to *Myth and Miracle* had been more than courtesy was witnessed during the same year, 1930, when he sent me his *Marina*, inscribed 'for' me as 'with, I hope, some appropriateness'", *T. S. Eliot: Some Literary Impressions* in *Tate ed.* 247. TSE to Wilson Knight, 30 Oct 1930: "Thank you very much for your letter: few people would take the trouble to analyse a little poem like *Marina* so carefully, and few, I dare say, will care for it. I rather wanted you to like it, as you know the reference so well; I suspect that few persons in my acquaintance can remember *Pericles* at all clearly. I do not know whether you understand that the quotation is from Seneca's *Hercules Furens*; and that I wanted a crisscross between Hercules waking up to find that he had slain his children, and Pericles waking up to find his child alive. I did not add the reference *Hercules Furens* for fear of misleading people who had not read the play itself." TSE wrote to M. E. Cameron Watson, 29 June 1939, that the only criticism he knew of *Marina* specifically was by Wilson Knight, referring to "A Note on T. S. Eliot" in *The Christian Renaissance* (1933), which had "interested me very much".

To Michael Sadler, 9 May 1930, enclosing drafts of *Marina* for the Bodleian Library. "I intend a crisscross between Pericles finding alive, and Hercules finding dead—the two extremes of the recognition scene—but I thought that if I labelled the quotation it might lead readers astray rather than direct them. It is only an accident that I know Seneca better than I know Euripides."

To E. McKnight Kauffer, 24 July 1930: "I was relieved to hear from [Richard] De la Mare that he had confided my *Marina* to you. I had meant to ask him to do so, before he went away, and was afraid that it had gone elsewhere. Yours is the only kind of decoration that I can endure ··· The theme is paternity; with a crisscross between the text and the quotation. The theme is a comment on the Recognition Motive in Shakespeare's later plays, and particularly of course the recognition of Pericles. The quotation is from *Hercules Furens*, where Hercules, having killed his children in a fit of madness induced by an angry god, comes to without remembering what he has done. (I didn't give the reference for fear it might be more distracting than helpful to the reader who did not grasp the exact point: the contrast of death and life in Hercules and Pericles). I wonder whether this sort of explanation is useful or rather a bother to the artist? The scenery in which it is dressed up is Casco Bay, Maine. I am afraid no scenery except the Mississippi, the prairie and the North East Coast has ever made much impression on me." (For Maine, see note to 3^4 *variant* "Roque Island".)

To Kauffer, 8 Aug 1930: "Since I wrote to you I have seen your illustrations, which I like very much, except for the one point about which I spoke to de la Mare. It seems to me a pity that de la Mare did not shew me the drawing when he received it, as it might have saved you considerable trouble. My criticism was not of the drawing at all, but merely meant that I don't want what I write to have *The Waste Land* stamped upon it" (see Textual History).

To Kauffer [end of Sept 1930]: "I am delighted to have the beautiful drawing, with the inscription, and shall have it framed to match the other (*Simeon*) which I appropriated. I had not seen the original when in de la Mare's hands and was surprised by the difference. I must say that I like the colouring of the drawing you have given me very much better than that of the printed *Marina*. I wish that the poem had been printed according to this one." In June 1938, TSE opened an exhibition of advertising by Shell-Mex and BP, where Kauffer was a leading designer, and in 1940 he wrote what became *Defence of the Islands* to accompany an exhibition organised by Kauffer in New York. Asked to contribute to a profile of Kauffer in 1949, he wrote: "I think it was at the end, or shortly after the end of the first World War that I met McKnight Kauffer, who was already, I think, better known and remarked among the younger artists than I was amongst the men of letters. He was in appearance very much the same figure that he is to-day: tall, slender and elegantly-dressed, and wearing whatever he wore with a grace that would make the best of the best efforts of the best tailor. (I cannot venture to say much about his appearance, because there is said to be a facial resemblance between Kauffer and myself—at any rate, when I have asked for him at the building in which he lives, several successive porters have taken for granted that I was his brother)."

On 28 Oct 1958, TSE wrote to F. D. Hoeniger (editor of the second Arden ed. of the play, 1963): "Yes, *Marina* was suggested by the recognition scene in Shakespeare's *Pericles* and has to do, of course, with the same father–daughter relationship. I had no daughter, but the relationship interested me and, of course, recognition, in my experience, is something that comes repeatedly in life. [*Added note*: One can have fresh 'recognition' of the same person.] (A fresh recognition of the familiar would be an interesting theme, but perhaps impossible to express in terms of the theatre). The quotation from Seneca was intended to express the reverse. As you know, Hercules, in the play of Seneca, came to his senses to see his children dead in front of him, before he realized that they were dead by his own hand. That is merely an antithetical form or recognition. I think that an interest not only in *Pericles* but in all Shakespeare's late plays has increased during the last twenty years. Some of the merit for calling attention to the beauty of the later plays is due, I think, to Professor Wilson Knight. The old assumption that Shakespeare was merely trying to adapt himself to a changing taste and compete with Beaumont and Fletcher is, I should imagine, now generally rejected."

To Hayward, 29 Nov 1939: "I have no family, no career, and nothing particular to look forward to in this world. I doubt the permanent value of everything I have written; I never lay with a woman I liked, loved or ever felt any strong physical attraction to; I no longer even regret this lack of experience; I no longer even feel acutely the desire for progeny which was very acute once."

Frank Herrmann recorded how in the late 1950s his wife would leave their infant daughter outside Faber. "After a particularly prolonged visit on a wintery day, Patricia came down stairs to find the *pram missing*! Panic! Miss Swann was endlessly on the phone. 'Where has the pram gone?' Patricia finally shouted. 'Oh', said Miss Swann, 'Camilla had kicked off all her blankets when Mr. Eliot came by on his way out to lunch. So he tucked her up and is pushing the pram round the Square.' TSE was gone for forty-five minutes while Patricia went back into the office. Pram pushing was not a role in which one easily envisaged Mr. Eliot. We often wondered whether the experience was a vicarious substitute for unfulfilled parenthood", *Faber's Forty-Five Years Ago* part III in *Antiquarian Book Monthly Review* Nov 1992.

In 1932: "He also told me that *Marina* is the poem that he likes best of all he has written", Aurelia Hodgson notes on TSE from conversations (Bryn Mawr).

Title ***Marina***: PERICLES: "my gentle babe *Marina*, | Whom, for she was born at sea, I have named so, | Here I charge your charity withal" (III iii).

Epigraph] [What place is this? what region? or of the world what coast?], Seneca, *Hercules Furens* 1138; tr. Jasper Heywood (1561); see note to *Burbank with a Baedeker: Bleistein with a Cigar* 7–12. To John Hayward, 30 Oct 1930: "I wonder if the reference at the head of the poem to the *Hercules Furens* (Hercules coming to and finding that he has killed his children) gets over to the few people who have read either Euripides or Seneca." In conversation with William Empson, 12 May 1959: "Seneca isn't in the school syllabus, so all the classical men were caught out", reported in *Argufying* 365. Empson: "Hercules' first words in Seneca when he is recovering from the madness in which he has killed his children: a madness sent from heaven, through no fault of his own, after a successful descent into hell and a successful killing of his enemies", *Argufying* 360.

1 **What ··· what ··· what ··· what:** *Pericles* V ii: "What pageantry, what feats, what shows, | What minstrelsy and pretty din" (Jason Harding, *EinC* Apr 2012). TSE, ms contribution to *Letters of the Moment* I (1924) by "F. M.": "What happy meetings, what luminous conversations in twilight rooms filled with the scent of hyacinths, await me now?" (c. 624 fol. 100). **What ··· shores:** *Pericles* V i: "What countrywoman? | Here of these shores?"

1–4 **What seas what shores what grey rocks and what islands ··· What images:** Whitman: "What widens within you Walt Whitman? | What waves and soils exuding? | What climes? ··· What rivers are these? what forests and fruits are these? | What are the mountains call'd that rise so high in the mists?" *Salut au Monde!* 5–12 (*Musgrove* 27).

1, 5, 21 **What seas what shores ··· what islands ··· O my daughter ··· where all the waters meet:** From the same year *Moody* 114 points to:

> O my people what have I done unto thee
> In this pool all the waves are silent
> In this pool all the seas are still
> All the waves die against this island
> Our life is in the world's decease
> Our peace
> In his will.
> Suffer me not to be separated
> O my people
>
> *Ash-Wednesday* VI 19–35 *variant*

3–4 **the woodthrush singing through the fog | What images return**: "Why, for all of us, out of all that we have heard, seen, felt, in a lifetime, do certain images recur, charged with emotion, rather than others? The song of one bird", *The Use of Poetry and the Use of Criticism* 148. **woodthrush singing:** see *Burnt Norton* I 22–27 and note on Whitman.

3^4 *variant* **Roque Island**: to Robert L. Beare, 25 Oct 1955: "The place to which you refer as 'Rogue Island' is presumably 'Roque Island' not far from Jonesport, Maine. The localisation is certainly something that I did well to omit from the final version." (The word is not clearly written in ms, and Grover Smith made the same error.)

3, 15, 22 **pine ··· singing ··· pine, and the woodsong ··· Bowsprit cracked with**

ice and paint cracked with heat: Kipling: "hemp and singing pine for to stand against the brine ··· Our paint is flaked ··· no vigil at the bow", *The Second Voyage* 6, 10, 15.

5 **O my daughter**: ms reading also of the final line. *Pericles*: "O royal Pericles", "O let me look!", "O my lord" (all V iii); "O, attend, my daughter" (II iii) (*Stephen Matthews* 151). *Cymbeline* V v: "yet (Oh my daughter)".

5–6 **daughter ··· sharpen the tooth**: KING LEAR (to his daughter Goneril): "sharper than a serpent's tooth it is | To have a thankless child!" (I iv). **sharpen the tooth**: "toothed ··· shark", *Ash-Wednesday* III 11 (see note). *Pericles* I iv: "so sharp are hunger's teeth".

6–7 **who sharpen the tooth of the dog, meaning | Death**: dog-fighting was outlawed in England and Wales in 1835. "Men! polish your teeth on rising and retiring; | Women! polish your fingernails: | You polish the tooth of the dog and the talon of the cat ··· Death", *Choruses from "The Rock"* VI 14–16, 18. "Who clipped the lion's wings | And flea'd his rump and pared his claws", *Burbank with a Baedeker: Bleistein with a Cigar* 29–30.

6, 8, 10, 12 **Those who ··· Those who**: "those who collect quails in the wrinkled land, those who hunt among the furze for the green-speckled eggs, those who dismount to pick things up", *Anabasis* X vii (*Abel*).

6–13 **meaning | Death ··· meaning | Death**: Romans 6: 23: "The wages of sin is death" (*Grover Smith* 132). TSE: "an accumulation of old buildings, however beautiful, means death unless we can also make beautiful new buildings", *A Commentary* in *Criterion* Oct 1934.

7, 9, 11, 13 **Death**: "death" occurs seven times at line-endings in *Pericles*. TSE of Donne's *The First Anniversary* and *The Second Anniversary*: "nowhere did he rise to greater heights of verbal and metrical beauty ··· Compare, for instance, the funeral sermon in which recurs so persistently the word 'DEAD', as a musical bar by itself ··· with the recurrence in variation in the *First Anniversary* of 'Shee, shee is dead; she's dead: when thou know'st this, | Thou know'st how lame a cripple this world is . . . Shee, shee is dead; shee's dead: when thou know'st this, | Thou know'st how ugly a monster this world is'", *The Varieties of Metaphysical Poetry* 157–58 (Clark Lecture V). Donne: "When you shall find that hand that had signed to one of you a *Patent* for *Title*, to another for *Pension*, to another for *Pardon*, to another for *Dispensation*, *Dead*: That hand that settled Possessions by his *Seale*, in the *Keeper*, and rectified *Honours* by the *sword*, in his *Marshall*, and distributed relief to the *Poore*, in his *Almoner*, and *Health* to the *Diseased*, by his *immediate Touch*, Dead ··· Dead ··· Dead ··· dead", Sermon on the death of King James, 26 Apr 1625 (*Sermons* ed. Pearsall Smith, 57–58).

8 **glitter with the glory of the hummingbird**: Mayne Reid: "Listen to his whirring wings, like the hum of a great bee. It is from that he takes his name of 'humming-bird.' See his throat, how it glitters—just like a ruby!" *The Boy Hunters* 140 (*Crawford* 21–22).

8–9 **glitter ··· the hummingbird, meaning | Death**: D. H. Lawrence quotes Crèvecoeur on hummingbirds: "They often fight with the fury of lions, and one of the combatants falls a sacrifice and dies", adding "they start and flash their wings like little devils, and stab each other with egoistic sharp bills", *Studies in Classic American Literature* ch. 3.

10 **sty:** *Pericles* IV vi (Quarto; the brothel scene): MARINA: "most ungentle Fortune have plac't mee in this Stie." TSE on his own spelling, to Robert L. Beare, 25 Oct 1955: "*sty* is misspelt in every edition. Pig's sty is s-t-y, and it is curious that I gave it the extra 'e' which gives the word an entirely different meaning." See Textual History to *Mr. Pugstyles: The Elegant Pig* 27 and to *Little Gidding* I 29 for "sty" again misspelt and corrected.

10–12 **the sty of contentment, meaning | Death ··· the animals:** Irving Babbitt quoted Sainte-Beuve: "never be able to treat man in exactly the same way as plants or animals", followed at once by Emerson on scientific materialism: "one lives in a sty of sensualism, and would soon come to suicide", *The Masters of Modern French Criticism* (1912) 246.

13–15 **Death ··· unsubstantial, reduced by a wind, | A breath:** OED "unsubstantial" 2: "Having no bodily or material substance", begins with Shakespeare: "Shall I beleeue that unsubstantiall death is amorous?" (*Romeo and Juliet* V iii) and "Welcome then, | Thou unsubstantiall ayre that I embrace" (*King Lear* IV i). Likewise, "insubstantial" 1: "Not existing in substance or reality", begins with Shakespeare: "And like this insubstantiall Pageant faded | Leaue not a racke behinde" (*The Tempest* IV i). TSE: "My life is light, waiting for the death wind", *A Song for Simeon* 4. See note to *WLComposite* 175–76, "Carrying | Away the little light dead people".

14–21 **reduced by a wind, | A breath of pine ··· nearer than the eye ··· between leaves and hurrying feet | Under sleep:** Pound: "All night, and as the wind lieth among | The cypress trees, he lay ··· light as leaves | And closer me than air", *Speech for Psyche in the Golden Book of Apuleius* (1911); included by TSE in Pound's *Selected Poems*. **breath of the pine:** Vachel Lindsay: "*Yea, from the breath of the pine!*", *The Black Hawk War of the Artists* 12, 54 in *Poetry* July 1914. **woodsong:** OED has no definition but three citations: "Fall to your wod-songs" (1601); "The sweet wood-song's penetrating flow" (Felicia Hemans, 1834); and TSE.

16 *variant* **The world in chase:** OED "chase" *n.*[1] e: "*in chase* is said both of the chaser and of the chase".

16–17 **this grace ··· place ··· face:** Herbert: "The soldiers also spit upon that face, | Which Angels did desire to have the grace | And Prophets once to see, but found no place", *The Sacrifice* 181–83. Kipling: "Not for Prophecies, Visions, Gifts, or Graces", rhyming with "places" and "faces", *The Supports* (TSE: "Given", 19). Kipling's poem speaks of the ocean, a ship, a bulkhead, fathers, our children, and the shore.

17 **face, less clear and clearer:** 1 Corinthians 13: 12: "For now we see through a glass, darkly, but then face to face" (*Jain 1991*).

18 **The pulse in the arm:** *Pericles* V i: "But are you flesh and blood? | Have you a working pulse?" (*Grover Smith* 313).

19 **Given or lent:** Tennyson: "God gives us love. Something to love | He lends us", *To J. S.* 13–14. Alice Meynell: "Given, not lent, | And not withdrawn—once sent", *Unto us a Son is Given* 1–2 (*Grover Smith* 132). Kipling: "Our loves are not given, but only lent", *The Power of the Dog* 27 (Jennifer Formichelli, personal communication).

19–20 **more distant than stars and nearer than the eye ··· feet:** Tennyson: "Closer is He than breathing, and nearer than hands and feet ··· the eye of man cannot see", *The Higher Pantheism* 12, 17 (TSE: "breath", 15). TSE: "More distant and more solemn | Than a fading star", *The Hollow Men* II 9–10.

20 **small laughter between leaves:** Pound: "The laugh they wake amid the border rushes. | This is our home, the trees are full of laughter", "and all the leaves are full of voices", Canto I (first version, *Poetry* June 1917) 58–59, 128. This canto quotes and names *Pericles* (William Harmon, *Yeats Eliot Review* Spring 1978). TSE: "the leaves were full of children, | Hidden excitedly, containing laughter", "hidden laughter | Of children in the foliage", *Burnt Norton* I 40–41, V 35–36. **laughter between leaves and hurrying feet:** John Davidson: "the tread; | Burst of laughter from the shuffled leaves", *November* III. **laughter ··· and hurrying feet:** Conrad Aiken: "clamor of music and hurrying feet", *The Jig of Forslin* (1916), V vi. TSE: "weary feet, | Forever hurrying", *On a Portrait* 2–3.

20–21 **Whispers and small laughter between leaves ··· sleep, where all the waters meet:** "Laughter and apple-blossom floating on the water, | Singing at nightfall, whispering", *Murder in the Cathedral* I.

20–21 *variant* **in a new world:** "O brave new world", *The Tempest* V i.

22 **Bowsprit:** pronounced by TSE in his 1933 recording as in *rainbow* (the English manner), but in 1955 as in *bough*. *The Columbiad* had rhymed "bowsprit" with "cowshit". At the end of his *Lines Addressed to Geoffrey Faber Esq*. TSE makes comic play where "avow | bow" turns out to be only an eye-rhyme because the meaning is longbow. **cracked with ice ··· cracked with heat:** Baudelaire: "La glace qui les mord, les soleils qui les cuivrent, | Effacent lentement la marque des baisers" [the ice's tooth, the suns that burn them bronze, gradually efface the stigmata of kisses], *Le Voyage* I 15–16 (*Kenner* 234). "Where's a cocktail shaker, Ben, here's plenty of cracked ice", *WLComposite* 554.

27 **unknown, my own:** *Pericles* V i: "rise: thou art my child: | Give me fresh garments. Mine own, Helicanus", quoted by TSE in *The Development of Shakespeare's Verse* (1937) (Iman Javadi, personal communication).

28 **The garboard strake leaks, the seams need caulking:** in his *Life of Dryden*, Dr. Johnson deplored Dryden's use of "nautical language" in *Annus Mirabilis* 581–92, the description of repairs after the battle at sea. He italicised a dozen words in the dozen lines, including *calking-iron* and *seams* and commented: "I suppose here is not one term which every reader does not wish away." (Johnson's objection was disputed in an essay, *Poetic Diction of English Classicists*, by Raymond Dexter Havens, in the Harvard Festschrift for George Kittredge: see note to *The Waste Land* [V] 399–422.) For the garboard-strake and Kipling see note to *WLComposite* 501: "And then the garboard-strake began to leak". TSE: "the mizzen top-gallant shrouds had been repeatedly belayed to the fore staysail, and the flying jib-boom cleared, and lashed to the monkey-rail", *A Tale of a Whale* (1905). **caulking:** *Pericles* III i: "we have a chest beneath the hatches, caulked and bitumed ready".

30–31 **a world of time ··· Resign my life for this life:** "the hand of time ··· Unable to resign or to insist", *Animula* 24, 26 *variant*. **Resign my life:** *Titus Andronicus* I i: "Tomorrow yield up rule, resign my life" (Jason Harding, *EinC* Apr 2012).

32 **The awakened:** believing her dead, Pericles commits his wife Thaisa to the sea

during the storm, but when her casket comes ashore she revives (III ii). TSE to Virginia Woolf, 28 Dec 1939, on reading William Archer's translation of Ibsen's *When we Dead Awaken*: "(Why does Archer say 'awaken' instead of 'awake'?) (I thought that awaken was transitive)." See note to *Sweeney Agonistes: Fragment of an Agon* 160, "you waked up".

33–34 **What seas what shores what granite islands ··· fog:** Roy Campbell's hundred-line *Tristan da Cunha* has "mist ··· An island of the sea ··· suns that sink and shores that fade ··· granite". TSE praised the poem on publication: "His control of the metre is remarkable, and his language stronger and less flamboyant than in some of his earlier work", *Tristan da Cunha* (1927). In 1930 he became its publisher when Campbell collected it in his first Faber book, *Adamastor* (*McCue 2014d*).

The Cultivation of Christmas Trees

Published separately in distinct editions in New York (8 Oct 1954) and London (26 Oct 1954), with no variants. British ed. illustrated by David Jones (see end of notes). American ed. with "Typography, binding and decorations by Enrico Arno". Added to "Ariel Poems", *1963+* (the only poem ever added to an existing section). No recording known.

Written in 1952 (see letter to Curtis quoted below) and "more or less to order" (Columbia reading, 28 Apr 1958, *Columbia U. Forum* Fall 1958, 14).

"I do not consider it very well executed, but I hope that the idea is a right one", *Levy* 53. Inscribed copies: "for Anne Ridler | an F. & F. pot boiler— | the doctrine is better | than the verse. | T. S. Eliot | 1954" (Blackwell's catalogue, 2010); "to Martin d'Arcy S. J. | —Perhaps not poetry, but—I hope—sound. | T. S. Eliot | Christmas 1954" (Berg).

Moody 361: "In Eliot's own collection of photographs as preserved in the Hayward Collection [King's] there is a faded poor snapshot of a Christmas tree."

Speech on modern religious drama, after a performance of Charles Williams's *The Seed of Adam*, 9 Dec 1936: "Religious drama is not there to give you the effect of the mass-manufactured plaster saint, or the comfortable deadness of the second-rate religious Christmas card. Religious drama ought to supply something in the religious life of the community that cannot be supplied in any other way and when it is fine drama and poetry, it can have a missionary power that is incalculable", quoted in Hayward's *London Letter* in *New York Sun* 23 Jan 1937.

To Geoffrey Curtis, 21 Dec 1944: "The non-religious observances of Christmas, except when one can be among little children—little Christian children, I mean, for with children there is a seemly congruity between the religious and the non-religious—become harder to bear, require more patience, every year as I grow older." To Curtis, 24 Nov 1953: "your note reminded me of a set of verses I wrote a year ago ··· I shall be interested to know whether you think I have brought the same idea which you make clear in your note, i.e. the implication of the *parousia* [Second Coming] in the Incarnation." He was referring to a review of *The Coming of the Lord* by A Religious of C.S.M.V. (the Community of St. Mary the Virgin), in which Curtis wrote: "We are shown the Second Coming in relation to the whole, and made to realize that there is but 'One Coming; in the Incarnation, in the Spirit, in the Sacraments, in the Judgement; and that a Coming to heaven'" (*Books: An Occasional Paper for Church People*, Mowbray, Autumn 1953). On 28 Dec TSE wrote again, enclosing the second carbon of *ts7*: "In clearing up papers, I discovered an *early draft* of the verses which I mentioned to you—which will, presumably, be an 'Ariel Poem' for 1954—and send it herewith. Please, this is not a good enough poem, so don't show it to anyone." When the poem was published, he inscribed a copy: "My dear Geoffrey I hasten to send you the final version" (Christie's, 23–24 Nov 2009).

Bold line numbering refers to the draft text printed in the Textual History.

1, 4, 9, 18, 22, 29 **attitudes towards Christmas ··· The rowdy (the pubs being open till midnight) ··· The child wonders at the Christmas Tree ··· the reverence and the gaiety** (*first full draft*: **the proper levity**) **··· piety ··· annual emotion**: of mediaeval religious drama: "I suppose that their feeling was a fusion of piety with the excitement of the child's annual Christmas pantomime, and the larking spirit of a bank holiday ··· recover the right attitude ··· using the word 'amuse' in a wide sense, and one in which the notion of merriment need not enter ··· levity—and perhaps unusual seriousness as well—are unsuitable to the twentieth century", *Religious Drama: Mediaeval and Modern* (1937).

1–4 **attitudes towards Christmas · · · The social, the torpid, the patently commercial, | The rowdy**: to Godfrey Childe, 17 Dec 1928: "with the responsibilities, the business interruptions, and the pagan ceremonies which turn Christmas into a hideous farce, I cannot make any engagements till after the festival is behind us".

4, 26 **midnight ··· St. Lucy**: "the exquisite line which ends Donne's *Nocturnall upon S. Lucies Day*: 'Both the yeares, and the dayes deep midnight is'", *George Herbert* (1962) 32.

8 **not only a decoration, but an angel**: "It ought to be explained for the benefit of the reader to whom angels mean little more than Christmas cards, that M. Maritain's view ··· is equally tenable whether you believe in the existence of angels or not", *Three Reformers* (1928). To Edward J. H. Greene, 19 Apr 1940: "I think that I first heard of Maritain about 1925, when I think I came across *Art et Scholastique* ··· I first met him in July 1926."

14 **delight in new possessions**: to Polly Tandy, 23 Dec 1941: "I know that the pleasure of unwrapping the parcels is almost greater, while it lasts, than that of having the contents."

21 *ts6 variant* **to the final Tree**: Herbert: "Man stole the fruit, but I must climb the tree; | The tree of life to all, but only me", *The Sacrifice* 202–203. (For Herbert's poem, see note to *Marina* 16–17.)

26 **St. Lucy, her carol, and her crown of fire**: *Hands*: "In Sweden (the home of the Christmas tree) St. Lucy (Lucia) is the saint associated with Christmas. She underwent many tortures which she miraculously survived, among them being burnt alive: the flames did not consume her but formed a crown of fire upon her head." Her Saint's Day is 13 Dec. In 1948 TSE was in Stockholm to collect

his Nobel Prize. To Marion Cushing Eliot, 18 Dec: "That was the 13th—St. Lucy's Day, which is celebrated in Sweden with peculiar ceremonies. While I was shaving · · · I heard a chorus of young female voices piping a carol in the corridor." TSE inscribed a copy of the poem "for Lucia Praz for St. Lucy's Day and for Christmas T. S. Eliot 1954". **crown of fire:** "the crowned knot of fire", *Little Gidding* V 45.

32 **When fear came upon every soul:** Acts 2: 42–44: "And they continued stedfastly in the apostles' doctrine and fellowship, and in breaking of bread, and in prayers. And fear came upon every soul: and many wonders and signs were done by the apostles. And all that believed were together, and had all things common."

40–41 *ms2* **Is this the kind of message you want to send? | Is it the kind that you care to receive?:** "people are often disappointed if they don't get what they expect, even if they don't want it", reported *Wellesley College News* 8 May 1947 (see headnote to *La Figlia Che Piange*). To his brother Henry, 1 Jan 1936: "As for my address to the Unitarian clergy of Boston, I did not want to address them at all, and I only acceded to repeated invitation. I gave them exactly what I was asked for, and I did not get fair treatment either." Of Kipling the moralist: "He was well aware that the moral is unwelcome, and must be insinuated, or conveyed (as we say nowadays) subliminally", *"The Unfading Genius of Rudyard Kipling"* (1959).

At the foot of the last page of the poem in *1954* is an inscription by David Jones:

CVM LVCIA
ET OMNIBUS
SANCTIS TVIS
INTRA QVORVM
NOS CONSORTIVM
VENIÆ LARGITOR
A · ADMITTE · Ω
ΕΙΡΗΝΗΙ ΘΑΛΛΟΥΣΑ ΚΑΙ ΗΠΙΟΧΕΙΡ ΥΓΙΕΙΗΙ

[WITH LUCY AND ALL YOUR SAINTS INTO WHOSE COMPANY ADMIT US, BESTOWER OF FORGIVENESS | IN PEACE FLOURISHING AND IN GENTLE-HANDED WHOLENESS], tr. Nicolete Gray, *The Painted Inscriptions of David Jones* (1981). Gray: "from the Canon of the Mass (now Eucharistic Prayer 1). The Greek is from the Orphic hymn to Persephone XXIX . . . St Lucy was martyred in Sicily where Persephone gathered her flowers."

David Jones was later to create a bookplate lettered "E · LIBRIS | ELIOT | | THOMAS · STEARNS | | ESME · VALERIE", showing the head of an elephant holding an arrow by his trunk, and encircled, in green, by an inscription which plays with beginnings and ends: "THE · CERTAINTY · OF · UNCHANGING · LOVE ·"

Unfinished Poems

Section introduced, with half-title, *1936+*. (None of the poems was ever added to *Sel Poems*.) The contents appear in the order of first publication:

Sweeney Agonistes

Fragment of a Prologue	*Criterion*	Oct 1926
Fragment of an Agon	*Criterion*	Jan 1927

(The two collected in 1932 as *Sweeney Agonistes*.)

Coriolan

I. *Triumphal March*	as an Ariel Poem	Oct 1931
II. *Difficulties of a Statesman*	*Commerce*	Winter [1931/]1932

Sweeney Agonistes

1. An Uncompleted Work 2. Aristophanes 3. Conception
4. Jazz 5. Arnold Bennett's Advice 6. *The Superior Landlord*
7. Delays and *Criterion* Publication of the two Fragments
8. Volume Publication 9. After Publication
10. Première in America: Enter an Old Gentleman
11. British Performances

The two Fragments were published in the *Criterion* without further reference to a larger design: first, *Fragment of a Prologue* in Oct 1926, then *Fragment of an Agon* in Jan 1927. (To Marguerite Caetani, 21 Aug 1926: "putting my own pseudo-dramatic verse into the *Criterion* means that for the next two numbers I can use so much the less of other people".) There was no authorised American publication until 1936. However, Samuel Roth exploited US copyright law to reprint the Fragments in *Two Worlds Monthly*, NY, in Jan 1927 and May–June 1927 respectively (having also used part of Joyce's *Work in Progress* and a story by D. H. Lawrence from previous issues of the *Criterion*: see *Spoo* 88). The second Fragment was legitimately reprinted in *Profile: Ezra Pound: An Anthology Collected in MCMXXXI* (Milan, 1932).

In a letter to Charles Williams, 2 Apr 1929, TSE referred to "the two fragments of *Sweeney Agonistes* (published in the *Criterion*)", and the full title *Sweeney Agonistes: Fragments of an Aristophanic Melodrama* was used for the volume published in Dec 1932, and in *1936+*. *Sweeney Agonistes* was reprinted in *From the Modern Repertoire: Series One* ed. Eric Bentley (U. Denver, 1949). It was performed, with "an unpublished last scene" (see 10. PREMIÈRE IN AMERICA: ENTER AN OLD GENTLEMAN), as part of *Homage to T. S. Eliot: A Programme of Poetry Drama and Music* on 13 June 1965, at the Globe Theatre, Blackfriars Road; the music was by John Dankworth and the "settings" were by Bridget Riley. In 1969 Riley proposed to Faber a limited edition version of no more than 75 portfolios, and Charles Monteith suggested that it should include "that final short scene which doesn't appear in the *Collected Poems*" (Faber archive). No such portfolios were produced.

No recording by TSE of *Fragment of a Prologue* is known. He recorded *Fragment of an Agon* (in two parts) in May 1947 for the Harvard Poetry Room; released by Harvard Vocarium Records, 1948.

On 27 Jan 1947 the BBC Third Programme broadcast "Robert Beatty and Margaret Leighton in *Sweeney Agonistes*. Produced by Patric Dickinson" (*Radio Times*).

1. AN UNCOMPLETED WORK

Fragments. James Macpherson: *Fragments of Ancient Poetry* (1760). A. E. Housman, *Fragment of a Greek Tragedy* (a comic poem). TSE to R. J. G. Johnson, 1 Apr 1935: "You must remember that *Sweeney Agonistes* really *is* a fragment from my point of view, and that my intention was a full length play on an Aristophanic model. The present fragments would have looked very different in a complete text from what they appear to be in isolation; and they are consequently, even after ten years' interval, still a different thing in my mind from what they can be in the mind of any producer. In order to be produced at all, in fact, with any effect, the fragments have to be interpreted differently from my original meaning ··· I think it is worth making the point that a fragment like this is a very different matter for the producer than a complete play." When the text was reprinted in the revised edition of *Twenty-four One-Act Plays* ed. John Hampden (1954), TSE added a note: "The author wishes to point out that *Sweeney Agonistes* is not a one-act play and was never designed as such. It consists of two fragments. But as the author has abandoned any intention of completing them, these two fragmentary scenes have frequently been produced as a one-act play."

Unger (1961) 28: "*Sweeney Agonistes* is not actually an 'unfinished' work. Each part and the two parts together are deliberate ironical parodies of surviving fragments of classical texts, and thus the fragmentariness is a justifiable aspect of the finished product." Although TSE's comments show this to have been wrong, he acknowledged something of their heritage in a letter to Mary C. Petrella, 7 Nov 1957: "The Sweeney fragments were written in 1924 although not published in book form until 1932. They are, therefore, in a sense, pre-Christian fragments." (For Fragments of the Pre-Socratic philosophers, see note on the epigraphs to *Four Quartets*. TSE was received into the Church of England in 1927.)

TSE was almost certainly referring to *Sweeney Agonistes* when he wrote to E. McKnight Kauffer on 15 Dec 1929 that some of the illustrations Kauffer had done for *Robinson Crusoe* "have a quality which reminds me of Chirico, and which remind me that it is my duty to finish the play, so that the world may have the benefit of your scenery for it." To Kauffer, 6 Jan 1930: "I am afraid that my play is still no further forward than those two fragments published in the *Criterion*." To Hallie Flanagan, the first director of the Fragments, 9 Feb 1934: "I cannot tell you when or whether there will be more of *Sweeney.*" To A. L. Rowse, 13 June 1934, of *The Rock*: "Except for the abortive *Sweeney Agonistes* it is my first complete attempt on a major scale".

In *1936* and *1963*, *Sweeney Agonistes* appeared within "Unfinished Poems", along with *Coriolan*. Of books unfinished by writer or reader: to Desmond MacCarthy, 14 Nov 1947: "The answer about *Finnegans Wake* is certainly NO, I have not read it. (It is also true that I have never read the whole of Rabelais, or of *The Faery Queen*, or *The Excursion*; and I am not sure that I have even read all of the Canterbury Tales; and I certainly do not know the later poems of Browning as you do)."

2. ARISTOPHANES

During the correspondence about the final shape of *The Waste Land*, Pound and TSE discussed Aristophanes, apparently as an inspiration for new work. Pound to TSE, [28? Jan] 1922: "Aristophanes probably depressing, and the native negro phoque [folk] melodies of Dixee more calculated to lift the ball-encumbered phallus of man" (see headnote to *The Waste Land*, 1. COMPOSITION). TSE to Pound, 3 Sept 1923: "have mapt out Aristophanic comedy, but must devote study to phallic songs, also agons." (This was immediately followed in the letter by "King Bolo's big black basstart queen"; see "Improper Rhymes".) The term "phallic songs" is used in S. H. Butcher's tr. of Aristotle's *Poetics* (3rd ed., rev., 1902) 3.3.

The alternative title on TSE's trial leaf is "HOMAGE TO ARISTOPHANES: A FRAGMENT". Jacob Isaacs recalling TSE's love of music hall: "Mr. Eliot had written his first dramatic piece, *Sweeney Agonistes* ··· He had had his Comic Purgation ··· Whether this purgation came directly from Aristophanes or indirectly from Ernie Lotinga, who is not only bawdy but a direct descendant of the phallic comedy of Greece and Rome, I do not know. This I do know, that if I have done nothing else for literature, I did at least take Mr. Eliot to see Mr. Ernie Lotinga at the Islington Empire", *An Assessment of Twentieth-Century Literature* (1951) 147. For *The Rock* as a "revue", see letter to the *Spectator*, 1 June 1934, in headnote to *Choruses from "The Rock"*, 7. AFTERWARDS. After a performance of *Beyond the Fringe* (1961), TSE wrote in his programme "An amazingly vigorous quartet of young men: their show well produced and fast moving, a mixture of brilliance, juvenility and bad taste ··· Still, it is pleasant to see this *type* of entertainment so successful" (Alan Bennett, *LRB* 3 Jan 2013).

Carol H. Smith: "Eliot gives abundant evidence throughout his essays of having noted closely the work of another group of Frazer's followers, the Cambridge School of Classical Anthropology", *Smith 1963* 43. Among the "fixed forms" of Greek tragedy summarised in 1912 by Gilbert Murray was first "An *Agon* or Contest, the Year against its Enemy, Light against Darkness, Summer against Winter". OED adds Francis Macdonald Cornford, *The Origin of Attic Comedy* (1914, dedicated to Murray). TSE had previously written *The Little Passion: From "An Agony in the Garret"* in the *March Hare* Notebook.

Although TSE cited Cornford in his seminar paper *The Interpretation of Primitive Ritual* (1913), he appears not to have bought *The Origin of Attic Comedy* until after writing *The Waste Land*, for his copy contains advertisements for the publisher's list for Autumn 1922 and therefore cannot have been bought earlier than that summer. (His attention may have been drawn to it by *From Ritual to Romance* by Jessie L. Weston, who quotes Cornford several times and takes from him one of her two title-page epigraphs.) TSE wrote to his mother [mid-Oct? 1923], that he wanted "to work in a desultory way on preparations for my play, which involves studying Aristophanes and learning all I can about the Greek theatre". Both Murray and Cornford are cited in *The Beating of a Drum* (1923), in *Nation & Athenæum* 6 Oct.

Cornford's ch. IV, "Some Types of Dramatic Fertility Ritual", begins with Frazer's *The Golden Bough* (and also mentions Xenophon's *Anabasis*). Cornford explains "the *Parabasis* of the Chorus—a long passage which cuts the play in two about half way through its course and completely suspends the action. It is delivered by the Chorus and its Leaders, and it normally opens with a farewell to the actors, who leave the stage clear till it is over, and then return to carry on the business of the piece to the end. The Chorus, meanwhile, turn their backs on the scene of action and advance across the orchestra to address the audience directly—the movement from which the *Parabasis* takes its name. The action of the play is thus divided into two parts. Of these two parts, the first normally consists of the *Prologue*, or exposition scenes; the Entrance of the Chorus (*Parados*); and what is now generally called the *Agon*, a fierce 'contest' between the representatives of two parties or principles, which are in effect the hero and villain of the whole piece."

Chapter V describes Attic comedy in terms closely followed by TSE in the Synopsis to *The Superior Landlord* (this headnote, 6. *THE SUPERIOR LANDLORD*); the nature of the *Agon*: "The *Agon*, which, together with the scenes leading up to it, normally occupies the first half of the play between *Parados* and *Parabasis*, stands in a fixed relation to the concluding marriage, in that the bridegroom in that marriage is usually the victor in the *Agon*. Here, however, the resemblance [to modern comedies] ends. For, in the Comedy of Aristophanes, as we have seen, there is no romantic plot, no complication of intrigue to be straightened out in a dénouement, no pair of lovers separated and reunited by turns of fortune. The contest, the *Agon*, is not with a favoured rival for the hand of the bride; nor are its dangers and difficulties occasioned by the morose old father who exists in later Comedy to see that the course of true love shall not run smooth. On the contrary, the hero is often himself a morose old father, and the *Agon* turns, not upon his love affairs, but upon his political and social views. The normal plan is that the action of the play should begin with a quarrel or fight, which leads as quickly as possible to the *Agon* proper. This is not, as in the romantic plot, a whole train of action with well-laid schemes and counter-machinations prolonged to a dénouement. It is more like a sort of trial, with a strict rule of procedure. The hero, who has been attacked and even threatened with death, is put upon his defence. He makes out his case and turns the tables upon his accuser. The debate lasts for, perhaps, two hundred lines, during which the action does not advance. Then, in the second half of the play, after the *Parabasis*, we are shown the hero enjoying the fruits of his victory · · · Three, or sometimes four rôles are involved in the *Agon*: never more than four. First there are the two Adversaries (as we shall call them). For the sake of convenience, we shall distinguish them as the 'Agonist' and the 'Antagonist.' The Agonist is the hero, who is attacked, is put on his defence, and comes off victorious. The Antagonist is the villain, who is in the stronger position at first, but is worsted and beaten from the field. Besides these there is the Chorus, whose Leader directs the trial and sometimes pronounces the verdict; the rest of the Chorus sing their *Ode* and *Antode* at the proper moment. Finally, there is in some cases a minor character, a friend or companion of the Agonist, who plays the part of Buffoon, interjecting remarks and anecdotes, naïve, humorous, or obscene, aside to the audience."

TSE to Harry Crosby, 26 Oct 1927: "As for 'agon', you will find a full discussion of the word in Liddell and Scott's Greek-English Lexicon. I use the word in accordance with an analysis of F. M. Cornford in his very interesting book on the origins of Greek comedy." On Middleton's *A Game at Chesse*: "Swinburne called it 'complete and exquisite,' and 'the only work of English poetry which may properly be called Aristophanic.' We must take 'Aristophanic,' of course, in a Swinburnian sense; but even so this is high and deserved praise", *A Game at Chesse* (1930).

Among TSE's copies of Aristophanes were the Greek texts *Aristophanis Comoediae* ed. Augustus Meineke (Tauchnitz, 1840, vol II), signed by TSE and dated 1909 (Pierpont Morgan), and *Aristophanis Comoediae* ed. Immanuel Bekker 5 vols (1829), which is included among *TSE's books: Bodleian list* (1934). The front endpapers of his schoolboy copy of *The Acharnians* bear his notes, ending: "Was a conservative, admirer of Aeschylus, opponent of demagogues who followed Pericles. Cleon had Aristophanes whipped by ruffians. Arist. opposed Sophists and Euripides. *Clouds* (423) took off Socrates ··· *Acharnians* (425), *Knights* (424), *Clouds* (423), *Wasps* (422), *Peace* (421), *Birds* (414) are earliest examples of European comedy, are full of attacks on his time. Arist. never held public office, never offered any suggestions for betterment of Athenian polity. After Peace of Nicias he became altered. Radical democracy run out. Reaction, new laws restrained mention of public characters in plays. *Frogs* (405) was last great play. *Plutus* (388) was forerunner of modern drama of popular manners."

Richard Aldington on Laurent Tailhade, *Egoist* 1 Oct 1915: "He may elect Aristophanes as his master—his great book is called *Poèmes Aristophanesques*—but his true kin is Catullus and Martial." Under the aegis of the Greek comic playwright Aristophanes, Tailhade had ridiculed the political and military élites of France in the wake of the Dreyfus affair (see note to *Mr. Apollinax* 6–7 and headnote to *Cousin Nancy*). TSE to the Dean of Chichester, 10 Jan 1935: "I simply can't see a Church pageant about Peace making any impression ··· The only possibility that I can envisage for handling the subject at all is in the form of Aristophanic farce, which certainly could not be produced under official auspices and which would probably be too libellous to be produced at all. But what use is there in dealing with the subject unless one can deal frankly and freely with the whole swindle?"

3. CONCEPTION

Virginia Woolf, *Diary* 20 Sept 1920: "He wants to write a verse play in which the 4 characters of Sweeny act the parts. A personal upheaval of some kind came after Prufrock, & turned him aside from his inclination—to develop in the manner of Henry James. Now he wants to describe externals." Grover Smith takes Woolf's first sentence to refer not, for instance, to the four characters from *Sweeney Among the Nightingales* (which had been included in the Hogarth Press *Poems* of the previous year), but to four constituents of the personality of Sweeney. He relates TSE's enterprise to *Happy Families*, Aldous Huxley's closet drama about seduction, published in Feb 1920 in *Limbo: Six Stories and a Play*: "Huxley's mischievous and often hilarious scene pairs up two sets of personages, one set being male, the other female, each consisting of four subordinate elements of a single personality. With exact differentiation between the sexes as to traits, the four in each set consist of a Freudian Superego, Ego and Id, and a ventriloquist's dummy for exchanges of sex-neutral small-talk" (*Grover Smith 1998*). Such ideas, he suggests, helped to evolve the Tiresias figure, and "it was in *The Waste Land* that Eliot exhausted the attractions of the device" (*Grover Smith 1983* 102). Again: "*Sweeney Agonistes*, still in the future, was not to mature the plan portended by Mrs. Woolf's words"; and on parallels between Huxley's play and *Sweeney Agonistes*: "The minstrel personage Bones relates to a character in *Happy Families* who clicks percussion bones. The tropic isle of the songs faintly recalls Huxley's setting for his play, a conservatory of exotic plant species of erotic scent or cannibal reputation, described in fantastic travesty. The subtle distribution of the four sets of characters in *Sweeney Agonistes* into card suits replicates the card-pack origin of *Happy Families*" (*Grover Smith 1998*). (For Huxley's own debt in *Happy Families* to TSE's previous poems, see note to *The Waste*

Land [I] 112–113, 126 and *McCue 2013b*.) Huxley published another play at Easter 1920, in *Coterie*, entitled *Permutations Among the Nightingales*. TSE was embarrassed in May 1937 when John Hayward sent him a bookseller's catalogue entry offering one of only 50 or so copies of Huxley's *Jonah* (1917), inscribed to TSE at Christmas 1917, for not only had TSE disposed of it, but its pages had not been cut open. TSE's annotated copy of Huxley's *The Defeat of Youth* (1918) is at Colgate U. TSE: "The way to deal with Huxley is exactly to sneer at him, and for this purpose there is, I think, a chance for a good pamphlet by some real ruffian—not a gentleman, and preferably not even an Etonian, but, let us say, one who has plumbed life to the very dregs of Carlton House Terrace · · · in short, I can think of no one except Wyndham Lewis or myself", *"Aldous Huxley and the Christian Religion"* by Roger Lloyd, reader's report (1931).

The day TSE first saw *The Waste Land* in the *Dial*, 12 Nov 1922, he wrote to Gilbert Seldes: "I find this poem as far behind me as *Prufrock* now: my present ideas are very different." On 20 Jan 1932, he wrote to Erik Mesterton, translator of *The Waste Land* into Swedish, that "horns and motors, which shall bring | Sweeney to Mrs. Porter in the spring" ([III] 197–98) "refers certainly to the Sweeney poems, but not by intention to the dialogues which I have renamed *Sweeney Agonistes*, because they were not written at the time. A reference to it is suitable, however".

To Wyndham Lewis, 26 Sept 1923: "I understand that you encourage me to go on with the Sweeney play—I hope that is what you mean." But *Sweeney Agonistes* was abandoned in 1925. *Laverty* records that in 1936 TSE told her that *Sweeney Agonistes* had been "written in two nights. Working from ten o'clock at night until five the next morning I succeeded, with the aid of youthful enthusiasm and a bottle of gin, in completing the work in what I believe must have been record time. Unfortunately, as one grows older, gin and enthusiasm seem to lose some of their value as mental stimulants." (See headnote *Journey of the Magi* for TSE's claim to have written the poem "in three quarters of an hour · · · with the assistance of half a bottle of Booth's gin".)

4. JAZZ

Jazz, so named, is documented from *c.* 1915, and was widely regarded as degenerate. In Jan 1921, the *Contemporary Review* commented: "The frank barbarism began its appeal with the nigger minstrels and has landed us in 'jazz'." Vivien Eliot to Mary Hutchinson, [Dec? 1917]: "One day you really must try Tom's Negro rag-time" (see note to *The Waste Land* [II] 128, "Rag"). In 1922, as widespread radio broadcasting was beginning in America, F. Scott Fitzgerald published *Tales of the Jazz Age*.

To Alfred Kreymborg, 23 Aug 1923, on his book (published by Martin Secker Ltd.): "I have not told you yet how much I enjoyed the Secker *Puppet Plays*. I think you have really got hold of something new and fruitful in rhythm—at any rate they have been a great stimulation to me and I have read them several times. They are very different indeed from what I have in my mind to attempt, yet they are more like it than anything else I know. I am trying to get at a dominant rhythm and subordinated rhythms for the thing—I expect it will be called jazz drama. Anyway, you encourage me to continue." Kreymborg to TSE, 14 Jan 1924: "That you are planning plays of your own—also with puppets—was and is an exciting bit of news." The following year, in his autobiography, Kreymborg mentioned TSE's asking him about writing for puppets (*Troubadour* 397). See *Grover Smith* 113–14 for what he calls "the tragic side of the vapid jazz age", and correspondences between *Sweeney Agonistes* and F. Scott Fitzgerald's *The Great Gatsby* (1925), which TSE read three times. TSE to John Hall Wheelock of Scribner's, concerning *Tender is the Night* (1934): "I read *The Great Gatsby* when it first appeared. At the time I knew nothing about the author; but I remember saying that it interested me more than any American novel I had read since Henry James's. Since then I have been waiting impatiently for another book by Mr. Scott Fitzgerald; with more eagerness and curiosity than I should feel towards the work of any of his contemporaries, except that of Mr. Ernest Hemingway. ¶ Is the foregoing paragraph of any use to you?" (A slightly abbreviated form of the third sentence was used by Scribner's on the jacket.)

TSE to Gilbert Seldes, 6 Nov 1923: "I enjoyed very much your article on jazz music [*Toujours Jazz* in *Dial* Aug 1923]. My play, if it is ever written, will certainly appear as a text, although I intend it for production with an orchestra consisting exclusively of drums." Seldes had quoted Henry Edward Krehbiel: "Berlioz in his supremest effort with his army of drummers produced nothing to compare in artistic interest with harmonious drumming of these savages. The fundamental effect was a combination of double and triple time, the former kept by the singers, the latter by the drummers, but it is impossible to convey the idea of the wealth of detail achieved by the drummers by means of exchange of the rhythms, syncopation of both simultaneously, and dynamic devices · · · I was forced to the conclusion that in their command of the element, which in the musical art of the ancient Greeks stood higher than either melody or harmony, the best composers of to-day were the veriest tyros compared with these black savages", *Afro-American Folksongs* (1914) 65 (Shawn Worthington, personal communication). TSE: "Poetry begins, I dare say, with a savage beating a drum in the jungle, and it retains that essential of percussion and rhythm", *The Use of Poetry and the Use of Criticism* 155. On Gertrude Stein's work: "its rhythms have a peculiar hypnotic power not met with before. It has a kinship with the saxophone. If this is the future, then the future is, as it very likely is, of the barbarians", *Charleston, Hey! Hey!* (1927). (TSE's title is from *I'm Gonna Charleston back to Charleston* by C. A. Coon and J. L. Sanders, recorded 1925.)

"The primitive jazz rhythm may have been a 'mere direct' expression of a type of ecstasy, but it is not necessarily 'more perfect' than its later developments. The work of Duke Ellington etc. whether you like it or not is not simply a deteriorated version of the negro spiritual. *Old Man River* is of course a brilliant fake, and part of the pleasure in it comes from the awareness that it is a fake", *Comments on Mannheim's Letter* (1944). For *Ol' Man River*, composed in the style of a folksong for *Show Boat* (Kern and Hammerstein, 1927), see letter to Theodora Eliot, 4 Jan 1937, quoted in note to the unadopted part title to *Ash-Wednesday* I, "*All Aboard for Natchez Cairo and St. Louis*".

On Stravinsky's music for *Le Sacre du Printemps*: "it did seem to transform the rhythms of the steppes into the scream of the motor horn, the rattle of machinery, the grind of wheels, the beating of iron and steel, the roar of the underground railway, and the other barbaric cries of modern life; and to transform these despairing noises into music", *London Letter* in *Dial* Oct 1921.

To Hayward, 5 Aug 1941, on Disney's *Fantasia*: "it is a curious and often very ingenious adaptation of Modern Art, including surrealism, for the popolo, and makes me think that perhaps surrealism is just the kind of art for the lower middle classes, when they get used to it. What goes into a surrealist picture has a strong affinity with the junk in a small Best Parlour, barring the obscenity, and they will get that in time. To provide the necessary element of the expected, you have Mickey Mouse as the Dukas Sorcerer's Apprentice: that part is good in the Snow White way. The dinosaurs in the Sacre de Printemps (when I think of the derision with which a popular audience at the Coliseum greeted that music when the ballet was first produced, it provides interesting reflections on the popularisation of Art: anything that is not first rate, however unpopular at first, becomes acceptable to the popolo in time). The only really poisonous part was the picturization of the Pastoral Symphony, a real degradation of that music, with comic female centaurs and baby Pegasuses, and a character called Bacchus who is really Silenus. It makes you think."

To John Gordon Caffey, 5 Oct 1944: "when I started to write many years ago a kind of play which I never finished called *Sweeney Agonistes*, I had designed that the speech should have an accompaniment of percussion instruments, various drums, and also the bones."

5. ARNOLD BENNETT'S ADVICE

To Arnold Bennett, 13 July 1924, requesting help: "I have a scheme in view, concerning which yours is the only advice which would be of any help. So I hope that it will not be impossible for you to see me." Bennett was away until August, but recorded a visit by TSE on 10 Sept 1924: "He wanted to write a drama of modern life (furnished flat sort of people) in a rhythmic prose 'perhaps with certain things in it accentuated by drum-beats.' And he wanted my advice. We arranged that he should do the scenario and some sample pages of dialogue", *Journals III, 1921–1928* ed. Newman Flower (1933). Bennett (1867–1931) had made TSE's acquaintance when impressed by a reading which included *The Hippopotamus*, at a charity event on 12 Dec 1917. Bennett's *The Author's Craft* (1914) covered both fiction and drama, and he had enjoyed stage success, notably with *Milestones* (1912) and *Sacred and Profane Love* (1920). Three parts of his *Florentine Journal* appeared in the *Criterion* (Dec 1927, Jan and Feb 1928).

To Bennett 8 Oct 1924: "I have five or six typed pages of dialogue, and a very brief scenario, which I should now like to submit to you · · · I could come to see you either Monday, Tuesday or Thursday evenings of next week · · · Perhaps I shall have a little more dialogue by then." To Bennett, 23 Oct 1924, after their second meeting: "I am reconstructing my play according to all of your suggestions · · · I shall feel that the play will be as much yours as mine." 19 Apr 1925: "I came to see you last in *November* with the outline & some dialogue of my play. I am writing now to explain that since December either I or my wife has been continually ill—I have had two months lately on end;—and my wife three months, of critical illness which is not ended; and I have had to let everything go. I do not want you to think that I have troubled you for nothing. The help you gave me determined me to carry out this play: I have thought of it a great deal, & I shall finish it next winter."

What he had drafted is not certain, but it probably included what he called *The Superior Landlord*, a five-page outline, of which the ribbon copy and carbon are preserved at King's. The ribbon copy has pencil estimate of length: "Say 4000 words" and later endorsement "Early typescript T. S. Eliot". Both copies are misbound, with the character list following the first page of text. *Grover Smith 1983* 62 claims that *The Superior Landlord* dates from 1933. *Sidnell* 100–101, 264–65 detects the influence of Auden's *The Dance of Death* (1933) and argues that *The Superior Landlord* dates from 1934. *Madden* disputes this, and it is improbable because these foolscap leaves (watermarked "Dickinson Bond 1804") precisely match those of the Fragments published in 1926 and 1927. The mention in *The Superior Landlord* of "Badinage ··· leading up to Fragment II" suggests that the Fragments were already written.

6. *THE SUPERIOR LANDLORD*

Manuscript Synopsis

Prologue.	Doris & Dusty.
Parados.	Arrival of Wauchope, Horsfall, Klipstein [*1st reading*: Klepstein], Krumpacker, Swarts, Snow. FIGHT between Swarts & Snow. Sweeney arrives.
Agon.	Sweeney monologues.
Parabasis.	Chorus "The Terrors of the Night". anapests—pnigos
Scene.	Entrance of Mrs Porter. Debate with Sweeney. Murder of Mrs Porter.

Parados: the arrival of the chorus, singing and dancing, in Aristophanic comedy.

Agon ··· Parabasis: see headnote, 2. ARISTOPHANES. TSE scored a sentence in Cornford's ch. VI, "The Chorus in Agon and Parabasis": "It has been doubted whether the poet's oration on his own behalf was an original feature of the *Parabasis*."

anapests—pnigos: discussing the form of the *Parabasis*, Cornford writes of "an address to the audience, composed in the long anapaestic measure, and called by Aristophanes 'the *Anapaests*.' Here the mask is dropt and with it all pretence of dramatic illusion. The Leader delivers a message from the poet to the Athenian people, setting the transcendant merits of the author in contrast with the ridiculous inferiority of his rivals, and claiming credit for the services he has rendered in exposing those abominable rogues, his political opponents and prophets of contemporary culture. The speech appropriately ends in a peroration called *pnigos*, because it was to be delivered in one breath with increasing rapidity, the voice, perhaps, rising to a scream capable of drowning any demonstrations of disapproval from the adherents of demagogue or sophist" (121). TSE scored the last sentence. For bombastic political rhetoric, see *Mr. Pugstyles.*

Murder of Mrs Porter: TSE to his Swedish translator, Erik Mesterton, 25 Oct 1948: "I do not know why you should think that Sweeney was going to murder Doris. The intended victim was Mrs. Porter, who had not made her appearance at the point where I abandoned the attempt. She was, however, to prove invulnerable or else to come to life again, being in some shadowy way a kind of vegetation goddess. I do not know why the dream songs were given that title or whether I had any original intention of incorporating one or more into the play so you see that I am almost as much in the dark as anyone can be." (For *Dream Songs*, see headnote to *Eyes that last I saw in tears*.)

Interruption by A. L. Old Clothes man

A. L. ~~Boy Scouts~~ Dustman.

A. L. Tenant Below.

A. L. Pereira

Parabasis II. Theological discussion.

Contemporary Politics.

Ode Antode Epyrheme

Chorikon. Half-choruses. *αισχρολογια*

Invocation of the Muse.

Scene Sweeney begins scrambling eggs. Distribution of eggs.

Return of Mrs Porter.

Exodus.

After Theological discussion *TSE wrote "p.122", referring to Cornford. In the left margin are his approximate word-counts:* Prologue, 150; Parados, 300; Agon, 250; Parabasis, 100; Scene, 350 [*emended from 300?*]; Parabasis II, 100; Ehurikon, 50; *total at foot of first leaf*: 1300; Scene, 250; Exodus, 50. Total, 1600 [*emended from 1650*].

A. L.: *Crawford* 163: "Interruptions of the action by figures of the *Alazon* (Impostor) type, scored 'AL.' by Cornford, were also common." TSE scored the first sentence of Cornford's ch. VII, "The Impostor" (132): "There is one more constant motive in Aristophanes' comedies still to be accounted for—the unwelcome intruders who so often thrust themselves upon the hero in the second part of the play." He also scored a paragraph headed "The Impostor a double of the Antagonist" (148): "The Impostor in Aristophanes, as we have seen, has three essentials: (1) he interrupts the sacrifice or wedding-feast, and claims a share in the fruits of the Agonist's victory; (2) he has a vaunting, boastful, swaggering disposition; (3) he is regularly mocked, beaten, or otherwise mishandled, and driven away. We have also found reason to suggest that he may be in some way a double of the Antagonist. We naturally look for further light to Dionysiac myth and ritual, where, I believe, we shall find the figure we seek to identify."

Ode Antode Epyrheme: the Ode and Antode are usually a symmetrical pair of songs. The "epirrhema" is that which is said besides or afterwards, addressed to the audience.

Chorikon: a choral interlude such as that in Aristophanes' *The Birds*. ***αισχρολογια***: vulgar language.

Dramatis Personae and Scenario: *The Superior Landlord*

[*Half-title page*]

Be absolute for death, either death or life
Shall thereby seem the sweeter: reason thus with life—

[*Title page*]

THE SUPERIOR LANDLORD

~~PEREIRA~~

~~or~~

~~THE MARRIAGE OF LIFE AND DEATH~~

~~A Dream~~

Between the acting of a dreadful thing
And the first motion, all the interim is
Like a miasma, or a hideous dream.

[*new page*]

CHARACTERS.

Doris Dusty	Sub-tenants
Lieut. Sam Wauchope Capt. Harvey Horsfall	Canadian Officers

Epigraph on half-title page **Be absolute · · · reason thus with life**: see note on unadopted epigraphs to *Sweeney Agonistes* (below).

Title ***THE SUPERIOR LANDLORD***: pencil addition above the four typed lines "PEREIRA · · · A Dream". (Though the pencil deletion cancelled only the middle two, the intention was probably to delete all four.) In law, a superior landlord is a person to whom the ownership of a property may later revert. *Grover Smith 1983*: "The action was conceived · · · as the dream-vision of an insignificant man—called, in Expressionistic style, 'the Tenant Downstairs', Sweeney being 'the Superior Landlord' · · · In this dream Pereira, the lessee or subordinate landlord, has allowed two young women, Doris and Dusty, to occupy the upstairs flat, which he rents from Sweeney." (For "any other superior bank clerk", see note to *The Waste Land* [I] 69.) OED "landlord" 1b: "*fig.* of God", with Richard Corbett: "It wounded mee the Landlord of all times | Should let long lives, and leases to their crimes", *An Elegy on the Death of Dr. Ravis, Bishop of London.*

Deleted subtitle **THE MARRIAGE OF LIFE AND DEATH**: Blake, *The Marriage of Heaven and Hell* (title).

Epigraph **Between the acting · · · a hideous dream**: *Julius Caesar* II i, with "miasma," for Shakespeare's "phantasma". See note to *The Hollow Men* V 7–8. "miasmal mist", *The Hippopotamus* 36. "Phantasmal gnomes", *WLComposite* **341**.

Klipstein Krumpacker	American Gentlemen
Lincoln Snow	Negro Jazz Drummer
Milton Swarts	Jewish Jazz Drummer
Sweeney	
Pereira	
The Tenant Downstairs	
Mrs. Porter	

[*new page*]

Doris and Dusty in a furnished flat. Conversation about Pereira, who telephones to say that he wishes to come to see them, but is put off. Cutting the cards. Wauchope is heard outside. Enter Wauchope, Horsfall, Klipstein and Krumpacker. Enter Swarts and Snow with banjos. Expecting Sweeney and Mrs. Porter. Sweeney enters. Preparations for supper. All take their places round the table as follows:

Sweeney
Doris Dusty
Klipstein Krumpacker
Horsfall Wauchope
Snow Swarts.

Snow and Swarts in dinner jackets, Horsfall and Wauchope in lounge suits and motoring gabardines, Klipstein and Krumpacker in evening dress. Sweeney in brown jacket, green trousers, canary waistcoat and brown bowler which he keeps on throughout the evening. On either side of Sweeney, on the table, is a chafing dish, with materials—eggs, milk, toast, beer, cheese, etc.—for making welsh rarebit and scrambled eggs. Bottles of various wines and spirits on the table, brought by the various guests. As they take their places the quartette (K., K., H. and W.) burst into a convivial chorus. Badinage between Sweeney and Doris, leading up to conversation of Fragment II. At the end of this a KNOCK. Mrs. Porter is expected. It turns out

---

Preparations for supper. All take their places round the table as follows: staging would presumably require the actors to be arranged so as to be seen by the audience, as in Leonardo's *Last Supper*, where the disciples use only one long side of the table. (For Leonardo's fresco, see *Lune de Miel* 13, "la Cène, et un restaurant pas cher".) The characters are paired, and because they do not surround the table, Snow (White) and Swarts (Black) are at extremes.

chafing dish: OED: "A vessel to hold burning charcoal or other fuel ··· a portable grate."

to be THE FIRST INTRUDER. This is a Boy Scout, a Postman, or anything you like, soliciting contributions. He is quickly expelled. No sooner has he gone than there is another KNOCK. Mrs. Porter is expected. This turns out to be THE SECOND INTRUDER—Pereira. He has been suspicious and decided to come and see for himself. He addresses the girls with exaggerated sarcastic politeness, is baited by the others, and psychoanalysed by Klipstein and Krumpacker. He finally intimates his intention of evicting the two girls—the flat is his and he has lent it to them. Sweeney here takes the matter up. He points out that Pereira took the flat for his own occupation, and that he has in effect sub-let it, and draws Pereira's attention to Section 6 of the Rent and Mortgage Interest Restrictions Act 1923 (13 & 14 Geo.5). What is that to do with Sweeney. Sweeney reveals himself as the Superior Landlord. Pereira withdraws routed. Presently there is another KNOCK. Is it Pereira again or Mrs. Porter? It is the Tenant Downstairs, a small insignificant man in spectacles, a mackintosh over pink striped pyjamas, red slippers and a walking stick. He has come to complain of the noise. Noise denied—no one been there all day, they only just came in. Sweeney tells him that any complaints must be referred to the owner of the flat—Mr. Pereira. He retires. [~~Chorus.~~] Sweeney starts cooking. Chorus.

End of Part I.

INTERLUDE. As the chorus ends a Viennese walz is heard beginning very softly. The actors assume fixed positions, and the stage becomes dimmer and the scene melts away. The music becomes louder. A bright sky blue drop scene descends, and two dancers (male and female) drift across in a ballet, in period-costumes. Ballet lasts only about 3 minutes. After they have left the stage a diseuse (hidden) recites a passage of poetry which will be in complete contrast to the verse of the play. The whole scene is completely in contrast in setting and mood to the play itself, but melts into it at beginning and end. The scene rises on

[*Interlude deleted in top copy*]

THE FIRST INTRUDER · · · THE SECOND INTRUDER: see TSE's letter of 6 Nov 1932 in headnote, 8. VOLUME PUBLICATION: "expulsion of three *Intruders*".

Postman · · · soliciting contributions · · · suspicious: OED "solicit" 2a: "To entreat or petition". 4d: "Of women: To accost and importune (men) for immoral purposes" (quoting "Means could easily be adopted to prevent soldiers being solicited by women", 1869). Since postmen do not ordinarily solicit contributions, presumably blackmail or a protection racket.

Section 6 of the Rent and Mortgage Interest Restrictions Act 1923: clause (3) provides that "Where the interest of the tenant of a dwelling-house · · · is determined, either as the result of an order or judgment for possession or ejectment, or for any other reason, any sub-tenant to whom the premises or any part thereof have been lawfully sub-let shall · · · be deemed to become the tenant of the landlord on the same terms". To A. E. James, 9 Apr 1927: "The Rent due from the Sub-Tenant has just been paid by the Agent, by cheque in favour of the Executors."

(13 & 14 Geo.5): the 13th and 14th years of the reign of George V, which began in 1910.

diseuse: OED: "A female artiste who specializes in monologue", from 1896.

Part II.

The party has been going on for some time, many empty bottles, remains of food on plates. The end of the Interlude music overlaps the gramophone of the party. The men are sitting about stolidly, while Doris and Dusty are walzing together like two automatic dolls. [*Top copy has a marginal arrow-link from "walzing" sentence to mention of ballet in previous paragraph, with "Query—too near together?"*] As the record ends and the girls return to their seats, a strong soprano voice is heard outside

"Casey Jones was a fireman's name;
In the red-light district he won his fame"

It is Mrs. Porter. Presently she is heard again on the stairs, as Snow holds the door open—

"And the neighbours knew by the shrieks and groans
That the man at the throttle was Casey Jones".

Mrs. Porter enters. She is very tall, very thin, very old, as you see from her face, but immensely vigorous, good figure, and carries herself like a young woman. Very fashionably and expensively dressed. She is greeted with great enthusiasm. She takes her seat at the head of the table beside Sweeney. Here there is a CONTEST of some length between Sweeney and Mrs. Porter, each supporting a different point of view. They are evidently antipathetic and hostile, but drawn together simply because each is the only person [*1st reading*: person's] on the other's plane of vitality. There is no logical victory at the end, and indeed no end, but Sweeney speaks less and less, more and more briefly and sullenly, and goes on drinking, so that you are given the impression that he is having the worst of it and is getting into an ugly mood. As they continue the others become a bit uncomfortable, someone puts on the gramaphone and the two girls dance again, but this time becoming more and more frightened and hysterical. Suddenly Sweeney pulls something out of his pocket, gives a dull roar, the girls shriek, and Mrs. Porter falls on the floor. She is carried out for dead into the next room. Sweeney sits drinking, the only one who is quite collected. At the height of the confusion there is a KNOCK—it is the Tenant returned to complain again. Contrast between the confusion of the party this time and the cheeky reception given him the first time. All talk at once, apologise, promise, anything to get rid of him. He becomes more confident, threatens them boldly, and goes away. Silence. Sweeney goes on drinking. Suddenly a voice is heard from the next room

"Said Casey Jones before he died:
There's two more women I wish I'd tried—"

---

the gramophone ··· walzing together like two automatic dolls ··· puts on the gramaphone: "with automatic hand, | And puts a record on the gramophone", *The Waste Land* [III] 255–56, and note to 255 for "gramaphone".

Casey Jones: railway driver killed in an accident. Engine wiper Wallace Saunders is said to have made up *The Ballad of Casey Jones* in 1900. Versions vary, but the lyrics of Billy Murray's Blue Amberol cylinder of 1910 have: "The switchman knew by the engine's moan | That the man at the throttle was Casey Jones. || Casey Jones said just before he died, | There's two more roads that I'd like to ride."

RESURRECTION of Mrs. Porter who returns as lively as ever. The only person who is not amazed and who receives this quite calmly is Sweeney, and you know that he knew everything in advance, as did she, and that the two are accepting the roles given them by fate. She ascends to her former place beside Sweeney, stichomythia between the two, all stand and raise wineglasses, and a sort of hymenaeal hymn is sung. All form two by two in procession singing. Drop scene: the procession still singing is seen descending the stairs of the building. This scene gives time for the backscene to be changed. As they drift away singing more faintly the scene is raised and as the familiar KNOCK is heard—

The Tenant is discovered in bed. Eight A.M. The knock is the knock of his servant. He raises himself dully, still half asleep, and looks dazedly about him. It has been his DREAM. [*This last paragraph deleted in top copy*]

Curtain.

---

stichomythia: "The next stage also was reached with the help of a hint from Seneca. Several scholars, Butler in particular, have called attention to a trick of Seneca of repeating one word of a phrase in the next phrase, especially in stichomythia, where the sentence of one speaker is caught up and twisted by the next", *Seneca in Elizabethan Translation* (1927).

a sort of hymenaeal hymn: OED "Hymen" 1. "The God of marriage". 3. "A wedding-hymn, hymeneal song. rare." TSE: "(Io Hymen, Hymenæe)", *Ode* ("Tired. | Subterrene") 13 and note.

the familiar KNOCK ··· The Tenant is discovered in bed ··· The knock is the knock ··· half asleep ··· It has been his DREAM: De Quincey, *On the Knocking at the Gate in Macbeth*: "From my boyish days I had always felt a great perplexity on one point in *Macbeth*. It was this: the knocking at the gate, which succeeds to the murder of Duncan, produced to my feelings an effect for which I never could account ··· At length, in 1812, Mr. Williams made his *début* on the stage of Ratcliffe Highway, and executed those unparalleled murders which have procured for him such a brilliant and undying reputation ··· Now it will be remembered that in the first of these murders (that of the Marrs) the same incident (of a knocking at the door soon after the work of extermination was complete) did actually occur, which the genius of Shakespeare has invented ··· we must be made sensible that the world of ordinary life is suddenly arrested—laid asleep—tranced ··· Hence it is that, when the deed is done, when the work of darkness is perfect, then the world of darkness passes away like a pageantry in the clouds: the knocking at the gate is heard; and it makes known audibly that the reaction has commenced: the human has made its reflux upon the fiendish; the pulses of life are beginning to beat again; and the re-establishment of the goings-on of the world in which we live, first makes us profoundly sensible of the awful parenthesis that had suspended them." For TSE on this essay, see note to *Fragment of an Agon* 161–73.

7. DELAYS AND *CRITERION* PUBLICATION OF THE TWO FRAGMENTS

Henry Eliot to their mother, Charlotte, 6 Apr 1926: "Tom says he is writing a play of modern life, in which some of the characters of his poems appear again." The previous month had seen publication of Charlotte Eliot's *Savonarola*. TSE's Introduction had declared (xi): "The next form of drama will have to be a verse drama but in new verse forms. Perhaps the conditions of modern life (think how large a part is now played in our sensory life by the internal combustion engine!) have altered our perception of rhythms. At any rate, the recognised forms of speech-verse are not as efficient as they should be; probably a new form will be devised out of colloquial speech."

To Mrs. Hugh Fraser Stewart, 9 June 1926: "The only difficulty about my play is the tense. It is true that I am going to write it, it is partly true that I have partly written it and it is wholly untrue to say that it is written. Were the whole play in existence, I should have had no hesitation; it would be the A.D.C. [the Amateur Dramatic Club, Cambridge] who would hesitate. But two or three unfinished scenes are of no use to anybody."

In *Criterion* Oct 1926, *Fragment of a Prologue* ended: "(*To be continued*.)" In *Criterion* Jan 1927, the title *Fragment of an Agon* is followed by "[From *Wanna Go Home, Baby?*]" Untraced as a specific title, the spelling of "Wanna Go Home, Baby?" suggests American song lyrics of the era.

8. VOLUME PUBLICATION

After receiving an approach for publication of a limited edition of the two Fragments in Guy Chapman's "King's Printers" series, TSE wrote to David Higham, 28 Nov 1929: "I will confirm what I said to you on the telephone about Guy Chapman's offer. It is certainly tempting, but I had already considered (for my own firm) and dismissed the possibility of publishing the two 'Fragments' by themselves. I have not yet given up the hope of finishing the play of *Sweeney Agonistes*; if I do, it means considerably revising these fragments; and if I finish the play, I have, as I said, definite notions about the form of publication. I think that you will be able to put my reasons to Chapmans in such a way that they will not suppose that I object to them; for indeed I am pleased and flattered by the offer."

Volume publication of *Sweeney Agonistes* was proposed again—by Faber—while TSE was in America in 1932. Frank Morley, who was compiling the *Criterion* in the editor's absence, sent a telegram:

> PUBLISHING TWO JOYCE TALES AS XMAS HALFCROWN BOOK WANT SAME TIME PRICE PUBLISH FRAGMENTS PROLOGUE AGON TOGETHER CABLE PERMISSION TITLE STOP NOT TIME SEND PROOFS WOULD COLLATE CRITERION TEXT MORLEY

and followed with a letter on 8 Nov: "it occurred to us that it would be very helpful to rake in some badly needed cash by producing the Two Fragments of *Sweeney Agonistes* as a 2/6 item simultaneously with the two *Shem and Shaun* tales." Meanwhile TSE had replied with a telegram of his own, 2 Nov:

> PERMISSION MUST BE GIVEN I SUPPOSE STOP TITLE SWEENEY AGONISTES FRAGMENTS OF AN ARISTOPHANIC MELODRAMA DONT MAKE IT ARTY ELIOT.

On 6 Nov, TSE wrote confirming his permission, adding:

> I don't know what you mean by collating texts as there is only one text, that in *The Criterion*, however, collate it if you can and emend it if you will. I should have liked a short preface something like this:
>
> The author has decided to reprint these two fragments, originally published in two numbers of *The Criterion*, only because such a long time has elapsed since the work was designed, that he has become reconciled to the probability that it will never be completed. Had the drama ever been continued, he is sure that the first fragment, which he recognises to be inferior, would have been much altered or even superseded. He reprints it only because it may help to give some notion of the original scheme, which was based upon the account of Aristophanic drama by F. M. Cornford in his *Origins of Attic Comedy*. At the close of the second scene, after the expulsion of three *Intruders* (two ticket-sellers and the tenant of the flat below) Mrs. Porter was to have appeared.

No preface appeared in the book. The sheets were printed on 16 Nov (Faber archive), using the typeface Bodoni, and TSE acknowledged receipt of finished copies in a letter to Morley from Eliot House at Harvard dated "St. Stephen Protomartyr 1932": "*Sweeney Agonistes* is nicely printed, I like the type; please send SIX more copies and debit my account. I hope I draw some royalties."

9. AFTER PUBLICATION

In 1933: "I once designed and drafted a couple of scenes of a verse play. My intention was to have one character whose sensibility and intelligence should be on the plane of the most sensitive and intelligent members of the audience; his speeches should be addressed to them as much as to the other personages in the play—or rather, should be addressed to the latter, who were to be material, literal-minded and visionless, with the consciousness of being overheard by the former. There was to be an understanding between this protagonist and a small number of the audience, while the rest of the audience would share the responses of the other characters in the play. Perhaps this is all too deliberate, but one must experiment as one can", *The Use of Poetry and the Use of Criticism* 153–54. Although TSE's readers could not know it when they read this, the protagonist in his mind may have been not Sweeney but the disturbed Tenant who appears in *The Superior Landlord* and who, in the first drafting, dreams the whole thing, with whom TSE would have sympathised. For TSE's sensitivity to noise, see note to *Morning at the Window* title, 1, 3. In an unpublished memoir, *T. S. Eliot* (Texas), Osbert Sitwell records that the flat below the Eliots' at 18 Crawford Mansions (where they lived 1916–20), was occupied by two "actresses" who spent their time "playing the piano, singing, or putting some particularly loud record on the gramophone". This often went on "far into the small hours and without interval", and at midnight they tended to shout out loudly to "gentleman friends" down on the pavement. When TSE eventually complained to the landlord, he was told "Well, you see, Sir, it's the Artistic Temperament" (see *Letters 1* 334).

To Paul Elmer More, 28 Apr 1936: "I think myself that it is the most *original* thing that I have done. It is useless to speculate whether, if circumstances had permitted my finishing that play at the time, it would have been equally good as a whole; the only thing that is certain is that twelve years have made too great a difference in me for me to touch it now." *Smidt* 61: "I asked Eliot in 1948 why he never finished *Sweeney Agonistes* and had the following reply: 'Because when time lapses before a work is completed you change in the meantime and your inspiration changes. I don't believe in rewriting poetry, it usually spoils it; or in continuing to work on older things. Most readers by now will have acquired some idea of what *Sweeney Agonistes* forms a fragment of, and I wouldn't like to disturb that idea.' Introducing *Fragment of an Agon*, Columbia, 28 Apr 1958: "This was a work I never finished because it has to be spoken too quickly to be possible on the stage, to convey the sort of rhythm that I intended. It was much too fast for dialogue, really" (*Columbia University Forum* Fall 1958, 14).

E. M. W. Tillyard: "Some years ago, when *Sweeney Agonistes* was performed in London, Sweeney was represented as a rather tired business man. I had the chance of asking the author whether this unexpected representation had his approval. He answered *No*, and that his own picture of his Sweeney was of a retired professional boxer who kept a pub", *EinC* July 1953. Also after the first production, Nevill Coghill asked "Who *is* Sweeney? How do you see him? What sort of man is he?" TSE: "I think of him as a man who in younger days was perhaps a professional pugilist, mildly successful; who then grew older and retired to keep a pub", *March & Tambimuttu eds.* 86. Conrad Aiken recalled TSE taking boxing lessons as a form of self-discipline: "The boxing lessons, meanwhile, took place at a toughish gymnasium in Boston's South End, where, under the tutelage of an ex-pugilist with some such monicker as Steve O'Donnell, he learned not only the rudiments of boxing, but also, as he put it, 'how to swarm with passion up a rope' · · · Was Steve O'Donnell the prototype of Sweeney, as some have suggested?" *March & Tambimuttu eds.* 21. For the name, see note on the title *Sweeney Erect.* (TSE took Geoffrey and Enid Faber to a boxing match at the Albert Hall in Apr 1927.)

TSE to Roberto Sanesi, 10 Dec 1959, responding to list of poems Sanesi wished to translate into Italian: "I entirely agree with you that *Sweeney Agonistes* would probably prove very difficult. A prose translation would not do, and the rhythms are probably possible in the English language only."

10. PREMIÈRE IN AMERICA: ENTER AN OLD GENTLEMAN

In reply to a request for permission to stage *Sweeney Agonistes*, TSE not only acceded, but provided new material. To Professor Hallie Flanagan of Vassar College, 18 Mar 1933:

> I have no objection to your doing *Sweeney*, what there is of him, though I cannot imagine what anybody can do without me there to direct it. The action should be stylised as in the Noh drama—see Ezra Pound's book and Yeats' preface and notes to *The Hawk's Well.* Characters *ought* to wear masks; the ones wearing old masks ought to give the impression of being young persons (as actors) and vice versa. Diction should not have too much expression. I had intended the whole play to be accompanied by light drum taps to accentuate the beats (esp. the chorus, which ought to have a noise like a street drill). The characters should be in a shabby flat, seated at a refectory table, facing the audience; Sweeney in the middle with a chafing dish, scrambling eggs. (See "you see this egg.") (See also F. M. Cornford: *Origins of Attic Comedy*, which is important to read before you do the play.) I am talking about the *second* fragment of course; the other one is not much good. The second should end as follows: there should be 18 knocks like the angelus, and then

Enter an old gentleman. He is in full evening dress with a carnation, but otherwise resembles closely Father Christmas. In one hand he carries an empty champagne bottle, in the other an alarum clock.

THE OLD GENTLEMAN. Good evening. My name is Time. The time by the exchange clock is now nine-forty-five (or whatever it is). I come from the vacant lot in front of the Grand Union Depot, where there is the heroic equestrian statue of General Diego Cierra of Paraguay. Nobody knows why General Cierra is there. Nobody knows why I am there. Nobody knows anything. I wait for the lost trains that bring in the last souls after midnight. The time by the exchange clock is now 9:46.

SWEENEY. Have you nothing else to say?
OLD GENTLEMAN. Have you nothing to ask me?
SWEENEY. Yes.
OLD GENTLEMAN. Good.
SWEENEY. When will the barnfowl fly before morning?
When will the owl be operated on for cataracts?
When will the eagle get out of his barrel-roll?
OLD GENTLEMAN. When the camel is too tired to walk farther
Then shall the pigeon-pie blossom in the desert
At the wedding-breakfast of life and death.
SWEENEY. Thank you.
OLD GENTLEMAN. Good night.

(*As Old Gentleman leaves, the alarum clock in his hand goes off.*)

The following year, TSE was not sure whether he would continue with the play. To Hallie Flanagan, 9 Feb 1934: "I cannot tell you when or whether there will be more of *Sweeney* but in any case I hope to start something new of the same kind as soon as I have finished with a dramatic pageant which is to be produced in the early summer" (*The Rock*). In the event he wrote no more. It was not until 1943 that Flanagan printed the extra dialogue from his letter of ten years before (*Flanagan* 82–84), with a photograph of the cast on the set, adding that in time for the première in 1933, "The alarum clock went off and Mr. Eliot arrived on May 6". The extra dialogue was printed again in Carol H. Smith's *T. S. Eliot's Dramatic Theory and Practice* (1963) and in the programme for the Stage Sixty Theatre Club's *Homage to T. S. Eliot* (1965).

My name is Time: in *The Winter's Tale*, Time appears at the start of Act IV as chorus. Act V includes three Gentlemen. TSE sent a telegram to Flanagan, 27 Nov 1941: "CANT IDENTIFY FATHER TIME KINDEST REGARDS ELIOT".

General Diego Cierra: apparently TSE's invention.

the lost trains that bring in the last souls after midnight: Laforgue: "les trains manqués", *Dimanches* ("J'aurai passé") 4, quoted in *Baudelaire* (1930).

barrel-roll OED: "an aeronautical feat in which an aeroplane makes a complete revolution about the longitudinal axis", recorded from 1927, then in Auden's *The Orators* (1932).

the wedding-breakfast of life and death: *Hamlet* I ii: "The funeral bak'd meats | Did coldly furnish forth the marriage tables." (See deleted subtitle.)

TSE to Virginia Woolf, 25 Apr 1933: "Next week I go to Poughkeepsie N.Y. where the young ladies of Vassar College are to perform *Sweeney Agonistes* in treble pipe." (OED "pipelet": "a weak piping voice", with 1885, "in a soft treble pipe".) Directed by Flanagan, the première took place on 6 May 1933, as part of *Now I Know Love—A Mime Sequence*, the rest of which consisted of idylls by Theocritus, *Telephone* by Dorothy Parker and *Pent House* by Vassar student Mary Morley Crapo (later Mary Hyde Eccles).

Before the performance, *Vassar Miscellany News* reported on 3 May: "The music for the production, which has been composed by Quincy Porter, is thematic rather than historical; yet the three Theocritus idylls are pastoral in tone, while the Sweeney [music] is as mad and contemporary as the text ··· The construction used for the plays is based upon no tenet of stage craft, but is designed to provide a playing space which must defy time and space in their leap through twenty-one centuries."

The following week, Frani Blough reported that the music "was written for string quartet, with a percussion section behind scenes, which it seems was someone rubbing sandpaper together ··· the strings were perfect for the mournful love themes and the exotic Crocodile Isle music of *Sweeney* ··· the music for *Under the Bamboo Tree* in *Sweeney Agonistes* contained snatches of the popular song ··· Sweeney is the disillusioned and tired man, who toys with the idea that life on a cannibal isle, getting back to the old primitive instincts, might be the solution of the modern problem. He really knows perfectly well it wouldn't be however, and so does Dusty who says 'I'd be bored' and 'I don't like eggs, I don't like life on your Crocodile Isle.' But it is she who finally goes out with him at the end—to a coffin instead of an idyllic island—not Doris who always picked up his ideas too quickly to understand them, sings *Under the Bamboo Tree*, and does a native dance. The 'fragment' was beautifully reproduced; the acting was a rarely seen combination of finish and spontaneity, especially on the part of Carolyn Hoysradt and Elizabeth Carey as Dusty and Doris ··· A rhythmic motif was carried through the play from the opening when Dusty is cutting the cards to tell her fortune to the last grim knocks off-stage (the knocks have been variously interpreted as hammering the nails in the coffin, and the knocks of the policeman on the door) and the motif seemed not studied but quite inevitable."

After the performance: "'Yes, *Sweeney* was entirely different from my previous conception of it,' said Mr. Eliot, discussing the Experimental Theatre's production of his play. 'But I liked it very, very much. In fact, I am inclined to think Mrs. Flanagan's way of presentation was better than my own might have been. *Sweeney* is still a fragment to me, I can only see it as part of a longer play, but Mrs. Flanagan successfully produced it as a complete dramatic unit.' Mr. Eliot was so encouraged by the success of the fragment to which *Sweeney* belongs that he is planning to complete the play. 'The first option on the dramatic performance of the finished work will go to Mrs. Flanagan,' he promised", *Vassar Miscellany News* 10 May 1933. Elsewhere in the same issue: "'I have always wanted to experiment with new forms of verse plays,' he answered when asked about the actual starting point of *Sweeney Agonistes*. The blank verse Elizabethan forms are exhausted for the modern dramatic writer, but strongly rhythmic forms, and rhymed verses may have a future on the stage. He mentioned particularly *Four Plays for Dancers* by William Butler Yeats as being one of the early experiments of the sort. The relation of *Sweeney* to the agons of Aristophanes was rather by unconscious influence than any deliberate planning. 'I wanted to *soak* myself in Aristophanes,' Mr. Eliot said, and whatever characteristics may have come out in *Sweeney* were due to that rather than to any direct design. It will come, perhaps, as a surprise to the classics majors that Mr. Eliot bases all his analysis of Aristophanes on that familiar volume, F. M. Cornford's *Origins of Greek Comedy*."

Flanagan 84–85 recalled that the day after the performance, "by request of the student body, Mr. Eliot discussed poetry in the theatre. Roaming about the setting of his own play, he talked about poetry with impersonal lucidity. 'My poetry is simple and straightforward,' he declared; and when the audience laughed he looked pained. 'It is dubious whether the purpose of poetry is to communicate anyway. Poetry ought simply to record the fusion of a number of experiences' ··· To student questions from the crowded house he was painstakingly exact, though sometimes cryptic. 'Was the production what you expected?' 'The moment expected may be unforeseen when it arrives.' (This line he later used in *Murder in the Cathedral*.)" See TSE to J. Bramwell, 11 July 1945: "The first question about a poem is not whether it is intelligible but whether it is readable" (in headnote to *The Waste Land*, 9. AFTER PUBLICATION).

11. BRITISH PERFORMANCES

To I. A. Richards, 18 May 1934: "Rupert Doone ··· is anxious to put on a performance, which will include *Sweeney Agonistes* and *Fulgens et Lucres*, somewhere in Cambridge during this term ··· While I can make no promises for the future of the Group Theatre, it seems to me an experiment worth while trying out." (The only copy of Henry Medwall's *Fulgens and Lucres*, the earliest surviving English secular play, had been sold at auction in 1919 and reproduced in facsimile in 1920.) Despite Doone's initial plan, the first British performance of *Sweeney Agonistes* was given privately in London, by his Group Theatre, of which TSE was a literary director, on 11 Nov 1934. John Hayward, *London Letter* in *New York Sun* 23 Nov 1934:

> If you ··· are interested in the more intimate activities of contemporary literature, the most important event I can record is a private performance of T. S. Eliot's *Sweeney Agonistes*, which took place on the evening of Armistice Day. Originally printed in Eliot's *Criterion* quarterly, these two *Fragments of an Aristophanic Melodrama* have since been published together by Faber & Faber of London (1932). They mark an important stage in the evolution of Eliot's poetry as his first experiment in a new form of verse-drama. Unfortunately I was unable to attend the performance, but Eliot has given me some notes which may interest you. He tells me that *Sweeney Agonistes* was actually performed for the first time at Vassar College in May, 1933, under the direction of Mrs. Flanagan. The opportunity for a London performance was given by the Group Theater, a small company of enthusiasts, led by Rupert Doone, formerly one of Diaghilev's dancers. Doone, incidentally, has already produced a miming version of Auden's *Dance of Death*. *Sweeney Agonistes* was played before a small but distinguished Bloomsbury audience—including Aldous Huxley, Virginia Woolf and Lady Ottoline Morrell—in the small attic rooms of the Group Theater in Great Newport street, round the corner from Leicester Square. All the performers, except Sweeney, wore masks, and there was no stage, the actors and audience being situated in relation to each other in such a way as to give the spectators the impression that they were minor characters in the drama, an informal setting, which has been used successfully in Russia. The complete performance lasted about half an hour—rather longer than I supposed—but it appears that the tempo was deliberately slowed up in order to create an atmosphere of suspense. Eliot, at any rate, was satisfied with it all, and particularly with the second of the two scenes. He admits, however, that Sweeney himself was conceived after a different plan from the one he

> imagined. If he really looked like Crippen, as Eliot says he did, then he is not the same never-to-be-forgotten apenecked Sweeney of the early poems.

A second private performance followed on 25 Nov (prompt copy, Berg). A third performance, in December, was attended by Yeats and Brecht. TSE to Yeats, 6 Dec: "although the presentation was in important respects entirely alien to my intentions, I was very much pleased with the skill and intelligence of the production". Desmond MacCarthy: "I found myself in an L-shaped room on the third floor, round which seats had been arranged, leaving an empty space in the middle, where stood a table with some drinks on it and some unoccupied chairs. It was in this space that the performance took place. We, the spectators, were in the position of Elizabethan swells; we were sitting on the stage itself ··· Into the darkened room, or rather into a little pool of light created by one lamp overhead, came two young women wearing masks; their masks bore a grotesque resemblance to a commonplace kind of prettiness", *Listener* 9 Jan 1935. A newspaper cutting at Harvard reads "All the characters but one are masked. The unmasked is a real man. The masked are symbols ··· The suggestion is that life is a hopeless business", against which TSE wrote: "This production was *completely* the reverse of what *I* meant!"

Sweeney Agonistes was licensed for public performance in Britain by the Lord Chamberlain's Office on 25 July 1935, after inspection of the printed text. The reader's report on it by G. S. Street (BL) summarises: "This 'fragments of an Aristophanic melodrama' consist of 'fragment of a prologue' and 'fragment of an agon'. In the former two girls tell their fortunes by cards and one of them, Doris, draws a coffin. They are joined by Sam Wauchope and three American friends who talk about London. In the second fragment besides these five there are Sweeney, Swarts and Snow, the last two merely playing nigger instruments. Sweeney talks in free verse about carrying Doris off to a cannibal island and eating her. Later he tells, also in verse, about a man who 'did in' a girl in a bath and was not found out but apparently went mad. Then they all sing a chorus about dreaming they are going to be hanged. Serious poets are seldom happy when they relax—Swinburne's limericks are a notable exception—and I don't think this nonsense amusing. There is no harm in it. The word 'copulation' is used on pp. 24 and 25. I don't think it is a necessarily banned word and think it would be rather absurd to cut it out of an eminent poet's verses, even comic ones: it is not indecent. Recommended for Licence, G. S. Street."

In Oct 1935, *Sweeney Agonistes* and Auden's *The Dance of Death* opened at the Westminster Theatre for 15 public performances (see *Malamud*). The programme contained a Producer's Note by Doone: "My production is concerned with morals as well as aesthetics. I have sought to criticise the conventionalities of modern behaviour with its empty code and heartiness—immoral but never immoral enough—decaying, but so long in dying. I see Sweeney himself as a modern Orestes (the only three-dimensional character in the play). The rest are conventionalised conventional characters—the Eumenides or Bogies of Sweeney's persecution. RD."

*

TSE, on Hofmannsthal's *The Tower*: "the play is essentially poetic drama. I do not know whether it has ever been presented on the stage; but the latter part ··· becomes so phantasmagoric that one can only imagine its representation in terms of a dream-film such as Jean Cocteau might devise · · · and if *The Tower* is unplayable, we must attribute this not to failure of skill but to the fact that what the author wished here to express exceeded the limits within which the man of the theatre must work. For the surface meaning, the real or apparent reason for human behaviour which must be immediately apprehensible by the audience if the play is to hold their interest, Hofmannsthal cares less and less as the play proceeds. He seems to have loaded this play, in symbolism which perhaps has more than one level of significance, with all the burden of his feelings about the catastrophe of the Europe to which he belonged, the Europe which went down in the wreck of empires between 1914 and 1918. As Herr Meyer-Sichting justly says, there is much in the play which cannot be 'understood', but only 'intuited'. The play expresses not only the author's suffering during those years that remained to him, but also his ultimate Christian hope. I find it interesting to compare the message of *The Tower*, so far as I have succeeded in grasping it, with that of the masterly essay which Paul Valéry wrote in 1919, called *La Crise de l'esprit*: an essay which, because so much of its prophecy has already come to pass, is more terrifying since the second World War than it was at the date of its first publication. Both men were poets; both had their formation and first practised their art in the world before 1914; both lived on—the French poet eighteen years after the death of the Austrian—into a waning civilization", *A Note on "The Tower"* (1963).

To Erich Alport, 5 Oct 1929, on Hofmannsthal: "I have long had the idea myself of trying to translate one of his Jacobean plays into more or less Jacobean English; but I don't know when I could get that done." To Herbert Read, "Friday" [6 Dec 1929] (with specific reference to Hofmannsthal's *Die Hochzeit der Sobeide* and *Die Frau im Fenster*): "I feel emboldened to try my hand at translating one or two of Hofmannsthal's Jacobean verse plays back into Jacobean. Do you think it is possible and worth while?" To Read, 20 Mar 1936: "It is true that I have always had a high opinion of Hofmannsthal, and that I did at one time entertain the notion of translating one of his plays · · · It seems to me the sort of occupation that we might well take up after we are seventy. That of course is the dilemma about such works of translation, that the most suitable people to do them are also the people who ought not to spend the time on them · · · I am all for postponing it for another 20 or 25 years."

*

Unadopted epigraphs] (See headnote to Textual History of *Sweeney Agonistes*, description of drafts. **Junius**: *The Letters of Junius* Letter 7. Faber published C. W. Everett's edition in 1927 (*Schuchard* 219). In a letter to the *TLS*, 6 Dec 1926, TSE apologised for having mistaken the 17th-century scholar Francis Junius "who was only a name in an obscure corner of my memory for a Junius with whom I am on more intimate terms", the 18th-century author whom he ranked among the "masters of English prose". **St. John of the Cross**: see note to second epigraph of final text. ***Measure for Measure***: III i, with "seem" for Shakespeare's "be". From the same speech by the Duke, disguised as a Friar, as the epigraph to *Gerontion*. **LES CHOEPHORES**: see note to first epigraph of final text. **Casey Jones**: see headnote 6. *THE SUPERIOR LANDLORD*.

Title ***Sweeney Agonistes***: since 1932. ***Agonistes***: "In Greek the word can mean a contestant in the games · · · or a champion · · · and in the Christian tradition · · · 'saint' or 'martyr'", note to *Samson Agonistes* in *Milton: Complete Shorter Poems*, ed. John Carey (rev. ed. 1997). In 1930, Nevill Coghill staged Milton's play in Oxford and invited TSE, who replied on 17 May: "It is very thoughtful of you to offer me tickets for your production of *Samson Agonistes*—a play which I admire immensely, and which—if there ever has been a performance before—I have never had the opportunity of seeing—and I wish indeed that I could come; but the latter part of May and the beginning of June finds me very rushed indeed · · · I shall have to content myself with reading any accounts of the performances afterwards." To Hugh Gordon Porteus, 5 Nov 1931: "I was very much pleased, particularly because you mentioned one piece of mine which I very much like, and which everybody ignores, that is the two fragments which I now call *Sweeney Agonistes*. You perhaps remember the quotation 'at the mill with slaves'?" (Milton: "Ask for this great Deliverer now, and find him | Eyeless in Gaza at the mill with slaves, | Himself in bonds under Philistian yoke", *Samson Agonistes* 40–42.) To Marcus S. Crouch, 15 May 1939: "if a play is not intended to be produced, it is not worth writing". Milton, prefacing *Samson Agonistes*: "Division into act and scene referring chiefly to the stage (to which this work was never intended) is here omitted", *Of that Sort of Dramatic Poem which is Called Tragedy*.

Subtitle ***Aristophanic Melodrama***: *Smith 1963* 58: "His play is Aristophanic in that it combines a comic surface of social satire with the ritualistic celebration of death and rebirth which Cornford found to underlie comedy · · · It is melodramatic in the older sense of the term, a play combining music and drama, because it is in the music hall tradition, but it is also melodramatic in another sense." ***Melodrama***: OED ("Gk. song, music + F. *drame*") 1: "In early 19th c. use, a stage-play (usually romantic and sensational in plot and incident) in which songs were interspersed".

First epigraph] TSE gave Paul Mazon's French translation of these two Greek lines as the epigraph to "FRAGMENT OF A MELOCOMIC MINSTRELSY", one of two typescript titles on a separate leaf (see headnote to Textual History, drafts from King's: 2. TYPESCRIPT TITLES). ***Choephoroi***: Iphigenia, the daughter of Clytemnestra and Agamemnon, has been sacrificed by him to the gods, to secure favourable winds to Troy. On his return from Troy, Agamemnon is killed by Clytemnestra and her lover Aegisthus. Orestes, the son of Clytemnestra and Agamemnon, is urged by Apollo to avenge his father, and so kills his mother as well as Aegisthus. *Lemprière*: "Orestes is tormented by the Furies, and exiles himself to Argos, where he is still pursued by the avengeful goddesses." Aeschylus' trilogy, *Oresteia*, depicts in *Agamemnon* the king's return and his murder; in *Choephoroi* (*The Libation Bearers*), the return of Orestes avenging his father; and in *Eumenides* (*The Kindly Ones*, meaning the Furies), the pursuit and prosecution of Orestes by the Furies, and his final acquittal. *The Family Reunion* I i: HARRY: "Look there! | Can't you see them? *You* don't see them, but I see them, | And they see me." To Hayward, 2 May 1935, when Vivien was desperate to see her husband again: "I have not yet got over the feeling of being hunted: in my sleep I am pursued like Orestes, though I feel with less reason than that hero · · · I don't know how much ground there is for this feeling, but it is something *plus fort que moi*, of the character of nightmare, and I have to give way to it." 25 Feb 1936: "I have more than one kind of nightmare: hence my interest in Orestes."

Second epigraph] St. John of the Cross: *Ascent of Mount Carmel* I IV 1. Apparently TSE's own translation from J. P. Migne's French as quoted in Gonzague Truc, *Les Mystiques espagñols: Saint Térèse—Jean de le Croiz* [1921] (Jennifer Formichelli, personal communication). TSE recommended Truc's book at the end of his first Clark Lecture (*The Varieties of Metaphysical Poetry* 65). See note to *Ash-Wednesday* I 1–3, 5. "During the sixteenth century, Spain experienced an extraordinary outburst of mysticism: in other words, she produced at least three great mystics and saints, and probably several hundred pathological ecstatics. The greatest were St. Theresa, and St. John of the Cross, both Carmelites. I think that St. John was the greater writer, or rather that his writings are very much more important than St. Theresa's; but probably Theresa had the greater influence", *Thinking in Verse* (1930). TSE had made a note of St. John of the Cross, *Dark Night of the Soul*, in 1914 (*Harvard index cards*); see note to *Burnt Norton* III 25–32. He acknowledged a copy of William Force Stead's book *The Shadow of Mount Carmel* on 13 Nov 1926. For St. John of the Cross and the doctrine that "one must divest oneself of the love of created beings", see note to *East Coker* III 35–46. TSE, contributing for the first time to *Christendom*: "But unless this humanity is considered always in relation to God, we may expect to find an excessive love of created beings, in other words humanitarianism, leading to a genuine oppression of human beings in what is conceived by other human beings to be their interest", *Catholicism and International Order* (1933). For the Buddhist text "he becomes divested of passion, and by the absence of passion he becomes free", see note to *The Waste Land* part title "III. *The Fire Sermon*".

To Geoffrey Faber, 10 May 1936: "I quite agree that the exaltation of love (which is only incidentally but necessarily 'physical') is an illusion, in being the illusion of a unity of two *persons* as well as the transient identification of sensation in two bodies. Between any two people (and the more intimate their relations the more important this becomes) there is always an unresolvable element of hostility which may be only further incubated by the dominance of one over the other. A man in love has moments at least when he feels his condition, with resentment, to be one of slavery rather than of self-realisation. (It is I think, a coming to terms between the elements of attraction and repulsion that constitutes permanent affection, but I am not talking about affection) ··· I've tried to express something of my belief at the end of *Burnt Norton*. I mean that the 'illusion' of love is something to pass forward through, not to dash into and out of again, like a bath. You will have to put up with a little mystical theology—I can't help that, because I can't talk about the subject without bringing it in. The 'illusion' is merely a degree of reality, then, essentially different from hallucination; and love of created beings should lead us to the only love that is wholly satisfactory and final, the love of God—even though for 99% of parsons this is only a stock phrase: it is *ciò che per l'universo si squaderna*" [the scattered leaves of all the universe], *Paradiso* XXXIII 87.

Fragment of a Prologue

From a ms by TSE relating to a sketch by Vivien Eliot ("Felice at the Card Table"), *c.* 1924: "Felise gives parties as a stimulant to stir up her own sluggish torpor. The party: Fanny, her brother Horace, a dago, an American, a German, the central figures (& Fresca). Play a mad kind of bridge. Fanny & Horace, with a *little* whisky (they are abstemious people) whip themselves up into a kind of frenzy in which they develop the most witty conversation & gestures, malapropisms with several meanings" (U. Maryland).

Characters] Given at the head of *Fragment of an Agon*. **WAUCHOPE:** Charles Ware Waughop, Joseph Louis Swarts and Louis Frederick Klipstein were contemporaries of TSE's at Smith Academy (Smith Academy Yearbooks, Washington U.; *Stayer*). Lt. Gen. Sir Arthur Wauchope was High Commissioner for Palestine, 1931–38. (TSE's Wauchope is a Lieutenant.) **HORSFALL:** perhaps *horseplay* + *pratfall* (OED: "*Theatr.* A comedy fall", from 1939) (*Stayer*). **KLIPSTEIN. KRUMPACKER:** Otto H. Schwarz to TSE, 5 Mar 1950, recalling their schooldays: "I know there is only one source from which you get the name Klipstein, the football player at Smith, what a character" (see note to *Fragment of a Prologue* 128, "Klip"). TSE to Schwarz, 20 Apr: "you were right about Klipstein, I remember him well, and how he looked the part. Krumpacker was a name and character I collected later at Harvard." To Lewis Morris, 24 Oct 1929, on a contemporary who had died: "but for my stout Anglo-Saxon constitution I suppose I should be in a box too. Krumpacker too: well, well." **SWARTS. SNOW:** *Smith 1963* 61: "entertainers brought in to provide jazz song and dance routines so popular at parties in the nineteen-twenties". *The Superior Landlord* specifies: "Lincoln Snow Negro Jazz Drummer" and "Milton Swarts Jewish Jazz Drummer". (Ger. *Schwarze* = negro.) **DORIS:** for "Doris, towelled from the bath", see note to *Sweeney Erect* 41. The subtitle of *The Superior Landlord* is *A Dream*. For *Doris's Dream Songs*, see headnote to *The Hollow Men*. **DUSTY:** *Partridge*: "Penniless; lower classes', from ca. 1870".

Stage direction (*ts1*) **Doris playing patience**: asked by Auden why he liked playing patience, TSE replied: "Because it's the nearest thing to being dead" (*Spender* 240). TSE: "He is skilful at solitaire patience", *How to Pick a Possum* 19 (in *Noctes Binanianæ*), and note.

1 **Pereira:** Bishop Henry Horace Pereira, Hon. Chaplain to Queen Victoria, died in Jan 1926 and was remembered in an obituary and correspondence in *The Times*. In 1905 he had published both *Intemperance* and *Intemperance as a Hindrance to Spiritual Life* (*Jayne*). Robert Speaight recalled reading *Sweeney Agonistes* in Colombo (Ceylon), "where practically everyone is called Pereira, and where the banyan trees composed an embarrassing background", *Braybrooke ed.* 78. Jonathan Pereira helped to pioneer pharmacology, publishing the standard *Elements of Materia Medica* in 1839. ("a medicine made from the bark of a Brazilian tree and used to mitigate or remove fever", *Grover Smith 1963* 65.)

21–27 **Ting a ling ling · · · That's Pereira | Yes that's Pereira · · · Pick up the receiver:** the technology did not allow the caller to be identified until he or she spoke.

31 **Miss Dorrance's *flat***: the italics perhaps mark a distinction from an "apartment" (Michael Field, *American Literary History* Spring 1992); or perhaps, since Pereira is not obviously American, from rooms for entertaining gentlemen on business. "Grishkin has a maisonnette", *Whispers of Immortality* 24. For a change by "F. M." from "Ellison & Antony lived in a flat", to "Ellison and Antony lived in 'Mansions' · · · It was not apparently sordid, any more than all 'Mansions' are sordid", see *McCue 2016*.

43, 52, 61 **She's got her feet in mustard and water · · · Sweeney · · · Mrs. Porter**: "The sound of horns and motors, which shall bring | Sweeney to Mrs. Porter in the spring. | O the moon shone bright on Mrs. Porter | And on her daughter | They wash their feet in soda water", *The Waste Land* [III] 199–201 (see note). Footbaths of mustard and water were recommended for everything from bunions to dyspepsia, sometimes together with "Female corrective mixture". Soda-water was solely for drinking.

49 **Now I'm going to cut the cards for to-night**: Vivien Eliot, for a story by "F. M." with songs, dancing and record-playing: "For two months Sibylla and Felice stayed in the high up sea-side flat · · · They cut the cards at all hours to discover their fortunes for the day, for each other, and for everyone they knew. Sibylla took great stock of the results" and "'Draw a card' said Felice, spreading out the other pack on her lap. Sibylla drew one. 'Nine of diamonds,' said Felice, 'you're in luck.' 'Let me see what does that mean?' 'Good luck, prosperity or business success', Felice replied promptly" (c. 624 fols. 62, 109).

97 **co*in*cidence** (as also **inter*est*ed** *Fragment of an Agon* 102): "F. M.": "'Come and try these *ex*cellent strawberries and cream *un*der the apple-tree,' he boomed · · · '*Per*-fectly en*chant*ing,' said the critic", *Fête Galante* (1925). For words partially italicised in Alfred Kreymborg's *Lima Beans*, see note to *Sweeney Among the Nightingales* 18–20.

110–14 **Knock · · · Knock**: see note to *Fragment of an Agon* 161–73. OED knocking-shop: "*slang*. A brothel" (1860).

116 **How come? how come?**: OED "how" 19: "*colloq*. (orig. *U.S.*) phr.: how did (or does) it come about (that)?" with this as first citation from a British publication. The sense of this Canadian speaker, though, appears closer to "What's up?" Joel Chandler Harris: "'How come, Brer Rabbit—how come?'" *Nights with Uncle Remus* (1883) ch. XLVII. Janet Adam Smith records that TSE's visits to Michael Roberts's family were marked by "the pleasant ritual of reading *Uncle Remus*" (*Olney ed.*).

124, 128 **Loot · · · Cap**: Lieutenant (pronounced *loo-tènant*, as opposed to the British *lef-tènant*), Captain.

125 **the Canadian Expeditionary Force**: with more than half a million men enlisting, the Canadian Corps were, in Lloyd George's words, "marked out as Storm Troops", the élite of the allied forces.

126–28 **klipstein · · · Klip**: "Sir Ferdinand || Klein. Who clipped", *Burbank with a Baedeker: Bleistein with a Cigar* 28–29 (pronunciation of *-stein* being variable).

129 **Yes we did our bit, as you folks say**: OED "bit" 4h: "*to do one's bit*: to make one's contribution to a cause or the like, esp. by serving in the armed forces" (1915),

with "Every man beyond the military age can and should do his 'bit'", *Ladies' Home Journal*, 1917. OED then quotes Galsworthy and TSE's line.

130 **I'll tell the world we got the Hun on the run:** C. B. Elderkin's song *We've Got the Hun on the Run* was published in 1918, but the phrase was common.

137, 158–59 **We hit this town last night for the first time ··· Sam of course is at *home* in London, | And he's promised to show us around:** "Now for a peek about the town ··· When you're out for an afternoon | Find somebody with money to spend", *Suite Clownesque* II 12, 15–16.

156 **real live:** OED "live" 1c: "frequent in jocular use, esp. in 'a real live —'", from 1887. 2b: "(orig *U.S.*). Of persons: Full of energy and alertness; 'wide-awake', up-to-date", with first British citation from 1932. In *The Superior Landlord* Part II, Sweeney and Mrs. Porter share a "plane of vitality", and after her resurrection Mrs. Porter "returns as lively as ever". **Britisher:** *Fowler*: "a word made in America, but now discountenanced in American dictionaries as 'in jocose use only' or as 'almost disused'; if these phrases give the actual & not merely the desirable American usage ··· it is time that British writers reconciled themselves to relinquishing the word in its convenient function of announcing that the user of it is American."

Fragment of an Agon

Vassar College performance programme: "When the curtain rises the company is seated in a shabby kitchen, in front of a refectory table. Sweeney, wearing a mask of an old man which makes him appear young, is scrambling an egg in a chafing dish. The time is 9:46 by the Exchange clock" (see headnote, 10. PREMIÈRE IN AMERICA: ENTER AN OLD GENTLEMAN). Yet *Flanagan* 84, recalling the première: "As the illustrations indicate, there was no shabby flat, no refectory table, and no chafing dish. The egg, however, was present in the setting itself and Mr. Eliot found it a satisfactory egg."

1–39] From his early years, TSE adopted the Tennysonian tradition of idealising exotic islands: "Ligarcia Huskchobornza the great plant. This fine flower was discovered in the South Sea Islands by a convict, 'Mickey' Dennisson, sent there for murder", *Eliot's Floral Magazine* (Houghton). To Conrad Aiken, 31 Dec 1914: "Come, let us desert our wives, and fly to a land where there are no Medici prints, nothing but concubinage and conversation." See note to *To Walter de la Mare* 2.

6–11 **I'll be the cannibal ··· I'll be the missionary ··· Into a stew. | A nice little, white little, missionary stew:** Joyce: "Dignam's potted meat. Cannibals would with lemon and rice. White missionary too salty", *Ulysses* episode VIII (Lestrygonians), with "—One stew" shortly before (Shawn Worthington, personal communication). TSE in 1948: "The man who, in order to understand the inner world of a cannibal tribe, has partaken of the practice of cannibalism, has probably gone too far: he can never quite be one of his own folk again. [*Footnote*: Joseph Conrad's *Heart of Darkness* gives a hint of something similar]", *Notes Towards the Definition of Culture* 41. "I find it difficult to believe that I ever said I 'enjoyed' my friends. I may have said that I enjoyed the society of my friends or I enjoyed friendships, but I am not a cannibal", memo to Peter du Sautoy about Louis Untermeyer's biographical notes for *Makers of the Modern World* (Faber archive). **I'll convert *you*! | Into a stew:** Cornford: "The Cook is a magician, a dealer in enchanted herbs, a medicine man. As such he is not, in origin, distinct from the Learned Doctor" (*Smith 1963* 68). On Cornford's phrasing, see Commentary to *The Waste Land* [III] 218 *TSE's Note.* **A nice little, white little, missionary stew:** Charles Dibdin:

> Says Freedom, "Why that's my own little island!"
> Oh, it's a snug little island!
> A right little, tight little island,
> Search the globe round, none can be found
> So happy as this little island.

Dickens quotes this as "our right little, tight little, island" at the beginning of ch. VI of *Little Dorrit.*

18–31 **no telephones · · · no gramophones · · · no motor cars · · · You'd be bored:** "In an interesting essay in the volume of *Essays on the Depopulation of Melanesia*, the psychologist W. H. R. Rivers adduced evidence which has led him to believe that the natives of that unfortunate archipelago are dying out principally for the reason that the 'Civilization' forced upon them has deprived them of all interest in life. They are dying from pure boredom. When every theatre has been replaced by 100 cinemas, when every musical instrument has been replaced by 100 gramophones, when every horse has been replaced by 100 cheap motor-cars, when electrical ingenuity has made it possible for every child to hear its bedtime stories from a loudspeaker, when applied science has done everything possible with the materials on this earth to make life as interesting as possible, it will not be surprising if the population of the entire civilized world rapidly follows the fate of the Melanesians", *Marie Lloyd* (1922). ("the essential advantage for a poet is · · · to see the boredom, and the horror, and the glory", *The Use of Poetry and the Use of Criticism* 106.) Rivers: "in the Solomon Islands the rulers stopped the special kind of warfare known as head-hunting, without at all appreciating the vast place it took in the religious and ceremonial lives of the people, without realising the gap it would leave in their daily interests, a blank far more extensive than that due to the mere cessation of a mode of warfare · · · I have now to suggest that this loss of interest forms one of the reasons, if indeed it be not the most potent of all the reasons, to which the native decadence is due", *Rivers ed.* 93–94. TSE, asked in 1945 about technology separating man from the artistic and creative crafts: "sooner or later · · · there will be a general rebellion against that · · · human beings will just become bored with the kind of life they have from it—and I think that boredom is a very powerful force in life and that people will do the most extraordinary things to escape from it · · · they are likely to be driven to wars of one kind or another, simply · · · to escape from boredom" (*Hodin*).

To J. H. Oldham, 14 Dec 1943: "I have lived to see many things working together, labouring and travailing to bring forth a degraded culture—the bioscope, the B.B.C., Bloomsbury, and now this monstrous regiment of Free Churchmen." Poetic drama should "enter into overt competition with prose drama" with verse spoken by people "dressed like ourselves, living in houses and apartments like ours, and using telephones and motorcars and radio sets",

Poetry and Drama (1951) 26. "There's a deterioration, it seems to me, in the quality of amusement as it becomes more mass entertainment and as the media for mass entertainment become more highly developed. The cinema first; now television. It's profitable to appeal to the largest audience and therefore to the lowest common denominator. I think that the end of a purely materialistic civilization with all its technical achievements and its mass amusements is—if, of course, there's no actual destruction by explosives—simply boredom. A people without religion will in the end find that it has nothing to live for. I did touch on this problem a good many years ago in an essay I wrote on the death of a great music-hall artist, Marie Lloyd", *A Conversation, recorded in 1958, between T. S. Eliot and Leslie Paul* ([1964]/1965). For "boring ··· automatism", see note to 108–112.

22 **Citroën**: three full syllables in TSE's recording.

34–35 **Birth, and copulation, and death. | That's all the facts when you come to brass tacks**: to Henry Eliot, 29 July 1926: "Unitarianism is a bad preparation for brass tacks like birth, copulation, death, hell, heaven and insanity: they all fall within the classification of Bad Form."

37, 39 **I've been born, and once is enough ··· Once is enough**: John 3: 3: "Except a man be born again, he cannot see the kingdom of God." In *The Superior Landlord* Part II: "Mrs. Porter falls on the floor. She is carried out for dead into the next room ··· RESURRECTION of Mrs. Porter who returns as lively as ever."

40 *stage direction* **TAMBO ··· BONES**: foils for the more educated master of ceremonies in minstrel shows in 19th-century America. "The two players, one on tambourine, the other on bones, who take seats opposite one another during the main part of the minstrel show. These 'endmen' were usually more heavily made-up than the other performers, used a more exaggerated dialect, and were called upon to perform more ludicrous and demeaning gyrations", Michael Field in *American Literary History* Spring 1992. Huxley, *Happy Families* (stage direction): "CAIN WASHINGTON TYRRELL, ASTON's negro brother—for the TYRRELLS, I regret to say, have a lick of the tar-brush in them and CAIN is a Mendelian throwback to the pure Jamaican type. CAIN is stout and his black face shines with grease." TSE: "Here let a clownesque be sounded | on the sandboard and bones", *Suite Clownesque* III 14^15 *stage direction*. On the blackface comedy duo Two Black Crows, see note to *Ash-Wednesday* I unadopted title (*"All Aboard for Natchez Cairo and St. Louis"*). Frank Morley's *Fable XIV* in *Noctes Binanianæ* contains a duet for TSE and Hayward with "*NIGGER MINSTRELS*" and ending "See them roll and see them go | See | Them | Ro-holl | And see | Them | *GO*."

40–48 ***Under the bamboo ··· Under the bamboo tree***:

> If you lak-a-me, lak I lak-a-you;
> And we lak-a both the same,
> I lak-a say, this very day,
> I lak-a change your name;
> 'Cause I love-a-you and love-a-you true
> And if you-a love-a-me,
> One live as two, two live as one
> Under the bamboo tree.

Bob Cole and Rosamond Johnson, *Under the Bamboo Tree* (1902) performed by

Marie Cahill ("the top song of the Cole and Johnson partnership", *The Fireside Book of Favorite American Songs* ed. Margaret Bradford Boni, 1952).

TSE to his Swedish translator, Erik Mesterton, 16 Nov 1948: "I had in mind the actual melody which went with it." TSE is said to have sung *Under the Bamboo Tree* at the party to celebrate his Nobel Prize (Cyril Connolly, *Sunday Times* 10 Jan 1965). Longfellow: "Under a spreading chestnut-tree", *The Village Blacksmith* 1.

40, 73 ***Under the bamboo ··· My little island girl***: on adapting and imagining popular songs, see note to *The Waste Land* [II] 128–30.

43–45 ***Two live as one | One live as two | Two live as three***: J. M. Barrie: "Are you and I one? Or are you and Joanna one? Or are the three of us two?" *Dear Brutus* (1922) III (*Grover Smith 1996* 78). Ring Lardner: "they say two can live as cheap as one", *Big Town* (1921).

55 ***Gauguin maids***: *Under the Bamboo Tree* begins "Down in the jungle lived a maid | Of royal blood though dusky shade." On TSE's return to Harvard from Paris in 1911: "He would bring back from his travels a nude by Gauguin, and proudly display it in his new rooms in Ash Street", *Sencourt* 37.

62–64 ***Do you want to flirt with me? | Under the ··· banyan ··· tree***: John Fryer: "Under the Banyan Tree, an Altar with a Dildo in the middle being erected, they offer Rice and Cocoe-Nuts to the Devil", *A New Account of East-India and Persia* (1698).

63–64 ***Under the ··· banyan ··· Or under the bamboo tree***: "It is under the banyan tree that a village used to meet every evening to hear complaints from aggrieved parties. A sort of justice was done", *Back Under the Banyan Tree* in *Economic Weekly* (India), 1 Sept 1956 (recalling an old apocryphal phrase). ***bamboo***: OED *v.*[1]: "To beat or 'cane' with a bamboo."

92 **what life is**: Arnold Bennett: *The Old Wives' Tale* (1908) bk. 4, "What Life Is".

102–103 **I assure you, Sir, we are very interested ··· girl**: Huxley, *Happy Families*, ASTON: "··· this girl really interests me." SIR JASPER: "Oh yes, I know, I know. She interests you too, Cain, doesn't she?"

104 **Any man might do a girl in**: OED "do" 46c: "do in": "do a great injury to ··· often, to murder, kill. *slang*", from 1905. TSE to Dorothy Pound, 27 Oct [1923]: "I don't think I will give you the name [of the doctor] unless you ask me again, or unless you want to do somebody in." The night after the première of *Sweeney Agonistes*, TSE answered questions from Vassar students, one of whom asked "Mr. Eliot, did you ever do a girl in?" *Flanagan* 85: "Mr. Eliot looked apologetic and said, 'I am not the type'." Vivien Eliot wrote to Middleton Murry, [Sunday] 1926, of her fears: "Sometimes that he is mad or else that he is most *frightfully* & subtly *wicked* and *dangerous*. That he is a terrible *menace*" (*Letters 3* 223). TSE had written to Middleton Murry of Vivien, probably in Apr 1925: "Must I kill her or kill myself?" (*Letters 2* 628) and "I know that the spring is Fear—a fear which I cannot account for. And I know that I have killed *her*. And this terrible sense of the most subtle form of *guilt* is itself paralysing and deadening" (*Letters 2* 632). To Frank Morley, 17 Feb 1938, on Harry's guilt, in *The Family Reunion*, about his wife's death at sea: "Don't agree with you yet about PUSHED, because I *wanted* the comic associations. Besides, how else, without a good deal of machinery ··· can you get something on the borderline where it might have been murder,

might have been an accident, or might have been imaginary? For all we know, he may have been standing several feet away thinking about this or that but with the lower level of day-dream mind fancying himself pushing her over. When you want to kill somebody the imagination of doing it, in a particular way, can be very vivid; and everyone knows that a realistic dream can come back to the mind later and you can wonder indefinitely whether it was dream or actuality."

104–106 **Any man might do a girl in ··· Once in a lifetime**: Hermann Hesse: "Each one of us must in one hour of his life stand on the threshold of the borderland where Myshkin stood", *Thoughts on the Idiot of Dostoevsky*, tr. Stephen Hudson [Sydney Schiff], *Dial* Aug 1922. *Tomlin* 90, recalling a meeting with TSE on 25 May 1937: "He then gave me a slight shock by lapsing into a brief sort of reverie, and saying that if one had ever felt like 'murdering someone', one could never do anything about it. Something had been registered in the past and in one's own being." To Robert Waller, 19 Oct 1942: 'Doesn't everyone who has enough imagination ··· belong to the criminal classes as well as to other classes? No, one can have a great deal of imagination and yet be undeveloped on the criminal side."

107–108 **kept her there in a bath | With a gallon of lysol**: in 1910, after murdering his wife, Dr. Crippen dissolved her organs in acid in a bathtub; see note on title *Sweeney Erect*. *Grover Smith 1963* 71: "lysol is a cleansing agent, albeit a violent one." Huxley, *Happy Families*, ASTON: "I ought to have warned you in time of the chloroform flower." BELLE: "But it's such a lovely feeling now—like being in a very hot bath with lots of verbena bath-salts, and hardly able to move with limpness."

108–112 **lysol in a bath ··· Epsom ··· I seen that in the papers**: "Baudelaire has perceived that what distinguishes the relations of man and woman from the copulation of beasts is the knowledge of Good and Evil ··· he was at least able to understand that the sexual act as evil is more dignified, less boring, than as the natural, 'life-giving', cheery automatism of the modern world. For Baudelaire, sexual operation is at least something not analogous to Kruschen Salts ··· he was capable of a damnation denied to the politicians and the newspaper editors of Paris", *Baudelaire* (1930). OED quotes the newspaper slogan "That Kruschen feeling" for this laxative. Epsom salts, also a laxative, are primarily bath salts. (Baudelaire: "Les directeurs de Journaux ··· Liste de canailles" [The directors of newspapers ··· A list of guttersnipes], *Mon Cœur mis à nu* in *Journaux Intimes*.) For "Birth, and copulation, and death", see 28 and note.

129–31 **SWEENEY: I'd give him a drink and cheer him up. | DORIS: Cheer him up? DUSTY: Cheer him up? | SWEENEY: Well here again that don't apply**: TSE on Othello's "Soft you; a word or two before you go" (V ii): "What Othello seems to me to be doing in making this speech is *cheering himself up*. He is endeavouring to escape reality, he has ceased to think about Desdemona, and is thinking about himself". (Othello has done her in.) Stoicism "is the permanent substratum of a number of versions of cheering oneself up. Nietzsche is the most conspicuous modern instance of cheering oneself up", *Shakespeare and the Stoicism of Seneca* (1927).

132 **I've gotta use words when I talk to you**: *Fête Galante* (1925) by "F. M.": "when

she tried to speak to him her words conveyed nothing", following "under the apple-tree" (as here "*Under the bamboo tree*").

134–35 **He didn't know if he was alive | and the girl was dead | He didn't know if the girl was alive | and he was dead:** Conrad: "Then he tried to imagine himself dead, and Carlier sitting in his chair watching him; and his attempt met with such unexpected success, that in a few moments he became not at all sure who was dead and who was alive", *An Outpost of Progress* II (*Unger 1956* 233); for Conrad's story see note to *Journey of the Magi* 8–10. TSE: "In Gopsum Street a man murders his mistress. The important fact is that for the man the act is eternal, and that for the brief space he has to live, he is already dead ··· something is done which can not be undone", *Eeldrop and Appleplex* I; see also note to *The Waste Land* [V] 403, 405. "'I feel | As if I'd been a long time dead'", *The Little Passion: From "An Agony in the Garrett" ms1* 7–8. "I was neither | Living nor dead", *The Waste Land* [I] 39–40 (see note for source in Dante). "'Are you alive, or not?'", *The Waste Land* [II] 126.

139, 140 **joint:** OED 14: "slang or colloq. (chiefly U.S.) ··· applied to illicit drinking-saloons". For Prohibition, see note to *WLComposite* 2. TSE: "Marm Brown's joint, and the girls and gin", *WLComposite* 524.

145–46 **Death or life or life or death | Death is life and life is death:** *Cornford* 82 quotes the Euripidean question "Who knows if to be living be not death?" (*Crawford* 151).

156–61 **When you're alone in the middle of the night ··· waiting for you:** Gilbert and Sullivan: "When you're lying awake | With a dismal headache, | And repose is taboo'd by anxiety", Lord Chancellor's patter song, *Iolanthe* (Henry W. Wells, *New Poets from Old*, 1940, 75).

158 **the hoo-ha's:** OED "hoo-ha": "[Orig. unknown]. A commotion, a rumpus, a row", from 1931 (*Punch*). OED comments on TSE's plural usage that it "seems to be without parallel" (but compare *heebie-jeebies*). TSE to his Swedish translator, Erik Mesterton, 16 Nov 1948: "As for 'hoo-ha's', it is merely intended to be an inarticulate noise suggesting terror and impending doom. I seem to remember in Cockney speech some such phrase as 'that gives me the "hoo-ha's"' meaning, in more modern and general terms, the jitters, otherwise shivers of nervousness and apprehension, but for my purpose you need take it only as a noise."

160 **you waked up:** *Fowler* writes that the past tense is *woke*, and only rarely *waked* (and then usually in the transitive). See note to *Marina* 32, "the awakened".

161 **you wait for a knock and the turning of a lock for you know the hangman's waiting:** "waiting for a knock upon the door", *The Death of the Duchess* [II] 49, becoming *The Waste Land* [II] 138. "'You have the key ··· sleep, prepare for life.' || The last twist of the knife", *Rhapsody on a Windy Night* 73–77.

161–73 **knock and the turning of a lock ··· hangman's waiting ··· KNOCK | KNOCK | KNOCK:** *Macbeth* II ii ends with the stage direction "*Knock*" three times, followed immediately by II iii:

Enter a Porter

Knocking within.
PORTER. Here's a knocking indeed: if a man were Porter of Hell Gate, he should have old turning the Key. *Knock.* Knock, Knock, Knock.

Then the Porter to Macduff: "much drink may be said to be an equivocator with lechery". (See *The Superior Landlord* for "*Scene* ··· Murder of Mrs Porter" and, several times, the stage direction KNOCK.)

TSE: "I have attempted a *croquis* [rough draft] of a play (*Sweeney Agonistes*) to indicate that *our* tragic feelings are best expressed not through 'tragedy' but through farce", footnote to a lecture, *Shakespeare Criticism* (*Excerpts from Lectures 1932–1933*). "For to those who have experienced the full horror of life, tragedy is still inadequate ··· In the end, horror and laughter may be one—only when horror and laughter have become as horrible and laughable as they can be ··· there is potential comedy in Sophocles and potential tragedy in Aristophanes, and otherwise they would not be such good tragedians or comedians as they are ··· De Quincey's *Knocking on the Gate in Macbeth* is perhaps the best known single piece of criticism of Shakespeare that has been written", *Shakespearian Criticism I: From Dryden to Coleridge* (1934). For De Quincey's essay, see final note to *The Superior Landlord* (*Sweeney Agonistes* headnote, 6. THE SUPERIOR LANDLORD).

Coriolan

1. Composition 2. After Publication

Triumphal March was published separately as Ariel Poem 35, with drawings by E. McKnight Kauffer, 8 Oct 1931 (with 300 signed large-paper copies, 29 Oct); then in *Recent Poetry 1923–1933*, ed. Alida Monro (1933); and in *Modern Things*, ed. Parker Tyler (1934), its first US publication. Before the publication of *Triumphal March*, TSE had written *Difficulties of a Statesman*, which was published in *Commerce* Winter [1931/]1932, with a facing French translation by Georges Limbour. *Difficulties of a Statesman* (without the translation) then appeared in *Hound & Horn* Oct–Dec 1932, its first US publication. The two were published in succession but as independent poems, not as *Coriolan*, in *The Faber Book of Modern Verse*, ed. Michael Roberts (1936), a month before the publication of *1936*, where the title *Coriolan* was first used.

A proof copy of the 1931 Ariel Poem sold by Glenn Horowitz (cat. 22, 1990, item 50) bears a note in an unknown hand: "Mr. Eliot didn't like this type so Mr. Simon is consulting with Mr. Kauffer before he sets it again." Rather than a roman typeface, Oliver Simon of the Curwen Press finally used the strikingly modern typeface Kabel (1926–27), by the German typographer Rudolf Koch. This was the only Ariel poem by any poet set in a sans serif type.

Although TSE recorded *Triumphal March* four times and *Difficulties of a Statesman* twice, he never recorded them together.

Triumphal March was recorded May 1933, Columbia U. Second: 1946, Levy's Sound Studios, London for the Writers Group of the Society for Cultural Relations between the Peoples of the British Commonwealth and the USSR. Third: 13 May 1947, Harvard, as part of the Morris Gray Poetry Reading. Fourth: 26 Sept 1955, London; released by Caedmon 1955 (US), 1959 (UK).

Difficulties of a Statesman was recorded May 1947, for the Harvard Poetry Room;

released 1948 by Harvard Vocarium Records (alternative take recovered at Harvard, 2014). Second: 12 Nov 1950, for U. Chicago Round Table, broadcast by NBC.

1. COMPOSITION

Like *The Hollow Men* (and probably *Ash-Wednesday*)—and by contrast with *Four Quartets*—*Coriolan* was intended from the start to be a series of constituent parts.

To Lincoln Kirstein of *Hound and Horn*, 12 June 1931: "Had I had any verse to offer you, you would have received it, but I am not likely to have anything this year except a piece which I am working on for the *Ariel Poems*." To Marguerite Caetani, 23 June 1931: "I have done a part of a projected long poem, but this part must be used for our 'Ariel' series in the autumn, so I cannot give you use of the English text; but when I have done another section, I can offer you that if it proves suitable." (For the purposes of the Ariel series, the title of *ts1* was changed from *Coriolan: Part I* to *Triumphal March*.) To Caetani, 31 Aug 1931: "I have a section of a much longer poem which I should be glad to let you see for *Commerce*, though I do not know whether it is translatable or whether you will like it. But as there is some remote possibility that I may finish the poem some day, I should like to know, in the event of your accepting it, when you would be likely to use it." 14 Sept: "As for my poem, you shall have it as soon as I have time to type out a copy." 30 Oct: "I should ··· be glad to have a cheque for £15 for the poem." 31 Dec: "You speak as if you were enclosing corrected proofs, but perhaps you mean that you want me to return them as soon as I get them." 24 Feb 1932: "I look forward to the forthcoming issue of *Commerce*." (*Sencourt* 118 claims that TSE read *Difficulties of a Statesman* at a gathering with Lady Ottoline Morrell in 1930, but this cannot have taken place before 1931.)

After publication of *Difficulties of a Statesman* in France and the United States, TSE wrote to J. Clifford Turner, 8 Mar 1935: "I have your letter of the 4th, and will send you copies of *Mr. Pugstyles* and *The Difficulties of a Statesman* as soon as I have time to make copies, or have copies made. The former is unpublished, and the latter has never been published in this country. Meanwhile, I am sending Miss Thirburn the only available copy of the former. Perhaps she would let you take a copy off that."

Hugh Ross Williamson on "the new masterpiece which 1932 sees in the making": "It is not yet completed; even its title and plan, I believe, tentative and subject to modification ··· At the moment (July, 1932), the first two sections of this projected work (which is to be slightly longer than *The Waste Land*) are in print—*Triumphal March* ··· and *Difficulties of a Statesman* ··· The titles themselves suggest that, as *The Waste Land* was the post-War world, so here is the post-Peace world ··· As in *The Waste Land*, there is a world-conspectus and a simultaneity of action. The triumphal march is not only the Great War (ironically compressed into a catalogue of fighting weapons), but all processions which the mob wildly and foolishly acclaims", *The Poetry of T. S. Eliot* (1932) 181–84. Williamson prints one acknowledgement only: "I should like to express my gratitude to Mr. Eliot for his kindness in supplying certain facts of which I have made use in this book, and for the stimulus of his conversation."

For TSE's work at Lloyds Bank on settlement of international loans and on John Maynard Keynes's *The Economic Consequences of the Peace*, see note to *The Waste Land* [III] 277–78, 290–91. "The present age, a singularly stupid one, is the age of a mistaken nationalism and of an equally mistaken internationalism", letter to the editor, *Transatlantic Review* Jan 1924.

2. AFTER PUBLICATION

To John Middleton Murry, 20 Oct 1931, of *Triumphal March*: "consciously, I had in mind the ordinary chatter of a crowd, and also the general state of paganism in this country; but in any such phrase, there are undertones only audible to the writer, and other undertones ignored by the writer but audible to readers like yourself. Anyway, I can't do anything about it; except to mention that this is a part of a much longer piece, of which the second part is already written, of which the third part is I think writable, and of which I doubt whether I am able to write the fourth part—which must be largely derivative from S. John of the Cross—at all."

To Mary Hutchinson, 28 Oct 1931: "It is a great satisfaction to me if you do like the poem—or a part of a poem, for it is merely the first of four sections of which only one other is written. I have found it an interesting problem to try to work out how to write a poem which should be in one aspect, and that the most obvious, a political satire. So far, I do not seem to have succeeded, because one reader—quite an intelligent German—wrote to me of this fragment as being 'militarist'—I should have thought that if anything it was distinctly the contrary."

I. A. Richards to TSE, 6 Nov 1931, on *Triumphal March*: "it comes off for me perfectly—but seems an easy thing, for *you*, to be writing. Still, the pounding of the hoofs and the central swoon of significance so soon forgotten and the sacred trivial winding it off all come so easily into the reader's mind that he doesn't measure the poet's problem with them. But do you consciously dovetail into your other poems—or is that just the pathetic critic's whim? crumpets/eagles and *Cooking Egg.* So many people come to me and point these things out because I once mentioned some such puzzling correspondences, that I'd like to know." TSE, 11 Nov 1931: "I shall be interested to know what further impression you will get from the second part of this poem, which I have finished, and from the third and fourth parts which are not yet written. But I should like to show you the second part when I see you. As for the allusions you mention, that is perfectly deliberate, and it was my intention that the reader should recognize them. As for the question why I made the allusions at all, that seems to me definitely a matter which should not concern the reader. That, as you know, is a theory of mine, that very often it is possible to increase the effect for the reader by letting him know a reference or a meaning; but that if the reader knew more, the poetic effect would actually be diminished; that if the reader knows too much about the crude material in the author's mind, his own reaction may tend to become at best merely a kind of feeble image of the author's feelings, whereas a good poem should have a potentiality of evoking feelings and associations in the reader of which the author is wholly ignorant. I am rather inclined to believe for myself that my best poems are possibly those which evoke the greatest number and variety of interpretations surprising to myself. What do you think about this?"

To Miss M. Swann, 10 Dec 1937: "I am very interested to know that you have been experimenting with *Triumphal March*, because it is particularly amongst my poems one which is very much better aloud than when read to oneself. I do not quite see in what way it is susceptible of choral treatment in the ordinary sense, but it obviously could profit by being apportioned between several voices." (See note to *The Waste*

Land [III] 218 for TSE's "strong dislike of dividing up for voices poems which were conceived in terms of one voice".)

Reading *Triumphal March* at Harvard, 13 May 1947, TSE introduced it as "one of the most difficult of my poems for me or anyone else to read aloud, but for that reason, if for that reason only, I think one of those best worth trying to read. It is of course complete in itelf, but it was to have been part of a much longer poem in which the character persisting throughout was a certain Cyril Parker." Of the Ariel Poems: "*Triumphal March* originally appeared in this series too; but I took it out of the series because I meant it to be the first of a sequence in the life of a character who appears in the first part as Young Cyril. It is rather difficult to read: I ought always to go into training for several weeks before attempting it", *Chicago Round Table* (1950). Then, after reading *Difficulties of a Statesman*: "And that was as far as I got with *that* poem."

Title **Coriolan**: present in *Triumphal March ts1*, but not used in print until *1936*. "*Coriolanus* may be not as 'interesting' as *Hamlet*, but it is, with *Antony and Cleopatra*, Shakespeare's most assured artistic success", *Hamlet* (1919). To G. Wilson Knight, 30 Oct 1930 (after discussing *Marina*): "I have been rereading *Coriolanus*. I wonder if you will agree with me—it is rather important—I feel now that the political criticism, so much mentioned, is a very surface pattern; and that the real motive of the play is the astonishing study of the mother–son relation: 'he did it to please his mother . . .' I think of writing a poem on this and on Beethoven's version *Coriolan*." (In his copy of the Temple ed. of the play, which he dated 1903, TSE underlined "he did it to please his mother and to be partly proud", I i.) TSE's mother's *Savonarola: A Dramatic Poem* [1926] describes the French Army "passing through the Porta Romana · · · watching the movement of the troops · · · yonder march the French · · · 'Tis he! He comes! See, yonder rides the King · · · Yet with indifferent glances passing by · · · How fine they look! Who'd ask a braver sight? | How proudly rides each plumed and jewelled knight · · · The pride and pomp of war" (29–30); "The chivalry | And flower of France have all passed by. | Here come the herd" (32); "What sudden cry of triumph rings without? | How joyously and loud the people shout!" (34); "throw those weapons down | And take the cross" (70). TSE's introduction speaks of "the heroes of Shakespeare and Corneille" (ix).

TSE's view of Beethoven may have derived from *Beethoven: His Spiritual Development* by J. W. N. Sullivan (see headnote to *Four Quartets*, 7. MUSIC).

Interlude: in a Bar 11, "Broken and scarred", had taken up "broke | And scarred" from *Coriolanus* IV v. (TSE: "Revive for a moment a broken Coriolanus", *The Waste Land* [V] 426.) Shakespeare's scene, which gave TSE the epigraph to *Ode* ("Tired. | Subterrene"), shows the reconciliation of the enemies Coriolanus and Aufidius, and ends with the servants looking forward to new battles against Rome, now that Coriolanus has changed sides. Second Servant: "Why, then we shall have a stirring world again. This peace is nothing, but to rust iron, increase tailors and breed ballad-makers." First Servant: "Let me have war, say I; it exceeds peace as far as day does night. Peace is a very apoplexy · · · it makes men hate one another." Third Servant: "· · · The wars for my money."

Against a newspaper announcement in Jan 1935 that Robert Speaight would play Coriolanus in a black shirt at the Mercury Theatre, TSE wrote: "I have told Speaight that Coriolanus was a patrician ◁ would have nothing to do with anything so plebeian as fascism" (Houghton). "I have at hand a book containing statements by Sir Oswald Mosley, which anyone with the merest smattering of theology can recognize to be not only puerile but anathema", *The Church and Society* (1935).

Challenging Wyndham Lewis: "'We possess a great deal of evidence,' says Mr. Lewis, 'as to what Shakespeare thought of military glory and martial events.' Do we? Or rather, did Shakespeare think anything at all?" *Shakespeare and the Stoicism of Seneca* (1927). Against this in his copy of the first American edition of *Selected Essays*, TSE wrote, probably in the 1960s: "cf. my opinion later (the chronicle plays)". In the course of reviewing Lewis: "*Coriolanus* is not a defence of aristocracy, or a mere attack on the mob. Shakespeare is, in fact, completely critical and detached from any partisanship: in this play his own emotion is very strong indeed, but cannot be associated with that of any character or group in the play", *The Lion and the Fox* (1937). "The fact is that the situation of belief in the modern world is more analogous to that of the later Roman Empire than to any other period that we know", *Revelation* (1937). "We are all, so far as we inherit the civilization of Europe, still citizens of the Roman Empire ··· But, of course, the Roman Empire which Virgil imagined and for which Aeneas worked out his destiny was not exactly the same as the Roman Empire of the legionnaires, the pro-consuls and governors, the business men and speculators, the demagogues and generals", *Virgil and the Christian World* (1951).

"I noticed in the 1930s that *Troilus and Cressida*, with its bitter view of public affairs, and *Timon of Athens*, with its mood of disillusion, were revived several times. In some circumstances—certainly in Paris in 1934—even *Coriolanus* may arouse a wider interest. But for the most part, these and the other later plays are plays for a limited public, and that doesn't mean, in my opinion, that they are less great, or less dramatic, or that Shakespeare did not continue to develop", *The Development of Shakespeare's Verse* (recorded version, 1950).

I. *Triumphal March*

To Gregor Ziemer, 10 Feb 1937, referring to *Matthiessen*: "*Triumphal March* was not concerned with contemporary politics. I am afraid that I cannot give you any more explanation than the very exhaustive one of Mr. Matthiessen, who I think already explains a little too much."

Title ***Triumphal March***: OED "triumph" 1: "*Rom. Hist.* The entrance of a victorious commander with his army and spoils in solemn procession into Rome, permission for which was granted by the senate in honour of an important achievement in war." *The Oxford Companion to Classical Literature*: "To be granted a triumph it was at first necessary ··· to have won a great victory over a foreign enemy, with at least 5,000 of the enemy killed, and to have brought home at least a token army to show that the war was won ··· the *triumphator* ··· stood, richly dressed and wreathed in bay, on a four-horse chariot ··· The procession was joined by the magistrates and senators, captives, spoils, and sacrificial animals. It proceeded from the Triumphal Gate ··· along the Via Sacra to the Capitol." (TSE: "triumphal cars", *East Coker* II 9.)

North's Plutarch on the triumph of Paulus Æmilius: "First, the people having set up sundry scaffolds · · · about the market-place, and in other streets of the city · · · the sight of this triumph was to continue three days, whereof the first was scant sufficient to see the passing by of the images, tables, and pictures, and statues of wonderful bigness, all won and gotten of their enemies, and drawn in the show upon two hundred and fifty charrets. The second day, there were carried upon a number of carts, all the fairest and richest armour of the Macedonians, as well of copper, as also of iron and steel, all glistering bright · · · fair burganets upon targets: habergions, or brigantines and corselets, upon greaves: round targets of the Cretans, and javelins of the Thracians, and arrows amongst the armed pikes · · · there followed three thousand men, which carried the ready money in seven hundred and fifty vessels · · · The third day early in the morning, the trumpets began to sound · · · After them followed six-score goodly fat oxen · · · young men · · · who led them to the sacrifice · · · he came himself in his charret triumphing · · · It was a noble sight to behold: and yet the person of himself only was worth the looking on, without all that great pomp and magnificence. For he · · · carried in his right hand a laurel bough, as all his army did besides: the which being divided by bands and companies, followed the triumphing charret of their captain."

Cornford: "The marching songs of various English regiments, with their ribald satire on the officers, still perpetuate the fescennine tradition of the Roman triumph. [*Footnote*: Similar customs lived on through the Middle Ages at church festivals, especially those which perpetuated the Roman *Kalends*. Thus, the Synod held at Rome in 826 · · · speaks of bad Christians who go to church on feast days]", *The Origin of Attic Comedy* 40–41. In hospital in 1962, TSE sang Fred Gilbert's music hall song of 1892, *The Man Who Broke the Bank at Monte Carlo*: "my daily walk | To the great Triumphal Arch is one grand triumphal march" (*T. S. Matthews* 171).

Kenner 221: the poem's "interminable pageant · · · incorporates a Roman general's triumph, Christ's entry into Jerusalem, the Lord Mayor's show, the pageant in *Purgatorio* Canto XXIX, the viceregal cavalcade in *Ulysses*" (episode XI, Sirens). *Kojecky* 101 invokes Mussolini's coup and the March on Rome in Oct 1922 as enthusiastically reported in the *Daily Mail* and collected in *The "Red" Dragon and the Black Shirts: How Italy Found her Soul* by Sir Percival Phillips (57): "The three columns of Fascisti assembled at the Villa Borghese · · · There were 117,000 in all · · · For seven hours they defiled before the impressive Victor Emmanuel Memorial · · · As the units finished their triumphal march they went to the railway station, where trains were waiting to take them home." The *Daily Mail* was owned by Lord Rothermere, whose estranged wife was funding the *Criterion*, which was first published in the month of the March on Rome. TSE to Grover Smith, 4 July 1949: "My ability to forget dates in connection with my own work is, I should think, somewhat exceptional. My impression however is that according to the silly calendar which was somewhat pretentiously and vainly adopted after Mussolini's march on Rome, the year 1922 and not 1921 was Anno I."

Six weeks after the Allied victory in the Great War, Vivien Eliot described to Charlotte Eliot, 30 Dec 1918, the visit of President Woodrow Wilson: "London was looking its *most* beautiful when Wilson drove through the streets. Although very tired after Xmas day, Tom and I went early and stood in the best place we could find, for over two hours. Even then we had quite thirty *rows* deep of people in front of us—and I should have seen nothing at all if Tom had not lifted me up just as they passed."

France especially celebrated the defeat of an old enemy. A stereoscopic photograph of the Victory Day Celebrations at the "Arch of Triumph" Paris, on Bastille Day, 14 July 1919, published by the Keystone View Company, gave a summary: "On this great day Paris was almost delirious with joy and pride. The terrible war which had strained the resources and taxed the spirit of France almost to the limit had ended in glorious victory; the dreaded enemy beyond the Rhine whose threats and menaces had for half a century hung like a black cloud over the nation, was humbled in the dust. Today the victory celebration; today countless thousands are out in holiday attire, lining the sidewalks as the veterans who have won the war march by; today, for the first time in the history of France, foreign soldiers, allies in the glorious struggle, march in triumph under the Arc de Triomphe ··· From its summit 155 feet high, one has a wonderful view—the city spreads out interminably in every direction, at one's feet these magnificent avenues lined with stately buildings and bordered with handsome trees; near by the Seine, its winding course spanned by bronze, stone and marble bridges; in the distance the great cathedral of Notre Dame, the stately Palace of the Louvre and other great buildings. The Arc de Triomphe was erected to commemorate the victories of the Great Napoleon ··· On the inner side of the arch are inscribed the names of those great victories which made France so powerful and which stamped Napoleon as the greatest military commander of his age." "F. M.": "behind us the huge grey mass of the Louvre ··· impending, magnificent, imperial—triumphant symbol of ··· the one people which has supreme belief in its own power and its own destiny", *A Diary of the Rive Gauche* II (1925). For TSE's "depression caused by the hollow gaiety of the public celebrating" at the end of the Second World War, see note to *The Hollow Men* V 28–31.

Keynes on Clemenceau, the French Prime Minister, in 1919: "His philosophy had ··· no place for 'sentimentality' in international relations ··· In spite, therefore, of France's victorious issue from the present struggle ··· her future position remained precarious in the eyes of one who took the view that European civil war is ··· a normal, or at least a recurrent, state of affairs for the future, and that the sort of conflicts between organised Great Powers which have occupied the past hundred years will also engage the next ··· For a Peace of magnanimity or of fair and equal treatment ··· could only have the effect of shortening the interval of Germany's recovery and hastening the day when she will once again hurl at France her greater numbers and her superior resources ··· as soon as this view of the world is adopted ··· a demand for a Carthaginian Peace is inevitable", *The Economic Consequences of the Peace* ch. 3. "Clemenceau's aim was to weaken and destroy Germany in every possible way", ch. 5. For Keynes on the Carthaginian Peace at Versailles, see note to *The Waste Land* [III] 277–78, 290–91. TSE to his mother, 2 Oct 1919: "it is certain that at the Peace Conference the one strong figure was Clemenceau ··· and that Wilson went down utterly before European diplomacy. It is obviously a bad peace, in which the major European powers tried to get as much as they could, and appease or ingratiate as far as possible the various puppet nationalities which they have constituted and will try to dominate."

"We cannot, after the treaty of Versailles, believe that any war will end war; we believe rather that war breeds war: certainly that a bad peace breeds war", *The Christian in the Modern World* (1935). "That the French should be in constant apprehension of German aggression ··· is quite natural", *A Commentary* in *Criterion* Jan 1936. For TSE in 1939 on "many among the enemy who are inspired by no worthier ambition than that of reversing the situation of 1918", see note to *East Coker* V 2, "the years of *l'entre deux guerres*".

To Stephen Spender, 9 June 1932: "What really matters is not what I think about the Church to-day, or about Capitalism, or military processions, or about Communism: what matters is whether I believe in Original Sin."

1–5 **Stone, bronze, stone ··· the City**: "Foundation of the City. Stone and bronze ··· stones", *Anabasis* IV i, iii (*Abel* 222–23). **stone, oakleaves**: "The Church shall protect her own, in her own way, not | As oak and stone; stone and oak decay", *Murder in the Cathedral* II. **oakleaves**: *Coriolanus*: "His brows bound with oak"; "he comes the third time home with the oaken garland"; "brow-bound with the oak" (I iii, II i, II ii). Oakleaves are variously used in military decorations. *London Gazette* 29 Dec 1922: "laurel leaves for gallantry, or with oak leaves for meritorious service." **horses' heels**: CORIOLANUS: "Let them pull all about mine ears, present me | Death on the wheel, or at wild horses' heels", opening of III ii.

1–2 **Stone, bronze, stone, steel, stone, oakleaves, horses' heels | Over the paving**: Joyce: "Bronze by gold heard the hoofirons, steelyringing", *Ulysses*, opening of episode XI (Sirens). Achille Delaroche, tr. Stuart Merrill: "to trample under the steel of their horses' hoofs the prostrate", *The Conquering Dream* in *Pastels in Prose*. TSE: "dead leaves still rattled on like tin | Over the asphalt ··· metal leaves", *Little Gidding* II 30–31, 34. "stone and steel", *WLComposite* 341.

2–3 **paving. | And the flags**: "flagstones" are etymologically unrelated to "flags".

4–5 **people ··· the City**: *Coriolanus* III i, SICINIUS: "What is the city, but the people?" ALL: "True, the people are the city" (with "the city" two dozen times in the play).

4, 13–17 **Count them ··· 5,800,000 rifles and carbines ··· 53,000 field and heavy guns, | I cannot tell how many projectiles**: *Atkins* 22: the speaker "cannot have counted so many and so specifically (even if the numbers be rounded off)".

4–46 **such a press of people ··· so many crowding the way ··· our sausages ··· indifferent ··· the temple ··· the country ··· to church ··· sausage**: Shelley, *Swellfoot the Tyrant* II i: *The Public Sty. The Boars in full Assembly.* PURGANAX: "religion, morals, peace and plenty ··· The patronage, and pensions, and by-payments, | Which free-born Pigs regard with jealous eyes ··· the failure of a foreign market for | Sausages, bristles and blood-puddings ··· a state-necessity— | Temporary of course ··· Irreverent mockery of the genuflexions | Inculcated by the arch-priest. *A loud cry from the* PIGS." TSE to the Rev. Desmond Morse-Boycott, 17 June 1930: "a large public which is indifferent ··· a much smaller public which is hostile, and there is another public which is rejoiced, when the Anglo-Catholic Congress takes place ··· a great many others, scattered about the country ··· I hope that I may take advantage of your hospitable sausages at 4d. per lb." **And such a press of people ··· and we**

so many crowding the way: "What of the crowds that ran, | Pushed, stared, and huddled, at his feet, | Keen to appropriate the man?" *Mandarins* I 3–5.

8–9 **Are they coming? ··· Here they come. Is he coming?**: *Coriolanus*: "Ha? Martius coming home? ··· Martius coming home?"; "He's coming"; "Now he's coming" (II i, III iii, IV vi).

10 **The natural wakeful life of our Ego is a perceiving**: Edmund Husserl: "The natural wakeful life of our Ego is a continuous perceiving, actual or potential", *Ideas* tr. W. R. Boyce Gibson (1931) 127. TSE to James Haughton Woods, professor of philosophy at Harvard, 5 Oct 1914: "I have been plugging away at Husserl, and find it terribly hard, but very interesting; and I like very much what I think I understand of it." TSE's annotated copy of Husserl's *Logische Untersuchungen* (which he gave to Michael Roberts) is dated "Marburg 1914". To Martin D'Arcy, 19 Aug 1931, of Husserl: "it proved to be about the most difficult German that I have ever read, with occasional flashes of clarity. But I do think that he is a really important man." (TSE: "Losskij's essay reaches us through the cumbrous constructions of the German language", *"Der Sinn der Ikonen"* by L. Ouspensky and V. Losskij, reader's report, 1952.)

10–11 **The natural wakeful life of our Ego is a perceiving ··· our sausages**: "a poet's mind is ··· constantly amalgamating disparate experience; the ordinary man's experience is chaotic, irregular, fragmentary. The latter falls in love, or reads Spinoza, and these two experiences have nothing to do with each other, or with the noise of the typewriter or the smell of cooking; in the mind of the poet these experiences are always forming new wholes", *The Metaphysical Poets* (1921). **Ego**: pronounced *eggo* in TSE's recordings.

11–12 **We can wait with our stools and our sausages | What comes first? Can you see?**: "timid plugs 50 yrs hence will be lining up with campstools to see the 1st performance of the old favorite", jotting on *"Timidity"* (c. 624 fol. 104). (OED "plug", 6b: "An incompetent or undistinguished person".)

11–15 **our sausages ··· 28,000 trench mortars**: OED "sausage" 2e: "*slang*. A German trench-mortar bomb, so called because of its shape", with 1918: "At first we called them 'sausages', then ··· they became 'flying pigs'." In 1915, Harry Champion recorded the song *My Old Iron Cross*: "All at once a thousand Germans shouted 'Give us meat' | I gave them a sausage that I'd dug up for a treat". OED "sausage" 2d: "*slang*. A German", from 1890. In 1914, Mark Sheridan recorded the song *When Belgium put the Kibosh on the Kaiser*: "A silly German sausage | Dreamt Napoleon he'd be ··· he talked of peace | While he prepared for war". Robert Graves: "Sausages are easy to see and dodge ··· the faint plop! of the mortar that sends off the sausage ··· we pick out at once", *Good-Bye to All That* (1929) ch. XIII.

A sausage-seller is one of the adversaries in the agon of Aristophanes' *Knights*. TSE told Richard Eberhart, 30 Mar 1933, "that the sausage is of Aristophanic origin, besides being phallic" (*Harvard Advocate* Dec 1938). Eberhart: "I read Christ into Caesar, which he said was not intended; but one could have it if one liked" (Joel Roache, *Richard Eberhart*, 1971, 96).

11, 46 **sausages ··· sausage**: pronounced *saussages* in TSE's recordings of 1933 and 1955, but *sorsages* in 1947.

13–23] Both the inventory and the layout of these lines derive from *The Coming*

War by General Erich Ludendorff published by Faber in June 1931 (*Grover Smith* 162). This was Christopher Turner's translation of *Weltkrieg droht auf deutschem Boden*, published in Munich earlier the same year (*jacket*: "Ludendorff forecasts the events of a second world war, which he tells us is immediately impending"). Ludendorff: "The world war has proved a disappointment to the supernational forces in many ways. They are too affected by superstition, their Jewish mentality, or the teaching of Christianity to understand that the nations are governed by spiritual laws of the highest import" (12). The book was a call to the German people to "take the sword to regain their liberty" (175) as they had before (67–68):

> It is with feelings of shame and indignation that I transcribe the details of our self-emasculation. We surrendered:
>
> 5,800,000 rifles and carbines,
> 102,000 machine-guns,
> 28,000 trench mortars,
> 53,000 field and heavy guns,
> nearly all our projectiles, mines and fuses, to the amount of many millions,
> 13,000 aeroplanes,
> 24,000 aeroplane engines,
> 50,000 ammunition wagons,
> 55,000 army wagons,
> 11,000 field kitchens,
> 1,150 field bakeries,
> 1,800 pontoons, as well as a large amount of miscellaneous war material.
>
> Our enemies to-day are supplied with war material on a similar scale, enough, indeed to enable them to equip every fit man.

See note to title *Triumphal March* for the punitive terms demanded at Versailles. **102,000 ··· 1,150**: spoken as "a hundred two thousand ··· a thousand a hundred and fifty" in TSE's recordings of 1933 and 1947, but as "a hundred and two thousand ··· a thousand one hundred and fifty" in 1955. (There is no known recording of TSE reading *Five-Finger Exercises* IV. *Lines to Ralph Hodgson Esqre.*, with its "999 canaries".)

24 **What a time that took**: Roman triumphs were notoriously long. Suetonius reports that "upon his triumph day", Vespasian was "wearied with the slow march and tædious traine of the pompe", *Life of Vespasian* §12 (tr. Holland, Tudor Translations, introduction by Charles Whibley, 1899).

25–27 **the Scouts ··· the Mayor and the Liverymen**: *The Times* of 30 Mar 1929 reported celebrations of the 25th anniversary of the Entente Cordiale, at which Lord Mayors and Lady Mayoresses and officials of the United Associations of France and Great Britain were met by the Sub-Prefect of Grasse ··· the Deputy Mayor of Cannes and "a cordon of Boy Scouts ··· Then followed a drive through the triumphal arch framing the Rue Maréchal Foch, and along streets ablaze with banners ··· and thronged with citizens and people from the country." **Scouts**: "A troop of well-disciplined helpful boy-scouts", *The Old Gumbie Cat* 34. Robert Baden-Powell, the founder of the Scouting movement, had successfully defended the town in the Siege of Mafeking during the Boer

War. TSE: "The first part ··· a documented account of the Boy Scouts ··· and such 'movements', contains valuable material and is horrid reading", *"Totem: The Exploitation of Youth"* by Harold Stovin (1936), review.

26 ***société gymnastique de Poissy***: many French athletics societies had a para-military side.

28–31 **There he is now, look: | There is no interrogation in his eyes | Or in the hands, quiet over the horse's neck, | And the eyes watchful, waiting, perceiving, indifferent**: "He merely stands and waits | Upon his own intrepid dignity; | With fixed regardless eyes— | Looking neither out nor in— | The centre of formalities", *Mandarins* I 8–12.

29 **There is no interrogation in his eyes**: MACBETH (to Banquo's ghost): "Thou hast no speculation in those eyes" (III iv), following "our stools" and "hide" (TSE: "our stools", 11; "hidden ··· hidden", 32). Arthur Machen: "in a mad hurry, with an awful interrogation in his eyes", *The London Adventure* (1924) 85 (Andrew Roberts, personal communication).

30–33 **horse's ··· dove's ··· palmtree**: "I have halted my horse by the tree of the doves, I whistle a note so sweet", *Anabasis* closing *Song* i (*Abel* 225).

31 **indifferent**: *Coriolanus* II ii: "he waved indifferently". For Charlotte Eliot, "with indifferent glances passing by" (from her *Savonarola*) see note to title *Coriolan*. To Stephen Spender, 9 May 1935: "One has got at the same time to unite oneself with humanity, and to isolate oneself completely; and to be equally indifferent to the 'audience' and to oneself as one's own audience. So that humility and freedom are the same thing." See note to *Little Gidding* III 4, "indifference".

31–32 **eyes ··· under the dove's wing ··· breast**: Ernest Dowson: "Dove-eyed, with the breast | Of a dove, to my side", *Chanson sans paroles* 18–19 (see note to *So through the evening, through the violet air* 1). Swinburne: "Breasts more soft than a dove's ··· And all the wings of the Loves", *Hymn to Proserpine* 25–26. For Swinburne's poem see notes to *Mr. Eliot's Sunday Morning Service* 13–14, *The Waste Land* [I] 6–7 and *Ash-Wednesday* III 11.

31, 32, 42 **eyes ··· dove's ··· eagles**: *Coriolanus*: "those doves' eyes"; "That like an eagle in a dove-cote, I | Flutter'd your Volscians in Corioles" (V iii, V vi). For the second of these speeches see *Noctes Binanianæ*, note to *Three Sonnets* [III] 3.

32 **O hidden under the dove's wing, hidden in the turtle's breast**: after mention of the March on Rome: "The deterioration of democracy has placed upon men burdens greater than they could bear, and surreptitiously relieved them of those they could bear ··· in this state of mind and spirit human beings are inclined to welcome any regime which relieves us from the burden of pretended democracy. Possibly also, hidden in many breasts, is a craving for a regime which will relieve us of thought and at the same time give us excitement and military salutes", *The Literature of Fascism* (1928). *Hidden under the heron's wing* (title).

32–33 **O hidden under the dove's wing ··· breast, | Under the palmtree at noon**: see note to *Coriolan* II. *Difficulties of a Statesman* 32–33, "O hidden under the . . . Hidden under the".

34 **At the still point of the turning world**: Conrad Aiken: "I seek the unmoving centre— | But is it moveless or are all things turning?" *The Jig of Forslin* (1916)

120. Karl Barth: "Faith ··· is the affirmation of resurrection as the turning-point of the world", *The Epistle to the Romans*, tr. Edwyn C. Hoskyns (1933) 39 (Ben de la Mare, personal communication). "At the still point of the turning world. Neither flesh nor fleshless", *Burnt Norton* II 18. "The world turns and the world changes", *Choruses from "The Rock"* I 60.

35–36 **temple ··· the sacrifice. | Now come the virgins bearing urns, urns:** Keats: "Who are these coming to the sacrifice? ··· altar ··· priest", *Ode on a Grecian Urn* 31–32.

37–39, 48–50 **Dust | Dust | Dust of dust, and now ··· Give us a light? | Light | Light:** Poe's *Ulalume* has line-endings "dust ··· dust ··· dust" (st. 6) followed by "Light! ··· Light!" (st. 7). TSE commended Poe's poem for its "power of incantation", *"A Dream within a Dream"* (1943).

42–45 **how many eagles! and how many trumpets! | (And Easter Day ··· we took young Cyril to church ··· And he said right out loud, *crumpets*:** "Mr. Symons seems to us like a sensitive child, who has been taken into a church, and has been entranced with the effigies, and the candles, and the incense. *Such rugs and jugs and candle lights!* ··· a Roman", *Baudelaire in Our Time* (1927), quoting Edward Lear's *The Daddy Long-legs and the Fly* 22. **eagles:** for use as a military ensign, see note to *A Cooking Egg* 29–30. **Cyril ··· a bell:** Tennyson: "Cyril, with whom the bell-mouthed glass had wrought", *The Princess* IV 137. **they rang a bell:** bells that have been silent since Holy Thursday are sounded again during the Easter Vigil. **a bell ··· *crumpets*:** a Wellesley College examination paper of 1936 using this poem included a note: "on the streets of London itinerant peddlars of crumpets push little carts with an attachment which rings a bell"—against which TSE wrote: "O Montreal" (King's). (Samuel Butler's *Psalm of Montreal*, with its refrain "*O God, O Montreal!*", satirises cultural ignorance.) To Elizabeth Manwaring, 26 Feb 1936: "I was ··· horrified by the examination paper you sent. I hope I am not too much influenced by the fact that I should be unable to answer most of the questions, and that I was irritated by the examiner's remark about the Sacring Bell, and by his ignorance of crumpet sellers. No, what horrifies me is that your young people should actually be set to study contemporary verse in qualification for the degree of B.A. [*Footnote*: But I am to believe that the same thing goes on here.] They ought to be reading Aristophanes." (The Sacring Bell is rung when the Host is elevated during High Mass.) *Grover Smith 1996* 80: "The bell, recalling the crumpet-man's clanging in the street, arouses a reflex as in I. P. Pavlov's ··· *Conditioned Reflexes* (1927) and *Lectures on Conditioned Reflexes* (1928)." (*Smart* 110 quotes John Hayward: "The muffin man, one of the relics of old London, has just passed ··· jangling his bell", *New York Sun* 23 Mar 1935.) **eagles! ··· trumpets! ··· *crumpets*:** "where are the eagles and the trumpets? ··· buttered scones and crumpets", *A Cooking Egg* 29–31 (for TSE's letter to I. A. Richards, acknowledging this allusion, see headnote, 2. AFTER PUBLICATION).

44–47 **young Cyril ··· sausage ··· He's artful:** Dickens, of his young pickpocket: "Dodger, take off the sausages"; "The Artful's a deal too artful", *Oliver Twist* ch. VIII, XXXIX. For "artful Dodger" and Julius Caesar see "Other Verses", *Dearest Mary | Je suis très affairé* 8, with note to 14–15.

46–47, 51 **Don't throw away that sausage, | It'll come in handy ··· *Et les soldats*:** in 1920, Lt.-Col. Charles à Court Repington published his Great War memoirs under the controversial title *The First World War*, implying that there might be a need to fight again, and that weapons should not be thrown away but kept at hand. OED: "first" *a.* 2a. 1931: "what a dear dead ··· colonel preferred to call the First World War". In *1936* TSE placed *Coriolan* among the poems that are "Unfinished". **throw ··· sausage:** sausage gun = *Minenwerfer*, literally mine thrower ("28,000 trench mortars", 15). "There is a sausage gun | Over the way. | Fired by a bloody Hun | Three times a day. | You should see the Tommies run | When they hear the sausage gun", to the tune of *There is a Happy Land Far Far Away*. **come in handy:** "Some years ago I wrote a poem called *Triumphal March*. In it I included a list of war material ··· It was prose, certainly, but it came in very handily for my purpose", transcript of tape for the interview *Talking Freely* (1961) (Valerie Eliot collection); for Ludendorff's term "war material", see note to 13–23. Before publication of the interview, TSE changed "handily" to "effectively". To Polly Tandy, Ash-Wednesday [26 Feb] 1936: "If you any needs sistance to help keep the Ole Man peaceable you say the word, sister, say the word, and Ill be along with a mighty powerful monkey-wrench I got handy." **come in:** Ludendorff, *The Coming War* (see note to 8–9, "come ··· come ··· coming").

48–50 **Give us a light? | Light | Light:** Louis MacNeice: "lights a cigarette ··· Give me a cigarette, another cigarette", *Homo Sum* (1929) 4, 16 (the last line). Jack London: "'Hey, Bo, give us a light,' some one calls to you. Now this is an advertisement that that particular man has tobacco on him", *The Road*, 1907. TSE: "Lights, lights", *Burbank with a Baedeker: Bleistein with a Cigar* 27. "Light of Light, very God of very God", Nicene Creed (to Paul Elmer More, 17 Feb 1932: "your preference for the Apostles Creed over the Nicene does not seem to me wholly justified"). "Darkness now, then | Light. || Light", *The Rock* 48 (closing lines of Part I); "the lifting light, || Light || Light || The visible reminder of Invisible Light", *Choruses from "The Rock"* IX 41–43. "Light | Light | Light of light || Gone", *Burnt Norton* V 39 *variant* (see Textual History).

51 ***Et les soldats ··· ILS LA FAISAIENT*:** *Matthiessen* 82–83 points to Charles Maurras, *L'Avenir de l'Intelligence* (1905):

> Un écrivain bien médiocre, mais représentatif, est devenu presque fameux pour ses crises d'enthousiasme toutes les fois qu'un membre de la République de lettres se trouve touché, mort ou vif, par les honneurs officiels. Tout lui sert de prétexte, remise de médaille, érection de statue, ou pose de plaque. Pourvu que la cérémonie ait comporté des uniformes et des habites brodés, sa joie naïve éclate en applaudissements.
>
> 'Y avez-vous pris garde? dit-il, les yeux serrés, le chef de l'État s'était fait représenter. Nous avions la moitié du Conseil des ministres et les deux préfets. Tant de généraux! Des régiments avec drapeau, des musicians et leur bannière. Sans compter beaucoup de magistrates en hermine et des professeurs, ces derniers sans leur toge, ce qui est malheureux.—Et les soldats faisaient la haie?—Ils la faisaient.—En armes?—Vous l'avez dit.—Mais que disait le peuple?—Il n'en croyait pas ses cent yeux!
>
> [A writer, fairly mediocre but representative, has become almost famous for his crises of enthusiasm every time a member of the Republic of letters finds himself

touched dead or alive by official honours. Everything serves him as a pretext, the award of a medal, the raising of a statue, or the installation of a plaque. Provided that the ceremony calls for uniforms and braided costumes, his naive joy bursts out in applause.

—Have you spotted what's over there? he says, with serried eyes, the head of state has had himself portrayed. We had half of the Council of Ministers and the two Prefects. How many generals! Regiments with flags, musicians and their colours. That's without counting the magistrates in ermine and the professors, though they were not in their robes, which is a pity.—And the soldiers, were they lining the streets?—They were lining the streets.—Armed?—You've said it.—But what did people say?—A hundred eyes, and they couldn't believe them!]

Alongside TSE's lines, Valerie Eliot wrote in *VE 1951*: "c.f. first essay in *L'Avenir de l'Intelligence* by Charles Maurras. (TSE)". The essay's title is "*L'Illusion*", these being the opening paragraphs. TSE to Dudley Sheppard, 11 Mar 1935: "The final line in French about which you ask is a quotation from a passage ··· concerned with an ironic description of the public funeral of a distinguished man of letters. I believe there is some other colloquial shade of meaning attached to 'Ils la faisaient', but I have forgotten what it is, and it does not matter for my purposes." *L'Avenir de l'Intelligence* had been reprinted in Maurras's *Romantisme et révolution* (1922), and TSE listed it among several books likely to clarify his assertion that "there is a tendency—discernable even in art—toward a higher and clearer conception of Reason, and a more severe and serene control of the emotions by Reason", *The Idea of a Literary Review* (1926).

II. *Difficulties of a Statesman*

Title ***Difficulties of a Statesman***: "What I want to read you is the second section, which is called *Difficulties of a Statesman*—a subject of interest to everybody", *Chicago Round Table* (1950). Noting that in his "brilliant book *The Endless Adventure*", Frederick Scott Oliver had approvingly quoted "a sentence attributed to Disraeli: 'Real statesmen are inspired by nothing else than their instinct for power and love of country'", TSE asked: "In the difficulty that I have stated, that the Christian cannot accept the world as it is ··· should he not withdraw from the world altogether?" *The Christian in the Modern World* (1935). ***Statesman***: to A. L. Rowse, 11 Apr 1931: "how many great statesmen have been great men?" Charles Whibley: "Politics is the profession of the second-rate. The man of genius strays into it by accident. We do not need the fingers of both hands to count the statesmen who have served England since the seventeenth century ··· It is not an extravagant claim that they should have some mastery of literary expression. Words are the material of their craft", *The Trimmer* in *Political Portraits: Second Series* (1923). Quoting this, TSE wrote: "the relation of a statesman's statesmanship to his prose style is not negligible; we can find interesting laboratory material in the writing of Mr. [Ramsay] MacDonald, Mr. Lloyd George, and particularly Mr. Winston Churchill", *Charles Whibley* (1931). Under the heading "The Conditions of Statesmanship": "what people want from their statesmen ··· is not merely energy, efficiency and ability, but a right sense of values; they do not want the values of a class to which they do not themselves belong, or even merely those of the class to which they do belong, but of the nation as a whole. These should not be values imposed by the power of a personality or the doctrines of a 'party', but elicited by a kind of representative character; and should have reference not necessarily to what people think they want, but to what they really want and what they can recognise that they ought to want—to people not always just as they are, but as they would like to be. The late King George V came to have some of this representative character: so that the humblest individual could imagine himself almost as in the same position—but not doing the job so well. Mr. Churchill has gained something of this authority", *Christian News-Letter* 14 Aug 1940. On Keynes: "And at last the brilliant man ··· was transformed into the great statesman. Perhaps the word 'statesman' is too near the word 'politician' for my purpose; but the word 'public servant' on the other hand connotes the official and the pro-consul", *John Maynard Keynes* (1946). "The obvious secularist solution for muddle is to subordinate everything to political power: and in so far as this involves the subordination of the money-making interests to those of the nation as a whole, it offers some immediate, though perhaps illusory relief: a people feels at least more dignified if its hero is the statesman however unscrupulous, or the warrior however brutal, rather than the financier", *The Idea of a Christian Society* 41–42. "great statesmen will somehow typify the whole nation, at the same time that they surpass it", *Letter from T. S. Eliot* 29 July 1944, a paper for The Moot. To Desideria Pasolini, Italian translator of *The Elder Statesman*, 9 July 1952: "There is in the English title an ironic intimation, since my hero had hardly distinguished himself to the degree necessary to justify the title [*added:* of *Statesman* which is much more dignified than 'politician']." The letter then turns to a speech by Mrs. Cargill in act II:

> You wanted to pose
> As a man of the world. And now you're posing
> As what? I presume, as an elder statesman;
> And the difference between being an elder statesman
> And posing successfully as an elder statesman
> Is practically negligible.

The *New Statesman*, to which TSE had contributed often before 1920, was known as "the Statesman". Pound, reviewing *Prufrock and Other Observations*: "Mr Appolinax' laughter 'submarine and profound' transports him from the desiccated new-statesmanly atmosphere of Professor Channing-Cheetah's", *Drunken Helots and Mr. Eliot* in *Egoist* June 1917.

1–2 **CRY what shall I cry? | All flesh is grass:** Isaiah 40: 6–8: "The voice said, Cry. And he said, What shall I cry? All flesh is grass, and all the goodliness thereof is as the flower of the field. The grass withereth, the flower fadeth: because the spirit of the Lord bloweth upon it: surely the people is grass. The grass withereth, the flower fadeth: but the word of our God shall stand for ever" (*Grover Smith 1965* 165). TSE to Marguerite Caetani, 29 Sept 1931: "The only point that I should like to make to any possible translator is that the refrain at the beginning, which is from Isaiah ··· should be translated into the usual French version." For "the post-Peace world", see headnote to *Coriolan*, 1. COMPOSITION. "To cry for peace, but ignore the causes of war that are capable of being dealt with by intelligence alone, is worse than folly", *The Christian in the*

Modern World (1935). **CRY what shall I cry?**: Beddoes: "A bodiless childfull of life in the gloom, | Crying with frog voice, 'What shall I be?'", *Death's Jest-Book* III iii 329–30, Isbrand's Song; quoted in *The Three Voices of Poetry* (*Grover Smith* 316). Swinburne had turned Beddoes's words against him as a description of *Death's Jest-Book* (*Essay on the Poetical and Dramatic Works of George Chapman*, prefixed to *Poems and Minor Translations*, 1875, xxxv). For Beddoes's song, again at the beginning of a poem by TSE, see note to *Animula* 1. **CRY**: matched in *Later Poems* by capitalising of the first word of *Triumphal March* (as also some other poems).

3 **Companions**: *Coriolanus*: "such Companions"; "You Companion!" (IV v, V ii).

3–4 **Knights of the British Empire ··· Honour**: to Laurence Binyon, 16 May 1930, on his Dante translation: "'Old honoured father': should one not give more the allusion to the pietas of Aeneas? I confess that 'honoured' has to me the devilish suggestion of a K.B.E. or something of that sort." ("honour stains", *Little Gidding* II 90.) **Cavaliers, | O Cavaliers!**: Whitman: *Pioneers! O Pioneers!* (title) in *Birds of Passage* (*Musgrove* 10). **Cavaliers ··· of the Legion of Honour**: members of the highest rank in France's *Légion d'honneur*, which Napoleon based loosely on the Roman legions.

5 **Order of the Black Eagle**: highest order of chivalry in the former Kingdom of Prussia, which had come to an end in 1918. For Roman and Napoleonic eagles, see note to *A Cooking Egg* 29–30.

6 **Order of the Rising Sun**: Japanese order of chivalry, established 1875.

8–18 **form the committees ··· standing committees, select committees and sub-committees ··· secretary ··· committees ··· commission ··· commission**: to the Bishop of Brechin, 5 July 1939, on the book committee of the Church Literature Association: "I acted as secretary of the committee ··· the committee was reorganised in a somewhat elaborate scheme, in such a way—if I remember rightly—that I remained secretary of the general committee ··· the inmost committee was really handled by Dr. F. L. Cross ··· I believe that you are still chairman of the whole committee, and I suppose that I am still secretary." To Mary Trevelyan [29 June] 1942: "In my father's family is an hereditary taint, going back for centuries, which expresses itself in an irresistible tendency to sit on committees." "We have seen so many Boards, Commissions and Conferences already", *A Commentary* in *Criterion* Jan 1932. "one can hardly be expected to brighten at the suggestion of setting up more 'fact-finding commissions'", *A Commentary* in *Criterion* Oct 1936. "not to be accomplished by appointing commissions to do our thinking for us", *The Christian Conception of Education* (1942). "I have given you my Law, and you set up commissions", *Choruses from "The Rock"* III 8.

13 **one pound ten a week ··· thirty shillings**: in each case, "thirty bob". John Davidson: "I'm a clerk at thirty bob as you can see ··· To come the daily dull official round", *Thirty Bob a Week* st. 1, 3. TSE: "I am sure that I found inspiration in the content of the poem ··· The personage that Davidson created in this poem has haunted me all my life, and the poem is to me a great poem for ever", *John Davidson* (1961). The poem was one of ten TSE chose for *A Personal Anthology* (1947).

15 **And one's week's leave a year:** OED "leave" 1e: "In military, naval, and official use (also sometimes in schools and gen. in offices, etc.)"

16–21 **commission ··· commission ··· commission ··· Volscian commission:** "commission", in the other sense of authority conferred, occurs three times in *Coriolanus*.

21–23 **confer with a Volscian commission | About perpetual peace: the fletchers and javelin-makers and smiths ··· protest against the reduction of orders:** international disarmament talks had popular support at the time of the poem, but *The Times* 26 Mar 1929 reported the chairman of Vickers-Armstrong saying that the company was "dependent on the amount of armament orders available, without which we cannot hope to make profits." For Ludendorff's protest at the loss of Germany's armaments, see note to *Coriolan* I. *Triumphal March* 13–23. TSE: "the politicians, the bankers, the armament makers ··· I believe that modern war is chiefly caused by some immorality of competition which is always with us in times of 'peace'; and that until this evil is cured, no leagues or disarmaments or collective security or conferences or conventions or treaties will suffice to prevent it ··· And here is the perpetual message of the Church ··· The Church has perpetually to answer this question: to what purpose were we born?" *The Church's Message* (1937). **perpetual peace:** *Richard III* V ii: "To reap the harvest of perpetual peace, | By this one bloody trial of sharp war". *Coriolanus* II ii: "Run reeking o'er the lives of men as if 'twere | A perpetual spoil". Immanuel Kant *Project for a Perpetual Peace* (1795) (Mark Thompson, personal communication). **fletchers:** OED: "One who makes or deals in arrows; occasionally, one who makes bows and arrows. *Obs.* exc. *Hist.* or *arch.*"

24 **marches:** OED "march" *n.* 3, 1a: "a tract of land on the border of a country, or a tract of debatable land separating one country from another. Often *collect. pl.*, esp. with reference to the portions of England bordering respectively on Scotland and on Wales. Now *Hist.* and *arch.*" TSE: "men from the marches", *Anabasis* I xv. Housman: "They cease not fighting, east and west, | On the marches of my breast", *A Shropshire Lad* XXVIII, *The Welsh Marches* 23–24. (TSE: "the hills | That lie on the border of Shropshire and Wales", *Pollicle Dogs and Jellicle Cats* 22–23.) M. Bland of Faber, memo to printer, 18 Aug 1947: "In *The Difficulties of a Statesman* the line 'The guards shake dice on the marshes' should read 'The guards shake dice on the marches'. 'Marshes' at the end of the following line is correct" (Faber archive).

25 **And the frogs ··· croak in the marshes:** Virgil: "Et veterem in limo ranae cecinere querelam" [And the frogs in the mud croak their ancient lament], *Georgics* I 378 (*Grover Smith* 166). **O Mantuan:** *Purg.* VI 74–78: "'O Mantuan, I am Sordello of thy city' ··· Ah Italy, thou slave, hostel of woe, vessel without pilot in a mighty storm, no mistress of provinces, but a brothel!" (*Stormon*). *Moody* 167: "Sordello's greeting to Virgil ··· moved Dante to cry out against the falling away of the Italian city-states from the ideal of the Holy Roman Empire."

26 *variant* **lightning in nights of July:** the month was so named in honour of the month of Julius Caesar's birth. *Julius Caesar* I iii begins with thunder and lightning: "the cross blue lightning ··· this dreadful night | That thunders, lightens, opens graves". July is the "Thunder Month" (*The Oxford Companion*

to the Year, quoting 1696: "With the great bell to drive away thunder and lightning"). It is also the month of Bastille Day, for which see headnote to *Triumphal March*. In the United States it is the anniversary of the signing of the Declaration of Independence; see *Ode* ("Tired. | Subterrene"), which in *ts1* was titled *Ode on Independence Day, July 4th 1918* and which has an epigraph from *Coriolanus*.

28, 36, 40, 50 **Mother mother ··· O mother ··· Mother ··· O mother**: the crisis in *Coriolanus* V iii: "O Mother, Mother! | What have you done? ··· Oh my Mother, Mother: Oh! ··· Most dangerously you have with him prevail'd." D. H. Lawrence "gave his best to his mother", TSE's *Lecture Notes as Norton Professor* (1933).

31 **sweaty torchbearer**: OED's first citation for "torch-bearer" is from Sir Thomas Elyot, 1538. "After the torchlight red on sweaty faces", *The Waste Land* [V] 322.

32 **the dove's foot rested**: Genesis 8: 8–9: "He sent forth a dove from him, to see if the waters were abated from off the face of the ground; but the dove found no rest for the sole of her foot, and she returned unto him into the ark."

32–33 **O hidden under the ... Hidden under the ... Where the dove's foot rested ··· repose of noon, set under the upper branches of noon's widest tree**: "O hidden under the dove's wing ··· breast, | Under the palmtree at noon", *Coriolan* I. *Triumphal March* 32–33 (same line-numbers as in this part). "Hidden under coral islands", *Mr. Apollinax* 10. "Hidden under the heron's wing ··· the lotos-birds", *Hidden under the heron's wing* 1–2. (For TSE and exotic islands, see note to *Sweeney Agonistes* II. *Fragment of an Agon* 1–39.)

35 **the cyclamen spreads its wings**: "Wreathed in the wingèd cyclamen", *Elegy* 4.

39 **Noses strong to break the wind**: Massinger: "Here he comes, | His nose held up; he hath something in the wind", *The Roman Actor* IV i (*Hands*). Quoting the lines in *Philip Massinger* (1920), TSE called them "hardly comparable to 'the Cardinal lifts up his nose like a foul porpoise before a storm'" (Webster, *The Duchess of Malfi* III iii). Holland's Suetonius: "he would give folke leave to breake winde downward ··· having certaine intelligence, that there was one who for manners and modestie sake, by holding it in, endaungered his owne life", *Life of Tiberius* §32 (Tudor Translations, introduction by Charles Whibley, 1899).

42 **mactations, immolations, oblations, impetrations**: Maurice de la Taille's *The Mystery of Faith and Human Opinion Contrasted and Defined* (1930) discusses Christ as the property of God: "And all this in current language will be expressed in terms of prayer, of supplication, of impetration" (54). It also contains an essay, *Distinction between Oblation and Immolation in Traditional Theology*, which asks "whether we ought to use the word *immolation* to signify explicitly (*in recto*) the killing or mactation of the animal, inasmuch as that killing has in view the sacerdotal oblation of the sacrifice, or whether we should not rather keep the word *immolation* for the sacerdotal oblation itelf, as connoting (*in obliquo*) the aforesaid killing or mactation" (349). TSE to Lord Halifax (born 1839, President of the English Church Union), 27 Mar 1931, acknowledging loan of the volume: "Thank you very much for lending me *De la Taille*". At Easter [5 Apr] 1931: "On some points he confirmed what I already believed—as the unity of the Passion and sacrifice—and he provides valuable suggestion on one point that had puzzled me, the Agony of Gethsemane after the Last Supper ··· the 'symbolism' in the Eucharist seems to me *sui generis*, and in danger of confusion with

ordinary types of symbolism." In his copy of *G.Jones*, against quotations of this line and 33, TSE wrote "from some book on the Eucharist recommended to me by Will Spens [Master of Corpus Christi College, Cambridge]" and "See Halifax and La Taille" (Valerie Eliot collection). In a copy of *1963* 2nd imp. (1965), Valerie Eliot wrote: "P. de la Taille on the Eucharist". **mactations:** OED: "The action of killing, *esp.* the slaughtering of a sacrificial victim". **oblations:** OED: "The action of solemnly offering or presenting something to God or to a deity; the offering of a sacrifice". In the drafts of *The Rock*, a priest speaks words attributed in Foxe's Book of Martyrs to Hugh Latimer: "The very marrow bones of the mass are altogether detestable, and therefore by no means to be borne withal, so that of necessity the mending of it is to abolish it for ever. For if you take away oblation and adoration, which do hang upon consecration and transubstantiation, the most papists of them all will not set a button by the mass, as a thing which they esteem not, but for the gain that followeth thereon" (ts, Lord Chamberlain's Papers, BL). **impetrations:** OED: "The action of obtaining or procuring by request or entreaty. (Chiefly *Theol.*)"

48 **"Rising and falling, crowned with dust":** Kipling: "Who is the happy man? He that sees in his own house at home little children crowned with dust, leaping and falling and crying", epigraph to *The Story of Muhammad Din* (*Grover Smith* 316, informed by TSE). See *To the Indians who Died in Africa* 1–5.

Minor Poems

Section introduced, with half-title, *1936+*. (None of the poems was ever added to *Sel Poems*.)

CONTENTS IN ORDER OF FIRST PUBLICATION:

Eyes that last I saw in tears	*Chapbook* [Nov] 1924
The wind sprang up at four o'clock	*Chapbook* [Nov] 1924
Five-Finger Exercises I–V	*Criterion* Jan 1933
Landscapes I. *New Hampshire*	*Virginia Quarterly Review* Apr 1934
Landscapes II. *Virginia*	*Virginia Quarterly Review* Apr 1934
Landscapes IV. *Rannoch, by Glencoe*	*NEW* 17 Oct 1935
Lines for an Old Man	*NEW* 28 Nov 1935
Landscapes V. *Cape Ann*	*New Democracy* 15 Dec 1935
Landscapes III. *Usk*	*1936*

Section title ***Minor Poems***: "I admit that my own experience, as a minor poet, may have jaundiced my outlook", *Shakespeare and the Stoicism of Seneca* (1927). "I do not pretend to offer Vaughan, or Southwell, or George Herbert, or Hopkins as major poets: I feel sure that the first three, at least, are poets of this limited awareness", *Religion and Literature* (1935). Adding this essay to *Selected Essays* in 1950 (in the US) and 1951 (in Britain), TSE added a footnote after "major poets": "I note that in an address delivered in Swansea some years later (subsequently published in *The Welsh Review* under the title of *What Is Minor Poetry?*) I stated with some emphasis my opinion that Herbert is a major, not a minor poet. I agree with my later opinion. [1949]".

Eyes that last I saw in tears

Eyes that last I saw in tears and *The wind sprang up at four o'clock* were "I" and "II" of *Doris's Dream Songs*, published in *Chapbook* [Nov] 1924, then in America as *Three Dream Songs* in *American Poetry 1925* ed. Louis Untermeyer (1925). (The third "Dream Song" became *The Hollow Men* III.) *Eyes that last I saw in tears* was also printed as "II" of *Three Poems* in *Criterion* Jan 1925, with a footnote: "The second of these poems appeared in the *Chapbook* 1924, but is here reproduced because of the different context." Omitted from *1925*, *Eyes that last I saw in tears* reappeared, among the "Minor Poems", *1936+*. When Conrad Aiken asked why it was not in *1925*, TSE replied, 22 Jan 1926: "The answer to paragraph 3 of your letter is that I did not think it was good enough and that it did not seem to fit in very well with the rest."

The private printing for Frederick Prokosch ("Venice", "1939") is a later forgery (see Nicolas Barker, *The Butterfly Books*, 1987).

No recording known.

In his interview with TSE, Donald Hall asked: "Are any of your minor poems actually sections cut out of longer works? There are two that sound like *The Hollow Men.*" TSE: "Oh, those were the preliminary sketches. Those things were earlier. Others I published in periodicals but not in my collected poems. You don't want to say the same thing twice in one book", *Paris Review* (1959).

To Roberto Sanesi, in response to a list of 29 poems Sanesi wished to translate into Italian, 10 Dec 1959: "I should suggest omitting also *Eyes that last I saw in tears* and *The Wind sprang up at Four o'clock* in as much as these were merely preliminary sketches before *The Hollow Men.*"

1, 3, 5 **Eyes that last I saw in tears · · · death's dream kingdom · · · the eyes:** Dante, *Vita Nuova* [XXXI], tr. Rossetti: "The eyes that weep for pity of the heart · · · Beatrice is gone up into high Heaven, | The kingdom where the angels are at peace · · · and to her friends is dead", *The Early Italian Poets* 288 (*Bush* 88). TSE: "And I have known the eyes already", *The Love Song of J. Alfred Prufrock* 55, with "decisions and revisions", 48 (here: "decision | Eyes I shall not see · · · hold us in derision", 9–10, 15) (*Bush* 89).

1–4, 15 **Eyes · · · death's dream · · · vision · · · in derision:** Swinburne, three times: "to derision · · · death and division", *Dolores* 157–59. "In his eyes foreknowledge of death · · · with derision · · · vision | Between a sleep and a sleep", *Atalanta in Calydon* 357–61. "The grave's mouth laughs unto derision | Desire and dread and dream and vision", *Ilicet* 34–35.

2–3 **division · · · kingdom:** *King Lear* I i: "in the division of the kingdom."

7, 15 **my affliction · · · in derision:** Psalm 119: 50: "This is my comfort in my affliction: for thy word hath quickened me. The proud have had me greatly in derision."

13–14 **eyes · · · a little while | A little while · · · tears:** Job 24: 23: "his eyes are upon their ways. They are exalted for a little while." Psalm 37: 10: "For yet a little while, and the wicked shall not be." John 7: 33: "yet a little while am I with you" (similarly 12: 35, 13: 33). John 14: 19: "Yet a little while, and the world seeth me no more". John 16: 16–20: "A little while, and ye shall not see me; and again, a little while, and ye shall see me · · · ye shall weep and lament."

13, 15 **eyes · · · hold us in derision:** Cavalcanti, tr. Pound: "hold me not in derision · · · And then toward me they so turned their eyes", *Ballata VII* 9, 13. For Cavalcanti, Dante's close friend, see note to *Ash-Wednesday* I 1. **hold us in derision:** Job 30: 1: "have me in derision." Psalm 2: 4: "The Lord shall have them in derision." Psalm 59: 8: "thou shalt have all the heathen in derision."

The wind sprang up at four o'clock

Publication: see headnote to *Eyes that last I saw in tears.* Seven lines are taken, slightly revised, from *Song* ("The golden foot I may not kiss or clutch"); see headnote to that poem. Omitted from *1925*, *The wind sprang up at four o'clock* reappeared, among the "Minor Poems", *1936+*.

No recording known.

G. Jones 19: "A large structure of allusion moves behind these lines condensing Cantos VII–XII of the *Inferno* ··· The Tartar horsemen ··· are the Centaurs (horsemen) of *Inferno* XII ··· this canto occurs at 4 a.m. on Holy Saturday morning; and Dante signifies the time by saying that the Great Bear is lying over the abode of Caurus, the north-west wind. It is across the river Phlegethon that these creatures shake their spears at Virgil and Dante." See headnote to *The Waste Land*, 1. COMPOSITION, for its relations to this poem.

1 **The wind sprang up**: "The world of contact sprang up like a blow | The winds", *Bacchus and Ariadne: 2nd Debate between the Body and Soul* 11 (see note). "then sprang up a little damp dead breeze", *Oh little voices of the throats of men* 45. "The wind sprang up and broke the bells", *Song* ("The golden foot I may not kiss or clutch") 7.

1, 5 **four o'clock ··· waking**: "—And we are moved into these strange opinions | By four-o'clock-in-the-morning thoughts", *Preludes* IV *additional lines after* 16 *in ms1*. "The lamp said, 'Four o'clock ··· prepare for life'", *Rhapsody on a Windy Night* 69–77.

2 **broke the bells**: OED "break" 6. *intr.*: "To crack without complete separation. Formerly said of a bell".

3 **Swinging between life and death**: "Swinging from life to death", *Song* ("The golden foot I may not kiss or clutch") 4.

5 **confusing strife**: James 3: 16: "For where envying and strife is, there is confusion."

5, 7 **strife ··· river**: Ezekiel 47: 19: "from Tamar even to the waters of strife in Kadesh, the river to the great sea" (again at 28: 48). Psalm 106: 32: "They angered him also at the waters of strife."

7 **the blackened river**: the Styx. Dryden's Virgil: "by *Styx* he swore, | The Lake of liquid Pitch" and "Styx, th'Inviolable Flood, | And the black Regions", *Aeneid* IX 120–21, X 173–74.

10, 12 **shake ··· spears**: Job 41: 29: "He laugheth at the shaking of a spear." TSE: "the mind shakes its tumult of spears", *Anabasis* I xii.

12 **Tartar**: OED *n.*² 1: "A native inhabitant of the region of Central Asia extending eastward from the Caspian Sea, and formerly known as Independent and Chinese Tartary. First known in the West as applied to the mingled host of Mongols, Tartars, Turks, etc., which under the leadership of Jenghiz Khan (1202–1227) overran and devastated much of Asia and Eastern Europe; hence vaguely applied to the descendants of these now dwelling in Asia or Europe"; *n.*⁴ *Obs.*: "= Tartarus; the infernal regions; hell." Perhaps prompted here by "Tamar"; see note to 5, 7.

Five-Finger Exercises

Published in *Criterion* Jan 1933. TSE returned the proofs to his secretary Miss B. Wilberforce, 18 Oct 1932, in a letter from America with a PS: "There seem to be very few dogs in this country."

No recording known.

Title **Five-Finger Exercises**: OED: "a piece of music written for the purpose of affording practice in the movement of the fingers in pianoforte playing; also *transf.* and *fig.*, something very easy", from 1903.

I and II: Aurelia Hodgson, wife of Ralph Hodgson, made notes on TSE: "During the spring he wrote two short poems, one *Lines to a Cat*, the other *To a Dog*. Vivienne told me he had written the former the day before, and after dinner she asked him to read it to me. He found it and said, 'I will if you'll stay in the room. The more people there are, the easier it is to read.' I felt very honoured. When R. was present a few days later we asked him to read it again. By then he had the two, and he felt the latter [*with* former *written above*] was the better. R. said, 'Read both, and we can see.' He did, tho after the first he opened Blake and read a poem about the three nuns, which was *remotely* suggestive. T.S.E. said, 'A poem is nothing, if it isn't unique, and this one isn't!' The second one came to him while he was in a tube train, and he passed up his station in his haste to put it on paper" (Bryn Mawr, box 25, nbk 7). For Blake, see note to I 1.

IV and V recall Edward Lear's *"How pleasant to know Mr. Lear!"* (Also: "How delightful to meet the O'Possum", *How to Pick a Possum* 3.) TSE alluded to Lear's poem when writing to Hayward [18 Jan 1937]: "Possibly my taste for Marsala is due to my admiration for Edward Lear, but I do like it, and like Mr. Lear, I never get Tipsy at all." In *The Aims of Education* (1950), he cited "runcible hat" from Lear's poem. The last of TSE's extension lectures in 1917–18 on Victorian literature was *The Laureates of Nonsense—Edward Lear, Lewis Carroll, and the Makers of Light Verse*. On 2 Oct 1932, shortly after arriving at Harvard, he wrote to his secretary asking her to send him a copy of Lear's poems "with also the *Four Little People & the Quangle Wangle's Hat*" (*The Story of the Four Little Children who Went Round the World*), and he discussed Lear again in *The Music of Poetry* (1942). When Faber published Holbrook Jackson's edition of *The Complete Nonsense of Edward Lear* (1947), it was reviewed in the *Sunday Times* by Richard Jennings, to whom TSE wrote on 24 Nov:

> I note in passing that you make no reference to the celebrated McTaggart Theory. You will remember that McTaggart of Trinity (Cambridge) held the preposterous view that *runcible* meant *tortoise-shell*. But the essay I have been intending for years to write—*The Concept of Runcibility, or McTaggart Refuted*, is still in the womb of time. And meanwhile
>
> "Romantic England's dead and gone:
> It's with Ed. Leary in the grave."

(Yeats: "Romantic Ireland's dead and gone, | It's with O'Leary in the grave", *September 1913* 7–8.) In later life TSE owned both a drawing by Edward Lear and Augustus John's etching of Lear (Stephen Spender, *New York Times* 29 Sept 1963). For Lear's "Old Man of", see note to *Gerontion* 70–72.

Frank Morley recalled Hodgson in 1923 or 1924: "I stood with Hodgson on the steps of St. Paul's and received his remark: 'Don't sell short those compatriots of yours, Pound and Eliot'", *Morley 1966* 95.

The Eliots had been introduced to Hodgson on 11 Dec 1931 by Ottoline Morrell. Aurelia Hodgson recorded her husband's diffidence: "To me he explained later that it was quite possible that TSE might not care to know *him*" (notes on TSE, Bryn Mawr).

Hodgson inscribed a copy of the 1930 reprint of his *Poems* (1917) "to his dear friend Vivienne Haigh Eliot" (Clodd collection, Maggs catalogue 2004, 876). TSE to Morrell, from Harvard, 10 Apr 1933: "I have a letter from Vivienne, in which she mentions that your comment upon my jingle about Hodgson was that Hodgson must be a very Cruel Man. Of course I know how effectually V. can garble reports, but to be quite sure, I write to say that I have found Hodgson one of the gentlest of men, and the stanza was meant to indicate that." In 1935 TSE offered Hodgson the opportunity to publish his poems with Faber, and Hodgson replied that "the association would be particularly pleasing" (9 Apr 1935), but Macmillan remained Hodgson's publisher. As well as their correspondence, Bryn Mawr has a photograph of the two poets together in 1932, each with a pipe and with a dog on a leash (comparable to the drawing of Hodgson by TSE, see notes to IV. *Lines to Ralph Hodgson Esqre.*). Writing to the Hodgsons on 6 Apr 1962, TSE called himself "a great admirer" of Hodgson's poems.

I. *Lines to a Persian Cat*

Title ***Lines to***: TSE's first use of this unassuming formula, which he adopted for I–V, as also for *Lines to an Old Man* (originally published as *Words for an Old Man*). Although TSE intended it as prose, *Defence of the Islands* was first printed under the heading *LINES WRITTEN BY T. S. ELIOT* (see headnote).

I 1–2 **songsters of the air repair | To the green fields of Russell Square**: Horace "now suddenly burst loudly into song, in the hoarse, quavering voice which is used by songsters in the streets of London", *On the Eve* (1925); TSE's authorship uncertain, see Index of Identifying Titles. Blake: "the green woods · · · the air · · · the green hill", *Songs of Innocence: Laughing Song* 1–4; "Farewell green fields", *Night* 9.

I 2–9 **Russell Square · · · the dull brain · · · the quick eyes · · · delay**: "One sits delaying in the vacant square · · · The eye retains the images | The sluggish brain · · · dull", *First Debate between the Body and Soul* 9, 22–25. **the dull brain**: Keats, *Ode to a Nightingale* 34. Shelley: "the dullest brains", *Letter to Maria Gisborne* 220.

I 3 **Beneath the trees there is no ease**: Keats: "There are plenty of trees, | And plenty of ease", *The Gothic looks solemn* 13–14 (Archie Burnett, personal communication).

I 5 **Woolly Bear**: not the caterpillar, but the name of the Persian cat (see headnote to V. *Lines for Cuscuscaraway and Mirza Murad Ali Beg*).

I 6 **There is no relief but in grief**: F. A. Paley, footnote on Plato's *Philebus* 47e: "though tears give *relief* in grief, and in this sense 'there's bliss in tears;' yet Plato seems rather to have been thinking of tears of joy", *The Philebus of Plato* tr. Paley (1873) 78. "Their faces relax from grief into relief", *The Dry Salvages* III 12.

I 7–8, 10 **when will · · · When will · · · *When* will Time**: "When will the fountain of my tears be dry? | When will my sighs be spent? | When will desire agree to let me die?" anonymous lyric repr. in 1888 in *More Lyrics from the Song-Books of the Elizabethan Age* ed. A. H. Bullen (*Grover Smith* 250). In the supplementary scene for *Sweeney Agonistes* sent to Hallie Flanagan, the old gentleman introduces himself as "Time", and Sweeney asks him: "When will the barnfowl fly before morning? | When will the owl be operated on for cataracts? | When will the eagle get out of his barrel-roll?" (see headnote, 10. PREMIÈRE IN AMERICA: ENTER AN OLD GENTLEMAN).

I 9–10 **Why will the summer day delay? | *When* will Time flow away**: "Children and cats in the alley ··· (Somewhat impatient of delay) | On the doorstep of the Absolute", *Spleen* 8, 15–16 (likewise concluding lines). For "delaying" in another *March Hare* poem, see note to I 2–9.

I 10 ***When* will Time flow away?**: Tennyson: "When will the stream be aweary of flowing | Under my eye?" *Nothing Will Die* 1–2 (*Musgrove* 89). TSE: "time is time, and runs away", *Song* ("If space and time, as sages say") 7.

II. *Lines to a Yorkshire Terrier*

"I've never done any dogs. Of course dogs don't seem to lend themselves to verse quite so well, collectively, as cats", *Paris Review* (1959). For the Eliots' first Yorkshire terrier, named Dinah Brooks, see letter to his mother, 23 Apr 1919. Two other Yorkshire terriers, Peter and Polly Louise, can be seen in the photograph album kept by Vivien 1924–29 (Bodleian).

On notepaper from the Emerald Beach Hotel in the Bahamas, in the winter of 1963–64, when in frail health, TSE wrote out Lionel Johnson's poem *Dead*: "In Merioneth, over the sad moor | Drives the rain, the cold wind blows ··· lightly down she lies ··· the wind lives and wails ··· A spirit cries *Be strong!* and cries *Be still!*" (On a second sheet, he wrote out Kipling's *The Appeal*: "Let me lie quiet in that night | Which shall be yours anon ··· Seek not to question other than | The books I leave behind.") Lionel Johnson's poem had featured as the last item in *A Personal Anthology* (1947): "I do not think it is a perfect poem; there are lines in it which I should like to alter, it is a poem which you do not find in anthologies, but which has something in it, a tone, a few lines and phrases, which re-echo in the mind for a lifetime."

II 2–4 **tree ··· In a black sky, from a green cloud | Natural forces shriek'd aloud**: John Davidson: "Motionless, leaden cloud, | The region roofed and walled; | Beneath, a tempest shrieked aloud", *Winter Rain* 1–4 (*Grover Smith 1974* 254). TSE: "three trees on a low sky", *Journey of the Magi* 24 (Donald Sommerville, personal communication).

II 4–6 **Natural forces shriek'd aloud, | Screamed, rattled, muttered endlessly. | Little dog was safe and warm**: Poe (in *For Annie* 19–23, 79–80; see description of *ts1* in Textual History), likewise of a dead pet:

> The moaning and groaning,
>   The sighing and sobbing,
> Are quieted now,
>   With that horrible throbbing
> At heart ···
>
> When the light was extinguished,
>   She covered me warm

TSE read from Poe's poem on the BBC in the talk published as *"A Dream within a Dream"* (1943).

II 4, 10–12 **Natural forces shriek'd aloud · · · Pollicle dogs and cats all must · · · Like undertakers, come to dust:** *Cymbeline* IV ii: "Fear no more the heat o'th'Sun, | Nor the furious Winter's rages · · · Golden lads, and girls all must, | As chimney-sweepers come to dust."

II 7 **cretonne:** OED: "French name of a strong fabric of hempen warp and linen woof; applied in England to a stout unglazed cotton cloth printed on one or both sides with a pattern".

II 7, 12, 15 **eiderdown · · · dust · · · sleep endlessly:** Herbert: "we can go die as sleep · · · Making our pillows either down, or dust", *Death* 21, 24 (see note to final line of *Five-Finger Exercises*).

II 8–9, 12 **cracked and brown · · · dry · · · dust:** "drink · · · dry · · · without rain · · · mudcracked · · · If there were water · · · A spring · · · the sound of water", *The Waste Land* [V] 335–50. Poe, *For Annie* 31–40:

> And oh! of all tortures
>   *That* torture the worst
> Has abated—the terrible
>   Torture of thirst · · ·
> I have drank of a water
>   That quenches all thirst:—
>
> Of a water that flows,
>   With a lullaby sound,
> From a spring but a very few
>   Feet under ground

cracked and brown: "The wilderness is cracked and browned", *Mr. Eliot's Sunday Morning Service* 12.

II 10–11 **Pollicle dogs and · · · Jellicle cats:** see headnote to *The Marching Song of the Pollicle Dogs.*

II 13–14 **Here a little dog I pause | Heaving up my prior paws:** Herrick: "Here a little child I stand | Heaving up my either hand", *Another Grace for a Child* (*Grover Smith* 250). Corbière: "ne pas connaître | Ton écuelle ni ton maître, | Ne jamais marcher sur les mains, | Chien!" [Not to recognise your bowl or your master, never to pad about on my hands, | Dog!], *A Mon Chien Pope* [To My Dog Pope] 6–9.

II 14 **prior:** OED specifies "Preceding (in time or order)".

III. *Lines to a Duck in the Park*

Ralph Hodgson to Aurelia Bolliger (c/o T. S. Eliot), 8 June 1932: "Ducks, yes, tell Eliot, worms, newts and pretty nearly anything that they can find." Bolliger, who married Hodgson the following year, was staying with the Eliots at 68 Clarence Gate Gardens.

III 1 **The long light shakes across the lake:** Tennyson: "The long light shakes across the lakes", *The Princess*: "The splendour falls" (1850) [III ^ IV] 3 (*Grover Smith* 250).

III 4 **no eft or mortal snake:** Tennyson: "A bedmate of the snail and eft and snake", *The Holy Grail* 569 (*Grover Smith* 250). **eft:** OED *n.*1: "A small lizard or lizard-like animal" (also "newt").

III 5, 7 **duck and drake · · · I have had the Bread and Wine:** Yeats: "O'Driscoll drove with a song | The wild duck and the drake · · · The bread and the wine had a doom", *The Host of the Air* 1–2, 25 (*Grover Smith* 250).

III 13–14 **the enquiring worm shall try | Our well-preserved complacency:** Marvell: "then Worms shall try | That long preserved virginity", *To His Coy Mistress* 27–28. **enquiring worm:** HAMLET: "A certain convocation of politic worms are e'en at him" (IV iii); see note to *The Love Song of J. Alfred Prufrock* 113, 116.

IV. *Lines to Ralph Hodgson Esqre.*

IV 4 **Baskerville Hound:** Conan Doyle: "an enormous coal-black hound, but not such a hound as mortal eyes have ever seen. Fire burst from its open mouth, its eyes glowed with a smouldering glare, its muzzle and hackles and dewlap were outlined in flickering flame. Never in the delirious dream of a disordered brain could anything more savage, more appalling, more hellish be conceived than that dark form and savage face which broke upon us out of the wall of fog", *The Hound of the Baskervilles* (1902) ch. 14.

IV 4–7 **Hound · · · tear you limb from limb:** Maud Stessor described Hodgson as "an uncouth, untidy man with strange blazing eyes and a shock of hair, invariably escorted on his walks abroad by a retinue of six or seven huge bull terriers", *Bookman* 31 Apr 1931. TSE in childhood: "Poor Mosly felt badly at this, when an immense bull-dog came tearing after him. [*continued:*] The bull-dog ran and catching Mosly's pants tore a large piece out", *Mosly Wrags: The adventures of a hobo* by Gabbee Tahkers, *Fireside* Nos. 5–6. "Do you wear pants! If so wear *NeverRip*, fine for hobos! Bulldogs cannot tear them", *Eliot's Floral Magazine*. "I cannot afford yachting, but I should like to breed bull terriers", *Harvard College Class of 1910, Seventh Report* (1935) 221.

IV 5–6 **from his master | Will follow you faster and faster:** Poe: "Caught from some unhappy master whom unmerciful Disaster | Followed fast and followed faster", *The Raven* 63–64 (*Grover Smith* 250).

IV 7 **tear you limb from limb**: Aurelia Hodgson: "Late in the spring he told me he had heard a story of Ralph Hodgson's once being given 5 ~~summons~~ complaints by the police because a maid had one of the dogs on a[n] elastic Whiteley's Exerciser instead of a proper leader, and he had gone about attacking people in the dark. We agreed that the story sounded apocryphal. [*Footnote*: Actually it is true, and there were 7 complaints]", notes on TSE from his conversation, 1930s.

IV 11 **his palate fine**: Keats: "him whose strenuous tongue | Can burst Joy's grape against his palate fine", *Ode on Melancholy* 27–28 (*Grover Smith* 250).

IV 12 **gooseberry tart**: to Hodgson, 31 Oct 1934: "The gooseberries in Japan must have an especially sour flavour to make you like this chattering in your delirium". 11 May 1935: "no use worrying about the future till you get back to Ridgeways and we can fill you up with gooseberry tarts." Postcard, 4 Nov 1938: "Saddle of mutton arranged, but I cannot promise gooseberry tart."

IV 15 **999 canaries**: Vivien Eliot to Aurelia Hodgson, undated: "I got your postcard this morning about the canaries etc" (Beinecke). Kochi Doi, a colleague at Sendai U., recorded that Hodgson was given a roller canary, and bought a second. The two mated and there were soon more than 30 (Robert H. Sykes, *Explicator* May 1972).

IV 16–17 **round his head finches and fairies | In jubilant rapture skim**: *Grover Smith* 250 points to Hodgson:

> When flighting time is on I go
> With clap-net and decoy,
> A-fowling after goldfinches
> And other birds of joy.
>
> I lurk among the thickets of
> The Heart where they are bred,
> And catch the twittering beauties as
> They fly into my Head.
>
> *The Birdcatcher* (1917)

IV 18–19 **How delightful to meet Mr. Hodgson! | (Everyone wants to meet *him*)**: "You hear everyone remark | Look at him!" *Suite Clownesque* III 16–17.

V. *Lines for Cuscuscaraway and Mirza Murad Ali Beg*

"E is for Eliot, a very stern man. | His prose is severe, and his poems don't scan", page heading in Faber's Christmas Books catalogue 1933 (author unknown). In a comic letter to Geoffrey Faber, 7 July 1936, TSE characterises himself: "I would point out that my emoluments from the publishing house of Faber are not only ridiculously inadequate in consideration of the burden of responsibility that I bear, but are only just sufficient to enable me to dress neatly and modestly and to entertain the innumerable bores at whom I should be able to snap my fingers were I not connected with a publishing house." The poem's first publication, in the *Criterion*, used frequent capitals in 18th-century style; see Textual History.

Title ***Cuscuscaraway***: OED "cuscus" 2: "aromatic root of an Indian grass" + "caraway": "umbelliferous plant · · · aromatic and carminative". Also "cuscus"

3: "a genus of marsupial quadrupeds found in New Guinea" (citing H. H. Romilly: "The opossums and cuscus tribe taste strongly of gum leaves on which they feed"). For TSE, a cur: "I would tell you about our Cus Cus Praps except that I can't Draw Dogs so well as Cats", to Tom Faber, 20 Jan 1931. ***Mirza Murad Ali Beg***: author of the historical romance *Lalun the Beragun: or The Battle of Paniput* (Bombay, 1884). TSE had heard of this "Legend of Hindoostan" from Kipling's story *To Be Filed for Reference* within *Plain Tales from the Hills* (1888), where the dying McIntosh boasts of his writings: "'What Mirza Murad Ali Beg's book is to all other books on native life, will my work be to Mirza Murad Ali Beg's!'" (*Grover Smith* 250). TSE: "in *Plain Tales from the Hills* he has given the one perfect picture of a society of English, narrow, snobbish, spiteful, ignorant and vulgar, set down absurdly in a continent of which they are unconscious. What Mirza Murad Ali Beg's book is to all other books of native life, so is Mr. Kipling's to all other books of Anglo-Indian life", *Kipling Redivivus* (1919). To Hayward, 3 Jan 1941: "Your outline of the old ladies of Wimbledon is very promising, and I hope will be developed in the great work which is to be to Mirza Murad Ali Beg's book what Mirza Murad Ali Beg's book is to all other books of native life." Again, to the Faber committee: "I think it no exaggeration that what Mirza Murad Ali Beg's book is to all other books, so is this book to Mirza Murad Ali Beg's", *"All and Everything"* by G. Gurdjieff, reader's report (1949). Kipling retold Beg's story in his poem *With Scindia to Delhi* (1890).

TSE to Anne Ridler, 25 June 1945: "It was kind of you to let me see your broadcast. A few comments. 1. I wonder whether your Hindus will understand that Cuscuscaraway and Mirza Murad Ali Beg were the cur and the cat referred to in the poem? The former was not the original Pollicle (Dinah, who attached herself to me one evening in Eastbourne, and after a few nights at the police station became mine for the fee of five shillings) but a successor of known antecedents. The latter was a Persian kitten given me by Alida Monro, nervous and rather dull-witted—a descendant of the well-known prizewinner Woolly Bear." (For Dinah, see TSE to his mother, 23 Apr 1919, quoted in headnote to II. *Lines to a Yorkshire Terrier.* For "Woolly Bear", see note to I. *Lines to a Persian Cat* 5.) Proposing a toast for the Kipling Society: "I leave you to guess why a Persian cat I once possessed was dignified by the name of Mirza Murad Ali Beg", *"The Unfading Genius of Rudyard Kipling"* (1959). For TSE's description of Mirza Murad Ali Beg to Tom Faber, 28 Dec 1931, see headnote to *Practical Cats*: 8. APROPOS OF *PRACTICAL CATS* BY VALERIE ELIOT.

V 1 **How unpleasant to meet Mr. Eliot!** (*variant* **to know**): Edward Lear: *"How pleasant to know Mr. Lear!"* with its fifth line: "His mind is concrete and fastidious". In his copy of *The Spiritual Letters of Dom John Chapman* (1935) 156, TSE scored "We all have one unpleasant person to live with, whom we can't get away from—ourself" (King's). *Tomlin* 89 reports TSE on 25 May 1937: "Looking back he said he realised how clumsily he had behaved in certain situations, and indeed what an 'unpleasant' person (that was the adjective he used) he knew he had sometimes been." TSE to Frank and Christina Morley, 3 Feb 1947, after the death of Vivien (23 Jan): "I feel as if I had descended into depths such that there was a great gulf fixed. The shock of looking at a rather unpleasant stranger, and finding that it is oneself in a mirror; the shock of finding, at 58, the greatest crisis of one's life—but I can't, and probably shouldn't try, to express myself at present." (See *Portrait of a Lady* III 16–17, "I feel like one who smiles, and turning shall remark | Suddenly, his expression in a glass", and note.) "Sometimes my poems turn out to be much more unpleasant than I thought they were", *T. S. Eliot Talks about His Poetry* (1958). **unpleasant**: on *Georgian Poetry*: "What nearly all the writers have in common is the quality of pleasantness. There are two varieties of pleasantness: (1) The insidiously didactic, or Wordsworthian (a rainbow and a cuckoo's song); (2) the decorative, playful or solemn, minor-Keatsian, too happy, happy brook, or lucent sirops ··· Another variety of the pleasant, by the way, is the unpleasant", *Verse Pleasant and Unpleasant* (1918). (Shaw published *Plays Pleasant and Unpleasant* in two vols. in 1898. *TSE's books: Bodleian list* (1934) includes *Plays Unpleasant.*) On the "peculiarity" of Blake: "It is merely a peculiar honesty ··· against which the whole world conspires, because it is unpleasant. Blake's poetry has the unpleasantness of great poetry", *William Blake* (1920) I. Of the mature poet: "He is not, my poet, altogether a pleasant character ··· I must say for myself lest I should be misunderstood, that I am not talking about myself", *Modern Tendencies in Poetry* (1920). On Dryden: "It is harder to be natural than to be artificial, it requires a great deal more work, and is painful and unpleasant because sincerity is always painful and unpleasant. Well, Dryden did the work, and experienced no doubt the pain and unpleasantness, and he restored English verse to the condition of speech", *Dryden the Poet* (1931). On Yeats's *The Spur*: "These lines are very impressive and not very pleasant ··· I do not read them as a personal confession of a man who differed from other men, but of a man who was essentially the same as most other men; the only difference is in the greater clarity, honesty and vigour ··· Similarly, the play *Purgatory* is not very pleasant, either", *Yeats* (1940). On Leonardo: "that formidable and unpleasant personality", *A Note on "Monstre Gai"* (1955). **to meet Mr. Eliot**: to his mother, 6 Jan 1920, of his cousin Abigail Eliot: "we were both much taken with her. She seems intelligent, and has a sense of humour, and charming manners. She and Vivien found each other very congenial. Vivien had always longed to meet an Eliot." **Mr. Eliot**: among TSE's various identities (T. S. Eliot, TSE, Possum, Uncle Tom, T.P.), this was the formal name used among the junior ranks at Faber, and in publicity for his books and the firm's other activities—there being no need for further identification. To W. H. Auden, 30 Jan 1934: "Dear Auden (I think that we might drop the Mr)". To George Every, 4 Jan 1937: "Dear George, (Please drop Mr.)" To Charles Madge, 28 Oct 1940: "Dear Madge, (I think we might 'drop the mister')." After thirteen years of "Dear Gallup" and "Dear Mr. Gallup", "My dear Mr. Gallup" and "My dear Gallup", TSE addressed a letter to "Dear Donald Gallup" (10 Aug 1949), before the final step, on 19 Oct 1949: "Dear Donald, (I think that we might become rather more informal)"—yet he did not sign himself "Tom" until 1951. See notes on the titles *Mr. Eliot's Sunday Morning Service* and *The Love Song of J. Alfred Prufrock.*

V 2 **of clerical cut**: OED "cut" 17: "The shape to which, or style in which a thing is cut", quoting *As You Like It* II vii: "With eyes severe, and beard of formal cut", and "A broad-brimmed hat and coat of Quakerish cut" (1883). TSE: "a clerical hat and an apron and gaiters | For a Possum who dresses in Style", *A Practical Possum* 4–5.

V 2 *variant* **figure of corpulent size:** Lear: "His body is perfectly spherical", *"How Pleasant to Know Mr. Lear!"* 19.

V 3 *variant* **his nose inflamed:** Lear: "His nose is remarkably big", *"How Pleasant to Know Mr. Lear!"* 6 (author also of *The Dong with the Luminous Nose*).

V 5 **nicely:** obsolete or rare senses in OED include 1: "Foolishly, unwisely"; 3a: "Finely, elegantly, refinedly, daintily"; 4a: "sparingly, grudgingly"; 4b: "Fastidiously, squeamishly"; 4c: "Scrupulously, punctiliously"; 5a: "With insistence on detail". *Fowler*, "nice": "Everyone who uses it in its more proper senses, which fill most of the space given to it in any dictionary, & avoids the modern one that tends to oust them all, does a real if small service to the language."

V 5–7 **so nicely | Restricted to What Precisely | And If and Perhaps and But:** Alfred Kreymborg: "back to the starting-point, | with if or suppose or providing or but—", *Pianissimo* (published in *Poetry* in 1922, and perhaps known to TSE from *Prize Poems 1913–1929*, ed. Charles A. Wagner, with an introduction by Mark Van Doren, in which *The Waste Land* was reprinted). Aurelia Hodgson: "In spite of Lady Ottoline's story of Mr. Eliot's careful speech and the legend of 'Just-what-do-you-mean-by-the-second-"very"' type, his conversation was wholly free from pedanticisms. He always said, 'Who'll have sauce on *their* meat?' ··· he told us of a phrase on which he had become self-conscious in Eng[land]. When he was working in Lloyds Bank, a superior drew to his attention 'under the circumstances' ··· he told me of a legend about himself, which had never occurred and wasn't uncomplimentary—he could wish it *were* true. The story goes that he was at dinner, with a gushing young woman beside him. She turned to him and said, 'Don't you find D. H. Lawrence's latest book [whatever it was] is *too* amusing?' Mr. Eliot is reported to have thought this over in silence, and then to have replied, 'And just what do you mean by "*too*"?'", notes on TSE from his conversation, 1930s (Bryn Mawr). Asked about sub-clauses and parentheses in his prose: "The reason for the syntactical complications is a passion for avoiding over-simplifications and over-emphasis", *T. S. Eliot Answers Questions* (1949). "As I have a reputation ~~for pedantic precision~~ ~~for a pedantic affectation of precision~~ ~~for affecting pedantic precisions~~ for being pedantic, which I do not want to lose ···" *American Literature and the American Language* (1953), draft (King's).

V 6 **What Precisely:** "'Mother, why *precisely* does the refrigerator drip?'" are the supposed first words of Jeremy Cibber in Richard Aldington's satire on TSE, *Stepping Heavenward* (1931) 5 (*T. S. Matthews* 105).

V 7 **And If and Perhaps and But:** "offends and perplexes more | With the imperatives of 'is' and 'seems' | And 'may' and 'may not'", *Animula* 18–20 variant. To Desmond MacCarthy, 28 Dec 1942: "avoidance of repetition of words (even *ofs* and *ands* and *buts* have to be carefully watched)".

V 11 **porpentine cat:** OED "porcupine": "*Porpentine* was the form known to Shakes. who uses it 7 times", citing no examples between 1657 and this of TSE's. *Hamlet* I v: "And each particular hair to stand on end | Like quills upon the fretful porpentine".

V 12 **wopsical:** Edward Lear has "a runcible hat" in *"How Pleasant to Know Mr. Lear!"* and used his invented adjective in other contexts. For TSE on "pollicle" and "jellicle", see headnote to *Practical Cats*, 3. COMPOSITION; for "moley", see note to *Billy M'Caw: The Remarkable Parrot* 41. TSE to E. Foxall, 3 Feb 1932: "the confection of new words · · · is not a device which particularly commends itself to me. The idea, of course, is not a new one, and an argument in its favour may be found in *Alice in Wonderland*. Of course I admit that a similar technology has been extensively employed by Mr. James Joyce, but you must remember that Mr. Joyce has only arrived at it after a very long process of literary toil · · · I think that in the verses you have shown, the composite words stand out far too conspicuously." To Hugh Ross Williamson, 18 May 1932: "I have come across in Walter de la Mare's *Lewis Carroll* a quotation from a letter which Carroll wrote about *The Hunting of the Snark*. 'I am very much afraid', he said, 'I didn't mean anything but nonsense . . . But since these words mean more than we mean to express when we use them . . . whatever good meanings are in the book I am very glad to accept as the meaning of the book.'" (De la Mare's *Lewis Carroll* was published by Faber in 1932. TSE and de la Mare both admired Carroll and Ralph Hodgson; but see *To Walter de la Mare* headnote.) "non-sense is not vacuity of sense: it is a parody of sense, and that is the sense of it", *The Music of Poetry* (1942).

V 14 **Whether his mouth be open or shut:** Herbert: "Thy mouth was open, but thou couldst not sing", *Death* 4. (For Swinburne's "The grave's mouth", see note to *The wind sprang up at four o'clock* 1–15.)

Landscapes

New Hampshire and *Virginia* were published as *Words for Music* in *Virginia Quarterly Review* Apr 1934 and in Britain in *The Best Poems of 1934* ed. Thomas Moult (1934). (Yeats had published his *Words for Music Perhaps* in 1932.) A small number of copies of the pair was privately printed that year as a "Butterfly Book" for Frederick Prokosch, still under the title *Words for Music*. Prokosch sent several copies to TSE, who replied, 20 Feb 1935: "Very many thanks for your kind gift, and for printing my two poems in such a charming way. I am sure that no one could raise any objection to your printing poems in this way which are not for sale, and I am very pleased by the gifts. It occurs to me that a short poem produced in this way would make a very nice Christmas card, and if you cared to produce something in this way for next Christmas for me, I would write a poem for the purpose. Of course, an arrangement of that sort would naturally involve my paying for your expense and time." TSE may have had in mind the Ariel Poems series which had finished in 1931. He sent copies of the Butterfly Book to W. H. Auden, I. A. Richards and others. To Stephen Spender, 22 Feb 1935: "I haven't the slightest idea who Prokosch is, but he seems a very amiable person. I printed one of his own poems last year, and he has just sent me another, which

I also like." (Prokosch's poems *The Voyage* and *Going Southward* appeared in *Criterion* July 1934, July 1935.)

Rannoch, by Glencoe was published in *NEW* 17 Oct 1935 and in *New Democracy* (NY) 15 Dec 1935.

Cape Ann was published in *New Democracy* 15 Dec 1935.

"Twenty-two copies" of *Cape Ann* and *Usk* were privately printed for Prokosch as the Butterfly Book *Two Poems*, for distribution by the author at Christmas 1935.

The five *Landscapes* were collected in *1936+* and *New Hampshire*, *Virginia* and *Usk* appeared in *Sesame.*

Recorded 26 July 1946, NBC (NY) for the Library of Congress. Second: 13 May 1947, Harvard, as part of the Morris Gray Poetry Reading. Third: 23 May 1947, Washington. Fourth: 12 Nov 1950, for U. Chicago Round Table, broadcast by NBC. Additionally: I and II were recorded after the lecture *From Poe to Valéry*, 19 Nov 1948, at the Library of Congress.

TSE was probably referring to *Landscapes* when he wrote to John Lehmann, 22 Aug 1935, about a request for new work for an anthology: "I have a few small and trifling pieces, but the difficulty is that I contemplate bringing out a new collected edition of my poems in the spring, and as my output is so small I cannot offer to print separately any unedited verse which is likely to go into that book."

To William Force Stead, 9 Aug 1930, on Stead's poems *The House on the Wold*: "the transitions between the Umbrian and the Oxfordshire background enhance the effect. This leads to the second point: my admiration, as a fellowcountryman, at the degree to which you have absorbed these two landscapes. I do not think I am wholly deficient in the 'feeling for nature'; it is either that I have lived for many years almost exclusively in towns, or else that I only have it in association with strong human emotions—I don't think the latter—however that may be, I know I have to go back to Missouri and New England for natural imagery." See TSE's Preface to *This American World* (1928)—"In New England I missed the long dark river · · · in Missouri I missed the fir trees"—quoted in headnote to *The Dry Salvages*, the poem in which New England and the American South were finally combined, as were seas and rivers.

Publication of *New Hampshire* and *Virginia* in *Virginia Quarterly Review* was a result of TSE's difficulties with what became *After Strange Gods*. After speaking in public some seventy or eighty times in the United States (letter to Hayward, 19 July 1933), and being obliged to publish his Charles Eliot Norton Lectures given at Harvard (*The Use of Poetry and the Use of Criticism*), he delayed publishing those given in Virginia. Returning to London he wrote to F. S. Barr, U. Virginia, 27 Aug 1933:

> I must apologise for letting you down over the lecture. What happened was, that on re-reading the set I found that they need very much more re-writing than they should, and that I was unwilling to let even one appear in periodical form until I had been able to revise it; and until now I have had to concentrate on preparing my Harvard lectures for press for this autumn. I hope to get to work on the Page-Barbour lectures in about

> ten days; I will send you a revise of number III as soon as ready and hope that there will be time, if it fits your editorial plans, to have it appear in the *Quarterly*.
>
> Meanwhile, as a peace-offering, I enclose two small songs—if you don't want them for the *Quarterly* return them. I am not likely to use them elsewhere; some day I may add a few more, or else tear them up. I may add that they have no political significance whatever.

In the deposition he prepared for the obscenity case concerning *Lady Chatterley's Lover*, TSE wrote of *After Strange Gods*: "It was expressly by my own wish that there were no further impressions after 1934" and, in a paragraph he then crossed out: "I should have realised that I as well as he [Lawrence] should have been described as 'a sick soul'", *Lady Chatterley Deposition* (1960). Again: "It should be mentioned somewhere that I became dis-satisfied with *After Strange Gods*, which I came to consider rather intemperate, especially in speaking of Thomas Hardy, and no longer keep in print in this country", *Northrop Frye corrigenda* (1963). The first edition of *After Strange Gods: A Primer of Modern Heresy* consisted of 3,000 copies, published 22 Feb 1934; a 2nd imp. of 1,500 copies followed in Dec 1934. The US ed., from Harcourt Brace, was of 1,500 copies, published 19 Apr 1934. Faber's 2nd imp. continued to be advertised on the rear panel of *The Idea of a Christian Society* (Oct 1939), but the book went out of print on 3 Aug 1944 and TSE prevented further printings, although part, including a page about Hardy, appeared in John Hayward's two selections from TSE, *Points of View* (1941) and *Selected Prose* (1953). For Hardy and "self-expression", see headnote to *Opera*.

Moody 183: "The three American *Landscapes* were probably written during Eliot's visit there in 1933; the Welsh and Scottish probably after his return to England in 1934 or 1935." Valerie Eliot dated *Virginia* "1933" in her copy of 14th imp. of *1936* (1951).

To I. A. Richards, 4 June 1935 (having sent *New Hampshire* and *Virginia* in the Butterfly Book *Words for Music* on 20 Feb 1935): "I have done two more 'words for music', but I believe they are not as good as those you have seen." To Richards, 24 Sept 1935, with *Usk* and *Cape Ann*: "I enclose two more *Landscapes* (these are obviously *not* Words for Music): are they too different in method to go together?"

Hayward to TSE 3 Mar 1942, of a Red Cross auction: "I suggested to Mary [Hutchinson] that you might be kind enough to copy out in your own hand one of your *Landscapes*—*Rannoch by Glencoe*, for example—with a note to the effect that it was specially so transcribed for the Sale"; TSE presented instead the typescript of a lecture.

At the Morris Gray Poetry Reading at Harvard, 13 May 1947: "I would like to read ··· not because there's any demand for it, a series of little poems called *Landscapes* of which nobody takes much notice, but which I rather like. On the one hand I am reassured by two friends of mine both of whose judgments I trust in these matters. One, a Southerner, told me that the *Landscape* called *Virginia* was the best, and another, a Scot, assured me that *Rannoch, by Glencoe* is the best. I have had no reports from New Hampshire or Massachusetts, and nothing definite from Wales, but I have recently acquired a Welsh godson, with a name that I cannot pronounce." *Lehmann* on TSE's reading at Bryn Mawr in Oct 1948: "he read especially for the American audience two landscape poems: *New Hampshire* and *Virginia*. He introduced these two poems with the words: 'And, now to you people here, as a relief—not for you but for my soul'—and he may well have alluded to his departure from America, which has been criticized by many and which he himself perhaps does not regard as right in every aspect, albeit necessary for him." TSE at U. Chicago on 12 Nov 1950 (after reading *Coriolan* II. *Difficulties of a Statesman*): "I'll give you the short *Landscapes*, as being something in a lighter vein."

To Jean Mambrino, 24 July 1952, on translation into French (perhaps unsent):

> I must say that the poems you have chosen strike me as the most untranslatable of all my verse, since they are the most purely lyrical and the effect and meaning depend so very much upon the particular arrangement of syllables which is found in the English. You have, on the whole, made a fairly close literal translation, although it seems to me, especially in the case of the first two, that the value of the poems evaporates completely, and must evaporate completely in any translation.
>
> I note, however, a few small points. In *New Hampshire* it would be better to put the five verbs at the end in the imperative mood, although in English they have the advantage of ambiguity between the imperative and the indicative. In *Virginia*, I do not think that "tranquille" quite renders "still". As one has to select out of the meaning of the word in one language only a part of its meaning for translation, I should say that what should be emphasised is the fact that the hills, in contrast to the river, give the impression of immobility. This poem, by the way, is modelled on the Spanish copla form. For *Usk*, I think an understanding of this poem depends partly on the immediate evocation of the scenery of *The Mabinogion*, Welsh tales belonging to the Arthurian cycle. In *Rannoch*, I do not think that "tendre" is quite the right rendering of "soft". It might almost be "mou". As for the birds, these particular varieties of singing sparrows are only known in America, and I do not know what you can do about them as there is probably no French equivalent. All you can do, is to substitute known European song birds for unknown American birds. I have never known what difference there is, if any, between "le goéland" and "la mouette", both of which are given in the dictionary as the equivalent of "sea-gull", and I am not quite sure that "bavardage" is right for "palaver". A "palaver" is more a discussion or conference. You have in French the verb "palabrer".

Alongside the quotation of II 1–4 in *G. Jones* (202), TSE wrote "This is a *copla*". The Spanish *copla* is a light song, usually a love song. The word derives from *cuplé*, a short, often playful song for the stage. (See Margaret Greaves, *Journal of Modern Literature* Summer 2014.)

Title **Landscapes**: to Geoffrey Faber, 29 Sept 1952:

> The mountains of Vermont are amazingly beautiful · · · and would be so even if they were not now adorned by forest foliage of the most brilliant colours: every shade from light yellow and brown through scarlet to deep heather purple, according to the species of tree. But the towns, the villages and the scattered homesteads are sordid and *mesquin* [mean]; the country is almost a desert; and you [would] not believe that man could have inhabited a territory for a good three hundred years and made so shallow an impression upon it. He has not improved nature or in any way come to terms with it—as in England or in Italy you feel an intimate relation between the life of nature and the life of the race · · · you feel that every house and sign of human life might be swept away and leave exactly the same inhuman natural beauty that was there before.

To Bonamy Dobrée [28 Oct] 1932: "I envy you · · · your prospect over the mellow fields & mists of Norfolk. The New England landscape is very beautiful in autumn, with its beeches and maples in full blaze and clamour over the rugged hills; but the *paysage* is, after all, not humanised."

I. *New Hampshire*

In June 1933 TSE visited Emily Hale in New Hampshire before sailing back to Britain. He returned to New Hampshire on holiday in Sept 1936.

Title ***New Hampshire***: Robert Frost was awarded a Pulitzer Prize for his *New Hampshire* (1923), a collection Jeffrey Hart considered "a rejoinder to the author of *The Waste Land*" (*Sewanee Review* Summer 1976). TSE: "it was only in 1915, after I came to England, that I heard the name of Robert Frost", *Ezra Pound* (1946). Toast to Robert Frost, *Books across the Sea*, June 1957: "I have a special weakness—no, I shouldn't call it a weakness—a special understanding, of a great deal of his work because I also have the New England background. But I think that there are two kinds of local feeling in poetry. There is the kind which makes that poetry only accessible to people who have the same background, to whom it means a great deal; and there is another kind which can go with universality: the relation of Dante to Florence, of Shakespeare to Warwickshire, of Goethe to the Rhineland: the relation of Robert Frost to New England" (transcript by Beatrice Warde, Faber archive). To Glenway Westcott, 24 Mar 1961: "I should have been glad to add my voice to those recommending Robert Frost for the Nobel Prize, but unfortunately I have already put forward another candidate writing in another language from ours, and also suggested that at some future date the name of Mr. Ezra Pound might be considered."

I 1 **Children's voices in the orchard**: *Coriolanus* III i: "Have I had children's voices?" Blake: "When the voices of children are heard on the green | And whisperings are in the dale, | The days of youth rise fresh in my mind", *When the voices of children*. TSE: "children's voices, ended in a wail", *First Caprice in North Cambridge* 4. "Children's voices in little corners | Whimper whimper", *The Burnt Dancer* 20–21. "Children singing in the orchard", *Ode* ("Tired. | Subterrene") 12. "*Et O ces voix d'enfants*", *The Waste Land* [III] 202.

I 1, 8, 12 **Children's voices in the orchard ··· light-in-leaves ··· apple-tree**: Pound: "This is our home, the trees are full of laughter ··· and the Mounts Balde and Riva | Are alive with song, and all the leaves are full of voices", *Three Cantos* (I), *Poetry* June 1917. TSE: "the leaves were full of children, | Hidden excitedly, containing laughter", *Burnt Norton* I 40–41. "The voice ··· And the children in the apple-tree", *Little Gidding* V 34–35 (see note).

I 2 **Between the blossom- and the fruit-time**: Swinburne: "between the blossom and the grass", *Laus Veneris* 309; one of the Swinburne poems which a volume of selections "should certainly contain", *Swinburne as Poet* (1920).

I 3 **crimson head**: "In New England I missed the long dark river, the ailanthus trees, the flaming cardinal birds", *This American World* (1928). The cardinal is the state bird of Virginia.

I 7–8 **grieves, | Cover me over, light-in-leaves**: Ralph Caldecott: "Till death did end their grief ··· Till Robin-redbreast painfully | Did cover them with leaves", *The Babes in the Wood* [1879] (*Grover Smith* 247).

I 10–12 **swing ··· Swing up into the apple-tree**: "There, is a tree swinging", *The Hollow*

Men II 6. "Or I could take sanctuary | In any oak or apple tree", *The Country Walk* 33–34.

II. *Virginia*

II 1 **Red river:** Charlottesville's Albemarle clay sometimes stains red the Rivenna River, Virginia. "the river | Is a strong brown god", *The Dry Salvages* I 1–2.

II 2, 4, 11 **heat · · · heat · · · Iron thoughts:** Kipling: "the thoughts that burn like iron if you think", *The Song of the Banjo* 68. For lines from the same stanza, see note to *Portrait of a Lady* I 15–19.

II 5 **mocking-bird:** to Ralph Hodgson, 11 May 1935: "The Nightingales HAVE been something extra this year · · · though you know my convictions a good mockingbird can beat the nightingale all holler" (see note to *Sweeney Among the Nightingales* 35).

III. *Usk*

Introduced as "Usk in Wales", *Chicago Round Table* (1950). Hayward: "The Usk · · · is an English river, in Monmouthshire, on the border of Wales, which Eliot visited last summer", *London Letter* in *New York Sun*, 28 Mar 1936. As well as being the Arthurian country of legend, the Usk valley was home to Henry Vaughan, who, in the first poem of *Olor Iscanus* [Swan of Usk] (1651), bids "all *Bards* born after me | (When I am *ashes*) sing of thee!" *To the River Isca* 35–36. TSE took holidays with the Fabers at their Welsh home, Ty Glyn Aeron, each year from 1933 to 1936 (two sheets of photographs survive; Houghton). To Fr. Mervyn Sweet, 24 May 1949: "As for what you ask about my small poem—which in spite of its slightness is one of my favourites amongst my own work—I am almost never inspired to write anything descriptive or evocative on the spot. It is only out of memories that I can do anything of the sort. No, the poem was written in London and probably sometime after I had motored from Cardiganshire back to London through that delightful and rather magical landscape."

III 3 **The white hart behind the white well:** Philip Edwards suggests this refers to the beehive-shaped village well, said formerly to have been whitewashed, a hundred yards from the White Hart Inn, Llangybi. The Inn is said to have been used as a local headquarters by Cromwell (see reports, *Guardian* and *Independent* 6 Aug 2003).

III 4 **lance:** Jessie L. Weston: "the Waste Land, the Fisher King, the Hidden Castle with its solemn Feast, and mysterious Feeding Vessel, the Bleeding Lance and Cup", *From Ritual to Romance* 3. The lance is prominent in the Arthurian cycle and in the *Mabinogion.*

III 5 *variant* **mantrams:** OED "mantra", also "mantram": "A sacred text or passage, esp. one from the Vedas used as a prayer or incantation." For the Vedic mantra "Shantih", see note to *The Waste Land* [V] 433.

III 6 **Gently dip, but not too deep:** George Peele: "Gently dip, but not too deep, | For fear you make the golden bird to weep, | Fair maiden white and red, | Stroke me smooth, and combe my head", *The Old Wives' Tale* 664–67 (*Grover Smith* 247).

IV. *Rannoch, by Glencoe*

Introduced as "Rannoch, by Glencoe, in the Scottish Highlands", *Chicago Round Table* (1950).

TSE to F. S. Oliver, 3 Nov 1931: "I still hope that I may some day, like Dr. Johnson, pay a visit to your country." Frank Morley: "On November 10 [1933], Tom and Donald Brace and I went off to Scotland—we were met by George Blake at Glasgow to drive over Rannoch Moor to and from Inverness", *Morley 1966* 107. And, recalling the Scottish writer Neil M. Gunn (who became a Faber author in 1939): "Neil Gunn ··· was living at Inverness in the years between the two world wars when George Blake and I, and on one occasion T. S. Eliot, were privileged to stay ··· One item I remember from that between-wars drive from Glasgow to Inverness with Eliot was the pause we made on Rannoch Moor. It was some weeks later that Eliot handed me his short poem, one of the few *Landscapes* that he cared to preserve, called *Rannoch, by Glencoe*", *Morley 1980* 463. TSE to Hayward, 17 Aug 1942, on an affectionate regard: "I have a peculiar *tendre* for everything Scotch which psychology may be able to explain but I can't." (For "*tendre*", see letter to Jean Mambrino, 24 July 1952, in headnote to *Landscapes*.)

This was the first of TSE's poems to appear in *NEW*, for which he wrote often 1934–48 and which was also to publish *Words for an Old Man* (*Lines for an Old Man*) and the last three of the *Four Quartets*. To McKnight Kauffer, 29 Mar 1940: "I did not wish to make you feel that you needed to write to me about the poem—which was why I had it sent to you in that impersonal way wrapt up in the N.E.W. (of which, however, I am a member of the Editorial Committee, and to which I contribute from time to time, sometimes anonymously in the editorial notes—as a rule, you can assume that any note attacking bishops or a bishop is from my Corona [typewriter])."

Title **by**: Henry Vaughan's letter of dedication in *Olor Iscanus* is subscribed "*Newton* by *Usk*".

IV 1 **the crow starves ··· patient**: "The starved crow sits in the field, attentive", *Murder in the Cathedral* II, opening chorus, added 2nd ed. (1936). **the crow ··· the stag**: Lucilius: "If thou livest the long years of a stag or crow", *The Greek Anthology* IV [389], tr. W. R. Paton (Loeb, 1918).

IV 6 **ancient war**: the Roman Catholic MacDonalds were overwhelmed by the Protestant Campbells at the Massacre of Glencoe, 1692.

IV 11–12 **in the long pass | No concurrence of bone**: OED "concurrence" 1: "Running together, confluence, meeting. *Obs.*" b: "Confluence of people". c: "meeting of lines, surfaces, etc", with 1658: "there is a concurrence of sinews and muscles". 4: "Accordance, agreement". For "those who opposed ··· and those whom they opposed ··· are folded in a single party", see *Little Gidding* III 39–42.

V. *Cape Ann*

"And finally, Cape Ann in Massachusetts", *Chicago Round Table* (1950).

In 1896 TSE's father built a house at Gloucester, Cape Ann, where the family spent part of each summer. "I have never returned to Cape Ann or to Gloucester Mass. since 1915", ts note dated 14 Aug 1947 (*CompositionFQ* 34); TSE did later return to Cape Ann with Valerie Eliot. To Bonamy Dobrée [28 Oct] 1932: "The bird life of New England is the most wonderful in creation, except that since my time the countryside has become infested with Starlings, a sordid and squalid immigrant who is driving out the natives." On 3 Dec 1935, at Magdalen College, Oxford, TSE read *Cape Ann* "with great gusto", commenting that he had written it "to show that I know something about birds" (*Tomlin* 70).

V 1 **O quick quick quick, quick hear the song-sparrow**: William Allingham on the thrush: "Be quick! be quick! Here, here, here!" *The Lover and Birds* 27 (Allingham's first line, "Within a budding grove", had been adopted by C. K. Scott Moncrieff for his translation of the second volume of Proust in 1924); see note to V 10. TSE: "Quick, said the bird", *Burnt Norton* I 19. "Quickens to recover | The cry of quail and the whirling plover", *Ash-Wednesday* VI 15–16.

V 1–3 **O quick quick quick, quick hear the song-sparrow, | Swamp-sparrow, fox-sparrow, vesper-sparrow | At dawn and dusk**: Frank M. Chapman: "SONG SPARROW ··· Its irrepressible vitality and good spirits in spite of all circumstances are aptly illustrated by the fact that its song may be heard in every month of the year and in all weathers; also by night as well as by day ··· Its alarm note is a simple metallic *chip*, which is very distinctive once learned. But its merry chant ··· its best-known note ··· it will be found forming a part of a long scattered migrating train that usually includes a number of different species"; "VESPER SPARROW ··· if you quicken your steps and try to overtake him, he will rise and bound on before you ··· Early morning and late afternoon are his favourite hours, but he can be heard at other times", *Handbook of Birds of Eastern North America*. Chapman distinguished thirty-one species of sparrow in all, and in his copy TSE checked each of the four named in the poem, plus the yellow-winged sparrow. The volume is inscribed "Thomas Stearns Eliot Sept. 26th 1902" by his mother, with TSE's identifying note: "In my mother's handwriting. A much coveted birthday present on my 14th birthday. T. S. Eliot. 18 June 1928." See the author's Notes on the Waste Land 356.

V 3–4 **dance | Of the goldfinch**: Chapman's *Handbook* includes a drawing of the weaving flight of the American goldfinch (marked in TSE's copy).

V 5 **Blackburnian warbler**: Chapman's *Handbook*: "uncommon enough to make us appreciate his unusual beauty ··· in the spring its notes may be likened to *wee-see-wee-see, tsee-tsee, tsee, tsee, tsee-tsee, tsee, tsee.*"

V 6 **With shrill whistle the note of the quail, the bob-white**: Chapman's *Handbook*: "BOB-WHITE; QUAIL ··· The name 'Bob-white' originated in the spring call of the male ··· he whistles the two clear musical, ringing notes *Bob-white!*" (Marked in TSE's copy, as is "water-thrush", 8.)

V 9–10 **Greet | In silence the bullbat:** Chapman's *Handbook*: "NIGHTHAWK; BULL-BAT ··· Batlike he flies erratically about, and at more or less regular intervals utters a loud nasal *peent* ··· after calling several times in close succession the bird on half-closed wings dives earthward with such speed that one fears for his safety ··· At the moment the turn is made one may hear a rushing, booming sound, which ··· can be imitated in tone by blowing across the bung-hole of any empty barrel."

V 10 *variant* **Some are archaic. Sweet:** "'Some are archaic' refers to the use of 'delectable' and the extinction of the quail; but I am not sure that it does not sound too self-conscious", note on the envelope sending *ts2* to Richards.

V 10 **Sweet sweet sweet:** Allingham: "Scream'd Chaffinch, 'Sweet, sweet, sweet!'" *The Lover and Birds* 9.

V 13 **The palaver is finished:** "I have given you speech, for endless palaver", *Choruses from "The Rock"* III 7. **palaver:** OED: "Palavra appears to have been used by Portuguese traders on the coast of Africa for a talk or colloquy with the natives ··· to have been there picked up by English sailors ··· and to have passed from nautical slang into colloquial use." TSE was aware of the nationality of many in Cape Ann: "witness in New England alone, the Portuguese in the fishing industry", *This American World* (1928). To C. S. Lewis, 8 Mar 1943: "I wish that my knowledge of Portuguese was beyond the mere deciphering stage, for I find the *Lusiads*, even in translation, in some respects more satisfactory [than *Paradise Lost*]—though also disfigured in at least one episode by absurdity." (*The Lusiad* by Luís de Camoens, tr. Richard Fanshawe, 1655.)

Lines for an Old Man

Published in *NEW* 28 Nov 1935, then *1936+*. No recording known. The private printing as *Old Man's Song* ("Salzburg", "1936") is a later forgery by Prokosch. Copy "alpha" (Sotheby's, 1–2 May 1972) contains a note by Prokosch: "In the typescript which Eliot sent me this poem was titled (in pencil) *Old Man's Song*." No such typescript has been found.

Frederick Tomlin discussed the poem with TSE and Michael Cullis on 3 Dec 1935: "First, what was the exact meaning of the title? Was it 'Lines *in the mouth of* an old man'? 'Yes.' Secondly, what did 'writhing in the *essential* blood' mean? ··· Michael recalls him as saying that the notion was suggested by a detective story by R. Austin Freeman, which concerned a negro knocking his brow against a bar, so that the blood issuing forth was 'essential'. Michael: 'A Homeric epithet, in other words'. Eliot (with some deliberation and slowly crumbling his cake): 'Yes, you could say that.' My recollection was that the detective story was one of E. Phillips Oppenheim's, and that it concerned a horrific murder whereby the victim was, so to speak, liquefied and poured down the sink, so that the 'essence' of him was thus disposed of ··· Our last question concerned 'inaccessible *by* the young'; and Eliot replied that, according to the OED, 'by' was a permissible use with 'inaccessible' as well as 'to', and in his opinion its presence in the last line sounded better", *Tomlin* 66–67.

Title ***an Old Man***: frequent in TSE's poems, with four iterations of "an old man" in

Gerontion; Tiresias twice in *The Waste Land* [III] 219, 228; "an old man's mouth drivelling", *Ash-Wednesday* III 10; "Ash on an old man's sleeve", *Little Gidding* II 1. Also: "blind old man", *First Debate between the Body and the Soul* 2; "drunken old man", *The Death of Saint Narcissus* 29; "laughter ··· Like the old man of the sea's", *Mr. Apollinax* 8–9. "old men on winter evenings", *Ash-Wednesday* VIII 32; "the wisdom of old men", *East Coker* II 44; "Old men ought to be explorers", *East Coker* V 31.

Unadopted dedication **to Stéphane Mallarmé**: both *ts1* and *ts2* derive two lines at the end of the poem from a sonnet by Mallarmé: "Garlic and sapphires in the mud | Clot the bedded axle-tree" (see Textual History; also *Burnt Norton* II 1–2 and note). "Hopkins can be called a difficult poet, but not, as is Mallarmé, an *opaque* poet", *Types of English Religious Verse* (1939).

1 **The tiger**: to Philip Mairet, 1 Jan 1936: "P.S. I wasn't thinking of the younger generation at all. I was thinking about the tiger at Whipsnade." (For the zoo, see note to *Choruses from "The Rock"* II 16 and note.)

1–2, 10 **The tiger ··· Is not more irritable than I ··· youth**: Wordsworth: "He was a lovely youth! I guess | The panther in the wilderness | Was not so fair as he", *Ruth* 37–39 (in *The Golden Treasury*). Tennyson: "The lion on your old stone gates | Is not more cold to you than I", *Lady Clara Vere de Vere* 23–24 (*Grover Smith 1996* 157).

1–2, 12 **The tiger ··· than I ··· my golden eye**: Blake: "Tyger Tyger, burning bright ··· Burnt the fire of thine eyes!" *The Tyger.* Tennyson: "golden ··· golden ··· burning eyes", *The Poet* 1–2, 39. TSE: "the serpent's golden eyes", *Choruses from "The Rock"* X 10 (*G. Jones* 229). "The golden vision reappears | I see the eyes", *Eyes that last I saw in tears* 4–5.

5–6 **Writhing ··· essential blood ··· tree**: for "F. M." and "bursting ··· misshapen bloom ··· the essential spring", see note to *A Song for Simeon* 1–2.

8–11 *variant* **My hate is more than hate of hate, | More bitter than the love of youth**: Tennyson: "The poet in a golden clime was born, | With golden stars above; | Dowered with the hate of hate, the scorn of scorn, | The love of love", *The Poet* 1–4 (with "Youth", 28). From his addition to *ts1*, TSE retained in *ts2* "the love of youth", and, at 12, adopted Tennyson's "golden", while dropping "hate of hate".

14 **Tell me if I am not glad**: to Ralf Rudeloff, 2 Oct 1956, on this line and *Burnt Norton* II 1–2: "As for *Garlic and Sapphires*, that is a conscious adaptation of a line of Mallarmé, *Tonnerre et rubis aux moyeux!*; just as another line from the same sonnet is adapted at the end of a short poem of mine called *Lines for an Old Man*: *Dire si je ne suis pas joyeux!*" See note to *Burnt Norton* II 1–2.

Choruses from "The Rock"

"I say that the consummation of the drama, the perfect and ideal drama, is to be found in the ceremony of the Mass ··· And the only dramatic satisfaction that I find now is in a High Mass well performed." ("E." in *A Dialogue on Dramatic Poetry*, 1928)

1. "If I were a Dean" 2. The Commission 3. Authorship of the Pageant 4. Composition 5. Performance 6. Apropos of Performance and Publication 7. Afterwards

Section introduced, with half-title, *1936+*.

The Rock was published 31 May 1934, after which all ten choruses were printed in *1936+* and *Guild*. In 1940, *Sesame* printed only Choruses I and X (numbering the latter II). Choruses I–III, VII, IX and X were included in *Penguin / Sel Poems*. None of the other contents of *Penguin / Sel Poems* (first published in 1948) were more recent than 1930 (*Ash-Wednesday* and *Marina*), and without any of the *Choruses*, there would have been fewer than a hundred pages of verse. Yet to maintain sales of his *Collected Poems 1909–1935*, TSE was concerned to restrict the proportion of them represented in selection (perhaps particularly when it was in the hands of another publisher). Similarly he was concerned to exclude *Four Quartets* from his collected poems, adding them only in *1963*.

In Sept 1955 TSE recorded X 17–46; released by Caedmon, 1955 (US), 1960 (UK).

1. "IF I WERE A DEAN"

A contribution by TSE to the *Chichester Diocesan Gazette* May 1931:

> My first thought of "If I were a Dean" is not of what I should want to do, but of what I should *not* want to do: and I make no apology. I have nothing but admiration and pity for those Deans who have toiled unceasingly, made appeals and collected subscriptions year after year, for—what? Merely to keep their minsters from tumbling about their ears. To me a cathedral is primarily a place of worship, the focus of devotion of its diocese, and not a National Monument: but I think—the State being already so far Socialised, and the position of the Church in the State being what it is—that the structural repair of cathedrals, and perhaps also of all those churches which have historic and architectural importance, ought to be at the cost of the State ··· The nation as a whole, I contend, should be made to pay for their mere *preservation*, rather than that part of the nation for which they are primarily places of worship and devotion.
>
> I am quite well aware of all the difficulties involved in carrying out such a drastic proposal; and if I were a Dean under the settlement I suggest, I dare say I might in the end prefer to be buried by the collapse of the roof of my own cathedral, rather than buried under a mass of correspondence, memoranda and instructions from the Office of Works, to say nothing of the visits of committees and inquisitory officials. To my irresponsible vision, however, these difficulties are details to be settled by ingenious compromise; the point is that in my Utopian deanery there will be no anxiety about the framework of the cathedral.

> I should thus hope to be free to collect, and to use, funds not for the mere preservation of the bones of my cathedral, but for the interior beautification of its living body. And I should try to avoid the fault of making my interior a period piece, of being overawed by the designs of its remote builders. I have seen old and beautiful churches which modern hands seemed afraid to touch, and which therefore remained mere remains; and I have also seen modern churches in which the decorator seems fearful of departing by a decade, in the least ornament or altar cloth, from the period style in which the church was built. I prefer rather a church which shows the loving attempts of generation after generation, each according to its own notions of beauty, to leave visible testimony of its devotion. I should like to be able to encourage the best contemporary artists in stone, metal, paint and wood, to apply themselves to the decoration of my cathedral; and the best musicians to make music for its offices · · ·
>
> My cathedral, then, would be richly decorated inside: with tapestries (as, for example, they hang round the bases of columns in the cathedral of Toulouse), with modern religious paintings, with memorial tablets (but only to good churchmen), with chapels and church furniture. I hold also the theory, that it is chiefly in the life of such a centre as a cathedral that art can vitally affect us. Who, except the technical expert, can really enjoy a visit to an art museum or an evening in a concert room? · · · a cathedral where art—not merely archaeology—is dedicated to God, seems to me the best place in which art can flourish · · ·
>
> I should devise as many cathedral ceremonies as possible · · · I should pay particular attention to the performance of religious drama. I do not underrate the beauty of our mediaeval religious drama, and I should try, not I hope, to "revive" it, but to keep it alive; but at the same time I should still more encourage the composition and the performance of plays by contemporary authors. Some people maintain that a good religious play cannot be written nowadays; I believe, as I believe of religious painting and sculpture, that if the opportunity is given, the work will be done. We must expect that the early attempts will be imperfect; but I am sure that in time poets and dramatists, as well as painters and sculptors and artisans, will not be lacking.
>
> But in no two cathedrals would or should conditions be quite the same; and, wherever my deanery is situated, I should wish to encourage and stimulate first the local spirit of that part of England · · · And for such activities as religious drama, I should want to have them performed, as far as possible, *within* the cathedral itself.
>
> But besides all these interests and duties · · · I maintain that a Dean should have sufficient continuous leisure to be able to apply himself to some considerable work of scholarship or of original theological and philosophical writing · · · There is a book which I have never been able to buy, and which I have never had room to accommodate even could I buy it, and which I have never had the time to read even could I buy it and house it. If I were a Dean, I should hope that I might be able to have it, to have shelves for it, and to read as much of it as one man can reasonably expect to read in a lifetime: it is Migne's *Patrologia Latina et Graeca*.

(J. P. Migne's collection of the Latin and Greek writings of the Church Fathers was published in 161 volumes, 1857–66.)

After writing *The Rock* and *Murder in the Cathedral* (1935), TSE considered Charles Williams's latest novel: "The plot is a good enough one: the production of a new poetic drama (a great one, so the author must be either Williams or myself, I cant make out which, perhaps both; anyway he is a very wise and fine character named Stanhope and he is what would be the local squire except that the place has become a London suburb) by a local amateur society", *"Descent into Hell"* by Charles Williams, reader's report (1937).

2. THE COMMISSION

TSE discussed *The Coming of Christ*, John Masefield's festival play for Canterbury, in his *Commentary* in *Criterion* June 1928: "We venture to counsel our spiritual pastors, that they should see to it either that they employ artists who are definite in their theology, or else who are really good artists."

As president of the Religious Drama Society (formed 1929), George Bell wrote to TSE in 1932 inviting him to a conference on the subject. TSE sent his regrets on 12 July: "I am leaving for America on September 17 and shall not be back until next May." E. Martin Browne, the society's director of religious drama, later recorded that the impulse for *The Rock* came in Mar 1933 from the Rev. R. Webb-Odell, director of the Forty-Five Churches Fund, which aimed to build and endow new churches in the rapidly growing suburbs in the diocese of London (*Browne* 3). On 9 Mar 1933, Webb-Odell wrote to TSE offering the fee of a hundred guineas for his "invaluable service" and recommending sources for the study of Bishop Blomfield and Peter the Hermit.

TSE to Webb-Odell, 5 Feb 1934:

> I think that Mr. Browne and I shared the desire, even before we had begun to discuss the matter, to escape as far as possible from the conventional conception of an "historical pageant". I mean that a pageant which should merely be a brilliant review of the more picturesque or impressive episodes in the history of London church-building, however pleasing to the old or instructive to the young, was never in question. The past is employed only because of its relevance to the present, and to bring the attention to the very urgent and anxious problems with which the Church to-day is concerned. There is no problem of a community to which the presence or absence of a church is irrelevant: and he who is concerned that a church should be built is committed to a concern with all the problems of the community which the church is intended to serve. The problem of church-building is integral with the problem of more and better housing in general. The employment of men for building churches suggests the whole problem of unemployment. There are many who will say that "in these times" the money and the labour might be put to better purpose, or at least to satisfy more pressing needs; and, while repudiating the assumptions on which such objections are made, we must assert that these needs are all one need, and that they can all be satisfied. There is sufficient stone, clay, lime, and other materials in the country for all the building of every kind that is wanted; there is sufficient unemployed labour. The world is ready enough to employ money for the purpose of making more money, or for the purpose of destroying competition: it needs more *non-productive* activity.
>
> In the ordinary sense, the pageant is true enough to the pageant form in having no "plot"; it endeavours to get its coherence from a significance such as I have tried to suggest above; while the separate scenes, it is hoped, will be enjoyed also for their own sake. A continuity of tone is aimed at through the recurrence of the Chorus and the symbolic figure of The Rock; while the modern and the historical scenes are purposely juxtaposed and blended to enhance the effect of contemporaneity. I have not been so ambitious as to hope that what I contribute might be great poetry, but I have tried to write efficient verse of a kind simple and straightforward for the stage, and I think I have succeeded in writing something that is at least wholly lucid and understandable, and have not spared the use of rhetorical devices of great antiquity.

To Michael Roberts, 14 Jan 1935: "I should be glad to think that the writing of occasional poetry is a justifiable activity, because that is all that the choruses in the Rock can pretend to be." To Mary Dunlop, 30 Nov 1943: "The fact is that from the beginning I had no intention of allowing the full text of *The Rock* to remain in print: all that I wanted to preserve were the choruses which are in my *Collected Poems*, and as for the rest of the text, it was merely a bit of hack-work for a special occasion according to a design which was given to me to complete. I do not consider it of any value whatever and even at the time it only contained a few gags which I thought amusing."

3. AUTHORSHIP OF THE PAGEANT

To Webb-Odell, 5 Feb 1934: "I do not wish to be described as the Author of this Pageant. I am the writer of the Words, so far as these are original, and compiler of the speeches of certain historical personages out of their own works. I have written the choruses, the song, and some modern dialogue. I do not wish to disclaim responsibility, but to give credit where it is due. And, having no experience of writing for the theatre, I am very grateful to have had the opportunity of this collaboration; which also has made it possible for me to concentrate upon the problem, new to me, of trying to write a kind of verse which should produce the intended effect when declaimed from a stage to an audience unfamiliar with it."

Although the original title page and jacket of *The Rock* specified "Book of Words by T. S. Eliot", the volume was listed as being by TSE and a part of the Faber poetry list, for instance on the jacket to Spender's *Vienna* (1934). Faber's regular advertisement on the front cover of *New Verse* was devoted in June 1934 to a single book:

> *The Rock* is the text written by Mr. Eliot for a pageant produced at Sadler's Wells on behalf of the Forty-Five Churches Fund of the Diocese of London. In form it approximates to a play. It contains nearly eight hundred lines of verse, mostly choruses. The dialogue is chiefly in prose, and consists of scenes ancient and modern, with a continuity provided by three bricklayers.

Peter du Sautoy to Helene Ritzerfeld of the German publishers Suhrkamp Verlag, 15 Feb 1965: "about republication of *The Rock* ··· the parts of the play which are really Mr. Eliot's are already in the *Collected Poems*, namely *Choruses from "The Rock"*, whereas a great deal of the rest of the play was not written by him but contributed by various people. He never felt that the play as a whole was his and that is why he didn't want it reprinted as part of his collected work."

4. COMPOSITION

To Paul Elmer More, 7 Nov 1933: "I am working on something which amuses me more: the writing of some verse choruses and dialogues for a sort of play to be given to advertise the campaign for raising money for 45 new churches in London diocese. If I have a free hand I shall enjoy it. I am trying to combine the simplicity and immediate intelligibility necessary for dramatic verse with concentration, under the inspiration of, chiefly, Isaiah and Ezekiel." The same day, TSE wrote to the Archbishop of York, about a memorandum on the Church's social policy: "it seems to me that while any greater relief for the unemployed is unlikely, and will be said by politicians to be impossible—as in the present state of things it may be—the important point is to gain an admission of the fact that the unemployed *ought* to be better looked after than they are." Enclosed were his notes: "I do not feel satisfied with the gospel of leisure as preached for instance by the disciples of Major

Douglas. It seems to me that the proportion of time that the vast majority of human beings can well occupy in amusement, games, hobbies, self-education etc. is very limited; and that we need a new conception of 'work'. What every one needs, surely, is to be able to feel that his activity is of a special character: that his work has some other function, from his own point of view, than merely to support him; and that, if he has much spare time, that time may be spent for some larger purpose than merely to occupy his own body and mind. What the unemployed need is not merely occupation, but occupation useful to society." The Social Credit system advocated, from 1919, by Major C. H. Douglas aimed to overcome problems of unemployment caused by mechanisation and the consequent imbalance between increased output of goods and falling income to pay for them. Douglas had been promoted by Pound since 1920, and TSE considered one of his books for Faber in 1932. (In the three years following the Wall Street Crash of 1929, unemployment in Britain had risen dramatically.) TSE to Donald Main, 14 Mar 1934: "It would be interesting if you would develop your ideas about Major Douglas, with whom, so far as I understand his ideas, I do not think I can agree." To *Social Credit*, 27 Aug 1934 (pub. 7 Sept): "While I do not pretend that I understand Major Douglas's theory yet, I cannot see that his opponents are in a strong position, so long as they support a system which simply does not work." To John Maynard Keynes, 5 Apr 1934, after declining to comment on Social Credit: "it would ··· weaken my case if I attached it to any particular vision of economic paradise ··· I venture to hope that you may come to see my church pageant at Sadler's Wells in June. I have taken the liberty of engaging two of my characters ··· in a discussion concerning yourself" (*The Rock* 33).

The Sadler's Wells programme for *The Rock* had a foreword by G. Vernon Willesden and Bertram F. Kensington which describes the enterprise:

> the Pageant Play ··· will succeed not in proportion to the financial result, but just in so far as the spiritual needs of our new districts are brought home to those who live in the older London ··· Out in Middlesex, to the North and West of London, you will find suburb after suburb where ten years ago were large country estates, lanes and fields. They cluster round railway lines and 'bus routes like leaves upon a branch ··· You will see young married people, proud of their labour-saving houses and their district, settling down to bring up children in the clearer air and more open surroundings of outer London ··· But often you will look in vain for what hitherto has been the heart and centre of each English community, the parish Church. It can make no profit and can call for no compulsory tax; it can be provided solely by the goodwill and sacrifice of those who believe it to be the great essential of human life ··· our real concern is with the deeper issue: the religious education of the children, the spiritual provision for those who are building homes and families in new areas, the claim of God on our new London.
>
> That is the burden of responsibility which this Play asks older London to share with us. We want to send clergy, we want to secure sites, we want to build halls, and eventually, probably with financial help from demolished churches from central London, to build parish churches. But first our work is to advertise the need, and to ask all the Church people of older London to share the responsibility laid upon the Diocese.

A list of elements to be written, prepared probably by Browne (Bodleian ms Don. d.44 fol.67) includes:

CHORUSES.
5 min. A. Discounting of religion in modern thought.
2 min. B. The Building of Nehemiah.
2 min. C. The Church shall suffer again and again.
Part II.
3 min. D. The Crusades.
4 min. E. Puritans. Argument of service of Art to Faith.
4 min. F. Preparation for Dedication.

The first four of these are ticked in pencil. The list concludes with "BUILDERS' SONG", also ticked.

TSE sent Bonamy Dobrée part of the dialogue on 27 Mar 1934: "HERE is my dialogue do not laugh at my simplicity: I am told to have Wren talking to Pepys and Evelyn (First, does this too far violate probability) and saying he is designing St. Paul. His predicting jerrybuilding of future is MY idea and I should like to keep it—please PLEASE try to put this into good period language for me and hash it about as you will, shall be grateful and will acknowledge in preface." As the report for the Lord Chamberlain shows (see 5. PERFORMANCE, below), it was well known that

Sir Christopher Wren
Said, "I am going to dine with some men.
If anybody calls
Say I am designing St. Paul's."
E. C. Bentley, *Biography for Beginners* (1905),
illustrated by G. K. Chesterton

The joke survived in the dialogue (*The Rock* 83). Bentley gave his middle name, Clerihew, to such profiles in verse (see "Uncollected Poems" for TSE's clerihews). Bentley's son Nicolas drew the pictures for a subsequent collection, *Baseless Biography*, in 1939, and for *Old Possum's Book of Practical Cats* in 1940.

TSE's original draft of a cockney scene at the beginning of *The Rock* was respectfully but forcefully criticised by the Rev. Vincent Howson of "The East End Amateurs" in a letter to Martin Browne, 29 Mar 1934: "he is dealing with something which he has not yet mastered, the cockney mind, and with London papers, like the *Daily Mail*, and others who make a big thing of cockney dialect, he must get this part true to life" (Bodleian); see TSE's acknowledgement of Howson in Prefatory Note (below).

TSE to Donald Brace, 2 June 1934: "I am sending you four copies of my latest production, a kind of play called *The Rock*, which was written for performance on a specific occasion here in London ··· The only point about it worth making is that the choruses do represent a new verse experiment on my part; and taken together, make a sequence of verses about twice the length of *The Waste Land*." To A. L. Rowse, 13 June 1934: "I was deliberately trying to strike out a new line, which I felt might alienate some of my earlier supporters. Except for the abortive *Sweeney Agonistes* it is my first complete attempt on a major scale, and I often felt, while working on the pageant, that I had bitten off more than I could chew. I hope at least that it will put an end to the nonsense about 'intellectualism' and 'obscurity'. I am anything but an intellectual; more nearly a pure *émotif*. And nobody with anything to say *wants* to be obscure. But one isn't naturally simple or lucid; it takes work and experience to get there. One has to shed a great deal, or work out a lot of poison; and perhaps simplicity only comes through a gradual mastery of one's own emotions. But perhaps when I say 'simplicity' here I mean objectivity."

5. PERFORMANCE

The Rock was licensed for public performance at Sadler's Wells by the Lord Chamberlain's Office, 12 Apr 1934 (BL). As with *Sweeney Agonistes*, the official reader was G. S. Street, who reported:

> There are a multitude of scenes in this "pageant play" but they succeed one another without pause. A serious study of it would take a day's hard reading, not that it is obscure—as I find much of the author's other poetry—but because the incidents and characters and the ideas expressed by them are so numerous. It is partly in verse and partly in prose dialogue: in the case of the modern workmen introduced slangy and topical. It goes to and fro in time and I think T. S. Eliot has attempted to cram too much into it. The scene is an open space, we learn from inference on the banks of the Thames. A male and female chorus begin and resume at intervals: it expresses the poet's point of view, I suppose. Then "The Rock" comes on. It is not until the end of the pageant that The Rock is identified with St. Peter. He speaks of man's labours. We then have some modern workmen who are building a church. Rahere, who built St. Bartholomew, appears to them and his workmen lend a hand. I think that not to weary the Lord Chamberlain I had better from this point merely give a list of the personages who appear: he will readily imagine the ideas and arguments for which they stand. A Modern Agitator. The Jews rebuilding Jerusalem. A crowd incited by the Agitator against the workmen. The Danish invasion. Shock Troops and Black Shirts. A Plutocrat with a long speech to them. The Rock again. Part II The Chorus and The Rock. Bishop Blomfield. Young men setting out in Richard's Crusade, with a Latin service for them and investment with their Crosses. An argument between modern people about art and religion. Very long sermons by a Reformation preacher, ending in a Priest's going to be burnt. The Rock, or St. Peter, again. A ballet of Dick Whittington and his Cat(!) Pepys, Evelyn and Wren conversing after dinner and Mr Eliot positively gets in the Chesterton [and Bentley] joke about Wren. St. Peter again and a Benediction by the Bishop—of London?
>
> The author's religious views and the auspices of the Bishop of London guarantee the reverence of the religious portions of the pageant, nor would anyone object to the lighter passages. I think Mr Eliot goes out of his way to exaggerate the views of "The Blackshirts", if he means the followers of Sir Oswald Mosley and this introduction of political animus seems a great pity. I should be inclined at least to suggest to the author the excision of these passages. See I, 34. There is a conversational bloody (I, 4) but I should not interfere with that. Recommended for Licence.

Beneath this is a comment by the Lord Chamberlain, the Earl of Cromer: "This is a curious play to receive the blessing of the Bishop of London, but as it seems to be the case I hardly think any interference necessary."

The Rock was first performed at the Sadler's Wells Theatre on 28 May 1934 (Ralph Vaughan Williams sending a congratulatory postcard to the composer, Martin Shaw, on 30 May). Each scene featured performers and directors from several different London churches. The Finale: Blessing of the New Church (AD 1934) featured "Representatives of churches built in London in every decade, 1834–1934, and of former scenes." The Chorus consisted of "seven male and ten female figures" who "speak as the voice of the Church of God". Choruses I–VI appear in Part I, choruses VII–X in Part II.

6. APROPOS OF PERFORMANCE AND PUBLICATION

T. S. Eliot and Martin Browne, *The Story of the Pageant*, Sadler's Wells programme:

> *The Rock* is not a pageant in the usual sense. It does not consist of a number of historical scenes or tableaux in order of time. The aim is not merely to remind people that churches have been built in the past, but to employ the historical scenes to reinforce, in appropriate places, the emphasis upon the needs of the present · · ·
>
> A Chorus, as in Greek Tragedy, comments in verse from time to time upon the needs and troubles of the Church to-day, and upon the action. This Chorus opens both parts of the play, and from time to time appeals to "The Rock," who, though he takes little part in the action, symbolizes the permanence and continuity of the Church of God, and its resistance to the forces of evil and dissolution.
>
> After the opening chorus, and some words of encouragement and consolation by "The Rock," a chant of Builders is heard, followed by a chant of the Unemployed, to which the Builders reply. The light then discovers the modern bricklayers discussing their work and many other things as well. A remark by one of them leads to an "experiment with time," in which the builders find themselves spectators of the conversion of Sabert, King of London, and his Saxon followers, by the Roman missionary Mellitus.

(For TSE on J. W. Dunne's *An Experiment with Time*, see headnote to *Burnt Norton*: 2. GENESIS.) TSE to Webb-Odell, 8 Feb 1934: "I seem to have mislaid the letter in which you gave me bibliography for Rahere, nor do I remember whether you made any suggestion of whence to draw the material for a sermon by Mellitus (I imagine that there is none recorded, from what I find out of that saint, but perhaps there are early sermons which would do). Would you be so kind as to tell me what you can?" (Rahere founded St. Bartholomew's Hospital in 1123. St. Mellitus, first Bishop of London and third Archbishop of Canterbury, was part of the mission sent by Pope Gregory the Great in 595 to convert the pagan Anglo-Saxons to Christianity.)

Prefatory Note:

> I cannot consider myself the author of the "play", but only of the words which are printed here. The scenario, incorporating some historical scenes suggested by the Rev. R. Webb-Odell, is by Mr. E. Martin Browne, under whose direction I wrote the choruses and dialogues, and submissive to whose expert criticism I rewrote much of them. Of only one scene am I literally the author: for this scene and of course for the sentiments expressed in the choruses I must assume the responsibility.
>
> I should like to make grateful acknowledgment of the collaboration of Dr. Martin Shaw, who composed the music. To Mr. F. V. Morley I am indebted for one speech for which technical knowledge of bricklaying was required; to Major Bonamy Dobrée for correcting the diction of the Christopher Wren scene; to Mr. W. F. Cachemaille-Day for information concerning the relations of architects, contractors and foremen. The Rev. Vincent Howson has so completely rewritten, amplified and condensed the dialogue between himself ("Bert") and his mates, that he deserves the title of joint author.
>
> T. S. E.
>
> *April* 1934

The title-page of Faber's edition read: "THE ROCK | A PAGEANT PLAY | WRITTEN FOR PERFORMANCE | AT SADLER'S WELLS THEATRE | 28 MAY — 9 JUNE 1934 | ON BEHALF OF THE | FORTY-FIVE CHURCHES FUND | OF THE DIOCESE OF | LONDON | | BOOK OF WORDS BY | T. S. ELIOT". TSE wrote the jacket material:

> *The Rock*, recently performed at Sadler's Wells, is a work of collaboration between Mr. Eliot and Mr. Martin Browne, the producer of the play: Mr. Browne providing the scenario, and Mr. Eliot the words. The action turns upon the efforts and difficulties of a group of London masons in building a church. Incidentally a number of historical scenes, illustrative of church-building, are introduced. The recent production on behalf of the Forty-Five Churches Fund of the Diocese of London, included much pageantry, mimetic action, and ballet; with music by Dr. Martin Shaw. This is the text provided by Mr. Eliot. The dialogue is mostly in prose; but the choruses, in considerable variety, constitute a piece of work in verse much longer than any of his previously published poems. The author has experimented in the attempt to find modern forms of verse suitable for the stage.

Grover Smith 1956 316 notes, as *Gallup* does not, a slip "prepared for insertion in copies of the first English edition": "In the Iconoclasm scene, all the incidents are taken from London history. St. Uncumber's statue was divested of its 'gay gown silver shoes'; the Maypole from St. Andrew's Undershaft was destroyed by Puritans who objected to the name of the church being derived from it; the Rood of St. Paul's was broken up in the street and the head desecrated. The sermons are extracts from those of Latimer and others."

US jacket material:

> The choruses in this pageant play represent a new verse experiment on Mr. Eliot's part; and taken together make a sequence of verses about twice the length of *The Waste Land.* Mr. Eliot has written the words; the scenario and design of the play were provided by a collaborator, and the purpose was to provide a pageant of the Church of England for presentation on a particular occasion. The action turns upon the efforts and difficulties of a group of London masons in building a church. Incidentally a number of historical scenes, illustrative of church-building, are introduced. The play, enthusiastically greeted, was first presented in England, at Sadler's Wells; the production included much pageantry, mimetic action, and ballet, with music by Dr. Martin Shaw. Immediately after the production of this play in England, Francis Birrell wrote in *The New Statesman*: "The magnificent verse, the crashing Hebraic choruses which Mr. Eliot has written had best be studied in the book. *The Rock* is certainly one of the most interesting artistic experiments to be given in recent times." The *Times Literary Supplement* also spoke with high praise: "The choruses exceed in length any of his previous poetry; and on the stage they prove the most vital part of the performance. They combine the sweep of psalmody with the exact employment of colloquial words. They are lightly written, as though whispered to the paper, yet are forcible to enunciate ··· There is exhibited a command of novel and musical dramatic speech which, considered alone, is an exceptional achievement."

7. AFTERWARDS

To the Editor of *The Spectator*, 1 June 1934 (pub. 8 June):

> Mr. Verschoyle's amiable review of *The Rock* in your issue of to-day leaves me wondering what he thinks that the production was intended to be. The "play" makes no pretence of being a "contribution to English dramatic literature": it is a revue. My only seriously dramatic aim was to show that there is a possible *rôle* for the Chorus: an aim which would have failed completely without the aid of a perfectly trained group of speakers like Miss Fogerty's. And to consider *The Rock* as an "official apologia" for church-building is to lay a weight upon it which this rock was never intended to bear. It is

not an apologia for the campaign, but an advertisement. If I had meant to write an apologia—I do not know whether any other people besides Mr. Verschoyle think that one is needed—I should have written a prose pamphlet.

I also wonder what Mr. Verschoyle wanted, when he speaks of my "reluctance to commit myself to logical justification" and my "unwillingness to substantiate my beliefs". He does not make matters clearer by referring to "despair of the Church's attitude towards such questions as Housing and Population"—a despair which we are to believe has helped to convert people to Communism or Fascism. Let me recommend for reading, to Communists, Fascists, and Mr. Verschoyle, the Archbishop of Canterbury's speech at the Guildhall on March 12th, on the subject of Housing. And as for Population, would Mr. Verschoyle have wished me to tax my poetic resources by making my Chorus declaim about Birth-Control?

In conclusion, may I repeat what every author knows: that criticism is only valuable to an author when it is particularised.

Religious dramas and pageants. "I suspect that, for the most part, people still tend to regard the performance of a religious play as something to be attended, like a bazaar or a jumble sale, from a sense of duty rather than for the purpose of enjoyment. You may even feel that you have fulfilled your duty if you buy tickets and manage to give them away to somebody who will go in your place. You may even think of them as you may think of pageants—as performances which give a great deal more pleasure to the people taking part in them (especially if the costumes are interesting) than to the audience", *Religious Drama: Mediaeval and Modern* (1937).

After *The Rock*, TSE was surprised by requests for permission to perform it in other dioceses. To S. Eley, 24 June 1938: "I have personally no wish to see *The Rock* revived, and but for not wishing to stand in the way of any public cause, I would hardly give my consent. The fact that I have allowed the text to go out of print, and have only preserved the choruses, is sufficient indication of my own attitude." (There had been a second impression in June, and would be a third in September.)

TSE was asked to write or contribute to several new pageants, including one by Martin Browne about Peace and the League of Nations (see headnote to *Sweeney Agonistes*, 2. ARISTOPHANES). In addition he was asked to comment on pageants by, among others, Rodney Bax, Mary Boutwood, Christopher Fry, Gertrude Leigh and Vernon Watkins. To John Hayward, 13 July 1939: "in my opinion no pageant will ever surpass that ··· at the Albert Hall for the Mothers' Union Annual Festival ··· Enid [Faber] promises me the unusual treat of TWO Agricultural, cattle, flower, vegetable, cake and corgie shows this year. I like local Shows almost as much as pageants." To the Rev. Richard Roseveare, 24 June 1942: "Pageantry is a matter on which I cannot be a very helpful adviser; I detest pageants of all sorts. Of course, I do not know the particular group of youth to which you hope to appeal, but I think that a pageant would have to be a real work of genius in order to captivate the minds of young people of any critical intelligence."

Dramatic and choral writing. To Paul Elmer More, 20 June 1934: "You must by this time have received the copy of *The Rock* which I sent you. It represents, so far at least as the verse choruses go, a venture on a wider sea than before; and I shall be curious to know whether you find as deep a fissure between 'actuality of form' and 'actuality of content' as you do in its predecessors."

To I. A. Richards, 20 July 1934: "I think that the verse in *The Rock* does at times get too near to what I have called literalness, to be really important—perhaps very often. And one had to stick to very crude symbols."

To Christopher Fry, 9 Mar 1939, about *Thursday's Child*, a collaboration with Martin Shaw: "I am apprehensive lest your choruses become too elaborate and difficult for the purpose they are to serve. The necessity for simplification is so great in chorus that you can hardly go too far in that direction in writing. The simplification must go farther according to the number of speakers: a chorus of eight voices must be much simpler than one for four, and so on. Furthermore, as your choruses are to be spoken in the open air, they must be simpler still, and the great thing is that each chorus should represent a definite emotional tone, as that is about all that most of the audience will get. To adopt the figure of speech used by Cocteau, I feel that this chorus tends to a delicate lacework where what is needed is a large simple pattern in coarse rope. I am sure you can do this if you keep in mind that a chorus is a kind of poster art, and that the details of beauty which are possible in verse to be read or to be recited as chamber music by a single voice, are quite lost in verse for this purpose. The rhythm is very important; the general emotional tone should be unmistakeable; and the key has to be given by a few verses and iterated words of the simplest kind. If a chorus is not immediately intelligible to a very simple mind on reading, it is probably too elaborate." (In the Introduction to *Seneca: His Tenne Tragedies* in 1927, TSE had written: "The art of dramatic language, we must remember, is as near to oratory as to ordinary speech or to other poetry. On the stage, M. Jean Cocteau reminds us, we must weave a pattern of coarse rope that can be apprehended from the back of the pit, not a pattern of lace that can only be apprehended from the printed page. We are not entitled to try fine effects unless we achieve the coarse ones." Revising this for *Selected Essays* as *Seneca in Elizabethan Translation*, TSE dropped the sentence about Cocteau, who had been describing his libretto for the ballet *Les mariés de la Tour Eiffel*, 1921.)

To E. M. Stephenson, 21 Nov 1941: "choral verse is a very different thing from straight 'poetry'. The choice and order of words is affected when the verse is written to be spoken by a number of voices. The more voices you have in view, the greater the simplification has to be; and the appeal has to be much less intellectual and more simply emotional, if the chorus is to affect an audience at all. The result is something that in some respects is more crude than poetry intended to be read or recited by one voice."

"I shall begin with 1933: that is a good date for me, as that is the year in which I broke into Show Business. In that year I was commissioned to write the text for a mammoth Pageant to advertise the need for 45 new churches in the outer suburbs of London. The Pageant was produced at Sadler's Wells in the summer of 1934 with great success and so many amateur actors that the Clerkenwell Town Hall had to be adapted temporarily as a dressing room", *Harvard Class of 1910, Fiftieth Anniversary Report* (1960).

On the timeliness of the commission: "Twenty years ago I was commissioned to write a pageant play to be called *The Rock*. The invitation to write the words for this spectacle ··· came at a moment when I seemed to myself to have exhausted my meagre poetic gifts, and to have nothing more to say. To be, at such a moment, commissioned to write something which, good or bad, must be delivered by a certain date, may have the effect that vigorous cranking sometimes has upon a motor car when the battery is run down. The task was clearly laid out: I had only to write the words of prose dialogue for scenes of the usual historical pageant pattern, for which I had been given a scenario. I had also to provide a number of choral passages in verse, the content of which was left to my own devices: except for the reasonable stipulation that all the choruses were expected to have some relevance to the purpose of the pageant, and that each chorus was to occupy a precise number of minutes of stage time ··· This chorus of *The Rock* was not a dramatic voice; though many lines were distributed, the personages were unindividuated. Its members were speaking *for me*, not uttering words that really represented any supposed character of their own", *The Three Voices of Poetry* (1953).

Title **The Rock**: to Webb-Odell, 5 Feb 1934: "I have tried various 'fancy' titles, but they usually suffer from obscurity, and I think that a simple straightforward title which gives some clue to the subject matter is what is wanted. It ought to include both 'London' and 'Church' or 'Churches', I take it. Is *The Church Bells of London* too flat, or too clumsy, or anything else? 'Bells' has a merry sound, and perhaps [Martin] Shaw could introduce a few chimes here and there—that would be a good thing anyway, I think ··· A title which had some simple familiar allusion would be more pat, but I cant think of one. I wish I could get a more 'catchy' title." Webb-Odell replied on the same day: "As to Title, frankly I hate *Church Bells*. It reminds me of some transpontine melodrama of my youth. Martin Browne to-day suggests, *Many Mansions*, which doesn't seem bad. What is wrong with the title Lady Keeble gave it, *vide* yesterday's *Observer—The Rock*?" (OED "transpontine": "across or over a bridge; *spec.* ··· south of the Thames ··· of drama in vogue in the 19th century at the 'Surrey-side' theatres".) TSE replied, 8 Feb: "Browne's *Many Mansions* seems to me quite good. My only objection to *The Rock* is that the Rock himself, if he gives the title to the production, will be identified by most people as St. Peter pure and simple, which does directly conjure up to my mind the Petrine Claims—which are hardly appropriate. Do you think this is a considerable objection or not? If not, then perhaps this is the best title. Another point. I saw a poster to-day which describes me as 'the author'. This is not correct, and gives me what is not due. I should be glad if posters could in future read 'Produced by Martin Browne. Words by T. S. Eliot. Music by Martin Shaw.' or something like that?" (OED "Petrine": "*Petrine claims*, claims of the Popes, based on their traditional succession from St. Peter.")

The opening stage direction introduces the Chorus: "*The scene is an open place, with an irregular rocky hill in the middle. The* CHORUS, *seven male and ten female figures, are discovered. They speak as the voice of the Church of God.*"

I

I 1 **The Eagle:** the constellation Aquila.

I 2 **The Hunter with his dogs pursues his circuit**: see note to *Sweeney Among the Nightingales* 9.

I 8, 15 **knowledge of motion, but not of stillness ··· the wisdom we have lost in knowledge**: Tennyson: "Knowledge comes, but wisdom lingers ··· Knowledge comes, but wisdom lingers ··· moving toward the stillness", *Locksley Hall* 141, 143–44.

I 11 **All our knowledge brings us nearer to our ignorance:** see note to *East Coker* III 38–39, and for St. John of the Cross see note to *East Coker* III 35–46.

I 14 **Where is the Life we have lost in living:** "But where is the penny world I bought", *A Cooking Egg* 25. "this life | Living to live in a world of time beyond me", *Marina* 29–30.

I 15–16 **the wisdom that we have lost in knowledge ··· the knowledge we have lost in information:** "The vast accumulations of knowledge—or at least of information—deposited by the nineteenth century have been responsible for an equally vast ignorance. When there is so much to be known ··· it becomes increasingly difficult for anyone to know whether he knows what he is talking about or not", *The Perfect Critic* II (1920). Aristotle, whom TSE cites in the same paragraph, ranked knowledge (*episteme*) below wisdom (*sophia*) in the scale of consciousness at the beginning of the *Metaphysics* bk. 1. TSE: "What we need is not information but knowledge", *Dante* (1929) III. "in the mere matter of information, there are nowadays so many subjects about which we should like to know something, that we are in danger of knowing too little about too many things", *Leadership and Letters* (1949). To T. J. Wood, 19 Apr 1940: "I should be willing to admit that modern science has displaced earlier views of the nature of the world, but I am not quite prepared to admit that it has put anything in their place ··· I am by no means clear as to what philosophies are outworn, or indeed whether any philosophy wears out."

I 19 **timekept:** OED has this example only (the word recurs at III 29).

I 21 **we have too many churches:** for the proposal to demolish nineteen City churches, see Commentary on *The Waste Land* [III] 264, "Magnus Martyr".

I 22 **chop-houses:** OED quotes Johnson's Dictionary, "a mean house of entertainment, where provision ready dressed is sold" and Clough, "Dines in a dingy chop-house".

I 24–29 **spend their Sundays. | In the City ··· We toil for six days, on the seventh we must motor | To Hindhead, or Maidenhead:** Exodus 23: 12: "Six days thou shalt do thy work, and on the seventh day thou shalt rest." MacNeice: "Man's heart expands to tinker with his car | For this is Sunday ··· drive beyond Hindhead ··· Escape from the weekday time", *Sunday Morning* in *Criterion* Jan 1934. TSE: "You say that the hundreds of thousands, who listen in or ride about in Morris cars on Sunday because they are too British in their 'shyness' to go to Church ··· constitute the Church of England ··· not a visible Church of communicants, but a wholly invisible Church of shy schoolboys", *Parliament and the New Prayer Book* (1928). "I do not know how much pleasure is enjoyed by the man who drives a car the machinery of which he understands no better than he understands his own stomach, in a stream of similar cars along a monotonous road on a Sunday afternoon", *The Search for Moral Sanction* (1932). "The world seemed futile—like a Sunday outing", *After the turning of the inspired days* 13. ("The inhabitants of Hampstead have silk hats | On Sunday afternoon go out to tea ··· On Monday to the city, and then tea ··· They have another Sunday when the last is gone", *The Death of the Duchess* I 1–7.) To Frank Morley, 4 Aug 1938: "people who are saved from the abyss by religion would be saved by anything, say a Sunday excursion to Scarborough". **Hindhead, or Maidenhead:** Vivien Eliot to Aurelia Bolliger, 12 May 1932: "on *Monday* let us all go down to the country in the car to see my Aunt Lillia at Hindhead". Aurelia Hodgson, notes on TSE (1932?): "Trip to Maidenhead: Tom watch roadsigns | I watch map | V[ivien] drives | Derby Day" (Bryn Mawr).

I 34 **the country now is only fit for picnics**: "much of the change of a destructive kind · · · seems to result from the over-development of town life and the atrophy of the country. It is from a population habituated to town life, a population to which the countryside represents holidays, whether on an elaborate or a simple scale, that the countryside has to be protected", *A Commentary* in *Criterion* Oct 1934.

I 46–47 **ceaseless labour, | Or ceaseless idleness** : "One effect of industrialisation is that many of those who have work must work too hard or too long, and most of those who have no work must be idle", *The Seach for Moral Sanction* (1932).

I 49 **I have trodden the winepress alone**: see note to VIII 6–7.

I 57 ***Make perfect your will***: see note to VIII 46–48.

I 58 **take no thought of the harvest**: Matthew 6: 25–26: "Take no thought for your life, what ye shall eat, or what ye shall drink · · · Behold the fowls of the air: for they sow not, neither do they reap, nor gather into barns; yet your heavenly Father feedeth them."

I 64 **perpetual struggle of Good and Evil**: "the perception of Good and Evil—whatever choice we make—is the first requisite of spiritual life", *Personality and Demonic Possession* (1934).

I 72^73 *variant* **Squeezed like tooth-paste in the tube-train**: toothpaste was first sold in collapsible tubes in the 1890s.

I 75 **I will show you the things · · · done**: "Come in under the shadow of this gray rock, | And I will show you", *The Death of Saint Narcissus* 2–3. "I will show you something different · · · I will show you fear in a handful of dust", *The Waste Land* [I] 27–30.

I 78 **the work of the humble**: "the very word 'work' has altered its meaning in an industrial society. Truly, for me, 'work' means work primarily for the benefit of others and for the community as a whole; and such work includes giving pleasure or amusement to others. Nowadays 'work' means rather making money; either a little money by tending a machine, or more money by manipulating money", *The Search for Moral Sanction* (1932).

I 92–93 ***And a job for each | Every man to his work***: "every worker must learn his job: what the artist has to learn is to do it the way it has been done in the past; and then to do it in a different way", Note for The Moot, sent to J. H. Oldham, 11 Nov 1944.

I 94, 106, VII 39 ***No man has hired us***: Matthew 20: 6–7: "about the eleventh hour he went out, and found others standing idle, and saith unto them, Why stand ye here all the day idle? They say unto him, Because no man hath hired us" (*Grover Smith 1956* 173).

I 115–16 ***They shall not die in a shortened bed | And a narrow sheet***: Isaiah 28: 20: "For the bed is shorter than that a man can stretch himself on it: and the covering narrower than that he can wrap himself in it" (*Grover Smith 1956* 173).

II

Heading in ts **CHORUS AA**: indicating that this was composed after Chorus III, which was originally headed "CHORUS I" but changed to "CHORUS A".

II 2–3 **citizens of the saints ··· chief cornerstone**: Ephesians 2: 19–20: "ye are no more strangers and foreigners, but fellowcitizens with the saints, and of the household of God; And are built upon the foundation of the apostles and prophets, Jesus Christ himself being the chief corner stone."

II 7 **Your building not fitly framed together**: Ephesians 2: 21: "In whom all the building fitly framed together groweth unto an holy temple." **the Spirit which moved on the face of the waters like a lantern**: Genesis 1: 2–3: "And the Spirit of God moved upon the face of the waters. And God said, Let there be light: and there was light." TSE in 1941: "I find that I share Micklem's difficulty about the use of 'the Spirit' with a capital and 'the spirit' in lower case; and I wonder whether this does spring from a desire to be comprehensive and make room for all the shades of Christian belief and of non-Christian belief and of those who show the 'awareness' of 'spiritual issues' ··· The word 'spirit' has a very wide network of meanings, and a network which may always become an entanglement", *Letter from T. S. Eliot* Mar 1941, a paper for The Moot. **set on the back of a tortoise**: the Church Missionary Society: "the great body of the Hindoos ··· believe that the Earth was actually drawn up by the tusks of a Boar, and rests to this hour on the back of a Tortoise!" *Ignorance and Superstition of the Hindoos* in *Missionary Papers* Michaelmas 1820.

II 8 **How can we love our neighbour?**: Leviticus 19: 18: "thou shalt love thy neighbour as thyself". Mark 12: 31: "Thou shalt love thy neighbour as thyself. There is none other commandment greater than these."

II 16 **a kind of**: "*A kind of* is a phrase only to be used in extremity", *Charleston, Hey! Hey!* (1927). **Whipsnade**: the zoo park in Bedfordshire opened in 1931, proving immediately popular.

II 26 **the Church ··· always decaying, and always being restored**: culture "is always decaying and always has to be reborn", *Notes on Mannheim's Paper* (1941).

II 33 **expiating the sins of your fathers**: Nehemiah 9: 2: "confessed their sins, and the iniquities of their fathers."

II 43–44 **Body of Christ incarnate. | And now you live dispersed**: for "Parcel Resurrection", see headnote to *Ash-Wednesday* II.

II 44 **ribbon roads**: OED's earliest citation is from *The Times* in 1929 (TSE's line being cited next), but *The Old Inn* by TSE's friend W. G. Tinckom-Fernandez had "Out on the ribbon-road ··· the motor's acrid smoke | Assails", in *The Nation* 3 Dec 1914. TSE used the term in the first ed. of *Anabasis* (X vi, *1930*) and wrote to A. L. Rowse, 7 Mar 1931: "When one observes the By Passes of London: mile after mile of suburban house each with its attendant Private Garage: this is merely planting out clerks and functionaries in places in which they could not possibly live unless each had his Small Car; it seems to me that the whole present settlement of England is being made to encourage the motor car industry." He also made the point publicly: "when I see the tendency for the village to be replaced, not by the suburb, for which there is much to be said, but by an endless line of houses along a ribbon road over which passes a ceaseless stream of cars, I wonder what sort of organic unity can be left", *The Search for Moral Sanction* (1932). The Ribbon Development Act was passed in 1935. For "by-pass way", see VII 37.

II 49–51 **Nor does the family even move about together, | But every son would have his motor cycle, | And daughters ride away on casual pillions**: Middleton: "A fine journey in the Whitsun holydays, i'faith, to ride with a number of citizens and their wives, some upon pillions, some upon side-saddles, I and little Thomasine i' the middle, our son and heir, Sim", *Michaelmas Term* IV i, quoted in *Thomas Middleton* (1927). TSE to L. C. Knights, 14 July 1936: "I think that your criticisms of some of my remarks about Middleton are quite justified. I really was not thoroughly at home in Middleton's comedies, although I once prepared a text of *Michaelmas Term*". To Stephen Spender, 9 June 1932: "for one person who escapes through religion into a 'sentimental dreamland', there are thousands who escape by reading novels, by looking at films, or best of all, by driving very fast on land or in air, which makes even dreams unnecessary."

III

III 25–26 **peeled ··· iron ··· In a street of scattered brick where the goat climbs**: against this line quoted in *G. Jones*, TSE wrote "Shadwell". Rather than the 17th-century dramatist, Thomas Shadwell, this probably referred to the run-down district of East London. ("Shadwell and Stepney are picturesque", *A Commentary* in *Criterion* Jan 1927, questioning "picturesque" as a principle for preservation. Of Bina Gardens: "Il n'est pas lieu moins pittoresque" [There is no less picturesque place], *Vers pour la Foulque* 8 in *Noctes Binanianæ*.) "patched and peeled in London. | The goat coughs at night in the field overhead", *Gerontion* 10–11.

III 31–36 **tennis flannels ··· godless people ··· golf**: "an evening journal has published a photograph of the Bishop of London, complete with golf-bag and tennis racket, leaving for New Zealand ··· at the same time as renewed rumours of the design to destroy the City Churches", *A Commentary* (deploring an industrial construction beside St. Magnus Martyr) in *Criterion* Oct 1926. For TSE's association of bankers, golf clubs and unemployment, see *A Commentary* in *Criterion* July 1931.

III 32–33 **the thorn revisit, | The nettle shall flourish on the gravel court**: Isaiah 34: 13: "And thorns shall come up in her palaces, nettles and brambles in the fortresses thereof: and it shall be an habitation of dragons, and a court for owls."

III 34–36 **decent godless people ··· the asphalt road | And a thousand lost golf balls**: to Bonamy Dobrée, 21 Aug 1926: "What I meant was that after Disestablishment the Church of England will lose its whole reason for existence; and that its more serious members will gradually go over to Rome. Some will fall into nonconformity; the majority will content itself with civil marriages and individual Gods (my God, my dog, my pipe, my golf-tools and my allotment garden, your god for yours)." Golf again: "Everyone would be affected: the man who regularly has a run in his car and a round of golf on Sunday, quite as much as the punctilious churchgoer", *Thoughts After Lambeth* (1931). "people who ··· believe that in a perfect world those who like golf could play golf, and those who like religion could go to church", *Catholicism and International Order* (1933). The weekend for many consisted only of Sunday (see notes to I 24–29 and *The Waste Land* [I] 68).

III 37–38 **We build in vain unless the LORD build with us. | Can you keep the City that the LORD keeps not with you**: Psalm 127: 1: "Except the Lord build the house, they labour in vain that build it: except the Lord keep the city, the watchman waketh but in vain."

III 41 **active marmots**: as opposed to in hibernation.

III 44 **I have loved the beauty of Thy House**: Psalm 26: 8 (Douay tr.).

III 45 **I have swept the floors and garnished the altars**: Luke 11: 24–25: "my house ··· swept and garnished". TSE: "Swept and set in order", *Easter: Sensations of April* II 4. To Ezra Pound, 19 Dec 1934: "dambitall, you just cant keep things straight very long in this place; just when you got it swepngarnished in bust the amateurs again".

III 52 **the Stranger**: Deuteronomy 29: 22–26: "the stranger that shall come from a far land, shall say, when they see the plagues of that land, and the sicknesses which the Lord hath laid upon it ··· what meaneth the heat of this great anger? Then men shall say, Because they have forsaken the covenant of the Lord God ··· For they went and served other gods."

III 52–55 **the meaning ··· a community?**: to J. H. Oldham, 14 Sept 1939: "What does the term 'community' convey to most people nowadays?" The word does not appear in the King James Bible.

III 57–75] Taken as an extract in "The Choice of Life" section of Geoffrey Faber's anthology *The Pattern of Freedom* (1940), which also included the five lines which were dropped from the end of Chorus VI (see Textual History).

III 65 **common and preferred**: like shares on the stock market. See note to *East Coker* III 1–7.

IV

IV 5 **In Shushan the palace**: Nehemiah 1: 1.

IV 5–13 **in the month of Nisan ··· consumed with fire**: Nehemiah 2: 1: "in the month Nisan, in the twentieth year of Artaxerxes the king, that wine was before him: and I took up the wine, and gave it unto the king ··· And said unto the king ··· why should not my countenance be sad, when the city, the place of my fathers' sepulchres, lieth waste, and the gates thereof are consumed with fire?"

IV 10 **with a few, to Jerusalem**: Nehemiah 2: 11–12: "So I came to Jerusalem ··· I and some few men with me."

IV 14 **No place for a beast to pass**: Nehemiah 2: 14: "there was no place for the beast that was under me to pass."

IV 19, V 4 **With the sword in one hand and the trowel in the other ··· "The trowel in hand, and the gun rather loose in the holster"**: Nehemiah 4: 17–18: "every one with one of his hands wrought in the work, and with the other hand held a weapon. For the builders, every one had his sword girded by his side, and so builded" (*Grover Smith 1956* 174). TSE to Theodore Spencer, 7 Nov 1933, quoting VI 14–16:

> Now (after a hurried visit to Inverness and Paris this week) I am to start work seriously on the text of the Revue for the 45 Churches, and am working myself up into the temper of a Prophet of Israel—
>
> Men! polish your teeth on rising and retiring;
> Women! polish your finger-nails:
> You polish the tooth of the dog and the talon of the cat.
>
> If they don't mind my writing that sort of thing I believe I can do it—
>
> Remembering the words of Nehemiah the Prophet: the trowel in hand, and the gun rather loose in the holster.

gun rather loose in the holster: William Howard Russell: "revolver loose in the holster", *My Diary in India* (1860) I 408. Dillon Wallace: "a good old single-action ··· keep it prominent and handy, and loose in the holster", *Beyond the Mexican Sierra* (1910) 193.

V

V 1 **the heart is deceitful above all things, and desperately wicked:** Jeremiah 17: 9.

V 2 **Sanballat ··· Tobiah ··· Geshem:** officials who tried to prevent the Jews rebuilding Jerusalem (Nehemiah 2–6).

V 5 **snakes that lie on mouldering stairs:** "Along the garden stairs | The sluggish python lies", *Circe's Palace* 10–11 (*Hands*).

VI

VI 4–6 **those who live near a Bank ··· those who live near a Police Station:**

> Eeldrop and Appleplex commanded from their windows the entrance of a police station across the way ··· [Eeldrop:] "I am, I confess to you, in private life, a bank-clerk . . ."
>
> "And should, according to your own view, have a wife, three children and a vegetable garden in a suburb," said Appleplex.
>
> "Such is precisely the case," returned Eeldrop ··· "As it is Saturday night, I shall return to my suburb. Tomorrow will be spent in that garden.'"
>
> *Eeldrop and Appleplex* I

("where they spend their Sundays ··· the suburbs", Chorus I 24–26.) TSE joined Lloyds Bank in 1917, the year of *Eeldrop and Appleplex*. For "The suburban garden", see note to *The Waste Land* [I] 71–75, "the Dog ··· that's friend to men".

VI 16–18 **You polish the tooth of the dog ··· Death:** "who sharpen the tooth of the dog, meaning | Death", *Marina* 6–7 (for dog-fighting, see note).

VI 20 **Evil and Sin, and other unpleasant facts:** TSE jotting among Vivien Eliot's papers: "There are only 2 things—Puritanism & Catholicism. You are one or the other. You either believe in the reality of *sin* or you don't. *That* is *the* important moral distinction—not whether you are good or bad. Puritanism does not believe in Sin: it merely believes that certain things must not be done" (c. 624 fol. 44).

VI 23 **dreaming of systems so perfect that no one will need to be good:** "No perfect scheme can work perfectly with imperfect men; if the Russian scheme ever comes to 'work' perfectly with what *I* call imperfect men, then to me the Russian system will be condemned by its very efficiency ··· no system that continues to repeat, and must repeat, the words *'be ye perfect'* can be expected to work perfectly", *Christianity and Communism* (1932), citing Matthew 5: 48: "Be ye therefore perfect, even as your Father which is in heaven is perfect." In the same series of *Listener* articles, TSE condemned "the pursuit of the mirage of the Earthly Paradise—the illusion that we can be made happy and perfect by the application of legislation or force of the results of scientific discovery", *The Search for Moral Sanction* (1932). "one of the dangerous delusions that the Christian must avoid is that of the perfect human society situated somewhere in the future. It was one of the limitations of Judaism that it dreamt of such a future, a limitation that Christianity outgrew, and which we now see returning ··· Communism looks ··· to an eventual perfection of human nature to be brought about exclusively from outside", *The Christian in the Modern World* (1935). To Leonard Woolf, 13 Jan 1940:

> you will never get a society of complete automata or one of perfectly enlightened free men. However, your ideal democracy is more nearly compatible with Christianity than the ideal (at least as you put it) of totalitarianism, for the latter commits the fundamental error of an assertion of Human Infallibility incarnated in a Ruler ··· what is more difficult is to put one's finger on the errors of a system of education which has failed to educate.

"Do we agree ··· that we must choose socialism in order to avoid fascism? [Friedrich] Hayek would maintain that the distinction ··· is largely illusory, and that once you commit yourself to a unitary plan, very similar consequences must follow in both cases", *"The Collective Commonwealth and the Christian"* (1944), response to a paper by H. A. Hodges for The Moot. "The other direction in which the confusion of culture and politics may lead, is towards the ideal of a world state in which there will, in the end, be only one uniform world culture. I am not here criticising any schemes for world organisation. Such schemes belong to the plane of engineering, of devising machinery. Machinery is necessary, and the more perfect the machine the better. But a culture is something that must grow ··· a political structure is partly construction, and partly growth; partly machinery, and the same machinery, even if good, is not necessarily equally good for all peoples", *Culture and Politics* (1947).

VI *after* 34 *variant* [4–5] **There are always the young ··· The enthusiasts:** Johnson: "The young Enthusiast quits his Ease for Fame", *The Vanity of Human Wishes* 136.

VII

VII 1 **In the beginning ··· Waste and void ··· darkness was upon the face of the deep:** Genesis 1: 1–2 ("waste and void" being the wording of the Revised Version, 1885).

VII 3 **seed ··· lodgement and germination:** frequent in American agricultural writing concerning seeds, spores etc.

VII 3 *variant*, 16 **man ··· a feather on the wind | Driven this way or that ··· the snow:** "Gull against the wind, in the windy straits ··· feathers in the snow ··· old man driven", *Gerontion* 69–72. See note to VII 16 *variant.*

VII 5, 7 *variants* **Crying for life beyond this life, for ecstasy not of the flesh ··· the waters:** "ecstasy of the animals ··· the waters ··· this life ··· beyond me ··· this life ··· lips parted", *Marina* 12, 21, 29–32.

VII 7–8 **And the spirit moved ··· the light**: for Genesis 1: 2–3, see note to II 7.

VII 9 **Invented the Higher Religions; and the Higher Religions**: William James: "as all the higher religions have assumed", *Is Life Worth Living?* (1896). Frazer: "magic steals up to higher standpoints too, and insinuates itself into higher religions", *The Golden Bough* I 424. TSE: "that there is such a thing as 'religion' above the various particular religions, seems to me very doubtful", *The Return of Foxy Grandpa* (*c.* 1927).

VII 11 **light was ever surrounded and shot with darkness**: Genesis 1: 4: "God divided the light from the darkness." OED "shot" *ppl.* 5a: "Woven with warp-threads of one colour and weft-threads of another, so that the fabric (usually silk) changes in tint when viewed from different points."

VII 16 *variant* **the windy places**: "windy spaces", *Gerontion* 16. (See Textual History, VII 15–17.)

VII 19 **A moment not out of time, but in time, in what we call history: transecting, bisecting the world of time**: "the author's purpose ··· is not to produce something which might have been written and performed in the fifteenth century; it is merely to arouse in the audience the kind of feeling towards the divine story which a fifteenth century audience might have enjoyed. Such an audience would have been innocent of 'historical accuracy' of place or time; a modern audience is far too aware of these things. Nowadays every 'historical' film is staged in the original setting, when possible: if religious films become popular, the Holy Land will be over-run with film studios. On the other hand, we have already had Shakespeare in modern dress ··· Both of these methods are mistaken, because they both make the audience more conscious of what they should forget, the differences of place and time", *"The Merry Masque of Our Lady in London Town"* (1928).

VII 27 **not for other gods, they say, but for no god; and this has never happened before**: to the Editor, *Manchester Guardian* 20 Jan 1940 (responding to a letter from H. G. Wells): "Since early times men have arisen to proclaim that there was no God: it is quite a different thing to assert that the word 'God' 'conveys no positive meaning at all'." Of Twain: "It is as a native that he accepts the River God, and it is the subjection of Man that gives to Man his dignity. For without some kind of God, Man is not even very interesting", *The Adventures of Huckleberry Finn* (1950), Introduction. "you can never fight a religion except with another religion", *Christianity and Communism* (1932). "one only ceases to be a Christian by being something else definite—a Buddhist, a Mohammedan, a Brahmin", *Why Mr. Russell Is a Christian* (1927). "The World is trying the experiment of attempting to form a civilized but non-Christian mentality. The experiment will fail; but we must be very patient in awaiting its collapse", *Thoughts After Lambeth* (1931). **no god**: Psalm 14: 1: "The fool hath said in his heart, There is no God." Clough: "'There is no God,' the wicked saith", *Dipsychus* VI 154.

VII 28–29 **gods ··· Dialectic**: "what remote frontier of heaven and hell ··· I have searched the world through dialectic ways", *Oh little voices of the throats of men* 7, 16. **Dialectic**: OED *a* and *n.*[2] 1: "Of, or pertaining to, or of the nature of logical disputation". 2: "In Marxist theory used specifically in relation to materialism."

VII 28 *variant* **professing first Reason, as in seventeen hundred and eighty nine**: first year of the French Revolution.

VII 31 **with empty hands and palms turned upwards**: "those who would build and restore turn out the palms of their hands", II 6. See note to *Burbank with a Baedeker: Bleistein with a Cigar* 14–15, 17.

VII 41 **Has the Church failed mankind, or has mankind failed the Church?**: "the True Church can never fail", *The Hippopotamus* 7. To C. M. Ady, 3 Jan 1940: "It is not clear just what, in your opinion, has failed, but the suggestion is alternatively that the Church has failed the modern world, or that the modern world has failed the Church. I think that whatever you mean could be put more clearly."

VII 42–43 **the Church is no longer regarded ··· and men have forgotten | All gods except Usury**: "I seem to be a petty usurer in a world manipulated largely by big usurers. And I know that the Church once condemned these things", *The Church's Message* (1937). "would you yourself advocate ··· excommunication of persons practising usury?" *Liberal Manifesto* (1939). For usury, see note to *A Cooking Egg* 15–16, "a five per cent. Exchequer Bond".

VIII

VIII 4–5] Psalm 79: 1: "the heathen are come into thine inheritances; thy holy temple have they defiled".

VIII 6–7 **Who is this that cometh from Edom? || He has trodden the wine-press alone** (7 *variant* **With dyed garments from Bosra?**): Isaiah 63: 1–4: "Who is this that cometh from Edom, with dyed garments from Bozrah? ··· I have trodden the winepress alone ··· the day of vengeance is in mine heart, and the year of my redeemed is come."

VIII 10 **Peter the Hermit**: instigator, in 1096, of the People's Crusade.

VIII 15–18 **Some went for love of glory, | Some went who were restless and curious, | Some were rapacious ··· Many left their bodies**: Pound, *Hugh Selwyn Mauberley* IV (George Simmers, personal communication):

> Some quick to arm,
> some for adventure,
> some from fear of weakness,
> some from fear of censure,
> some for love of slaughter, in imagination,
> learning later . . .
> some in fear, learning love of slaughter;
>
> Died some, pro patria,
> non "dulce" non "et decor" . . .

TSE included the poem in Pound's *Selected Poems*. In his copy of Smart's translation of Horace's Odes, TSE underlined "It is sweet and glorious to die for one's country" (III ii), and wrote "Dulce et decorum &c".

VIII 18 **Many left their bodies to the kites**: TSE's first printed story tells of a wounded soldier, "not more than two-thirds dead", waiting to be devoured by a vulture. In the final paragraph, as the bird flies off, the soldier "lost consciousness, and when he came to himself, it was to find that he was in the carriage of the rescuing hospital corps", *The Birds of Prey* (1905).

VIII 19 **sea-strewn along the routes:** "Along the wet paths of the sea", *Goldfish* IV 10.

VIII 27 **our King did well at Acre:** Richard I (Richard the Lionheart) captured the city of Acre in Western Galilee in 1191 during the Third Crusade. **did well:** the New Testament has "do well" repeatedly. "unto governors ··· for the punishment of evildoers, and for the praise of them that do well", 1 Peter 2: 14.

VIII 36, 42–43 **avarice ··· Our age ··· vice:** "Perhaps the dominant vice of our time ··· will be proved to be Avarice", *The Church's Message* (1937); in the broadcast, TSE said not "vice", but "sin".

VIII 38 **the Crusades:** "I am not prepared to admit that the nominal motives (which were probably in part the actual motives) of a great many participants in the Crusades were wrong. I do not see how at the time anything could have checked me from a whole-hearted support of the Crusades, except such knowledge of the human heart as would lead one to anticipate what did happen; for actually, of course, the Crusades turned out a thoroughgoing disgrace to Christian Europe", *Notes on the Way* (12 Jan 1935).

VIII 46–48 **nothing is impossible, nothing, | To men of faith and conviction. | Let us therefore make perfect our will:** Romans 12: 2: "be not conformed to this world, but be ye transformed ··· that ye may prove what is that good, and acceptable, and perfect, will of God" (*Hands*). Garvie's ed. of Romans, which TSE owned, glosses: "*good*, the morally right; *acceptable*, the religiously fit; *perfect*, what realizes the ideal, whether moral or religious". **make perfect our will:** "*Make perfect your will*", I 57. *Murder in the Cathedral* II, THOMAS: "if I am worthy, there is no danger. | I have therefore only to make perfect my will". For "Our peace in His will", see note to *Ash-Wednesday* VI 30–33.

IX

IX 1–2 **Son of Man ··· show thee:** Ezekiel 40: 4: "Son of man ··· set thine heart upon all that I shall shew thee". TSE: "Son of man ··· you know only | A heap of broken images", *The Waste Land* [I] 20–22.

IX 32–36 **spirit and body ··· spirit and body ··· His Temple ··· must not deny the body:** 1 Corinthians 6: 19: "Your body is the temple of the Holy Ghost." TSE: "'Body' may suggest either 'incarnation' or 'vile body', and so set the mind off in quite different directions", *Christianity and the Secular* (1944), a paper for The Moot. **Visible and invisible must meet in His Temple:** see notes to I 24–29 and X 3, 6.

IX 37 **Now you shall see the Temple completed:** a scrapbook kept by TSE's mother (Houghton) contains a hymn she wrote for the dedication of the mission house of the Mission Free School of St. Louis, beginning:

> The workman's task is at an end,
> The dwelling stands complete
> Whose walls shall echo to the tread
> Of happy children's feet.

X

TSE resisted musical settings of his poems (see letter to the Master of Magdalene and Francis Turner, 9 Nov 1962, quoted at the end of "This Edition", 6. TSE ON TREATMENTS OF HIS POEMS). However, he gave Martin Shaw permission to use Chorus X from *The Rock* in *The Greater Light*, an anthem for tenor solo, double choir and orchestra. The anthem was published in 1966 to mark the first anniversary of TSE's death. A copy is at Magdalene (Eliotiana II).

For the early ms draft of this Chorus, see Textual History.

ms draft [6–14] For the snake in the Antistrophe, see *Introspection.*

ms draft [12–14] **What fellowship hath Righteousness with Unrighteousness, & light with darkness?**: 2 Corinthians 6: 14.

ms draft [29–30] **Light through the water showing the | seagods the passing shadow of Argo**: see note to X 32–33.

X 2 **By one who came in the night**: 1 Thessalonians 5: 2: "the day of the Lord so cometh as a thief in the night" (*Hands*).

X 3 **a visible church, one more light set on a hill**: Matthew 5: 14: "Ye are the light of the world. A city that is set on an hill cannot be hid." John Winthrop (one of the founders of the Massachusetts Bay Colony): "we must consider that we shall be as a city upon a hill. The eyes of all people are upon us", *A Model of Christian Charity* (1630).

X 3, 6 **a visible church ··· the Visible Church**: of the Church: "In one use of the word, it means the 'visible Church' founded by Jesus Christ and living continuously since its foundation ··· In another use, it means 'the invisible Church,' consisting of all true believers, living and dead and to come ··· Those who use the term exclusively in the second sense, tend to think of the visible churches rather as societies or associations, of a voluntary nature ··· But for those to whom the first meaning is paramount, the Church is something which lives: as a tree may be encumbered by parasites, warped and mutilated by tempest, crippled by disease, so the Church lives, sustained by the Holy Ghost, Who causes the sap to flow through its living limbs", *Reunion by Destruction* (1943) 12–13.

X 7–8 **The great snake ··· moving his head to right and to left**: "He sways [*variant:* moves] his head from side to side, with movements like a snake", *Macavity: The Mystery Cat* 15.

X 9 **the Mystery of Iniquity**: 2 Thessalonians 2: 7.

X 12 **be ye separate**: 2 Corinthians 6: 17: "Wherefore come out from among them, and be ye separate, saith the Lord."

X 14 **Seek not to count the future waves of Time**: Kipling: "Seek not to question other than | The books I leave behind", *The Appeal* 7–8. Included in *A Choice of Kipling's Verse* and written out by TSE late in life on notepaper of the Emerald Beach Hotel, Nassau.

X 17 **O Light Invisible, we praise Thee**: Francis Thompson: "O world invisible, we view thee", *The Kingdom of God* 1 (*Grover Smith 1956* 175). **Light invisible**: *Paradise Lost* I 63: "darkness visible".

X 17–18 **Light · · · Too bright for mortal vision:** *Paradise Lost* III 375–76, 380: "Light, thyself invisible | Amidst the glorious brightness · · · Dark with excessive bright".

X 24, 28 **Glow-worm glowlight on a grassblade · · · small lights of those who meditate:** Marvell: "whose dear light · · · meditate · · · Grasses fall", *The Mower to the Glowworms* 1–8.

X 29–33 **coloured panes · · · light reflected from the polished stone, | The gilded carven wood · · · fresco · · · submarine · · · light that fractures through unquiet water:** "Reflecting light · · · coloured glass · · · drowned · · · window · · · ascended · · · Stirring · · · sea-wood · · · In which sad light a carvèd [*variant*: carven] dolphin swam", *The Waste Land* [II] 83–96.

X 32–33 **our eyes look upward | And see the light that fractures through unquiet water:** Dante compares the astonishment of the eternal light to the sight of Jason's ship, the *Argo*, from below: "che fe' Nettuno ammirar l'ombra d'Argo" [that erst threw Neptune in amaze at *Argo*'s shadow], *Paradiso* XXXIII 96 (*Matthiessen* 153). TSE: "Nowhere in poetry has experience so remote from ordinary experience been expressed so concretely, by a masterly use of that imagery of *light* which is the form of certain types of mystical experience · · · I do not know anywhere in poetry more authentic sign of greatness than the power of association which could in the last line, when the poet is speaking of the Divine vision, yet introduce the Argo passing over the head of wondering Neptune", *Dante* (1929) II. To Laurence Binyon, 7 July 1941, on his translation of this canto: "only one criticism, but that bothers me a good deal · · · A good deal is lost by rendering 'Nettuno' as 'ancient seas'. To me the image has always meant Neptune looking up through clear water and seeing the light darkened by the hull of Argo passing over and there is something extraordinarily impressive about this sudden appearance of the old god in such a canto as this. And is 'forgetfulness' right for 'letargo'? The precise feeling suggested here seems very difficult to render." (Temple translates "letargo" as "lethargy".) Hawthorne, *The Blithedale Romance* ch. XXVII, on Zenobia's death by water: "there, perhaps, she lay, with her face upward, while the shadow of the boat, and my own face peering downward, passed slowly betwixt her and the sky!"

Four Quartets: Headnote

1. First Publication 2. A Quartet of Four
3. Composition 4. "Not Merely More of the Same" 5. The War
6. Title 7. Music 8. Publication 9. TSE on *Four Quartets*

1. FIRST PUBLICATION

Burnt Norton	*Collected Poems 1909–1935*	2 Apr 1936
East Coker	*NEW*	21 Mar 1940
The Dry Salvages	*NEW*	27 Feb 1941
Little Gidding	*NEW*	15 Oct 1942

Burnt Norton was originally published as the last section, and longest new poem, in *1936*. It then appeared separately as a pamphlet after the success of *East Coker* in this form. Like *East Coker*, the remaining two Quartets were each published first in *NEW* and then as pamphlets. The four were collected as the American edition *US 1943* and subsequently in Britain in *1944*. TSE to Hans Feist, 6 Dec 1945, of a proposed German translation of all his poems: "I do not, however, wish to publish at the present time all of my poems in one volume. That is to say, I wish to keep the *Four Quartets* in a separate volume by themselves."

It was in the US likewise that a section called *Four Quartets* first figured within a larger collection of TSE's poems: in *US 1952*. (*Burnt Norton* therefore appeared as a separate publication, as the opening of a publication, in the middle of a publication, and as the close of a publication: pamphlet, *Four Quartets*, *US 1952*, *1936*.) After twelve impressions of *1944*, the Quartets were gathered into the British *Collected Poems* in *1963*. An edition of 290 signed copies of *Four Quartets*, finely printed by Giovanni Mardersteig in Verona, was published by Faber in 1960.

To Charles Williams, 31 Mar 1943: "As you have observed that *Burnt Norton* is included in the volume entitled *Poems 1909–1935*, your acumen will no doubt have led you to the conclusion that *Burnt Norton* was probably not composed later than 1936, which is exactly the fact. For the sake of consistency and in defiance of the truth I should prefer the date of *Burnt Norton* to be given as 1935. In any case, this departure from veracity does not affect the critical issue very much for the main point is that *Burnt Norton* is the first of these poems by some four years and that it is meant to be read first by anyone reading all four poems and that it will appear first in the volume consisting of all four together which will probably appear next year."

To Richard Church, 24 Nov 1943: "The four poems together are intended to form a whole and we propose to publish them all together in a volume in the spring. Until this volume has appeared and made what impression it can, I feel that I should be doing myself a disservice in allowing *Burnt Norton* which I now consider simply as a section of a much longer poem to be published in any anthology." To Norman Foerster, 20 Mar 1946: "I am still very anxious to establish the *Four Quartets* as one poem, and I still think that the publication of any one of the four parts in an anthology obstructs the establishing of that view, but I should like to come to a compromise, so I am writing to ask whether it would go to any degree toward meeting your wishes if I consent to your choosing separate sections from different poems in the volume. This, by fracturing the unity still further, would be better from my point of view since it would be clear that what appeared in the anthology were merely selections from the book and not a whole poem in itself."

On *In Memoriam*: "Tennyson took a long time over the poem: perhaps there were superfluous passages, or stretches below his sustained level—if so, he eliminated and improved. The structure is designed with great care. Each section (some are very short and some longer) is a complete poem in itself—that is to say, represents a particular mood realised in its appropriate imagery: but the moods represented by the sections follow according to a logic of the emotions to form a continuous meditation on life and death", *"The Voice of His Time"* (1942).

To H. W. Heckstall-Smith, 17 Sept 1947, on the recording of *Four Quartets*: "I am much interested in what you say further about the evidence of different degrees of intensity in my own reading of the poems. I think that you are certainly right on the whole although I was not altogether conscious of it. There are, however, passages in the poems which are deliberately intended to give an effect of flatness for purposes of contrast, and one should perhaps distinguish my own flatness in reading these passages from that of reading passages in which I do not feel complete conviction."

To John D. Stephenson, 13 July 1945: "Burnt Norton is a manor house in Gloucestershire. I know nothing of the history of the house or of its owners. I merely happened to walk through the grounds one summer day at a time when the house had evidently been unoccupied for at least several years. East Coker is the small village in Somerset where my family lived for six or seven generations. Little Gidding is the chapel which is all that remains of the religious community run by the Ferrars in the seventeenth century. The best impression of it, any rate the best known, is that to be found in the first part of *John Inglesant*" (by J. Henry Shorthouse, 1881); see individual headnotes.

Four Quartets was recorded by the HMV Gramophone Co. Ltd. under the auspices of the British Council in London, and released in 1947. Six sessions were required: 22 Oct 1946 (*Burnt Norton*), 12 Nov (*East Coker*), 19 Nov (*The Dry Salvages*), 28 Nov (*Little Gidding*), 2 Dec (*Burnt Norton, East Coker*), 13 Mar 1947 (*Burnt Norton*).

Additionally: *East Coker* V only, May 1942 in Stockholm for the Swedish Broadcasting System; *East Coker* in full, before Nov 1945, for the BBC Indian Service (letter to Desmond Hawkins, 2 Nov 1945), and again 23 May 1947, at the National Gallery of Art, Washington; *Little Gidding* in full 13 May 1947, Harvard, as part of the Morris Gray Poetry Reading; and *Little Gidding* IV only 12 Nov 1950, for U. Chicago Round Table, broadcast by NBC.

2. A QUARTET OF FOUR

TSE to William Matchett, 19 Jan 1949: "The idea of the whole sequence emerged gradually. I should say during the composition of *East Coker.* Certainly by the time that poem was finished I envisaged the whole work as having four parts which gradually began to assume, perhaps only for convenience sake, a relation to the four seasons and the four elements. But certainly *Burnt Norton* at the time of writing was a solitary experiment, and I had nothing in mind for the next step."

However, as early as 1938, when Geoffrey Tandy suggested an adaptation of *Burnt Norton* as voices for radio, TSE had revealed that he had something fourfold in mind.

To Tandy, 10 Feb 1938: "About *Burnt Norton*. I do not feel quite sure about this idea of yours, although I recognise its profundity in principle. I had rather wait until I can manage to do something that I have had in mind for some time past: write a few pieces of Chamber Music, somewhat on the same lines, but deliberately with the intention of distribution between a definite number of voices, probably four. It may turn out that the stuff does not look any different from *Burnt Norton*, I mean that one kind will be as suitable or as unsuitable for several voices as the other, but there may turn out to be a difference, and as that seems just possible I had rather wait, and not confuse myself by bothering at present with an adaptation. However, I will go on thinking about the matter." (For "chamber music", see below, 7. MUSIC.)

3. COMPOSITION

Approximate dates of composition:

Burnt Norton	late 1935–Feb 1936
East Coker	Oct 1939–Mar 1940
The Dry Salvages	July 1940–Feb 1941
Little Gidding	early 1941–Sept 1942

Burnt Norton began with lines previously written. A version of the opening lines of Part I had been written for the Second Priest in *Murder in the Cathedral* (see Textual History description of *tsMinC*), and the opening two lines of Part II had been written for *Lines for an Old Man*. TSE later told John Lehmann how he adapted the dramatic fragments: "I thought pure, unapplied poetry was in the past for me, until a curious thing happened. There were lines and fragments that were discarded in the course of the production of *Murder in the Cathedral*. 'Can't get them over on the stage,' said the producer, and I humbly bowed to his judgment. However, these fragments stayed in my mind, and gradually I saw a poem shaping itself round them: in the end it came out as *Burnt Norton*. Even *Burnt Norton* might have remained by itself if it hadn't been for the war, because I had become very much absorbed in the problems of writing for the stage and might have gone straight on from *The Family Reunion* to another play. The war destroyed that interest for a time: you remember how the conditions of our lives changed, how much we were thrown in on ourselves in the early days? *East Coker* was the result—and it was only in writing *East Coker* that I began to see the Quartets as a set of four", *T. S. Eliot Talks about Himself and the Drive to Create* (1953).

When TSE sent setting copy for *Collected Poems 1909–1935* to his American publisher Donald Brace, 31 Dec 1935, it was "with the exception of one poem which is unfinished, and which I will forward if I can finish it within the next fortnight. This poem would come at the end in any case". To Mary Hutchinson, 19 Jan 1936: "except that I can't get the last four lines right, I think I have written rather a nice poem to conclude my Collected Poetical Works." In his *London Letter* in the *New York Sun* for 28 Mar 1936, John Hayward writes that *Burnt Norton* was "completed only a month or so ago".

Sylvia Beach wrote to TSE, 21 Mar 1936, requesting that he read at her bookshop in Paris: "Is it true that you are working on a new long poem, and would you consent to read from it? We would love to hear even a small piece of it." *1936* appeared the following month, and TSE read at Shakespeare & Co. on 6 June, with Joyce, Gide and

Valéry in the audience (*NY Herald Tribune* 15 June). According to Noel Riley Fitch's *Sylvia Beach and the Lost Generation* (1983), the reading included *The Waste Land* and "early written parts" of *Burnt Norton.*

Anne Ridler on her time as TSE's secretary: "I have often wished that I had known, when I was working for him, and he wrote in that summer of 1937 to Sir Matthew Nathan at West Coker saying he would like to pay him a visit—I wish that I had known whether he had poetry in his mind. Of course it didn't mean anything to me, it was just a letter proposing a visit. I think I knew that his family came from those parts, and I supposed he was perhaps going to do a bit of family hunting, but that was what gave rise to the poem · · · All this must have begun with a summer visit to Chipping Campden", interview with Kieron Winn, 9 Feb 2000.

TSE to Stephen Spender, 5 Oct 1939: "This autumn, I am divided between the notion of a poem about the length of *Burnt Norton*, which has been at the back of my mind for a long time, and seeing whether I can devise a play suitable for Martin Browne's project of a caravan company to play without scenery in small villages."

To Hayward, 8 Feb 1940: "I hope I can get away in time to have a rest at the club, and to get on with my new poem in succession to *Burnt Norton*—the second of the three quatuors—provisionally entitled *East Coker*; of which I have drafted the first two out of the five sections—it may be quite worthless, because most of it looks to me like an imitation of myself, and as for the rest, well, Blake and Clough kept getting into it, and I have been trying to rub them out—I *have* got rid of the line 'The Archer's bow and Taurus' ire', which however did not look quite so silly as all that in its context" (presumably the first section of II). OED "quatuor": "*Mus.* = *quartet* 1. [A composition for four voices or instruments, esp. one for four stringed instruments]. The current term in Fr., but not now in Eng. use. 1726 BAILEY, *Quatuor* (in Musick Books) signifies Musick composed for 4 Voices." Last citation 1811.

Hayward to Frank Morley, Feb 1940: "I am relieved to hear that Tom has picked up his tablets again after all these months—almost a year—of silence · · · He now writes to say that he is making a little progress with a new poem in succession to *Burnt Norton*" (King's).

TSE to Hayward, 20 Feb 1940, on the *Christian News Letter*: "my association with the C.N.L. is giving me a lot of subject-matter for another Tract for the Times · · · Federal Union, Rights of Man, Education, Mass Observation—enough cokernut shies to give 6s. of entertainment. And speaking of cokernuts, I enclose a Poem. I don't know whether it is worth tinkering with or not: but you might keep it to yourself, and return it in a week or two in enclosed stamped envelope with the expected neat faint pencil marks. Part IV worries me: that kind of tour de force is always dangerous, because the only good phrases may prove to be reminiscences. It looks like quite clever pseudo-post-Benlowes; I can't bother to re-read the whole of Saintsbury's Caroline Poets, to say nothing of the major sources; but if your nose tells you that I have pinched a line without knowing it, let me know." (George Saintsbury's three volumes of *Minor Caroline Poets*, 1905–21, include Benlowes, Cleveland and Henry King.)

TSE to Frank Morley, 12 Mar 1940: "you may have noticed that I sent you last week a carbon copy of a poem · · · I am giving it to Philip Mairet to publish at Easter in the *New English Weekly*, and it has therefore occurred to me that if it is going to be printed here I ought to have it published in an American periodical as soon as possible, in order to cover the copyright. So would you be willing to undertake to pass it on to any suitable periodical that would care to publish it within the necessary period? I don't know whether I can trust you in a matter like this, because your first impulse, if you think the poem good enough to print at all, would probably be to get as much money for it for me as you can. But one ought not to sell anything of this sort, whether it is good or bad. I would rather get it into a really respectable periodical, even if it could not pay, than be paid some derisory sum like 500 or 1,000 dollars by one of your disreputable reviews with money. My idea was something like the *Southern Review* or the *Kenyon Review* or that kind of heavy magazine, preferably published south of Mason and Dixon's line. Definitely not *Poetry* or any magazine that makes a feature of poetry. Perhaps it doesn't matter whether it is published or not, but in case you think fit to take any steps and have the time to do so, I enclose a sheet of corrections, which please incorporate in the text I gave you."

To Morley, 18 Apr 1940: "I had in fact had in my head the notion of eventually printing these two poems and the unwritten one together in one book, and I am very glad that the idea has occurred to you. But if the third poem is to swing its weight with the other two, it is probably not due till 1943 at the earliest. These are, in that sense, time poems."

Hayward sent a regular newsletter—"Tarantula's Special News-Service"—to Morley in the US, keeping him abreast of British publishing and gossip. That of Apr 1940 urged Harcourt Brace to issue *East Coker* "separately in the manner of an outsize 'Ariel' poem", adding that TSE would probably wish "to wait until *East Coker*, *Burnt Norton* and the two other pieces he has in mind to complete the series with" could all appear together. (The large paper issues of the Ariel Poems series are the same format as the 1937 pamphlet of Auden's *Spain*, which in turn was the model for Faber's pamphlets of the Quartets.) In the margin of Hayward's letter, Morley noted: "I have suggested, & TSE very pleased, that when the 3rd and/if 4th poem in the sequence is ready, we'll make a book of them. Am against publication of *E.C.* on its own." Hayward was more successful with Faber, and he wrote to Morley in June: "Energetic intervention on my part has led to the Book Committee deciding to print *East Coker* at once as a separate piece. I hope you will follow suit. Tom has undertaken to write a third and concluding poem of about 200 lines, and all three poems will them be printed in small-book form—towards autumn, if we are spared."

TSE to E. M. W. Tillyard, 6 June 1940: "what you say for yourself and others heartens me and encourages me in the project of writing a third poem in progression from *Burnt Norton* and *East Coker*."

Writing to TSE on 20 June 1940, Hayward expressed the hope that the mood in which TSE had been able to write *East Coker* would return, "so that the third and last part of the work will be written". TSE, 23 June: "If, after the Summer School in July, I find that conditions give me the right time and conditions necessary, I intend to try to write poem III. That might just be done: in these days one cannot look far enough ahead to contemplate the year's steady work which a play would demand." TSE to Morley, 15 July: "You are too reasonable, I expect, to hope for a third poem by any definite date. I shall be thinking about it and it is possible that I might write it this summer but very likely not. In any case you won't count upon it for the autumn season." Hayward to Morley, Aug 1940: "The third poem of the trilogy has not yet been written."

The eventual title *Four Quartets* was hinted at by the announcement of *East Coker* among the Autumn Books for 1940: "This is a poem of the same length and in the same form—described by the author as a 'quartet'—as *Burnt Norton*, which was published in his *Collected Poems 1909–1935*. These two poems, and at least one yet unwritten, are intended to form a kind of sequence."

In autumn 1940, TSE changed his domestic arrangements, for reasons he explained to Richard Jennings, 25 Feb 1941: "I had to leave Kensington because I found being a warden there that I couldn't keep my mind on literary composition during an alerte, besides I had to sit up two nights a week waiting for Incidents and was too sleepy in the daytime; and the only graceful way to stop being a warden was to leave Kensington: so now I live with some people in Surrey and with the Fabers in Hampstead when in town."

To Morley, 9 Oct 1940: "I *want* to do another *quartet*—provisionally entitled *The Dry Salvages* (accent on the *vages*—see chart of Cape Ann)." This Anglo-American Quartet was to coincide with the Lend-Lease scheme enacted in Mar 1941. (The USA entered the war in Dec 1941.) When completed, the sequence comprised one Quartet named after an American place and three after English places. Although the title "Kensington Quartets" had been abandoned (see below, 6. TITLE), war may have affected the balance in the years since TSE wrote to Nelson Lansdale, 22 June 1938:

> I have your letter of 13 June, asking me whether I am an American or an English writer. That is a very difficult question to decide, and I submit that I am in no better position to answer it than is anyone else in possession of the published facts. I take it that the question of legal status is not raised, but only that of literary status. If one is to appeal to the year books, I can point out that for several years I appeared in both the British and the American *Who's Who*. The editors of the American *Who's Who* eventually dropped me without any notification. Possibly their opinion on this vexed question might be of some value ··· It might be argued that this question is one which cannot be decided by itself, but is only a special case in a general category. Is Napoleon, for instance, to be considered as an Italian or a Frenchman? We know that his native language was Italian, and that his Corsican family were probably of Genoese extraction. His case however is not quite parallel to mine, because he changed the spelling of his name, which I have not done.
>
> A case perhaps more pertinent is that of Cardinal Newman. Is Cardinal Newman to be considered an Anglican or a Roman writer? One notes of both these men that they are claimed or repudiated according to the disposition of the individual critic.

Hayward wrote to TSE on 9 Nov 1940 to say that Morley was "very anxious to know if there is any likelihood of the third poem being written before the end of the year, so that he can publish the trilogy in the Spring." TSE to Hayward, 10 Dec 1940: "I have been working this morning at a poem to follow *E. Coker*, and on a first section dealing with Water, as the previous first section dealt with Earth, or with Autumn instead of Summer: and at this stage it seems to me very unpromising." Hayward to TSE, "Christmastide 1940": "I'm glad to hear that you've begun a sequel to *West Croaker.*"

TSE to Geoffrey Curtis, 31 Dec 1940: "I have just completed another poem to go with *East Coker*, and contemplate a fourth to complete the series. The unwritten one is provisionally, *Little Gidding*." Hayward received "the typescript of the first draft of the third poem of Tom's trilogy" on 1 Jan 1941, having had "No warning that it was even begun" (Hayward to Morley, Jan 1941). TSE to Philip Mairet (editor of *NEW* 1934–49), 5 Jan, sending *The Dry Salvages*: "I enclose for your private examination a copy of my new poem. Any criticisms will be appreciated. I may have other changes to make before releasing it for publication. I am least certain about the last section. I am also uncertain about the title—whether it will carry: so I won't explain it as

I wish to find out what kind of misconception it arouses. The word 'groaner' may be too obscure also."

To Clive Bell, 3 Jan 1941: "Such encouragement as you convey is all the more welcome at a time when one needs encouragement, if one is to persist in this odd occupation of making patterns with words. It will require only a little more such flattery, however (so exquisitely concentrated) to persuade me to complete work on my scheme of a set of four. I may even take in hand the long neglected task of putting in order the epical ballad on the life of Chris Columbo (the famous Portuguese navigator) and his friends King Bolo and his Big Black Queen."

Requesting that Geoffrey Faber have the typescript of *The Dry Salvages* copied and that copies be sent to Morley "by two different mails, so that he can get copyright in America", TSE explained, 21 Jan 1941: "I never feel safe about a poem in these days until I get a copy safely evacuated to the U.S.A. Meanwhile you could help me by looking through it for any musical flaws, and any incorrect or inexact words. John Hayward is pretty good at the latter, and made some useful comments on Draft 2: but I trust hardly anyone nowadays to *hear* a poem and criticise it from that point of view. Neither John, nor Mairet who has seen Draft 3 (this is Draft 4) seemed to be bothered by obscurity. It is impossible for me to know about that myself; for the emotional charge comes from my last visit to that coast (where we had a seaside house) in 1915, after which I never saw my father again. Neither religious nor artistic treatment of past agony is, in my experience, a pain killer: they don't let you off the rock—but they do make you get the vultures into some kind of pattern." (For TSE's vulture and Gide's eagle, see note to *Dans le Restaurant* 20.) To Faber again, 3 Feb: "your criticisms are precisely what I want. I have marked seven of them for immediate change; some others I want to keep in mind and perhaps use after the *N.E.W.* publication, and two or three I have the satisfaction of rejecting with scorn. So what could be better?"

On 24 Feb 1941 TSE wrote to the Librarian of Magdalene College, Cambridge, offering the "manuscripts" of *The Dry Salvages* and future poems. His Harvard friend Harold Peters, with whom he had sailed the Gloucester coast, was injured in a boating accident and died in Feb 1941 (*Soldo* 80), but this is not mentioned in TSE's known correspondence from that year (he wrote to Hayward on 8 Nov 1942 of receiving some news of "Lt. Commander Peters, who was a pal of mine at Harvard"). To Herbert Read, 1 Mar 1941: "I take it you see the *N.E.W.* I should be interested to have any comments on my salVAGES: especially as there is time for tinkering before we publish it" (as a Faber pamphlet).

To Anne Ridler, 17 May 1941: "I don't think I want any of the three quartets [in *A Little Book of Modern Verse*] because they are to make a separate volume as soon as, and if, I complete the fourth. But authors must not make their own choice: one has too much tenderness for the little poems of one's own which have always sat about in corners and never been asked for a dance by anybody." To M. J. Tambimuttu, 21 June: "I cannot release *East Coker* for anthology purposes yet. You see, I am working on a fourth poem in the same form, and we intend to bring out the four as one volume, making, I hope, something like a coherent poem sequence, next year." To Gerald D. Saunders, 25 Sept: "You see, the poem is designed as one of a sequence of four poems which Harcourt Brace will publish in New York as soon as the last poem is ready." Henry Eliot, presenting *The Dry Salvages* to the Sawyer Free Library, Gloucester: "The poem has been published only in this form, and only in England, though later it will be published in a volume with three other poems, one of which is not yet finished" (*Gloucester Daily Times and Cape Ann Advertiser* 27 Feb 1942).

Hayward to Morley, June 1941: "Tom · · · wants if possible to complete the cycle with a fourth poem—Earth, Air, Water, *Fire*—and has got as far as making a rough, preliminary draft".

Sending a draft of *Little Gidding* to Hayward on 7 July 1941, TSE wrote: "you will understand my being worried and diffident and depressed at this writing · · · If however I can wring victory out of defeat, the question will arise whether I should let them publish this separately uniform with the other three, and make a book after a season (i.e. autumn 1942) or not publish this separately, so as to have something new in the book."

To Hayward, 14 July 1941: "I have pushed on with *Little Gidding*, and enclose provisional results · · · My suspicions about the poem are partly due to the fact that as it is written to complete a series, and not solely for itself, it may be too much from the head and may show signs of flagging. That is a dilemma. Anyway, however doubtful of it I have been, I had to finish it somehow or it would have stuck in my crop and prevented me from turning to other tasks. The question is not so much whether it is as good as the others (I am pretty sure it is not) but whether it is good enough to keep company with them to complete the shape. If the problem is more than one of improving details, it will have to go into storage for some time to come." To Theodore Spencer, 21 July: "I was very pleased by your expression of enjoyment of *The Dry Salvages*. I think myself that it is the best of the poems that I have done in this form: a thought which at the moment does not give me unqualified pleasure, because I have just written a fourth, I hope final, quartet to go with the three you know. I am awaiting John Hayward's impressions: I am in that uncomfortable state when I am dissatisfied without knowing quite what is wrong."

Hayward to Morley, July 1941: "Tom has completed the first rough draft of the final poem of the Quadrologue—*Little Gidding* · · · Tom is exercised to know whether to print the poem separately and postpone the publication of the quartet until the autumn of 1942, or to publish the poems as a collection this autumn with *Little Gidding* as the novelty to attract purchasers who already possess the earlier pieces. My own view is that in these times the less delay the better in bringing into the world the kind of work that consolidates one's faith in the continuity of thought and sensibility when heaven is falling and earth's foundations fail." (Housman: "These, in the day when heaven was falling, | The hour when earth's foundations fled", *Epitaph on an Army of Mercenaries.*)

Hayward to TSE, 22 July 1941: "As yet I have done no more than read through the draft of the pome · · · I await your order to comment · · · your last most entertaining newsletter with which additional fragments of the pome were included."

Hayward to Montgomery Belgion (then a prisoner-of-war), 29 July: "A fourth and final poem in the group is in preparation & I have a draft in front of me. It is to be called *Little Gidding.*"

TSE to George Every, 30 July: "I have actually written a fourth poem (*Little Gidding*) but at present I am deeply dissatisfied with it."

Hayward to Morley, Aug 1941: "I have not yet had an acknowledgement of my observations on the poem *Little Gidding*. He fears that it is uninspired and mechanically repetitive of the earlier poems in the group, but says that he must get it off his mind before he can turn to other work."

TSE to Hayward, 17 Oct 1941: "Two points have constantly slipped out of my letters. One is my curious lapse in failing to thank you for your careful notes on Spittle-Skidding. which WILL be most useful to me in revision. I have probably forgotten to mention them before simply because I had determined to put the whole thing out of my mind until December. Your notes are carefully preserved against my resumption of that toil."

Hayward to Morley, July 1942: "My tactful feelers about the poem's progress have been without effect and, as from past experience I know that he finds the summer an unfruitful time for composition, I fear that he may not get down to it before the autumn. He was, as I think I told you in an earlier letter, dissatisfied with the first draft, considering it to be generally inferior to the first three poems which, by the way, have been as highly praised over here as anything he has written and have more than rehabilitated his current poetic reputation which was in some danger of becoming temporarily dimmed by the vapourings of the young. I think myself that he underrates the fundamental strength and beauty of the poem in its first crystallization, though I believe he is at any rate half persuaded now that it is better material to work on than he had at first supposed ··· His chief fear was that he was simply repeating himself and so running into the risk of producing an elegant parody of the earlier poems in the group." (*Levy* 106 recalls showing TSE two pages in Dylan Thomas's handwriting, including *Chard Whitlow*, Henry Reed's parody of *Burnt Norton*. At the foot of the second, TSE wrote: "Not bad. But I think I could write a better parody myself! T. S. Eliot, 27.iv.58".)

TSE to Hayward, 21 July 1942: "I have put Part II of *Little Gidding* into the melting pot, but nothing has solidified yet." 17 Aug: "obstinately my mind refuses to do its best at the rechauffé of *Murder*, until it has eased itself of *Little Gidding.* So here is a rescension of Part II, which seemed to me the centre of weakness. Even if this is better than the first version (which I assume you still have by you) it may not be good enough; and if it is not good enough (minor improvements, of course, apart) then I fear that the poem must simply be allowed to disintegrate. If this is fundamentally all right, then an improvement of the other sections does not seem to be beyond the bounds of possibility. I submit it (together with another edition of Part III) with some trepidation."

Hayward to Morley, 7 Sept 1942: "*Little Gidding* is almost completed. After almost exactly a year's delay, Tom took it in hand about three weeks ago and since then I have received three revisions and expect to receive the final text this week."

TSE to Herbert Read, 18 Sept 1942: "I *think* that *Little Gidding* is now about as good as I can make it: at any rate I have sent a copy to Mairet—though I have already made two more improvements since posting it." (The following day he wrote to Hayward with some final changes and dissatisfactions: see headnote to *Little Gidding*, 2. COMPOSITION.) In a copy of *NEW* inscribed for Valerie Eliot, TSE wrote: "The poem was given to help a weekly which, alas, was dying from lack of support. Mairet had been, I maintain, a great editor, and not bound to the social-credit chariot wheels." In a letter to W. Travers Symons, 1 Oct 1958, TSE paid tribute to Mairet's contribution to Neville Braybrooke's symposium for TSE's 70th birthday, and recalled their "work together on the *New English Weekly* ··· But with the disappearance of the *New English Weekly*, which was, while it lasted, the best weekly published in this country, something of great value went out of my life."

TSE to the Master of Magdalene, A. B. Ramsay, 31 Oct 1942: "It would be a pleasure to me to be allowed to add to the manuscripts and other papers connected with my poem *The Dry Salvages* which you kindly accepted on behalf of the College, the manuscripts and papers of my latest poem, *Little Gidding*, a poem of about the same length which completes the series to which the other belongs. These papers are of the same description and of about the same bulk."

The drafts of *Four Quartets* were almost all published, along with a selection of the correspondence with Hayward, in Helen Gardner's *The Composition of "Four Quartets"*. The appendix on *The Writing of "Little Gidding"* in *Smart* is, as he writes, based upon her scholarship.

4. "NOT MERELY MORE OF THE SAME"

TSE's letter of advice to George Barker of 24 Jan 1938 turns repeatedly upon words and phrases that had figured in *Burnt Norton* or were to do so in the three further Quartets:

> I do not think that these poems make a volume which it is advisable to print as it stands. To you, no doubt, these poems appear new, and a development of your previous work: but they will not so appear to the reader. I do not say that they are not, take them all round, just as good as your first volume: the point is, that after two volumes they are not the right stuff for a third. There comes a point, and it comes very quickly, where the reader of poetry—and I mean the most intelligent and sensitive reader—demands not merely more of the same, but something new. The ordinary novel reader is quite happy to have "another Edgar Wallace" or "another Ethel Mannin" as the case may be; and would be annoyed if he got anything very different from the last. He is not going to re-read the author's previous novels, and he wants the same thing made to look just different enough. But in publishing poetry you are publishing primarily for the hundred or so best readers—if you get a larger public, that is all to the good, but it can't be aimed at. And the best poetry readers don't want more of the same: until you do something quite new they prefer to re-read what you have done already.
>
> Whether you stop writing poetry for a time, or merely stop printing it, is a point upon which no one can advise you; but I do feel that for the present you should stop publishing: except, of course, for "trying things out" in periodicals. Poetry is either a matter of a brief outburst, or it is a matter of a lifetime's work: in either case it is a nuisance to be a poet. When it is a life work, you are sure to find from time to time that your inspiration is exhausted, and that you either repeat yourself, or stop writing. These are painful, but necessary periods. I do not say that this has happened to everybody who has been accounted a great poet. A few men, like Shakespeare, have gone on growing so fast that they simply could not repeat themselves; you could almost say that Shakespeare was a new man every time he started a new play. But more often a poet has gone on writing without knowing that he has not developed sufficiently to justify it. Swinburne wrote many good poems in later life—poems that nobody else could have written. But at the same time it is not *necessary* to read them, in a world crammed with reading-matter. In the long run, it is only *necessary* poems that count, and only the necessary poems that will be read.
>
> I think, as I say, that it is a right part of the labour of going on writing poetry, to have these periods of sterility and bafflement of which I speak. They should recur throughout one's active life. There have been several periods of considerable extent in my own life, when I have felt *almost* convinced that I should never be able to write again; or when I have produced something with great labour and found it still-born. In fact, these periods seem to make up the greater part of my life. My published work might be much larger than it is, if I had not kept in mind that *nothing is worth doing*

twice. It is quite possible that my later work is not so good as my earlier—I must prepare myself not to be too depressed if I ever see that to be so; but at any rate I can make sure that it shall be *different*. Whether we develop or not is a mysterious business, not directly under our control. But one must try to be clear about this: in what way do I feel things differently from last year? and let one's work be faithful to the change. One's emotional life is in constant change; one wakes up astonished to find that one does not feel the same about something as one did yesterday; feelings disappear from which we part with regret; but there is always the fascination of the new, or perpetually adapting oneself as an artist to the change in oneself as a man, and as one grows older restating the problems of life from the older point of view.

Now in these periods of sterility one has to have recourse partly to patience and waiting: that is the passive side. But one can also do much by filling up one's mind—partly from books, from interesting oneself in new subjects in the outside world, and partly from one's experience and study of human beings. Also, one can do much by widening one's taste in poetry, and saturating oneself in authors who are not immediately congenial; and by technical experiments in verse of various kinds. All these activities will help to preserve you from the common danger—which I see in your own verse—of diffuseness; and help you to gain concentration.

Ever yours,
T. S. Eliot

P.S. There is a common error nowadays of making a distinction between poetry for "the few" and poetry for "the many". This is introducing an irrelevance based on political premises. Poetry should be written, not for the "few" in the sense of a small group of highly refined, or socially superior, triflers who are trained to enjoy the obscure and the eccentric and the perverse: but for the "few" in the sense that there are never more than a very small number of people who are competent to judge poetry at all. One must aim to satisfy the *best* readers of poetry—whoever they may be, because one only knows a *very* few oneself; the rest are scattered and often obscure; and not more than a very small percentage of newspaper critics—sometimes none—is included among them. And the larger public, or "the people", is only the shadow of this unknown or only partly known élite. To aim directly at "the people" is to aim to write the ephemeral, because that is what the people wants.

5. THE WAR

A week after Britain declared war on Germany, and shortly before publication of *Old Possum's Book of Practical Cats*, TSE wrote to John Hayward, 11 Sept 1939: "My financial future* [* or sh[d.] I say *foutse*?] seems to depend upon Cats." (Fr. *foutre* = fuck-up; *fou* = mad, + *tse* = TSE.) 21 Nov: "The two small books are still selling very well, the *X. Society* [*The Idea of a Christian Society*] now more rapidly than the *Cats*; But I can't think of anything more serious (in the way of poetry and drama) to write next."

Stephen Spender: "Although some painters were reserved to paint war pictures, no poet was reserved for the purpose of writing war poetry or any other kind of poetry. It would be impossible, of course, for a poet to enter into an undertaking to write poetry about war in the same way that a painter can paint scenes of war. It would also have been impossible for a government in conducting total war to give poets complete freedom without any obligation to write propaganda or, indeed, to write anything", in *Poetry Since 1939* (1946), "II. Conditions in which Poets have Worked".

The magazine *Time* reported, 7 June 1943, TSE's comment on writing in wartime: "Of these quartets their author has said, 'each represents the maximum length of a poem which I have been able to get continuous time to do under these conditions.'"

To Frederick Tomlin, 15 May 1957: "it was war-time conditions which produced three of my *Four Quartets. The Family Reunion* was produced in the spring of 1939; when I saw it on the stage and realised all the errors and defects of technique, I was determined to start another play which should be free of the same faults. The war prevented this owing to the impossibility of sitting down morning after morning to a task which would occupy me for a couple of years. The quartet form was the solution because I could concentrate on the five sections of each poem separately" (*Tomlin* 200). By comparison with play-writing, "The form of the *Quartets* fitted in very nicely to the conditions under which I was writing, or could write at all. I could write them in sections and I didn't have to have quite the same continuity. It didn't matter if a day or two elapsed when I did not write, as they frequently did, while I did war jobs", *Paris Review* (1959). Each Quartet is longer than that which precedes it.

"The last three of my quartets are primarily patriotic poems", draft of *The Three Voices of Poetry* (1959) (*Moody* 203). "All the last three Quartets are in a sense war poems—increasingly. *East Coker* belongs to the period of what we called the 'phony war'", *T. S. Eliot Talks about His Poetry* (1958). After Janet Adam Smith reviewed the 1952 edition of *Gallup* in *New Statesman* 24 Jan 1953, TSE sent her a postcard, 8 Feb, "to complain of your finding nothing Toppicle in the 4 4tets. If L. G. isn't Toppicle: well, it was *meant* to be the best Patriotic Poem in the language."

To Anne Ridler, 9 Nov 1940: "I now sleep in comfort in the Fabers' basement shelter, instead of sitting up in uniform in the wardens' room ··· the rest of the time, in Surrey, I live in absolute luxury. Unless I can produce some work of value this winter, I shall not feel justified in this life."

To Henry Eliot, 1 June 1942, describing a lecture tour in Sweden: "What is accomplished by this sort of cultural warfare is impossible to say: but it [is] a part of total warfare which one must, as an individual, accept one's part in." In this spirit, during 1943, TSE agreed to act as temporary president of "Books Across the Sea" (slogan: "All readers of books in English are freemen of one common realm"), and was using its notepaper for letters (perhaps to conserve Faber's ration). To Mary Trevelyan, 30 Oct 1944: "I have just recorded a wee broadcast of 1½ minutes on the Responsibility of Men of Letters for the European Service, and am trying to repeat it in French and German."

To E. Martin Browne, 20 Oct 1942: "It is hard, when you sit down at a desk, to feel confident that morning after morning spent fiddling with words and rhythms is a justified activity—especially as there is never any certainty that the whole thing won't have to be scrapped" (*Browne* 158). (TSE included Marianne Moore's *Poetry*, beginning "I, too, dislike it: there are things that are important beyond all this fiddle", in her *Selected Poems*, 1935.) "Of what use is this experimenting with rhythms and words, this effort to find the precise metric and the exact image to set down feelings which, if communicable at all, can be communicated to so few that the result seems insignificant compared to the labour?" *Christianity and Communism* (1932). "the intolerable wrestle | With words and meanings. The poetry does not matter", *East Coker* II 20–21.

To Neville Braybrooke, 25 Nov 1958: "At the time when I wrote *East Coker* I had been living for some years in South Kensington and travelled daily on the Underground between Gloucester Road and Russell Square, and *East Coker* itself was composed before the Blitzkrieg began. There is some reference to the Blitz, of course, in *Little Gidding*."

6. TITLE

To E. M. Stephenson, 12 Mar 1941: "you are on the right line when you speak of the musical phrase because I tend to think of my own work in building it up more in terms of an analogy of musical form than in any other. I say analogy because I think it is dangerous to press the resemblance between poetry and music too far."

TSE to Hayward, 7 July 1941: "I have wanted to call the book Kensington Quartets, but this may not find favour." 3 Sept 1942: "The title I have always had in mind for it was KENSINGTON QUARTETS. I have had a fancy to have Kensington in it." Hayward to Morley, 7 Sept 1942: "I'm afraid that 'Kensington' is too likely to suggest to the uninformed majority of readers a private joke of some kind or an allusive jibe at all that 'Kensington' is commonly thought to stand for—the decaying rentier, frayed respectability and the keeping up of outmoded conventions. (You remember me in Bina Gardens?)" TSE to Hayward, 9 Sept 1942: "I see your objection to KENSINGTON." (To Virginia Woolf, 31 Oct [1933]: "I have not done much more about lodgings; but my present intention is to look at a room in Kensington (a district which I dislike) . . . while I am looking about elsewhere.")

To Hayward, 3 Sept 1942: "How great is the resistance to 'quartets'? I am aware of general objections to these ~~usual~~ musical analogies: there was a period when people were writing long poems and calling them, with no excuse, 'symphonies' (J. Gould Fletcher even did a 'Symphony in Blue' I think, thus achieving a greater confusion des genres). But I should like to indicate that these poems are all in a particular set form which I have elaborated, and the word 'quartet' does seem to me to start people on the right tack for understanding them ('sonata' in any case is *too* musical). It suggests to me the notion of making a poem by weaving in together three or four superficially unrelated themes: the 'poem' being the degree of success in making a new whole out of them." (John Gould Fletcher's *The Blue Symphony* appeared in *Poetry* Sept 1914; George Gershwin's *Rhapsody in Blue* was first performed in 1924. Conrad Aiken's *The House of Dust*, 1920, was subtitled *A Symphony.* For John Addington Symonds's *In the Key of Blue*, see note to *Goldfish* I 13–15. On musical titles, see note to the title *Preludes*.)

Morley looked more favourably upon the use of "Kensington" than Hayward (Hayward to Morley, 8 Nov 1942, *Composition FQ* 26–27). On 7 Dec, however, TSE wrote to I. A. Richards: "I fear that 'Kensington' will have to go, as all the opinions taken have been adverse: but I can't think of anything better, and they may have to go out plainly as *Four Quartets*—rather a pity, as a name might have given the impression of unity which I should like to establish." Valerie Eliot, *TLS* 16 July 1971: "T. S. Eliot's wish to call his four poems 'Kensington Quartets' is not so surprising as Mr Carswell seems to think (July 2). *Burnt Norton* and *East Coker* were written in the Royal Borough, in Grenville Place and Emperor's Gate respectively, and contain local allusions—for example 'a place of disaffection' is Gloucester Road Underground Station. And in *Little Gidding* the line 'We trod the pavement . . .' is a reference to the surface of the Cromwell Road."

TSE to Montgomery Belgion, 9 Feb 1943: "Frank is publishing the four quartets in one volume in the spring." Although not as part of the title, TSE continued often to use the definite article: "the *Four Quartets*" (occasionally "the four *Quartets*"; also "my *Four Quartets*", "these *Four Quartets*").

7. MUSIC

To Pamela Murray, 4 Feb 1938: "What interests me is the dramatic, and I think that the chief interest in the best of my early poems is the sketching, however slightly, of character; you will observe a middle period (*Ash Wednesday*) in which there is no dramatic interest; and now I am chiefly interested in the theatre. But I am also interested (*Burnt Norton*) in possible approximations to musical form and musical effect."

"The use of recurrent themes is as natural to poetry as to music. There are possibilities for verse which bear some analogy to the development of a theme by different groups of instruments; there are possibilities of transitions in a poem comparable to the different movements of a symphony or a quartet; there are possibilities of contrapuntal arrangement of subject-matter", *The Music of Poetry* (1942); see Thomas R. Rees, *Journal of Aesthetics and Art Criticism* Autumn 1969.

To H. W. Heckstall-Smith, 25 Apr 1946: "There is no suggestion that my *Four Quartets* are intended for four voices or indeed for any voice except the author's, as most lyrical poetry is. As soon as the author has a different voice in mind than his own the poem becomes to that extent dramatic. I meant simply chamber music with distinct themes and movements."

In *English Letter Writers* (1933), TSE quotes D. H. Lawrence to Catherine Carswell, 11 Jan 1916: "the essence of poetry with us in this age of stark and unlovely actualities is a stark directness, without a shadow of a lie, or a shadow of deflection anywhere. Everything can go but this stark, bare, rocky directness of statement, this alone makes poetry, to-day". TSE comments: "This speaks to me of that at which I have long aimed, in writing poetry; to write poetry which should be essentially poetry, with nothing poetic about it, poetry standing naked in its bare bones, or poetry so transparent that we should not see the poetry, but that which we are meant to see through the poetry, poetry so transparent that in reading it we are intent on what the poem *points at*, and not on the poetry, this seems to me the thing to try for. To get *beyond poetry*, as Beethoven, in his later works, strove to get *beyond music.* We never succeed, perhaps, but Lawrence's words mean this to me, that they express to me what I think that the forty or fifty original lines that I have written strive towards." (To Ford Madox Ford, 14 Aug 1923: "There are *I* think about thirty *good* lines in *The Waste Land*, can you find them? The rest is ephemeral"; see note to [V] 331–58.)

When J. Shepherd enquired why the five-part poems were not "quintets", TSE's secretary replied, 24 Aug 1961: "the form had originally been suggested to him by musical quartets, which are so called because they are scored for four instruments ··· and he had particularly in mind the late quartets of Beethoven." When Brigid Brophy questioned what the four instruments were in each Quartet (*New Statesman* 23 Apr, 14 May 1965), Hugh Heckstall-Smith recalled writing to TSE in 1944 asking "what the four of his Quartets were four of, and he answered that it had nothing to do with anything except that 'quartet' suggested Chamber Music composed for close attention by a small audience who had a fair understanding of what they were listening to", *New Statesman* 21 May 1965.

Musical influences. "Those of us who love Beethoven find in his music something that we call its meaning, though we cannot confine it in words; but it is this meaning which fits it in, somehow, to our whole life; which makes it an emotional exercise and discipline, and not merely an appreciation of virtuosity", *Poetry and Propaganda* (1930). *Howarth* 286–89 suggests that TSE had read J. W. N. Sullivan's *Beethoven: His Spiritual Development* (1927). For TSE's acquaintance with Sullivan, see letter to Aldous Huxley, 8 Jan 1925. In 1927, however, TSE declined a request from the Beethoven Centennial committee that he write about the composer. To Frederick N. Sard, 15 Jan 1927: "Of course I am familiar as an ordinary listener with a great deal of his work, but I have no special knowledge of his chamber music or of his later work."

To Stephen Spender, 28 Mar 1931, on Beethoven's Op. 132: "I am delighted to hear that you have been at the late Beethoven—I have the A minor quartet on the gramophone, and find it quite inexhaustible to study. There is a sort of heavenly or at least more than human gaiety about some of his later things which one imagines might come to oneself as the fruit of reconciliation and relief after immense suffering; I should like to get something of that into verse once before I die" (*Spender* 128–29). Again, 30 May 1931: "I fear that you exaggerate the precision and detail of my knowledge of Beethoven: I am quite unconscious of any of the parallels you mention, and one or two of the works I do not know, or at least do not remember. I can claim nothing but a profound impression, mostly from the better known symphonies, sonatas and overtures, but dating certainly from an early time and my eldest sister was playing Beethoven incessantly before I was out of the cradle. But my theory of writing verse is that one gets a rhythm, and a movement first, and fills it in with some approximation to sense later." Spender referred to Sullivan's book in an essay on TSE in *The Destructive Element* (1935). His wife, the pianist Natasha Spender, played Beethoven to TSE in Aug 1942 and later recalled discussing the composer with him during the writing of *Four Quartets* (personal communication). TSE to Edwin Muir, 24 Feb 1943, of *Little Gidding*: "thank you very much for your kind and penetrating review in *The New Statesman*. You are quite right in supposing that the Beethoven late quartets were present in the background." See notes to the title *Coriolan* and to *East Coker* V 12 and 31.

Kenner 261 claims that the string quartets most in TSE's mind were Bartok's nos. 2–6. *Moody* 198 compares *Burnt Norton* to no. 4 and *Jones* 265 proposes no. 6. Of these, the most probable influence is no. 4, which is structured as a chiasmus, of the kind for which Bartok is famous. In the Philharmonia pocket score, Bartok wrote: "The slow movement forms the kernel of the work. The other movements are stratified around it · · · the first and fifth movements providing the external layer, and the second and fourth, the internal layer." ("In my beginning is my end · · · In my end is my beginning", *East Coker*.)

Memo from M. I. Drage of Faber to Basil Douglas of the Apollo Society, 3 Feb 1967: "Mrs. Eliot says she hesitates to declare that any particular quartet, either by Beethoven or Bartok, could be held a preeminent influence in the writing of the *Four Quartets* · · · Eliot was especially fond of Beethoven's 132nd [the A minor, Op. 132], but she would not like this one to be given any categoric position in his preferences" (Faber archive).

8. PUBLICATION

The announcement of *Collected Poems 1909–1935* in Faber's Autumn List 1936 calls it "The definitive edition to date, with a new long poem" (*Burnt Norton*). TSE to Paul Elmer More, 27 Mar 1936: "I am just sending you my volume of collected poems, which is due to appear next week. Having produced this book so close on the heels of the volume of essays makes me feel for the moment as if I had been preparing for a dignified retirement, or at least postponing further literary work until another janma." (*Essays Ancient and Modern* had been published less than a month before. Sanskrit *janma* = birth, state of existence, lifetime; see note to *The Dry Salvages* V 1–12.)

To Louis MacNeice, 19 July 1935: "It never seems to me desirable to date poems at this stage [first book publication]. It might be desirable later with a large collected edition, although even in that case I think it is better to date poems in blocks according to what the author recognises to be the important periods in his development, rather than individually."

The pamphlet of *East Coker* appeared in Sept 1940. *Burnt Norton* followed in a matching pamphlet in Feb 1941, Richard de la Mare having briefed the printers, 28 Nov 1940, that it was "the first of a series of four or five poems that Eliot is writing, of which *East Coker* is the second, and the others will also be published separately in pamphlet form" (Faber archive). (The colophon of the *Burnt Norton* pamphlet read "First published in February 1941", with later impressions interpolating "in this form".) *The Dry Salvages* pamphlet followed the first two in Sept 1941; Hayward's copy was acknowledged on 5 Sept (although inscribed "for John Hayward whose suggestions somewhat altered this poem T. S. Eliot 10.ix.41").

Little Gidding cost TSE the most effort. John Hayward wrote in his "Letter from London" published in Swedish in *Bonniers Litterara Magasin* in May 1942 that TSE "had hoped to complete by last autumn the poetic tetralogy of which only the first three sections—*Burnt Norton*, *East Coker* and *The Dry Salvages*—have been published. But the fourth and concluding poem—*Little Gidding*—has not progressed beyond a first draft. Fine as it seems to me to be, it has been laid aside until he feels that he can improve it." (Later, believing that *Bonniers Litterara Magasin* had published a Swedish translation of *Little Gidding* without his knowledge—it was in fact *The Dry Salvages*—TSE wrote to George Svenson, 17 Apr 1945, in protest: "I am not prepared to acknowledge Mr. Warburton's translation as authoritative ··· There must have been—at least there should have been—some places where he was not quite sure of what I meant: if I had been given the opportunity to explain any doubtful points, the translation would have been by so much the more faithful.")

Little Gidding was published in *NEW* 15 Oct 1942, and as a Faber pamphlet on 1 Dec 1942, the date inscribed in Hayward's copy. TSE to Hayward, 27 Nov 1942: "You shall have an advance copy next week: they are poorly bound" (in printed card covers, as opposed to the card with printed paper wrappers of the other three). To Alan Rook, 24 Sept 1943, declining his poem *Green Mountain*: "We simply cannot, especially in present times, undertake to publish single poems in this way ··· You may think that I am not myself in a very strong position to urge this consideration, but that is an exceptional privilege of mine and even for myself that would not have been possible for my firm to publish my poems in this way ten years ago."

Four Quartets was published in the USA on 11 May 1943 and in Britain in Oct 1944. TSE to Hayward, 17 May 1943: "I hope Frank [Morley] has sent you a copy of *Four*

Quartets. I haven't received any myself; but I understand from the London office of *Time* that the book is out." 21 May: "I gather that the first impression of *Four Quartets* was a mess, and that Frank has admitted to my brother (who always flings himself to the defense of my interests) that they would not have produced it but for having to preserve the copyright." Hayward acknowledged his copy of the US edition on 4 June 1943: "It is, to judge by my copy, the most wretchedly printed book produced by a firm with all the resources of modern typography I've seen. Even the amateur Hogarth *Waste Land* is hardly worse. The choice of type on the cover and for the text is deplorable. The inking is bad. The lay-out is contemptible—just look at the spacing of the textual paragraphs. The imposition is appalling."

Gallup: "There were two impressions of this book before publication. Only the first bears the words 'first American edition' on the verso of the title-leaf. In this first impression, the margins of many pages were incorrect because of faulty imposition of the formes as a result of the use of unskilled war-time labour. The entire impression would have been destroyed except that it was necessary to meet the announced publication date in order to preserve copyright, and consequently 788 copies for review and other purposes were distributed before the corrected impression was ready. On 5 May 1943, the 3377 copies then remaining of the first impression were destroyed and replaced by the second impression of 3500 copies. These do not carry the edition note on the verso of the title-leaf." Many subsequent impressions are identified by code designations within brackets on the verso of the title-leaf (Archie Henderson, personal communication).

US 1943 jacket material:

> These are four long poems, in a new form described by Mr. Eliot as 'quartets.' The first of the four poems is *Burnt Norton*, which was published as the concluding poem of Mr. Eliot's *Collected Poems, 1909–1935*. *Burnt Norton* heralded a sequence; in due course it was followed by *East Coker*, which was published in this country in *The Partisan Review* in 1940, and by *The Dry Salvages*, published in the same magazine in 1941. The sequence has now been completed by *Little Gidding*, a fourth poem of the same length and in the same form, which appears in this country for the first time in this volume. A distinct phase of Mr. Eliot's poetry, the product of the last seven years, is here presented.

To John Lehmann, 17 Aug 1944: "As for when my four Quartets will appear together, you, as a publisher, know as well as I do how undependable dates have become. The publication was originally fixed for last spring. Then it was altered to September 1st, and the date at the moment is ~~September 29th~~ Oct. 3!" Hayward to TSE, 18 June 1944, of the Faber edition: "I am very glad the Quartets are at last ready for publication ··· Thank you very much for the set of proofs which shall be treasured among ye Archives."

1944 jacket material:

> The four poems which make up this volume have all appeared separately: *Burnt Norton* first in 1936, *East Coker* in 1940, *The Dry Salvages* in 1941, and *Little Gidding* in 1942. The author, however, has always intended them to be published as one volume, and to be judged as a single work.

This was later changed (removing the implication that four poems had been planned from the start, and warning purchasers of TSE's *Collected Poems* that they were paying a second time for part of the contents), and from the 8th imp. (1950) to the 12th (1963) read:

> The four poems which make up this volume—*Burnt Norton*, *East Coker*, *The Dry Salvages* and *Little Gidding*—first appeared separately in this order. The first of them, *Burnt Norton*, was included by the author in his *Collected Poems, 1909–1935*. But it led to three successors, and the author wishes the four poems to be judged as a single work.

The words on the Faber contents page, "I wish to acknowledge my obligation to friends for their criticism, and particularly to Mr John Hayward for improvements of phrase and construction" had been slightly different in the American edition (see Textual History). In *The Cocktail Party* (1949), TSE acknowledged his indebtedness to E. Martin Browne "And to Mr. John Hayward, for continuous criticism and correction of vocabulary, idiom and manners." Hayward was also acknowledged in *The Confidential Clerk* (1954) and *The Elder Statesman* (1959). *Collected Poems 1909–1963* included no acknowledgements: for this and other instances, see headnote to *Prufrock and Other Observations*, 4. TITLE, DEDICATION AND EPIGRAPH TO THE VOLUME.

Valerie Eliot to Barbara Hardy, 30 June 1977: "My husband would often quote passages of Dickens to me from memory, especially when he was happy. You may be interested to know that his original epigraph for *Four Quartets* was 'What a rum thing Time is, ain't it, Neddy', but he was afraid it might be misunderstood" (*Pickwick Papers* ch. XLII; *Composition FQ* 28; the unadopted heading to Parts I and II of *The Waste Land*, "HE DO THE POLICE IN DIFFERENT VOICES", was from *Our Mutual Friend*). TSE to his Aunt Susie (Mrs. Hinkley), 28 Dec 1931: "I suppose you are all engrossed with Barbara junior's wedding. Barbara and Chardy bring home to me the 'flight of time'. As the Fleet gate keeper in *Pickwick* said:—'What a rum thing time is, ain't it, Neddy?'" TSE's "Pickwick Paper (Advanced)", sent to the Fabers and Hodgsons in Feb 1939, asked examinees to identify this Dickens quotation. ("flight of time", Virginia Woolf: "The flight of time which hurries us so tragically along", *Jacob's Room*, 1922, ch. XII.)

9. TSE ON *FOUR QUARTETS*

To Hayward, 12 June 1944, sending a proof of *Four Quartets*: "Going through them again, I am depressed by a certain imprecision of word and phrase, especially in *Burnt Norton*, but also in *East Coker*: my only solace is that I *do* think the writing improves toward the latter part of the book." *Lehmann* on TSE's reading *Four Quartets* at Bryn Mawr in Oct 1948: "According to him, they are by far the best thing he has written up to now. He read the third part, *The Dry Salvages*."

Henry Eliot to Henry B. Harvey, 10 Oct 1946: "Best evening we had was at Dublin [New Hampshire], when he read two of his Quartets to us, with some commentary. In re the title, asked him why Four Quartets; pointed out that a musical quartet has four voices, also four or perhaps three parts, whereas each of TSE's quartets has five parts. I mentioned having bought one of Beethoven's quartets on having read a review which attempted to draw parallels (not evident to me). Well, TSE said, there wasn't that much of a parallel. Asked whether in Dry Salvages the river was the individual (or his soul) and the sea the world (or universe) ··· he said, well, no, he hadn't thought of that. Asked whether the silent motto (E. Coker) referred to the Eliot motto Tace et Fac, said yes, he had thought of that. Rose garden (Burnt Norton, I), Alice in Wonderland" (Wilson Library, U. North Carolina).

To E. R. Curtius, 16 Feb 1946: "I am deeply shocked that my poem should have presented itself to you in that light. Whatever its merits or demerits, to me it seems to express much more of Christian hope than any of my previous work. I have had opinions from theologians both Anglican and Roman, and I am sure that to none of them, English or French, has it appeared to depict a 'Welt ohne Gott' [world without God]. Three criticisms have been made of the pertinence of which I am sensible: 1. that the second poem is excessively influenced by the negative way of St. John of the Cross; 2. in relation to the first, that I am too deeply influenced by Indian thought; 3. that I have grasped the Incarnation but not the Resurrection. But I must protest against your interpretation! I cannot but feel that there enters into it a good deal of your own vision at the present time. For that I can only condole in silence." 13 Mar: "I was not so surprised that you should have found my *Four Quartets* depressing as that you should have found them depressing in comparison to my earlier work. To me it seems that viewed in relation to my earlier poetry these four poems represent as a whole a considerable degree of progress in the direction you desire. I have always been very anxious to write only from the stage I had actually reached and not to fall into the temptation of writing from a more advanced stage of spiritual life than I had mastered. I also admit to a natural tendency to Jansenism which no doubt is partly individual temperament and partly the reflex of a strong element of Calvinism on both sides of my family in the seventeenth century, but it does seem to me that I have kept on moving, although perhaps at a very slow pace." For Jansenism and Calvinism, see headnote to *East Coker* 4. AFTER PUBLICATION.

To Anne Ridler, 15 Aug 1949, on her revision of *The Faber Book of Modern Verse* (1951) and Michael Roberts's wish, before his death, to drop *Ash-Wednesday* but add a Quartet: "I suppose I shall have to release single 'Quartets' eventually, and I should prefer to do it first in a volume of our own." To F. O. Matthiessen, 19 Aug 1949: "We are now willing to release for the first time one of the later quartets for the *Oxford Book of American Verse*. But I have personal and sentimental reasons for asking you to take *The Dry Salvages*. In the first place this is the only one of the Quartets in which the scenery is American, referring to the Mississippi and the New England coast. In the second place *Little Gidding* is particularly English, and if it appeared in any Oxford collection I would want it to be in the *Oxford Book of English Verse*. It is not only East Anglian in scenery but historical in content and is in fact essentially a patriotic war poem of 1942." *The Oxford Book of American Verse* included *The Dry Salvages*.

"If the last two *Quartets* seem obscure to some, then the obscurity there is inherent in the ideas expressed", *T. S. Eliot Answers Questions* (1949). "I see the later *Quartets* as being much simpler and easier to understand than *The Waste Land* and *Ash-Wednesday*. Sometimes the thing I'm trying to say, the subject matter, may be difficult, but it seems to me that I'm saying it in a simpler way", *Paris Review* (1959). "I cannot explain the *Four Quartets*. Any attempt on my part to explain would merely be saying something else. One can say that *Little Gidding* is a patriotic poem—it was written during the dark days of 1942—but that is only one aspect of it. It was after writing the first two that I saw the pattern required four in all. I associated them with the four elements: air, earth, water and fire, in that order", *Grantite Review* (1962). In his copy of Charles M. Bakewell's *Source Book in Ancient Philosophy* (1907), TSE had scored: "For with earth we perceive earth, with water, water, with air, the air divine, and with fire, the devouring fire, and love we perceive by means of love, hate by means of dismal hate" (46).

Smidt 34: "Eliot told me in 1948 that it was during the writing of *East Coker* that the whole sequence began to emerge, with the symbolism of the four seasons and the four elements. *Burnt Norton* then had to stand for spring in the sequence, though its imagery was perhaps more summery."

Hayward's notes for Leyris's French translation (1950) began by recommending Helen Gardner's *The Art of T. S. Eliot*, "but more helpful and suggestive than any critical study is the background of knowledge provided by the poet's own earlier writings, in prose as well as verse. Only with this knowledge can the evolution of much of the meaning of the *Four Quartets* be properly understood ··· In a letter to an American student Mr. Eliot states that the four poems 'gradually began to assume, perhaps only for convenience, a relationship to the four seasons and the four elements'. This relationship is merely implied and should not be stressed. Viz. *Burnt Norton*: air; early summer. *East Coker*: earth; late summer. *The Dry Salvages*: water; autumn. *Little Gidding*: fire; winter."

Translations. To Paul Flamand, 29 Jan 1946: "in the course of the last few years, translations of all of these *Four Quartets* have appeared separately in one or another French review, all by different translators mainly of mediocre quality and none of them under my supervision." To Jean Mambrino, 25 Nov 1946: "As for the *Four Quartets*, I must admit that I am not really satisfied with any of the translations which I have so far seen in magazines, though that done by Madame Bosco and Monsieur Gide is certainly the best." To E. R. Curtius, 30 June 1947: "it seems to me that if poetry is to be translated at all it should appear in several translations and not be restricted to the interpretation of one translator". To the Public Orator of Oxford University, Thomas Higham, 27 June 1948, after receiving an honorary D.Litt: "I have been able to appreciate the virtuosity, and relish the wit, of your words in reading them at leisure: and I can only say that I would gladly confide to you the authority, which you would less gladly accept, to translate—or restore—the whole of my works into Latin. I am convinced that I should be better served, than I have been by some of my translators into other tongues."

Copies of the French translations of *East Coker* by Roger Montandon (*Lettres* 31 May 1944) and of *Little Gidding* by André Gide and Madeleine Bosco (*Aguedal* Dec 1943) and then by Pierre Leyris (*Dieu Vivant* 13, 1949) are at King's with annotations by TSE. The more important of his comments are recorded below. The pages of the Leyris have not been cut open, so TSE did not read the entire translation in this copy. On 24 Oct 1949, however, he wrote to Leyris's publisher to secure Hayward a £30 fee for his work on it, offering if necessary to reduce his own royalties.

In Sept 1947, HMV issued TSE's recording of *Four Quartets* with, as a Leaflet, an Author's Note. This had been submitted to Evelyn Donald of the British Council on 10 Apr, and had been slightly revised. It was subsequently printed on the record sleeve.

> A recording of a poem read by its author is no more definitive an "interpretation" than a recording of a symphony conducted by the composer. The [*draft*: A] poem, if it is of any depth and complexity, will have meanings in it concealed from the author, and should be capable of being read in many ways, and with a variety of emotional emphases.

A good poem, indeed, is one which even [*draft*: the most inexpert reading cannot wholly ruin, and which even] the most accomplished reading cannot exhaust.

What the recording of a poem by its author can and should preserve, is the way that poem sounded to the author when he had finished it. The disposition of lines on the page, and the punctuation (which includes the *absence* of punctuation marks, when they are omitted where the reader would expect them) can never give an exact notation of the author's metric. The chief value of the author's record, then, is as a guide to the rhythms.

Another reader, reciting the poem, need not feel bound to reproduce these rhythms; but, if he has studied the author's version, he can assure himself that he is departing from it deliberately, and not from ignorance.

Four Quartets: Commentary

Burnt Norton

1. The House and TSE's Visit   2. Genesis

Published within *1936*. No independent reprint was envisaged until the success of the Faber pamphlet of *East Coker* prompted a similar pamphlet of *Burnt Norton*, 20 Feb 1941 (five impressions to 1943). No separate US publication. Within *Four Quartets* in *US 1943*, *1944+*.

1. THE HOUSE AND TSE'S VISIT

Hayward: "The poem takes its title from the chateau Burnt Norton, near Campden in Gloucestershire, the property of Viscount Sandon, elder son of the Earl of Harrowby. The chateau was uninhabited when the poet visited it as a stranger in the summer of 1934 during a holiday in Campden."

Overlooking the Vale of Evesham, a mile north-west of Chipping Campden in Gloucestershire, Norton House was enhanced in the 18th century with extensive gardens by Sir William Keyt, but in Sept 1741, after a week of drinking, he set fire to the house and immolated himself. The ruins were pulled down in 1789, and the 17th-century farmhouse, subsequently expanded, became known as Burnt Norton. The estate was acquired by the Earls of Harrowby, and in 1902 the 5th Earl extended the rose-garden and constructed a swimming pool and a semi-circular amphitheatre. TSE to Raymond Preston, 9 Aug 1945: "I know nothing of the history of the house and what you tell me about Sir William Keyt is news to me. I daresay that I found some obscure attraction in the name, but otherwise I am afraid this house was only a point of departure for my poem. Indeed I suspect that anyone visiting the house with my poem in mind might find the house and gardens disappointingly commonplace." To Hermann Peschmann, 12 Sept 1945: "You are quite correct in identifying the manor house Burnt Norton, and no doubt when you saw the house you were disappointed. The poetry—if any—is in the poem and not in the house. It is a perfectly third-rate manor house built on the site of an older one which had been destroyed by fire. I merely happened upon it one day when it was unoccupied; I think there was someone living in the lodge but I wandered through the grounds quite freely and it provided the suggestion for a deserted house."

During his year in the US, 1932–33, TSE had met Dr. John Carroll Perkins, Minister of the Unitarian Chapel in Boston, and his wife, the aunt of TSE's friend Emily Hale. In 1934—and for the next two summers—the Perkinses rented a house in Chipping Campden in the Cotswolds, where Emily Hale stayed with them. Soon after their arrival TSE was invited for the weekend. TSE to Mrs. Perkins, 30 July 1934: "I should like to formulate, if not express, my appreciation of a delightful weekend". He visited again a month or so later, writing with renewed thanks on 4 Sept. Although none of his letters of 1934 is known to mention Burnt Norton, it is likely that he and Emily came upon it in late August or early September.

Jeanette McPherrin, a friend of Emily Hale's, later wrote to Judy Sahak, Librarian of Scripps College, 6 July 1980, that her own letters contained "no revelations about the relationship between Mr. Eliot and Miss Hale ··· which modern readers would find unbelievably 'proper' in the Victorian sense." For TSE's visit to the Perkinses, 26–29 Sept 1935, see headnote to *A Valedictory Forbidding Mourning*.

In *The Recent Poetry of T. S. Eliot* (in *New Writing and Daylight*, ed. John Lehmann, 1942), Helen Gardner gave a history of the house. On 2 Dec 1942, TSE wrote to her: "I have no such connection as you suggest with the house at Burnt Norton. It would not be worth while mentioning this except that it seemed to me to make a difference to the feeling that it should be merely a deserted house and garden wandered into without knowing anything whatsoever about the history of the house or who had lived in it. I am afraid, however, reading your comments, that anyone who visited the place would be disappointed by the mediocrity of both house and garden" (*Composition FQ* 37).

2. GENESIS

"For instance, the first of my *Quartets* is *Burnt Norton*: the inspiration for that was certain lines which were cut out of the beginning of *Murder in the Cathedral.* The lines are not identically reproduced, but essentially they are the same ··· the producer pointed out to me that the lines were strictly irrelevant to the action and didn't get things forward. Well, those lines led to *Burnt Norton*", *A Conversation, recorded in 1958, between T. S. Eliot and Leslie Paul* ([1964/]1965). *Composition FQ* 39: "The opening ··· was originally written as a comment by the Second Priest after the exit of the Second Tempter. The second of Thomas's temptations is the temptation to attempt to retrace one's steps, to try to go back to the moment when a choice was made and make a different choice." The lines were cut before the first performance:

> Time present and time past
> Are both perhaps present in the future.
> Time future is contained in time past.
> If all time is eternally present
> All time is unredeemable.
> What might have been is a conjecture
> Remaining a permanent possibility
> Only in a world of speculation.
> What might have been and what has been
> Point to one end, which is always present.
> Footfalls echo in the memory
> Down the passage which we did not take
> Into the rose-garden.
> (Published in *Composition FQ* 82, omitting lines 4–5, 9–10)

For the context of a poem as opposed to a play, see Chad Schrock, *EinC* Jan 2014. TSE: "I was not writing verse of the same kind as my own lyric poems: but it struck me that I was using a verse which would serve my purpose for this one play and subject, and for no other", *The Aims of Poetic Drama* (Nov 1949).

Grover Smith 1996 94–98 discusses the possible influence on Part I of Frederic H. W. Myers's *Human Personality and Its Survival of Bodily Death* (1903, notably the sentence "In dealing with Time Past we have memory and written record, in dealing with Time Future we have forethought, drawing inferences from the past"); as also

An Adventure by Anne Moberly and Eleanor Jourdain (1911, re-issued by Faber 1931) and *An Experiment with Time* by J. W. Dunne (1927, re-issued by Faber 1934). TSE to R. L. Mégroz, 26 Oct 1927, after the first appearance of Dunne's book: "In view of a recent book on the subject, which has aroused a good deal of interest, I suggest that if you could get together an anthology of anticipation dreams it would go particularly well. I have never had any such myself, but I think that they are not uncommon."

In the year of the Faber re-issue of *An Experiment with Time*, Ethelbert in *The Rock* (15–16) referred to its theory of serialism: "There's some new notion about time, what says that the past— what's be'ind you—is what's goin' to 'appen in the future, bein' as the future 'as already 'appened. I 'aven't 'ad time to get the 'ang of it yet; but when I read about all those old blokes they seems much like us." *Burnt Norton* was composed the following year. TSE to Bonamy Dobrée, 7 Feb 1934: "Thats rather odd your Saying you may be in London from the 18th to the 17th it sounds to me like an Experiment with time nevertheless huzza."

In a letter to Hayward, 5 Aug 1941, TSE acknowledged three literary sources for *Burnt Norton*: his own *Landscapes* I. *New Hampshire*, Elizabeth Barrett Browning's *The Lost Bower* (see note to *Little Gidding* II 67–96, *first venture in verse* [22]) and Kipling's *"They"* (see note to *Burnt Norton* I 30–38). Kipling's story (in *Traffics and Discoveries*, 1904) tells of an unplanned visit to a secluded garden, a child's "laugh among the yew-peacocks", "the silver of a fountain behind a hedge thrown up against the sun", "the utterly happy chuckle of a child absorbed in some light mischief", and a "broad stone path where the fountain-basin lay like one star-sapphire".

N. Parkinson (*N&Q* Jan 1955) was the first of several commentators to invoke Frances Hodgson Burnett's story *The Secret Garden*: "The ivy hung thick over the door, the key was buried under the shrubs, no human being had passed that portal for ten lonely years—and yet inside the garden there were sounds. They were the sounds of running, scuffling feet seeming to chase round and round under the trees, they were strange sounds of lowered, suppressed voices—exclamations and smothered, joyous cries. It seemed actually like the laughter of young things, the uncontrollable laughter of children who were trying not to be heard, but who in a moment or two—as their excitement mounted—would burst forth · · · Was he losing his reason and thinking he heard things which were not for human ears?", final chapter, "In the Garden". Parkinson quotes *Burnt Norton* I 11–14, I 40–41 and V 35–36 (see note below); *East Coker* III 31–33, *The Family Reunion* (see note to *Burnt Norton* I 13–46) and *The Confidential Clerk* II.

Epigraphs] The two Greek quotations originally appeared on the part-title page, when *Burnt Norton* was published within *1936*, but were omitted from all five impressions of *Burnt Norton* as a separate pamphlet (1941–43). See Textual History. They appeared opposite the opening of *Burnt Norton* in *1944*, but before the newly introduced section title page, as epigraphs to the whole book, in *1979*. **Diels:** Hermann Diels's Greek and German edition of the Fragments of the Pre-Socratic philosophers was published in Berlin, 1903–10, and regularly reprinted. TSE to Bonamy Dobrée, 11 Apr 1927: "I have sent for the translation of Diehl's book · · · I attended Diehl's lectures years ago, and have read a couple of his books. Do you know his *Manual*? It has a lot of interesting illustrations." **Herakleitos:** *Hayward*: "The epigraphs from Heraclitus may be translated as follows: 1. 'Although the Word (Logos) is common to all, most men live as though they had each a private wisdom of his own'. 2. 'The way up and the way down are one and the same'." Philip Wheelwright: "'The way up' meant to Heraclitus, outwardly, the qualitative movement from rock and earth through the intermediate stages of mud, water, cloud, air, and aether, to the rarest and uttermost of all states, which is fire; 'the way down' meant the contrary movement. Both the movements are in process all the time in all things that exist, hence they are said to be 'the same'. Existence thus involves unceasing tension between upward and downward pulls—toward the realm of rarity, warmth, light and toward the realm of density, cold, dark. The pull is not only observed in physical phenomena, it operates too in our souls", *Rajan ed.* 100. In his copy of Charles M. Bakewell's *Source Book in Ancient Philosophy*, TSE underlined and marked the translation "The way up and the way down is one and the same." His student notes of 1911–12 include scholars' opinions of Heraclitus gleaned from G. T. W. Patrick's *Heraclitus of Ephesus* (1889) (*Jain* 198). He quoted Heraclitus in Greek again in *Gordon Craig's Socratic Dialogues* (1955). To E. M. Stephenson, 8 Oct 1945, of the first epigraph:

> Diels' *Fragmente der Vorsokratiker* is, I believe, still considered the standard text of the pre-Socratic philosophers; at any rate it was when I was a student of these matters. His text is accompanied by a German translation ··· "Aber obschon das Wort allen gemein ist, leben die meisten doch so, als ob sie eine eigene Einsicht haetten."
>
> I should say that Herakleitos meant a great deal more than simply "the word is in common use". I think he meant rather that the reason, the Logos, or the rational understanding of the nature of things is common or available to all men. Most people live as if they had a peculiar and individual insight. No one translation, however, can be considered as anything more than a limited interpretation since the meanings of key words in Greek philosophy can never be completely rendered in a modern language. That is the reason for my putting the Greek text instead of an English translation of it.

TSE underlined the Greek and put a pencil mark against the German in his copy of Diels (vol 1, 77). For Heraclitus and Villon, see headnote to *Mr. Apollinax.*

To Henry Eliot, 28 Apr 1936: "I think that there is something to be said for your suspicion of epigraphs: that is, I am aware that they may appear to be there for the wrong reason. The purpose is to give a clue to the tone and mood of the poem, rather than to the literal meaning. The word LOGOS was important in this way, suggesting the current of Greek thought uniting with the Gospels, coming down to the hermits of the Thebaid, to St. John of the Cross, and to an item of individual experience in the world to-day. But the immediate effect on most readers is very likely wrong." To Raymond Preston, 9 Aug 1945: "I should not wish to pin myself down to any particular interpretation of a phrase from Herakleitos. The value of such an epigraph is partly due to the ambiguity and the variety of possible interpretations. The fragments of Herakleitos as we know them have extraordinarily poetic suggestiveness and I have sometimes wondered whether his essays would not lose in value if we had his complete works and saw the sentences in their context." To Hermann Peschmann, 12 Sept 1945: "As for the quotations of Heraclitus, the reason for presenting them in the original Greek is that it preserves their delightful obscurity. Any translation must be a personal interpretation and I had no wish to interpret. But the meaning is something as follows: the word Logos is almost untranslateable.

It may mean reason or explanation or it may mean word in the sense which was developed for the first chapter of St. John. 'Logos being common to all men was universal' or 'Although the Logos is common the majority of men live as if they had an individual understanding'. This is a very rough translation and not good enough to use, and people can differ indefinitely as to what it means. The translation of the second fragment is perfectly straight-forward: 'the way up and the way down are the same', but as to what Heraclitus meant by it, that is a very different matter."

To Hans Paeschke, 6 Feb 1947, about a typescript essay by Hans Egon Holthusen: "there are many · · · valuable points · · · for instance, the distinction between the connotation of the word *time* in English and the word *zeit* in German. While Dr. Holthusen is right in mentioning the philosophers as well as Heracleitos it is obvious that there is much more influence of the latter than of the former, and the reconciliation, identification, or however one chooses to phrase it and the temporal and the timeless probably spring much more from Indian philosophy, insofar as it is not Christian, such as the commentary of Patanjali." (Perhaps referring to Pada III, Sutra 52: "Two moments cannot occur together; for no order is possible for any two things occurring simultaneously. Order is the sequence of the following moment from the preceding one. Therefore the present is the only moment, there being none either past or future; and as such there is no collective term for it (as *Time*). The future and the past moments (those that are popularly so called) are to be explained as referring to the different modifications", *The Yoga-Darsana: The Sutras of Patanjali*, tr. Ganganatha Jha [Bombay, 1907], the text used by James Haughton Woods at Harvard.)

To Dr. Nicola Coppola, 28 Jan 1960: "I was certainly in my youth very much influenced by Herakleitos, and I think that this influence has been a permanent one. The quotations at the beginning of *Burnt Norton* are a tribute to my debt to this great philosopher."

I

I 1–2] Ecclesiastes 3: 15: "That which hath been is now; and that which is to be hath already been; and God requireth that which is past." Augustine: "in the Eternal nothing passeth, but the whole is present; whereas no time is all at once present: and that all time past, is driven on by time to come, and all to come followeth upon the past; and all past and to come · · · flows out of that which is ever present"; "if times past and to come be, I would know where they be · · · time past · · · is not: but now when I recall its image · · · I behold it in the present, because it is still in my memory", *Confessions* bk. XI 11, 18 (TSE: "memory", I 11). Bradley: "In morality the past is real because it is present in the will; and conversely, what is not present in the will is only past", *Ethical Studies* Essay I; "If there is not, present in this passing 'now', a Reality which contains all 'nows' future and past, the whole of our truth and knowledge must be limited to the 'now' that we perceive", *Essays on Truth and Reality* 332. William James: "The past, the present, and the future in perception, for example, are absent from one another, while in imagination they are present or absent as the case may be. If the time-content of the world be not one monistic block of being, if some part, at least, of the future, is added to the past without being virtually one therewith ··· then it is absent really as well as phenomenally and may be called an absolute novelty", *Some Problems of Philosophy* ch. VIII. TSE: "Past, present and future are one, which abstraction decomposes", *Notes in French on Bergson's Lectures* (1910–11) (tr., *Marx* 29). Among his notes in the front of his copy of Hegel's *Lectures on the Philosophy of History*, TSE wrote: "Time?", "Is there any present connection between ourselves and the past?", "The past exists to us as present", "Can we argue about anything but the present?" and "Have we *anything* but the present?"

To his mother, 30 Dec 1917, on a photograph album: "It gives one a strange feeling that Time is not before and after, but all at once, present and future and all the periods of the past, an album like this" (see *East Coker* V 28). "the historical sense involves a perception, not only of the pastness of the past, but of its presence ··· Whoever has approved this idea of order ··· will not find it preposterous that the past should be altered by the present as much as the present is directed by the past", *Tradition and the Individual Talent* I (1919). "the present consists of a great deal of the past and a little of the future", *A Preface to Modern Literature* (1923). "as the age is not an instant, but an indefinite span of time including part of both past and future, we can still, with our retrospective selves, appreciate such acting as that of Bernhardt", *Dramatis Personæ* (1923).

In Henry James's *The Sense of the Past* bk. II, Pendrel has been bequeathed an old house, and dreams of "Recovering the lost ··· to that extent was he not, by his deepening penetration, contemporaneous and present? 'Present' was a word used by him in a sense of his own and meaning as regards most things about him markedly absent." TSE to W. K. Lowther Clarke, 16 Mar 1934: "I have always been an admirer to James, and particularly of *The Sense of the Past.*" See notes to I 13 and to *Little Gidding* II 42 and II 47. "I am the old house | With the noxious smell and the sorrow before morning, | In which all past is present", *The Family Reunion* I i.

I 1 **Time present:** *The Cloud of Unknowing* ch. 4: "time is precious: for God, that is the giver of time, giveth never two times together, but each one after other" (scored in TSE's copy). Lancelot Andrewes: "when all is done, we shall have somewhat to do, to bring this to a *Nunc*, to a *time present* ··· *Now*, is the only sure part of our *time*. That which is *past*, is come and gone. That which is *to come*, may peradventure never come", Ash-Wednesday Sermon 1619. TSE: "reason counsels us to avoid surrendering ourselves either to a present which is already past or to a future which is unknown", *Education in a Christian Society* (1940).

I 4–8 **all time ··· Only in a world of speculation:** "that which is purely in time cannot be said to exist at all", *Knowledge and Experience* 110.

I 5 **All time is unredeemable:** Ephesians 5: 15–16: "See then that ye walk circumspectly, not as fools, but as wise, redeeming the time, because the days are evil." TSE: "Redeem | The time", *Ash-Wednesday* IV 18–19. "not redeemed from time", *Little Gidding* V 21. "all past is present, all degradation | Is unredeemable. As for what happens— | Of the past you can only see what is past, | Not what is always present", *The Family Reunion* I i (*Bush* 188). See note to *The Waste Land* [V] 402–404.

I 6, 34 **abstraction ··· dry concrete:** "The confused distinction which exists in most heads between 'abstract' and 'concrete' is due not so much to a manifest fact of the existence of two types of mind, an abstract and a concrete, as to the existence of another type of mind, the verbal, or philosophic", *The Perfect Critic* II (1920) (*Ricks* 257).

I 7–8 **Remaining a · · · possibility | Only in a world of speculation:** for I. A. Richards, "he has realised what might otherwise have remained largely a speculative possibility", see headnote to *The Waste Land*, 9. AFTER PUBLICATION. For "speculation", see note to *The Dry Salvages* II 39–40.

I 8, 11, 12, 14, 17 **world of speculation · · · echo · · · Down · · · echo · · · I do not know · · · echoes:** Tennyson: "Echo · · · down? who knows? for a vast speculation had failed · · · worldling", *Maud* I [i] 4, 9, 11.

I 11, 14–15 **echo in the memory · · · My words echo | Thus, in your mind:** Lionel Johnson's *Dead* has "something in it, a tone, a few lines and phrases, which re-echo in the mind for a lifetime", *A Personal Anthology* (1947). See headnote to *Five-Finger Exercises* II. *Lines to a Yorkshire Terrier.* On Andrewes, Donne and Jeremy Taylor: "Their words linger and echo in the mind", *John Bramhall* (1927).

I 11, 16 **echo in the memory · · · rose-leaves:** Shelley: "Music, when soft voices die, | Vibrates in the memory · · · Rose leaves, when the rose is dead", *To* ——, quoted in *Swinburne* (1920).

I 12–14 **Down the passage which we did not take | Towards the door we never opened | Into the rose-garden:** a childhood friend recalled the position of the Eliots' house beside a girls' school: "They lived on Locust Street, adjoining the building then occupied by the Mary Institute · · · Beside the school building there was a big yard, grass-grown, with a number of trees. From this yard a door opened into the school gymnasium and the Eliots had a key. Tom and I usually played in this yard and in the gymnasium", Thomas McKittrick to Harford Powel, 19 June 1953 (see note to I 28–29).

Alice's Adventures in Wonderland ch. I: "Alice opened the door and found that it led into a small passage · · · she knelt down and looked along the passage into the loveliest garden you ever saw. How she longed to get out of that dark hall, and wander about among those beds of bright flowers and those cool fountains, but she could not even get her head through the doorway." Louis L. Martz: "Mr Eliot has remarked in conversation upon the importance of *Alice in Wonderland* here", *Unger ed.* Conrad: "One closes behind one the little gate of mere boyishness—and enters an enchanted garden. Its very shades glow with promise. Every turn of the path has its seduction · · · One goes on. And the time, too, goes on, till one perceives ahead a shadow-line warning one that the region of early youth, too, must be left behind. This is the period of life in which such moments of which I have spoken are likely to come. What moments? Why the moments of boredom, of weariness, of dissatisfaction", *The Shadow-Line* I (*Unger 1956* 237–38). TSE: "Children singing in the orchard", *Ode* ("Tired. | Subterrene") 12. Frost: *The Road Not Taken* (Donald Sommerville, personal communication).

I 13 **Towards:** pronounced *t'ords* in TSE's recording of 1946–47. **the door we never opened:** Henry James: "if life was · · · but a chain of open doors through which endless connections danced there was yet no knowledge in the world on which one should wish a door closed", *The Sense of the Past* bk. II. James's notes, published with the unfinished novel in 1917: "on opening the door of the house with his latchkey he let himself into the Past".

I 13–19 **the door we never opened ··· Quick, said the bird:** MacNeice: "And we wait in vain, expecting a door that never opens, | But have you heard the mocking-bird, the mocking-bird, the mocking-bird?" *Adam's Legacy* in *Blind Fireworks* (1929).

I 13–46 **the door we never opened ··· Other echoes | Inhabit the garden ··· the first gate ··· dead leaves ··· vibrant air, | And the bird called ··· dry concrete ··· What might have been and what has been | Point to one end:** *The Family Reunion* II ii:

AGATHA I only looked through the little door
When the sun was shining on the rose-garden:
And heard in the distance tiny voices
And then a black raven flew over.
And then I was only my own feet walking
Away, down a concrete corridor
In a dead air ···
HARRY ··· I was not there, you were not there, only our phantasms
And what did not happen is as true as what did happen
O my dear, and you walked through the little door
And I ran to meet you in the rose-garden.
AGATHA This is the next moment. This is the beginning.
We do not pass twice through the same door
Or return to the door through which we did not pass.

I 16 **Disturbing the dust on a bowl of rose-leaves:** Austin Dobson: "I plunge my hand among the leaves: | (An alien touch but dust perceives, | Nought else supposes;) ··· memory of the vanished days | When they were roses", *Pot-Pourri* 1–6 (see note to *Portrait of a Lady* II 4–5). TSE: "And dusty roses, crickets, sunlight on the sea", *Goldfish* III 7. Ferris Greenslet on Pater: "almost the sole luxury he allowed himself was a bowl of rose-leaves, preserved by an old lady in the country from a special receipt, and sent every year as a present to him, as a reminder of her friendship", *Walter Pater* (1903) 30. TSE to Greenslet, 13 Jan 1932: "When I had to leave Germany rather hurriedly in 1914 one of the books ··· I had to leave behind ··· was your essay on Walter Pater." TSE's *Arnold and Pater* (1930) may have been prompted by Greenslet's comparison of the two Victorians (69–72). To Pierre Geffroy, 14 June 1944, on his translation of *Burnt Norton*: "I had forgotten, I admit, that the English usage of the word *potpourri* was so completely different from the French. I suppose then that a bowl of dried rose leaves is a particularly English institution for which there is no French word. It would be rather a wider dish I think than is indicated by the word *coupe* but you must exercise liberty in that respect in order to preserve the rhythm of your line." OED "pot-pourri" 2: "A mixture of dried petals of different flowers mixed with spices, kept in a jar for its perfume." Fr. medley.

I 19 **Quick, said the bird:** *Stevenson* 80 reports TSE as explaining, 24 Nov 1943, that this represents "the quick movement of birds to be instantly on the spot and as quickly gone." TSE: "O quick quick quick, quick hear the song-sparrow", *Landscapes* V. *Cape Ann* 1 (see note to I 42, below).

I 21–22 **our first world ··· our first world:** J. E. Adamson's *The Individual and the Environment* (1921) proposed a division into "the physical world ··· the first world", "the second world, the social fabric", and "the third world, the moral order". Vaughan: "Happy those early days! ··· Before I understood this place | Appointed for my second race ··· my first love", *The Retreat* 1–8. Quoting

Vaughan's opening, TSE wrote: "I think it is a reference to some particular experience or experiences at some early period; just as I think that very different work, the *New Life* of Dante, also refers to a particular experience of childhood", *Mystic and Politician as Poet* (1930) (*Bush* 189).

I 22 **deception of the thrush**: among the thrushes are mocking birds: "When tamed, he mocks every sound he hears, with equal exactness, and it is often very amusing to witness the effect of this deception", J. L. Comstock, *Natural History of Birds* (1850). "But sound of water over a rock | Where the hermit-thrush sings in the pine trees | Drip drop drip drop drop drop drop | But there is no water", *The Waste Land* [V] 355–58.

I 22–27 **thrush ··· music hidden in the shrubbery**: Whitman: "in secluded recesses, | A shy and hidden bird is warbling ··· Solitary the thrush, | The hermit withdrawn to himself ··· Sings by himself a song", *When Lilacs Last in the Dooryard Bloom'd* 18–22 (*Musgrove* 67).

I 24–26, 40 **over the dead leaves | In the autumn heat ··· the bird called ··· for the leaves were full of children**: Kipling: "the wood was so full of noises of summer (though the birds had mated) that I could not at first distinguish these from the tread of small curious feet stealing across the dead leaves", *"They"*. See note to I 30–38.

I 27 **unheard music**: Keats: "Heard melodies are sweet, but those unheard | Are sweeter", *Ode on a Grecian Urn* 11–12. **music hidden**: "in the early plays of Shakespeare there are only occasional hints of what I may call the *hidden music*, the under and overtones", *The Development of Shakespeare's Verse* (1937).

I 28 **unseen eyebeam crossed**: Donne: "Our eye-beames twisted, and did thred | Our eyes, upon one double string", *The Extasie* 7–8 (*Grover Smith* 256). TSE: "as for the threading of the eyes like buttons on a double thread, one thread proceeding from each eye to the other, it not only fails to render the sense of losing oneself in an ecstacy of gazing into the eyes of a loved person, it actually aggravates the difficulty of finding out what it is all about", *The Varieties of Metaphysical Poetry* 109–10 (Clark Lecture III).

I 28–29 **the unseen eyebeam ··· the look of flowers that are looked at**: alongside these lines in *VE's 1951*, Valerie Eliot wrote Mallarmé's "Rien, ni les vieux jardins reflétés par les yeux | Ne retiendra ce cœur" [Nothing—not old gardens reflected in the eyes—will keep back this heart], *Brise Marine* [*Sea Breeze*], attributing the comparison to F. R. Leavis. D. H. Lawrence: "the very flowers, in the shops or parks | are being deflowered by being looked at by so many unclean eyes", *Shows* in *Last Poems* (1933). TSE: "in the awareness of the observing eye", *WLComposite* 339. A childhood memory: "Once I entered the school yard before the last girls had left. When I looked in a school window and saw a girl looking out at me, I fled out of there in a hurry", TSE to Mary Institute, St. Louis, 11 Nov 1959, quoted in *St. Louis Post-Dispatch* 12 Nov 1959 (Walter J. Ong, *American Literature* Jan 1962).

I 30–38 **There they were ··· and they ··· The surface glittered out of heart of light, | And they were behind us**: to his French translator Claude Vigée, 1 Feb 1946: "*They.* They has no expressed antecedent. It is used almost as if it was a substantive. You may recall that there is a short story by Kipling called *They* and my use of the word here will present less difficulty to readers who know that story. *They* are undefined wraiths or presences of persons of former times who had known the garden and for whom it was sufficiently associated with their emotions to have left impressions of them upon it. I think that *scintillait* is nearer to the image in my mind. I agree that this is a very difficult line to translate." (*Scintiller*: to sparkle, glitter.) For the story, see *Burnt Norton* headnote, 2. GENESIS. **accepted and accepting ··· pattern ··· sunlight**: "the kind of pattern which we perceive in our own lives only at rare moments of inattention and detachment, drowsing in sunlight", *John Marston* (1934) (*Moody* 164). See note to V 32–33, and for "retire into a sunlit stupor" see note to *Portrait of a Lady* I 1–14. **accepted and accepting**: Lancelot Andrewes: "Let us then make this so accepted a time in itself twice acceptable by our accepting, which, He will acceptably take at our hands", Christmas Sermon 1610, quoted in *Lancelot Andrewes* (1926) (*Matthiessen* 194).

I 36 **the lotos rose**: OED "lotus" (also "lotos") 3a: "The water-lily of Egypt and Asia" (*Nymphæa lotus*). H. Bourne: "Some species ··· expand the flower about sunrise in the morning, while floating on the surface of the water, and close it at an early hour in the afternoon ··· consecrated by the Egyptians to *Isis* and *Osiris*, or the Sun and Moon", *Flores Poetici* (1833) 122–23. Sir William Jones: "on the placid waters blooming ··· An opening lotos rose", *To Bhavani* 11–13.

Often confused with the lotos of Homer's *Odyssey* IX and Tennyson's *The Lotos-Eaters* (OED 1: "The plant yielding the fruit which was the food of the Lotophagi ··· producing in those who ate it a state of dreamy forgetfulness", with first citation from Sir Thomas Elyot). Bourne: "supposed to have been the Sugar-Cane ··· because those were said ··· to lose relish for every thing else, who had once tasted of the Lotus." **quietly, quietly**: Browning: "Quietly, quietly the evening through", *Andrea del Sarto* 17 (*Blamires* 14).

I 37 **glittered out of heart of light**: *Paradiso* XII 28: "del cor dell'una delle luci nuove" [from out of the heart of one of the new lights] (*Hayward*). Henry James: "out of the heart of which a light flashed", *The Wings of the Dove* bk. IV II (Christopher Ohge, personal communication). **heart of light**: Conrad (title): *Heart of Darkness*; the story was the source of the first epigraph to *The Hollow Men*.

I 37, 39 **heart of light ··· Then a cloud passed**: "Light of light || Gone", *Burnt Norton variant after the closing lines of* V (see Textual History).

I 37, 40, 42–43 **heart of light ··· children ··· human kind | Cannot bear very much reality**: "We are tired children ··· and can endure only a little light", *Choruses from "The Rock"* X *ms draft* [42–44]. "Pascal's disillusioned analysis of human bondage is sometimes interpreted to mean that Pascal was ··· incapable of enduring reality", *The "Pensées" of Pascal* (1931). "Looking into the heart of light, the silence", *The Waste Land* [I] 41 (see note). **human kind | Cannot bear very much reality**: *Murder in the Cathedral* II, THOMAS: "Human kind cannot bear very much reality" (*Hayward*). "the spectacle of the *whole* of human stupidity ··· is more than any human mind can endure", *Views and Reviews* in *NEW* 6 June 1935. **human kind | Cannot**: "The insupportable shirt of flame | Which human kind cannot remove", *Little Gidding* IV 8–14, *2nd draft* [5] *variant.*

I 40 **Go ··· children**: alongside this line quoted in *G. Jones* (130), TSE wrote "Engraving 'Cache-cache' on my mother's mantelpiece". (Fr., hide and seek.)

I 42 **Go, go, go:** "Twit twit twit | Jug jug jug jug jug jug", "Drip drop drip drop drop drop drop", "Co co rico co co rico", *The Waste Land* [III] 205–06, [V] 358, 392; "Quick quick quick quick", "Sweet sweet sweet", *Landscapes* V. *Cape Ann* 1, 10 (see note to *Cape Ann* V 1 for Allingham: "Be quick! be quick! Here, here, here!")

II

II 1–2 **Garlic and sapphires in the mud | Clot the bedded axle-tree:** alongside these lines, Valerie Eliot wrote in *VE's 1951*: "omitted from *Words for an Old Man*". These two lines formed the ending in the first drafts of that poem (which became *Lines for an Old Man*), "Garlic" having initially read "Thunder" (see Textual History). TSE told Raymond Preston that he had in mind Mallarmé's "Tonnerre et rubis aux moyeux" [Thunder and rubies at the axles], from the sonnet *M'introduire dans ton histoire* [*To introduce myself into your story*] (*Preston* 16). In his second Turnbull Lecture he returned to this sonnet:

> It is a mistake to suppose that a simile or a metaphor is always something meant to be *visible* to the imagination; and even when it is meant to be visible, that all its parts are meant to be visible at once. Examine a sonnet by a modern poet ··· and you will find in the fourteen lines four or five images which it is quite impossible to imagine or conceive simultaneously, and at least one which cannot be visualized at all:
>
> Dis si je ne suis pas joyeux
> Tonnerre et rubis aux moyeux
> De voir en l'air que ce feu troue
>
> Avec des royaumes épars
> Comme mourir pourpre la roue
> Du seul vespéral de mes chars.
>
> "Thunder and rubies up to the wheel hub" is just as difficult to figure out as the career of Crashaw's tear; and it is only when you have an impression of the sonnet as a whole that it comes into place, and has meaning. The poet's business is to know what effect he intends to produce, and then to get it by fair means or foul. There is the element of rationality, the element of precision, and there is also the element of vagueness which may be used; and we must remember that one distinction between poetry and prose is this, that in poetry the word, each word by itself, though only being fully itself in context, has absolute value. Poetry is *incantation*, as well as imagery. "Thunder and rubies" cannot be seen, heard or thought together, but their collocation here brings out the connotation of each word.
>
> *The Varieties of Metaphysical Poetry* 271–72

[Mallarmé: Say if I am not glad, thunder and rubies at the axles, to see, in the air pierced by this fire, with scattered kingdoms, as if dying in purple the wheel of the only vesperal one among my chariots]. TSE: "Roses and bitumen, gift of song, thunder and fluting in the rooms", *Anabasis* preliminary *Song* iii. Perse: "*Bitumen et roses, don du chant! Tonnerre et flûtes dans les chambres!*" ("fluting in the room" might be heard or seen, but Fr. "*flûte*" does not have the architectural sense).

In Proust's *À la recherche du temps perdu: Albertine Disparue* (1925), the narrator's farewell letter to Albertine quotes Mallarmé's sestet "which you said you could not understand" (*Composition FQ* 80); in Scott Moncrieff's translation of Proust it remained in French (XI 54). TSE on Mallarmé: "he called attention to the fact that the actual writing of poetry, the accidence and syntax, is a very difficult part of the problem. Mallarmé gets his modernity, his sincerity, simply by close attention to the actual writing", *Modern Tendencies in Poetry* (1920). TSE to Philip Mairet, 31 Oct 1956: "'Garlic and Sapphires in the mud' is an echo of a line in a sonnet by Mallarmé ··· with probable recollection also of Charles Péguy's description of the Battle of Waterloo." Péguy: "Alors la bataille a commencé trop tard. Des fondrières, quoi ··· Alors il y avait de la boue, de la boue ordinaire, de la boue comme il y en a tous les jours, jusqu'aux essieux" [So, the battle began too late. Pot-holes, eh? ··· So there was mud, ordinary mud, mud as there always is, up to the axles], *À nos amis, à nos abonnés* [*To Our Friends, To Our Subscribers* (tr. eds)]. (For this passage see note to *A Cooking Egg* 25, 29.) TSE described Péguy as "one of the most illustrious of the dead who have fallen in this war", *Charles Péguy* (1916). See Jean Verdenal's letter to TSE of mid-July 1911 in *Letters 1* and note to the dedication of *Prufrock and Other Observations*. In his notes for the translation of *Four Quartets* by Pierre Leyris, Hayward pointed also to Mallarmé's "bavant boue et rubis" [slobbering mud and rubies] from *Le Tombeau de Charles Baudelaire*. TSE to Pound, 2 Apr 1936: "you do hide your gems in about as much muck of disorderly mss. as Possible and a neat ms. is better than rubies". (Rubies and sapphires are often found together, embedded in sediments, at the same sites.) **sapphires in the mud:** TSE on Donne's prose: "There is no question of ··· digging jewels out of mud", *Prose and Verse* (1921). **in the mud | Clot the bedded axle-tree:** Edgar Lee Masters: "sons amid the rolling thunder | Of cannon stand in trenches where the dead | Clog the ensanguined ice", *O Glorious France* (1916). Masters' "rolling thunder" as well as Mallarmé's "Tonnerre" contributed not only to the earlier form of the lines, "Thunder and sapphires", but to the astrological reprise at the start of part II of *East Coker* (see notes there to II 7–17 and II 8–9, and *McCue 2014a*). Wilfred Owen: "much blood had clogged their chariot-wheels", *Strange Meeting* 34 (wr. 1918, pub. 1919). TSE to Emily Hale, 6 Oct 1930, on Owen: "he belonged to no group, and his interesting technical innovations are all his own, though he may have known the work of Gerard Hopkins." Again: "there is one poem of his at least, *Strange Meeting*, which is of permanent value and, I think, will never be forgotten, and which is not only one of the most moving pieces of verse inspired by the war of 1914–18, but also a technical achievement of great originality", *A Tribute to Wilfred Owen* (1964). **mud | Clot:** OED ("blood" VI) has "blood-clot" from 1859.

II 1 *variant*, 2, 15 **Thunder ··· axle-tree ··· reconciled:** Chapman's Bussy speaks in successive speeches of "The burning axletree ··· thunder" (see note to *Burbank with a Baedeker: Bleistein with a Cigar* 7–12) and "be reconciled | With all forgiveness", *Bussy d'Ambois* V i (Mermaid ed., commonly V iii).

II 1, 3 **sapphires in the mud ··· blood:** Lovelace: "Flowing both through soul and blood ··· 'Tis a diamond in mud", *To Lucasta: Ode Lyric* 18–20.

II 2–3, 12 **Clot ··· trilling wire in the blood | Sings below inveterate scars ··· the sodden floor:** the entertainer Harry Lauder was said to have raised funds for 12,000 Great War troops. An advertisement for his book *A Minstrel in France* was illustrated with "German barb-wire with a bit of Scotch tartan held fast in deadly prongs". The text told how he "sang to the soldiers ··· in the mud and blood soggy trenches", *The Rotarian* May 1918. **trilling wire in the blood | Sings:** *Knickerbocker* Nov 1852: "trilling wires of a telegraph". Poe: "The trembling living wire", *Israfel* 21–22. TSE: "the fever sings in mental wires", *East Coker* IV 17. For TSE in 1930 to Laurence Binyon on "'Flame' within 'my veins'" as a violent "collocation of the metaphor and of the physiology", see headnote to *Little Gidding*, 3. DANTE. **inveterate scars ··· wars:** "after the last war ··· inveterate sin", *Reunion by Destruction* (1943) 7. *The Rotarian* July 1918: "French war veterans ··· to be our guests ··· so that these battle-scarred veterans might be made to feel at home". **inveterate:** pronounced *inveterert* in TSE's recording of 1946–47.

II 3–5, 12–13 **blood ··· inveterate scars ··· wars ··· And hear upon the sodden floor | Below, the boarhound and the boar:** Chapman: "One drop of his most precious blood ··· Descending to that noisome sink, | Where every hour hell's horrid Boar | Lies plunged, and drown'd ··· Raze, Lord, my sins' inveterate scars ··· see my will's sharp wars", *Petrarch's Seven Penitential Psalms* II iii–v (John Shand, *Nineteenth Century* Sept 1944). **the sodden floor:** Ford Madox Ford: "that clutter of sodden corses | On the sodden Belgian grass— | That is a strange new beauty", *Antwerp* III 13–15; TSE of this poem, published in *The New Poetry: An Anthology* ed. Harriet Monroe (1917): "Mr. Hueffer [Ford] is well illustrated by the only good poem I have met with on the subject of the war", *Reflections on Contemporary Poetry* III (1917).

II 5 **Appeasing long forgotten wars:** OED "appease" 1: "To bring to peace, pacify, quiet, or settle". Frazer: "to perpetuate the memory or to appease the ghosts of large numbers of men who had perished on the field of battle", *The Golden Bough* IV 95 (Mark Thompson, personal communication). OED "appeasement" 4: "Freely used in political contexts in the 20th century." Often with the sense of soothing or assuaging. Churchill: "I counsel prudence and appeasement" (1920). *The Times*: "The policy of international appeasement must of course be pressed forward ··· With the policy of appeasement must go the policy of preparation—preparation not so much for war as against war" (1938). However, OED continues: "since 1938 often used disparagingly with allusion to the attempts at conciliation by concession ··· before the outbreak of war with Germany in 1939." TSE to his mother, 2 Oct 1919: "It is obviously a bad peace, in which the major European powers tried to ··· appease or ingratiate as far as possible the various puppet nationalities". Reginald Snell, reviewing *Four Quartets*: "the only significant alteration from the pamphlet form of the poems ··· is the appearance of the word 'appeasing' instead of 'reconciling,' in connection with 'forgotten wars'—a risky change, considering the emotional overtones to which the newer word now gives rise", *NEW* 14 Dec 1944. (The change avoided the repetition "reconciling ··· reconciled", II 5, 15.) TSE: "He is quite correct, and correct also in suggesting that one of the changes was of doubtful value", *NEW* 25 Jan 1945. No further change was made. **appeasing ··· forgotten:** TSE "distasteful as a story of suffering which is past, as an inventory of grief which cannot now be appeased, and therefore might as well be forgotten", *The Dark Side of the Moon* (1946), Preface. The book, which was anonymous, is "a history of the relations between Poland and the U.S.S.R. from 1939 to 1945".

II 5, 8 **forgotten wars ··· stars:** Wordsworth: "Wreck of forgotten wars ··· stars", Sonnet *Composed among the Ruins of a Castle in North Wales* (Shawn Worthington, personal communication).

II 6 **The dance along the artery:** Sir John Davies: "those blew vaines ··· Observe a daunce" and "Love daunceth in your pulses and your vaines", *Orchestra* st. 52, 106 (*Schmidt 2007*). See note on the dancing in *East Coker* I 25–45.

II 6, 8 **dance ··· stars:** *Inside the gloom* initially imagined Ursa Major as "The dancing bear" (13 *variant*).

II 7 **The circulation of the lymph:** Rimbaud: "La circulation des sèves inouïes" [The circulation of unheard-of saps], *Le Bateau ivre* 39 [*The Drunken Boat*] (Iman Javadi, personal communication). For Rimbaud's poem, see note to *Mr. Apollinax* 10–12. **lymph:** OED 2: "*Bot.* A colourless fluid in plants; the sap." *Obs.*, citing Cowper: "That moved | The pure and subtle lymph | Through th' imperceptible meand'ring veins | Of leaf and flow'r", *The Task* VI 136. OED 3: "*Phys.* A colourless alkaline fluid, derived from various tissues and organs of the body, resembling blood but containing no red corpuscles."

II 8 **drift of stars:** fig. 10 of Richard A. Proctor's *Other Worlds than Ours* (NY, 1870; often repr.) illustrates the "Drift of the Stars in the Constellations Cancer and Gemini". TSE: "death and the raven drift above", *Sweeney Among the Nightingales* 7. "It is not essential that the allegory or the almost unintelligible astronomy should be understood—only that its presence should be justified", *Dante* (1920).

II 8–15 **stars ··· above ··· the figured leaf ··· floor | Below ··· stars:** Clough: "the figured ceiling overhead, | With cunning diagrams bestarred", *Uranus* 10–11. **figured leaf:** *In Memoriam* XLIII: "that still garden of the souls | In many a figured leaf enrolls | The total world since life began" (*Musgrove* 89).

II 9–13 **tree ··· tree ··· boarhound:** see note to "the boarhound slain between the yew trees", *Animula* 36.

II 13–15 **boarhound and the boar ··· among the stars:** see note to *WLComposite* 519, "Hyades". "The Hunter with his dogs pursues his circuit", *Choruses from "The Rock"* I 2.

II 16 **At the still point of the turning world:** Aristotle: "all animals move by pushing and pulling, and accordingly there must be in them a fixed point, like the centre in a circle, and from this the motion must begin", *De Anima* III ch. 10 (*Kenner* 254). See note to V 27–28.

II 16–21 **At the still point of the turning world ··· Except for the point, the still point, | There would be no dance, and there is only the dance:** *Hayward*: "The image was suggested to the poet by the description of the dance of the Tarot figures in the novel, *The Greater Trumps*, by Charles Williams (1932). It is, incidentally, the aim of all magic to find the still centre or point of equilibrium." Williams: "imagine that everything which exists takes part in the movement of a great dance—everything, the electrons ··· everything that changes, and there is nothing anywhere that does not change. That change—that's what we know of the immortal dance", ch. 7. TSE told Helen Gardner too that Williams was the source of the image (*Composition FQ* 85). TSE wrote the jacket copy for Faber's "standard edition" of Williams's novels (1954). **movement ···**

fixity ··· movement: "in a healthy society there must be an element of fixity *and* an element of mobility", *Education in a Christian Society* (1940). See note to *Ash-Wednesday* I 39. **there the dance is ··· There would be no dance, and there is only the dance:** "So with walking or running: our purpose is to get to a destination. The only value of our movement has been to achieve some end that we have set ourselves. But the purpose of the dance is the dance itself. Similarly with poetry: the poem is for its own sake", TSE's Introduction to *The Art of Poetry* by Paul Valéry (1958). A great dancer "is a being who exists only during the performances ··· a personality, a vital flame which appears from nowhere, disappears into nothing and is complete and sufficient in its appearance ··· a being which exists only in and for the work of art which is the ballet", *Four Elizabethan Dramatists* (1924).

II 28 ***Erhebung***: the Higher (Ger.); Hegelian terminology. See the synonym—elevation—"Emporheben", used of mountaineering, *Mélange Adultère de Tout* 11.

II 28–30 **concentration | Without elimination, both a new world | And the old made explicit:** "interesting oneself in new subjects in the outside world ··· to gain concentration", to George Barker, 24 Jan 1938 (see headnote to *Four Quartets*, 4. "NOT MERELY MORE OF THE SAME").

II 31–32 **ecstasy ··· horror:** "the intensity of the vision of its own ecstasies or horrors", *Cyril Tourneur* (1930).

II 35 **Protects mankind from heaven and damnation:** to Geoffrey Curtis, 14 Feb 1936: "don't imagine that the 'fear of Hell' is not capital in my theology. It is only balanced by that 'fear of Heaven' so well expressed in one of Newman's Oxford sermons." (Newman: "If then a man without religion (supposing it possible) were admitted into heaven, doubtless he would sustain a great disappointment ··· Nay, I will venture to say more than this;—it is fearful, but it is right to say it;—that if we wished to imagine a punishment for an unholy, reprobate soul, we perhaps could not fancy a greater than to *summon it to heaven*. Heaven would be hell to an irreligious man ··· And so heaven itself would be fire to those, who would fain escape across the great gulf from the torments of hell", *Parochial and Plain Sermons*, 1834, I.)

II 41 **smokefall:** OED, "after NIGHTFALL *rare*". TSE as sole citation, glossed with Helen Gardner's "the moment when the wind drops and smoke that had ascended descends".

III

III 1–37] *Hayward*: "The setting of this section is the London Tube." *Kenner* 256–57: "its locale, Eliot noted, sharing a private joke with his brother in Massachusetts, is specifically the Gloucester Road Station", near TSE's home in Emperor's Gate. *Composition FQ* 86: "Eliot travelled daily from Gloucester Road Station, whose two means of descent, by the stairs or by the lift, suggested to him the movement down and the 'abstention from movement' [III 35], while being carried down." The staircase is a spiral. As well as the Piccadilly Line, which TSE took to Russell Square, Gloucester Road station is on what was informally known as the Inner Circle (since 1949, the Circle Line).

III 3 **in a dim light:** "the crowd in Hell who peered at him and his guide under a dim light", *Dante* (1929) I. Milton: "Casting a dim religious light", *Il Penseroso* 160. (*The Rock* II, MRS. POULTRIDGE: "What is that lovely line of Keats, *dim religious light*? Or is it George Herbert?")

III 10 **plenitude:** pronounced *pleenitude* in TSE's recording of 1946–47, despite the OED's short *e.*

III 10–12, 14 **a flicker | Over the strained time-ridden faces | Distracted from distraction by distraction · · · no concentration:** "It is not true that the craving which has possessed most peoples at most times, for seeing human actions represented with mime and voice, is simply a craving for amusement and distraction. I think that the cinema comes nearer to pure distraction, to 'taking our minds off . . .' the things they ought to be on as well as the things they need at times to be taken off from", *Religious Drama: Mediaeval and Modern* (1937). "We tire of distraction or concentration · · · We thank Thee", *Choruses from "The Rock"* X 38. "that perpetual distraction from God", *The Church's Message* (1937); see note to III 13–21. **time-ridden · · · Distracted from distraction by distraction:** "time · · · Time can only distract", *The Dry Salvages* III 5–7 *msA* [5].

III 12, 13 **Distracted from · · · empty of meaning:** "Distracted from · · · but not with human meaning", *The Burnt Dancer* 6, 28. "Distraction · · · of the mind", *Ash-Wednesday* III 19 and note.

III 12, 14, 31–32 **Distracted · · · no concentration · · · fancy · · · spirit:** for Donne on being distracted from prayer, see note to V 13–22.

III 13 **Filled with fancies:** Johnson's Dictionary: "FANTASIED *adj.* Filled with fancies or wild imaginations."

III 15 **Men and bits of paper, whirled by the cold wind:** against this line quoted by *G. Jones*, TSE wrote: "tube-station of course, as the train approaches. Cf. W. Lewis: 'the cold tube wind'" (perhaps pointing to *The Enemy of the Stars*: "A gust, such as is met in the corridors of the tube, makes their clothes shiver or flap", *Blast* 1 60).

III 17 **of unwholesome lungs:** John Bascom: "God gives a pure atmosphere to the inhalation of the most unwholesome lungs", *A Philosophy of Religion* (1876). TSE to H. W. Heckstall-Smith, 7 Oct 1947: "it is not always possible to give a cogent reason for the use of what may be literally not the right word. A more curious case than 'refracted' is the phrase 'unwholesome lungs' in *Burnt Norton*. I knew at the time that I should obviously have written unhealthy, but that seemed to me to have undescribable associations which the uncorrect 'unwholesome' escaped. I think that unhealthy seemed to limit the associations too closely to mere physical health." (For "unwholesome", see note to *East Coker* V 26–31. For "refracted", see note to *East Coker* I 21.)

III 19 **Eructation:** pronounced *ear-uctation* in TSE's recording of 1946–47.

III 21–23 **hills of London, | Hampstead · · · Ludgate:** Blake, *Jerusalem* ch. 4, pl. 84 1–5:

> "Highgate's heights & Hampstead's, to Poplar, Hackney & Bow,
> "To Islington & Paddington & the Brook of Albion's River.
> "We builded Jerusalem as a City & a Temple; from Lambeth
> "We began our Foundations, lovely Lambeth. O lovely Hills
> "Of Camberwell"

III 22–23 **Hampstead ··· Ludgate:** "7 hills", noted by Hayward in his copy of *1944* (suggesting comparison with Rome). **Campden:** not the London borough of Camden (created 1965, named after Camden Town), but Campden Hill in Kensington. To Edith Sitwell, 8 July 1935: "I have to go to an event of the same kind on Campden Hill."

III 23–24 **Highgate ··· twittering:** "Francis Bacon, Earl of Verulam and Viscount St. Albans, whose life twittered out at Highgate in 1626", *The Genesis of Philosophic Prose* (1929). **Not here | Not here the darkness, in this twittering world:** "Not here, O Ademantus, but in another world", *WLComposite* 348. **the darkness, in this twittering world:** *Hayward*: "Cf. the description of the twittering ghosts in Hades. Homer, *Odyssey* XXIV 5–9". George Musgrave tr. (1865), XXIV 10–16: "as when in the inmost cavernous depths | Of some mysterious cave the flitting bats | Twitter in air ··· The shades of the defunct ··· With murmurs shrill but voiceless." Hayward to TSE, 14 Oct 1941: "civil-service typists ··· keeping up an incessant aimless twitter". TSE to Hayward, 20 Feb 1943: "that strange gathering of twittering ghosts and goblins on Saturday night". Edgar Lee Masters: "To twitter amid cold winds and falling leaves!" *Thomas Trevelyan* in *Spoon River Anthology* (TSE: "cold wind", III 15).

III 25–26 **Descend lower, descend only | Into the world of perpetual solitude:** *Inf.* IV 13: "'Or discendiam quaggiù nel cieco mondo'" ["Now let us descend into the blind world here below"] (*Servotte and Grene*).

III 25–32 **Descend lower ··· Internal darkness, deprivation | And destitution ··· Desiccation of the world of sense, | Evacuation of the world of fancy, | Inoperancy of the world of spirit:** St. John of the Cross: "God here purges the soul according to the substance of its sense and spirit, and according to the interior and exterior faculties, the soul must needs be in all its parts reduced to a state of emptiness, poverty and abandonment and must be left dry and empty and in darkness", *Dark Night of the Soul* II VI 4. TSE: "the only poetry that I can think of which belongs to quite the same class as Herbert—as expression of purity and intensity of religious feeling, and, as I am told by those who can appreciate Spanish literature more accurately than I, for literary excellence—is St. John of the Cross. Although, of course, both in their racial and in their personal temperaments the two men are very different", *Mr. T. S. Eliot on "George Herbert"* (1938). To Paul Elmer More, 17 Feb 1932: "perhaps the best subject for discussion which we could begin when you come over here in the spring is St. John of the Cross. I really feel that you are over-bold in your criticism of one who is crowned with so much authority." For St. John of the Cross, see notes to the second epigraph to *Sweeney Agonistes* and to *Ash-Wednesday* I 1–3, 5.

III 27 **that which:** five times within *Four Quartets*; characteristically philosophical, occurring in TSE's *Oxford notes on Aristotle* (1914–15).

III 30 **Desiccation of the world of sense:** Bertrand Russell: *The World of Physics and the World of Sense*, lecture IV of *Our Knowledge of the External World* (1914). TSE: "I have lost my sight, smell, hearing, taste and touch", *Gerontion* 59. "First, the cold friction of expiring sense", *Little Gidding* II 78.

III 32 **Inoperancy of the world of spirit:** "The spreading potency of the unclean; the inoperancy of the holy are sorrowfully acknowledged by Haggai", *Report on the 46th Annual Meeting of the Church Congress* (1906) 399 (Archie Henderson, personal communication). **Inoperancy:** not in first ed. of OED but later added with this line as sole citation.

III 33–34 **This is the one way, and the other | Is the same:** Herakleitos: "*ὁδὸς ἄνω κάτω μία καὶ ὡυτή*" [The way up and the way down are one and the same]; the second epigraph at the head of *Burnt Norton*. St. John of the Cross: "For, upon this road, to go down is to go up, and to go up to go down, for he that humbles himself is exalted and he that exalts himself is humbled", *Dark Night of the Soul* II xviii 2 (*Preston* 20).

III 36 **appetency, on its metalled ways:** "an adumbration of the universe of material atoms regulated by laws of motion ··· there is quite naturally no place in Hobbes's universe for the human will ··· mechanistic psychology. There is a modern theory, closely akin ··· I cite ··· one of the most acute of younger psychologists: 'Anything is valuable which will satisfy an appetency without involving the frustration of some equal or more important appetency'", *John Bramhall* (1927), quoting I. A. Richards, *Principles of Literary Criticism* (1926) ch. VII. (TSE's secretary returned Richards's *Practical Criticism* and *Principles of Literary Criticism* to the London Library in Oct 1933.) **appetency:** OED: 1: "*strictly*, The state of longing for, desiring, craving; appetite, passion"; 2: "Instinctive inclination or propensity." 3: "Of things inanimate: Natural tendency, affinity." 4: "*Metaph.* Suggested term including both desire and volition, as distinguished from cognition and feeling." Stressed on the first syllable. Corresponding to Aristotle's *ὄρεξις* (*Grover Smith* 260), and frequent in the translation of *De Anima* by R. D. Hicks (1907), where it is contrasted with intelligence and used twenty times in III ch. 10.

IV

IV 1–2 **Time and the bell have buried the day, | The black cloud carries the sun away:** adapting the proverbial "Bell, To bear (*or* carry away) = to be first", *Oxford Dictionary of English Proverbs*. Mark Reinsberg adduced "The bailey beareth the bell away" from an anonymous lyric (*American Literature* Nov 1949), but when Genesius Jones cited this, TSE underlined "based on a fifteenth- or sixteenth-century lyric" and wrote "?" (*G. Jones* 131). Richard Barnfield: "you have lost your light; | The Sunne and Moone, beare witnesse of my mone: | The cleere is turnd to clouds; the day to night ··· When *Bounty* liv'd, I bore the Bell away", *The Complaint of Poetrie, for the Death of Liberalitie* st. I–II. For Barnfield, see note to *The Waste Land* [II] 98–104.

IV 3–5 **Will the sunflower turn to us, will the clematis | Stray down, bend to us; tendril and spray | Clutch and cling:** Tennyson, *The Window* 21–27:

> Vine, vine and eglantine,
> Clasp her window, trail and twine!
> Rose, rose and clematis,
> Trail and twine and clasp and kiss,
> Kiss, kiss; and make her a bower
> All of flowers, and drop me a flower,
> Drop me a flower.

(TSE to I. A. Richards, 23 July 1936: "I am extremely happy to have your commendation of *Burnt Norton*. You are quite right about Tennyson. I had to reread Tennyson in the autumn in order to do a preface to a Nelson cheap edition, and I expanded this into an essay included in *Essays Ancient and Modern*.") TSE: "there the clematis droops over the lintel", *Coriolan* II. *Difficulties of a Statesman* 35. "clings ··· and clutch", *Whispers of Immortality* 7, 11.

IV 3, 7, 8 **clematis ··· yew ··· kingfisher's wing**: alongside IV 8–9 quoted in *G. Jones*, TSE wrote "On the Trent, near Kelham" (headquarters of the Society of the Sacred Mission). *Composition FQ* 38: "on a hot day in the summer of 1935 when Eliot was staying at Kelham he saw a kingfisher on a stream running into the Trent by Averham Church ··· there is a yew in the churchyard there and masses of clematis in the rectory garden."

IV 8–9 **After the kingfisher's wing | Has answered light to light**: *Paradiso* XII 23–24: "sì del cantare e sì del fiammeggiarsi | luce con luce gaudiose e blande" [alike of song and flashing light with light, gladsome and benign] (*Preston* 21). *Bush* 204–205 compares, from the previous year, "O Greater Light, we praise Thee for the less ··· our little light" (*Choruses from "The Rock"* X 19, 42), where a distinction is made by capitalisation (as *Ash-Wednesday* V distinguishes "the word" from "the Word"). Tennyson: "The splendour falls ··· The long light shakes across the lakes ··· echoes flying ··· answer, echoes ··· answer, echoes ··· answer, echoes, answer", *The Princess* III^V (TSE's *Lines to a Duck in the Park* begins "The long light shakes across the lake").

IV 9–10 **answered light to light, and is silent, the light is still | At the still point of the turning world**: Valéry: "et lui rendent lumière pour lumière, et silence pour silence, se donnant et se recevant sans rien emprunter à la matière du monde" [and returned to it light for light and silence for silence, giving and receiving without borrowing anything from the material world], *Eupalinos ou l'Architecte* (1921) (Stephen Romer, personal communication). TSE: "And the light shone in darkness and | Against the Word the unstilled world still whirled | About the centre of the silent Word", *Ash-Wednesday* V 7–9.

V

V 4–7 **Only by the form, the pattern, | Can words or music reach | The stillness, as a Chinese jar still | Moves perpetually in its stillness**: to Sherrie Waites, 10 Aug 1962: "I did not have Keats' *Ode* [*on a Grecian Urn*] in mind. What I attempted to convey about the Chinese jar occurred to me some years ago when there was a Chinese exhibition, I think at the Royal Academy." (Many of the three thousand exhibits at the *International Exhibition of Chinese Art*, 1935–36, were vases and jars.) In the first act of *The Confidential Clerk*, Sir Claude explains his passion for "form and colour" embodied in "china or porcelain", and his longing for "a world where the form is the reality, | Of which the substantial is only a shadow". Colby replies: "All the time you've been speaking, I've been translating | Into terms of music." Pater in "The School of Giorgione": "All art constantly aspires towards the condition of music", *Studies in the History of the Renaissance* (1873). TSE: "'All the arts *approach* the condition of music.' Yes! but not by being less themselves", *The Borderline of Prose* (1917). "This peculiar range of sensibility can be expressed by dramatic poetry, at its moments of greatest intensity. At such moments, we touch the border of those feelings which only music can express", *Poetry and Drama* (1951). "Music itself may be conceived as striving towards an unattainable timelessness; and if the other arts may be thought of as yearning for duration, so Music may be thought of as yearning for the stillness of painting or sculpture", TSE's Introduction to *The Art of Poetry* by Paul Valéry (1958). For "that intensity at which language strives to become silence", see note to *East Coker* I 13.

V 13–16 **Words · · · Decay with imprecision:** "Out of the slimy mud of words, out of the sleet and hail of verbal imprecisions, | Approximate thoughts and feelings", *Choruses from "The Rock"* IX 22–23 (*Hayward*). "the general mess of imprecision of feeling", *East Coker* V 10. "When the language degenerates, the capacity of the people for thinking, feeling, and adapting itself to new conditions also degenerates", *The Writer as Artist* (1940).

V 1–22 **Words · · · chattering · · · The Word · · · Is most attacked by voices · · · the disconsolate chimera:** Donne, on distractions from prayer: "Sometimes I finde that I had forgot what I was about, but when I began to forget it, I cannot tell. A memory of yesterdays pleasures, a feare of to morrows dangers, a straw under my knee, a noise in mine eare, a light in mine eye, an any thing, a nothing, a fancy, a Chimera in my braine, troubles me in my prayer. So certainely is there nothing, nothing in spirituall things, perfect in this world", Sermon Preached at the funerals of Sir William Cokayne, 12 Dec 1626 (*Sermons* ed. Logan Pearsall Smith, 4). Quoting this in *Lancelot Andrewes* (1926), TSE commends the editor for juxtaposing it with the extract that Pearsall Smith calls "I am Not all Here"; see note to *East Coker* I 49–50. F. P. Harton: "The imagination is constantly at work presenting to the mind thoughts of all kinds · · · It is impossible to prevent wrong suggestions of the imagination, but it is possible to reject them · · · interest in the things of God implies constant rejection of all imaginings which are contrary or dangerous to them, which is mortification, and such mortification must not be confined to the imagination, but extend also to the intellect · · · God asks not only for acute, but also, and chiefly, for consecrated thinking", *The Elements of the Spiritual Life* (1932) 177; in his copy (Magdalene), TSE scored the whole paragraph, as also another on the "dangers of prayers recited out of books" (311). For Krishna's "He whose mind does not wander, and who is engaged in constant meditation", see note to *The Dry Salvages* III 33–44.

V 17–19 **Shrieking voices · · · in the desert:** "shrieking forms in a circular desert", *The Family Reunion* II ii (*Preston* 22).

V 19–20 **The Word in the desert · · · voices of temptation:** Matthew 4: 1–3: "Then was Jesus led up of the Spirit into the wilderness to be tempted of the devil". *Hayward*: "John 1 and Flaubert, *La Tentation de Sainte Antoine*", ch. 7. (John 1: 1, 23: "In the beginning was the Word · · · the voice of one crying in the wilderness".) **The Word in the desert:** "Phrases such as · · · 'the word within a word, unable to speak a word', do not desert us", *Lancelot Andrewes* (1926); see note to *Gerontion* 18, 20.

V 19, 22 **The Word in the desert · · · chimera:** Irving Babbitt on "the quest of the absolute" in Republican France (quoting Edmond Scherer): "It has concentrated upon a chimera all the powers of idealism that formerly found expression in religion. 'Our generation is pursuing a mirage vainer than that of the desert'", *The Masters of Modern French Criticism* (1912) 205. Babbitt's next paragraph twice has "chimeras". **disconsolate chimera:** *Lemprière* "Chimæra":

"a celebrated monster ··· which had three heads, that of a lion, a goat, and a dragon ··· Bellerophon, mounted on the horse Pegasus, overcame it". And "Pirene": "Pirene was so disconsolate at the death of her son Cenchrius ··· that she pined away, and was dissolved by her continual weeping into a fountain of the same name ··· the horse Pegasus was then drinking some of its waters, when Bellerophon took it to go and conquer the Chimæra." OED 3b: "An unreal creature of the imagination ··· an unfounded conception. (The ordinary modern use.)" *Knowledge and Experience* 128–29 discusses the meaning in this sense of a "real chimera". **disconsolate:** St. John of the Cross: "Strive always to prefer, not that which is easiest, but that which is most difficult ··· Not that which is a consolation, but rather that which is disconsolateness", *Ascent of Mount Carmel* I XIII 5–6 (see note to *Ash-Wednesday* I 1–3, 5). **chimera:** pronounced *ky-meera* by TSE in his recording of 1946–47, whereas *Fowler* recommends *kim-eera*.

V 19, 21, 33 **The Word in the desert ··· funeral ··· a shaft of sunlight:** "To the death in the desert, the prayer in forgotten places by the broken imperial column", *Murder in the Cathedral* closing chorus. "Sunlight on a broken column", *The Hollow Men* II 23. See note to V 32–33, below.

V 24 **The figure of the ten stairs:** to E. M. Stephenson, 19 Aug 1943: "A reference to a passage in *The Ascent of Mount Carmel* by St. John of the Cross of which I regret I cannot give the exact place." St. John of the Cross on "the ten steps of the mystic ladder of Divine love": "The tenth and last step of this secret ladder of love causes the soul to become wholly assimilated to God", *Dark Night of the Soul* II XIX–XX (*Moody* 240; *Preston* 22). TSE to Hayward, 16 Oct [1942]: "One of the commoner forms of nuisance now ··· is the request from some 'student' or schoolchild for elucidation of some line in one of my earlier poems. An easy favourite, up to the moment, is 'as in the figure of the ten stairs': Miss Melton [his secretary] can deal with that now without asking me."

V 25–39] See note on second epigraph to *Sweeney Agonistes*, for "I've tried to express something of my belief at the end of *Burnt Norton*."

V 26 **Not in itself desirable:** Bradley: "In order to have the sum of pleasures, I must have them all *now*, which is impossible. Thus you can not reach the end, and the effort to reach it is not in itself desirable", *Ethical Studies* Essay III.

V 27–28 **itself unmoving, | Only the cause and end of movement:** Aristotle: "The final cause, then, produces motion as being loved, but all other things move by being moved", *Metaphysics* (in *Works* ed. W. D. Ross, 1928, VIII) 1072a. TSE: "There is a type of religious mysticism which found expression in the twelfth century, and which is taken up into the system of Aquinas. Its origin is in the *Metaphysics* of Aristotle 1072b and elsewhere", *The Varieties of Metaphysical Poetry* 99 (Clark Lecture III; see note). Dryden: "that *UNIVERSAL HE* ··· *Unmade, unmov'd*; yet *making, moving All*", *Religio Laici* 15–17 (*Donoghue* 240).

V 32–33 **Between un-being and being. | Sudden in a shaft of sunlight:** "shaping the still un-shapen: | I have seen these things in a shaft of sunlight", *Murder in the Cathedral* opening chorus. "lost in a shaft of sunlight", *The Dry Salvages* V 25.

V 35–36 **hidden laughter | Of children in the foliage:** "unheard music hidden in the shrubbery", I 27; "The voice of the hidden waterfall | And the children in the apple-tree", *Little Gidding* V 34–35 (*Hayward*). "Whispers and small laughter between leaves", *Marina* 20 (see note).

V 37 **Quick now, here, now, always:** also *Little Gidding* V 39. "Neither matter nor form in the abstract is sufficient to explain the this-here-now", *Matter and Form in Aristotle's "Metaphysics"* (1915).

V 38–39 **Ridiculous the waste sad time | Stretching before and after:** Shelley: "We look before and after, | And pine for what is not", *To a Skylark* 86–87, included in *The Golden Treasury* and quoted by TSE in *A Note on Richard Crashaw* (1928). TSE: "before and after time · · · Time before and time after", *Burnt Norton* III 16, 18. "Not the intense moment | Isolated, with no before and after", *East Coker* V 21–22 (and see note to V 22–24). "the past is all deception, | The future futureless", *The Dry Salvages* I 43–44. "nowhere, no before and after", *Little Gidding* V 22.

after V 39] See Textual History for three or four deleted lines not recorded in *Composition FQ*, which are presumably what TSE meant when he told Mary Hutchinson, 19 Jan 1936, "I can't get the last four lines right."

East Coker

1. The Village and the Eliot Connection 2. TSE's Visits
3. Composition 4. After Publication

Published in *NEW* 21 Mar 1940. Labelled "Supplement", the poem occupied the central four pages so as to be readily detachable. Some extra copies of these pages were printed afterwards (*Gallup* A36a). First US publication in *Partisan Review* May–June 1940 (although V 1–18 had been quoted from *NEW* in *Poetry* (Chicago) May 1940, with no variants). The first printing with its own title page was *NEW leaflet* (*Gallup* A36b), which was followed by the Faber pamphlet, 12 Sept 1940 (six impressions to Feb 1942). No separate US publication. Within *Four Quartets* in *US 1943*, *1944+*. A reading by Robert Speaight was broadcast on 21 July 1941.

1. THE VILLAGE AND THE ELIOT CONNECTION

Hayward: "The poem takes its title from the village of East Coker, near Yeovil in Somersetshire, some twenty miles from the Channel coast. It was from this village, the home of the poet's ancestors, that Andrew Eliot emigrated in 1667 to found the American branch of the Eliot family from which the poet is directly descended."

Walter Graeme Eliot, *A Sketch of the Eliot Family* (1887) 11: "Nestled among the hills and meadows of the heart of Somersetshire, the garden spot of England, is the little hamlet of East Coker, three or four miles S. W. from Yeovil, on the London & Southwestern Railway. Here, almost under the shadows of a fine old parish church, dating back to the fifteenth century, was the home for a century or more of the Eliot family, previous to their departure for America and liberty." TSE to Hermann Peschmann, 12 Sept 1945: "East Coker may certainly be described as a hamlet. Three miles south-west of Yeovil there are three tiny villages of North, East and West Coker. They are all very small indeed."

To R. P. de Menasce, 31 May 1940: "The poem is of course serial to *Burnt Norton* which is also the name of a place. The names have perhaps no 'figurative' meaning for the reader, who certainly does not need to know anything more about them than is indicated by the poems. The 'place' serves as a concrete localisation of a mood and a train of meditations, that is all. East Coker, however, is a small village in Somerset, whereby my family lived from about the middle of the fifteenth century until 1671 when they went to New England. It serves, accordingly, for the author's purpose, as a place for a meditation on beginnings and ends."

TSE was inconsistent about the date of the emigration, which Helen Gardner gives as "around 1669" (*Composition FQ* 42). (*Walter Graeme Eliot* 15: "Andrew Eliott, baptized in East Coker, England, in 1627, was last mentioned there in 1668, and appears next in America, as joining the first church of Beverly [Mass.], 1670.") To Gilbert H. Phelps of BBC Bristol, 26 Nov 1945: "Some of the verses are intended to be evocative of that village but it must be admitted that they would do equally well for any number of other villages in other parts of England. There is, of course, the personal association which is that my family lived there for something over 200 years before they went to America in 1669 and that they therefore seem to have lived longer there than anywhere else before or since. There is also an allusion, of course, to

Sir Thomas Elyot who was a West Country worthy although he died in Cambridgeshire." But to Neville Braybrooke, 25 Nov 1958: "Andrew Eliot left for America I think in 1667".

To T. W. Cole, 25 Sept 1941: "Andrew Eliot · · · was descended from Thomas Elyot's grandfather who was himself a native of East Coker. We may therefore claim Thomas Elyot in a way for East Coker as I presume that his father, Richard Elyot, was born there." (Sir Thomas Elyot's association with Sir Thomas More, according to TSE's *More and Tudor Drama* (1926), "laid him for a time under suspicion of excessive orthodoxy".) On Sir Thomas Elyot's *The Governour*, see notes to I 13 and I 28–33.

To his brother, 7 Feb 1939: "I could copy out Eliot data in the British Museum Library, which has a copy of the *Sketch of the Eliot Family* (2nd edition) but you ought to have the copy that father had · · · I think William de Aliot is wholly, or so far as we are concerned, apocryphal; anyway, if he existed, there is a gap of three hundred years". TSE had no doubt, however, about his own pedigree, claiming, in *"The Unfading Genius of Rudyard Kipling"* (1959), to come "from wholly British stock".

2. TSE'S VISITS

Although Valerie Eliot reported that TSE visited East Coker "for the first and only time in early August 1937, when he was staying with Sir Matthew Nathan at West Coker" (*Composition FQ* 42), he had visited also in the previous year. To Polly Tandy, 18 June 1936, describing a visit from Yeovil: "By foot to the pretty village of East Coker, the only blemish of which is a memorial stained glass window, the ugliest that I ever saw, Faith Hope & Love with malignant faces, Love a little higher than her villainous sisters by reason of standing upon the family arms incorrectly inscribed, which has been put in only this year by an American cousin."

Writing to Hayward the following year [31 Mar 1937], TSE signed himself "Your oblgd obt servt | Th. Eliot | of Somerset", and on 27 July 1937 he wrote to introduce himself to Sir Matthew Nathan (later the author of *The Annals of West Coker*, 1957): "My friend Dorothy Bussy informs me that you are engaged on a history of the Coker parishes. I am expecting to come to East Coker for the night of August 3rd, as I shall have been staying with the Richmonds at Salisbury, and it would be a great pleasure to me to call on you on that day." To Lady Richmond, 5 Aug 1937: "I walked from East to West Coker in great heat and saw Sir Matthew Nathan, who struck me as a remarkable man, even in discussing matters of moment no greater than local feuds during the Wars of the Roses."

Frank Morley: "Eliot visited East Coker with thoughts of the house, in the double sense of that word, started by his ancestor, the Sir Thomas Elyot who was born (some editors estimate) exactly four hundred years before the Thomas Eliot whose birth had come about in 1888 in St Louis. After 'our' Eliot, the male line of that house—of his particular branch—was to become extinct. I know that Eliot had feelings that the former Elyot was the beginning of an era of which he was the ending · · · they were the beginning and end of the same house", *Literary Britain* (1980) 196.

Against a speculation in *G. Jones* about TSE's feelings of family reunion on visiting "the family home from which the Eliots had migrated hundreds of years before" (133), TSE wrote: "No house there. Said to have been destroyed by fire."

3. COMPOSITION

To James J. Angleton and E. Reed Whittemore, 31 Jan 1939: "I have had to decline all invitations to contribute poetry to periodicals on the one final ground that I have not written any poems. All the verse that I have composed in the last two years forms part of a play which is about to be published" (*The Family Reunion*).

Stephen Spender recorded TSE's conversation on 11 Sept 1939: "He said it was very important that one should, at all costs, go on writing now. 'It doesn't seem to me to matter very much whether, at the moment, it is or isn't very good. The important thing is to keep going. Probably it's impossible to do excellent work while things are so disturbed ··· Just writing every day is a way of keeping the engine running' ··· Eliot said that he did not care to listen to Beethoven so much as formerly just now ··· I said I was at once attracted by, and sick of, public events being dealt with in a public manner in poetic plays. He agreed that the problem was to write about a smaller theme—perhaps family life—which had all the implications of what is going on in the world outside", *Horizon* May 1940. (TSE: "Mostly the individual | Experience is too large, or too small", *A Note on War Poetry* 10–11.)

4. AFTER PUBLICATION

To Frank Morley, 5 Apr 1940, on comments by George Every: "Every says (but not in a damaging way) that the tone is Jansenist rather than Calvinist: which you ought to appreciate, having (it seems) read Pascal's *Thoughts*." (John Calvin, 1509–64. Cornelius Jansen, d. 1638.) TSE: "Jansenism ··· was morally a Puritan movement ··· at least as severe as those of any Puritanism in England or America ··· Calvinists emphasized the degradation of man through Original Sin, and considered mankind so corrupt that the will was of no avail; and thus fell into the doctrine of predestination ··· It was upon the doctrine of grace according to St. Augustine that the Jansenists relied", *The "Pensées of Pascal"* (1931).

To Morley, 9 Apr: "your commentary on E. Coker is being digested. You are an old sly boots to bring in Beethoven, to get me so mollified as to agree to every criticism you make. But your comment is of two kinds (1) slight: most of which I violently disagree with; but then if I accepted it at once that would be evidence that I hadnt taken my job seriously (2) serious: which means waiting to see whether there is anything I can do. Your serious criticism could not be acted upon just in a spare hour or more; if you are right (and I think likely you are) it means waiting to make a new leap at the thing, and that cannot be predicted or arranged. I may have the leap in me, or I may be off on something else ··· Gravest criticism that of opening paragraph of Part II. You are probably right. The question is, am I up to doing anything about it?"

To Desmond Hawkins, 7 Mar 1941: "I see no objection to broadcasting *East Coker* to the Hindus if they want it ··· I should think that if they want to hear short-wave English poets at all they would rather hear them do a bit of their own stuff than giving thumbnail introductions to Shakespeare."

TSE to Anne Ridler, 10 Mar 1941, replying to a letter after publication of *The Dry Salvages*: "I don't think the ordinary reader will like it so much as *E. Coker*—in fact, the success of that poem is a little disconcerting: I find it hard to believe that a poem of mine which sells nearly 12,000 copies can be really good. (I am glad, by the way, that you like part IV [of *East Coker*], which is in a way the heart of the matter. My intention was to avoid a pastiche of George Herbert or Crashaw—it would be folly to try—and to do something in the style of Cleveland or Benlowes, only better; and I liked the use of this so English XVII [17th-century] form with a content so very un-English—which George Every calls Jansenist. But the poem as a whole—this five part form—is an attempt to weave several quite unrelated strands together in an emotional whole, so that really there isn't any heart of the matter.)" In his fourth Clark Lecture, TSE had commented: "Cleveland is not very remunerative; Benlowes' verses, like those of Miss Gertrude Stein, can, for anyone whose taste has already been disciplined elsewhere, provide an extremely valuable exercise for unused parts of the mind", *The Varieties of Metaphysical Poetry* 137.

Title] To Andrew Gilchrist, 13 May 1944: "I hear indirectly that another periodical, which I don't know at all, *l'Arche*, is going to produce *East Coker*—which will probably become something like 'la houillère orientale'" (= Eastern coke mine).

I

I 1 **In my beginning is my end**: in his copy of Charles M. Bakewell's *Source Book in Ancient Philosophy*, TSE scored Heraclitus' frag. 103: "In the circumference of a circle beginning and end coincide." (For Heraclitus, see epigraph at the head of *Burnt Norton*.) The motto "En ma fin est mon commencement" was embroidered on the chair-of-state of Mary, Queen of Scots, as TSE knew, perhaps from Maurice Baring's biography *In My End Is My Beginning* (1931) (*Sweeney 1941*). To E. M. Stephenson, 19 Aug 1943: "Yes, this device was of course in my mind, but there was no particular relevance about Mary Stuart except that she had her place in the sixteenth century" (*Stephenson* 87). To R. J. Schoeck, 27 Jan 1947, on the suggestion that he had in mind de Machaut's *Ma fin est mon commencement*: "Guillaume de Machaut has never been more than a name to me and I had certainly never read the poem you quote. The parallel is not only interesting but gratifying as it is always a pleasure to me to find that any idea of my own has been anticipated long ago without my knowledge. It appears to me to give my own statement greater validity." Charlotte Eliot (in 1890) on Giordano Bruno: "In the beginning seest thou the end, | And in the end a mere beginning still", scrapbooks in Missouri Historical Society library (*Howarth* 31). Bradley: "the end lies hid in that which is assumed at the beginning", *Appearance and Reality* ch. XXV (see note to *Little Gidding* V 27–32). Lancelot Andrewes: "a manger for His cradle, poor clouts for His array. This was His beginning. Follow Him farther · · · Is His end any better?" Christmas Sermon 1611 (the paragraph of the *Verbum infans*; see notes to I 13 and *Gerontion* 17–19). TSE: "The crudest experience and the abstrusest theory end in identity, and this identity I call the absolute. If you choose to call it nothing, I will not dispute the point. But whichever it is, it is both beginning and end", *Degrees of Reality* (1913). "(But our beginnings never know our ends!)" *Portrait of a Lady* III 14. "the end precedes the beginning, | And the end and the beginning were always there", *Burnt Norton* V 10–11. "What we think a beginning is often an end | And to make an end is to make a beginning. | The end is where we start from. For every moment | Is both beginning and end", *Little Gidding* V 1–3 *verse draft msC* [1–4].

Herbert of Cherbury: "O that our love might take no end, | Or never had beginning took!" *Ode upon a Question moved, Whether Love should continue for ever?* 39–40. In Grierson's Introduction to *Metaphysical Lyrics and Poems of the Seventeenth Century* (1921) xxxvi, TSE scored the sentence that called the poem "the finest thing inspired by Donne's *Ecstasy*". On Shaw's *Back to Methuselah*: "Even the author appears to be conscious of the question whether the beginning and the end are not the same ··· The pessimism of the conclusion of his last book ··· is pessimism only because he has not realized that at the end he has only approached a beginning, that his end is only the starting point towards the knowledge of life", *London Letter* in *Dial* Oct 1921. "In ending we must go back to the beginning and remember", *In Memoriam* (1936). In Montandon's tr. of *East Coker*, "Dans ma principe est ma fin", TSE underlined "principe" with "!" **in succession:** *Old Deuteronomy* 2 (at line-end).

I 2 **Houses rise and fall:** Poe: "the 'House of Usher'—an appellation which seemed to include ··· both the family and the family mansion", *The Fall of the House of Usher* (1839). Likewise Hawthorne's *The House of the Seven Gables* (1851). See Frank Morley quoted in headnote, 2. TSE'S VISITS. The de Courtenays were feudal holders of the East and West Coker manors from the 13th to the 16th centuries and enjoyed mixed fortunes over generations (Marcus Fysh, personal communication). TSE: "forever building, and always decaying, and always being restored", *Choruses from "The Rock"* II 26.

I 2–4 **Houses rise and fall ··· in their place | Is an open field:** Virginia Woolf: "Buildings fall; even the earth perishes. What was yesterday a cornfield is today a bungalow", *Craftsmanship* (broadcast 29 Apr 1937, *Listener* 5 May; see notes to V 18 and *Little Gidding* V 4–11). *Grover Smith 1996* 100: "Eliot, in the late 1940s, told me that he did not remember any talk. I think that he may, nevertheless, have read it." Tennyson, *Aylmer's Field* final lines:

> Then the great Hall was wholly broken down,
> And the broad woodland parcelled into farms ···
> The slow-worm creeps, and the thin weasel there
> Follows the mouse, and all is open field.

(TSE: "field-mouse", I 12). **open field:** (as also 15, 23); to Morley, 9 Apr 1940: "'Playing field'—no. Too heavy an emphasis on the modern. Want something more colourless there. Open field is right, I think." The open field system of farming was "especially associated with medieval manorial estates", *Blamires* 44. **by-pass:** to Frank Morley, 9 Apr 1940: "Dont understand what you mean by 'by-pass'. Do you mean that the term is not used in U.S.A. or that it jars?" (OED's first citation is 1922; *Choruses from "The Rock"* VII 37 has "by-pass way".) In Montandon's tr., "Est un champ, ou une fabrique, ou un passage", TSE underlined "passage" with "?"

I 3 *variant* **replaced ··· place:** to Hayward, 27 Feb 1940: "*Replaced* and *place*. It was intentional, but Hebert also objects, so I had better do something about it." For Fr. Hebert see Textual History headnote on *ts1b*.

I 5 **new building:** to Herbert Read, 18 Sept 1942: "it's only possible to do tinkering when one is not possessed with the desire for new building" (see headnote to *Little Gidding*, 2. COMPOSITION).

I 7–8 **flesh, fur and faeces, | Bone of man and beast, cornstalk and leaf:** Hopkins: "Flesh and fleece, fur and feather, | Grass and greenworld all together", *The*

May Magnificat 17–18. ("Hopkins is a fine poet · · · His innovations · · · are easily imitated though not adaptable for many purposes", *After Strange Gods* 47. To Wolfgang Clemen, 7 Mar 1949, on Hopkins: "I did not become acquainted with his work until the publication of the second edition of the poems which I think was subsequent to 1925 [1930]. My impression is that my reading of Gerard Hopkins came too late for me to be influenced by him.")

I 9–11 **there is a time for building | And a time for living and for generation | And a time for the wind:** Ecclesiastes 3: 1–8: "To every thing there is a season, and a time to every purpose under the heaven: a time to be born, and a time to die; a time to plant, and a time to pluck up that which is planted; a time to kill and a time to heal; a time to break down, and a time to build up; a time to weep, and a time to laugh; a time to mourn, and a time to dance; a time to cast away stones, and a time to gather stones together; a time to embrace, and a time to refrain from embracing; a time to get, and a time to lose; a time to keep, and a time to cast away; a time to rend, and a time to sew; a time to keep silence, and a time to speak; a time to love, and a time to hate; a time of war, and a time of peace" (*Hayward*). TSE: "And when to prune, and when to bind | And when to cut, and when to move", *A Valedictory* 28–29. Ecclesiastes 1: 4: "One generation passeth away, and another generation cometh: but the earth abideth for ever" (*Kenner 1960* 266). Swinburne: "From the winds of the north and the south · · · A time for labour and thought, | A time to serve and to sin", *Atalanta in Calydon* 342, 348–49, a chorus quoted by TSE in *Swinburne as Poet* (1920). *The Love Song of J. Alfred Prufrock* 23–48 has "time for" and "time to" repeatedly.

I 9–13 **Houses live and die · · · field-mouse · · · arras:** Byron "on mutability": "that antique house · · · a mouse, | Whose little nibbling rustle will embarrass | Most people as it plays along the arras", *Don Juan* XVI xx.

I 11–13 **the wind to break the loosened pane | And to shake the wainscot where the field-mouse trots | And to shake the tattered arras:** Tennyson: "The blue fly sung in the pane; the mouse | Behind the mouldering wainscot shrieked", *Mariana* 63–64 (with "winds · · · wind", 54, 75). TSE quoted these lines in *In Memoriam* (1936). Also "the shrieking rush of the wainscot mouse", *Maud* I [vi] 260 (both *Blamires* 43). TSE to Hayward, 27 Feb 1940: "*Fieldmice.* They *did* get into our country house in New England, and very pretty little creatures too: we always restored them to the Land, and only slew the housemice. But the particular point here is that the house is supposed to have been long deserted or empty. Do housemice go on living in an unoccupied house? If so, I had better alter this; because I admit that in a tenanted house the fieldmouse is an *exception*" (*Composition FQ* 97).

I 12 **wainscot · · · field-mouse trots:** "Speaking of the Elizabethans, I think of a figure used in one of the Martin Marprelate tracts, which I can never forget; when the author, speaking of his adversary, Bishop Cooper, says that he 'Has a face like old wainscot, and would lie as fast as a dog would trot.' As for the bishop's veracity, there is no doubt something to be said on both sides, but in my memory, that simile sticks to him like wax; he will never be free of it. These are properly, rhetorical images; they emphasise rather than elucidate; and in strict reason, it is meaningless to compare rapidity of lying, even, to rapidity of dog's trotting. And the image of old wainscot is a variable one: that is to say, it may have effect equally on various minds to which it suggests different things. To me it means an old, weatherbeaten, pitted as if worm-eaten, brown face; and in juxtaposition with the dogtrot, suggests great villainy. This variable margin of suggestion is what I call rhetorical effect. But it is quite different from the well-known figure of Dante when he is trying to make you visualise exactly that dolorous twilight in which moved the form of Brunetto Latini", *The Varieties of Metaphysical Poetry* 121–22 (Clark Lecture IV), where the Marprelate quotation is corrected (James T. Bratcher, *N&Q* June 2007). "The wall, the wainscot and the mouse ··· brown baked features", *Little Gidding* II 6, 41. **wainscot**: pronounced *wainsk't* in TSE's recordings of 1946–47. See Textual History. **field-mouse trots**: Verlaine: "Dame souris trotte", *Impression Fausse* 1, 3 (*Grover Smith 1996* 101).

I 13 **tattered arras ··· motto**: Pound: "Mantegna painted the wall. | Silk tatters, 'Nec Spe Nec Metu'", *Cantos* III (*Harmon 1976a*). **arras**: TSE defended to Hayward the archaic spelling of his typescripts, 27 Feb 1940: "*Aresse*. This early Tudor spelling is O.K." To Frank Morley, 5 Apr 1940: "'Aresse' you may be sure I had got taped (I know where to get it even if it isn't in the *O.E.D.*)" Again, 9 Apr: "'Aresse' as I cabled is O.K. Out of *The Governour*." After publication in *NEW* (with "aresse"), TSE emended to "arras" in the *NEW 2nd proof* he sent to Montgomery Belgion, commenting: "the early Tudor spelling seemed to bother readers". Recalling a request that the American edition use the later spelling, Morley wrote: "At Harcourt, Brace we had a standing order to follow, exactly, the Faber spelling. The Faber spelling, and therefore the 'H,B' spelling (in 1943), was *arras*", *Tate ed.* 111. In fact, the proof for *US 1943* was set from *NEW* and had the antique spelling, until TSE wrote to Morley, 20 Feb 1943, with proof corrections including "Read *Arras* for *Aresse*." See note to I 28–33. **silent motto**: the family motto *Tace et fac*, "Be silent and act", was used by Sir Thomas Elyot and adapted for TSE's dedication of *The Sacred Wood* to his recently deceased father: "TACUIT ET FECIT" (see headnote to *Prufrock and Other Observations*, 4. TITLE, DEDICATION AND EPIGRAPH TO THE VOLUME). Henry Eliot to Henry B. Harvey, 10 Oct 1946: "Asked whether the silent motto (E. Coker) referred to the Eliot motto Tace et Fac, said yes, he had thought of that." It also appears on TSE's bookplate, and was written by him against "silent" in a copy of *G. Jones*, where this line is quoted (211).

The derivation of "motto" from "mot", aligns "silent motto" with Lancelot Andrewes's *Verbum infans* (Christmas Sermon 1611) and the "silent Word" of *Ash-Wednesday* V 9 (*Harmon 1976a*). *Ricks* 247: "silent ··· because any motto woven upon an arras is silent; because in the decaying house there is no one to hear ··· because the motto is not revealed here in the poem, the line itself keeping silent; because, if you do know the motto, it is in a dead language, in Latin, not in our speaking language; and because it is a silent motto, as enjoining silence". TSE: "that intensity at which language strives to become silence", *The Poetic Drama* (1920). "Words, after speech, reach | Into the silence", *Burnt Norton* V 3–4.

I 15–16 **the deep lane | Shuttered with branches**: East Coker has many such "holloways" of antiquity. Six photographs of East Coker taken on TSE's visit in Aug 1937 include three of its lanes; two are captioned by TSE "Road from Yeovil to E. Coker", the third "E. Coker—W. Coker road" (Houghton). He sent similar photographs to Hayward, 2 June 1940: "I enclose two views of East Coeker which I have discovered: you will note just that touch of artistry which distinguishes my work always from that of the ordinary amateur photographer." Before turning to his next Quartet, TSE wrote: "those again for whom the paths of glory are the lanes and the streets of Britain", *Defence of the Islands* [18–19].

I 19 **Into the village, in the electric heat:** to Lady Richmond, 5 Aug 1937: "I walked from East to West Coker in great heat." **electric:** to Hayward, 27 Feb 1940: "*Electric.* I will think about alternatives."

I 21 **refracted:** OED: "To break the course of (light or other waves) and turn (it or them) out of the direct line; esp. to deflect at a certain angle at the point of passage from one medium into another of different density" (L. *frangere* = to break). TSE to H. W. Heckstall-Smith, 8 Sept 1947: "You are perfectly right, and my use of the word 'refracted' has puzzled and bothered me for a long time. I was pained by it ··· when I heard a B.B.C. recording of the poem. I think that I must have preferred the vowel sound of 'refracted'. It is, no doubt, for this same reason that I made the slip of writing 'hermit crab' instead of 'horseshoe crab'. This latter I have corrected. I think I shall have to do something about the line in the next impression." 17 Sept: "I have thought—I was about to say reflected—further about this verbal difficulty. I now recall the fact that I discarded the verb reflect simply because it suggested the brightness and glare of a mirror, which is not at all the right effect that I had in mind. I therefore used the word refracted, which incidentally had a better vowel sound for my purpose, in the hope that the reader might accept it as intended in its original sense as broken back. Since writing to you I have discussed this point with Professor I. A. Richards who advises me to retain the word refracted. It appears to be a case in which if I discarded this word I should be obliged to renounce any attempt whatever to convey the right effect that I had in mind." No alteration was made. For "hermit crab" see note to *The Dry Salvages* I 19.

I 22 **dahlias:** pronounced *daylias* in TSE's recordings of 1946–47, as endorsed by *Fowler* and OED (though the formal pronunciation, after the botanist Dahl, is also mentioned by OED).

I 24–25 **If you ··· On a summer midnight:** Kipling: "Yet, if you enter the woods | Of a summer evening late", *The Way Through the Woods* 13–14 (*Raine* 105). TSE praised the poem in *Rudyard Kipling* (1941). **If you do not come too close ··· you can hear the music:** "if it is a great play, and you do not try too hard to hear them, you may discern the other voices too", *The Three Voices of Poetry* (*Ricks* 259).

I 25–45 **On a summer midnight ··· daunsinge ··· Feet rising and falling:** Sir John Davies:

> *Dauncing* (bright Lady) then began to be,
> When the first seedes whereof the world did spring,
> The Fire, Ayre, Earth and Water did agree,
> By Loves perswasion, Natures mighty King,
> To leave their first disordered combating
>
> *Orchestra, or a Poeme of Dauncing* st. 17

In his Introduction to *Some Longer Elizabethan Poems* (1903), A. H. Bullen quoted these lines as an example of Davies's debts to Jasper Mayne's tr. of Lucian. (The epigraph to *Mr. Apollinax*, in Greek, is from Lucian. For *Orchestra* see notes to *Gerontion* 67–71, *Ash-Wednesday* V 8 and *Burnt Norton* II 6.) *Paradise*

Lost I 781–87: "faerie elves, | Whose midnight revels, by a forest side | Or fountain some belated peasant sees, | Or dreams he sees · · · they on their mirth and dance | Intent, with jocund music charm his ear" (*Grover Smith* 35). Helen Gardner: "as the Ordnance Survey map shows, there is an ancient dancing circle", *Composition FQ* 42. **midnight · · · music · · · dancing around the bonfire · · · betokeneth concorde. Round and round the fire | Leaping through the flames · · · Rustically solemn or in rustic laughter · · · country mirth · · · Keeping time, | Keeping the rhythm · · · man and woman**: Poe: "merriment · · · musically wells · · · harmony · · · clamorous appealing to the mercy of the fire · · · Leaping higher, higher, higher · · · *What* a world of solemn thought their monody compels! | In the silence of the night · · · neither man nor woman · · · Keeping time, time, time", *The Bells*. TSE to Rolf Gardiner, 6 Apr 1942: "I am as keen about the 'cultural' (and even religious, in a wider and even more fundamental sense than people are accustomed to use the word) aspects of 'agrarianism' as anybody; but · · · I am aware of a stubborn resistance and persistence in regarding such ideas as fantastic. They immediately suggest 'folk-dancing'—or what the ordinary person ridicules under that title."

I 28–33 **The association · · · concorde**: Sir Thomas Elyot, *The Governour* (1531) bk. I xxi (*Sweeney 1941*):

> It is diligently to be noted that the associatinge of man and woman in daunsing, they bothe obseruinge one nombre and tyme in their meuynges [movings], was nat begonne without a speciall consideration, as well for the necessarye coniunction of those two persones, as for the intimation of sondry vertues, whiche be by them represented. And for as moche as by the association of a man and a woman in daunsinge may be signified matrimonie, I coulde in declarynge the dignitie and commoditie of that sacrament make intiere volumes, if it were nat so communely knowen to all men, that almoste euery frere lymitour carieth it writen in his bosom · · · In euery daunse, of a moste auncient custome, there daunseth to gether a man and a woman, holding eche other by the hande or the arme, which betokeneth concorde.

(TSE to Theodore Spencer, 21 July 1941: "there is an admirable piece of detective research into East Coker by one J. J. Sweeney in the *Southern Review*. Only he is under the delusion that I have read *all* the works of Sir T. Elyot, and he is ignorant of Chas. Williams's *The Greater Trumps*.")

To R. P. de Menasce, OP, 31 May 1940: "The lines in archaic spelling have the public purpose of localising in time the fairy-like vision. They have also the private association of being quoted from *The Governour* of Sir Thomas Elyot, published I believe in 1531. He is not personally associated with the village, but was a grandson of Simon Eliot of that place. I think that it is right to translate them into language of a Renaissance flavour." To Frank Morley, 9 Apr 1940: "Now as to the antic spelling, that is not, as you suppose, an Ezra touch. The situation is much more like that between Geoffrey and Bruce. Geoffrey wanted all old spelling modernised; Bruce [Richmond] didn't want to. So they compromised by chucking Sir. T. Elyot out. But I won't, because it is a quotation: *The Governour* is always printed with that spelling, even in the Everyman edition. Public justification: to put the visionary scene at some definite historical period: and I think the Early Tudor helps to make it definite. Private: T. Elyot was a grandson of Simon E. of East Coker. You may say all this doesnt matter; but it does to me. (ob. 1546 . . . ob. 1946? beginning & end of A epoch)." Morley in *Tate ed.* 111: "I gathered there had been a row about it · · · Tom yielded, but it rankled." (TSE yielded only by changing the spelling of "aresse", 13; Sir Thomas's spelling was retained.) The prose recommendations in TSE's *Syllabus: Elizabethan Literature* (1918) begin: "Sir Thomas Elyot's *Gouvernour*, Edward VI.'s Prayer Books, are in the 'Everyman' edition." To Hayward on 27 Feb 1940, TSE quoted "And for as moche · · · his bosome", adding: "The public intention is to give an early Tudor setting, the private, that the author of *The Governour* sprang from E. Coker (apparently born in Wilts. but his father was the son of Simon E. of E.C.)" To I. A. Richards [4] June 1940: "it AIN'T Chaucerian: it is quoted direct from a book published in 1531 (*The Governour*) and I hoped that that bit would help to give the imagery in that section a local habitation in time. And the book has a certain relation to the place—which is not, as some have thought, in Massachusetts, but in Somerset." (*A Midsummer Night's Dream* V i: "imagination · · · gives to airy nothing | A local habitation and a name". Theseus goes on to ask "what dances shall we have · · · ?" TSE: "summer midnight", I 25.) TSE: "The ideals of *The Governour*, the ideals of John Locke, those of Thomas Arnold, are all equally exhausted and inapplicable to any future Christian society", *Education in a Christian Society* (1940).

I 29 **daunsinge:** pronounced simply *dancing* in TSE's recordings of 1946–47.

I 30] For TSE to Hayward on this line, see Textual History I 46^47.

I 33–34 **Round and round · · · circles:** "Round and round the circle | Completing the charm", *The Family Reunion* final speech. "*Here we go round the prickly pear · · · Here we go round the prickly pear*", *The Hollow Men* V 1, 3.

I 34–36 **Leaping · · · Lifting heavy feet in clumsy shoes:** Auden: "The shuffling couples in their heavy boots, | The young men leaping", *Letter to R. H. S. Crossman, Esq.* 13–14, in Auden and MacNeice's *Letters from Iceland* (1937; the first of these lines repeated as caption to a photograph). TSE: "Shall we lift up our feet among perpetual ruins?" *Choruses from "The Rock"* III 43.

I 37 **country mirth:** Dryden: "With wholesome Food and Country Mirth", *From Horace, Epod. 2d.* 95 (*Grover Smith 1996* 157–58).

I 38–39 **those long since under earth | Nourishing the corn:** Kipling "aims I think to give at once a sense of the antiquity of England, of the number of generations and peoples who have laboured the soil and in turn been buried beneath it, and of the contemporaneity of the past", *Rudyard Kipling* (1941). "our temporal reversion nourish · · · The life of significant soil", *The Dry Salvages* V 48–50 (see note).

I 42–46 **The time of · · · Eating and drinking:** Ecclesiastes: see note to I 9–11.

I 44 **the coupling of man and woman:** "the love of man and woman · · · is only explained and made reasonable by the higher love, or else is simply the coupling of animals", *Dante* (1929) III. "Baudelaire has perceived that what distinguishes the relations of man and woman from the copulation of beasts is the knowledge of Good and Evil", *Baudelaire* (1930). "to ravish a woman · · · coupling of beasts", *Anabasis* X viii.

I 47 **Dawn points:** F. R. Leavis: "The 'points' clearly come from the French (*poindre* and *point du jour*). It is a *trouvaille* because of the suggestion · · · of the regularly punctuating recurrences of time", *Scrutiny* Summer 1942. Milton: "Or ere the point of dawn", *On the Morning of Christ's Nativity* 86 (*Williamson* 218).

I 47 *variant* **points and the star fades**: to Hayward, 27 Feb 1940: "*Star fades*. You are right." *Composition FQ* 99: "Probably Hayward pointed out that the morning star does not fade at dawn."

I 48–49 **Out at sea the dawn wind | Wrinkles and slides**: *Purg.* I 115–17: "The dawn was vanquishing the breath of morn which fled before her, so that from afar I recognised the trembling of the sea" (*Servotte and Grene*). *Paradise Lost* XI 842–43: "a keen north-wind, that blowing dry | Wrinkled the face of Deluge" (for the same passage, see note to *Silence* 3–4). Tennyson: "The wrinkled sea beneath him crawls", *The Eagle* 4. Symons: "The fountain wrinkles under a faint wind", *From Paul Verlaine: Fêtes Galantes* V: *À la Promenade* 5 in *Knave of Hearts* (1913). TSE: "breakers of camp in the little dawn wind, seekers of watercourses over the wrinkled rind of the world", *Anabasis* I xv. "the urban dawn wind", *Little Gidding* II 35.

I 49–50 **I am here | Or there, or elsewhere**: "Everyone knows a passage from a sermon of Donne's, which is given by Mr. Pearsall Smith under the title of 'I am Not all Here'", *Lancelot Andrewes* (1926). Donne: "I am not all here, I am here now preaching upon this text, and I am at home in my Library considering whether *S. Gregory*, or *S. Hierome*, have said best of this text, before. I am here speaking to you, and yet I consider by the way, in the same instant, what it is likely you will say to one another, when I have done, you are not all here neither; you are here now, hearing me, and yet you are thinking that you have heard a better Sermon somewhere else", *Sermons* ed. Logan Pearsall Smith 3–4. See note to *Burnt Norton* V 13–22. TSE: "We stand before a beautiful painting, and if we are sufficiently carried away, our feeling is a whole · · · The feeling is neither here nor anywhere", *Knowledge and Experience* 20. For "Here or there", see note to V 30, 32.

II

To Montgomery Belgion, 19 July 1940: "I don't know whether it strikes a reader (what I intended) that the first passage of section II is meant to be a kind of parody of the earlier Yeats influenced by Blake (some of his poems are very much so); but that at the same time I use the word 'parody' only because I can think of no other: the effect of a very small pinch of irony is not intended to be comic, and in any case the irony is not directed against Yeats—is not literary criticism—but a part of something going on within my own mind at that point." To Geoffrey Curtis, 31 Dec 1940: "The first movement of part II is a *serious* kind of parody of early Yeats under the influence of Blake. Otherwise I should have thought that Yeats was chiefly apparent in the references to old age (with a difference)."

II 1 **What is the late November doing**: Blake: "What are those golden Builders doing | Near mournful ever-weeping Paddington", *Jerusalem* Plate 27, *To the Jews*, 25–26. For Blake's lines, see note to *A Cooking Egg* 27–32.

II 1–7 **What is the late November doing · · · summer heat · · · Late roses filled with early snow**: temperatures in England in Nov 1938 reached a record-breaking 70 °F. Snow then fell from 17 Dec until Christmas. To his brother, 23 Dec: "The weather has been phenomenal for London: it snowed this week for three days on end." **Late roses filled with early snow:** Campion: "like rose-buds fill'd with snow", *There is a garden in her face* 10 (*Grover Smith* 323).

II 1, 13 **November · · · Leonids:** OED: "a group of meteors which appear to radiate from the constellation Leo." Under the heading "November Leonids", *The Times* 15 Nov 1929 told readers: "During the next few years we may reasonably anticipate increasing numbers of these November meteors and they ought to be interestingly abundant about 1933, 1934, and 1935", and explained: "The meteors owe their origin to a periodical comet which visits our parts of space every 33 years · · · they are generally bright, and leave streaks of glowing light along their paths. Of all the displays which gild our nocturnal skies the November Leonids have perhaps furnished the grandest spectacles." *The Times* 14 Nov 1931: "The date of the earth's passage through the stream becomes slowly later"; accordingly the "Stars of the Month" columns of 1 Nov 1937 and 1 Nov 1939 expected the comets to be especially visible in "late November" (II 1).

II 7–17 **snow? | Thunder rolled by the rolling stars · · · fights · · · Comets · · · Hunt the heavens · · · that destructive fire | Which burns before the ice-cap reigns:** Edgar Lee Masters: "You have become a forge of snow white fire · · · Your sons are stars · · · meteor changes · · · the rolling thunder | Of cannon stand in trenches where the dead | Clog the ensanguined ice · · · Flaming to heaven", *O Glorious France*. Masters's poem appeared in *Songs and Satires*, which TSE reviewed in *Mr. Lee Masters* (1916). See *Burnt Norton* II 1–2 and note, and *McCue 2014a*. Aerial warfare during the Great War had included the bombing of London and the use of anti-aircraft guns. (MacNeice: "searchlights probe the heavens", *Autumn Journal*, 1938, vii.) TSE and his wife sheltered in a cellar (see her letter to Charlotte Eliot, 22 Oct 1917, in *Letters 1*). For TSE in 1933 recalling "the time of the air-raids in London", see headnote to *Sweeney Among the Nightingales*.

II 8–9 **Thunder rolled by the rolling stars | Simulates triumphal cars:** Mallarmé: "Tonnerre et rubis aux moyeux · · · Du seul vespéral de mes chars" [Thunder and rubies at the axles · · · of the only vesperal one among my chariots], *M'introduire dans ton histoire* [*To introduce myself into your story*] 10, 14 (*Composition FQ* 101). See note to *Burnt Norton* II 1–2 for TSE quoting Mallarmé's sonnet. ("drift of stars · · · among the stars", *Burnt Norton* II 8, 15.) **rolling stars:** Cicero on the nine spheres: "one is the celestial · · · in which are fixed the sempiternal courses of the rolling stars", *Somnium Scipionis*, cited in a discussion of Dante's cosmology in *A Triad of Great Poets* [Aeschylus, Dante, Milton], *Tait's Edinburgh Magazine* Oct 1853, 584 (tr. probably by the article's author). Cicero was among TSE's Latin school texts for several years both at Smith Academy and at Milton Academy. **triumphal cars:** for the four-horse chariot of the *triumphator* in a Roman triumph, see headnote to *Coriolan* I. *Triumphal March*. OED "chariot" 1b: "a triumphal car · · · Now chiefly *poet.*, and applied *fig.* to the car in which the sun, moon, night, etc., are represented as pursuing their course."

II 8–19 **stars · · · constellated · · · the heavens · · · That was a way of putting it—not very satisfactory: | A periphrastic study in a worn-out poetical fashion:** to Ian Cox, 21 Apr 1937, on his *Desire Provoketh*: "one ought to be able to look at what you have set down out of the margins of one's eye · · · just as one can count more of the Pleiades on a clear night when one is not looking directly at them. This is a periphrastical way of putting it · · · published just as it is, it would fall into a category of literature ··· very much below its level of intensity; that of the quiet meditative observation of nature plus reflection, say." For this letter see "The End of All Our Exploring", 3. PUBLISHER AND POET.

II 11 **Scorpion fights against the Sun**: the sun is in Scorpio from about 23 Oct to 21 Nov.

II 16–17 **fire | Which burns before the ice-cap reigns**: Newman: "thou tell'st of space, and time ··· Of fire, and of refreshment after fire ··· As ice which blisters may be said to burn", *The Dream of Gerontius* §4 152–54, 157. TSE: "Moving alone through flames of ice", *The Family Reunion* II iii.

II 18 **a way of putting it—not very satisfactory**: "a very satisfactory intimacy ··· Not a happy way of putting it", *The Use of Poetry and the Use of Criticism* 112. "it was (you may say) satisfactory", *Journey of the Magi* 31.

II 20–21 **the intolerable wrestle | With words and meanings**: "the word is not merely the sound with a meaning; the word becomes interesting for its meaning elsewhere as well as for its meaning in the context; for its own meaning as well as what the writer means to mean by it", *The Varieties of Metaphysical Poetry* 272–73 (Turnbull Lecture II).

II 21 **The poetry does not matter**: "but a poem is not poetry", *A Note on War Poetry* 15 (see note). For "poetry ··· with nothing poetic about it", see *Four Quartets* headnote, 7. MUSIC. **does not matter**: on Kipling: "There are deeper and darker caverns into which he penetrated—whether through experience or through imagination does not matter", *Rudyard Kipling* (1941). On the Victorian attitude to evolution: "It is an attitude of vague hopefulness which I believe to be mistaken. But that does not matter: what matters is that Tennyson felt it and gave it expression", *"The Voice of His Time"* (1942). "One positive contribution towards poetry is all that one can hope to make; beyond that it does not matter whether one is Shakespeare or Jules Laforgue; whether one is 'original' or 'derivative'", *The Varieties of Metaphysical Poetry* 289 (Turnbull Lecture III). "neither division nor unity | Matters", *Ash-Wednesday* II 53–54.

II 22–26 **(to start again) ··· the wisdom of age? Had they deceived us, | Or deceived themselves**: "some of us devote our later years to trying to express the same ideas better ··· Alas! if there is no truth that has not been discovered by our ancestors, then there is also no possible error by which they have not been deceived", *The Three Voices of Poetry* (1954; preliminary remarks omitted from *On Poetry and Poets*). **And the wisdom of age**: Browning: "The wisdom of age and the folly of youth, at once", *The Flight of the Duchess* XI. See note to II 43–44.

II 22, 37: **what one had expected ··· undeceived**: "We have been undeceived about developments ··· expected to bring unity", *Catholicism and International Order* (1933).

II 25–26 **Had they deceived us, | Or deceived themselves**: Hugh Latimer, of the clergy: "This is your generation ··· Have you thus deceived me? or, have you rather deceived yourselves?", First Sermon to the Convocation before the Parliament began, 9 June 1536. TSE put extracts from Latimer's Second Sermon into the mouth of the Preacher in the drafts of *The Rock*.

II 25–31 **deceived ··· deceived ··· the quiet-voiced elders ··· deceit ··· the knowledge of dead secrets ··· from which they turned their eyes**: the History of Susanna (four pages, set apart from the Book of Daniel in the Apocrypha): "And the two elders saw her going in every day, and walking; so that their lust was inflamed toward her. And they perverted their own mind, and turned away their eyes, that they might not look unto heaven ··· Then Susanna cried out with a loud voice, and said, O everlasting God, that knowest the secrets, and knowest ··· that they have borne false witness against me ··· And the Lord heard her voice ··· the holy spirit of a young youth, whose name was Daniel: who cried with a loud voice ··· beauty hath deceived thee, and lust ··· With that all the assembly cried out with a loud voice, and praised God." **deceived themselves ··· elders ··· deceit**: "The elders have had the satisfaction ··· of persuading themselves that the way they want to behave is the only moral way", *Thoughts After Lambeth* (1931). **quiet-voiced**: Henry Adams on Garibaldi: "a quiet-featured, quiet-voiced man in a red flannel shirt", *The Education of Henry Adams* ch. VI.

II 27 **receipt**: to Hayward, 27 Feb 1940, who had marked this word with "X": "*Receipt*. I mean of course in the sense of a *recipe* or formula. Is there any objection to bequeathing a formula? You can bequeath a copyright or a patent. I don't quite see your point." *Composition FQ* 101: "Hayward's objection may have been to the rhyming of 'receipt' and 'deceit'." See quotation from Andrewes in note to IV 1.

II 28 **hebetude**: OED: "The condition or state of being blunt or dull; dullness, bluntness, obtuseness, lethargy", citing Pound to Quinn, 3 Apr 1918: "not the hebetude of a lignified cerebrum."

II 31–33 **There is, it seems to us, | At best, only a limited value | In the knowledge derived from experience**: "We need a constant reminder, too, of how little we remember, and therefore of how little we learn from experience", *A Commentary* in *Criterion* Jan 1937. See note to *A Cooking Egg* 20, and see note to its epigraph for TSE writing at the age of thirty on the value of experience.

II 33–37 **experience ··· the pattern is new in every moment | And every moment is a new and shocking | Valuation of all we have been**: "The experience of a poem is the experience both of a moment and of a lifetime. It is very much like our intenser experiences of other human beings. There is a first, or an early moment which is unique, of shock and surprise", *Dante* (1929) I. (For "the intense moment", see note to V 21–23.) "a lifetime burning in every moment", *East Coker* V 23. "(And the time of death is every moment)", *The Dry Salvages* III 36. "every moment is a fresh beginning", *The Cocktail Party* III. (For "Every moment is a new problem", see note to V 3–4.) "the *whole* existing order must be, if ever so slightly, altered; and so the relations, proportions, values of each work of art toward the whole are readjusted", *Tradition and the Individual Talent* I (1919). Bergson: "l'intelligence laisse échapper ce qu'il y a de *nouveau* à chaque moment d'une histoire" [the intellect lets what is *new* in each moment of a history escape], *L'Evolution créatrice* ch. II (Philip Le Brun, *RES* May 1967). "For every moment | Is both beginning and end", *Little Gidding* V *verse draft msC* [3–4].

II 39–40 **in the middle of the way ··· in a dark wood**: Dante: "Nel mezzo del cammin di nostra vita | mi ritrovai per una selva oscura" [In the middle of the journey of our life I came to myself in a dark wood], *Inf.* I 1–2 (*Hayward*); see V 1.

II 41 **grimpen**: Conan Doyle: "life has become like that great Grimpen Mire, with little green patches everywhere into which one may sink and with no guide to point the track", *The Hound of the Baskervilles* (1902) ch. VII (*Sweeney 1941*). The Grimpen Mire is a bog that claims the lives of men and horses. OED (since 1972) "grimpen": "? A marshy area", quoting Conan Doyle, then TSE. For Lawrence Durrell on TSE's pleasure in his borrowing going undetected, see headnote to *Macavity: The Mystery Cat*. TSE makes a common noun of Conan Doyle's proper noun; similarly "grannoch", *Whan Cam ye fra the Kirk?* 3 (see note).

TSE to Hayward, 15 Nov 1939: "My movements must be as carefully calculated as if I was walking in the famous Grimpen Mire: at any moment you may hear a wild shriek, and I shall disappear like one of those unfortunate Dartmoor Ponies." To Christopher Morley, 10 Nov 1950, regretting he cannot dine with the Baker Street Irregulars, "as I should have been delighted to participate, and, especially, if I had time to prepare a short travelogue with lantern slides on the topography of the Great Grimpen". Pronounced *grimpin* in TSE's recordings.

II 41–42 **grimpen ··· fancy lights:** Milton, describing Satan as an *ignis fatuus* leading Eve: "Hovering and blazing with delusive light, | Misleads the amazed night-wanderer from his way | To bogs and mires", *Paradise Lost* IX 639–41. For *ignis fatuus*, see note to *Conversation Galante* 1–5.

II 43–44 **Do not let me hear | Of the wisdom of old men:** Kipling: "Oh, do not despise the advice of the wise, | Learn wisdom from those that are older", *Love-O'-Women* (*Ricks 1998*). Lionel Johnson: "Wisdom of ages! wisdom of old age! | Written, and spoken of, and prophesied", *Experience*; see note to *Little Gidding* II 88. **the wisdom of old men ··· their folly:** Pound: "I was a gaunt, grave councillor | Being in all things wise, and very old, | But I have put aside this folly", *La Fraisne* (included by TSE in Pound's *Selected Poems*). **folly:** against Montandon's tr. "folie" [madness], TSE wrote "bêtise!" [foolishness].

II 44–45 **old men ··· fear and frenzy:** Yeats: "Grant me an old man's frenzy, | Myself must I remake ··· Or inspired by frenzy ··· An old man's eagle mind", *An Acre of Grass*, 1938, in *Last Poems* (1939) (*Composition FQ* 68). Earlier, in *Modern Poetry* (broadcast 11 Oct 1936), Yeats had said: "It was in Eliot that certain revolutionary War poets, young men who felt that they had been dragged away from their studies, from their pleasant life, by the blundering frenzy of old men, found the greater part of their style" (*Essays and Introductions*, 1961, 500).

II 46 **belonging to another, or to others, or to God:** "But anyone who would write must let himself go, in one way or the other, for there are only four ways of thinking: to talk to others, or to one other, or to talk to oneself, or to talk to God", *Charles Whibley* (1931).

II 47 **The only wisdom we can hope to acquire:** for "the wisdom which we shall have acquired", see note to *Little Gidding* V 27–28.

II 48 **humility is endless:** Pascal: "Discourses on humility are a source of pride in the vain, and of humility in the humble ··· Few men speak humbly of humility", *Pensées* 377. Lancelot Andrewes: "what was this sign a sign of? There needs no straining at all—of humility clear; *signum humile, signum humilis* ··· Humility then: we shall find Him by that sign where we find humility ··· Such a sign of humility as never was. Signs are taken for wonders", Christmas Sermon 1618 (see *Gerontion* 17). TSE: "Humility is the most difficult of all virtues to achieve; nothing dies harder than the desire to think well of oneself", *Shakespeare and* *the Stoicism of Seneca* (1927). To Jeanette McPherrin, 9 May 1935: "I have tried to suggest that there is a wrong way of being humble as well as a right way."

II 49–50] TSE probably had these two lines in mind when he quoted the first to Sherrie Waites, 10 Aug 1962, saying that it had "no bearing on the history of the West of England [*with note*: Germelshausen]", adding "I thought that this line and the line which precedes it were melodious." **houses ··· under the hill**: in a squib on the name *Trevelyan*: "It means 'public house under the hill'", *Miss Mary Trevelyan* (in "Other Verses"). **under the sea ··· under the hill**: Tennyson: "O Sea! ··· the stately ships go on | To their haven under the hill", *Break, break, break* 9-12 (TSE: "dark dark dark", III i).

II 50 **dancers ··· gone under the hill**: Blake: "The lost Traveller's Dream under the Hill", *Epilogue: To the Accuser Who is the God of This World* 8. Pound: "Quick eyes gone under earth's lid", *Hugh Selwyn Mauberley* (1920) V 6. Friedrich Gerstäcker: "Der Tanz ist aus—die Tänzer werden jetzt zu Hause gehen" [The dance is over—the dancers have all gone home], *Germelshausen* (see headnote to III).

III

To H. W. Häusermann, 24 May 1940: "The third section contains several lines [35–46] adapted from the *Ascent of Mount Carmel*. I think that the imagery of the first section (though taken from the village itself) may have been influenced by recollections of *Germelshausen*, which I have not read for many years. I don't think the poem needs or can give rise to further explanation than that" (quoted in *English Studies* Aug 1941 by Häusermann, who added that Friedrich Gerstäcker's story *Germelshausen* was "frequently used in American schools as a text-book for beginners in German"). In the story (pub. 1860), a young artist meets and falls in love with a girl who takes him to Germelshausen, a village not found on his map, but which appears for one day every century. At midnight the village disappears, and the young man is separated forever from his love. *Composition FQ* 43: "What seems to have remained in Eliot's mind is merely the idea of a man from another age encountering the revelry of the long dead." TSE to Lady Richmond, 18 June 1936: "East Coker was delightful, with a sort of Germelshausen effect."

III 1–7 **O dark dark dark ··· The vacant interstellar spaces ··· dark the Sun and Moon**: Milton: "O dark, dark, dark, amid the blaze of noon, | Irrecoverably dark, total Eclipse | Without all hope of day! ··· The Sun to me is dark | And silent as the Moon, | When she deserts the night | Hid in her vacant interlunar cave", *Samson Agonistes* 80–89 (*Hayward*, also G. W. Stonier, *New Statesman* 14 Sept 1940). TSE had quoted Milton's lines, and commented: "Here *interlunar* is certainly a stroke of genius, but is merely combined with 'vacant' and 'cave', rather than giving and receiving life from them", *Milton* I (1936). (To Hayward, 3 Mar 1941: "while I retire into the interlunar cave.") "lunar incantations ··· through the spaces of the dark", *Rhapsody on a Windy Night* 4, 10. TSE had come across "O dark, dark, dark!" as the epigraph to ch. VIII of A. C. Green's *The Leavenworth Case* (1878), a detective story he read as a boy (*Crawford* 29). **O dark dark dark**: James Thomson: "Oh, dark, dark, dark, withdrawn from joy and light!" *The City of Dreadful Night* XIV 30 (*Crawford* 51). **They all go into the dark**: Henry Vaughan: "They are all gone into the world of light!" *Silex Scintillans* (*Grover Smith* 268). Arnold: "the last sparkle of flame before we are all in the dark, the last glimpse of colour before we all go into the drab", *Essays in Criticism*, Preface. TSE: "They vanish, the individuals, and our feeling for them sinks into the flame which refines", earliest notes for *Little Gidding* (*msA* fol. 77; see headnote to *Little Gidding* in Textual History).

III 2 **The vacant interstellar spaces, the vacant into the vacant**: H. L. Mencken on the culture of the American South: "It is, indeed, amazing to contemplate so vast a vacuity. One thinks of the interstellar spaces", *The Sahara of the Bozart* in *Prejudices: Second Series* (1920). (TSE: "'our own vacuity'", *Conversation Galante* 10.) **interstellar spaces**: an astronomical term at least since Francis Bacon: "we must first inquire, whether there be a collective vacuum in the interstellar spaces?" *Descriptio Globi Intellectualis* (1612). For Pascal on "The eternal silence of these infinite spaces", see note to *Silence* 15 ("I am terrified"). Before writing his introduction to Pascal's *Pensées* (1931), TSE had contributed an introduction to *The Wheel of Fire* (1930), where in his essay on Hamlet, G. Wilson Knight had written, "Between the sick soul and the knowledge of love there are all the interstellar spaces that divide Hell from Heaven", 27 (*Stephen Matthews* 162). To Hope Mirrlees, 16 Sept 1953: "astronomy bores me—it seems to me a study that interests chiefly people with no precise Christian faith: they like to wander about in the vast interstellar spaces." ("A dull head among windy spaces. || Signs are taken for wonders", *Gerontion* 16–17.)

III 2–8 **interstellar ··· merchant bankers ··· the Sun and Moon ··· the Stock Exchange Gazette**: likening stars to stocks and shares: "Dividing the stars into common and preferred", *Choruses from "The Rock"* III 65. The City had been associated with the heavens in the earliest ts of *The Rock*:

> Since building and destruction find their only
> Justification in the dividends
> On which the whole creation seems to move,
> Which move the sun and all the other stars ···
> Your capital is always unproductive
> Which brings no increment to the investor;
> You purchase shares which will never be quoted.
>
> Bodleian, MS Don. d. 44 fol. 162, *1st reading*

Tennyson: "And one far-off divine event, | To which the whole creation moves", *In Memoriam*, last lines. Dante: "the Love that moves the sun and the other stars", *Paradiso*, last line.

III 3 **eminent men of letters**: of Shaw and Wells: "We are in agreement with the eminent men of letters mentioned, in wishing to see the strengthening of central authority", *A Commentary* in *Criterion* Apr 1929.

III 3–8 **The captains, merchant bankers ··· all go into the dark, | And dark the Sun and Moon ··· the Directory of Directors**: Revelation 6: 15: "And the kings of the earth, and the great men, and the rich men, and the chief captains, and the mighty men, and every bondman, and every free man, hid themselves in the dens and in the rocks of the mountains" (*Preston* 29). Henry James: "capitalists and bankers, retired men of business, illustrious collectors", *The Golden Bowl* bk. III IV. TSE: "Those are the golf club Captains, these the Scouts, | And now the *société gymnastique de Poissy* | And now come the Mayor and the Liverymen", *Coriolan* I. *Triumphal March* 25–27. To Ezra Pound, Michaelmas [29 Sept] 1933 (concerning primarily Cantos XIV, XV): "there aint anythink real about blokes like Rothermere Beaverbrook Mellon and Henri Deterding I don't know who Lawrence is [Sir Herbert Lawrence] No matter and you cant make them real Its beyond Shakesp. etc. to give them individuality there are just types politicians profiteers financiers newspapersprops. & pressgangs, Calvin, the English, Vicecrusaders, liars, stupids pedants preachers bishops lady golfers Fabians conservatives imperialists & people who dont believe Major Douglas etc. I dont see what you can do with Hell without Sin & sinners This is not a theologgical argument its just the way it seems to me things hang together or dont It may be allright just as an interlude in Limbo but it wants to be supported by a real Hell underneath with real people in it Put me in if you Like". In 1934: "This is exactly what we find of the society which Mr. Pound puts in Hell, in his *Draft of XXX Cantos*. It consists (I may have overlooked one or two species) of politicians, profiteers, financiers, newspaper proprietors and their hired men, *agents provocateurs*, Calvin, St. Clement of Alexandria, the English, vice-crusaders, liars, the stupid, pedants, preachers, those who do not believe in Social Credit, bishops, lady golfers, Fabians, conservatives and imperialists", *After Strange Gods* 42–43. To Virginia Woolf, 22 Apr 1937: "I wondered whether you had not risen completely above literary and academic society, and were not moving in a world consisting of K.C.'s, belted surgeons, chartered accountants, generals, admirals of the blue, retired pro-consuls (e.g. Ronald Storrs), and higher ecclesiastics."

III 6–8 **all go into the dark ··· Directors:** to Geoffrey Curtis, 31 Dec 1940: "I hope I do not give the impression that the 'dark' into which the company directors go is the spiritual darkness of the mystic."

III 7 **the Sun and Moon:** regular meeting place of the revolutionists in James's *The Princess Casamassima*: "The Princess listened intently ··· Among other things our young man mentioned that he didn't go to the 'Sun and Moon' any more ··· this particular temple of their faith ··· was a hopeless sham", ch. XXIV. Casamassima *née* Christina Light.

III 7–8 **Almanach de Gotha:** annual directory of European royalty and higher nobility, published 1763–1944. Pronounced *Allmanack de Goater* in TSE's recordings of 1946–47. **Stock Exchange Gazette:** weekly journal, first pub. 1901. **Directory of Directors:** annual guide to the City, first pub. 1879.

III 8–9 **the Stock Exchange Gazette, the Directory of Directors ··· lost the motive of action:** "to live without words which convey, or which stimulate, emotion would be suicide, for it would mean dispensing with desires and motives for action ··· more conscious use of language ··· should help to protect us against the newspapers, the wireless, and everything else that is comprehended under the term propaganda", *Poetical and Prosaic Use of Words* (1943). **cold the sense:** "The cold craving when the sense is gone", *Little Gidding* II 76–93 *prose synopsis* [2–3]. **lost the motive of action:** HAMLET: "and lose the name of action" (III i).

III 12–14 **let the dark come upon you ··· the darkness of God ··· The lights:** John 12: 35–36: "Walk while ye have the light, lest darkness come upon you ··· believe in the light".

III 13–17 **darkness of God. As, in a theatre, | The lights are extinguished ··· rumble**

of wings ··· darkness on darkness ··· panorama ··· being rolled away: Poe: "in a theatre ··· in the form of God ··· mumble low, | And hither and thither fly ··· vast formless things | That shift the scenery to and fro ··· Condor wings ··· Out—out are the lights ··· The curtain ··· Comes down with the rush of a storm", *The Conqueror Worm* 5, 9–15, 33, 36 within the tale *Ligeia*. For Poe's poem, see *Mandarins* 1 13–15, "merely shifting scenes" (Conrad Aiken drew on the same description in *The Jig of Forslin*: see *Grover Smith* 268). For Poe's tale, see note to *The Waste Land* [II] 79–118. **As, in a theatre, | The**: *Richard II* V ii: "As in a theatre, the eyes of men | After a well-graced actor leaves the stage". **The lights are extinguished**: black-out instructions circulated from July 1939, evoking memories of Sir Edward Grey's remark on the eve of the Great War: "The lamps are going out all over Europe; we shall not see them lit again in our lifetime." OED "black-out" 1: "*Theatr.* The darkening of a stage during a performance", quoting first Shaw 1913, then the memoir in Rupert Brooke's *Collected Poems* (1918). OED 3: "The action of extinguishing, covering, or obscuring lights as a precaution against air-raids", from 1935: "instructions for compulsory 'black-outs' in districts where experiments were being carried out against air attacks". For Hayward to TSE, 12 Dec 1940, "rising in the black-out", see note to *Little Gidding* II 25–28, and for TSE on the distinction between the topical and the universal senses of "blackout", see letter to Hayward, 9 Sept 1941, in note to *Little Gidding* II 38. To Hope Mirrlees, 12 Apr 1946: "I really must do the complete Holy Week this year, for the first time since 1940 (and we didn't have Tenebrae then, because of the blackout)."

III 15–19 **underground ··· stations**: during both world wars, hundreds of thousands of Londoners took nightly shelter from air-raids, on the platforms of the Underground until trains stopped running, and then on the tracks and escalators too. (During the Great War, TSE and his wife sheltered in a cellar; see her letter to Charlotte Eliot, 22 Oct 1917, in *Letters 1*.) One of Henry Moore's "Shelter Drawings" appeared in *Britain at War* (1941), along with TSE's *Defence of the Islands*.

III 23 **wait without hope**: for "being separated ··· even from Hope" and "a recognition of the fact that one can do without all these things", see letter to Geoffrey Faber [18 Sept 1927] quoted in note to *The Dry Salvages* II 42–47. "Without haste without hope without fear", *In silent corridors of death* 6.

III 24 **hope for the wrong thing**: "Having hoped for the wrong things or dreaded the wrong things", *The Dry Salvages* II 58. "Conservatism is too often conservation of the wrong things", *The Church's Message* (1937). To Frank Morley, 4 Aug 1938: "Coleridge cannot mean very much for one, or is likely to mean the wrong things, unless one knows a fair amount of what Coleridge knew". "Radicalism then proceeds to organize the 'vital issues', and reject what is not vital ··· In short, while liberalism did not know what it wanted of education, radicalism does know; and it wants the wrong thing", *Modern Education and the Classics* (1933). "Unless society can exercise some unconscious pressure upon its members to want the right things, the right life, the opportunity given may be merely the opportunity to follow false lights", *Education in a Christian Society* (1940) ("fancy lights", II 42, and see note to III 40–41). To Egon Vietta, 23 Feb 1947: "we have largely learned the wrong things". "how many of those who call themselves 'conservative' · · · are concerned with conserving the right things", *"The Conservative Mind"* by Russell Kirk, reader's report (1954).

III 26–34 **all in the waiting. | Wait without thought · · · You say I am repeating | Something I have said before**: to George Barker, 24 Jan 1938: "from time to time · · · inspiration is exhausted · · · you either repeat yourself, or stop writing · · · A few men · · · simply could not repeat themselves · · · *nothing is worth doing twice* · · · in these periods of sterility one has to have recourse partly to patience and waiting" (see headnote to *Four Quartets*, 4. "NOT MERELY MORE OF THE SAME"). Shakespeare had "the gift of never doing the same thing twice", *The Development of Shakespeare's Verse* (1950 text). "critical ability, that power of self-criticism, without which the poet will do no more than repeat himself to the end of his life", *Goethe as the Sage* (1955).

III 29–30 **winter lightning, | The wild thyme unseen**: John Day: "winter lightening or Christmas thunder", *Law-Trickes* act V (for Day, see note to *The Waste Land* [III] 197). *A Midsummer Night's Dream* II i: "I know a bank where the wild thyme blows". TSE: "The wild thyme unseen, or the winter lightning", *The Dry Salvages* V 26. For *A Midsummer Night's Dream*, see note to I 28–33.

III 33–35 **You say I am repeating | Something I have said before. I shall say it again. | Shall I say it again?**: "I may often repeat what I have said before, and I may often contradict myself", *The Music of Poetry* (1942). Whitman: "If you do not say any thing how can I say any thing? · · · Do I contradict myself? | Very well then I contradict myself", *Song of Myself* 1324–26 (both *Musgrove* 20–21). TSE: "The debt of every poet to his predecessors and contemporaries is a scent eagerly sniffed and followed by every critic; but the debts of poets to their own earlier work are apt to be overlooked. Yet any intelligent psychologist ought to see at once that any poet, even the greatest, will tend to use his own impressions over and over again. It is by no means a matter of poverty of inspiration. Every man who writes poetry has a certain number of impressions and emotions which are particularly important to him. Every man who writes poetry will be inclined to seek endlessly for a final expression of these, and will be dissatisfied with his expressions and will want to employ the initial feeling, the original image or rhythm, once more in order to satisfy himself", *Poets' Borrowings* (1928). To Montgomery Belgion, 19 July 1940: "As for repeating myself, I am not sure that I have your meaning clear. I only *meant* repeating just at that point (for several lines the imagery is very suggestive of *Burnt Norton*): because the whole subject matter (so far as there is any) of the total poem I thought was pretty different, only not so firmly grasped." For "certain images recur", see note to *Journey of the Magi* 23–27. To H. Warner Allen, 12 Dec 1949: "One has to take account of the fact that to many people, every writer on mystical subjects appears not only to be saying the same things as other writers, but himself to be saying the same things again and again. So I think he needs to be clear in advising people on the matter that is coming." On two aims in lecturing: "One is, to avoid saying anything that I have said before; the other is, to avoid saying anything that somebody else has said before—and probably said better · · · some of us devote our later years to trying to express the same ideas better", *The Three Voices of Poetry* (1954; preliminary remarks omitted from *On Poetry and Poets*). "this poet of torrential imagination recognized many of his best bits · · · saved them, and reproduced them more than once", *Christopher Marlowe* (1919).

III 35 **again?**: this reading was changed on a late ts to "here and now?" and twice printed so. But when Frank Morley objected, TSE wrote to him, 5 Apr 1940: "I will think about 'again' instead of 'here and now' and I tend to believe that you are right". (The words "here and now" appear at V 30.) The reading "again?" was restored in time for Faber's pamphlet, *EC*.

III 35–46 **In order to arrive there · · · where you are not:** *Hayward* and *Sweeney 1941* point to St. John of the Cross:

> In order to arrive at having pleasure in everything,
> Desire to have pleasure in nothing.
> In order to arrive at possessing everything,
> Desire to possess nothing.
> In order to arrive at being everything,
> Desire to be nothing.
> In order to arrive at knowing everything,
> Desire to know nothing.
> In order to arrive at that wherein thou hast no pleasure,
> Thou must go by a way wherein thou hast no pleasure.
> In order to arrive at that which thou knowest not,
> Thou must go by a way that thou knowest not.
> In order to arrive at that which thou possessest not,
> Thou must go by a way that thou possessest not.
> In order to arrive at that which thou art not,
> Thou must go through that which thou art not
>
> *Ascent of Mount Carmel* I XIII 1

William James had quoted the passage in "Saintliness" in *The Varieties of Religious Experience*. TSE mentioned St. John of the Cross to his brother in connection with the epigraphs to *Burnt Norton* (see note), and wrote in the same month to Bonamy Dobrée, 17 Apr 1936: "The doctrine that in order to arrive at the love of God one must divest oneself of the love of created beings was thus expressed by St. John of the Cross, you know: i.e. a man who was writing primarily not for you and me, but for people seriously engaged in pursuing the Way of Contemplation. It is only to be read in relation to that Way: i.e. merely to kill one's human affections will get one nowhere, it would be only to become rather more completely a living corpse than most people are. But the doctrine is fundamentally true, I believe. Or to put your belief in your way, that only through the love of created beings can we approach the love of God, that I do believe to be UNTRUE. Whether we mean by that domestic and friendly affections, or a more comprehensive love of the 'neighbour', of humanity in general. I don't think that ordinary human affections are capable of leading us to the love of God, but rather that the love of God is capable of informing, intensifying and elevating our human affections, which otherwise may have little to distinguish them from the 'natural' affections of animals. Try looking at it from that end of the glass!" (For St. John of the Cross, see note to *Sweeney Agonistes* second epigraph. For "the coupling of animals", see note to I 44.) On Paul Elmer More: "What is significant to me · · · is not simply the conclusions at which he has arrived, but the fact that he *arrived* there from somewhere else; and not simply that he came from somewhere else, but that he took a particular route. And conversely, the point at which he has arrived gives an importance to the stages of the journey", *Paul Elmer More* (1937). Pater: "For the way to perfection is through a series of disgusts", *Studies in the History of the Renaissance* ch. VI (scored in TSE's copy).

Reluctantly granting permission for performance of a musical setting using *East Coker*, TSE explained to the Master of Magdalene Sir Henry Willink, and the Pepys Librarian Francis Turner, 9 Nov 1962, that he was making an exception: "it is not one of the parts which I would normally allow a composer to make use of. The passage he wants is, of course, based on St. John of the Cross; unfortunately it is from St. John's prose and not from his verse." (For the letter, see "This Edition", 6. TSE ON TREATMENTS OF HIS POEMS.)

III 36–41 **To arrive where you are, to get from where you are not ··· In order to possess what you do not possess | You must go by the way of dispossession:** Whitman: "To see nothing anywhere but what you may reach it and pass it ··· To look up or down no road but it stretches and waits for you ··· To see no possession but you may possess it", *Song of the Open Road* XIII 170–74 (*Musgrove* 54). **where you are not:** Baudelaire, tr. Stuart Merrill: "It always seems to me that I will be better where I am not", *Anywhere Out of the World* in *Pastels in Prose*.

III 38–39 **to arrive at what you do not know | You must go by a way which is the way of ignorance:** Pascal: "The other extreme is that reached by great intellects, who, having run through all that men can know, find they know nothing, and come back again to that same ignorance which is conscious of itself", *Pensées* 327. TSE: "By being 'educated' I mean ··· being able to allow for all the books one has not read and the things one does not understand—it means some understanding of one's own ignorance", *Revelation* (1937). Clough: "I also know not, and I need not know ··· Come all to this true ignorance and thee", *The Questioning Spirit* 46–50 (*Murray*).

III 40–41 **In order to possess what you do not possess | You must go by the way of dispossession:** "the way leads towards possession | Of what you have sought for in the wrong place", *The Cocktail Party* II.

III 44 **And what you do not know is the only thing you know:** Socrates: *ἓν οἶδα ὅτι οὐδὲν οἶδα* [I know that I know nothing], quoted by Diogenes Laertius, *Lives of Eminent Philosophers* bk. II §32.

IV

Raymond Preston reported discussing the lines of "the Good Friday poem in *East Coker*" in 1951 with TSE, who said he was "occupied with the craftsman's problems ··· he then added that he thought they were probably influenced by the practice of the rosary and in particular by the Sorrowful Mysteries", *Braybrooke ed.* The five Sorrowful Mysteries are five divisions of the rosary, suitable for prayer and meditation: the Agony in the Garden, the Scourging of Christ, the Crowning with Thorns, the Carrying of the Cross, and the Crucifixion. On the rosary, see the note to *Burnt Norton* V 13–22.

IV 1–12] *Hayward*: "In this pastiche of a 17th-century 'metaphysical' poem on the Passion, the 'wounded surgeon', 'the dying nurse', and 'the ruined millionaire' are metaphorical allusions to Christ crucified, the Church, and Adam after the Fall, respectively. *East Coker* was written for Good Friday 1940" (see IV 25).

Noting the French translation of "dying nurse" as "l'infirmière moribonde", the German translator of *Four Quartets*, Nora Wydenbruck, wrote to TSE, 8 May 1953: "I took both the surgeon and the nurse to mean Christ · · · What disturbs me is the implication that the Church is moribund". TSE, 19 May: "The majority of the authorities on the subject whose work I have consulted, seem to hold the opinion that the 'dying nurse' is the Church. On this subject I can throw no light myself, but we will have to think of some justification for the phrase. This happens to be one of the cases in which an uninflected language has an advantage—there are, of course, other situations in which the lack of inflection is distinctly disadvantageous." Helen Gardner:

> In his book *"Four Quartets" Rehearsed* (1946), Mr. Raymond Preston provided an allegorical interpretation of the lyric, identifying the "wounded surgeon" with Christ, the "dying nurse" with the Church Militant, and the "ruined millionaire" with Adam; and in a footnote reported that he had originally thought "that the ruined millionaire was the Fallen Angel" and that he was "indebted to Mr. Eliot for the correction". In *The Art of T. S. Eliot* (1949) I contested this interpretation, in spite of Mr. Preston giving the author as his authority, on the grounds that to endow a hospital is an act of charity hardly to be compared with endowing the world with Original Sin. I took all three figures, surgeon, nurse, millionaire as types of Christ.
>
> [*Footnote*:] I have to own that Hayward · · · gives the same allegorical interpretation as Mr. Preston · · · I regret that I never summoned up the nerve to ask Eliot whether I was wrong to query at some length the identification of the millionaire with Adam. But he would probably have evaded siding with either of his readers.
>
> *Composition FQ* 43–44

IV 1 **the wounded surgeon plies the steel**: Thackeray: "The wounded writhe · · · The out-worn surgeon plies his knife", *The Due of the Dead* 19, 21 (Marcia Karp, personal communication). Isaiah 53: 5: "he was wounded for our transgressions · · · and with his stripes we are healed" (*Cook*). Luke 4: 23: "Physician, heal thyself." OED "physician" 2: "One who practises the healing art, including medicine and surgery" (as distinguished from 2b: "One legally qualified to practise the healing art · · · *esp.* as distinguished from one qualified as a surgeon only"). Andrewes: "The Physician slain, and of His Flesh and Blood a receipt made that the patient might recover", Sermon of the Nativity 1612 (*Grover Smith* 269–70) (TSE: "receipt", II 27). Herbert: "his condition | Though it be ill, makes him no ill Physician", *The Church-Porch* 443–44. Valéry compared himself to a surgeon: "j'ai coutume de procéder à la mode des chirurgiens qui purifient d'abord leurs mains et préparent leur champ opératoire. C'est ce que j'appelle le *nettoyage de la situation verbale*. Pardonnez-moi cette expression qui assimile les mots et les formes du discours aux mains et aux instruments d'un opérateur" [I generally proceed like a surgeon who sterilises his hands and prepares the area to be operated on. This is what I call *cleaning up the verbal situation*. You must excuse this expression equating the words and forms of speech with the hands and instruments of a surgeon], *Poésie et pensée abstraite* (tr. Denise Folliot as *Poetry and Abstract Thought* in *The Art of Poetry*, 1958). TSE: "I am convinced of the capital importance of a preliminary *nettoyage de la situation verbale*", *UNESCO and Its Aims* (1947). But in his Introduction to Valéry's *The Art of Poetry*: "it may be the fact that I cannot identify, under the disguise of this metaphor, any experience of my own, that makes me suspect that 'cleaning up the verbal situation' is, in plain English, eyewash." For "*la plaie et le couteau!*" [the wound and the knife!], see note to *I am the Resurrection and the Life* 4–5, "the victim and the sacrificial knife".

IV 1–2 **surgeon plies the steel | That questions**: in 1934: "'the hereditary body of religious faith and moral practice.' And, in order not to limit my instances to theology, I will quote from another contemporary Liberal practitioner, a literary critic this time: '··· exposing them with the scalpel of a surgeon rather than that of a philosopher'", *After Strange Gods* 22–23, quoting V. F. Calverton, *Contemporary Literature: A Study in Pathology in Our Neurotic Age* ed. S. D. Schmalhausen (1932). Benlowes: "here lance me, Lord ··· piercing blade", *Theophila's Love-Sacrifice* XIII lxxiii, lxxv (see note to IV 16–24). In a ts submitted to TSE, Keith Douglas wrote of a swordfish that "yielded to the sharp enquiring blade", *The Marvel* 1–4. TSE, on Douglas's ts (in 1941?): "the *surgeon's* blade is 'enquiring', but I am not sure about this word" (BL Add. mss 53773).

IV 2 **distempered**: OED 3: "Disordered, diseased". 2: "Of the bodily humours ··· disturbed in humour, temper, or feelings ··· vexed, troubled. *Obs.*" *Paradise Lost* IX 1128–32: "in subjection now | To sensual appetite ··· from thus distempered breast, | Adam, estranged in look and altered style".

IV 3–25 **bleeding ··· the fever chart ··· fever ··· blood ··· good**: Kipling: "Our blood 'as truly mixed with yours—all down the Red Cross train ··· The same old saw-backed fever-chart. Good-bye—good luck to you!" *The Parting of the Columns* 13–16.

IV 6 **disease**: to Eleanor Hinkley, 13 Sept 1939: "Psychology may help us to distinguish between disease and sin, but that does not abolish either. To do away with the sense of sin is to do away with civilisation."

IV 9–10 **Adam's curse | And that, to be restored**: Clough: "That to forget is not to be restored", *Adam and Eve* XIII 35 (*Murray*).

IV 11 **The whole earth is our hospital**: Bach, Cantata 25 (words anon.): "Die ganze Welt ist nur ein Hospital ··· einen quälet in der Brust | Ein hitzges Fieber böser Lust; | Der andre lieget krank | An eigner Ehre hässlichem Gestank; | Den dritten zehrt die Geldsucht ab | Und stürzt ihn vor der Zeit ins Grab. | Der erste Fall hat jedermann beflecket | Und mit dem Sündenaussatz angestecket. | Ach! dieses Gift durchwühlt auch meine Glieder ··· Wer ist mein Arzt, wer hilft mir wieder?" [The whole world is but a hospital ··· For one quakes in his breast with the burning fever of evil pleasure; another lies ill in the putrid smell of his pride; a third is a slave to gold and is thrust before his time into the grave. The first Fall has stained everyone and infected them with the leprosy of sin. Ah! This poison rages so through my limbs ··· Who is my doctor, who will heal me?] (TSE: "the healer's art ··· Our only health is the disease ··· Adam's curse ··· the ruined millionaire", IV 4–12). Bach's high baroque setting was composed for the 14th Sunday after Trinity 1723, with the prescribed text Luke 17: 11–19, the cleansing of the lepers (Richard Luckett, personal communication). Andrewes: "'What is man, that Thou shouldest visit him?' Visit him;—not as 'the day spring from on high' doth the earth; but visit him, as if a great prince should go into an hospital", Sermon of the Nativity 1612 (*Grover Smith* 269–70). Sir Thomas Browne: "For the world, I count it not an Inn, but an Hospital, and a place, not to live, but die in", *Religio Medici* II 12 (*Hayward*). Pater: "the whole world seemed to present itself as a hospital", *Marius the Epicurean* ch. XXV (*Janowitz*, who also quotes Pater's essay on Browne: "to Browne the whole world is a museum; all the grace and beauty it has being of a somewhat mortified kind"). For Browne, Raleigh and Pater, see note to *Little Gidding* III 35–36. Baudelaire, tr. Stuart Merrill: "This life is a hospital", *Anywhere Out of the World* in *Pastels in Prose*.

IV 15 **prevents:** including OED 4. *Theol.*, etc: "To go before with spiritual guidance and help: said of God, or of his grace, anticipating human action or need. *arch.*", citing 1548–49 Bk. of Common Prayer, "That thy grace maye alwayes prevente and folowe us." An alteration by TSE, from "torments", made only after first publication in *NEW* (see Textual History).

IV 16 **chill ascends from feet to knees:** death of Falstaff: "bade me lay more clothes on his feet: I put my hand into the bed, and felt them, and they were as cold as any stone: then I felt to his knees, and so upward, and upward and all was as cold as any stone", *Henry V* II iii. TSE: "upward at the knees ··· from nape to base", *Sweeney Erect* 17, 22.

IV 16–24 **chill ··· freeze ··· frigid ··· blood:** Benlowes: "When blood does freeze to ice of death", *Theophila* X xxxv ("modelled on Benlowes" wrote TSE in a copy of *G. Jones*, alongside the quoted lines 18–20). **blood ··· drink ··· bloody flesh ··· food ··· flesh and blood:** "food they need; | Christ's flesh, their meat; blood, drink indeed", *Theophila* III lxxxvi. TSE: "I confess myself to a mild partiality to this man's verse ··· I have spoken of Benlowes ··· in order to show how a versifier of much above the ordinary level ··· can bring a good idiom to such a point that a drastic reform of language is needed", *The Minor Metaphysicals: From Cowley to Dryden* (1930). TSE had quoted *Theophila* I xxxvi–xxxvii in his fourth Clark Lecture (*The Varieties of Metaphysical Poetry* 137); see headnote to *Four Quartets*, 3. COMPOSITION. **freeze | And quake in frigid purgatorial fires:** Webster: "sweat in ice and freeze in fire", *The Duchess of Malfi* IV ii. For Webster's scene, see note to *The Waste Land* [II] 117–23.

IV 17 **sings in mental wires:** William C. Scott: "Poetry essentially consists in ··· those electric trains of thought that kindle admiration and sympathy in their communication—those far-reaching mental wires that come in contact with the beautiful", *Poetry and Religion* (1853). Harry Jones: "the mental wires that have been out of tune", *Recreation* in *Good Words* magazine (1881). TSE: "The trilling wire in the blood", *Burnt Norton* II 3.

IV 21–25 **blood ··· food ··· blood ··· we call:** Hopkins: "We scarcely call that banquet food, | But even our Saviour's and our blood", *Barnfloor and Winepress* 31–32. **good:** OED 8c: "of a day or season observed as holy by the church", citing Quarles, "One bad good-Friday", *Emblems* V vii. *East Coker* was published in *NEW* on 21 Mar 1940, the day before Good Friday (*Preston* 34). In these years, TSE occasionally dated his letters simply "Easter", "Holy Innocents' Day", or used saints' days, explaining to Kathleen Bliss, 10 Mar 1945 (St. Blanche): "Mary Trevelyan sent me a Belgian diary full of saints I never heard of".

IV 24 **substantial flesh and blood:** Glocester Ridley, paraphrasing the 9th-century monk Bertram: "Think not so grossly, as that I will give my substantial flesh and blood to be eaten and drank by you (which indeed were a wicked and ungodly act for you to do)", *Life of Dr Nicholas Ridley* (1763) 167. Passages from the sermons of the 16th-century martyr Nicholas Ridley are quoted in the typescript of *The Rock* submitted to the Lord Chamberlain's office (BL), but were later cut. "Flesh and blood is weak and frail, | Susceptible", *The Hippopotamus* (*Preston* 36).

V

V 1–2 **So here I am, in the middle way, having had twenty years— | Twenty years largely wasted:** Clough: "Here am I yet, another twelvemonth spent, | One-third departed of the mortal span", *"Blank Misgivings of a Creature moving about in Worlds not realised"* 1–2 (*Murray*). *Composition FQ* 18: "Eliot's rueful confession that Blake and Clough kept 'getting into' *East Coker* · · · the opening of Part V might have come straight out of *Amours de Voyage*." See headnote to *Four Quartets*, 4. COMPOSITION. "Here I am", *Gerontion* 1 (written twenty years earlier). **in the middle way:** *Inf.* I 1: "Nel mezzo del cammin di nostra vita" [In the middle of the journey of our life]. TSE: "In the middle, not only in the middle of the way", II 39. "Britain is the bridge between Latin culture and Germanic culture in both of which she shares. But Britain is not only the bridge, the middle way, between two parts of western Europe; she is, or should be · · · not only European but the connection between Europe and the rest of the world", *A Commentary* in *Criterion* Mar 1928.

V 1–2, 4 **here I am · · · having had twenty years— | Twenty years · · · a wholly new start:** "I am bidden · · · Twenty years after · · · not wholly inappropriate", *The Cultivation of Christmas Trees ms2* 1–3.

V 2 **Twenty years largely wasted, the years of *l'entre deux guerres*:** Léon Daudet, opening paragraph of *L'Entre-deux-guerres: Souvenirs des milieux littéraires, politiques, artistiques et medicaux de 1880 à 1905* (1915): "La grande crise qui vient de fonder sur l'Europe, et notamment sur la France, ne changera en rien l'inclinaison de ces modestes souvenirs. Mais il me paraît que ce titre, *l'Entre-deux-guerres*, caractérise bien la morne période qui va de 1890 à 1904, de l'échec du boulangisme à la fin de la ligue de la Patrie Française. Nous sommes à vingt ans de distance du désastre de 70–71" [The great crisis which has just fallen upon Europe, and particularly upon France, will not change in the slightest the bent of these modest reminiscences, but it seemed to me that this title, *l'Entre-deux-guerres*, well characterises the grim period 1890–1904, from the check to *boulangisme* to the end of the league of the Patrie Française. We are twenty years away from the disaster of 1870–71], (*boulangisme* = a political movement; 1870–71 = the Franco-Prussian War, for which see note to *The Waste Land* [I] 8–17). Daudet was among the leaders of *l'Action Française*. In 1927, TSE unsuccessfully recommended Daudet's book *Le Stupide XIXe Siècle* for publication by Faber. TSE to Hayward, 23 June 1940 (enclosing the drafts of *East Coker*): "I agree that the state of exhaustion which will follow our winning this war is hardly likely to favour the arts of civilisation in our time: yet the last twenty years was not a period which I regard as a specially noble one; and unless things are simply worse, they might be made better."

"In the last twenty years we have been more unsettled by events, than we could be by two generations of prophets", *The Christian in the Modern World* (1935). In 1943: "No generous mind can welcome the task of denouncing the results of twenty years of devoted labour, on the part of such Christian men as the designers of the South India Scheme; no ingenuous heart can fail to be moved by the spectacle of such waste. Twenty patient years to build what is only an elaborate artifice! Twenty years to construct a pantomime horse! Yet, on a longer view, we can assure ourselves that no such efforts are wasted", *Reunion by Destruction* 21. "Twenty years and the spring is over", *Landscapes* I. *New Hampshire* 6. ***l'entre deux guerres***: on the outbreak of the Second World War: "The clear formulation of our own aims cannot be arrived at without a deal of hard thinking by our best minds over a considerable period of time. There must be many ··· visited by the suspicion that this expense of spirit, body and natural resources may only lead to another uneasy interim *entre deux guerres*; there may be many among the enemy who are inspired by no worthier ambition than that of reversing the situation of 1918. We have the obligation to reassure the one group, and to undeceive the other", *Truth and Propaganda* (1939) (Ricks 269). TSE on Hayward's projected book, 11 Sept 1939: "I am happy to think that the Recherche du temps perdu is stirring in your mind. You ought to begin taking notes ··· Anyway, get on with it. Forgotten epochs, l'entre deux guerres." 9 Nov: "As for the future of civilisation, let us avoid that subject, but do try to train your mind occasionally on the subject of le temps perdu of l'entre deux guerres, of which you are to be the definitive social chronicler." 29 Nov: "I expect from you something in the way of a permanent document on the age of l'entre deux guerres". Hayward wrote to Anne Ridler, 28 Feb 1940, that his schooldays were during "the twilight of the sad interim *entre deux guerres*" (BL Add. ms 71225 fol. 20). TSE: "I think ··· the seventeen volumes of *The Criterion* constitute a valuable record of the thought of that period between two wars", *A Note on The Criterion* (1966).

V 2] In *ts1b*, TSE wrote, slantwise: "20 yrs / l'entre 2 guerres / 20 yrs. or 600 upwards / Home is where we start from". The conflicts between England and France known as the Hundred Years' War began in 1337. (For the Battle of Poitiers, see note to *Little Gidding* II 67–96 *drafts first venture in verse* [6].)

V 2–3 **Twenty years ··· Trying to learn to use words**: "if the work of the last twenty years is worthy of being classified at all, it is as belonging to a period of search for a proper modern colloquial idiom", *The Music of Poetry* (1942). It had also been a period of trying to use words instead of weapons (see next note). To Pamela Murray, 4 Feb 1938: "It is perhaps useful to remember that there are three generations of poets alive, each with its own characteristics. The oldest is Mr. Yeats; the middle generation may be represented by Mr. Ezra Pound and myself; and the third by Mr. Auden and Mr. Spender. Of course there are younger poets still, but there has not yet been time for a distinct 'fourth' generation to be established. One may take 'generation' as meaning a space of about twenty years in age between each. But it is a mistake to treat all the poets of any one generation as if they were very much alike—if they are any good they are very different from each other. And of course they vary according to the forms in which they prefer to express themselves."

V 2–15 ***guerres*** **··· get the better of words ··· raid on the inarticulate ··· Undisciplined squads ··· fight**: to the *Times Educational Supplement*, 26 Oct 1942 (unpublished): "the battle of words often seems to be being fought with words which have not been properly trained for the very difficult military operations which they are expected to carry out".

V 3–4 **Trying to learn to use words, and every attempt | Is a wholly new start, and**

a different kind of failure: "As one goes on, writing verse, into middle age, one can only do well by becoming more and more conscious of one's limitations: of what one can do well, and of what one cannot do; learning to use one's abilities to the best and to avoid overstraining oneself where weakest. And I think that some of what I have said about the practice of poetry is applicable to the greatest and most general profession of all—that of marriage. For, just as a poet can never be sure that he knows how to write poetry, but must constantly start as if afresh, so, I think, married people must always regard each other as a mysterious person whom they are gradually getting to know, in a process which must go on to the end of the life of one or the other · · · Every moment is a new problem, and you cannot succeed, in the best meaning of 'success', unless you approach the new poem, or the familiar husband or wife, with a feeling that there is a great deal for you to learn", *On Poetry* (1947), passage omitted from published text (ts Hay Library, Brown U.). **a wholly new start**: on Symons: "if we can recall the time when we were ignorant of the French symbolists, and met with *The Symbolist Movement in Literature*, we remember that book as an introduction to wholly new feelings, as a revelation", *The Perfect Critic* I (1920).

V 5–6 **one has only learnt to get the better of words | For the thing one no longer has to say**: "the more your work is praised · · · the more difficult it becomes to write the next thing so that it shall be the thing you have it in you to write, instead of the thing that you know people expect", *On Poetry* (1947) 9.

V 8 **raid on the inarticulate**: Santayana on William James: "His excursions into philosophy were accordingly in the nature of raids", *Character and Opinion in the United States* (1920) 67. Jacques Rivière: "'It is only with the advent of Romanticism that the literary act came to be conceived as a sort of raid on the absolute and its result as a revelation'", quoted in *The Use of Poetry and the Use of Criticism* 128–29 (*Crawford* 200).

V 8–9 **raid · · · shabby equipment**: "There are points, certainly, upon which even I, with an incomparably inferior equipment and ability for theological thinking, would venture to disagree", *Paul Elmer More* (1937). To Colin Robinson, 6 Dec 1945: "it seems to me that you are trying to express rather difficult ideas which are just beyond your grasp, with an equipment of vocabulary and prosody which is inadequate for poetic expression." **shabby**: Frank Morley urged restoration of the original reading, "worn-out" (see Textual History), but TSE replied, 5 Apr 1940, drawing attention to "worn-out" at II 19: "as for 'shabby', well I couldn't say 'worn out' again, having used it once, and I feel that an adjective is necessary there, both for the metre and for the reason that otherwise you get too heavy a stress on 'equipment'." ("some worn-out common song", *Portrait of a Lady* II 40.)

V 9–10 **deteriorating | In the general mess of imprecision of feeling**: to Hayward, 12 June 1944, sending a proof of *Four Quartets*: "Going through them again, I am depressed by a certain imprecision of word and phrase, especially in *Burnt Norton*, but also in *East Coker*." "Out of the slimy mud of words, out of the sleet and hail of verbal imprecisions, | Approximate thoughts and feelings", *Choruses from "The Rock"* IX 22–23. "Words · · · Decay with imprecision", *Burnt Norton* V 13–16.

V 11 **Undisciplined squads of emotion**: "belief in the undisciplined imagination and emotions", *An American Critic* (1916). Given the "disorganized and hysterical state" of Europe in 1918, the League of Nations seemed "to illustrate that exaggerated faith in human reason to which people of undisciplined emotions are prone", *Catholicism and International Order* (1933). For the *Vita Nuova* and "the discipline of the emotions", see letter to Paul Elmer More, 2 June 1930, quoted in headnote to *Ash-Wednesday*, 3. AFTER PUBLICATION. "every precise emotion tends towards intellectual formulation", *Shakespeare and the Stoicism of Seneca* (1927). Clark Lecture VI (1926): "In Dante, as I have said again and again, you get a system of thought and feeling; every part of the system felt and thought in its place, and the whole system felt and thought; and you cannot say that it is primarily 'intellectual' or primarily 'emotional', for the thought and the emotion are reverse sides of the same thing", *The Varieties of Metaphysical Poetry* 182–83. (Bradley: "That which is mainly intellectual ··· would probably be admitted ··· to fall outside religion", *Appearance and Reality* ch. XXV, footnote; in his copy TSE underlined "mainly" and wrote: "And you cannot determine at what point it is *mainly*." *The Sacred Wood*, Preface to the 1928 edition: "in criticizing poetry, we are right if we begin, with what sensibility and what knowledge of other poetry we possess, with poetry as excellent words in excellent arrangement and excellent metre. That is what is called the technique of verse. But we observe that we cannot define even the technique of verse; we cannot say at what point 'technique' begins or where it ends.") To A. L. Rowse, 3 Mar 1941: "I am disturbed, I may say, however, by the constant tuffiness that creeps into Auden's work: an abuse of emphatic adjectives which are impressive on a first reading but after two or three readings comes to appear empty and superfluous. The adjective is always a danger."

V 11–18 **what there is to conquer ··· has already been discovered ··· There is only the fight to recover what has been lost ··· under conditions | That seem unpropitious ··· trying**: "poetry ··· must be constantly exploring 'the frontiers of the spirit.' But these frontiers are not ··· conquered once and for all and settled ··· Our effort is as much to regain, under very different conditions, what was known to men writing at remote times and in alien languages ··· emotions themselves are constantly being lost; they can never be merely preserved, but must be always re-discovered", *That Poetry is Made with Words* (1939). (See note to V 26–31, and for the poet's "duty to arouse feelings which hadn't been discovered before", see note to *Little Gidding* II 74.) "You are attempting the same thing in conditions still more difficult", *A Message from T. S. Eliot* (1949). Clark Lecture VII: "If you cease to be able to express feelings you cease to be able to have them, and sensibility is replaced by sentiment", *The Varieties of Metaphysical Poetry* 200. To I. A. Richards, 20 Feb 1944, on Basic English: "If Basic is *too* efficient will English disappear? Will humanity perhaps be only too glad to be excused from the sort of thoughts and feelings which can only be expressed in English, or some other complete language of a natural growth?" (Clark Lecture I: "Not that I suggest that the history of human emotion has been a steady accumulation ··· Many feelings have to be abandoned, many are mislaid, many are corrupted, some seem to have disappeared", *The Varieties of Metaphysical Poetry* 52.) "The business of the poet is not to find new emotions, but to use the ordinary ones and, in working them up into poetry, to express feelings which are not in actual emotions at all", *Tradition and the Individual*

Talent II (1919); in his copy of the American first edition of *Selected Essays*, TSE scored the last phrase, with "?" For "some emotions have been purified away", see quotation from *The Development of Shakespeare's Verse* (1937) in headnote to *Marina*. **lost | And found and lost again**: on the Jacobean-Caroline period: "On all sides, it was an age of lost causes, and unpopular names, and forsaken beliefs, and impossible loyalties, as Matthew Arnold would have said; the beauty of life and the shadow of martyrdom are the background ··· I sometimes wonder whether the generation succeeding my own may not be also a generation which has lost faith in lost causes", *The Minor Metaphysicals* (1930). (For Arnold on Oxford as "Home of lost causes", see note to *Little Gidding* III 36–45.) Of Arnold: "if he were our exact contemporary, he would find all his labour to perform again", *The Sacred Wood* (1920), Introduction. "It is not to say that Arnold's work was vain if we say that it is to be done again; for we must know in advance, if we are prepared for that conflict, that the combat may have truces but never a peace. If we take the widest and wisest view of a Cause, there is no such thing as a Lost Cause because there is no such thing as a Gained Cause. We fight for lost causes because we know that our defeat and dismay may be the preface to our successors' victory, though that victory itself will be temporary; we fight rather to keep something alive than in the expectation that anything will triumph", *Francis Herbert Bradley* (1927). "We cannot revive old factions", *Little Gidding* III 36. **under conditions | That seem unpropitious ··· trying**: to J. H. Woods, 23 Mar 1917: "I will send you a copy of an article I wrote for the *Monist*—I fear not a very good one, done under trying conditions—on Leibniz and Aristotle."

V 12 **By strength and submission**: J. W. N. Sullivan: "Beethoven is one of the very few musicians who can really be compared with a great and profound poet ··· an expression of the reconciliation of Freedom and Necessity, or of Assertion and Submission", *Beethoven: His Spiritual Development* (1927; 1936) 124–26. *Sullivan* 170 quotes Beethoven's journal 1812–13: "Submission, absolute submission to your fate, only this can give you the sacrifice . . . to the servitude—O, hard struggle!" (*Howarth* 288). See note to V 31. **discovered**: to Geoffrey Faber, 25 Mar 1941, on "modern poetry": "I am always inclined to think of the development of an art analogously to that of an experimental science ··· To 'discover' has always been the word for me, rather than to 'invent'; to reveal or release something which is in a sense already 'there'; and to do something new, however small, not for the sake of novelty, but because the other things have already been done perfectly and there is no point in repetition."

V 13–14 **men whom one cannot hope | To emulate**: "in the verse of George Herbert this simplicity is carried as far as it can go—a simplicity emulated without success by numerous modern poets", *The Metaphysical Poets* (1921); in his American first ed. of *Selected Essays*, TSE scored this sentence and the next. On Yeats: "Development to this extent is not merely genius, it is character; and it sets a standard which his juniors should seek to emulate, without hoping to equal", *A Commentary* in *Criterion* July 1935. "The path of poetry through the ages is strewn with wreckage of attempts to emulate great masters by imitating them", *Royal Academy Speech* (1960). To Anne Ridler, 19 June 1942: "thank you for your news and your charming letter which I cannot attempt to emulate". To Rev. J. W. Welch, 25 May 1944, declining to write a dramatisation: "One cannot hope to emulate the poetry of the Prophets, nor indeed would there by any point in doing so."

V 15–16 **only the fight to recover what has been lost | And found and lost again and again:** *Fire and Gas in World War* in *Popular Mechanics* July 1915: "in some places the trenches are less than 30 yd. apart · · · in the process of continual attack and counter attack." *New York Herald* 11 Sept 1918: "Huns fail to recover ground but will still fight."

V 17 **neither gain nor loss:** "the one thing that time is ever sure to bring about is the loss: gain or compensation is almost always conceivable but never certain", *Notes towards the Definition of Culture* 25. "between the profit and the loss", *Ash-Wednesday* VI 4. "And the profit and loss", *The Waste Land* [IV] 314 (see note).

V 18 **The rest is not our business:** Valéry: "Mas ces naufrages, après tout, n'étaient pas notre affaire" [But these shipwrecks, after all, are not our business], *La Crise de l'esprit* (for which see *A Note on "The Tower"* (1963), quoted in headnote to *Sweeney Agonistes*, 11. BRITISH PERFORMANCES). TSE: "It is our business, as Christians, *as well as* readers of literature, to know what we ought to like", *Religion and Literature* (1930). "I do not want to let my words be twisted to suggest that we should take no concern with the lives of future generations. It is very much our business · · · we must affirm the eternal against the transient; the eternal which has been realized in the past, can be realized in the present; and it is our business to try to bring about a future in which the obstacles to this realization will be less", *Literature and the Modern World* (1935). To Meg Nason, 29 Sept 1939: "You are very right, I think, in what you say about thinking about the present, or eternity, but not about the middle distance. Thinking about our immediate tasks, and about eternity, are what make the difference to what we do and are; the rest is not our business." Virginia Woolf: "In order to use new words properly you would have to invent a whole new language; and that, though no doubt we shall come to it, is not at the moment our business. Our business is to see what we can do with the old English language as it is", *Craftsmanship* (1937; see note to I 2–4). MacNeice: "But that, we thought to ourselves, is not our business", *Autumn Journal* (1938) vi. **The rest is:** "The rest is merely shifting scenes", *Mandarins* 1 15 (see note).

V 19–20 **As we grow older · · · the pattern more complicated:** "a recognition of the truth that not our feelings, but the pattern which we may make of our feelings, is the centre of value", *A Brief Introduction to the Method of Paul Valéry* (1924); for "feelings which are not in actual emotions at all", see note to V 11–18. "we perceive a pattern behind the pattern into which the characters deliberately involve themselves; the kind of pattern which we perceive in our own lives only at rare moments of inattention and detachment, drowsing in sunlight. It is the pattern drawn by what the ancient world called Fate", *John Marston* (1934), on *Sophonisba*. "as one becomes older · · · the past has another pattern", *The Dry Salvages* II 37–38.

V 20–25 **the pattern more complicated | Of dead and living · · · not the lifetime of one man only | But of:** "No poet, no artist of any art, has his complete meaning alone. His significance, his appreciation is the appreciation of his relation to the dead poets and artists. You cannot value him alone; you must set him, for contrast and comparison, among the dead", *Tradition and the Individual Talent*

I (1919). "the creation of any form cannot be the work of one man or of one generation of men working together, but has to evolve", *The Need for Poetic Drama* (1936). "The Church ··· consists not only of the living but of the dead", *The Church as Action* (1936). "not the experience of one life only | But of many generations", *The Dry Salvages* II 50–51. "a provincialism, not of space, but of time ··· one for which the world is the property solely of the living, a property in which the dead hold no shares", *What is a Classic?* 30.

TSE: "C'est l'aperçu d'Auguste Comte ··· que nous devons admettre la solidarité entre les morts, les vivants, et ceux qui vivront après nous" [It is the insight of Auguste Comte ··· that we must grant the solidarity of the dead, the living, and those who will live after us], *Autour d'une Traduction d'Euripide* (1916).

V 20–21, 34 **pattern ··· intense ··· another intensity**: "I have in mind ··· Imagination as capacity for experience ··· in which 'experience' is spiritual experience, and as capacity for experiencing not merely the immediate but the immediate with its relations—so that the highest imagination will combine the maximum intensity of immediacy with the maximum implication of pattern", *Letter to Dr. Oldham from T. S. Eliot* (1941), a paper for The Moot.

V 21 **Of dead and living. Not the intense moment**: Bradley: "It would be so even if the pleasures did not die; but in addition the past pleasures have died ··· the assertion that happiness is completed in one intense moment, or the confession that happiness is impossible", *Ethical Studies* Essay III.

V 21–23 **Not the intense moment | Isolated, with no before and after, | But a lifetime burning in every moment**: to Henry Eliot, 18 Feb [1924]: "not merely a question of the moment but of the whole future, as it is a result not of the moment only but of the whole past" (Mark Thompson, personal communication). "The experience of a poem is the experience both of a moment and of a lifetime", *Dante* (1929) I. **Not the intense moment | Isolated, with no before and after**: Karl Barth, tr. Edwyn C. Hoskyns: "We have done no more than make room for the 'Moment' which has no before and no after", *The Epistle to the Romans* (1933) 137 (Ben de la Mare, personal communication). Barth was a contributor to *Revelation* (1937), which had an introductory essay by TSE. For "every moment" see note to II 33–37.

V 21–24 **dead and living ··· lifetime ··· lifetime**: Thomas Jefferson to James Madison, 6 Sept 1789: "I set out on this ground, which I suppose to be self evident, *that the earth belongs in usufruct to the living*: that the dead have neither powers nor rights over it"; to John W. Eppes, 24 June 1813: "The earth belongs to the living". Pound took the second as epigraph to his pamphlet *Social Credit* in 1935, and quoted it in Canto LXXVII (*The Pisan Cantos*, 1949). He cited both in his Italian broadcast of 27 Apr 1943.

V 22–24 **before and after ··· lifetime of one man**: *Hamlet* IV iv: "What is a man ··· his time ··· Looking before and after." See note to *Burnt Norton* V 38–39.

V 22–28 **before and after ··· The evening with the photograph album**: to his mother, 30 Dec 1917: "It gives one a strange feeling that Time is not before and after, but all at once, present and future and all the periods of the past, an album like this." For "your album of souvenirs", see *Inoubliable France* in note to *The Dry Salvages* II 56–66, III 3–15.

V 23–24 **a lifetime burning in every moment | And not the lifetime of one man only:** to George Barker, 24 Jan 1938: "Poetry is either a matter of a brief outburst, or it is a matter of a lifetime's work" (see headnote to *Four Quartets*, 4. "NOT MERELY MORE OF THE SAME").

V 25 **old stones:** a note by TSE alongside the line in his copy of *G. Jones* (136) reads "churchyard at E. Coker", and another alongside its quotation again (218) reads "Thinking of E. Coker churchyard". *Hayward*: "There is a particular allusion in this line to the village churchyard at East Coker, where the old gravestones are now indecipherable". TSE: "an illegible stone", *Little Gidding* V 14.

V 26–31 **There is a time for · · · to be explorers:** "the craving for continual novelty of diction and metric is as unwholesome as an obstinate adherence to the idiom of our grandfathers. There are times for exploration and times for the development of the territory acquired", *The Music of Poetry* (1942).

V 30, 32 **here and now · · · Here or there:** Edward Marsh's *Rupert Brooke: A Memoir* (1918) printed: "She is not here, or now— | She is here, and now, yet nowhere—" (see note to *Little Gidding* I 53). **here and now:** "To believe in the supernatural is · · · to believe that the supernatural is the greatest reality here and now", *The Modern Dilemma* (1933). **Here or there:** Hermann Peschmann pointed out the erroneous reading "and" for "or" (in all collected printings of *Four Quartets* from *US 1943* until finally corrected in *1974*; TSE's two recordings of 1946–47 also have "and"). TSE replied, 7 Mar 1950: "How very odd. Thanks for calling my attention to it. What I prefer is *Here or there does not matter* (Here-or-there—i.e. an abbreviation of 'whether here or there') is the subject of the singular *does*" (*Composition FQ* 113). OED "here" *adv.* 12: "neither here nor there: Of no account either one way or the other". FitzGerald: "'Fools! your Reward is neither Here nor There'", *The Rubáiyát of Omar Khayyám* xxv.

V 31 **Old men ought to be explorers:** *Sullivan* 229 on Beethoven's last quartets: "The middle three quartets are the greatest of the five and it is here that Beethoven the explorer is most clearly revealed", (*Howarth* 288). TSE: "the end of all our exploring | Will be to arrive where we started", *Little Gidding* V 27–28 (see note).

V 36 **desolation:** pronounced *dezolation* in TSE's recordings.

V 36 *variant* **Aranyaka, the forest:** Sanskrit holy books of which the Upanishads are part. *Composition FQ* 113: "sacred books whose name can be interpreted as meaning either that they were written in the forests by forest hermits, or that they were written for those who, after a life of action, had retired to the forests."

V 36–38 **Through the dark cold and the empty desolation, | The wave cry, the wind cry, the vast waters | Of the petrel:** the Battle of the Atlantic began on 3 Sept 1939 with the sinking of the British S.S. *Athenia* and continued throughout the war. Alexander Wilson et al.: "The stormy petrel · · · is found over the whole Atlantic Ocean, from Europe to North America, at all distances from land, and in all weathers", *American Ornithology* (1831). **cry · · · cry · · · end:** Psalms 61: 1, 102: 1: "From the end of the earth will I cry unto thee", "let my cry come unto thee" (Mark Thompson, personal communication).

V 37 **the wind cry, the vast waters:** Virgil, tr. Joseph Warton: "Whither vast waters drive before the wind", *Georgics* IV 496. TSE had underlined the conclusion of Smart's translation of Horace's Ode I vii, "to-morrow we will re-visit the vast ocean", adding the Latin: "Cras ingens iterabimus aequor".

V 38 **petrel**: OED quotes from the *Voyages* (1703) of the explorer William Dampier: "they pat the Water alternately with their Feet, as if they walkt upon it; tho' still upon the Wing. And from hence the Seamen give them the name of Petrels, in allusion to St. Peter's walking upon the Lake of Gennesareth". Dampier, the first person to circumnavigate the world three times, is commemorated in the church of the parish where he was born in 1651, East Coker. **porpoise**: to Ian Cox, 14 Oct 1938, declining to take place in a broadcast of *Moby-Dick*: "It is true that my great-grandfather was an owner of whaling ships in New Bedford ··· that is as near as I come to a connexion with Nantucket ··· it is so long since I have even heard my own North Shore speech, that I should be in danger of confusing even that with the speech to the Eastward of Cape Porpoise" (in Maine, sixty miles north of the Dry Salvages).

The Dry Salvages

Published in *NEW* 27 Feb 1941. Although not labelled "Supplement", the poem occupied the central four pages so as to be readily detachable. First US publication in *Partisan Review* May–June 1941. Separately as a Faber pamphlet, 4 Sept 1941 (four impressions to Feb 1944). No separate US publication. Within *Four Quartets* in *US 1943*, *1944+*.

BBC memo from George Barnes to the Director of Talks, 12 Mar 1942: "I saw Eliot last night and spoke to him [about] *The Dry Salvages*. He is very anxious that the first public reading of the poem should be done by Robert Speaight" (BBC Written Archives). Speaight broadcast the poem on 21 Apr 1942.

The cover of *Partisan Review* lists "*The Dry Salvages* | a long poem by | T. S. Eliot". In the copy he presented to Geoffrey and Enid Faber, TSE underlined "long" (Rick Gekoski, personal communication).

TSE gave erroneous dates to Norman Foerster, 30 Apr 1946: "I was working on the whole poem of *The Dry Salvages* during the latter part of 1942 and the beginning of 1943. The last section, like all the others, was drafted in the summer of 1942 and I was revising this section, like the others, up to the time of its publication, first in *The New English Weekly* and second in the *Partisan Review*."

1. THE DRY SALVAGES: GEOGRAPHY AND HISTORY

Faber Autumn List 1941: "*The Dry Salvages* is the third of a sequence of four long poems. The first two were *Burnt Norton* and *East Coker*, both of which are well understood to mark a new stage in Mr. Eliot's poetic achievement. The fourth is still to come. The title of the poem, like the titles of the two earlier poems, is a place-name. 'The Dry Salvages' are a group of rocks off the American coast well known to sailors. The name is a corruption of 'Les Trois Sauvages'. The word 'Salvages' is locally pronounced to rhyme with 'ages', and this pronunciation is intended in the title of the poem."

The Dry Salvages are north of Gloucester, Massachusetts, three miles from Rockport Harbor, off the coast of Cape Ann. *Hands*: "The Dry Salvages are a line of black granite rocks some hundred yards long which rise up sheer from the sea bed 100 feet below. They project about 20 feet above the sea at low tide and half that at high tide. They are white above the tide-mark from the droppings of sea birds. A bell-buoy is located some quarter-mile to seaward ([I] 37) and there is a foghorn on Cape Ann itself ([I] 33). The Dry Salvages, seen from the seaward side through the fog ··· resemble a jagged line of teeth ([I] 30)."

Presenting a copy of the Faber pamphlet to the Sawyer Library in Gloucester, Henry Eliot wrote: "My brother ··· spent some 20 summers as a child and youth at Eastern

Point, where my father had a house at the top of the hill back of the old Beachcroft hotel · · · I do not myself remember the reefs being called anything but 'Dry Salvags,' nor did I ever hear 'Salvages' accented on the second syllable." This was printed in *Gloucester Daily Times* 27 Feb 1942, with a comment: "Rockport folks do accent the later syllable in 'Salvages,' even though the name appears to be a corruption of the word 'savages'." In late 1946, Gunnar Ekelof wrote to TSE suggesting that the name might be corrupted from "droit(s) de salvages", a kind of informal salvage tax. TSE, 5 Nov: "Your suggestion of the origin of *Salvages* strikes me as extremely plausible. I admit that I have no reason for supposing that the original name was *Les Trois Sauvages* beyond my own ingenuity. Your explanation seems to me very much more likely." However, *Worthen* 242–43 cites a map of 1785 at Yale where "they are simply named the 'Salvage Rocks' ('salvage' being a common English spelling of 'savage' in the 17th and 18th centuries) while the appellation 'Dry' dates only from the mid-19th century, when French (or German) influence on the name would have been extremely unlikely." The derivation had previously been challenged by TSE's relative, Rear-Admiral Samuel Eliot Morison, to whom TSE wrote in 1964: "I imagine that it was to my brother that I owe the explanation of the title, and I seem to remember that the rocks were known to the local fishermen as the 'Dry Salvages'. But I myself can give no further explanation and it may be that mine owes more to my imagination than to any explanation that I heard." Morison also pointed out that TSE appeared, over the years, to have confused his ancestor Andrew Eliot of East Coker with "Mr. William Eliot, sometime of New Sarum", who was lost in a famous wreck in the 1630s (see Morison, *The American Neptune* Oct 1965, *Howarth* 118 and *Composition FQ* 51–54, 120–21).

2. "THE RIVER IS WITHIN US, THE SEA IS ALL ABOUT US"

A century after the end of the Colonial Period with the defeat of TSE's distant cousin, President John Quincy Adams, TSE wrote to Herbert Read, "St. George's Day" [23 Apr 1928]: "Some day I want to write an essay about the point of view of an American who wasnt an American, because his America ended in 1829; and who wasnt a Yankee, because he was born in the South and went to school in New England as a small boy with a nigger drawl, but who wasnt a southerner in the South because his people were northerners in a border state and looked down on all southerners and Virginians, and who so was never anything anywhere and who therefore felt himself to be more a Frenchman than an American and more an Englishman than a Frenchman and yet felt that the U.S.A. up to a hundred years ago was a family extension. It is almost too difficult even for H. J. [Henry James] who for that matter, wasnt an American at all, in that sense." Quoting this in *Tate ed.*, Read adds that "on one or two later occasions when in a mood of solemn gaiety he would sing a ballad like *The Reconstructed Rebel*" (chorus: "I'm a reconstructed rebel and I don't give a damn, | I hate the reconstruction and I hate Uncle Sam"). Ian Cox to TSE, 14 Oct 1938: "I kept recalling the sound of conversations between Frank Morley and yourself, varied with *Frankie and Johnnie* and *The reconstructed rebel*" (BBC Written Archives). (Such songs would have appalled TSE's grandfather, William Greenleaf Eliot, the "unflinching supporter of the temperance cause, of woman suffrage, and of all movements to elevate the poor and ignorant · · · one of the staunchest supporters of the Union", *Walter Graeme Eliot* 110.)

TSE's Preface for *This American World* (1928) calls up much of the land- and seascape that figures in the poems: "My family were New Englanders, who had been settled—my branch of it—for two generations in the South West—which was, in my own time, rapidly becoming merely the Middle West. The family guarded jealously its connexions with New England; but it was not until years of maturity that I perceived that I myself had always been a New Englander in the South West, and a South Westerner in New England; when I was sent to school in New England I lost my southern accent without ever acquiring the accent of the native Bostonian. In New England I missed the long dark river, the ailanthus trees, the flaming cardinal birds, the high limestone bluffs where we searched for fossil shell-fish; in Missouri I missed the fir trees, the bay and goldenrod, the song-sparrows, the red granite and the blue sea of Massachusetts." To Marquis W. Childs, Missouri Historical Society, 8 Aug 1930: "Of course my people were Northerners and New Englanders, and of course I have spent many years out of America altogether; but Missouri and the Mississippi have made a deeper impression on me than any other part of the world", quoted in *From a Distinguished Former St. Louisan* (1930). TSE wrote, anonymously, of Gloucester as "the most beautiful harbour for small ships on the whole of that coast", *Fishermen of the Banks* by James B. Connolly (1928), Publisher's Preface. When he was 15, his mother "hired a retired mariner to teach her two sons sailing", according to *Braybrooke*.

To Herbert Read, 15 Sept 1932, on his prose memoir of childhood, *The Innocent Eye*: "Long ago I had the half formed opinion of trying something of the same sort myself which I was going to call *The River and the Sea*, but I think that my point of view would have been more definitely, or shall we say less subtly symbolical." *Ash-Wednesday* VI 32–34:

> Sister, mother
> And spirit of the river, spirit of the sea,
> Suffer me not to be separated

In 1952: "Au dix-septième siècle, mes aieux ont quitté, un peu précipitamment, l'Ouest de l'Angleterre pour se refugier aux côtes de la Nouvelle Ang[le]terre. À ma première vue des côtes de la terre armoricaine, j'ai cru constater une ressemblance au paysage de mon enfance. Côtes granitiques, exposées aux orages de l'Atlantique, pays de marins hardis, habiles et courageux. Et au dix-septième, une autre ressemblance: la Nouv. Angl. hébergeant aussi bon nombre de sorcières—que mon aieul s'est mis immédiatement à exterminer" [In the 17th century my ancestors left, rather hurriedly, the west of England to seek refuge on the New England coast. When I first saw the coast of the Armorican land, I thought I noticed a resemblance to the landscape of my childhood. Granite coastlines, exposed to the tempests from the Atlantic, land of daring sailors, skilful and brave. And in the 17th century, another similarity: New England providing shelter also for a number of witches whom my forebear set out right away to exterminate"], notes for a speech at U. Rennes, 21 Apr 1952 (King's; tr. Javadi).

3. COMPOSITION

TSE complimented Roy Campbell on his poem *Tristan da Cunha* in a letter on the day of its publication to the *New Statesman* (15 Oct; pub. 22 Oct 1927): "The poem has a curious resemblance—not in detail, but in rhythm and in general spirit—to a German poem which is almost unknown even in Germany, the *Tristan da Cunha* of

Johannes Th. Kuhlemann (*Der Strom*, Cologne, 1919). I once attempted to translate this poem, which is very fine, but abandoned the attempt." Campbell's poem has: "mist about your shoulders", 2 (TSE: "fogs conceal it", II 71); "gulls" 6 (TSE, I 6); "shattered mast", 72 (TSE: "shattered lobsterpot", I 23); "you have no hope or fear", 31 (TSE: "Having hoped for the wrong things or dreaded the wrong things", II 58); "thunder swings its bells", 50 (TSE: "the ground swell · · · Clangs | The bell", I 46–48); "what long regrets", 43 (TSE: "regret · · · regret", III 4); "Plunge forward · · · Plunge forward", 61–65 (TSE: "Fare forward", III 14, 26, 39, 45); "granite", 93 (TSE, I 16); "generations" 102 (TSE, II 51); see *McCue 2014d*.

As well as John Hayward's archive of drafts, King's has the letters between TSE and Hayward, and a professional photograph of the Dry Salvages.

In response to this first sight of the poem, on receiving *ts2* in Dec 1940, Hayward jotted a sheet of notes (King's HB/V14b). He evidently set his thoughts down for TSE, who replied on 4 Jan 1941: "Thank you very much for your helpful letter, and for its promptitude: I was surprised at hearing from you so soon. There are some, perhaps most, of your suggestions which I accept at once; some which I must think about; some which my first impulse is to reject. That is the normal and proper mixture. One or two ('spell lasts') I had discovered for myself in the meantime" (see V 29). These notes by Hayward for TSE during composition are printed either in the Commentary below or, where variants are crucial, in the Textual History (designated *Hayward's Queries*). They are distinct from Hayward's later notes of 1950 for readers of Pierre Leyris's French translation *Quatre Quatuors* (designated *Hayward*).

For TSE's letter to Philip Mairet, 5 Jan 1941, enclosing *ts3b*, see headnote to *Four Quartets*, 3. COMPOSITION.

NEW 13 Feb 1941 ran an advertisement: "A New Poem by T. S. Eliot similar in form to *East Coker* (which was printed in our Easter Number of last year) will appear in our issue of February 27. Will readers who wish to obtain extra copies of this number please send in their orders now. We are unable in present circumstances to print a very much larger edition. Those who book extra copies now will not only be lending us useful co-operation, but will prevent disappointment to themselves."

4. AFTER PUBLICATION

Hayward to TSE, 5 Mar 1941: "*The Dry Salvages*, with its revisions and additions—particularly the extra lines where I hoped you might add something—is a splendid piece and I long to see it dressed up to match *Burnt Norton* & *East Coker* of which there are substantial piles prominently displayed at Bowes & Bowes and Heffer's [bookshops]. When the poem is published separately I think the note should be removed to the verso of the leaf facing the first page of the text."

TSE to Desmond MacCarthy, 10 Dec 1941: "it seems to me a much better poem than *East Coker* · · · I have been puzzled by the suggestion of lassitude which the reviewers so far seem to have found in its rhythm."

To Marguerite Caetani [late Sept 1941]: "It matters much to me that what I write at this time should be good, because I think that a good poem is more important now than at any previous time, and on the other hand a second-rate one seems to have less excuse than ever. But it is hard to maintain the conviction that one is right in spending so much time and energy on writing verse! I have written a final poem with which I am not satisfied, and to which I shall return when other duties permit" (*Little Gidding*).

In 1953: "the Mississippi of Mark Twain is not only the river known to those who voyage on it or live beside it, but the universal river of human life", *American Literature and the American Language* 17.

Title] *Hayward's Queries*: "Title (Dry Salvages is a quotation?)" TSE to Hayward, 4 Jan 1941: "'The Dry Salvages' *is* a place name (rhymes with 'rampages'). It is ('Les trois sauvages') the name of a group of three rocks off the eastern corner of Cape Ann, Massachusetts, with a beacon: convenient for laying a course to the eastward, Maine or Nova Scotia. It happens to have just the right denotation and association for my purpose; and therefore I am the more disturbed by your comment. It doesnt matter that it should be obscure, but if it is going to lead people quite on the wrong track, then something must be done. I dont like the idea of a note of explanation. Please advise." Hayward to TSE, 7 Jan: "I deplore my ignorance ··· But I took Dry Salvages—for you omitted the inverted commas that might have suggested to me that it was a place name—to be in some sense a reference to what the sea gives up—the torn seine and the dead, and, by extension, memories of a dead life ··· I think the least you can do is to place single quotation marks round the title. This, I think, should at once suggest a proper name—and one that, perhaps, requires to be defined in this way ··· because it is not, like East Coker, a place-name so much as the name of a place ··· (Cf 'The Hard' Lyme Regis: 'Fastnet' &c.) You could, alternatively, add Cape Ann, viz. 'The Dry Salvages' Cape Ann ··· I do think there is a danger of some people making my mistake about wet & dry salvage, so I hope you will consider adopting one or other of my suggestions if none better occurs to you." The exchange prompted TSE's parenthetical note at the head of the poem.

Prefatory note **Cape Ann, Massachusetts**: "We beat around the cape and laid our course | From the Dry Salvages to the eastern banks", *WLComposite* 489–90. *Cape Ann* is the last of TSE's *Landscapes*. **with a beacon**: it was removed in 1945 (*Boyd*). **Groaner**: see note to I 32.

I 1–14] *Hayward*: "The poet was born and brought up in St. Louis, Mo., U.S.A., which lies below the confluence of the Mississippi and Missouri rivers. It is clear from 11–14 how deeply the presence of this great waterway was felt in his own home." The confluence gives the water a visible brownness (*Worthen* 6). Sherwood Anderson: "land of many rivers running down to the brown slow strong mother of rivers ··· the river powerful as ever, strange as ever, but silent now, forgotten, neglected", *Dark Laughter*, quoted by Wyndham Lewis in *Paleface* (1929) 213, 215 (E. W. F. Tomlin, *N&Q* June 1980). TSE to Allen Tate, 18 May 1933, after visiting Charlottesville: "I hope to return in 1935 and visit Richmond, Charleston, Savannah, and so on via Tennessee to New Orleans and then up the River to St. Loouss." On Mark Twain: "A river, a very big and powerful river, is the only natural force that can wholly determine the course of human peregrination ··· the river with its strong, swift current is the dictator to the raft or to the steamboat. It is a treacherous and capricious dictator ··· Twain is a native, and the River God is his God. It is as a native that he accepts the River God, and it is the subjection of Man that gives to Man his dignity. For without some kind of God, Man is not even very interesting", *The Adventures of Huckleberry Finn* (1950), Introduction.

I 1 **I do not know much about gods; but I think**: to Bonamy Dobrée, 20 Mar 1928: "I do not know about Ramadan very much but am writing in mid-lent." On discussing problems in a vacuum: "I do not know much about Man, but I am sure that our minds do not work like that", *The Aims of Education* (1950) (*Ricks* 274).

I 1–3 **gods · · · the river · · · a strong brown god · · · intractable · · · recognised as a frontier**: Alexis de Tocqueville: "The Mississippi takes its source at the boundary of the two great regions · · · like a god of antiquity · · · inexhaustible", *Democracy in America* (tr. Henry Reeve, rev. Francis Bowen, 1876) ch. I (Owen Boynton, personal communication). **the river | Is a strong brown god**: Hindus regard the Ganges as a goddess; the river carries millions of tons of fertilising sediment ("Ganga was sunken", *The Waste Land* [V] 395). J. Milton Hayes's poem *The Green Eye of the Little Yellow God* (1911), with its Indian setting and the phrase "the little yellow god", 24 (after "strong", 14), was a music hall favourite.

I 3 **a frontier**: the Mississippi formed the western boundary of the United States until the Louisiana Purchase of 1803–04, and is still part of the boundaries of ten states.

I 3 *variant* **for a time**: *Hayward's Queries*: "for a *while* (time confusing)".

I 5 **a problem confronting the builder of bridges**: innovative engineering was required to build the Eads Bridge, St. Louis (1874), then the world's longest arch bridge. See note to I 11. Another bridge was constructed in the city in the 1890s. *Raine* 106 compares Kipling's story *The Bridge Builders*, with its line "The end shall be as it was in the beginning" ("In my end is my beginning", *East Coker* V 38).

I 5–6 **only a problem · · · solved**: TSE told A. L. Rowse that "he could never write a poem unless he tricked himself into the belief that it was only a technical problem to be solved" (Rowse, *A Cornish Childhood*, 1942, 218).

I 6–7 **the brown god is almost forgotten | By the dwellers in cities—ever, however, implacable**: St. Louis was flooded in 1892 and 1903. In 1927, down the length of the Mississippi, some 26,000 square miles were flooded.

I 7 **ever, however, implacable**: to A. L. Rowse, 22 Mar 1941: "The two internal rhymes had already been commented on adversely by Geoffrey and John Hayward, but (although I accepted most of their suggestions) I remained obdurate · · · I can't defend them except by affirming that they seem to my ear the right hiccup in the right place." Geoffrey Faber had commented on "ever, however" (see Textual History) and Hayward had marked "tosses up our losses" ([I] 22), though neither marked "reaches, the beaches" ([I] 17). To Rowse, 25 Feb 1943, on his poem *Invocation to a Cornish House*: "I am bothered by the rhymes (and especially one triple rhyme) in an unrhymed poem. I mean that it should have no rhymes, or regular rhyme, or, what is most difficult of all, rhymes just where they have a particular justification in *altering the tone* for a moment. The rhymes here seem to me to come just because they happened so, and therefore jar."

I 9–10 **Unhonoured, unpropitiated · · · waiting, watching and waiting**: Clough: "Ah, let me look, let me watch, let me wait, unhurried, unprompted! · · · Waiting, and watching, and looking!" *Amours de Voyage* II xii (*Murray*). **unpropitiated**: pronounced *unpropissiated* in TSE's recording of 1946–47.

I 10 **worshippers of the machine**: J. H. B. De St. Pierre: "a savage ··· feels himself disposed to fall down and worship the machine", *Studies of Nature* (tr. L. T. Rede, 1803) 322. TSE: "It is impossible, certainly, for the Christian *not* to strive and hope for a better state of things on earth, though without that false assumption of the *excessive value of the future* which communism inherits from nineteenth century Liberalism, and without that worship of the machine, that faith in gadgets and inventions", *The Christian and the Modern World* (1935).

I 11 **His rhythm was present in the nursery bedroom**: to Marquis W. Childs, 8 Aug 1930: "The River also made a deep impression on me; and it *was* a great treat to be taken down to the Eads Bridge in flood time ··· I feel that there is something in having passed one's childhood beside the big river, which is incommunicable to those who have not", quoted in *From a Distinguished Former St. Louisan* (1930).

I 11–14 **the nursery bedroom, | In the rank ailanthus of the April dooryard ··· the evening**: of his childhood home at 2635 Locust Street and the Mary Institute schoolyard: "There was at the front of our house a sort of picket fence which divided our front yard from the schoolyard. This picket fence merged a little later ··· into a high brick wall which concealed our back garden from the schoolyard and also concealed the schoolyard from our back garden. There was a door in this wall and there was a key to this door. Now, when the young ladies had left the school in the afternoon ··· When the girls had left in the afternoon, the schoolyard was mine for a playground, first of all under the supervision of my nurse ··· I remember a mound on which stood a huge ailanthus tree ··· I have a photograph of myself standing against this ailanthus tree at the age of seven or eight", *From Mary to You* (1959; after delivering this centennial address at the school, TSE read *The Dry Salvages*). Henry James: "following the nursery-maid with unequal step and sniffing up the strange odour of the ailantus-trees"; "the ailantus-trees beyond the wooden paling. The peculiar fragrance of this vegetation used to diffuse itself in the evening air", *Washington Square* ch. III, ch. XXXIV. **the rank ailanthus of the April dooryard**: Whitman: *When Lilacs Last in the Dooryard Bloom'd* (title and first line); see notes to IV 14–15. **ailanthus**: OED: "said to mean 'Tree of the gods'" ("gods", I 1). Pronounced *al-anthus* in TSE's recording of 1946–47. **dooryard**: OED (with this line as latest citation): "*U.S.* A yard or garden-patch about the door of a house."

I 13–14 **grapes on the autumn table, | And the evening circle in the winter gaslight**: to his mother, 14 Oct 1917: "I always think of return to St. Louis as meaning Concord grapes on the table in the blue fruit basket." To Hayward, 27 Dec 1939: "One of my strongest associations is that of the smell of grapes and of the charwoman (an old family retainer) which always greeted me on returning in the autumn to our house in St. Louis, after the summer at 'The Downs', Eastern Point, Gloucester, Mass." Emma D. E. N. Southworth: "events of the day had thrown a shade of seriousness over the evening circle ··· gathered around the centre-table", *The Two Sisters* (1859) 299. TSE: "circles of the stormy moon ··· table cloth ··· hothouse grapes", *Sweeney Among the Nightingales* 5, 13, 20. "The evening with the photograph album", *East Coker* V 28.

I 15 **the sea is all about us**: Kipling: "The Jungle is all about us!" *The King's Ankus.*

I 19 **horseshoe crab**: to Hayward, 12 Jan 1945: "At the bottom of the first page of *The Dry Salvages* in the four Quartets please alter *hermit* crab to *horse-shoe* crab. I do not know how I came to make such a blunder (though obviously the wrong crab scans better). I have written a letter to the *New English Weekly* to point this out, and I shall have it altered in the next printing, whenever that is, and send you a copy. How could one find the remains of a hermit crab on a beach? All there could be would be the shell of some other crustacean. I am surprised that neither you nor anyone else has spotted this." *NEW* 25 Jan 1945:

> In his review of my *Four Quartets* in *The New English Weekly* several weeks ago, Mr. Snell mentioned my note of acknowledgement to friends for their help, and observed that he could find only three or four minor changes from the text as originally printed in your columns. He is quite correct, and correct also in suggesting that one of the changes was of doubtful value [*Burnt Norton* II 5]. But the "improvements of word and phrase" for which I made acknowledgement were incorporated before the poems were printed in any form, and therefore remain invisible.
>
> There is, however, one error in the text which has escaped the observation of any of my friends or critics, and of which I have only just myself become aware. In the first section of *The Dry Salvages*, "hermit crab" should be "horse-shoe crab." It was, of course, the horse-shoe crab that I had in mind: the slip must have been due to the fact that I did not want a spondee in that place. What is more curious is that the term "hermit crab" should have continued to do duty for "horse-shoe crab" in my mind, in this context, from the date of original publication of the poem until last week. I shall be grateful to any of your readers who may possess the poem, if they will kindly make the alteration.

To Richard de la Mare, 6 Feb 1945: "There is an error of my own to be corrected the next time the Quartets are reprinted. I know that there is a new impression which has not yet come in, so that this may be some time ahead, but if I do not put it in writing now I shall forget when the time comes. At the bottom of the first page of *The Dry Salvages*, I want 'Hermit Crab' changed to HORSE-SHOE CRAB [*with*: 'but *not* in capitals']. This was a curious slip because I meant Horse-shoe Crab the whole time. I want to get it put right before somebody accuses me of ignorance" (Faber archive). TSE corrected Alton Peters's copy of the pamphlet *The Dry Salvages* (Pierpont Morgan).

Henry Eliot wrote to Henry B. Harvey, 10 Oct 1946, that TSE was still "much worried because he meant to write 'horse-shoe crab' instead of hermit crab." TSE had not forgotten the mistake in 1952: "On re-reading the poem some time after the final text had been published, I was horrified to observe that I had referred to the wrong kind of crab—the *hermit* crab which has no shell of its own, but takes for a habitation the shell of some other deceased crustacean. The hermit crab, having no shell of its own, could hardly be identified by a shell on the beach; and indeed, I am not sure that I have ever seen a hermit crab. The crab I had in mind was the *horseshoe* crab. I knew the difference perfectly well: how was it that after spending months in re-writing and revising that poem, I had failed to notice that I continued to associate the name of one kind of crab with the mental picture of another? Simply because the sound of the word *hermit* fitted perfectly for my line, and the sound of *horseshoe* was harsh. In such a dilemma, there was only one choice: to put in the right crab, and sacrifice the right sound", *Scylla and Charybdis* (1952). To Robert Beare, 10 Mar 1953: "One difference between a New York and London edition is that I corrected the English edition of *The Dry Salvages* but have left an error in the New York edition which also occurs in the first English edition: 'hermit crab'; the correct text is '*horseshoe* crab'." American impressions of *Four Quartets* were still appearing with the error later than 1948. A typed note apparently by TSE in the back of Hayward's copy of *1944* (King's) reads: "HORSESHOE CRAB, according to Manson: Crabe des Moluques, *or* limule. According to Manson also, crabe des Moluques *or* limule is KING-CRAB." Henry Adams: "One was almost glad to act the part of horseshoe crab in Quincy Bay, and admit that all was uniform—that nothing ever changed—and that the woman would swim about the ocean of future time, as she had swum in the past ··· unable to change", *The Education of Henry Adams* ch. XXX (George M. Spangler, *N&Q* Aug 1968). Irving Babbitt wrote of Descartes having conceived of the soul as "living quite apart from the body, having its seat in the pineal gland, in much the same way, to quote a recent writer, 'as the hermit crab resides in its borrowed shell'", *The Masters of Modern French Criticism* (1912) 236. (Frederic Burk: "The fundamental conception of the soul which flourished when men believed that it resided in the pineal gland, as the hermit crab resides in its borrowed shell, dominates our education to-day. The new conception of the child is radically different from the old ··· the child is made up of blind instincts and impulses which well up from within", *The Training of Teachers: The Old View of Childhood and the New* in *Atlantic Monthly* Oct 1897. For "a child of ten ··· peering through sea-water", see note to I 20–21.) **crab**: TSE: "I should have been a pair of ragged claws | Scuttling across the floors of silent seas", *The Love Song of J. Alfred Prufrock* 73–74.

I 20 **The pools ··· curiosity**: "It would almost seem that the one object of his curiosity was—himself. He reminds us of Narcissus gazing into the pool", Introduction to *The Art of Poetry* by Paul Valéry (1958) (*Ricks* 276).

I 20–21 **The pools where it offers to our curiosity ··· algae ··· sea-anemone**: "The sea-anemone which accepts or rejects a proffered morsel is thereby relating an idea to the sea-anemone's world", *Knowledge and Experience in the Philosophy of F. H. Bradley* 44 (*Ricks* 279). For some poets, arriving at originality is "a progressive absorption in, and absorption of, and rejection (but never a total rejection) of other writers. Others, like Crosby, have little of this absorptive and rejective faculty", *Transit of Venus: Poems by Harry Crosby* (1931), Preface. *Levy 1965*: "He summed up experiences with a rare brevity, as in this comment on the Germans after six weeks of formal and informal meetings: 'They are like sponges or sea anemones, soaking up foreign influence for a while, then rejecting it all.'" For "reject", see note to *Ash-Wednesday* II 16.

TSE quoted with approval Marianne Moore, "the sea when it proffers flattery in exchange for hemp, rye, flax, horses, platinum, timber and fur" (*My Apish Cousins*) in *Marianne Moore* (1923). TSE: "I should say that the mind of any poet would be magnetised in its own way, to select automatically, in his reading (from picture papers and cheap novels, indeed, as well as serious books, and least likely from works of an abstract nature, though even these are aliment for some poetic minds) the material—an image, a phrase, a word—which may be of use to him later. And this selection probably runs through the whole of his sensitive life. There might be the experience of a child of ten, a small boy peering through sea-water in a rock-pool, and finding a sea-anemone for the first time: the simple experience (not so simple, for an exceptional child, as it looks) might lie dormant in his mind for twenty years, and re-appear transformed in some verse-context charged with great imaginative pressure", *The Use of Poetry and the Use of Criticism* 78–79. *Murder in the Cathedral* II chorus: "I have lain on the floor of the sea and breathed with the breathing of the sea-anenome, swallowed with ingurgitation of the sponge."

William James: "Had we no concepts we should live simply 'getting' each successive moment of experience, as the sessile sea-anemone on its rock receives whatever nourishment the wash of the waves may bring", *Some Problems of Philosophy* ch. IV. TSE: "Truth on our level is a different thing from truth for the jellyfish, and there must certainly be analogies for truth and error in jellyfish life", *Knowledge and Experience* 166. "We are not to say that there is one real world to which the system corresponds, for so far as the system is complete and exact, it *is* the real world. But it is not the same world as that of the plowboy or the jellyfish, except *for* the metaphysician who is inside of his own system", *Content, Objectivity and Existence* (1914).

Bradley: "It is no human ideal to lead 'the life of an oyster'. We have no right first to find out just what we happen to be and to have, and then to contract our wants to that limit", *Ethical Studies* Essay II. TSE to Geoffrey Faber [18 Sept 1927]: "Plato has something valuable to say about the theory of value. Remember his oyster" (Plato: "if you had no memory you would not recollect that you had ever been pleased ··· your life would be the life, not of a man, but of an oyster", *Philebus* 21c, tr. Benjamin Jowett. For a different translation, see note to *Five-Finger Exercises* I. *Lines to a Persian Cat* 6.) TSE: "Then he knew that he had been a fish", *The Death of Saint Narcissus* 24. TSE praised unspecified lines in Rupert Brooke's *The Fish* for "a really amazing felicity and command of language", *Reflections on Contemporary Poetry* I (1917). For fear of or longing for the submarine, see notes to *Mr. Apollinax* 11–15.

I 20–34 **pools ··· sea-anemone ··· fog ··· wave ··· sea voices ··· groaner ··· seagull ··· fog**: Archibald MacLeish: "fog ··· pools among | The sea anemones ··· gulls ··· the wave sound ··· moan ··· Cry of gulls", *Land's End* III in *Criterion* July 1927 (see note to *Ash-Wednesday* III 17–19).

I 21 **delicate algae**: Pound: "And one gropes in these things as delicate | Algæ reach up and out beneath | Pale slow green surgings of the underwave", *Sub Mare*, included by TSE in Pound's *Selected Poems*. **algae**: pronounced *al-ghee* in TSE's recording of 1946–47. (OED recommends a soft *g*.) After reading three new cantos, TSE had "only one query" for Pound, 22 Oct 1936: "'see weed' etc. To one raised on the shore of the manymermaidcrowded sea, this collocation suggest algae such as a child I dried and classified on the shores of Massachusetts" (*Crawford* 32).

I 21–22 **algae ··· torn**: "the torn algae", *Those are pearls that were his eyes. See!* 3.

I 22 **tosses up our losses**: *Hayward's Queries*: "Tosses—losses—flotsam, jetsam, wrack. ×5 times earlier spinithrift—". **tosses ··· losses ··· torn**: see note to *Ash-Wednesday* V 22, VI 4. **our losses**: for these words in Elizabeth Barrett Browning, see note to *Little Gidding* II 67–96, *first venture in verse* [22]. **seine**: OED: "A fishing net designed to hang vertically in the water, the ends being drawn together to inclose the fish". Within yards of the Eliots' summer house in Gloucester was Seine Field, where fishermen mended nets (Jayme Stayer, personal communication).

I 24 **the gear of foreign dead men**: "the army gear", *Anabasis* VI x.

I 24–25 **The sea has many voices, | Many gods and many voices**: Tennyson: "the deep | Moans round with many voices", *Ulysses* 55–56. TSE called the second of Tennyson's lines "a true specimen of Tennyson-Virgilianism ··· too *poetical* in comparison with Dante, to be the highest poetry", *Dante* (1929) I (see Virgil's *Aeneid* in note to II 70–75). "the sea with many voices | Moaned all about us", *WLComposite* 516–17.

I 28 **Often together heard: the whine**: Milton: "We ··· both together heard | What time the grey-fly winds her sultry horn", *Lycidas* 27–28. **together heard**: *Hayward's Queries*: "(inversion)". For "as though together fused" in the Temple translation of *Paradiso*, see note to *Little Gidding* V 44–46. TSE to A. L. Rowse, 3 Jan 1936, of a typescript by Rowse: "'This protest make' seems to me a bad inversion. There are good inversions as well as bad ones, but the good ones are uncommon. This seems to me quite bad."

I 28–32 *variant* **rigging ··· soothing menace ··· wailing warning ··· approaching ··· heaving**: participle endings underlined by Geoffrey Faber in *ts4*, with "rather a lot of -ing terminations". TSE marked this and emended "soothing menace" to "menace and caress". See note to II 1–4.

I 30 **rote**: OED *n.* 6: "Now *U.S.* The roaring of the sea or surf", with this line among the citations.

I 31 **wailing warning**: "to warn of rocks which lie below", *To the Class of 1905* 5.

I 32 **heaving groaner**: *Hayward's Queries*: "rote? – groaner?? groiner??" TSE to Hayward, 4 Jan 1941: "'Groaner'. Yes, I was waiting to see what you would make of this. It is the New England word for a 'whistling buoy', which by some arrangement of valves, makes a groaning noise as it rises and falls on the swell. There must be some English equivalent, but that would give the wrong effect. I noted absence from O.E.D. This is a pretty problem too." Hayward, 7 Jan: "My first reaction to 'groaner' was that it was a buoy of some kind. Then O.E.D. shook me and I assumed it must be a type of vessel (though still with a local name) on account of the following words: rounded homewards—which I then took to refer to the creaking, groaning play of the ship's timbers as, turning the headland, she set a course for home; the springing of timber being a characteristic sea-voice. This is a bit of a problem. At the moment I can only suggest changing the qualifying adjective to one that would, by implication, suggest that 'groaner' is a navigational signal and not a vessel. What about 'warning groaner'? ('moaning' would be a good word but for the repetition of the broad 'o' sound). The trouble is that 'heaving' is too good to lose. But something may occur to you along the line of my suggestion that 'groaner' should be explained by its epithet." TSE explained the word in his parenthetical note at the head of the poem. OED has added "groaner", with first citation from 1903, then this line.

I 32, 35 **heaving groaner ··· tolling bell**: *Hayward*: The groaner "should not be confused with the bell-buoy."

I 34, 39 *variant* **stillness of the silent fog ··· anxious worried women**: Geoffrey Faber in *ts4*: "does 'silent' add enough to 'stillness'? / ⁊ does 'worried' add enough to 'anxious'?" TSE marked I 34 in *ts4* and changed "stillness" to "oppression".

I 35–41 **bell · · · swell · · · anxious worried women | Lying awake · · · unweave, unwind, unravel**: William Morris: "Sister, let the measure swell | Not too loud; for you sing not well | If you drown the faint boom of the bell · · · Will he come back again, or is he dead?" *The Blue Closet* 9–11, 53. (In *The Music of Poetry* (1942), TSE wrote that Morris's poem "has an effect somewhat like that of a rune or charm.") TSE (anonymously): "Gloucester has many widows, and no trip is without anxiety for those at home", *Fishermen of the Banks* by James B. Connolly (1928), Publishers' Preface. *Lemprière* on Penelope and the Trojan War: "when Ulysses did not return like the other princes of Greece at the conclusion of the war, her fears and her anxiety were increased · · · she was soon beset by a number of importuning suitors · · · she declared that she would make choice of one of them, as soon as she had finished a piece of tapestry, on which she was employed · · · she baffled their eager expectations by undoing in the night what she had done in the daytime." TSE: "Penelope would not have gone on weaving and un-weaving unless she had maintained the hope of Ulysses' return", *Religious Drama: Mediaeval and Modern* (1937). For "worried" and drowning, see note to *Mr. Apollinax* 11.

I 44 *variant* **at the same time**: *Hayward's Queries*: "'at the same *time*' (tricky pun)".

I 44–45 **before the morning watch · · · and time is never ending**: Psalm 130: 6 (Bk. of Common Prayer): "My soul fleeth unto the Lord before the morning watch, I say, before the morning watch" (*Hayward*, *Grover Smith* 275). TSE: "before the morning | Near the ending of interminable night", *Little Gidding* II 25–26.

I 45 **When time stops**: *1 Henry IV* V iv: "And Time, that takes survey of all the world, | Must have a stop."

I 46 **that is and was from the beginning**: *Hayward*: "*Cf.* the doxology in the Anglican service: 'As it was in the beginning, is now, and ever shall be . . .'"

I 46 *variant* **And through the fog the pretemporal ground swell**: Geoffrey Faber underlined "pretemporal" in *ts4* with "A difficult image—not *quite* sure I get its implication, or rather the implication of the prefix 'pre-'. It's all right, if *you* are sure of it. On the sound aspect, I confess I don't like the '-al' ending with its (to my ear) weakening anticipation of the sound which concludes the line."

I 47–48 **Clangs | The bell**: *Cook*: "the bell · · · aurally links itself to a 'calamitous annunciation', and etymologically associates itself with prayer. Its clang becomes a 'Clamour'; the clamour, as *clamare*, becomes prayer · · · section IV will again evoke the Annunciation · · · in its reference to 'the sound of the sea bell's | Perpetual angelus'" (IV 14–15). Hayward to TSE, 5 Mar 1941: "I'm slightly sorry that in the final version 'the bell' · · · has become an object from being a subject; I liked the sonorous emphasis of 'bell' coming after the intransitive 'clangs'. Clang as a transitive verb seems to me to be the weaker."

II

II 1–4 **wailing · · · withering · · · Dropping · · · remaining · · · drifting**: Geoffrey Faber in *ts4*: "the run of participles seems right here" (see note to I 28–32 *variant*, and line endings of *The Waste Land* [I] 1–6). **wailing · · · flowers · · · wreckage:**

Conrad Aiken: "Wailing I heard, but also I heard joy. | Wreckage I saw, but also I saw flowers", *Prelude for Memnon* (1931) XIV (*Grover Smith* 275).

II 5 **The prayer of the bone on the beach**: Yeats: "Sang a bone upon the shore", *Three Things* (1929), an Ariel poem (*Grover Smith* 275).

II 5, 35 **unprayable ··· prayable**: OED "unprayable" 2: "That cannot be uttered as a prayer. *rare*", citing only this line. "prayable" b: "Of a prayer: that may be made", citing only this line.

II 8–9 **further ··· emotionless**: to his French translator Claude Vigée, 1 Feb 1946: "*Further*. I think that I prefer the less emphatic *à venir* to *successives*. I think that your original translation *impassibles* is the best. It is *emotionless* rather in the sense of emotion dominated and kept below the threshold of consciousness."

II 19–20 **the fishermen sailing | Into the wind's tail**: *Hayward*: "The fishermen in question are those engaged in cod-fishing on the famous fogbound 'Grand Banks' off the coast of Newfoundland."

II 21–23 **We cannot think of a time that is oceanless ··· future**: Revelation 21: 1: "for the first heaven and the first earth were passed away; and there was no more sea". Tennyson: "There was no more *sea*, says St. John in Revelation ··· I remember reading that when I was a child, and not being able to reconcile myself to a future when there should be no more sea", Hallam Tennyson, *Tennyson: A Memoir* (1897) I 234. **oceanless**: OED: "devoid of or lacking an ocean", citing only this line.

II 25–30 **We have to think of them as forever bailing, | Setting and hauling ··· drying sails ··· Not as making a trip ··· For a haul that will not bear examination**: as the draft of TSE's preliminary note had explained, the way of life was under threat: "The Gloucester fishing fleet of schooners ··· has been superseded by motor trawlers." Noting that the *Gloucester Daily Times* "devoted whole pages" as early as 1911 to falling fish stocks, Mark Kurlansky writes: "By the 1930s, British engine-powered vessels were traveling ever farther to find fish, and the British government was discussing an endemic problem in their fishing fleet causing the disappearance of fish stocks. But, incredibly, in Gloucester there were fishermen still working under sail power until 1960", *The Last Fish Tale: The Fate of the Atlantic and Our Disappearing Fisheries* (2008). **forever bailing**: "forever building", *Choruses from "The Rock"* II 26.

II 26 **lowers**: OED "lour, lower": "when said of clouds, lower [rhyming with *flower*] to look threatening, has some affinity in sense with lower [rhyming with *mower*] to descend". Pronounced to rhyme with *flowers* in TSE's recording of 1946–47. A pencilled note by TSE tipped into Hayward's copy of *1944* reads: "LOUR (more usual, apparently than LOWER) Se renfrogner, froncer les sourcils. S'assombrir, s'obscurcir, se couvrir, menacer" (King's).

II 27 **Over shallow banks**: Clough: "Over the low sea-banks", *Amours de Voyage* III iv (*Murray*).

II 32 **No end to the withering of withered flowers**: "This is the case even ··· let us say, when a withered flower is the sign of a particular moment in our history", *Knowledge and Experience* 48.

II 36 **Prayer of the one Annunciation**: spoken by Mary after the conception of Christ has been announced to her by the angel Gabriel: "Behold the handmaid of the Lord; be it unto me according to thy word", Luke 1: 38.

II 37–66 **It seems, as one becomes older, | That the past has another pattern · · · the moments of agony · · · We appreciate this better | In the agony of others · · · the agony abides**: to Hayward, who had muscular dystrophy, 2 Feb 1931: "As for suffering, it is very queer indeed. Of course, I admit that I know little, perhaps less than most, of physical suffering, and I am sure that you know much of both. But I have had considerable mental agony at one time or another, and once or twice have felt on the verge of insanity or imbecility (I mean two quite different experiences) · · · If I had died even five years ago, everything that I had suffered up to then would, so far as I can see, have been just waste and muddle. Then a pattern suddenly emerges from it, without one's seeming to have done anything about it oneself. And I don't suppose it is ever the same pattern for any two people."

II 39–40 **development · · · notions of evolution**: OED "development" 3b: "Of races of plants and animals: The same as evolution" (1844). TSE in 1948: "I am anxious to avoid speaking as if the evolution of primitive culture to higher forms was a process which we knew by observation. We *observe* the differences, we *infer* that some have developed from a stage similar to that of the lower stages which we observe · · · I am here not concerned with that development", *Notes Towards the Definition of Culture* 35. Bradley: "Potential existence can, in brief, be used only where 'development' or 'evolution' retains its proper meaning", *Appearance and Reality* ch. XXIV; scored by TSE. In the drafts of the poem, TSE originally enclosed "development" in quotation marks (see note to II 47–48). TSE: "Christianity will probably continue to modify itself, as in the past, into something that can be believed in (I do not mean *conscious* modifications like modernism, etc., which always have the opposite effect)", *A Note on Poetry and Belief* (1927). "Darwin's *Origin of Species* · · · was to start more speculation on the origin and destiny of man—speculation both wise and foolish, scientific and unscientific, relevant and irrelevant—than any book of the century · · · a doctrine of the almost automatic progress of the human race no longer seems credible", *"The Voice of His Time"* (1942). See note to *East Coker* II 21. (TSE's copy of Darwin's book is autographed "T. S. Eliot London 1911"; Houghton.) For "Progress!", see *To the Class of 1905* 78 and note.

II 42 *variant* **I don't mean**: *Hayward's Queries*: "I don't mean · · · ? = not merely".

II 42–45 **moments of · · · sudden illumination · · · experience**: "states of soul · · · which can be experienced only in moments of illumination", *Thoughts for Meditation* (1951).

II 42–47 **The moments of happiness · · · a very good dinner · · · restores the experience | In a different form**: to Geoffrey Faber [18 Sept 1927]: "There is another 'good thing' of life too, which I have only had in flashes. It is the sudden realisation of being separated from all enjoyment, from all things of this earth, even from Hope; a sudden separation and isolation from *everything*; and at that moment of illumination, a recognition of the fact that one can do without all these things, a joyful recognition of what John of the Cross means when he says that the soul cannot be possessed of the divine union until it has divested itself of the craving for all created beings. And after this one returns (I do anyway) to the *canard aux oranges* or the *moules marinières* or whatever it be with a keener pleasure, because one is less limited to these things ··· If we are rightly directed, a good dinner can lead us towards God, and God can help us to enjoy a good dinner." For St. John of the Cross on the peril of attachment to "a person, a garment, a book ··· a particular kind of food", see note to *Little Gidding* III 3. TSE: "without the sanctions of religious faith, it is doubtful whether 'human nature' is able to preserve its values. And by values here I mean appreciation of right and wrong in something wider than an ordinary moral sense: I include health and recreation, artistic appreciation, and a proper *cuisine*: I include everything necessary for salvation and everything necessary for the preparation and enjoyment of a good soup or salad. For the modern British do not even know what to eat and drink: their minds are too lazy", *Notes on Social Philosophy* (1941). In another mood: "The practised salad-maker ··· will not expect to succeed equally well every time, because it is a matter of inspiration, and a number of imponderable and incalculable elements enter into the preparation of any salad. But it is this uncertainty that makes the preparation of salad so exciting, and that renders the great salad so memorable. Personality plays a large part", *How to Prepare a Salad* (1936). **fulfilment ··· a very good dinner**: "the concept of 'fullness of life' for all men, which is set before us, is not much more comprehensive than that of fullness of stomach", *Full Employment and the Responsibility of Christians* (1945). "you've got to give me a very good dinner", *The Confidential Clerk* II. To Edward J. H. Greene, 19 Apr 1940, of Paris in 1926: "It was a very good dinner, and I remember the *canard aux oranges* with permanent pleasure." To Ashley Dukes, [18 Feb 1948]: "This was an evening which will rank in my memory with a dinner given by Léon Daudet in 1926." To Hayward, 19 May [1941]: "I shall have pleasure in supping with you (the term 'dinner' having dropped out of the language)." To Dorothea Richards, 9 Jan 1943: "people who think of the pleasures of taste as transitory have no palate: I get solid satisfaction still from the memory of meals eaten many years ago."

II 42, 45 *variants*, 48 **I don't mean ··· One had the experience ··· We can assign**: *Hayward's Queries*: "*I—One—We*".

II 45–49 **We had the experience but missed the meaning ··· meaning ··· experience ··· the past experience revived in the meaning**: I. A. Richards: "Many people are endowed with memories of marble upon which time can do little to efface even the slightest mark, but they benefit little from the endowment ··· To be able to revive an experience is not to remember when and where and how it occurred, but merely to have that peculiar state of mind available", *Principles of Literary Criticism* ch. XXII. Against the first sentence TSE wrote, "But *what* do they remember." The second he scored, underlining "revive".

II 47–48 **beyond any meaning | We can assign to happiness**: in draft, "happiness" was enclosed in quotation marks. To Hayward, 2 Feb 1931: "faith is not a *substitute* for anything: it does not give the things that life has refused, but something else; and in the ordinary sense, it does not make one 'happier'. Perhaps it makes it more possible to dispense with 'happiness'." For "substitute", see note *Whispers of Immortality* 10–12.

II 48, 56 *variants*, 60 **I have suggested also ··· Now, the point is ··· We appreciate this better**: putting "X" beside each of these phrases in *ts4*, Geoffrey Faber wrote at the head of the leaf (II 42–67): "I find all this passage very impressive: and all the more, for that reason, I dislike the 'lecture-stigmata' you (as it seems to me) wilfully give to it! The Xs mark my points of resentment!" TSE added his own "X" beside II 48 in *ts4*. *Hayward's Queries* included "'I have suggested also . . .'?"

II 52 **probably quite ineffable**: to A. L. Rowse, 22 Mar 1941: "you may prefer 'hardly expressible', but it does not say the same thing. I mean much more than that: I don't mean that you can't express it very well, but that *I* can't express it at all and I therefore doubt whether it can be brought into relation to words at all, and I know that my words are not approximate at all." On Logan Pearsall Smith's saying that there remains something "baffling and enigmatic" about Donne's sermons: "We may cavil at the word 'incommunicable', and pause to ask whether the incommunicable is not often the vague and unformed; but the statement is essentially right", *Lancelot Andrewes* (1926).

II 53 **the backward look**: "the backward glance may yield regrets for our adventurousness, or may even change us to salt, but can bring out no information", *The Validity of Artificial Distinctions* (1914). (Genesis 19: 26, of Lot's wife: "But his wife looked back from behind him, and she became a pillar of salt.")

II 56–62 **the moments of agony · · · are likewise permanent · · · We appreciate this better | In the agony of others, nearly experienced, | Involving ourselves, than in our own**: Aristotle: "men pity when the danger is near themselves · · · all things, which we fear for ourselves, we pity when they happen to others. And since it is when they seem near that sufferings are piteous, (while things which are ten thousand years off in the past or the future · · · are not pitied at all, or pitied in a less degree), it follows that those who aid the effect with gesture, voice, dress,—in a word those who dramatise it are more piteous · · · Hence we are moved by the tokens and by the actions of sufferers", *Rhetoric* II viii. TSE: "every poet who has made poetry of some experience not previously given poetic expression, has made a permanent contribution to our awareness of life. I would also note that the poet is not necessarily limited to his own experience. It seems probable that a man who has had strong emotions, and who has been more conscious than most men of the feelings he has experienced, is thereby better equipped for writing poetry; but he may, or may not, limit himself to his own experience. He may be concerned with emotions he has never himself suffered, but only observed and imagined", *Poetical and Prosaic Use of Words* (1943).

II 56–66, III 3–15 **agony · · · permanent · · · permanence · · · agony · · · experienced · · · experience · · · people change · · · agony · · · the future · · · a book that has never been opened · · · those who · · · the past · · · different lives · · · future**: "To the Reader" from *Inoubliable France* [*title page translation*: *France Remembered*] (1944):

> Those who open this book, to study the photographs, of scenes so familiar and so strange, and to read the evocative text, are likely to be drawn to it first by its power of awakening memories from their own past lives. Whether these are memories of six or seven years ago, or out of a more remote past, it makes no difference. To most English lovers of France, the most recent visit now appears in as distant a perspective as the first recollections. To some, this book will bring memories of holidays, or of visits to French friends; to some, memories of studies pursued with the ardour and curiosity of youth; to some, memories of still more intense experience. The views of familiar places will recall the moments of our lives which

were passed there; those of places unvisited, will be assimilated to other scenes of French landscape which we have known.

The picture of a place, however, as it evokes personal memories, may identify that place too closely with a life that is buried, or a chapter that is closed. I would remind you therefore that these photographs do not come from your album of souvenirs, they record the expression of their subjects, the demeanour of the monuments and streets and countryside, under actual conditions. Yet with the passing of the horde they have little concern. They are of the present, and also of the permanent France; they will remind you that the France you loved did not die when you parted from her; and they will, I hope, help to span the gulf between the France you knew and the France you look forward to knowing, between the thoughts and sentiments and experience of the past and those of the future. So, when we receive a recent photograph, of a friend who has passed through agonies since our last meeting, we may say first "how little changed!" and presently, "Yes, changed, certainly, and I am glad to think that I have changed too; for unless we both change, and change in harmony, how can our affection survive?"

II 60–62 **We appreciate this better | In the agony of others · · · than in our own**: after reading TSE's description of Shakespeare's struggle "to transmute his personal and private agonies into something rich and strange", in *Shakespeare and the Stoicism of Seneca* (1927), Geoffrey Faber wrote to TSE, 15 Sept 1927: "I often suspect that storm and stress exhaust the desire, if not the power, to write greatly; and that an imaginative apprehension of other men's distress, rather than a distressful life of his own, is the real qualification of the great Dramatist."

II 63 **the currents of action**: *Hamlet* III i: "their currents turn awry | And lose the name of action" (*Blamires* 102).

II 66 **the agony abides**: to Geoffrey Faber, 21 Jan 1941: "Neither religious nor artistic treatment of past agony is · · · a pain killer"; see headnote, 2. "THE RIVER IS WITHIN US, THE SEA IS ALL ABOUT US".

II 67 **Time the destroyer is time the preserver**: Shelley: "Wild Spirit, which art moving everywhere; | Destroyer and preserver; hear, oh, hear!" *Ode to the West Wind* 13–14 (*Blamires* 99).

II 68 **Like the river with its cargo of dead negroes, cows and chicken coops**: "At such times, it carries down human bodies, cattle and houses", *The Adventures of Huckleberry Finn* (1950), Introduction. "The river bears no empty bottles, sandwich papers, | Silk handkerchiefs, cardboard boxes, cigarette ends | Or other testimony of summer nights", *The Waste Land* [III] 177–79. "in this deadwater where floats a dead ass · · · river", *Anabasis* IV ix. **negroes**: to Frank Morley, 19 July 1943, on receipt of the first American ed. of *Four Quartets*: "I don't know why you spell negroes with a capital N: that's the only error I have so far detected." To Robert Beare, 10 Mar 1953: "One difference between editions at least, arises from a difference in practices in English and American typography. In the United States, I understand that 'negro' always appears with a capital 'N'. In this country, 'negro' is always in lower case."

II 69 **the bite in the apple**: *Hayward*: "The apple is used as a symbol of the Fall."

II 70–75 **the ragged rock in the restless waters · · · a seamark · · · is what it always was**: Dryden: "Far in the Sea, against the foaming Shoar, | There stands a Rock; the raging Billows roar | Above his Head in Storms; but when 'tis clear, | Uncurl their ridgy Backs, and at his Foot appear. | In Peace below the gentle Waters run

··· The mark to guide the Mariners aright ··· Then round the rock they steer", *Aeneid* V 164–73. "Round and round the rugged rock | The ragged rascal ran", tongue-twister, *The Oxford Nursery Rhyme Book* (1955). TSE: "No light to warn of rocks which lie below, | But let us yet put forth courageously", *To the Class of 1905* 3–6. **a seamark:** *Coriolanus* V iii: "Like a great sea-mark standing every flaw | And saving those that eye thee!" (*Blamires* 101). **lay a course**: see TSE to Hayward, 4 Jan 1941, in note to the title *The Dry Salvages*. **what it always was:** *Hayward's Queries*: "Abrupt end to sect. II?" *The Family Reunion* II ii: "John will recover, be what he always was."

II 72 **halcyon day:** OED "halcyon" 1: "A bird of which the ancients fabled that it bred about the time of the winter solstice in a nest floating on the sea, and that it charmed the wind and waves so that the sea was specially calm during the period: usually identified with a species of kingfisher, hence a poetic name of this bird", with Shenstone: "So smiles the surface of the treach'rous main | As o'er its waves the peaceful halcyons play." 2: "Calm, quiet ··· (Usually qualifying *days*.)" TSE to Hayward, 6 June 1937: "exhilarated this afternoon by the halcyon weather".

III

Hayward: "Part III, which is mainly concerned with the right end of action, recalls the famous dialogue in the Bhagavad-Gita between Krishna, the God, an avatar of Vishnu, and Arjuna, his warrior-disciple, on the field of battle. 'There Arjuna is concerned with the problem of the innate sinfulness of human action, and Krishna replies to his doubts by insisting on the necessity of disinterestedness'" (*Gardner* 173). When TSE took Charles Lanman's Harvard course "Elementary Sanskrit" in 1911–12, the *Gita* was assigned reading. His earliest copy (tr. Lionel D. Barnett, Temple Classics, 1905) is signed on title page "T. S. Eliot Cambridge 1912" (see headnote to *I am the Resurrection and the Life*). "My own scholarship is very slender, but I learnt to distrust people who talk about the *Bhagavad Gita* without mentioning that it is a syncretism of half a dozen philosophical systems", *"The Poems of Dadu"*, reader's report (1926). TSE called the *Gita* "the next greatest philosophical poem to the *Divine Comedy* in my experience", *Dante* (1929) II.

To A. Frank-Duchesne, 5 Nov 1945: "I have been sometimes told, however, that the influence of Indian thought and sensibility in my poetry has sometimes led me at least very near the edge of heterodoxy." To Egon Vietta, 23 Feb 1947: "Long before I was a Christian, I was a student of Indian philosophy, and of the Buddhist scriptures in Pali: both from study of some original texts, under teachers of Indic philology and philosophy at Harvard, and from an early interest in Schopenhauer and Deussen also in connexion with Sanskrit. I have thought that as the scholastics, notably St. Thomas, incorporated Aristotelianism into Christian thought, so the task remains for some still more encyclopaedic scholar (who would need also an encyclopaedic *imagination*) to reconcile and incorporate Eastern religious thought into that of Christianity. So far, most students of the East have known little, and cared less about their own western tradition of thought; or else have started from the assumption that the East had nothing to teach us. The result is, that we have largely learned the wrong things. (The late Dr. Coomaraswamy had some qualifications and much learning, but he approached the synthesis from an Indian point of view). This is outside of my competence, and I have little learning; but I do think that some of my poetry is peculiar in a kind of poetic fusion of Eastern and Western currents of feeling." (See TSE to I. A. Richards, 9 Aug 1930, quoted in headnote to "*Poems* (1920)", 5. TSE'S PROFICIENCY IN FRENCH.) TSE's jacket copy for Purohit Swami and Yeats's translation of *The Ten Principal Upanishads* (1937) referred to "that body of literature which is as important for the study of the religion of India as the Old Testament is for Judaism and Christianity".

Against the suggestion in the ts of *Beare* that *The Dry Salvages* quoted "from the Yeats–Purohit translation", TSE wrote: "nonsense! Do you suggest that I had never read the *Gita* until I published Purohit Swami?" (ts, U. Maryland). Yet he wrote to Beare, 17 Nov 1955: "while it is true that I knew the *Bhagavad-Gita* long before Purohit Swami made his translation, and did indeed, at one time read it in the original (I have long since even forgotten the alphabet), I should mention that when I came to quote from the *Bhagavad-Gita* in *The Dry Salvages*, I quoted from the Swami's translation. It seemed to me a good translation, which is the reason why we published it, and it was the translation which I had to hand." For the Upanishads, see note to *The Waste Land* [V] 399–422.

III 2, 4 **one way of putting the same thing · · · wistful regret · · · regret**: to George Barker, 24 Jan 1938: "the same · · · the same thing · · · one does not feel the same about something as one did yesterday; feelings disappear from which we part with regret" (see headnote to *Four Quartets*, 4. "NOT MERELY MORE OF THE SAME"). "That was a way of putting it", *East Coker* II 18.

III 3–4 **a Royal Rose or a lavender spray | Of wistful regret**: Ibsen, tr. William Archer: "the rooms all seem to smell of lavender and dried rose-leaves · · · It reminds me of a bouquet—the day after the ball", *Hedda Gabler* act II. In a letter to Virginia Woolf, [28 Dec] 1939, TSE described reading Archer's Ibsen. **Royal Rose**: not a specific variety of plant. To William Matchett, 14 June 1949, on *Four Quartets*: "'Rose' when spelt with a capital has always some reference to Charles the 1st. There is in the background certainly the memory of the Wars of the Roses, but its primary context is the seventeenth century" (see headnote to *Little Gidding*, 1. HISTORY OF LITTLE GIDDING).

In the Wars of the Roses, Henry VII of the House of Lancaster won the throne when Richard III of the House of York was killed at Bosworth Field on 22 Aug 1485, the red rose succeeding the white. To Anne Ridler, 19 Aug 1949, anticipating the opening of *The Cocktail Party*: "I hope it is not ominous that the play should open on the anniversary of Bosworth; and I hope that I shall not have bad dreams before the battle; but I shall saddle white Surrey and try to get the white rose that I habitually wear on that day, and pray for the soul of King Richard as usual." (*Richard III* V iii, RICHARD: "Saddle white Surrey for the field tomorrow.") King Henry later united the two roses by marrying Princess Elizabeth of the House of York. Charles MacFarlane, on their son Henry VIII: "Popular songs magnified the exploits of the Henries and Edwards, his royal predecessors, and anticipated his own great victories. '· · · And save this flower which is our king, | This Rose, this Rose, this royal Rose'", *The Great Battles of the British Army* (1833, new ed. 1860) 45–46. TSE to Henry Sherek, 27 July 1954: "I have always been a stout supporter of the Yorkist cause in general and of Richard III in particular, and for some years have made a point of hearing Mass on the anniversary of the Battle of Bosworth." To Geoffrey Curtis, 19 Aug 1943:

"Say a Hail Mary on Sunday for Richard III." See note to *Little Gidding* III 46–50 *3rd draft* [1–2].

III 5 **yellow leaves:** Shakespeare: "That time of year thou mayst in me behold | When yellow leaves, or none, or few, do hang | Upon those boughs which shake against the cold", Sonnet 73.

III 5–7 *msA* [7] **For what alters the past to fit the present, can alter the present to fit the past:** "Whoever has approved this idea of order · · · will not find it preposterous that the past should be altered by the present as much as the present is directed by the past", *Tradition and the Individual Talent* I (1919).

III 6 **the way up is the way down:** *Hayward*: "*Vide* epigraph to *Burnt Norton*". Heraclitus: "The road up and the road down is one and the same", frag. 69 (Elizabeth S. Dallas, *Comparative Literature* Summer 1965). TSE: "Reality, though I should judge *one* at bottom, divides itself into a Cartesian dichotomy—the way up, consciousness, and the way down, matter", *Inconsistencies in Bergson's Idealism* (1913) (*Childs* 151). D. H. Lawrence on Dana's *Two Years Before the Mast*: "The way up, and the way down. The strange ways of life", *Studies in Classic American Literature* ch. 9.

III 7 **this thing is sure:** *Hayward's Queries*: "this is certain (too many monosyllables at present)".

III 9–19 **When the train starts, and the passengers are settled | To fruit, periodicals · · · letters · · · sleepy rhythm · · · not escaping from the past · · · terminus · · · the drumming liner:** Clough: "we travel along in the railway-carriage, or steamer, | And, *pour passer le temps*, till the tedious journey be ended, | Lay aside paper or book · · · terminus · · · did we really believe that the Present indeed is the Only!" *Amours de Voyage* III vi (*Murray*). **passengers · · · Their faces relax from grief into relief:** Herbert: "till the grief | Of pleasures brought me to him, ready there | To be all passengers' most sweet relief", *Christmas*. TSE: "There is no relief but in grief", *Five-Finger Exercises* I. *Lines to a Persian Cat* 6.

III 12–13 **grief into relief · · · sleepy:** Coleridge: "drowsy, unimpassioned grief · · · relief", *Dejection* 22–23 (for TSE's marked copy of this poem see notes to *Do I know how I feel? Do I know what I think?* 1 and *Little Gidding* II 3–16).

III 13 **To the sleepy rhythm of a hundred hours:** "I know that a poem, or a passage of a poem, may tend to realize itself first as a particular rhythm before it reaches expression in words, and that this rhythm may bring to birth the idea and the image", *The Music of Poetry* (1942) ("passengers", 9). "He was stifled and soothed by his own rhythm. | By the river", *The Death of Saint Narcissus* 8–9. "In our rhythm of earthly life we tire of light · · · We are children quickly tired: children who are up in the night · · · we sleep and are glad to sleep, | Controlled by the rhythm of blood and the day and the night and the seasons", *Choruses from "The Rock"* X 36–39. "Keeping the rhythm in their dancing", *East Coker* I 40. Of the river: "Keeping his seasons · · · the machine · · · His rhythm was present in the nursery bedroom · · · April · · · autumn · · · winter", *The Dry Salvages* I 8–14. "hammered and hummed · · · The machine · · · the engine · · · I lay in bed · · · endless geological periods · · · the machine", *The Engine* I, II. "And the rhythm that governs the repose of our sleepingtime, | The breathing in unison", *A Dedication to my Wife* 3–4.

III 14–31 **Fare forward, travellers! not escaping from the past | Into different lives**

··· **While time is withdrawn, consider the future | And the past:** "put forth courageously. || As colonists embarking from the strand | To seek their fortunes on some foreign shore | Well know they lose what time shall not restore", *To the Class of 1905* 6–9. **time is withdrawn:** MacNeice: "I am glad to have known them, | The people or events apparently withdrawn", *Autumn Journal* xxi; "Time was away and somewhere else", *Meeting Point* in *Plant and Phantom* (1941).

III 14, 26, 39, 45 **Fare forward:** see note to III 44–45.

III 16 **You are not the same people:** "The *I* who saw the ghost is not the *I* who had the attack of indigestion", *Knowledge and Experience* 121. To Stephen Spender, 9 May 1935: "Of course the self recovered is never the same as the self before it was given" (see note to *Gerontion* 65–66 for this letter). "You would have found that she was another woman | And that you were another man"; "What we know of other people | Is only our memory of the moments | During which we knew them. And they have changed since then ··· at every meeting we are meeting a stranger", *The Cocktail Party* I i, I iii. "I'm not the same person as a moment ago", *The Elder Statesman* I. Introducing his Morris Gray Poetry Reading Harvard, 13 May 1947: "one becomes rather out of touch with one's very early work. It's not as if it were written by somebody else; that would be comparatively easy. But it seems to have been written by a young person with whom one is intimately and rather embarrassingly associated and of whom one is slightly ashamed. Furthermore as time goes on, one sees more and more flaws in one's early work, which it's too late to repair because one isn't enough the same person to have the right to tamper with the early poems." See headnote to *Sweeney Agonistes*, 9. AFTER PUBLICATION, for "when time lapses before a work is completed you change in the meantime". "F. M.": "I am not the same person who once played—as it seems to one—a leading part in those spring fantasies", *Letters of the Moment* I (1924). On a draft, TSE had written: "was it really me in those past springs" (c. 624 fol. 28v).

III 16–37 **You are not the same people who left that station | Or who will arrive at any terminus ··· 'the past is finished' ··· in any language ··· fructify in the lives of others:** on Valéry's remark "L'Europe est finie": "something will remain operative, on the further generations ··· every language, to retain its vitality, must perpetually depart and return ··· We have to return to where we started from, but the journey has altered the starting place: so that the place we left and the place we return to are the same and also different ··· Now the journey has to be taken by new travellers ··· it is by this perpetual departure and return that the great languages of Europe can be kept alive; and if they can be kept alive, then Europe is not finished", *"Leçon de Valéry"* (1946).

III 19 **the deck of the drumming liner:** D. H. Lawrence: "I hear the steamer drumming", *A Bad Beginning*; quoted by John Middleton Murry in *Son of Woman: The Story of D. H. Lawrence* (1931), which TSE reviewed in *Criterion* July 1931 (C. E. Baron, *Cambridge Quarterly* Spring 1971).

III 19–20 **the deck ··· Watching the furrow that widens behind you:** Clough: "far behind ··· the deck ··· watch below | The foaming wake far widening as we go", *Where lies the land to which the ship would go?*

III 19, 29–31 **drumming ··· the hither and the farther shore | While time is withdrawn, consider the future | And the past with an equal mind:** Clough:

"from the tumult escaping, 'tis pleasant, of drumming and shouting, | Hither, oblivious awhile, to withdraw ··· Yield to the calm", *Amours de Voyage* III ix (*Murray*).

III 21–22 **You shall not think "the past is finished" | Or "the future is before us":** Bradley on time: "It is taken as a stream, and past and future are regarded as parts of it, which presumably do not co-exist, but are often talked of as if they did", *Appearance and Reality* ch. IV.

III 26, 31, 35 **voyaging ··· with an equal mind ··· death:** Dryden: "With equal Mind, what happens, let us bear, | Nor joy, nor grieve too much for Things beyond our Care. | Like Pilgrims, to th'appointed Place we tend; | The World's an Inn, and Death the Journeys End", *Palamon and Arcite* III 885–88. **with an equal mind:** Horace: *Æquam mentem* (Odes II iii). Arnold: "Nature, with equal mind, | Sees all her sons at play", *Empedocles on Etna* I ii.

III 29 **the hither and the farther shore:** the Buddha calls desire and nirvana the two shores: "The man for whom there is neither this nor that shore, nor both—him, the fearless and unshackled, I call indeed a Brahman", *Dhammapada* Upanishad, tr. Irving Babbitt, ch. XXVI st. 385 (*Grover Smith* 323). For TSE on "works like the Dhammapada", see note to *The Waste Land* [V] 433. "Attain at length the farther shore", *Airs of Palestine, No. 2* 34.

III 33–44 **"on whatever sphere ··· time of death" ··· field of battle:** *Gita* 8. 5–8: "Whosoever at the time of death thinks only of Me, and thinking thus leaves the body and goes forth, assuredly he will know Me. On whatever sphere of being the mind of a man may be intent at the time of death, thither he will go. Therefore meditate always on Me, and fight; if thy mind and thy reason be fixed on Me, to Me shalt thou surely come. He whose mind does not wander, and who is engaged in constant meditation, attains the Supreme Spirit", *The Geeta* tr. Shri Purohit Swami (Faber, 1935). *Preston* 44: "Arjuna is required to engage in battle against a hostile but related clan; but at the sight of his near relatives in the opposing army he hesitates to begin the fight, and is recalled to a sense of duty by Krishna ··· The way of salvation, he says, lies in action performed in fulfilment of duty, but action performed in complete freedom from personal desires or interest." For the significance, see *Composition FQ* 56–57, and on TSE's fusion of many verses from the *Gita* see *Kearns* 248–50.

Asked to offer a comment for *Authors take sides on the Spanish War* (1937), TSE declined: "While I am naturally sympathetic, I still feel convinced that it is best that at least a few men of letters should remain isolated, and take no part in these collective activities." His demurral was itself printed in the section headed "Neutral". "Now an ideally unprejudiced person, with an intimate knowledge of Spain, its history, its racial characteristics, and its contemporary personalities, might be in a position to come to the conclusion that he should, in the longest view that could be seen, support one side rather than the other. But so long as we are not compelled in our own interest to take sides, I do not see why we should do so on insufficient knowledge: and even any eventual partisanship should be held with reservations, humility and misgiving. That balance of mind which a few highly-civilized individuals, such as Arjuna, the hero of the *Bhagavad Gita*, can maintain in action, is difficult for most of us even as observers, and, as I say, is not encouraged by the greater part of the Press", *A Commentary* in *Criterion* Jan 1937 ("of the press", *The Dry Salvages* V 12).

III 34–35 **the mind · · · the time of death**: "Who knows, Mrs. Chamberlayne, | The difference that made to the natives who were dying | Or the state of mind in which they died?" *The Cocktail Party* III.

III 38 **do not think of the fruit of action**: *Gita* 2.47: "But thou hast only the right to work, but none to the fruit thereof. Let not the fruit of thy action be thy motive; nor yet be thou enamoured of inaction" (*Hayward*, quoting Purohit Swami's translation. *Hayward*: "It is perhaps relevant to recall that the poet devoted two years at Harvard to the study of Sanskrit and Hindu metaphysics"). Pater: "Not the fruit of experience, but experience itself is the end", *Studies in the History of the Renaissance* Conclusion. (In 1929, TSE collated editions of this final chapter of Pater on Montgomery Belgion's behalf.)

III 42 **real destination**: "to what purpose were we born? For what destination do we die? What is the end of man?" *The Church's Message* (1937) broadcast text (the printings omitted the second question). "working by means of mathematical symbols · · · we start at a real place and arrive at a real place but haven't been in real places on the journey", *Comments on Mannheim's Letter* (1944).

III 43 **Arjuna**: stressed on the first syllable in TSE's recording of 1946–47.

III 44–45 **Not fare well, | But fare forward**: Thomas Hodgkin: "When the blessing was given, the youth said: 'Farewell.' 'Not farewell, but fare forward' answered Severinus", *Theodoric the Goth: The Barbarian Champion of Civilisation* (1891) 99 (*footnote*: "L. *Vale* = farewell; *Vade* = fare forward").

Hayward's Queries: "Fare forward?—Browning". TSE to Hayward, 4 Jan 1941:

> I had quite forgotten the Browning, and I don't even remember it now. I was thinking of the words of the sibyl to Alaric (wasn't it?) on his way to Rome: "not fare well but fare forward". This point bothers me.

Hayward to TSE, 7 Jan 1941:

> As to the Browning "canard" (as it turns out to be) I hasten to put your mind at ease. It's the old story of a half-remembered and unchecked tag floating in and out of one's memory. The hortatory phrase "Fare Forward" struck, as they say, a chord—or what I took to be a chord. I recalled at once the familiar *Epilogue to Asolando*, but recalled it inaccurately, thinking the last words were: "Cry 'Speed,—fight on, fare forward | There as here'". Browning in fact wrote "Fare ever" · · · I apologize.

Not fare well, | But fare forward, voyagers: TSE: "Unable to fare forward or retreat", *Animula* 26. "Fare forward to the end", *Murder in the Cathedral* I (*Kenner* 237). "VII. Decision to fare forth", *Anabasis* Preface, original summary of the sections.

IV

IV 1 **Lady, whose shrine stands on the promontory**: on 14 June 1947 Charles Olson sent Pound a postcard of the life-size statue of the Lady which stands atop the Church of Our Lady of Good Voyage, Gloucester, with right arm outstretched and a fishing vessel nestling in her left hand, suggesting that she was the original "Lady, whose shrine stands on the promontory". Presumably it was sent to TSE and so to Hayward, for it is now at King's, with a note by TSE, 14 Aug 1947: "Mr. Olson or Olsen is in error. I have never returned to Cape Ann or Gloucester

Mass. since 1915. Presumably this statue tops the facade of the R.C. church in Gloucester. I do not think it was there in my time: anyway I had no knowledge of its existence when I wrote *The Dry Salvages*. But I thought that there *ought* to be a shrine of the B V M [Blessed Virgin Mary] at the harbour mouth of a fishing port." According to Henry Eliot's widow, TSE did not revisit the Gloucester area until 1960. *Boyd* points out that the original church burnt down in 1914, and that TSE might have seen this statue on the new church in 1915, but *Levy* 121 reports TSE as saying on 12 Mar 1961: "Notre Dame de la Gard [Marseilles] is the church I had in mind when I wrote that line." **promontory**: pronounced with four full syllables in TSE's recording of 1946–47.

IV 2–5 **all those who are in ships, those | Whose business has to do with fish ··· And those who conduct them**: Psalm 107: 23: "They that go down to the sea in ships, that do business in great waters" (*Cook*). Revelation 18: 17: "And every shipmaster, and all the company in ships, and sailors, and as many as trade by sea." TSE: "princes paid in currency of fish", *Anabasis* IV x.

IV 9 **Figlia del tuo figlio**: *Paradiso* XXXIII 1: "Vergine madre, figlia del tuo figlio" [Virgin mother, daughter of thy son]. The pronoun "suo", in TSE's drafts and earliest printings, is the polite form of address (usually capitalised) in modern Italian (in Dante's day, "vostro"). No edition of the *Commedia* prints "suo". "for some years, I was able to recite a large part of one canto or another to myself, lying in bed or on a railway journey", *What Dante Means to Me* (1950). In his copy of *The Student's Chaucer*, alongside "Thou mayde and mooder, doghter of thy sone" (*Seconde Nonnes Tale* 36), TSE wrote in 1908–09: "from Dante".

IV 10 **Queen of Heaven**: *Paradiso* XXXI, 100–101: "la Regina del cielo, ond'i' ardo | tutto d'amor" [the Queen of heaven for whom I am all burning with love] (*Hayward*).

IV 11–13 **those who were in ships, and | Ended their voyage on the sand, in the sea's lips | Or in the dark throat**: Harriet Monroe:

> In ships they went down to the sea.
> And the sea had a million lips
> And she laughed in her throat for glee.
> And the floor of the sea was strewn
> With tempest trophies dread
>
> *The Ocean Liner* 35–39 in *You and I* (1914)

IV 14 **wherever cannot reach them the sound of**: *Hayward's Queries* (of "cannot reach"): "c.r. inversion".

IV 14–15 **the sea bell's | Perpetual angelus**: Whitman: "the tolling tolling bells' perpetual clang", *When Lilacs Last in the Dooryard Bloom'd* 43 (*Musgrove* 73) (TSE: "Clangs | The bell", I 47–48). **angelus**: Roman Catholic devotions at morning, noon and sunset, beginning "Angelus domini nuntiavit Mariæ" and commemorating the Incarnation; also the bell rung to announce these.

V

V 1–12 **To communicate with Mars ··· features of the press**: Faber had an active list of titles such as *Healing Ritual* (1935); *Moons, Myths and Man* (1936); *This World and That: An Analytical Study of Psychic Communication* (1940); *Astrology in Everyday Life* (1940); *Magic and Divination* (1941). TSE, "*Vers un Nouveau*

Prophetisme" [*Toward a New Prophetism*] by Raymond Abellio, reader's report (1955); quoted in *Monteith*:

> I yield to no one in my relish for signs and wonders, omens, portents, sibylline utterances, prophecies, the Flood, rains of blood, loess and frogs, powers & principalities, leprechauns & kelpies, undines, kobolds, apsaras, yakshinis, Hiram Abiff, Rosy Crosses, catharism, the Great Pyramid, Zen, Sufism, Lemuria, Atlantis, janmas, yugas, samsara, Cyril Connolly, the Loch Ness Monster, giants, dwarfs, cynocephali, jettatura, doppelganger, the evil eye, divination by cards, sand or knucklebones, cheiromancy, necromancy, little green men swarming out of flying saucers in North Dakota talking Japanese, and such like, but I like 'em one at a time.

("Never has the printing-press been so busy, and never have such varieties of buncombe and false doctrine come from it", *After Strange Gods* 61.)

V 1–19 **To communicate with Mars ··· Pastimes ··· the press ··· When there is distress ··· time:** the year after *The Dry Salvages*, TSE took an interest in "a recent correspondence in *The Times* concerned with the increased addiction to astrology and divination—always a tendency in times of stress", *Christian News-Letter* 8 July 1942. On behalf of the London Spiritualist Alliance, Arthur Conan Doyle had written to *The Times* on 26 July 1928 claiming that "mediums are essential ··· for the conduct of our Churches" and again on 6 Aug 1928, suggesting Parliament "sweep away the obsolete Fortune-Telling Act".

V 2 **To report:** *Hayward's Queries*: "(Tó) Report" (suggesting that the first word be omitted). **behaviour:** Hayward to TSE, 5 Mar 1941: "I prefer the original 'appearance' ··· It is always the appearance of the Loch Ness monster and its fellows that excites the vulgar mobile."

V 3 **haruspicate:** not in OED, although it has "haruspex": "One of a class of ancient Roman soothsayers, of Etruscan origin, who performed divination by inspection of the entrails of victims, and in other ways." (For "mactations, immolations, oblations, impetrations", see note to *Coriolan* II. *Difficulties of a Statesman* 42.) To Adrienne Monnier, 29 Apr 1925: "Que les haruspices soient favorables à votre revue!" [May the omens be favourable for your review!] To John W. Nance, 19 Dec 1929, "I must record my disgust with the foul word *modernist*" (see note to *Cousin Nancy* 8–10). Nance replied, 20 Dec, apologising and regretting that the better word "Futurist" would have been misleading: "Cras ingens haruspex—that is what you are." (For Horace's "Cras ingens", see note to *East Coker* V 37.) TSE to Hayward, 11 Aug 1939: "So far as the augurs, soothsayers and haruspices can determine, assisted by all the arts of geomancy, horoscopy, the entrails of birds and Old Moore, the autumn season should open ··· on September 10th." **scry:** OED: "To see images in pieces of crystal, water, etc. which reveal the future or secrets of the past or present."

V 3 *variant* **horoscope, haruspicate with sand:** *Hayward's Queries*: "haruspicate—coscinomancy" (= divination by the turning of a sieve). TSE to Hayward, 4 Jan 1941: "'Haruspicate'. Gross carelessness on my part. I wonder whether haruspicate with guts would do. I dont think it would." Hayward to TSE, 7 Jan 1941: "No I don't think 'with guts' is quite nice! Is'nt it a pleonasm anyhow? I should not like to lose the conjunction of horoscope-haruspicate ··· I should like to keep 'sand' (or sieves)."

V 3–8 **Describe the horoscope ··· evoke | Biography ··· fiddle with pentagrams:** to Theodore Spencer, 19 July 1948, of requests to view the TSE collection at Eliot House: "Theresa has at least wisely refused permission to a lady, I believe of the usual foreign origin, who said she wanted access to the collection to make a psycho-analytic study of my work. I should particularly wish the exclusion of psycho-analysts, casters of horoscopes and other practitioners of magic."

V 3, 6, 15–16 **Describe the horoscope ··· release omens ··· in the Edgware Road. | Men's curiosity searches past and future:** "consulting the oracles and having our horoscopes cast in the Tottenham Court Road ··· There are, of course, two futures: there is the future of the present ··· and there is the future of the future ··· omens ··· *ominous* ··· If this is of the future, then the future is, as it very likely is, of the barbarians. But this is the future in which we ought not to be interested", *Charleston, Hey! Hey!* (1927).

V 4 **disease in signatures:** to C. A. Bodelsen, 19 Dec 1958: "I was not thinking of Shakespeare's signature or that of anyone else, but was using the word in a much more obscure and possibly not permissible sense. The definition is found in the large Oxford Dictionary as no. 4 of the meanings of signature ['A distinctive mark, a peculiarity in form or colouring, etc., on a plant or other natural object, formerly supposed to be an indication of its qualities, esp. for medicinal purposes'], and I would quote this example which is given there. 1697 'Whether men, as they say of plants, have signatures to discover their nature by, is hard to determine.' Another example from 1748, 'There are some which think that herbs the fittest for curing those parts of man's body, to which they bear some sort of resemblance, commonly called a signature'." (TSE slightly misquotes OED, which reads "that think those Herbs" and "a Man's Body".)

V 7 **sortilege:** OED: "casting lots in order to decide something or to forecast the future; divination". Laforgue: "O géraniums diaphanes, guerroyeurs sortilèges" [O diaphanous geraniums, prophetic warriors] (first line); quoted in *The Metaphysical Poets* (1921).

V 9 **barbituric acids:** used as hypnotic and sedative drugs. **barbituric:** stressed on the third syllable in TSE's recording of 1946–47.

V 10 **recurrent:** pronounced as in *recur* at this point in TSE's recording of 1946–47, but as in *current* at *Little Gidding* II 27.

V 11–12, 32 **explore the womb, or tomb, or dreams ··· features of the press ··· The hint half guessed, the gift half understood, is Incarnation:** "The Incarnation was to him an essential dogma ··· a word half understood ··· some alien or half-formed science, as of psychology ··· the dogmas of sciences of which we have read in the newspapers", *Lancelot Andrewes* (1926).

V 12 **Pastimes:** pronounced with short *a* in TSE's recording of 1946–47.

V 14 **distress of nations and perplexity:** Luke 21: 25: "And there shall be signs in the sun, and in the moon, and in the stars; and upon the earth distress of nations, with perplexity" (*Grover Smith* 280) ("horoscope", 3).

V 15 **Whether on the shores of Asia, or in the Edgware Road:** "whether in Argos or in England", *The Family Reunion* II i chorus. "It is not immediately obvious that events in places so remote as Tinevelly and Dornakal may have consequences in every parish in England", *Reunion by Destruction: Reflections on a Scheme* *for Church Union in South India* (1943) 2. **Asia:** pronounced *Aisha* in TSE's recording of 1946–47. **the Edgware Road:** to Bonamy Dobrée, Monday [Sept 1927?]: "walk smartly up Brompton (or is it The Brompton, like The Edgware?) Road". TSE and Vivien lived near Edgware Road underground station, 1916–20. For "the Tottenham Court Road", see note to V 3, 6, 15–16.

V 15–18 **Asia ··· past and future ··· timeless:** to Frederic Prokosch, 9 Feb 1938, of an ode submitted to the *Criterion*: "I am a bit bothered by 'the infinite magic of human memory' in connexion with Asia ··· indifference to time seems more characteristic of the past of Asia than memory."

V 16 **Men's curiosity:** "What has since happened to M. Bourget, in fact, has been the disappearance of the sense of curiosity. Curiosity is suppleness, it is tolerance, it is the source of unbiased judgment as well as of enthusiasm and feeling", *M. Bourget's Last Novel* (1917). In *Revelation* (1937), TSE quoted Gerald Heard's prediction that "Humanity will be bored" while deploring his opinion that curiosity might save it: "*Curiosity the finest of the passions!* Vanity of vanities!" For Milton's "unprofitable Sin of Curiosity", see note to *Little Gidding* IV *three-stanza ts drafts* [10, 12–14]. OED "curiosity" 5a: "undue or inquisitive desire to know or learn. *Obs.*" c: "Inquisitiveness in reference to trifles or matters which do not concern one." 8: "A desire to make trial or experience of anything novel ··· *Obs.*"

V 18–19 **The point of intersection of the timeless | With time:** Karl Barth: "In this name two worlds meet and go apart, two planes intersect ··· The point on the line of intersection at which the relation becomes observable and observed is Jesus"; "In such knowledge men love God, not before or after, but in the 'Moment' which is no moment in a series, and which is the meaning of every moment in time", *The Epistle to the Romans* (tr. Edwyn C. Hoskyns, 1933) 29, 319. (TSE had a particular interest in this Epistle. His copy of A. E. Garvie's *Romans: Introduction, Authorized Version* (1901) is at Harvard.)

TSE: "In every moment of time you live where two worlds cross, | In every moment you live at a point of intersection", *The Rock* 52. "transecting, bisecting the world of time", *Choruses from "The Rock"* VII 18. "language ··· the intersection of the timeless moment", *Little Gidding* I 52. "That which is called by the Christian mystics 'the mystic union' or Union with God, is defined as 'the timeless moment', a glimpse of pure self-consciousness and as it were an instant of eternity", *The Timeless Moment* by Warner Allen (1946), jacket material (initialled by TSE in Faber catalogue, King's). Henry Hewes recorded of TSE: "He does not believe we can really grasp the concept of the timeless, although he himself has had intuitive flashes which he's hinted at in the *Quartets*. He feels these will only be communicable to those who have had similar flashes", *Eliot on Eliot: "I feel younger than I did at 60"* (1958); see note to V 24. To F. C. Happold, 18 Nov 1958: "I shall be pleased to answer any questions I can about the *Four Quartets*, but you must not think of me as a mystic or contemplative. I have had a few flashes during my life, though there must be many people whose experience has taken them farther. Tennyson, for instance, knew more about certain types of experience than I do." **point of intersection:** "The music of a word is, so to speak, at a point of intersection", *The Music of Poetry* (1942).

V 19–20 **an occupation for the saint— | No occupation either:** "an occupation for prophets and makers of almanacks, of whom I am not one," *The Varieties of Metaphysical Poetry* 159 (Clark Lecture V). "the conscious occupation | Of the praying mind", *Little Gidding* I 47–48.

V 22–24 **selflessness and self-surrender ··· Moment**: "What happens is a continual surrender of himself as he is at the moment to something which is more valuable. The progress of an artist is a continual self-sacrifice, a continual extinction of personality", *Tradition and the Individual Talent* I (1919). In TSE's first American ed. of *Selected Essays*, he later scored the second sentence, with "?" (In the same volume he drew a wavy line under "sacrifice", with "?", in the passage "the artist ··· must surrender and sacrifice himself", *The Function of Criticism* (1923) I.) **self-surrender**: on Communism: "M. Gide turns to a doctrine which, while it has nothing to say to the question: what is the end of man? can say a good deal about the self-surrender of the individual to society. The *âme collective* does duty for God", *Revelation* (1937). "The awful daring of a moment's surrender", *The Waste Land* [V] 403 (see note). For letter to Stephen Spender, 9 May 1935, on recovery and surrender, see note to *Little Gidding* III 15.

V 23, 43–44 **For most of us ··· For most of us ··· Never here to be realised**: "For most of us the occasion of the great betrayal on the clear issue will never come", *A Sermon Preached in Magdalene College Chapel* (1948). (For Paul Elmer More's *The Great Refusal* (1894), see note to *The Waste Land* [I] 60–63.)

V 24 **the moment in and out of time**: "a moment in time and of time, | A moment not out of time, but in time", *Choruses from "The Rock"* VII 18–19 (*Hayward*). "The real issue is ··· between those who believe only in values realizable in time and on earth, and those who believe also in values realized only out of time", *A Commentary* in *Criterion* Oct 1936.

V 25 **distraction fit, lost in a shaft of sunlight**: "the kind of pattern which we perceive in our own lives only at rare moments of inattention and detachment, drowsing in sunlight", *John Marston* (1934). For "retire into a sunlit stupor", see note to *Portrait of a Lady* I 1–14. For distraction from prayer, see note to *Burnt Norton* V 13–22. "hysteric fits ··· distract her brain", *WLComposite* 287, 290.

V 27–29 **music heard so deeply ··· you are the music | While the music lasts**: Edwin Diller Starbuck: "a musician may suddenly reach a point at which pleasure in the technique ··· falls away and ··· he becomes the instrument through which the music flows", *The Psychology of Religion* (1899) 385; title mentioned in *Harvard index cards* (1914) (Joshua Richards, personal communication). Graham Greene: "When music plays, one does not see or think; one hardly hears. A bowl—and the music is poured in until there is no 'I', I *am* the music", *The Man Within* (1929) ch. IV (J. C. Maxwell, *N&Q* Oct 1964). (Writing to Hayward, 7 May 1943, about a British Council exhibition, TSE noted the absence of Graham Greene's name.)

V 29 *variant* **the music lasts, the spell lasts**: *Hayward's Queries*: "spell lasts".

V 29–32 **hints and guesses, | Hints followed by guesses ··· discipline ··· The hint half guessed, the gift half understood, is Incarnation**: Andrewes "tried to confine himself in his sermons to the elucidation of ··· dogma ··· The Incarnation was to him an essential dogma ··· a word half understood ··· an undisciplined mysticism", *Lancelot Andrewes* (1926). Half a dozen paragraphs later TSE describes how, "In this extraordinary prose, which appears to repeat, to stand still, but is nevertheless proceeding in the most deliberate and orderly manner, there are often flashing phrases which never desert the memory." He quotes the passages from Andrewes that are behind *Gerontion* 18–20 and *Journey of the Magi* 1–5, before quoting the Donne behind *Burnt Norton* V 13–22 and *East Coker* I 49–50.

V 32 *variant* **unguessed ··· not understood ··· Incarnation**: Geoffrey Faber in *ts4*: "Isn't this in want of *some* qualification? *You* must guess & understand, or you couldn't say it; & you wouldn't claim to be the only percipient wld. you? Does 'Incarnation' mean '*The* Incarnation' (of Christ) or the incarnation of every human spirit?" TSE: "I take for granted that Christian revelation is the only full revelation; and that the fullness of Christian revelation resides in the essential fact of the Incarnation", *Revelation* (1937).

V 40 **dæmonic**: pronounced *de'monic* in TSE's recording of 1946–47. **chthonic**: OED recommends pronunciation *kthonnic*. In his recording TSE minimises the opening consonant. *Hayward's Queries*: "chthonic (sound)". OED: "dwelling in or beneath the surface of the earth" (particularly of pagan deities); from 1882 (now citing this line). Edgar Jepson: Eliot's poetry "is as autochthonic as Theocritus", *Recent United States Poetry* in *English Review* May 1918.

V 41–42 **And right action is freedom | From past and future also**: on Gide: "exploring all possibilities, willing to try anything—the slave, not of the past, but of the future", *A Commentary* in *Criterion* Jan 1933 (*Ricks* 261). "More, like Babbitt, seems almost to have been born in a state of emancipation from the prejudices of his time and place. Many people give the appearance of progress by shedding the prejudices ··· of one generation only to acquire those of the next ··· 'keeping up to date'", *Paul Elmer More* (1937). "liberation | From the future as well as the past", *Little Gidding* III 9–10.

V 43–44 **the aim | Never here to be realised**: "we have to remember that the Kingdom of Christ on earth will never be realised, and also that it is always being realised", *The Idea of a Christian Society* 59.

V 45, 49 **undefeated ··· yew-tree**: to William Matchett, 14 June 1949: "With regard to 'Yew' it may be both a death symbol, and because it is a very long lived tree, a symbol of the everlasting. But the chief point of the yew in the concluding passage of *The Dry Salvages* is the simple fact that so many old grave-yards have a yew tree. I believe that the cause of this frequency was a medieval edict made with a view to insuring an adequate supply of wood for the bows of the archers; in other words the yew tree was a kind of munitions factory."

V 46 **we have gone on trying**: "meanwhile we have gone on living", *Murder in the Cathedral* I.

V 47 *variant* **We content**: *Hayward's Queries*: "We [*added*: ?] content". Geoffrey Faber in *ts4*: "Does the rhythm demand the elliptical 'We content'? It is difficult for me to take it without jibbing a bit and searching for a lost auxiliary!!" See Textual History.

V 48–50 **our temporal reversion nourish ··· The life of significant soil**: to the Moot: "I quite agree that 'real culture is something that has to be produced again and again, etc.' but the same thing is true of real potatoes: out of the same soil, fertilised by the excrement of men and animals (some of which have eaten potatoes) and by decaying vegetation ··· Soil and vegetables are two different things, but what I mean by culture is neither one nor the other, but that which includes both", *Notes on Mannheim's Paper* (1941). "The culture of a people is not a construction, but a growth. Like *agri*culture, it is something formed over a long period of time by co-operation of man with his environment—not by exploitation of the soil", *Civilization: The Nature of Cultural Relations* (1943). To V. V. C. Collum, 24 Mar 1943: "We are particularly interested ··· in publishing books dealing with agricultural problems, both from the most practical and the most theoretical end of the scale." Wartime Faber titles included *Soil and Sense* (1941) and *The Living Soil* (1944). "without the life of the soil from which to draw its strength, the urban culture must lose its source of strength and rejuvenescence", *The Man of Letters and the Future of Europe* (1944).

To A. L. Rowse, 3 Mar 1941: "I did much appreciate your offer of your house at St. Austell's ··· I don't know whether an old Tory like you ever deigns to look at the *New English Weekly* ··· but if you do you may have observed that I have finally tackled the sea from the coast of it which I know best. Besides, I should feel an impostor in Cornwall, as I do in Galloway ··· So my sea poem returns to Somerset (or if you like Devon, but at any rate England and not Cornwall) at the end." (Rowse's *Tudor Cornwall,* 1941, was part of a lifelong insistence that he was Cornish, not English.) TSE described his "composite" personal landscape before reading *The Dry Salvages*: "You will notice ··· that this poem begins where I began, with the Mississippi; and that it ends, where I and my wife expect to end, at the parish church of a tiny village in Somerset", *The Influence of Landscape upon the Poet* (1960).

Little Gidding

1. History of Little Gidding 2. Composition 3. Dante 4. After Publication

Published in *NEW* 15 Oct 1942 and broadcast by Robert Speaight on 12 Nov before publication as a separate Faber pamphlet on 20 Nov (three impressions to Sept 1943). No separate publication in the US, where *Little Gidding* appeared first in May 1943 within *Four Quartets* in *US 1943*. Then *1944+*.

1. HISTORY OF LITTLE GIDDING

Hayward: "The poem takes its title from the remote village of Little Gidding in Huntingdonshire, ten miles north-west of the county town, once celebrated for the religious community based on the Christian family established there in 1626 for contemplation and prayer by Nicholas Ferrar, the friend of the poet George Herbert. The community was dispersed 21 years later by Cromwell's troops. The chapel, which they ransacked and ruined, was restored for worship in the 19th century, and was visited by the poet in the company of Dr. H. F. Stewart, the Pascalian scholar, and his wife Jessie, on May 25, 1936. There is an interesting account of the Little Gidding community in J. H. Shorthouse's historical novel *John Inglesant* (1880)." Helen Gardner suggests that TSE would have known this very popular romantic tale as a boy, noting that the edition in his library was "published by Macmillan in 1927 in 'The Caravan Library'. Mrs. Valerie Eliot tells me she cannot say whether he actually read this copy, as he often borrowed books from the London Library and purchased them much later" (*Composition FQ* 61).

The Little Gidding community was known for devising and compiling harmonies of the four gospels and other books of the Bible—allowing them to be read as unified narratives. Among the recipients of copies was Charles I, who visited the community in 1633 and 1642. Other visitors included George Herbert and Richard Crashaw, and when Herbert died the manuscript of *The Temple* was sent to Ferrar, who organised its publication. On the night of 1 May 1646, after a series of defeats in the First Civil War, the King sought shelter at Little Gidding, and was taken to nearby Coppingford where he stayed two nights. Later that year the community was vandalised by Parliamentary troops, and in 1657 it closed. (For the history see *Composition FQ* 58–63 and Appendix to the Victoria County History of Huntingdon.) The title page of *The Arminian Nunnery or A Briefe Description and Relation of · · · Little Gidding* (1641) was used by the *Listener* to illustrate TSE's *The Devotional Poets of the Seventeenth Century* (1930), although he made no reference there to the book or the place.

Reviewing Mario Praz's *Secentismo e marinismo in Inghilterra: John Donne–Richard Crashaw*, TSE wrote that the section "which deals with Roman activity and with the extreme Right of the Anglican Church under Laud, with Crashaw's connexion with the retreat of Little Gidding and with the misfortunes of Peterhouse makes extremely good reading", *An Italian Critic on Donne and Crashaw* (1925). TSE referred to Crashaw and the "cloistral society of Little Gidding" in his sixth Clark Lecture (*The Varieties of Metaphysical Poetry* 164).

To Mrs. John Carroll Perkins, 10 July 1936, recalling that spring: "The only really lovely day that I remember was a day at the end of May when I was motored over from Cambridge to Little Gidding" (*Composition FQ* 35). That year, TSE read in draft a play about King Charles and Little Gidding entitled *Stalemate: The King at Little Gidding* by George Every (*Composition FQ* vii, 62–63). He also acted as a "referee" for a Cambridge doctorate about Little Gidding by Bernard Blackstone, writing to the Secretary of the English Faculty Board, T. R. Henn, 6 Mar 1936: "I do not think, however, that I ought to do this unless the other referee is someone possessed of exact scholarship in the literature and history of the period. While I did at one time study the work of George Herbert pretty carefully, I am unfamiliar with Nicholas Ferrar."

Schuchard 182: "When A. L. Maycock, the Cambridge author and librarian, published his *Nicholas Ferrar of Little Gidding* (1938), Eliot had Blackstone review it for the *Criterion* in October. Maycock's book, wrote Blackstone, erases myths and distorted views of Ferrar and lays the groundwork for a much-needed scholarly study. Later in the year, Blackstone brought out the materials for such a study in his *Ferrar Papers*, declaring Ferrar to be 'in singleness of vision and completeness of achievement · · · the most original genius in the church during the vital period of her post-Reformation history' [xi]. Eliot had the book reviewed by another Kelham friend, Charles Smyth, who praised Blackstone's sense of the spiritual complexity of Ferrar's writings" (*Criterion* Jan 1939). In 1946 TSE became a patron of the newly inaugurated Society of the Friends of Little Gidding.

2. COMPOSITION

TSE began planning the fourth Quartet before the third was complete. To Geoffrey Curtis, 31 Dec 1940: "The unwritten one is provisionally, *Little Gidding*." Early jottings and drafts were made in the same pad as those for *The Dry Salvages* (*msA*), in a matching hand and on closely succeeding pages (see *Composition FQ* 237–38).

After a trial typescript of Part I, TSE made another typescript of all five parts (*ts2*), showing them in various states of development. He wrote to Hayward, 27 June 1941: "I have had to buy a new copy of Kipling's Poems · · · I am to edit a selection · · · it is also (as a little reflection will remind you) a kind of War Work · · · I am not getting on very well with *Little Gidding*: there have been too many interruptions." On 7 July 1941, he sent Hayward a copy of his third typing, *ts3b*: "I am taking the liberty of enclosing what I have already done in the way of *Little Gidding* · · · you will understand my being worried and diffident and depressed at this writing. BUT I do not want ANY comments at this stage. You cannot form any opinion of it as a whole until you see the whole; and as for details, I want to do more polishing myself before I receive hints from the Critick. I feel especially that Part II doesn't come off."

Hayward designated *ts3b* the "First Complete Draft", and *ts9b* (sent 17 and 27 Aug 1942) the "First Revision", but in the meantime he was consulted about intermediate stages. TSE wrote on 14 July 1941: "I have pushed on with *Little Gidding*, and enclose provisional results." Hayward acknowledged "additional fragments of the pome" (now untraced) on 22 July, and on 1 Aug he sent his reaction. (The text as he describes it sometimes precedes the readings of *ts4*, but the pagination he gives is not that of a complete fair copy.) In his letter of 14 July, TSE discussed changes he was making: "You will observe that I have had to remove 'cancel' from Part I, because I wanted the word further on: I have also had some trouble with the words 'broken' and 'common'." Because of the phrase "Or cancelled by the Paraclete" in a draft stanza of IV (later deleted), he wished to avoid reading "or cancel curiosity" (I 44), so after toying with "instruct" in his retained ribbon copy of *ts3*, he typed "or inform curiosity" in *ts4*. After typing "broken" at II 23 in *ts4*, he revised it to "crumbled" in his ribbon copy (*ts4a*), because of the repetition from "a broken king" at I 26. As for "common", it appears three times in the final text, which may have been what was troubling him. Neither "a common genius" (III 24) nor "The common word" (V 8) was emended after *ts3*. At III 41–42, TSE had tried out "common silence" in both manuscript and typescript before the lines reached their final form in *ts3*:

> Accept the constitution of silence
> And are folded in a single party.

However, in his carbon (*ts3b*), Hayward put an "X" against the second of these lines. This may have been to signal an emendation made by TSE in the missing "additional fragments", or it may have been an objection of his own. At any rate, TSE again typed "common" in *ts4*, before immediately deleting it and reverting to "single party". In these weeks TSE worked intensively on *Little Gidding*, writing again to Hayward on 28 July: "I have I think improved the poem a little by cutting out the second stanza of Part IV and also the Anima Christi lines at the end of Part III (too heavy, I think)." TSE wrote these changes on his ribbon copy (*ts4a*). The carbon of this new typescript, *ts4b*, was given to Geoffrey Faber. Hayward did not receive a fresh typescript until Aug 1942.

TSE had warned Hayward on 14 July 1941: "The question is not so much whether it is as good as the others (I am pretty sure it is not) but whether it is good enough to keep company with them to complete the shape. If the problem is more than one of improving details, it will have to go into storage for some time to come." To Frank Morley, two days later: "The fourth poem has been written and is now being examined by Geoffrey [Faber] and John Hayward but my own suspicion about it is that it is a flop and that I shall have to put it aside and make a fresh start if I can toward the end of the year, but it is yet too soon to be quite sure what is wrong with it and how much."

Hayward's letter of 1 Aug offered reassurance and detailed criticism, still based on *ts3* (see Textual History): "I agree with you that the poem, in the *unfinished and unpolished* state in which you have allowed me to see it, is not quite up to the standard of the others in the group. But it does not seem to me to be, potentially, inferior to them; nor do I think that it shows signs of fatigue or that, as you seem to fear, it is merely a mechanical exercise; I am sure that it only requires to be revised and perhaps rewritten in certain passages, to which I shall refer, to be brought to perfection as the culminating poem of the series ··· My general impression is that Parts I, II, V and all but the first paragraph of Part III are all right. Part IV seems to me to break down. The first fifteen lines of Part III—the didactic passage—strike me as being imperfectly resolved into poetry, in fact rather laboured and prosy. I think I appreciate the difficulty of this kind of expository writing. It may be that it is too easy to cast such philosophic and ethical statements into the kind of long, fluid lines you use so ingeniously. But this particular passage does seem to me to drag; to need fusing: possibly to be presented to the reader in a less didactic and uncompromising form. As for Part IV, I can't fit it into the scheme of the poem as a whole. Now that you have discarded (and rightly so, I think) the 2nd. stanza ("Till death shall bring the audit in . . .") it consists of only two short stanzas ["Between the initial watery sign" and "The dove descending breaks the air"] and their point has escaped me ··· these two stanzas seem to me scarcely to justify a section to themselves. My own view, for the little that it is worth, is that this section should be extended rather than rewritten, or if this is not possible, that it should be so reorganized as to be capable of being incorporated in some way either at the end of Part III or at the beginning of Part V · · · I approve of the omission of the last four lines of Part III" (the *Anima Christi* lines, "Soul of Christ · · · incinerate them"). After many "niggling details" (discussed in the Commentary and Textual History) his letter continued: "assure me that you intend to add *Little Gidding* to the group. You *must not* discard it just because you have the natural misgivings of a poet bringing a movement to its close—misgivings doubtless exacerbated by the miserable time you have had with your teeth."

TSE, 5 Aug 1941: "I agree that the first part of Part III needs thorough re-writing · · · I am especially puzzled about Part IV · · · The defect of the whole poem, I feel, is the lack of some acute personal reminiscence (never to be explicated, of course, but to give power from well below the surface) and I can *perhaps* supply this in Part II. It is whatever is wrong with Part IV that bothers me most."

Bonamy Dobrée was also consulted around this time, and may have been sent the carbon of *ts5* (not traced). On 6 Aug 1941 TSE replied to his comments: "I seem to need other people's opinions (or those of a small number of people) more than I once did: I suppose it comes partly from the different way of working appropriate to middle age, which becomes more deliberate and painstaking. And I feel the need for it especially just now, when I have been conscious of working, so to speak, against time. One sees certain things that one wants to do, and everyone must have a feeling of precariousness of the future; and as my natural way of writing verse seems to require a long period of germination for each poem, before I address myself to the machine, I have been afraid that I have been overproducing, and at last trying to make poetry out of unseasoned material. On the other hand, excellent as your comment appears to me to be, I must say that I think my private critics improve with practice. John Hayward, who has had the longest training in this difficult and exacting art, has now got to the point of making quite drastic criticism; and Faber is improving. It is practice in criticising the work of a particular author in this particular way that is needed, before the mind releases itself to say what it really thinks: and I therefore allow for the leniency of the beginning. I have come to the conclusion that the first two lines of Part II are not right; that the first section of Part III is not well worked out; and that Part II needs a spark, a line or two somewhere, to set it alight. John also finds Part IV a failure: but I cannot yet see just what is wrong. However, you have given me the main assurance that I want: that the poem appears to you to have an organic relation to the others, and is not merely a wooden leg. And for this in particular I am grateful."

To Geoffrey Faber, 22 Aug 1941, arranging a visit to the Fabers in Wales: "I shall also bring John Hayward's criticisms of *Little Gidding*, because I find it useful, not merely to conscript three or four friends (not more) to criticise, but to get them to criticise each other's criticisms. Thus one gets something like a notion of how the thing might strike a person of equal intelligence and sensibility who did not know the author. I have only made a few minor corrections so far, of which the most important is the omission of Part III. I think Part IV will have to be completely recast." (*Geoffrey Faber's notes*, given below, accompany *ts4b*; see Textual History headnote.)

To McKnight Kauffer, 29 Aug 1941: "I have written a fourth poem to complete the series from *Burnt Norton*; but I am not satisfied with it, and am putting it aside to work on in the winter after I have got two or three other jobs off. John has made a number of useful criticisms."

Thanking Hayward belatedly for "your careful notes on 'Spittle-Skidding'", TSE told him, 17 Oct 1941, that he had "determined to put the whole thing out of mind until December". More than a year now passed before the next letter that Hayward bound into his volume of typescripts, and in this period TSE drafted the revised ending to Part II. (To Robert Waller, 19 Oct 1942: "Fortunately for me, my mind ticks rather slowly, so that I can spend a year or more, off and on, over the same poem and perhaps get it finished before I have outgrown it.") Hayward to Anne Ridler, 24 Nov 1941: "*Little Gidding*, the last poem of T. S. E.'s tetralogy, has been put aside for revision in December" (BL Add. ms 71225 fol. 53v).

Hayward to TSE, 16 Jan 1942: "I am anxious to hear that *Little Gidding* is not forgotten." TSE to Marion Dorn, 2 Feb 1942: "I am stuck with my last poem: I have done a draft of it, but felt quite dissatisfied and put it aside since November." Hayward to Belgion, 27 Apr 1942: "he promises to complete as soon as possible the fourth & last poem of the tetralogy, a draft of which—it's called *Little Gidding*—I have had by me for more than 6 months."

TSE to Hayward, 21 July 1942: "Mr. Hoellering of Film Traders Ltd. comes to see me once a week about *Murder in the Cathedral*. I have put Part II of *Little Gidding* into the melting pot, but nothing has solidified yet." 26 July: "I shall have no peace until I have written in a few bits for the film version of *Murder in the C.* · · · This film titan, and *Little Gidding*, are both on my mind · · · When I copy them out I shall let you have a copy of my SET OF VERSES which I composed for Storm Jameson to oblige Bonamy" (*A Note on War Poetry*). To Hayward, 17 Aug, enclosing *ts9b* (Parts II and III): "my mind refuses to do its best at the *rechauffé* of *Murder*, until it has eased itself of *Little Gidding*. So here is a recension of Part II, which seemed to me the centre of weakness. Even if this is better than the first version (which I assume you still have by you) it may not be good enough; and if it is not good enough (minor improvements, of course, apart) then I fear that the poem must simply be allowed to disintegrate. If this is fundamentally all right, then an improvement of the other sections does not seem to be beyond the bounds of possibility. I submit it (together with another edition of Part III) with some trepidation."

He wrote again to Hayward on 27 Aug 1942, enclosing *ts9b* (Parts I and V) and *ts10b* (Part II): "this letter is merely to send you another revision of Part II and a slightly altered I and V and to answer a few questions implied or expressed. You will find that in several cases I have followed your advice negatively if not positively." Then 2 Sept, enclosing *ts12*: "I send you herewith a new fair copy, having dealt with your criticisms. I think that it is much easier to judge of changes when you have a fresh copy incorporating them, and moreover I find it advisable, as did Virginia [Woolf], to type out anything again and again. Each time I find something that I had previously overlooked and this time I think I have picked up two points which neither you nor I noticed. According to my figures, I have altered nine passages according to your suggestions, rejected six suggestions and remained uncertain about two others. As for Part IV, which I now include, I am as yet too close to this new version to be able to tell whether it is fundamentally right or fundamentally wrong."

On 7 Sept 1942, TSE sent Hayward a two-page report on small points in *Little Gidding* (see Commentary, especially II 38). A lost letter from Hayward of 8 Sept may have crossed with this, but was more probably a prompt reply. TSE acknowledged it on 9 Sept: "This time I accept nearly everything: perhaps it means that my resistance is weakening, at this stage; but chiefly I think because I perceive that these belong to that almost inevitable residue of items, in a poem of any length, for which the ideal is unattainable." Again his principal concern was with Part II.

Accordingly, he now retyped the entire poem one final time, sending a carbon of *ts13* to Hayward on 19 Sept 1942, accepting "waning dusk" in the Dantesque lines in Part II: "You will also find that I have made other alterations in the same section. This type of verse appears to present the greatest difficulties. Every word sticks out, and the tax upon one's vocabulary is immense. Syllables and terminations also give one great trouble. If it is as difficult in Italian as in English (which I find it hard to credit) then my admiration for Dante should have no bounds. I am still unsatisfied: 'enchantment' and 're-enactment' in the same passage are unpleasing. But I think that there is a point beyond which one cannot go without sacrifice of meaning to euphony, and I think I have nearly reached it. Anyway, I have sent a copy to Mairet for the *N.E.W.,* and I propose to give a copy of the enclosed to Dick [de la Mare]. There will still be the possibility for [*margin*: ? of] alterations in proof. But to spend much more time over this poem might be dangerous. After a time one loses the original feeling of the impulse, and then it is no longer safe to alter. It is time to close the chapter." Even then, after a paragraph of personal news, there was a postscript: "I don't like 'strode' and 'patrol' either. But you can't have a verb with a labial termination -ed or -t before 'together', and I don't want to give up 'patrol'. Is 'strode' ever pronounced 'strod'?" (see note to II 54). He returned to II 79, 85 in a further note, dated by Hayward 22 Sept: "I cannot find any alternative for either 'enchantment' or 're-enactment' which doesn't either lose or alter meaning. 'Re-enacting' is weak as a substantive; and I want to preserve the association of 'enact'—to take the part of oneself on a stage for oneself as the audience."

To Frank Morley, as his American publisher, 10 Sept 1942: "I think that I may have finished *Little Gidding*. At the moment at any rate I only appear to be held up by the problems presented by two lines and I think it is likely that these may turn out to belong to that small residue of insoluble problems which remain as a sediment in any but the most perfect poem of this length. The whole thing has given me far more trouble than any of its predecessors, which may, of course, mean that it is not so good · · · We propose to give it here a run of a year or more before producing the final volume of all four poems together, but knowing your repeated wishes, the Board are willing to let you publish the collection of four poems together ahead of us. That is to say, you would have to publish it, I presume, within six months of its appearance in the *New English Weekly*, in order to preserve the copyright, but of course from our point of view, we should prefer you to publish it toward the end rather than the beginning of this period of grace · · · In any case, I shall post you two successive copies of the typescript by air mail as soon as ready." To Herbert Read, 18 Sept 1942: "I *think* that *Little Gidding* is now about as good as I can make it: at any rate I have sent a copy to Mairet [editor of *NEW*]—though I have already made two more improvements since posting it. This defecation OUGHT to make it possible to attend to *Murder*: it's only possible to do tinkering when one is not possessed with the desire for new building" (see *East Coker* I 9: "there is a time for building" and note to *First Debate between the Body and Soul* 49). To W. H. Auden, 15 Oct 1942: "*Little Gidding* I think will be published in November. At any rate I have decided that I am going stale on it after a year and a half, and that nothing further I can do will improve it."

Faber Autumn List 1942: "*Little Gidding* is the fourth and concluding poem of the series in which *Burnt Norton*, *East Coker*, and *The Dry Salvages* have already been published."

3. DANTE

After their mother's death in 1929, Henry Eliot acquired the books that TSE had owned in his school years. In the 1940s he gave them to Eliot House at Harvard. The three volumes of Dante are now in the Houghton Library.

TSE: "I have found no other poet than Dante to whom I could apply continually, for many purposes, and with much profit, during a familiarity of twenty years. I am not a Dante scholar; my Italian is chiefly self-taught, and learnt primarily in order to read Dante; I need still to make constant reference to the translations · · · The reader whom I have kept in mind · · · is the reader who commences his reading of Dante with Messrs. Dent's invaluable *Temple Classics* edition · · · For this reason I have in quotation followed the *Temple Classics* text, and have followed pretty closely the translation in the same volumes", *Dante* (1929), Preface (which is omitted from the text in *Selected Essays*). "I read Dante only with a prose translation beside the text. Forty years ago I began to puzzle out the Divine Comedy in this way; and when I thought I had grasped the meaning of a passage which especially delighted me, I committed it to memory; so that, for some years, I was able to recite a large part of one canto or another to myself, lying in bed or on a railway journey. Heaven knows what it would have sounded like, had I recited it aloud; but it was by this means that I steeped myself in Dante's poetry", *What Dante Means to Me* (1950).

In *Dante* (1929) II, TSE quoted *Purg.* XXI 135, "quando dismento nostra vanitate", but replaced the Temple translation, "when I forget our nothingness", with his own: "so that I forget our vanity". To Sir Frederick Pollock, 6 Jan 1930: "I agree that the Temple is often unsatisfactory, either as graceful English or as exact translation. Yet for the passage you mention I still feel that 'vanity' is right. The word may convey a greater range of meaning to me than to others; but I should have thought that the reader who was ignorant of the original meaning of 'vanitas' might be ignored! The word—with the allusion to Ecclesiastes—is so much richer than 'emptiness' is."

Laurence Binyon was assisted by Pound in making his translations of Dante's *Inferno* (1933), *Purgatorio* (1938) and *Paradiso* (1943). TSE also offered comment, writing to Binyon, 16 May 1930:

> Who am I to criticise translations of Dante? The only attempts at any translation that I have made, suggest to me that it is quite impossible to translate anything; and I feel that in my small essay on Dante, I may lead readers to the erroneous impression that Dante is translatable.
>
> But I do like your translations, and I cannot believe that you are as ignorant of Dante as I am. I like your metric, and I think you are right to stress (as it seems to me you do) the Teutonic element in English: I believe that we can only approach the divine informality of Dante's Latin speech through our own origins.
>
> If I may make a few unimportant criticisms:
>
> Will "Galahalt" do for "Galeotto": the implications of "Galahad" are so strong for us.
>
> I am not quite satisfied with "As if of Hell asserting great disdain" because "asserting" seems to me to weaken the contempt: possibly I am affected by "despitto" sounding like "spit".

> "Ancestors" seems to me a weak word in English for family Pride: I wish that it might have been "Forebears". Ulysses: the Italian gives me somehow the notion of a *licking* tongue, i.e. the metaphor seems in the Italian more closely welded to the image.
>
> "Sweet son": is it not rather The sweetness of having a son?
>
> "Old honoured father": should one not give more the allusion to the pietas of Aeneas? I confess that "honoured" has to me the devilish suggestion of a K.B.E. or something of that sort.
>
> "Debito amore" does not suggest to me "overdue": I may be quite irrelevant, but I think of it as being merely "due" to Penelope who was a boring person.
>
> "Tardi", I cant think of the right word, but it suggests to me that the physical reflexes were not as immediate as they had been.
>
> Isn't "bruti" enough, without "of the field". "You weren't made to lie down with the animals".
>
> "Them" (Ugolino) rather suggests to me that there were more children, but these were all that were with him.
>
> P.24. Is "Flame" within "my veins" right? Isnt "veins" suggested to you by the preceding? and isnt the collocation of the metaphor and the physiology a little violent?
>
> I hope you will not consider this sort of comment impertinent. It is the sort that I should like to have myself; and I shall send you my *Ash Wednesday*, which is merely an attempt to do the verse of the *Vita Nuova* in English, so that you may have me at your mercy. Any way, I am sure that Praz is right, and I do hope you will some time complete the translation. [H. F.] Cary is painful; Longfellow is weary; and my cousin [Charles Eliot] Norton is dull. And I do not know of anyone living who could translate Dante as well as that. Ezra could do parts, but he will never understand the whole pattern.

Pound: "One was thankful in 1906 to Dent for the Temple bilingual edtn., it saved one from consulting Witte, Toynbee, god knows whom, but at any rate from painfully digging in with a dictionary, a Dante dictionary etc. . . . and one (I believe more— I can not believe my experience unique) never got through to the essential fact that it is really THERE ON THE PAGE", review of *Dante's Inferno translated into English Triple Rhyme* by Laurence Binyon (*Criterion* Apr 1934). TSE offered Binyon comments on his translation of *Paradiso* XXX and XXXIII in a letter of 7 July 1941 (see note to *Choruses from "The Rock"* X 32–33). For TSE's later praise of Binyon's Dante, see note to II 25–96. TSE wrote to Binyon, 22 Nov 1940, requesting a volume of selected poems for Faber's Sesame series, but Binyon's publisher, Macmillan, refused permission. Macmillan also prevented Binyon offering new poems to Faber (TSE to Binyon, 10 Feb 1941).

4. AFTER PUBLICATION

To Desmond MacCarthy, 28 Dec 1942: "I do think that the poem shows progress in simplification towards direct statement. How far the slowness and round-aboutness of my movement in this direction may be due to some difficulty in communication in the present age, and how far merely to an initial tangle of knots in my own temperament, I am not in a position to discover. I like to think, in any case, that the difference from *Burnt Norton* to *Little Gidding* represents some degree of clarification of thought and feeling."

To Montgomery Belgion, 9 Feb 1943: "The best notices of it were in *The Tablet* and the *Catholic Herald*! But Desmond MacCarthy, in the *Sunday Times*, was very laudatory yesterday: so far about 12,000 copies sold."

To F. O. Matthiessen, 29 July 1943: "The only point that occurs to me—of course, I can only speak of my intentions and am unable to say how far I have succeeded—is the deliberate introduction of a refrain from Juliana of Norwich and a line from the *Cloud of Unknowing* in the last poems. For one thing, I wanted the poem to escape any suggestion of historical sentimentality about the seventeenth century by this reiterated reference to the fourteenth century and therefore to get more bearing on the present than would be possible if the relation was merely between the present and one particular period of the past. Juliana is also appropriate, of course, because the atmosphere of this poem is intended to be distinctly East Anglian. I don't want to develop these associations further into anything that might seem wire-drawn and remote." To E. M. Stephenson, 9 Dec 1942, of V 25: "as you have drawn so much attention to Juliana of Norwich it might be as well to mention that another line 'With the drawing of this Love and the voice of this Calling' is taken from a mystical work of the same period of antithetical type, *The Cloud of Unknowing*." Julian of Norwich lived *c.* 1342–*c.* 1416 and *The Cloud of Unknowing*, which is anonymous, is thought to date from the late 14th century. (In Schofield's *English Literature from the Norman Conquest to Chaucer* 99, TSE underlined "The fourteenth century was the age of nationalism.") "you must expect something in a seventeenth century form but with a fourteenth century spirit", *"The Merry Masque of Our Lady in London Town"* (1928).

To Jean Mambrino, 25 Nov 1946, who had translated the poem into French: "I have also read your translation of *Little Gidding* which, so far as I am competent to judge, seems to me for the most part accurate, though I regret in places the lack of indication of some of the brusque changes from one metre to another, the effect of which is an important part of the design of the poem. I feel in Part II, for instance, that the effect of the original might be better rendered by taking greater liberties with the literal meaning, and that the more formal rhymed pattern of the first three stanzas might be more effective even at the cost of somewhat altering the content. Then for what follows in this section, a great deal is lost by abandoning the *terza rima*, the purpose of which was to put the reader in the frame of mind of the *Inferno* or *Purgatorio*. I wonder whether a verse might be found best somewhat on the line used by Valéry in *Le Cimetière Marin*." TSE sent a copy of *Little Gidding* to Laurence Binyon *c.* 1 Dec 1942, inscribed: "I have felt some diffidence about offering this: but any experiment in an English variation of *terza rima* ought to be submitted to the censure of you who know more about it than any of us!"

To Mary Trevelyan [14 Feb] 1949: "Little Gidding doit être le nom d'un petit garçon très cher à M. Eliot, says a French critic."

A newspaper interview, *Eliot on Eliot: "I feel younger than I did at 60"* (1958), reported: "He claims not to be conscious of any diminution of his mental faculties and is, in fact, planning to write one more verse play, and some literary or social criticism in prose. 'I'm curious,' he adds, 'to see if I shan't also want to write a few more poems in a rather different style. I feel I reached the end of something with *Four Quartets*, and that anything new will have to be expressed in a different idiom.' . . . the one work with which he is most satisfied is the last of the *Four Quartets*."

Joseph L. Featherstone reports of a reading at Boston College, 4 Dec 1961, that TSE read *Little Gidding* and referred to it as "my best" (*Harvard Crimson* 6 Dec 1961). On a similar occasion at Boston College three years before he had explained that every poet considered his most recent poems the best, "though not as good as the ones he is going to write" (*Harvard Crimson* 15 May 1958).

TSE's comments on the tr. by André Gide and Madeleine Bosco (*Aguedal* Dec 1943) are from the copy at King's and were published by *Tilby*. To Kathleen Raine, 10 May 1944: "I have just seen and read with mixed feelings the translation of *Little Gidding* by Gide and Madame Bosco."

I

I 1–16 **Midwinter spring · · · The brief sun flames the ice, on pond and ditches · · · The soul's sap quivers · · · transitory blossom | Of snow:** *Murder in the Cathedral* I:

> Spring has come in winter. Snow in the branches
> Shall float as sweet as blossoms. Ice along the ditches
> Mirror the sunlight. Love in the orchard
> Send the sap shooting.

"What is the late November doing | With the disturbance of the spring", *East Coker* II 1–2. "F. M.": "this is the essential spring—spring in winter", *Letters of the Moment* I (1924) (*Loretta Johnson 1988*). For Edgar Lee Masters' "forge of snow white fire · · · ensanguined ice · · · Flaming", see note to *East Coker* II 7–17. **Midwinter spring · · · brightest, with frost and fire · · · windless cold · · · glare · · · early afternoon · · · transitory blossom:** undated jotting by TSE for "F. M.": "*SPRING*. The pitiless glare of early morning ushering in a merciless frosty glaring day—*exposure* of spring · · · this glare · · · cold wind red nose in the country · · · primroses · · · what matters?" (c. 624 fol. 106); see *McCue 2016*. **Midwinter spring is its own season:** *A Midsummer Night's Dream* II i: "And never since the middle summer's spring." TSE: "And cheat the winter into spring", *A Valedictory Forbidding Mourning* 19–20. In the Gide/Bosco tr., "Ce printemps, au cœur de l'hiver, est la vraie saison de ces lieux", TSE queried "Ce" and "de ces lieux".

I 1–2 **spring · · · Sempiternal:** *Paradiso* XXVIII 116: "primavera sempiterna" [eternal spring] (Robin Kirkpatrick, personal communication). **Sempiternal:** OED: "everlasting, eternal", citing North's Plutarch: "the sempiternall fire". TSE to Anne Ridler, 3 Apr 1948, on a play for radio: "why 'sempiternal'—it seems a very heavy word for the occasion?"

I 2–5 **Sempiternal · · · sundown · · · When the short day is brightest, with frost and fire, | The brief sun flames the ice:** Pater: "To burn always with this hard, gemlike flame · · · Not to discriminate every moment some passionate attitude in those about us, and in the brilliancy of their gifts · · · is, on this short day of frost and sun, to sleep before evening", *Studies in the History of the Renaissance* Conclusion (*Janowitz*). For Pater's Conclusion, see note to *The Dry Salvages* III 38.

I 8 **A glare that is blindness in the early afternoon:** Shelley: "a cold glare, intenser than the noon, | But icy cold, obscured with blinding light", *The Triumph of Life* 77–79 (*Grover Smith* 283). TSE: "dark in the afternoon", *East Coker* I 16.

I 10 **pentecostal fire:** see headnote to IV.

I 11 **In the dark time of the year:** Donne: "Christmas · · · that dark time of the year", Sermon at St. Paul's, 13 Oct 1622. TSE to Hayward, 26 Oct 1936, parodying Chatterton: "That bird wych in the dark time of the yeerë | Sitteth in dudgeon on the aspen bouwe | And cryeth *arsehole arsehole* lhoude and cleerë", (Iman Javadi, personal communication).

I 12 **The soul's sap · · · earth smell:** Donne: "The worlds whole sap is sunke: | The generall balme th'hydroptique earth hath drunk", *A Nocturnall upon S. Lucies Day, Being the shortest day* 5–6 (*Grover Smith* 282); see note to *The Cultivation of Christmas Trees* 4, 26. **The soul's sap:** Babbitt on Hippolyte Taine: "The word for which he has the greatest predilection is probably sap (*sève*). What most delights him is the vigorous rising of the sap in the human vegetation", *The Masters of Modern French Criticism* (1912) 232.

I 12–13 **There is no earth smell | Or smell of living thing:** *Geoffrey Faber's notes*: "Is this so? (Query not criticism. I do seem to remember a tangy kind of smell.)" TSE to Ottoline Morrell, from Harvard, 14 Mar 1933: "nothing here smells right; especially the countryside lacks that deep damp earthy smell of England." **smell:** in the Gide/Bosco tr., TSE twice underlined "parfum".

I 13–14 **This is the spring time | But not in time's covenant:** Herrick: "give the honour to this Day, | That sees *December* turn'd to *May* · · · the Spring-time of the year", *A Christmas Carol* 9–13 (*Grover Smith* 323, pointing out that this verse was quoted by TSE in a printed Christmas card, and that the conceit is common in 17th-century verse). TSE's earliest draft, *msA*, begins "Winter scene. May." At *East Coker* I 25, "May" turned to "summer" during drafting.

I 14 **time's covenant:** God's covenant with Noah, Genesis 8: 22: "While the earth remaineth, seedtime and harvest, and cold and heat, and summer and winter, and day and night shall not cease" (*Composition FQ* 161). **hedgerow:** beside the Gide/Bosco tr. "qui clôt le jardin", TSE wrote "no—along the road side".

I 14–16 **the hedgerow | Is blanched for an hour with transitory blossom | Of snow:** in Coleridge's *Poetical Works* (1907), TSE marked the lines "Betwixt the tufts of snow on the bare branch | Of mossy apple-tree", *Frost at Midnight* 68–69 and the four succeeding lines which end the poem. To Hayward, 5 Aug 1941: "Geoffrey found that the comparison of May blossom and snow on the hedges did not ring true: but I am awaiting his written comment which I hope will make clear why he feels thus." "Late roses filled with early snow", *East Coker* II 7.

I 15–17 **transitory blossom · · · neither budding nor fading:** Clough: "Budding, unfolding, and falling, decaying and flowering ever · · · the transient blossom of Knowledge", *Amours de Voyage* III iv (*Murray*). **transitory:** pronounced with four full syllables in TSE's recording of 1946–47.

I 15–16, 24 **blanched · · · blossom | Of snow · · · White again:** Housman: "Loveliest of trees, the cherry now | Is hung with bloom along the bough · · · come again · · · in bloom · · · I will go | To see the cherry hung with snow", *A Shropshire Lad* II.

I 19–20 **the unimaginable | Zero summer:** "such a (complete) explanation would not be an explanation *of* anything; it would be (absolute) zero", *Report on the Relation of Kant's Criticism to Agnosticism* (1913). Russell: "the problem concerning infinity is the same as that concerning continuity and the infinitesimal. For this purpose, we shall find it convenient to ignore the absolute zero, and to mean, when we speak of any kind of magnitudes, all the magnitudes of the kind except zero", *Principles of Mathematics* (1903) ch. XXIII. Hayward to TSE, 1 Aug 1941: "Is this an allusive reference to the Absolute Zero of physics? I feel a little uneasy about the epithet—slightly Clevelandish?" OED does not record "zero summer", though it has "zero hour" ("the hour at which an attack or operation is timed to begin") from 1917.

I 19^20 *variant* **Summer beyond sense, the inapprehensible:** this line was present in all typescripts except the last and was printed in *NEW*. Helen Gardner on *ts13a*, the typescript sent to the printer of the *Little Gidding* pamphlet: "It is possible that Eliot overlooked the fact that in this version the line had been omitted and failed to restore it", *Composition FQ* 161. Hayward added it to his copy of the final typescript. Yet TSE's having initially typed "S" for "Summer" and then typed "Zero" over it suggests a deliberate change of mind. **inapprehensible:** to Ian Cox, 21 Apr 1937: "You have put in a great deal of the inapprehensible and unnameable emotion and feeling which one wants to get in to any work of poetry or imaginative prose". For this letter see "The End of All Our Exploring", 3. PUBLISHER AND POET.

I 23–24 **If you came this way in may time, you would find the hedges | White again, in May · · · sweetness:** Arnold on Clough: "next year he will return, | And we shall have him in the sweet spring-days, | With whitening hedges", *Thyrsis* 72–74 (*Murray*).

I 24^25 *variant* **In the may time, the play time:** for Hayward's warning about this "dangerous conjunction", see Textual History. *As You Like It* V iii, Song: "In the spring-time, the only pretty ring-time".

I 26 **like a broken king:** *Hayward*, quoting J. F. M. Carter, *Nicholas Ferrar, his Household and Friends* (1892) 310: "Charles I, a fugitive from Cromwell, after his final defeat at the battle of Naseby, found temporary refuge at Little Gidding in 1646; 'Very privately, in the darkness of night, he came once more to Gidding'." See note to "a king at nightfall", III 26–27. An armorial window in the church has the inscription "Insignia Caroli Regis qui latitabat apud Ferrarios 2do Maii A.S. 1646" [Arms of King Charles who refreshed himself at the Ferrar house 2nd May 1646] (*Composition FQ* 62). *Richard II* II i: "The king's grown bankrout like a broken man". For Kipling's *The Broken Men*, see note to the title *The Hollow Men*. In the Gide/Bosco tr., "en roi dépossédé", TSE underlined "en", with a tick.

I 29 **behind the pig-sty:** "sty of contentment", *Marina* 10 (likewise originally spelt "stye"). To Hayward, 16 Oct [1942]: "You did not point out to me, what you will see is the fact, that I did not know how to spell 'pig-sty'. However, I will forgive you that, in view of your innumerable and much more important benefactions." OED lists "stye" as an alternative spelling, and it occurs in *The Education of Henry Adams* ch. III, but TSE misspelt the plural in *Mr. Pugstyles: The Elegant Pig* 27, changing his 1930s spelling "stys" to the also incorrect "styes" when retyping the poem in 1946 (OED: "sties"). Alongside the Gide/Bosco tr., "l'étable", TSE wrote "sty ?" **dull façade:** added to the chapel in 1714.

I 32 **from which the purpose breaks:** in the Gide/Bosco tr., "D'où le dessein essentiel ne s'échappe en brisant sa coque", TSE underlined "s'échappe · · · coque".

I 35–37 **other places · · · the sea jaws, | Or over a dark lake, in a desert or a city:** *Hayward*: "Although 'the sea jaws' recall *The Dry Salvages* IV 12 ['the sea's lips'], they are specifically associated in this passage with the Scottish island of Iona in the Inner Hebrides (*cf. Murder in the Cathedral*) where St. Columba founded a monastery, and with the island of Lindisfarne off the Northumbrian coast to which St. Cuthbert retired to die. The 'dark lake' is lake Glendalough in county

Wicklow, Ireland, where St. Kerin (or Coerugen) made a hermitage above the lake which is still a place of pilgrimage. The 'desert' is the Thebaid, associated with the Egyptian St. Anthony and other solitaries (*cf. Burnt Norton* V 19–20). The 'city' is Padua, associated with the other St. Anthony." Expressing regret, 4 July 1940, at having missed C. P. Curran while visiting Dublin to deliver the Yeats Memorial Lecture, TSE recalled his previous stay in the city and "that excursion to Glendalough three years ago". Writing to Curran on 4 May 1960, he again mentioned the occasion "when we went to see St. Kevin's cave (to which I later referred in a poem called *Little Gidding*)."

I 39 **Now and in England**: Browning: "In England—now!" *Home-Thoughts, from Abroad* 8 (*Loucks 1993*). For "*Little Gidding* is particularly English", see letter to F. O. Matthiessen, 19 Aug 1949, in headnote to *Four Quartets*, 9. TSE ON *FOUR QUARTETS*.

I 39 *variant* **Tragedy transcending**: Yeats: "Hamlet and Lear are gay; | Gaiety transfiguring all that dread", *Lapis Lazuli* 16–17. TSE: "transfigured, in another pattern", III 16. OED 1: "change in outward form".

I 45 **to kneel**: against the Gide/Bosco tr., "tomber à genoux", TSE wrote: "? over-stresses the physical attitude".

I 45–46 **to kneel | Where prayer has been valid**: *Levy* 41–42 reports TSE, 29 June 1953: "What I mean is that for some of us, a sense of place is compelling. If it is a religious place, a place made special by the sacrifice of a martyrdom, then it retains an aura · · · I am aware that not all persons have a sense of place (as I describe it), nor is it necessary for it to exist to make prayer valid." George Every recalled TSE describing the impression made on him by seeing people praying: "He suddenly realised that prayer still went on and could be made. It wasn't simply of historic and cultural interest. People did pray and he might", *Eliot as a Friend and a Man of Prayer* (unpublished), quoted *Spurr* 37.

I 48 **or the sound of the voice praying**: in *The Spiritual Letters of Dom John Chapman* (1935) 120, TSE scored a passage about prayer: "The strangest part is when we begin to wonder whether we mean anything at all, and if we are addressing anybody, or merely using a formula without sense. The word 'God' seems to mean nothing. If we feel this, we are starting on the right road."

I 49–51 **what the dead had no speech for, when living · · · beyond the language of the living**: *Levy* 128–29 reports TSE, 2 Jan 1962: "I had chiefly in mind that we cannot fully understand a person, grasp the totality of his being, until he is dead. Once he is dead, the acts of his life fall into their proper perspective and we can see what he was tending toward. Also, with the living presence removed, it is easier to make an impartial judgment, free of the personality of the individual." (See TSE on A. R. Orage's mysticism in note to III 40–41.)

I 50 **They can tell you, being dead**: Yeats: "But now she knows it all, being dead", *Purgatory* (1938) (*Grover Smith 1996* 164). MacNeice: "Our mind, being dead, wishes to have time die · · · ghosts", *August* in *Poems* (1935) (TSE: "timeless", 52). TSE: "come from the dead, | Come back to tell you all", *The Love Song of J. Alfred Prufrock* 94–95. Hebrews 11: 4: "he being dead yet speaketh".

I 50–51 **the communication | Of the dead is tongued with fire beyond the language of the living**: Conrad: "as mute as the faces of the dead who are possessed of a knowledge beyond the comprehension of the living", *Amy Foster* (*Unger 1956*

242). Auden: "The words of a dead man | Are modified in the guts of the living", *In Memory of W. B. Yeats* (1939) 22–23 (*Grover Smith 1996* 106). TSE: "No dead voices speak through the living voice; no reincarnation, no re-creation. Not even the *saturation* which sometimes combusts spontaneously into originality", *Reflections on Contemporary Poetry* IV (1919). For "saturation", see note to *Burbank with a Baedeker: Bleistein with a Cigar* 7–12. **tongued with fire**: for Acts 2: 1–6, see headnote to *Little Gidding* IV. *Hayward*: "Fire is used variously throughout the poem as a symbol for Pentecost, for Purgatory, for Hell, and for Divine Love." Hawthorne: "These fathers ··· lacked ··· the Tongue of Flame", *The Scarlet Letter* ch. XI.

I 51 *variant* **touched with fire**: Tennyson: "If the lips were touched with fire from off a pure Pierian altar", *Parnassus* 17. (Isaiah 6: 6–7: "Then flew one of the seraphims unto me, having a live coal ··· laid it upon my mouth, and said, Lo, this hath touched thy lips.")

I 51^52 *variant* **the speech of the living is wind in dry grass**: "wind in dry grass ··· And voices are | In the wind's singing", *The Hollow Men* 8, 25–26. "the grass is singing", *The Waste Land* [V] 386.

I 52 **the intersection of the timeless moment**: see note to *The Dry Salvages* V 18–19.

I 53 **England and nowhere. Never and always**: Edward Marsh's *Rupert Brooke: A Memoir* (1918) printed fragments of a projected long poem which Brooke described as being "about the existence—and non-locality—of England", including the lines "She is not here, or now— | She is here, and now, yet nowhere—" (*Loucks 1993*).

II

II 1–4 **Ash ··· Dust in the air suspended | Marks the place where a story ended**: on 10 May 1941 London was choked with burning paper from two bombed warehouses of books, including Hayward's editions of Donne and Swift (Phyllis Rowell, *Dr Johnson's House During the War* 21; Hayward to Frank Morley, May 1941). The raid of 29 Dec 1941 destroyed five million books in Paternoster Row. The possibility of a pun on "storey" is supported by TSE's uncertainty about spelling in letters to Hayward: "the second story ?storey bedrooms" (27 June 1941) and "It is one story above the lift" (9 Mar 1943).

II 1–8 **Ash ··· suspended ··· the death of air**: *Levy* 15 reports TSE, 26 July 1948, describing his firewatching duties at Faber: "During the Blitz the accumulated debris was suspended in the London air for hours after a bombing. Then it would slowly descend and cover one's sleeves and coat with a fine white ash. I often experienced this effect during the long night hours on the roof." Faber's register has no record of TSE firewatching at Russell Square before 12 Nov 1942, by which time *Little Gidding* was written (pub. 1 Dec), but he had undertaken such duties in Kensington, writing to Polly Tandy, 3 July 1940: "I have just 'listed for a Air Warden". (Housman: "I 'listed at home for a lancer", *Last Poems* VI.) *Levy* 14 reports TSE's recollection: "We had to watch the fires and report them as quickly as they occurred. You will be interested to know that the lines from *Little Gidding* came out of this experience." On 24 Aug 1972, David Jones recalled TSE's telling him "that he had a system whereby he could get through several books while watching" (Thomas Dilworth in *Sewanee Review* Winter 1994).

II 1–24 **Ash ··· water and fire**: Heraclitus frag. 76 (tr. Bakewell): "Fire lives the death of air, and air the death of fire; water lives the death of earth, and earth the death of water." See epigraphs at head of *Burnt Norton*.

II 2 **all the ash the burnt roses leave**: "isolating culture from religion, politics and philosophy we seem to be left with something no more apprehensible than the scent of last year's roses", *The Idea of a Christian Society* 77. Hayward to TSE, 1 Aug 1941: "Compared with the other lines in the stanza this one seems to me to have too much weight at the end. The heavy stress on 'burnt' could be lightened by omitting the definite article and this would lay a shade more stress on 'roses'. As it is, this line takes something from the essential 'airiness' of the stanza—dust, breath, air: the death of air—as if the ash of burnt roses was not an imponderable but a tombstone." TSE, 5 Aug: "I am also unhappy about the first two lines of Part II (lyric)."

II 3–16 **suspended ··· hope ··· without mirth ··· earth**: Coleridge: "hope ··· earth ··· rob me of my mirth ··· Suspends", *Dejection* 80–85, quoted in *The Use of Poetry and the Use of Criticism* 68: "one of the saddest of confessions that I have ever read." In Coleridge's *Poetical Works* (1907), TSE marked *Dejection* 87–90.

II 6 **the wainscot and the mouse**: Tennyson: "the mouse | Behind the mouldering wainscot", *Mariana* 63–64. "the wainscot where the field-mouse trots", *East Coker* I 12. **wainscot**: pronounced *wainsk't* in TSE's recording of 1946–47. The spelling "wainscote", used by TSE in *msA*, is given by OED as 16th–17th century.

II 6, 18 **The wall, the wainscot and the mouse ··· The town, the pasture and the weed**: H. W. Heckstall-Smith wrote to TSE, 15 Jan 1943, comparing these lines to Herbert Trench's line "The vine, the woman, and the rose" (*Requiem of Archangels for the World*, collected 1919). TSE, 22 Jan: "it is possible to find similar constructions much earlier than in the work of Herbert Trench. There is, for instance, the line 'the viol, the violet and the vine' which I think is Edgar Poe" (*The City in the Sea* 23).

II 8–9 **the death of air ··· flood and drouth**: Milton: "Summer drouth, or singèd air | Never scorch thy tresses fair", Attendant Spirit's song in *Comus* (928–31) with "flood ··· mud" (water and earth, completing the four elements). TSE: "the desert | Of drouth", *Ash-Wednesday* V 35–36.

II 9–10 **drouth ··· in the mouth**: Tennyson: "I thirsted for the brooks, the showers: | I rolled among the tender flowers: | I crushed them on my breast, my mouth; | I looked athwart the burning drouth | Of that long desert to the south", *Fatima* 10–14 (*Musgrove* 88). Swinburne: "in his mouth, | Made of grave's mould and deadly drouth", *After Death* 3–4; "drouth, | And as the air which is death ··· The breath came forth of her mouth | And the fire came forth of her breath", *Atalanta in Calydon* 1978–82 (TSE: "the air", "inbreathed", "death of air", "and fire", 3, 5, 8, 17).

II 10–11 **the mouth, | Dead water and dead sand**: "dead mouths ··· thirst and drunk the waters of the sands ··· dead waters", *Anabasis* I xii, xiii, xvi (with "deadwater", IV ix).

II 11–16 **Dead water and dead sand ··· The parched eviscerate soil ··· This is the death of earth**: on dearth from the death of earth: "the organisation of society on the principle of private profit ··· is leading both to the deformation of humanity by unregulated industrialism, and to the exhaustion of natural resources ··· immediate benefits leading to dearth and desert", *The Idea of a Christian Society* 61 (*Ricks* 256).

II 14–16 **toil ··· without mirth ··· earth**: Kipling: "They take their mirth in the joy of the Earth—they dare not grieve for her pain. | They know of toil and the end of toil", *Dedication from "Barrack-Room Ballads"* (in TSE's *A Choice of Kipling's Verse*).

II 17–27 *variant* **Water and fire succeed ··· the pasture ··· fire ··· scarred foundations ··· fire ··· skeletons ··· Fire without and fire within ··· This is the place where we begin**: "In my beginning ··· In succession | Houses rise and fall ··· or in their place | Is an open field ··· old timber to new fires, | Old fires to ashes ··· Bone", *East Coker* I 1–6.

II 19–24 **Water and fire deride | The sacrifice that we denied. | Water and fire shall rot | The marred foundations we forgot, | Of sanctuary and choir, | This is the death of water and fire**: in the 1920s, the planned demolition of nineteen City churches was prevented by protestors (see Commentary on *The Waste Land* [III] 264), but ten Wren churches were ruined by the Blitz on 29 Dec 1940 alone. What was not burnt was often irreparably soaked. A documentary film called it "almost like the day of judgment." **deride | The sacrifice that we denied**: "the Commission on Christian Doctrine [1938] ··· devoted fifteen pages to the concept of Sacrifice: the present Bishop of Truro, in a recent pamphlet entitled *The Gospel for To-morrow*, giving a page to the Communion Service, dismisses the matter with the words: 'absurd notions about sacrifice have crept in, notions which discredit both God and man'", *Reunion by Destruction* (1941) 16.

II 23 **sanctuary**: OED 1: "A building or place set apart for the worship of God", 2b: "*Eccl.* That part of a church round the altar". Pronounced with four full syllables in TSE's recording of 1946–47. TSE had written of the City churches as refuges "to receive the solitary visitor at noon from the dust and tumult of Lombard Street", *London Letter* in *Dial* June 1921 ("Or I could take sanctuary | In any oak or apple tree", *The Country Walk* 33–34).

II 25–96] *Hayward*: "The setting of this Dantesque section is a street in the Kensington district of London just before dawn and after a bombing attack. The narrator is on duty as an air-raid warden. There are allusions throughout to Dante's meeting with Brunetto Latini, *Inf.* XV." The recognition scene combines this with two of Dante's other encounters: with the shades of Guido Cavalcanti and Arnaut Daniel (*Purg.* XXVI), and with that of Forese Donati (*Purg.* XXIII). For Brunetto, see note to *East Coker* I 12; for Arnaut Daniel, see note to title *Ara Vos Prec* in headnote to "*Poems* (1920)", 7. PUBLICATION OF *ARA VOS PREC*. C. H. Grandgent:

> Just as, in Hell, Dante's old master, Brunetto Latini, scorched almost beyond recognition, suddenly greets his former disciple with the exclamation "Qual maraviglia!" ["What a wonder!" XV 24] so ··· in Purgatory one of the souls [Forese] ··· reveals himself by the cry "Qual grazia m'è questa?" ["What grace is this to me?" XXIII 42].

(TSE: "I should like to mention one book which has been of use to me: the *Dante* of Professor Charles Grandgent of Harvard", *Dante* (1929) Preface. TSE's mother had sent him Grandgent's address in Cambridge on 23 Aug 1922.) TSE to Eudo C. Mason, 23 Jan 1946: "I am surprised by the opinion of Dr. Leavis and your friend in Basel. They seem to me to have come to the conclusion that that particular passage is the same sort of thing as Henry James' *The Jolly Corner*. Your interpretation is in my opinion nearer to the truth. There is, of course, as I am aware, a certain confusion about his status because the literary landscape is for the most part that of Brunetto Latini, whereas at the end it becomes that of Arnaut Daniel. However, the reference to Hamlet's ghost may help and it is, I hope, clear enough that the figure appears not from hell but from Purgatory, and therefore is by no means condemned nor rejected. You can find in his features, if you like, some traces of Yeats, Swift, Mallarmé and Poe, and there are as well touches of humanist teachers who have less to do with poetry."

On the *Commedia*: "the *simple* style of which Dante is the greatest master is a very difficult style. In twenty years I have written about a dozen lines in that style successfully; and compared to the dullest passage of the *Divine Comedy*, they are 'as straw'. So I believe that it is difficult", *Dante* (1929) II (paragraph omitted in *Selected Essays*), alluding to Job 41: 27: "He esteemeth iron as straw, and brass as rotten wood" (*Ricks 2003* 33–34). *Lehmann* records TSE's reading at Bryn Mawr in Oct 1948, when, asked about *The Waste Land*, he replied that Part V had been written quickly, and went on: "*Little Gidding* II, where I used Dante's *terza rima*, was the hardest piece of work I've ever written. It had to be done in a straightforward manner, the wrong word showed up so much in that style." Also on the poetic challenge: "Twenty years after writing *The Waste Land*, I wrote, in *Little Gidding*, a passage which is intended to be the nearest equivalent to a canto of the *Inferno* or the *Purgatorio*, in style as well as content, that I could achieve. The intention · · · was to present to the mind of the reader a parallel, by means of contrast, between the Inferno and the Purgatorio, which Dante visited, and a hallucinated scene after an air-raid. But the method is different: here I was debarred from quoting or adapting at length—I borrowed and adapted freely only a few phrases—because I was *imitating*. My first problem was to find an approximation to the *terza rima* without rhyming · · · This section of a poem—not the length of one canto of the *Divine Comedy*—cost me far more time and trouble and vexation than any passage of the same length that I have ever written. It was not simply that I was limited to the Dantesque type of imagery, simile and figure of speech. It was chiefly that in this very bare and austere style, in which every word has to be 'functional', the slightest vagueness or imprecision is immediately noticeable. The language has to be very direct; the line, and the single word, must be completely disciplined to the purpose of the whole; and, when you are using simple words and simple phrases, any repetition of the most common idiom, or of the most frequently needed word, becomes a glaring blemish", *What Dante Means to Me* (1950) ("every word is at home", V 4). "when I came to attempt one brief imitation of Dante I was fifty-five years old and knew exactly what I was doing", *To Criticize the Critic* (1961) 128.

To Bonamy Dobrée, 23 Aug 1961: "I call my tercets *terza rima* simply because this alternation of weak and strong endings is, in my opinion, the closest equivalent to *terza rima* possible in English. I am familiar with several translations of Dante in *terza rima*, of course, especially Binyon's, which is the best I know. But I feel very strongly that rhymes in English are too emphatic, and in a passage of any length this form of verse becomes tiring. In Italian the rhymes seem to come quite naturally and lightly. This cannot be reproduced by English rhymes." Robert Bridges had alternated feminine and masculine endings, in combination with full rhyme, in another cityscape of night into morning, *London Snow* (1880; included in Faber's *Selected Poems of Robert Bridges*, 1941). His first five lines end "flying | brown | lying | town | failing" (*Ricks 2010* 195–96). TSE on Bridges: "it is certain that his experimentation has served a valuable purpose. It has helped to accustom readers of verse to a more liberal conception of verse technique, and to the notion that the development of technique is a serious and unceasing subject of study among verse writers", *A Commentary* in *Criterion* July 1930. Recalling his own early days, in *Paris Review* (1959): "One really ignored poet laureates as such, the Robert Bridges."

The Dantesque vision is in some ways a re-imagination of *First Debate between the Body and Soul*, constituting TSE's final such debate ("As body and soul begin to fall asunder", *Little Gidding* II 81).

First Debate	*Little Gidding*
The withered leaves (6)	the dead leaves (II 30)
wind is shambling down the street (1)	the urban dawn wind (II 35)
The eye (22)	the eyes (II 42)
pure (15)	purify (II 74)
sense (26)	sense (II 78)
a shabby square (39)	the shabby road (II 94 *variant*)
dies (15)	dying (II 83 *variant*)
patience · · · turpitude · · · fact · · · nature (5, 12, 25, 41)	impatience · · · turpitude · · · fact · · · nature (*prose draft*)

The encounter in the street with "A blind old man" in *First Debate between the Body and Soul* may suggest Milton and Joyce within the "familiar compound ghost". A memory of the earlier quatrains rhyming on *-ations* may have contributed to *Little Gidding*, where the ms drafts have as line-endings "revelation", "observation", "desolation", "expectation" and "salutation" (plus, within lines, "desolations", "precipitation" and "preparation"). However, the only such ending in the final version of *Little Gidding* II, "laceration", was suggested by Hayward. Coleridge: "But oh! each visitation | Suspends what nature gave me at my birth, | My shaping spirit of Imagination", *Dejection* 84–86. For TSE on *Dejection* see note to II 3–16.

II 25–28 **In the uncertain hour before the morning · · · At the recurrent end of the unending | After the dark dove with the flickering tongue:** *Blamires* 142: "the last bombers have gone, but the *All Clear* has not yet sounded" (see note to II 96). Hayward to TSE, 12 Dec 1940: "what now passes for morning, for rising in the black-out is a queer business and makes me feel as if it were still deep midnight." (For Donne's "Both the yeares, and the dayes deep midnight", *A Nocturnall upon S. Lucies Day, Being the shortest day* 45, see note to *The Cultivation of Christmas Trees* 4, 26.) TSE: "Between midnight and dawn · · · When time stops and time is never ending", *The Dry Salvages* I 43–45. *Purg.* IX 52: "Dianzi, nell'alba che precede al giorno" [Erewhile in the dawn which precedes the day] (*Praz* 373). Swinburne: "It is an hour before the hour of dawn", *Tiresias*, likewise an opening line (*Hands*). Paul Elmer More: "in the night hours just before dawn, when the noise of the city has died away and belated men look questioningly at each other as they meet", *The Great Refusal* 128 (TSE: "pointed scrutiny ··· The first-met stranger", II 37–38. For More's account, see note to *The Waste Land* [I] 60–63). Kipling: "Even in that certain hour before the fall", *The Fabulists* (*Grover Smith 1950* 419). TSE: "Before the certain hour of maternal sorrow", *A Song for Simeon* 20 (*Grover Smith 1950* 419). **uncertain hour:** Coleridge: "at an uncertain hour | That agony returns: | And till my ghastly tale is told, | This heart within me burns", *The Rime of the Ancient Mariner* Part VII (K. Narayana Chandran, *ANQ* Winter 1997). **ending of interminable night | At the recurrent end of the unending:** James Thomson: "In their recurrence with recurrent changes", *The City of Dreadful Night* I 19 (Michael O'Neill in *Harding ed.* 206). TSE: "End of the endless | Journey to no end | Conclusion of all that | Is inconclusible", *Ash-Wednesday* II 39–42. **the dark dove:** Germany's first military plane (obsolete since the start of the Great War) was the Taube, or "Dove" (*Grover Smith* 287). For "The dove descending", see note to IV 1. For iconography of the dove, see note to *Mr. Eliot's Sunday Morning Service* 9–16. **dove ··· flickering tongue:** Matthew 10: 16: "be ye therefore wise as serpents, and harmless as doves". Shelley: "unassailed ··· the great City, veiled | In virtue's adamantine eloquence, | 'Gainst scorn and death and pain thus trebly mailed, | And blending in the smiles of that defence | The Serpent and the Dove, Wisdom and Innocence", *The Revolt of Islam* IV xix. **flickering tongue:** William Morris: "of serpents ··· The burning eyes with flecks of blood and streaks of fire are stained, | Their mouths with hisses all fulfilled are licked by flickering tongue", *The Æneids of Virgil* II 204, 210–11.

II 26 *variant* **restless night:** "restless nights in one-night cheap hotels", *The Love Song of J. Alfred Prufrock* 6.

II 28–29 **dove ··· passed below the horizon of his homing:** TSE underlined the Gide/Bosco tr., "plus bas que son horizon habituel", with "?" *Tilby* comments that the translators failed to see the comparison of German bombers to homing pigeons. (RAF bombers carried homing pigeons as a last resort for communication.)

II 29, 37 **horizon ··· pointed scrutiny:** to Hayward, 5 Aug 1941: "the American freshwater college sleuth would here discover some innuendo about Spender & Connolly, but none intended". (OED "freshwater" 1b. *U.S.*: "further inland ··· freshwater colleges, the adjective carrying with it some implication of rusticity and provincialism", from 1925.) *Horizon* (1940–49) was edited by Cyril Connolly, with Stephen Spender as a frequent contributor. *Scrutiny* (1932–53) was edited by F. R. Leavis.

II 30 **dead leaves:** *Burnt Norton* I 24. To Ian Cox, 13 Oct 1937, on his poetry: "the imagery of the dead leaves is something which is very real to you, which is not conscious invention, but a real experience. Yet I find that you seem rather obsessed by it than making use of it."

II 30, 34–35 **dead leaves ··· blown towards me like the metal leaves | Before the urban dawn wind:** Shelley: "numerous as the dead leaves blown", *The Triumph of Life* 528. Also:

> O wild West Wind, thou breath of Autumn's being,
> Thou, from whose unseen presence the leaves dead
> Are driven, like ghosts from an enchanter fleeing
>
> *Ode to the West Wind* 1–3

("enchantment", II 79.) TSE misquoted this when he wrote that "the image of the leaves whirling in the wind *Like stricken ghosts from an enchanter fleeing* would have been impossible but for the *Inferno*—in which the various manifestations of *wind*, and the various sensations of *air*, are as important as are the aspects of *light* in the *Paradiso*", *What Dante Means to Me* (1950).

II 31 **asphalt:** pronounced assonantally with *lass* and *pal* in TSE's recording of 1946–47.

II 32 **Between three districts whence**: Gérard de Nerval: "Arrivé cependant au confluent de trois rues, je ne voulus pas aller plus loin" [Having arrived nevertheless at where three roads meet, I wished to go no further], *Aurélia* I ii (*Hands*). James Thomson: "a spot whence three close lanes led down", *The City of Dreadful Night* XVIII 2 (*Grover Smith* 324). The Metropolitan Boroughs of Kensington, Chelsea and Westminster converge at Knightsbridge Station on the Cromwell Road, in the area where TSE worked as a firewatcher during the poem's composition ("patrol", II 54: see note). However, London's different kinds of "district"—administrative, postal and ecclesiastical—are not congruent, and common usage blurs their boundaries (Bruce Hunt, personal communication). TSE: "where three dreams cross", *Ash-Wednesday* VI 21.

II 33 **one**: OED 20a: "*simply* = A person; some one" is marked "*arch.* or *obs.*" Wilfred Owen: "as I probed them, one sprang up", *Strange Meeting* 6 (see notes to II 51–53 and to *Burnt Norton* II 1–2).

II 33–47 **I met one walking · · · the sudden look of some dead master · · · Both one and many · · · a familiar compound ghost · · · And heard another's voice cry: "What! are *you* here?" · · · I was still the same, | Knowing myself yet being someone other**: Herbert Read: "A soldier passed me · · · His footsteps muffled, his face unearthly grey; | And my heart gave a sudden leap · · · a ghost · · · I shouted Halt! and my voice had the old accustomed ring · · · He turned towards me and I said: | 'I am one of those who went before you · · · one of the many who never returned, | Of the many who returned and yet were dead · · ·'", *To a Conscript of 1940*. In Read's poem the encountered soldier is not a ghost and it is the officer who is ambiguous. TSE to Read, 7 June 1940, on the arrangement of Read's *Thirty Five Poems*: "I like the *Conscript of 1940* better than ever in its present position." Faber published the book in its Sesame series in Nov 1940, with this poem first. See *The Waste Land* [I] 69–70: "There I saw one I knew, and stopped him, crying: 'Stetson!' | 'You who were with me in the ships at Mylae! · · ·'" and see note to *The Waste Land* [I] 69.

II 33–52 **I met one walking · · · dawn · · · familiar · · · a double part · · · strange · · · at this intersection time:** "Gently at twilight, gently go at dawn · · · When the familiar scene is suddenly strange | Or the well known is what we have yet to learn, | And two worlds meet, and intersect, and change", *To Walter de la Mare* 14–18, with "presences walk with us, when alone" in the drafts (sonnet II 3). For Karl Barth, "two planes intersect", see note to *The Dry Salvages* V 18–19. **I met · · · face · · · the eyes · · · another's · · · face · · · each other:** for "I met my own eyes | In another face", *Perque Domos Ditis Vacuas* by "F. M.", see headnote to *In silent corridors of death*. ("F. M." also has "deathly airlessness"; TSE: "the death of air" II 8.)

II 34 **towards:** pronounced *to'rd* (with no *s*) in TSE's recording of 1946–47 (see notes to *Burnt Norton* I 13 and *The Love Song of J. Alfred Prufrock* 93).

II 35 *variant* **little dawn wind:** "breakers of camp in the little dawn wind", *Anabasis* I xv (*Abel* 224). "Out at sea the little | Dawn wind slides", *East Coker* I 48–49 *variant*.

II 36–37 **I fixed upon the down-turned face | That pointed scrutiny:** *Inf.* XV 44–45 (Brunetto): "ma il capo chino | tenea" [kept my head bent down] (*Grover Smith* 286). *Purg.* XXIII 41 (Forese): "volse a me gli occhi un'ombra, e guardò fiso" [a shade turned its eyes to me and fixedly did gaze] (Iman Javadi, personal communication). **down-turned ··· scrutiny:** TSE, 27 Aug 1942, replying to Hayward's suggestion: "I am afraid that 'down-cast', that is, with a hyphen between 'down' and 'cast', would hardly do because the word will be spoken much the same whether there is a hyphen or not." 7 Sept: "I had already changed to 'And as I fixed upon the down-turned face' so that's allright, but you seem to object also to 'scrutiny'? I admit that the sense is late: the first example is from Fanny Burney" (OED "scrutiny" 3: "In recent use: The action of looking searchingly at something; a searching gaze", quoting Burney, 1796).

II 36–47 **I fixed upon the down-turned face | That pointed scrutiny ··· eyes of a familiar ··· So I assumed a double part ··· someone other:** TSE on Wyndham Lewis's second portrait of him: "he knows the history of one's face as well as the expression assumed for the sitting—an expression which is sometimes a defensive or bogus one when exposed to the sustained scrutiny of an unfamiliar pair of eyes on the other side of the easel", *Time* 30 May 1949.

II 37–38 **That pointed scrutiny with which we challenge | The first-met stranger in the waning dusk:** *Inf.* XV 17–21 (Brunetto): "and each looked at us, as in the evening men are wont to look at one another under a new moon; and towards us sharpened their vision, as an aged tailor does at the eye of his needle." (In the copy given to him by his mother, TSE scored XV 16–21 in the Italian.) In *Dante* (1929) I, TSE commended Matthew Arnold for singling out the simile (see note to *In the Department Store* 4), but this is untraced in Arnold, so TSE may have been confusing C. H. Grandgent's praise for it in his *Dante* (1916) 267 (see note to II 25–96) with Arnold's repeated praise for "e la sua volontade è nostra pace" (*Paradiso* III 85), for which see note to *Ash-Wednesday* VI 30–33. For Dante "trying to make you visualise exactly that dolorous twilight in which moved the form of Brunetto Latini", see note to *Burnt Norton* I 12. **pointed scrutiny:** "F. M.": "looking again at the young man with a well-disguised but very sharp scrutiny", *Night Club* (1925).

II 37–38 *variant* **With which we face the first-met stranger at dawn:** "To prepare a face to meet the faces that we meet", *The Love Song of J. Alfred Prufrock* 27. **stranger at dawn:** Hayward to TSE, 1 Aug 1941: "I wish the two stressed monosyllables had'nt got to complete this line; but I don't see how to alter this. It's not important." See Textual History.

II 38 **waning dusk:** to Hayward, 3 Mar 1941: *Points of View* "will have a different and superior status if the choice is known to have been made by you, while I retire into the interlunar cave (there is a lovely word I found in the O.E.D. and want to use as soon as I can: 'antelucan')." Hayward, 5 Mar: "in these times no hones or stones should be left unturned if our antelucan operations are to proceed smoothly." TSE to Hayward, 7 Sept 1942, on the lines that gave him most difficulty: "I am glad you objected to 'First Faint' because it calls my attention to that fact that 'light' will not do either, as it comes too close (being terminal) to 'night' a few lines before. It is surprisingly difficult to find words for the shades before morning; we seem to be richer in words and phrases for the end of day. And I don't want a phrase which might mean *either*. I am inclined to put 'The first-met stranger after lantern-end' unless it seems to you too quaint. I do mean just the moment at which we should put out a lantern, if we were carrying one. 'End' because 'time' or 'hour' might as well mean 'lighting-up time'. There is very likely some dialect word for this degree of dawn; but even if I could find it it probably wouldnt do." After a page of other details, the letter ends: "No, I dont think 'lantern-end' will do, because there is so much ending at the beginning. Is 'lantern-out' too strained? I reckon it is. But it is better than 'lantern-down'." 9 Sept: "I am still however wrestling with the demon of that precise degree of light at that precise time of day. I want something more *universal* than black-out (for even if the blackout goes on forever, I want something holding good for the past also—something as universal as Dante's old tailor threading his needle). On the other hand, any reference to the reverberes wd. take the mind directly to *pre-war* London, which would be unfortunate. It must therefore be a country image or a general one. I have been fiddling with something like this:

The stranger in the antelucan dusk

The stranger at the antelucan hour

Perhaps it is too self-conscious, and belongs rather to a Miltonic than to a Dantesque passage? If so, I shall fall back on one of your versions. But I did rather like 'lantern-end' (more suitable there than a heavy latinism, for the image should be both sudden and homely, with the precision of country terminology for these phenomena) if only 'end' hadn't clashed. (What is quite interesting is to find that this austere Dantesque style is more difficult, and offers more pitfalls, than any other)." 19 Sept: "You will observe that I have accepted 'waning dusk', and my observation conducted during the last few days leads me to believe that it will wear. I cannot find words to express a proper manifestation of my gratitude for your invaluable assistance." Tennyson, on "dusk" in the morning: "now the doubtful dusk reveal'd | The knolls once more", *In Memoriam* XCV. Also: "With all the varied changes of the dark, | And either twilight and the day between", *Edwin Morris* 36–37. Charlotte Brontë: "for it was evening and now waxing dusk", *Villette* ch. 10.

Recalling his struggle for the exact word: "I found myself in great difficulties for a word to express *twilight before dawn*, as distinct and different from *twilight before night*. The word *dusk*, in English, means either: but its immediate denotation, to every English speaking person, is the evening · · · I believe that I could have found one word meaning the dusk of morning, in one or more English country dialects, because country people are more likely to need such a word than townsfolk. But a dialect word—apart from the fact that its obscurity would probably have required a footnote—would have aroused the wrong associations. The scene I was describing was in a London street; the personages in the scene were not people who would express themselves in country dialect; and any uncommon word would have been most unsuitable. So, after giving up the hope of finding one word, I had to try to find two words. The substantive could only be *dusk*; there would have to be an adjective to indicate *which* dusk I meant; and if necessary I should have to support it with some other indication of the time of day. I first hit upon a word which seemed to me, for a short time, to be a real *trouvaille*: the adjective *antelucan*—'before the light'; in the great Oxford Dictionary it is defined as: 'of or pertaining to the hours just before dawn'. Its meaning was exactly what I required, and I was much taken by the *sound* of the word ··· But here was a word with the right meaning and a very agreeable sound which nevertheless would not do. It is a rare word. Though its meaning is clear enough, such a word is appropriate only for an *ornate* style; and the passage into which I wished to insert it was in a very deliberately *plain* style: the word would have attracted attention to itself, and away from the task it had to perform. It might have been a suitable word if I had been writing in the style of Milton ··· So I had in the end to put 'waning dusk'. It was not what I wanted: but it was, I believe, the best that the English language could do for me", *Scylla and Charybdis* (1952). TSE appears to have forgotten Dante's "splendori antelucani" [brightness ere dayspring born], *Purg.* XXVII 109 and Pound's "The antelucanal glamour", *The Spirit of Romance* 13 (Iman Javadi, personal communication). "It may sometimes happen that the word which has the exact meaning you want, has the wrong sound. The perfect word in its place would always satisfy both demands", *Poetical and Prosaic Use of Words* (1943).

II 39–45 **I caught the sudden look ··· in the brown baked features ··· "What! are *you* here?"**: *Hayward* points to *Inf.* XV 25–30 (Brunetto):

> Ed io, quando il suo braccio a me distese,
> ficcai gli occhi per lo cotto aspetto
> sì che il viso abbruciato non disfese
> la conoscenza sua al mio intelletto;
> e chinando la mia alla sua faccia,
> risposi: "Siete voi qui, ser Brunetto?"

> [And I, when he stretched out his arm to me, fixed my eyes on his baked aspect, so that the scorching of his visage hindered not my mind from knowing him; and bending my face to his, I answered: "Are you here, Ser Brunetto?"]
>
> *Hayward*

The verb "Siete voi" is the second person plural, the archaic respectful form (Iman Javadi, personal communication). **some dead master | Whom I had known**: "some dead sage, which no one has understood before; which ··· has lain unknown", *After Strange Gods* 33. **some dead master**: in Leyris's translation, "certain maître mort", TSE underlined "certain" with "?" **dead master**: "we should ··· study very carefully the work of those dead masters whose poetry has a special appeal to us; and carefully, in a different spirit, the work of some of those masters whose work does not", *Royal Academy Speech* (1960) *1st draft*. See "The End of All Our Exploring", 3. PUBLISHER AND POET. From Dec 1920 until Mar 1922, TSE began letters to Pound with "Cher Maître". Of a different art: "a painter of the Umbrian school ··· cracked and browned", *Mr. Eliot's Sunday Morning Service* 9, 12. **brown baked features**: *Composition FQ* 175: "The 'scorched brown features' of the manuscript renders '*il viso abbruciato*'. Eliot probably changed 'scorched' to avoid a repetition of the word [from II 13 *variant*] ··· He first tried 'scarred' and then took 'baked' from another phrase of Dante's: '*lo cotto aspetto*'" (see Textual History). Alongside II 40–43 in the Gide/Bosco translation, TSE wrote: "where is the cotto aspetto?"

TSE on Corbière: "when he describes the procession of mendicants and cripples to the shrine of the Virgin, and says: 'Là, ce tronc d'homme où croît l'ulcère, | Contre un tronc d'arbre où croît le gui' the phrase burns itself in like the *cotto aspetto* of Dante's Brunetto Latini", *Modern Tendencies in Poetry* (1920); during the Blitz, firemen were known as "heroes with grimy faces" (TSE: "scorched brown", *variant*; also "scorched eviscerate soil", II 13 *variant*). Thomas Hood: "His cheek was baked and brown", *The Sub-Marine* 2. James Hook: "whose face he recollected Pen had compared to a brown baked pie-crust", *Pen Owen* (1822) III 407. For "an old, weatherbeaten, pitted as if worm-eaten, brown face", see note to *Burnt Norton* I 12.

II 41 **Both one and many**: "At what point in its course does the Mississippi become what the Mississippi *means*? It is both one and many", *The Adventures of Huckleberry Finn* (1950), Introduction.

II 42 **familiar compound ghost**: to Hayward, 20 Feb 1943: "Perhaps your visitor who spotted the Dante allusions had been reading a painstaking article in the Cambridge Magazine which went into that very thoroughly [probably D. W. Harding, *Scrutiny* Spring 1943]. But why the phrase 'compound ghost' 'both one and many' should still leave people convinced that the stranger was one particular person, I don't understand." Poe: "the tones in the voice of the shadow were not the tones of any one being, but of a multitude of beings ··· in the well-remembered and familiar accents of many thousand departed friends", *Shadow—A Parable* (end).

TSE to Henry Eliot, 25 Mar 1943: "There is in the end of the section an allusion to a late poem of Yeats—'you wonder much that lust and rage | should dance attendance on my old age' or something like that, and the word 'laceration' is intended to remind of Swift, of whom of course Yeats was much aware, but the words 'one and many' and 'compound ghost' are intended to prevent the identification of the figure with any one person." On Swift's epitaph, see note to II 82–84. Yeats's *The Spur* reads, in full:

> You think it horrible that lust and rage
> Should dance attendance upon my old age;
> They were not such a plague when I was young:
> What else have I to spur me into song?
>
> (*Last Poems*, posthumous, 1939)

Quoting this, TSE commented: "The tragedy of Yeats's epigram is all in the last line", *Yeats* (1940) (*Composition FQ* 186). To Donald Hall, 16 Apr 1959: "Of course I had met Yeats many times. Yeats was always very gracious when one met him and had the art of treating younger writers as if they were his equals and contemporaries." To Kristian Smidt, 25 Sept 1961: "I must confess I was not thinking of Robert Browning when I refer to a 'familiar compound ghost'. I was thinking primarily of William Yeats, whose body was of course brought back to Ireland after the war. I also had in mind Swift, as the word 'laceration' suggests, and naturally Mallarmé, whose line I translated [see note to II 74]. But the body on the foreign shore was William Yeats's."

Other writers are spectrally present. For Milton and Joyce, see note to II 25–96. Ralph Pendrel's ghostly encounter with the portrait at the end of bk. II of James's

The Sense of the Past is compared in bk. III with Hawthorne's *The House of Seven Gables* and with "poor Hamlet". See notes to II 47 and *Burnt Norton* I 13. To Charles Williams, 24 Dec 1942: "You are right about Latini but of course it is also Arnaut Daniel, Yeats and Swift and you will not have missed the point of one line referring to Mallarmé and Edgar Poe. However, if anybody is well acquainted with Juliana and *The Cloud of Unknowing* it must be yourself." **compound**: pronounced *cumpound* in TSE's recording of 1946–47.

II 42 *variant* **a vague familiar ghost**: Shakespeare: "that affable familiar ghost", Sonnet 86 (*Grover Smith* 286). TSE: "gardens have long memories; | Like houses, have familiar ghosts", *A Valedictory Forbidding Mourning* 46–47. ("unfamiliar gust", *WLComposite* 526.)

II 42, 44 **ghost ··· a double part**: to Richard de la Mare, 7 Feb 1941, on TSE's alteration to the text of W. H. Auden's *New Year Letter*, previously published in the US as *The Double Man*: "please have it altered to read 'So condition his ears as to keep the Song | That is not a sorrow from the invisible twin'." (Auden's line originally ended "the Double Man".) To Auden, 19 Apr: "You gave me ··· no end of trouble over the doubleness of your man. I understand that you have returned the proof without comment on my substitution of 'the invisible twin', a small forgery of which I was rather proud ··· If you ever want somebody to ghost poetry for you, I think I could fill the position satisfactorily, for a suitable fee."

II 42, 47 **ghost ··· myself yet ··· someone other**: TSE at Milton Academy: "it occurred to me that as I had to talk to somebody, I would take more or less a metaphorical figure and make him as real as I could—that is, it occurred to me to say a few words to the ghost of myself at the age of seventeen or thereabouts, whom we may suppose to be skulking somewhere about this hall", *Address by T. S. Eliot, '06, to the Class of '33* (1933).

II 43–47 **Both intimate and unidentifiable ··· Knowing myself yet being someone other**: Bergson: "la fausse reconnaissance peut ébrauler la personalité entière ··· Celui qui l'éprouve est souvent en proie à une émotion caractéristique; il devient plus ou moins étranger à lui-même" [false recognition may disturb our whole personality ··· Whoever experiences it is often the prey of a characteristic emotion becoming more or less a stranger to himself], *L'Energie spirituelle* ch. V.

II 44–48 **I assumed a double part, and cried | And heard another's voice cry: "What! are *you* here?" | Although we were not. I was still the same, | Knowing myself yet being someone other— | And he a face still forming**: Clough: "She spoke, nor speaking ceased, I listening; but | I was alone—yet not alone—with her | As she with me ··· As at the first, and yet not wholly ··· The fusion and mutation and return | Seemed in my substance working too", *Adam and Eve* Scene XIV 29–35 (*Murray*). **I assumed a double part, and cried | And heard another's voice**: Shelley's meeting with the ghost of Rousseau: "ere he could resume, I cried: | 'First, who art thou?'" *The Triumph of Life* 198–99 (TSE: "I cried", II 44 *variant*). These were among thirty consecutive lines of Shelley's poem quoted by TSE in *What Dante Means to Me* (1950); see note to *The Waste Land* [I] 60–63. John Buchan: "I seemed to be another person, standing aside and listening to my own voice", *The Thirty-Nine Steps* (1915) IV (George Simmers, personal communication). An unpublished poem by "F. M." (c. 624 fol. 10) has "I met my own eyes | In another face", *Perque Domos Ditis Vacuas* (TSE: "first-met ··· eyes ··· face", [II] 38–48). "perque domos ditis vacuas" [through the empty halls of Dis], *Aeneid* VI 269.

II 45 **heard another's voice cry**: alongside the Gide/Bosco translation, "j'entendis une autre voix crier", TSE wrote: "ambiguous". For Dante, "as pleased Another", see note to *WLComposite* 475–557. **"What! are *you* here?"**: Blake: "Pliny & Trajan! what are you here?" *I will tell you what Joseph of Arimathea* 3. TSE to Bonamy Dobrée, This Tuesday after the 9th Sunday after Trinity [1927]: "Italics are bad in poetry. Abused by M. Arnold."

II 45 *variant* **And heard my voice: "Are you here, Ser Brunetto?"**: the works of the 13th-century Florentine scholar Brunetto Latini greatly influenced Dante. In Brunetto's *Tesoretto*, he condemned sodomites as "contra natura", yet it is among them that Dante encounters him. Brunetto bids Dante farewell: "'sieti raccomandato il mio *Tesoro*, | nel quale io vivo ancora; e più non cheggio.' | Poi si rivolse" ["let my *Treasure*, in which I still live, be commended to thee; and more I ask not." Then he turned back], *Inf.* XV 119–21. TSE to Hayward, 27 Aug 1942: "I think you will recognise that it was necessary to get rid of Brunetto for two reasons. The first is that the visionary figure has now become somewhat more definite and will no doubt be identified by some readers with Yeats though I do not mean anything so precise as that. However, I do not wish to take the responsibility of putting Yeats or anybody else into Hell and I do not want to impute to him the particular vice which took Brunetto there. Secondly, although reference to that Canto is intended to be explicit, I wished the effect of the whole to be Purgatorial which is much more appropriate." (To Peter du Sautoy: "I had rather be damned in the company of Yeats, Hofmannsthal, Claudel and Cocteau than praised by this extraordinary American", *"The Death of Tragedy"* by George Steiner, reader's report [1961]. Faber published the book.)

Inscribing a copy of *Ara Vos Prec* for Emily Hale, dated "5.ix.23" (Sotheby's, 20 Oct 2011), TSE quoted Brunetto: "sieti racommendato il mio tesoro | nello qual vivo ancor e non più chieggio. | Poi si rivolse". This does not match the Temple Classics text, but is similar to the inscription in a copy of the Hogarth Press ed. of *The Waste Land* which TSE presented to Geoffrey Faber, dated "27.v.25" (within days of their first meeting): "'Sieti racommendato il mio tesoro | Nel quale io vivo ancor—'" (Bonhams, 20 Sept 2005).

II 45–46 **"What! are *you* here?" | Although we were not**: "I was not there, you were not there, only our phantasms", *The Family Reunion* II ii.

II 46–47 **I was still the same, | Knowing myself yet being someone other**: "dans ma préface, peux-je dire que St. J. Perse et St. Leger Leger, l'auteur d'*Anabase* et l'auteur d'*Éloges*, sont identiques, ou voulez-vous garder votre anonymat fragile?" [in my preface, may I say that St. J. Perse and St. Leger Leger, the author of *Anabase* and the author of *Éloges*, are identical, or do you wish to preserve your fragile anonymity?] ("And no identity", II 50 *variant.*) Lucien Fabre had reviewed *Anabase* in *Les Nouvelles Littéraires* Aug 1924: "Saint-Leger Leger a disparu; et son fantôme ne semoie pas trop inquiéter Saint-John Perse. Réunissons donc Saint-Leger Leger et Saint-John Perse dans la même admiration" [Saint-Leger Leger has disappeared, and his ghost does not seem to be causing St.-John Perse any uneasiness. So let us reunite Saint-Leger Leger and Saint-John Perse in the same admiration]. TSE used Fabre's (separate) "note" in his own Preface to *Anabasis* (1930) and had it translated so as to print it in the final edition (*1959*).

II 47 **Knowing myself yet being someone other:** James: "'The point is that I'm not myself.' ··· 'I'm somebody else'", *The Sense of the Past* bk. III. See note to II 42 above. **yet being someone other:** Jean de Bosschère: "Et dans chaque ville il est un autre personnage" [And in each town he is another person], quoted in *Reflections on Contemporary Poetry* II (1917); see headnote to *Mélange Adultère de Tout*. "I was someone else", *The Family Reunion* I ii.

II 48–49 **he a face still forming; yet the words sufficed | To compel the recognition they preceded:** *Purg.* XXIII 43–45 (Forese): "Mai non l'avrei riconosciuto al viso; | ma nella voce sua mi fu palese | ciò che l'aspetto in sè avea conquiso" [Never had I recognised him by the face, but in his voice was revealed to me that which was blotted out in his countenance] (*Griffiths and Reynolds* 320).

II 49 **To compel the recognition they preceded:** to Natalie Clifford Barney, 11 May 1923: "April is indeed the cruellest month, and the fact follows the word." To Hayward, 7 Sept 1942: "I am inclined to stick to 'preceded', because the words you suggest [*predicted*, *portended*] convey a different meaning from what I want. I mean, to be aware that it is someone you know (and to be surprised by his being there) before you have identified him. *Recognition* surely is the full identification of the person." Writing to Robert Sencourt, 19 Jan 1967, John Betjeman recorded that TSE had been "very amused by ··· things like mistaken identity".

II 51–52 *variant* **cross of purpose | In:** *Macbeth* II ii: "Infirm of purpose."

II 51–53 **Too strange ··· meeting nowhere:** Harold Monro's volume of poems *Strange Meetings* (1917) preceded the writing of Wilfred Owen's poem *Strange Meeting*. See note to *Burnt Norton* II 1–2.

II 51, 69 **Too strange to each other for misunderstanding ··· Between two worlds become much like each other:** "a world too strange for", *The Burnt Dancer* 9, repeated in 10.

II 54 **trod ··· pavement ··· dead patrol:** Paul Elmer More: "shadows of night drift past us on the silent pavement ··· souls of the generations before us who trod this same way in their life", *The Great Refusal* 128. TSE to Hayward [22 Sept 1942] (after *ts13*): "Read 'trod the pavement' for 'strode together'. The idea of togetherness is, I think, in the word 'patrol', so that 'together' is superfluous, whereas a reminder of the surface of the Cromwell Road is timely." **dead patrol:** in the Gide/Bosco tr., TSE underlined the last three words of "patrouilles de la mort". **dead:** OED 2b: "deathlike, insensible, in a swoon. *Obs.*" 16: "Without vigour or animation". 26: "Of calm or silence: Profound, deep".

II 55–56, 67 **easy ··· ease ··· as the passage now presents no hindrance:** replying to a suggestion of Hayward's, 9 Sept 1942: "'Easeful' will never be any use until Keats's trade-mark has worn off. Also it means something else. There was nothing ease-giving about this transit." (Keats: "half in love with easeful Death", *Ode to a Nightingale* 52.)

II 57 **I may not comprehend, may not remember:** in the Gide/Bosco tr., "Je ne pourrai ni comprendre", TSE inserted "peut-être" after "pourrai", with "!"

II 57–60 **remember ··· you have forgotten ··· their purpose:** *Hamlet* III iv, Ghost:

"Do not forget. This visitation | Is but to whet thy almost blunted purpose" (after "Remember" repeatedly in I v).

II 58 **And he: :** Alan Seeger: "And he:" *Dante. Inferno, Canto XXVI* (five lines after "'Master,' I said"). The translation is in Seeger's *Poems* (1916), which TSE reviewed; see note to *Whispers of Immortality* 19.

II 58 *variant* **I am not eager to recall:** "Ugolino found his greatest grief in recalling past error and sin", *Mr. Middleton Murry's Synthesis* (1927), quoting *Inf.* XXXIII 4–6.

II 60–65 **These things have served their purpose ··· last year's words belong to last year's language:** "There are a great many words in the English language ··· and a great many of these words are now dead, have served their purpose and will not come into use again", *The Writer as Artist* (1940). For "no more apprehensible than the scent of last year's roses", see note to II 2.

II 61–62 **pray they be forgiven | By others, as I pray you to forgive:** the Lord's Prayer: "Forgive us our trespasses, as we forgive them that trespass against us."

II 63, 65–66 **Last season's fruit ··· last year's words belong to last year's language | And next year's words await another voice:** *Hayward*: "Oderisi of Gubbio's lament for the transitoriness of human fame" (*Purg.* XI 97–101: "one Guido hath taken from the other the glory of our tongue; and perchance one is born who shall chase both from the nest. Earthly fame is naught but a breath of wind"). TSE: "What we want is ··· To point out that every generation, every turn of time when the work of four or five men who count has reached middle age, is a *crisis* ··· the intelligence of a nation must go on developing, or it will deteriorate; and that every writer who does not help to develop the language is ··· a positive agent of deterioration", *Observations* (1918). In the final issue of the *Criterion*: "If a similar review is needed, then it will be far better for someone else to start a new review with a new title. New conditions will very likely require new methods and somewhat different aims", *Last Words*, Jan 1939. "My language is finished, for me, when I have come to the end of my resources, in endeavouring to extend and develop that language (and for a poet, his language represents his country, and Europe too). For an artist who comes at the end of a period, art ends with himself ··· I hope, in any case, that something will remain operative, on the further generations who will have different criteria, and who will adapt verse to different purposes",*"Leçon de Valéry"* (1946); see note to V 16–18. "let me | Resign my life for this life, my speech for that unspoken", *Marina* 30–31.

To the Rev. Luke Turner, 16 Feb 1943: "I hope I shall not seem ungrateful for your ··· flattering notice of *Little Gidding* in the *Blackfriars* literary supplement ··· but I am moved to express my distress at your referring to English as a dying language. Some centuries hence if the English language has in the meantime actually died, a philologist of the future may be in a position to look back and give reasons for believing that in the year 1942 the English language was indeed moribund, but I don't see why we should make that assumption so long as the language has any life left and therefore must be believed capable of being restored to full animation. I am quite aware of all the degeneration which has taken place and of the further decline which is likely to set in if all the mad reformers of education have their way, but I believe that to allow readers to assume that the language is dying may be to accelerate by inviting acquiescence a process we deplore." (See note to III 36–45, "cannot revive".) "The symptom of approaching death of a language and a civilisation is when men go on writing poetry in a style and vocabulary which has become meaningless to their less learned contemporaries", *The Last Twenty-Five Years of English Poetry* (1939).

II 67–71 **the passage now presents no hindrance | To the spirit · · · two worlds become much like each other · · · In streets:** Paul Elmer More: "we are dismayed to find our advance checked at a certain point beyond which this guide cannot take us. Then our perception is deepened. The material world is seen in its naked reality. Two paths are open to us. Either with the followers of the Vedanta we look upon matter as pure illusion · · · or else, with the school of the Sankhya, we deem it eternal and self-existent · · · I do not know how better to express that stage of our spiritual progress when the material world becomes in every aspect a hindrance to us. Whichever way our reason leads us—and the two systems are morally one—beauty to the enlightened mind becomes above all things the most dangerous illusion", *The Great Refusal* 6–7. (TSE: "More's early education was received in the schools and University · · · of St. Louis, Missouri. His religious upbringing, from which he early rebelled, was that of an antiquated and provincial American Presbyterianism. He distinguished himself as a classical scholar, and for several years was a Greek master in a local school. It is possible that one or two elder scholars in St. Louis gave him his first curiosity about Indian philosophy and Sanskrit literature · · · his eventual Anglicanism cannot be evaluated without reference to the process by which he arrived at it", *An Anglican Platonist: The Conversion of Elmer More* (1937), anonymously in the *TLS*.) For More, see notes to III 3–12 and *The Waste Land* [IV] 314.

II 67–96 *drafts* (A–E)

A) **Remember rather the essential moments** (*first venture in verse*)

[3] **The agony and the solitary vigil:** *The Little Passion: From "An Agony in the Garret"* (in *March Hare* Notebook).

[3] *variant* **The dark night in the solitary bedroom:** "The agony in the curtained bedroom", "the chilly pretences in the silent bedroom", *The Family Reunion* II i, II iii.

[6] **Remember Poitiers, and the Anjou wine:** to Edward Forbes 22 May [1911]: "At Christmas I travelled for two weeks in France, and saw several things not often visited—including Poitiers, Angoulême, Toulouse, Albi, Moissac, and other places in the south west." In Aug 1919 TSE and the Pounds visited the area again, on a walking tour (see TSE to his mother, 3 Sept). Pound to TSE [? 1919]: "Don't know what to suggest re/ country. unless you try Angers & Poitiers. = or environs of Tours & will ask Miss Barney · · · Angers only place much nearer than Brantôme, except Tours & Poitiers" (Valerie Eliot collection). The Battle of Poitiers (1356) was an English victory in the Hundred Years War. TSE: "Let the Angevin | Destroy himself, fighting in Anjou", *Murder in the Cathedral* I. **the Anjou wine:** to Hayward, 13

July 1939: "Scudamore Griffiths · · · likes to ask us over for a bottle of vin d'Anjou before lunch."

[6–8] **Anjou wine · · · the smell of varnish | On the clean oar, the drying of the sails:** the sonnet *Heureux qui, comme Ulysse* by Joachim du Bellay (1522–60) ends: "Et plus que l'air marin la douceur Angevine" [And more than the sea air, the softness of Anjou] (*Composition FQ* 184).

[14–21] **(After many seas and after many lands) · · · nearer · · · faces · · · place · · · grace:** "What seas what shores · · · nearer · · · faces · · · place · · · grace", *Marina* 1–15.

[22] **He turned away, and in the autumn weather:** Hayward to TSE, 1 Aug 1941: "I do not get the significance of autumn? It struck me as having a greater significance than you intended it to have". TSE, 5 Aug (referring to "She turned away, but with the autumn weather", *La Figlia Che Piange* 17): "'Autumn weather' only because it *was* autumn weather—it is supposed to be an *early* air raid—and to throw back to *Figlia che piange* (but not having my Poems by me I may be misquoting) but with less point than the children in the appletree [V 35] meaning to tie up with *New Hampshire* and *Burnt Norton* (with a touch, as I discovered in the train, of *They* which I don't think I had read for 30 years, but the quotation from E. B. Browning has always stuck in my head, and that may be due to *They* rather than to the Bardess herself)." Elizabeth Barrett Browning's *The Lost Bower*, about a paradisal spot which the poet can no longer find, was on the syllabus for TSE's Southall evening classes, 1916 (*Schuchard*). Its first four lines are quoted in Kipling's story:

> In the pleasant orchard closes,
> "God bless all our gains", say we;
> But "May God bless all our losses",
> Better suits with our degree.

Helen Gardner notes that TSE had incorporated "our losses" in *The Dry Salvages* I 22. **He turned away:** *Inf.* XV 121, of Brunetto's return to the infernal flames: "Poi si rivolse" [Then he turned back]. TSE had praised Dante's image of Brunetto turning back "like one of those who run for the green cloth at Verona" in *Tradition and the Individual Talent* II (1919) and quoted it in *The Post-Georgians* (1919), in his fourth Clark Lecture (*The Varities of Metaphysical Poetry* 122), and in *Dante* (1929) I. Rather than Brunetto in the *Inferno*, TSE's published text ("He left me") invokes Marco Lombardo in the *Purgatorio*; see note to II 94–95 below.

Pound, *The Return* 8–9:

> And murmur in the wind,
> and half turn back;

For Pound's poem see *Ricks 2010* 197–200, notes to *Ash-Wednesday* VI 3–4 and *Little Gidding* V 18.

[22] *variant* **He turned away, and with his motion of dismissal:** for "she turned away" and "dismissal" in Hawthorne's *The Blithedale Romance*, see notes to *La Figlia Che Piange* 14–22 and 17–18, 20.

[22–23] **He turned away, and · · · I heard a distant dull deferred report:** Tennyson: "He spoke; and, high above, I heard them blast | The steep slate-quarry, and the great echo flap | And buffet round the hills, from bluff to bluff", *The Golden Year* final three lines.

B and C) **Then, changing face and accent** (*prose exposition and verse fragment*)

B) *msB* fol 1. *prose*

[6] **My alien people**: "an alien people", *Journey of the Magi* 42.

[9–10] **I fought some evil the darkness**: "the evening fought itself awake ··· evil ··· Pointed a ribald finger at me in the darkness ··· chuckled at me in the darkness ··· the darkness", *Prufrock's Pervigilium* [10, 15–19].

C) *msB* fol 2. *verse fragment*

[2] **after many seasons**: "(After many seas and many lands)", *first venture in verse* [14].

D) **Then, changing form and feature** (*second venture in verse*)

[20–21] **even with the true defend the false | And with the eternal truth the local error?**: Bradley: "We cannot, on the one hand, accept anything between non-existence and reality, while, on the other hand, error obstinately refuses to be either. It persistently attempts to maintain a third position, which appears nowhere to exist, and yet somehow is occupied ··· error, because it is false, cannot belong to the Absolute; and, again, it cannot appertain to the finite subject", *Appearance and Reality* ch. XVI; the whole paragraph scored by TSE, who wrote at the head of the next chapter: "Error and evil imply absolute perfection, but the perfection wh. they imply is not the same as the perfection at which they aim." **And with the eternal truth the local error?**: to Bonamy Dobrée, 12 Nov 1927: "if there is no fixed truth, there is no fixed object for the will to tend to. If truth is always changing, then there is nothing to do but sit down and watch the pictures ··· I should say that it was at any rate essential for Religion that we should have the conception of an immutable object or Reality the knowledge of which shall be the final object of that will; and there can be no permanent reality if there is no permanent truth." **eternal truth**: "guesses at eternal truths", *Goldfish* III 5.

E) **Consider what are the gifts of age—** (*prose draft of intervening passage*, II 76–93)

[8–11] **retrospection of past motives ··· that one was moved while believing oneself to be the mover**: "past and future ··· Where action were otherwise movement | Of that which is only moved | And has in it no source of movement", *Ash-Wednesday* V 35–39.

Published text resumes

II 68 **spirit unappeased and peregrine**: Dante: "che per lo suo splendore | lo peregrino spirito la mira", *Vita Nuova* [XLI] final sonnet; tr. Rossetti: "Abash'd, the pilgrim spirit stands at gaze", *The Early Italian Poets* 308. Rossetti translates Dante's commentary: "I then call it a 'Pilgrim Spirit,' because it goes up spiritually, and like a pilgrim who is out of his known country." TSE: "the *Divine Comedy* has been shown to be closely similar to similar supernatural peregrination stories in Arabic and in old Persian literature", *Dante* (1929) III. Pound: "She hath clad her soul in fashions peregrine", *Sonnets and Ballate of Guido Cavalcanti* (1912), *Sonnet* XII. Dante's "persona umile e peregrina" [a lowly and an alien man], *Paradiso* VI 135, was repeatedly invoked by TSE in self-description: apropos of his role as translator of St.-John Perse (to Marguerite Caetani, 21 Jan 1930); in his *Speech at Aix-en-Provence* (1947); and in *Christ Church, Oxford*, Speech (1948). **peregrine**: pronounced *peregryne* in TSE's recording of 1946–47.

II 68–69 **peregrine ··· Between two worlds**: on Bradley: "a transmigration from one world to another, and such a pilgrimage involves an act of faith", *Knowledge and Experience* 163.

II 69 **Between two worlds**: Byron: "Between two worlds life hovers like a star", *Don Juan* XV xcix; quoted twice in *Byron* (1937). Arnold: "Wandering between two worlds, one dead, | The other powerless to be born", *Stanzas from the Grande Chartreuse* 85–86. TSE: "Mr. Clive Bell, lingering between two worlds, one dead, is in some respects the Matthew Arnold of his time", *Potboilers* (1918), review. "wanderings in the neutral territory | Between two worlds", *The Family Reunion* II iii (*Preston* 58). Shelley: "Ere Babylon was dust, | The Magus Zoroaster, my dead child, | Met his own image walking in the garden. | That apparition, sole of men, he saw. | For know there are two worlds of life and death: | One that which thou beholdest; but the other | Is underneath the grave, where do inhabit | The shadows of all forms that think and live | Till death unite them and they part no more", *Prometheus Unbound* I 191–99; quoted by Reilly in *The Cocktail Party* act II. TSE to D. W. Evans, 23 Sept 1954: "the passage from Shelley is one that had stuck in my mind since I first read *Prometheus Unbound* at the age of fifteen, and I was startled to find [Charles] Williams making use of it in *Descent into Hell*" (Faber, 1937) ch. 4. "where two worlds cross, | In every moment you live at a point of intersection", *The Rock* 52. Joyce: "Between two roaring worlds, where they swirl, I", *Ulysses* episode X (Wandering Rocks) (Shawn Worthington, personal communication). For Barth, "two worlds meet", see note to *The Dry Salvages* II V 18–19. **two worlds become much like each other**: "I have known two worlds, I have known two worlds of death", *The Rock* 47.

II 69, 72 **Between two worlds ··· I left my body on a distant shore**: Paul Elmer More: "Between the two lies the world of the indifferent, and, I begin to surmise, the world of the artist ··· leaving his body in the new ocean", *The Great Refusal* 75–76, 78. For More, see note to II 67–71.

II 70–71 **words I never thought to speak | In streets I never thought I should revisit**: *Inf.* XXVII 61–62: "If I thought my answer were to one who ever could return to the world"; see epigraph to *The Love Song of J. Alfred Prufrock*.

II 72 **body on a distant shore**: see note to II 42. Yeats died in the South of France on 28 Jan 1939 and was buried at Roquebrune-Cap-Martin (exhumed 1948 and returned to Ireland). Virgil, of the shades in the underworld: "Tendebantque manus ripae ulterioris amore" [stretched out hands in yearning for the farther shore], *Aeneid* VI 314 (*Hayward*). Tourneur: "Walking next day upon the fatal shore, | Among the slaughtered bodies of their men", *The Atheist's Tragedy* II i, quoted in *Cyril Tourneur* (1930) (*Grover Smith 1950* 418). TSE on *In Memoriam*: "Hallam died young, and died abroad: in the ninth section Tennyson's thoughts revert to the bringing back of Hallam's body—'Fair ship, that from the Italian shore'", *"The Voice of His Time"* (1942). ("those who were in ships, and | Ended their voyage on the sand", *The Dry Salvages* IV 11–12.)

II 73 **our concern was speech**: *Lehmann* records TSE's answers to questions after a reading at Bryn Mawr in Oct 1948: Q. "Do you think that the poet can concern himself just with his own feelings? Has he not a responsibility for his country, humanity, etc.?" A. "His responsibility is towards the language." (It was at Bryn Mawr that in 1905 Henry James had given his address *The Question of Our Speech*.) See TSE on the artist's job, "to prevent the language from deteriorating", in *The Writer as Artist* (1940) quoted in "The End of All Our Exploring". **speech**: "Donne invented an idiom, a language which less original men could learn to talk ··· and Dryden imposed a new way of speech on the next hundred years", *The Minor Metaphysicals* (1930). "Of Jules Laforgue ··· I can say that he was the first to teach me how to speak, to teach me the poetic possibilities of my own idiom of speech", *What Dante Means to Me* (1950). "But what is overlooked is that an *identical* spoken and written language would be practically intolerable. If we spoke as we write we should find no one to listen; and if we wrote as we speak we should find no one to read", *Charles Whibley* (1931).

II 73–74 **speech impelled us | To purify the dialect of the tribe**: Coleridge: "few have guarded the purity of their native tongue with that jealous care, which the sublime Dante in his tract *De la nobile volgare eloquenza* declares to be the first duty of a poet", *Biographia Literaria* ch. XVI (R. Bates, *N&Q* Nov 1953). In a letter to Madame Elsa Gress, 30 Oct 1946, TSE sent an 80th birthday tribute to Johannes Jørgensen (Danish poet, and biographer of Catholic saints): "The poet is the servant of his own language; yet ··· We have a common task and a common loyalty, transcending our local loyalty ··· the great stream of European tradition. We owe allegiance to a common civilisation, and to its sources in Greece, Rome and Israel; each of us must struggle to preserve, and, if he may, enrich that inheritance. In acknowledgement of your contribution I salute you, the elder master" ("master", II 39; "common", II 50).

II 74 **To purify the dialect of the tribe**: Mallarmé: "donner un sens plus pur aux mots de la tribu", *Le Tombeau d'Edgar Poe* (*Hayward*; also Delmore Schwartz, *Matthiessen* 192). The Gide/Bosco tr. gives Mallarmé's own words, beside which TSE wrote "Good!" To William Matchett, 14 June 1949: "I wonder whether a pertinent distinction could be made between *allusion* and *borrowing*. The two may somewhat overlap or indeed the same quotation may serve both purposes. In the line taken from Mallarmé, for instance, my direct intention was merely to borrow. It seemed to me a very happy translation of his line and it gave me exactly the words that I wanted to say. The secondary purpose in this case is the allusion. If readers recognize the source, so much the better. One might be able to find other quotations of which the primary purpose is allusion and borrowing the secondary."

TSE praised Mallarmé's poem *Le Tombeau de Charles Baudelaire*:

> L'effort pour restituer la puissance du Mot, qui inspire la syntaxe de l'un et de l'autre et leur fait écarter le sonore pur ou le pur mélodieux (qu'ils pourraient,

tous les deux, s'ils le voulaient, si bien exploiter), cet effort, qui empêche le lecteur d'*avaler d'un coup* leur phrase ou leur vers, est une des qualités qui rapprochent le mieux les deux poètes. Il y a aussi la fermeté de leur pas lorsqu'ils passent du monde tangible au monde des fantômes.

[The effort to restore the power of the Word, which inspires the syntax of both and makes them set aside resonant purity or melodious purity (that they could both, if they wished, exploit so well)—this effort, which prevents the reader of their prose or verse from gulping it down, is one of the qualities which the two poets have in common. There is also the firmness of their step as they pass from the tangible world to the world of ghosts.]

Note sur Mallarmé et Poe (1926)

In *Lancelot Andrewes* (1926), TSE likened reading Andrewes to "listening to a great Hellenist expounding a text of the *Posterior Analytics*: altering the punctuation, inserting or removing a comma or a semi-colon to make an obscure passage suddenly luminous, dwelling on a single word, comparing its use in its nearer and in its most remote contexts, purifying a disturbed or cryptic lecture-note into lucid profundity. To persons whose minds are habituated to feed on the vague jargon of our time ···" (To the Editor of *The Times*, 4 Aug 1938, supplementing the obituary of H. H. Joachim: "To his *explication de texte* of the *Posterior Analytics* I owe an appreciation of the importance of punctuation.") Turnbull Lecture III: "In looking at the history of poetry ··· the important poets will be those who have taught the people speech; and the people had in every generation to be taught to speak: the function of the poet at every moment is to make the inarticulate folk articulate; and as the inarticulate folk is almost always mumbling the speech, become jargon, of its ancestors or of its newspaper editors, the new language is never learnt without a certain resistance, even resentment ··· this purification of language is not so much a progress, as it is a perpetual return to the real", *The Varieties of Metaphysical Poetry* 289–90. "the man of letters, especially if his vehicle is one of the great languages, such as French or English—the man who knows what a precious instrument he possesses, how many centuries have gone to its development, with what difficulty and toil its excellence is maintained, and with what ease its strength and purity may be destroyed, must be concerned with the preservation of his language, rather than with its exploitation", *The Unity of European Writers* (1944). Of Twain: "I should place him, in this respect, even with Dryden and Swift, as one of those rare writers who have brought their language up to date, and in so doing, 'purified the dialect of the tribe'", *American Literature and the American Language* (1953). TSE (tr. Iman Javadi): "Naturally the poet has a deep affection for words, he is in love with words; and I feel that he has a duty towards his native language and his own poetic idiom to cultivate this affection. It is his duty, when he can, to offer words that no one knew before, to arouse feelings which hadn't been discovered before. He must find new ways to use the language and always try to preserve its peculiarity and its purity", *Ein Gespräch mit T. S. Eliot* (1964). On Huxley: "I was delighted to find that in his last brief book, *Literature and Science*, he quotes a line of Mallarmé which had impressed me so deeply that I paraphrased it in *Little Gidding*: *donner un sens plus pur aux mots de la tribu*", *Aldous Huxley* (1965).

II 76–77 **Let me disclose ··· lifetime's effort**: in the Gide/Bosco tr., TSE braced with

"!" the lines "J'userai des dons réservés à l'âge | Pour poser une couronne sur les labeurs de votre vie." To George Barker, 24 Jan 1938: "Poetry is either a matter of a brief outburst, or it is a matter of a lifetime's work" (see headnote to *Four Quartets*, 4. "NOT MERELY MORE OF THE SAME").

II 76–77 *variant* **gifts ··· prizes:** to Hayward, 7 Sept: "I now think 'prizes' is rather heavy-handed after 'gifts'." To Mrs. Elsmith, 4 Sept 1942: "she is able to know and to prize the best gifts of friendship".

II 76–93 *prose draft* (*msC*) **the gifts of age—The cold craving when the sense is gone ··· doubt of self which springs from retrospection of past motives:** "I was neither ··· craving ··· I have lost my sight, smell, hearing, taste and touch ··· chilled delirium ··· when the sense has cooled", *Gerontion* 39, 57, 62–63 (with "*age*", epigraph).

II 77 **To set a crown upon your lifetime's effort:** *Purg.* XXVII 142, Virgil's final words to Dante: "'per ch'io te sopra te corono e mitrio'" ["wherefore I do crown and mitre thee over thyself"] (*Grover Smith* 286). In the penultimate typescript, Hayward underlined three assonantal vowels in this line, which then read "The final prizes of your lifetime's effort", writing "X X X" in the margin, and *"finis coronat opus".* Hayward had used the same phrase to describe *Little Gidding* in a letter of Aug 1941 to Frank Morley (*Smart* 301). TSE: "what is more common is for the critic to assume that one's work is finished, that the last piece one wrote represents the crowning effort of a lifetime: very often, indeed, it evidences the certain decline of the author's powers", *Author and Critic* (1955). "the poet is the least abstract of men, because he is the most bound by his own language: he cannot even afford to know another language equally well, because it is, for the poet, a lifetime's work to explore the resources of his own", *Goethe as the Sage* (1955).

II 78 **cold ··· expiring sense:** Conrad: "I remember my youth and the feeling that will never come back any more—the feeling that I could last forever ··· the deceitful feeling that lures us on ··· the triumphant conviction of strength, the heat of life in a handful of dust, the glow in the heart that with every year grows dim, grows cold, grows small, and expires—and expires, too soon, too soon, before life itself", *Youth* (*Unger 1956* 240). For "in a handful of dust", see note to *The Waste Land* [I] 30.

II 78–80 **expiring sense ··· bitter tastelessness of shadow fruit:** *Paradise Lost* XI 532–38: "So mayst thou live, till like ripe fruit thou drop ··· thou must outlive | Thy youth, thy strength, thy beauty, which will change | To withered weak and gray; thy senses then | Obtuse, all taste of pleasure must forgo"; also X 563–66: "but taste | Deceived; they fondly thinking to allay | Their appetite with gust, instead of fruit | Chewed bitter ashes" (*Hands*). Tourneur: "Your gravity becomes your perished soul | As hoary mouldiness does rotten fruit", *The Atheist's Tragedy* I iv; quoted in *Cyril Tourneur* (1930) (*Grover Smith 1983* 114). Arthur Symons: "tired with age and grief ··· shadowy fruit", *Faint Love* (TSE: "age", II 76).

II 79, 82, 84 **enchantment ··· impotence of rage ··· to amuse:** Symons: "My life is like a music-hall, | Where, in the impotence of rage, | Chained by enchantment to my stall, | I see myself upon the stage | Dance to amuse a music-hall", *Prologue: In the Stalls* 1–5 (1895).

II 79, 85 **enchantment ··· re-enactment:** for TSE on these words, see letter to

Hayward, 19 Sept 1942, in *Little Gidding* headnote, 2. COMPOSITION. To Desmond MacCarthy, 28 Dec 1942: "I am particularly glad that you liked the Ghost passage, because I found that piece gave me the greatest trouble. The simplicity of language at which one must aim, in this kind of verse, requires the avoidance of repetition of words (even *ofs* and *ands* and *buts* have to be carefully watched) and even the avoidance of words of similar formation too near together—I am not happy about enchant*ment* and re-enact*ment* so close together, but I could find no substitute for either word."

II 82–84 **impotence of rage | At human folly, and the laceration | Of laughter at what ceases to amuse**: alongside these lines quoted in *G. Jones*, TSE wrote "Cf. Swift". *Hayward* pointed to Swift's epitaph on himself: "Ubi sæva Indignatio Ulterius Cor lacerare nequit" [Savage indignation there | Cannot lacerate his breast], tr. Yeats, *The Winding Stair and Other Poems* (1933). (Hayward transposed "Ulterius" and "Cor", having previously jotted them correctly beside 83 in *ts9b*, before, in *ts12b*, he suggested "laceration", which TSE accepted.) TSE to Mrs. J. J. Hawkes, 22 Oct 1947, rejecting a UNESCO proposal that the classics should be translated into all languages: Swift "would have admitted the impotence of imagination, when confronted with human activity so much more fantastic than anything he could invent. If not wholly overcome by vertigo, he would have had to find some other medium in which to express his laceration of heart. But, as you might justly have observed, Eire is not a United Nation, and the voice of the Dean would not have been heard."

To Geoffrey Faber, [27 Aug 1927], on Swift: "I never knew that he meant so much to you; he has always been one of the very great men to me; indeed *Gulliver*, and especially the last chapter of the Houhynyms, is to me with *King Lear* as one of the most tragic things ever written ··· I have always felt a particular sympathy and (probably) illusory understanding of Swift in connexion with Stella and Vanessa ··· I should like even to collaborate, to a small extent, on Swift. Do you know the *Drapier's Letters* well? They are magnificent. But I think I could do better justice to the poetry (without vanity) than has yet been done. Swift's obscenity is as little understood as Baudelaire's blasphemy." **rage | At human folly ··· laceration**: Johnson's *The Vanity of Human Wishes* has "the rage of power ··· heady rage ··· lacerated Friendship claims a tear", 33, 281, 304 (see note to II 90).

II 82, 86, 88 **conscious impotence ··· shame ··· things ill done**: "consciousness of death, of shame and of failure", *The Cultivation of Christmas Trees ts3* 29 *variant.*

II 85 **the rending pain of re-enactment**: Conrad: "Did he live his life again in every detail of desire, temptation, and surrender during that supreme moment of complete knowledge?" *Heart of Darkness* pt. 3. For the passage from Conrad, see note to *The Hollow Men* first epigraph.

II 86–87 **the shame | Of motives late revealed**: Lancelot Andrewes: "look back upon our sins past ··· consider the motives, the base motives, and weigh the circumstances, the grievous circumstances, and tell over our many flittings, our often relapsing, our wretched continuing in them", Ash-Wednesday Sermon 1619. TSE: "About Donne there hangs the shadow of the impure motive", *Lancelot Andrewes* (1926). To Conrad Aiken, 10 Aug 1929: "My progress, if I ever make any, will be in purging myself of a large number of impure motives." On Pascal: "the magnificent analysis of human motives and occupations which was to have constituted the early part of his book ··· seeing through human beings and observing the vanity of their thoughts and of their avocations, their dishonesty and self-deception, the insincerity of their emotions, their cowardice, the pettiness of their real ambitions", *The "Pensées" of Pascal* (1931). "I am doubtful whether the right procedure is to attempt to yoke together commitments to the development of the 'spiritual life' ··· and social-political interests, if there is any suspicion that the motive—or one of the motives—for this union is an attempt to make room for everybody", *Moot Paper* 50 (1941). (See note to III 49, "purification of the motive".)

"The last temptation is the greatest treason: | To do the right deed for the wrong reason", *Murder in the Cathedral* I (within final speech). TSE characterised the sceptic as "the man who suspects the origins of his own beliefs ··· who suspects other people's motives because he has learned the deceitfulness of his own" (*Notes on the Way*, 5 Jan 1935). Henry Eliot took up both of these when he deplored TSE's *The Modern Dilemma* (1933) in a letter to his brother, 12 Sept 1935:

> I am not sure whether it is your past motives alone that you question, or your present motives also; I mean your motives for embracing the Church ··· People commonly speak as if motives were always single; whereas they are usually multiple; and often nearly as obscure to oneself as to others. But a great many secondary motives can be classified under the primary motive of wishing to appear well in the eyes of others ··· how came you to address to the clergy of Boston, a city saturated with associations of your ancestors, immediate and distant, what seems to me in all truth a fanatically intolerant and shocking tirade? ··· I cannot agree that one's supposed duty to one's church absolves one from the ordinary decencies; furthermore, even the Roman Church approves the injunction, "Honor thy father and mother."

TSE replied, 1 Jan 1936: "It seems a little hard that a man's questioning of his own motives should be taken, as you seem to take it, as evidence of their insincerity."

II 87–88 **awareness | Of things ill done**: Yeats, *Vacillation* V in *The Winding Stair and Other Poems* (1933), quoted in *After Strange Gods* 46 (*Smidt 1973*):

> Things said or done long years ago,
> Or things I did not do or say
> But thought that I might say or do,
> Weigh me down, and not a day
> But something is recalled,
> My conscience or my vanity appalled.

For Yeats's collection, see note to II 82–84.

II 88 **things ill done**: John Ford: "Sigh out a lamentable tale of things | Done long ago, and ill done", *The Lover's Melancholy* IV ii (*Grover Smith* 286). TSE regarded this as one of the three plays by Ford in which "we find some of the best 'poetical' passages", *John Ford* (1932). Kipling quoted Ford's two lines as the epigraph to *Love-O'-Women*, a story of repentance and of "more that was worst than any repentince" (*Ricks 1998*). Norman Cameron's nine-line poem *All Things Ill Done* (*The Winter House*, 1935) closely resembles TSE's lines (*Ricks 1998*). TSE: "Ill done and undone, | London so fair", *The Builders* 1–2 (*Ricks* 141). **done to others' harm**: *Purg.* XVII 123: "il male altrui impronti" [seeks another's hurt].

TSE scored this line in the copy of the *Purgatorio* given to him by his mother (Iman Javadi, personal communication).

II 88, 90 **things ill done and done ··· fools' approval stings:** Lionel Johnson: "miserable things | Done long ago, not done with: the live stings | Left by old joys, follies", *Experience* (*Ricks 1998*). TSE: "In a verse or a line here or there of Lionel Johnson, there is a ring of the spoken voice", *The Last Twenty-Five Years of English Poetry* (1940). (For Lionel Johnson, see headnote to *Five-Finger Exercises* II. *Lines to a Yorkshire Terrier*.)

II 89 **which once you took for:** *Pedro and Segovia*: "the brilliancy of her wit was impertinence and what once she took for modesty, was sheepishness", *Lady's Magazine* 1780. **took for:** to Hayward, 7 Sept 1942, in reply to his suggested emendation of the original reading: "*Felt* is not strong enough: I mean not simply something not questioned, but something consciously approved."

II 90 **fools' approval stings:** Dr. Johnson: "Grief aids disease, remember'd folly stings", *The Vanity of Human Wishes* 117 (*Grover Smith 1950* 420). **honour stains:** Pope: "Or stain her Honour, or her new Brocade", *The Rape of the Lock* II 107.

II 92 **that refining fire:** *Purg.* XXVI 148 (Arnaut): "Poi s'ascose nel foco che gli affina" [Then he hid him in the fire which refines them]. TSE to Hayward, 27 Aug 1942: "the reference to swimming in fire which you will remember at the end of Purgatorio 26 where the poets are found. The active co-operation is, I think, sound theology and is certainly sound Dante, because the people who talk to him at that point are represented as not wanting to waste time in conversation but wishing to dive back into the fire to accomplish their expiation." (See note to title *Ara Vos Prec* in headnote to "*Poems* (1920)", 7. PUBLICATION OF *ARA VOS PREC*.) Malachi 3: 2: "But who may abide the day of his coming ··· for he is like a refiner's fire" (*Cook*); famously set within Handel's *Messiah*.

II 92–93 **fire | Where you must move in measure, like a dancer:** F. E. Brightman, introduction to his 1903 edition of Lancelot Andrewes's *Preces Privatæ*: "His single thoughts are no doubt often suggested by the words he borrows, but the thoughts are made his own, and the constructive force, the fire that fuses them, is his own ··· The prayers are arranged, not merely in paragraphs, but in lines advanced and recessed, so as in a measure to mark the inner structure and the steps and stages of the movement." TSE recommended the edition and quoted "this excellent piece of criticism" in *Lancelot Andrewes* (1926); see note to *Ash-Wednesday* III 19 ("stops and steps of the mind over the third stair"). "The differences between a great dancer and a merely competent dancer is in the vital flame, that impersonal, and, if you like, inhuman force which transpires between each of the great dancer's movements", *Four Elizabethan Dramatists* (1924). See IV 13–14, "only suspire | Consumed by either fire or fire", and note. "deceptive cadences | Wherewith the common measure is refined", *To Walter de la Mare* 28–29. *The Burnt Dancer* (title; *March Hare* Notebook). Shelley: "feet which kissed | The dancing foam ··· And her feet, ever to the ceaseless song | Of leaves ··· moved in a measure new", *The Triumph of Life* 370–71, 375–77 (with "faded" 248, TSE: II 96). TSE: "When I read poetry I put myself into a kind of trance and move in rhythm to the rhythm of the piece in question", *T. S. Eliot Answers Questions* (1949).

II 93 **move in measure, like a dancer:** Sir John Davies: "*Time the measure of all moving is*; | And Dauncing is a moving all in measure", *Orchestra* st. 23 (*Schmidt 2007*). For Sir John Davies see note to *East Coker* I 25–45. Johnson's Dictionary "Dance": "To move in measure". TSE: "the dance would be brought to life in all its complexity ··· each having its proper part in the measure", *The Greater Trumps* by Charles Williams (1954), jacket material. **like a dancer:** to Hayward, 27 Aug 1942 (enclosing *ts9b*): "I ··· rather like the suggestion of the new line which carries some reminder of a line, I think it is about Mark Antony." *Antony and Cleopatra* III xi: "he at Philippi kept | His sword e'en like a dancer": used not about Antony but by him of Octavius (*Composition FQ* 31).

II 94 **The day was breaking. In the disfigured street:** Tennyson: "the long unlovely street ··· On the bald street breaks the blank day", the close of *In Memoriam* VII, quoted in full by TSE, *In Memoriam* (1936): "This is great poetry, economical of words, a universal emotion related to a particular place."

II 94–95 **The day was breaking ··· He left me, with a kind of valediction:** *Purg.* XVI 142–45 (Marco Lombardo): "'Vedi l'albòr, che per lo fummo raia, | già biancheggiare, e me convien partirmi, | l'angelo è ivi, prima ch'io gli appaia.' | Così tornò, e più non volle udirmi" ["See the light, that beams through the smoke, now waxing bright; the angel is there, and it behoves me to depart ere I am seen of him." So turned he back and no more would hear me], Iman Javadi, personal communication. For "turned away" and "turned back", see note to II 67–96, *first venture in verse* [22].

II 95 *variant* **salutation:** see note to unadopted title to *Ash-Wednesday* II.

II 96 **faded on the blowing of the horn:** *Hamlet* I i, on the disappearance of the Ghost: "It faded on the crowing of the cock." *Hayward*: "The blowing of the horn here suggests, with all the associations of the horn's melancholy and stirring notes ('Dieu, comme le son du cor est triste') the sounding of the 'All Clear' siren after the end of an air-raid." Alfred de Vigny, "Dieu! que le son du Cor est triste au fond des bois!" [God! how sad the Horn's sound is in the depth of the woods!], *Le Cor* [*The Horn*], closing line. Hawthorne: "The horn sounded at daybreak ··· as if ··· the trump of doom", *The Blithedale Romance* ch. VI.

III

III 1 **There are three conditions:** Henry Clarke Warren's tr. of the *Anguttara-Nikaya*: "There are three conditions, O priests, under which deeds are produced. And what are the three? Covetousness is a condition under which deeds are produced; hatred is a condition under which deeds are produced; infatuation is a condition under which deeds are produced", *Buddhism in Translations* (1896) 215–16 (*Howarth* 372).

III 1–2 **There are three conditions ··· flourish in the same hedgerow:** sonnet attrib. Sir Walter Raleigh: "Three things there be that prosper up apace | And flourish, while they grow asunder far" (K. Narayana Chandran, *N&Q* Dec 2008). TSE: "Since the time of Rousseau, men's attitude toward life has vacillated between two points of view which are really complementary and which flourish in the same soil", *An American Critic* (1916).

III 1–7 **There are three conditions ··· indifference ··· the live and the dead nettle:** to Hayward, 27 Aug 1942, on his suggested emendation "The live nettle and the dead": "I cannot fall in with your suggestion of an inversion of 'dead nettle'. You know as well as I do that the dead nettle is the family of flowering plant of which the White Archangel is one of the commonest and closely resembles the stinging nettle and is found in its company. If I wrote 'the live nettle and the dead' it would tend to suggest a dead stinging nettle instead of a quite different plant, so I don't see that anything can be done about that." *Composition FQ* 200, citing this letter: "The image is very apt, when explained: indifference, that neither stings nor bears a flower." But this is qualified by Gardner in a footnote: "Mrs. Ridler pointed out to me that Eliot has confused two plants of the same family: White Deadnettle (*Lamium album*) and Yellow Archangel (*Galeobdolon luteum*). I suppose he would have rejected the suggestion of a hyphen in 'dead-nettle' on the same grounds as he rejected Hayward's suggestion of 'down-cast'" (see note to II 36–37).

TSE to Desmond MacCarthy, 28 Dec 1942:

> In the "nettle" passage, you put your finger on a bit which I was myself dissatisfied with: I do not think that the operation has been completed, and your difficulty confirms my suspicion. I do not mean that Attachment resembles Indifference; but that Attachment *can* resemble Detachment, and that Detachment *can* be mistaken for Indifference. You will not agree about the first: but surely, on a more familiar plane, a selfish love of a person and an unselfish love of a person can easily be mistaken for each other, or at least the first can be mistaken for the second? But the image of the nettle is not happy, because it assumes the existence of a third kind of plant, which does not exist, which might be mistaken for both. By "dead nettle", by the way, I do not mean a nettle which has died, but the "dead nettle", the unstinging flowering plant which is found together with the stinging nettle, and belongs, I believe, to another species or genus.

In *Noctes Binanianæ*: "When the flowering nettle's in blossom", *How to Pick a Possum* 1.

III 1–11 **There are three conditions ··· growing between them, indifference ··· action**: Clough: "There are two different kinds ··· I do not wish to be moved, but growing where I was growing, | There more truly to grow, to live where as yet I had languished ··· action | Is a most dangerous thing", *Amours de Voyage* II xi (*Murray*).

III 3 **Attachment to self and to things and to persons**: St. John of the Cross:

> These habitual imperfections are, for example, a common custom of much speaking, or some attachment which we never wish entirely to conquer—such as that to a person, a garment, a book, a cell, a particular kind of food, tittle-tattle, fancies for tasting, knowing or hearing certain things, and suchlike. Any one of these imperfections, if the soul has become attached and habituated to it, is of as great harm to its growth and progress in virtue as though it were to fall daily into many other imperfections and casual venial sins which proceed not from a common indulgence in any common and harmful attachment, and will not hinder it so much as when it has attachment to anything. For while it has this there is no possibility that it will make progress in perfection, even though the imperfection be extremely small. And thus the soul that has attachment to anything, however much virtue it possess, will not attain to the liberty of Divine union.
>
> *Ascent of Mount Carmel* I xi 4

TSE scored the entire passage in his copy. See his letter to Geoffrey Faber

[18 Sept 1927] quoted in note to *The Dry Salvages* II 42–47. "It seems to me that all of us, so far as we attach ourselves to created objects and surrender our wills to temporal ends, are eaten by the same worm", *Nightwood* by Djuna Barnes, Preface (1937).

III 3–12 **Attachment to self and to things ··· The live and the dead ··· attachment ··· action ··· action:** "To live as if tomorrow might bring any worldly disaster, or illness or death, and yet live serenely, without attachment to material objects, and giving to human beings that love which is proper after the love of God; that is hard work. And if we repudiate non-Christian philosophies of life in the name of Christianity, then we have a great responsibility to repudiate them in that name alone, and not in the name of worldly attachments. And worldly attachments may be just as much to prejudices and mental habits, as to possessions. This is one side of the Christian attitude. The other is that of action", *The Christian in the Modern World* (1935). For Arnold's words "attachment to so many beaten causes", see note to III 36–45. **detachment | From self and from things and from persons ··· not less of love but expanding | Of love beyond desire ··· love of a country | Begins as attachment to our own field of action:** Paul Elmer More: "The true aim of the philosopher is not morality ··· but isolation and inattachment ··· From the individual we extend this love to our neighbors, from them to the world at large in ever widening circles ··· beyond this ··· we strive to loose ourselves from all attachment whatsoever", *The Great Refusal* 7–8. For More, see note to II 67–71. **detachment ··· action ··· action:** "The detached observer, by the way, is likely to be anything but a dispassionate observer; he probably *suffers* more acutely than the various apostles of immediate action", *The Lion and the Fox* (1937).

III 4 **persons:** as distinct from "people"; on ambition: "For most people, in most occupations, it is a very good thing ··· so long as it does not lead them to sacrifice persons and spiritual values", *On Poetry* (1947) 8. **indifference:** "few men have the energy to follow the middle way in government ··· there is only extremity or apathy: dictatorship or communism, with enthusiasm or with indifference", *John Bramhall* (1927). "We are really, you see, up against the very difficult problem of the *spiritual* and the *temporal* ··· The danger, for those who start from the spiritual end, is Indifferentism; neglect the affairs of the world and save as many souls out of the wreckage as possible", *A Commentary* in *Criterion* Jan 1935. OED "indifferentism" b: "*esp.* The principle that differences of religious belief are of no importance" (last citation from 1856).

III 4–6 **growing between them, indifference ··· life | Being between two lives:** More: "we who walk in the shadow of doubt, we know not which is the sadder and which is the wiser, the fortitude and disdain of the stoic who contemns pleasure and pain alike, or the anguish and humiliation of the monk who deliberately loses his life to gain life. Between the two lies the world of indifference", *The Great Refusal* 75. See note to II 69, 72.

III 5–6 **as death resembles life, | Being between two lives:** "Swinging from life to death | Bleeding between two lives", *Song* ("The golden foot I may not kiss or clutch") 4–5. "throbbing between two lives", *The Waste Land* [III] 218. "to keep two lives together", *A Note on War Poetry* 13 *variant.*

III 6, 8–9 **two lives ··· not less of love but expanding | Of love:** Donne: "Our two soules ··· endure not yet | A breach, but an expansion", *A Valediction Forbidding Mourning* 21–23.

III 9 **love beyond desire**: "Our obligation, certainly, is to *love*—to love *without desire* (for the latter is to seek oneself in the beloved object, see St. John of the Cross quoted above)—or I might say to love beyond desire—for such love is not effected by the mere quenching of desire. *The soul, by resigning itself to the divine light, that is, by removing every spot and stain of the creature, which is to keep the will perfectly united to the will of God—for to love Him is to labour to detach ourselves from, and to divest ourselves of, everything which is not God's for God's sake—becomes immediately enlightened by, and transformed in, God*", end of *Notes on the Way* in *Time & Tide* 19 Jan 1935. The closing sentence, from *Ascent of Mount Carmel* (tr. David Lewis), II v, is quoted from *The Mystical Doctrine of St. John of the Cross* (1934), the edition TSE reviewed in the *Criterion* July 1934. The previous passage referred to, from ch. vii, reads: "*this is not that other course which is nothing but to seek oneself in God, which is the very opposite of love*", and appears in the abridgment under the heading "Detachment and Freedom are Necessary".

III 9–10 **liberation | From the future as well as the past**: "And right action is freedom | From past and future also", *The Dry Salvages* V 41–42. The earliest outline of *The Dry Salvages* had "Liberation from the past is liberation from the future" (*msA* fol. 65).

III 10–11 **love of a country | Begins as attachment to our own field of action**: Burke: "To be attached to the subdivision, to love the little platoon we belong to in society, is the first principle ··· of public affections. It is the first link in the series by which we proceed towards a love to our country, and to mankind", *Reflections on the Revolution in France* (1790) 68–69. TSE to Willard Thorp, 1937: "It is difficult anyway to be sure except when two people have a common knowledge of one field of political action." To Hayward, 4 Aug 1940: "So much for local patriotism." At the end of the war: "the duty to 'take action' ··· will vary according to the position, the influence, the intelligence and the knowledge of the individual Christian; but ··· it is the duty of the individual to do what he can in his own sphere of action", *Full Employment and the Responsibility of Christians* (1945).

III 13 **indifferent:** pronounced as four full syllables in TSE's recording of 1946–47.

III 13–14 **History may be servitude, | History may be freedom:** Keynes: "The policy of reducing Germany to servitude for a generation ··· should be abhorrent ··· In the great events of man's history ··· Justice is not so simple", *The Economic Consequences of the Peace* ch. V. TSE: "Assuming that the individual has political and economic freedom, is that enough to guarantee his liberty? ··· How easy it is to see the servitude of others, their obedience to prejudice ··· and how difficult to recognize and face our own!" *Notes on the Way* in *Time & Tide* 19 Jan 1935. **History ··· History**: the word pronounced as three full syllables in TSE's recording of 1946–47. **servitude ··· freedom**: "There is all the difference in the world between imitation and influence. Imitation is servitude; influence can mean liberation", *Royal Academy Speech* (1960).

III 15 **with the self which, as it could, loved them**: Bradley: "the self which, as identified ··· the self which", *Ethical Studies* Essay VII ("Selfishness and

Self-Sacrifice"). **the self which, as**: to Stephen Spender, 9 May 1935: "you have to give yourself up, and then recover yourself, and the third movement is having something to say, before you have wholly forgotten both surrender and recovery. Of course the self recovered is never the same as the self before it was given".

III 17–19 **Sin is Behovely · · · shall be well**: the words of Jesus, in a vision, to Juliana of Norwich, who adds: "In this naked word sin, our Lord brought to my mind generally all that is not good; and the shameful despite, and the uttermost tribulation that he bare for us in this life, and his dying, and all his pains and passion", *XVI Revelations of Divine Love* XIII ch. 27. TSE to Hayward, 2 Sept 1942: "I forgot in my previous letter to give an explanation which bears on your query of *behovely.* This line and the two which follow and which occur twice later constitute a quotation from Juliana of Norwich. The beautiful line the presence of which puzzles you toward the end of page 11 comes out of *The Cloud of Unknowing* ["the drawing of this Love and the voice of this Calling", V 25]. My purpose was this: there is so much 17th century in the poem that I was afraid of a certain romantic Bonnie Dundee period effect and I wanted to check this and at the same time give greater historical depth to the poem by allusions to the other great period, i.e. the 14th century. Juliana and *The Cloud of Unknowing* represent pretty well the two mystical extremes or, one might say, the male and female of this literature. I might have dragged in Walter Hilton and Richard Rolle, I daresay, but for one thing I don't know them so well and for another I think that would be overdoing it. Does it seem to you possible that the passages in question ought to be put in inverted commas?" (For *Bonnie Dundee* see note to III 33 and the headnote to *Whan cam ye fra the Kirk?* in "Other Verses".) For the 14th and 17th centuries, see headnote 4. AFTER PUBLICATION.) To Hayward, 7 Sept 1942: "I'm afraid I don't like capitalising the quotes. Too much like headlines: slightly comic. I thought better of restoring the spelling; but I read the texts in modern versions, and the London Library seems to possess *no* texts with the xiii [*margin*: ? xiv] century spelling · · · I now incline to put between guillemets 'Sin is behovely,' etc. on its first appearance, but *not* the two repetitions. This means putting 'With the drawing of this love . . .' in quotes also. [*added*: Or not?]" 9 Sept: "I accept the more limited capitalisation." Hayward to TSE, 21 Sept 1942 (after *ts13*):

> There is no one I can send to the University Library and I can only get a Chairman [pilot for his wheelchair] now after sunset, otherwise I should have investigated for you the original spelling and capitalization of the texts of Juliana and William Rolle. I still hope to be able to do this, if only to satisfy my own curiosity · · · Meanwhile the good Miss Flack has procured · · · the best edition of Juliana's *Revelations* · · · The Sloane MS. follows almost exactly the only other extant · · · and both preserve pretty well the 14th cent. English of the lost prototype. What may be of interest to you is the reproduction, given by the editor in a footnote, of the exact form (from the Sloane MS.) of the passage you quote. *Viz.*—
>
> "Synne is behovabil, but al shal be wel & al shal be wel
> & al manner of thyng shal be wele."
>
> · · · I am curious to know where you got the reading "behovely".

TSE explained to Desmond MacCarthy, 28 Dec 1942, that his source was "Juliana of Norwich, *Revelations*, Cressy's edition, which is the only one I know or have access to, and 'behovely' there means 'unescapeable', inevitable, and not the modern 'useful'. I hesitated over putting the whole sentence into quotation marks; John Hayward persuaded me to introduce the capital B instead, as in the later quotation from the *Cloud of Unknowing* ('With the Drawing of this love'). My motive for forcing these XIV century references was to give greater historical depth and avoid the sentimentality which concentration on the XVII might arouse (for a somewhat similar reason, the crossing of Thomas Browne with Nijinsky). This is an explanation, *not* a defence." (For Browne and Nijinsky, see note to III 35–36.) To Henry Eliot, 8 Jan 1943: "After much thought and discussion, I put in the capitals instead of quotation marks, which one critic thought would be more irritating to the reader." To Henry Eliot, 25 Mar 1943: "'Behovely', by the way, means *inevitable*, *unescapable*. This is the XIV century use; later it came to mean 'useful'. The three lines are quoted from the Revelations of Juliana of Norwich, Cressy's edition; the copy which I have and which I bought in London, was published in St. Louis, Mo." (1920, reprinting the original ed. of 1670). In 1373, the anchoret and mystic, then aged about 30, "received 16 'shewings' of the Passion in the form of words spoken to her from the Cross. In her 13th revelation she quotes the mystical voice reassuring her about the nature of sin" (*Hayward*).

TSE emphasised "the probable importance of the mystics of the fourteenth century—of Richard Rolle and Julian of Norwich for instance—as late as the time of Lancelot Andrewes and George Herbert", *Paul Elmer More* (1937). "no one could confuse the mysticism of Spain with that of Germany, or the mysticism of the twelfth and thirteenth centuries ··· with that of the seventeenth", *Letter to Dr. Oldham from T. S. Eliot* (1941), a paper for The Moot. "Some have accused the Reformed Church of England of having been, even at its best, of a golden mediocrity now somewhat tarnished: certainly it is a long way from Juliana of Norwich to George Herbert", *Reunion by Destruction* (1943) 19 (earlier in the pamphlet: "It behoves us to come to a judgment upon the merits of the Scheme for South India"). **sin is Behovely**: OED "behovely": "Of use; useful, profitable; needful, necessary", *Obs.* except *arch.*, with these lines as the first citation since Gower in 1393. Pronounced *behoovely* in TSE's recording of 1946–47. TSE to J. H. Oldham, 14 Aug 1942, on the bombing of German towns: "The difficult problem to present in short is that of what one might call the necessity of sin ··· we have got into the position—indeed, that humanity is chronically more or less deeply in the position—in which it is necessary to do what is wrong ··· consent to the action and at the same time feel the necessity for penitence." On "just wars": "it is almost impossible to say anything about the subject without being misunderstood by one or both parties of *simplifiers*. (Yet Æschylus, at least, understood that it may be a man's duty to commit a crime, and to accomplish his expiation for it.) The whole notion of justice is travestied when we draw too sharp a distinction between war and peace", *A Commentary* in *Criterion* July 1936. **Behovely**: alongside the Gide/Bosco tr., "ce qui convient, car", TSE wrote: "fatale / inévitable", and underlining "car", he wrote "mais". For "it behoves him" in St. John of the Cross, see note to *Ash-Wednesday* II 1.

III 18 **All shall be well**: "All will be well" was a habitual phrase of Winston Churchill's, occurring dozens of times in his wartime speeches. Hayward to TSE, 20 June

1940: "I don't mean that I'm not hopeful, as Mr Churchill is, that all will be well ··· *East Coker* says this and much more far better than I can." In his "Give us the tools" broadcast of 9 Feb 1941, Churchill spoke of receiving from President Roosevelt a copy of Longfellow's poem *Thou, too, sail on, O Ship of State!* and declared that his reply was "Put your confidence in us. Give us your faith and your blessing, and under Providence, all will be well." TSE to Christina Morley, 27 July 1942: "I am still pottering with *Little Gidding*, and think that when I have got Part II right all will be well, though not very well."

III 20, 23–24 **this place ··· peculiar genius ··· a common genius:** OED "genius" 3c: "Of a language, law, or institution: Prevailing character or spirit"; d: "With reference to a place: The body of associations connected with, or inspirations that may be derived from it".

III 20–25 **I think, again, of this place, | And of people, not wholly commendable ··· But some of peculiar genius ··· United:** "A wholly Christian society ··· communal ··· a community of men and women, not individually better than they are now, except for the capital difference of holding the Christian faith ··· the religious life ··· given its due place", *The Idea of a Christian Society* 60. **not wholly commendable:** Bernard Blackstone's doctoral dissertation, for which TSE acted as a "referee", revealed the "singularly unpleasant" behaviour of John Ferrar's wife, Bathsheba (see Blackstone's *Discord at Little Gidding* in *TLS* 1 Aug 1936). **commendable:** *Hamlet* I ii: "'Tis sweet and commendable in your nature, Hamlet" (*Blamires* 166). (But in TSE's recording of 1946–47 pronounced *commèndable*, not as Shakespeare's *còm'ndable*.) Underlining the Gide/Bosco tr. "peu louables", TSE wrote: "too strong".

III 22 **kin or kindness:** *Hamlet* I ii: "A little more than kin, and less than kind", (*Blamires* 166).

III 26 **king at nightfall:** when Charles I ("a broken king", I 26) reached Little Gidding in secret in May 1646, it was "the very last place where this most unfortunate Prince was in the hands of those whom he might safely trust" (P. Peckard, *Memoirs of the Life of Mr. Nicholas Ferrar*, 1790, 232–33). TSE: "Only at nightfall ··· a broken Coriolanus", *The Waste Land* [V] 415–16. TSE informed Pound in a letter of 19 Feb 1937 that the "day you wrote on was properly speaking CHARLES KING & MARTYR"—and used the phrase to date letters in 1930, 1939 and 1940. In a ms, Vivien Eliot wrote: "there is no Jacobite like your Bostonian", and TSE added: "Descendants of complacent rebels, bourgeois revolutionists against taxations, they mourn annually for the martyred Charles" (misc. c. 624 fol. 112). *Walter Graeme Eliot* 12: "Being members of the Established Church of England at the period of Cromwell's accession to power, and when Roundhead intolerance had become as oppressive as had previously been the Romish influence, it would not be surprising if the Eliots had found emigration ··· necessary."

III 27–29 **three men, and more ··· here and abroad:** *Hayward*: "Charles I, Archbishop Laud, and the Earl of Strafford, amongst other Royalists condemned to execution by Cromwell's party during the Civil War." *Grover Smith* 289: "He remembers Ferrar, King Charles here and in his death, Laud, Strafford, and even perhaps Sir John Eliot, who was imprisoned before the Civil War for contumacy of the King; he remembers others such as Crashaw, who died abroad."

III 30–38, 44 **one who died blind and quiet ··· old factions ··· old policies ··· an**

antique drum · · · defeated: "Milton in old age, blind and poor, having given his best years to a cause which was partly defeated and partly out of date", *"The Voice of His Time"* (1942; this passage in ts only, Texas). *Hayward* (of Milton): "'Hee dy'd', according to his nephew, John Phillips, 'in a fitt of the Gout, with so little pain or Emotion, that the time of his expiring was not perceiv'd by those in the room. And though hee had bin long troubl'd with that disease · · · yet was hee not ever observ'd to be very impatient.'" (The author is now thought to be Cyriack Skinner.)

III 33–34 **not · · · Nor**: to John Hayward, 31 May 1943, on redrafting a lecture: "I have not chosen good illustrations, nor have I made their pertinence clear, or just on what grounds I was criticising them (this seems to me a sentence in which the construction *not . . . nor* is permissible)."

III 33–38 **to ring the bell backward · · · We cannot revive old factions · · · an antique drum**: OED: "to ring bells backward: to ring them beginning with the bass bell, in order to give alarm of fire or invasion, or express dismay" (from *c.* 1500). (Not possible with a single bell: see *Composition FQ* 204–205.) Walter Scott: "Dundee he is mounted, he rides up the street, | The bells are rung backward, the drums they are beat", *Bonny Dundee* II. For the Jacobite Viscount Dundee, see *Clerihews IV*. (Where III 33–34 were quoted in *G. Jones* (144), TSE wrote "Cf. *Bonnie Dundee*".) To Henry Eliot, 25 Mar 1943: "'ring the bells backward' refers to *Bonnie Dundee* and incidentally but not intentionally *Bonnie Dundee* suggests the parody of it at the end of *Alice Through the Looking-Glass*, which takes one back to the deliberate reminder of *Alice in Wonderland* at the beginning of *Burnt Norton*—where, also, I had been affected, I think, by Kipling's *They.*" (*Through the Looking-Glass* ch. IX: "To the Looking-Glass world it was Alice that said, | 'I've a sceptre in hand, I've a crown on my head'".) Charles Lamb to George Dyer, 20 Dec 1830, on arson: "the great fire was blazing last night · · · a bonfire visible to London, alarming her guilty towers, and shaking the monument · · · Alas! can we ring the bells backward? Can we unlearn the arts that pretend to civilize, and then burn the world? There is a march of science; but who shall beat the drums for its retreat?" Beaumont and Fletcher: "like bells rung backwards, | Nothing but noise and giddiness", *Wit without Money* IV i. Marianne Moore: "If in Ireland | they play the harp backward at need", *Spenser's Ireland* in *What Are Years* (1941).

III 35 **summon the spectre of a Rose**: when Pierre Leyris, in an introductory note to his translation of *Little Gidding*, associated this passage with the Wars of the Roses, TSE wrote in the margin: "He seems to have missed the Rose of Charles KM" (King and Martyr). **Rose**: To Bonamy Dobrée, 6 Aug 1941: "There are really three roses in the set of poems: the sensuous rose, the socio-political Rose (always appearing with a capital letter) and the spiritual rose: and the three have got to be in some way identified as one."

III 35–36 **summon the spectre of a Rose · · · old factions**: Hayward to TSE, 9 Nov 1940: "MADAME RAMBERT · · · is also in these parts, persuading the youth of East Anglia to put on tights and chase the Spectre of the Rose." Hayward, 17 Feb 1941: "cf. Sir Th. Browne · · · 'nor in ye bed of Cleopatra raise up the ghost of a rose'." (Browne: "Nor will the sweetest delight of Gardens afford much comfort in sleep; wherein the dulnesse of that sense shakes hands with delectable odours; and though in the Bed of *Cleopatra*, can hardly with any delight raise up the ghost of a Rose", *Garden of Cyrus* antepenultimate paragraph). Hayward again, 1 Aug: "I can't resist expressing a regret that, having quoted so far, you did'nt follow Sir T. B. and put 'raise up the ghost of a rose'. I do wish you would consider making this alteration. It is an exquisite evocation." TSE, 5 Aug, referring instead to *Le Spectre de la Rose*, which he had seen Nijinsky dance: "Damn Sir T. Browne, a writer I never got much kick from: I suppose it *is* a reminiscence, though I was thinking of the Ballet and perhaps it would be better to go all out for the quotation, as the reference back to the Royal Rose [*The Dry Salvages* III 3] must be retained because of the two or three other rose connotations." To Bonamy Dobrée, 6 Aug: "John had called my attention to the Browne pinch, of which I had been cheerfully unconscious: I am now thinking that perhaps I had better go all out and take Sir Thomas's phrase directly—'raise up' instead of 'summon'." (For TSE in 1925 to Herbert Read, "does it raise the spectre of a Gunpowder Plot?", see note to the epigraph to *The Hollow Men.*) Sceptical of "any attempt in prose that appears to strive toward the condition of 'poetry'", TSE associated Browne with Raleigh and Pater: "I only wish to take the precaution of looking upon the Monna Lisas of prose, the drums and tramplings of three conquests, the eloquent just and mightie deaths [*Urn Burial* ch. V], with a suspicious and interrogating eye, and making quite certain what, if any, solid and genuine bit of life they have pounced upon and raised to the dignity of poetry", *Prose and Verse* (1921).

III 36–45 **We cannot revive old factions · · · taken from the defeated | What they had to leave us**: Arnold: "our sentiment for beauty and sweetness, our sentiment against hideousness and rawness, has been at the bottom of our attachment to so many beaten causes, of our opposition to so many triumphant movements. And the sentiment is true, and has never been wholly defeated, and has shown its power even in its defeat. We have not won our political battles, we have not carried our main points, we have not stopped our adversaries' advance, we have not marched victoriously with the modern world; but we have told silently upon the mind of the country, we have prepared currents of feeling which sap our adversaries' position when it seems gained, we have kept up our own communications with the future", *Culture and Anarchy* (1869) I; quoted by TSE as "eloquent of the importance which Arnold has for the present time", *A Commentary* in *Criterion* Jan 1925. (See *Defence of the Islands* [15–22].) Arnold on Oxford: "Beautiful city! · · · Home of lost causes, and forsaken beliefs, and unpopular names, and impossible loyalties", *Essays in Criticism* First Series (1865). TSE: "Bolingbroke would stand higher with posterity and deserve far more of his country had he been prepared to stick to a lost cause", *Augustan Age Tories* (1928). "I have myself no great taste for lost causes. I mean that if I believe in a cause I find it impossible to believe that the cause is lost. If it really appears to me to be lost, then I must stop and examine, whether I have really cared purely for its essence, or whether I have attached myself as much to an impermanent form", *A Commentary* in *Criterion* July 1932. "I think that the phrase 'lost cause' is itself wrong. There are such things as dead issues. But there is no such thing as a lost, or as a securely gained cause", *Christ Church, Oxford*, Speech (1948). **cannot revive**: on Cecil Sharp's hope for a native ballet: "you cannot *revive* a ritual without reviving a faith. You can *continue* a ritual after the faith is dead—that is not a conscious, 'pretty' piece of archæology—but you cannot *revive* it", *The Ballet* (1925). "I am not, certainly, in favour of attempting to revive a language which is nearly dead. By the time that it is preserved only among a few country peasantry, the culture which it represents is unlikely to be more than a mutilated relic", *Cultural Diversity and European Unity* (1945); see note to II 63, 65–66.

III 38 **antique:** pronounced *an-teek* by TSE in his recording of 1946–47 (as opposed to the Elizabethan *antic*).

III 40–41 **opposed | Accept:** of A. R. Orage's mysticism: "while it was something that I think should be opposed if he were still alive, it is something that I think we should, in a fashion, accept now that he is dead", *A Commentary* in *Criterion* Jan 1935.

III 41 **the constitution of silence:** Virginia Woolf: "To combine new words with old is fatal to the constitution of a sentence", *Craftsmanship* (1937; see note to V 4–11, and note to *East Coker* I 2–4).

III 42^43 *variant* **The victory no longer a victory:** "The dangerous militarism of the present time is that which believes, either from natural 'aggressive instinct' or from sheer exhaustion of patience, that communism can be put an end to by a victorious war against Russia (still, probably, cherishing a long out-of-date notion of 'victory')", *"Education for Peace"* by Herbert Read, reader's report, Sept 1948.

III 44 **the defeated:** Auden: "History to the defeated | May say Alas but cannot help nor pardon", closing lines of *Spain.* (Auden's poem of 1937 was the printers' model for the *Four Quartets* pamphlets.)

III 46 **perfected:** pronounced with stress on the second syllable in TSE's recording of 1946–47 (as opposed to the Elizabethan *pèrfected*, which TSE used at the end of his recording in 1950 of *The Development of Shakespeare's Verse*).

III 46–50 *3rd draft* [1–2] **The damaged crown on the thornbush | The Duke with his iron shutters:** Richard III and Duke of Wellington. *Composition FQ* 209–10: "The chroniclers report that the crown which Richard III wore on the battle field at Bosworth was found with the spoil of battle by Lord Stanley, who crowned the victor, Henry Tudor, there and then. The legend that the crown was found hanging in a thornbush arose in the sixteenth century. In a television programme on Eliot his friend Miss Hope Mirrlees reported that he always wore a white rose on the anniversary of Bosworth "'in memory of 'the last English king' ··· I suppose Eliot thought of Bosworth as 'the end of the Middle Ages' and of Richard as representing an old order that was passing. In the same way, Wellington, with the windows of Apsley House twice broken by the London mob, which regarded him as the chief opponent of the Reform Bill, represented pre-industrial England." For TSE on how his America "ended in 1829", see headnote to *The Dry Salvages*, 2. "THE RIVER IS WITHIN US, THE SEA IS ALL ABOUT US".

III 49 **purification of the motive:** "About Donne there hangs the shadow of the impure motive", *Lancelot Andrewes* (1926). To George Hoellering, 30 Oct 1944, on a speech added to *Murder in the Cathedral* for the film version: "I have endeavoured to give it a flavour of pride and arrogance and impurity of motive" ("To purify the dialect ··· motives late revealed", II 74, 87). The speech begins

"My Lord the King, I am guilty of no treason", *The Film of "Murder in the Cathedral"* (1952) 25 (Iman Javadi, personal communication).

III 50 **In the ground of our beseeching:** Juliana of Norwich: "in the sweet words where he saith full merrily, 'I am ground of thy beseeching.' For truly, I saw and understood in our Lords meaning, that he shewed it", final paragraph of the last of her *Revelations* (see IV 8 and note).

after III 50, *msA* [1–4] **Soul of Christ ··· incinerate them:** adapted from the first four lines of the prayer *Anima Christi sanctifica me* (*Composition FQ* 69). See Textual History.

IV

To the Rev. Arthur MacGillivray, 4 Feb 1946: "I did not know that my Pentecost poem had been reprinted in the *New York Times Book Review* ··· This section of *Little Gidding* certainly stands more by itself than any other section of the poem". Selecting a reading for broadcast: "I choose the fourth section out of *Little Gidding* as the one I think the best", *Chicago Round Table* (1950).

Acts 2: 1–6: "And when the day of Pentecost was fully come, they were all with one accord in one place. And suddenly there came a sound from heaven as of a rushing mighty wind, and it filled all the house where they were sitting. And there appeared unto them cloven tongues like as of fire, and it sat upon each of them. And they were all filled with the Holy Ghost, and began to speak with other tongues, as the Spirit gave them utterance ··· Now when this was noised abroad, the multitude came together, and were confounded, because that every man heard them speak in his own language."

IV *msA draft* [2] **crepitative:** OED "crepitation" 1: "A crackling noise; crackling."

IV *msA draft* [5–7] **expectation, doubt, despair ··· never resting feet ··· aspirations:** Henry James Pye, parodying Gray's *Ode on a Distant Prospect of Eton College*: "Ambition ··· And false report that glides along | With never-resting feet", *Ode on Ranelagh* 71, 79–80.

IV *msA draft* [6, 8] **never resting feet ··· watery:** "through the water ··· shine the unoffending feet", *Mr. Eliot's Sunday Morning Service* 13–14.

IV *msA draft* [12] **votary of Soledos:** *Composition FQ* 213: "It may be that Eliot who did not know Spanish wrote 'Soledos' for '*Soledad*', solitude." Gongora: "Hangs as votive rod | In the dank temple of the ocean god", *Las Soledades* (1612–13) I 464–65, tr. Edward Meryon Wilson as *The Solitudes of Don Luis de Gongora* (1931). (*A Fragment from the Solitudes* appeared in the *Criterion* in July 1930.) A note to the second of the *Soledades* (that "of the Shores") reads: "The daughters might be either land or sea nymphs, votaries of Diana or Tethys."

IV *msA draft* [12] *variant* **thanatos:** OED: "death-instinct", with first citation (referring to Freud) from 1935. OED does not record TSE's first thought, "athanatos" [immortal].

IV *msA revised draft* [4–5] **pay the dues ··· beneath the line:** OED "line" *n.*[2] 17d: "In phrases indicating the boundary between a debit and a credit in one's account" (the first citation, from 1940, has "below the line" in quotation marks).

IV *three-stanza ts drafts* [8] *variant* **Till death shall bring the audit in:** MacNeice:

"To-night we sleep | On the banks of the Rubicon—the die is cast; | There will be time to audit | The accounts later", *Autumn Journal* xxiv.

IV *three-stanza ts drafts* [10, 12–14] ***Unprofitable Sin* ··· The assets that we think to win | By *Prudence*, and by *Worldly Cares* | Figure as gilt-edged stocks and shares:** Milton: "with Gaine, Pride and Ambition ··· unprofitable Sin of Curiosity", *Letter to a Friend* (1633). TSE: "It reads like the prospectus for a company flotation: and indeed that is what the South India Church, in its initial stages, is—a holding company, framed to control the shares in three distinct operating companies", *Reunion by Destruction* (1943) 12.

IV 1 **The dove descending:** to Hayward, 5 Aug 1941: "I am especially puzzled about Part IV. It may be that the attempt to give a XVII century flavour is a mistake (having previously done it successfully) but I feel that some explicit attack on the Descent of the Dove of the Holy Ghost (which is an undertone throughout) is necessary at this point". Matthew 3: 16: "And Jesus, when he was baptized, went up straightway out of the water: and, lo, the heavens were opened unto him, and he saw the Spirit of God descending like a dove, and lighting upon him." John 1: 32: "I saw the Spirit descending from heaven like a dove." (In the Middle Ages, many churches had a "Holy Ghost hole" in the vault, through which at Pentecost the figure of a dove could be lowered.) Herbert: "Listen sweet Dove unto my song, | And spread thy golden wings in me ··· Where is that fire which once descended | On thy Apostles?" *Whitsunday*. Herbert's poem was read by TSE as part of the address printed as *Mr. T. S. Eliot on "George Herbert"* (1938). Charles Williams: "and there was communicated to that group of Jews, in a rush of wind and a dazzle of tongued flames, the secret of the Paraclete", *The Descent of the Dove: A Short History of the Holy Spirit in the Church* (1939) 3, reviewed by TSE in *A Lay Theologian* (1939). TSE to Bonamy Dobrée, 12 Nov 1927: "The Dove dove down" (see "Improper Rhymes"). George Meredith's *The Lark Ascending* inspired Vaughan Williams's piece, which had its première in 1921 (*Moody* 256).

IV 1–10 **descending ··· terror ··· sin and error ··· fire ··· torment ··· hands:** Herbert: "terror ··· When sin and error ··· torturing ··· Thy hand above did burn ··· Thy hand ··· descend", *Justice* (2). Webster: "Sin ··· error, | Their death a hideous storm of terror", *The Duchess of Malfi* IV ii.

IV 1–14 **air ··· despair ··· Love. | Love ··· suspire ··· fire:** Swinburne: "two loves ··· Two loves ··· Their breath is fire upon the amorous air, | Fire in thine eyes and where thy lips suspire ··· fire ··· despair ··· despair", *Hermaphroditus* 6–14 (partly quoted in OED "suspire").

IV 2 **incandescent:** Mallarmé: "Le soleil que sa halte | Surnaturelle exalte | Aussitôt redescend | Incandescent" [The sun which its supernatural stay raises up comes down at once burning], *Cantique de saint Jean* [*Canticle of Saint John*] 1–4 (*Greene* 138).

IV 8 **Who then devised the torment? Love:** *Hayward*: Juliana of Norwich: "I desired oftentimes to wit in what was our Lords meaning: and fifteen year after and more, I was answered in ghostly understanding, saying thus; 'What? wouldest thou wit thy Lords meaning in this thing? Wit it well: love was his meaning. Who sheweth it thee? Love. Wherefore sheweth he it thee? For love' ··· Thus was I learned that love is our Lords meaning. And I saw full surely that ere

God made us He loved us; which love was never slacked, nor ever shall be. And in this love He hath done all His works; and in this love He hath made all things profitable to us; and in this love is our life everlasting. In our making we had beginning; but the love wherein He made us was in Him from without beginning: in which love we have our beginning. And all this shall we see in God, without end", final paragraph of the last of her *Revelations*. Dante, *Inf.* V 100–102: "Love, which is quickly caught in gentle heart, took him with the fair body of which I was bereft; and the manner still afflicts me" (with "torments", 116); see note to *Ash-Wednesday* II 34–38. **devised**: to Hayward, 9 Sept 1942: "first draft, 'devised' rejected as too self-conscious"; yet after alternating between this and "designed", in successive drafts, it was "designed" that TSE finally rejected. **torment? Love**: Samuel Daniel: "Love is a torment of the mind", *Song* from *Hymen's Triumph* (in *Oxf Bk of English Verse*). TSE: "torment | Of love unsatisfied | The greater torment | Of love satisfied", *Ash-Wednesday* II 35–38. To Hayward, 9 Sept 1942: "I had hesitated already between 'torture' and 'torment'". In 1956, revising for a new edition his critical note from 1933 on Harold Monro's *Collected Poems*, TSE emended "tortured" to "tormented" in the phrase "one variety of the infinite number of possible expressions of tortured human consciousness". He also changed "tormented" to "harassed" in the phrase "sincere and tormented introspection" (King's).

IV 8 *variant* **Who heaped the brittle rose leaves?**: Pentecostal customs in Italy traditionally included the strewing of rose petals.

IV 8–9, 11 **Love. | Love ··· shirt of flame**: Alexander Smith: "clad in love, | Like a pale martyr in his shirt of fire", *A Life-Drama* (1859) ii 220–21 (Archie Burnett, personal communication).

IV 11–12 **The intolerable shirt of flame | Which human power cannot remove**: the centaur Nessus assaulted Dejanira and was killed by an arrow shot by her husband, Hercules. As he died, he gave her a tunic, saying it had "the power of recalling a husband from unlawful love". When Dejanira heard of Hercules' wooing of Iole, she sent him the tunic, "and Hercules as soon as he had put it on fell into a desperate distemper, and found the poison of the Lernæan hydra penetrate through his bones. He attempted to pull off the fatal dress, but it was too late ··· As the distemper was incurable, he ··· erected a large burning pile on the top of mount Œta ··· laid himself down upon it ··· and the hero saw himself on a sudden surrounded with the flames without betraying any marks of fear or astonishment", *Lemprière* ("Hercules"). *Antony and Cleopatra* IV xii, ANTONY: "The shirt of Nessus is upon me." **cannot**: pronounced *can nòt* in TSE's recording of 1946–47. "And can not be confused", *How to Pick a Possum* 47 (*Noctes Binanianæ*).

IV 13–14 **only suspire | Consumed by either fire or fire**: OED "suspire" *v.* 3. *intr*: "To breathe", cites Elizabeth Barrett Browning: "fire-flies, that suspire | In short soft lapses of transported flame", *Aurora Leigh* VII 1061–62. TSE quotes Dante's "sospiri" (*Inf.* IV 27) in Notes on the Waste Land 64. "Sullen succuba suspired", *Ode* ("Tired. | Subterrene") 14 *variant.*

V

V *verse draft* (*msC*) [8–11] **the end ··· The only obituary ··· every word ··· Every poem ··· every action | A step on the scaffold:** "The only end to the battle, if we live to the end, is holiness; the only escape is stupidity ··· the first step is to find the least incredible belief ··· everything ··· Everyone, in a sense, believes in something; for every action involving any moral decision implies a belief", *A Commentary* in *Criterion* Apr 1933.

V *verse draft* (*msC*) [13–15] **The dying die for us | And we die with them. But to speak of regret || Is to outlive regret:** Tennyson: "O last regret, regret can die", *In Memoriam* LXXVIII 17. Emerson: "The persons who make up a nation to-day, next year die, and their experience dies with them", *Self-Reliance*.

V 4–5 **every word is at home, | Taking its place:** Swift: "Proper words in proper places, makes the true definition of a style", *A Letter to a Young Gentleman, Lately Entered into Holy Orders*. TSE: "The ideal literary critic ··· should be primarily concerned with the word and the incantation; with the question whether the poet has used the right word in the right place, the rightness depending upon both the explicit intention and an indefinite radiation of sound and sense", *The Varieties of Metaphysical Poetry* 287 (Turnbull Lecture III); for sound and sense, see note to V 9 and note to *To Walter de la Mare* 19, 23, 30, 32. "The ugly words are the words not fitted for the company in which they find themselves", *The Music of Poetry* (Iman Javadi, personal communication).

V 4–11 **every word is at home ··· the old and the new ··· the complete consort ··· every sentence:** Virginia Woolf: "You cannot use a brand new word in an old language because of the very obvious yet always mysterious fact that a word is not a single and separate entity, but ··· part of a sentence ··· How can we combine the old words in new orders ··· That is the question", *Craftsmanship* (1937; see note to III 41, and note to *East Coker* I 2–4).

V 5, 6, 8, 21 **Taking its place ··· The word ··· exact ··· pattern:** for "the word ··· in its place ··· exact and comprehensive ··· a fusion and a pattern with the word", see *Transit of Venus: Poems by Harry Crosby* (1931), TSE's Preface.

V 6–9 **neither diffident nor ostentatious ··· exact without vulgarity ··· precise but not pedantic:** "Nor intellectual nor mean, | And graceful, not too gay", *Mandarins* 4 12–13. TSE on 18th-century prose: "style neither strained nor relaxed, neither ascetic nor luxurious", *Views and Reviews* in *NEW* 20 June 1935. For the pedantic Polonius, "rich not gaudy", see note to *Mandarins* 2 13 "(rich not crude)".   **exact without vulgarity ··· precise but not pedantic:** Denham on the Thames as "My great example": "Though deep, yet clear; though gentle, yet not dull; | Strong without rage, without o'erflowing full", *Cooper's Hill* 188–89.   **pedantic:** to A. L. Rowse, 3 Mar 1941: "You know that my pencil has a chronic itch to comment on the margins. But as you know me for Pedant (and proud of it, mind you: Pedant and Puritan) you will not be ruffled by that." See note to *Five-Finger Exercises* V 5–7.

V 7 **An easy commerce of the old and the new:** Pound: "I am old enough now to make friends. | It was you who broke the new wood ··· Let there be commerce between us", *A Pact* (1913) 5–6, 9. TSE included the poem, which begins "I make a pact with you, Walt Whitman", in Pound's *Selected Poems* (1928), and wrote to Pound, 8 Dec 1936: "I am quite Willin to make a Pact with you" (Shawn

Worthington, personal communication). TSE: "I have, in recent years, cursed Mr Pound often enough; for I am never sure that I can call my verse my own; just when I am most pleased with myself, I find that I have only caught up some echo from a verse of Pound's", *Isolated Superiority* (1928). See note to V 18.

V 8–9 **Without vulgarity ··· The formal word precise but not pedantic**: in *ts9b* Hayward marked the stress "withōut vulgarity" and suggested "būt unpedāntic". In a memoir of Hayward, Kathleen Raine quoted V 9 as "a line of *Little Gidding* whose authorship he claimed", *Book Collector* Winter 1965. TSE: "We are, of course, accustomed to think of the poet as spending a good deal of time fussing over 'the right word', and yet to think of poetry as concerned with material essentially vague. Our notions of 'precision' are measured by the precision of the physical sciences ··· I do not pretend that poetry aims at precision of the same kind, or of an analogous kind"; later, giving an example from Poe: "he is sacrificing sense to sound ··· This sacrifice is not so illegitimate as might at first seem, because ··· precision of sound is as important as precision of sense. But it is an imperfection, though the poem as a whole is the precise expression of a peculiar, though vague emotion", *Poetical and Prosaic Use of Words* (1943).

V 8–10 **without vulgarity ··· dancing together**: "the poem is for its own sake—we enjoy a poem as we enjoy dancing; and as for the words, instead of looking *through* them, so to speak, we are looking *at* them ··· When the written language remains fixed, while the spoken language, the vulgar speech, is undergoing changes, it must ultimately be replaced by a new written language", Introduction to *The Art of Poetry* by Paul Valéry (1958).

V 12 **Every poem an epitaph**: Vaughan: "every book is thy large epitaph", *On Sir Thomas Bodley's Library; The Author Being Then in Oxford* (K. Narayana Chandran, *N&Q* Dec 1993).

V 12–13 **And any action | Is a step to the block**: Henry King: "And ev'ry houre a step towards thee", *An Exequy To his Matchless never to be forgotten Friend* 96. TSE quoted 89–100, 111–14 in *The Metaphysical Poets* (1921). He recalled the poem in *Personal Choice* (1957). For his discovery of the poem as a boy, see headnote to *Burbank with a Baedeker: Bleistein with a Cigar.* **to the block**: Johnson: "And fatal Learning leads him to the Block", *The Vanity of Human Wishes* 172. TSE's first thought was "on the scaffold" (see Textual History).

V 13 **the sea's throat**: see notes to I 35–37 and to *The Dry Salvages* IV 11–13.

V 16–18, 27–28 **See, they depart, and we go with them ··· See, they return, and bring us with them ··· the end ··· Will be to arrive where we started**: "every language, to retain its vitality, must perpetually depart and return upon itself; but without the departure there is no return and the returning is as important as the arrival", *"Leçon de Valéry"* (1946) (*Ricks* 106).

V 18 **See, they return, and bring us with them**: Pound: "See, they return; ah, see the tentative | Movements", *The Return* (1912) 1–2 (Mary T. Shea, 1942, *Grover Smith* 325). TSE quotes the first four lines of the poem in *Ezra Pound: His Metric and Poetry* (1917) (*Ricks* 260). For Pound's poem, see note to *Ash-Wednesday* VI 3–4.

V 19–20 **The moment ··· equal duration**: used by TSE for occasional inscriptions, as in Lee Anderson's commonplace book signed and dated 4. v. 60 (*Album of Gems*, Washington U.), and on a Faber postcard signed and dated 15. ix. 60, laid into Mardersteig copy no. 171.

V 19–22 **The moment ··· not redeemed from time, for history is a pattern | Of timeless moments:** "A moment not out of time, but in time, in what we call history: transecting, bisecting the world of time, a moment in time but not like a moment of time", *Choruses from "The Rock"* VII 19 (noted by Hayward in his copy of *1944*). "This historical sense, which is a sense of the timeless as well as of the temporal and of the timeless and of the temporal together, is what makes a writer traditional", *Tradition and the Individual Talent* I (1919).

V 24 **History is now and England:** "there are some words, the history of which is almost the history of England", *The Writer as Artist* (1940) ("every word is at home", V 4). See notes on I 39 ("Now and in England") and I 52–53 ("Here, the intersection of the timeless moment | Is England and nowhere. Never and always"). "The critical moment | That is always now, and here", *Murder in the Cathedral* II.

V 25 **with the drawing of this Love and the voice of this Calling:** *The Cloud of Unknowing* ch. 2: "What weary wretched heart and sleeping in sloth is that, the which is not wakened with the drawing of this love and the voice of this calling?" ch. 9: "therefore lift up thy love to that cloud. Or rather (if I shall say thee sooth) let God draw thy love up to that cloud; and strive thou through help of its grace to forget all other things" (scored in TSE's copy). See letter to Hayward, 2 Sept 1942, quoted in note to III 17–19. For *The Cloud of Unknowing*, see note to *Ash-Wednesday* I 39. (To Hayward, 2 Oct: "My edition of *Cloud of Unknowing* IS m'Cann's, the most recent"; see Bibliography.) For Lancelot Andrewes on spiritual procrastination, see note to *Gerontion* 18, 20.

V 27–28 **the end ··· Will be to arrive where we started:** returning to a thought from long before: "The token that a philosophy is true is, I think, the fact that it brings us to the exact point from which we started. We shall be enriched, I trust, by our experience on the Grand Tour, but we shall not have been allowed to convey any material treasures through the Custom House. And the wisdom which we shall have acquired will not be part of the argument which brings us to the conclusion; it is not part of the book, but it is written in pencil on the fly-leaf. For the point to which we return should be the same, but somehow is not, but is a higher stage of reality", *The Validity of Artificial Distinctions* (1914). "A man's destination is his own village, | His own fire, and his wife's cooking", *To the Indians who Died in Africa* 1–2.

V 27–32 **the end ··· to arrive where we started ··· the last of earth left to discover | Is that which was the beginning:** Bradley: "truth-seeking scepticism pushes questions to the end, and knows that the end lies hid in that which is assumed at the beginning", *Appearance and Reality* ch. XV (*Ricks* 106).

V 31–32 **When the last ··· Is that which was the beginning:** Matthew 20: 16: "So the last shall be first, and the first last".

V 34–35 **The voice ··· And the children in the apple-tree:** *Hayward*: "A recollection of the poet's childhood in general and not of any specific incident in it." TSE told Hayward, 5 Aug 1941, that "the children in the appletree ··· tie up with *New Hampshire* and *Burnt Norton*". ("Children's voices in the orchard ··· Swing up into the apple-tree", *Landscapes* I. *New Hampshire*; and "for the leaves were full of children", *Burnt Norton* I 40. Also: "Children singing in the orchard",

Ode ("Tired. | Subterrene") 12. "Whispers and small laughter between leaves", *Marina* 20.)

V 34–38 **voice of the hidden waterfall · · · children in the apple-tree · · · the stillness | Between two waves of the sea**: *Hayward*: "the distant waterfall in the forest, | Inaccessible, half-heard. | And I hear your voice as in the silence | Between two storms, one hears the moderate usual noises | In the grass and leaves, of life persisting", *The Family Reunion* (1939) I ii. It was Hayward who suggested "stillness" as an alternative to the earlier reading, "silence". TSE replied, 7 Sept 1942: "I *think* silence will have to stand, because I was using a line from the *Family Reunion*. And surely the (relative) silence between two waves is when they are breaking *on* something. Should I say 'Between two waves on the shore'?"

V 36 **Not known, because not looked for**: TSE put a question mark against the Gide/Bosco tr., "Que nos yeux ne virent jamais".

V 40 **complete simplicity**: "Great simplicity is only won by an intense moment or by years of intelligent effort, or by both. It represents one of the most arduous conquests of the human spirit: the triumph of feeling and thought over the natural sin of language", *The Post-Georgians* (1919). Of a poet's progress: "Simplicity and naturalness of speech are not necessarily his gift at the beginning; he is more likely to arrive at them in his maturity by years of hard work", *The Development of Shakespeare's Verse* (1937). To A. L. Rowse, 13 June 1934: "perhaps simplicity only comes through a gradual mastery of one's own emotions" (see headnote to *Choruses from "The Rock"*, 4. COMPOSITION).

V 41 **Costing not less than everything**: against the Gide/Bosco tr., "(Plus chèrement rien ne s'acquiert)", TSE wrote "weak".

V 44–46] *Paradiso* XXXIII 85–93 (last canto of the *Commedia*):

Nel suo profundo vidi che s'interna,
   legato con amore in un volume,
   ciò che per l'universo si squaderna;
sustanzia ed accidenti, e lor costume,
   quasi conflati insieme per tal modo,
   che ciò ch'io dico è un semplice lume.
La forma universal di questo nodo
   credo ch'io vidi, perchè più di largo,
   dicendo questo, mi sento ch'io godo.

[Within its depths I saw ingathered, bound by love in one volume, the scattered leaves of all the universe; substance and accidents and their relations, as though together fused, after such fashion that what I tell of is one simple flame. The universal form of this complex I think that I beheld, because more largely, as I say this, I feel that I rejoice.]

Temple ed. with sidenote: "The form of the universe".

(Literally, *nodo* = knot.) Quoted by TSE, with one further tercet and slightly emended translation, in *Dante* (1929) II. (The "eternal rose" and "a white rose" are introduced at *Paradiso* XXX 124 and XXXI 1.)

V 45 **crowned knot of fire**: *The Cloud of Unknowing* ch. 47: "knit the ghostly knot of burning love betwixt thee and thy God, in ghostly onehead and according of will" (*Drew* 239). **crowned knot**: a crown is "a knot formed by tucking the strands of a rope's ends over and under each other to lock them and prevent them unravelling", *The Oxford Companion to Ships and the Sea*. OED "crown" *v.*1 14 (*Naut.*) does not specify three strands, but E. M. Stephenson may have consulted TSE before she wrote: "The crowned knot, used by sailors, has the particular significance of three strands representing the Trinity", *Stephenson* 92.

V 46 **And the fire and the rose are one**: in Aug 1917, while TSE was its assistant editor, the *Egoist* printed B. Durak's *The Unseen Attendant*: "As the rose-fire of the hidden sun dawning over a winter sea, there comes to you the love that is enflaming, enlightening." Gérard de Nerval: "Et la treille où le Pampre à la Rose s'allie" [And the arbour where the vine joins with the rose], *El Desdichado* [*The Disinherited*]. For the same sonnet, see notes to *The Love Song of J. Alfred Prufrock* 124–29 and *The Waste Land* [V] 429. TSE: "fires | Of which the flame is roses", *East Coker* IV 19–20. For "three roses in the set of poems ··· have got to be ··· identified as one", see note to III 35. For Hayward's contribution to the line, see Textual History. **rose**: for "Rosa mystica", see note to *Ash-Wednesday* II 28.

Occasional Verses

Section introduced, with half-title, *1963+*. These poems were not collected in *US 1952*. None of the poems was ever added to *Sel Poems*.

CONTENTS

Defence of the Islands	1941
A Note on War Poetry	1942
To the Indians who Died in Africa	1943
To Walter de la Mare	1948
A Dedication to my Wife	1959, rev. 1963

On the top sheet to *tsW* (prepared for the printer of *1963* in connection with *Washington copy 1954*), TSE headed these "Occasional Poems", but when adding to the Contents pages, he wrote: "*Occasional ~~Poems~~ Verses*". (For *A Valedictory Forbidding Mourning: to the Lady of the House* as an Occasional Poem, see headnote to that poem, in "Uncollected Poems".)

Dr. Johnson: "In an occasional performance no height of excellence can be expected from any mind, however fertile ··· The occasional poet is circumscribed by the narrowness of his subject ··· Not only matter but time is wanting. The poem must not be delayed till the occasion is forgotten. The lucky moments of animated imagination cannot be attended; elegances and illustrations cannot be multiplied by gradual accumulation: the composition must be dispatched while conversation is yet busy", *Life of Dryden*.

To Michael Roberts, 14 Jan 1935: "I should be glad to think that the writing of occasional poetry is a justifiable activity, because that is all that the choruses in the Rock can pretend to be." To Lawrence Durrell, 13 Feb 1942, who had requested a contribution to a "select magazine": "I don't know what to send you unless it is a set of verses which I have just done for the Indian Red Cross book. I only hesitate because although I have endeavoured to clear up the point a bit, I find that people are still very confused about the distinction between verse and poetry, so that what I offer as good verse might be judged as a bad poem." (Rudyard Kipling always used the term "verse" of his own work, as acknowledged by the title of TSE's selection, *A Choice of Kipling's Verse*. This formula was used by Faber only once more during TSE's lifetime, for *A Choice of Walter de la Mare's Verse*.)

To John Nerber, 12 Oct 1948, assenting in principle to a request to reprint *To Walter de la Mare*: "I would ask you also to put in a note between the title and the poem stating that these verses were contributed to the volume of *Tribute to Walter De la Mare upon his Seventy-fifth Birthday*. I am always anxious to draw a clear distinction between my poems proper and my poems written for special occasions. Of the latter there are, of course, only a very few". *To Walter de la Mare* was reprinted in *Tiger's Eye* (NY) 15 Dec 1948.

To Walter McElroy, 11 Feb 1949: "As for the poem to Walter de la Mare, this was like two others which I published during the war, an occasional poem, and I do not wish to be represented in anthologies by any poems written for particular occasions. Indeed I no longer possess copies of the two poems written during the war and I have not copies of the volumes in which they appeared." (The "two others" were *A Note on War Poetry* and *To the Indians Who Died in Africa.*) To McElroy, 28 Feb 1949, declining permission for any of the *Four Quartets* to appear in an anthology of Forties poetry: "If, however, you have the public texts of the three war poems you mention, and if you will give them as a general title, *Three Occasional Poems*, I am willing to let you use these as a compensation." To McElroy, 19 Apr 1949: "I am glad you mentioned *Defence of the Islands* because I was rather distressed when I found that people regarded it as a poem. I had no idea of writing a poem and I do not wish to reprint it. These words were written for a particular purpose in 1940 to accompany an exhibition of photographs of British war-work to be displayed in New York. Each one of the sentences was meant to apply to and to appear in large letters on the wall together with an appropriate group of photographs, and to my way of thinking the words themselves lose a great deal of their meaning without the photographs they were designed to accompany." McElroy's planned anthology appears not to have been published. See headnote to *Choruses from "The Rock"*, 2. THE COMMISSION, for TSE's view of his contributions as "occasional poetry" (or "hack-work").

To W. P. Watt, 5 Jan 1945, returning a typescript of poetry: "The author's description, 'occasional poetry', is quite correct. It is good and accomplished occasional verse, eminently worthy of a periodical but not sufficiently of our type to justify our considering the book." TSE's jacket copy for A. L. Rowse's *Poems of Deliverance* (1946) reads: "These poems, though spoken with the tones of the patriot, are not in the limited sense 'occasional verse'. For, as must always be true of verse that can claim to be poetry, the occasional approaches the universal in expressing also the particular experience of the poet" (initialled in Faber catalogue, King's). In letters, TSE also speaks of "*vers d'occasion*" and "*vers de circonstance*".

Defence of the Islands

Defence of the Islands was written at the request of E. McKnight Kauffer, who was then working for Britain's Ministry of Information. TSE explained to Hayward [11 June 1940], that it would appear as an inscription "to go round the walls of a room of war photographs for the New York [World's] Fair. You walk round in a determined order, so that you only see one clause at a time, and necessarily in that order. I should like your criticism, and especially of the last line. Is it too much like the epitaph of the Lacedemonians after ~~Marathon?~~ Thermopylae? I thought that if the resemblance seeped in to the minds of the better educated American readers, they might draw for themselves the analogy of these people in the pictures keeping the gates for *them*." There followed a PS: "It is to be *ANONYMOUS.*" To Bernard Iddings Bell, 9 July 1940: "your ··· assertion that 'resistance to Germany's theology cannot be carried out by dead men' seems to me very doubtful. St. Thomas of Canterbury's resistance to the ideology of Henry II was far more operative after his death than before, and something might be said about the Lacedemonians after Thermopylae. Certainly, I would say that resistance to Germany's ideology cannot be carried out by men who are unwilling to die, or to sacrifice everything individually dear to them, including social privileges. I do not see how it can be carried out by succumbing to German domination." (See note to "the hot gates", *Gerontion* 3.)

To Hayward, 3 July 1940: Mary Hutchinson "astonished me with the information that the Kauffers are said to have left for America." Some fifty copies of a broadside, *LINES WRITTEN BY T. S. ELIOT* TO ACCOMPANY THIS EXHIBITION OF PHOTOGRAPHS (ending "T. S. ELIOT | *9th June, 1940*") were hand-printed in London to send to the World's Fair.

A second exhibition, the following year, was selected by the Director of London's National Gallery, Kenneth Clark, and featured work by Britain's official War Artists. After showing at the Museum of Modern Art, NY (22 May–2 Sept 1941), it toured the US. A press release stated that "In conjunction with the exhibition the Museum of Modern Art published a catalog *Britain at War* to which T. S. Eliot has contributed a poem entitled *Defense of the Islands.*" The acknowledgements in the catalogue, *Britain at War*, ed. Monroe Wheeler (New York, 1941), thanked TSE "for contributing his poem", which appeared facing the introduction. *Britain at War* anticipates *Inoubliable France*, a book of photographs to which TSE contributed the Preface, for which see note to *The Dry Salvages* II 56–66.

TSE to Hayward, 14 July 1941: "About that Kauffer affair. I had always supposed that the screed I wrote (you remember for the M.o.I.) was prose. Ted [Kauffer] had cabled briefly to ask permission to print it in some volume, which I gathered was of a propaganda kind: but I was disconcerted to find it featured as a *poem*. And I fear that without the photos scattered in between (*Times* type of photos of Canterbury, snowdrops in Devon, ploughing in Berkshire etc. besides the air, army, navy and ARP scenes) it will not look very coherent. I have not yet seen the book. I shall be grateful if you will inform any American correspondents that it really is prose." *No Mean Heritage* ed. S. N. Ritchie (Melbourne, 1946) used paragraphs which ignore TSE's lineation.

To Basil N. Bass, 29 Apr 1953: "I have always declined to republish these lines as they are not self-explanatory, and furthermore, I did not intend them to be considered as poetry. They are merely a kind of prose commentary on a series of photographs of the war effort in Britain, which was exhibited in New York in 1940." To Charles Norman, 1 May 1957: "I was indeed very glad to receive from you a copy of the lines I wrote in 1940 as I did not possess a copy until then. I should explain that it never occurred to me at the time of writing that my lines would be spoken of later as a 'poem' ··· I still think of the pieces rather as a collection of captions than as a poem", with "captions" typed over "quotations".

First collected by TSE in *1963*, after Kauffer's death in 1954.

Title ***Defence of the Islands***: Winston Churchill: "I have, myself, full confidence that if all do their duty, if nothing is neglected, and if the best arrangements are made, as they are being made, we shall prove ourselves once again able to defend our Island home ··· We shall go on to the end, we shall fight in France, we shall fight on the seas and oceans, we shall fight with growing confidence and growing strength in the air, we shall defend our Island, whatever the cost may be", House of Commons, 4 June 1940 (*McCue 2013a*). (In a broadcast speech on 17 May, Churchill had said: "We shall defend our Island home, and with the British Empire we shall fight on unconquerable until the curse of Hitler is lifted from the brows of mankind.") TSE: "if we proceed from bad to worse, we arrive at length at the prose style of Mr. Winston Churchill", *A Commentary* in *Criterion* Apr 1929. Three pages of *A Commentary* in Jan 1934 were devoted to Churchill's style, "which consists in constantly pitching the tone a little too high". TSE's attitude changed, however, in wartime. To Hayward, 19 June 1940, on the speech "This was their finest hour" (see note to [21–22]): "Incidentally, did you listen to Winston's speech last night? the particularly husky after dinner one? Whatever else one thinks, my dear John, you will agree that it is a pleasure to realise that we have, what has not before happened in our time (mine or yours) · · · a Prime Minister who is, as Henry James would have said, had he been one of us (for he was, as a matter of fact, the grandson of an Irishman) in some respects, and with certain qualifications, what one might call roughly, in these days, a social equal: and a further pleasure (which I invite you to share with me) to reflect that the Churchill family, in earlier times, had an association with the county of Somerset" (as had the Eliots, see headnote to *East Coker*). Churchill knows "how to speak English which is pure but not pasteurized", *Christian News-Letter* 14 Aug 1940 (see "The conditions of statesmanship" in note to the title *Difficulties of a Statesman*). To Philip Mairet, 10 Mar 1941, on preparing to broadcast *Towards a Christian Britain* (1941): "I was, and am · · · wanting to give them blood and sweat, and not promise them a Christian happy land as the reward for the Churchill blood and sweat." ***Defence***: "There are perhaps those who will admit to expression in poetry patriotism on the defensive: Shakespeare's Henry V is acceptable, in his otherwise embarrassing grandiloquence, because the French army was a good deal bigger than the English force", *Rudyard Kipling* (1941).

[1–2] **memorials of built stone—music's enduring instrument**: legend has it that Troy was built by the music of Apollo. Tennyson: "the song-built towers and gates | Reel, bruised and butted with the shuddering | War-thunder", *Tiresias* 96–98 (of Thebes, built to the music of Amphion). Tennyson on Camelot: "For an ye heard a music, like enow | They are building still, seeing the city is built | To music, therefore never built at all, | And therefore built for ever", *Gareth and Lynette* 271–74 (for which see note to *The Waste Land* [V] 382). **music's enduring instrument**: to Kauffer [10 June 1940]: "I think that '—music's enduring instrument' ought to come out. It blemishes the simple straightforwardness of the phrase."

[1–2] *variant* **music's timeless instrument**: "timeless · · · moment in and out of time · · · music | While the music lasts", *The Dry Salvages* V 18–29.

[1–4] **memorials of built stone · · · of English verse**: Waller: "When Architects have done their Part · · · Time, if we use ill-chosen Stone, | Soon brings a well-built Palace down", *Of English Verse* st. 3.

[1–2, 5–6] *variant* **timeless instrument · · · with the defence of this island**: "timeless moments · · · With the drawing of this Love and the voice of this Calling", *Little Gidding* V 22, 25.

[2–4] **many centuries · · · of English verse**: for "a collection of quotations", see TSE to Charles Norman, 1 May 1957, in headnote.

[6] *variant* **this Island**: Waller: "Rome (tho' her Eagle thro' the World had flown) | Cou'd never make this Island all her own", *Panegyrick to my Lord Protector* st. 17.

[8] **battleship, merchantman, trawler**: according to Churchill, the Dunkirk evacuation of 21 May–3 June 1940 (just days before this poem was written) involved "countless merchant seamen ··· 220 light warships and 650 other vessels".

[9–10] **pavement of British bone**: "a solid pavement of bone-bed", G. E. Roberts in *Proceedings of the Geologists' Association* 1859–65.

[11–12] **man's ··· death ··· the power of darkness in air**: Housman: "The Queen of air and darkness | Begins to shrill and cry. | 'O young man, O my slayer, | To-morrow you shall die'", *Last Poems* III.

[14, 17] **forebears ··· ancestors**: to Laurence Binyon, 16 May 1930: "'Ancestors' seems to me a weak word in English for family Pride: I wish that it might have been 'Forbears'."

[15] **Flanders**: Waller: "Flanders hath receiv'd our Yoke", *Upon the Death of the Lord Protector* 20. Sterne: "what prodigious armies we had in Flanders", *Tristram Shandy* bk. II ch. 18. John McCrae: "We shall not sleep, though poppies grow | In Flanders fields", *In Flanders Fields* (1915).

[15–16] **Flanders and France ··· undefeated in defeat**: "Who are only undefeated | Because we have gone on trying", *The Dry Salvages* V 45–46. Churchill: "our thankfulness at the escape of our Army and so many men, whose loved ones have passed through an agonising week, must not blind us to the fact that what has happened in France and Belgium is a colossal military disaster", House of Commons, 4 June 1940.

[15–22] **those undefeated in defeat ··· changing nothing ··· to say, to the past and the future generations ··· we took up our positions**: see Arnold, *Culture and Anarchy*, quoted in note to *Little Gidding* III 36–45.

[16–17, 20] **changing nothing of their ancestors' ways but the weapons ··· the past and the future generations**: on behalf of the Classical Association to the Greek Ambassador (George Seferis), 21 Oct 1941, "on this anniversary of the Italo-German assault upon your country": "As your people have maintained the glory of their ancestors in war and in endurance, so we believe that they will in the future be worthy also of their ancestors in victory and in peace."

[18] **the paths of glory**: Pope: "With equal steps the paths of glory trace", *Odyssey* I 392. Gray: "The paths of glory lead but to the grave", *An Elegy Written in a Country Church Yard* 36 (with "isle" = aisle, 39). Tennyson: "Not once or twice in our rough island-story, | The path of duty was the way to glory", *Ode on the Death of the Duke of Wellington* 201–202, 209–10. (Tennyson urges Wellington's vigilance about the threat of invasion from France: "He bade you guard the sacred coasts", 172.)

[19] **the lanes and the streets of Britain** (*variant* **the field and streets of our homes**): Churchill: "we shall fight in the fields and in the streets", House of Commons, 4 June 1940.

[19] *variant* **is a field at home**: "attachment to our own field", *Little Gidding* III 11.

[21–22] **we took up our positions**: Churchill: "Let us therefore brace ourselves to our duties, and ··· men will say, 'This was their finest hour'", House of Commons, 18 June 1940. TSE: "The constellations | Took up their stations", *Inside the gloom* 3–4. "we returned to our places", *Journey of the Magi* 40.

[22] To McKnight Kauffer [11 June 1940]: "I don't think the last line will do: it is one of those awkward cases in which each word separately is what you want, but they won't all go together. 'Positions' and 'instructions' so close together is disagreeable to the ear. So it must either be 'we took up our places, in obedience to instructions' or 'we took up our positions, in obedience to orders'. I rather like 'instructions' better than 'orders', because it suggests voluntary cooperation, rather than mere discipline; but on the other hand I prefer 'positions' to 'places', because it has a more precise military sound. So I should like you to try them out on a few people of sufficient sensitivity to words and sounds, and decide this for me. Yours T.S.E. ¶ I don't know how urgent this is: I am sending a copy to John [Hayward] for his opinion. I can get Herbert Read's view when I see him on Thursday, and I think his would be valuable."

[22] *variant* **in obedience to orders**: Simonides: "Stranger, tell the Lacedemonians that we lie here obedient to their orders", *Anthologia Palatina* VII 249 (*Grover Smith* 324); see headnote. TSE on postwar renewal of literary relations: "there is much that we shall have to come to understand, in our diverse experience in these last three years. For this we do not need to be given orders, but we need facilities", *The Unity of European Writers* (1944). "the element of unquestioning obedience should be as small as the situation admits—for always, in peace as well as war, some orders must be carried out whether they are understood and approved or not", *Leadership and Letters* (1949).

A Note on War Poetry

Published in *London Calling*, ed. Storm Jameson (New York, 1942), then *1963+*.

Written during the revising of *Little Gidding*. TSE, who had contributed *The Marching Song of the Pollicle Dogs* and *Billy M'Caw: The Remarkable Parrot* to *The Queen's Book of the Red Cross* (1939), wrote to Storm Jameson, 12 Feb 1942: "Thank you for your letter of the 7th. These Red Cross books are very troubling. For the first Red Cross book I was able to provide two children's poems which were the only unpublished work that I had to offer. The second book was the Indian Red Cross book for which I have written some verses about the Indian troops. Now comes your American Red Cross book and I am rather at a loss what to do. I never have anything unpublished on hand except things that I don't want to publish at all and if I do anything for this book it would have to be specially written for the occasion. While I should be quite glad to do that if I could think of an appropriate subject, I am in a position in which I have already undertaken rather more than I can carry out between now and June, so I am afraid that if you want a contribution immediately I cannot be one of the contributors. If there were no hurry I should be able to begin thinking about it at the beginning of June." To Bonamy Dobrée, 13 July: "Now about your friend Hurricane Jim. I put my mind on the problems of a Red Cross Poem (or Bun) for her · · · and finally it occurred to me that if I could not write a poem I might at least do something on the subject of the difficulty of writing a poem. So I send you the enclosed first for your opinion as a friend (candid): if you think it is good enough send it on to her; if not, return it to me. Perhaps the idea is wrong, perhaps it is injudicious, perhaps the composition will do me no credit. I leave that to your judgement. But if you transmit it to your friend, do not let her regard it as a POEM: it is a SET OF VERSES."

To Hayward, 21 July: "I have written a set of verses for Bonamy's friend Hurricane Jim (M. Storm Jameson) who has badgered me for her American Red Cross Book. Will the Mexican Red Cross Book turn up next? I am to address the Swedes, radio-telegraphically, on Friday night, about War Poetry: I understand that it will be arranged in the form of a dialogue, my interlocutor speaking in Swedish for the better instruction of the Swedes in outlying farms, so it should be pretty rum." Along with *Little Gidding*, the broadcast and these verses were mentioned in the next letter to Hayward, 26 July: "I provided three pages of text on WAR POETRY, out of which Mr. Ohlsson arranged an ingenious dialogue: he taking everything in Swedish, and giving me a few interjections such as 'Well, that is very much what I think' etc · · · When I copy them out I shall let you have a copy of my SET OF VERSES which I composed for Storm Jameson to oblige Bonamy." To Hayward, 10 Oct: "I cannot wholly suppress in my mind the suspicion, which, however, I do not wish to pass on to any wider public than the recipient of this letter, that all these Red Cross levies upon literature serve chiefly to give otherwise unoccupied people a sense that they are 'doing something'."

To M. J. Tambimuttu, 22 Apr 1941, on selections for *Poetry in Wartime* (Faber, 1942): "I should not like it to be a collection of 'war poems' in the narrower sense, although the best that are written should certainly be included. In the first place, I do not think that there have yet been enough first-rate poems directly concerned with the war; and in the second place I believe that while people want poetry they do not want 'war poetry' in such a concentrated dose. I should like to consider an anthology of poems written during the war, whatever their subject matter." *T. S. Eliot on Poetry in Wartime* (1942), from his radio broadcast to Sweden:

> Not very long after the present war began, people were writing to the newspapers asking: "Where are the war poets?" · · · I think that the question is worth considering for a moment, if only to show why it should not be asked. For it does not concern this war only, but all wars; not this country alone, but all countries which pride themselves on their poetry.
>
> When we ask for "war poetry," we may be asking for one or the other of two different things. We may mean patriotic poetry · · · which expresses and stimulates pride in the military virtues of a people. Or we may be asking for poets to write poetry arising out of their experience of war. As for the first, we must consider, how very little first-rate poetry of this kind there is in any language—and how little of that has ever been written in the middle of a great war. The greatest war poem of Europe is Homer's *Iliad*: it was not written during the Trojan War; and, although Homer was a Greek, I think that he makes the Greeks appear rather more unpleasant than the Trojans · · ·
>
> So in general, I should say that while a poet, as a man, should be no less devoted to his country than other men, I distinguish between his duty as a man and his duty as a poet. His first duty as a poet is towards his native language, to preserve and develop that language · · · The beginning of the last war produced an outburst of excellent verse: but the men who were thus stimulated to write were not, I think, any of them real poets. The later stages of the war produced some verse of more permanent value: such as that of Isaac Rosenberg and Wilfred Owen, and the more bitter verse of Siegfried Sassoon. This was "war poetry" in its material: but its spirit was more that of sadness and pity than of military glory · · ·

> I am impressed by the number of young British poets whose work has begun to appear during this war; and I am glad that so little of what they write gives an answer to satisfy the sort of people who ask "where are our war poets?" ··· When these poets write about the war, it is mostly about some limited experience, even trivial experience, such as cold, discomfort, or the boredom of waiting at an isolated post ··· the bigger experiences need time, perhaps a long time, before we can make poetry of them ··· when, after the war, the experience has become a part of a man's whole past, it is likely to bear fruit in something very different from what, during time of war, people call "war poetry".

(Rosenberg had been a friend of the Schiffs. TSE considered writing a preface to his poems in 1935, but the Faber board dissuaded him; see TSE to D. W. Harding, 17 May 1935. Faber published Sassoon's *Poems Newly Selected* in 1940.)

To Desmond Hawkins, 5 July 1940, declining to campaign for the exemption of writers from war service: "I can't see the exemption of writers merely for the sake of preserving them. So far as they can make a better contribution to the war (in its largest sense) in some job in which they can employ their talents, instead of being merely atoms in the ranks, I am all for finding them that sort of job. The example to which you refer, of artists being kept to 'paint a record of the war' at least fulfils the letter of that principle. But I cannot see why writers should desire any exceptional immunity, *qua* writers: if they are really conscientious Conscious Objectors, that is a different matter ··· I hope you will understand that I, as a person who owing to physical inferiority was rejected in the last war, am most loth to dogmatise or make any public expression of opinion of what younger men placed very differently from the way I was, should do or should not do now."

To Dr. Alfred Weber, 15 Jan 1958: "I have your letter of 6th January and am so much touched by the amiability with which you accept my prohibitions that the asperity of my earlier communications is transformed and I am inclined, if so wished, to mitigate the sentence. If there are any two poems from which you have agreed to take four lines which you would care to print in full (with the exception of *Ode* which I do not like) you are welcome to do so. I should in fact rather welcome the printing complete of *A Note on War Poetry.*"

Title **A Note on**: a dozen pieces of TSE's prose use this formula. "any book, any essay, any note in *Notes and Queries*, which produces a fact even of the lowest order about a work of art is a better piece of work than nine-tenths of the most pretentious critical journalism", *The Function of Criticism* (1923) IV. The earliest ms title for this poem had been *Notes on Poetry in Wartime.* In drafts, *The Cultivation of Christmas Trees* enjoyed several introductory formulae: *A Preamble to*, *A Comment Upon* and *A Note on* (see Textual History). In *1963*, "Notes on the Waste Land" had its own entry in the "Index of Titles of Poems". ***War Poetry***: to A. L. Rowse, 17 June 1944, on a proposed title: "NOT *War Poems*, ever! If the war stops, it kills the book; if the war goes on, it is meaningless."

1, 3 **expression of collective emotion ··· individual**: Jane Ellen Harrison: "Art, as Tolstoy divined, is social, not individual ··· The dance from which the drama rose was a choral dance ··· what the Greeks called a *thiasos*. The word means a *band* and a *thing of devotion*; and reverence, devotion, collective emotion, is social in its very being", *Ancient Art and Ritual* (1913) 240. TSE wrote to Harrison on 29 May 1923 inviting her to contribute to the *Criterion*, but she never did. "The only way of expressing emotion in the form of art is by finding an 'objective correlative'", *Hamlet* (1919).

6–7 **To create the universal, originate a symbol | Out of the impact:** "A symbol created by death", *Little Gidding* III 46 *variant*.

12–13 **"incidents" ··· the effort to keep day and night together:** OED "incident" 1b: "An occurrence or event, sometimes comparatively trivial in itself, which precipitates or could precipitate political unrest, open warfare, etc. Also, a particular episode (air-raid, skirmish, etc.) in war." Several of OED's citations, like TSE, have the word in quotation marks. (See headnote to *Four Quartets* 3. COMPOSITION for TSE on "an alerte ··· waiting for Incidents" in 1941.) *Service Slang* (1943): "There are no occasions, occurrences, or events in an airman's life. Anything that happens to him is an 'incident' .. why, nobody knows." To J. H. Oldham, 27 Aug 1943: "We all tend much more to employ military terms and metaphors nowadays: but I wonder whether there is too much a suggestion of wiliness for material ends about the word 'strategy'. Incidentally, I think that there is a moderation to be observed in the use of military figures: the Church Militant should not become the Panzerkirche." **the effort:** OED "war effort": from 1919, "the effort of a nation to win a war, or of an individual group to contribute to that end" (see "the war effort", in TSE's prefatory note to *Defence of the Islands*).

13–15 **In the effort to keep day and night together. | It seems just possible that a poem might happen | To a very young man** (13 *variant*: **With the struggle to keep two lives together**): Faber catalogue 1936 (of TSE): "if he did not have to read so many manuscripts he would have more time for writing poetry. To which our reply has always been that after all we make it possible for him to keep body and soul together" (see headnote to Textual History, 3. KEY TO EDITIONS, *1936*). "As body and soul begin to fall asunder", *Little Gidding* II 81.

12–17 **"incidents" ··· That is a life. || War:** Van Wyck Brooks: "it seems as if religion too were an incident ··· these countless ism's ··· are all absolutely separate. And being incidents they do not mix together to form a background from which we look out upon life in general ··· warring ··· warring", *The Wine of the Puritans* 78 (reviewed by TSE in 1909).

13 *variant*, 19 **two lives ··· War is not a life:** "as death resembles life, | Being between two lives ··· liberation ··· love of a country", *Little Gidding* III 5–6, 9–10.

15 **but a poem is not poetry:** Marianne Moore: "I, too, dislike it: there are things that are important beyond all this fiddle ··· the result is not poetry", *Poetry* in *Observations* (1924) and included by TSE in *Selected Poems of Marianne Moore* (1935). In the introduction, he wrote: "If you aim only at the poetry in poetry, there is no poetry either." TSE: "The poetry does not matter", *East Coker* II 21. Wilfred Owen: "The Poetry is in the pity", Preface for an unpublished collection, printed in *The Poems of Wilfred Owen* ed. Edmund Blunden (1931).

21–22 **The enduring is not a substitute for the transient, | Neither one for the other:** "nothing in this world or the next is a substitute for anything else; and if you find that you must do without something, such as religious faith or philosophic belief, then you must just do without it", *The Use of Poetry and the Use of Criticism* 113. "no substitute for sense", *Whispers of Immortality* 10 (see note).

24–25 **"poetry" ··· verse:** see headnote to "Occasional Verses".

To the Indians who Died in Africa

Published in *Queen Mary's Book for India* (foreword by the Right Hon. L. S. Amery), 1943. (Queen Mary, 1867–1953, had been Empress of India during the reign of her husband, George V, from 1910 to 1936.) Reprinted in *The Tiger Triumphs: The Story of Three Great Divisions in Italy* (London, for the Government of India, 1946) without title or author's name (though TSE's publishers are thanked), set entirely in small capitals and with 11–15 omitted. After being collected in *1963*, the verses were reprinted in *Of Books and Humankind: Essays and Poems Presented to Bonamy Dobrée* ed. John Butt (1964), where the explanatory paragraph is dropped and the title is preceded by the dedication "To Bonamy Dobrée because he likes it".

To Cornelia Sorabji (1866–1954, barrister and social reformer), 9 Apr 1941: "I should be very happy to do anything in my power to forward the increase of the Indian Troops Comfort Fund ··· As for a contribution to the book, you do not say by what date such contributions must be received. You see, I have absolutely nothing on hand at the moment and I should have to try to write something specially as soon as I can make the time ··· I cannot definitely promise anything in prose or verse." 26 Jan 1942: "I never have anything on hand, unpublished, that I can contribute for such collections as yours, and no poem anywhere near completion. What I had in mind, as a token—for it will be a disappointment if I do not have the honour of my name in the book—was to try to write a short epigrammatic poem in homage to the gallantry of the Indian troops in Africa. If I can do this, in the next ten days or so, I will send it to you: if I fail, I shall write to offer my humble apologies." 11 Feb: "As earnest of my good intentions I send you herewith some verses which I have composed with your book in view. I shall be grateful if you will let me know in time up to what date I can alter, substitute or withdraw, because I am not at all certain that I am satisfied with what I have done. I shall also be grateful if you will let me know your opinion of the suitability of these lines or any detail in them from the point of view of the people about whom and for whom they are written. There may be possibilities of misunderstanding of which I am unaware ··· PS. I am sorry the paper is a bit crumpled but the dog sat on it." To Hayward [1 Mar 1942]: "I enclose a copy of the *verses* which I have composed to order for Cornelia Sorabji's Indian Red Cross Book: I had to do it as she is in hospital with fractured hips. I have to make sure that there is nothing in it offensive to the Punjabis and Pathans." Hayward, 3 Mar: "I venture to express the faintest possible uneasiness about the use of the word 'graveyard' in the last stanza. I do so because you say that you have been careful not to offend the Punjabis and the Pathans. It occurs to me that as Indians are consumed after death on Gats or Ghats or Gahts and are not buried in graves it may be inappropriate to suggest that interment is practised." (TSE to Henry Eliot, 19 Oct 1929, after their mother's death: "I have a perfectly irrational (not theological) dislike of cremation".) TSE to Sorabji, 9 Mar 1942: "In the verses I sent you, I have been worried lest the phrase 'the same graveyard' in the last stanza should give offense to devout Moslems, or others. Do you think it would be better to change it to 'may have the same memories'? which would do for the versification equally well. And if there is anything unacceptable about 'the dog's great grandson' playing with the child, please let me know" (see Textual History). His letter concluded: "P.S. And does 'the moment after death' sound too soon for some believers? I may change that." On this letter are notes, dated 16 Mar, apparently for a reply by Sorabji: "need not change—but if he wd rather (a) 'graveyard' sug[gestio]n safer [i.e. that it would be safer to substitute 'memories'] (b) Indian Moslems do keep dogs, old fashioned ones—village *watch*dogs: in parts goats ⁊ cows more usual". Meanwhile, Lady Richmond wrote to TSE, 13 Mar: "Miss Sorabji sent word that you would like to see your Poem ⁊ here it is—I am getting all the contributions to The BOOK typed here ⁊ am keeping them till she gets home, as we hope she will do very soon—as she has no facilities for keeping them in the Hospital. May I diffidently say how much I like the Poem? It, at least, will remain true, whatever the changes may be with which we may be faced by the time the book is ready." TSE to Lady Richmond, 21 Mar: "This, I think, is the final version. After several consultations I have, I hope, expunged everything that might disturb the orthodox of any faith—at the expense of the only striking phrases, to be sure: but this sort of composition isn't poetry, and has its own rules."

During the Great War, TSE's friend W. G. Tinckom-Fernandez had discussed the strategic importance to Western Imperialism of India's participation: "For the first time in modern history ··· dark-skinned troops of India and the Far East, black troops of the hinterlands of Africa, have fought for and against Europeans, and have espoused a quarrel that is not their own ··· a new *morale* must be substituted and imposed if the fetich of a legendary supremacy is to be maintained throughout the harems and bazaars of the East", *India and the War* in *Nation* 10 June 1915. For a commission for TSE to review "several books on contemporary Indian politics" in 1916, see headnote to *Airs of Palestine, No. 2.*

Writing to Edward Thompson on 11 Oct 1930, TSE described himself as "a director of Faber & Faber who happens to be particularly interested in India" and proposed a meeting "not because I am one of the publishers of your last book, but because what you said to me about India was so congenial to my own prejudices or intuitions ··· I have had Indian friends, and my interest in India was enough to make me spend two or three years, at one more leisured period, in the study of Sanskrit and Pali."

To Raja Rao, writer and philosopher, 27 Apr 1939: "I have read your short stories with much interest and appreciation, and it does seem to me that you have unusual success in communicating the life of an Indian village ··· I sincerely hope that you may find some other publisher to take the risk, as I should like to see them in print."

TSE remained interested in Indian affairs and wartime loyalties, telling Hayward on 12 July 1943 that he had been reading Sir Reginald Coupland's report on the lack of realism in plans to partition the Punjab (1943). In Nov 1943 the Council for the Defence of Church Principles published TSE's *Reunion by Destruction: Reflections on a Scheme for Church Union in South India.*

Of G. T. Wrench: "He argues that it is impossible to superimpose the British pattern of life upon the Indian. A purely Indian solution must be sought—and sought, not in the westernized towns, but in the rural communities and in the development of the soil and countryside", *Land and Motherland* (1947), jacket copy (initialled by TSE in Faber catalogue, King's).

K. S. Narayana Rao's *T. S. Eliot and the Bhagavad-Gita* (*American Quarterly* Winter 1963; Addendum, Spring 1964) explains TSE's evocation of specific stanzas of the *Gita*, especially II 37–38 and II 46, and compares the dilemma of Indians who fought for the British Empire with that of Arjuna in the epic (see note to *The Dry Salvages* III 33–44 for *Preston* on Arjuna's dilemma).

Title] Thousands of Indian troops took part in Operation Crusader, Nov–Dec 1941, which relieved the eight-month Siege of Tobruk. This victory over Rommel was the first by British-led forces over German ground forces during the Second World War.

1–3 **A man's destination ··· His own fire ··· To sit in front of his own door at sunset**: "The man who has builded during the day would return to his hearth at nightfall", *Choruses from "The Rock"* V 10. "the evening hour that strives | Homeward", *The Waste Land* [III] 220–21 (see note).

1–5 **A man's destination ··· Playing in the dust**: Kipling: "Who is the happy man? He that sees in his own house at home little children crowned with dust, leaping and falling and crying", epigraph to *The Story of Muhammad Din*. See *Coriolan* II. *Difficulties of a Statesman* 48 and note.

1–6 **A man's ··· village, | His own fire ··· his own door at sunset ··· his grandson, and his neighbour's grandson | Playing ··· Scarred but secure, he has many memories**: Longfellow: "The village smithy stands ··· When the evening sun is low. || And children coming home from school | Look in at the open door ··· the flaming forge ··· burning", *The Village Blacksmith* 2–23. (For Longfellow's poem, see notes to *Sweeney Agonistes: Fragment of an Agon* 42, "*Under the bamboo tree*" and to *The Columbiad* st. 28.)

3–4 **in front of his own door at sunset | And see his grandson, and his neighbour's grandson | Playing in the dust together**: Southey: "It was a summer evening, | Old Kaspar's work was done, | And he before his cottage door | Was sitting in the sun; | And by him sported on the green | His little grandchild Wilhelmine", *After Blenheim*, on "the famous victory" (K. N. Chandran, *Journal of Modern Literature* Spring 2007).

3–5 **in front of his own door ··· his grandson, and his neighbour's grandson | Playing in the dust together**: "and children tumble in front of the door", *Murder in the Cathedral* II opening chorus, added in 2nd ed. (1936).

16–17 **the Midlands ··· the Five Rivers**: to Mons. J. Simon, 9 Oct 1945, offering *To the Indians who Died in Africa* for translation into French for the journal *Presence*: "I wish to make it quite clear that the enclosed poem is *vers d'occasion* ··· I should not propose to include it in any collection, but I have no objection to its appearing as such in a periodical. If you use it I should be glad if you would append the date, 1943. In case you use this poem, I should like to point out for the benefit of the translator that the Midlands means a certain number of counties in the centre of England, and that the Five Rivers means the part of India known as the Punjab, Five Rivers being the translation of the Indian name. It is from this part of India that some of the most notable fighting troops have come." (Punjab, "land of five rivers", Sanskrit.)

17 **graveyard:** more controversial than the pre-*1963* reading, "memories", because

the Hindu custom is not to bury the dead (Rao, *American Quarterly* Spring 1964); see headnote.

21 **judgment after death**: when Alan Clodd protested that the new reading in *1963*, "moment after death", made the lines "less Christian", TSE replied, 19 June 1964: "I shall certainly go back to 'judgment after death' instead of 'moment after death' as it is, I agree, more serious and immensely superior." The emendation was made in *1963* 4th imp. (1968), but "moment" continued to appear in US printings (see Textual History).

21–22 *variant* **the moment after death ··· the fruit of action**: "At the moment which is not of action or inaction ··· the fruit of action", *The Dry Salvages* III 32–38.

To Walter de la Mare

Published in *Tribute to Walter de la Mare on his Seventy-fifth Birthday* [ed. W. R. Bett], Faber, 1948. Bett wrote asking for a contribution on 18 Feb 1947, and TSE replied on 5 Mar: "I find myself too much in the dark as to what kind of compilation you have in mind to be able to reply definitely ··· I should be unable to write anything of critical value by the end of June as I have to pay a visit to America next month. It is possible that I might be able to write a few verses in Walter de la Mare's honour, but this would only be a small contribution to a volume which needs very much more solid matter than that." (Robert Lowell to Elizabeth Bishop, 14 Jan [1949]: "The Eliot poem was charming—not very strenuous though. A couple of years ago, when he'd just finished it, he said to me that verse allowed one to be much more uncritically enthusiastic, or something of the sort.") TSE's first venture in writing a tribute for the Festschrift may have been *Montpelier Row* (see headnote to that poem), followed by the draft sonnets from which *To Walter de la Mare* emerged (see Textual History). At Easter 1947 he wrote again to Bett enclosing the final text, "which is not yet quite what I should like it to be: but I am afraid I simply cannot devote any more time to improving it, as I have to leave for America in a fortnight".

To George Rylands, 6 July 1926, inviting him to review for the *Criterion*: "I do not know whether you have ever read any of de la Mare's prose—the books which I have for review are all prose—or what you think of it. My opinion is that although he is over-rated he has certain original and valuable qualities, especially in *The Memoirs of a Midget*, and I do not think it is worth while for anyone to tackle him who does not care for what he has to give. One must be critical of course, but I do not think it is necessary to be quite so harsh as was Leonard Woolf in the last *Nation*. Or rather, I think that what Leonard said was all perfectly true, but there are other things in de la Mare's work worth praise." Rylands reviewed four volumes of de la Mare's prose (along these lines) in *Criterion* Oct 1926.

Walter de la Mare's son Richard was one of the founding directors of Faber (and later chairman). One of the best-selling of established poets, Walter de la Mare was an early addition to the firm's list. As well as six Ariel poems apiece, he and TSE each contributed two poems to *The Queen's Book of the Red Cross* in 1939.

After sending *Journey of the Magi* to de la Mare in 1927, TSE asked for a contribution to the *Criterion*, where de la Mare's story *The Picnic* appeared in Apr 1930.

In 1929, de la Mare invited TSE to write for *The Eighteen-Eighties: Essays by Fellows of the Royal Society of Literature* (1930). TSE replied that he was unable to write on Aesthetics or Vernon Lee, but could write about Pater. To de la Mare, 6 Jan 1930: "Many thanks both for your letter about the 80s, and for the honour which you have, I suspect, inveigled others into agreeing to bestow upon me. I must confess that the Royal Society of Literature, like the British Academy, is terra incognita on my map; and it is an honour I had never dreamed of—it is not so very many years since I was called a literary bolshevik (in the *Morning Post*, to be sure). But I am highly pleased at being elected to the fellowship." TSE's essay appeared in the book as *The Place of Pater* and was reprinted in *Selected Essays* as *Arnold and Pater*. TSE was also represented in a volume of de la Mare's in 1930, the anthology *Desert Islands*, which includes within a running sequence the lines that became *Ash-Wednesday* I (see Textual History).

In a note to Geoffrey Faber, TSE wrote: "a publisher has got to pursue a certain consistency in the kind of verse he publishes, if he is going to market any of it. Of course, there are awkward exceptions! Of which Walter de la Mare is the most conspicuous example", *"Thames Symphony"* by Oliffe Richmond, reader's report, 7 Oct 1945. On 7 May 1946, TSE went to tea at Walter de la Mare's house, where he met Owen Barfield (whose name he did not catch). To Hope Mirrlees: "This afternoon I have to make a pilgrimage to Twickenham, to see Walter de la Mare. It takes an hour to get there, and presumably an hour to get back; I shall probably get off the bus at the wrong stop and no one will be able to direct me; and I think it is very conscientious of me to go". Later that year he wrote the jacket copy for de la Mare's *The Traveller*.

For TSE's sixtieth birthday in 1948, Richard March and Tambimuttu edited *A Symposium*. TSE complained to I. A. Richards, 10 May 1948, that Tambimuttu had been "poisoning my relations with all of my friends; thank God for one who has refused to have anything to do with this offensive tombstone. I intend to be on the s.s. *America* on my birthday, at least. Even Walter is too young to have such a *festschrift*, and perhaps it will be the death of both of us; but I couldn't well not appear in Walter's book could I?"

Two days after his 75th birthday, de la Mare wrote a sonnet, *To Light You to Bed*, dedicated to TSE and dated "April 25 1948" (the ms, "bearing Eliot's marginal notes critical of the romantic diction", is reproduced in *Sackton* 261). "Here at his hornbook sits a drowsy child | Lit by a guttering candle's fickle beams | So heavy is his eye each letter seems | An imp endowed with grins and antics wild."

De la Mare was appointed a Companion of Honour in 1948, six months after TSE's appointment to the Order of Merit. TSE to de la Mare, 12 June 1948: "I permit myself to write a line to express my pleasure in learning of your Companionship of Honour, and in thinking of the pleasure that it will give to those who love you and to innumerable admirers of your work; in thinking also of the dignity which is added to the order. Thinking least of all, in a way, of yourself; for your fame will survive and orders and degrees will be forgotten." In Nov 1948, TSE was awarded the Nobel Prize.

In 1951 de la Mare was to tell Laurence Whistler, "What I have against T.S.E. is that in *The Waste Land* he felt it necessary to give precise meanings and correspondences" (*Theresa Whistler* 401). Laurence Whistler was the brother of Rex Whistler, who had drawn the decorations for de la Mare's *Desert Islands*. Later, Laurence Whistler would engrave on glass TSE's poems *Amaz'd astronomers did descry* (for Geoffrey Faber) and *Long may this Glass endure, and brim with wine* (for the Faber family).

TSE to Theresa Whistler, 21 Nov 1962, of de la Mare: "I did not know him intimately and saw him on very few occasions but I have at least one memory of a visit to him which is worth recording and will let you have it in due course." No further letter arrived.

2 **A desert island**: to de la Mare, 8 May 1930, thanking him for an inscribed copy of *Desert Islands*: "it is written in a siren style that might charm even the dullest of subjects into animation; but who does not like this subject?"

5 **kinkajou · · · mangabey** (*with variants* **capybara, coati, peccary**): small mammals. J. G. Wood: "The Kinkajou is also an inhabitant of Southern America. It is not unlike the Coati in its habits"; "The Common, or Collared Peccary, is an inhabitant of South America"; "The Mangabeys, as these monkeys are called, are all inhabitants of Western Africa." For Wood, see note to *Burbank with a Baedeker: Bleistein with a Cigar* 22–24. To Ezra Pound, 12 Mar 1934: "if he dont look out he will be reincarnate as a Capybara". 4 May 1936: "Now Then, Ez, mon capybara, hydrochaerus, you know zwellz I do that a prince should before all else watch over his own rational and moral motivation".

9 **the nursery tea**: "The nursery tea, the school holiday", *The Family Reunion* I i.

13 **ghosts return**: de la Mare published two poems entitled *The Ghost*, and one called *The Ghost Chase*. TSE: "Story of Turn of Screw. Good visible ghosts not dela Mare shivers", *Lecture Notes as Norton Professor* (1933) fol. 37.

13 **ghosts** (*variant* <u>they</u>): for Kipling's *They*, see note to *Burnt Norton* I 30–38.

18 **two worlds meet, and intersect**: Byron: "Between two worlds life hovers like a star", *Don Juan* XV xcix, quoted twice in TSE's *Byron* (1937). TSE: "bisecting the world of time", *Choruses from "The Rock"* VII 19. THE ROCK: "I have known two worlds, I have known two worlds of death", *The Rock* 47 (last speech of Part I). "The point of intersection of the timeless | With time", *The Dry Salvages* V 18–19. "the intersection of the timeless moment"; "In concord at this intersection time | Of meeting", *Little Gidding* I 52, II 52–53.

19 **cats · · · moonlight dance**: Edward Lear: "They danced by the light of the moon", *The Owl and the Pussy-Cat*. TSE: "Reserving their terpsichorean powers | To dance by the light of the Jellicle Moon", *The Song of the Jellicles* 27–28.

19, 23, 30, 32 **dance · · · chance · · · By conscious art practised with natural ease · · · sound**: Pope: "True ease in writing comes from art, not chance, | As those move easiest who have learn'd to dance · · · The sound must seem an echo to the sense", *An Essay on Criticism* 362–65.

19, 22–24 **"moonlight · · · the nocturnal traveller · · · an empty house**: de la Mare: "'Is there anybody there?' said the Traveller, | Knocking on the moonlit door · · · But only a host of phantom listeners | That dwelt in the lone house then | Stood listening in the quiet of the moonlight | To that voice from the world of men", *The Listeners*.

29 **Wherewith**: TSE's indecision over "By which" / "Wherein" / "Whereby" (see Textual History) resembles that over "Wherefrom" / "From which", *The Waste Land* [II] 80.

30 **conscious art practised with natural ease**: "Of all poets, Valéry has been the

most completely conscious (perhaps I should say the most nearly conscious) of what he was doing", *"Leçon de Valéry"* (1947).

Draft sonnets (printed in Textual History)

I.

1, 3 **children ··· inaccessible ··· not a tiger. There's no room for him:** "The tiger in the tiger-pit | Is not ··· And inaccessible by the young", *Lines for an Old Man* 1–2, 11.

6 **from limb to limb:** "tear you limb from limb", *Five-Finger Exercises* IV. *Lines to Ralph Hodgson Esqre.* 7.

9 **Spanish Gold:** de la Mare's *Desert Islands* (1930), in which *Marina* was reprinted, includes descriptions of several treasure hoards, including one of a wreck on the Spanish Main.

10, 13 **nursery ··· to be read to:** "an old man ··· Being read to by a boy", *Gerontion* 1–2.

14 **de la Mare:** pronounced as if rhyming with Delaware (having been spelt as one word by his father and grandfather).

II.

1–3 **familiar ··· Or when the strange is one already known, | And presences walk with us, when alone:** "There is always another one walking beside you", *The Waste Land* [V] 362 (and see Commentary). "I met one walking ··· stranger ··· known, forgotten, half recalled ··· familiar", *Little Gidding* II 33–42.

5, 7–8 **moonlight dance ··· midnight hour | The witches' sabbath of the maiden aunts:** Pope: "As Hags hold Sabbaths, less for joy than spight, | So these their merry miserable Night; | Still round and round the Ghosts of Beauty glide", *Of the Characters of Women* 239–41. William Empson discussed Pope's lines in *Seven Types of Ambiguity* (1930) ch. IV, and alluded to them again in ch. VIII ("to maintain one's defences and equilibrium and live as well as one can; it is not only maiden aunts who are placed like this"). TSE's first note to *Montpelier Row* makes play with *Seven Types*.

7 **Under ··· at the midnight hour:** Stanley Holloway, monologue on the ghost of Anne Boleyn (1934): "With her head tucked underneath her arm | She walks the Bloody Tower! | With her head tucked underneath her arm | At the midnight hour."

A Dedication to my Wife

An earlier text appeared as *To My Wife*, the dedication to *The Elder Statesman* (1959), reprinted at the head of that play in *Collected Plays* (1962). The final version first appeared in *1963*. On its prominent positioning there, see Textual History. See also *Dedication II* ("Uncollected Poems").

"This copy no. 1 is of course for my darling bedfellow with whom I sink into blissful silence, my beloved Valerie, my wife, the wife of | T. S. Eliot | 6.xi.60", inscription in Mardersteig edition of *Four Quartets* (Valerie Eliot collection). Earlier, on 26 Apr 1946, TSE had inscribed for her a copy of *1936* 5th imp. (1942). He subsequently added, on its title page: "Inscribed eleven years ago, at the request of Collin Brooks, for a young lady whom I had never met & whose name was that of a complete stranger. We did not meet until the 29th August 1949. I married her on the 10th January 1957. I inscribe this book again, to my beloved & adored wife. Good Friday 1957. T. S. Eliot." Enclosed is a letter, 30 Sept 1946, thanking her for her "kind letter and birthday wishes, both of which gave me much pleasure" (Valerie Eliot collection).

To Cyril Connolly: "I was particularly touched by the way in which you referred, in reviewing my *Collected Poems*, to my last dedicatory poem to my wife. You were the first sympathetic reader and critic to call attention to the unusual fact that I had at last written a poem of love and of happiness. It would almost seem that some readers were shocked that I should be happy" (quoted by Connolly, *Sunday Times* 10 Jan 1965). To Pound, 28 Dec 1959: "She gives me the first happiness I have ever known."

"Without the satisfaction of this happy marriage no achievement or honour could give me satisfaction at all", *Harvard Class of 1910, Fiftieth Anniversary Report* (1960).

2–3 **wakingtime ··· sleepingtime**: OED "waking" *vbl.n.* 5: "waking-time, the time when one is awake; the moment at which one wakes up". OED "sleeping" 1e quotes 1833 E. B. Browning tr. *Prometheus Bound*: "From work-times, diet-times, and sleeping-times." TSE: "One who moves in the time between sleep and waking", *Ash-Wednesday* IV 14. In *The Elder Statesman* III, Lord Claverton hears a voice of conscience "between waking and sleeping".

5 **lovers whose bodies smell of each other**: TSE inscribed a copy of *The Sacred Wood* "for my Valerie", adding: "the touch and smell of whom intoxicates her husband T. S. Eliot" (Magdalene). **each other**: twelve times in *The Elder Statesman* including "in love with each other", twice, and "love each other". See "each other", four times in *Dedication II* ("Uncollected Poems"). "among each other ··· among each other", *The Death of Saint Narcissus* 22–23.

8 **No peevish winter wind**: OED "peevish" 2b: "Of the wind: Piercing, 'shrewd'."

9–10 **No sullen tropic sun shall wither | The roses**: "Have you no brighter tropic flowers | With scarlet lips, for me?" *Song* ("The moonflower opens to the moth") 7–8. "The sun which does not feel decay ··· withered", *A Lyric* 3, 11.

11–12 **But this dedication is for others to read: | These are private words addressed to you in public**: "my opinion is, that a good love poem, though it may be addressed to one person, is always meant to be overheard by other people. Surely, the proper language of love—that is, of communication to the beloved and to no one else—is prose", *The Three Voices of Poetry* 6.

Uncollected Poems

1. POEMS NOT COLLECTED BY TSE: ARRANGEMENT IN THE PRESENT EDITION

Many of TSE's poems were not included by him in his final *Collected Poems* of 1963. Among the exclusions were two volumes: *Old Possum's Book of Practical Cats* (1939) had been included in 1952 in the American *Complete Poems and Plays* (a volume he disliked), whereas *Anabasis* (1930), his translation of St.-John Perse's *Anabase*, had not. Also excluded were his contributions to *Noctes Binanianæ* (1939), which had been for private circulation. Each of these three has a separate section in Vol. II of the present edition.

Likewise absent from *1963* were the poems he had written as a schoolboy and undergraduate, which had been privately printed in *The Undergraduate Poems of T. S. Eliot* [1949] and *Poems Written in Early Youth* (1950). Had he known of their survival, TSE would undoubtedly also have excluded the poems in *Inventions of the March Hare* (1996) and the materials associated with *The Waste Land* (published in *WLFacs* in 1971).

Of individual poems, the only one to have been published in a volume of his own but excluded from *1963* was *Ode* ("Tired. | Subterrene") from *Ara Vos Prec*, but also absent were *Song* ("The golden foot I may not kiss or clutch"), which had been published anonymously in Spring 1921 in *Tyro* but never collected and *The Death of Saint Narcissus*, which had been submitted for publication to *Poetry* but not printed (and which he wished not to see printed in his lifetime, see headnote). He also omitted from *1963* some contributions to anthologies: *The Marching Song of the Pollicle Dogs* and *Billy M'Caw: The Remarkable Parrot*, poems for children printed in *The Queen's Book of the Red Cross* (1939), and *Let quacks, empirics, dolts debate*, printed in *Gala Day London* (1953). All of these appear in the present section, along with miscellaneous private poems and unfinished poems.

"Other Verses" such as need to be presented within their immediate context—juvenilia, poems in letters or written as the addresses of envelopes, and other forms of light and comic verse—are printed in Vol. II, as are "Improper Rhymes".

The contents of this section are arranged chronologically, so far as can be determined. TSE to Geoffrey Faber, 28 Apr 1941, on Faber's *The Buried Stream: Collected Poems 1908–1941*: "*any* order of poems written over a long space of time is more or less at best the best of a bad job, I think; and so I prefer the chronological". Despite his writing to Grover Smith, 4 July 1949, "My ability to forget dates in connection with my own work is, I should think, somewhat exceptional", his memory and concern for dates were enduring.

Many poems in the *March Hare* Notebook were dated by TSE, mostly in pencil and (it appears from the hand) around the time of composition. The dates range from Nov 1909 to Apr 1911, but do not match the order of the poems. Some later poems in this section are also dated on the drafts. In other cases, dates are apparent from letters or from date of publication. With different degrees of confidence, dates can be assigned to most of the other poems on the basis of reference to known events, or the paper on which they were written (for which, see *Rainey*), or the handwriting or typewriter. Information on each appears in the individual headnotes.

2. *POEMS WRITTEN IN EARLY YOUTH*

TSE: "I began I think about the age of fourteen, under the inspiration of FitzGerald's *Omar Khayyam*, to write a number of very gloomy and atheistical and despairing quatrains in the same style, which fortunately I suppressed completely—so completely that they don't exist. I never showed them to anybody", *Paris Review* (1959). On Blake: "His early poems show what the poems of a boy of genius ought to show, immense power of assimilation. Such early poems are not, as usually supposed, crude attempts to do something beyond the boy's capacity; they are, in the case of a boy of real promise, more likely to be quite mature and successful attempts to do something small," *William Blake* (1920).

TSE was one of the editors of the *Harvard Advocate* 1909–10. "I was known as a poet as an undergraduate; I was an editor of the *Harvard Advocate* the chief undergraduate literary paper and I wrote the ode for the graduation ceremonies for my class in 1910", *Northrop Frye corrigenda* (1963).

After their first appearances, most of the *Poems Written in Early Youth* were reprinted in special issues of the *Harvard Advocate* in 1938 and 1948 and in *The Harvard Advocate Anthology* (1950). The note on the author on the back of his *Selected Poems* (Penguin, 1948) included the information that "His first poems were printed in *The Smith Academy Record* and the *Harvard Advocate* (1905–1909)."

An unauthorised separate printing, *The Undergraduate Poems of T. S. Eliot* [1949], was suppressed but was followed by an authorised edition of 12 copies only of *Poems Written in Early Youth* (1950). This was reprinted in 1967 in a trade edition, and the poems appeared in an appendix to *1969*.

Adv 1938: "Eight Poems" reprinted in the *Harvard Advocate* Dec 1938, special number for T. S. Eliot (TSE's corrected copy, King's). To Donald Brace, 18 Nov 1938: "I enclose a copy of the letter which I have just written to Harry Brown of the *Harvard Advocate*. The editors of the *Advocate* have been designing a special number for my jubilee [fiftieth birthday], including a number of articles about me, to appear in December; and for this I naturally raised no objection to their reprinting eight undergraduate poems of mine, which appeared in that periodical (of which I was an editor) between 1906 and 1910. But a possibility which Cap Pierce brought to Frank's attention seems now to be in danger of sprouting: a literary agent has persuaded them into thinking of reprinting the whole issue as a pamphlet, and trying to get some publisher here to undertake it · · · I wanted to let you know at once that I definitely object to having these poems reprinted except in the *Advocate*. If they choose to reprint the articles about me, that is their affair and I cannot object, but I have no desire to have my old undergraduate verse broadcast. Mr. Harry Brown appears to be under the impression that the *Advocate* holds all rights. They can hardly maintain this after receiving my veto: if they should, we must come down on them. I shall be glad and grateful if you will take steps if you hear any rumours of such a pamphlet being published." To Henry Eliot, 23 Dec 1938: "I hope that Mr.

Harry Brown was not downcast by my putting a veto upon the re-issue of the *Advocate* number in England, which he had ingenuously undertaken. My point was simply that I did not want this undergraduate verse to re-appear except as a part of a number of the *Advocate*, not in a pamphlet form ··· He replied very respectfully, but seemed to think that I did not even want the poems mentioned or quoted in any review of the *Advocate* in any other periodical—which far exceeded my prohibition."

Adv 1948: nine poems—now including *Ode* ("For the hour that is left us Fair Harvard")—reprinted *Harvard Advocate* Nov 1948. To the editors of the *Harvard Advocate*, 2 Feb 1949: "May I say without offence that I am surprised that you should reprint these poems without asking my permission. It may not have occurred to you that if I had thought these poems good enough I should long ago have included them in my Collected Works. Authors do not always like to see in circulation the poems which they have themselves rejected. These were reprinted in a special number of the *Advocate* some years ago, but that was a rather different occasion as that number was entirely in my honour and there was that special justification for exhuming my own contribution to the *Advocate*."

Undergraduate Poems: ten poems, as *The Undergraduate Poems of T. S. Eliot* [1949], now including *Song* ("The moonflower opens to the moth"). Hayward's Introduction to *Early Youth 1950* wrongly dated this unauthorised pamphlet 1948.

As the error at *Nocturne* 14 shows, this is a re-impression of the type from *Adv 1948*, with the addition of the extra poem and with two lines in *Spleen* accidentally transposed. In 1947, TSE had protested about the eighty copies of *A Practical Possum* printed at Harvard (see headnote to that poem), so when some 1,000 copies of *Undergraduate Poems* were printed, he wrote to the editor of the *Harvard Advocate*, 29 Nov 1949, to say that he was "exasperated by the circulation of this pamphlet". It was, nevertheless, included in *Gallup*, who corrected the date and added that "about 750 were withdrawn from circulation in December 1949, but at least some—and possibly all—of these appear to have found their way back into the market". (*Gallup 1988* 108 explains how withdrawn copies "were put away in a closet, and promptly began to disappear, as each departing editor took a few copies as souvenirs. *The Undergraduate Poems of T. S. Eliot* soon acquired for those in the know the status of a presumably rare, 'suppressed' item. In the 1960s, an undergraduate who had access to the *Advocate* office appropriated for himself a good many more than just the winked-at few, selling them at very substantial prices to dealers in Cambridge, New Haven and New York. The thief was soon caught; and the *Advocate* editors profited by the lesson he had taught them, making their own arrangements with a rare book firm in England to handle most of the copies that remained.")

Adv Anth: eight poems reprinted, together with *Gentlemen and Seamen* (a prose piece from May 1909), in *The Harvard Advocate Anthology* ed. Donald Hall [1950]. TSE to Hall, 29 Dec 1949: "I must thank you for your very handsome apology without any date. After all, part of the experience of editing university magazines is the experience of finding out what the etiquette of publication is. However, while I am ready to forgive your predecessors for their ignorance of the rules, I think that it is more difficult to excuse their publishing my verses with so many misprints as to be practically garbled." Acceding then to a request to print the poems in *The Harvard Advocate Anthology*, he added: "The only thing I ask is that you should not want *all* of my undergraduate poems, but leave out at least one. I don't care which. Make up your minds as to which is the worst, and leave that out." Accordingly, the anthology omitted *Song* ("If time and space as sages say") as "probably the poorest". Hall to TSE, 5 July 1950: "Mr. Donald Gallup ··· tells me that your *Humouresque*, even as printed in 1910, contained two errors. (The *Advocate* seems to have had similar faults over a forty year period.) Perhaps you would like to rectify these errors in the *Advocate Anthology.*" TSE, 10 July: "I cannot lay my hand on a copy at the moment, so would you be so kind as to ask Mr. Donald Gallup for the corrections, as I am sure that you may take any corrections he gives you as authoritative." For the *Advocate* in 1957, see *Your cablegram arrived too late* ("Other Poems").

Early Youth 1950: *Poems Written in Early Youth* [ed. with notes by John Hayward, and with Introduction initialled by him] (1950). To the ten poems of *Undergraduate Poems* are added two from *Smith Academy Record* (*A Fable for Feasters* and *A Lyric*), the recital piece *To the Class of 1905* and the later poem *The Death of Saint Narcissus.* Gallup received a letter from Hayward, June 1950: "Eliot has agreed to allow Bonniers, his Swedish publishers, to produce a tremendously private edition of 12 copies (including one for you) of his verse *Juvenilia.* Bonniers will keep 5–6 copies for themselves (one for each of the directors) on the understanding that they must never be sold or alienated. No copies will be available to the public & as the edition will not be 'published', no copies will be sent to 'copyright' libraries in Sweden or abroad. I have undertaken to supply the material & do any necessary editing. I want your help." Gallup's account goes on: "I sent him photocopies of the texts as originally printed between 1907 and 1910 in the *Advocate* and suggested that Eliot might be willing to allow the inclusion of *The Death of Saint Narcissus* ··· I sent Hayward a Photostat, and he reported to me in July that Eliot hadn't 'the foggiest recollection' of the poem, but agreed that it could be included in 'the rare booklet'. *Poems Written in Early Youth* (Stockholm, 1950) appeared in December and stirred up a good deal of interest" (*Gallup 1988* 108–109). Georg Svensson of Bonniers to Peter du Sautoy, 3 Dec 1965: "Eliot was so strict about this that although a copy was sent to the Swedish Academy [where he had received the Nobel Prize in Dec 1948], the Royal Librarian and the university libraries never got any although they can claim to have one free copy of every book printed." The title *Poems Written in Early Youth* may have been influenced by "Poems written in Youth", a section of Edgar Allan Poe's *Poems* (TSE dated his copy 1906).

Hayward's copies of pages from the original *Harvard Advocate* printings are at King's. They are bound with his manuscript transcript, the typescript made from that and one of his two proofs. Those intermediate stages are not collated in the present edition. Information from the notes not given elsewhere is designated "(*Hayward*)", although Valerie Eliot wrote in a letter of 26 May 1966 to Peter du Sautoy that they "were in fact provided by Tom" (Faber archive).

TSE to D. E. S. Maxwell, 22 May 1951: "I am averse to any further republication of my juvenile poems. If I did agree to publish them, it would have to be under the imprint of Faber & Faber, in any case, but I have no intention or design to do so ··· I think they are verse of a kind which is much better printed, if at all, some time after the author's death." To Wilder Penfield, 1 May 1964: "I don't think I produced any memorable verse during my undergraduate days ··· the various poems which appeared in the *Harvard Advocate* are now only of biographical interest." The first trade collections of the poems followed TSE's death:

Early Youth 1967: *Poems Written in Early Youth* (1967). Follows *Early Youth 1950* except where stated. Published reluctantly by Valerie Eliot so as to retain rights, because of fears of unofficial publication in Germany. Four of the poems were reprinted using this text in *First Flowering: The Best of the Harvard Advocate* ed. Richard M. Smoley (1971).

1969: as an appendix to the edition.

Except where noted, the present text is that of *Early Youth 1950*, which had TSE's imprimatur.

Note (by Valerie Eliot) from *Early Youth 1967*:

> These early poems were collected by John Hayward and privately printed in an edition limited to twelve copies by Albert Bonniers of Stockholm in 1950. So much interest has been expressed in this collection, which was supervised by the author, that it seems wise to make it generally available as a corrective to the inaccurate, pirated versions.
>
> These appear to be the only juvenilia of my husband that survive. At the age of nine or ten, he told me, he wrote "a few little verses about the sadness of having to start school again every Monday morning". He gave them to his Mother and hoped they had not been preserved. At about fourteen he wrote "some very gloomy quatrains in the form of the *Rubáiyát*" which had "captured my imagination". These he showed to no one and presumed he destroyed.
>
> Two incidents connected with *A Lyric* (which is given on page 17) remained in the poet's mind. These stanzas in imitation of Ben Jonson were done as a school exercise when he was sixteen. "My English master, who had set his class the task of producing some verse, was much impressed and asked whether I had had any help from some elder person. Surprised, I assured him that they were wholly unaided". They were printed in the school paper, *Smith Academy Record*, but he did not mention them to his family. "Some time later the issue was shown to my Mother, and she remarked (we were walking along Beaumont Street in St. Louis) that she thought them better than anything in verse she had ever written. I knew what her verse meant to her. We did not discuss the matter further".
>
> 1966, V.E.
>
> Acknowledgements and thanks are due to the late John Hayward's sister, Mrs. Oakeley, for her permission to reproduce his introduction and notes.

(The jacket material for *Early Youth 1967* derives closely from this note: "These early poems were collected by John Hayward and privately printed in 1950 by Bonniers of Stockholm in an edition limited to twelve copies. So much interest has been expressed in the poems that it has been decided to re-issue them in order that correct versions may be made generally available. The collection was prepared under the supervision of the author.")

Introduction (by Hayward) from *Early Youth 1950*, *1967*:

> Apart from a few unrecorded *jeux d'esprit*, this collection contains all the surviving poems written by T. S. Eliot between the winter of 1904 and the spring of 1910; that is to say, between his sixteenth and twenty-second birthdays, while he was a day-boy at Smith Academy, St. Louis, or an undergraduate at Harvard. *The Death of Saint Narcissus*, which was suppressed in proof and never published, is of a slightly later date.
>
> The first two schoolboy poems were originally published in *Smith Academy Record*; the third was publicly recited by the poet on Graduation Day, 1905, and is here printed for the first time from the only known copy. The nine undergraduate poems, together with a variant version of the *Lyric* printed in *Smith Academy Record*, were originally published between 1907 and 1910 in *The Harvard Advocate*, of which the poet was an associate-editor from 1909 to 1910. Eight of these ten poems were reprinted together in *The Harvard Advocate* in 1938; and, without permission, with the addition of the second *Song*, in the same periodical in 1948. The ten poems were reissued in the same year by the editors of the *Advocate*, again without permission, and with many misprints, in a pamphlet entitled *The Undergraduate Poems of T. S. Eliot.*
>
> The sources of the text of the present authorized collection are given in the Notes at the end.
>
> J. H. [*Early Youth 1967 spells out*: JOHN HAYWARD]

To A. H. Cooke, 18 Sept 1929: "At nineteen, I wrote some verse worth publishing, but I did not get anyone to publish it until I was twenty-eight."

3. *INVENTIONS OF THE MARCH HARE*

To Keith Douglas, 15 Feb 1941: "My impression so far is that you have completed one phase which begins with the very accomplished *juvénilité*, and that you have started on another which you have not yet mastered. Of the first phase I feel that, as might be expected, there is a certain musical monotony in the rhythms. That does not matter in itself because it is a good thing to go on doing one thing until you are sure that its use is exhausted, but from the point of view of collective publication it is a very good monotony, and I think you have definitely an ear. What I should like to see is the second phase which you have begun developed to the point of formal mastery."

OED "Invention" 11: "*Mus.* A short piece of music in which a single idea is worked out in a simple manner." Kipling: "and I must even piece out what he had told me with my own poor inventions while Charlie wrote of the ways of bank-clerks", *The Finest Story in the World*. This story was collected in Kipling's *Many Inventions* (1893), and TSE referred to it, together with *Alice's Adventures in Wonderland*, in a footnote to *Rudyard Kipling* (1941). Carroll's Haigha and Hatta appear together in *Through the Looking-Glass*, in which the White Knight repeatedly says "It's my own invention". TSE to J. H. Oldham, 4 Nov 1944, on The Moot: "I anticipate that even without that, members will tend to disperse all over the place each chasing his own March Hare, and I don't want this to become an educational discussion." Grover Smith to Christopher Ricks, 15 Mar 1997: "Once, when I was quizzing Eliot on some supposed allusions in his poems, he wrote at the end of a long reply: 'And please don't hunt so many March Hares!'"

For the history and contents of the Notebook and accompanying leaves, and for *Valerie's Own Book*, see the Textual History headnote, 5. THE *MARCH HARE* NOTEBOOK

AND ACCOMPANYING LEAVES and 6. *VALERIE'S OWN BOOK*. For the history of the other poems in this section, see individual headnotes.

A Lyric ("If Time and Space, as Sages say") and *Song* ("If space and time, as sages say")

The first, printed in *Smith Academy Record* Apr 1905, then *Early Youth* (1950) and reprinted in 1957 in *Powel*, then *Early Youth* (1967)+. Written Jan 1905.

The second, printed in *Harvard Advocate* 3 June 1907, then *Adv 1938, Adv 1948, Undergraduate Poems, Early Youth* (1950)+.

For TSE's mother's reaction to seeing *A Lyric* in *Smith Academy Record*, see headnote to "Uncollected Poems", 2. *POEMS WRITTEN IN EARLY YOUTH*. TSE wrote an introduction to his mother's dramatic poem *Savonarola* and arranged its publication in 1926. Following her death he wrote to his brother, Henry, 19 Oct 1929:

> About mother's poems. I should very much like them to be published. I have a few, but not many. It would be a great pleasure to me to write an introduction or preface for the book, and perhaps if I did so a publisher, or a publisher of limited editions particularly, might be ready to bear part or all of the cost of production. It would be a delicate and possibly invidious task, as whatever I wrote would have to have the approval of all members of the immediate family before it appeared, but I should be glad to do it. Some of them, indeed all of them in some degree, are good poems. I remember when I wrote a poem at Smith Academy, when I was 16, I learned to my surprise that she had had copies typed and distributed (I only heard that from Aunt Rose) and then mother said to me that it was a better poem than any she had written. It wasn't; but even then I had some perception of what such a statement meant.

Imitation of Ben Jonson's *Song. To Celia* ("Drinke to me, onely, with thine eyes").

The line-numbered lemmata below give preference to TSE's second version, *Song*.

Titles **A Lyric** | **Song**: in early notes for what became his essay *The Nature of Metaphysical Poetry* (*Criterion* Apr 1923), Herbert Read claimed that "the lyric has the essential quality of 'emotion' but its distinction seems to rest on its connection with visual sensibility". TSE objected: "? Why not stick to the meaning—to accompany music, to be sung" (Read papers, U. Victoria).

1–2 **If space and time, as sages say, | Are things that cannot be**: the poem was written months before Einstein revolutionised the physics of space, time and matter with the special theory of relativity. In Sept 1904 Henri Poincaré lectured on the emerging ideas at the St. Louis World's Fair (to which Smith Academy sent a troop: *Yearbook 1903–04*). In his paper for the Fair, *The Principles of Mathematical Physics*, Poincaré described contemporary challenges to the Newtonian laws of time and space (vol 1 of *Congress of Arts and Science: Universal Exposition, St. Louis, 1904* ed. Howard J. Rogers, 1905). Josiah Royce of Harvard also spoke at the Congress. Charles Mauron's *On Reading Einstein*, which TSE translated for *Criterion* Oct 1930, described how "before the first relativists (Lorentz, Poincaré) two vast things-in-themselves dwelt quietly at the very heart of abstract science: Space and Time", and how in the new theory, "Time and Space in themselves vanish". For Poincaré and Einstein, see headnote to *Mr. Apollinax.* TSE to Pound, 23 July 1934: "a Little Animil wich I understan does illustrate the Quantum Theory by bein at two Places at once even if he dont understand it".

Emerson: "Time and space are but physiological colors which the eye makes", *Self-Reliance*. TSE's *Knowledge and Experience* 110 quotes Bradley's *Appearance and Reality* ch. IV, "Space and Time": "And time so far, like space, has turned out to be appearance" (*Lockerd* 16). Two of TSE's anonymous reviews in *Monist* Oct 1917 mention Time and Space. Summarising essays in *Mind* Apr 1917, he wrote: "Time and space are both objective"; and summarising B. M. Laing: "This perversion of the Kantian doctrine leads Schopenhauer to hold (in contrast to Kant) that the world of space and time is an illusion." Kipling: "the soul had passed beyond the illusion of Time and Space of Things", *Kim* ch. XV (two pages from the end) (*Crawford* 31). TSE: "his maturest work on India, and his greatest book, is *Kim*", *Rudyard Kipling* (1941); a copy appears in *TSE's books: Bodleian list* (1934).

7 **time is time, and runs away**: "*When* will time flow away", *Five-Finger Exercises* I. *Lines to a Persian Cat* 10.

9 **flowers I sent thee**: Jonson: "I sent thee, late, a rosie wreath", *Song* 9.

9, 11 **flowers · · · withered**: TSE: "Fresh flowers, withered flowers, flowers of dawn", *Before Morning* 4.

11 **withered · · · bee**: Jonson: "It could not withered bee", *Song* 12 (original spelling).

A Fable for Feasters

Printed in *Smith Academy Record* Feb 1905, signed "T. E. '05", then *Early Youth* (1950)+.

Hayward: "This Byronic exercise was Eliot's first appearance in print" (though perhaps written after *A Lyric*). TSE wrote that Byron was his "first boyhood enthusiasm · · · images come before the mind, and the recollection of some verses in the manner of *Don Juan*, tinged with that disillusion and cynicism only possible at the age of sixteen, which appeared in a school periodical", *Byron* (1937). *Moody* 352: "The verses were *A Fable for Feasters. Beppo* looks a likelier model." Ottava rima, Byron's stanzaic form in both *Don Juan* and *Beppo*, was adopted by Richard Barham for *The Ghost* in *The Ingoldsby Legends* (*Grover Smith* 3), a copy of which appears in *TSE's books: Bodleian list* (1934). TSE: "you cannot write satire in the line of Pope or the stanza of Byron", *After Strange Gods* 24. "No imitation of Alexander Pope's couplets, or of Byron's ottava rima can be more than a clever pastiche", *Royal Academy Speech* (1960). See note to *WLComposite* **229–300**.

An address at Chichester Cathedral: "In my schooldays, we were given to understand that, before the Reformation, England was groaning under the burden of supporting innumerable idle monks; and that Henry VIII sent them all packing, except a small number of the least incorrigible, whom he turned into deans and canons", *The Value and Use of Cathedrals in England Today* (1951). In William Henry Schofield's *English Literature from the Norman Conquest to Chaucer* 128, TSE underlined "keenly satirised" in the sentence "The notorious vices of the monks were keenly satirised in an amusing piece, *L'Ordre de Bel Aise.*"

6 **travelers:** Valerie Eliot, 8 Oct 1969, answering a query: "it is the American spelling and Tom was living there at the time" (memo, Faber archive).

21 **He stole the fatter cows and left the thinner:** Peacock: "The mountain sheep are sweeter, | But the valley sheep are fatter; | We therefore deemed it meeter | To carry off the latter", *The War Song of Dinas Vawr* 1–4.

To the Class of 1905

Printed in *Early Youth* (1950)+ under a provided title, *At Graduation 1905*.

Written as a school graduation piece and recited at Memorial Hall, 13 June 1905. TSE was commencement poet of Smith Academy, according to *The Smith Academy Anvil*, Class of 1905 (Myerson, St. Louis), of which he was also associate editor. To Marquis W. Childs of Missouri Historical Society, he wrote on 8 Aug 1930 that he had graduated from Smith Academy "with some distinction, having produced the Class Poem, which even now seems to me not bad". In 1953: "my part in the ceremony was to deliver the valedictory poem of the year. I was informed afterwards, by one of my teachers, that the poem itself was excellent, as such poems go, but that my delivery was very bad indeed", *American Literature and the American Language* 3. This was perhaps his respected English teacher, Roger Conant Hatch, who contributed several rousing songs to *The School Songs of Smith Academy* [1907? ed.]. Also in the volume was the school song (words W. W. Gale, music W. H. Pommer, 1897): "When boyhood's past and we are men | Where'er or what we be, | We'll oft look back with feelings warm | To Smith Academy." The St. Louis World's Fair, 1904, epitomised high expectations for the new century. To Hayward, 19 Aug 1943: "I hope you will be impressed by the pathos of the hopes which I expressed for the twentieth century and for the future of a day school which was dissolved through lack of pupils a few years later." For "false assumption of the *excessive value of the future*", see note to *The Dry Salvages* I 10.

Title ***To the Class of 1905*:** this title, though not necessarily TSE's own, is from a printed programme discovered by Jayme Stayer at Washington U. TSE may later have agreed to the title *At Graduation 1905*, which Hayward printed in square brackets in *Early Youth* (1950).

3–4 **sail we | Across the harbor bar:** Tennyson, *Crossing the Bar* (title).

5 **to warn of rocks which lie below:** "the ragged rock in the restless waters", *The Dry Salvages* II 70.

15 **o'er:** to Ross E. Pierce, 9 Mar 1936: "Why use 'o'er' at all, in this century? People do not use it in the best conversation."

43–44 **when we are grown | Gray-haired and old:** "We'll call it back to mem'ry dear when we are gray and old", *The Red and the White* (music, W. H. Pommer) in *The School Songs of Smith Academy*.

50 **Incense of altar-smoke shall rise to thee**: "smoking incense, which had a most unpleasant odor", *The Man Who Was King* (1905).

57 **t'will**: Robert Giroux suggested the emendation "'twill", but in a memo to Peter du Sautoy, 23 Mar 1967, Valerie Eliot replied that "t'will" had been "confirmed by Tom in 1950".

77 **motto**: "This golden motto e'er shall stand. | Not for ourselves alone, | But for our friends and native land", *Non Nobis Solum: Our Motto* (words, Roger Conant Hatch; music, William John Hall) in *The School Songs of Smith Academy*. The Eliot family's close involvement with the school is evident from this title, for as Charlotte Eliot noted in her life of TSE's paternal grandfather, "The motto on Dr. Eliot's family crest was 'Tace et fac.' Another less commonly used in the family was, 'Non nobis solum,' and this he preferred", Charlotte C. Eliot, *William Greenleaf Eliot* (1904) 358. For "*Tace et fac*", see note to *East Coker* I 13.

78 **"Progress!"**: on Unitarianism: "I do not plan to deprecate the alcoholic or stimulant value of the idea of Progress. I belong to a church of which one of the tenets refers to the Progress of mankind onward and upward forever. I do not understand what this phrase means, but I acknowledge its value for enthusiasm", *The Relationship between Politics and Metaphysics* (1914), alluding to J. R. Lowell. For the Eliots and Unitarianism, see headnote to *Mr. Eliot's Sunday Morning Service*. "the doctrine of progress, while it can do little to make the future more real to us, has a very strong influence towards making the past less real to us. For it leads us to take for granted that the past, any part or the whole of it, has its meaning only in the present", *A Commentary* in *Criterion* Oct 1932. "The assumption of the inevitability of progress has, we all know, been discarded in its nineteenth century form: it is the butt of popular philosophers like Dean Inge ··· Nevertheless, we retain the essential of the doctrine of progress: we have no faith in the present", *Literature and the Modern World* (1935). For "superficial notions of evolution ··· in the popular mind", see *East Coker* II 40–41.

80–81 **"Farewell", | A word that echoes like a funeral bell**: Keats: "Forlorn! the very word is like a bell ··· Adieu!", *Ode to a Nightingale* 71, 73 (*Crawford 2015* 75).

Song ("When we came home across the hill")

Printed in *Harvard Advocate* 24 May 1907, then *Adv 1938, Adv 1948, Undergraduate Poems, Early Youth* (1950)+.

3 **The gentle fingers of the breeze**: "the last fingers of leaf", *The Waste Land* [III] 173. "fingers of surf", *Mr. Apollinax* 13. "Fingers of yew", *Burnt Norton* IV 7.

5 **The hedgerow bloomed with flowers still**: "the hedgerow | Is blanched for an hour with transitory blossom", *Little Gidding* I 14–15.

8 **and the leaves were brown**: Lewis Carroll: "In autumn, when the leaves are brown, | Take pen and ink, and write it down", *Through the Looking-Glass* ch. VI (TSE: "one more thought for pen and ink!" *Mandarins* 4 1).

Before Morning

Printed in *Harvard Advocate* 13 Nov 1908, then *Adv 1938, Adv 1948, Undergraduate Poems, Early Youth* (1950)+.

The month after publication, the *Harvard Lampoon* printed a parody (reprinted *Soldo* 99):

Before Morning

(With apologies to T.S.E. of the *Abdicate*)

While all the east was wearing red with gray,
The bottles on the backstep turned toward dawn,
Bottle on bottle waiting for the day,
Clean bottles, milk bottles, bottles of dawn.

This morning's bottles and bottles of yesterday,
Their contents drips across the steps of dawn,
Blobs of the fresh and curdles of decay,
Clean bottles, milk bottles, bottles of dawn.

Circe's Palace

Printed in *Harvard Advocate* 25 Nov 1908, reprinted *Cap and Gown: Some College Verse* ed. R. L. Paget (1931). Then *Adv 1938, Adv 1948, Undergraduate Poems, Early Youth* (1950)+.

Title] *Lemprière* on Circe: "Celebrated for her knowledge of magic and venomous herbs · · · Ulysses, at his return from the Trojan war, visited the place of residence; and all his companions, who ran headlong into pleasure and voluptuousness, were changed by Circe's potions into filthy swine. Ulysses, who was fortified against all enchantments by a herb called *moly*, which he had received from Mercury, went to Circe, and demanded, sword in hand, the restoration of his companions to their former state. She complied · · · For one whole year Ulysses forgot his glory in Circe's arms." *Odyssey* X; retold by Hawthorne in *Tanglewood Tales* (1853) under the heading "Circe's Palace".

12 **stately and slow**: Lionel Johnson: "Stately and slow, she went away", *The Troopship* 6 (*Crawford 2015* 103). Whittier: "Stately and slow, with thoughtful air", *The Prophecy of Samuel Sewall* 9 (Shawn Worthington, personal communication).

On a Portrait

Printed in *Harvard Advocate* 26 Jan 1909, then *Adv 1938, Adv 1948, Undergraduate Poems, Early Youth* (1950)+.

To J. Isaacs, 29 Dec 1948: the poem "is of course inspired by the Manet portrait" (*La Dame au Perroquet*, in the Metropolitan Museum, NY, since 1889). Harford Powel, Jr.: "Tinckom-Fernandez says ··· that Eliot saw a reproduction of it in an English book on French Impressionist art", *Notes on the Life of T. S. Eliot, 1888–1910* (Brown University thesis, 1954) 78.

2–3 **restless brain and weary feet, | Forever hurrying up and down**: *Symons* 108 on Laforgue's art: "There is in it all the restlessness of modern life, the haste to escape from whatever weighs too heavily on the liberty of the moment, that capricious liberty which demands only room enough to hurry itself weary" (*Mayer* 47). TSE: "hurrying feet", *Marina* 20.

2–4 **feet ··· hurrying up and down ··· stands at evening in the room alone**: "Paces about her room again, alone", *The Waste Land* [III] 254.

7 **lamia**: OED: "a fabulous monster supposed to have the body of a woman, and to prey upon human beings and suck the blood of children". Keats, *Lamia* (1820).

13–14 **The parrot on his bar**: "'Billy M'Caw! | Come give us a dance on the bar!'", *Billy M'Caw: The Remarkable Parrot* 17–18.

14 **Regards her ··· eye**: "'Regard that woman ··· And you see the corner of her eye ···", *Rhapsody on a Windy Night* 16–21.

Song ("The moonflower opens to the moth")

Printed in *Harvard Advocate* 26 Jan 1909, then *Undergraduate Poems*, *Early Youth* (1950)+.

1, 7 **Moonflower ··· tropic**: OED "moon-flower" 2: "tropical climbing plant, *Ipomœa alba*, of the family Convolvulaceæ, which bears fragrant, white, trumpet-shaped flowers opening at night".

7–8 **tropic flowers | With scarlet lips**: the flowers of the tropical *Psychotria elata* strikingly resemble scarlet lips.

Ballade of the Fox Dinner

Recited 15 May 1909. Privately printed for the Fox Club in *Fifty Years: William R. Castle* (1949) and reprinted in *Soldo*. The Digamma, or Fox Club, was an exclusive Harvard society with its own three-storey building. TSE was Treasurer 1908–09 (*Crawford 2015* 94–95).

Title ***Ballade***: the ballade form (three stanzas and a shorter envoi) was popular among later Victorians and Edwardians.

6 **Oblivious of bonds and stocks:** the bankers' panic on Wall Street in 1907 saw the share index fall almost 50 per cent from the previous year (Jayme Stayer, personal communication).

25 **temporize**: OED 4: "to arrange or make terms, to effect a compromise". The

Women's Christian Temperance Union ("white ribboners") was founded in 1874, and led the way to Prohibition in 1919. Harvard had its own Temperance Society in the 19th century (Jayme Stayer), and Cambridge became a "dry" city in 1886 (see note to *WLComposite* 2). **demon Rum**: used generically for alcohol. O. Henry: "'demon rum'—as the white ribboners miscall whiskey", *The Trimmed Lamp* (1907).

Nocturne

Published in *Harvard Advocate* 12 Nov 1909. After being reprinted in *Adv 1938*, the poem appeared in a non-Harvard publication, *Time* 2 Jan 1939, against TSE's wishes. Then *Adv 1948, Undergraduate Poems, Early Youth* (1950)+.

Moody 18–19: "Laforgue could rewrite *Hamlet* · · · with the ironic condescension of one who knows it all. His Hamlet reflects that at least he has saved Ophelia from a life worse than death; and then is himself saved from the banalities of a passionate elopement when Laertes stabs him. Eliot, in *Nocturne*, applied that treatment to *Romeo and Juliet.*" (For Laforgue's *Hamlet*, see note to *Preludes* I 13 and related notes.)

1 **Romeo, *grand sérieux***: "Are we then so serious?" *Conversation Galante* 18 (with "nocturne", 8; and "moon", 1).

2 **Guitar and hat in hand**: *Symons* 109 on Laforgue: "He composes love-poems hat in hand, and smiles with an exasperating tolerance before all the transformations of the eternal feminine." TSE: "Waits, hat and gloves in hand", *Spleen* 13. "hat in hand", *Suite Clownesque* IV 6.

7–8 **Behind the wall I have some servant wait, | Stab**: for such uses of "have", see note to "You have the scene arrange itself", *Portrait of a Lady* I 2.

First Caprice in North Cambridge

Published in *March Hare.*

Dated Nov 1909 in Notebook.

Title ***Caprice in***: preposition perhaps coloured by a musical key (such as Caprice in C). Symons has a poem *Caprice*, Théodore de Banville *Les Caprices*, and Verlaine, *Caprices* I–V. W. D. Howells's *Caprice* was reprinted in *A Vers de Société Anthology* ed. Carolyn Wells (1907). For musical titles see note to the title *Preludes.* ***North Cambridge***: the distinctly non-Harvard part of Cambridge, Massachusetts.

1 **A street-piano, garrulous and frail**: John Davidson, *To the Street Piano* (1894); see note to *Preludes* II 1–4. TSE: "when a street-piano, mechanical and tired | Reiterates some worn-out common song", *Portrait of a Lady* II 39–40. (*First Debate between the Body and Soul* has "street-pianos through the trees" four times.) Laforgue has *Complainte de l'orgue de Barbarie* [Complaint of the

Barrel-Organ] and *Autre complainte de l'orgue de Barbarie.* Symons: "Enigmatical, tremulous, | Voice of the troubled wires ··· Wail to me", *The Barrel-Organ* 1–4 (TSE: "voices ··· wail", 4). W. G. Tinckom-Fernandez's *The Street Organ* (*Harvard Advocate* 25 June 1908) had "spring shyly taps the window-pane" (TSE: "against the panes ··· windows", 2–3). For Tinckom-Fernandez, see note to *Cousin Nancy* 2. **street- ··· garrulous:** "Along the city streets ··· garrulous waves of life", *Silence* 1–3.

1–3 **-piano ··· frail ··· yellow evening ··· windows:** Verlaine: "Le piano que baise une main frêle ··· le soir rose et gris ··· la fenêtre" [The piano that a frail hand kisses ··· the evening rose and grey ··· the window], *Romances sans paroles* [*Romances without Words*] V.

1, 4 **garrulous and frail ··· wail:** John Gray: "wail ··· tremulous and frail", *Sonnet: Translated from Paul Verlaine* (1890). **garrulous and frail:** Laforgue: "Les Jeunes Filles inviolables et frêles" [the frail inviolable Young Ladies], *Dimanches: C'est l'automne* [*Sundays: It's Autumn*] 9 (see note to *Easter: Sensations of April* I 13–14). TSE to Paul Elmer More, 2 June 1930: "having met the mild blond garrulous and frail stripling Tate, your news made me explode with laughter". **frail ··· evening flung ··· voices:** Hardy: "At once a voice arose ··· In a full-hearted evensong ··· An aged thrush, frail ··· thus to fling his soul", *The Darkling Thrush* 17–23. For Hardy, see headnote to *Opera*.

1–8 **garrulous and frail ··· children's ··· grass ··· sparrows:** John Gray: "The garrulous sparrows ··· child ··· grass", *Poem* (1893).

2 **The yellow evening flung against the panes:** "When the evening is spread out against the sky", *The Love Song of J. Alfred Prufrock* 2 (with "yellow ··· panes", 15, 16). **yellow evening:** "a sunset yellow and rose", *Second Caprice in North Cambridge* 17. "evening yellow and rose", *Portrait of a Lady* III 32.

2–3 **flung against the panes ··· windows:** Van Wyck Brooks: "if humour is discredited ··· it will have its fling at the windows", *The Wine of the Puritans* 103. TSE: "window ··· Flung their smoke", *The Waste Land* [II] 90, 92.

2–10 **evening ··· mud and grass ··· Delve in the gutter with sordid patience:** "Rocks, moss, stonecrop ··· at evening, poking the peevish gutter", *Gerontion* 12, 14. **sparrows ··· gutter with sordid:** "The thousand sordid images ··· And you heard the sparrows in the gutters", *Preludes* III 4, 9 (for "images", see note to 7). **gutter with sordid patience ··· considerations:** "gutters ··· With senile patience | The withered leaves | Of our sensations", *First Debate between the Body and Soul* 3–7. "reverberation ··· With a little patience", *The Waste Land* [V] 326, 330. **with sordid patience:** *Paradise Lost* II 569: "With stubborn patience".

4 **children's voices:** see note to "Children's voices in the orchard", *Landscapes* I. *New Hampshire* 1.

4–6 **voices ··· broken glass ··· grass:** "Our dried voices ··· As wind in dry grass | Or rats' feet over broken glass", *The Hollow Men* I 5–9.

6 **Trampled:** Shelley: "Would trample out, for any slight caprice", *The Cenci* III I 235 (TSE's title: *Caprice*).

7 **A heap of broken barrows:** "A heap of broken images", *The Waste Land* [I] 22.

11 **minor considerations:** to Aiken, 30 Sept 1914: "sometimes I think—if I could

only get back to Paris · · · I'm in the worry way now. Too many minor considerations. Does anything kill as petty worries do?" Laforgue: "Je me sens fou d'un tas de petites misères" [I'm driven mad by a heap of little miseries], *Complainte d'une convalescence en mai* 13.

Second Caprice in North Cambridge

Published in *March Hare.*

Dated Nov 1909 in Notebook.

1 **This charm of:** Tennyson: "this charm | Of woven paces", *Merlin and Vivien* 327–28. *Paradise Lost* IV 651–52: "With charm of earliest birds, nor rising sun | On this delightful land".

1, 7 **vacant lots · · · bricks:** Virginia Woolf on TSE: "His father was a brick merchant in St Louis; & they lived in the slums among vacant lots", *Diary* 10 Sept 1933. TSE: "my father, from filial piety, did not wish to leave the house that he [William Greenleaf Eliot] had built · · · so it came to be that we lived on in a neighbourhood which had become shabby to a degree approaching slumminess · · · for nine months of the year my scenery was almost exclusively urban, and a good deal of it seedily, drably urban at that. My urban imagery was that of St. Louis, upon which that of Paris and London have been superimposed", *The Influence of Landscape upon the Poet* (1960). "*In the vacant places | We will build with new bricks*", *Choruses from "The Rock"* I 79–80. For "vacant lots", see *Preludes* IV 16 and note.

1–17 **This charm of vacant lots · · · tins in piles · · · December · · · sunset yellow and rose:** Henry James: "the red sunsets of winter · · · boards and tin and frozen earth · · · loose fences, vacant lots · · · as the afternoon closed, the ugly picture was tinted with a clear, cold rosiness", *The Bostonians* ch. XX.

2–4 **fields that lie · · · eye:** Milton: "climes that lie | Where day never shuts his eye, | Up in the broad fields of the sky", *Comus* 977–79.

3–4 **Sinister, sterile · · · Entreat the eye:** Job 24: 21: "He evil entreateth the barren that beareth not" (with "his eyes", 24: 24). **Entreat the eye:** *Romeo and Juliet* II ii: "Two of the fairest stars in all the heaven, | Having some business, do entreat her eyes | To twinkle in their spheres till they return." TSE remarked "some artificiality" there: "For it seems unlikely that a man standing below in the garden, even on a very bright moonlight night, would see the eyes of the lady above flashing so brilliantly as to justify such a comparison", Note added to *Poetry and Drama* (1951) as reprinted in *On Poetry and Poets*, adapted from *The Development of Shakespeare's Verse* (1937, 1950).

6–7, 9 **tins · · · bricks · · · Far from our definitions:** "such words as 'world' or 'self' denote objects which are by no means simple · · · Towards objects of this type there are two points of view which seem to me mistaken. One is to hypostasise them, to treat them as more real, or as manifestations of a higher reality, than such objects as bricks and tin cans", *Comments on T. H. Green* (*c.* 1914).

7–8 **Shattered bricks and tiles | And the debris of a city:** C. F. G. Masterman: "broken bottles, and the refuse of the city", *From the Abyss* (1902) 12. (For Masterman's social study see note to the title *Easter: Sensations of April.*) **bricks and tiles:** Verlaine: "Briques et tuiles, | O les charmants" [bricks and tiles, | O the charm of them], *Walcourt* 1–2 (TSE: "charm", 1, 14).

9 **definitions:** recognising the etymology. The title-page of *Notes towards the Definition of Culture* has the epigraph: "DEFINITION: 1. The setting of bounds; | limitation (rare)—1483 | —*Oxford English Dictionary*".

14, 16–17 **charm ··· evening ··· sunset yellow and rose:** Tennyson: "The charmèd sunset lingered low adown | In the red West ··· rosy flame", *The Lotos-Eaters* 19–20, 26.

Opera

Published in *March Hare.*

Dated Nov 1909 in Notebook.

Nietzsche deplored opera while praising *Tristan und Isolde.* "The man incapable of art ··· dreams himself into a time when passion suffices to generate songs and poems: as if emotion had ever been able to create anything artistic. The postulate of the opera is a false belief concerning the artistic process, in fact, the idyllic belief that every sentient man is an artist", *The Birth of Tragedy* §19. TSE on Hardy: "He seems to me to have written as nearly for the sake of 'self-expression' as a man well can ··· interested not at all in men's minds, but only in their emotions; and perhaps only in men as vehicles for emotions. It is only, indeed, in their emotional paroxysms that most of Hardy's characters come alive ··· a refined form of torture on the part of the writer, and a refined form of self-torture on the part of the reader", *After Strange Gods* 54–56. However: "It should be mentioned somewhere that I became dis-satisfied with *After Strange Gods*, which I came to consider rather intemperate, especially in speaking of Thomas Hardy, and no longer keep in print in this country", *Northrop Frye corrigenda* (1963).

1 **Tristan and Isolde:** *Ackroyd* 38: the poem "seems to have been written after he had seen a performance in Boston ··· When he was in his sixties he discussed this opera with Stravinsky, and from that conversation Stravinsky inferred that it must have been 'one of the most passionate experiences of his life'", quoting Igor Stravinsky, *Memories of T. S. Eliot* in *Esquire* Aug 1965. Jean Verdenal to TSE, 5 Feb 1912: "Tristan et Y., du premier coup vous émeuvent atrocement, et vous laissent aplati d'extase, avec une soif d'y revenir" [*Tristan and Isolde* is terribly moving at the first hearing, and leaves you prostrate with ecstasy and thirsting to get back to it again]. TSE was to see it again at the Boston Opera in Dec 1913 (*Crawford 2015* 197). TSE phrases from the opera appear in *The Waste Land* [I] 31–34 and 42. TSE on Laforgue: "It is noticeable how often ··· such philosophical terms from the vocabulary of Schopenhauer and Hartmann, the Valkyrie, and such properties from the dramas of Wagner, recur. Laforgue is the nearest verse equivalent to the philosophies of Schopenhauer

and Hartmann, the philosophy of the unconscious and of annihilation, just as Wagner is the nearest music equivalent to the same philosophies, though apart from this approximation to a similar philosophic mood, it would be difficult to say what there is in common between Wagner and Laforgue. But in Laforgue there is continuous war between the feelings implied by his ideas, and the ideas implied by his feelings. The system of Schopenhauer collapses, but in a different ruin from that of *Tristan und Isolde*", *The Varieties of Metaphysical Poetry* 215 (Clark Lecture VIII).

1–2 **Tristan and Isolde · · · fatalistic**: "an attraction as fatal as that indicated by the love-potion motif in *Tristan und Isolde*", *John Ford* (1932).

2 **And the fatalistic horns**: "Beats like a fatalistic drum", *Rhapsody on a Windy Night* 9. Laforgue: "sur un mode allègre et fataliste, un orchestre aux instruments d'ivoire improvisait une petite ouverture unanime" [In an allegro and fatalist mode, an orchestra of ivory instruments was improvising an astonishingly unanimous overture], *Salomé* III. Laforgue again: "cette éternelle valse de Chopin usée comme l'amour—ô délices poignantes, ô bon fatalisme!" [this eternal waltz of Chopin's employed as though it were love—oh poignant delights, oh happy fatalism!], *Paysages et Impressions* in *Mélanges posthumes* [*Posthumous Miscellanies*] (1903) 30.

2–4 **the fatalistic horns | The passionate violins | And ominous clarinet**: "Among the windings of the violins | And the ariettes | Of cracked cornets | Inside my brain a dull tom-tom begins", *Portrait of a Lady* I 29–32. French symbolists had characterised musical instruments (Verlaine: "la flûte impure", *Il parle encore* 18), but so had Dryden: "The trumpet's loud clangour", "The soft complaining flute", "Sharp violins proclaim | Their jealous pangs, and desperation", *A Song for St. Cecilia's Day* 25, 33, 37–38. Eric Griffiths (personal communication): "TSE was perhaps thinking especially of act II of *Tristan und Isolde* with its paroxysmic love-duet preceded by sequences for six horns (bar 76ff.) and solo clarinet (bar 126ff.), and with its 'passionate violins'."

3, 5–6 **passionate · · · And love torturing itself | To emotion for all there is in it**: "To be in love with emotion has been our affliction since Rousseau · · · Strong passions do not need explanation; but just as a man who is not very much in love excuses the follies which he has committed for the purpose of appearing passionate, so the philosophical Christian apologizes for the religion in which he would like to believe", *"Religion and Science: A Philosophical Essay"* by John Theodore Merz (1918), review. **torturing itself**: likewise of music, Laforgue: "Dans l'orgue qui par déchirements se châtie" [In the church-organ which tortures itself with heart-rendings], *Complainte propitiatoire à l'Inconscient* [*Propitiatory complaint to the Unconscious*] 9.

5–6, 10 **love torturing itself | To emotion for all there is in it · · · self-expression**:

> Oh, spare these reminiscences!
> How you prolong the pose!
> These emotional concupiscences
> Tinctured attar of rose.
> (The need for self-expression
> Will pardon this digression).
>
> *Portrait of a Lady* II 15^16 *variant*

10 **self-expression:** in 1909, still a fairly recent compound. OED first citation, 1892, *Nation*: "This doctrine of unbounded self-indulgence—or, as his [Walt Whitman's] admirers would prefer to call it, self-expression." TSE conveyed his suspicions twice in one year, writing of J. E. Spingarn: "For Mr. Spingarn the phrase 'self-expression' appears to be completely adequate", *Creative Criticism* (1926), and of Donne: "his sermons, one feels, are a 'means of self-expression'", *Lancelot Andrewes* (1926). For Hardy and "self-expression", see headnote.

11 **We have the tragic? oh no!:** Nietzsche, on *Tristan* act III: "Here there interpose between our highest musical excitement and the music in question the tragic myth and the tragic hero", *The Birth of Tragedy* §21. TSE to Aiken, 19 July 1914: "For when you have all those little things you cease to fret about them, and have room for a sort of divine dissatisfaction and *goût* for the tragic which is quite harmless, *d'ailleurs*, and compatible with a bank account. I think perhaps that only the happy can appreciate the tragic, or that the tragic only exists for the happy." 30 Sept: "That, in fact, is I think the great use of suffering, if it's *tragic* suffering—it takes you away from yourself—and petty suffering does exactly the reverse, and kills your inspiration. I think now that all my good stuff was done before I had begun to worry—three years ago." On suffering and a "pattern", see note to *The Dry Salvages* II 37–66. Quoting Pound's Canto XIV: "It is, in its way, an admirable Hell, 'without dignity, without tragedy'", *After Strange Gods* 43. "A man is only important as he is classed. Hence there is no tragedy, or no appreciation of tragedy, which is the same thing", *Eeldrop and Appleplex* I (1917).

12 **Life departs with a feeble smile:** "Till life evaporates into a smile", *First Debate between the Body and Soul* 44. "And Life, a little bald and gray, | Languid, fastidious, and bland, | Waits, hat and gloves in hand", *Spleen* 11–13.

16 **I feel like the ghost of youth:** *Symons* 73 on Rimbaud: "there is a certain irony, which comes into that youthful work as if youth were already reminiscent of itself, so conscious is it that youth is youth, and that youth is passing." James Thomson: "I felt a ghost already", *Insomnia* 270 (*Crawford* 49). TSE at Milton Academy, 27 years after his own graduation: "it occurred to me that as I had to talk to somebody, I would take more or less a metaphorical figure and make him as real as I could—that is, it occurred to me to say a few words to the ghost of myself at the age of seventeen or thereabouts, whom we may suppose to be skulking somewhere about this hall", *Address by T. S. Eliot, '06, to the Class of '33* (1933).

16–17 **ghost of youth | At the undertakers' ball:** in *Departmental Ditties*, Kipling followed *The Undertaker's Horse* with *One Viceroy Resigns*, which has "O Youth, Youth, Youth!" (6) and "That ghost has haunted me for twenty years" (18). TSE has "the Whore House Ball" in the refrain of *Ballade pour la grosse Lulu* and *The Columbiad* st. 15 (where it appears to be a tune).

Humouresque

Printed in *Harvard Advocate* 12 Jan 1910, then *Adv 1938, Adv 1948, Undergraduate Poems, Early Youth* (1950)+. Text of *ms1* published in *March Hare.*

Dated Nov 1909 in Notebook.

Hayward: "The theme of this exercise in the manner of Laforgue was suggested by the second stanza of his *Locutions de Pierrot* XII: 'Encore un de mes pierrots mort; | Mort d'un chronique orphelinisme; | C'était un cœur plein de dandysme | Lunaire, en un drôle de corps" [Another of my pierrots dead. Dead of chronic orphanism; his was a heart full of lunar dandyism, in a freakish body]; Hayward's spelling of the French as "dandyisme", is here corrected. Laforgue's lines had been quoted in *Symons* 108. In the *commedia dell'arte* tradition, poor little Pierrot is the deadpan, downtrodden clown, often berated by Harlequin.

Title **Humouresque**: OED "humoresque": "*Mus.* A composition of a humorous or capricious character", 1880. Adjectivally: "Of a humorous style", quoting Gosse, 1896: "the old tradition of humoresque literature". See note to the title *Suite Clownesque.*

6, 7, 10 **face ··· face ··· Mouth twisted to**: "Twisted faces from", *Morning at the Window* 6.

15 **The snappiest fashion since last spring's**: "And in spring he affects such sartorial | Display as the fashion allows", *How to Pick a Possum* 27–28. **snappiest**: OED "snappy" 6b: "Neat and elegant; smart, 'natty'", 1881.

18 **(Feebly contemptuous of nose)**: Symons: "although of nose not neat", *From Catullus. Chiefly Concerning Lesbia* XLIII.

Convictions (Curtain Raiser)

Published in *March Hare.*

Dated Jan 1910 (changed from Nov 1909) in Notebook.

Title ***Convictions***: Irving Babbitt on Ferdinand Brunetière: "He had convictions and insisted on judging with reference to them at a time when convictions, at least among the educated classes, had almost completely gone out of fashion. He possessed something of the power that usually belongs to those who have convictions to impose themselves on those who have none", *The Masters of Modern French Criticism* (1912) 303–304. ***Curtain Raiser***: originally slang. OED: "The slight opening pieces, or 'curtain raisers' as they are profanely styled", from 1886. Laforgue's *Hamlet*: "Un héros! et que tout le reste fût des levers de rideau!" [To be the hero of a play! And to reduce all of the other plays to little curtain-raisers!]; see note to *Mandarins* 1 13–15.

1 **Among my marionettes:** *Symons* 154 on Maeterlinck: "a drama so precise, so curt, so arbitrary in its limits, that it can safely be confided to the masks and feigned voices of marionettes ··· Are we not all puppets, in a theatre of marionettes, in which the parts we play, the dresses we wear, the very emotion whose dominance gives its express form to our faces, have all been chosen for us ···? And as our parts have been chosen for us, our motions controlled from

behind the curtain, so the words we seem to speak are but spoken through us, and we do but utter fragments of some elaborate invention." (For "a function assigned", see note to *He said: this universe is very clever* 2–3.) Symons on Jarry's *Ubu Roi*: "a generation which has exhausted every intoxicant, every soluble preparation of the artificial, may well seek a last sensation in the wire-pulled passions, the wooden faces of marionettes, and, by a further illusion, of marionettes who are living people; living people pretending to be those wooden images of life which pretend to be living people", *Studies in Seven Arts* (1906) 374–75. *An Apology for Puppets* was moved to the front of the 1909 edition of Symons's *Plays, Acting and Music* (1903): "The marionette may be relied upon. He will respond to an indication without reserve or revolt; an error on his part (we are all human) will certainly be the fault of the author; he can be trained to perfection ··· I assure you, you will find it quite easy to fall in love with a marionette ··· In our marionettes, then, we get personified gesture, and the gesture, like all other forms of emotion, generalized." For TSE and Symons, see "A Beginner in 1908". Irving Babbitt on Anatole France:

> His underlying mood is always that of contemptuous pity for beings who even in their most serious concerns are the dupes of mobile appearances.
>
> Les petites marionnettes
> Font, font, font
> Trois petits tours,
> Et puis s'en vont.
>
> [The little marionnettes, they make they make they make three little turns, and then they depart.] But the little marionettes, as M. France sees them, are thoroughly vicious and depraved, the playthings of hunger and the reproductive instinct.
>
> *The Masters of Modern French Criticism* 319

Marionettes are everywhere in German romantic literature too, notably in Kleist. For TSE's admiration for Alfred Kreymborg's *Puppet Plays* (1923), see headnote to *Sweeney Agonistes*, 4. JAZZ. In 1923 he told Kreymborg that he was planning puppet plays of his own (*Crawford* 161). "I do not by any means intend the actor to be an automaton, nor would I admit that the human actor can be replaced by a marionette", *Four Elizabethan Dramatists* (1924). TSE: "One of my marionettes is dead", *Humouresque* 1. See also note to 14.

2 **enthusiasm**: to Frank Morley, 15 Sept 1932: "I am incorrigibly distrustful of enthusiasm." (Pater: "High passions give one this quickened sense ··· the 'enthusiasm of humanity'", *Studies in the History of the Renaissance* Conclusion.) For "Progress" and "enthusiasm", see note to *To the Class of 1905* 78.

3 **They see the outlines of their stage**: "Who see their outlines on the screen", *Mandarins* 4 4.

3–5 **stage ··· later age**: Milton: "the tale of Troy divine, | Or what (though rare) of later age, | Ennobled hath the buskined stage", *Il Penseroso* 100–102.

4, 6–7 **immense ··· an audience ··· suspense**: "immense ··· the audience | Who still continue in suspense", *Suite Clownesque* I 14, 17–18.

6 **an audience open-mouthed**: "the close rabble in the cinema ··· Wide mouthed, in charmed rapture worship from afar", *WLComposite* Part III *ms1* [25–27].

9–10 **tissue paper roses ··· alone**: "Her hand twists a paper rose ··· alone", *Rhapsody on a Windy Night* 57–59 (see note).

9, 13 **roses ··· supposes**: rhymed in Austin Dobson, *Pot-Pourri* 3, 6 (see note to *Burnt Norton* I 16).

11 **The monotone**: "Capricious monotone", *Portrait of a Lady* I 34. The French romantic and symbolist poets reiterate "monotone".

13 **supposes**: as a noun ("an act of supposing"), archaic, though not apparently obsolete, by 1910; OED's two latest citations, 1875 and 1897, have the word within inverted commas, as archaic or self-conscious. Jonson: "Fatted with Supposes of fine Hopes", *A Tale of a Tub* III vii.

14 **over there my Paladins**: W. S. Gilbert: "Overflowing, | Easy-going | Paladin", *The Gondoliers* I. **Paladins**: OED: "In modern forms of the Charlemagne romances, one of the Twelve Peers or famous warriors of Charlemagne's court, of whom the Count Palatine was the foremost; hence sometimes *transf.* a Knight of the Round Table; also *fig.* a knightly hero, renowned champion, knight-errant." Samuel Daniel: "Let others sing of Knights and Paladins", *Delia* XLVI (1592; in *Oxf Bk of English Verse*). W. W. [Watson White] in *Harvard Advocate* 25 Nov 1908, on *Il Teatro Marionetti*: "If you have read the board outside, and are somewhat familiar with Italian, you recognize in this puppet no other than *Orlando*—known as '*Furioso*,' and you know that he must be waiting for *Rinaldo* or for his sister *Bradamante* ··· Presently *Orlando* may be joined by *Carlamagno*, gorgeously caparisoned as befits the ruler of the Holy Roman Empire." Rimbaud repeats "paladins" three lines before "pantins" (puppets), in *Bal des pendus* [*Dance of the Hanged*] 2–3, 6. TSE on talkers of cant: "One characteristic which increased my suspicion of the scientific paladins of religion is that they are all Englishmen, or at least all Anglo-Saxons", *Thoughts After Lambeth* (1931).

15 **talking of effect and cause**: "we will talk of cause and effect whenever a phenomenon or group of phenomena is thought of as lived through and not as contemplated", and "I agree thoroughly with Mr. Russell when he speaks of cause as a superstition: I only question whether we could live without superstitions", *Cause as Ideal Construction* (1914). **effect and cause**: Bradley: "I may be told that in causation a succession is involved with a direction not reversible ··· even in our own world, how unsatisfactory the succession laid down in causation!" *Appearance and Reality* ch. XXIII. TSE: "A *totality* of causes is of course the effect itself, or freedom. But freedom is subject to the same alteration: complete freedom is identity of effect and cause", *Report on the Ethics of Kant's Critique of Practical Reason* (1913). "Many years ago I was given to understand that science had dispensed with the notion of causality, and that the recurrence of the same events in the same order, and predictability, was all that it had to do with. The notion of cause and effect was to be left to man in his everyday common activities", *Poetical and Prosaic Use of Words* (1943).

15–16 **effect and cause ··· laws**: Clough: "Repose upon effect and cause, | And action of unvarying laws", *Say, will it, when our hairs are grey* 12–13.

16 **"learn to live by nature's laws!"**: Stoic doctrine, quizzed by Horace, *Epistles* I x 12. T. H. Green: "They seek to discover what are the laws—the modes of operation of natural forces—under which we have come to be what we are, in order that they may counsel us how to seek our happiness by living according

to those laws. Now it is obvious that to a being who is simply a result of natural forces an injunction to conform to their laws is unmeaning", *Prolegomena to Ethics* 10; TSE marked the second sentence here.

19 **Reason**: "Mr. Foerster's 'reason' seems to me to differ from any Greek equivalent (*λόγος*) by being exclusively human; whereas to the Greek there was something inexplicable about *λόγος* so that it was a participation of man in the divine", *Second Thoughts about Humanism* (1929). **nothing to excess**: proverbial in Greek; written in the temple at Delphi by Cleobulus, and quoted by Plato in *Protagoras.* TSE: "Romanticism stands for *excess* in any direction", *Syllabus: Modern French Literature* (1916) Lecture I.

25–26 **I'd throw my heart beneath his feet. | I'd give my life to his control**: "my heart | Under my feet"; "your heart would have responded | Gaily, when invited, beating obedient | To controlling hands", *The Waste Land* [III] 296–97, [V] 420–22.

28–29 **marionettes ··· keen**: HAMLET: "I could interpret between you and your love, if I could see the puppets dallying." OPHELIA: "You are keen, my lord, you are keen" (III ii).

Spleen

Printed in *Harvard Advocate* 26 Jan 1910, then *Adv 1938*, *Adv 1948*, *Undergraduate Poems*, *Early Youth* (1950)+.

Title] Four successive poems in the section *Spleen et Idéal* in Baudelaire's *Fleurs du Mal* share this title. Laforgue on Baudelaire: "Le premier qui ait apporté dans notre literature l'ennui dans la volupté ··· le spleen et la maladie (non la Phtisie poétique mais la névrose)" [The first to bring our literature the boredom implicit in sensuality ··· spleen and illness (not the poetic aspects of consumption but rather neurosis)], *Littérature* in *Mélanges posthumes* (1903) 112. Verlaine too has *Spleen*, and Symons has *From "Romances sans Paroles"* VII. *Spleen.* In English, "spleen" was taken up by Ernest Dowson.

2–5 **Sunday faces; | Bonnets, silk hats and conscious graces ··· mental self-possession**: Isaac Taylor: "Sunday dresses and Sunday faces, illuminated by a Sunday summer sky, give to the scene the liveliness and grace that so well befit Christianity, where Christianity is free, intelligent, and sincere", *Unitarianism in England* in *Logic in Theology and Other Essays* (1859).

3 **silk hats**: Conrad Aiken to TSE, 23 Feb 1913, on their friend Harry Wehle: "Write and tell me ··· how Silk Hat Harry demeans himself". TSE: "a silk hat on a Bradford millionaire", *The Waste Land* [III] 234.

6 **unwarranted digression**: "Is it perfume from a dress | That makes me so digress?" *The Love Song of J. Alfred Prufrock* 65–66.

11–14 **a little bald ··· fastidious ··· Waits, hat and gloves in hand, | Punctilious of tie and suit**: "slightly bald ··· hold my coat ··· attendant lord ··· meticulous", *The Love Song of J. Alfred Prufrock* 82, 85, 112, 116.

16 **On the doorstep of the Absolute**: likewise concluding *Afternoon*: "the absolute"

(there rhyming at a distance with "suits", as here with "suit"). On the philosophical term, see note to *Conversation Galante* 14.

First Debate between the Body and Soul

Published in *March Hare.*

Dated Jan 1910, *ms1.*

Title **First Debate between the Body and Soul**: Marvell, *A Dialogue between the Soul and Body.* Laforgue wrote debate-poems with antiphonal effects similar to the intercalated quatrains here all ending with "our sensations". TSE on Laforgue: "What he wants, of course, is some way of salvation in which both the mind and the feelings, the soul and the body, shall cooperate towards fulness of life", *The Varieties of Metaphysical Poetry* 285 (Turnbull Lecture III). Bradley: "Can we say that bare soul ever acts upon body, and can soul exist at all without matter · · ·? In our experience assuredly bare soul is not found. Its existence there, and its action, are inseparable from matter", *Appearance and Reality* ch. XXIII, "Body and Soul". TSE scored the passage and underlined the middle sentence. He persistently put his mind to this question. At Harvard in 1912–13 he took Hugo Munsterberg's "Seminary in Psychology" (subject for the year: "Mind and Body"), and two courses by Charles Bakewell, "The Kantian Philosophy" and "Seminary in Metaphysics". In his copy of Bakewell's *Source Book in Ancient Philosophy* 241–42, he underlined in the account of Aristotle the remark that the "soul may be regarded as a sort of form and idea"; the previous sentence had spoken of "our sensation" ("our sensations", 7), and on the next page TSE jotted down six terms, including sensation and Imagination. Bergson's *Matière et mémoire* (1896) is subtitled *Essai sur la relation du corps à l'esprit.* TSE's Clark Lectures in 1926 were devoted to body and soul, as in the dismissal of Descartes' Meditation VI (*Of the Existence of Material Things, and of the real distinction between the Soul and Body of Man*), *The Varieties of Metaphysical Poetry* 81–82 (Lecture II). Annotating the fourth Ennead in his Plotinus, TSE wrote: "He looks at soul 1st as possessed of faculties wh. refer to sensible world (Aristotle) 2 as rising above the world to union with God · · · Plotinus is a two substance man as against Aristotle's reduction of the soul to functions of the body" (quoted in notes to *The Varieties of Metaphysical Poetry* 114). "As the soul leaves the body torn and bruised, | As the mind deserts the body it has used", *La Figlia Che Piange* 11–12, where the internal rhyme "imagination · · · cogitations" (18, 23) recalls the refrain here. See *March Hare* 230 for TSE's engagement with body and soul in Leibniz, Bradley, Donne and Sir John Davies. ***Debate***: Ronald Bush wrote that TSE "was still thinking of going on with the 'Debate' as late as March 1918" (*Bush* 19), but in the letter he cites, "my dialogue" refers to *Eeldrop and Appleplex.*

Unadopted title ***Reflections in a Square***: the following year TSE wrote *Entretien dans un parc.*

2–4 **A blind old man who coughs and spits sputters | Stumbling among the alleys**

and the gutters || He pokes: Henry Adams: "one fumbled over it as feebly as ever. In such labyrinths, the staff is a force almost more necessary than the legs; the pen becomes a sort of blind-man's dog, to keep him from falling into the gutters", *The Education of Henry Adams* ch. XXV. TSE: "A blind old drunken man who sings and mutters, | With broken boot heels stained in many gutters", *Prufrock's Pervigilium* [30–31]. "poking the peevish gutter. | I an old man", *Gerontion* 14–15.

3, 5, 7 **gutters · · · With senile patience · · · sensations:** "gutter with sordid patience · · · considerations", *First Caprice in North Cambridge* 9–10. "patience · · · irritations", *O lord, have patience* 1, 3. "With a little patience · · · reverberation", *The Waste Land* [V] 330, 336. **With senile patience:** *Paradise Lost* II 569: "With stubborn patience" (in Hell).

6–7 **The withered leaves | Of our sensations:** Hawthorne: "On the soil of thought and in the garden of the heart, as well as in the sensual world, lie withered leaves—the ideas and feelings that we have done with", *Buds and Bird Voices* (*Mosses from an Old Manse*) (TSE: "Idea", 15). Shelley: "Like withered leaves to quicken a new birth! | And, by the incantation of this verse", *Ode to the West Wind* 64–65 (TSE: "August wind", 1). Keats: "blown vagrant in the wind · · · blind · · · throw | Himself on withered leaves · · · muttered", *Endymion* II 562–67 (TSE: "blind", 2, 10; "mutters", 2 *variant*). Byron: "the languid rout | Of our Sensations", *Don Juan* IX lxxv. **sensations:** Bergson: "si l'art qui ne donne que des sensations est un art inférieur, c'est que l'analyse ne démêle pas souvent dans une sensation autre chose que cette sensation même" [If the art which gives only sensations is an inferior art, the reason is that analysis often fails to discover in a sensation anything beyond the sensation itself], *Essai sur les données immédiates de la conscience* (1889) ch. I; tr. F. L. Pogson as *Time and Free Will* (1910). TSE referred to the translation in *The Relationship Between Politics and Metaphysics* (1914).

6, 9 **withered leaves · · · vacant square:** "Of withered leaves about your feet | And newspapers from vacant lots", *Preludes* I 7–8.

8 **devoted to the pure idea:** for Remy de Gourmont's fascination with "l'idée pure", see *March Hare* 232. "Explained the Pure Idea", *Inside the gloom* 12. "the idea pure as salt", *Anabasis* I ix (*variant* "the pure idea").

9–10 **in the vacant square · · · blind:** Cavalcanti, tr. Rossetti: "Over the curse of blindness she prevails, | And heals sick languors in the public squares", *To Guido Orlandi: Sonnet. Of a consecrated Image resembling his Lady* (in *The Early Italian Poets*). TSE's *Syllabus: Elizabethan Literature* (1918) told his students "Read: A few translations of Italian Sonnets in Rossetti's *Early Italian Poets*, and sonnets in *Golden Treasury* or in the *Oxford Book of English Verse*" (elided in *Schuchard* as "Italian sonnets in *Golden Treasury* or in the *Oxford Book of English Verse*").

10 **inconscient:** adapting Laforgue; see note to *Afternoon* 9.

11–12 **exude | The odour:** OED "exude": *ex-sudare*, "To ooze out like sweat". TSE: "La sueur aestivale, et une forte odeur", *Lune de Miel* 4.

12 **turpitude:** markedly sexual in French. Remy de Gourmont describes marriage as "la bonté de Dieu à la turpitude humaine" [God's grace towards human turpitude], and "La vieille opposition entre la virginité et la turpitude" [the old

conflict between chastity and turpitude], *La Morale de l'amour* in *La Culture des idées*. In Flaubert's *Bouvard et Pécuchet* ch. VII, "sa turpitude" reveals itself in syphilis, "une maladie secrète". *TSE's books: Bodleian list* (1934) includes both these French titles. TSE: "Francis Bacon is neither the first nor the last man to combine intellectual power with moral turpitude", *Elizabeth and Essex* (1928). "these abominations, the turpitudes", *Choruses from "The Rock"* V 7. "the soul & body ··· human folly & turpitude & pusillanimity", *Little Gidding* II 76–93 *prose draft* (for affinities with this poem, see note to *Little Gidding* II 25–96).

13 **And a street piano through the dusty trees:** "A street-piano, garrulous and frail", *First Caprice in North Cambridge* 1 (see note).

15 **The pure Idea dies of inanition:** Emerson: "Give me truths; | For I am weary of the surfaces, | And die of inanition", *Blight* 1–3. Louis Bertrand, tr. Stuart Merrill: "the salamander died of inanition", *The Salamander* in *Pastels in Prose*. (For Merrill, see headnote to "*Poems* (1920)", 5. TSE'S PROFICIENCY IN FRENCH.) TSE: "idealism, having sold his mess of pottage for a birth-right, is perhaps beginning to show signs of inanition", *The Relativity of the Moral Judgment* (1915). **inanition:** OED: "The action or process of emptying; the condition of being empty; *spec.* the exhausted condition resulting from want or insufficiency of nourishment."

15, 23 **dies of inanition ··· brain:** Bergson: "chez des animaux morts de faim, on trouve le cerveau à peu près intact" [in animals that have died of hunger the brain is found to be almost unimpaired]; with note: "Récemment, des observations analogues ont été faites sur un homme mort d'inanition" [Recently, analogous observations have been made on a man who died of inanition], *L'Evolution créatrice* (1907) ch. II.

18 **Imaginations:** *The Merry Wives of Windsor* IV ii: "you must pray, and not follow the imaginations of your own heart". *Hamlet* III ii: "And my imaginations are as foul | As Vulcan's stithy". *King Lear* IV vi: "wrong imaginations".

18–19 **Imaginations | Masturbations:** "took their recreation ··· And practiced masturbation", *The Columbiad* st. 16. Byron to John Murray, 9 Nov 1820: "such writing is a sort of mental **** — ******** his *Imagination.*—I don't mean he is *indecent*, but viciously soliciting his own ideas into a state", *Letters and Journals* ed. R. E. Prothero, V (1901) 117. The expurgated text was expanded in Leslie Marchand's edition: "mental masturbation—he is always f—gg—g his *Imagination*", *Byron's Letters and Journals*, vol. 7, 1977. TSE to Aiken, 19 July 1914, "Dr. Hans Frigger (the celebrated poet)".

27 **The cosmic smudge of an enormous thumb:** Henry James: "Charming places, charming objects, languish, all round him, under designations that seem to leave on them the smudge of a great vulgar thumb", *New England: An Autumn Impression* III in *The American Scene*. TSE to his mother, 2 June 1918: "James was a fine writer—his book of impressions of America, written about 1907 I think, is wonderfully well written." James again: "the month of August; a spectacle that I am far from speaking of as the finest flower of my old and perhaps even a little faded cluster of impressions, but which smudges that special sojourn as with the big thumb-mark", *Siena Early and Late* II in *Italian Hours* (TSE: "August", 1).

29 *variant* **the sanctuary of the soul:** Samuel Rogers: "And may the secret of thy soul | Remain within its sanctuary!" *The Sleeping Beauty* 15–16. The poem is

in *The Golden Treasury*, which was a set text for TSE at Smith Academy in 1905 (*Stayer*). TSE: "For in the sanctuaries of the soul", *To the Class of 1905* 49.

32–33 **Imagination's | Poor Relations**: see Bradley on "The relation of body to soul" in note on title. Henry James has "poor relation" and "imagination" in the second paragraph of *The Beast in the Jungle* (1903). OED "poor" 8: *poor relation* "relative or kinsman in humble circumstances (also *transf.*)", from 1720.

32–37 **Imagination's ··· Absolute! ··· supersubtle**: "The Absolute, we find, does not fall within any of the classes of objects: it is neither real nor unreal nor imaginary. But I do not think that supersubtle defence is necessary", *Knowledge and Experience* 169.

33, 35 **Relations ··· our sensations**: T. H. Green: "A sensation is the unalterable effect of its conditions, whatever those conditions may be. It is unalterably related to other sensations. Our opinion about its conditions or relations may vary, but not the conditions or relations themselves, or the sensation determined by them", *Prolegomena to Ethics* (1906) 30. TSE marked the first two of these sentences in his copy.

36–37 **Absolute! complete idealist ··· peasant**: *Symons* 53, on Villiers de l'Isle-Adam: "too sincere an idealist, too absolute in his idealism, to hesitate", a dozen lines after "a peasant".

37 **A supersubtle peasant**: *Othello* I iii: "a super-subtle Venetian". Henry James is very fond of "supersubtle". TSE: "Donne, or a supersubtle heroine of one of Racine's tragedies"; "I am not presenting Marino as a supersubtle Italian who led the simple Englishman Crashaw astray", *The Varieties of Metaphysical Poetry* 88, 177–78 (Clark Lectures II, VI).

37 *variant* **supersensitive**: Tennyson: "a supersensual sensual bond", *Merlin and Vivien* 107. TSE: "a supersensuous experience", "many super-sensuous feelings", *The Varieties of Metaphysical Poetry* 120, 133 (Clark Lecture IV). For Madame Blavatsky's "super-sensuous status", see note to *A Cooking Egg* 21–23.

42–43 **a little while | Standing**: Wordsworth: "A little while I stood", *Nutting* 21, with "withered leaves", 18 (TSE, four times) and "the trees", 25 (TSE, 46).

42, 44 **a little while ··· life ··· a smile**: Shelley: "My father lived a little while, | But all might see that he was dying, | He smiled with such a woeful smile!" *Rosalind and Helen* 315–17.

42, 44–45 **a little while ··· a smile | Simple and profound**: Laforgue's *Hamlet*:

> "Oh! cloître-toi! L'amour, l'amour
> S'échange, par le temps qui court,
> Simple et sans foi comme un bonjour"
> —C'est en effet bien curieux, assure l'acteur.
> Et Hamlet, prince de Danemark et créature infortunée, exulte!

["Oh! cloister yourself ! Love, love is spoken and returned, during this time that is current, simply and faithlessly as good morning."—"Really, it is extremely unusual," the actor assures the author. And Hamlet, Prince of Denmark and unfortunate creature, exults!]

Emile Verhaeren: "Et réunir notre esprit et le monde, | Dans les deux mains d'une très simple loi profonde" [And reunite our spirit with the world, in the two hands of a very simple profound law], *L'Attente* [*Waiting*] closing lines.

TSE's books: Bodleian list (1934) includes this volume of Verhaeren's, *Les Visages de la vie* (1899). TSE: "simple and faithless as a smile", *La Figlia Che Piange* 16. "His laughter was submarine and profound", *Mr. Apollinax* 8.

44 **Till life evaporates into a smile**: "Life departs with a feeble smile", *Opera* 12. "An aimless smile that hovers in the air | And vanishes", *Morning at the Window* 8–9 (see note).

49 **Defecations:** OED 2: "Purification of the mind or soul from what is gross or low"; with Jeremy Taylor (1649): "A defecation of his faculties and an opportunity of Prayer". Two lines of Coleridge's *Reason* gained particular currency because Matthew Arnold applied them to one form of poetic achievement in *On Translating Homer* I:

> Coleridge says, in his strange language, speaking of the union of the human soul with the divine essence, that this takes place
>
> > Whene'er the mist, which stands 'twixt God and thee,
> > Defecates to a pure transparency;
>
> and so, too, it may be said of the translator with his original, which alone can produce a good translation, that it takes place when the mist which stands between them—the mist of alien modes of thinking, speaking, and feeling on the translator's part—"defecates to a pure transparency," and disappears.

TSE: "Mind in this pure and defecated state is a figment; and true as these laws may be of mind, they are not true of the world as *I* experience it, at least, for this world contains many things besides mind, and it does not even contain mind unadulterated", *The Relativity of the Moral Judgment* (1915). "the world would be pure form defecated of particularity", *Thought and Reality in Aristotle's "Metaphysics"* (1915). To Robert Nichols, 8 Aug 1917: "This struggle to preserve the advantages of practice and at the same time to defecate the emotions one has expressed already is one of the hardest I know." To Herbert Read, 18 Sept 1942: "I *think* that *Little Gidding* is now about as good as I can make it ··· This defecation OUGHT to make it possible to attend to *Murder* [*in the Cathedral*]." Again: "I think that what stimulates me to write a poem is that I have something inside me that I want to get rid of. I have to get it out. It is almost a kind of defecation, if you like", *Talking Freely* (1961). OED has "defecation" 3: "discharging of the fæces" from 1830.

49 *variant* **desquamations**: OED 1: "The removal of scales or of any scaly crust." 2: "A coming off in scales or scaly patches", but also the more positive aspect of this "removal of scales". TSE: "The scales are fallen from their eyes", *Airs of Palestine, No. 2* 39.

Easter: Sensations of April

Published in *March Hare.* Part II had been printed in the limited edition of *Letters* (1988), with a facsimile of the leaf that was laid into the Notebook.

Part I dated Apr 1910 in Notebook; Part II dated May 1910 in *ms1*.

Beginning "The little negro girl", TSE's poem asks comparison with Blake's *The Little*

Black Boy, which four times mentions the "heat" (TSE, 7), and twice "God" (TSE, 3); it too has "flowers" (TSE: "geranium", 2, 13). Blake's poem is about being "taught" a childlike religious lesson (TSE: "Sunday school", 14).

The opening of ch. VII of C. F. G. Masterman's *From the Abyss* (1902) has many elements of TSE's poem: "It is Sunday evening, and the tinkling of numerous church bells is fretfully protesting the desirability of public worship. The temperature has been anything over a hundred and twenty in the sunshine, the asphalt has become soft and bubbly, and in the narrow street", with "the heat", "upper windows" and "children, the girls in white" in the next few lines. (James Kissane proposed *From the Abyss* as a source for *The Waste Land*; *Yeats Eliot Review* Spring 1979.) John Gray's sonnet *Poem* (1893), beginning "Geranium", has "A wistful child" and "The asphalt burns".

Title **Easter**: Valerie Eliot noted that TSE's mother, Charlotte Eliot, "throughout her life wrote poems, some of which, like *Easter Songs*, were printed in the *Christian Register*", *Letters* (1988) 5. Houghton has a copy of *Easter Songs* (1899). ***Sensations of April***: Laforgue: "O paria!—Et revoici les sympathies de mai" [Pariah!—And the sympathies of May are back again], *Simple agonie* 1 (with "se crucifie", 17). Also Rimbaud on "les soirs bleus d'été", "la fraîcheur" and "l'amour infini" [blue summer evenings, its coolness, endless love], *Sensation* 1–6. TSE (on Dadaism, loosely): "It prefers in fact, things which are not art, because the sensation of enjoying something ugly is more amusing than the worn out enjoyment of something beautiful ··· and in the end, if we pursue only sensation, we shall cease to have even sensation", *Modern Tendencies in Poetry* (1920). Lytton Strachey "has invented new sensations from history, as Bergson has invented new sensations from metaphysics", *London Letter* in *Dial* Aug 1921. TSE's final Clark Lecture: "Humanity reaches its higher civilisation levels not chiefly by improvement of thought or by increase and variety of sensation, but by the extent of co-operation between acute sensation and acute thought", *The Varieties of Metaphysical Poetry* 220–21.

I

I 1 **The little negro girl who lives across the alley**: for "The married girl who lives across the street", see headnote to *The Love Song of St. Sebastian.*

I 3 **formulae**: OED "formula" 1a: "A set form of words ··· to be used on some ceremonial occasion". TSE: "to reduce the world to a set of formulae is to let it slip through our fingers in a fine dust", *The Relativity of the Moral Judgment* (1915). Of Paul Elmer More: "The fundamental beliefs of an intellectual conservatism, that man requires an askesis, a *formula* to be imposed upon him from above", *An American Critic* (1916). "The true critic is a scrupulous avoider of formulae ··· The things of which we are collectively certain, we may say our common formulae, are certainly not true", *Knowledge and Experience* 164–65. "The world is not quite given up to diplomacy, | Combinations and finding of formulas", *Choruses from "The Rock"* VI *after* 34 *variant* [2–3].

I 4 **Geraniums**: see headnote to *Rhapsody on a Windy Night* for TSE's debt to Laforgue. "a dead geranium ··· sunless dry geraniums", *Rhapsody on a Windy Night* 12, 63 (here: "Withered and dry", 10).

I 7–8 **smell ··· street:** "smells of chestnuts in the streets", *Rhapsody on a Windy Night* 65.

I 9–13 **Geraniums geraniums | Withered and dry | Long laid by | In the sweepings of the memory || The little negro girl:** Apollinaire: "yeux d'une mulâtresse ··· Et les roses de l'électricité s'ouvrent encore | Dans le jardin de ma mémoire" [the eyes of a mulatto woman ··· and the roses of electricity still open themselves in the garden of my memory], *J'ai eu le courage* [*I have had the courage*] (Nov–Dec 1908).

I 10, 12 **Withered ··· memory:** Shelley: "votive wreaths of withered memory", *Epipsychidion* 4. **dry ··· sweepings:** Tennyson: "so I triumphed ere my passion sweeping through me left me dry", *Locksley Hall* 131.

I 13–14 **girl ··· Brings a geranium from Sunday school:** Laforgue: "Les Jeunes Filles inviolables et frêles | Descendent vers la petite chapelle" [The frail inviolable Young Ladies descend toward the little chapel], *Dimanches: C'est l'automne* [*Sundays: It's autumn*] 9–10, quoted in *The Varieties of Metaphysical Poetry* 214–15 (Clark Lecture VIII); see note to *First Caprice in North Cambridge* 1.

following I 14 *in draft* **She is very sure of God:** *Symons* 57–58, on Villiers de l'Isle-Adam: "He affirms; he 'believes in soul, is very sure of God;' requires no witness to the spiritual world of which he is always the inhabitant; and is content to lose his way in the material world, brushing off its mud from time to time with a disdainful gesture, as he goes on his way (to apply a significant word of Pater) 'like one on a secret errand.'" In the same chapter: "'I am far from sure,' wrote Verlaine, 'that the philosophy of Villiers will not one day become the formula of our century'", *Symons* 41 (TSE: "formulae of God", 3). *Bacchus and Ariadne* ends "I am sure".

II.

Title, II 1 ***Easter*** **··· Daffodils:** Housman: "And bear from hill and valley | The daffodil away | That dies on Easter day", *A Shropshire Lad* XXIX. TSE to Miss St. Clare Byrne, 7 Apr 1931: "Housman was certainly a great influence twenty or thirty years ago, and I only just escaped his influence myself." On *The Name and Nature of Poetry*: "'I have seldom,' he says, 'written poetry unless I was rather out of health.' I believe that I understand that sentence. If I do, it is a guarantee—if any guarantee of that nature is wanted—of the quality of Mr. Housman's poetry", *Housman on Poetry* (1933). To Cyril Clemens, 8 July 1936: "I have never been a very warm admirer of Mr. Housman's poetry." On a copy of the drawing she had made of TSE delivering the Clark Lectures at Trinity, Cambridge, TSE's sister-in-law Theresa noted, that at dinner "Housman sat at high table, an honor to T.S.E.", *The Varieties of Metaphysical Poetry* 16.

II 1, 3 **Daffodils ··· The cool secluded room** Van Wyck Brooks: "the kind of criticism which one receives from a bowl of daffodils on one's desk or the breeze that rustles in the window curtains", *The Wine of the Puritans* 27.

II 1, 9 **Daffodils ··· imagination:** in *Oxf Bk of English Verse*, Quiller-Couch printed Wordsworth's "I wandered lonely as a cloud" as *Daffodils* among "Poems of the Imagination".

II 2–3, 7 **sunlight fills ··· cool ··· room ··· perfume**: Keats: "Filling the chilly room with perfume light", *The Eve of St. Agnes* 275.

II 4 **Swept and set in order**: Luke 11: 25, the house "swept and garnished". TSE: "I have swept the floors and garnished the altars", *Choruses from "The Rock"* III 45. Herbert: "Who sweeps a room, as for thy laws", *The Elixir* 19. **set in order**: Exodus 39: 37–38: "even with the lamps to be set in order ··· the oil for light ··· the sweet incense" (TSE: "sunlight ··· sweet perfume", II 2, 7). TSE: "Shall I at least set my lands in order?" *The Waste Land* [V] 425 (see note).

II 4–5 **in order— | Smelling**: *Paradise Regained* II 351: "That fragrant smell diffused, in order stood".

II 5 **Smelling of earth and rain**: Herbert: "I once more smell the dew and rain", *The Flower* 38, likewise rhyming with "again". TSE praised Herbert's stanza as "itself a miracle of phrasing", *George Herbert* 26. Tennyson: "Smelling of musk and of insolence", *Maud* I [vi] 234 (TSE: "insistent sweet perfume", II 7). TSE: "smelling of vegetation", *Journey of the Magi* 22.

II 6–7 **again | The insistent**: "returns like the insistent out-of-tune", *Portrait of a Lady* II 16.

II 7 **perfume**: stressed here on the second syllable (unlike I 6).

II 9–10 **Irritate ··· the nerves**: Hawthorne: "It irritated my nerves; it affected me with a kind of heart-sickness", *The Blithedale Romance* ch. XVIII. TSE to his mother, 31 Oct 1920: "I have simply not had the time to do a single piece of work, and when one has in mind a great many things that one wants to do, that irritates the nerves more and more." **the imagination | Or the nerves**: Henry James: "the imagination, for the nerves", *New York: Social Notes* V in *The American Scene*. *Symons* 24, of Gérard de Nerval: "Every artist lives a double life, in which he is for the most part conscious of the illusions of the imagination. He is conscious also of the illusions of the nerves, which he shares with every man of imaginative mind." Similarly, Symons, *A New Art of the Stage*: "The imagination has been caught; a suggestion has been given which strikes straight to 'the nerves of delight'; and be sure those nerves, that imagination, will do the rest", *Studies in Seven Arts* (1906) 354. TSE: "threw the nerves in patterns on a screen", *The Love Song of J. Alfred Prufrock* 105 (see note).

Ode ("For the hour that is left us Fair Harvard, with thee")

Written for Harvard Commencement, 1910. Printed in *Harvard Class Day*, programme of events for 24 June 1910, beneath a photogravure of Memorial Hall, and in *Harvard Advocate* the same day. Also printed in the *Boston Evening Transcript* and *Boston Evening Herald*. Under the headline "St. Louisans in Class Day" and subheading "T. S. Elliott's Ode is Sung by Harvard Graduates", the *St. Louis Republic or Post Dispatch* reported: "The exercises in Sanders' Theater began with the singing of the class ode by Thomas Stearns Elliott of St. Louis, class odist." (The tune was that of *Fair Harvard*.) Reprinted in *Adv 1948*, *Undergraduate Poems*, *Early Youth* (1950)+.

Hayward: "As 'Odist' of the Harvard Class of 1910 T. S. Eliot recited his 'Class Ode' in the Sanders Theater at Harvard in the forenoon of Class Day. The 'Poet' of the Harvard Class of 1910 was Edward Eyre Hunt of Mechanicsburg, Ohio."

1 **the hour that is left us:** Emerson: "To fill the hour,—that is happiness", *Experience* in *Essays: Second Series*. For Emerson, a Harvard man, see note to *Sweeney Erect* 25–26.

2 **the importunate years:** George Hodges: "the importunate months", *The Human Nature of the Saints* (1904). Hodges was Dean of the Episcopal Theological School at Cambridge, Massachusetts.

7 **ambitions that sprang at thy feet:** A. R. Eagar: "amaranths sprang at my feet", *The Invocation of Venus* (1877).

13 **efface and destroy:** a pious commonplace since the 18th century.

16 **to thine and to thee:** poetic diction. Edward B. Osborne: "A new page is opening ··· to thine and to thee", New Year's Address, 1871, in *Letters from the Woods* (1893). S. B. Rockwell: "Threat'ning ruin and death to thine and to thee", *Apostrophe to Colonel E. D. Baker* in *Green Mountain Poets* ed. Albert J. Sanborn (1872).

Silence

Published in *March Hare*.

Dated June 1910 in Notebook.

Title ***Silence*:** Laforgue on Baudelaire: "La Beauté c'est le Silence éternel. Tout notre tapage de passions, de discussions, d'orages, d'art, c'est pour, par le bruit, nous faire croire que le *Silence n'existe pas.* Mais quand nous retombons las, nous l'écoutons restagner de partout et nous sommes plus tristes, pas assez forts pour un tapage éternel ou pour nous faire au Silence éternel" [Beauty is eternal Silence. All our uproar of passions, of arguments, of storms, of art, is in order (by means of the noise) to make us believe that *Silence does not exist.* But when we lapse into being tired, we hear it become stagnant again everywhere, and we are more sad, not strong enough for an eternal uproar or to conduct ourselves in the face of an eternal Silence], *Littérature* in *Mélanges posthumes* (1903) 116–17 (tr. eds). TSE: "the heart of light, the silence", *The Waste Land* [I] 41.

Title, 15 ***Silence*** **··· I am terrified:** Pascal: "Le silence éternel de ces espaces infinis m'effraye" [The eternal silence of these infinite spaces terrifies me], *Pensées* 206. Pater quoted this in *Studies in the History of the Renaissance* ch. I, and TSE marked it in his copy. TSE: "For chance is merely absence of explanation, and a gigantic hand organ of atoms, grinding out predictable variations on the same tune, would fill the vast silences which idealism leaves empty", *The Relativity of the Moral Judgment* (1915). TSE dissented from I. A. Richards ("The inconceivable immensity of the Universe"): "It was not, we remember, the 'immense spaces' themselves but their *eternal silence* that terrified Pascal. With a definite religious background this is intelligible. But the effect of popular astronomy books (like Sir James Jeans's) upon me is only of the insignificance of vast space", *The Use of*

Poetry and the Use of Criticism 133 (referring to Jeans's *The Mysterious Universe*, 1930). For "the vacant interstellar spaces", see *East Coker* III 2 and note.

1 **Along the city streets:** "If he walked in city streets", *The Death of Saint Narcissus* 18.

1–3 **Along the city streets ··· high tide ··· the garrulous waves of life:** Tennyson: "There where the long street roars, hath been | The stillness of the central sea", *In Memoriam* CXXIII 3–4. Dr. Johnson: "Why, Sir, Fleet-street has a very animated appearance; but I think the full tide of human existence is at Charing-cross", *Boswell* II 337 (2 Apr 1775). Hawthorne: "From the street came the tumult of the pavements ··· I felt a hesitation about plunging into this muddy tide of human activity", *The Blithedale Romance* ch. XVII; see headnote to *Morning at the Window* (and its "waves of fog", 5).

3–4 **waves ··· Shrink:** "and hushed the shrunken seas", *Sweeney Among the Nightingales* 10 ("hushed" being a contrast to these "garrulous waves"). *Paradise Lost* XI 845–46, after the Flood: "the fresh wave ··· their flowing shrink". **divide:** as in the miracle at the Red Sea; *Paradise Lost* VII 262–63, which—like TSE's lines—has "divide" at the line-division: "let it divide | The waters from the waters".

4, 9–10 **divide ··· justified. | The seas of experience:** a poem by TSE's mother, Charlotte Eliot, has: "No longer shall the law thy tribes divide, | Through faith and love shall all be justified. | Let me go forth, O Lord!" *Saint Barnabas: A Missionary Hymn* 8–10 (undated, King's).

5 **With a thousand incidents:** Henri Bergson: "notre vie psychologique est pleine d'imprévu. Mille incidents surgissent" [our psychic life is full of the unforeseen. A thousand incidents arise], *L'Evolution créatrice* ch. 1 (in the same paragraph as "la masse fluide ··· un écoulement sans fin" [the fluid mass ··· an endless flow]; TSE: "tide ··· waves ··· seas", 2–3, 10). Bergson's *Introduction à la metaphysique* has "les milles incidents"; also "indivisible" (TSE: "divide", 4). Shelley: "with a thousand motions", *Prometheus Unbound* IV 247.

6 **Vexed and debated:** OED "vex" 7: "To subject (a matter) to prolonged or severe examination or discussion; to debate at excessive length"; citing first Donne, *Biathanatos*: "The best way to finde the truth in this matter, was to debate and vexe it".

7–8 **the hour ··· the ··· hour:** "Pray for us sinners now and at the hour of our death | Pray for us now and at the hour of our death", *Ash-Wednesday* I 40–41.

9 **life is justified:** Psalm 143: 2: "For in thy sight shall no man living be justified." Nietzsche: "only as an *aesthetic phenomenon* is existence and the world eternally *justified*", *The Birth of Tragedy* §5.

10, 12 **experience ··· So immediate:** TSE's *Knowledge and Experience* (completed 1916, pub. 1964) ch. 1, "On Our Knowledge of Immediate Experience".

10–11 **The seas of experience | That were so broad and deep:** Arnold: "The Sea of Faith | Was once, too, at the full", *Dover Beach* 21–22 (David Chinitz, personal communication).

11–12 **That were so broad and deep, | So immediate and steep:** *Paradise Lost* VII 288–89, after the dividing of the waters (see note to 3–4): "So high as heaved the tumid hills, so low | Down sunk a hollow bottom broad and deep".

12–14 **and steep ··· what you will**: Donne: "On a huge hill, | Cragged, and steep, Truth stands, and he that will", *Satire* III 79–80 (David Coleman, personal communication).

16 **There is nothing else beside**: in Laforgue's *Le Concile féerique*, Le Monsieur ends his set speech: "Vrai, il n'y a pas autre chose" [Truly, there is nothing else]; the setting of the playlet, announced at the beginning, is "Nuit d'Etoiles" [Night of Stars]. Laforgue adapted the line for the end of his poem *Esthétique*: "Car il n'y a pas autre chose" [Because there is nothing else].

Mandarins

Published in *March Hare.*

Dated Aug 1910—"the 4" (poems under this title) in Notebook.

Title ***Mandarins***: Laforgue mentions mandarins three times, once as "le Grand Mandarin", in his *Salomé*, which begins: "Il faisait ce jour-là deux mille canicules qu'une simple révolution rythmique des Mandarins du Palais avait porté le premier Tétrarque ··· sur ce trône" [Two thousand dog-stars ago that very day, a simple rhythmic revolution of the Palace Mandarins had placed the first Tetrarch on the throne]. Gustave Kahn: "vos oiseaux, vos tasses et vos mandarins" [your birds, your cups and your mandarins], *Votre domaine est terre de petite fée* [*Your Realm is the Land of the Little Fairy*] (printed in the anthology *Poètes d'aujourd'hui*, for which see headnote to "*Poems* (1920)", 4. WHAT FRANCE MEANT TO TSE). In a run of four stanzas in Byron's *Don Juan* (XIII xxxiii–xxxvi), the Mandarin is taken as a type of cultivated indifference. In the issue of the *Harvard Advocate* that printed TSE's *Circe's Palace*, 25 Nov 1908, an essay by W. W. [Watson White] described *Il Teatro Marionetti* in Boston, quoting twice from *Hamlet*: "But 'the play's the thing' and we are here to see it. Presently, announced by a burst of chords from the mandolins, the curtain laboriously and unevenly ascends. Behold! There stands a martial figure 'armed ··· cap-a-pie,' its remarkably small head turned so as to present the audience with a staring, blank expression in shiny paint. Firmly planted on ridiculously fat legs—spread wide apart—it brandishes its tin sword." (OED "mandarin": "obs. variant of mandolin".) For W. W.'s essay, see note to *Convictions* 14. Irving Babbitt on Gautier: "As time went on the means employed by the different schools to arrive at a titillation of the æsthetic faculty became increasingly complex and incomprehensible to the uninitiated. 'Literature,' wrote M. Lemaître at the height of the symbolistic movement, 'tends more and more to become a mysterious diversion of mandarins'", *The Masters of Modern French Criticism* (1912) 308.

1

1 1 **complete**: TSE argued that Hamlet's tragedy was not "intelligible, self-complete, in the sunlight", *Hamlet* (1919). OED "complete" 5: "Of persons: Fully equipped or endowed; perfect, accomplished, consummate." *Henry VIII*

I ii: "This man so complete". *Troilus and Cressida* III iii: "marvel not, thou great and complete man".

1 2 **addressed:** OED 2: "Well-ordered, accomplished. *Obs.*"; 4: "Arrayed, attired, trimmed, dressed. *arch.*" **addressed with sword:** *Pericles* II iii: "Even in your armours, as you are addressed, | Will well become a soldier's dance." TSE: "Sweeney addressed full length to shave"; *Sweeney Erect* 21 (see note).

1 5 **Keen to appropriate the man:** *The Merchant of Venice* III ii: "so keen and greedy to confound a man".

1 6 **all these baits:** Milton: "vice with all her baits", *Areopagitica*; "Yet have they many baits" and "lickerish baits", *Comus* 537, 700.

1 7 **popular:** *Coriolanus* four times has the pejorative sense (OED 5a: "studious of, or designed to gain, the favour of the common people. *Obs.*"). TSE's jacket copy for Louis MacNeice's *Poems* (1935): "his work is intelligible but unpopular".

1 8 **merely stands and waits:** in his copy of Milton's *Paradise Regained, Samson Agonistes, & Other Poems*, TSE marked the sonnet *When I consider how my light is spent*, with its last line "They also serve who only stand and wait" (see *The O'Possum Strikes Back* 33, "when considering how his life is spent", in *Noctes Binanianæ*). *Paradise Lost* V 351–55:

> without more train
> Accompanied than with his own complete
> Perfections, in himself was all his state,
> More solemn than the tedious pomp that waits
> On princes

(TSE: "his own", 9; "complete", 1, also at the line-ending).

1 8–12 **He merely stands and waits | Upon his own intrepid dignity; | With fixed regardless eyes— | Looking neither out nor in— | The centre of formalities:** TSE in *Coriolan* I. *Triumphal March* 28–31:

> There he is now, look:
> There is no interrogation in his eyes
> Or in the hands, quiet over the horse's neck,
> And the eyes watchful, waiting, perceiving, indifferent

With "such a press of people · · · so many crowding the way", 4–6 (here: "the crowds that ran", 3).

1 10 **With fixed regardless eyes:** Keats: "she danced along with vague, regardless eyes", *The Eve of St. Agnes* 64.

1 12 **centre of formalities:** "centre of operation", *Mungojerrie and Rumpelteazer* 4 (and note to 3–4). ("Centre" remained as a formal spelling in the US.)

1 13–15 **A hero! and how much it means; | How much— | The rest is merely shifting scenes:** "A hero!—Where would he belong?" *Humouresque* 23. In his *Hamlet*, Laforgue has the Prince brood upon shifting scenes: "Un héros! et que tout le reste fût des levers de rideau!" [To be the hero of a play! And to reduce all of the other plays to little curtain-raisers!] TSE: "It has often been said that no man is a hero to his own valet; what is much more important is that no honest man can be a hero to himself; for he must be aware how many causes in world history, outside of abilities and genius, have been responsible for greatness", *The Varieties of Metaphysical Poetry* 289 (Turnbull Lecture III). **means**

··· **shifting scenes:** Tennyson: "the shifting scenes ··· what this wild Drama means", *The Play* 2, 4. **The rest is:** *Hamlet* V ii: "the rest is silence" (TSE's immediately preceding poem in the Notebook is *Silence*). "The rest is not our business", *East Coker* V 18. "The rest is grace", *Little Gidding* II 67–96 *first venture in verse* [21]. As an ending, Verlaine: "Et tout le reste est littérature", *Art poétique*. Théodore de Banville: "Aimer le vin, | La beauté, le printemps divin, | Cela suffit. Le reste est vain", *À Adolphe Gaïffe* 4–6; quoted by Symons in *Studies in Two Literatures* (1897) 265. **merely shifting scenes:** Poe: "Mere puppets they, who come and go | At the bidding of vast formless things | That shift the scenery to and fro", *The Conqueror Worm* 14, within *Ligeia* (see notes to *East Coker* III 13–17). TSE: "Prince Hamlet ··· start a scene or two", *The Love Song of J. Alfred Prufrock* 111–13 (with "come and go", 13, 35). Hawthorne: "in lieu of these shifting scenes, came back ··· all the townspeople assembled and levelling their stern regards", *The Scarlet Letter* ch. XI (TSE: "the crowds ··· fixed regardless eyes", 3, 10).

2

2 1 **ladies of uncertain age:** Byron: "She was not old, nor young, nor at the years | Which certain people call a '*certain age*', | Which yet the most uncertain age appears", *Beppo* xxii. OED "certain" II 7e: "sometimes euphemistically: Which it is not polite or necessary further to define. *a certain age:* an age when one is no longer young, but which politeness forbids to be specified too minutely: usually, referring to some age between forty and sixty (mostly said of women)." TSE: "A lady of almost any age", *The smoke that gathers blue and sinks* 16.

2 3 **persiflage:** OED cites Hannah More, 1799: "The cold compound of irony, irreligion, selfishness, and sneer, which make up what the French .. so well express by the term *persiflage*". Byron: "Whether the mode be persiflage or piety, | But wear the newest mantle of hypocrisy", *Don Juan* XVI lii. Rhymed here with "age"; *Fowler* recommends as though rhyming with *badinage*.

2 4–6 **tranquillity ··· sea:** Shelley: "an isle 'twixt Heaven, Air, Earth, and Sea, | Cradled, and hung in clear tranquillity", *Epipsychidion* 457–58; "the full and weary sea | To the depths of its tranquillity", *Rosalind and Helen* 971–72.

2 5 **Regard:** equivocally indicative ("Two ladies ··· Regard ···"), or imperative, with French inflection ("Regard that woman ··· Regard the moon", *Rhapsody on a Windy Night* 16, 50). Laforgue: "Penche, penche ta chère tête, va, | Regarde les grappes des premiers lilas" [Bend, bend your darling head—come, look at the bunches of the first lilacs], *Dimanches: C'est l'automne* 61–62. For Laforgue's poem see note to *La Figlia Che Piange* 2–3, 7; for Laforgue elsewhere in the present poem see notes in *March Hare*.

2 6 **A distant prospect of:** Thomas Gray, *Ode on a Distant Prospect of Eton College*. Byron: "a distant prospect", *Childe Harold's Pilgrimage* IV 285.

2 6, 9–10 **the sea ··· patterns ··· the floor:** "the sea; | Studies the sunlit pattern on the floor", *Animula* 10–11.

2 7 **outlines delicate and hard:** *Symons* 71 on Rimbaud: "in whom dream is swift, hard in outline". **delicate and hard:** "Visionary, and yet hard", *Interlude: in a Bar* 8.

2 8 **gowns that fall from neck and knee**: "Arms that lie along a table ··· skirts that trail along the floor", *The Love Song of J. Alfred Prufrock* 67, 102.

2 9 **Grey and yellow**: "Afternoon grey and smoky, evening yellow and rose", *Portrait of a Lady* III 32 (with "sunsets", II 12; here "sunset", 13).

2 12–13 **they approve | The abstract sunset**: OED "approve" 6: "To pronounce to be good, commend". Pope: "For fools admire, but men of sense approve", *An Essay on Criticism* 391.

2 13 **The abstract sunset (rich**: Tennyson: "Rich was the rose of sunset there", *The Wreck* 136. **(rich, not crude)**: on apparel, *Hamlet* I iii, POLONIUS: "But not expressed in fancy; rich, not gaudy". TSE: "rich and modest", *The Love Song of J. Alfred Prufrock* 43 (and note to 113, 116). **abstract**: OED 4d: "In the fine arts, characterized by lack of or freedom from representational qualities"; the first citation is 1915, *Forum* (N.Y.), but the *New Shorter* OED (1993) amalgamates 4d and 4e, adding 1868: "treated after a thoroughly abstract fashion" (on decorative wood carving). The *Trésor de la langue française* gives "abstrait", of fine art, in opposition to "expressioniste", with a 1904 citation. The OED entry of 2014 gives 6: "*Fine Art*. Designating art which is not founded on an attempt to represent external reality, but rather seeks to achieve an effect on the viewer purely by the use of shape, colour, and texture; of or relating to art of this kind. Also (of an artist, esp. a painter): producing art with these characteristics", with earliest citation 1851: "Abstract painting, which admits of no faithful imitation of nature, but whose forms and colors, though they have their basis in nature, are yet reduced or invented traditionally or conventionally, or by individual caprice or fancy." *Axis* magazine (1935–37) described itself as "A Magazine of Contemporary 'Abstract' Painting and Sculpture" until its penultimate issue (Autumn 1936), when the quotation marks around "Abstract" were dropped (Brian Webb and Peyton Skipwith, *John Piper*, 2013, 32–33).

2 16–17 **porcelain, | Murmurs a word**: "Among the porcelain, among some talk of you and me", *The Love Song of J. Alfred Prufrock* 89.

3

3 1 **the mandarins**: see note to title. OED 1e: "*transf.* A person of much influence, a great man. Often used *colloq.* of Government officials, leading politicians or writers, etc." with 1908: the "mandarins of London letters". 1b: "A toy representing a grotesque seated figure in Chinese costume, so contrived as to continue nodding for a long time after it is shaken."

3 1–4 **eldest ··· in obese repose ··· Regards**: Thomas Gray: "Youth on the prow, and Pleasure at the helm; | Regardless of the sweeping Whirlwind's sway, | That, hushed in grim repose", *The Bard* 74–76 (in *The Golden Treasury*). **repose ··· intellectual double chins ··· nose**: Byron: "(dogs have such intellectual noses!)" *Don Juan* II lviii, rhyming with "reposes". TSE rhymes "nose" with "repose" in *Suite Clownesque* I 8–11, again of someone obese ("His belly sparkling and immense", 14). *A Practical Possum* 60 *variant alts*: "repose / Nose". **repose**: OED 5b: "*Painting*, etc. Harmonious arrangement of figures or colours, having a restful effect upon the eye", from 1695, Dryden. Irving Babbitt praised "vital repose" and defended it against "the romanticists", *The New Laokoon* (1910) 229–33 (TSE dated his copy 1910).

3 4 **Regards the corner of his nose:** "see the corner of her eye", *Rhapsody on a Windy Night* 21.

3 5 **The cranes that fly:** TSE quoted *Inf.* V 46–48 (tr. diverging from Temple Classics): "And as the cranes go chanting their lays, making themselves a long streak in the air, so I saw the wailing shadows come, wailing, carried on the striving wind", *Dante* (1929) I.

3 6 **Pert, alert:** Pertelote, Chaucer's hen in *The Nun's Priest's Tale.* Laforgue rhymes "Meurtres, alertes ··· pertes" [murders, alerts ··· losses] in *Complainte de l'automne monotone* 29, 33.

3 8 *variant* **Attentive intuitionist:** in *Eeldrop and Appleplex* I (1917), Appleplex reports: "Mrs. Howexden recommends me to read Bergson", and Eeldrop replies that "A philosophy about intuition is somewhat less likely to be intuitive than any other." In Sept 1927, the *Criterion* published TSE's (signed) translation of Charles Mauron's *Concerning "Intuition"*, an attack on Middleton Murry's "new antinomy ··· Intuition and Intelligence". Calling Murry "a perfect pupil of his master, Bergson", TSE wrote in the next *Criterion*: "I mean that intuition must have its place in a world of discourse; there may be room for intuitions both at the top and the bottom, or at the beginning and the end; but that intuition must always be tested, and capable of test, in a whole of experience in which intellect plays a large part", *Mr. Middleton Murry's Synthesis* (1927).

3 8 *variant* **intellectualist:** "just as Bergson is an intellectualist", *Eeldrop and Appleplex* I (1917).

3 9 **World in fist:** OED "fist" 1b: 1400, of Christ: "He .. hooldith the world in his feest". In iconography there is, for instance, Emile Verhaeren, *L'Ivresse* [*Drunkenness*] 7: "Des aigles noirs, tenant le globe entre leurs pattes" [black eagles, holding the globe between their claws]. *TSE's books: Bodleian list* (1934) includes this volume of Verhaeren, *Les Visages de la vie* (1899).

3 10 **Screen and cranes:** as though punning with Fr. *écran* = screen. Laforgue: "l'écran des horizons" [the screen of horizons], *Complainte des Mounis du Mont-Martre* [*Complaint of the Hindu Ascetics from Montmartre*] 50.

3 11 **And what of all that one has missed!:** Laforgue: "Oh, qu'ils sont pittoresques les trains manqués!" [Missed trains! Oh, how picturesque they are!], *O géraniums diaphanes* 51. TSE quoted from the poem in *The Metaphysical Poets* (1921).

3 12 **And how life goes on different planes!:** "the errors in question are *not* simple error, but are formed by the compounding of theories belonging to different planes", *The Relationship between Politics and Metaphysics* (1914). **different planes:** Bergson: "S'il y a ainsi des *plans différents*, en nombre indéfini" [Just as there are these *different planes*, indefinite in number], *Matière et mémoire* (1896) ch. III. The running head for these pages was "Les divers plans de conscience". TSE: "But 'the greatest poetry', like the greatest prose, has a doubleness; the poet is talking to you on two planes at once", *The Wheel of Fire* by G. Wilson Knight (1930), Introduction. "The perception of life as on several different planes at once, noticeable in Chapman and Dostoevski ··· Keeping dif. planes intersecting. Intersection of planes of reality has been problem of fiction ever since *Bleak House* & [Wilkie Collins's novel] *Armadale*. Became final with Joyce", *Lecture Notes as Norton Professor* (1933) fols. 37–38. "We sometimes feel, in following the words and behaviour of some of the characters of Dostoevsky,

that they are living at once on the plane that we know and on some other plane of reality from which we are shut out", *John Marston* (1934). *The Family Reunion* II i: "They don't understand what it is to be awake, | To be living on several planes at once | Though one cannot speak with several voices at once." For other instances, see notes to this poem in *March Hare*.

4

4 1 **pen and ink**: to his mother, 19 Jan 1919: "little, very little, can ever filter through to pen and ink of what one feels".

4 1–2 **thought ··· spleen**: on Donne: "in this loose and desultory form of Satire he found a type of poetry which could convey his random thoughts and reflections, exercise his gift for phrasing, his interest in the streets of London, his irritability and spleen", *The Varieties of Metaphysical Poetry* 144 (Clark Lecture V). Donne's *Satire III* begins: "Kind pity chokes my spleen". See note on title *Spleen*. Laforgue: "Puis rien ne | Saurait faire | Que mon spleen ne chemine | Sous les spleens insulaires | De petites pluies fines" [Besides nothing could prevent my gloom following its course under the individual glooms of the fine drizzle], *Le brave, brave automne!* 17–20. Austin Dobson:

> "That is why, in a mist of spleen,
> I mourn on this Nankin Plate.
> Ah me, but it might have been!"—
> Quoth the little blue mandarin.
>
> *On a Nankin Plate* 16–19

4 1–3 **thought for pen and ink ··· How ··· think**: Thomas Hood: "Pray only think for pen and ink | How hard to get along", *Lines in a Young Lady's Album* 9–10 (repr. in *A Vers de Société Anthology* ed. Carolyn Wells, 1907).

4 4 **Who see their outlines on the screen**: "They see the outlines of their stage", *Convictions* 3. "But as if a magic lantern threw the nerves in patterns on a screen", *The Love Song of J. Alfred Prufrock* 105. "sees on the screen", *WLComposite* 285^286 [14] *variant.* OED 1d has, as its first cinematic citation, *Moving Picture World* (1910): "People .. like to see on the screen what they read about".

4 4 *variant* **Arrange and comprehend the scene**: "You have the scene arrange itself", *Portrait of a Lady* I 2.

4 4 *variant* **conscient**: *Symons* 107, of Laforgue: "He sees what he calls *l'Inconscient* in every gesture." Symons quoted *Autre complainte de Lord Pierrot* II: "d'un oeil qui vers l'Inconscient s'emballe" [an eye transported towards the Inconscient], tr. eds. TSE of Laforgue: "It is noticeable how often the words 'inconscient', 'néant', 'L'absolu' and such philosophical terms from the vocabulary of Schopenhauer and Hartmann ··· recur", *The Varieties of Metaphysical Poetry* 215 (Clark Lecture VIII).

4 5–7 **good ··· demoiselles**: Byron: "A dashing demoiselle of good estate", *Don Juan* XV xlii.

4 7–9 **demoiselles ··· dragons**: OED "demoiselle" 2b: "A dragon-fly", with 1816: "The name given to them in England, 'Dragon flies', seems much more applicable than 'Demoiselles' by which the French distinguish them", and Gosse, 1844: "an acquaintance with these *demoiselles*". Corbière has the double sense

in *Idylle coupée* 85 and *Rondel* II. Remy de Gourmont: "La libellule, joliment appelée la demoiselle" [The dragon-fly, gracefully called "la demoiselle"], *Physique de l'amour* ch. XIII.

4 8–9 **cherry · · · dragons**: Tennyson: "To catch a dragon in a cherry net", *The Princess* V 162.

4 10 **Expanded by the breeze**: Pope: "expand thy sails · · · and catch the nimble gales", *Odyssey* XII 104–105. Shelley: "the expanded sail", *Alastor* 398.

4 10–13 **by the breeze · · · gay**: Tennyson: "gay · · · by the breeze", *Maud* I [iv] 103–104.

4 12 **Nor intellectual nor mean**: Marvell: "He nothing common did or mean", *An Horatian Ode* 57. **Nor · · · nor**: *Measure for Measure* III i: "Thou hast nor youth nor age" (epigraph to *Gerontion*). OED 2b: "Chiefly *poet.*"; no instance after 1832. For "not . . . nor", see note to *Little Gidding* III 33–34.

4 12–13 **Nor intellectual nor mean, | And graceful, not too gay**: Wordsworth: "An intellectual ruler in the haunts | Of social vanity, he walked the world, | Gay, and affecting graceful gaiety", *The Excursion* II 180–82. **not too gay**: "London's a little too gay for us", *Sweeney Agonistes: Fragment of a Prologue* 148 and 150 (David Chinitz, personal communication).

4 15 **How life goes well in pink and green!**: "in blue and green", "green | Going in white and blue", *Ash-Wednesday* III 15, IV 3–4.

Goldfish (Essence of Summer Magazines)

Published in *March Hare.*

Goldfish is dated Sept 1910 at the end, in Notebook.

Title ***Goldfish***: Henry James: "As for the younger persons, of whom there were many, as for the young girls in especial, they were as perfectly in their element as goldfish in a crystal jar: a form of exhibition suggesting but one question or mystery. Was it they who had invented it, or had it inscrutably invented *them*?" *Florida* V in *The American Scene*. (See note to *First Debate between the Body and Soul* 27.)

I

Title I, I 1 ***Summer Magazines*** **· · · August evenings**: Francis Jammes: "J'aime dans les temps Clara · · · qui allait, les soirs chauds · · · lire les *magazines* d'autrefois" [Through the years I go on loving Clara · · · who walked, on warm evenings · · · reading magazines of bygone days], *J'aime dans les temps* 1–4 (with "des fins d'Eté" [the ends of summer], 12). In this volume, *De l'Angelus de l'aube à l'Angelus du soir* (1898)—which appears in *TSE's books: Bodleian list* (1934)—Jammes describes himself as "moi qui chante les anciens magazines" [I who hymn the ancient magazines], *On m'éreinte* [*They criticise me savagely*] 2. (W. G. Tinckom-Fernandez: "It was Eliot who first told me of the Vers Libre movement, of the work of Paul Fort and Francis Jammes", *Harvard Advocate* Dec 1938. Both French poets appeared in *Poètes d'aujourd'hui.*)

I 1–2 **Always the August evenings come | With**: "The winter evening settles down | With", *Preludes* I 1–2. Laforgue: "Aux soirs d'août", *Clair de lune* 4; "ce soir d'août", *Dimanches* 23; "En ce soir d'août", *Complainte des blackboulés* 15; and "O crépuscules d'août!" *Les deux Pigeons.*

I 2 **With preparation for the waltz**: "An *Invitation to the Dance*", *A Cooking Egg* 8 (see note).

I 1–2; IV 7, 17, 20, 37 **the August evenings come | With preparation for the waltz ··· October ··· the news from either Pole ··· soul ··· street pianos and small beers!**: "Pole ··· soul ··· drink our bocks ··· Reading the comics and the sporting page ··· a Polish dance ··· street piano ··· The October night comes down", *Portrait of a Lady* I 8, 10, 40; II 32, 35, 39; III 1.

I 1, 4, 6–8 **evenings ··· all ··· call, recall | So many nights and afternoons ··· all**: "For I have known them all already, known them all— | Have known the evenings, mornings, afternoons", *The Love Song of J. Alfred Prufrock* 49–50.

I 5 **The *Merry Widow***: by Franz Lehar, 1905. Valerie Eliot noted that TSE's brother "took him to his first Broadway musical, *The Merry Widow*, which remained a favourite", *Letters* (1988) 54. E. N. P. (unidentified) in *Harvard Advocate* 13 Nov 1908 (which included TSE's *Before Morning*): "Now a word about the *Merry Widow Waltz.* We have always liked this waltz, and we like it still. It is melodious, graceful, seductive. But no mere amateur should attempt it ··· It requires a complete mastery of all the resources of the piano, and an ideal grasp of the aesthetic principle, to interpret it adequately before an intelligent audience."

I 8 **August, with all its faults!**: Cowper: "England, with all thy faults, I love thee *still*— | My country!" *The Task* II 206–207. Byron: "'England! with all thy faults I love thee still', | I said at Calais, and have not forgot it", *Beppo* xlvii.

I 8–9 **all its faults ··· waltzes**: Byron, on Germany: "Who sent us—so be pardoned all her faults, | A dozen Dukes—some Kings, a Queen—and 'Waltz'", *The Waltz* 53–54. **all its faults ··· turn, return**: *Hamlet* IV vii: "all his faults ··· turneth wood to stone" (David Coleman, personal communication).

I 9–10 **the waltzes turn, return; | The *Chocolate Soldier* assaults**: Byron: "*sans armour* thou shalt take the field, | And own—impregnable to *most* assaults, | Thy not too lawfully begotten 'Waltz'", *The Waltz* 12–14. **The *Chocolate Soldier***: operetta by Oskar Straus (performed in Vienna, 1908), adapting Shaw's *Arms and the Man.* TSE to Henry Sherek, 3 May 1957: "I sometimes think that Shaw is best at musical comedy for *The Chocolate Soldier* and *My Fair Lady* are the only two of his works which I should like to see again and again."

I 10–11 ***Soldier* assaults | The ··· sphinx**: popular belief had it that a French soldier shot off the nose of the Sphinx during Napoleon's Egyptian campaign of 1798. Byron's *The Waltz* mentions both "Buonaparte" and Egypt (56, 127). James Thomson: "A warrior leaning on his sword alone | Now watched the sphinx", *The City of Dreadful Night* XX 27–28. **assaults | The tired**: "she is bored and tired ··· he assaults", *The Waste Land* [III] 236–39.

I 11 **tired Sphinx**: Gautier: "Des sphinx, lassés de l'attitude" [Of sphinxes, tired by the pose], *Nostalgies d'obélisques* II 31. Emerson: "The Sphinx is drowsy", *The Sphinx* 1. Wilde: "my lovely languorous Sphinx!" *The Sphinx* 13. (In his

Introduction to *Selected Poems of Marianne Moore* (1935), TSE speaks of the "typographical caprice" of internal rhyme in Wilde's poem.)

I 12 *variant* **that we not discern**: syntactically closer than the final reading ("We cannot discern") to Dante's "non discerno" (*Purg* XXVII 129; "discern no further") with which TSE ended *What is a Classic?* (1944). *Paradiso* IX 103: "Non però qui si pente, ma si ride" [Yet here we not repent, but smile]; TSE scored the Italian in the copy his mother gave him.

I 13–15 **turn ··· Float and fall, | Like the cigarettes**: Tennyson: "The folded leaf ··· turning yellow | Falls, and floats", *The Lotos-Eaters* 71–76. **Float and fall**: John Addington Symonds: "Where dingy lamplight floats and falls", *In the Key of Blue* 38.

I 15–16 **cigarettes ··· marionettes**: Wilde: "Sometimes a horrible marionette | Came out, and smoked its cigarette", *The Harlot's House* (1908) 22–23 (with "waltz", 32).

II

Title ***Embarquement pour Cythère***: Watteau's painting (Louvre, submitted 1717) initiated the term *fête galante*. Baudelaire: "Watteau, ce carnaval où bien des cœurs illustres, | Comme des papillons, errent en flamboyant, | Décors frais et légers éclairés par des lustres | Qui versent la folie à ce bal tournoyant" [Watteau, that carnival in which so many illustrious hearts wander incandescent like butterflies, in cool and frivolous settings, where chandeliers pour down the garish light of madness on the swirling dance], *Les Phares* [*The Beacons*] 21–24. Watteau's *Embarquement pour l'Ile de Cythère* became Baudelaire's *Un Voyage à Cythère*, from which TSE quoted "well-known lines" in *Baudelaire in Our Time* (1927). TSE queried Symons's translation of the Baudelaire: "We wonder even whether Mr Symons has not confused ··· Cythera with Cytherea" (this stricture was dropped when TSE reprinted his review in *For Lancelot Andrewes*).

Symons 107: "In his acceptance of the fragility of things as actually a principle of art, Laforgue is a sort of transformed Watteau, showing his disdain for the world which fascinates him, in quite a different way." Laforgue: "Et comment quelques couples vraiment distingués | Un soir ici ont débarqué" [and how several really refined couples disembarked here one evening], *Cythère* 11–12. Also: "Allez, hup! à Cythère!" [Mount! We are leaving this island for an island ruled by the Goddess of Love!], *Persée et Andromède*; for which, see headnote to *Ode* ("Tired. | Subterrene"). In Laforgue's *Pierrot Fumiste*, Pierrot exclaims: "'Cochers! Tous à Cythère! Au pays de Watteau!' (Il remonte dans la voiture. La noce qui était redescendue remonte. On va partir)" ["Coachmen! Everybody to the island ruled by the Goddess of Love! To the land of Watteau!" (He ascends the carriage again. Having once descended, the wedding party ascended again. They are departing)]. Austin Dobson's *After Watteau* begins "*Embarquons-nous!*" and ends:

> "*Allons, embarquons pour Cythère*";
> You will not? Press her, then, PIERROT,—
> "*Embarquons-nous!*"

II 4–5 **let us embark— | The night is anything but dark**: "Let us go then, you and I, | When the evening is spread out against the sky", *The Love Song of J. Alfred Prufrock* 1–2.

II 5–6 **The night is anything but dark, | Almost as clear as day:** André Salmon: "ô nuit tendre | Où je vois si clair en mon coeur" [oh tender night where I see so clearly within my heart], *Le Festin sous la lune* [*The Banquet beneath the Moon*] (1910) 43–44; with "Des artistes boivent et mangent" [artists drink and eat] 3.

II 11–12 **cigarette ··· light it at the evening star:** Salmon: "Parmi le clair de lune bleu, | L'autre, moins fou, ne se propose | Que d'allumer sa pipe aux cieux" [In the light of the blue moon, the other, less mad, proposes only to light his pipe at the heavens], *Le Festin sous la lune* 10–12. *Paradise Lost* VIII 519–20: "bid haste the evening star | On his hill top, to light the bridal lamp." **evening star:** Tennyson: "Sunset and evening star", *Crossing the Bar*; with "Turns again ··· dark ··· embark" (TSE: "*Embarquement* ··· dark ··· return", *title*, 5, 9).

II 12–13 **star) | To porcelain land, what avatar:** Browning: "Oh, never star | Was lost here but it rose afar! ··· In Vishnu-land what Avatar?" conclusion of *Waring*, a story of embarkation. **porcelain land:** "the porcelain department", *In the Department Store* 1 (see note).

II 13–14 **land ··· blue-:** Jean Lorrain (embarking for "Cythère"): "bleu pays", *Embarquement* (1887) 5, 26. The poem is in the edition of *Poètes d'aujourd'hui* that TSE owned.

II 13, 15 **avatar ··· Philosophy:** "It becomes clear after a little inspection that this type of thought, the *Word made Flesh*, so to speak, is more restricted in the times and places of its avatar than is immediately evident", *The Varieties of Metaphysical Poetry* 54 (Clark Lecture I).

II 14 **blue-delft-romance:** blue delft is invoked in Laforgue's mockery of romance, *Le Miracle des roses*, as the heroine's inkwell: "Ruth était exorcisée de ses hallucinations, et pouvait désormais s'adonner sans partage au seul et pur travail de sa tuberculose, dont elle reprit le journal d'une plume trempée dans un encrier à fleurs bleues genre Delft" [Ruth was exorcised of her hallucinations, and from that day she could give herself entirely to the duties of her consumption, whose record she began again with a pen dipped in a blue-flowered ink-well manufactured at Delft].

II 15 **Philosophy through a paper straw:** Swinburne: "and she | Drank lightly deep of his philosophy | In that warm wine of amorous words which is | Sweet with all truths of all philosophies", *The Queen's Pleasance.* Meredith: "through, | To teach philosophers the thirst of thieves", *A Ballad of Fair Ladies in Revolt* 4–5 (TSE: "Ladies" II 1). For Meredith's poem, see note to III 7. TSE: "the philosophy of Aristotle strained through the schools", *Dante* (1920). "Even *philosophy*, when divorced from *theology* and from the knowledge of life and of ascertainable facts, is but a famishing pabulum, or a draught stimulating for a moment, leaving behind drought and disillusion", *Modern Education and the Classics* (1932). Conrad Aiken recalled the sing-song of their Harvard friend W. G. Tinckom-Fernandez with his "exquisite English diction—'a cup of chocolate—one farthing is the rate—you suck it through a straw, a straw, a straw'", *Ushant* (1952) 135.

III

III 2 **have the call:** OED "call" 14b: "to be in chief or greatest demand; to be the favourite: in *Long Whist*, to be entitled to 'call honours'"; from 1840: "Youth has the call".

III 3 **White flannel ceremonial:** "I shall wear white flannel trousers", *The Love Song of J. Alfred Prufrock* 123. **ceremonial:** including OED 4: "A robe or garment worn on some ceremonial occasion (*obs.*)"

III 4 **With cakes and tea:** "after tea and cakes and ices", *The Love Song of J. Alfred Prufrock* 79.

III 5 **guesses at eternal truths:** *Guesses at Truth* by Two Brothers (Augustus William Hare and Julius Charles Hare, 1827, much reprinted). Symons on Réjane's acting: "It is like an accusing confirmation of some of one's guesses at truth, before the realities of the flesh and of the affections of the flesh. Scepticism is no longer possible", *Plays, Acting, and Music* (1903) 45. **eternal truths:** "And with the eternal truth the local error", *Little Gidding* II 67–96 *second venture in verse* (*msB*) [21]. **eternal:** for "*infinite* and *eternal*", see note to *Ash-Wednesday* IV 6.

III 6 **Sounding the depths with a silver spoon:** "I have measured out my life with coffee spoons", *The Love Song of J. Alfred Prufrock* 51. TSE to Frank Morley, 4 Aug 1938: "I hope you liked the spoon ··· S. Paul, S. Augustine, and of course S. John of the Cross ··· I should be glad to think that that spoon might be of use ··· S. John of the Cross (I hope that you can make some use of that spoon) ··· As for the abyss (do you think you can make any use of that spoon?) the ordinary mistake is to think that 'Religion' saves one from it." **with a silver spoon:** OED "spoon" 3c: "to be born with a silver spoon in one's mouth, to be born in affluent or lucky auspices" from 1801 (the first citation being American).

III 7 **And dusty roses ··· sunlight:** "a paper rose, | That smells of dust", *Rhapsody on a Windy Night* 57–58. "Dust in sunlight", *A Song for Simeon* 6. "Sudden in a shaft of sunlight | Even while the dust moves", *Burnt Norton* V 33–34. "Disturbing the dust on a bowl of rose-leaves", *Burnt Norton* I 17. **sunlight on the sea:** Meredith: "But now they dream like sunlight on a sea", *A Ballad of Fair Ladies in Revolt* 22. TSE: "Pleasure in the wind, the sunlight and the sea", *Animula* 10.

III 11 **Essence of summer magazines:** Laforgue: "deux dames-jeannes d'essences-bouquets de printemps et d'automne" [two demijohns of essence of spring and autumn], *Salomé*.

III 13–15 **How much ··· How much ··· How much one means:** "A hero! and how much it means; | How much—", *Mandarins* 1 13–14. "'You do not know how much they mean to me, my friends, | And how, how rare ···'", *Portrait of a Lady* I 19–20. **knows ··· means:** Tennyson: "Tears, idle tears, I know not what they mean", *The Princess* IV 21.

III 18, 20 **Play ··· conscience ··· crown:** HAMLET: "The play's the thing | Wherein I'll catch the conscience of the King" (II ii).

III 19 **means and ways:** OED "ways" records that "ways and means" formerly took this form (last citation, 1561: Hoby tr. Castiglione's *Courtyer* "Ech honest louer..vseth so manye meanes and wayes to please the woman whome hee loueth").

III 20 **wear the crown:** Tennyson: "Of those that wear the Poet's crown", *To ——, After Reading a Life and Letters* 10.

III 20, 22 **crown of your ideal ··· rose:** Tennyson: "as though there were | One rose in all the world, your Highness that, | He worships your ideal", *The Princess* II 36–38.

IV

IV 3, 6 **Old letters, programmes, unpaid bills ··· The limbo of a bureau drawer:** Baudelaire: "Un gros meuble à tiroirs encombré de bilans, | De vers, de billets doux, de procés, de romances, | Avec de lourds cheveux roulés dans des quittances, | Cache moins de secrets que mon triste cerveau" [Even an enormous chest of drawers stuffed with accounts and verses, love-letters and law-suits, drawing-room ballads, and heavy plaits of hair rolled in receipts, has fewer secrets to hide than has my unhappy brain], *Spleen* ("J'ai plus de souvenirs") 1–5. **bureau drawer:** at the line-ending: "He likes to lie in the bureau drawer", *The Rum Tum Tugger* 16.

IV 9 **Barcarolle:** OED: "A song sung by Venetian *barcaruoli* as they row their gondolas; a song or piece of music composed in imitation or reminiscence of such songs." Often invoked by 19th-century French poets. Gautier has *Barcarolle*; the first poem in the first book of poems by Villiers de l'Isle-Adam is *Barcarolle*; and Verlaine's *A Clymène* begins: "Mystiques barcarolles". Laurent Tailhade: "Combien qu'autour d'eux la Seine | Regorge de chiens crevés" [How often around them the Seine throws up dead dogs], *Barcarolle* 5–6, included in the anthology *Poètes d'aujourd'hui* (TSE: "barking", IV 11). Apollinaire: "La barque au barcarols chantants" [The barque with barcarolles being sung], *La Chanson du Mal-Aimé* [*Song of the Ill-loved*] final section, 22 (TSE: "barking", 11). For Apollinaire's poem, see note to *Interlude in London* 1. Eric Griffiths (personal communication): "Given his other allusions in this period to Chopin, TSE may have had in mind Op. 60, but the Barcarolle from act IV of Offenbach's *Les Contes d'Hoffmann* may also be relevant, with the mechanical doll in act II ('marionettes', 15) and the resurrected mother of act III ('leave their graves', 15)."

IV 10 **wet paths:** Homeric. Shelley: "watery paths", and shapes "Which walk upon the sea", *Prometheus Unbound* II v 106, 110.

IV 10–11, 14 **the sea ··· barking waves ··· the neuropathic:** *Symons* 12–13 on Gérard de Nerval: "and when, one day, he was found in the Palais-Royal, leading a lobster at the end of a blue ribbon (because, he said, it does not bark, and knows the secrets of the sea), the visionary had simply lost control of his visions, and had to be sent to Dr. Blanche's asylum." **barking waves:** Milton: "Scylla wept, | And chid her barking waves into attention", *Comus* 257–58. Kirke White: "He had words | To soothe the barking waves", *Christmas-Day* (*c.* 1800, OED). **waves pursue:** Milton: "Like waves they me pursue", Psalm LXXXVIII 68.

IV 14 **neuropathic winds:** Apollinaire: "au vent dément" [in the mad wind], *Les Colchiques* [*The Crocuses*] (1907) 12. OED: "Relating to, or caused or distinguished by nervous disease or functional weakness of the nervous system", from 1857; the citations are strictly medical. Laforgue has "les névropathes" four times within four paragraphs of *Le Miracle des roses*. **renew:** Shelley: "The earth doth like a snake renew | Her winter weeds outworn" and "Although a subtler

Sphinx renew | Riddles of death Thebes never knew", *Chorus*, *Hellas* 1062–63, 1082–83, the first quoted by TSE in *John Dryden* (1921) and *The Varieties of Metaphysical Poetry* 174 (Clark Lecture VI). Shelley's *Chorus* ("The world's great age begins anew") was printed on its own in *Oxf Bk of English Verse.*

IV 16 **Walking the waves:** Milton: "Through the dear might of him that walked the waves", *Lycidas* 173.

IV 17 **Bringing the news from:** OED "evangelize" 1a: "To bring or tell good tidings". Browning: *How They Brought the Good News from Ghent to Aix.* **from either Pole:** Herbert, *Content* 18. Tennyson: "to either pole she smiles, | Universal ocean softly washing all her warless Isles", *Locksley Hall Sixty Years After* 169–70. *Mayer* 61: "news of the polar explorations of Peary, Amundsen, and Shackleton ··· made headlines in 1909–1910." Kipling: "PICCIOLA—Both Poles have been overdone in Art and Literature. Leave them to Science for the next twenty years. You did not send a stamp with your verses", "Answers to Correspondents", appended to *With the Night Mail: A Story of 2000 A.D.* (1909). In *Homage to Wilkie Collins* (1927), TSE foresaw a similar danger: "'the destruction of the atom' will probably flourish for several years in bad detective stories".

IV 18 **fourth dimension:** OED from 1875 (G. H. Lewes) and citing Bertrand Russell, 1904: "The merit of speculations on the fourth dimension .. is chiefly that they stimulate the imagination, and free the intellect from the shackles of the actual." Much pondered at the time, in, for instance, C. H. Hinton's *The Fourth Dimension* (1904), early P. D. Ouspensky, and C. B. Patterson's "thought studies in the fourth dimension", *A New Heaven and a New Earth* (1909). Thomas Hardy: "A fourth dimension, say the guides, | To matter is conceivable", *A Dream Question* 22–23 in *Time's Laughing-Stocks* (1909).

IV 21, 23 **neat ··· complete:** "Neat, complete", *Suite Clownesque* III 22. For "complete", see note to *Mandarins* 1 1.

IV 28 **aged sibyl:** see note to *The Waste Land*, epigraph.

IV 28, 34 **eyes ··· assuring certainties:** "and eyes | Assured of certain certainties", *Preludes* IV 6–7.

IV 29 **four crossroads:** Thomas Hood: "And they buried Ben in four cross-roads", *Faithless Nelly Gray* 67 (Donald Gallup, personal communication).

IV 29–30 **crossroads ··· oracle:** perhaps invoking the story of Oedipus, though that takes place not at a crossroads but at a fork in the road. **oracle:** "The task of philosophy, it appears to me, is largely one of simplification: to disentangle the riddling oracles of the world, to paragraph and punctuate them and insert the emphases", *The Relativity of the Moral Judgment* (1915).

IV 33 **theoretic:** "It must be remembered that the French mind is highly theoretic—directed by theories—and that no theory ever remains merely a theory of art, or a theory of religion, or a theory of politics", *Syllabus: Modern French Literature* (1916) Lecture II, *The Reaction against Romanticism.*

IV 33, 36 **seas ··· Hesperides:** *Lemprière* "Hesperides": "three celebrated nymphs ··· appointed to guard the golden apples which Juno gave to Jupiter on the day of their nuptials ··· the place of their residence, placed beyond the ocean by Hesiod, is now believed to be near mount Atlas ··· This celebrated place or garden abounded with fruits of the most delicious kind". **some**

Hesperides: Kipling's concluding stanza to *The Second Voyage* (1903) likewise rhymes "New prows that seek the old Hesperides!" with "seas". TSE quoted thirty lines of Tennyson's unreprinted early poem *The Hesperides*, praising it highly, in *In Memoriam* (1936).

IV 37 **small beers**: OED "small beer" 1: "Beer of a weak, poor, or inferior quality". 2. *transf.* "Trivial occupations, affairs, etc.; matters or persons of little or no consequence or importance". *Othello* II i: "To suckle fools, and chronicle small beer."

Suite Clownesque

Published in *March Hare.*

Suite Clownesque is dated Oct 1910 at the end, in Notebook.

Title ***Suite***: OED 2d: "*Mus.* A set of instrumental compositions (orig. of movements in dance style) to be played in succession". TSE to L. A. G. Strong, 30 June 1925, on *The Hollow Men*: "I am still in doubt as to how I wish this suite to be arranged". ***Clownesque***: added in pencil to the original title *Suite.* Fr., clown-like; see III 14^15 and note; also *Humouresque.* Laforgue: "La bouche clownesque ensorcèle | Comme un singulier géranium" [The clownish mouth casts a spell like a singular geranium], *Pierrots* I 7–8 (see note to *Rhapsody on a Windy Night* 12, 63). Laforgue wrote of "les virtuosités clownesques" (*L'Art moderne en Allemagne* II), and to his sister Marie, 14 May 1883: "Je trouve stupide de faire la grosse voix et de jouer de l'éloquence. Aujourd'hui que je suis plus sceptique et que je m'emballe moins aisément et que, d'autre part, je possède ma langue d'une façon plus minutieuse, plus clownesque, j'écris de petits poèmes de fantaisie, n'ayant qu'un but: faire de l'original à tout prix" [I find it stupid to speak loudly and to play with eloquence. These days I'm more sceptical and I launch myself less readily. On the other hand, I'm master of my speech in a way that's more minute, more clownesque. I write little fantasy poems, with only one aim, to be original at any price].

I

I 1 **Across the painted colonnades**: Pope: "Beneath the pompous Colonnade", *Odyssey* III 511.

I 1, 4 **colonnades ··· serenades**: Villiers de l'Isle-Adam: "Voici l'heure des sérénades | Où brille, loin des colonnades" [Here is the hour of serenades where there shines, far from the colonnades], *Guitare* (1859) 1–2. Stuart Merrill (the American who made himself a French symbolist) rhymed "colonnades ··· serenades", *Le Palais désert* 6, 9.

I 1, 12 **Across the painted colonnades ··· across the orchestra**: "across the wall ··· across the floors", *Prufrock's Pervigilium* [22–34]. "live across the window panes", *Interlude in London* 2 (see note to 2–8). "feet passing across the skies", *Paysage Triste* 12. "stretched tight across the skies", *Preludes* IV 1. "Strode across the hills", *Cousin Nancy* 2. For "drips across the steps", see the parody of TSE in headnote to *Before Morning*.

I 2–4 **the terra cotta fawns · · · lawns · · · serenades**: a fawn is not a faun, but Verlaine: "Un vieux faune de terre cuite | Rit au centre des boulingrins, | Présageant sans doute une suite | Mauvaise à ces instants sereins" [An old terra cotta faun is laughing in the middle of the lawns, no doubt foreseeing an unhappy outcome to these happy moments], *Le Faune* 1–4 (TSE: "*Suite* · · · lawns · · · comedian", *title*, 3 5). John Gray's version of Verlaine, from the same sequence: "The fountains tall that leap upon the lawns | Amid the garden gods, the marble fauns", *Claire de Lune* 12–13. (For Hawthorne's *The Marble Faun*, see note to *Mr. Apollinax* 19. Here, terra cotta fawns. *Mr. Apollinax* 4 *variant*: "Priapus, terra cotta in the shrubbery".) Laforgue brings together terra cotta, music and clowns: "Les virtuoses en musique, en terre cuite, en langues, en peinture, etc · · · en plastique personnelle (les clowns)" [Virtuosos in music, in terra cotta, in painting, etc · · · in bodily sculpture (the clowns)], *Critique d'art* in *Mélanges posthumes* (1903) 178.

I 3 **Among the potted palms, the lawns**: Tennyson: "Among the palms and ferns", *Enoch Arden* 589.

I 3, 5 **lawns · · · comedian**: "Like amateur comedians across a lawn", *Afternoon* 8.

I 4 **cigarettes and serenades**: Tennyson: "canzonets and serenades", *The Princess* IV 117.

I 4, 6, 14 **serenades · · · vest · · · sparkling**: Symons: "singers of serenades · · · short vests, silken and bright", *From Paul Verlaine: Fêtes Galantes* XV. *Mandoline* 1, 9.

I 5–8 **comedian · · · nose | Nose · · · nose**: "the propriety of Cyrano on Noses · · · in the particular case of Cyrano on Noses, the character, the situation, the occasion were perfectly suited and combined", *"Rhetoric" and Poetic Drama* (1919). Rostand's *Cyrano de Bergerac* (1897) had been promptly translated, and in 1898–99 Richard Mansfield starred in the first English-language performances in the US. When he was ten, TSE's magazine *Fireside* had a note on *The Theatre*: "Cryno de Bergerac has created a great sensation" (No. 1, 28 Jan 1899; ms, Houghton). TSE supplied "an picture by our funny artist", of Cryno (with nose in profile, hat, and sword). "The men (their names were Comtes de Soke and de Nose) drew their swords and began to pink", *Fireside* no. 3 (Jan 1899). **Nose that interrogates the stars**: "(Feebly contemptuous of nose)", *Humouresque* 18. *Coriolan* has "There is no interrogation in his eyes" (I. *Triumphal March* 29) and "Noses strong to break the wind" (II. *Difficulties of a Statesman* 39). Rimbaud: "Fantasque, un nez poursuit Vénus au ciel profond" [Fantastic, a nose follows Venus in the deep sky], *Accroupissements* [*Squattings*], last line. TSE compared Massinger with Webster, to Massinger's disadvantage: "'Here he comes, | His nose held up; he hath something in the wind', is hardly comparable to 'the Cardinal lifts up his nose like a foul porpoise before a storm'", *Philip Massinger* (1920). For "Possum's Nose", see note to *A Practical Possum* 60.

I 6 **broad dogmatic**: OED "Broad Church": admitting "variety of opinion in matters of dogma and ritual · · · According to the Master of Balliol (Prof. Jowett), the term was first proposed in conversation, in his hearing, by A. H. Clough, and became colloquially familiar in Oxford circles, a few years before 1850." **vest**: OED "vest" 3b: "a waistcoat. Now *N. Amer.*" 2: "An ecclesiastical vestment. *rare.*"

I 6–10 **vest · · · scarlet · · · real · · · jellyfish:** Byron: "No real likeness,—like the old Tyrian vest | Dyed purple, none at present can tell how, | If from a shell-fish", *Don Juan* XVI x. **jellyfish:** OED 2 *fig.*, from 1883: "A person of 'flabby' character, or deficient in energy, steadfastness, or 'backbone'". For "truth and error in jellyfish life", see note to *The Dry Salvages* I 20–21.

I 6, 10, 23 **nose · · · jellyfish · · · toes:** Carroll: "when you've cleared all the jelly-fish out of the way" and "so he with his nose | Trims his belt and his buttons, and turns out his toes", both from *Alice's Adventures in Wonderland* ch. X, "The Lobster-Quadrille". *TSE's books: Bodleian list* (1934) includes "*Alice in Wonderland* (early ed.)"

I 8 **scarlet nose:** the bulbous prop essential to a clown.

I 11 **without repose:** Shelley: "Outspeed the chariot, and without repose", *The Triumph of Life* 140 (with "ribald crowd · · · obscene · · · wild dance · · · savage music", 136–42). Théodore de Banville, tr. Stuart Merrill: "his red shoes · · · trace without repose the figure of a lawless dance", *Harlequin* in *Pastels in Prose*.

I 14–15, 24 **His belly sparkling and immense: | It's all philosophy · · · his soul:** Wordsworth: "Thou, whose exterior semblance doth belie | Thy Soul's immensity; | Thou best Philosopher", *Ode: Intimations of Immortality* 109–11.

I 14, 17–18 **immense · · · the audience · · · suspense:** "immense · · · an audience open-mouthed | At climax and suspense", *Convictions* 4, 6–7.

I 15, 19 **philosophy and art · · · entities:** "the Abstract Entities", *Whispers of Immortality* 29 (see note).

I 20–21 **lights! · · · the world at rights:** "lights · · · sets the room to rights", *WLComposite* 358–360. OED 14, "to rights" ("to or into a proper condition"), gives "at rights" as rare (one instance, 1641: "to set all things at rights").

I 20, 25 **a ring of lights · · · Concentred:** *Paradise Lost* IX 105–107: "Light above light, for thee alone, as seems, | In thee concentring all their precious beams | Of sacred influence."

I 22 **Here's one who gets away with it:** TSE of *The Giaour*: Byron "not only gets away with it, but gets away with it *as narrative*", *Byron* (1937).

I 23 **spreading of the toes:** Henry Ware Eliot Jr (TSE's brother), of a debonnaire figure "on the Square": "He has a truly high-life way | Of turning out his toes", *Pierre* in *Harvard Celebrities: A Book of Caricatures* (1901).

I 23, 25 **spreading of the toes · · · vest and nose:** Lear: "And it's perfectly known that a Pobble's toes | Are safe,—provided he minds his nose", *The Pobble Who Has No Toes*, with "scarlet", 12, 28 (TSE, 8) and "The World · · · the world", 7, 20 (TSE: "the world", 21). For Lewis Carroll, see note to I 6, 10, 23. TSE: "Nose · · · toes" is the concluding rhyme of *A Practical Possum* and appears again in *Dirge*.

I 24–25 **self- · · · Concentred:** Scott: "The wretch, concentred all in self", *Breathes there the man with soul so dead* 12. (TSE to John Hayward [1 Mar 1942]: "how pleasant it is to cross the Tweed Bridge in a southerly direction and breathe the famous lines of Walter Scott, Breathes there etc." The poem is in *Oxf Bk of English Verse*.) TSE: "The interest of a performer is almost certain to be centred in himself: a very slight acquaintance with actors and musicians will testify", *The Possibility of a Poetic Drama* (1920).

II

II 1 **with a skirt just down to the ancle**: *Fowler*: "ankle, ancle. The -k- is usual." TSE has "ancle" twice, to Eleanor Hinkley, 27 Nov 1914. As to the fashion in skirts: "Ankle-length ones have gained votaries across the Channel", *Daily Chronicle* 1903, is OED's first citation for the compound.

II 7 **linger · · · finger**: "Smoothed by long fingers, | Asleep . . . tired . . . or it malingers", *The Love Song of J. Alfred Prufrock* 76–77.

II 11 **Seven little girls run away from school**: Gilbert, *The Mikado* (prod. 1885), act I:

> Three little maids from school are we,
> Pert as a school-girl well can be,
> Filled to the brim with girlish glee,
> Three little maids from school!
> Everything is a source of fun · · ·
> From three little maids take one away.

(TSE: "Everybody is under age", II 2.) Wordsworth's *We are Seven* is also about a little maid.

II 11, 14 **little · · · descend**: "Burbank crossed a little bridge | Descending at a small hotel", *Burbank with a Baedeker: Bleistein with a Cigar* 1–2 (see note on "Descending").

II 13 **street car**: OED 1, from 1862: "*N. Amer.* A passenger car, running through the streets, usually on rails; a tram-car."

II 21–22 **text · · · next?**: Byron ends, not a poem, but a stanza: "Men should know why | They write, and for what end; but, note or text, | I never know the word which will come next", *Don Juan* IX xli. Kipling ends a poem with a question:

> But to insult, jibe, and quest, I've
> Still the hideously suggestive
> Trot that hammers out the unrelenting text,
> And I hear it hard behind me
> In what place soe'er I find me:—
> "'Sure to catch you soon or later. Who's the next?"
>
> *The Undertaker's Horse* (1886)

II 22 **"Where shall we go to next?"**: "What is there for us to do?" *The Death of the Duchess* 12. "'What shall we ever do?'", *The Waste Land* [II] 134.

III

III 1 **walking down the avenue**: Paul Elmer More: "I was walking down the Avenue where the Park stretches away to your right · · · when my attention was caught by a lady just ahead", *The Great Refusal* 100. **the avenue**: Henry James: "Hadn't it been above all, in its good faith, the Age of Beauties—the blessed age when it was so easy to *be*, 'on the Avenue', a Beauty, and when it was so easy, not less, not to doubt of the unsurpassability of such as appeared there?" *The Sense of Newport* II in *The American Scene*. TSE: "The next I know the old cab was hauled up on the avenue", *WLComposite* **49**.

III 3–4 **meet you · · · greet you**: *The Cubanola Glide* (1909), quoted by TSE: "Tease, Squeeze lovin' & wooin' | Say Kid what're y' doin'", *WLComposite* **10–11** *variant*. For TSE and popular songs, see note to *The Waste Land* [III] 128–30.

III 6–7 **Broadway ··· moon:** Nathaniel Parker Willis: "The moon hangs just over Broadway", *City Lyrics* (1844).

III 7 **Under the light of the silvery moon**: the song *By the light of the silvery moon* (words, Edward Madden; music, Gus Edwards) was introduced in 1909 by the child singer Georgie Prince. It formed part of Edwards's vaudeville sketch "School Boys and Girls" (TSE: "the girls", 9, 16). TSE: "by the light of the Jellicle Moon", *The Song of the Jellicles* 24.

III 8–9 **You may find me | All the girls behind me**: for the rhyme see the ending of Kipling's *The Undertaker's Horse*, quoted in note to II 21–22. TSE: "'*Throw your arms around me—Aint you glad you found me*'", *The smoke that gathers blue* 18.

III 10 **Euphorion**: (i) Greek poet in the age of Antiochus; (ii) son of Aeschylus the tragedian; (iii) son of Faust in the Second Part of Goethe's *Faust*. Santayana: "Faust retires with her [Helen] to Arcadia,—the land of intentional and mid-summer idleness. Here a son, Euphorion, is born to them, a young genius, classic in aspect, but wildly romantic and ungovernable in temper. He scales the highest peaks, pursues by preference the nymphs that flee from him, loves violence and unreason, and finally, thinking to fly, falls headlong, like Icarus, and perishes", *Three Philosophical Poets* (1910) 177. (For Santayana's essay, see note to *Gerontion* 69.) Pater: "Goethe illustrates a union of the Romantic spirit, in its adventure, its variety, its profound subjectivity of soul, with Hellenism, in its transparency, its rationality, its desire of beauty—that marriage of Faust and Helena, of which the art of the nineteenth century is the child, the beautiful lad Euphorion, as Goethe conceives him, on the crags, in the 'splendour of battle and in harness as for victory', his brows bound with light", *Studies in the History of the Renaissance* ch. VIII. For ambiguous names, see note to *The Love Song of J. Alfred Prufrock* 94, "Lazarus". **Euphorion of the modern time**: one such Euphorion is George Eliot's plagiarist in *The Wasp Credited with the Honeycomb* (within *Theophrastus Such*).

III 10–11 **of the modern time | Improved and up to date—sublime**: Tennyson: "If, in thy second state sublime ··· The perfect flower of human time", *In Memoriam* LXI 1, 4. TSE: "Tennyson lived in a time which was already acutely time-conscious ··· a time busy in keeping up to date", *In Memoriam* (1936). TSE knew the rhyme also in *The Subway Express* (words, James O'Dea; music, Jerome Kern), which he quoted to Virginia Woolf, [6 Jan] 1935:

> I have another good song, it goes:
>
> I met you first at Spring St.
> And then upon my word
> I thought I'd known you all my life
> When we reached 23d.
> I won your heart at Haarlem,
> At the Bronx you murmured Yes:
> We lost no time
> On that ride sublime
> On the Subway
> Ex*press*.

III 11 **up to date:** recent in the slangy sense. OED "date" 7, from 1890, with 1893: "who invented the Gaiety burlesque 'up to date'—and gave this detestable phrase to the language". OED "up to date": "abreast of the times", citing W. S. Gilbert, *The Gondoliers* (1889), "A Grand Inquisitor is always up to date"; and *Daily News* (1894), "keep them, as the odious modern phrase is, up to date" (1894). TSE: "In a world which is chiefly occupied with the task of keeping up to date with itself", *Imperfect Critics* (1919). "Many people give the appearance of progress by shedding the prejudices and irrational postulates of one generation only to acquire those of the next: by 'keeping up to date'", *Paul Elmer More* (1937). But the *Criterion* of May 1927, announcing a change to monthly publication, declared that it was to be "up-to-time in its appreciation of modern literature".

III 12 **Quite at home in the universe**: Tennyson: "Quite sundered from the moving Universe", *The Princess* VII 37, with "Deeper", 36 (TSE: "depths", 12^13 *variant*). TSE: "Do I dare | Disturb the universe?" *The Love Song of J. Alfred Prufrock* 45–46. **at home**: OED 11c: "At one's ease", citing Tindale, 1528: "The mayde was at home also in heuenly pleasures." (Hegel: "Nature is a system of known and recognized Laws; Man is at home in it, and that only passes for truth in which he finds himself at home", *Lectures on the Philosophy of History* 459. TSE underlined "that ··· home" in his copy.)

III 12^13 *variant* **Seen from the depths of**: Tennyson: "Tears from the depth of some divine despair", *The Princess* IV 22.

III 13 **Shaking cocktails on a hearse**: Wilde: "The troubled plumes of midnight shook | The plumes upon a hearse: | And bitter wine", *The Ballad of Reading Gaol* III xviii (for which, see notes to *Rhapsody on a Windy Night* 9–12 and 11). TSE: "Where's a cocktail shaker, Ben, here's plenty of cracked ice", *WLComposite* 554. To Polly Tandy, 31 May 1935: "Jellicle cats & dogs all must | Like cocktail mixers, come to dust" (see *Five-Finger Exercises* II. *Lines to a Yorkshire Terrier* 10–12).

III 14^15 *stage direction* **sandboard**: not given as a musical instrument in OED or *Webster's Dictionary*, so perhaps part of the hearse: OED 2: "*Mech.* On a vehicle: a sturdy wooden bar running parallel to and above an axle", 1867, with "in car-building, a spring-plank", 1895. For music, also "washboard", OED 3c: "used as a percussion instrument". **bones**: OED: "pieces of bone struck or rattled, to make rude music; *esp.* two pieces of bone or ivory held between the fingers of each hand and rattled together as an accompaniment to the banjo or other instrument; chiefly used by 'nigger minstrels'". *Sweeney Agonistes: Fragment of an Agon*, Song, stage-direction: "Swarts as Tambo. Snow as Bones". W. S. Gilbert in *The Bab Ballads*: "The first was a highly-accomplished 'bones'", *The Three Kings of Chickeraboo* 5.

III 15, 16, 23 **walking on the beach ··· the girls ··· flannel suit**: "I shall wear white flannel trousers, and walk upon the beach ··· sea-girls", *The Love Song of J. Alfred Prufrock* 123, 130.

III 21 **the absolute**: see notes to *Conversation Galante* 14 and *Afternoon* 9.

III 21, 23 **First born child ··· quintessential**: *Paradise Lost* III 1, 6: "offspring of Heaven first-born ··· bright essence". Milton has "quintessence", both at III 716, "And this ethereal quintessence of Heaven", and (with "first") at VII 244–45: "Ethereal, first of things, quintessence pure | Sprung from the deep" (TSE: "depths", 12^13 *variant*). **quintessential**: slangy, OED: "Eldon's quintessential Toryism", 1887.

III 22 **complete**: see note to the opening line of *Mandarins*, "Stands there, complete".

III 24–25 **nothing the matter with us! | —But say, just be serious:** Laforgue: "J'aurai un: 'Ah ça, mais, nous avions De Quoi vivre! | C'était donc sérieux?'" [I'll react with a: "Drat it, we had the Wherewithal to live on! Was it serious after all?"], closing *Autre complainte de Lord Pierrot* (see note to *Portrait of a Lady* III 31). In his *Hamlet*, Laforgue follows "devenu si sérieux" with "soyons sérieux ici!" TSE's *Nocturne* begins: "Romeo, *grand sérieux*". *Conversation Galante* ends "And—'Are we then so serious?'"

IV

IV 5 **Columbine:** OED: "A character in Italian Comedy, the mistress of Harlequin, transferred to our Pantomime or Harlequinade". Verlaine's *Colombine* is from the same sequence—*Fêtes galantes* (1869)—as *Le Faune*, which influenced *Suite Clownesque* I (see note to I 2–4).

IV 6 **hat in hand:** *Symons* 109, on Laforgue: "He composes love-poems hat in hand." TSE: "Guitar and hat in hand", *Nocturne* 2. "hat and gloves in hand", *Spleen* 13.

IV 6, 8 **hand ··· saraband:** Lovelace: "So you but with a touch from your fair hand, | Turn all to saraband", *To Lucasta: I laugh and sing.* When it was suggested that the name Lucasta Angel in *The Confidential Clerk* should be changed, TSE cited Lovelace (*Sackton* H75–79).

IV 6, 9 **hand ··· The discovered masquerades:** "the other masquerades ··· hands", *Preludes* II 6–8 (David Chinitz, personal communication).

IV 12 **dense:** "It is this contrast between the tenuous and the dense which is the contrast between thought and reality ··· a loss of density and richness ··· the greatest philosophies have themselves something of this density and richness, and consequently are ··· almost as difficult and inexhaustible as the world itself", *The Validity of Artificial Distinctions* (1914), the first remark being added in the margin.

IV 14 **Explodes in laughter:** OED "explode" 5b ("To 'go off' with a loud noise ··· *trans.* and *fig.*") has this idiom from 1867: "made the crowd explode with laughter". OED 1a. (*Obs.*): "To clap and hoot (a player, play, etc.) off the stage". *Paradise Lost* X 545–46: "Thus was the applause they meant, | Turned to exploding hiss, triumph to shame".

The Triumph of Bullshit

Published in *March Hare.*

Dated Nov. 1910, *ms1.*

Wyndham Lewis to Pound, [Jan 1915]: "Eliot has sent me Bullshit & the Ballad for Big Louise [*Ballade pour la grosse Lulu*]. They are excellent bits of scholarly ribaldry. I am longing to print them in *Blast*; but stick to my naif determination to have no 'Words Ending in -Uck, -Unt and -Ugger.'" Pound replied, [Jan 1915]: "I dare say Eliot will consent to having blanks for the offending words", but neither poem was published. (Three lines of Pound's *Fratres Minores* had been inked over by hand in each copy of the first issue of *Blast* (June 1914) at the insistence of the publisher, John Lane; *O'Keeffe* 155–56.)

Consisting (strictly) of three stanzas with the same final line and a shorter envoi, the ballade form was scabrously used by François Villon.

Title ***Triumph of***: invoking the tradition of Petrarch's *Triumphs*, and then Shelley's *The Triumph of Life* and Swinburne's *The Triumph of Time*. ***Bullshit***: OED records this first from Wyndham Lewis's letter to Pound. *Partridge*: "mostly Australian". In his copy of Hegel's *Lectures on the Philosophy of History* 431, TSE underlined the words here italicised: "The time-honoured and cherished *sincerity of the German people* is destined to effect this revolution out of the honest truth and simplicity of its heart", and wrote in the margin: "BULL".

6 **galamatias**: OED "galimatias": "Confused language, meaningless talk, nonsense", citing 1653 Urquhart's *Rabelais* I ii, "A Galimatia of extravagant conceits."

9–13] Ottoline Morrell on TSE in 1916: "highly polite and conventional and decorous, and meticulous. I tried to get him to talk more freely by talking French to him, as I thought he might feel freer doing so, but I don't think it was a great success, although better than English. He speaks French very perfectly, slowly and correctly" (*Morrell 1974* 101–102). See headnote to "*Poems* (1920)", 5. TSE'S PROFICIENCY IN FRENCH.

10, 12 **gauche** ··· ***brioche***: Laforgue liked off-rhymes on "brioche": "crèche ··· brioche", *Lunes en détresse* 6, 8; "dimanches ··· blanches ··· brioches", *Dimanches: Bref, j'allais* 23, 24, 26.

14 **attenuate**: as participial, Meredith: "The idea is too exquisitely attenuate", *The Egoist* (OED).

15 ***isiculous***: formed from an icicle (OED records the obsolete spelling "isicle").

18 **cabotin**: OED: "A low-class actor", 1903. Laforgue of Corbière: "Jamais Cabotin, jamais", *Dragées: Charles Baudelaire, Tristan Corbière* (1920) 168. Irving Babbitt on Ernest Renan: "Literature seemed to him to have been invaded by that instinct for posing and stage effect to which, in its lower forms, the French give the name of *cabotinage*. It would not be easy to exaggerate this element in French character, especially since Rousseau and the romanticists ··· Nero—the imperial *cabotin*", *The Masters of Modern French Criticism* (1912) 294.

25–28] FitzGerald's *Rubáiyát of Omar Khayyám*:

> And when Thyself with shining Foot shall pass
> Among the Guests Star-scatter'd on the Grass,
> And in thy joyous Errand reach the Spot
> Where I made one—turn down an empty Glass!

(Likewise the concluding lines.) TSE's first reading had "Among the guests star-scattered on the grass" (see Textual History). For his writing "gloomy quatrains in the form of the *Rubáiyát*", see headnote to "Uncollected Poems", 2. *POEMS WRITTEN IN EARLY YOUTH*.

26 **Theories scattered**: the world "swarms with inchoate theories which ultimately perhaps mean the same thing—at the point where all meanings are lost", *The Validity of Artificial Distinctions* (1914).

25, 28 *variant* **And when Thyself with shining Foot shall pass ··· You have the right to stick them up my ass:** "Now that we talk of dying— | And should I have the right to smile?" *Portrait of a Lady*, likewise as the conclusion. All three full stanzas of *The Triumph of Bullshit* begin with ladies.

Fourth Caprice in Montparnasse

Published in *March Hare.*

Dated Dec 1910 in Notebook.

Title ***Fourth*:** TSE either did not write or did not preserve a Third Caprice. ***Caprice in Montparnasse*:** Charles-Louis Philippe on married men thinking of the prostitutes of Montparnasse: "Une petite aventure, un sourire, un caprice pour celle qui passe" [A little adventure, a smile, a moment's caprice with the girl passing by], *Bubu de Montparnasse* ch. VII.

1 **We turn the corner of the street:** Philippe: "Every street-corner spoke to them of memories", *Bubu of Montparnasse* ch. VII. TSE: "And at the corner of the street", *Preludes* I 11.

1, 7 **street ··· blackened trees:** "The conscience of a blackened street", *Preludes* IV 8.

1, 11 **We turn the corner of the street ··· Hand in pocket:** Apollinaire: "mains dans les poches ··· Au tournant d'une rue brûlant" [hand in pockets ··· at the corner of a street that was burning hot], *La Chanson du Mal-Aimé* [*The Song of the Ill-Loved*] 7, 16. See note to *Rhapsody on a Windy Night* 16–21.

9 **Like mendicants without regrets:** Baudelaire: "Et nous alimentons nos aimables remords, | Comme les mendiants nourrissent leur vermine" [And we nourish our fond remorses as beggars suckle their own lice], *Au lecteur* [*To the Reader*] 3–4; see *The Waste Land* [I] 76.

9, 13 **regrets ··· Among such scattered thoughts:** "Among velleities and carefully caught regrets", *Portrait of a Lady* I 15.

11 **Hand in pocket, undecided:** Laforgue: "Les mains dans les poches, | Le long de la route ··· Sans que tu t'en doutes!" [Hands in pockets, right down the road ··· though you don't expect it!], *Locutions des Pierrots* XIV.

11, 15 **undecided ··· hard to please:** Scott: "O Woman! in our hours of ease, | Uncertain, coy, and hard to please", *Marmion* VI xxx.

12 **Indifferent if derided:** "Which still are unreproved, if undesired ··· And makes a welcome of indifference", *The Waste Land* [III] 238, 242.

13–14 **scattered ··· corner ··· street:** Donne: "scattered in corners of each street do lye", *The Lamentations of Jeremy* 272 (with "stand ··· hand", 275–76; TSE, 8, 11).

15, *draft lines after* 15 **why are we so hard to please? | The world is full of:** Robert Louis Stevenson: "The world is so full of a number of things, | I'm sure we should all be as happy as kings", *Happy Thought* in *A Child's Garden of Verses*, a collection listed by TSE on his *Syllabus: Modern English Literature: Second*

Year's Work (1917). "while the mind of man has altered [since 1890], verse has stood still; and the majority of our poets can only touch us as a *Child's Garden of Verses*, a heavy trifling; they have nothing to say to the adult, sophisticated, civilized mind; are quite unaware of its tragedies and ecstasies", *A Note on Ezra Pound* (1918). **why are we so hard to please ··· universities:** Laforgue: "l'Université ··· Je m'ennuie, nous nous ennuyons tant! n'est-ce pas, messieurs?" [the University ··· I am tired. All of us are so tired, aren't we, Gentlemen?], *Salomé.*

draft lines after 15 **The world is ··· full of universities:** on William James: "But James has an exceptional quality of always leaving his reader with the feeling that the world is full of possibilities—in a philosopher, a rare and valuable quality", *William James on Immortality* (1917). To Conrad Aiken, 16 Nov 1914: "University towns, my dear fellow, are the same all over the world; only they order these matters better in Oxford." (Sterne: "—They order, said I, these matters better in France—", *A Sentimental Journey* opening words.) 31 Dec: "As you know, I hate university towns and university people, who are the same everywhere". **journalists ··· universities:** "En Amérique, professeur; | En Angleterre, journaliste", *Mélange Adultère de Tout* 1–2.

Inside the gloom

Published in *March Hare.*

The handwriting suggests a date at the end of 1910.

Laforgue similarly contemplates the heavens in fourteen sardonic couplets, with a rhythm resembling that of TSE's opening couplets:

Lune bénie
Des insomnies,

Blanc médaillon
Des Endymions,

Astre fossile
Que tout exile

[Blessed moon of insomnias, | White medallion of Endymions, | Fossil star which everything banishes] *Litanies des premiers quartiers de la lune* [*Litanies of the first two quarters of the moon*].

TSE returned to the constellations and to gloom: "Death and the Raven drift above ··· Gloomy Orion and the Dog", *Sweeney Among the Nightingales* 7–9. Again: "the drift of stars ··· the boarhound and the boar ··· among the stars", *Burnt Norton* II 8–15, and "rolling stars ··· and Leonids fly", *East Coker* II 8–13.

1–2 **Inside the gloom ··· room:** "in its ··· gloom ··· drawing-room", *Whispers of Immortality* 26–28. "in its own gloom ··· in a dusty room", *Animula* 29–30.

1, 3, 4 **gloom ··· constellations ··· stations:** W. S. Gilbert's *Thespis*, or *The Gods Grown Old* (prod. 1871), begins with a Chorus of Stars: "Throughout the night |

The constellations | Have given light | From various stations ··· midnight gloom".

4 **Took up their stations**: "we took up | Our positions", *Defence of the Islands* [21–22].

9 **tail on fire**: legend has it that when ringed with fire, the scorpion stings itself to death with its tail.

11 **Cassiopea**: mentioned, along with the Great Bear and other constellations, at the close of Laforgue's *Persée et Andromède*, which TSE adapted in *Ode* ("Tired. | Subterrene").

11–12 **Cassiopea | Explained the Pure Idea**: *Paradise Lost* VII 557, the Creation: "Answering his great idea". Tennyson: "Ida, Ida, Ida ··· Ida ··· Cassiopeia", *The Princess* IV 413–18. **the Pure Idea**: "And yet devoted to the pure idea ··· The pure Idea dies of inanition", *First Debate between the Body and Soul* 8, 15 (see notes).

13 **Major Bear**: Ursa Major. See note to *Gerontion* 68, "the shuddering Bear". When he was ten, TSE's magazine *Fireside* (No. 13–14, Feb 1899) included chapters of *A Voyage to the Great Bear.*

13 *variant*, 27 **The dancing bear ··· chattered**: "Like a dancing bear ··· chatter", *Portrait of a Lady* III 28–29.

14 **Balanced a chair**: as at a circus, balancing a chair on its nose. *Paradise Lost* IV 1000: "balanced air", with the astronomical "scorpion" two lines earlier (TSE, 7). **chair**: Cassiopeia, invoked in the previous couplet, is the Lady's Chair (rhymed by Hardy with "Greater Bear" in *Shut out that moon*, 1909).

16 **intellection**: OED 1: "the exercise or activity of the intellect". 1b: "Applied *spec.* to the kind of immediate knowledge or intelligence ascribed to divine or angelic beings. *Obs.*" Common to English and French. Berkeley, 1732: "As reason is of kind peculiar to man, so by intellection he [Pico of Mirandola] understands a kind or manner of knowledge peculiar to angels". TSE on Marianne Moore: "To the moderately intellectual the poems may appear to be intellectual exercises; only to those whose intellection moves more easily will they immediately appear to have emotional value", *Selected Poems of Marianne Moore* (1935), Introduction.

18 **Vital Force**: OED has citations from 1702. Emerson: "In certain men, digestion and sex absorb the vital force"; "Only so can ··· vital force accumulate", *The Conduct of Life* ch. I, II. OED has a separate entry for Bergson's *élan vital* in *L'Evolution créatrice* (1907), often tr. as "vital force" (though in Arthur Mitchell's translation of 1911, only so in the index). TSE: "in spite of the appearance of Bergson ··· I am inclined to believe that philosophies which admit the inclusion ··· of anything which eludes rational grasp—such as *vitalism*—are more natural to non-'Latin' countries", *Revelation* (1937). "*Vers libre* does not exist, and it is time that this preposterous fiction followed the *élan vital* and the eighty thousand Russians into oblivion", *Reflections on "vers libre"* (1917).

19 **Cetus**: constellation, the Whale.

20 **the relation of life to matter**: Bergson: "la vie est, avant tout, une tendance à agir sur la matière brute" [life is, more than anything else, a tendency to act on

inert matter], *L'Evolution créatrice* ch. I. See *The smoke that gathers blue and sinks* 6–7 and note.

21–22 *variant* **a fork and knife** ··· **Place:** "If you look for a knife or a fork | And you think it is merely misplaced—", *Mr. Mistoffelees* 33–34.

23 **Bootes:** OED: "A northern constellation, the Wagoner, situated at the tail of the Great Bear and containing the bright star Arcturus". Pope: "When clouds conceal Boötes' golden wain", *Thebais* 521.

23, 25–26 **unsettled** ··· **questions** ··· **indigestions:** "ours is an unsettled age ··· conscious of these questions as a man with indigestion is conscious of his stomach", *The Idealism of Julien Benda* (1928). Byron: "For ever and anon comes Indigestion ··· and perplexes | Our soarings with another sort of question ··· confusion of the sorts and sexes, | Of being, stars, and this unriddled wonder, | The World ··· a glorious blunder", *Don Juan* XI iii. W. S. Gilbert: "Commencing with a gentle pain | Scarce worth a question, | It grows apace, till you complain | Of indigestion", *The Mountebanks* (prod. 1890) act I. Austin Dobson rhymes "Your cynic question" with "due | To indigestion", *A Gage d'Amour* 16, 11–12.

27–28 **chattered** ··· **mattered:** "Oh, Lady Kleinwurm's monde—no one that mattered— | Somebody sang, and Lady Kleinwurm chattered", *WLComposite* 255–56.

Entretien dans un parc

Published in *March Hare.*

Dated Feb 1911 in Notebook.

Title ***Entretien dans un parc***: [Conversation in a Park]. J.-B. Pater's painting *Conversation galante dans un parc* was then in the Rothschild collection, Paris. (TSE's *Conversation Galante* was also drafted in the Notebook.) Watteau's *Assemblée dans un parc* (Louvre) has, on the left, a couple moving away; on the right, a seated couple talking; and a woman in tension with a suitor. The painting anticipates Watteau's *L'Embarquement pour l'Ile de Cythère*, for which see headnote to *Goldfish* II. *Embarquement pour Cythère.* Verlaine: "Dans le vieux parc solitaire et glacé | Deux formes ont tout à l'heure passé" [In the old lonely icy park two figures have passed right on time], *Colloque sentimental* 1–2. TSE's cancelled title for *First Debate between the Body and Soul* was *Reflections in a Square.*   ***dans un parc***: "From April to middle-December | He is apt to occur in the parks", *How to Pick a Possum* 21–22 (here: "April", 3).

Unadopted title ***Situation***: "Here is Belladonna, the Lady of the Rocks, | The lady of situations", *The Waste Land* [I] 49–50. OED 1: "place, position, or location"; 9a: "Position of affairs"; 9b: "A particular conjunction of circumstances (*esp.* one of a striking or exciting nature) under which the characters are presented in the course of a novel or play"; 9c, without article, has Sheridan, *The Critic* (1779): "This scene goes entirely for what we call situation and stage effect ··· There's situation for you! there's an heroic group!" (TSE: "All the scene's absurd!" 19). For TSE on "Situation" in Henry James, see note to *Portrait of a Lady* II 9. Pater repeatedly used the word "situation" of Browning: "His poetry is pre-eminently the poetry of situations ··· His gift is shown by the way in which he accepts such a character, throws it into some situation ··· [In *Dis Aliter Visum: or, Le Byron de Nos Jours*, the two jaded Parisians] begin to interest us only when thrown into a choice situation ··· what an artificial light is constructed and broken over the chosen situation", *Studies in the History of the Renaissance* ch. VIII. Browning's failed lovers invoke Paris, so theirs would be an *Entretien*; and like TSE's title, Browning's subtitle is in French. TSE's cancelled title, *Situation*, might or might not be French.

Unadopted title, 13 ***Situation* ··· She smiles**: "smiles at situations ··· I smile, of course", *Portrait of a Lady* II 9–10.

1, 6–7 **afternoon ··· I wonder if it is too late or soon ··· our lives** : "Well! and what if she should die some afternoon ··· should die ··· tardy or too soon ··· Now that we talk of dying", *Portrait of a Lady* III 31–40. On hearing that his brother Henry had only months to live, TSE wrote to Frank Morley, 10 Nov 1946: "One doesn't want to arrive too soon, or too late. That is the invariable problem in such cases." (To Anne Ridler, 30 June 1947: "Your father must have been very proud of your success as both a poet and a mother. My own father died too soon to be able to see me as anything but a son who had taken the wrong course in life. Those are fortunate who die at the right time.") **too late or soon**: "Gives too late | What's not believed in, or ··· Gives too soon", *Gerontion* 39–41.

3 **We walked along**: "through which we walked along", *So through the evening, through the violet air* 12 *variant*.

3–4 **April ··· uncertainties**: *Two Gentlemen of Verona* I iii: "O, how this spring of love resembleth | The uncertain glory of an April day, | Which now shows all the beauty of the sun, | And by and by a cloud takes all away!"

4 *variant* **certain uncertainties**: "Assured of certain certainties", *Preludes* IV 7.

5 **becomes intense**: Browning: "While, oh, how all the more will love become intense", *Fifine at the Fair* 881.

5, 18, 21, 28 **Struggling intention that becomes intense ··· a bit ridiculous ··· And what we feel, or not ··· But if we could have given ourselves the slip**: Bradley: "a kindred difficulty attaching to what is called Introspection. Can I observe my own present state, and, if not that, what in the end can I observe? ··· when I try to observe exhaustively, say, some internal sensations, the idea that I am struggling to remember them seems even ridiculous ··· What I feel, that surely I may still feel", *On Our Knowledge of Immediate Experience* (Jan 1909), *Essays on Truth and Reality* 166.

6, 11 **late or soon ··· the world has not been changed:** Wordsworth has Proteus, the changer, in his sonnet *The world is too much with us; late and soon.*

12, 15 **revision ··· decision**: "indecisions ··· revisions", *The Love Song of J. Alfred Prufrock* 32–33.

14 **So little**: Miltonic, particularly at the head of the line: "So little here, nay lost; but Eve was Eve", *Paradise Regained* IV 6; "So little is our loss, | So little is thy gain", *On Time* 7–8.

17 **And yet this while we have not spoken a word**: Browning: "And yet—she has not

spoke so long!" *The Last Ride Together* 100; "And yet God has not said a word!" *Porphyria's Lover*, last line.

18 **It becomes at last a bit ridiculous**: "At times, indeed, almost ridiculous", *The Love Song of J. Alfred Prufrock* 118.

19–20 **All the scene's absurd! | She and myself**: *As You Like It* II vii: "All the world's a stage, | And all the men and women merely players".

21 **And what we feel, or not**: see note to *Do I know how I feel? Do I know what I think?* 1.

22–25 **Round and round, as in a bubbling pot ··· cool ··· fire ··· fire**: *Macbeth* IV i: "Round about the cauldron go ··· pot ··· Fire burn and cauldron bubble ··· Cool". Augustine: "To Carthage I came, where a cauldron of unholy loves bubbled up all around me", *Confessions*, tr. J. G. Pilkington (1871), opening of bk. III. TSE's Note to *The Waste Land* [III] 307 quotes a different translation of the same sentence. On Walter Lippmann: "When ··· describing fact or criticising human affairs, he is apt to be right; when he philosophises, he is not wholly wrong. When he stirs the two ingredients together in his witches' cauldron, a foul vapour rises", *The Relationship between Politics and Metaphysics* (1914). **pot ··· ridicule**: Ecclesiastes 7: 6: "For as the crackling of thorns under a pot, so is the laughter of the fool: this also is vanity".

26 **blind alley**: "the blind alleys of taboo and superstition", *The Relativity of the Moral Judgment* (1915). Of logical positivism: "even if some of its avenues turn out to be blind alleys, it is, after all, worth while exploring a blind alley, if only to discover that it *is* blind", TSE's Introduction to *Leisure the Basis of Culture* by Josef Pieper (1952). **stopped with**: *King John* IV ii: "stopped with dust: the first of April" (TSE: "April", 3; "dusty", 34).

26–27 **Up a blind alley ··· childish scrawls!**: to Robert Waller, 21 Sept 1942: "I do fear that Dylan Thomas has been up a blind alley, an alley choked with rather rank vegetation of verbiage." **walls ··· chalked with childish scrawls**: Shelley: "a brick house or wall | Fencing some lonely court, white with the scrawl | Of our unhappy politics", *Letter to Maria Gisborne* 266–68.

30 **No stumbling**: 1 John 2: 10: "He that loveth his brother abideth in the light, and there is none occasion of stumbling in him". **ends unshaped**: *Hamlet* V ii: "There's a divinity that shapes our ends" (with "unshaped", *Hamlet* IV v). Shelley: "Who shaped us to His ends and not our own", *The Boat on the Serchio* 31. TSE: "ends unknown", *The Engine* I.

30, 32 **ends ··· moles**: "The mole digs and the eagle flies, but their end is the same, to exist", *Selected Poems of Ezra Pound* (1928), Introduction. Blake: "Does the Eagle know what is in the pit? | Or wilt thou go ask the Mole?" *The Book of Thel*, *Thel's Motto* 1–2.

32 **keep ··· ants or moles**: Webster's Dirge, from *The White Devil* V iv:

> The ant, the field-mouse, and the mole
> To rear him hillocks that shall keep him warm
> And (when gay tombs are robbed) sustain no harm;
> But keep the wolf far thence, that's foe to men,
> For with his nails he'll dig them up again

(In Palgrave's *Golden Treasury*; see note to *The Waste Land* [I] 71–76.) For ants and moles in an erotic context, see Remy de Gourmont, *Physique de l'amour*.

The ant, ch. X: "Il meurt sur place, la femelle se relève, gagne son nid, pond, avant d'accueillir la mort. Les noces des fourmis, c'est toute une fourmilière à la fois; la chute des amants simule une cascade dorée et la résurrection des femelles jaillit au soleil comme une écume rousse" [He dies on the spot, the female gets up, returns to the nest, lays, before dying. The fêtes of the ant are of the whole ant hill at once, the fall of the lovers like a golden cascade, and the resurrection of the females gleams in the sun like a russet foam]. The mole, ch. IX: "il n'est peut-être aucune femelle qui ait, autant que la taupe, de justes motifs pour craindre le mâle ··· il ··· finit par l'acculer dans une impasse, et, tandis qu'elle enfonce dans la terre son museau aveugle, il l'agrippe, l'opère et la féconde ··· Et quelle vierge humaine montra jamais une telle constance à garder sa vertu? Et laquelle, seule dans la nuit d'un palais souterrain, userait ses mains à ouvrir les murs, toute sa force à fuire son amant?" [there is perhaps no female who has better reason than the mole for fearing the male ··· he ··· ends by catching her in an impasse, and while she is still ramming her blind muzzle into the earth, he grips, operates, fecundates ··· What human virgin would show such constancy in the defence of her virtue? Who, alone in the night, in a subterranean palace, would use her hands to open the walls, all her strength to flee from her suitor?]

34 **But then, what opening out of dusty souls!**: Meredith: "Ah, what a dusty answer gets the soul | When hot for certainties in this our life!" *Modern Love* L (TSE: "uncertainties", 4; "life", 15). TSE's "moles ··· souls": Meredith ended *Hard Weather* with the rhyme "soul ··· mole". For TSE and Meredith, see headnote to *Cousin Nancy.* TSE: "damp souls of housemaids | Sprouting", *Morning at the Window* 3–4.

Interlude: in a Bar

Published in *March Hare.*

Dated Feb 1911 in Notebook.

2, 5–6 **forms that pass ··· broken glass || The walls ··· scattered:** Tennyson: "forms that passed at windows ··· the wall ··· wind-scattered", *A Dream of Fair Women* 23, 27, 31. TSE: "rats' feet over broken glass ··· form", *The Hollow Men* I 9–11.

4–5 **floors that ··· glass:** Tennyson: "That crashed the glass and beat the floor", *In Memoriam* LXXXVII 20. TSE: "I lie on the floor a bottle's broken glass", *Hidden under the heron's wing* 7.

6–8 **fling back the scattered streams ··· Visionary, and yet hard:** Shelley: "flung | Its green arms round the bosom of the stream", *The Question* 6–7 (with "visionary", 33). **the ··· streams | Of life ··· Visionary**: Wordsworth: "the sister streams of Life and Death", *The Prelude* (1850) VI 439 (recreating his *Descriptive Sketches* 72: "the mystic streams of Life and Death"). **scattered streams | Of life:** Byron: "Whose scattered streams from granite basins burst, | Leap into life", *The Corsair* I 127–28.

11 **Broken and scarred:** *Coriolanus* IV v: "broke | And scarred". TSE: "a broken Coriolanus", *The Waste Land* [V] 416.

12–13 **fingernails | Tapping the bar:** Tennyson: "a tap | Of my finger-nail on the sand", *Maud* II [ii] 69–70, with his "the sand" and TSE's "the bar" oddly combining as the sand-bar of Tennyson's *Crossing the Bar* (for which see note to *Goldfish* II. *Embarquement pour Cythère* 11–12).

Bacchus and Ariadne: 2nd Debate between the Body and Soul

Published in *March Hare.*

Dated Feb 1911, *ms1.*

Title ***Bacchus and Ariadne***: *Lemprière* "Ariadne": "According to some writers, Bacchus loved her after Theseus had forsaken her, and he gave her a crown of seven stars, which, after her death, was made a constellation." *Moody* 61 suggests that the final stanza of *Sweeney Erect* "may allude to a variant of Ariadne's tale, which has it that she did not die of a broken heart, but was loved by Bacchus". *Crawford* 108 links this with the present poem, "probably inspired by Titian's painting in the National Gallery. He [TSE] ticked this picture in his London *Baedeker*, whose commentary singles it out for its great 'exuberance'":

> *Titian*, Bacchus and Ariadne, painted in 1514 for Alphonso, Duke of Ferrara. "This is one of the pictures which once seen can never be forgotten ··· Rich harmony of drapery tints and soft modelling, depth of shade and warm flesh all combine to produce a highly coloured glow; yet in the midst of this glow the form of Ariadne seems incomparably fair. Nature was never reproduced more kindly or with greater exuberance than it is in every part of this picture. What splendour in the contrasts of colour, what wealth and diversity of scale in air and vegetation; how infinite is the space—how varied yet mellow the gradations of light and shade!"
>
> (quoting Joseph Crowe and Giovanni Battista Cavalcaselle, *The Life and Times of Titian*, 1877, 2nd ed. 1881)

TSE, slightly later than this poem, on the interior of the Doge's Palace, Venice: "Only painting that I note is the Bacchus & Ariadne of Tintoretto. As near to feeling as T. ever came", notes on Italy, summer 1911 (Houghton).

1 **lives ··· like a wave:** Shelley: "Oh, lift me as a wave, a leaf, a cloud! | I fall upon the thorns of life!" *Ode to the West Wind* 53–54. TSE on Donne's *The Extasie* 2 ("A pregnant banke swel'd up"): "he means rather, 'was swollen' or perhaps swells like a wave", *The Varieties of Metaphysical Poetry* 269 (Turnbull Lecture II).

1, 3 **their lives curl ··· wave ··· grave:** Ernest Dowson: "Beneath the long curled wave, | So quiet a grave. || And they sleep well | These peasant-folk, who told their lives away", *In a Breton Cemetery* 5–8. TSE on his childhood reading: "nothing that was recommended to me served the purpose of what I found for myself. Byron and Shelley, Omar Khayyám, Rossetti, Swinburne—and smaller men too, like Ernest Dowson: I seemed to get suddenly a personal intimacy with these poets whom I read for myself; and perhaps the feeling that some of them would not be approved by my elders added to the pleasure", *Prize Day Address, Penzance* (1938). **curl ··· wave ··· break**: "a wave of excitement curled into the street and broke", *Eeldrop and Appleplex* I (1917).

4–5 **tendencies unknown ··· drums**: "hammered and hummed ··· ends unknown", *The Engine* I.

5–6, 9 **The drums of life were beating on their skulls | The floods of life were swaying in their brains ··· desert**: TSE ended *The Beating of a Drum* (1923): "It is equally possible to assert that primitive man acted in a certain way and then found a reason for it. An unoccupied person, finding a drum, may be seized with a desire to beat it; but unless he is an imbecile he will be unable to continue beating it, and thereby satisfying a need (rather than a 'desire'), without finding a reason for so doing. The reason may be the long continued drought. The next generation or the next civilization will find a more plausible reason for beating a drum. Shakespeare and Racine—or rather the developments which led up to them—each found his own reason. The reasons may be divided into tragedy and comedy. We still have similar reasons, but we have lost the drum." In the Introduction to his mother's play *Savonarola* (1926): "the meaning of the series of acts is to the performers themselves an interpretation; the same ritual remaining practically unchanged may assume different meanings for different generations of performers; and the rite may even have originated before 'meaning' meant anything at all. The persons concerned may believe that the ritual is performed in order to induce a fall of rain" (*Crawford* 117). **drums ··· brains**: "Inside my brain a dull tom-tom begins", *Portrait of a Lady* I 32.

9 **Like railway-engines over desert plains**: often in Kipling, as "skirting the edge of the desert on a narrow-gauge railway", *William the Conqueror* (1898). For "the rhythms of the steppes ··· the grind of wheels ··· the roar of the underground railway", see headnote to *Sweeney Agonistes*, 4. JAZZ. **over desert plains**: "Over endless plains, stumbling in cracked earth", *The Waste Land* [V] 369.

10 **The world of contact sprang up**: Tennyson: "sprang up for ever at a touch ··· And world-wide fluctuation swayed | In vassal tides that followed thought", *In Memoriam* CXII 10, 15–16 (TSE: "like a wave", 1; "swaying", 6). See note to *The wind sprang up at four o'clock* 1.

10–17 **The world ··· the world ··· chrysalis**: "The world is not simply there, for metaphysics to play upon; it is itself metaphysical, and meditating upon its own nature, spins itself out of its own belly", *The Validity of Artificial Distinctions* (1914). **pure ··· purity ··· chrysalis**: Laforgue: "chrysalide ··· Purs" [chrysalis ··· innocent], *Complainte des crépuscules célibataires* [*Complaint of bachelor twilights*] 28–30.

11 **The wind beyond the world**: *TSE's books: Bodleian list* (1934) includes William Morris's *The Wood Beyond the World* (1894). TSE perhaps combined this title with Kipling's phrase "The Wind that blows between the Worlds", which comes three times in his poem *Tomlinson* (1892; in *A Choice of Kipling's Verse*). (*Tomlinson* mentions "a caddis-case"; TSE: "chrysalis", 17.) On combining Morris and Kipling, see note to the title *The Hollow Men*. **the world had passed without a trace**: Laforgue: "La terre crève aux cieux, sans laisser nulle trace" [The earth breaks open to the skies, without leaving any trace whatsoever], *Soir de carnaval* 8.

14, 16 **ingenuous · · · set free:** *Symons* 89, on Verlaine: "The verse murmurs, with such an ingenuous confidence, such intimate secrets. That 'setting free' of verse".

17–18 **cautious midnight of its chrysalis · · · meditates its wings:** Bergson: "la conscience a dû s'assoupir, comme la chrysalide dans l'enveloppe où elle se prépare des ailes" [consciousness has had to fall asleep, like the chrysalis in the envelope in which it is preparing for itself wings], *L'Evolution créatrice,* ch. II. TSE: "Small lights of those who meditate at midnight", *Choruses from "The Rock"* X 28. **cautious midnight · · · meditates:** *Paradise Lost* IX 55, 58–59: "meditated · · · and at midnight returned | From compassing the earth, cautious of day". TSE: "nights · · · cautious", *WLComposite* 292–94. **midnight · · · meditates its wings:** Marvell on the nightingale: "And studying all the summer night, | Her matchless songs does meditate", *The Mower to the Glowworms* 3–4. Meredith: "She flew on it, then folded wings, | In meditation", *The Night-Walk* 31–32. Coleridge: "Meditation's heaven-ward wing", *Religious Musings* 413. TSE: "Who clipped the lion's wings · · · Thought Burbank, meditating on | Time's ruins", *Burbank with a Baedeker: Bleistein with a Cigar* 29–32.

19 **Nourished · · · by manure:** Browning: "nourished with manure", *The Inn Album* 711. **stimulated by manure:** OED "stimulating", 1842, *Suburban Horticulture*: "hence this manure is stimulating as well as enriching".

20–22 **I am sure it is like this | I am sure it is this | I am sure:** for such iterations in TSE, see note to *The Waste Land* [III] 277–78, 290–91, 306. **I am sure:** "She is very sure of God", *Easter: Sensations of April, draft line after* [I] 14.

The smoke that gathers blue and sinks

Published in *March Hare.*

Dated Feb 1911, *ms1.*

1–2 **The smoke that gathers blue · · · cigars:** Kipling's story *A Conference of the Powers* opens: "The room was blue with the smoke of three pipes and a cigar", *Soldiers Three* (1888). **gathers blue:** Joel 2: 6: "all faces shall gather blacknesse". Tennyson: "that beech will gather brown, | This maple burn itself away", *In Memoriam* CI 3–4; "The topmost elm-tree gathered green", *Sir Launcelot and Queen Guinevere* 8.

3, 5 **after-dinner drinks · · · insolence:** *Paradise Lost* I 502: "flown with insolence and wine". FitzGerald: "Oh, many a Cup of this forbidden Wine | Must drown the memory of that insolence!" *Rubáiyát of Omar Khayyám* XXX.

3, 16 **torpid after-dinner · · · of almost any age:** *Measure for Measure* III i: "Thou hast nor youth, nor age | But as it were an after-dinner's sleep | Dreaming on both" (which TSE modified as the epigraph to *Gerontion*; see also note to *Mandarins* 4 12). Laforgue's prose vignette *Après-dîner torride et stagnante* has "la cigarette · · · des seins · · · ces musiciens · · · une vieille fille" (TSE: "cigars", 2; "chiefly breast", 17; his musicians, 14; "A lady of almost any age", 16).

6 **matter "going by itself"**: Bertrand Russell: "Blind to good and evil, reckless of destruction, omnipotent matter rolls on its relentless way", closing paragraph of *The Free Man's Worship* (1903), later *A Free Man's Worship*. TSE of the science writer Gerald Heard: "Readers will be reminded, by the turgid style rather than by the ill-constructed sentences, of that remarkable effusion of twenty years ago, Mr. Bertrand Russell's essay, *A Free Man's Worship*", *Revelation* (1937). "One may become a Christian partly by pursuing scepticism to the utmost limit. I owe much, in this way, to Montaigne; something, in this way, to Bertrand Russell's essay *A Free Man's Worship*: the effect this essay had upon me was certainly the reverse of anything the author intended", *A Sermon preached in Magdalene College Chapel* (1948) 5. T. H. Green: "If it could be admitted that matter and motion had an existence *in themselves*, or otherwise than as related to a consciousness, it would still not be by *such* matter and motion, but by the matter and motion which we know, that the functions of the soul, or anything else, can for us be explained", *Prolegomena to Ethics* (1906) 13; scored by TSE. **"going by itself"**: Louis Büchner: "Dogmatic writers call it an unworthy view of God, to regard the world as clockwork going by itself", *Force and Matter: Empirico-Philosophical Studies, Intelligibly Rendered* ed. J. Frederick Collingwood (1864) 38.

8 **Stifled with glutinous liqueurs**: Milton: "smeared with gums of glutinous heat"; *Comus* 917. Keats: "Or where God Bacchus drains his cups divine, | Stretched out, at ease, beneath a glutinous pine", *Lamia* I 209–10.

9 **sensation**: see note to *First Debate between the Body and Soul* 6–7.

10 **overoiled machinery**: Van Wyck Brooks: "Efficiency is the well-oiled machinery", *The Wine of the Puritans* (see *The Engine* I and notes). **overoiled**: including "oiled", OED 3: "*slang.* Drunk", from 1737. TSE to Virginia Woolf, [6 Jan] 1935, from one of the songs he liked to sing, about drinking Wurzburger: "It's allright to oil up a sewing-machine". See headnote to *Among the various middle classes* (in "Other Verses"). **machinery**: including OED 1: "*Theatr. and literary*" from 1687, with Pope, Dedication to *The Rape of the Lock*, 1714: "a term invented by the Critics, to signify that Part which the Deities, Angels, or Daemons, are made to act in a Poem" (TSE: "action", 11).

16 **A lady of almost any age**: "Two ladies of uncertain age", *Mandarins* 2 1 (see note).

18 ***"Throw your arms around me—Aint you glad you found me"***: From *The Cubanola Glide* (1909) (David Chinitz, *ANQ* Summer 1998, correcting *March Hare* which cited an earlier song):

> Throw your arms around me
> Ain't you glad you found me,
> Tease, squeeze, lovin' and wooin',
> Oh babe, what are you doin',
> Ride to glory by your baby's side
> When you do de Cubanola glide.

For this song, see *WLComposite* **10–11** and note; and for TSE and popular songs, see note to *The Waste Land* [II] 128–30.

20–21 **a negro (teeth and smile) | Has a dance:** Van Wyck Brooks: "she *danced* · · · a negro · · · Negroes grin", *The Wine of the Puritans* 109.

22 **That's the stuff!**: OED "stuff" 7f: "that's the stuff (to give them *or* to give the

troops)", from 1923 only; but in 1766 Colman and Garrick had "Money, money!—that's the stuff that makes the great man", *The Clandestine Marriage* I, and *The Oxford Magazine* Dec 1768 had "do not squander time—for that's the stuff life is made of."

He said: this universe is very clever

Published in *March Hare.*

Dated Mar 1911, *ms1.*

1–3 **this universe is very clever ··· Each atom goes on working out its law:** to Norbert Wiener, 6 Jan 1915: "The only way in which we can talk about the 'universe' at all, it seems to me, is with reference to the universe of physical science" ("matter going by itself", *The smoke that gathers blue and sinks* 6).

3 *variant* **Each atom has its Place in Life:** "The young person enters the society, & waits to have a function assigned him. Then 1st disaster: they dont allot him any function, unless he is an absolute mollusc. If so, he gets a function, & never needs to think again ··· Put a higher person into this milieu, they probably find a function & for a time all goes well. *The Rebel*—the individual—is of a kind that insists on growing (whereas to have a *function* means that you are not to grow—which is much more comfortable)", *Principles of Growth: & How to Avoid It* (*c.* 1925). (*The Family Reunion* I i, first chorus: "like amateur actors who have not been assigned their parts?" See note to *Convictions* 1.) "Explained the use of a Place in Life", *Inside the gloom* 22. "We returned to our places", *Journey of the Magi* 40.

2, 4 **paper ··· cut an unintentioned caper:** Byron: "In taking up this paltry sheet of paper, | My bosom underwent a glorious glow, | And my internal Spirit cut a caper", *Don Juan* X iii. Gilbert and Sullivan: "Paragraphs got into all the papers. | We only cut respectable capers", *Ruddigore* (prod. 1887) act II. The first act of Gilbert's *The Grand Duke* (prod. 1896) has "wall-papers ··· capers" (and, in the same song, "spiders ··· insiders"; TSE: "spider ··· inside her", 6, 8). **unintentioned:** Elizabeth Barrett Browning: "As little children take up a high strain | With unintentioned voices", *Casa Guidi Windows* II 10–11.

6 **syphilitic spider:** Donne: "The spider love", *Twicknam Garden* 6; TSE quoted this in *Rhyme and Reason: The Poetry of John Donne* (1930). TSE: "'~~Fuck Spiders' was his chief remark~~", *The Columbiad* st. 5. Emerson: "That devil-spider that devours her mate | Scarce freed from her embraces", *Philosophers* 11–12. Remy de Gourmont on the epirus spider: "A peine la fécondation est-elle opérée que l'ogresse se retourne, bondissante, et dévore l'amant sur le lieu même de ses amours" [Scarcely has the fecundation been finished when the ogress turns, leaping, and devours the suitor on the very spot of his amours], *Physique de l'amour* ch. XIII. TSE asked Pound on 28 July 1922 about obtaining a copy of his translation, *The Natural Philosophy of Love* (Boni & Liveright, 1922). Translating his own *Vers pour la Foulque* (in *Noctes Binanianæ*), TSE rendered "la Tarentule ··· au vénin sûr" (25–26) as "spider with ··· deadly poison", and "des chats

avariés" (19) at first as "syphilitic cats", emended in the printed text to the more accurate "damaged cats". **syphilitic**: Byron has "pseudo-syphilis", *Don Juan* I cxxxi, with "intentions" in the next stanza (TSE: "unintentioned", 4).

6–7 **in the middle like a syphilitic spider | The Absolute sits waiting**: Bergson's Absolute more than Bradley's (for philosophers' use of the term, see note to *Conversation Galante* 14). In Paris "during the first decade and more of this century", TSE recalled, "over all swung the spider-like figure of Bergson", *A Commentary* in *Criterion* Apr 1934. Aiken to TSE, [23 Nov 1913] on Bergson: "I always wax impatient with these withered little spiders who spin endless subtleties out of their own inner consciousness, merely using the external world as attacking-points, or points of suspension." TSE: "The world is not simply there, for metaphysics to play upon; it is itself metaphysical, and meditating upon its own nature, spins itself out of its own belly", *The Validity of Artificial Distinctions* (1914). To Edward J. H. Greene, 19 Apr 1940: "So far as I can see, Bergson had no influence on either my verse or my prose. It was only during the years 1910 and 11 that I was greatly impressed by his work." **in the middle, like a syphilitic spider · · · sits**: Sir John Davies:

> Much like a subtill Spider which doth sit,
> In middle of her Web which spreadeth wide;
> If ought do touch the utmost threed of it,
> She feeles it instantly on every side
>
> *Nosce Teipsum* 1061–64

TSE compares these lines favourably with a couplet from Pope (*An Essay on Man* I 217–18), and describes Davies's poem as "a long discussion in verse of the nature of the soul and its relation to the body", but adds of Davies's theories that "we cannot take them very seriously", *Sir John Davies* (1926).

6, 8 **spider · · · inside her**: "spider inside her inside", *Oxf Dictionary of Nursery Rhymes.*

9–10 **crucifixion · · · officechairs**: Aiken on TSE at the end of 1911: "He had taken a room in Ash Street, installing in it a small stove—'something to point the chairs at'—and a Gauguin *Crucifixion,* brought from Paris", *March & Tambimuttu eds.* 21.

10 **passed his life on officechairs**: "measured out my life with coffee spoons", *The Love Song of J. Alfred Prufrock* 51.

12 **abysmal**: OED 1: "Of, pertaining to, or resembling an abyss". 2: "In weakened sense: of an exceptionally poor standard or quality; extremely bad", with first citation from James, *The Golden Bowl* bk. II xxviii.

15 **an article**: Byron: "'Tis strange the mind, that *very* fiery particle, | Should let itself be snuffed out by an Article", *Don Juan* XI lx (a stanza about "the Gods" and a "Poor fellow"). TSE: "Is personality equivalent to this totality of experience, or is it only a (very fiery) particle?", *"Religion and Science: A Philosophical Essay"* by John Theodore Merz (1916), review.

Interlude in London

Published in *March Hare.*

Dated Apr 1911 in Notebook.

This April poem, with its "hibernate ··· live ··· sudden rains ··· garden plots ··· spring", has affinities with the opening and closing of *The Waste Land* I. "F. M.": "pots ··· the essential spring—spring in winter, spring in London ··· flower women at street crossings ··· one's face in the glass ··· One's soul stirs stiffly out of the dead endurance of the winter—but toward what spring?" *Letters of the Moment* I (1924).

Title **Interlude**: the predominant sense is "usually of a light or humorous character", but OED 2b is more solemn: "*Music.* An instrumental piece played between the verses of a psalm or hymn, or in the intervals of a church-service, etc." Also OED 3: "An interval in the course of some action or event; an intervening time or space of a different character or sort." See *Interlude: in a Bar.*

1 **We hibernate among the bricks**: to Eleanor Hinkley, 26 Apr 1911: "I just came back from London last night ··· Paris has burst out, during my absence, into full spring; and it is such a revelation that I feel that I ought to make it known. At London, one pretended that it was spring, and tried to coax the spring, and talk of the beautiful weather; but one continued to hibernate amongst the bricks. And one looked through the windows, and the waiter brought in eggs and coffee, and the *Graphic* (which I conscientiously tried to read, to please them)". Laforgue: "Ah! quel juillet nous avons hiverné" [Ah, what a July we have hibernated], epigraph to the volume *L'Imitation de Notre-Dame la Lune* [*The Imitation of Our Lady the Moon*]. Apollinaire: "j'ai hiverné", *La Chanson du Mal-Aimé* [*The Song of the Ill-Loved*] 46 (in *Mercure de France* 1 May 1909), with "briques", 11 (at the line-ending) and "L'année dernière", 59 (TSE: "last year's", 6). See notes to *Goldfish* IV 9 and *Fourth Caprice in Montparnasse* 1, 11. **hibernate**: OED: "Of persons: To winter in a milder locality", from 1865. **among the bricks**: TSE's father was president, then chairman of the Hydraulic-Press Brick Company in St. Louis (see note to *Second Caprice in North Cambridge* 1, 7). "among the bric-à-brac", *Portrait of a Lady* III 9.

1, 5–6 **hibernate among the bricks ··· sudden rains | Softening last year's garden plots**: Hawthorne: "she had reminded me of plants that one sometimes observes doing their best to vegetate among the bricks of an enclosed court, where there is scanty soil, and never any sunshine", *The Blithedale Romance* ch. VII. TSE to Conrad Aiken, 21 Aug 1916: "We are vegetating". See note to *Morning at the Window* 3–4.

1–9 **bricks ··· six ··· sudden rains ··· mouldy flowerpots**: Tennyson: "the mouldering bricks ··· six ··· showers ··· a flower among the flowers", *Locksley Hall Sixty Years After* 257–60.

2–8 **And live across the window panes ··· the wind ··· the spring goes**: W. G. Tinckom-Fernandez: "Spring shyly taps the window-pane, | And all the winds of heaven sigh | With hope for June-sun-scented days—", *The Street Organ* 1–3 (see notes to *First Caprice in North Cambridge* 1 and *Do I know how I feel? Do I know what I think?* 21–22). **across the window panes:** *Oh little voices of the throats of men* 37. "upon the window-panes ··· on the window-panes ··· across the window-panes", *The Love Song of J. Alfred Prufrock* 15–16, 25. "Drift across the window-panes", *Mr. Eliot's Sunday Morning Service* 3.

4–5 **Indifferent ··· Indifferent:** frequent in Symons's early poems. TSE: "With your air indifferent and imperious", *Conversation Galante* 16. "And the eyes watchful, waiting, perceiving, indifferent", *Coriolan* I. *Triumphal March* 31.

5–6 **sudden rains ··· last year's garden plots:**

> "That corpse you planted last year in your garden,
> "Has it begun to sprout? Will it bloom this year?
> "Or has the sudden frost disturbed its bed?
>
> *The Waste Land* [I] 71–73

last year's: frequent in Swinburne: "last year's rose" (*The Two Dreams*), "last year's leaf" (*Thalassius*), "last year's birds" and "last year's roses" (*Pastiche*).

5, 8–10 **sudden rains ··· down the street ··· flowerpots ··· broken:** "The showers beat | On broken blinds and chimney-pots, | And at the corner of the street", *Preludes* I 9–11.

6, 9, 10 **garden plots ··· flowerpots ··· broken:** Tennyson: "With blackest moss the flower-plots ··· broken", *Mariana* 1–5 (often misquoted as "flower-pots").

8 **Careless:** including OED 1: "Free from care, anxiety, or apprehension. (Since *c.* 1650, *archaic, poetic,* or *nonce-word*)."

10 **broken flutes:** OED "flute" 4: "*Arch.* A channel or furrow in a pillar"; but the musical sense may be heard (*Portrait of a Lady* II 17: "a broken violin"). André Salmon: "La flûte s'est brisée sur mes dents, | La flûte est brisée! La flûte est brisée! | C'était un tuyau d'ivoire et rien dedans. | Mais le vent qui passait? ··· Le vent a passé. || Mes dents l'ont brisée la flûte d'ivoire | Et le vent chanteur a fui je ne sais où" [The flute is cracked upon my teeth, the flute is cracked! The flute is cracked! It's an ivory pipe with nothing inside but the wind which was passing? ··· The wind has passed. My teeth have cracked the ivory flute and the singing wind has gone I know not where], *La flûte brisée* (1905) 1–6. The poem ends: "Tout ce qui n'a pas fui avec le vent | Je l'ai brisé avec mes dents" [Everything that has not gone with the wind I have cracked with my teeth]. Writing to Scofield Thayer, 14 Feb 1920, on poets in France, TSE listed Salmon among "the more important men there".

Ballade pour la grosse Lulu

Published in *March Hare.*

Dated July 1911, *ms1*. *Grover Smith* 30: "About 1913 a piece called *The Ballade of the Outlook*" was seen by Conrad Aiken. *Ballade pour la grosse Lulu* (each verse of which begins "*The Outlook* ···") was untraced when Grover Smith wrote, so Aiken was presumably his source. For dealings with Wyndham Lewis over the poem, see headnote to *The Triumph of Bullshit.*

Title] Villon, *La Ballade de la Grosse Margot* (title). Lulu the woman of the streets was made famous by Frank Wedekind's Lulu play *Erdgeist* (1909) (*Loretta Johnson*).

1–2 **The Outlook ··· Lyman Abbot:** Abbott (1835–1922), pastor and editor of the NY weekly *The Outlook* (formerly *The Christian Union*). "He championed a modern rational outlook in American Christianity", *The New Columbia Encyclopaedia*. The jacket flap of the first US edition of *1925*, issued in 1932, featured an endorsement from *The Outlook*: "In Mr. Eliot we have one of those renewals of poetry which happen roughly once in a century, and which spring from direct and deliberately made contact with the common life and speech of the moment."

4 **God is in his Firmament:** Browning: "God's in his heaven— | All's right with the world!" *Pippa Passes* I 227–28.

5–6 **"300 Boers | On Roosevelt have paid a call":** two Boer representatives were received at the White House by Theodore Roosevelt on 5 Mar 1902. Roosevelt, US President 1901–09, was Contributing Editor of *The Outlook* and had an article in each of the five issues of July 1911. In a letter to Maynard Keynes, 23 Mar 1945, TSE mentioned having kept "a scrap-book of the Boer War".

8 **the Whore House Ball:** "the band struck up 'The Whore House Ball'", *The Columbiad* st. 15. The White House Ball was a regular fixture in the fashionable calendar.

10–12 **Booker T. ··· "How I set the nigger free!":** *Up from Slavery* (1901), the autobiography of Booker T. Washington (1856–1915), was serialised in *The Outlook*. Between 6 May and 1 July 1911 it had published *The Man Farthest Down*, his series of six articles ending: "in Europe the man farthest down is woman".

10 *variant* **Edward Bok:** editor of *The Ladies' Home Journal* 1889–1919.

11 **"Up from Possum Stew!":** see headnote to *Practical Cats*, 1. POSSUM.

13–14 **"the learned horse | Jim Key, was murdered in his stall":** having apparently been trained by his owner Bill Key (a former slave) to read, write, use a telephone and perform other marvels, the learned horse Beautiful Jim Key performed in front of millions, 1897–1906, and was the biggest earner at the St. Louis World's Fair. He died peacefully in 1912.

18–20 **Rockefellar ··· Money ··· "Jesus as a Savings Bank":** John D. Rockefeller famously said "God gave me my money." His gift of $1.5 million to U. Chicago for the building of a chapel was reported by *The Outlook* 31 Dec 1910.

26 **Harvard's great ex-president:** Charles W. Eliot, president of the university 1869–1909. A letter from him to TSE, 25 July 1919, is printed in *Letters 1*. He was related not only to TSE but to the Lymans, and so to the Roosevelts. While he headed Harvard, Theodore Roosevelt was a student there, Booker T. Washington was awarded an honorary degree, and John D. Rockefeller helped to build the medical school.

The Little Passion: From "An Agony in the Garret"

Published in *March Hare*.

Assigned to 1915 by *Gallup 1970* 37. The hand of *ms1*, however, resembles that of poems from Paris, 1911 (when TSE lived in a garret), and the diction recalls that of *Goldfish*, *Inside the gloom*, *He said: this universe is very clever*, *Portrait of a Lady*, *Preludes* and *Rhapsody on a Windy Night*, all poems of 1910–11 (see notes below).

The stifling frustration of the streets is recalled in a letter to Aiken on the last day of 1914 (see note to 2), but TSE is unlikely to have used "our souls are spread out" and "washed-out" later than the publication of *Preludes* and *Rhapsody on a Windy Night* in *Blast* in July 1915 (see below, notes to *ms1* **16** and **19**, **21**).

In Notebook, *ms2* follows *Suppressed Complex* and *Morning at the Window* and precedes twenty-eight blank leaves and three stubs.

An alternative title to the putative sequence *An Agony in the Garret* may have been *The Descent from the Cross*. TSE to Aiken, 25 July 1914: "I enclose some *stuff*—the *thing* I showed you some time ago, and some of the themes for the *Descent from the Cross* or whatever I may call it" ("cross", 7, **15**). To Otto Heller, 5 Oct 1923 on *The Waste Land*: "The poem is neither a success nor a failure—simply a struggle. Practically, one crucifies oneself and entertains drawing rooms and lounges" (see headnote to *The Waste Land*, 9. AFTER PUBLICATION).

Title ***The Little Passion***: Corbière's *Petit mort pour rire* [*Little dead one for fun*] is among the poems TSE transcribed on leaves laid into the Notebook (see headnote to *Tristan Corbière*). ***Passion · · · Agony***: TSE corrected the Theological Editor of *NEW*, 29 Mar 1934: "when he speaks of 'agony and passion' he is transferring to the Incarnation two terms which are properly applicable to the Atonement". ***Agony in***: "After the frosty silence in the gardens | After the agony in stony places", *The Waste Land* [V] 323–24. *The Family Reunion* I iii: "The agony in the dark"; and II i: "The agony in the curtained bedroom". *Little Gidding* had in draft "The agony and the solitary vigil" (II 67–96, *first venture in verse* [3]). ***in the Garret***: "They did not crucify him in an attic", *He said: this universe is very clever* 11. "in a little low dry garret", *The Waste Land* [III] 194. Mantegna, *The Agony in the Garden*, National Gallery, London.

1 **Upon those stifling August nights**: "Always the August evenings come", *Goldfish* I 1.

2 **I know he used to walk the streets**: to Conrad Aiken, 31 Dec 1914: "One walks about the street with one's desires, and one's refinement rises up like a wall whenever opportunity approaches."

3, 5, 7 **the lines of lights · · · the lines of lights · · · cross**: Byron: "The line of lights too up to Charing Cross", *Don Juan* XI xxvi, with immediately a description of those hanged on lamp-posts during the French Revolution. **cross**: "He said: 'this crucifixion was dramatic'", *He said: this universe is very clever* 9.

ms1 (printed in Textual History)

1 **those ideas:** (*Gallup 1968* erroneously reads "these ideas".) "Are these ideas right or wrong?" *Portrait of a Lady* II 43.

1, 3 **ideas · · · seldom well digested:** "Are not all these questions | Brought up by indigestions?" *Inside the gloom* 25–26.

6 **That spun around him like a wheel:** with the martyrdom in 15–16 suggesting St. Catherine. "The inhabitants of Hampstead are bound forever on the wheel", *The Death of the Duchess* I 9. "London, your people is bound upon the wheel", *WLComposite* 340.

7–8 **"I feel | As if I'd been a long time dead":** Shelley: "I walked about like a corpse alive", *Rosalind and Helen* 312. TSE: "A man lay flat upon his back, and cried | 'It seems that I have been a long time dead'", *So through the evening, through the violet air* 24–25. To Aiken, 31 Dec 1914: "In Oxford I have the feeling that I am not quite alive—that my body is walking about with a bit of my brain inside it, and nothing else." *The Family Reunion* II iii: "It takes so many years | To learn that one is dead!"

16 **our souls are spread:** "His soul stretched tight", *Preludes* IV 1.

17 **across the bar:** Tennyson, *Crossing the Bar* (title).

18–19 **hopeless · · · withered face:** Wordsworth: "his withered face. | Reverence the hope", *The Old Cumberland Beggar* 176–77.

19, 21 **face · · · A washed-out:** "A washed-out smallpox cracks her face", *Rhapsody on a Windy Night* 56.

21 *variant* **unconscious half-disgrace:** James Thomson: "Unconscious of the deep disgrace", *In the Room* 190, with "hopeless" 198 (TSE, 18); for the poem see note to *The Waste Land* [III] 215–18.

The Burnt Dancer

Published in *March Hare.*

Dated June 1914, *ts1.*

Title] St. John of the Cross: "Of little use are its eyes to a moth, since desire for the beauty of the light dazzles it and leads it into the flame", *Ascent of Mount Carmel* I viii 3. Shelley: "The desire of the moth for the star, | Of the night for the morrow", *One word is too often profaned* 13–14; "sweet Lamp! my moth-like Muse has burned its wings", *Epipsychidion* 53; "plumes of fire, | And towards the lodestar of my one desire, | I flitted, like a dizzy moth · · · A radiant death, a fiery sepulchre, | As if it were a lamp of earthly flame", *Epipsychidion* 218–24. Symons:

> I am the torch, she saith, and what to me
> If the moth die of me? I am the flame
> Of Beauty, and I burn that all may see
> Beauty, and I have neither joy nor shame,

But live with that dear life of perfect fire
Which is to men the death of their desire.

Modern Beauty (1899) 1–6

(TSE: "the end of his desire", 36.) TSE: "but became a dancer before God", *The Death of Saint Narcissus* 17. "that refining fire | Where you must move in measure, like a dancer", *Little Gidding* II 92–93.

Epigraph **sotta la pioggia dell' aspro martiro:** [beneath the rain of the sharp torment], *Inf* XVI 6 (Temple Classics: "sotto"). In the copy given to him by his mother, TSE scored the line. The Argument of the Canto makes clear that this is "burning rain". Shelley: "the agony of the flame", *The Revolt of Islam* X xxi.

1–2 **flame | A black moth**: *Bhagavad-Gita* xi 29: "As moths with exceeding speed pass into a lighted fire to perish, so pass the worlds with exceeding speed into Thy mouths to perish." (The previous verse has "Thy blazing mouths", and the next verse "flaming mouths"; TSE: "the ragged teeth of flame", 17.) For the *Gita* see headnotes to *I am the Resurrection and the Life* and *The Dry Salvages* III.

3 **Caught in the circle of desire**: as Arnaut Daniel is caught in the circle of lust, *Purg.* XXVI 133–48, and Paolo and Francesca in the circle of the carnal sinners, *Inf.* V 73–142.

3, 5 **desire ··· that do not tire**: Tennyson: "But mine the love that will not tire, | And, born of love, the vague desire", *In Memoriam* CX 18–19. Cavalcanti tr. Rossetti: "The devastating flame ··· desire ··· that shall not tire ··· fire", *Canzone: He laments the Presumption and Incontinence of his Youth* 1, 4, 8–9 (in *The Early Italian Poets*). Christina G. Rossetti: "O Love exhaust, fulfilling my desire: | Uphold me with the strength that cannot tire, | Nerve me to labour till Thou bid me rest, | Kindle my fire from Thine unkindled fire", *Later Life* 5.

4 **Expiates**: see letter to Hayward, 27 Aug 1942, in note to *Little Gidding* II 92.

5–13 **wings ··· golden ··· pride ··· mirthless dance and ··· revel**: *Paradise Lost* IV 763–70: "golden ··· lights | His constant lamp ··· wings ··· loveless, joyless ··· court amours | Mixed dance, or wanton mask ··· proud".

6, 28 **Distracted from ··· but not with human meaning**: "Distracted from distraction by distraction | Filled with fancies and empty of meaning", *Burnt Norton* III 12–13.

9, 10 **a world too strange for**: "Too strange to each other for misunderstanding ··· Between two worlds become much like each other", *Little Gidding* II 51, 69. Pater: "in a world too coarse", in *Studies in the History of the Renaissance* ch. V, with "strange" in the previous sentence.

13 **mirthless dance**: Chaucer: "Daunseth he murye [merry] that is myrtheles", *The Parlement of Foules* 592.

14, 41 **O danse danse mon papillon noir**: David Augustin de Bruéys: "Ma femme, chasse, chasse ces papillons noirs" [My lady, chase, chase these black butterflies], *L'Avocat Patelin* [*The Crafty Lawyer*] II iii. Laforgue: "On y danse, on y danse", *Complainte de cette bonne Lune* 3, after the nursery rhyme *Sur le pont d'Avignon.* **papillon noir**: in the plural, *papillons noirs* are dark thoughts. Flaubert: "Elle le regarda brûler ··· les corolles de papier, racornies, se balançant le long de la plaque comme des papillons noirs, enfin s'envolèrent par la cheminée" [She watched it burn ··· the shrivelled paper petals hovered along the fireback like black butterflies and finally flew away up the chimney], *Madame Bovary* penultimate paragraph of pt. I. Flaubert to Hippolyte Taine, 1 Dec 1866: "ce qu'on appelle 'les papillons noirs', c'est-à-dire ces rondelles de satin que certaines personnes voient flotter dans l'air, quand le ciel est grisâtre et qu'elles ont la vue fatiguée" [what are called "black butterflies", which is to say those discs of satin that certain people see floating in the air, when the sky is grey and they have tired sight] (Henry Gott, personal communication). *TSE's books: Bodleian list* (1934) lists among the "Paper Books" both "Flaubert Correspondence" and "Flaubert Corresp. 2 vols." Verlaine: "Et le chagrin mettait un papillon noir | A son cher front tout brûlant d'orfèvreries" [And sorrow set a black butterfly on his beloved forehead, burning so with the works of goldsmiths], *Crimen Amoris* 26–27 (Florian Gargaillo, personal communication).

15 **odours of your name**: *Romeo and Juliet* II ii (First Quarto): "That which we call a rose | By any other name would smell as sweet."

15–16 **odours · · · Mozambique**: *Paradise Lost* IV 160–62: "past | Mozambic, off at sea north-east winds blow | Sabaean odours from the spicy shore."

16 **Nicobar**: the Nicobar Islands, in the Bay of Bengal, often mentioned by Frazer in *The Golden Bough*.

15, 17 **name · · · teeth of flame**: Wilde: "teeth of flame · · · name", *The Ballad of Reading Gaol* VI i.

15, 20–21 **name · · · in little corners | Whimper**: Tennyson: "And my own sad name in corners cried", *Maud* I [vi] 261.

17–18 **the ragged teeth of · · · upon the waters**: Symons: "he saw | The ragged teeth of the sharp Apennines | Shut on the sea", *Giovanni Malatesta at Rimini* (1906) 14–16. Symons's poem is about Paolo and Francesca (see note to 3). **flame · · · perfumed · · · upon the waters**: *Antony and Cleopatra* II ii: "Burned on the water · · · so perfumed". For this speech by Enobarbus, see notes to *Burbank with a Baedeker: Bleistein with a Cigar* 11–12 and *The Waste Land* [II] 77–110.

18 **perfumed oil**: Sir Edwin Arnold: "perfumed oils", *The Light of Asia* Book the Fourth 83. For TSE's admiration for the poem, see note to *The Waste Land* [V] 399–422. **oil upon the waters**: *Oxf Dictionary of English Proverbs* "to pour oil upon the waters": "to smooth matters over". **upon the waters**: Tennyson, *Enoch Arden* 590 and 592, describing the tropical island (TSE: "tropic", 15).

18–19 **upon the waters · · · secret**: Ecclesiastes 11: 1: "Cast thy bread upon the waters". Proverbs 9: 17: "stolen waters are sweet, And bread eaten in secret is pleasant".

20 **Children's voices in little corners**: see note to *Landscapes* I. *New Hampshire* 1, "Children's voices in the orchard".

23 **Agony nearest to delight**: John Davidson: "The Seraph at his head was Agony: | Delight, more terrible, stood at his feet", *Insomnia* (1905) 10–11.

24–25 **Dance fast dance faster · · · mortal disaster**: Poe: "whom unmerciful Disaster | Followed fast and followed faster · · · perfume", *The Raven* 63–64, 79 (TSE: "perfumed", 18). Christina G. Rossetti: "He danced indeed, but danced in dudgeon, | Capered in fury fast and faster:— | Ah, could he once but hug his master | And perish in one joint disaster!" *Brother Bruin* 22–25. TSE:

"Which, just at a word from his master | Will follow you faster and faster | And tear you limb from limb", *Five-Finger Exercises* IV. *Lines to Ralph Hodgson Esqre.* 5–7. **disaster:** OED: "f. *des-* + *astre* ··· unfavourable aspect of a star or planet" ("evil ··· star", 11–12).

28 **but not with human:** *Paradise Lost* IX 561: "but not with human voice endued" (TSE: "voices", 20).

30 **Within the circle of my brain:** *Hamlet* I v: "Within the book and volume of my brain" (six lines after "globe").

32 **acolyte:** OED 1: "*Eccl.* An inferior officer in the church who ··· performed subordinate duties, as lighting and bearing candles, etc". The candle duties are stressed throughout the OED instances. **of pain:** Swinburne's *Dolores* has "Our Lady of Pain" concluding every other stanza of the fifty-five.

34 **The singèd reveller:** Matthew Arnold, *The Strayed Reveller* (title). **reveller:** Edward Young: "For other ends they shine, | Than to light revellers from shame to shame", *Night Thoughts* IX 679–80. See headnote to *Whispers of Immortality*.

34–37 **fire ··· Losing the end of his desire | Desires completion of his loss:** "the death of desire ··· completion", *Little Gidding* III 9–11 *draft* (*msA*). "fire ··· The culmination of desire", *Little Gidding* IV *first draft of* 1–7 (*msA*) [2, 4]. **fire ··· loss:** 1 Corinthians 3: 15: "If any man's work shall be burned, he shall suffer loss: but he himself shall be saved; yet so as by fire."

35 **Caught on those horns that toss and toss:** (i) "horns ··· toss": those of a bull. "bullocks have horns (and they toss 'em)", *How to Pick a Possum* 5. (ii) 1 Kings 2: 28: "caught hold on the horns of the altar". (iii) the horns of the monster, Daniel 7: 7, and Revelation 17: 16: "And the ten horns which thou sawest upon the beast, these shall hate the whore, and shall make her desolate and naked, and shall eat her flesh, and burn her with fire" (TSE: "fire ··· horns", 34–35, and "burn", 38). Revelation has "golden" (TSE, 7), and "strength" (TSE: "strong", 33). (iv) *Inf.* XXVI 85, which TSE quoted in *Dante* (1929) I:

> So Ulysses, unseen in the hornèd wave of flame,
>
> *Lo maggior corno della fiamma antica* ···
>
> *The greater horn of the ancient flame.*

35, 37 **Caught on those horns ··· his loss:** "torn on the horn ··· loss", *Ash-Wednesday* V 22, VI 4 (*Jain* 187).

35, 38 **Caught on those horns ··· whiter flames:** Keats: "I looked upon the altar, and its horns | Whitened with ashes, and its languorous flame", *The Fall of Hyperion* I 237–38.

36–37 **the end of his desire | Desires completion:** Tennyson: "That my desire, like all strongest hopes, | By its own energy fulfilled itself, | Merged in completion?" *The Gardener's Daughter* 232–34. **the end of his desire:** *Paradiso* XXXIII 46: "al fine di tutti i disii" [the goal of all my longings]. **desire | Desires:** Luke 22: 15: "With desire! have desired". Christina G. Rossetti: "Thy Will I will, I Thy desire desire", *A Martyr* 34 (rhyming with "fire", in martyrdom); see note to *Ash-Wednesday* VI 30–33, "Our peace in His will".

37–38 **Desires ··· whiter flames that burn:** Symons: "I dance, and as I dance |

Desires as fires burn white | To fan the flame delight", *The Armenian Dancer* 16–18.

38–39 **strayed · · · vagrant:** Pope, of birds: "Vagrants of air, and unforeboding stray", *Odyssey* II 212. **vagrant · · · star:** Kipling: "vagrant star-dust", *Dedication* to *Barrack-Room Ballads* (in *A Choice of Kipling's Verse*). Kipling's next two lines have: "our world. || They are purged of pride" (TSE: "world too strange for pride", 9).

38, 40 **burn not · · · return not:** Swinburne rhymes, for instance, "know not · · · flow not · · · grow not" (*Anima Anceps*); "falls not · · · calls not" (*A Forsaken Garden*); "bent not · · · lent not", "give not · · · forgive not", "give not · · · live not" (*A Song in Season*).

40 **broken guest:** Donne: "When my grave is broke up againe | Some second ghest to entertaine," *The Relique* 1–2. TSE cited Donne's stanza in *Reflections on Contemporary Poetry* I (1917), *The Metaphysical Poets* (1921) and *The Varieties of Metaphysical Poetry* 125 (Clark Lecture IV).

Oh little voices of the throats of men

Published in *Letters* (1988); then *March Hare*.

Sent in a letter to Conrad Aiken, from Marburg, 25 July 1914, with *The Love Song of St. Sebastian*. In this ts (which lacks 6), TSE marked the margin in three places. Bracing 1–14, he wrote: "Introduction. To be amplified at the end also". Beside 15–34, he wrote: "This [*added*: theme] to recur twice, in variations." Bracing 37–end, he wrote: "finale to the foregoing". For subsequent comments to Aiken see headnote to *The Love Song of St. Sebastian*.

1 **little voices:** as in two successive poems by Symons in *Images of Good and Evil* (1899): *The Coming of Spring* I and *September Idyl* 2. Verlaine's "Le choeur des petites voix" (*Romances sans paroles* I 6) was translated by Symons (1913) as "Little voices that sing" (TSE: "song", 2). In *The Symbolist Movement in Literature* 155, Symons quoted, in translation, from Maeterlinck "the little voice of light" (from *Le tragique quotidien*). For TSE on frequent use of "little", see note to *Burbank with a Baedeker: Bleistein with a Cigar* 1–2.

3–4 **hands · · · rend the beautiful and curse:** *Richard III* I ii: "These nails should rend that beauty" with "Curse" six lines later and, a dozen lines further on, "Why dost thou spit at me?" (TSE: "spit", 12).

3–8 **men · · · undirected feet · · · ways · · · paths:** Proverbs 3: 6: "In all thy ways acknowledge him, And he shall direct thy paths". Proverbs 16: 9: "A man's heart deviseth his way: But the Lord directeth his steps."

5 **Impatient tireless · · · feet:** Sir Edwin Arnold: "To tread its paths with patient, stainless feet", *The Light of Asia*, Book the Fourth (TSE: "paths", 8).

5, 7–9 **feet · · · heaven and hell · · · paths · · · do well:** Rossetti: "those stairs | Which, of all paths his feet knew well, | Were steeper found than Heaven or Hell", *Dante at Verona*, closing lines (TSE: "stair", 48).

7 **frontier of heaven and hell:** *Symons* 20–21 on Gérard de Nerval: "so sharp an awakening was but like the passage from one state to another, across that little bridge of one step which lies between heaven and hell, to which he was so used in his dreams." Pascal: "Entre nous, et l'enfer ou le ciel, il n'y a que la vie entre deux, qui est la chose du monde le plus fragile" [Between us and heaven or hell there is only life, which is the frailest thing in the world], *Pensées* 213.

7, 11–12 **hell ··· pleasure and pain ··· wind ··· rain:** *Paradise Lost* II 586–89: "Forgets both joy and grief, pleasure and pain. | Beyond this flood a frozen continent | Lies dark and wild, beat with perpetual storms | Of whirlwind and dire hail".

8 **divers:** OED 3: "Now somewhat *archaic,* but well known in legal and scriptural phraseology".

10 **to keep the ways you keep:** "to meet the faces that you meet", *The Love Song of J. Alfred Prufrock* 27.

11–13 **balance pleasure and pain ··· rain ··· sun:** Tennyson, *Sir Launcelot and Queen Guinevere* 1–4:

> Like souls that balance joy and pain,
> With tears and smiles from heaven again
> The maiden Spring upon the plain
> Came in a sun-lit fall of rain.

(TSE: "heaven", 7); with "fear of wrong", 13 (TSE: "ways of wrong", 6). Bradley discussed "a balance of pain" and "a balance of pleasure", and concluded: "In the world, which we observe, an impartial scrutiny will discover more pleasure than pain, though it is difficult to estimate, and easy to exaggerate, the amount of the balance", *Appearance and Reality* ch. XIV, XVII.

12 **blow against the wind and spit against the rain:** Blake: "Mock on, mock on, Voltaire, Rousseau! | Mock on, mock on—'tis all in vain! | You throw the sand against the wind, | And the wind blows it back again", *Mock on* 1–4. **blow against the wind:** *Paradise Lost* XI 311–13: "But prayer against his absolute decree | No more avails than breath against the wind | Blown stifling back on him that breathes it forth."

13 **more real than:** Shelley: "Forms more real than living man", *Prometheus Unbound* I 1748.

15 **Appearances appearances:** religious, philosophical, artistic and social.

(i) 1 Samuel 16: 7: "for man looketh on the outward appearance, but the Lord looketh on the heart". John 7: 24: "Judge not according to the appearance".

(ii) Kant: "For the truth is, that, however far we may carry our investigations into the world of sense, we never can come into contact with aught but appearances", *The Philosophy of Kant* ed. John Watson 37; underlined by TSE in his copy. TSE on F. H. Bradley, notably on *Appearance and Reality*: "The attitude of science, then, involves the constitution of a larger and larger limbo of appearance ··· Economics is appearance for the biologist, biology for the chemist. Similarly, social psychology is appearance to the individual psychologist"; "This seems to me essentially the position of the critical philosophy: the thing is known through its appearances, but as soon as the distinction is made appearance and thing fall apart, and appearance replaces thing as a point of attention", *Knowledge and Experience* 73, 96. "Whenever we desire to *explain* we will think of a reality which causes the appearance, but as soon as we have clearly formulated it, it turns out to be itself appearances", *Cause as Ideal Construction* (1914). On Bradley's understanding of appearance, see Richard Wollheim, *F. H. Bradley* (1959) 211–32.

(iii) *Symons* 170: "Knowing so much less than nothing, for we are entrapped in smiling and many-coloured appearances". TSE, Introduction to G. Wilson Knight's *The Wheel of Fire* (1930): "in a work of art, as truly as anywhere, reality only exists in and through appearances ··· The work of Shakespeare is like life itself something to be lived through. If we lived it completely we should need no interpretation; but on our plane of appearances our interpretations themselves are a part of our living." Turnbull Lecture III: "The artist is the only genuine and profound revolutionist, in the following sense. The world always has, and always will, tend to substitute appearance for reality. The artist, being always alone, being heterodox when everyone else is orthodox, and orthodox when everyone else is heterodox, is the perpetual upsetter of conventional values, the restorer of the real", *The Varieties of Metaphysical Poetry* 288–89.

(iv) TSE's brother Henry to their mother, 12 Dec 1921: "he spoke of always having to be keyed up, alert to the importance of appearances, always wearing a mask among people ··· like a man playing a part."

15, 21–22 **Appearances appearances ··· Contradiction ··· contradiction**: Nietzsche, on Raphael: "we shall then have to regard the dream as an *appearance of appearance* ··· Raphael ··· has represented to us this depotentiating of appearance to appearance ··· the 'appearance' here is the counter-appearance of eternal Contradiction, the father of things", *The Birth of Tragedy* §4.

16 **world through dialectic**: "it is only by an abuse of transcendental dialectic that he can reduce the world to the one or the other", *The Ethics of Green and Sidgwick* (1914). On *Purgatorio*: "It is the philosophy of that world of poetry which we have entered. But with the XXVIIth canto we have left behind the stage of punishment and the stage of dialectic", *Dante* (1929) II. **dialectic ways**: Nietzsche: Kant "entices us into the dialectic by-ways that lead ··· to his 'categorical imperative'", *Beyond Good and Evil* §5. Bradley: "I wish simply to consider what sort of operation is performed by Dialectic, assuming that it has a real way of its own", *The Principles of Logic* bk. III, pt. I, ch. ii. TSE: "Much of idealism ··· consists in an attempt to take the delicate and evasive truths of historical and literary criticism ··· and dragoon them into the goose-step of dialectic ··· And in spite of the irresistible current of dialectic, I find myself always returning to the feeling ··· that what we call the physical universe represents something much more real and permanent than all our structures of thought", *The Relativity of the Moral Judgment* (1915). "men both deny gods and worship gods, professing first Reason, | And then Money, and Power, and what they call Life, or Race, or Dialectic", *Choruses from "The Rock"* VII 28–29.

16–17 **world through dialectic ways ··· nights:** *Paradise Lost* III 543–45: "Of all this world at once. As when a scout | Through dark and desert ways with peril gone | All night".

16–18 **the world ··· I ··· questioned restless ··· every ··· where**: Shelley: "'Where?' —the world's echo answered 'where?' | And in that silence, and in my despair, | I questioned every tongueless wind that flew", *Epipsychidion* 234–36.

17–18 **questioned restless nights ··· followed ··· led:** "Of restless nights in one-night cheap hotels ··· Streets that follow like a tedious argument ··· To lead you to an overwhelming question", *The Love Song of J. Alfred Prufrock* 6–10. "When restless nights distract her brain from sleep", *WLComposite* **290**.

18 **led:** both typescripts have "lead". See note to *The Love Song of St. Sebastian* 11.

21 **Contradiction is the debt:** Bradley: "There is only one way to get rid of contradiction, and that way is by dissolution", *Appearance and Reality* ch. XVI. TSE: "Nothing is contradictory until it has been made a thing, and everything can be made a thing, and everything is contradictory", *Definition and Judgment in Bradley and His Critics* (1914). "the real world of practice is essentially vague, unprecise, swarming with what are, from a metaphysical point of view, insoluble contradictions", *Knowledge and Experience* 136.

22 **And still:** at the head of the line in Milton: "And still revolt when truth would set them free", *Sonnet: I did but prompt* (TSE: "truth", 31, 32, 33).

23 **know what else you seek:** *Paradise Lost* VII 639: "know; if else thou seek'st".

23, 28, 34 **you seek ··· whether you ··· no other place:** Clark Lecture III: "whether you seek the Absolute in marriage, adultery or debauchery, it is all one—you are seeking in the wrong place", *The Varieties of Metaphysical Poetry* 115.

26–27 **nowise real; unreal, and yet true; | Untrue, yet real:** "we have in no wise gained the right to say that the object has passed out of existence altogether", *On Real, Unreal, Ideal, and Imaginary Objects* (1914). **nowise:** a favourite word for Browning (more than 130 instances). Swinburne: "And these things nowise move me" and "But nowise through her living", *Atalanta in Calydon* 205, 937. **real; unreal:** "Unreal emotions, and real appetite", *WLComposite* **281**.

28 **Hopeful of what?:** at the head of the line, *Samson Agonistes* 1575: "Hopeful of his delivery."

29 **Or pray for earth on tired body and head:** Pascal: "On jette enfin de la terre sur la tête, et en voilà pour jamais" [at the last a little earth is thrown upon our head, and that is the end forever], *Pensées* 210. Swinburne: "Ah yet would God that stems and roots were bred | Out of my weary body and my head", *Laus Veneris* 57–58. **tired body and head:** "not yet tired of the game— | But weak in body as in head", *Humouresque* 2–3.

30–31 **all the paths you tread ··· said:** Deuteronomy 11: 25: "all the land that ye shall tread upon, as he hath said unto you".

30–33 **true ··· As true as truth ··· truth ··· truth:** *Troilus and Cressida* III ii has "true" four times and "truth" eight times in twenty lines, including "I am as true as truth's simplicity, | And simpler than the infancy of truth."

32 **no truth:** as in Hosea 4: 1: "no truth, nor mercy, nor knowledge of God in the land". John 8: 44: "there is no truth in him".

32–33 **among the living ··· the dead:** likewise both ending the lines, Shelley: "Thou wert the morning star among the living ··· New splendour to the dead", *To Stella (from the Greek of Plato)* 1, 4. See note to *East Coker* V 20–25, "the pattern ··· Of dead and living".

34 **No other ··· no other:** Keats: "Happy is England! I could be content | To see no other verdure than its own; | To feel no other breezes", *Sonnet* XVII 1–3.

36 **till the morning broke**: Shelley: "Until upon their path the morning broke", *The Revolt of Islam* VII ix.

36–44 **-chair · · · Stirred · · · crawled · · · leapt · · · crawled · · · lair:** Wilkie Collins: "I had stirred in its lair the serpent-hatred of years · · · Like a lurking reptile, it leaped up at me · · · Like a lurking reptile, it dropped out of sight again—as she instantly resumed her former position in the chair", *The Woman in White* The Third Epoch viii. TSE called this "the greatest of Collins's novels", *Wilkie Collins and Dickens* (1927).

37–38 **Across the window panes · · · Stirred by the morning air**: "stirred by the air | That freshened from the window", *The Waste Land* [II] 89–90. "morning stirred the long nasturtium", *Suppressed Complex* 7 *variant*. "Morning stirs the feet", *Sweeney Erect* 9. *The Family Reunion* II ii, HARRY: "Do you feel a kind of stirring underneath the air?"

38–40 **Stirred · · · the shadows crawled and crept · · · through the trees**: *The Picture of Dorian Gray* ch. XI: "shadows crawl into the corners of the room, and crouch there. Outside, there is the stirring of birds among the leaves · · · Out of the unreal shadows of the night comes back the real life that we had known" (TSE: "real; unreal", 26). For the same passage of Wilde, see note to *The Love Song of J. Alfred Prufrock* 17–22.

39 **Across the floor the shadows crawled and crept**: "the darkness | Crawling among the papers on the table | It leapt to the floor", [19–21], with "the darkness creep along the wall", *The Love Song of J. Alfred Prufrock* 74^75 [1].

39, 41 **the shadows · · · form**: Shelley: "there are two worlds of life and death: | One that which thou beholdest; but the other | Is underneath the grave, where do inhabit | The shadows of all forms that think and live", *Prometheus Unbound* I 195–98 (TSE: "the living · · · the dead", 32–33). Nine lines from the same passage of Shelley are quoted in *The Cocktail Party* III.

39–42 **shadows · · · trees | Around · · · muffled · · · knees:** Tennyson: "O muffle round thy knees with fern, | And shadow Sumner-chace!" *The Talking Oak* 149–50.

40 **thin light**: OED "thin" 3c: "Wanting depth or intensity; faint, weak, dim, pale. Formerly of light (*arch.*)", from 1649. TSE: "thin moonlight", *Humouresque* 19. **shivered:** OED "shiver" *v.*[1] 2: "To fly in pieces; to split"; and *v.*[2] 1b: "To tremble", including 1878, "The air shivered with noise."

40–41 **shivered through the trees · · · danced:** Tennyson: "Where I hear the dead at midday moan, | And the shrieking rush of the wainscot mouse, | And my own sad name in corners cried, | When the shiver of dancing leaves is thrown", *Maud* I [vi] 259–62 (TSE: "the dead", 33). For Tennyson's wainscot mouse, see note to *East Coker* I 11–13.

44, 48 **lair · · · along the stair**: "lairs · · · along the garden stairs", *Circe's Palace* 8, 10.

45 **sprang up a little damp dead breeze**: see note to *The wind sprang up at four o'clock* 1. **dead:** OED IV: "Without motion"; 22a: "Of water, air, etc.: Without motion or current", with 1861, "The wind had fallen dead". Bulwer Lytton: "The night said not a word. The breeze was dead", *A Night in Italy* 81 (in *Oxf Bk of English Verse*).

47 **human voices**: Tennyson: "Cried from the topmost summit with human

voices and words", *The Voyage of Maeldune* 28. TSE: "Till human voices wake us, and we drown", *The Love Song of J. Alfred Prufrock* 131.

47–49 **And had those been human voices in the chimneys · · · You had not known whether they laughed or wept:** *The Family Reunion* I i: "as you once explained the sobbing in the chimney" (David Chinitz, personal communication). **human voices · · · known:** *Paradise Lost* IX 560–61: "Thee, serpent, subtlest beast of all the field | I knew, but not with human voice endued". **chimneys · · · laughed:** Whittier: "The great throat of the chimney laughed", *Snow-Bound* 164 (TSE: "throats", 1). W. D. Howells: "Leaped loud in welcome from the hollow floors; || But gusts that blew all day with solemn laughter | From wide-mouthed chimney-places", *Forlorn* (1873) 48–50 (TSE: "leapt", 41; "floor", 39).

48 **along the stair:** OED "along" B. 1: "Through the whole or entire length of; from end to end of"; as Thomson, *Winter* 186: "The whirling Tempest raves along the plain". TSE's usage resists the feeling that "along" moves horizontally. For other uses of "along", see note to *Morning at the Window* 9. For "among", see note to *The Love Song of J. Alfred Prufrock* 89, and for "across", see note to *Suite Clownesque* I 1, 12.

The Love Song of St. Sebastian

Published in *Letters* (1988); then *March Hare*.

Sent in a letter to Conrad Aiken, from Marburg, 25 July 1914, with *Oh little voices of the throats of men*:

> I enclose some *stuff*—the *thing* I showed you some time ago, and some of the themes for the *Descent from the Cross* or whatever I may call it. I send them, even in their present form, because I am disappointed in them, and wonder whether I had better knock it off for a while—you will tell me what you think. Do you think that the *Love Song of St. Sebastian* part is morbid, or forced? Then there will be an Insane Section, and another love song (of a happier sort) and a recurring piece quite in the French style beginning
>
> "The married girl who lives across the street
> Wraps her soul in orange-coloured robes of Chopinese."—
>
> Then a mystical section,—and a Fool-House section beginning
>
> "Let us go to the masquerade and dance!
> I am going as St. John among the Rocks
> Attired in my underwear and socks . . ."
>
> Does it all seem very laboured and conscious? The S. Sebastian title I feel almost sure of; I have studied S. Sebastians—why should anyone paint a beautiful youth and stick him full of pins (or arrows) unless he felt a little as the hero of my verse? Only there's nothing homosexual about this—rather an important difference perhaps—but no one ever painted a female Sebastian, did they? So I give this title *faute de mieux.*

To Aiken 30 Sept, about this poem and *Oh little voices of the throats of men*: "The stuff I sent you is not good, is very forced in execution, though the idea was right, I think." 16 Nov: "I think that you criticise my verse too leniently. It still seems to me strained and intellectual. I know the kind of verse I want, and I know that this isn't it, and I know why. I shan't do anything that will satisfy me (as some of my old stuff *does* satisfy me—whether it be good or not) for years, I feel it more and more." (Aiken named *The Love Song of St. Sebastian* in print and quoted from the letter, "I think ··· intellectual", *March & Tambimuttu eds.* 23.)

Henry James had written of the Descent from the Cross as the masterpiece of the painter Sodoma (*Siena Early and Late* I in *Italian Hours*, for which see note to *The Love Song of J. Alfred Prufrock* 70, 72). TSE's reference to "St. John among the Rocks" suggests St. John the Divine, with not only the landscape of Patmos but Revelation 6: 15: "And the kings of the earth, and the great men, and the rich men, and the chief captains, and the mighty men, and every bondman, and every free man, hid themselves in the dens and in the rocks of the mountains." But St. John the Baptist should not be excluded (for dualities in names, see note to *The Love Song of J. Alfred Prufrock* 94, "Lazarus"). In his London *Baedeker*, TSE marked, 170: "*Leonardo da Vinci* (1452–1519), Madonna and Child, with John the Baptist and an angel, a studio-copy, with alterations, of *La Vierge aux Rochers* in the Louvre." He also marked, 168: "*Antonio Pollaiuolo* (d. 1498), Martyrdom of St. Sebastian" (both National Gallery). *Schuchard* 219: "As Eliot's lecture notes for his 1909 [1910] Harvard course, 'Florentine Painting' (Fine Arts 20b), reveal, he had begun his study of Sebastian with Antonio Pollaiuolo's 15th-century painting of the martyr." (See note to the title *Portrait of a Lady.*)

Title ***The Love Song of St. Sebastian***: whether imagined as the words of or as words addressed to St. Sebastian is not clear, unlike *The Love Song of J. Alfred Prufrock* with its self-communing and evident failure to address another. ***Love Song***: John Gray's *Spiritual Songs* (1896) includes *Lovesong to the Bridegroom*, tr. from Friedrich Spee, with "arrows", "shoots a thousand darts", "pain", and "sharp to kill". Spee (1591–1635) questioned the use of torture in witch trials. ***St. Sebastian***: John Gray, probably with Albrecht Altdorfer's painting in mind: "The stair they stand on ··· Their ears ··· Pale Sebastian's feet", *Saint Sebastian: On a Picture* 9, 35, 51 (TSE: "at the foot of your stair ··· your feet are white ··· your ears", 3, 12, 28). Ian Fletcher: "Homosexuals had a particular cult of Saint Sebastian. The combination of nudity and the phallic arrows was irresistible. Baron Corvo, for example, has two sonnets [1891] for a painting of the Saint by Guido Reni in the Capitoline Gallery at Rome", *The Poems of John Gray* (1988) 325. *Gordon* 91 points out that although the saint was sentenced to be shot by archers, "he did not die but was rescued by a woman and nursed in her lodgings." His later martyrdom by a mace occurs in Gray's other such poem, *Saint Sebastian* (1897). Wilde's *The Picture of Dorian Gray* ch. XI, has "medallions of many saints and martyrs, among whom was St. Sebastian" (for the chapter, see note to *The Love Song of J. Alfred Prufrock* 17–22). On the *fin de siècle* fascination with St. Sebastian, see Richard Kaye, *Voluptuous Immobility: St. Sebastian and the Decadent Imagination* (1997). Gabriele d'Annunzio's sensational dance-drama or mystery play *Le Martyre de Saint Sébastien* was staged in Paris, danced by Ida Rubinstein, with music by Debussy and sets by Léon Bakst, 29 May to 19 June 1911, when Eliot could have seen it (*Gross*). Pound to his mother [May or early June]: "I heard *St Sebastian* the new De Bussy opera. The music is very wonderful, & D'Anunzio's libretto quite the *worst* thing even he has perpetrated."

1 **shirt of hair**: OED 1c: "= hair-shirt", the last instance being Cowper, *Truth* (1782) 81: "In shirt of hair and weeds of canvas dress'd".

3 **at the foot of your stair:** "at the foot of the stair", *Do I know how I feel? Do I know what I think?* 4. "There will be no footsteps up and down the stair", *The Death of the Duchess* 29.

6 **And torture and delight:** "Agony nearest to delight", *The Burnt Dancer* 23, likewise rhyming with "night".

7 **Until my blood should ring the lamp:** to Aiken, TSE wrote of this line, in the margin: "Does this mean anything to you? I mean stand all about in a pool on the floor". **ring the lamp:** "The little lamp spreads a ring on the stair", *Rhapsody on a Windy Night* 74 (here: "stair", 3; "I would come with a little lamp in the night", 2 *variant*).

9 **neophyte:** OED: "Not in general use before the 19th c." 1a: "A new convert; one newly admitted to a church or religious body. Used chiefly with ref. to the primitive Christian, or the Roman Catholic, Church; in the latter, also applied to a newly ordained priest, or to a novice of a religious order."

10 **And then put out the light:** *Othello* V ii: "Put out the light, and then put out the light" (TSE: "You would love me because I should have strangled you", 34). Symons: "put out the light: | 'Tis morning, let the daylight come. | God! how the women's cheeks are white", *In Bohemia* (1892) 13–15 (TSE: "the morning came", 20; "your feet are white", 12). "And we must extinguish the candle, put out the light and relight it", *Choruses from "The Rock"* X 40.

11 *variant* **lead:** TSE wrote to Aiken in the margin: "preterite! not present". *Oh little voices of the throats of men* 18 likewise has "lead" for "led". In early papers on philosophy, TSE wrote "lead" and "mislead" instead of "led" and "misled". "the reader has been *mis*lead", *Poetry and Propaganda* (1930).

11–12 **To follow where ··· To follow where:** Shelley: "To follow where the kiss should guide it, | Oh, cruel I", *Kissing Helena (from the Greek of Plato)* 5–6.

16, 18 **you would take me in:** Symons: "And the light is night above, | You will let me in, | You will take me", *Alla Passeretta Bruna* (1891) last lines.

17 **hideous in your sight:** Job 18: 3: "Wherefore are we counted as beasts, and reputed vile in your sight?"

18 **without shame:** Shelley: "Naked they were from torture, without shame", *The Revolt of Islam* X xxi (TSE: "torture", 6).

19–23, 34–37 **Because I should be dead | And when the morning came | Between your breasts should lie my head. || I would come ··· your head ··· You would love me because ··· because you:** *Grover Smith 1996* 158 points to Yeats, *He Wishes His Beloved Were Dead* (1899) 1–6:

> Were you but lying cold and dead,
> And lights were paling out of the West,
> You would come hither, and bend your head,
> And I would lay my head on your breast;
> And you would murmur tender words,
> Forgiving me, because you were dead.

20–21 **And when the morning came | Between your breasts should lie my head:** Song of Solomon 1: 13: "He shall lie all night betwixt my breasts". Symons: "Nestle between your breasts to-night", *To Muriel: at the Opera* (1895) 2.

25 **no one's else:** to Aiken, 30 Sept 1914: "The thing is to be able to look at one's

life as if it were somebody's else (I much prefer to say somebody else's)." *Fowler*: "the usual possessive form is not *everyone's* &c. *else*, which is felt to be pedantic though correct, but *everyone else's.*"

26 **all the world shall melt**: Amos 9: 13: "all the hills shall melt". Burns: "Till a' the seas gang dry, my dear, | And the rocks melt wi' the sun!" *A Red, Red Rose* (*Crawford 2015* 204).

29–30 **linger · · · finger**: see note to *Suite Clownesque* II 7.

30 **follow the curve with my finger**: Aurelia Hodgson on a conversation in 1932 or 1934: "Ralph once mentioned how he'd like to relive repeatedly that moment of boyhood when he first discovered the curve of a girl's cheek. TSE couldn't agree. 'It was too painful'" (notebook 7, box 25, Bryn Mawr).

32 **I think that at last you would understand**: "some way we both should understand", *La Figlia Che Piange* 15.

34 **because I should have strangled you**: Browning: "And strangled her", *Porphyria's Lover* 41. Wilde: "Yet each man kills the thing he loves", *The Ballad of Reading Gaol* I vii. The line figures in translation in d'Annunzio's *Le Martyre de Saint Sébastien*: "Il faut que chacun tue son amour" (*Gross*). Laurence Hope: "I would have rather felt you round my throat, | Crushing out life, than waving me farewell!" *Kashmiri Song* (1901); see note to *The Death of Saint Narcissus* 12–15, 27.

34–37 **because**: see *Ash-Wednesday* I 1–3 and note.

35 **infamy**: *Inf.* XXVII 66: "senza tema d'infamia ti rispondo" [without fear of infamy I answer thee], last line of the epigraph to *The Love Song of J. Alfred Prufrock.*

35, 38 **infamy · · · me**: Beaumont and Fletcher: "Wilt thou, hereafter, when they talk of me, | As thou shalt hear nothing but infamy, | Remember some of these things?" *A King and No King* III i, quoted in *Ben Jonson* (1919).

Paysage Triste

Published in *March Hare.*

Assigned to 1914 by *Gallup 1970* 5 and to 1914–15 by *Rainey* 196.

Title] Verlaine has a sequence of seven poems, *Paysages tristes*. The fourth, *Nuit du Walpurgis classique*, mentions the opera *Tannhäuser* (TSE, 19), and three times "les cors", the horns (TSE, 15: but see note). For Verlaine's poem, see note to *The Love Song of J. Alfred Prufrock* 116, 118. Huysmans: "Jamais, sans que de nerveuses larmes lui montassent aux yeux, il n'avait pu se répéter 'les Plaintes de la jeune fille', car il y avait dans ce lamento, quelque chose de plus que de navré, quelque chose d'arraché qui lui fouillait les entrailles, quelque chose comme une fin d'amour dans un paysage triste" [He was never able to hum "The Young Girl's Lament" without nervous tears rising to his eyes, for in this *lamento* there was something more than sadness, a note of despair that tore at his heartstrings, something reminiscent of a dying love-affair in a melancholy landscape], *À rebours* [*Against Nature*] ch. XV, tr. Patrick

McGuinness (2003). ***Paysage***: OED: "a. A representation of rural scenery. b. A rural scene, landscape." (Described as "*Obs.* exc. as Fr.") See notes to the titles *The Waste Land* and *Landscapes.*

1 **mounted in the omnibus:** going upstairs within the omnibus, as distinct from "mounted the omnibus". *Baedeker* 20: "The 'garden seats' on the top (same fares as inside) are pleasant enough in fine weather and are freely patronized by ladies." **in the omnibus:** Nathaniel Parker Willis, *The Lady in the White Dress, Whom I Helped Into the Omnibus* (1844); Symons, *In an Omnibus* (1892). (Pound's French poem *Dans un Omnibus de Londres* is from 1916.) **omnibus:** not then affected, though formal; *Baedeker*, although it concedes "familiarly known as a '*bus*'" (20), regularly uses "omnibus". (See the ten-year-old TSE's verses "I thought I saw a elephant | A-riding on a 'bus" and "He thought he saw a Banker's Clerk | Descending from the bus" in "Other Verses".) OED 2a: "= omnibus-box" (at the theatre or opera) from 1844 (TSE: "the box · · · opera-glasses", 8, 19).

2 **a penny fare:** *Baedeker* 20: "The fares vary from *1d.* to *6d.* or *7d.*"

7 **An almost:** OED 2b: "qualifying a sb. with implied attribute", with Southey, 1808: "an almost Quaker". **denizen of Leicester Square:** Pope: "He summons strait his denizens of air", *The Rape of the Lock* II 55 (for Pope's poem, see *March Hare* notes to this poem).

7, 13 **Leicester Square · · · ease:** "ease · · · Bloomsbury Square", *Cat Morgan Introduces Himself* 3, 4 (all line-endings).

10–11 **eyes · · · loosened hair:** Browning: "thy sweet eyes, | And loosened hair". *Pauline* 2–3.

10–12 **I see her moving · · · her chamber | With naked feet passing across the skies:** Wyatt: "With naked foot stalking in my chamber. | I have seen them", *They flee from me that sometime did me seek* 2–3. In *OxfBk of English Verse*, Wyatt's line was smoothed: "With naked foot stalking within my chamber". TSE: "With evening feet walking across the grass", *Hidden under the heron's wing* 5. "With broken boot heels stained in many gutters", *Prufrock's Pervigilium* [31]. **With naked feet:** Sir Edwin Arnold: "With naked feet, amid the peering maids", *The Light of Asia*, Book the Seventh. **across the skies:** "His soul stretched tight across the skies", *Preludes* IV 1.

11 **with loosened hair:** Landor: "His chaplets mingled with her loosened hair", *Gebir* II 136. TSE: "I wonder whether many people ever read *Gebir*; and yet Landor, the author of that dignified long poem, was a very able poet indeed", *What is Minor Poetry?* (1944). D. G. Rossetti mentions the "loosened hair" of the prostitute, *Jenny* 47. TSE alluded to that poem in *WLComposite* 273: "The lazy laughing Jenny of the bard". Meredith has "loosened hair" in *Modern Love* XIII, a Meredithian sonnet which remarks: "she drops a look of fondness, and goes by" (TSE: "that · · · look", 4).

13–14 **crudely ill at ease · · · sit:** Symons: "We sat together, you and I; | Our hearts were sweetly ill at ease", *Fête Champêtre* (1895) 2–3. *The Family Reunion* I i, first chorus: "Why do we feel embarrassed, impatient, fretful, ill at ease, | Assembled like amateur actors who have not been assigned their parts?"

13, 16 **ill at ease ··· knees:** "ill at ease | I mount the stairs ··· mounted on my hands and knees", *Portrait of a Lady* III 2–4 ("mounted", 1; "stare", 3).

15 **when the lights went out and the horn began:** act II of *Tristan und Isolde* begins with horns (Kit Toda, personal communication).

18 **The smiling stripling with the pink soaped face:** *Paradise Lost* III 636–40: "And now a stripling cherub he appears, | Not of the prime, yet such as in his face | Youth smiled celestial ··· flowing hair" ("loosened hair", 11). Byron: "a handsome stripling with smooth face", *Don Juan* XI xxxv. For pink shaving soap, see note to *Sweeney Erect* 21–22.

19 **in his care:** *Paradise Lost* IX 318: "so spake domestic Adam in his care".

Afternoon

Published in *Letters* (1988) and in *March Hare.*

Assigned to 1914 by *Gallup 1970* 37. Sent to Aiken, 25 Feb 1915, together with *Suppressed Complex* on a folded ms leaf: "I will put one or two small verses into this letter." After making a typescript copy of the poems, Aiken sold TSE's ms, *c.* 1931, and it is now untraced (see Textual History).

Baedeker 290 on the British Museum: "Assyrian, and American Collections and the Waddesdon Room. The Museum is open on Sun. afternoon from 2 o'clock, but is shut on Good Friday and Christmas Day.—Sticks and umbrellas are left in the hall."

1–2 **The ladies who are interested in Assyrian art | Gather in the hall of the British Museum:** Laurent Tailhade: "Les femmes laides qui déchiffrent des sonates | Sortent de chez Erard" [The ugly women who decipher sonatas are leaving Erard's], first lines of *Place des Victoires*, which also ends with the women under the gaze of statuary. Since TSE's copy of Tailhade's *Poèmes aristophanesques* (1904) was not printed until 1915, he evidently read the poem in the anthology *Poètes d'aujourd'hui* (see headnote to "*Poems* (1920)", 4. WHAT FRANCE MEANT TO TSE). In the anthology the poem shared a page with *Musée du Louvre* (see *March Hare* notes), and both poems were quoted and discussed by Pound in *New Age* 2 Oct 1913. For Tailhade, see headnote to *Cousin Nancy* and note to *Mr. Apollinax* 6–7. For the subtitle *Feuillet d'album. à Laurent Tailhade, le maitre*, see *Vers pour la Foulque*, Textual History, at the end of *Noctes Binanianæ*. **The ladies ··· Assyrian art | Gather in the hall:** "In the room the women come and go | Talking of Michelangelo", *The Love Song of J. Alfred Prufrock* 13–14.

1, 4–5 **The ladies ··· steam from drying rubber overshoes ··· hats:** Henry James: "The ladies, who were much the more numerous, wore their bonnets ··· Two or three had retained their overshoes, and as you approached them the odour of the india-rubber was perceptible", *The Bostonians* ch. IV. (For the novel, see headnote to *Portrait of a Lady*.) **drying rubber overshoes:** *Baedeker* advises ("Disposition of Time", 81): "Rainy days had better be devoted to the galleries and museums." **overshoes:** OED has as its first citation *Moby-Dick* (1851): "Hat, coat, and overshoes were one by one removed".

1–5 **Assyrian ··· perfume ··· hats**: Tennyson on the Assyrian art of the British Museum: "That jewelled mass of millinery ··· Assyrian Bull | Smelling of musk and of insolence", *Maud* I [vi] 232–34. **Assyrian ··· purple**: Byron: "The Assyrian came down like the wolf on the fold, | And his cohorts were gleaming in purple and gold", *The Destruction of Sennacherib* 1–2.

3 **perfume**: stressed here on the second syllable; see note to *Easter* II 7. **last year's tailor suits**: a fashion (and new term) from the previous decade (see *March Hare* notes to this poem). OED from *Westminster Gazette* 1907: "We do not soar beyond the new tailor-suit for a week or two longer"; also *Westminster Gazette* 1906: "*Elégantes* of Paris who were tailor-suited".

3, 5, 9 **last year's tailor suits ··· hats ··· Towards the unconscious, the ineffable, the absolute**: TSE on philosophy in 1912: "the New Realism, like most pre-War philosophies, seems now as demoded as ladies' hats of the same period", *Views and Reviews* in *NEW* 6 June 1935. "hat and gloves in hand ··· suit ··· On the doorstep of the Absolute", *Spleen* 13–14, 16.

6 **sombre Sunday afternoon**: *Baedeker* 84: "The movement for the Sunday opening of museums, galleries, and other large public collections has recently made great strides in London: and that day need no longer count as practically a *dies non* in the traveller's itinerary."

6–7 **Vanish in ··· fade ··· statuary**: Keats: "Vanished in elemental passion", *Endymion* II 375 (at the head of the line); "I vanish in the heaven's blue", *Fairy's Song* 18; "fade away ··· Fade far away", *Ode to a Nightingale* 20–21; "she cannot fade", *Ode on a Grecian Urn* 19; "I marked the goddess in fair statuary", *The Fall of Hyperion* I 336 (at the line-ending).

8 **Like amateur comedians across a lawn**: "lawns ··· Here's the comedian again", *Suite Clownesque* I 3–5.

9 **Towards ··· the absolute**: the poem apparently has no final full stop. The last sentence of *Knowledge and Experience* as published reads: "And this emphasis upon practice—upon the relativity and the instrumentality of knowledge—is what impels us toward the Absolute." In the Preface, written in 1964, TSE explained of his Harvard doctoral dissertation (completed 1916): "The last page of the typescript ends with an unfinished sentence: *For if all objectivity and all knowledge is relative* ... I have omitted this exasperating clause: it is suitable that a dissertation on the work of Francis Herbert Bradley should end with the words 'the Absolute'." On A. R. Orage: "without this restless desire for the absolute, Orage ··· would have been merely a reasonable persuader towards the reasonable revolution", *A Commentary* in *Criterion* Jan 1935. **the unconscious ··· the absolute**: of Corbière: "he has less direct feeling of 'the absolute', 'the unconscious', and the other abstractions which aroused Laforgue's passion", *The Varieties of Metaphysical Poetry* 217 (Clark Lecture VIII). **the absolute**: TSE may have recalled one of the hugely popular Hans Breitmann ballads, in pidgin Germanic English, by Charles Godfrey Leland, whose *Wein Geist* (1871) ends: "In Madchenlieb or Schnapsenrausch | Das Absolut ist dein" [In a girl's love or a fit of drunkenness, the Absolute is yours]. For the philosophical term, see note to *Conversation Galante* 14.

Suppressed Complex

Published in *Letters* (1988), then *March Hare*.

Assigned to 1914 by *Gallup 1970* 37. Sent in letters by TSE from Oxford. First, to Pound, 2 Feb 1915: "I enclose one small verse. I know it is not good, but everything else I have done is worse. Besides, I am constipated and have a cold on the chest. Burn it." Second, to Aiken, 25 Feb 1915 (see headnote to *Afternoon*).

Gallup 1970 tentatively proposed that *Suppressed Complex* might have been the poem sent by Pound to Wyndham Lewis in 1915 for *Blast* 2, but Timothy Materer's *Pound/ Lewis* (1985) 12–13 makes clear that the poem Pound sent was *Portrait of a Lady*.

Title ***Suppressed***: OED "suppress" 2a: "*Psychol*: to consciously inhibit (an unacceptable thought, memory or desire)", citing Freud, 1913, *The Interpretation of Dreams* (tr. A. A. Brill): "During his waking state ·· he has made an effort to suppress the sinful thoughts as often as they arise." TSE to his brother Henry, 2 July 1915, about Vivien and himself: "I am much less suppressed, and more confident, than I ever have been." To A. L. Rowse, 3 Mar 1941: "the Autobiography impresses me very favourably (it is always a wonder to me how people can write an autobiography, but it is probably because they have less to suppress than I have)." ***Complex***: OED 3: "*Psychol.* A group of emotionally charged ideas or mental factors, unconsciously associated by the individual with a particular subject, arising from repressed instincts, fears, or desires", from 1907.

5–8 **She stirred in her sleep · · · She was very pale · · · I passed joyously out through the window**: Baudelaire, tr. Stuart Merrill: "looked through the windows as thou wert sleeping · · · passed noiselessly through the panes · · · extraordinarily pale · · · joy", *Les Bienfaits de la Lune* [*The Blessings of the Moon*] in *Pastels in Prose*. (Baudelaire: "La Lune · · · regarda par la fenêtre pendant que tu dormais · · · passa sans bruit à travers les vitres · · · extraordinairement pâles · · · sa joie".)

7 **morning shook the long nasturtium**: "madman shakes a dead geranium", *Rhapsody on a Windy Night* 12. **the tawny bowl**: Robert Stephen Hawker: "Drink-hael! in Jesu's name | We fill the tawny bowl; | But cover down the curving crest, | Mould of the Orient Lady's breast", *King Arthur's Waes-hael* 3–6 (in *Oxf Bk of English Verse*).

8 **I passed joyously · · · through**: Shelley: "where joyously | Sate my two younger babes at play, | In the court-yard through which I passed", *Rosalind and Helen* 525–27.

In the Department Store

Published in *March Hare*.

Assigned to 1915 by *Gallup 1970* 37 and to 1914–15 by *Rainey* 196.

TSE's poem belongs, in kind, with one by his Harvard friend, W. G. Tinckom-Fernandez, *The Waitress* in *Harvard Advocate* 31 Jan 1908; the poems share mention of the lady, her eyes, her hair, her smile, and her being business-like / busy.

Title **In the Department Store**: OED "department store": "orig. *U.S.*", from 1887. H. G. Wells in *Mr. Polly* (1910) still finds it necessary to explain the term: "One of those large, rather low-class establishments which sell everything from pianos and furniture to books and millinery—a department store." Henry James's love-story *In the Cage* (1898) has a similar setting. TSE's "The summer evenings in the park" (5) recalls James's central elaborated scene on a summer evening in the park; in James, the phrase "in the Park" comes half a dozen times. James's story contributed to the cancelled title of Part II of *The Waste Land*, "In the Cage".

1 **The lady of the porcelain department**: Whistler's *La Princesse du pays de la porcelaine* was painted in 1864 (Freer Gallery, Washington). TSE: "To porcelain land", *Goldfish* II. *Embarquement pour Cythère* 13 (with "Ladies", 1). The tower or pavilion of porcelain was much invoked in poetry and prose. Longfellow: "And yonder, by Nakin, behold! | The Tower of Porcelain, strange and old", *Kéramos* strophe 27. (TSE in his Preface to Leone Vivante's *English Poetry* (1950): "I myself consider Longfellow underrated.") Henry James's Princess contemplates her insufficiently happy marriage under the image of "some wonderful beautiful but outlandish pagoda, a structure plated with hard bright porcelain", with its "rare porcelain plates", *The Golden Bowl* bk. IV I. Théophile Gautier: "Celle que j'aime, à présent, est en Chine; | Elle demeure avec ses vieux parents, | Dans une tour de porcelaine fine" [She whom I love, just now, is in China; she is living with her aged parents in a fine porcelain tower], *Chinoiserie* 5–7; "Dans la Chine bizarre, aux tours de porcelaine" [In the bizarre land of China, with its porcelain towers], *Le Sommet de la tour* [*The Pinnacle of the Tower*] 113. Judith Gautier, tr. Stuart Merrill: "In her pavilion of porcelain ··· the Empress is sitting ··· the Emperor ··· walks towards the pavilion of porcelain, leaving the astonished Mandarins to stare at one another in silence", *The Emperor* (*After Thoo-Foo*) in *Pastels in Prose* (with "Mandarins" thrice). Also Merrill: "Past the porcelain towers of Keou-Kang", *Ballade of the Chinese Lover* 9. (The lady's "pencil in her hair" may suggest an oriental pin.) André Salmon: "Dans une tour de porcelaine | O n'être de rien occupé | Que des vers de Li-Taï-Pé | Et d'un petit magot obscene" [In a porcelain tower oh to be occupied with nothing other than the verses of Li-Taï-Pé and a little obscene figurine], *Odelette Chinoise* (1910) 33–36.

2 **Smiles at the world**: *Paradise Lost* V 124–31:

> "··· fair morning first smiles on the world,
> And let us to our fresh employments rise
> Among the groves, the fountains, and the flowers
> That open now their choicest bosomed smells
> Reserved from night, and kept for thee in store."
> So cheered he his fair spouse, and she was cheered,
> But silently a gentle tear let fall
> From either eye, and wiped them with her hair.

(TSE: "keeps ··· her hair", 3; "eyes", 4; "nights", 6.) Milton: "employments ··· in store".

4 **sharpened eyes:** Pope, *Odyssey* V 505. OED "sharpen" 2a: "To render more acute (a person's wits, sight ··· etc.)" TSE:

> There is a well-known comparison or simile in the great XVth canto of the *Inferno* [XV 20–21], which Matthew Arnold singled out, rightly, for high praise; which is characteristic of the way in which Dante employs these figures. He is speaking of the crowd in Hell who peered at him and his guide under a dim light:
>
> *e sì ver noi aguzzevan le ciglia,*
> *come vecchio sartor fa nella cruna.*
>
> *and sharpened their vision (knitted their brows) at us, like an old tailor peering at the eye of his needle.*
>
> *Dante* (1929) I

The Temple Classics translation is "sharpened their vision"; TSE's gloss is in parentheses. Adduced also (with a different translation) in *The Varieties of Metaphysical Poetry* 122 (Clark Lecture IV). See note to *Little Gidding* II 37–38.

4–6 **behind her sharpened eyes take flight ··· heated:** Henry James: "the fear that Mrs. Gereth, with sharpened eyes, might wonder why the deuce ··· she had grown so warm", *The Spoils of Poynton* ch. 7.

5, 7 **The summer evenings in the park ··· dark:** Clough: "(Written in London, standing in the Park, | An evening in July, just before dark)", *Dipsychus* IV 128–29. TSE: "any morning in the park", *Portrait of a Lady* II 31.

6 **second story:** OED "story" 1: "while in England [as against the U.S.] the term FIRST-FLOOR is applied to the floor above the ground floor, the numbering of 'stories' (so named) usually begins with the ground-floor, so that the 'first-floor' is identical with the 'second story'."

7 **Man's life is powerless and brief and dark:** Bertrand Russell: "Brief and powerless is Man's life; on him and all his race the slow, sure doom falls pitiless and dark", *The Free Man's Worship* (1903). (Russell owed something to Shelley's *Queen Mab* III 220–21: "Man's brief and frail authority | Is powerless".) TSE, quoting Russell's first six words: "It is quite as good prose as Pater's, but it is not Mr. Russell's best prose", *Style and Thought* (1918). Hobbes: "and the life of man, solitary, poor, nasty, brutish, and short", *Leviathan* ch. 13 (TSE's copy of a 1907 ed. was dated by him Feb 1914). *King Lear* II iv: "Man's life is cheap as beast's". Byron: "Man's love is of man's life a thing apart, | 'Tis woman's whole existence", *Don Juan* I cxciv.

Do I know how I feel? Do I know what I think?

Published in *March Hare.*

Assigned to Jan–Apr 1915 by *Rainey* 198.

1 **Do I know how I feel? Do I know what I think?:** "Not knowing what to feel", *Portrait of a Lady* III 36. "Knowing neither how to think, nor how to feel",

WLComposite 338. "They know what they are to feel and what to think ··· They know what to think and what to feel", *The Death of the Duchess* 5, 8. "And what we feel, or not", *Entretien dans un parc* 21. On Laforgue's intelligence: "a poet genuinely occupied with the relation of feeling and thought, not, like Browning and Meredith, playing with their mechanical combinations"; then: "I take as metaphysical poetry that in which what is ordinarily apprehensible only by thought is brought within the grasp of feeling, or that in which what is ordinarily only felt is transformed into thought without ceasing to be feeling", *The Varieties of Metaphysical Poetry* 217, 220 (Clark Lecture VIII). "a pattern ··· of speech expressing more than what the characters know or know they feel"; "It is in those later plays that one becomes most conscious of the fact that we know neither what we do nor what we feel", *The Development of Shakespeare's Verse* (1937).

Pater: "The peculiar strength of Marius was to have apprehended this weakness of the threshold of human knowledge ··· Our knowledge is limited to what we feel, he reflected: we need no proof that we feel. But can we be sure that things are at all like our feelings?" *Marius the Epicurean* ch. VIII. (For the chapter, see note to *A Cooking Egg* 20, "experience".) In his copy of Bernard Bosanquet's *The Essentials of Logic*, TSE underlined "whatever we are obliged to think" (11) and wrote "How can I know what I am obliged to think?" in the margin. TSE: "L'esprit historique, c'est le fondement de la culture, et étant aussi le moyen de nous connaître nous-mêmes, de connaître notre état d'âme à nous, de savoir ce que nous pensons" [The historical spirit, such is the foundation of culture, and at the same time the means by which we recognise ourselves, recognise the state of our souls, know what we think], *Autour d'une Traduction d'Euripide* (1916). TSE's *Syllabus: Modern French Literature* (1916) has it that one of Rousseau's main tendencies was "Emphasis on *feeling* rather than *thought*" (*Margolis* 10). In his copy of Coleridge's *Poetical Works* (1907), he scored *Dejection* 87–90: "For not to think of what I needs must feel, | But to be still and patient, all I can; | And haply by abstruse research to steal | From my own nature all the natural man—".

1–2 **Do I know how I feel? Do I know what I think? | Let me take ink and paper:** "If you want to write poetry, keep away from pencils and paper and typewriters until you have overcome the temptation ··· Whatever you think, be sure that it is what you think; whatever you want, be sure that it is what you want; whatever you feel, be sure that it is what you feel", *Address by T. S. Eliot, '06, to the Class of '33* (1933). **feel ··· think ··· pen and ink:** to his mother, 19 Jan 1919, after his father's death: "my thoughts have been with you every day, though it always seems that little, very little, can ever filter through to pen and ink of what one feels. I am waiting as patiently as I can for letters. One keeps thinking of little things—I have been longing to have some little drawings of father's" ("letters", 5; "little ··· little", 20, 24).

1–3 **Do I know ··· let me take pen and ink ··· with my hat ··· take the air:** "Let us take the air ··· you do not know, you do not know ··· I take my hat ··· Let us take the air ··· me sitting pen in hand", *Portrait of a Lady* I 36; II 4, 29; III 30, 33.

4 **at the foot of the stair:** "at the foot of your stair", *The Love Song of St. Sebastian* 3.

10 **so much beauty:** Tennyson, *The Lover's Tale* I 206.

10–12 **beauty spilled ··· | Or wasted ··· villages ··· darkened chambers:** Thomas Gray: "Full many a gem of purest ray serene, | The dark unfathom'd caves of ocean bear: | Full many a flower is born to blush unseen, | And waste its sweetness on the desert air. || Some village-", *Elegy Written in a Country Church Yard* 53–57. **beauty spilled ··· wasted ··· untasted:** Symons: "This beauty is vain, this, born to be wasted, | Poured on the ground like water, spilled, and by no man tasted", *Wasted Beauty* (1906) 1–2 (TSE: "water", 16 *variant*). **spilled on the open street | Or:** Symons: "Or spilt upon the streets", *Summer in Spring* (1913) 8. **on the open street ··· in darkened chambers:** "on the streets ··· in darkened rooms", *Rhapsody on a Windy Night* 63–64 *variant.* **street | Or wasted:** Kipling: "Our towns of wasted honour— | Our streets of lost delight!" *The Broken Men* (1903) 69–70. (On *The Broken Men*, see note to the title *The Hollow Men.*) **wasted ··· untasted:** Shelley: "From wide cities, famine-wasted; | Groans half heard, and blood untasted", *Prometheus Unbound* I 528–29.

12 **darkened chambers:** Wilde's opium-den: "a little staircase, leading to a darkened chamber", *The Picture of Dorian Gray* ch. XVI. For Wilde's paragraph see note to *Prufrock's Pervigilium* [23].

12 *variant* **neurasthetic:** not in OED, which has "neurasthenic" from 1876. Neurasthenia: "*Path.* An atonic condition of the nervous system; functional nervous weakness; nervous debility", from 1856.

13 **restless on winter nights:** "restless nights", *The Love Song of J. Alfred Prufrock* 6, as also *Oh little voices of the throats of men* 17. **who can blame us?:** Kipling: "Can you blame us if we soak ourselves in beer?" *Gentleman-Rankers* 28 (in *A Choice of Kipling's Verse*). TSE quoted four lines of Kipling's poem in *Kipling Redivivus* (1919).

15–16 **slips ··· at my finger tips ··· that drips:** of a pianist playing Chopin: "finger-tips ··· slips", *Portrait of a Lady* I 9, 14. Symons ends *The Chopin Player*: "drips ··· Dying delicately at my finger tips?" (TSE: "death", 19). Symons: "I see them in my brain ··· They die of a touch", 1, 6 (TSE: "in the brain", 20; "death ··· touch", 19, 22). Swinburne's *Laus Veneris* likewise rhymes "finger-tips" with "drips", in lines which twice speak of "death" (149–52). TSE quoted *Laus Veneris* in a letter to Aiken, 19 July 1914. "slippery ··· held tight in his own fingers ··· pink tips", *The Death of Saint Narcissus* 25, 27. "Slip from fingers slip | When freely fingered", *Bellegarde* 10–11.

16 **creolin:** a disinfectant; in OED within citations for Jeyes' fluid and lysol; 1891, as "creoline".

19 **Will investigate the cause of death:** "In Gopsum Street a man murders his mistress ··· For the man's neighbors the important fact is what the man killed her with? And at precisely what time? And who found the body? For the 'enlightened public' the case is merely evidence for the Drink question, or Unemployment, or some other category of things to be reformed. But the mediaeval world, insisting on the eternity of punishment, expressed something nearer the truth", *Eeldrop and Appleplex* I (1917). Corbière: "Car il est mort, de quoi?" [Because he is dead, of what?], *Pauvre Garçon* [*Poor Boy*] 11.

19–20 **life ··· in the brain:** Tennyson: "And life is darkened in the brain", *In Memoriam* CXXI 8 (TSE: "darkened", 12).

20, 24 **a little whisper in the brain · · · a little laughter**: Symons: "A little love within my heart, | A little wisdom in my brain", *The Dance of the Seven Sins* (1899).

21–22 **the ancient pain · · · touch**: W. G. Tinckom-Fernandez: "Still in my heart the ancient pain, | Where, in my heart, old memories lie, | Touched by the songs the organ plays", *The Street Organ* 4–6. For his poem, see headnote to *Interlude in London*. Shelley: "And its ancient pilot, Pain", *Lines Written Among the Euganean Hills* 333.

23 **My brain is twisted in a tangled skein**: "My thoughts in a tangled bunch of heads and tails", *The Death of the Duchess* 43.

23–24 **tangled · · · blinding light**: Milton: "In the blind mazes of this tangled wood", *Comus* 181; "twilight shade of tangled thickets", *On the Morning of Christ's Nativity* 188.

24, 26 **a little laughter · · · after**: Swinburne: "Though time rend after · · · A little laughter", *Anima Anceps* 33, 35.

25 **blackness of ether**: John Davidson: "Only the empty ether hovered black", *Insomnia* 4. **ether**: "Like a patient etherised upon a table", *The Love Song of J. Alfred Prufrock* 3 (see note).

26 **either**: the relation to "ether" at the end of the previous line may be clarified by TSE's recorded pronunciation of "either" in *The Waste Land* [I] 27, with a long *i*, not a long *e*. For another poem ending without a full stop, see *Afternoon* 9 and note.

The Death of Saint Narcissus

Printed in *Early Youth* (1950, 1967), anomalously, since this poem was not printed while TSE was at school or at Harvard; then *WLFacs*. (Lines 1–5 had been published in 1960 in *Kenner* 33.) See headnote to *The Waste Land*, 1. COMPOSITION, for relation to this poem.

TSE to Robert L. Beare, 29 Apr 1953: "That unfortunate fragmentary poem on *The Death of St. Narcissus*, which I very much regret not having destroyed at the time of writing it, was written, I think, in 1912 or 1913." A letter to TSE from Richard G. Stern, 4 June 1956, enquiring about the poem, is annotated in Valerie's hand: "TSE 'does not consider the verses v. g. & will not permit them to be printed in his lifetime' & wd prefer no quotations sd be made from it. Chief interest 1st seven lines obviously recast, condensed & in his opinion, vastly improved for *TWL* [*The Waste Land*]. Poem's date between 1912–14 never a part of *TWL* & therefore did not meet EP's blue pencil—at any rate in that context" (Faber archive).

Gordon 1974 noted that *The Death of Saint Narcissus* and *Mr. Apollinax* were both drafted on paper with the watermark "Excelsior Fine British Make". She quoted TSE to Pound, 2 Feb 1915, on writing for Wyndham Lewis's *Blast*: "I have corresponded with Lewis, but his puritanical principles seem to bar my way to Publicity. I fear that King Bolo and his Big Black Kween will never burst into print. I understand that Priapism, Narcissism etc are not approved of", taking "Priapism, Narcissism" to refer to this poem and *Mr. Apollinax*. However, *Rainey* 133 takes them to refer to the indecent rhymes. *Rainey* 13–15 assigns the drafts of *The Death of Saint Narcissus* respectively to Apr 1915 and May 1915 (misprinted as "May 1916", *Rainey* 34).

Hayward note:

> Text from the unique *Poetry* (Chicago) galley-proof, preserved in the Harriet Monroe Collection in the University of Chicago. The proof, which consists of two galleys (15 and 16), is printed on one side of a single slip headed "POEMS". The letterpress, which is broken after the line "If he walked in city streets" is scored through by hand with the manuscript directive "Kill" (i.e. suppress) in the margin of each section. In the top right-hand corner of the proof there is a manuscript editorial note: "Jewel file | This poem | never pub'd | T. S. Eliot". There is no evidence to show when this poem was submitted to *Poetry* (Chicago), of which Harriet Monroe was the founder and editor, or when it was set in type. There was an interval of five years between the Harvard *Class Ode* and Eliot's next appearance in print, with *The Love Song of J. Alfred Prufrock*, which was published, on the recommendation of Ezra Pound, in the June 1915 issue of *Poetry* (Chicago), though it had actually been completed in 1911. *The Death of Saint Narcissus* was probably written during this interval, but it was certainly not set in type with a view to publication until after the appearance of *Prufrock*. On the other hand, the fact that its opening lines were to be incorporated almost exactly in *The Waste Land* (1922) should not be taken to indicate a later date for its composition.

Evidence nonetheless does exist for the date of submission to *Poetry*. The archive of *Poetry* (U. Chicago) has a typescript which Hayward had not seen, and two manuscripts were discovered along with the drafts of *The Waste Land*. Correspondence, too, is revealing. After the publication of *The Love Song of J. Alfred Prufrock*, Pound wrote to the editor on TSE's behalf in [July 1915], promising a second submission: "I want you to hold two or three pages open for Eliot in either Sept. or Oct. ··· He has done three small (half page) jems and will have enough for three pages I should think." He wrote again, presumably in August, sending "the three jems of Eliot for September, and a fourth thing *Cousin Nancy* which may do to fill the second page". When D. D. Paige published this in Pound's *Letters*, he appended a note: "Only three of the four were printed: *The 'Boston Evening Transcript', Aunt Helen* and *Cousin Nancy*, *Poetry*, October 1915." Correctly noting that *The Death of Saint Narcissus* "was set up in type apparently for publication in *Poetry*, but was not printed", *Gallup* allocated it to C21, "Three Poems", *Poetry*, Oct 1915. Both *WLFacs* and *March Hare* accepted this allocation. But Pound's page count rules out *The Death of Saint Narcissus*, which at 39 lines would in itself occupy a page and a half (David Bernstein, *The Hebrew University Studies in Literature* Spring 1976).

The Death of Saint Narcissus was not in the second batch of TSE's poems for *Poetry*, but was sent in the third on 29 May 1916, when Pound wrote: "Here are five poems by Eliot." Only four—*Conversation Galante*, *La Figlia Che Piange*, *Mr. Apollinax* and *Morning at the Window*—appeared in *Poetry* Sept 1916 (see Textual History of *Morning at the Window*). The typescript of *The Death of Saint Narcissus* appears to have been pinned to the others and folded in three for posting. It is marked up for publication in the sequence, and at the head of *Conversation Galante*, Monroe's assistant, Henry B. Fuller, has written "23" (unexplained) followed by a calculation:

23
28) 139 (5
140

—meaning that the page depth of 28 lines would give 140 lines in five pages, which would just accommodate the 139 counted lines of the five poems. Including titles and spaces, the line count of the typescript of *The Death of Saint Narcissus* was 47 lines, while the others occupied, respectively, 22, 28, 25 and 12 lines, making a total of 134. To this, add space for the heading "Poems", which was inserted above *The Death of Saint Narcissus*, with perhaps two lines beneath, and, at the end, space for the author's name. When set in type, with several long lines needing to be turned, the total was rather more, but it is clear that *The Death of Saint Narcissus* was the unprinted poem from the third submission.

When *Prufrock and Other Observations* was published in 1917, all but one of its twelve poems had already appeared in a journal. The exception was *Hysteria*, which is brief enough to have fitted on the same page as, for instance, *Morning at the Window* and may well have been the unprinted item from the second submission. It was published in Pound's *Catholic Anthology* in Nov 1915, but that July, in his letter to Monroe about the second submission, Pound had written: "I want the stuff out in time for my anthology." This may have been intended to secure US copyright for the poems, which would otherwise be lost by prior publication in *Catholic Anthology* in Britain (see headnote to "*Poems* (1920)", 1. CONTENTS IN ORDER OF FIRST PUBLICATION and *Spoo* 97–103). Though it was not printed, and does not survive in the *Poetry* archive, *Hysteria* was perhaps among the "stuff" of the second submission.

Title **Saint Narcissus**: Bishop of Jerusalem towards the end of the 2nd century, a recluse in the desert for many years. **Narcissus**: the story of the self-love of the mythological Narcissus is told in Ovid's *Metamorphoses* III. TSE: "the Catholic practitioners were, I believe, with the possible exception of certain heretics, not palpitating Narcissi; the Catholic did not believe that God and himself were identical", *The Function of Criticism* (1923) II. Of Valéry: "He reminds us of Narcissus gazing into the pool, and partakes of the attraction and the mystery of Narcissus, the aloofness and frigidity of that spiritual celibate", Introduction to Valéry's *The Art of Poetry* (1958). Nijinksky danced the leading part in the Ballet Russe production of Fokine's *Narcisse* in Paris during TSE's time there in 1911. (*Bernstein* proposed Nijinsky's life as the source of numerous details in the poem, but datable events show that many of his speculations are wrong.) TSE to Anne Ridler, 30 Sept 1952: "St. Ishmael is a charming name (like St. Narcissus, of whom I know nothing)."

1 **the shadow of this gray rock**: Paul Elmer More: "those who rest here have found for themselves the shadow of a great rock in a weary land", *The Great Refusal* 127.

1–6 **gray rock · · · red rock: | I will show you**: reworked as *The Waste Land* [I] 26–30. Frazer: "prodigious precipices of red and grey rock", *The Golden Bough* V (*Adonis Attis Osiris* I) 120 (*Vickery* 251). TSE: "While all the East was weaving red with gray", *Before Morning* 1. "Go where the sunset reddens the last grey rock", *Murder in the Cathedral* II. To Aldous Huxley, 11 May 1923, of his essay *From the Grey Stone*: "I like your essay *From this Grey Rock* very much."

12–15, 27 **stifled and soothed · · · By the river · · · the pointed tips of his fingers · · · pink tips:** Laurence Hope: "Pale hands, pink tipped, like Lotus buds that float | On those cool waters where we used to dwell, | I would have rather felt you round my throat, | Crushing out life, than waving me farewell!" *Kashmiri*

Song (1901). Adapted for music by Amy Woodforde-Finden in 1902 and lastingly popular. (TSE: "pale" 19 *variant.*)

14 **the pointed corners of his eyes:** Nijinsky was mocked at the Imperial Ballet School because of the shape of his eyes, but after his successes in London and Paris these became fashionable (*Bernstein*).

14–15 **the pointed corners of his eyes ··· the pointed tips of his fingers:** "His pointed ears", *Mr. Apollinax* 19 (see note).

21 **he was sure that he had been a tree:** Herbert: "I reade, and sigh, and wish I were a tree", *Affliction* (I) 57. Pound: "I stood still and was a tree amid the wood ··· I have been a tree amid the wood", *The Tree* (1908).

23–26 **tangling its roots ··· clutch:** "What are the roots that clutch, what branches grow | Out of this stony rubbish?" *The Waste Land* [I] 19–20.

24–25 **fish | With slippery white belly held tight in his own fingers:** to Robert Sencourt, 30 Dec 1930, on Edith Wharton: "this poetry leaves me feeling as cold as if I had been ··· stroking a dead fish."

25 **slippery white belly:** "slimy belly", *The Waste Land* [III] 188.

25–27 **slippery ··· held tight in his own fingers ··· pink tips:** "grasped ··· Held in the hand ··· Slip from fingers slip | When freely fingered", *Bellegarde* 6–11.

33–34 **to God ··· his flesh was in love:** "the love of God is erotic: that is only a tautology after all", *The Varieties of Metaphysical Poetry* 276 (Turnbull Lecture II).

37 **his white skin:** "Is it white skin or perfume on a dress", *The Love Song of J. Alfred Prufrock* 65 *variant.*

37–39 **and satisfied him ··· With the shadow in his mouth:** Conrad: "opening his mouth voraciously as if to devour all the earth with all its mankind ··· a shadow insatiable of splendid appearances, of frightful realities; a shadow darker than the shadow of the night", *Heart of Darkness* pt. 3 (Shawn Worthington, personal communication).

To Helen

Published in *March Hare*.

Printed without title in *March Hare*, but in a letter to Christopher Ricks, 26 Sept 1996, Donald Gallup proposed that the title *To Helen* be adopted from *ms2*, which he considered the later of the two, as an emendation at 9 suggests. *Rainey* assigns *ms2* to Apr 1915.

Title ***To Helen***: writing to Olive Walker, 4 Feb 1946, Henry Eliot recalled of his brother that at twelve or thirteen "he liked best, of Poe's, the *To Helen*" (Houghton; Matthew Geary, personal communication). TSE on Poe: "His world is immaterial and ghostly, rather than spiritual. There are two poems entitled *To Helen*", *"A Dream within a Dream"* (1943). TSE went on to quote from *To Helen* ("I saw thee once"), for which see note to *The Waste Land* [I] 36, "hyacinth girl".

The other *To Helen* ("Helen, thy beauty is to me") is in *Oxf Bk of English Verse*; see note to *Three Sonnets* [III] 9 and variant (in *Noctes Binanianæ*). For Poe, see note to *Burbank with a Baedeker: Bleistein with a Cigar* 17.

1 **lavatory:** *Fowler*: "The euphemistic use, which will end in driving the word out of currency, is to be deprecated." OED 4: "An apartment furnished with apparatus for washing the hands and face. Now often including water-closets, etc" (from 1656), with 1845: "the gentlemen's room, denominated by a contemporary a Lavatory".

2–6 **a negro ··· Bringing a dish with oranges and bananas, | And another brought coffee and cigars ··· large mouth:** "The silent man in mocha brown | Sprawls at the window-sill and gapes; | The waiter brings in oranges | Bananas figs and hothouse grapes", *Sweeney Among the Nightingales* 17–20. To Eleanor Hinkley from Paris, 26 Apr 1911 (see note to *Interlude in London* 1): "And one looked through the windows, and the waiter brought in eggs and coffee, and the *Graphic* (which I conscientiously tried to read, to please them)." For a situation with a man, a waiter, a woman, a mouth, see *Hysteria*.

6–7 *variant* **wide mouth ··· suspended on the:** Shelley: "suspended on the sweep of the smooth wave ··· Yawned", *Alastor* 362–64. TSE: "the close rabble in the cinema ··· Wide mouthed", *WLComposite* **229–98** *ms1* [25–27]. (For Howells's "wide-mouthed chimney-places", see note to *Oh little voices of the throats of men* 47–49.)

6, 8 **large mouth ··· rabbit:** Tennyson: "A rabbit mouth that is ever agape", *Maud* I [x] 360. **white rabbit:** to Eleanor Hinkley, 3 Jan 1915, about his boarding-house: "Mrs. Nichols an elderly white rabbit with a very small timid daughter who plays solitaire when it rains".

8–9 **the corner ··· his nose:** "the corner of his nose", *Mandarins* 3 4.

After the turning of the inspired days

Published in *WLFacs.*

Assigned to Oct 1913 by *Rainey* 34. *Gordon* 87 proposes Harvard, 1914. Valerie Eliot: "The [hand]writing and the Laforguean ending indicate that it is an early poem", BBC broadcast 2 Nov 1971. The handwriting matches that of *I am the Resurrection and the Life* and that of *So through the evening, through the violet air*, which Valerie Eliot assigned to "1914 or even earlier" (see headnote), although it also matches TSE's letter to his father, 23 July 1915.

WLFacs 109 remarks that with the substitution of "After" for "And", 7 became *The Waste Land* [V] 322. *WLFacs* notes: Compare 1–10 with *The Waste Land* [V] 322–330. See headnote to *The Waste Land*, 1. COMPOSITION.

1–2, 5–6 **After the turning ··· After the praying and the silence and the crying ··· After the life and death ··· After the judges and the advocates and wardens:** "After the sunsets and the dooryards and the sprinkled streets, | After the novels, after the teacups, after the skirts that trail along the floor", *The Love Song of J. Alfred Prufrock* 101–102.

2, 10 **the silence and the crying ··· dying:** "silent sighing; | Somewhere the soul crying", *In silent corridors of death* 3–4.

4 **frosty vigil:** Arthur Lillie: "he has never known storm, shipwreck, captivity, fever, and wounds, the frosty vigil, and the burning march. He has never broken lance for the Holy cause", *The King of Topsy-Turvy* (1870) ch. II.

9 **shaking spears and flickering lights:** "The campfire shake the spears", *Song* ("The golden foot I may not kiss or clutch") 12. "I saw ··· The camp fire shake with alien spears", *The wind sprang up at four o'clock* 9–10.

13 **The world seemed futile:** G. T. W. Patrick: "This is the most costly and the most tragic of all the wars of history ··· modern wars are wholly futile ··· the whole European world has gone insane", *The Psychology of War* in *Popular Science* Aug 1915.

13 *variant* **The world was ended:** "*This is the way the world ends | Not with a bang but a whimper*", *The Hollow Men* V 28–31, and see note on warfare.

13 *variant* **The show was ended:** OED "show" *n.*[1] 15b: "*Mil. slang.* An engagement, battle, or raid; a war", with Kipling: "What was the end of all the show, Johnnie, Johnnie?" (*The Widow's Party*).

I am the Resurrection and the Life

Published in *WLFacs.*

Assigned to Oct 1913 by *Rainey* 34. *Gordon* 87 proposes Harvard, 1914. See headnote to *So through the evening, through the violet air.*

WLFacs notes: "This little poem was influenced by *The Bhagavad-Gita* (with perhaps a nod to Emerson's *Brahma*)", quoting *Bhagavad-Gita* ix 16, tr. R. C. Zaehner (1969). In Lionel D. Barnett's Temple Classics tr. (1905), the verse reads:

> I am the sacrifice. I am the offering.
> I am the father's oblation. I am the healing herb.
> I am the spell. I am the butter-libation,
> I am the fire, I am the offering.

(TSE's copy of this is dated by him "Cambridge 1912". For the *Gita*, see note to *The Burnt Dancer* 1–2 and headnote to *The Dry Salvages* III.) Emerson:

> They reckon ill who leave me out;
> When me they fly, I am the wings;
> I am the doubter and the doubt,
> And I the song the Brahmin sings.
>
> *Brahma* 9–12

(See notes to 4–5 and to *Ash-Wednesday* I 1.) Emerson's lines were quoted by Bradley in *Appearance and Reality* ch. XXVI, where they are compared with three stanzas of Baudelaire's *L'Héautontimorouménos* [*The Self-Punisher*]. *Gordon* 151 (acknowledging Michael Wood) points to the poem's penultimate stanza:

Je suis la plaie et le couteau!
Je suis le soufflet et la joue!
Je suis les membres et la roue,
Et la victime et le bourreau!

[I am the wound and the knife, I am the blow and the cheek, the limbs and the rack, the victim and the executioner!]

For Baudelaire's poem, see note to *Airs of Palestine, No. 2* 9.

Valerie Eliot: "Some Joyce scholars may think the poem was prompted by part of Stephen's soliloquy in the Scylla and Charybdis episode of *Ulysses* [IX], which, Eliot told John Quinn, he had lived on ever since he had read it; but I am inclined to believe that the influence was direct, because when my husband gave me his copy of the Hindu classic, he spoke of the fire and the butter", BBC broadcast 2 Nov 1971, referring to TSE's letter to Quinn [9 July 1919]. (*Ulysses*: "I am the fire upon the altar. I am the sacrificial butter", but this was not published until *Little Review* Apr 1919.) William James, comparing monism to "the Hindoo doctrine of the Brahman": "In the Bhagavat-gita the holy Krishna speaking for the One, says: 'I am the immolation. I am the sacrificial rite. I am the libation offered to ancestors. I am the drug. I am the incantation. I am the sacrificial butter also. I am the fire ··· Place thy heart on me, worshipping me, sacrificing to me, saluting me'", *Some Problems of Philosophy* ch. VII (see note to *The Love Song of J. Alfred Prufrock* 56–58). TSE to Egon Vietta, 23 Feb 1947: "Long before I was a Christian, I was a student of Indian philosophy, and of the Buddhist scriptures in Pali: both from study of some original texts, under teachers of Indic philology and philosophy at Harvard, and from an early interest in Schopenhauer and Deussen also in connexion with Sanskrit" (see headnote to *The Dry Salvages* III). See headnote to *The Waste Land*, 1. COMPOSITION, for relation of *I am the Resurrection and the Life* to Part V.

1 **I am the Resurrection and the Life**: John 11: 25.

3–4 **the wife ··· the sacrificial knife**: Henry James, of Mrs. Penniman: "to have the sacrificial knife ··· suddenly thrust into her hand", *Washington Square* ch. XXVIII.

4 **And the victim and the sacrificial knife**: TSE: "The victim and the sacrificial knife are perfectly adapted to each other", *"Son of Woman: The Story of D. H. Lawrence"* (1931), reviewing John Middleton Murry's study. (Valerie Eliot on this review: "he referred ironically to subject and author as 'the victim and the sacrificial knife'", BBC broadcast 2 Nov 1971.)

4–5 **the victim and the sacrificial knife ··· the butter also**: on an author who wrote "The victimiser and the victims are the same reality ··· this is tremendous truth", TSE wrote: "Tremendous, but yet a household word. It is our old acquaintance, the Red Slayer, *la plaie et le couteau!* [the wound and the knife!]", *"The World as Imagination"* (1918), reviewing Edward Douglas Fawcett.

5 **butter**: for the butter ("*gheé*") as used in sacrifice, see *Gita* iv 24 (*WLFacs* notes): "The process is Brahman, the clarified butter is Brahman, offered by Brahman in the fire of Brahman."

So through the evening, through the violet air

Published in *WLFacs.*

Assigned to Oct 1913 by *Rainey* 34. *Gordon* 87 proposes Harvard, 1914. Valerie Eliot: "Both the tone, reminiscent of the *Preludes*, and the [hand]writing suggest it is an early piece", BBC broadcast 2 Nov 1971. *WLFacs* notes, more specifically:

> In *An Anatomy of Melancholy*, Mr. Conrad Aiken mentioned that he had "long been familiar with such passages as 'A woman drew her long black hair out tight'" [13], which he "had seen as poems or part-poems, in themselves. And now saw inserted into *The Waste Land* as into a mosaic" (*The Sewanee Review* Winter 1966). It would seem from the handwriting that this poem, *After the turning*, and *I am the Resurrection* were written about 1914 or even earlier.

The Waste Land [V] 377–84 adapts 13–16 and 19–22. Additionally, the first line contributes to [V] 372 (see note), and the sixth to [V] 344–45. See headnote to *The Waste Land*, 1. COMPOSITION.

6 **sunbaked houses**: OED "adobe" 1: "An unburnt brick dried in the sun". 2: "A house made of adobe. *U.S.*" TSE: "brown baked features", *Little Gidding* II 41.

7–8, 16 **The ··· word that frees | The inspiration that delivers ··· wings**: "to set free the purity that clings ··· wings", *Bacchus and Ariadne* 16, 18.

9 **wrinkled road which twists**: "wrinkled ways", *Oh little voices of the throats of men* 6.

25 **It seems that I have been a long time dead**: "I feel | As if I'd been a long time dead", *The Little Passion: From "An Agony in the Garret" ms1* 7–8.

32 **about his hair the seaweed purple and brown**: "By sea-girls wreathed with seaweed red and brown", *The Love Song of J. Alfred Prufrock* 130.

Introspection

Published in *March Hare.*

Assigned to July–Aug 1915 by *Rainey* 198.

For prose poems, see *Hysteria* and headnote.

Title ***Introspection***: OED 2: "*spec.* (with no object expressed): The action of looking within, or into one's own mind"; anticipated by Dryden, 1695, "introspection into mine own mind", and then from 1807. Bradley: "I have set down ··· of Introspection that 'The one self-knowledge worth having is to know one's mind'", *Appearance and Reality*. TSE ruled the margins of this penultimate paragraph of the preface, and underlined Bradley's self-quotation. (For the same paragraph, see note to *Ash-Wednesday* II 36–38.) On "what is called Introspection", see Bradley in the note to *Entretien dans un parc* 5, 18, 21, 28.

TSE: "There is certainly an important field for psycho-physics and the study of behaviour, and there are even certain processes where introspection is not without value", *Knowledge and Experience* 82. To his mother, 11 Apr 1917: "I have some ideas for an Article on Introspective Consciousness." On Aiken's *The Charnel Rose*: "Mr. Aiken has gone in for psycho-analysis with a Swinburnian equipment; and he does not escape the fatal American introspectiveness; he is oversensitive and worried. He is tangled in himself", *Reflections on Contemporary Poetry* IV (1919). On 21 Aug 1916, TSE sent Aiken a Laforguean burlesque concluding "they turned a flip flop somersault and disappeared down their own throats, leaving the assembly in darkness". To I. A. Richards, 9 Aug 1930, on the impossible feat of "translating" Indian thought into the European tradition: "However, some such study (as far as one can) is I believe profitable, as getting outside of one's own skin, or jumping down one's own throat." Henry Adams: "society in America was always trying, almost as blindly as an earthworm, to realize and understand itself; to catch up with its own head, and to twist about in search of its tail"; "He knew no tragedy so heartrending as introspection ··· Ever since 1870 friends by scores had fallen victim to it. Within five-and-twenty years, a new library had grown out of it. Harvard College was a focus of the study; France supported hospitals for it; England published magazines of it", *The Education of Henry Adams* chs. XVI, XXIX.

six feet deep: traditional depth of a grave. **in a cistern and a brown snake:** *Antony and Cleopatra* II v: "So half my Egypt were submerged and made | A cistern for scaled snakes." **a brown snake ··· along the brick wall:** "Along the garden stairs | The sluggish python lies", *Circe's Palace* 10–11. **head having swallowed his tail:** "My thoughts in a tangled bunch of heads and tails", *The Death of the Duchess* II 28. The mythical snake that swallows its tail is Ouroboros.

The Engine

Published in *March Hare.*

The pencilled draft *ms1* is on notepaper from U.S.M.S. [United States Maritime Service] *St. Louis*, on which TSE sailed from Liverpool to New York, 24 July–1 Aug 1915. For wartime fears when crossing the Atlantic, see note to II, "if the ship goes down", and headnote to *Mr. Apollinax*.

Both drafts assigned to Apr 1915 by *Rainey* 198.

On TSE's prose poems, see *Introspection* and note, and *Hysteria. The Engine* has some likeness to Charles Vildrac's prose poems in *Découvertes* (1912). Aiken reported on the young TSE, back from Paris: "But what did we talk about? What to write, of course, and how to write, and what to read—Charles Louis Philippe and Vildrac, fresh from Paris—" (*March & Tambimuttu eds.* 22). Writing to Scofield Thayer, 14 Feb 1920, TSE listed Vildrac among half a dozen of the "more important men" (as poets) in France.

In Kipling's story *Bertran and Bimi* (1891), the first paragraph has "he roused himself", and "without ceasing" (TSE: "I roused myself" and "ceased"). On the next page, on board ship:

> Then we laid out our bedding in the bows · · · our forefoot · · · The ship · · · The trampling tune of the engines was very distinct, and the jarring of the ash-lift, as it was tipped into the sea, hurt the procession of hushed noise. Hans lay down by my side and lighted a good-night cigar. This was naturally the beginning of conversation. He owned a voice as soothing as the wash of the sea, and stores of experiences as vast as the sea itself; for his business in life was to wander up and down the world, collecting orchids and wild beasts and ethnological specimens for German and American dealers. I watched the glowing end of his cigar wax and wane in the gloom, as the sentences rose and fell, till I was nearly asleep.

(TSE: "The engine · · · American business men · · · cigar · · · life · · · smooth · · · I lay in bed · · · the wash · · · the scuffle of feet · · · the tune · · · the light · · · the ship · · · I thought drowsily".) For Kipling's story, see headnote to *Sweeney Among the Nightingales* and note to *Sweeney Erect* 9–12.

Title ***The Engine***: as a child of ten, TSE had included a train-story, *Bill's Escape*, in his magazine *Fireside* (No. 1, 28 Jan 1899, and No. 2, 29 Jan); ch. II: "He heard the toot of the engine, he did not know what to do. It was sure death"; and ch. III began: "The engine came on".

I

The engine hammered and hummed · · · The machine was hard, deliberate and alert: to Middleton Murry [mid-Apr? 1925]: "I have made myself into a *machine*. I have done it deliberately—in order to endure, in order not to feel—*but it has killed* V [Vivien]." Alice Corbin Henderson: "One can not turn oneself into a human machine", *The Rejection Slip* in *Poetry* July 1916. (TSE: "the human engine waits | Like a taxi throbbing waiting", *The Waste Land* [III] 216–17.) **American business men · · · The machine · · · The machine**: Van Wyck Brooks: "American civilization has not yet learned to accept the machinery of life as a premise. Your business man · · · really loves his business—which means that he loves the machine"; "An American · · · doesn't believe in impulses and intuitions, because they interfere with the silent, regular inexorable grinding of the machine"; "the machinery of life", *The Wine of the Puritans* 19, 29, 55 (TSE: "silent"); TSE reviewed the book in *Harvard Advocate* 7 May 1909. **American · · · motives**: Brooks 28: "America · · · simple motives". **American · · · machine · · · surface**: Brooks 37: "The American · · · makes a religion of the machine · · · appearance of being always on the surface". (TSE: "worshippers of the machine", *The Dry Salvages* I 10.) **Flat faces of American business men**: Henry James: "No impression so promptly assaults the arriving visitor of the United States as that of the overwhelming preponderance · · · of the unmitigated 'business man' face", *New York: An Autumn Impression* VIII in *The American Scene.* Vivien Eliot to Henry Eliot, 11 Oct [1916]: "dreadful people really—very very rich manufacturing people · · · my American friends tell me they are very much like Americans!! Tom has just met a few at Ilkley (in Yorkshire) · · · and he says the same—he was struck with how much more like Americans they are than the South of England people." TSE to Scofield Thayer, 30 June 1918: "pour the vials of contumely upon the fair flat face of the people" (the American people). "The white flat face of Death", *Murder in the Cathedral* II, third chorus. For *Flatland*, see note to *Animula* 2. **Flat faces of American business men ··· one plane, broken only by the salient ··· angle:** Henri Gaudier-Brzeska: "ECONOMIC ACTIVITIES BECOME NOXIOUS ··· I SHALL DERIVE MY EMOTIONS SOLELY FROM THE ARRANGEMENT OF SURFACES ··· THE PLACES AND LINES BY WHICH THEY ARE DEFINED ··· this hill where the Germans are solidly entrenched ··· broken up by earth-works", *Vortex* (Written from the Trenches) in *Blast* 2 (May 1915). OED "salient" 4: "Of an angle: Pointing outward", "chiefly in *Fortif.*" B. 2a: "a spur-like area of land, esp. one held by a line of offence or defence, as in trench-warfare; *spec.* (freq. with *the* and capital initial), that at Ypres in western Belgium, the scene of severe fighting in the war of 1914–18" (this sense from 1914). TSE to Isabella Stewart Gardner, 4 Apr [1915]: "I have been seeing a good deal of some of the modern artists whom the war has so far spared. One of the most interesting of the radicals—Gaudier-Brzeska—do you know of him?—is in the trenches, (as is the interesting T. E. Hulme); cubism is still represented by Wyndham Lewis, by Jacob Epstein, and a man whose work I like exceedingly, Edward Wadsworth. There has been an exhibition ··· Epstein's four things ··· are certainly extraordinarily *habile* ··· I do not know whether you have heard of a certain infamous soi-disant quarterly called *Blast* ··· I am thinking of sending you a copy." The art collector Isabella Stewart Gardner (sometimes known as "Mrs. Jack") was married to the American businessman John Lowell Gardner II. For a poem "like the time of the air-raids in London" and modern art with "planes and angles", see TSE's remarks at Vassar College, in headnote to *Sweeney Among the Nightingales.* An undated inventory at Yale of TSE's possessions includes "Wadsworth *Engine Room*". Inspired by Conrad's *Typhoon*, this large, angular woodcut (1914/15) may have been exhibited at the Doré Gallery's Vorticist Exhibition in June 1915. A scene from *Typhoon* IV, when the *Nan-Shan* is threatening to sink, provided a caption when the print was shown again in 1919: "the iron walls of the engine room. Painted white, they rose high into the dusk of the skylight, sloping like a roof: and the whole resembled the interior of a monument, divided by floors of iron grating, with lights flickering in the middle, within the columnar stir of the machinery" (for this print, and Gaudier-Brzeska's letters from the Front to Wadsworth, see Jonathan Black in *London, Modernism, and 1914* ed. Michael J. K. Walsh, 2010). Wadsworth designed the Ovid Press initials and colophon used in *Ara Vos Prec.* **magazine:** OED 2: *Mil.* "A building in which is stored a supply of arms, ammunition and provisions for an army in time of war." 3a: *Mil.* "Stores, provisions, munitions of war". 4. "A ship laden with stores" (*obs*). 6. "A chamber in a repeating rifle, machine-gun, etc." **The machine ··· having chosen with motives and ends unknown to cut ··· The machine was certain:** Epstein's sculpture *Rock Drill*, incorporating mechanical drill and abstract figure, was exhibited in the Second London Group exhibition, at the Goupil Gallery, in Mar 1915. TSE: "we have direct knowledge neither of our own nor of others' will; a simple man could no more have will than could a machine", *Cause as Ideal Construction* (1914). For "the chorus ··· ought to have a noise like a street drill", see headnote to *Sweeney Agonistes*, 10. PREMIÈRE IN AMERICA: ENTER AN OLD GENTLEMAN. **motives ··· unknown:** Pope: "Must act on motives powerful, though unknown", *An Epistle to Bathurst* 114 (with "men of pelf", 109; TSE: "business men"). **ends unknown:** "ends unshaped", *Entretien dans un parc* 30. "tendencies unknown",

Bacchus and Ariadne 4. **certain and sufficient as a rose bush:** Laforgue: "—Conséquemment, comme la rose | Est nécessaire à ses besoins" [—It follows, as the rose is necessary to its needs], *Dialogue avant le lever de la lune* [*Dialogue before the Rise of the Moon*] 19–20. "rosiers ··· suffisants" [roses ··· sufficient], *Complainte des pianos qu'on entend dans les quartiers aisés* [*Complaint of the Pianos that One Hears in the Comfortable Districts*] 35, 39.

II

the engine ··· I lay in bed ··· endless geological periods ··· the machine: "Keeping his seasons ··· the machine ··· His rhythm was present in the nursery bedroom ··· April ··· autumn ··· winter"; "The sleepy rhythm of a hundred hours", *The Dry Salvages* I 8–14; III 13 (see note). **the scuffle of feet ··· the music:** to Eleanor Hinkley, while crossing the Atlantic to Europe (postmark 7 July 1914): "we have great fun, especially when it comes to dancing to the sound of the captain's phonograph" (variant title for II: "*Machinery: Dancers*"). **taut as a drumhead:** perhaps assisted by the other, nautical, sense of drumhead: OED 3: "The circular top of a capstan". OED: "court martial" 1b: "*drumhead court-martial* ··· summoned round an upturned drum, for summary treatment of offenders during military operations". TSE: "the deck of the drumming liner", *The Dry Salvages* III 19 (see note). **if the ship goes down:** the passenger ship *Lusitania* was sunk by a German submarine, 7 May 1915, with more than a thousand dead, a hundred being Americans. See headnote to *Mr. Apollinax.*

Hidden under the heron's wing

Published in *March Hare.* Date unknown.

1 **Hidden under the heron's wing:** "hidden under the dove's wing", *Coriolan* I. *Triumphal March* 32; and "hidden under the ··· Hidden under the ···", *Coriolan* II. *Difficulties of a Statesman* 32. "After the kingfisher's wing", *Burnt Norton* IV 8. **heron's wing:** Edith Wharton: "the cleverly planted heron wing in her fur cap", *The Age of Innocence* (1920) ch. 31.

2 **song before daybreak:** Swinburne, *Songs before Sunrise.* TSE, *Before Morning* (title). Jean Verdenal to TSE, 22 Apr 1912: "Je suis comme si j'avais toujours vécu à l'aube et comme si bientôt le soleil allait paraître" [It is as if I had always lived before daybreak and the sun were just about to rise], printed in *Letters 1*.

2–4 **song before daybreak that the lotos-birds sing ··· my beloved what do you bring:** Song of Solomon 2: 12, 16–17: "The time of the singing of birds is come ··· My beloved is mine, and I am his: He feedeth among the lilies. Until the day break, and the shadows flee away, Turn, my beloved". OED, "lotos" 6: "The *Parra gallinacea,* which in Australia is called the lotus-bird. It sits on the leaves that float on the water, particularly those of the water-lily". (For "the lotos rose", see note to *Burnt Norton* I 36.) **daybreak ··· sing ··· stars together:** Job 38: 7: "When the morning stars sang together".

2–8 **song ··· sing ··· whisper of ··· mist. || I lie ··· crimson:** Tennyson: "Glow with the glow that slowly crimsoned all ··· while I lay, | Whispering ··· Like that strange song I heard Apollo sing, | While Ilion like a mist rose into towers", *Tithonus* 56–63.

3 **Evening whisper of stars together**: "in the darkness | Whispering all together", *Prufrock's Pervigilium* [16–17]. "whispers in darkness", *Murder in the Cathedral* opening chorus.

5 **With evening feet walking across the grass:** Wyatt: "With naked foot stalking in my chamber", *They flee from me that sometime did me seek* 2 (see note to *Paysage Triste* 10–12).

6 **fragile arms:** *Paradise Regained* III 387–89: "Much ostentation vain of fleshly arm, | And fragile arms, much instrument of war | Long in preparing, soon to nothing brought". **dividing the evening mist:** *Paradise Lost* XII 629: "Gliding meteorous, as evening mist".

6–8 **arms ··· crimson fist:** *Paradise Lost* II 173–4: "arm again | His red right hand". **I ··· the housemaid's crimson fist:** "I am aware of the damp souls of housemaids", *Morning at the Window* 3 (here, "daybreak", 2). The maid Amanda "With coarsened hand, and hard plebeian tread", *WLComposite* 235.

O lord, have patience

Published in *March Hare.* Date unknown.

The top two-thirds of the ms page are given to the three widely spaced lines of Dante, each underlined, with TSE's quatrain immediately following the third of them. TSE may have intended to supply verses to follow each of Dante's three lines. In *Dante* (1929) I, he quoted the second tercet of *Inferno* III:

> We cannot understand the inscription at Hell Gate:
>
> *Giustizia mosse il mio alto Fattore;*
> *fecemi la divina Potestate,*
> *la somma Sapienza e il primo Amore.*
>
> *Justice moved my high Maker; what made me were the divine Power, the supreme Wisdom, and* the primal Love.
>
> until we have ascended to the highest Heaven and returned.

(TSE emends the Temple Classics translation, and in *Selected Essays* put "the primal Love" in roman type for emphasis.) The opening of *Inferno* III is quoted again by TSE at the end of the first section of *Dante* (1929). In *Two Studies in Dante* (1928), he had written about "what is certainly the central idea of the Divine Comedy—the idea of Justice": "the importance of the conception of Justice in the Divine Comedy can hardly be over-estimated"; "The Aristotelian 'justice' as taken over by Dante is a term with progressive enlargement of meaning, from social or legal justice to Divine justice, which are related but not identical. It is largely due, we believe, to the romantic conception of justice that the Inferno has been, especially among Anglo-Saxon and Northern readers, the most popular and most apparently intelligible part of the Comedy." Paul Elmer More thought well of TSE's *Dante* essay, but TSE wrote to him, 2 June 1930: "I am perturbed by your comments on Hell. To me it *is giustizia, sapienza, amore.* And I cannot help saying, with all due respect of a (somewhat) younger and (much) more ignorant man, that I am really shocked by your assertion that God did not make Hell. It seems to me that you have lapsed into Humanitarianism. The Buddhist eliminates Hell · · · only by eliminating everything positive about Heaven (uttama paranibbana being obviously not heaven). Is your God Santa Claus?" *Crawford* 42–43 noted that TSE probably read Dante later than (and in some way in the light of) James Thomson, who twice adopts the inscription at Hell Gate: "They leave all hope behind who enter there", "Leave hope behind, all ye who enter here", *The City of Dreadful Night* I 78; VI 210.

1 **O lord, have patience**: Matthew 18: 26, 29: "The servant therefore fell down, and worshipped him, saying, Lord, have patience with me · · · Have patience."

2 **derelictions**: OED 1: "The action of leaving or forsaking (with intention not to resume); abandonment. (Now *rare* exc. in legal use.)" The religious application is clear from OED, in Donne: "Desertion, or Dereliction"; and in Jeremy Taylor: "Repentance and dereliction of sins". The modern use (OED 2), "implying a morally wrong or reprehensible abandonment or neglect; chiefly in the phr. *dereliction of duty*", dates from 1778, Burke.

2, 4 **derelictions · · · my · · · convictions**: Browning: "Let me enjoy my own conviction · · · Still spying there some dereliction | Of truth, perversity, forgetfulness!" *Christmas-Eve* 1144–47.

In silent corridors of death

Published in *March Hare.*

Undated. The manuscript at one time belonged to Vivien Eliot's brother, Maurice Haigh-Wood, who was commissioned 2nd lieutenant in the Manchester Regiment, 12 May 1915. It is likely that he was the author of the first-hand account of the Front which was published with TSE's introductory remarks as a letter in *Nation* 23 June 1917 (repr. TSE's *Letters 1*). Its author complained:

> It is hideously exasperating to hear people talking the glib commonplaces about the war and distributing cheap sympathy to its victims.
>
> Perhaps you are tempted to give them a picture of a leprous earth, scattered with the swollen and blackening corpses of hundreds of young men. The appalling stench of rotting carrion mingled with the sickening smell of exploded lyddite and ammonal. Mud like porridge, trenches like shallow and sloping cracks in the porridge—porridge that stinks in the sun · · · But these are only words, and probably convey only a fraction of their meaning to their hearers.

Among Vivien Eliot's papers and evidently typed at the same time as *Necesse est Perstare?* by "F. M." (*Criterion* Apr 1925; see note to *The Hollow Men* V 25–27) is a fair copy ts of a poem, *Perque Domos Ditis Vacuas*, also "by F. M.":

> It was after the acrobats
> And I left my box
> And ran along the corridor
> Fast
> Because I wanted to get into the air into the air

And in the suffused light of the empty corridor
In the stale air and soft suffused light of the corridor
In the deathly airlessness of the silent corridor
In the stifling scent of death and suffocation of the corridor
I met my own eyes
In another face.

(c. 624 fol. 10)

The title is from *Aeneid* VI 269 [through the empty halls of Dis], describing the entrance to Hades (see *McCue 2016*).

1 **silent corridors of death**: adapting T. E. Hulme, Pound's *Catholic Anthology* (1915) contains *Poem: Abbreviated from the Conversation of Mr. T. E. H.* (subscribed TRENCHES: ST. ELOI), which ends: "My mind is a corridor. The minds about me are corridors. | Nothing suggests itself. There is nothing to do but keep on" (George Simmers, personal communication). TSE, reviewing an anthology of war poets: "Mr. Osborn has omitted one dead soldier who was a real poet—T. E. Hulme", *The New Elizabethans and the Old* (1919).

1–2 **death | Short sighs**: "I had not thought death had undone so many. | Sighs, short and infrequent, were exhaled", *The Waste Land* [I] 63–64.

3–4 **silent sighing ··· crying**: likewise rhyming with "dying", *After the turning of the inspired days* 2: "the silence and the crying" (*1st reading*: "the silence and the sighing").

4 **the soul crying**: Proverbs 19: 18: "let not thy soul spare for his crying".

6 **without hope**: "I said to my soul, be still, and wait without hope", *East Coker* III 23. See note to *The Dry Salvages* II 42–47.

7, 9, 11–12 **Without pressure ··· dying ··· warm ··· airless**: "Moving without pressure, over the dead leaves, | In the autumn heat, through the vibrant air," *Burnt Norton* I 24–25.

12 **Dry airless**: "sunless dry", *Rhapsody on a Windy Night* 63. "air which is now thoroughly small and dry", *Ash-Wednesday* I 30.

12–13 **airless sweet scent | Of the alleys of death**: *Hamlet* I v, GHOST, of his death by poison: "alleys of the body" (after "scent the morning air"). *The Times* 28 Dec 1916, on "Christmas at the Front": "the battalion had been roused to the crisp, chill dawn to sniff the sickly sweet scent of the rolling gas-cloud" (for "scent of death and suffocation" in *Perque Domos Ditis Vacuas*, see headnote).

12, 14 **airless sweet scent ··· corridors of death**: "apprehension deeper than all sense, | Deeper than the sense of smell, but like a smell | In that it is indescribable, a sweet and bitter smell | From another world", Harry to Mary, *The Family Reunion* I ii, after speaking of "a corridor ··· every corridor". In II ii, Agatha speaks of walking "down a concrete corridor | In a dead air", and in her next speech: "Up and down, through the stone passages | Of an immense and empty hospital | Pervaded by a smell of disinfectant." *Murder in the Cathedral* I: "more pain than birth or death. | Sweet and cloying through the dark air | Falls the stifling scent of despair."

13 **Of the alleys of death**: Tennyson: "Into the valley of death", *The Charge of the Light Brigade*.

Airs of Palestine, No. 2

Published in *March Hare.*

Assigned to 1917 by *Rainey* 198.

TSE to Aiken, 21 Aug 1916: "I have been writing: philosophy for the *Monist* and the *International Journal of Ethics*, reviews for the *New Statesman*, the *Manchester Guardian* and the *Westminster Gazette* · · · Of poetry I have not written a line; I have been far too worried and nervous. I hope that the end of another year will see me in a position to think about verse a bit." To his mother, 6 Sept 1916: "The *Westminster* have given some novels to do." The following day, to J. H. Woods: "I am doing considerable reviewing for the *Westminster Gazette*—all sorts of things from Durkheim and Boutroux down to *Village Government in India* and even H. de Vere Stacpoole's novels. I got hold of their Indian books by telling them that I was a student of Sanskrit and Pali—whereupon they gave me several books on contemporary Indian politics." But on 30 Jan 1917, Pound wrote to Harriet Shaw Weaver: "I am afraid Eliot has split with *The Westminster.*" For TSE and newspapers, see headnote to *The "Boston Evening Transcript".*

In a letter to John Middleton Murry, [Nov?] 1919, TSE adapted the first and third stanzas to deplore J. C. Squire, active in the publications named by TSE:

God from a Cloud to Squire spoke
And breath'd command: take thou this Rod
And smite therewith the living Rock;
And Squire hearken'd unto God.

And Squire smote the living Rock,
And Lo! the living Rock was wet—
Whence issue, punctual as the clock
  Land and Water,
  The New Statesman,
  The Owl,
  The London Mercury,
  And the *Westminster Gazette*

Squire was literary editor of the *New Statesman* from its inception in 1913 and acting editor 1917–18. (TSE contributed 1916–18.) He was founding editor, 1919–34, of the *London Mercury*, and published widely. Reviewing *Georgian Poetry 1916–1917*, ed. Edward Marsh, TSE called Squire's *Lily of Malud* "an original and rather impressive poem which deserves better company", *Verse Pleasant and Unpleasant* (1918). TSE to John Quinn, 25 Jan 1920, of the *London Mercury*: "J. C. Squire, the editor, knows nothing about poetry; but he is the cleverest journalist in London. If he succeeds, it will be impossible to get anything good published. His influence controls or affects the literary contents and criticism of five or six periodicals already. The *Times* [*TLS*] always more or less apart, the *Athenaeum* (and, of less influence, *Art & Letters*) are the only important reviews outside of the Squire influence."

Squire wrote that after several readings of *The Waste Land*, he was "still unable to make head or tail of it", despite the impression that "Mr. Eliot does mean something by it, has been at great pains to express himself, and believes himself to be exploring a new avenue ··· Mr. Eliot believes the poem to be about the decay of Western civilisation and his own utter sickness with life ··· A grunt would serve equally well", *London Mercury* Oct 1923. For his review of *1925*, see headnote to *Ash-Wednesday* II.

Title ***Airs of Palestine***: John Pierpont, who had attended Harvard Divinity School, established his reputation as a poet with *Airs of Palestine* (1816, new ed. 1840); see note to 25. ***No. 2***: as a sequel to Pierpont and, in the context of journalism, as though an issue number. Also OED "number" 5f: "number one, a children's word or euphemism for 'urine'; similarly number two for 'fæces'", citing 1902, "*Number two.* (nursery). Evacuation."

1 **God from a Cloud to Spender spoke**: Exodus 24: 16: "and the seventh day he called unto Moses out of the midst of the cloud". J. A. Spender edited the *Westminster Gazette* (founded 1893) from 1896 to 1922: "one of the most remarkable editorships in British journalism", *DNB*. Spender in 1940: "Eliot, on his own showing, requires the reading of a whole reference library for the understanding of his *Waste Land*. I say to him, this may be a curious and interesting new literary product, but there is no definition of poetry to which it corresponds" (Wilson Harris, *J. A. Spender*, 1946, 60). Stephen Spender was his nephew.

2–3 **And breathed command: "Take thou this Rod, | And smite therewith the living Rock"**: Numbers 20: 8–11: "And the Lord spake unto Moses, saying, Take the rod ··· And Moses took the rod from before the Lord, as he commanded him ··· And Moses lifted up his hand, and with his rod he smote the rock twice: and the water came out abundantly." Exodus 17: 5–6: "thy rod ··· take in thine hand ··· and thou shalt smite the rock, and there shall come water out of it". Browning: "He who smites the rock and spreads the water | Bidding drink and live a crowd beneath him", *One Word More* [10] 74–75. TSE quoted from Browning's poem in a letter to Scofield Thayer, 7 May 1916. **the living Rock**: OED "living" 2d: "Of rock, stone: Native, in its native condition and site, as part of the earth's crust." Widespread, including Wordsworth, Joanna Baillie and Tennyson. From the living Rock there might have issued living waters (biblical; OED 2d (*a*): "constantly flowing; also refreshing").

5–6 **Cloud ··· the swart tempestuous blast**: Shakespeare: "clouds ··· the swart-complexioned night", Sonnet 28 (in *Oxf Bk of English Verse*).

6 **Riding the ··· blast**: *Macbeth* I vii: "striding the blast". For the same speech see note to *Ode* ("Tired. | Subterrene") 20 (*Mahaffey*).

9 **struck the ··· Rock**: Baudelaire: "Je te frapperai ··· Comme Moïse le rocher!" [I shall strike you ··· as Moses struck the rock], *L'Héautontimorouménos* [*The Self-Punisher*] 1, 3. Arnold: "Youth rambles on life's arid mount, | And strikes the rock, and finds the vein", *The Progress of Poesy* 1–2.

11–12 **henceforth at twelve o'clock | Issues**: the *Westminster Gazette* was issued at mid-day; *Baedeker* listed it first of the six "leading evening papers". *Paradise Lost* VI 9–10: "Light issues forth, and at the other door | Obsequious darkness enters, till her hour". Noon is the hour of the Fall in *Paradise Lost*. **Issues:**

Ezekiel 47: 1, 8, 12: "and, behold, waters issued out from under the threshold ··· These waters issue out toward the east country ··· because their waters they issued out of the sanctuary". TSE: "'Issues from the hand of God, the simple soul'", *Animula* 1.

13–15 **Swift ··· pen ··· viscid torrents ··· dogs:** Swift's *A Description of a City Shower*, published in *The Tatler*, has torrential floods in London's streets feeding into the notorious Fleet ditch at Holborn Bridge, with "Sweepings from Butcher's Stalls, Dung, Guts, and Blood, | Drown'd Puppies, stinking Sprats, all drench'd in Mud" (61–62). Pope:

> To where Fleet-ditch with disemboguing streams
> Rolls the large tribute of dead dogs to Thames,
> The King of dykes! than whom no sluice of mud
> With deeper sable blots the silver flood ···
> Who flings most filth, and wide pollutes around
> The stream, be his the Weekly Journals bound
> *The Dunciad* (1742) II 271–74, 279–80

Fleet ditch, the underground river, gave its name to Fleet Street and hence to "gutter journalism" and "gutter press" (OED, from 1888 and 1899). For the Thames and journalistic corruption (*The Spectator*) see *Le Directeur* 1–5 and notes. For Tailhade, "the Seine throws up dead dogs", see note to *Goldfish* IV 9.

14 **The viscid torrents:** the rivers of Hell, *Paradise Lost* II 577–81, particularly "Abhorred Styx the flood of deadly hate" and "fierce Phlegeton | Whose waves of torrent fire inflame with rage".

14–15 **torrents ··· dogs and men:** Pope: "streams ··· And men and dogs shall drink him till they burst", *Epistle to Bathurst* 177–78. **dogs and men:** frequently together in the *Iliad* (Pope's tr.: "dogs, and voice of men", XII 164; "dogs and men", XIII 600; "men and dogs", XV 308; "the dogs, the men", XVIII 673). TSE: "the Dog ··· that's friend to men", *The Waste Land* [I] 74.

14–20 **The viscid torrents ··· long lanes ··· Bubble those floods of bilious green:** Tennyson: "a tide of fierce | Invective seemed to wait behind her lips, | As waits a river level with the dam | Ready to burst and flood the world with foam ··· Long lanes of splendour slanted o'er a press", *The Princess* IV 450–57. TSE: "Subterrene laughter ··· bubbling ··· river", *Ode* ("Tired. | Subterrene") 2–5. **long lanes:** Long Lane runs through what was a working-class area of Southwark.

15–19 **of dogs ··· Canning Town and Rotherhithe ··· Bermondsey ··· Wapping Stair ··· Clapham Junction ··· Sheen ··· Leicester ··· Grosvenor Square:** on John Davidson: "I have a fellow feeling with the poet who could look with a poet's eye on the Isle of Dogs and Millwall Dock", *John Davidson* (1961). ("Down Greenwich reach | Past the Isle of Dogs", *The Waste Land* [III] 275–76.) **Wapping Stair:** see note to *Billy M'Caw: The Remarkable Parrot* 33–34.

18–21 **Sheen ··· green ··· street of gems:** Milton, *Comus* 893–97 (extracted in *Oxf Bk of English Verse*):

> Thick set with agate, and the azurn sheen
> Of turkis blue, and emerald green
>   That in the channel strays,
> Whilst from off the waters fleet
> Thus I set my printless feet

John Gray: "EMERALD, exceeding green, | Doth present an olive sheen", *The Twelve Precious Stones* (1896). **Sheen ··· green**: Shelley: "And bulrushes, and reeds of such deep green | As soothed the dazzled eye with sober sheen", *The Question* 31–32 (in *Oxf Bk of English Verse*).

20 **bilious green**: the *Westminster Gazette* was printed on green paper "which Carlyle would probably have considered a compliment to Robespierre's complexion" (*Spectator* 11 Feb 1893). William Morris: "Still beaten by the billows green", *The Life and Death of Jason* bk. IV 594, with "two fair streams ··· Drawn down unto the restless sea", 589–91 (extracted in *Oxf Bk English Verse*; see note to 27). Baudelaire's *Spleen* ("Je suis comme le roi") ends with: "l'eau verte du Léthé" [Lethe's green tide]. Pope: "what street, what lane but knows, | Our purgings ··· And the fresh vomit run for ever green", *The Dunciad* (1742) II 153–56 (TSE: "lanes"). Shelley: "London, that great sea, whose ebb and flow ··· Vomits its wrecks", *Letter to Maria Gisborne* 193–94.

21 **Old Bond Street, the street of gems**: home to many jewellery firms.

21, 23 **gems ··· Thames**: rhymed in Spenser's *Prothalamion* 11–14. For Spenser's refrain, "sweet Thames run softly, till I end my Song", see note to *The Waste Land* [III] 175–84.

21–27 **gems ··· the torrent flows ··· pearly wall ··· Mary's garden**: commonplaces of hymns such as *The New Jerusalem*: "Thy walls are made of precious stones ··· Thy gates are of right orient pearl ··· Thy gardens ··· Quite through the streets, with silver sound, | The flood of Life doth flow ··· Our Lady sings *Magnificat*" (in *Oxf Bk of English Verse*). For this anonymous hymn, derived from Revelation 21–22, see note to *The Waste Land* [III] 231.

25 **the torrent flows**: John Pierpont: "see at his foot, the cool Cephissus flow", "On Arno's bosom, as he calmly flows", *Airs of Palestine* 70, 569.

27 **Wherein, by Mary's garden close**: close by / garden close. In *Andrew Marvell* (1927), TSE quoted the first five lines of what, following *Oxf Bk of English Verse*, he called *The Nymph's Song to Hylas* by William Morris, beginning: "I know a little garden close | Set thick with lily and red rose" (*The Life and Death of Jason* bk. IV 577–79). OED "close" 2d: "The precinct of any sacred place", with pronunciation "as in the adj." Despite this, the rhyme "garden close ··· rose" appeared in both Wilde's *Panthea* and John Gray's *Fleurs: Imitated from the French of Stéphane Mallarmé*, and TSE here rhymes "flows ··· garden close".

31 **all their sin**: Milton, Psalm LXXXV 7.

32 **navel**: Proverbs 3: 7: "fear the Lord ··· it shall be health to thy navel".

34 **Attain ··· the farther shore**: OED "attain" 6: "to arrive at", with 1585: "We quickly shall attain the English shore"; 1854: "attained the opposite shore". Pope's Homer: "Now give thy hand, for to the farther shore", *Iliad* XXIII 93. Virgil, of the dead in the underworld: "stabant orantes primi transmittere cursum | tendebantque manus ripae ulterioris amore" [They stood, pleading to be the first ferried across, and stretched out hands in yearning for the farther shore], *Aeneid* VI 313–14. TSE: "Here between the hither and the farther shore", *The Dry Salvages* III 29.

35 **Cleansed and rejoiced**: "But every week we hear rejoice ··· Blood of the Lamb shall wash him clean", *The Hippopotamus* 19, 29.

35–36 **rejoiced ··· the Germans:** *The Education of Henry Adams* ch. XX: "Germany was never so powerful, and the Assistant Professor of History had nothing else as his stock in trade. He imposed Germany on his scholars with a heavy hand. He was rejoiced."

36 **hate the Germans:** this, despite Spender's having been considered a German sympathiser before the war.

37–38 **redeemed from ··· frowardness:** Tennyson: "Redeemed it from the charge of nothingness", *Morte d'Arthur: The Epic* 279. **frowardness:** Proverbs: "the frowardness of the wicked", 2: 14; "Frowardness is in his heart", 6: 14; "the mouth of the wicked speaketh frowardness", 10: 32.

39 **The scales are fallen from their eyes:** Acts 9: 18: "And immediately there fell from his eyes as it had been scales: and he received sight forthwith, and arose, and was baptized" (TSE: "Cleansed", 35).

Petit Epître

Published in *March Hare.*

Assigned to Mar–Oct 1917 by *Rainey* 198. TSE wrote to his mother, 11 Apr 1917, that besides his lectures and reviewing, he had "been doing some writing—mostly in French, curiously enough it has taken me that way—and some poems in French which will come out in the *Little Review* in Chicago". Of the four French poems published by TSE, three (*Le Directeur*, *Mélange Adultère de Tout* and *Lune de Miel*) appeared in the *Little Review* in July 1917, along with *The Hippopotamus* (which adapted a poem by Théophile Gautier). The fourth, *Dans le Restaurant*, appeared there in Sept 1918. See headnote to "*Poems* (1920)", 5. TSE'S PROFICIENCY IN FRENCH.

[*Little Epistle*]

[It's not to disgust everyone, or to sip from the sewer of my ego, that I made verses out of everyday trivia, smelling somewhat of sauerkraut. But what on earth have I done to bring out the jackals? I said that there's a male smell and also a female smell, and that these are not the same. (The other day, the third Thursday in Lent, I noted this, in company of one of the latter.) Which is what the priest says, but in other words. Above all in the rutting season. So they made a rumpus and broke both of my windows. What on earth have I done to stir up these crab-lice? I will tell you what I've done: I imagined a Paradise where goods were equally shared (where equally I would have yours). The honourable chief of police has had his fill of such vices, and mutters through his bespectacled nose: "This is promiscuity." So I had to pay him five hundred francs, by way of a fine. The gentlemen of the press and all the rest, blackmailers and the name-tag people one and all, have drawn up their questionnaires for me. "He makes fun of Equality?" —"But he's a proper reactionary." —"He bad-mouths our ministers?" —"Why he's a saboteur, the prig." —"Is he quoting some German here?" —"He belongs in hell!" —"Does he doubt the afterlife?" —"An immoralist, for sure." —"Does he not doubt the existence of God?" —"How superstitious of him!" —"Has he no children?" —"He's a eunuch, clearly."

—"Does he not demand the vote for women?" —"A pederast, undoubtedly." —"As for his book, who gives a shit!" The gibberish of these monkeys, I hear it wherever I go.]

Tristan Corbière has a sardonic self-portrait, with aggressive officials and gossips:

> Le curé se doutait que c'était un lépreux;
> Et le maire disait: —Moi, qu'est-ce que j'y peux,
> C'est plutôt un Anglais . . . un *Être.*
>
> Les femmes avaient su—sans doute par les buses—
> Qu'il *vivait en concubinage avec des Muses!* . . .
> Un hérétique enfin . . . Quelque *Parisien*
> De Paris ou d'ailleurs

[The parish priest suspected it was a leper; and the mayor said: "As for me, what can I do, it's pretty sure to be an Englishman . . . some *Being* or other". The women had known—no doubt from the buzzards—that he *was living in sin with the Muses!* A heretic, and there's an end of it . . . Some *Parisian* from Paris or somewhere else]

Le Poète contumace [*The Contumacious Poet*] 24–30

Similarly the interrogation in *Le Renégat* [*The Renegade*] 15, 22: "son nom?", "Coup de barre du vice?" [his name? Paying over the odds for vice?]

1–2 **dégoute | Ou gout d'égout**: Corbière: "—Son goût était dans le dégoût" [His taste was for the distasteful], *Epitaphe* 47. (For Corbière's poem see note on the title *Mélange Adultère de Tout.*) Corbière again: "Moi j'en suis dégoûté.— | Dans mes dégoûts surtout, j'ai des goûts élégants" [In my distastes above all, I have elegant tastes], *Le Poète contumace* [*The Contumacious Poet*] 82–83; "Pur, à force d'avoir purgé tous les dégoûts" [Pure, as a result of having purged all disgusts], ending of *Le Renégat* [*The Renegade*]. In his copy of Pater's *Studies in the History of the Renaissance* ch VI, TSE scored the words: "For the way to perfection is through a series of disgusts".

8 **une odeur fémelle**: see note to *Rhapsody on a Windy Night* 66, "female smells in shuttered rooms".

37 **un suppôt de Satan**: Hell-hound. To Paul Elmer More, 7 Nov 1933, about *After Strange Gods*: "Lawrence appears as a *suppôt de Satan*".

43 **eunuque**: often in Corbière, for instance: "nous avons la police | Et quelque chose en nous d'eunuque et de recors" [We have the police and in us something of the eunuch and of the minion of the law], *Féminin singulier* 7–8.

Tristan Corbière

Published in *March Hare*.

Assigned to 1917 by *Rainey* 198. See Pound to Joyce, 19 Apr 1917, on TSE's burst of "scurrilous french", quoted in headnote to "*Poems* (1920)", 5. TSE'S PROFICIENCY IN FRENCH.

Greene 62 reported that TSE first read Corbière in *Poètes d'aujourd'hui*, the anthology he acquired in 1909 or soon after, and that he deepened his study in the years 1915–20. Greene is probably incorrect in saying that TSE acquired his copy of Corbière's *Les Amours jaunes* during his stay in Paris in 1910, for the copy he kept is dated 1912. In the Table at the back, TSE has marked all six of the *Rondels pour après.* In the Notebook, after the final blank leaves and stubs, on versos of unnumbered leaves and upside down in relation to the front of the volume, TSE made copies in black ink of two of them, *Do, l'enfant do . . .* adding "T. C." at the end; and that beginning "Il fait noir, enfant" [It's getting dark, child], adding "Corbière". Two of the other *Rondels* are pencilled by TSE on separate leaves laid in at the back of the Notebook: *Mirliton* [*Doggerel*] and *Petit mort pour rire* [*Little dead one for fun*], the second with the addition of the name and Paris address of Albert Messein, publisher of the 1912 edition of *Les Amours jaunes*.

[*Tristan Corbière*]

["For a moment he became Parisian."]

[Sailor! I know you, rentier from the fifth floor, watching out the night like an old owl; clearing your throat, you whom they call *an Ankou*, crouched on a pallet, with pointed beard, ghost-faced. In the next room scandals are hatching, a Portuguese office-clerk and a ten-cent queen of the night: between the whisperings through various holes—the sea batters the Breton coast in gusts. On a warm afternoon in the Luxembourg Gardens, sunbeams show us grizzled gentlemen, frock-coated, winking at pomaded ladies. And Lieutenant Loti, looking very dapper, strolls through the pages of the complacent Reviews like an old retired tart taking up her post on the boulevard.]

Epigraph **"Il devint pour un instant parisien"**: adapting Verlaine's essay *Tristan Corbière* in *Les Poètes maudits* [*The Cursed Poets*]: "Il devint Parisien un instant, mais sans le sale esprit mesquin · · · de la bile et de la fièvre s'exaspérant en génie et jusqu'à quelle gaieté!" [He immediately became a Parisian, but in a shabby mean-minded frame of mind · · · bile and fever exacerbating themselves within him to the point of high spirits!] Corbière himself had written of "Quelque *Parisien* | De Paris ou d'ailleurs" [Some *Parisian* from Paris or somewhere else], *Le Poète contumace* [*The Contumacious Poet*] 29–30.

1 **Marin!**: Corbière was a sailor and the son of a sea-captain. His poem *Matelots* [*Sailors*] has its exclamation: "Matelots!" (97). The paragraph from Verlaine quoted by Le Goffic (see note to epigraph) began: "Tristan Corbière fut un Breton, un marin et le dédaigneux par excellence" [Tristan Corbière was a Breton, a sailor and the perfect disdainer]. **Marin! je te connais**: "There I saw one I knew, and stopped him, crying: 'Stetson! | 'You who were with me in the ships at Mylae! · · ·'" *The Waste Land* [I] 69–70. **je te connais**: Baudelaire: "Tu le connais, lecteur, ce monstre délicat, | —Hypocrite lecteur,—mon semblable,—mon frère!" [Dear Reader, you are well acquainted with that fastidious monster—hypocritical Reader—my second self—my brother!], the close of *Au lecteur* [*To the Reader*]; quoted as the close of *The Waste Land* I.

2 **Qui veillait dans la nuit comme un vieil hibou**: Corbière, of himself: "Lui, seul hibou payant" [He, the only paying owl], *Le Poète contumace* 19; and again: "Voleur de nuit, hibou d'amour" [Night-thief, owl of love], *Guitare* 7.

3 **toi qu'on nomme *an Ankou***: Le Goffic's preface to *Les Amours jaunes* began: "Le Ier mars 1875, dans la trentième année de son âge, s'éteignait à Morlaix

un pauvre être falot, rongé de phtisie, perclus de rheumatismes et si long et si maigre et si jaune que les marins bretons, ses amis, l'avaient baptisé *an Ankou* (la Mort)" [On the 1st of May 1875, in the thirtieth year of his age, there was becoming extinguished a poor lamp of a creature, eaten away by phthisis, crippled with rheumatism and so lanky and so thin and so yellow that the Breton sailors, his friends, had christened him *an Ankou* (a Dead Man)]. Again: "la maladie en fit une pauvre caricature d'homme, l'espèce d'*Ankou*, de spectre ambulant dont se moquaient les Roscovites" [sickness made him a poor caricature of a man, a kind of *Ankou*, a walking spectre whom the Bretons of Roscoff made mock of]. Pound on Corbière: "his personal appearance had earned him the nickname 'an Ankou' (the corpse)", *New Age* 2 Oct 1913. Corbière uses the word at the beginning of a prose poem: "Un pays,—non, ce sont des côtes brisées de la dure Bretagne: *Penmarc'h, Toul-Infern, Poul-Dahut, Stang-an-Ankou* · · · Des noms barbares hurlés par les rafales" [A country,—no, this is the shattered coast of harsh Brittany: *Penmarc'h, Toul-Infern, Poul-Dahut, Stang-an-Ankou* · · · Barbarous names squalled by the squalls], *Casino des trépassés* [*Casino of the Dead*], tr. Val Warner. (TSE: "Bat sur les côtes bretonnes la mer en rafales", 8).

4 **barbe pointue**: "with a pointed beard", *Do I know how I feel? Do I know what I think?* 17.

8 **rafales**: Corbière rhymes on this in *Mirliton*, which TSE copied out (see headnote).

9–10 **Des rayons de soleil · · · après-midi · · · au Luxembourg**: "I am willing to admit that my own retrospect is touched by a sentimental sunset, the memory of a friend coming across the Luxembourg Gardens in the late afternoon", *A Commentary* in *Criterion* Apr 1934. See notes on the dedication of *Prufrock and Other Observations* and *The Waste Land* [I] 2.

11 **poudre de riz**: Corbière: "Kh'ol, carmin et poudre de riz" [Kohl, carmine and facepowder], *Déjeuner de soleil* [*Lunch in the sun*] 6.

11–12 **la poudre de riz. | Et Lieutenant Loti**: Laurent Tailhade: "Loti, fleur des rizières", *Odelette* (1904) 22. Pierre Loti (1850–1923), naval officer, novelist and travel writer, was repeatedly Tailhade's butt in *Poèmes aristophanesques* (see *March Hare* notes to this poem).

12, 14 **Loti · · · grue**: Francis Jammes dedicated to Loti his poem *Les grues* [*The Whores*].

14 *variant* **Fait le trottoirs**: [walks the streets] (as does a street-walker). Corbière: "Là, sa pauvre Muse pucelle | Fit le trottoir en *demoiselle.* | Ils disaient: Qu'est-ce qu'elle vend?" [There his poor maid of a Muse walks the street like a *young lady*. They used to say, What has she for sale?] *Paris* I 9–11. **Fait le trottoirs · · · grue**: Corbière: "C'est très parisien, dans les rues, | Quand l'Aurore fait le trottoir, | De voir sortir toutes les Grues | Du violon, ou de leur boudoir" [It's very Parisian, along the thoroughfares, when Dawn walks the street, to see all the prostitutes come out from the lock-up or from their boudoir], *Idylle coupée* [*Idyll Cut Short*] 1–4. TSE: "une ancienne grue", *Vers pour la Foulque* 20 (in *Noctes Binanianæ*); translated by TSE as "a retired great coarse woman / a superannuated prostitute".

Ode ("Tired. | Subterrene")

Published in *AraVP* as the last of the poems newer than *Prufrock* (which is then reprinted as the book's second half). Not in *US 1920.* This is the only poem published by TSE in a volume of his poems but not then collected. Sending *AraVP* to his brother Henry, he wrote, 15 Feb 1920: "I have not sent this to Mother or told her about it. I thought of cutting out the page on which occurs a poem called *Ode* and sending the book as if there had been an error and an extra page put in. Will you read through the new poems and give your opinion. The *Ode* is *not* in the edition that Knopf is publishing, all the others are. And I suppose she will have to see that book. Do you think that *Sweeney Erect* will shock her?" *Ode* was reprinted in James E. Miller, *T. S. Eliot's Personal Waste Land: Exorcism of the Demons* (1977); Vicki Mahaffey in *American Literature* Jan 1979; H. A. Mason in *Cambridge Quarterly* Apr 1990; then *March Hare.*

To Dr. Alfred Weber, 15 Jan 1958: "If there are any two poems from which you have agreed to take four lines which you would care to print in full (with the exception of *Ode* which I do not like) you are welcome to do so."

TSE adapts Laforgue's *Persée et Andromède*, where the map of the heavens is scanned, and mention is made of Cassiopeia, the Great Bear and other constellations. (For Laforgue's poem see notes to *Inside the gloom* 11 and the title of *Goldfish* II. *Embarquement pour Cythère.*) Titian's *Perseus and Andromeda* is in the Wallace Collection, and in his *Baedeker* TSE marked the room in which it hung. (*Arrowsmith 1981* is in error in placing the picture in the National Gallery.) *Grover Smith* 37–38 explains the mythology of the poem.

Title **Ode**: The poem's three parts roughly correspond to the strophe, antistrophe and epode of a classical ode. TSE to Herbert Read, 6 Jan 1941, on a poem of Read's: "I agree that it would be better to call it just *Ode*, or else find another term than 'rhetoric', because 'rhetoric' means everything to everybody: and I am not quite sure that this comes under any definition of 'ode'. What is an ode, anyway?"

Unadopted title ***Ode | on Independence Day, July 4th 1918***: the date may or may not be that of writing. TSE wrote to his mother, 7 July 1918, that Independence Day had been celebrated in London "solemnly, more as a very serious act of international courtesy, something of gravity, than the hilarious 4th of boyhood. I think that the appetite for the noisier sort of fireworks should have died out for this generation." *Alexandria Gazette* 12 July 1843, on the irony of marrying on Independence Day: "One of the toasts offered was candid: 'State of Matrimony—Happiness to those who have this day assumed the only chain which freemen can wear'" ("the bridegroom", 9).

Epigraph] Coriolanus, on the wounds he has inflicted on Aufidius and the Volscians: "My name is Caius Marcius, who hath done | To thee particularly and to all the Volsces | Great hurt and mischief" (IV v). Three times in the play

Coriolanus is compared to a dragon (18). For the reconciliation of enemies as leading again to war, see note to the title *Coriolan*.

2 **Subterrene laughter:** "his laughter was submarine and profound", *Mr. Apollinax* 7. "under ground | Leaned backward with a lipless grin", *Whispers of Immortality* 3–4. "he shall hear | A breathless chuckle underground", *Exequy* 27–28.

3 **the sacred wood:** Virgil: "cum iam glandes atque arbuta sacrae | deficerent silvae et victum Dodona negaret" [when the acorns and arbutes of the sacred wood began to fail, and Dodona denied men food], *Georgic* I 148–49, referring to the oracular grove of oaks at Dodona (*Stormon*). TSE's *The Sacred Wood: Essays on Poetry and Criticism* was published on 4 Nov 1920, the title likening the poet-critic to Frazer's priest: "In the sacred grove there grew a certain tree round which at any time of the day, and probably far into the night, a grim figure might be seen to prowl. In his hand he carried a drawn sword, and he kept peering warily about him as if at every instant he expected to be set upon by an enemy. He was a priest and a murderer; and the man for whom he looked was sooner or later to murder him and hold the priesthood in his stead ··· A candidate for the priesthood could only succeed to office by slaying the priest, and ··· he retained office till he was himself slain by a stronger or a craftier", *The Golden Bough* I 8–9 (George Watson, *The Literary Critics*, 1962, ch. 9). (Frazer: "Perpetual fires, kindled with the wood of certain oak-trees ··· if such a fire went out, it was lighted again by friction of the sacred wood", *The Golden Bough* II 366.) *Sweeney Among the Nightingales* has "the Sacred ··· wood" across the final two stanzas (36–37). For "the sacred grove" in Frazer, see note to *Exequy* 6–7.

4–5 **bubbling of the ··· | Mephitic river:** Maurice de Guérin, tr. Stuart Merrill: "inarticulate as the bubbling of the rivers", *The Centaur* in *Pastels in Prose.*

5 **Mephitic:** OED: "offensive to the smell ··· pestilential, noxious, poisonous". Virgil: "fonte sonat saevamque exhalat opaca mephitim" [echoes with hallowed fountain, and breathes forth from her darkness a deadly vapour], *Aeneid* VII 84 (*Stormon*).

7 **Profession of the calamus:** writer ("calamus scriptorius", a sharpened reed used for writing). Whitman's *Calamus* is a series of forty-five poems. The second has: "Do not fold yourself so in your pink-tinged roots timid leaves! | Do not remain down there so ashamed, herbage of my breast!" *Scented Herbage of My Breast* 19–20; the third: "Here to put your lips upon mine I permit you, | With the comrade's long-dwelling kiss or the new husband's kiss, | For I am the new husband and I am the comrade", *Whoever You Are Holding Me Now in Hand* 19–21 (TSE: "the bridegroom", 9). TSE: "I did not read Whitman until much later in life, and had to conquer an aversion to his form, as well as to much of his matter, in order to do so", *Selected Poems of Ezra Pound* (1928), Introduction.

9 **the bridegroom:** when Coriolanus reveals himself as the enemy leader (see epigraph), he is welcomed by Aufidius: "more dances my rapt heart | Than when I first my wedded mistress saw | Bestride my threshold" (*Coriolanus* IV v).

9–10 **the bridegroom smoothed his hair ··· upon the bed:** "The features of the injured bride!" *Elegy* 12. "publication of the bride-sheets!" *Anabasis* X v.

9–10, 16 **the bridegroom smoothed his hair ··· upon the bed ··· Perseus:** Laforgue: "Persée ··· ramène les boucles blondes de sa chevelure" [Perseus ···

while he rearranges his golden curls], *Persée et Andromède*. TSE: "Enacted on this same divan or bed · · · smooths her hair", *The Waste Land* [III] 244, 255.

10–14 **blood upon the bed · · · Hymen · · · Succuba eviscerate**: in response to congratulations from Conrad Aiken on the publication of *1925*, TSE sent a page from the *Nursing Mirror and Midwives' Journal* 28 Nov 1925, on which were underlined the words "Blood, mucus, shreds of mucus, purulent offensive discharge." (Faber had recently taken over publication of the journal.) See *Letters 3* 43–44 and Conrad Aiken to Robert N. Linscott, 4 Jan 1926, in Aiken's *Selected Letters*.

12 **Children singing in the orchard**: see note to *Landscapes* I. *New Hampshire* 1, "Children's voices in the orchard".

13 **Hymen Hymenæe**: Catullus 61: "io Hymen Hymenæe io, | io Hymen Hymenæe". In this repeated refrain, the ritual cry *ὑμήν* is lengthened to *ὑμέναιε*, where the quantities are different, making the line notoriously difficult to scan. F. M. Cornford on the "form and content of the Phallic Song": "the Marriage Songs—hymenaeal and epithalamium—with their ribald stanzas and the refrain '*Hymen, O Hymenaee!*'", *The Origin of Attic Comedy* 39. TSE: "a sort of hymenaeal hymn is sung", *Sweeney Agonistes* draft, *The Superior Landlord* II. *Gordon* 125 points to Whitman:

> O hymen! O hymenee! why do you tantalize me thus?
> O why sting me for a swift moment only?
> Why can you not continue? O why do you now cease?
> Is it because if you continued beyond the swift moment you
> would soon certainly kill me?
>
> *O Hymen! O Hymenee!*

Hymen: OED "Hymen" 3, "Marriage; wedlock", citing Dryden's *Aeneid* VII 769–70: "A bloody Hymen shall th'Alliance join | Betwixt the Trojan and Ausonian line."

14 **Succuba eviscerate**: Jonson: "Then, my glasses | Cut in more subtle angles, to disperse | And multiply the figures, as I walk | Naked between my *succubæ*", *The Alchemist* II ii. TSE quoted these lines (but not the last—perhaps deleted by an editor at the *TLS*?) in *Ben Jonson* (1919). **Succuba**: OED "succubus" 1: "A demon in female form supposed to have carnal intercourse with men in their sleep". 2b: "A strumpet, a whore". **eviscerate**: see *Little Gidding* II 13.

14 *variant* **suspired**: see note to *Little Gidding* IV 13–14.

15 **Tortuous**: OED 1b: "*Astron.* Applied to the six signs of the zodiac from Capricornus to Gemini, which · · · rise more obliquely than the other six. *Obs.*"

16–17 **Perseus · · · dragon**: *Lemprière*: Perseus "discovered, on the coast of Ethiopia, the naked Andromeda, exposed to a sea monster. He was struck by the sight, and offered her father Cepheus to deliver her from instant death, if he obtained her in marriage as a reward of his labours. Cepheus consented, and immediately Perseus raised himself in the air, flew towards the monster · · · and plunged his dagger in his right shoulder, and destroyed it."

17, 22 **dragon · · · Charles' Wagon**: *Mahaffey*: "the constellation Draco · · · in spring and summer, lies beneath · · · Ursa Major" (Charles' Wagon). *King Lear* I ii, EDMUND: "My father compounded with my mother under the dragon's tail, and my nativity was under *Ursa Major*; so that it follows I am rough and lecherous". TSE: "the circuit of the shuddering Bear", *Gerontion* 68.

19 **Indignant:** Virgil: "vitaque cum gemitu fugit indignata sub umbras" [with a moan life passed indignant to the Shades below], *Aeneid* XII 952, the final line (*Stormon*).

20 **the cheap extinction of his taking-off:** *Macbeth* I vii: "his virtues | Will plead like angels, trumpet-tongu'd, against | The deep damnation of his taking off" (for the speech, see *Airs of Palestine, No. 2* 6).

21 **Now lies he there:** *Julius Caesar* III ii (*Grover Smith* 37).

22 **Tip to tip washed beneath Charles' Wagon:** published in 1898, the cartoon *Ten thousand miles from tip to tip* signified the extent of US domination—from Manilla to Puerto Rico—after the defeat of Spain in the Spanish-American War. **washed ··· Charles':** the Charles River runs through Boston. ("The barges wash", *The Waste Land* [III] 273.)

The Death of the Duchess

Published in *WLFacs.*

Gordon 158 explains that evidence for dating *The Death of the Duchess* from the paper "is inconclusive" because the same kind of paper was used both for *ts3* of *Gerontion* (1919) and for the unpublished review, *Autour d'une Traduction d'Euripide* (1916). On the basis of the paper, *Rainey* 34 assigns the poem to Sept 1916, despite assigning the review, which twice uses the date 1916, to Feb 1919.

Grover Smith 1983 16 calls the poem TSE's "companion piece" to *Gerontion* and persuasively assigns it to 1919, "perhaps dating from the autumn, when he reviewed a production of *The Duchess of Malfi*". Valerie Eliot's notes in *WLFacs* identified II 23–24 as deriving from Webster's *The Duchess of Malfi*, but did not specify that II 51–53 derive from the same passage (see note to II 23–24, 51–53). See headnote to *The Waste Land*, 1. COMPOSITION.

Gordon 158: "Valerie Eliot tells me there is a letter to Eliot, written in 1919, in which the correspondent refers to *The Death of the Duchess* and Mr. Bleistein (in *Dirge*)." The Bleistein poem, however, was probably *Burbank with a Baedeker: Bleistein with a Cigar* (published summer 1919). The letter was probably that from Sacheverell Sitwell described by Sarah Bradford. On 1 Mar 1919, she writes, TSE showed Sitwell *Burbank with a Baedeker: Bleistein with a Cigar* and another poem (*Bradford* 92). Three days later, Sitwell wrote to TSE saying he was "overwhelmed", referring to "the 'hillmen' of Hampstead" and quoting "They discuss the evening papers, and other bird-news" (see I 1 and II 16).

I

I 1–6 **The inhabitants of Hampstead ··· On Sunday afternoon go out to tea ··· They know what they are to feel and what to think, | They know it with the morning printer's ink:** "I journeyed to the suburbs, and there I was told: | We toil for six days, on the seventh we must motor | To Hindhead, or Maidenhead. | If the weather is foul we stay at home and read the papers", *Choruses from "The Rock"* I 28–31. **what they are to feel and what to think, | They know it with the morning printer's ink:** "Wakening the appetites of life in some | And to others bringing the *Boston Evening Transcript*", *The "Boston Evening Transcript"* 4–5.

I 1–4, II 1 **inhabitants of Hampstead ··· tea ··· tea ··· tea ··· people hang upon the bridge rail:** "F. M.": "unkempt sub-editors (of monthlies) goggling over the gallery rail, and ladies from Hampstead who have met there for a good talk and a cup of tea", *Letters of the Moment* I (1924).

I 5, 8 **They know what they are to feel and what to think ··· They know what to think and what to feel:** *Do I know how I feel? Do I know what I think?* (first line).

I 10 **what is there for you and me:** "you and I ··· time for you and time for me ··· among some talk of you and me", *The Love Song of J. Alfred Prufrock* 1, 31, 89.

I 12 **What is there for us to do:** "Where shall we go next?" *Suite Clownesque* II 22. "'What shall we do tomorrow? | 'What shall we ever do?'" *The Waste Land* [II] 133–34.

II

II 1 **In the evening people hang upon the bridge rail:** Tennyson: "I waited for the train at Coventry; | I hung with grooms and porters on the bridge", *Godiva* 1–2.

II 3, 15 **In the square they lean against each other ··· The people leaning against another in the square:** "evil houses leaning all together", *Prufrock's Pervigilium* [15]. "Leaning together", *The Hollow Men* I 3 (*WLFacs* notes). ("leaning against another" may be a mistyping of "people leaning against one another".)

II 4–5 **like ··· on a table ··· over the table:** "Like a patient etherised upon a table", *The Love Song of J. Alfred Prufrock* 3.

II 7–10, 16–17 **heads of birds | Beaks and no words, || What words have we? || I should like to be in a crowd of beaks without words ··· other bird things ··· but no wings :** Browning:

> As to catch a hawk, some falcon-lanner,
> And thrust her broad wings like a banner
> Into a coop for a vulgar pigeon;
> And if day by day and week by week
> You cut her claws, and sealed her eyes,
> And clipped her wings, and tied her beak,

and "For here her voice changed like a bird's; | There grew more of the music and less of the words", *The Flight of the Duchess* 269–74 and 690–91 (see Textual History description of *ts1*). Valerie Eliot may have been confusing this with Webster's Duchess or with the allusion to *The White Devil* (see note to II 34) when she said "There is a reflection of the bird imagery of *The White Devil*" (BBC broadcast 2 Nov 1971).

II 10–12 **I should like to be ··· marble floors:** "I should have been a pair of ragged claws | Scuttling across the floors of silent seas", *The Love Song of J. Alfred Prufrock* 73–74 (James Longenbach, *ELH* Summer 1985).

II 13 **firelight on your hair:** "(But in the lamplight, downed with light brown hair!)" *The Love Song of J. Alfred Prufrock* 64.

II 13–15, 20–22 **firelight on your hair · · · footsteps up and down the stair · · · people leaning · · · Under the brush · · · still:** "Leaned out, leaning · · · Footsteps shuffled on the stair. | Under the firelight, under the brush, her hair | Spread out in fiery points | Glowed into words, then would be savagely still", *The Waste Land* [II] 106–110.

II 20–21, 35 **Under the brush her hair | Spread out · · · the brush proceed:** in *The Duchess of Malfi* III ii, the Duchess brushes her hair; see note to II 54–58. (The scenic form of Webster's IV ii, in which Cariola attends the Duchess, is partly based on *Othello* IV iii, in which Emila unpins Desdemona's hair and, traditionally, brushes it as Desdemona sings. See note to II 26, 28.)

II 22 **suddenly still:** *Silence* 13.

II 23–24, 51–53] In *WLFacs* notes, Valerie Eliot points to *The Duchess of Malfi* III ii:

> DUCHESS: Doth not the colour of my hair 'gin to change?
> When I wax gray, I shall have all the court
> Powder their hair with arras, to be like me.
> You have cause to love me; I entered you into my heart
> Before you would vouchsafe to call for the keys.

TSE made use of this passage three times. The fourth and fifth lines appeared in *Reflections on "vers libre"* (1917), the fourth line being misquoted as "You have cause to love me, I did enter you in my heart". TSE then changed the order of Webster's lines for this poem, where

> "*You have cause to love me, I did enter you in my heart*
> *Before ever you vouchsafed to ask for the key*"
>
> (II 23–24)

is followed some thirty lines later by

> "*When I grow old I shall have all the court*
> *Powder their hair with arras, to be like me.*
> But I know you love me, it must be that you love me"
>
> (II 51–53).

Of these five lines, only II 52 is given accurately from Webster, with II 23 varying in the same way as in *Reflections on "vers libre"* (1917).

Finally, in *"The Duchess of Malfi" at the Lyric: and Poetic Drama* (1919/20), TSE gave three lines, criticising the actor for "interpreting" them:

> ". . . does not my hair 'gin to change?
> When I grow old, I shall have all the court
> Powder their hair with arras, to be like me."

Here the first line is compressed, the second varies from Webster in the same way (but for a comma) as in this poem, and the third is quoted accurately. For other departures from the texts of 17th-century drama, see notes to *Gerontion* 54–56 and its epigraph.

II 25–26 **her arms were bare | Fixed for a question, her hands behind her hair:** "fix · · · Arms that are braceleted and white and bare · · · hair", *The Love Song of J. Alfred Prufrock* 56, 63–64 (with "question" three times in the poem).

II 26, 28 **her hair · · · tangled:** *The Duchess of Malfi* III ii, DUCHESS: "When were we so merry?—My hair tangles."

II 28 **My thoughts in a tangled bunch of heads and tails:** "My brain is twisted in a tangled skein", *Do I know how I feel? Do I know what I think?* 23. "head having swallowed his tail", *Introspection* 3–4.

II 30 **One that I knew**: "There I saw one I knew", *The Waste Land* [I] 69.

II 31 **Time to regain the door**: *WLFacs* notes: "This is not a quotation from *Prufrock*, but another example of 'cadence reproduction'" (referring to Pound's annotation "Pruf—" on the ts, and quoting his comment from two lines later). The cadence is that of "Time to turn back and descend the stair", *The Love Song of J. Alfred Prufrock* 39.

II 33 **And if I said "I love you" should we breathe**: Pound comments "cadence reproduction from Pr.[ufrock] or Por[trait of a Lady]": the cadence is that of "if she should die · · · should I have the right to smile", *Portrait of a Lady* III 31, 41. Pound: "Let the candidate fill his mind with the finest cadences he can discover, preferably in a foreign language so that the meaning of the words may be less likely to divert his attention from the movement; e.g. Saxon charms, Hebridean folk songs, the verse of Dante, and the lyrics of Shakespeare—if he can dissociate the vocabulary from the cadence", *A Stray Document* (1912/13) collected in *Make It New* and quoted in TSE's *Ezra Pound* (1946).

II 34 **Hear music, go a-hunting, as before?**: Webster: "What do the dead do, uncle? do they eat, | Hear music, go a hunting, and be merry, | As we that live?" *The White Devil* III i (Mermaid ed.; commonly III ii) (*WLFacs* notes).

II 40–44 **If I said · · · We should say**: "If one · · · Should say", *The Love Song of J. Alfred Prufrock* 96–97.

II 43, 49 **knock upon the door · · · waiting for a knock upon the door**: *The Duchess of Malfi* III ii, ANTONIO: "How now? who knocks?" (perhaps also IV ii, where the Duchess awaits her executioners).

II 45–49] Adapted as *The Waste Land* [II] 136–39.

II 52 ***arras***: powdered orris-root, smelling of violets (*The Duchess of Malfi* IV ii: "Strew your hair with powders sweet").

II 54–58 **Then I suppose · · · I know she knew**: Valerie Eliot on *The Duchess of Malfi* III ii: "The Duchess and Antonio, formerly her steward, now her husband, are in her bed-chamber. She is brushing her hair, with her back to him, and for a joke he and the maid Cariola slip away unnoticed. She continues talking, and when there is no reply, turns with 'Have you lost your tongue?' to find that her brother Ferdinand, who is also her enemy, has been listening to her. Antonio and Cariola do not return until after he has left. Eliot remarked on the 'breathless tension' of this scene, and the poignancy of the Duchess's words in a talk he gave on the Indian Service of the B.B.C." (*WLFacs* notes); the talk was *"The Duchess of Malfy"* (1941).

Song ("The golden foot I may not kiss or clutch")

Published with the pseudonym "Gus Krutzsch" in *Tyro* Apr 1921 as *Song to the Opherian*; then *WLFacs* from *ts1*, which is tentatively assigned to Jan 1921 by *Rainey* 15–17, and is annotated by Pound. See headnote to *The Waste Land*, 1. COMPOSITION, for relation to this poem.

Originally entitled *Song for the Opherion*, *ts1* was probably not setting copy for the printer (which presumably included the pseudonym), and may have been made before or after publication of the poem in Wyndham Lewis's *Tyro*. The inaccuracies in *Blast*'s printing of other poems by TSE show that as an editor Lewis could be textually negligent. *Blast* had changed another of TSE's titles to *Rhapsody of a Windy Night*, so it is possible that in this case the variant preposition "*to*" and the spelling of "*Opherian*" were not as the author intended.

Pound's annotation was almost certainly subsequent to the poem's publication, for he deleted what was printed as the third line, "Perhaps it does not come to very much" (2^3), calling it "georgian". Two further lines, "Waiting that touch | After thirty years.", which concluded *ts1* but did not appear in *Tyro*, were also deleted, probably by Pound (although the deletion is attributed to TSE in *WLFacs* 98/99). Likewise, it was probably Pound who reduced the title to *Song*.

TSE to Donald Gallup, 26 Nov 1946: "I don't remember which verses I called *Song to the Opherian* but I think it was one of the short poems which were called the *Dream Songs*. It may or may not have been one of those included as interludes in the first draft of *The Waste Land*. It is impossible to settle this point now. I preserved no copies of those *Waste Land* lyrics; the copies that I know of were those with the original manuscript which was in the possession of John Quinn, and it disappeared from sight after Mr. Quinn's death." To Grover Smith, 4 July 1949: "I haven't the slightest idea now what the *Song to the Opherian* was and am extremely thankful from one point of view that the manuscript in which it occurs has disappeared without trace."

After its pseudonymous publication, TSE wished to re-use *Song* in *The Waste Land* but had difficulty finding a place for it. Probably one of the "interludes", it may first have been stationed between Part II and Part III. It was then moved to the end, but Pound urged abolition of everything but the five parts.

Pound to TSE, [24 Jan 1922]: "The song has only two lines which you can use in the body of the poem." These were presumably the lines he braced, "When the surface of the blackened river | Is a face that sweats with tears?" (although the transcript of *ts1* in *WLFacs* interprets this brace as spanning 8–11).

When TSE typed Part III of *The Waste Land*, he had not included the 25-line passage beginning "The river sweats | Oil and tar" (*ms2*), but his mention to Pound on [26? Jan] of "Drifting logs" confirms that it had since been incorporated. He needed to avoid the duplication of "the blackened river · · · sweats" (from *Song*) and "The river sweats | Oil and tar", and he wrote to Pound that he was "working sweats with tears etc. into nerves monologue" in Part II. It is not clear how the lines from *Song* could have been incorporated there, and on [28? Jan] Pound replied: "I dare say sweats with tears will wait."

Later TSE used the second stanza of *Song*, in modified form, in *The wind sprang up at four o'clock*, which was originally published as the second of *Doris's Dream Songs* in *Chapbook* [Nov] 1924. By pointing out the resemblance between that *Dream Song* and the "poem of two stanzas by 'Gus Krutzsch'" from "an old copy of · · · *The Tyro*", a hostile editorial in *Poetry: A Magazine of New Lyrics* Sept 1925 then effectively revealed the authorship of *Song to the Opherian*.

The present edition gives not the text published in *Tyro* but that of *ts1* as it was finally left by TSE and Pound.

Unadopted title **Song to the Opherian** (*variant* **Song for the Opherion**): *WLFacs* notes: "There is no such word as 'Opherian', and it is possible that Eliot meant 'Orpharion' (from Orpheus and Arion), 'an instrument of the cittern family ··· essentially the poor man's lute' (Grove's *Dictionary of Music and Musicians*, 1954)." OED gives variant spelling "orpherian", and quotes Drayton: "Set the Cornet with the Flute, | The Orpharion to the Lute", *Eclogues* III 111. The title page of John Dowland's *First Book of Songes* (1597) says they may be sung "to the Lute, Orpherian, or Viol de gambo" (Oliver Soden, personal communication). As the title of an interlude between Parts II and III of *The Waste Land*, this would have anticipated "The pleasant whining of a mandoline", [III] 261 (OED quotes Smollett: "An excellent performer on the lute and mandolin").

Pseudonym on first publication **Gus Krutzsch**: see note to *WLComposite* 45 *variant*. TSE to Gallup, 25 July 1962, denying authorship of *Café Cannibale*, by John Adams, which also appeared in *Tyro* Apr 1921: "I can throw no light whatever now upon the authorship ··· All I can tell you is that Gus Krutzsch was a pseudonym for T. S. Eliot, who decided later that the verses were not good enough for him to wish to acknowledge them under his own name." *Sencourt* 67 (giving no source): "In 1921 he was to add to these disguises that of Gus Krutzsch, the pedant who refused to go to China because it had no native cheese."

1 **The golden foot I may not kiss or clutch**: Kipling: "a-wastin' Christian kisses on an 'eathen idol's foot", *Mandalay* 14 (in *A Choice of Kipling's Verse*) (*Grover Smith* 101).

5 **between two lives**: *The Waste Land* [III] 218 (see note).

9–10 **the surface of the blackened river | Is a face that sweats with tears**: Blake: "I wander thro' each charter'd street, | Near where the charter'd Thames does flow ··· black'ning", *London* (*Songs of Experience*, 1794). "The river sweats | Oil and tar", *The Waste Land* [III] 266–67 (with "blackened wall", [V] 381). See headnote.

12 **The campfire shake the spears**: "the shaking spears and flickering lights", *After the turning of the inspired days* 9.

Elegy

Published in *WLFacs* 116/117. See headnote to *The Waste Land*, 1. COMPOSITION, for relation to this poem.

Pencilled manuscript with *ms1* of *Dirge* on verso. Assigned to Oct–Nov 1921 by *Rainey*.

The top of the leaf is slightly torn, but the lines begin so far up as to leave no space for a title (though TSE added one later in the top left corner). Apparently, then, not a new poem, but a continuation, although no preceding leaf survives. Given that the paper matches *ms1* and *ms2* of *The Waste Land* (torn off TSE's pad apparently at the same time as *ms2*), these lines were almost certainly drafted in Margate. If they were for Part III of *The Waste Land*, which TSE composed there, they may have been intended as its concluding lines, with the draft of *Dirge* on the verso following in sequence as an interlude between Part III and Part IV. (For TSE's word "interlude" and the arrangement of the poem, see headnote to *The Waste Land*, 1. COMPOSITION.) The leaf probably survived because *Dirge* is on the other side.

Valerie Eliot, BBC broadcast, 2 Nov 1971: "As a boy, Eliot read steadily through the works of Poe, kept in his dentist's waiting room, and *Elegy* is ··· infected by Poe the poet, as well as by Poe the teller of tales, who is mentioned. There is an allusion to *The Maid's Tragedy* and an echo of *The Hound of Heaven.*" (See headnote to *Burbank with a Baedeker: Bleistein with a Cigar* for TSE's reading of Poe at the dentist, where he first saw lines quoted from Henry King's *An Exequy To his Matchless never to be forgotten Friend.* King's poem includes the words "elegy" and "dirges".)

1–2 **Our prayers dismiss the parting shade | And breathe a hypocrites's amen**: "Our sighs pursue th' elusive shade ··· Our sighs pursue the vanishd shade | And breathe a sanctified amen", *Whispers of Immortality* 11, 21–22 *variants* (for "the hypocrite's amen" in Lancelot Andrewes, see note).

3 **Aspatia**: Beaumont and Fletcher, *The Maid's Tragedy.* Valerie Eliot: "Deserted by her lover, Amintor, for Evadne, Aspatia disguises herself as her brother seeking to avenge his sister's wrong, and forces Amintor to kill her in a duel. Eliot quoted Aspatia's words [from earlier in the play] as the epigraph to *Sweeney Erect*" (*WLFacs* notes). Joyce: "He gave them then a much admirable hymen minim by those delicate poets Master John Fletcher and Master Francis Beaumont that is in their *Maid's Tragedy* that was writ for a like twining of lovers: *To bed, to bed*, was the burden of it to be played with accompanable concent upon the virginals. Well met they were, said Master Dixon, but, harkee, better were they named Beau Mont and Lecher", *Ulysses* episode XIV (The Oxen of the Sun) in *Little Review* Sept–Dec 1920.

3–4 **The wronged Aspatia returned | Wreathed**: *The Maid's Tragedy* II i, ASPATIA: "With flattering ivy clasp my coffin round; | Write on my brow my fortune."

4 **the wingèd cyclamen**: "the cyclamen spreads its wings", *Coriolan* II. *Difficulties of a Statesman* 35 (*WLFacs* notes).

5–6 **I should have mourned**: "I should have lost", *La Figlia Che Piange* 22.

5–8, 11 **I should have mourned ··· Were't not for dreams: a dream restores | The always inconvenient dead ··· a tale by Poe**: *Schuchard* 126 identifies *Ligeia*, a tale of "marriages ill-omened", in which a grieving husband remarries unhappily and finds his second wife's deathbed haunted by memories of his first wife (see note to *The Waste Land* [II] 79–120). Ligeia—with "naturally-curling tresses, setting forth the full force of the Homeric epithet, 'hyacinthine!'"—is a Rhine maiden, in that her husband believes they met in a city on the Rhine (see note to *The Waste Land* [III] 277–78, 290–91). For *The Conqueror Worm*, the poem within the tale, see note to *East Coker* III 13–17.

9–10, 21–22 **The sweat transpirèd from my pores! | I saw sepulchral gates, flung wide ··· God in a rolling ball of fire | Pursues my errant feet**: Marvell: "But at my back I always hear | Time's wingèd chariot hurrying near ··· And while thy willing Soul transpires | At every pore with instant fires ··· Let us roll all our strength, and all | Our sweetness, up into one ball: | And tear our pleasures with rough strife, | Thorough the iron gates of life", *To His Coy Mistress* 21–44 (Shawn Worthington, personal communication).

13 **That hand, prophetical and slow:** *Paradise Lost*, penultimate line: "They hand in hand with wand'ring steps and slow".

15 **cerements:** correctly pronounced *serments*, but OED notes sometimes erroneously three syllables, because of *ceremony* (as TSE's metre asks). *Fowler*: "disyllabic".

15–16 **Tore the disordered cerements, | Around that head:** Poe: "she let fall from her head, unloosened, the ghastly cerements which had confined it, and there streamed forth, into the rushing atmosphere of the chamber, huge masses of long and dishevelled hair", *Ligeia*.

20 **charnel vault:** Poe: "the bandages and draperies of the grave still imparted their charnel character to the figure", *Ligeia.*

21 **God, in a rolling ball of fire:** Marlowe: "The golden ball of Heaven's eternal fire", *Tamburlaine Part II* II iv (Shawn Worthington, personal communication).

22 **errant feet:** poetic diction. William Watson: "secret influence to himself unknown | Guided the wandering of his errant feet", *The Prince's Quest* (1880) IX. Owen Innsly: "hold the errant feet that stray", *Service* in *Love Poems and Sonnets* (1881).

24 **consuming heat:** Francis Thompson: "commingling heat", *The Hound of Heaven* 89–93 (Shawn Worthington, personal communication); see headnote, "an echo". *TSE's books: Bodleian list* (1934) includes "The Hound of Heaven (paper)", but he wrote to Geoffrey Curtis, 23 Mar 1932, of Thompson: "I do not know his poetry very well, and if I do not know it very well it is probably because I do not like it very much · · · I am not sure that in his religious poetry he ever reaches a spirit of pure devotion. The only poem I remember at the moment is certainly a very good one, the lines *To the Dead Cardinal*, but as I remember that, it is rather fine rhetoric than piety."

Dirge

Published in *WLFacs.* See headnote to *The Waste Land*, 1. COMPOSITION.

Assigned to 1919 in *March Hare* xlii, but to Oct–Nov 1921 by *Rainey* 35, and to Nov 1921 by *Rainey* 200–201. See headnote to *The Death of the Duchess.*

The earlier of the two mss of *Dirge*, almost certainly drafted in Margate in Oct–Nov 1921, is on the verso of the quatrains to which TSE added the title *Elegy*. See headnote to *The Waste Land*, 1. COMPOSITION, for its relations to these two short poems.

A reworking of Ariel's song in *The Tempest* I ii:

Full fathom five thy father lies:
  Of his bones are coral made;
Those are pearls that were his eyes:
  Nothing of him that doth fade,

But doth suffer a sea-change
Into something rich and strange.
Sea-nymphs hourly ring his knell:
Hark! now I hear them,—
Ding, dong, bell.

printed thus as *A Sea Dirge* in *The Golden Treasury*, where it is paired with *A Land Dirge* from Webster's *The White Devil* (see note to *The Waste Land* [I] 71–75). TSE: "Shakespeare too, was occupied with the struggle—which alone constitutes life for a poet—to transmute his personal and private agonies into something rich and strange, something universal and impersonal", *Shakespeare and the Stoicism of Seneca* (1927). Pound: "Full many a fathomed sea-change in the eyes | That sought with him the salt-sea victories", *Three Cantos* (II) in *Poetry* July 1917, collected in *Lustra* (1919). Bleistein and Ariel's song are first associated in *Burbank with a Baedeker: Bleistein with a Cigar* 5–6. Valerie Eliot: "The parodying of Ariel's song may owe something to the Proteus episode of *Ulysses*", BBC broadcast 2 Nov 1971. Joyce, *Ulysses* episode III, in *Little Review* May 1918, repr. *Egoist* Mar–Apr 1919, during TSE's tenure as deputy editor:

> Five fathoms out there. Full fathom five thy father lies. At one he said. High water at Dublin bar. Driving before it a loose drift of rubble, fanshoals of fishes, silly shells. A corpse rising saltwhite from the undertow, bobbing landward. There he is. Hook it quick. Pull. We have him. Easy now.
>
> Bag of corpsegas sopping in foul brine. A quiver of minnows, fat of a spongy titbit ··· God becomes man becomes fish becomes barnacle goose becomes featherbed mountain. Dead breaths I living breathe, tread dead dust, devour a urinous offal from all dead. Hauled stark over the gunwale he breathes upward the stench of his green grave, his leprous nosehole snoring to the sun.
>
> A seachange this. Seadeath, mildest of all deaths known to man

Decomposition of bodies in water is discussed over several pages of Poe's detective story *The Mystery of Marie Rogêt*, which TSE he admired as "the most austere example of the type" (to Gilbert Seldes, 12 Apr 1927). For Poe, see headnote to *Elegy*.

3 **Graves' Disease in a dead jew's eyes!**: Coleridge: "the curse in a dead man's eye!" *The Rime of the Ancient Mariner* IV. TSE's *ms1* had "Jew's" and "man's" as alternate readings. *The Merchant of Venice* III i: "Hath not a Jew eyes? ··· subject to the same diseases" (*Julius* 125). **Graves' Disease**: exophthalmic goitre (*WLFacs* notes). **jew's eyes!**: *Oxf Dictionary of English Proverbs*: "To be worth a Jew's eye = to be of much value; *orig.* worth while for a Jewess's eye to look at", citing G. Harvey (1593): "As dear as a Jew's eye." *The Merchant of Venice* II v: 'There will come a Christian by, | Will be worth a Jewess's eye'." See note to *Burbank with a Baedeker: Bleistein with a Cigar* 23.

4 **When the crabs have eat the lids**: Corbière: "Un cadavre bossu, ballonné, démasqué | Par les crabes" [A hunchbacked corpse, swollen, laid open by the crabs], *Le Bossu Bitor* [*Bitor The Hunchback*], penultimate stanza. **eat**: *Fowler*: "The past is spelt *ate* (rarely *eat*) & pronounced ĕt (wrongly āt)."

6 **suffer a sea-change**: *Fowler*: "one of the most importunate & intrusive of IRRELEVANT ALLUSIONS, & HACKNEYED PHRASES." **sea-change**: OED "sea" 23a: "a change wrought by the sea; now freq. *transf.* with or without allusion to

Shakespeare's use ··· an alteration or metamorphosis, a radical change", with no citations between Shakespeare and Pound.

7 **rich and strange**: for Ariel's song, see headnote.

8, 10 **nose ··· toes**: see note to *Suite Clownesque* I 23–24.

16 *variant*, 17 **Sea nymphs nightly ··· Hark now I hear them scratch scratch scratch**: two songs in *The Tempest.* I ii, ARIEL: "Sea-nymphs hourly ring his knell | Hark! now I hear them,— | Ding, dong, bell" (see headnote). And II ii, STEPHANO:

> "The master, the swabber, the boat-swain and I,
> The gunner and his mate,
> Loved Mall, Meg and Marian, and Margery,
> But none of us cared for Kate.
> For she had a tongue with a tang,
> Would cry to a sailor go hang;
> She loved not the savour of tar nor of pitch,
> Yet a tailor might scratch her where'er he did itch.
> Then to sea boys and let her go hang.

17 **Hark! now I hear them scratch scratch scratch**: "Bark bark BARK BARK | Until you can hear them", *Of the Awefull Battle of the Pekes and the Pollicles* 9–10. **scratch scratch scratch**: "Shantih shantih shantih", *The Waste Land* last line. (The similarity is clearest in *Dirge ms1*, where the three words are lowered as though a separate line.)

Those are pearls that were his eyes. See!

Published in *WLFacs.*

Assigned to May 1921 by *Rainey* 35. *WLFacs* notes: "This poem may have been written in 1921." A footnote on the transcription page (*WLFacs* 123) adds: "The first line became *The Waste Land* [I] 48, with 'Look!' substituted for 'See!'" (see also [II] 125). Valerie Eliot on these five lines: "The final poem is really a continuation of *Dirge*", BBC broadcast 2 Nov 1971. See headnote to *The Waste Land*, 1. COMPOSITION.

1 **Those are pearls that were his eyes. See!**: *The Tempest* I ii: "Those are pearls that were his eyes ··· Sea-nymphs" (see headnote to *Dirge* and note to *The Waste Land* [I] 48).

3 *variant* **And the torn algae drift above him, purple, red**: Valerie Eliot: "I wonder if he heard the echo of 'And blossom in purple and red' from Tennyson's *Maud*", BBC broadcast 2 Nov 1971 (*Maud* I [xxii] 920–23: "My dust would hear her and beat | Had I lain for a century dead; | Would start and tremble under her feet, | And blossom in purple and red").

5 **Still & quiet brother are you still and quiet**: *WLFacs* notes: "Probably unconscious echo of *Othello* III i: 'of spirit | So still and quiet'."

Exequy

Published in *WLFacs.*

Assigned to Nov 1921 by *Rainey* 35.

WLFacs notes: "Discouraging Eliot from including this poem in *The Waste Land*, Pound wrote: 'even the sovegna doesnt hold with the rest'" [24 Jan 1922]. The reference is to the final line. See headnote to *The Waste Land*, 1. COMPOSITION.

1–2 **Persistent lovers will repair ··· to my suburban tomb:** Donne: "When my grave is broke up again ··· All women shall adore us, and some men", *The Relique* 1, 19. **suburban tomb:** OED "suburban" quotes "The Rich had stately Monuments on the sides of the publick ways in their own suburbane fields" (1673).

6 **sacred grove:** Frazer: "Beside the temple at Upsala there was a sacred grove", *The Golden Bough* II 364 (in a section discussing thunder gods). For *The Sacred Wood*, see note to *Ode* ("Tired. | Subterrene") 3.

8–12 **my athletic marble form | Forever lithe, forever young, | With grateful garlands shall be hung | And flowers of deflowered maids; | The cordial flame shall keep me warm:** Keats: "unravished bride ··· leaf-fringed legend haunts about thy shape ··· For ever warm and still to be enjoyed | For ever panting, and for ever young ··· with garlands dressed", *Ode on a Grecian Urn* (*Crawford* 129). For Keats's *Ode*, see note to *The Waste Land* [II] 102.

15–21 *pencil draft* [1] **Pudibund:** OED *rare* a: "That is a subject of shame; shameful. *Obs.*" b: "Modest, bashful, prudish." TSE to Conrad Aiken, from Marburg, 19 July 1914: "I find that I have only one (torn) pair of pajamas, and my dictionary does not give the word for them. *Que faire?* The dictionary, however, gives the German equivalents for *gracilent* and *pudibund*. *You* might do something with that, but I lack inspiration" (*WLFacs* notes).

15–21 *pencil draft* [5] **mel.:** for "melodious" (*WLFacs* notes).

15–21 *pencil draft* [6] **am.:** "for amorous" (*WLFacs* notes).

15 **melodious fountain falls:** Marlowe: "By shallow rivers, to whose falls | Melodious birds sing madrigals", *The Passionate Shepherd to His Love* 7–8; in *The Golden Treasury* (*Crawford* 129).

16 **Carved by the cunning Bolognese:** Giambologna, Renaissance sculptor of fountains in Bologna, the Boboli Gardens in Florence and elsewhere.

19–21 *Pound's annotation*: "This is Laforgue not XVIII"] For a return to the 18th century, see next note.

23 **disdainful or disdained:** Pope: "Disdain whatever Cornbury disdains", *To Mr. Murray* 61.

27 **Just at:** ringed by TSE but deleted by Pound, this original reading is better than the alternative TSE offered ("Upon") because the awkwardness of "on the Mound | Upon the crisis", would have asked further revision.

27–28 **he shall hear | A breathless chuckle underground**: for Marvell's *To His Coy Mistress*, see note to *The Waste Land* [III] 185, 196–97.

29 **SOVEGNA ··· DOLOR:** [be mindful in due time of my pain], *Purg.* XXVI 147 (*WLFacs* notes). For TSE's returns to this Arnaut Daniel passage, see note to the title *Ara Vos Prec* in headnote to "*Poems* (1920)", 7. PUBLICATION OF *ARA VOS PREC*.

29 *variant* **Consiros vei la pasada folor:** [in thought I see my past madness] *Purg.* XXVI 143 (*WLFacs* notes). The Italian spelling is "passada".

The Builders

Composed as part of *The Rock*, this song (with words by T. S. Eliot, music by Martin Shaw) was published separately in 1934 as no. 107 in Cramer's Library of Unison and Part-Songs by Modern Composers, ed. Martin Shaw.

Printed in *The Rock* 19 (first stanza) and 28–29 (third stanza). The second stanza of the musical setting did not appear in *The Rock*, and the refrain ("A Church ··· unto this last") is there set in prose. The first stanza is repeated at the end of *The Rock* and was printed at the end of the theatre programme, to be sung by the audience after the Bishop's Benediction. *Browne* (30): "It had been planned from the first that the revue should have a theme-song, to be introduced at various points during the show and, it was hoped, to be widely sung afterwards in London."

Two other stanzas appear elsewhere (*The Rock* 64):

We have worked and have fought
For this London of ours;
Our lives have been bought
By Our Lord on the Cross;
We are those who pay rent [5]
To the temporal powers;
Of our lives misspent
Our Lord bears the loss.
(*refrain*)

With the strength that was warmed
In verminous rooms, [10]
With hands that were formed
In resentful wombs,
We will build the new towers
And fashion the shrine
In this London of ours [15]
For the Bread and the Wine.
(*refrain*)

Martin Shaw to TSE, undated (Bodleian):

> V[erse] 3 One awkward musical place—last line really wants another syllable at beginning. This is pattern:—

In this London of ours
Oh of yours and of mine

> Without that syllable there is a *musical* hiatus. 3 has the only penultimate line with a masculine ending. Could this be done? Otherwise it won't sing well. "Ours" can't be sung like "towers" unfortunately. Shall we print 3 verses & say "go back to 1st verse to end with if you want to"? I think 3 enough for singing.

TSE sent two revised versions on 25 Jan 1934. To R. Webb-Odell, 11 May: "Here is a draft of a note for the programme · · · It does not seem to me worth while, in the space, to give an exact and complete synopsis of the play, but merely the hang of it. Perhaps you may think it desirable to add a note about the Builders' Song."

TSE to Theodore Spencer, 20 June 1934: "The performances went off well—houses quite well filled—bishops pleased as some money was made · · · we had a fellow come down from Stepney with a piano-accordeon to provide the accompaniment for the bricklayer's song." To C. H. Gibbs-Smith, 11 June 1935, probably of this song: "I have no objection to your using the lines · · · but as the song from which the words come is rather a poor piece of doggerel I should prefer that my name should not be attached unless you particularly insist upon it."

1–2, 6–7 **Ill done and undone | London · · · the Thames · · · Queen of · · · Water**: see note to *The Waste Land* [II] 77–110 for Enobarbus' description of Cleopatra's barge ("and what they undid did") and *The Waste Land* [III] 279–91 for Queen Elizabeth I on the Thames.

6, 7 **Thames bord · · · Water**: London's water authority, 1903–74, was the Metropolitan Water Board.

10, 20, 30 **unto this last**: in the parable of the labourers, the householder hires labourers at different hours. At the end of the day he pays all equally, saying to those who have worked the longest, "Take that thine is, and go thy way: I will give unto this last, even as unto thee" (Matthew 20: 14). Ruskin, *Unto This Last* (1862).

15–16 **Shall the fruit fall then | The harvest be waste**: Herbert: "all blasted? | All wasted? | Not so, my heart: but there is fruit", *The Collar* 15–17.

Mr. Pugstyles: The Elegant Pig

TSE to Frank Morley, 3 May 1933: "Dear Franck · · · What you need now is a Pig, A pig, tell Sussanna that his name is Mr. Pugstyles: the way to pick a good pig; the ones that look like Stanley [Baldwin] are better pigs than the ones that look like Winston [Churchill]; get one of Stanley's pigs." To Hayward, 26 July 1934: "I have finished my Poem about the Pig, and should like to recite it."

Broadside verses to stir up support were popular at elections in the 18th and 19th centuries. Alexander Baring, the Taunton MP 1806–26, was the subject, for instance, of *Baring's the Man*: "Baring deserves our highest praise, | Let ev'ry Briton him revere; | Extol his acts in raptrous lays, | And stedfastly to him adhere!" For

TSE pairing *Mr. Pugstyles* and *Difficulties of a Statesman*, see headnote to *Coriolan*, 1. COMPOSITION.

Title] In *Nicholas Nickleby* ch. XVI, Mr. Pugstyles is a "plump old gentleman" who leads a delegation of constituents. He accuses their MP, Mr. Gregsbury, of "rather too much of a 'gammon' tendency", but Gregsbury—"tough, burly, thickheaded"—refuses to resign (*Grover Smith* 33). Dickens also satirises elections in *Pickwick Papers* ch. XIII: "Some Account of Eatanswill ··· and of the Election of a Member to serve in Parliament for that ancient, loyal, and patriotic Borough". For Shelley, "*The Public Sty. The Boars in full Assembly*", see note to *Coriolan* I. *Triumphal March* 4–46.

2 **foreign bred pigs which our village disdains:** Shelley: "failure of a foreign market for | Sausages", *Swellfoot the Tyrant* II i. See notes to *Coriolan* I. *Triumphal March* 4–46 for *Swellfoot* and 44–47 for sausages and Dickens.

8 **heavyweight ··· Pugstyles:** OED "pugilist": "One who practises the art of boxing ··· *fig.* a vigorous controversialist", from 1790. "Jack Johnson ··· became the world's champion heavyweight pugilist", *Popular Mechanics* (1911).

11 **From the tips of his ears to the ends of his pedals:** "And the tips of his ears and his tail and his toes", *A Practical Possum* 61.

21–24 **Barn ··· Vale ··· Elms ··· Farm ··· Dale ··· Green:** names of pastoral origin, but districts of London by 1933.

25 **Minories ··· Old Jewry:** streets and districts within the City of London with historic Jewish communities. **Minories:** pronounced *Minn-ories.*

26–28 **along Lothbury glide ··· the lanes of Cheapside:** Wordsworth: "Bright volumes of vapour through Lothbury glide, | And a river flows on through the vale of Cheapside", *The Reverie of Poor Susan* 7–8 (*Grover Smith* 34). "the long lanes of dogs and men | To Canning Town and Rotherhithe", *Airs of Palestine, No.* 2 15–16.

27 **Old Drury:** tavern in Catherine Street, Covent Garden.

48 **cheering until you could hear us for miles:** "Bark bark BARK BARK | Until you can hear them all over the Park", *Of the Awefull Battle of the Pekes and the Pollicles* 9–10.

54 **chaired:** OED 1b: "To place in a chair or on a seat, and carry aloft in triumph, as an honour to a favourite, a successful competitor, and formerly often to the successful candidate at a parliamentary election." Housman: "We chaired you through the market-place", *A Shropshire Lad* XIX.

Bellegarde

The two typescript leaves of *Bellegarde* were sent by TSE to his brother Henry probably in 1935 or 1936 (Houghton MS Am 1691.9). The first has only seven typed lines, the second only four. TSE to Henry, 3 Mar 1937: "*Bellegarde* is merely a sketch which was never finished." As Henry noted, the name is from the character in Henry James's *The American.*

After receiving the *Bellegarde* typescript, Henry wrote to TSE, 5 Dec 1936, requesting material to present to Eliot House, Harvard. TSE replied, 30 Dec: "As for manuscripts, I do all my prose stuff straight onto the typewriter, so there is never anything of that; and as for verse, I usually make a few rough notes and then draft and redraft on the machine. Sometimes I start with a pencil and then when I have got going work straight on with the typewriter. I gave two mixed manuscripts of this kind, *Anabasis* and *The Rock*, to the Bodleian. I have about fourteen or sixteen pencilled sheets of part of *Murder* which I might send you: I only kept them in case of emergency as somebody told me that they might eventually fetch a considerable sum. But I ought to present something to Eliot House." He subsequently sent 17 leaves of this pencil outline draft of the play

About two months later, these were followed by a further leaf which at some time has apparently been pinned to fols. 4–7 of the *Murder in the Cathedral* manuscript draft (now MS Am. 1691.9 fol. 21). This pencilled draft includes six lines which appear to have been an earlier state of *Bellegarde*, immediately followed by nine draft lines of *Murder in the Cathedral* I, beginning "Power possessed grows to glory". In this pencil draft, the *Bellegarde* lines read:

> Leaping pleasures pass tunefully
> Follow futility easily [greedily *alt*] grasped
> Held in the hand matchless a moment
> Fade fast impaired by impotence
> Slip from fingers slip
> When fingered.

Henry wrote to Donald Gallup in Apr 1937 (quoted *Gallup 1989* 240–41):

> I received from my brother the other day another page of pencil MS of *Murder*. It was pinned to a letter from the *Sunday Times*, London thanking TSE for the loan of it for some exhibit. On this TSE had typed (to me): "Another scrap of *M in C.*" I read the first few lines and then combed both editions for them but I could not find them—despite the fact that they were familiar. Finally I found that these first lines had been taken by TSE and used in a short poem called *Bellegarde* which he never finished or published. The rest of the MS *was* from *Murder*—a speech of the Second Tempter ··· I then examined the *Bellegarde* MS (which is typed, not handwritten) again, and noted that the four lines on p.2 of it sounded very much as if meant for Becket [12–15]. So this *Bellegarde* is evidently discarded material from *Murder.*

On a slip accompanying the two ts leaves of *Bellegarde*, Henry wrote: "These lines are nearly identical with six lines written for *Murder in the Cathedral* but deleted by TSE before publication. See *Murder MS.*"

Lines unrelated to *Bellegarde*, from a separate draft of *Murder in the Cathedral*, were to provide TSE with the opening of *Burnt Norton* (ts, U. Maryland). See headnote to *Burnt Norton* 2. GENESIS, and description of *tsMinC* (*Burnt Norton* Textual History, headnote).

The Anniversary

Recited 6 June 1935. John Carroll Perkins was minister of King's Chapel, Boston, 1926–33. For the Perkinses, see headnote to next poem and headnote to *Burnt Norton*, 1. THE HOUSE AND TSE'S VISIT. To George Bell, 13 June 1934: "Dr. Perkins is a specimen of the almost extinct Right Wing American Unitarian Minister, and has read a good deal of Anglican theology."

6–7 **Mr. Mase- | field**: as Poet Laureate since 1930, John Masefield had written a good deal of patriotic verse. His third poem, for George V's silver jubilee in 1935, had appeared in April, and he had been appointed O.M. on 3 June.

19 **pipkins**: OED 1: "A small earthenware pot or pan, used chiefly in cookery." **panikins**: OED ("pannikin · · · Also · · · panikin"): "A small metal · · · drinking vessel". **firkins**: OED: "A small cask for liquids".

A Valedictory

Forbidding Mourning: To the Lady of the House.

Recited 28 Sept 1935.

Mrs. Carroll Perkins was TSE's hostess in Chipping Campden each summer from 1934 to 1939, except for 1936 (*Composition FQ* 35). TSE to Emily Hale's friend Jeanie McPherrin, 3 Oct 1935: "I went down to Campden that afternoon [26 Sept] · · · I had, of course, a perfectly delightful birthday party. Mrs. P. is (almost too consciously, malice would say) the perfect hostess—on Friday *The Yeomen of the Guard* · · · on Saturday evening a dinner arranged by Emily with great care in *her* honour—healths and tasteful speeches from and to the servants, and an Occasional Poem by myself which seemed to go down well · · · I would gladly put up with · · · the Perkins's in London permanently, for the sake of liberating E."

Concerned about Emily, he wrote again to McPherrin, 13 Dec 1934: "the Perkins's must be rather a drain on her vitality—I know that they are on mine, though I have never been with them any longer together than that weekend." To his Aunt Susie (Mrs. Hinkley), 7 June: "Mrs. Perkins strikes me as one of those gentle, stupid, kind, tyrannous, prejudiced, oppressive and tremendously powerful personalities who blight everyone about them · · · she makes my back hair bristle; and confound it one can't help trusting that bristle. Dr. Perkins is a very lovable, lazy-minded, muddleheaded man who is completely dominated by his wife, and who is really happier in Emily's company than he is with Mrs. Perkins, but he doesn't know it." (For Housman's "bristles", see headnote to *A Proclamation*.)

To Mrs. Perkins, 5 Mar 1945: "I wish you might return and restore the garden at Campden: the place seemed to be so peculiarly yours, that I should not want to visit it again without you there · · · many of the gardens in England that you knew, and some of which I remember so clearly visiting with you, must be sad vestiges of their former state · · · There are still those at Campden who hope for your return. [*footnote*: I would write a poem for you.]"

On Mrs. Perkins's behalf, TSE presented more than 400 of her colour slides of gardens of England and Scotland to the Royal Horticultural Society in London (*Evesham Journal* 13 Mar 1948). To Mrs. Perkins, 3 Mar 1948: "It all seemed symbolic of a beauty and order which is vanishing from the world."

To Gallup, 15 Sept 1961: "I remember composing a set of occasional verses for Mrs. Perkins. She and her husband had rented a house in Campden, Gloucestershire, for several summers, and they were just leaving I think, in 1939, after the outbreak of war, to return to the United States. Mrs. Perkins was a very keen gardener, and very much enjoyed the garden of the lady whose tenants they were. They never returned to England. After the war Dr. Perkins died and Mrs. Perkins went blind."

TSE's interest in flora dated back to his tenth year when he wrote *Eliot's Floral Magazine* (1899). Another hostess and friend, Hope Mirrlees, gave him a copy of *Wild Flowers of the Wayside and Woodland*, ed. T. H. Scott et al., 1936 (repr. 1940) in July 1941. For his nonsense botany, see headnote to *A Practical Possum.*

Title] Like *The Anniversary*, written for Dr. Perkins three months earlier, this title is reminiscent of Donne. Yet unlike *A Valediction: Forbidding Mourning*, which dramatises Donne's own leavetaking, this *Valedictory* marks the departure of the recipient. Two days after reciting the poem, TSE wrote to her: "I want now to thank you for all your kindness and sweetness to me during the past two summers · · · I had come to feel 'at home' at Campden in a way in which I had not felt at home for some twenty-one years, anywhere."

3–4 **autumn's season of · · · moister**: Keats: "Season of mists", *To Autumn* 1.

5 **tardy rose**: Horace: "Boy, ask not where the tardy Rose, | Secure from blighting Winter, blows", *Odes* I xxxviii (tr. William Duncombe in Dodsley's *Works of Horace in English Verse. By Several Hands* ed. Duncombe, 1757).

7–8, 49–50 **grief · · · leaf · · · grief | Revive · · · leaf**: Blake: "The Catterpiller on the Leaf | Repeats to thee thy Mothers grief", *Auguries of Innocence* 37–38.

9 **violas**: the plant, pronounced with stressed long *i* (as *violet*).

10, 41 **put off their coloured frocks · · · put on your gaudy jerkins**: John Norris: "The Woods shall put on their green Livery · · · And I a Violet Garland for my Offering", *A Pastoral upon the Blessed Virgin, gone from Nazareth to Visit Elizabeth* (1687). OED "jerkin": "A garment for the upper part of the body, worn by men in the sixteenth and seventeenth centuries."

11 **zinnia and marigold**: "experiences of gardenia or zinnia refine our experience of rose or sweet-pea", *John Marston* (1934).

16 **Clematis Jackmanii**: "will the clematis | Stray down, bend to us · · ·?" *Burnt Norton* IV 3–4 (*Composition FQ* 36). **Jackmanii**: four syllables ending *ee-eye*.

17–18 **myosotis · · · English name**: forget-me-not.

20 **cheat the winter into spring**: "Midwinter spring is its own season", *Little Gidding* I 1.

21 **O long procession, happy flowers**: Marvell: "See how the flow'rs, as at parade, | Under their Colours stand displayed: | Each Regiment in order grows, | That of the Tulip, Pink and Rose", *Upon Appleton House* XXXIX.

28–29 **And when to prune, and when to bind | And when to cut, and when to move:**

for "a time to be born, and a time to die; a time to plant, and a time to pluck up that which is planted", see note to *East Coker* I 9–11. *Paradise Lost* IX 210: "Lop overgrown, or prune, or prop, or bind".

36–38 *variant* **winter's dull ··· roots, that live beneath ··· death**: "dead ··· Dull roots ··· Winter ··· life", *The Waste Land* [I] 2–7.

39 **revolving year**: Dryden, *The Hind and the Panther* II 703; Thomson, *Autumn* 1305.

39–42 **shall bring | The sweet deception of the spring ··· Mrs. Perkins**: "The sound of horns and motors, which shall bring | Sweeney to Mrs. Porter in the spring", *The Waste Land* [III] 197–98. **deception of the spring**: "The deception of the thrush?" *Burnt Norton* I 22.

43–44 **man alone | Remembers in the singing bone**: "the bones sang ··· the bones sang ··· Forgetting themselves", *Ash-Wednesday* II 23, 48, 51.

45 **"Green earth forgets"**: Meredith: "how they sucked the teats | Of Carnage ··· Flushed the vext earth with blood, green earth forgets", *France.—December, 1870* V 21–24.

47 **familiar ghosts**: "a familiar compound ghost", *Little Gidding* II 42.

55 **human wishes**: after mentioning Erasmus Darwin's *The Botanic Garden* and quoting Henry Brooke's *Universal Beauty* in his Introduction to Johnson's *"London: A Poem" and "The Vanity of Human Wishes"* (1930), TSE wrote: "This is decadence ··· an age of retired country clergymen and schoolmasters ··· cursed with a Pastoral convention ··· intolerably poetic".

Pollicle Dogs and Jellicle Cats

Sent to Geoffrey Faber, 6 Mar 1936 (see headnote to *Practical Cats*, 3. COMPOSITION). A setting by Andrew Lloyd-Webber, and sung by him, was released on *Now & Forever* (2001).

For "Pollicle" and "Jellicle" see note to *The Marching Song of the Pollicle Dogs.* "Pollicle dogs and cats all must | Jellicle cats and dogs all must | Like undertakers, come to dust", *Five-Finger Exercises* II. *Lines to a Yorkshire Terrier* 10–12.

1 **The Princess Louise**: renowned for its elaborate Victorian interior; at 208 High Holborn, a short walk from Russell Square.

1, 8–10] See note to *WLComposite* 207–213 = **321–27**.

4 **talking of thisses and that's**: "the I is a construction out of experience, an abstraction from it; and the *thats*, the browns and hards and flats, are equally ideal constructions from experience", *Knowledge and Experience* 19.

6–19 **I have been ··· a jack of all trades ··· I have done ··· I have been ··· I invented an excellent specific for scurf ··· I bought ··· I once wrote ··· I travelled ··· in hats**: Lewis Carroll: "He said 'I look for butterflies ··· I make them into mutton pies ··· I hunt for haddocks' eyes ··· I sometimes dig for buttered rolls", the White Knight's song, *Through the Looking-Glass* ch. VIII ("It's My Own Invention"). See *Mélange Adultère de Tout.*

8–9 **life ··· and the profit and loss:** "dead ··· And the profit and loss", *The Waste Land* [IV] 312–14.

9 **fat and the lean:** Numbers 13: 20: "whether it be fat or lean".

11 **an agent for small furnished flats:** "A small house agent's clerk", *The Waste Land* [III] 232.

14–15 **Turf ··· Accountant:** euphemism for a bookmaker.

16 **scurf:** OED: "A morbid condition of the skin, especially of the head", *obs.*

16, 20 **specific ··· cure:** OED B. 1a: "A specific remedy", with 1671, "a specific for the cure of the Dropsie".

18 **Levantine:** stressed on the first syllable (the less common of the two pronunciations).

19 **I travelled (from Luton) in hats:** "One of the low on whom assurance sits | As a silk hat on a Bradford millionaire", *The Waste Land* [III] 233–34. **travelled ··· in hats:** commercial traveller, salesman.

34, 66 **actually:** to John Hayward, 12 June 1943: "it is always desirable to be reminded when one has slipped into using *actually*".

51 **Ingoldsby Oddie:** for *The Ingoldsby Legends*, see headnote to *A Fable for Feasters.*

64 **turned round with a look of surprise:** "with a pained surprise ··· and turn ··· turned", *La Figlia Che Piange* 4–5, 17.

The Country Walk

Published in *The Times* 6 June 2009, with the title *Cows.*

As the unadopted subtitle shows, TSE began this as an Epistle to Emily Hale. Their love for one another is manifest in his concern in letters when she was visiting England. See headnote to *Burnt Norton* for their visit to the house. TSE wrote to his Aunt Susie (Mrs. Hinkley), 7 June: "At present Emily is at Campden—a beauty-spot of England, or an eyesore, according as you look at it—with Dr. and Mrs. Perkins and Mrs. Philip Hale." (See headnote to *A Valedictory Forbidding Mourning.*)

To Dorothy Pound, 11 Aug [1925]: "I have a lovely p.c. for you but left it in London not knowing where you were: 6 cows killed by lightning under a tree in Gloucestershire." To Roy Campbell, 2 Sept 1929: "I don't know anything about bullfighting but it does not seem kind to the bulls or to your public. But I have a terror of bulls and even of cows, and was brought up to be amiable to animals, so I am prejudiced. I hope you will recover quickly. Who eats the bulls that are killed in this way? I am interested in the theories of the origin of the practice." To Theodore Spencer, 19 July 1933: "The worst of the country is that I am terrified of Cows. How does one get over that?" To Virginia Woolf, 3 Oct 1935: "last week end I was in Gloucestershire and ran away from a Bull down a hill into some blackberry bushes".

"I am afraid of high places and cows", *Harvard College Class of 1910, Seventh Report* (1935). To Anthea Tandy, 18 Oct 1956: "I had meant to send you a word of warning, lest you should begin breathing at Bulls too close. A friend of mine tried it on 3 bulls (all behind bars). Two of them, so far as she could judge, were rather annoyed than otherwise; the third responded with purrs of friendliness, but (she added) he is a most exceptionally sweet-tempered bull anyway."

Frank Morley of his son: "Donald at the age of nine in 1935 had begun to edit *The Family News*, a monthly periodical hand-published once a year. Tom submitted poems, but not until 1938 was a poem of Tom's accepted by Donald. That was a poem on Cows. Poems on Cats had been rejected. Donald had his own cat, which he had named Saucerer. Perhaps Donald as editor felt there was a spoof somewhere, about Tom's Cats. It did take a bit of knowing, always, to separate Tom's wit from his chaff", in *Tate ed.* 113.

The copy sent to Hayward in Dec 1936 (King's) is followed by *The cowlover's retort; or, an answer to the late poem, entitled "The country walk"*, a poem by Hayward with extensive criticisms and revisions by TSE (see *Smart* 103). TSE to Pound, 30 Dec (Beinecke): "for a Cow's best friend is her udder— | And the milk streamed in the pail | For the sake of dear old Yale".

Title] Aldous Huxley had published a story called *A Country Walk* in *Coterie* Autumn 1920, having in the previous issue, Easter 1920, published a play called *Permutations Among the Nightingales.* (*A Cooking Egg* was published in *Coterie* May 1919.) For Huxley's indebtedness to TSE's 1920 poems, see *McCue 2013b.*

Unadopted subtitle ***An Epistle to Miss E— H— with the humble Compliments of her obliged servant, the Author***: Popeian, as for instance *Epistle To Miss Blount on her leaving the Town, after the Coronation* ("As some fond virgin, whom her mother's care | Drags from the town to wholsom country air", 1–2); see *Burnt Norton* III 17, "Wind in and out of unwholesome lungs", and note. Substitution of dashes was frequent, as in *An Epistle to Mr. B—* by Francis Knapp (*c.* 1705). ***Miss E— H—***: Emily Hale. ***Tissington Tatlow***: general secretary of the Student Christian Movement, and rector of St. Nicholas, Acorns, in the City, in succession to H. H. Pereira.

2–3 **In England's green and pleasant land · · · the Cows**: Blake: "the holy Lamb · · · in England's green and pleasant land", from *Milton* ("And did those feet") 3, 16.

26 **horns · · · tossed**: "horns that toss and toss", *The Burnt Dancer* 35 (see note).

30, 32 **sober wishes never stray · · · away**: Thomas Gray: "Far from the madding crowd's ignoble strife | Their sober wishes never learn'd to stray · · · way", *Elegy Written in a Country Church Yard* 73–76.

33–34 **I could take sanctuary | In any oak or apple tree**: Marvell: "I · · · Take Sanctuary in the Wood", *Upon Appleton House* 481–82. After the Battle of Worcester in 1651, Charles II took sanctuary in an oak tree (the Royal Oak).

34 **In any oak or apple tree**: "Children's voices in the orchard · · · Swing up into the apple-tree", *Landscapes* I. *New Hampshire* 1, 12. "the children in the apple-tree", *Little Gidding* V 35. "the O'Possum | As he swings from a neighbouring tree", *How to Pick a Possum* 7–8.

I am asked by my friend, the Man in White Spats

To Alison Tandy, 6 Jan 1937, introducing *The Rum Tum Tugger* and signed "Your fexnite | Possum".

For the identity of the Man in White Spats, see note on the Preface to *Practical Cats.*

A Proclamation

With a letter to John Hayward, 27 Jan 1937, alluding to Housman's *The Name and Nature of Poetry* ("if a line of poetry strays into my memory, my skin bristles so that the razor ceases to act"): "You know my aversion to Modernism in all forms, and especially in Poetry; and you know that Movements like Surrealism are things that I cannot make Head or Tail of. But occasionally something comes my way, that makes me catch my breath, rub my eyes, pinch myself, sit up, cut myself shaving, and behave like Housman thinking of one of his poems—I mean that we old fogies have something to learn after all from the younger generation, and perhaps it's good for us to have a rude jolt now and again before we get too fossilised. Such a poem came my way yesterday, and I send it to you at once in the hope that you will be able to tell me whether I am awake or dreaming? Is this, or am I mistaken, the dawn of a new era, to which we must learn to adapt ourselves. I feel that what we old ones lack is Understanding, and I mean especially *sympathetic* Understanding. What I enclose is of the modern Allusive kind. I fear that I have not caught all its Allusions—though the subtle reference in line 23 to the 'Othello music' could escape no sensitive reader; it has that reference to 'old, forgotten far off things' that is so fascinating—with that vein of mocking irony running through it so characteristic of the Moderns—there must be many more allusions that you will be able to identify. Am I Right or am I Wrong? Please return it with any marginal notes you think fit to make. Perhaps you will laugh me to scorn, in your keen incisive Voltairean way, but it still seems to me that I have felt the authentic breath of genius. It was certainly a breath. But was it authentic? That is the question. Yours exaltedly, TP". (For Old Possum as "the real surrealist poet we have been waiting for", see the comic report supposedly by Herbert Read but actually by TSE about his own *Book of Practical Cats*, quoted in the headnote to the volume, 5. PUBLICATION.)

The editor and communist Roger Roughton, to whom *A Proclamation* is comically attributed, had just published *Sliding Scale*, a surrealist poem likewise in quatrains (*Poetry* Jan 1937).

TSE to Lawrence Durrell, July 1949: "It is refreshing always to find a poet who does understand that prose sense comes first, and that poetry is merely prose developed by a knowledge of aeronautics."

1 **Fair stood the wind for France:** Drayton, *To the Cambro-Britons. Agincourt* 1. (H. E. Bates's novel of this title was not published until 1944.)

2 **Cat jumped out:** "I knew how to let the cat out of the bag", *Gus: The Theatre Cat* 24. Roughton: "Hurrying kittens refer to the source", *Sliding Scale* 5. TSE to Tom

Faber, 7 Nov 1947, referring to Hugh Dalton's Budget of 12 Nov: "I reply with somewhat more than my usual promptitude · · · in response to your judicious observation about the necessity of spending as much money as possible before the odious Mr. Dalton lets his cats out of the bag."

3 **But O for the touch of a vanished hand**: Tennyson, *Break, break, break* 11.

4 **And sixpenny-worth of stout**: Roughton: "enclose a penny-halfpenny stamp; | For I must go at ten to one, | Ten to one it's guineas time", *Soluble Noughts and Crosses* 8–10 in *Contemporary Poetry and Prose* July 1936 (after the advertising slogan "Any time is Guinness time").

7, 19 **The face that launched a thousand ships · · · Helen of Troy set out to sea**: Marlowe: "Was this the face that launched a thousand ships | And burnt the topless towers of Ilium?" *Doctor Faustus* sc. XIV.

8 **Had a knowing look in its eye**: Dickens: "'And with *him?*' asked the boy, with a knowing look in his eye", *Howard's Son* in *All the Year Round* 7 Sept 1867.

9 **the mossy bank**: Amelia Welby, *The Green Mossy Bank where the Buttercups Grew* in *Poems* (1845).

9–10 **The toadstool on the mossy bank | Muttered aloud in its sleep**: Tennyson: "The white lake-blossom fell into the lake | As the pimpernel dozed on the lea", *Maud* I [xxii] 896–97.

12 **They sow and they also reap**: Galatians 6: 7: "whatsoever a man soweth, that shall he also reap".

13 **Once more unto the breach, dear friend**: *Henry V* III i: "Once more unto the breach, dear friends, once more."

14 **The Jellicle hosts proclaim**: "whom heav'n's high hosts proclaim", *Hark, a chorus in the skies*, no. 444 in *Psalms and Hymns* ed. J. Bickersteth (6th ed. 1838).

15 **Make wing at once to the rooky wood**: *Macbeth* III ii: "Light thickens, and the crow | Makes wing to the rooky wood."

17 **Ring out the old, ring in the new**: Tennyson, *In Memoriam* CVI 5.

18 **Jellicle Cats have got the vote**: suffrage was extended to all men in 1918 and to all women in 1928.

19–20 **set out to sea | In a beautiful pea-green boat:** Edward Lear: "The Owl and the Pussy-Cat went to sea | In a beautiful pea-green boat", *The Owl and the Pussy-Cat.*

21 **come blow up your horn**: "Little boy blue, come blow your horn", nursery rhyme.

22 **The year's at the spring**: Browning: "The year's at the spring | And day's at the morn · · · God's in his heaven— | All's right with the world!" *Pippa Passes*, Song (I 221–28). **too-wit too-woo**: *Love's Labour's Lost* V ii: "Tu-who · · · | Tu-whit to-who". To John Hayward, 26 Oct 1936: "Chatterton (the something boy who perisht in his pride), to wit (to who)". (Wordsworth: "I thought of Chatterton, the marvellous Boy, | The sleepless Soul that perished in its pride", *Resolution and Independence* 43–44.) See letter including *That bird wych in the dark time of the yeerë* in "Improper Rhymes".

23, 27 **Cassia buds and Venetian blinds · · · Cats**: *Othello, the Moor of Venice* I iii, IAGO: "drown cats and blind puppies" and "Cassio's a proper man, let me see now". See headnote for "the Othello music" (the title of an essay by G. Wilson Knight in *The Wheel of Fire*).

24 **And never a spray of rue**: Arnold: "Strew on her roses, roses, | And never a spray of yew!" *Requiescat* 1–2. (*Hamlet* IV v, OPHELIA: "There's rosemary · · · there's rue for you.")

25 **Let Jellicle joy be unconfined:** Byron: "On with the dance! let joy be unconfined", *Childe Harold's Pilgrimage* III 12.

26 **bring down the sky**: Wordsworth: "In some calm season, when these lofty rocks | At night's approach bring down the unclouded sky", *The Excursion* IV 1158.

27 **For Cats may come since Cats must go**: Tennyson: "For men may come and men may go, | But I go on for ever", *The Brook* 33–34.

28 **For an annual holiday**: the Holidays with Pay Bill was under discussion in 1937 (passed 1938).

after 28 ***Cetera desunt***: the rest is missing (L.) "*Cætera desunt——*" appears after the last line of Herrick's *The Country life, to the honoured M. End. Porter, Groome of the Bed-Chamber to His Maj.*, and "*Desunt cætera*" after the last lines of Donne's poems *Resurrection, imperfect* and *To the Countesse of Bedford. Begun in France but never perfected*.

A Practical Possum

Written Autumn 1940. To Polly Tandy, 22 Oct 1940: "I have been very evil not to write before · · · to thank Alison for the Lavender Bag" (used to freshen laundry). To Alison, 17 Dec: "I never thanked you properly either for the practical Lavender Bag, which is at work on my shirts". (TSE had signed himself "Lavender Possum" when writing to Polly Tandy, 4 Sept 1935.)

Colophon of the edition of 1947:

> This poem, one of Mr. Eliot's "occasional verse effusions," was composed as a letter to a little girl who had sent him a lavender bag. Mr. Eliot, who has already identified himself in "The Old Possum's Book of Practical Cats", needs no introduction as a poet.
>
> The very kind permission of the author of the verses, the owner of the manuscript, Mr. Henry Ware Eliot, and the Printing and Graphic Arts Department of Harvard Library makes possible this first printing · · · The edition is limited to eighty copies of which this is number [ ].

Donald Gallup later recalled that it was he who had suggested the poem for printing, and that the Houghton already owned "the original longhand draft", *Gallup 1988* 103.

TSE to Philip Hofer, 15 Aug 1947: "The printing seems to me an excellent piece of work · · · I must, however, raise a protest and a note of exclamation against their having printed as many as eighty copies. When you first raised the question and desired to sell some copies you suggested · · · that you would print sixty copies and send me twenty for myself. You were certainly very courteous when I declined to allow the poem to be printed for public circulation, but in your letter of December

3rd you said: 'The boys will print a few copies for private circulation solely and will send you some of these.' Well eighty copies does seem to me a good deal more than a few. It is almost certain that with as many as eighty copies released some of them will eventually get into the market and become collector's pieces, and I have no desire that this should come to pass. It really seems to me that you or your pupils have very considerably exceeded my licence and certainly there is a discrepancy between the original proposal to print sixty copies and send me twenty and the eventual printing of eighty copies and sending me only six."

To I. A. Richards, then teaching at Harvard, 8 Sept 1955: "The ··· incidents of the plot have pretty well vanished from my memory, but ··· I know that I was very annoyed, that I wrote him a letter ··· and that I subsequently received a list (either directly or indirectly) of the people to whom copies had been sent, and of those from whom copies had been retrieved. I remember remarking the fact that the people from whom he had recovered the copies were for the most part people like yourself, whom I didn't mind having copies, and I wished that he had got back some of the other copies instead ··· The point is that when I was in America in June, my cousin Aimée Lamb told me ··· that I had written a cruel letter ··· that Hofer had been deeply hurt; that there were circumstances which excused or extenuated his fault or error; and that my letter was so extreme as to make it impossible for him to explain these circumstances to me ··· If my cousin's assertion is correct, i.e. that my reproof was wholly out of proportion to the offense committed, I should like to apologise to this Mr. Hofer." (For TSE's "exasperation" in 1949 at the printing of his *Undergraduate Poems*, see headnote to "Uncollected Poems", 2. *POEMS WRITTEN IN EARLY YOUTH*.)

In TSE's nonsense botany series *Old Possum's "Children Shown to the Flowers"* (Faber archive), Plate 7 is "Possum Pie", with a coloured drawing at the head: "POSSUM PIE (*N. Possumus*): locally known in Bloomsbury as 'Humble Pie'; in Chelsea as 'Sweetie Pie'—many other local variants). The usual complaint against this undeservedly unpopular perennial is that its flowers are small and sparse, of irregular appearance, and of an uninteresting dull purple ··· Possum Pie benefits by transplantation, but even under the most scientific care takes from ten to twenty years to attain maturity. Nevertheless, under the most favourable conditions this is undoubtedly a handsome plant of decorative use." (OED: "*non possumus* [= we can not, L.] A statement or answer expressing inability to act or move in a matter.")

To Virginia Woolf, 1 Dec [1937]: "I suppose you will be off to Rodmell towards the end of the month to eat a Fortnum & Mason Yorkshire Pye". To Enid Faber, 24 Apr 1940: "I don't quite identify Tristram Pye. Is he one of the Hertfordshire Pyes? One of them was Poet Laureate some years ago." (Henry James Pye, Poet Laureate 1790–1813.) TSE to Enid Faber, 1 Oct 1942: "I was particularly sorry to postpone my introduction to Auntie Pye (if she meets with approval, she must be promoted to the honorary title of Sweetie Pye) ··· Does Auntie Pye smell of lavender?" To Tom Faber, 19 Aug 1943: "I hope that you slept soundly in an Auntie Pye Bed ··· picking lavender ··· I enclose a small Subscription so that you may purchase a sponge, a scrubbing brush, and a packet of Lux." (OED, "apple-pie bed": " a bed in which, as a practical joke, the sheets are so folded that a person cannot get his legs down".)

J. G. Wood, of the possum: "When captured it is easily tamed, and falls into the habit of domestication with great ease. It is, however, not very agreeable as a domestic companion, as it is gifted with a powerful and very unpleasant odour",

The Illustrated Natural History (see headnote to *Old Possum's Book of Practical Cats* 1. POSSUM).

1 **once lived in a Pye**: "Four and twenty blackbirds, | Baked in a pie", nursery rhyme. Byron: "A nest of tuneful persons, to my eye | Like 'four and twenty blackbirds in a pye;' || 'Which pye being open'd they began to sing'", Dedication to *Don Juan*, first two stanzas, referring to Robert Southey's appointment to succeed Henry James Pye as Poet Laureate.

2 **Surrounded by Gravy and Sweet Pertaters**: to Ezra Pound, 23 Dec 1937: "what can pore ole possum do to help except to allow himself to be baked with sweet pertaters which he is always ready to do, knowin what savoury gravoury he exudes under sufficient heat and with the judicious garnishments etc." (OED "potato": "*illit.* pertater".)

3 **Glass in his Eye**: another cat with a monocle (and cane) is Cumberleylaude, the Gourmet Cat.

4–8 **And a clerical hat and an apron and gaiters ··· And everyone said ··· isn't he Well Preserved**: "My morning coat, my collar mounting firmly to the chin ··· (They will say: 'But how his arms and legs are thin!')" *The Love Song of J. Alfred Prufrock* 41–44. **a clerical hat**: "features of clerical cut", *Five-Finger Exercises* V. *Lines for Cuscuscaraway and Mirza Murad Ali Beg* 1–2. *Tippett* 51 recorded a visit to Frank Morley, *c.* 1939: "mooching about on the grass I could see Eliot, wearing his famous clerical hat" (Oliver Soden, personal communication). **Well Preserved**: OED: "Often used to describe elderly persons who carry their years well."

28 **Condy's Fluid**: disinfectant. **Keating's Powder**: insecticide.

30 **Life Buoy**: soap; correctly "Lifebuoy" (see Textual History).

32–33 *variant* **But the Possum answered "No Sir," | And he winked his other eye**: Kipling: "The sergeant arst no questions, but 'e winked the other eye", *"Back to the Army Again"* (in *A Choice of Kipling's Verse*).

35 **Chemist (whose name was Boot)**: Boots the Chemist, est. John Boot, 1849.

39 **Eno's Salt**: digestive powder.

40 **iodoform**: OED: "A compound of iodine ··· having an odour of saffron and a sweet taste; used medicinally, and as an antiseptic".

60 **Possum's Nose**: to Polly Tandy, 14 Nov [1935]: "The great thing to begin with is that the Nose should be a Projection and not a Recession, because after that, once you have the material to work upon, it can be worked up into Roman or Norman by will power, prayer, absent treatment or manipulative surgery, but you cant make bricks without straw or a nose out of a dimple or a silk purse either ··· The main thing about a nose is that the bearer should be able to breathe through it, that is where I have always been a sufferer in life's handicap. If she can breathe through her nose, she has a chance; which I wish her, never having had a chance myself."

60–61 **Possum's Nose ··· his toes**: for Lear's Pobble, see note to *Suite Clownesque* I 23, 25.

61 **And the tips of his ears and his tail and his toes**: "From the tips of his ears to the ends of his pedals", *Mr. Pugstyles: The Elegant Pig* 11.

The Practical Cat

Sent to Alison Tandy, 15 Nov 1937.

For the title, see headnote to *Old Possum's Book of Practical Cats.* Before becoming one of the "4 kinds of Cat the Old Gumbie Cat the Practical Cat the Porpentine Cat and the Big Bravo Cat" (to Polly Tandy, 4 Nov 1934), the Practical Cat appears to have begun as companion to the Possum. To Tom Faber, 7 May 1931:

> Thank you for your Letters. I hope you like the Book, because it is a Poetry Book and I like it. I was very much Interested to hear about Ty Glyn Aeron, and the Island, and the Trout, and the Bees. I told the Practical Cat all about it, and the Practical Cat was so Excited that we finally said we would
>
> Go in for COUNTRY LIFE.
>
> For instance, there's

> Your uncle
>
> Tom

8 **Oopsa!**: "I greet him with an OOPSA CAT!" *The Ad-dressing of Cats* 49. OED "upsidaisy ··· Also oops-a-daisy", with 1912: "*Ups-a-daisy*, the tender words of the fond father when engaged in baby-jumping."

15 **He's always ready for fish on Fridays**: to Clive Bell, 11 Feb [1935]: "I cant eat Meat on Friday and it casts rather a damper on a British company to see a man eating eggs no matter how much he drinks."

The Jim Jum Bears

Written for young American relatives at Christmas [1937?].

3 **broken ··· scattered the bricks**: "shattered bricks", *Second Caprice in North Cambridge* 7.

7, 10 **Nurse ··· Jim ··· Nurse**: Belloc: "And always keep a-hold of Nurse | For fear of finding something worse", *Jim* in *Cautionary Tales* (1907).

16 **muddy feet**: "muddy feet that press | To early coffee-stands", *Preludes* II 4–5.

The Marching Song of the Pollicle Dogs

Published with *Billy M'Caw: The Remarkable Parrot* in *The Queen's Book of the Red Cross* (1939), introduced by an italicised note: "The publication of MR. T. S. ELIOT'S *The Waste Land* had as startling and decisive effect on English poetry as had the *Lyrical Ballads.* His more recent play, *Murder in the Cathedral*, had a similar impact upon the theatre. Quite lately he has confounded and delighted us with a collection of poems about cats. It is in such light-hearted vein that he is represented in these present verses." After this TSE has written on the galley proof, "Ha ha!" (At the front of the book, "The Authors and Their Contributions" explains: "T. S. Eliot writes two lilting poems: *The Marching Song of the Pollicle Dogs*, and *Billy M'Caw: The Remarkable Parrot.*")

Published at the beginning of the war, the book included a message from Queen Elizabeth, consort of George VI. TSE to Sir Frank Bowater (Lord Mayor of London), 4 Oct 1939: "I have your undated letter, kindly inviting me to contribute a poem to the Royal Red Cross book, to be published on behalf of your fund for the Red Cross. I should be delighted to contribute a poem, but unfortunately I have no unpublished poem on hand, and ··· I do not know when I can look forward to a time when I shall be able to write another poem. The only unpublished verses which I have on hand are a few poems written for children, not included in my forthcoming book of children's verse, which I fear are not of the quality which readers of the Royal Red Cross book are entitled to expect." To John Hayward, 12 Oct 1939: "I have been having some correspondence with Sir Frank Bowater, outgoing Lord Mayor, as a result of which he is being offered *The Marching Song of the Pollicle Dogs* for his Red Cross Book." The poems were sent to the publisher, Hodder & Stoughton, the following day. To Polly Tandy, 2 Nov 1939: "I enclose two Poems of Possum to be included in the Queen's Red Cross Book."

To John Hayward, 2 Apr 1936 describing his meeting with an "elderly Scottish gentleman" who claimed descent from the El(l)iot family, which he characterised as notable for blue eyes, hot temper and obduracy.

> Well, said he, do you mind the Elliot marching song? Yes said I, it begins
>
> My name it is little Jock Elliot
> And wha maun meddle wi' me?
>
> Ah ye ken it fine, said he, that shows that ye are a true Elliot. I am afraid that I read it somewhere, I said, I dont know the tune.

Valerie Eliot later wrote that "*The Marching Song of the Pollicle Dogs* was written to the tune of *The Elliots of Minto*" (see headnote to *Practical Cats*). TSE evidently knew the marching song, which is quoted in the notes to Walter Scott's *The Antiquary*.

On 14 Mar 1946 Arthur Rogers wrote to him about his poem: "In the last line why 'Wha *Maun* Meddle Wi' Me'? The original is surely '*Daur*' and what Scotsman would say Maun for Daur!" Recalling his mistake in quoting Arnaut Daniel (see headnote to "*Poems* (1920)", 7. PUBLICATION OF *ARA VOS PREC*), TSE replied to Rogers, 20 Mar 1946: "I do not pretend to be an expert in the Northern language and it may be that I have been guilty of a howler of the grossest kind. I was once guilty of a blunder of equal gravity with a quotation from the Provençal language. I only know that it was *maun* in a typed copy of the *Ballad of Little Jock Elliot* which somebody showed me some years ago. I admit that I was puzzled by this word which is certainly used much further South, and *daur* seems to me, on the face of it, much more probable. If I ever reprint my poem I shall certainly get it vetted by one of my Scottish friends." (TSE to Ian Cox, 14 Oct 1938, declining to take place in a broadcast about *Moby-Dick*: "it is so long since I have heard my own North Shore speech, that I should be in danger of confusing even that with the speech to the Eastward of Cape Porpoise. So it is evident that I know just enough about these matters not to dare to meddle with them.")

After the attribution in *Commerce* Autumn 1929 of *Som de l'escalina* (*Ash-Wednesday* III) to "T. S. Eliott", TSE wrote to Marguerite Caetani, 21 Jan 1930: "I was Angry about the spelling of my name, but it is a Venial rather than a Deadly Sin: Elyot, Eliott or Aliot have been used at various periods; the only real insult is to spell it Elliot or Elliott, which is Scotch." See headnote to *Whan Cam ye fra the Kirk?* and letter to H. J. C. Grierson, 15 Nov 1926. To Ottoline Morrell, from Harvard, 14 Mar 1933: "outside of Boston I am simply T. S. Eliot, but here I am an Eliot. There is a pleasure in anonymity—and that I am better able to enjoy in London than here, where I am still a news item; but after eighteen years of being merely oneself there is a pleasure in being just a member of one's family."

On 20 Nov 1936 he wrote to Polly Tandy of his hope that Possum might "become a regular Feature in the Children's Hour":

> I am toilin away trying to finish the Marching Song of the Pollicle Dogs, but the Scots dialect or language comes difficult to Me. It starts
>
> My name it is little Tom Pollicle
> And wha maun meddle wi me?
>
> but there I stuck so far.

TSE told Donald Hall: "I've never done any dogs. Of course dogs don't lend themselves to verse quite so well, collectively, as cats", *Paris Review* (1959), but see *Five-Finger Exercises* IV. *Lines to Ralph Hodgson Esqre.*

Title ***Marching Song***: to Hope Mirrlees [Oct 1944]: "I am sorry that I tore out the Marching Song of Portuguese Girlhood [from an enclosed booklet] to send to Faber, who is convalescing in Sussex and needs simple piano pieces." For F. M. Cornford, "The marching songs of various English regiments, with their ribald satire on the officers", see note to the title *Triumphal March* in *Coriolan*.

13 **sleeky and spurious**: Burns: "Wee, sleekit, cowrin, tim'rous beastie!" *To a Mouse* 1.

14 **mimsy**: Carroll: "All mimsy were the borogoves", *Jabberwocky*. For nonsense coinages, see notes to *Five-Finger Exercises* V. *Lines for Cuscuscaraway and Mirza Murad Ali Beg* 11 and 12, and to *Billy M'Caw: The Remarkable Parrot* 41.

27 **amphibolical**: OED: obsolete form of *amphibolic*, "of the nature of an amphiboly; ambiguous, equivocal" (citations all from the 1650s).

31 ***cave canem***: "Beware of the dog" (L.). ("O keep the Dog far hence", *The Waste Land* [I] 74.) ***canem***: pronounced to rhyme with "explain 'em". John Sargeaunt: "Of disyllables the penultimate vowel, if it be followed by a single consonant or by T and R or L, is sounded long, as *amo*, *scelus*, *Titus*, *onus*, *furor*, *lyra*, *patrem*, *triplex*", *Notes on the Westminster Pronunciation of Latin* in *Annals of Westminster School* (1898) (Kenneth Haynes, personal communication).

40 **WHA MAUN MEDDLE WI' ME**: the motto of the Order of the Thistle is *Nemo me impune lacessit* [No one provokes me with impunity] (31, "motto") (Donald Sommerville, personal communication).

Billy M'Caw: The Remarkable Parrot

For publication see headnote to *The Marching Song of the Pollicle Dogs.*

To Bonamy Dobrée, 29 July 1927: "I have to buy 1 young talking Parrot in Cage". 2 Sept: "Talking Parrot is off. My wife objects—says she had some friends who had four, and they made conversation impossible." 24 Jan 1928: "I am going to help the Flood sufferers by presenting a Young Talking Parret to the pub. in Hammersmith." To Frank Morley, 30 Jan 1928: "Dear Morleigh, What do you think I have just heard of a pub in the Roman Road Islington way this pub is called the ALBERT Well it Seems this pub has the most remarkable Parret You wouldnt believe ½ the Tales they tell about this Parret How it told the barman Off when he robbed the Till etc. Well I would have rung you up last night the minute I heard but it was Raining but anyway I think we ought to go down to Islington way and see about this Parret." (To Virginia Woolf, 9 Jan 1935: "I didnt try to tell you what Captain Eben Lake of Jonesport said to Captain Joe Tibbetts of East Machias · · · nor did I tell you what the Parrot in the Public in Islington said after seeing the barman rob the till.")

To Sally Cobden-Sanderson, 2 Feb 1928: "What I am going to write about is now what about this Parret I mean are you really ready to take delivery of this Parret Because if so it is essential to know clearly what are your wishes in the matter I mean to put it clearly do you want a Male or a Femaile Perret I mean it makes no Difference in so much As there Is no difference in Plumiage Noise etc. and you get a Cage in either case & a pkt. of birdseed, only This that if later on you wanted to make it a Pair it would make a difference which was which if you grasp my meaning you would want a Proper pair only this time it will only be a single Parret What I think is that as a Parret should be named Pansy but some say Alexander only tastes differ. Hoping to Hear from you on this small point I remain, yours faithfully."

TSE recalled a janitor, "Uncle Henry Jones", as "a romantic figure to me as a child, not only because he possessed a parrot which actually did a little talking but because he was reputed to have been a runaway slave", *From Mary to You* (1959). Hope Mirrlees, with whom TSE lodged during the war, had a parrot too. To John Hayward, 29 Aug 1943: "The Parrot died early this morning · · · for the last five weeks it had been looking like an elderly one-eyed pirate (parrot and pirate, that's good . . .) on the way to Execution Dock."

To J. Isaacs, 29 Dec 1948: "I am pleased that you liked the Parrot · · · I daresay it was composed about the same time as *The Rock* · · · it has no relation to the *Advocate* poem [*On a Portrait*] which is of course inspired by the Manet portrait, while the episodes in the Life of Billy m'Caw are entirely of my own invention. His figure was inspired by a very gifted parrot which used to belong to the licensee of a bar in Islington. The adventures of the real parrot were just as incredible as those of mine!"

1 **the old Bull and Bush**: music hall song sung by Florrie Forde: "Come, come, come and make eyes at me | Down at the Old Bull and Bush" (an 18th-century pub near Hampstead Heath).

9-11 **A very nice House it was · · · A very nice House. Ah, but it was the parret**: music hall song sung by Harry Fay: "Ours is a nice 'ouse ours is; | We never pay the rent and yet | The landlord never grouses, | We've got no windows in the house, | It's healthy, lets the air in, | It also lets the foul air out | When father he starts swearing." Parrots too were renowned for swearing. (TSE: "no one can possibly blaspheme in any sense except that in which a parrot may be said to curse, unless he profoundly believes in that which he profanes", *After Strange Gods* 52.)

16 **Lily La Rose**: "The bailey beareth the bell away; | The lily, the rose, the rose I lay", *The Bridal Morn* (anon, 15th–16th century). Swinburne: "change in a trice | The lilies and languors of virtue | For the raptures and roses of vice", *Dolores* 66–68. For Rose La Touche, see note to *A Cooking Egg* 9–24.

18 **on the bar**: "The parrot on the bar", *On a Portrait* 13.

22 **If it come to an argument, or a dispute**: "'I'll have the police if there's any uproar'", *Old Deuteronomy* 39 ("And what with the Station it being so near", 6).

24 **put her fist through your eye**: Charles-Louis Philippe: "'If you're fed up, I'll shove my fist through your face'", *Bubu of Montparnasse* ch. VI (1924).

31 **And then we'd feel balmy, in each eye a tear**: "All in the balmy moonlight it lay rocking on the tide— | And Growltiger was disposed to show his sentimental side", *Growltiger's Last Stand* 23–24.

33–34 **Robin Adairs · · · All in the Downs · · · Wapping Old Stairs**: Lady Caroline

Keppel's *Robin Adair* ("What's this dull town to me?"), Gay's *Sweet William's Farewell to Black-Eyed Susan* ("All in the Downs the fleet was moored") and the 19th-century *Wapping Old Stairs* ("Your Molly has never been false, she declares") are all sentimental ballads, the last two about sailors parting from their lovers. The "stairs" to the foreshore can still be seen in Wapping, East London. Dickens: "take a boat at Wapping Old Stairs", *The Uncommercial Traveller* II. TSE to Polly Tandy, 4 Apr 1941:

> It is so long since I have heard from you: I mean, since you have heard from me, that really, what you must think. Well I hope there is nothing really to think at all, except that
>
> Your Possum has never been false, he declares,
> Since last time he left you at Wapping Old Stairs.

41 **And Billy'd strike up on his moley guitar**: Edward Lear: "The Owl looked up to the stars above, | And sang to a small guitar", *The Owl and the Pussy Cat* 5–6. **moley**: TSE's own nonsense word. For others, see notes to *Five-Finger Exercises* V. *Lines for Cuscuscaraway and Mirza Murad Ali Beg* 11 and 12.

Grizabella: The Glamour Cat

Published in *Cats: The Book of the Musical* (1981). Text from *Valerie's Own Book*.

To Polly Tandy, 8 Dec 1939, two months before sending the eight lines that survive: "People have been Pestering me with suggestions: the Legal Cat—with an address at Gray's Inn; the Blue Water Cat (in contrast to Growltiger) etc. But what I incline to do is an idea of my own, and a very frightful one: the GLAMOUR CAT. The very thought of it makes me go shivery down the spine." 13 Feb 1940: "It is on my mind to pass by the shop in the Tottenham Court Road, where I dare say I shall find that the Shetland wool is unobtainable; but I do not doubt that you have had your hands full otherwise, and have been quite willing to postpone this extra chore which I imposed upon you without so much as asking leave. The Glamour Cat, I am sorry to say, is not turning out a suitable subject for edifying my juvenile audience; in fact, she came down in the world pretty far. The story is very sad, and also a bit sordid." TSE here quotes the poem, adding: "No, I fear that the story had better not be told." Later he reminisced: "there are one or two incomplete cats that probably will never be written. There's one about a glamour cat. It turned out too sad. This would never do. I can't make my children weep over a cat who's gone wrong. She had a very questionable career, did this cat. It wouldn't do for the audience of my previous volume of cats", *Paris Review* (1959).

Title ***Glamour Cat***: anticipating "glamor-puss". *Dictionary of American Slang* (ed. H. Wentworth and S. B. Flexner) cites Paul Gallico 1941: "we called them super-swoopers instead of glamorpusses".

1–2 **She haunted many a low resort | Near the grimy road of Tottenham Court**: "An almost denizen of Leicester Square", *Paysage Triste* 7. "having our horoscopes cast in the Tottenham Court Road", *Charleston, Hey! Hey!* (1927).

4 ***The Rising Sun***: a common name, but perhaps the Victorian pub at Smithfield

in the City of London. **The Friend at Hand**: historic pub, around the corner from Russell Square Tube station.

In Respect of Felines

Published in *Kenyon Review* Summer 1984, with B. R. Skinker's poem *To Mr T. S. Eliot, on reading "Old Possum's Book of Practical Cats"*, and an appraisal by Jeanne Campbell and John Reesman. Bertha Skinker attended Mary Institute, the school founded by TSE's grandfather, and her poem refers to their childhood days ("When the Eliots lived on Locust Street | Tom was pale and thin and shy") and to his supposed prejudice against cats ("But where,—Oh, where?—in this big round world | That is full of adorable pets | Did he ever have the bad luck to find | Such hateful pestiferous cats?") TSE sent her letter to Hayward, with "Ans[d] 1.6.40" (King's).

To J. R. Culpin, 4 Aug 1938, of the essays of "Mr. Singer" (unidentified): "His style shows a certain lack of ease: it reminds me somewhat of the epistolary style of a skilled and highly intelligent metal-worker whom I know; a man who can talk perfectly good and simple English, but who cannot put pen to paper without using words like *maelstrom* or *pandemonium*, a sort of language drawn I imagine from the leading articles of the penny press."

Recalling the lumbering, deferential couplets in Swift's *Mary the Cook-Maid's Letter to Dr. Sheridan* and *The Humble Petition of Frances Harris* (for which see note to *Possum now wishes to explain his silence* 16–17, in "Other Verses").

5 **Mousehole**: in Cornwall, five miles from Land's End.

LINES
Addressed to Geoffrey Faber Esquire, on his Return from a Voyage to the Bahamas, and the Parts about New Spain

Aug 1943. Geoffrey Faber had sent both TSE and Hayward a seven-page "Epistle" in heroic couplets (King's), to which each felt obliged to reply. TSE to Hayward [15 Aug]: "I have been cudgelling my brains, as I make no doubt you have also, under greater compulsion and I hope to better purpose, to discover what is the proper acknowledgement (without too great effluxion of energy) of a copy of verses (a carbon copy) addressed to J-hn H-yw-rd Esq. by the Rhyming Squire." Hayward to TSE, 22 Aug: "Though gratified I was not a little alarmed by ye Chairman's voluble *Pilgrimes*. It seemed, to say the least, churlish not to attempt an answer in kind; but the burden weighed heavily on me and I don't know how I managed as well as I did to turn out 96 lines of doggerel ··· I sent you a copy, for it seems that our efforts are meant to be circulated; but I rather hope that no further demands will be made upon my feeble ability." TSE to Hayward, 29 Aug: "Your Epistle to Geoffrey Faber Esq. does you no discredit. A much more witty, learned and ingenious riposte than my own, and I fear cost more labour. I have a suspicion, from a merry look in the

Chairman's eye, that this is not the end of it · · · unless the whisky gives out we may expect another elegant pass of pate. He considers your verses more Augustan than his own. I had entertained the notion of an account of the Banquet in the manner of *Paradise Lost*, with an enumeration of the places of origin of all the guests and all the *plats*, such as maize from *Orinokoo*, which with occidental pomp | Panoplied in *Quebec*, great Winston gnaw'd | With toothless gums etc., but dear me! one hasn't really time: how is [it] that one ever had time for these frisks, I wonder?" (*Hamlet* V i: "Cudgel thy brains no more". *The Tempest* IV i: "an excellent pass of pate".) Hayward to TSE, 16 Dec 1943: "Geoffrey has written me another set of jingles which I shall have to acknowledge in kind."

4 **feasts and frolicks and funereal games:** Geoffrey Faber's verses told of his late arrival at a dinner and the danger that this would "o'er the Feast spread the Funereal Pall". **funereal games:** athletic competitions held to mark the deaths of Greek heroes.

7 **He told of polyphemes, and clashing rocks:** "anfractuous rocks · · · (Nausicaa and Polypheme)", *Sweeney Erect* 3, 10. **polyphemes:** OED "polypheme": "Name of a Cyclops or one-eyed giant in Homer's *Odyssey*". **clashing rocks:** the Symplegades, at the entrance to the Bosphorus.

8 **darning and un-darning:** for "unweave, unwind, unravel" and Ulysses' wife Penelope, see note to *The Dry Salvages* I 35–41. To Enid Faber, 17 May 1943: "I look forward, as do you, to the return of Ulysses."

12 **ten years:** length of the Trojan War.

13 **FABRICIUS:** Roman consul and censor, admired for austerity, high principle and incorruptibility. In his verses Faber referred to himself as "thy *Fabius*". See letter to Hayward, 8 Feb 1940, quoted in note to *Clerihews* II (in "Other Verses").

16 **Which of the three could draw the longest bow:** only Ulysses could draw his unique bow, and it was by this that Penelope recognised him. OED "bow" *n.*[1] 4c: "*to draw the longbow*: to make exaggerated statements", with Byron: "At speaking truth perhaps they are less clever, | But draw the long bow better now than ever", *Don Juan* XVI i. The rhyme of "avow · · · bow" invites a theatrical comparison.

Morgan Tries Again

Date unknown, but after Mar 1944, when Morgan joined the strength at Faber & Faber. See headnote to *Cat Morgan Introduces Himself.*

12–13 **Miss 'Ile · · · Miss Swan:** as telephonist at Faber, Ethel Swan was renowned for her knowledge of the firm's workings. TSE to his secretary, 2 Aug 1933: "If there should be anything really urgent · · · put the call through yourself as there is no need for Miss Swan to be aware of my movements at present." A note on the typescript of this poem, probably added years later, reads: "The devoted receptionist for many years at Faber & Faber, 24 Russell Square, London, who welcomed me always on visits to the publishing house. Emily Hale".

16 **a kipper a line:** OED "penny-a-line": "to write at a penny a line", from 1849.

Montpelier Row

Date: Feb 1947.

Published with an Editor's Note by Joe Griffiths, *Walter de la Mare Society Magazine* July 2002, then *TLS* 16 Aug 2002. The notes below draw upon Griffiths.

Although this poem was published in 2002 as independent of TSE's *To Walter de la Mare* (and so appears independently here), the date indicates some relation between *Montpelier Row* and the published tribute. Since there is no evidence that de la Mare received *Montpelier Row* directly from TSE, it may have been a first venture, sent either to W. R. Bett (so subsequently reaching de la Mare?) or to one of TSE's friendly advisers such as Hayward or Dobrée. If so, the author's notes were probably not intended for print but for discussion, as suggested by the question "*Stream* is weak, but what can you do with *Thames*?" Hayward had heard such a question before, when TSE sent his clerihew "Mr. John Hayward", 8 Feb 1940: "I could not do anything better ··· But what can you do with a name like that?" (see *Clerihews* II in "Other Verses").

The observation that "a series of sonnets may ensue" anticipates the sonnets TSE drafted before *To Walter de la Mare* reached its final form (see Textual History).

Walter de la Mare lived at South End House, Montpelier Row, Twickenham, with a view of Marble Hill Park. TSE went to tea there, along with Owen Barfield, on 7 May 1946. See *To Walter de la Mare* and headnote.

1 **delicate:** "the delicate, invisible web you wove", *To Walter de la Mare* 31.

1–4 **delicate ··· tea and porcelain ··· window:** "Sit by a window drinking tea ··· translucent porcelain", *Mandarins* 2 16.

2–4 **tea ··· initiate ··· against the window pane:** "hibernate ··· across the window panes ··· and tea", *Interlude in London* 1–3.

7, 10 **the old enchanter ··· make real the dream:** de la Mare: "And all the enchanted realm of dream", *Sleep.* De la Mare was the author of *A Song of Enchantment* and *The Enchanted Hill.*

8 **marmoset:** "the scampering marmoset", *Whispers of Immortality* 22.

14 **there drifts the visible swan:** Yeats: "Where the swan drifts upon a darkening flood", *Coole Park and Ballylee, 1931* 48, in *The Winding Stair and Other Poems* (1933).

Notes 1 **both backwards and forwards:** Empson had written that according as lines 11 and 12 of *Whispers of Immortality* "go forwards or backwards, there are two versions of the syntax ··· Of course, you may say the lines are carefully punctuated, so that the grammar can only be taken one way, but in each case it is the less obvious grammar which is insisted on by the punctuation", *Seven Types of Ambiguity* ch. II.

Notes 5 **Hanoverian:** Alexander Pope and Lord Bathurst were among those who helped Henrietta Howard to plan the gardens at Marble Hill.

Notes 9 **habits of the amphisbaena:** in the epigraph to *The Amphisbæna: or The Limits of Human Knowledge*, Housman quotes "'Amphisbæna: a serpent supposed to have two heads, and by consequence to move with either end foremost'—JOHNSON" (revision of the Dictionary by H. J. Todd, 1818). Housman's poem was published anonymously in the *University College London Union Magazine* June 1906, then in *Three Poems: The Parallelogram The Amphisbaena The Crocodile*, privately printed at UCL (1935). TSE to Janet Adam Smith, 24 Feb 1947: "It was very kind of you to send the 'Parallelogram' poem, but how very odd that the Librarian did not know that Housman was the author ··· I cannot now remember who it was who showed me the copy of the periodical with the poem in it. Perhaps one day it will come to me in a flash. Meanwhile I hope the Librarian will unearth the 'Amphisbaena' for you." **habits of ichneumon:** in Conan Doyle's story *The Crooked Man*, Teddy the ichneumon has to be retrieved, having run up the curtain. TSE to Sally Cobden-Sanderson, 13 Dec 1927: "Mongeese (Ichneumons) are very *Usefull* (see Oxford Dictionary) for they eat Crocodiles' Eggs."

Let quacks, empirics, dolts debate

Published in *Gala Day London* (1953), accompanying one of the photographs by Izis Bidermanas, showing a cat on a park bench in Clarence Gardens, Regent's Park.

Mrs. M. Harari of the Harvill Press wrote to TSE in Feb 1952, enclosing photographs and asking him to choose one and return the others. TSE, 7 Mar: "As the photographs are not numbered or identified in any way, I can only say that a cat is sitting on a bench in a square. I will keep this in the hope of finding a few appropriate words, but that is a great difficulty."

1–2 **Let quacks, empirics, dolts debate ··· State:** Pope: "For Forms of Government let fools contest", *An Essay on Man* III 303. Johnson: "While Ladies interpose, and Slaves debate", *The Vanity of Human Wishes* 214. Browning: "The quack, the cheat, the liar ··· they are hooting the empiric, | The ignorant and incapable fool", *Paracelsus* V 142–49. **quacks:** OED *n.*[1] 1: "An ignorant pretender to medical or surgical skill; one who boasts to have a knowledge of wonderful remedies; an empiric". (TSE: "Henry VIII found out that monks were quacks", *A Fable for Feasters* 2.) *n.*[2]: "The harsh cry characteristic of a duck ··· *humorously*, A duck." **empirics:** OED 1: "A member of the sect among ancient physicians ··· who ··· drew their rules of practice entirely from experience, to the exclusion of philosophical theory." 2. "An untrained practitioner in physic or surgery; a quack." 2b: "*transf.* A pretender, impostor, charlatan." For ancient physicians, see note to *Whispers of Immortality* 19–20.

4 **Cultural Congress:** the Congress for Cultural Freedom was founded in 1950. "World conferences and congresses, European and local conferences and congresses, follow each other in endless succession: the public thirst for words about poetry, and for words from poets about almost anything—in contrast to its thirst for poetry itself—seems insatiable. In short, the compulsions and solicitations to a poet to write about poetry, and to talk about poetry, instead of

writing poetry, begin early in life and continue to the end", TSE's Introduction to *The Art of Poetry* by Paul Valéry (1958).

5 **Contemplative:** *The Cloud of Unknowing* ch. 8: "there be two manner of lives in Holy Church · · · Active is the lower, and contemplative is the higher · · · although they differ in part, yet neither of them may be had fully without some part of the other. Because that part that is the higher part of active life, that same part is the lower part of contemplative life. So that a man may not be fully active, except he be in part contemplative; nor yet fully contemplative · · · except he be in part active". TSE scored the central part of this passage.

7–8 **The Sage, disposed to sit and stare | With a vacant mind in a vacant square:** W. H. Davies: "What is this life if, full of care, | We have no time to stand and stare?" *Leisure*. (Although Davies was not a "Faber poet", the firm published his *Moss and Feather* as an Ariel Poem in 1928, and *Common Joys and Other Poems* as a Sesame Book in 1941.) TSE: "One sits delaying in the vacant square | Forced to endure the blind inconscient stare", *First Debate between the Body and Soul* 9–10. To John Hayward, 12 July 1943: "I have walked about · · · and, apart from reading Coupland's report on India, and the Lives of the Poets, have enjoyed vacancy of mind." **Sage:** "If Time and Space, as Sages say", *A Lyric* 1.

Inscriptions to Sir Geoffrey Faber on the occasion of his knighthood

The two "Inscriptions to Sir Geoffrey Faber on the occasion of his knighthood" (as Hayward phrased the half-title page which he bound with the drafts) were offered in 1954 as alternatives for a tribute to be engraved upon a commemorative glass. Beneath them on the first draft: "If the Second Attempt is preferred, and if it is too much for the Engraver, I ~~would~~ will attempt to shorten it. If neither is Acceptable, the Bard* will try Again. T.S.E. [*note*: Laureate of Russell Square.]" Then on another leaf: "P.S. In case of Doubt, or anything like Doubt, I would humbly suggest that the shorter set of Verses (or some lines to the same number) be inscribed upon the Glass; and that the longer set of Verses (for it impossible to do justice to such Merit in such a little space) should be Indicted upon fair paper of the most excellent quality, by one of our major Scribes (such as Bernard [Berthold] Wolpe) to be presented to the Chairman, and forcibly rehearsed in his presence by the Bard, on the Occasion of the Presentation of the Engraved Bathroom Glass. T. S. E." ("Bathroom Glass" was probably not a misapprehension but comic deprecation. Mary Trevelyan had given TSE an antique glass goblet for his birthday.)

The shorter verse was engraved by Laurence Whistler on a Georgian rummer presented to Sir Geoffrey by the Faber directors, and was published in the introduction of Whistler's *Engraved Glass 1952–1958* (1959), while the longer was declaimed by Charles Monteith "at a dinner given by Richard de la Mare and his wife, at Much Hadham Hall, Hertfordshire, to all the Directors and their wives, on the return of Sir Geoffrey and Lady Faber from their visit to South Africa, which coincided exactly with the knighthood" (Peter du Sautoy to Donald Gallup, 22 Mar 1961; Faber archive).

TSE to Sir Geoffrey, 5 June 1954: "If my verses satisfied, as they seemed to do, the desire of those whose affection and content, as well as my own, they were designed to express, and if they gave pleasure to the recipient, as I hoped they might do, then with your letter I am more than repaid. I think that the only proper subscription, however, is that of ANON., to indicate the collective rather than individual inspiration; and the artist has gone beyond my intention if he incised my initials beneath those on the beaker. I regret the presence of one appalling blemish in each set of verses: had I been allowed a month, instead of a weekend, in which to compose them, these faults would have been spotted and removed." (In the first, perhaps the ambiguity of subject and object, 5–6. In the second, perhaps the rhythm of "Eximious", 9.)

AMAZ'D astronomers did late descry

1–2 **AMAZ'D astronomers · · · A new great luminary in the sky:** Keats: "Then felt I like some watcher of the skies | When a new planet swims into his ken", *On First Looking into Chapman's Homer* 9–10.

3] Attrib. Alfred Austin: "Across the wires the electric message came | 'He is no better, he is much the same'", *On the Illness of the Prince of Wales, Afterwards Edward VII* (see *Possum now wishes to explain his silence* 17).

5 **"Sir Geoffrey let it be":** Pope: "Nature and Nature's Laws lay hid in Night: | God said, *Let Newton be!* and all was light", *Epitaph. Intended for Sir Isaac Newton, In Westminster-Abbey*.

VERSES

To Honour and Magnify Sir Geoffrey Faber Kt.

Title **Sir Geoffrey Faber Kt.:** see note to *Coriolan* II. *Difficulties of a Statesman* 3–4, "Knights of the British Empire". **Feodaries:** OED 1: "One who holds lands of an overlord on condition of homage". 2: "A subject, dependant, retainer, servant." 4: *obs.* "A confederate."

1–2 **A Man ſo various that he ſeem'd to be | A ſcore of Crichtons in epitome:** Dryden: "A man so various that he seem'd to be | Not one, but all Mankinds Epitome", *Absalom and Achitophel* 545–46, quoted in *John Dryden* (1930). *Monteith* refers to *VERSES To Honour and Magnify Sir Geoffrey Faber Kt.* as "an elegant Dryden pastiche".

2 **Crichtons:** the Scottish prodigy James Crichton (1560–82, pronounced *Cryton*) was described in John Johnson's *Heroes Scoti* (1603) as "omnibus in studiis admirabilis" and became known as "the Admirable Crichton". He was the subject of Sir Thomas Urquhart's *The Discovery of a most Exquisite Jewel* (1652). Though not historically related, J. M. Barrie's play *The Admirable Crichton* (1902) popularised the soubriquet. TSE to Philippa Whibley, 3 July 1930, proposing an editor for a ms of Urquhart's epigrams: "Hamish Miles occurs to me immediately · · · he edited or at least wrote an excellent introduction to Urquhart's *Admirable Crichton*, which was published by the Pleiad Press" (1927).

4 **Cunning:** OED 2a: "Possessing practical knowledge or skill; able, skilful, expert, dextrous, clever. (Formerly the prevailing sense; now only a literary archaism.)" TSE: "cunning with dice", *Mr. Mistoffelees* 28.

4 *footnote* **St. Jameſ's:** the monarch's diplomatic court. **Old Bailey:** the Central Criminal Court. Having won the Eldon Law Scholarship, Faber was called to the Bar in 1921, though he never practised.

4 *footnote variant* **Buck House:** knowing slang for Buckingham Palace (formerly Buckingham House).

6, 8, 10 **Country Squire ··· burſar ··· Compost-land to till:** Faber had been Estates Bursar of All Souls College, Oxford. TSE: "It has struck me that his knowledge of farm administration gained as Estates Bursar may have stood him in good stead when, as a country squire, he turned his attention to the breeding of pedigree cattle", *Geoffrey Faber 1889–1961* 15–16.

7–8 **And, in the Space of one revolving Moon, | As ſcholar, poet, burſar and patroon:** "But, in the course of one revolving Moon, | Was Chymist, Fidler, States-Man, and Buffoon", *Absalom and Achitophel* 549–50.

8 **patroon:** "to those who have easy access to the O.E.D. 'patroon' may not seem too inapt", *ts1*. OED 1: "Patron *Obs.*" 2: "A master (esp. of a slave) ··· *Obs.*" 3: "The captain, master, or officer in charge of a ship". 4: "In *U.S.* A possessor of a landed estate and certain manorial privileges granted under the old Dutch governments of New York". See Textual History.

9 **Eximious:** OED: "Excellent, distinguished, eminent", noting "Common in 17th c. literature: the few examples in 19th c. are humorously bombastic or pedantic."

10 **Or ſkies to ſcan:** as an amateur astronomer.

10–11 **ſcan ··· in mild affright:** Dryden: "looking backward with a wise afright, | Saw", *Absalom and Achitophel* 71–72.

Long may this Glass endure, and brim with wine

Written in Sept 1955, to be engraved by Laurence Whistler on a second Georgian rummer, for presentation to Geoffrey and Enid Faber by their children on their 35th wedding anniversary, 30 Dec 1955. The rummer was sold at Bonhams, 20 Sept 2005, but the verse appears to be unpublished. In addition, Whistler engraved two quatrains of his own verse and a fireworks display on a glass goblet for Geoffrey Faber to present to his wife on the same occasion.

TSE to Whistler, 28 Sept 1955:

> I enclose herewith my copy of the verses in its latest form, which has been passed by Faber. You will observe that I have omitted all punctuation at the end of lines. In the case of the triplet, I had in mind the fact that the three lines are to follow each other round the rim of the glass. I should have liked to make a triplet such that it would make sense equally well, no matter at which line you started. That is easy enough with a couplet, but with the triplet I have not wholly succeeded, inasmuch as if your eye strikes first the third line, you will observe that "Sev'rally charactered", which is apposite to

"Faber line", cannot qualify "this Glass". Nevertheless, I think that anyone can make out the sense of the triplet, no matter where he started. It struck me in any case that a full stop or a colon after "design" would look ungraceful, though I myself would not object to a little star or a dot like the upper part of a colon, being set between the three lines. On the other hand, I should rather like the prospective reader to know that when the verses are read in their proper order, they begin with "Long". I leave that problem entirely to you to solve.

With the three couplets, I had in mind that the emblems of the three grown-up children, together with the verses, were to be dispersed at equal intervals round the glass. There should, in any case, be no priority of age or sex, and the person looking at the glass can begin with anyone and turn round to the others. It would be impossible to put full stops after all of them, since none of them is a sentence in itself, and the alternative of having a comma after "mind", and after "parts", and a full stop after "lore" would defeat the continuity. It would seem to me best, therefore, to have no punctuation.

6 **subtile**: quoting Donne's "That subtile wreath of hair, which crowns my arm" (*The Funeral*), TSE comments: "the adjective 'subtile' is exact, though its exactness be not to us immediately apparent in the literal sense of the word which has so suffered from the abuse of the kindred word 'subtle'", *The Varieties of Metaphysical Poetry* 124 (Clark Lecture IV). However, TSE's usage here with this spelling—unique in his poems—is not OED 2, "Of fine or delicate texture", but 5: "Involving careful discrimination of fine points".

9 **secrets of hermetic lore**: as a physicist.

The gourmet cat was of course Cumberleylaude

In a letter of 8 July 1964 to Anthony Laude (of Neville Road, Cambridge), thanking him for dinner. "I also enjoyed meeting Cumberley a particularly fastidious eater without doubt, but a dignified and beautiful cat. I hope you will enjoy a few lines in honour of your feline companion, his character struck me so forcefully that I felt I had to write a few words in honour of him."

1 **Cumberleylaude**: OED "Cumberland": "a piquant sauce", quoting *Dinners at Home* (1878): "Cumberland Sauce for Game (Cold) · · · Cumberland Sauce (Hot)."

How the Tall Girl and I Play Together

Fair copy only, in *Valerie's Own Book*.

In 1953: "my opinion is, that a good love poem, though it may be addressed to one person, is always meant to be overheard by other people. Surely, the proper language of love—that is, of communication to the beloved and to no one else—is prose", *The Three Voices of Poetry* 6. Asked what he hoped he had achieved: "one always likes to think that one's last work is one's best so far · · · What I should like to do—I should like to write some poem that would give my wife as much delight as the poems which I have already written have given her", *Talking Freely* (1961).

12–13 **our middle parts · · · toes:** *Hamlet* II ii, GUILDENSTERN: "On Fortune's cap we are not the very button." HAMLET: "Nor the soles of her shoe?" ROSENCRANTZ: "Neither, my lord." HAMLET: "Then you live about her waist, or in the middle of her favours?" GUILDENSTERN: "Faith, her privates we." HAMLET: "In the secret parts of Fortune?" Frederic Manning rearranged Shakespeare's phrasing for the title of his Great War novel *The Middle Parts of Fortune* (1929; expurgated as *Her Privates We*, 1930).

13 **My toes play with her toes and my tongue with her tongue:** a copy of *Sweeney Agonistes* (Magdalene) is "Inscribed for my dear Valerie Eliot by T. S. Eliot; by Tom, for his beloved bedfellow Valerie, for her upon whom he relies and lies, touching her from mouth to toes."

Sleeping Together

Fair copy only, in *Valerie's Own Book.* Title from the list of Contents at the end of the first exercise book.

How the Tall Girl's Breasts Are

Fair copy only, on two pages, in *Valerie's Own Book.* Title above the poem has no apostrophe, but is correct in the Contents at the end of the first exercise book.

Dedication II

Fair copy only, in *Valerie's Own Book.* Beneath the poem TSE subsequently wrote: "(Rejected. See final version of *Dedication* in *Collected Poems: 1909–1962*)."

7–8 **To you I offer this dedication | In three words which for us are at one with each other: | Love adoration desire:** *The Waste Land*, closing lines:

Datta. Dayadhvam. Damyata.
Shantih shantih shantih

Love seeketh not Itself to please

Written for Valerie Eliot, in TSE's very late hand. Contesting Blake's *The Clod & the Pebble* (from *Songs of Experience*, 1794):

> "Love seeketh not Itself to please,
> "Nor for itself hath any care,
> "But for another gives its ease,
> "And builds a Heaven in Hell's despair."
>
> So sang a little Clod of Clay
> Trodden with the cattle's feet,
> But a Pebble of the brook
> Warbled out these metres meet:
>
> "Love seeketh only Self to please,
> "To bind another to Its delight,
> "Joys in another's loss of ease,
> "And builds a Hell in Heaven's despite."

(For *Songs of Experience*, see notes to *The Waste Land* [V] 322–26 and 379–81.) TSE: "The *Songs of Innocence and of Experience*, and the poems from the Rossetti manuscript, are the poems of a man with a profound interest in human emotions, and a profound knowledge of them. The emotions are presented in an extremely simplified, abstract form", *William Blake* (1920) I.

> But if there was nothing to distract him from sincerity there were, on the other hand, the dangers to which the naked man is exposed. His philosophy, like his visions, like his insight, like his technique, was his own. And accordingly he was inclined to attach more importance to it than an artist should; this is what makes him eccentric, and makes him inclined to formlessness.
>
> *But most through midnight streets I hear*
> *How the youthful harlot's curse*
> *Blasts the new-born infant's tear,*
> *And blights with plagues the marriage hearse,*
>
> is the naked vision;
>
> *Love seeketh only self to please,*
> *To bind another to its delight,*
> *Joys in another's loss of ease,*
> *And builds a Hell in Heaven's despite,*
>
> is the naked observation; and *The Marriage of Heaven and Hell* is naked philosophy, presented. But Blake's occasional marriages of poetry and philosophy are not so felicitous.
>
> *William Blake* (1920) II

(The unadopted subtitle to *The Superior Landlord* was *The Marriage of Life and Death*; see *Sweeney Agonistes* headnote, 6. *THE SUPERIOR LANDLORD*.)

On 9 Jan 1957, the day before his wedding, TSE had written to a friend to say that he and Valerie were keeping the ceremony very private "in view of the disparity of age and the obnoxiousness of most of the press · · · We love each other very much and are both sure that we are doing the right thing."

"The End of All Our Exploring"

"The whole of Shakespeare's work is *one* poem; and it is the poetry of it in this sense, not the poetry of isolated lines and passages or the poetry of the single figures which he created, that matters most. A man might, hypothetically, compose any number of fine passages or even of whole poems which would each give satisfaction, and yet not be a great poet, unless we felt them to be united by one significant, consistent, and developing personality." (*John Ford*, 1932)

1. Cumulation and Development 2. Experimentation 3. Publisher and Poet

1. CUMULATION AND DEVELOPMENT

To William Force Stead, 7 Jan 1927: "One may change one's ideas, sentiments and point of view from time to time; one would be rather atrophied if one did not; but change of mind is a very different thing from repudiation. Certainly I am 'dissatisfied' with everything I have done, but that also is a very different thing. I do not see why one should 'repudiate' anything that one has written provided that one continues to believe that the thing written was a sincere expression at the time of writing. One might as well repudiate infancy and childhood."

To Paul Elmer More, 27 Mar 1936: "I think that what appears to another person to be a change of attitude and even a recantation of former views must often appear to the author himself rather as part of a continuous and more or less consistent development."

"In the work of any major poet who does not repeat himself, the earlier part is necessary for understanding the later, and the later for understanding the earlier", new postscript, written 1948, for the *Selected Poems* of Ezra Pound. To Edith Sitwell, 20 Sept 1949, acknowledging a copy of her volume *The Canticle of the Rose*: "It is very useful too to have so much in one volume. I mean, that in a collection of the right length, representing all periods of a poet's work, one can grasp development so much better—the variety one is well aware of, but from the separate books as they appear one does not grasp the development as a whole. Also, the impression of the unity of the work, over twenty-seven years, is a great source of satisfaction; and the confirmation of validity is that the later poems make one understand the earlier poems better, as well as vice versa."

Yeats (1940): "Now, in theory, there is no reason why a poet's inspiration or material should fail, in middle age or at any time before senility. For a man who is capable of experience finds himself in a different world in every decade of his life; as he sees it with different eyes, the material of his art is constantly renewed. But in fact, very few poets have shown this capacity of adaptation to the years. It requires, indeed, an exceptional honesty and courage to face the change. Most men either cling to the experiences of youth, so that their writing becomes an insincere mimicry of their earlier work, or they leave their passion behind, and write only from the head, with a hollow and wasted virtuosity. There is another and even worse temptation: that of becoming dignified, of becoming public figures with only a public existence—coat-racks hung with decorations and distinctions, doing, saying, and even thinking and feeling only what they believe the public expects of them. Yeats was not that kind of poet."

2. EXPERIMENTATION

To Pamela Murray, 4 Feb 1938: "I do experiment consciously, in the sense that everything I undertake is like setting myself a new problem to solve. If one wants to say something that one has not said before, one must find a new way of saying it. It does not seem to me worth while ever to do the same thing twice. And as for the way of working, that depends upon the kind of poem. If it is only a little poem, well, it probably shapes itself quite quickly (though it may have been at the back of my head for a long time) and gets written in an hour or two at any time. If it is a long poem, or a play, then it is a matter of sitting down every morning after breakfast and working regularly for two or three hours a day at it, over a period of perhaps many months."

To Desmond MacCarthy, 14 Nov 1947: "assuming that an 'experiment' in the way of *Finnegans Wake* was worth making, was there any point in making it at such length? There will always, probably, be but few who will read the whole of it, in any generation: though everybody will have read *Anna Livia Plurabelle* (with the assistance, certainly very great, of the gramophone) just as all Frenchmen have read the propos torcheculatifs of Gargantua. I think the answer is that even such *morceaux* are a very different thing, if we know that they are fragments of a huge completed work, from what they would be if they were presented as sufficient in themselves · · · I don't think, therefore, that the 'unreadability' of *Finnegans Wake* makes it any the less a great literary 'monument' · · · The question remains, whether *Finnegans Wake* was worth doing; also the question, whether it must have a bad influence."

James Joyce 1882–1941, exhibition catalogue (1949): "One of the greatest capacities of genius is the power of development. The volume of a man's work should correspond to this capacity in him: what he leaves behind should be no more and no less than what is needed to realise each definite stage of his development. While an artist is still living and working, we see his development rather as change. According to our own capacities, we see this change as for the better or for the worse, in relation to that one of his works which we elect as 'the best'. Thus, there may have been readers of *Dubliners* who regarded the *Portrait* as an aberration, there were certainly admirers of the *Portrait* who deplored *Ulysses*; there were still more admirers of *Ulysses* who viewed *Finnegans Wake* as the raving of genius in decay, or as the futile effort of a man who had achieved his masterpiece, to find something new to say and a new way of saying it. But now at last, I think, the question 'which was Joyce's greatest work?' should appear as pointless as the question 'which is Shakespeare's greatest play?' Joyce's writings form a whole; we can neither reject the early work as stages, of no intrinsic interest, of his progress towards the latter, nor reject the later work as the outcome of decline. As with Shakespeare, his later work must be understood through the earlier, and the first through the last; it is the whole journey, not any one stage of it, that assures him his place among the great."

3. PUBLISHER AND POET

To Anne Ridler 28 Oct 1940, on contemporary poets: "There are only those who are of use to you, in one way or another, and those who are not: and as a rule, if people are trying to do something like what one is trying to do oneself, they are a nuisance; and if they are not, they are irrelevant."

To Geoffrey Faber, 25 Mar 1941:

> I suppose you must be allowed to keep that horrid term "modernist", which, as applied to poetry, was first used I think by Edith Sitwell, who never had the advantage of an education anyhow, and who meant, of course, poetry by Sitwells.
>
> I think that some positive case can be made out for the reaction against 19th century poets—something more respectable at least than the picayune destructiveness of a Lytton Strachey, if one looks at the poets whom some of us admired instead. The reaction was not literary criticism—it did not start from that impulse, though when we were young we did not see the distinction ourselves: it was rather one of affinities—"X is of more use to *me* than Y"—and a feeling that the creation of one literary generation cannot be nourished by that of the preceding. We had got into a different mood, and the 19th century seemed remote. It was also a reaction against meliorism—though that does not apply directly to Arnold. It is at least more interesting for what it tried to restore, than for what it disliked · · · My private view, which may shock you, is that the second phase of "modernist poetry"—I mean the "Faber poets"—is really the first phase of ~~the~~ *a* reaction. The revolution, if it deserves that name, which began *before* the last war, was abortive. The Leninists went out, and the Stalinists came in: Auden, Spender preserving external trappings of versification, allusiveness, obscurity, contemporary imagery, and adding the still more modern-seeming graces of homosexuality, leftwingery and an interim taste for Germans. Auden seems to drop with relief into the position of being a queer epigone of Kipling (no disrespect to the latter). (The quickest way to becoming old-fashioned is to be Modern). Of course this is not the meeting of the waters of which you speak. I am a bilious old Jeremiah, but the deadening of the auditory imagination, the slackness of craftsmanship in contemporary poetry, seems to me ominous.

To Robert Waller, 21 Sept 1942: "I doubt whether I get very much pleasure from any modern poetry, either by my contemporaries or by my juniors. That does not imply a comparative rating in which I put my own work very high. It is simply that if one writes oneself, interest in poetry is largely a matter of what can be of use to oneself, and I do not believe that living poets can be of much use to each other · · · I have had misgivings, in one direction or another, about everybody and about every tendency in the last twenty years. I don't feel that I have much in common with contemporary poetry. My own influence, so far as I have had any, has been purely negative—in helping to put one kind of poetical jargon out of date. But some of the fundamental attitudes which I disliked in 'Georgian' verse have seemed to me, from time to time, to creep back again in up-to-date disguises; as well as other attitudes which seemed to me mistaken. I cannot understand the fluency of many poets, or their inclination to write another poem rather than to spend time perfecting the one just written. Modern verse often seems to me to show a defective ear, and a lack of vitality in language · · · I do fear that Dylan Thomas has been up a blind alley, an alley choked with rather rank vegetation of verbiage. As for [Henry] Treece, I think that he has some real musical sense, and a great facility of striking imagery—some of which is really successful. I hope that he will discipline his language, and learn to put the right image in the right place and leave it to do its work, instead of making excess of imagery a substitute for structure · · · I have to go back to the dead to find poetry that I enjoy reading."

To Anne Ridler 30 Oct 1942: "I feel every year that I am becoming a little less confident of my own opinion of the first volumes of young poets."

To Diana Reeve, 29 Sept 1946:

> You have shown me a considerable mass of manuscript, which, if it consisted of finished poems, would be more than enough to constitute a life's work. Ordinarily, one would expect to find, in such a quantity, certain poems which one could say were worth preserving, some which could certainly be destroyed, and a great number in between of doubtful promise, some of which might be developed into finished verse.
>
> That is not what I find here. The later poems are, on the whole, firmer and clearer than the earlier ones; but all have something about them that strikes the reader, and none of them can be called a finished poem. You have, I should say, been writing hitherto, in order to set down certain experiences, and extrude certain obsessive images. These things are the material, or among the valid materials, of poetry: but to make poetry of them is another, and still more difficult task, requiring infinite patience. You are perhaps striving to communicate a message: but poetry does not work in quite that way. So far, you have been content to half-express what you have to say, and then pass on to say it again, or to say something a little different, in another poem. The effect is as if we overheard you talking to yourself, and could only catch a fragmentary phrase here and there. Now, to write poetry, one has to be interested in the form as well as the content, to be so much concerned with the form that, finally, the form itself represents the content, takes the content into itself. One has, first, to be interested in the surface, the immediate appearance; that is to be interested in words, for their own sake, until one finds a particular combination of words which, by being just right, conveys to the reader *some* immediate impression of the deeps of solitude out of which the poem emerges. For the poem, to be a poem, must emerge.
>
> It may surprise you to hear that what you need to exercise is a more *superficial* interest, so that you may give the pleasure of poetry to the reader before he quite understands the poem, and indeed to many readers who never will quite understand. The choice of words, both for their sound and for their precise sense and for their associations; the creation of a musical pattern, an effective metric: the sense for these qualities can only be exercised by a constant reading of poetry—and primarily for the immediate excitement of great verse, and by the concern with *how* the poet does it, more than with what he has to say to *you*. Also, one can try re-writing poems in different forms, and attending to all the different kinds of verse, so that, when the need comes, something like what you need for your own poem will come to your mind. Think for a time in terms of poetic technique; and for a time—if what you want is really to make a *poem*, read a good deal of poetry of all ages, and the best prose in subjects in which you may not be particularly interested, rather than the mystics. It is only, indeed, at a very advanced stage of the spiritual life—which few reach—that one can afford to concentrate on the mystics. We should all have some acquaintance with them (and I have suggested that you might, having gone so far, profitably study one or two mystics of a different type than those you have been attracted to); but in that direction, what we need most is just the apparently more humble exercise of learning how to pray.

To Pound, 4 Apr 1935, on Michael Roberts's *Faber Book of Modern Verse*: "It is a contemporary anthology in this sense that you and I & Yeats are there to show what good or harm we have done if either which I am inclined to doubt when I read what is turned out now a days. Furthermore it is to illustrate the development of English ENGLISH poetry such as it is for there is a point at which English and American divaricates. So far as I can make out American poetry consists of YOUR imitators from Macleith leish to Zukovsky etc. Robt. Fitzgerald and what not and Ame [Amy Lowell] I mean English poetry consists of the neo-pastoral and pylon-pastoral and practical joker schools. We leave the reader to judge for himself at what point gangrene sets in and draw his own moral ··· I dont like poetry much I mean what people write with now and then a canto from you or a canto from Binyan a canto here and a canto there and a occasional Beast from Marianne's menagerie a pangolin this time but I have to give the lads their chance I dont suppose Barker will appeal to you but there is something in that nevertheless I am more doubtful about Thomas (Dylan)."

To Christopher Hassall, 3 Jan 1936, of a long poem Hassall had submitted: "there is too much poetry in it, and not enough attention paid to the structure. One cannot afford to be so poetic as this in a poem of this length. One must begin by finding something which it might be misleading to call a plot. What I mean is a framework which will have its points of interest and excitement on a rather lower level than the poetic. I maintain that a long poem ought to be as interesting as a detective story, and this just isn't ··· If I pick it up and read a page by itself here or there I can get some enjoyment ··· But when one reads several pages continuously, the effect is of a diction very heavily clotted. It seems to me that you need to practise a more pedestrian style and the use of sparer and bonier language for the places where nothing more is required. Otherwise you lose intensity by aiming at intensity everywhere." To John Hayward, 25 Nov 1940, advising how to begin writing his novel of manners, "the RECHERCHE": "I think the thing is to start in a sort of middle style, the kind one can go on with indefinitely, and let it develop (as it will) into the Personal Idiom in the course of becoming a habit." 6 Dec 1940: "When I say Middle Style (or did I?) I mean such a fusion and confusion of *Sodome et Gomorrhe*, *Cranford*, *My Life and Hard Times* and the Duke of Portland's *Fifty Years at the Stage Door* as only you ··· can compound" (Proust; E. C. Gaskell; James Thurber; the Duke of Portland, *Fifty Years and More of Sport in Scotland*, Faber, 1933).

To Kenneth Allott, 18 Feb 1936: "Now I have been meditating the poems you sent me. They none of them seem quite so good as I think you might have made them with more time and trouble, and I wonder whether you always stopped to reflect on the meaning of each sentence when completed. I recognise a force and acidity that I like; all of the poems seem to me worth taking more trouble over than you seem to have taken. I return most with a few pencillings, and am keeping the first poem (four pages) to type out and see how it looks. It seems to me the best, and to need about 10 hours more work."

To Tom Burns, 9 Feb 1937, of verse by a friend (unidentified): "she ought to go on writing, although at the end of a lifetime's work her whole volume might not be very much bigger than it is now. But by that time she would have refined it as far as possible, and have developed her own critical faculty, which is so very important, to a degree at which she could distinguish very slight differences of quality which would enable her to select and reject with precision. Her themes are well worth dealing with again and again; in the end a great deal should be destroyed. I think that in a book such as hers would be it is almost more important to leave out what is not quite so good than it is to keep in the high spots."

To Ian Cox, 13 Oct 1937: "I have read your poem several times, and am very much interested in it, and as with your other work, I find it extremely difficult to put into words just what I feel about it. My feelings are however, very similar to those on reading your prose book. It is exciting and queerly disturbing, just as your prose is. It seems to me that you have the right material for poetry, but have not yet succeeded in making a poem out of it. To say that much is already to say a good deal, because people whose experience fabricates the right material inside them are by no means common. With most of the poetry that I see, not only is the workmanship bad, but the material itself is bogus. Your material and experience is quite real to me. Where I find the poem fails is both in rhythm and in the control of imagery. There is still a lack of musical pattern in the poem, and one does not feel inevitability in the line arrangement. This is one reason why my attention tends to wander from time to time. A poem, like anything else, must be constructed in such a way as to keep the reader's attention: I don't mean to keep it taut the whole time, because that itself is fatiguing and leads to inattention, but, in a poem of any length, by a right alternation of tension and relaxation. And when I say that a poem must keep the attention, I do not necessarily mean that it should be very simple and easy to understand. A poem can be very obscure and yet be extremely exciting to read."

To Mervyn Peake, 26 Jan 1940: "You speak in several poems of *singing*, but I think the first thing a poet needs to learn is how to talk. If you could absorb as influence a few poems by direct statement in the simplest and most austere language, I think that might be good for you. It is not necessary, in order to make a good poem, to have a very vast or sublime emotion to inspire it. It is not possible to make a good poem if the expression adopted is out of scale to the emotion felt, and a very commonplace feeling or insight, if honestly worked out, is as much as one needs or can expect to have."

The Writer as Artist (1940), a radio discussion with Desmond Hawkins:

> I believe that the writer as artist has a very vital social function, a social usefulness which goes far beyond the number of readers who consciously appreciate his artistry, which goes beyond the circle of those who read his work at all, which extends even, in time, to those people for whom he becomes merely a name on a public monument. He is useful, in the degree of his greatness, to all those who speak the same language, even if they never hear of him. As an artist, his job has been to use the right words in the right order: that is, he helps to prevent the language from deteriorating or from getting ossified; and I should like to make clear, if I can, why this is a matter of vital importance for everybody.
>
> A great language ··· is a marvellous social creation, dependent upon innumerable factors: history has not produced more than a very small number of great languages. A living language, one that people are using in all their daily affairs, is constantly changing: for every generation lives in a rather different world from its predecessor; it has new things and new situations to deal with, and it thinks and feels about them in a new way. But what people do not always remember is that a living language, being alive, can die ··· It will happen if the general level of culture, intelligence and energy declines, and if the nation ceases to produce individuals having just that pre-occupation with words which marks the writer as artist—a preoccupation with words which is at the same time a concern with the exploration of subtleties of thought and feeling. So if a nation to be great must have a great language, it is the business of the writer as artist to help to preserve and extend the resources of that language ···

When the language degenerates, the capacity of the people for thinking, feeling, and adapting itself to new conditions also degenerates; it is the ability of a people to produce the writer as artist that prevents it from sinking to a condition in which a short scale of farmyard noises will provide all the vehicle it needs for expression and communication.

Royal Academy Speech (1960):

I hold that a young poet, before taking liberties with versification, should aim at some proficiency in more formal and traditional kinds of verse. Let him try his hand at blank verse, the rhyming couplet, the sonnet and the villanelle. Let him find out in this way how difficult they are, and find out whether what he has to say can be said in one of the stricter forms or not. In so doing, the young poet may acquire some insight into the work of dead masters. And, in discovering that a traditional form does not fit what he has to say, he may learn also *why* it does not suit; and if he really has something to say, this may help him to find the way in which he can say it. To put it briefly, learn the rules before you start breaking them.

My second piece of advice is this: never aim at novelty. Novelty of form or idiom is not something that we should seek; it is something that should force itself upon us. It should force itself upon the poet simply because he has something to say which cannot be said in any other way—though of course no poet knows exactly what he has to say until he has said it. The startlingly new may come with a maximal or a minimal departure from an accepted convention of poetic speech: in either case it must appear *inevitable* so that the reader will understand that the poet has said something new and said it in the only way in which it could be said. The author who deliberately aims at originality of language is very often attempting to conceal, behind the eccentricity of his diction, the conventionality, the commonplaceness of his vision.

My third general piece of advice to the young poet is this: never attempt to do something that has been done, in your own language, as well as it can be done. In so doing, you are not only adopting a form, but mimicking the content. No imitation of Alexander Pope's couplets, or of Byron's *ottava rima*, can be more than a clever pastiche: for either the author had nothing original to say, or had something to say which he has not succeeded in saying—because it has not altered the form to the degree necessary for his individual communication. The path of poetry through the ages is strewn with the wreckage of attempts to emulate great masters by imitating them. When we are young, it is right that we should be carried away for a time by the work of some poet of another age or another language; but if the young writer has the real gift of nature, this enthusiasm will lead him away from imitation and make him more aware of what he has to say and the way in which he can say it. There is all the difference in the world between imitation and influence. Imitation is servitude; influence can mean liberation.

It may seem that I have indicated a very difficult road for the poet to follow, a road from which any deviation can lead to disaster. He must practise the accepted forms of verse, if he is to escape from them. He must avoid imitation, but not strive for originality. He must have something to say which will impose the proper way of saying it; but what he has to say cannot be abstracted from his way of saying it. It is this "something to say" which justifies the poem, giving it a "something to say" which may, in great poetry, touch the depths of human ecstasy or anguish. In other words, pure poetry—*la poésie pure*—is a goal which, if reached, would annihilate poetry.

Bibliography

Publishers are not noted, except when TSE's relation to them is important. Place of publication is not given when in Britain or America, or for French books published in Paris. Reference has often been made to editions used by TSE himself, and information about his own copies is included here, as are comments about his relation to some of the books about him.

Academic editions are listed by authors' names, not those of the editors:

Boswell, James, *Life of Johnson* ed. George Birkbeck Hill, rev. L. F. Powell (6 vols., 1934–50)

Anthologies and collections of essays are listed by the names of the editors:

Olney, James (ed.), *T. S. Eliot: Essays from the Southern Review* (1988)

TSE read many of the classics in Greek and Latin, but also knew great translations such as Golding's Ovid, Pope's Homer and Dryden's Virgil. Where more recent English translations are needed, original Loeb editions are mostly used, some of which are listed below.

In the editorial matter, references to collections of essays are given in the form "*Olney ed.*" References to books and articles are generally abbreviated to the author's name (*Greene*). If more than one title by an author is listed, the italicised name without date signifies the most important in this context, which is given first; references to other titles are then given with name and date. So *Gallup* signifies his *T. S. Eliot: A Bibliography* (1952, rev. ed. 1969), while *Gallup 1970* signifies his *T. S. Eliot & Ezra Pound: Collaborators in Letters* (1970). If more than one title from a single year is listed, then a letter is added, as for instance *Harmon 1976a*, *Harmon 1976b.*

Abel, Richard, *The Influence of St.-John Perse on T. S. Eliot* in *Contemporary Literature* Spring 1973

Ackerley, C. J., *"Who are These Hooded Hordes . . .": Eliot's "The Waste Land" and Hesse's "Blick ins Chaos"* in *Journal of the Australasian Universities Modern Language Association* Nov 1994

Ackroyd, Peter, *T. S. Eliot* (1984)

Adams, Henry, *The Education of Henry Adams* (1918); TSE's copy, Valerie Eliot collection.

Aiken, Conrad, *The Jig of Forslin* (1916)

—— *Ushant: An Essay* (1963)

—— *Selected Letters* ed. Joseph Killorin (1978)

Alexander, Michael, *The Dedication of "The Waste Land"* in *Scripsi* July 1986

Andrewes, Lancelot, *The Preces Privatae* tr. and ed. F. E. Brightman (1903); TSE's copy, Valerie Eliot Collection.

—— *Seventeen Sermons on the Nativity* [1887]. Recommended by TSE in *Lancelot Andrewes* (1926).

—— *Sermons* ed. G. M. Story (1967)

——*Selected Sermons and Lectures* ed. Peter E. McCullough (2006)

Apuleius, *Metamorphosen Libri XI* ed. J. van der Vliet (1897); TSE's copy, dated 1907, King's.

Aristophanes, *The Acharnians* [in Greek] ed. W. W. Merry (1880); TSE's copy with schoolboy notes (5th ed., 1901), Houghton.

——*Comoediae* [in Greek] ed. Augustus Meineke (Tauchnitz, 1860); TSE's copy, Vol. II only, dated 1909, Pierpont Morgan.

——*The Birds* [in Greek] ed. W. W. Merry (1889); TSE's annotated copy (4th ed., 1904), listed among books of his which were at Milton Academy in the 1930s.

Aristotle, *De Anima Libri III* [in Latin] ed. William Biehl (1911); TSE's annotated copy, King's. (TSE's note: "Copy used in 1914–15 with notes made during R. G. Collingwood's *explication de texte*, and extracts from Pacius' commentary on the *De Anima*, which Joachim made me read. TSE Presented to John Hayward Esqre 3.x.51.")

——*Nicomachean Ethics* tr. F. H. Peters (1881, 10th ed. 1906)

——*Poetics* tr. S. H. Butcher (1892, 3rd ed. 1902)

——*The Ethics of Aristotle* ed. John Burnet (1900); TSE's copy, heavily annotated while at Harvard and Oxford, Valerie Eliot collection.

——*De Anima* [On the Soul] tr. R. D. Hicks (1907)

——*Works* general ed. W. D. Ross (1908–52)

——*Rhetoric* tr. R. C. Jebb (1909)

Arrowsmith, William, *Daedal harmonies: A Dialogue on Eliot and the Classics* in *Southern Review* Jan 1977

——*The Poem as Palimpsest: A Dialogue on Eliot's "Sweeney Erect"* in *Southern Review* Winter 1981

——*Eros in Terre Haute: T. S. Eliot's "Lune de Miel"* in *New Criterion* Oct 1982

——*Grave Prattle: Eliot's "Le Directeur"* in *Yale Review* Winter 1989

Atkins, G. Douglas, *T. S. Eliot's Christmas Poems* (2014)

Augustine, *Confessions* rev. tr. E. B. Pusey (1838)

Babbitt, Irving, *The New Laokoon* (1910); TSE's copy, dated 1910, Houghton.

Badenhausen, Richard, *T. S. Eliot and the Art of Collaboration* (2004)

Baedeker, Karl, *London and Its Environs* (15th ed. 1908); TSE's copy, dated 14 Oct 1910, King's.

Bagchee, S. (ed.), *T. S. Eliot: A Voice Descanting* (1990)

Baker, George Pierce, *The Development of Shakespeare as a Dramatist* (1907); TSE's copy, dated 1909, offered for sale in 2011.

Bakewell, Charles M., *Source Book in Ancient Philosophy* (1907); TSE's annotated copy, Houghton.

Barker, Nicolas, *The Butterfly Books: An Enquiry into the Nature of Certain Twentieth Century Pamphlets* (1987)

Baron, C. E., *Lawrence's Influence on Eliot* in *Cambridge Quarterly* Spring 1971

Baudelaire, Charles, *"Les fleurs du mal", "Petits poèmes en prose", "Les paradis artificiels"* tr. Arthur Symons (1925). To Maurice Carpenter, 6 Oct 1934: "I quite agree with you about the inability of Arthur Symons to understand Baudelaire or to make a presentable translation . . . there is no tolerable translation of Baudelaire in English."

——*Intimate Journals* tr. Christopher Isherwood, with Introduction by TSE (1930)

——*Baudelaire: The Complete Verse* tr. Francis Scarfe (1986)

Beare, Robert L., *Notes on the Text of T. S. Eliot: Variants from Russell Square* in *Studies in Bibliography* 9 (1957). The ts (U. Maryland) has marginal comments by TSE. Beare's ts collation of poems, sent to TSE on 9 Apr 1955 (now King's), is not entirely accurate.

Beddoes, Thomas Lovell, *Plays and Poems* ed. H. W. Donner (1950)

Behr, Caroline, *T. S. Eliot: A Chronology of his Life and Works* (1983)

Benda, Julien, *Le Bergsonisme ou Une Philosophie de la Mobilité* (1912); TSE's copy with a letter of presentation from the author, 6 Jan 1921, Magdalene.

Benson, A. C., *Edward FitzGerald* (English Men of Letters, 1905)

Bergonzi, Bernard, *T. S. Eliot* (1972)

——(ed.), *Four Quartets: A Casebook* (1969)

Bergson, Henri, *Essai sur les données immédiates de la conscience* (1889); tr. F. L. Pogson as *Time and Free Will* (1910)

——*Matière et mémoire* (1896); 5th ed. (1908) tr. Nancy Margaret Paul and W. Scott Palmer as *Matter and Memory* (1911)

——*Introduction à la métaphysique* in *Revue de métaphysique* Jan 1903; rev. ed. tr. T. E. Hulme as *An Introduction to Metaphysics* (1912)

——*L'Evolution créatrice* (1907); tr. Arthur Mitchell as *Creative Evolution* (1911); TSE's copy of the translation, Houghton.

——*L'Energie spirituelle* (1919); tr. H. Wildon Carr as *Mind-Energy* (1920)

Bernstein, David, *The Story of Vaslav Nijinsky as a Source for T. S. Eliot's "The Death of Saint Narcissus"* in *The Hebrew University Studies in Literature* Spring 1976

Bhagavad-Gita tr. Lionel D. Barnett (1905); TSE's annotated copy, dated Cambridge, 1912, Houghton. (See also Purohit Swami, Shri.)

Bible. King James Version; TSE's annotated copy (undated but post-Victorian), King's. To the *Athenaeum* 16 May 1919: "Mr. Lytton Strachey informs me that in my review of Kipling's verse last week I referred to the 'Authorized Version' as the 'Revised Version.' I meant the Bible published by direction of King James I, and still in use in my childhood. Mr. Strachey says that there is a modern edition called the 'Revised Version.' I admit and apologize for the error."

Bishop, Elizabeth, and Robert Lowell, *Words in Air: The Complete Correspondence* ed. Thomas Travisano, with Saskia Hamilton (2008)

Blake, William, *The Poetical Works* ed. John Sampson (1913); TSE owned this ed. in 1934.

Blamires, Harry, *Word Unheard: A Guide through Eliot's "Four Quartets"* (1969)

Boodin, John Elof, *Truth and Reality* (1911); TSE's annotated copy, Houghton.

Bosanquet, Bernard, *Logic, or The Morphology of Knowledge* (1888); TSE's copy, (rev. ed., 1911; Vol. I only of two), Magdalene.

—— *The Essentials of Logic* (1895); TSE's annotated copy (1910 ed.), dated 16 Jan 1914, Houghton.

Boswell, James, *Life of Johnson* ed. George Birkbeck Hill, rev. L. F. Powell (6 vols., 1934–50)

Boyd, John D., *"The Dry Salvages": Topography as Symbol* in *Renascence* Spring 1968; repr. in *New Blackfriars* Apr and May 1970

Bradbrook, M. C., *T. S. Eliot: The Making of The Waste Land* (1972)

Braddon, Mary Elizabeth, *Lady Audley's Secret* (1862, rev. 8th ed. also 1862)

Bradford, Sarah, *Sacheverell Sitwell* (1993)

Bradley, F. H., *Ethical Studies* (1876); TSE's copy (2nd, rev. ed), Magdalene, inscribed "Property of Valerie and T. S. Eliot. This copy came from B. L. R. [Bruce Richmond] —Times Lit. Supp. 'as a peg' (as he used to say) for a front-page article on Bradley".

—— *The Principles of Logic* (1883)

—— *Appearance and Reality* (1893, 2nd ed. 1897); TSE's copy (5th imp., 1908), Magdalene.

—— *Essays on Truth and Reality* (1914)

Braybrooke, Neville (ed.), *T. S. Eliot: A Symposium for His Seventieth Birthday* (1958). TSE to Braybrooke, 25 Nov 1958: "The essays have, of course, affected me variously; some gave me great pleasure, a few rather puzzled me and the group of contributions by school children inspired me with awe and admiration · · · Among the essays which gave me particular pleasure I must mention those by Philip Mairet and Harold Nicolson and also your introduction."

—— *T. S. Eliot in the South Seas* in *Sewanee Review* Winter 1966

Brooks, Van Wyck, *The Wine of the Puritans: A Study of Present-Day America* (1908)

Browne, E. Martin, *The Making of T. S. Eliot's Plays* (1969)

Browning, Robert, *The Earlier Monologues* (1900); TSE's copy, Houghton.

Burnet, John, *Early Greek Philosophy* (1892); TSE's copy (2nd ed, 1908), Magdalene.

—— *Greek Philosophy. Part I: Thales to Plato* (1914); TSE's heavily annotated copy, Magdalene.

Burroughs, Franklin, *The Deception of the Thrush* in *Sewanee Review* Fall 2005

Bush, Ronald, *T. S. Eliot: A Study in Character and Style* (1983)

—— (ed.), *T. S. Eliot: The Modernist in History* (1991)

Carpenter, Humphrey, *Poor Tom: Mary Trevelyan's View of T. S. Eliot* in *English* Spring 1989.

Cauthen, I. B., Jr., *Another Webster Allusion in "The Waste Land"* in *MLN* Nov 1958

Chambers Slang Dictionary ed. Jonathon Green (1998, rev. ed. 2008)

Chandran, K. Narayana, *The Hawthorne Aspect of T. S. Eliot's "Coriolan": Allusive Journey as Errancy* in *Orbis Litterarum* Feb 2007 (a)

——*A Receipt for Deceit: T. S. Eliot's "To the Indians Who Died in Africa"* in *Journal of Modern Literature* Spring 2007 (b)

——*T. S. Eliot's Literary Adoption: "Animula" and "The Child" of H. E. Bates* in *English Studies* Aug 2007 (c)

Chapin, Katherine Garrison, *T. S. Eliot at the National Gallery* in *Poetry* Sept 1947

Chapman, Frank M., *Handbook of Birds of Eastern North America* (1895); TSE's copy (6th ed., 1902), King's. Inscribed by his mother "Thomas Stearns Eliot. Sept. 26th 1902", with additional note: "In my mother's handwriting. A much coveted birthday present on my 14th birthday. T. S. Eliot. 18 June 1928."

Chapman, George, *The Works: Poems and Minor Translations* with introduction by A. C. Swinburne (1904); TSE's copy, Valerie Eliot collection.

Chapman, Dom John, OSB, *The Spiritual Letters* (1935); TSE's copy, King's.

Chaucer, Geoffrey, *The Student's Chaucer* ed. W. W. Skeat (1894, 1908); TSE's annotated copy, Houghton.

Chiari, Joseph, *T. S. Eliot: A Memoir* (1982)

Childs, Donald J., *From Philosophy to Poetry: T. S. Eliot's Study of Knowledge and Experience* (2001)

Chinitz, David E., *T. S. Eliot and the Cultural Divide* (2003)

Clarke, Graham (ed.), *T. S. Eliot: Critical Assessments* (4 vols., 1990)

Clements, Keith (ed.), *The Moot Papers: Faith, Freedom and Society 1938–1944* (2009)

The Cloud of Unknowing ed. Dom Justin McCann (1924); TSE's lightly marked copy, dated 1942, Valerie Eliot collection.

Coleridge, S. T., *Poetical Works* ed. James Dykes Campbell (1893, repr. 1907); TSE's copy, with his bookplate, Houghton.

——*Poetical Works* ed. E. H. Coleridge (1912); TSE's annotated copy, Houghton.

Collingwood, R. G., *The Principles of Art* (1938)

Cook, Cornelia, *Fire and Spirit: Scripture's Shaping Presence in T. S. Eliot's "Four Quartets"* in *Literature & Theology* Mar 2001

Cook, Eleanor, *T. S. Eliot and the Carthaginian Peace* in *ELH* Summer 1979

Cookson, William, *A Guide to the Cantos of Ezra Pound* (1985)

Cooper, John Xiros, *T. S. Eliot and the Politics of Voice* (1987)

Corbière, Tristan, *Les Amours jaunes* (1873); TSE's copy (Édition définitive, Préface de Charles Le Goffic, 1912), Magdalene.

——*The Centenary Corbière* tr. Val Warner (1976)

Cornford, Francis Macdonald, *The Origin of Attic Comedy* (1914); TSE's annotated copy, Ian Patterson.

Costello, Harry T., *Josiah Royce's Seminar, 1913–1914, as recorded in the Notebooks of Harry T. Costello* ed. Grover Smith (1963)

Cowper, William, *Poems* ed. Robert Bell (3 vols., [1870]); TSE's copy, Magdalene.

Cox, C. B. and Hinchcliffe, Arnold P. (eds.), *T. S. Eliot: The Waste Land* (1968)

Crashaw, Richard, *Poems* ed. J. R. Tutin (Muses' Library, 1905); TSE's undated repr., Valerie Eliot collection.

Crawford, Robert, *The Savage and the City in the Work of T. S. Eliot* (1987)

—— *Young Eliot: From St Louis to "The Waste Land"* (2015)

Daiches, David, *English Literature* (1964)

D'Ambrosio, Vinnie-Marie, *Eliot Possessed* (1989)

Dante, *Le Opere di Dante* (Società Dantesca Italiana, Firenze, 1921); TSE's copy, dated "8. 5. 26", Magdalene.

—— *Vita Nuova* tr. Dante Gabriel Rossetti, in *The Early Italian Poets* (1861)

—— *Purgatorio*, Temple Classics ed. with Italian text and English tr. [by Thomas Okey, ed. H. Oelsner] (1899); TSE's copies: 1910 repr. inscribed "Thomas S. Eliot" by his mother, Houghton; 1912 and 1946 reprints, Valerie Eliot collection.

—— *Paradiso*, Temple Classics ed. with Italian text and English tr. [by P. H. Wicksteed, ed. H. Oelsner] (1899); TSE's copies: 1910 repr., Houghton; 1916 repr., Valerie Eliot collection.

—— *Inferno*, Temple Classics ed. with Italian text and English tr. [by John A. Carlyle, ed. H. Oelsner] (1900); TSE's copies: 1909 repr., Houghton; 1919 and 1941 reprints, Valerie Eliot collection.

—— *Convivio* [tr. P. H. Wicksteed] (1903); TSE's copy (1912), Valerie Eliot collection.

—— *Opere Minori* Vol. 2 (undated); TSE's copy, Valerie Eliot collection.

Dardis, Tom, *Firebrand: The Life of Horace Liveright* (1995)

Darwin, Charles, *The Origin of Species* (1859); TSE's annotated copy, dated "T. S. Eliot London 1911", Houghton.

—— *The Descent of Man* (1871); TSE's annotated copy (1913), Houghton.

Davidson, John, *John Davidson: A Selection of His Poems* ed. Maurice Lindsay (1961), with Preface by TSE

de Castro, Françoise, *Entretien avec T. S. Eliot*, ts memoir of a meeting on 23 Aug 1948 (King's).

Deussen, Paul, *Sechzig Upanishads* (Leipzig, 1897)

Dickens, Charles, TSE's New Century Library edition (17 vols., 1903), TSE's copy, Magdalene.

Dickey, Frances, *Parrot's Eye: A Portrait by Manet and two by T. S. Eliot* in *Twentieth-Century Literature* Summer 2006

A Dictionary of Surnames ed. Patrick Hanks and Patricia Hodges (1988)

Diels, Hermann, *Fragmente der Vorsokratiker* (3 vols., Berlin 1903–10); TSE's copy (1912), Valerie Eliot collection.

Dobrée, Bonamy, *A Personal Reminiscence* in *Tate ed.*

Donne, John, *Sermons: Selected Passages* ed. Logan Pearsall Smith (1919); TSE's annotated copy (unopened after 121), Magdalene.

Donoghue, Denis, *Words Alone: The Poet T. S. Eliot* (2000)

Donovan, Brigid, *The Love Song of T. S. Eliot's Secretary: A Memoir* in *Confrontation* (Long Island U.) Winter 1975

Doren, Mark Van, *John Dryden* (1920)

Dostoevski, Fyodor, [*Crime and Punishment*, pub. in Russian 1866], tr. into French by Victor Derély as *Le Crime et la châtiment* (1884)

——[*The Idiot*, pub. in Russian 1868], tr. into French by Victor Derély as *L'idiot* (1887)

——[*The Brothers Karamazov*, pub. in Russian 1880], tr. into French by Ély Halpérine-Kaminsky and Charles Morice as *Les Frères Karamazov* (1888)

Drew, Elizabeth, *T. S. Eliot: The Design of His Poetry* (NY 1949; London 1950). TSE to John Wheelock (Scribner's), 22 Mar 1949: "I have only been through it hurriedly, but it strikes me as a very competent piece of work indeed and although I am not qualified to judge it I am at least pleased with it."

Dryden, John, *Dramatic Essays* ed. W. H. Hudson (Everyman, 1912); TSE's copy, Valerie Eliot collection.

Durrell, Lawrence, *The Other T. S. Eliot* in *Atlantic Monthly* May 1965

Edwards, A. S. G., *T. S. Eliot and Friends: "Noctes Binanianæ"* in *Book Collector* Winter 2009

Egleston, Charles (ed.), *Boni & Liveright: A Documentary History* (2004), Vol. 288 of *A Dictionary of Literary Biography*

Eliot, Vivien, see headnote to Index of Identifying Titles for Prose by T. S. Eliot.

Eliot, Walter Graeme, *A Sketch of the Eliot Family* (1887); presentation copy from the author, with supplements, Library of Congress.

Emerson, Ralph Waldo, *Collected Poems and Translations* (Library of America, 1994)

Empson, William, *Argufying* ed. John Haffenden (1987)

——*Selected Letters* ed. John Haffenden (2006)

Field, Michael, *The Dialect in/of Modernism: Pound and Eliot's Racial Masquerade* in *American Literary History* Spring 1992

FitzGerald, Edward, *Rubáiyát of Omar Khayyám* (1859, 4th ed. 1879)

Flanagan, Hallie, *Dynamo: An Adventure in the College Theatre* (1943)

Flaubert, Gustave, *Madame Bovary* tr. Francis Steegmuller (1957)

Forster, E. M., *Abinger Harvest* (1936)

Fowler, H. W., *A Dictionary of Modern English Usage* (1926)

Frankau, Gilbert, *One of Us: A Novel in Verse* (1912)

Frazer, J. G., *The Golden Bough: A Study in Magic and Religion* (3rd ed. rev., 12 vols., 1906–1915)

——*The Golden Bough* (abbreviated ed., 1925); TSE's copy, Magdalene.

Friend, Albert C., *Parallel Passages to "The Waste Land"*, unpublished ts, 1932 (Houghton).

Frye, Northrop, *T. S. Eliot* (1963); TSE's corrigenda are in the Faber archive.

Gallup, Donald, *T. S. Eliot: A Bibliography* (1952, rev. ed. 1969)

——*The "Lost" Manuscripts of T. S. Eliot* in *Bulletin of the New York Public Library*, Dec 1968 (incorporating his *TLS* article of 7 Nov 1968)

——*T. S. Eliot & Ezra Pound: Collaborators in Letters* (1970)

——*Ezra Pound and His Contemporaries* (exhibition catalogue) in *Yale University Library Gazette* Jan 1976

——*Mr. Eliot at the Churchill Club* in *Southern Review* Oct 1985

——*Pigeons on the Granite: Memories of a Yale Librarian* (1988)

——*What Mad Pursuits: More Memories of a Yale Librarian* (1998)

Gardner, Helen, *The Art of T. S. Eliot* (1949). TSE to G. F. Higginson, 29 Nov 1952: "the best study of my poetry".

——*The Recent Poetry of T. S. Eliot* in *New Writing and Daylight* (1942)

——*T. S. Eliot and the English Poetic Tradition* (1965)

——*The Landscapes of Eliot's Poetry* in *Critical Quarterly* Winter 1968

——*The Composition of "Four Quartets"* (1978)

Gautier, Théophile, *Émaux et Camées* (1852, rev. and enlarged 1872); TSE's copy (1916), Magdalene.

Gewirtz, Isaac, *T. S. Eliot: Highlights from the Julius M. Cruse Collection* (1998)

Goldie, David, *A Critical Difference: T. S. Eliot and John Middleton Murry in English Literary Criticism, 1919–1928* (1998)

Gordon, Lyndall, *T. S. Eliot: An Imperfect Life* (1998)

——*The Waste Land Manuscript* in *American Literature* Jan 1974

——*Eliot's Early Years* (1977)

——*Eliot's New Life* (1988)

Gourmont, Remy de, *Physique de l'amour: essai sur l'instinct sexuel* (1903); tr. Ezra Pound as *The Natural Philosophy of Love* (Boni & Liveright, 1922).

Gray, Piers, *T. S. Eliot's Intellectual and Poetic Development 1909–1922* (1982)

Green, T. H., *Prolegomena to Ethics* ed. A. C. Bradley (1883), TSE's copy (5th ed., 1906), Houghton.

Greene, Edward J. H., *T. S. Eliot et la France* (Paris, 1951). Read in ts by TSE, who endorsed a printed copy "Lu et approuvé / T. S. Eliot / 2. xii. 51" (McCue collection).

Gregory, Horace, *The House on Jefferson Street: A Cycle of Memories* (1971)

Grierson, Herbert J. C. (ed.), *Metaphysical Lyrics and Poems of the Seventeenth Century* (1921); TSE's annotated copy, Magdalene.

Griffiths, Eric, and Reynolds, Matthew (eds.), *Dante in English* (2005)

Gross, Harvey, *The Figure of St. Sebastian* in *Southern Review* Autumn 1985, repr. in *Olney ed.*

Haffenden, John, *Vivien Eliot and "The Waste Land": The Forgotten Fragments* in *PN Review* May–June 2007

Hands, Anthony, *Sources for the Poetry of T. S. Eliot* (1993)

Harding, Jason, *The Criterion: Cultural Politics and Periodical Networks in Inter-War Britain* (2002)

—— (ed.), *T. S. Eliot in Context* (2011)

Harmon, William, *Eliot's Raids on the Inarticulate* in *PMLA* May 1976 (a)

—— *T. S. Eliot, Anthropologist and Primitive* in *American Anthropologist* Dec 1976 (b)

—— *Eliot and His Problems* in *Sewanee Review* Summer 1986

Harvard College Class of 1910. Secretary's Report. TSE submitted autobiographical notes to the Third (1917), Fourth (1921), Seventh (1935), Thirtieth Anniversary (1940), Fortieth Anniversary (1950), Fiftieth Anniversary (1950) and Fifty-fifth Anniversary (1965) reports.

Hayward, John, Notes to *The Waste Land* and to *Four Quartets* for Pierre Leyris's translations respectively in *Poèmes 1910–1930* [1947] and *Quatre Quatuors* [1950]. English ts, King's. The notes are designated *Hayward*. For the designation *Hayward Queries* among notes to *The Dry Salvages*, see headnote, 3. COMPOSITION.

—— (ed.), *The Penguin Book of English Verse* (1956), issued in hardback as *The Faber Book of English Verse* (1958)

Hegel, G. W. F., *Lectures on the Philosophy of History* tr. J. Sibree (1905); TSE's annotated copy, Houghton.

Herbert, George, *The Poems of George Herbert* (World's Classics, 1907); TSE's copy, Valerie Eliot collection.

Herrmann, Frank, *Faber's Forty-Five Years Ago* in *Antiquarian Book Monthly Review* Sept, Oct and Nov 1992

Hesse, Hermann, *Blick ins Chaos: drei Aufsätze* (1921); TSE's copy, King's.

—— *In Sight of Chaos* tr. Stephen Hudson (Zurich, 1923)

Heywood, Christopher, *"Lady Audley's Secret": A T. S. Eliot Source* in *RES* May 1976

Hobbes, Thomas, *Leviathan* (1651); TSE's copy (New Universal Library, [1907]) dated Feb 1914, Valerie Eliot collection.

Hodin, J. P., *T. S. Eliot on the Condition of Man Today*, interview in *Horizon* Aug 1945 (typescript read by TSE; letter, 25 Apr).

Homer, *The Odyssey* [in Greek] ed. John J. Owen (1859); TSE's copy, King's.

Hooker, Richard, *Of the Laws of Ecclesiastical Polity* (1593–97); TSE's copy (Everyman Vol. II only, 1907), Houghton.

—— *Works* ed. John Keble (3 vols., 1836); TSE's copy (2nd ed. 1841), Valerie Eliot collection.

Horace, *Works* tr. into prose by Christopher Smart (1756); TSE's undated 20th-century repr., with some annotation, Houghton.

Howarth, Herbert, *Notes on Some Figures Behind T. S. Eliot* (1965). TSE read this in ts in 1961 and insisted it be rewritten (see *Materer*).

Husserl, Edmund, *Logische Untersuchungen* (2 vols., 1900, 1901); TSE's annotated copy (Vol. I being 2nd ed., 1913), dated "Marburg 1914", London Library.

Huxley, Aldous, *Crome Yellow* (1921); TSE's copy, Houghton.

—— *Selected Letters* ed. James Sexton (2007)

Jain, Manju, *A Critical Reading of the "Selected Poems" of T. S. Eliot* (Delhi, 1991)

—— *T. S. Eliot and American Philosophy: The Harvard Years* (1992)

James, Henry: the fiction included in the New York Edition (1907–1909) is cited from there.

—— *Confidence* (1879)

—— *The Bostonians* (1886)

—— *In the Cage* (1898)

—— *The American Scene* (1907)

—— *Italian Hours* (1909)

—— *The Middle Years* (1917); autobiographical fragment

Janowitz, H. D., *"Marius the Epicurean" in T. S. Eliot's Poetry* in *Journal of Modern Literature* Spring 1989

Jayne, Sears, *Mr. Eliot's Agon* in *Philological Quarterly* Oct 1955, repr. in *Roby ed.*

Joachim, Harold, *The Nature of Truth* (1909); TSE's annotated copy, Magdalene.

John of the Cross, St., *The Complete Works* tr. and ed. E. Allison Peers (3 vols., 1934–35); TSE's set, Magdalene. Asked by the Bishop of Willesden to suggest a book he would like, TSE had proposed Vol. 1 of this, 15 June 1934: "Mrs. Stuart Moore tells me that it is much better than the previous Lewis translation." The first volume is inscribed to TSE as "A Helper of the Diocese and a True Friend of New London in Middlesex with gratitude from G. Vernon Willesden, Sadlers Wells June 1934".

—— *The Mystical Doctrine of St. John of the Cross* tr. David Lewis, rev. Dom Benedict Zimmerman, abridged R. H. J. Steuart (1934)

Johnson, Loretta, *A Temporary Marriage of Two Minds: T. S. and Vivien Eliot* in *Twentieth-Century Literature* Spring 1988

—— *T. S. Eliot's Bawdy Verse: Lulu, Bolo and More Ties* in *Journal of Modern Literature* Fall 2003

Johnson, Samuel, *Lives of the Most Eminent English Poets* (Chandos Classics selection, [1872]); TSE's copy, Valerie Eliot collection.

Jones, Florence, *T. S. Eliot among the Prophets* in *American Literature* Nov 1966

Jones, Genesius, *Approach to the Purpose: A Study of the Poetry of T. S. Eliot* (1964, 2nd ed. 1967). In the front of his copy TSE wrote: "A good deal of his interpretation seems to me to be fantastic over-interpretation. I wish he could just enjoy it as poetry! — But he does *like* it! Overrates my work" (Valerie Eliot collection).

Jonson, Ben, *The Works* ed. C. H. Herford, Percy Simpson and Evelyn Simpson (11 vols., 1925–52)

Joost, Nicholas, *Scofield Thayer and "The Dial": An Illustrated History* (1964)

Juliana of Norwich, *XVI Revelations of Divine Love* ed. R. F. S. Cressy (1670, repr. 1920)

Julius, Anthony, *T. S. Eliot, Anti-Semitism and Literary Form* (1995; 2nd ed. 2003)

Kant, Immanuel, *The Philosophy of Kant*, sel. and tr. John Watson (1908); TSE's copy, dated 3 Mar 1913, Houghton.

Kearns, Cleo McNelly, *T. S. Eliot and the Indic Tradition* (1987)

Kenner, Hugh, *The Invisible Poet: T. S. Eliot* (US 1959, UK 1960). TSE in 1958: "His chapter on F. H. Bradley contains the most valuable new information for the reader. I especially like the title of Kenner's book. I like the image; it's very appropriate" (*Levy* 105).

—— *The Pound Era: The Age of Ezra Pound, T. S. Eliot, James Joyce and Wyndham Lewis* (1972)

Keynes, John Maynard, *The Economic Consequences of the Peace* (1919)

Knight, G. Wilson, *My Romantic Tendencies* in *Studies in Romanticism* Winter 1982

Knowles, Sebastian D. G., *A Purgatorial Flame: Seven British Writers in the Second World War* (1990)

Kojecky, Roger, *T. S. Eliot's Social Criticism* (1971)

Laforgue, Jules, *Oeuvres Complètes* (4th ed., 2 vols., 1909); TSE's copy, dated 1909, Magdalene.

—— *Six Moral Tales* tr. Frances Newman (1928). This translation is used for prose, except where noted.

—— *Selected Poems with a Plain Prose Translation* tr. Graham Dunstan Martin (1998). This translation is used for poems, except where noted.

Lanman, Charles Rockwell, *A Sanskrit Reader* (1884); TSE's copy (5th imp., 1906), Magdalene.

Larisch, Marie, *My Past* (1913)

Latimer, Hugh, *Sermons* ed. Canon Beeching (1906); TSE mentioned his copy in a letter to his secretary in 1926.

Laverty, Maura, *Interview with Mr. T. S. Eliot*, unpublished ts of a broadcast on Radio Athlone, Republic of Ireland, 25 Jan 1936, with some annotation by TSE (Houghton).

Lawrence, D. H., *Letters* ed. Aldous Huxley (1932); TSE's annotated copy, dated "T. S. Eliot, Eliot House, January 1933", Houghton.

Le Brun, Philip, *T. S. Eliot and Henri Bergson* in *RES* May 1967 and Aug 1967

Leavis, F. R., *New Bearings in English Poetry* (1932)

Lee, Sidney, *A Life of William Shakespeare* (1907, new ed. 1909); TSE's copy offered for sale in 2011.

Lehmann, Irmgard, *Begegnung mit T. S. Eliot* in *Neuphilologische Zeitschrift* May 1949

Lemprière, John, *A Classical Dictionary* (1788; rev. F. A. Wright, 1948)

Lennard, John, *But I Digress* (1991)

Levy, William Turner, and Victor Scherle, *Affectionately, T. S. Eliot: The Story of a Friendship 1947–1965* (1968)

—— *Letter to the Editor: A Memoir of T. S. Eliot* in *New York Times Book Review* 31 Jan 1965

Lewis, Wyndham, *The Letters* ed. W. K. Rose (1963)

Leyris, Pierre (tr.), *Poèmes 1910–1930* by T. S. Eliot, bilingual edition with notes by John Hayward (1947)

Liddell, H. G. and Robert Scott, *A Greek–English Lexicon* (1843)

Lidderdale, Jane and Mary Nicholson (eds.), *Dear Miss Weaver: Harriet Shaw Weaver, 1876–1971* (1970)

Litz, A. Walton (ed.), *Eliot in his Time: Essays on the occasion of the fiftieth anniversary of "The Waste Land"* (1973)

Lockerd, Benjamin, *Aethereal Rumours: T. S. Eliot's Physics and Poetics* (1998)

Londraville, Richard and Janis, *Dear Yeats, Dear Pound, Dear Ford: Jeanne Robert Foster and Her Circle of Friends* (2001)

Loucks, James F., *A Second Browning Allusion in Eliot's "Burbank" Poem* in *N&Q* Jan 1976 (a)

—— *T. S. Eliot's "A Cooking Egg": An echo from Thomas Hood* in *N&Q* July 1976 (b)

—— *Pater and Carlyle in Eliot's "Little Gidding"?* in *N&Q* Dec 1993

Lowell, Robert, see Bishop, Elizabeth

McCue, Jim, *Editing Eliot* in *EinC* Jan 2006

—— *Dilemmas and Decisions in Editing Eliot* in *Literary Imagination* Mar 2012

—— *T. S. Eliot and the Roots that Clutch* in *New Criterion* Mar 2013 (a)

—— *Aldous Huxley and the Sweeney Family* in *N&Q* June 2013 (b)

—— *T. S. Eliot, Edgar Lee Masters and Glorious France* in *EinC* Jan 2014 (a)

—— *Appreciating the Rupee* in *N&Q* Mar 2014 (b)

—— *Did Eliot mis-ascribe the "water-dripping song" in "The Waste Land"?* in *N&Q* Mar 2014 (c)

—— *Roy Campbell and "The Dry Salvages"* in *N&Q* Mar 2014 (d)

—— [forthcoming, 2016, in *RES*]

McCue, Jim and Oliver Soden, *An Unknown Bird in the Early Faber Nest* in *N&Q* Mar 2014

McGreevy, Thomas, *Thomas Stearns Eliot: A Study* (1931). TSE to McGreevy, [14 Feb] 1931: "I feel impelled to say that you have produced I think an excellent piece of criticism. It is only disfigured (1) by your remarks about the Church of England, a subject of which you know nothing (2) a gross libel on page 20 of which I hope that as a gentleman you will make public retractation. I am not an Irishman, and can prove it." (See also headnote to *The Waste Land*, 9. AFTER PUBLICATION.)

McRae, Shannon, *"Glowed into Words": Vivien Eliot, Philomela, and the Poet's Tortured Corpse* in *Twentieth-Century Literature* Summer 2003

Madden, Benjamin, *Arnold Bennett and the Making of "Sweeney Agonistes"* in *N&Q* Mar 2011

Mahaffey, Vicki, *"The Death of Saint Narcissus" and "Ode": Two Suppressed Poems by T. S. Eliot* in *American Literature* Jan 1979

Major, John M., *Eliot's "Gerontion" and "As You Like It"* in *MLN* Jan 1959

Malamud, Randy, *T. S. Eliot's Drama: A Research and Production Sourcebook* (1992)

Mallarmé, Stéphane, *Vers et Prose: Morceaux Choisis*; TSE's copy (1901), Magdalene.

——*Mallarmé* tr. Anthony Hartley (1965)

Malory, Sir Thomas, see Morris, Charles

March, Richard, and M. J. Tambimuttu (eds.), *T. S. Eliot: A Symposium* (1948)

Margolis, John D., *T. S. Eliot's Intellectual Development 1922–1939* (1972)

Maritain, Jacques, *Réflexions sur L'Intelligence* (1924)

Marshall, William, *The Text of Gerontion* in *Studies in Bibliography* 4 (1951)

Marston, John, *The Works* ed. A. H. Bullen (3 vols., 1887)

Martin, Graham (ed.), *Eliot in Perspective* (1970)

Marvell, Andrew, *Poems* ed. G. A. Aitkin (Muses' Library [1904]); TSE's copy, Valerie Eliot collection.

Marx, William, *Paris* in *Harding ed.*

Massis, Henri, *Jugements* (1923–24); TSE's copy of the 15th imp., presentation copy from the author, Magdalene.

Materer, Timothy, *T. S. Eliot and his Biographical Critics* in *EinC* Jan 2012

Matthews, Stephen, *T. S. Eliot and Early Modern Literature* (2013)

Matthews, T. S., *Notes Towards the Definition of T. S. Eliot* (1974)

Matthiessen, F. O., *The Achievement of T. S. Eliot* (1935, 3rd ed. 1959). TSE to Charles Williams, 22 July 1944: "Matthiessen's book was, I think, a very good book of its date (1933): and he had the inestimable advantage, while working on it, of having me in daily view, at breakfast, lunch and dinner, and sometimes for bootleg evenings." TSE stayed with Matthiessen, of Eliot House, Harvard, in autumn 1932. To Matthiessen, 17 Sept 1934: "if meanwhile you have any questions to ask me, I will do my best to answer them." To I. A. Richards, 24 Sept 1935: "Matthiessen need hardly be mentioned. He is such a nice fellow, and his book was so depressing to me: I suppose he wrote it for his pupils: but should he have pupils?" To Itrat Hussain, 10 Feb 1939: "I think that on the whole Professor Mathiessen's book gives the fullest and most satisfactory analysis of my work, though I do not wish to derogate from the merit of other critics. I spent a year at Harvard five years ago, and was constantly in the company of Professor Mathiessen, and showed him a number of lectures which have since been destroyed, and also had a number of conversations with him about my work."

Mattingly, Ignatius G., *Mr. Eliot Visits the Elizabethan Club* in *Yale University Library Gazette* Oct 1987

Mayer, John T., *T. S. Eliot's Silent Voices* (1989)

Melchiori, Giorgio, *Echoes in "The Waste Land"* in *English Studies* Feb 1951

Menasce, Jean de, *La Terre mise à nu* (translation of *The Waste Land*) in *L'Esprit*, May 1926

Mermaid Plays, *The Best Plays of the Old Dramatists.* For the 21 titles, and for online facsimiles, see Wikipedia "Mermaid Series".

Merrill, Stuart, *Pastels in Prose* (1890); TSE's copy, Houghton.

Middleton Murry, John, *Son of Woman: The Story of D. H. Lawrence* (1931)

Miller, James E., *T. S. Eliot's Personal Waste Land* (1977)

Milton, John, *Paradise Regained, Samson Agonistes, & Other Poems* (1903); TSE's copy, Houghton.

Mirrlees, Hope, *Paris* (Hogarth Press, 1919)

Monteith, Charles, *Eliot in the Office* in *Grand Street* Spring 1990

Moody, A. David, *Thomas Stearns Eliot: Poet* (1979, rev. 1994)

—— (ed.), *The Waste Land in Different Voices* (1974)

—— (ed.), *The Cambridge Companion to T. S. Eliot* (1994)

—— *Ezra Pound: Poet* Vol. I, *The Young Genius* (2007); Vol. II, *The Epic Years* (2014)

Mordell, Albert, *T. S. Eliot's Deficiencies as a Social Critic / T. S. Eliot—Special Pleader as a Book Reviewer and Literary Critic* (1951)

More, Paul Elmer, *The Great Refusal: Letters of a Dreamer in Gotham* (1894)

Morley, Frank, *A Few Recollections of Eliot* in *Tate ed.*

—— *Literary Britain* (1980)

Morrell, Ottoline, *Ottoline: The Early Memoirs of Lady Ottoline Morrell* ed. Robert Gathorne-Hardy (1963)

—— *Ottoline at Garsington: Memoirs of Lady Ottoline Morrell 1915–1918* ed. Robert Gathorne-Hardy (1974)

Morris, Charles, *King Arthur and the Knights of the Round Table: A Modernized Version of the "Morte Darthur"* (1891); TSE's copy (one vol., 1896), autographed "T. S. Eliot, First Year Class. Smith Academy", Houghton.

Morris, George L. K., *Marie, Marie, Hold on Tight* in *Partisan Review* Mar–Apr 1954

Murray, Paul, *The Unidentified Ghost: Arthur Hugh Clough and T. S. Eliot's "Four Quartets"* in *Studies: An Irish Quarterly Review* Spring 1981

Musgrove, Sydney, *T. S. Eliot and Walt Whitman* (Wellington, 1952)

Newton-De Molina, David (ed.), *The Literary Criticism of T. S. Eliot* (1977)

Nietzsche, Friedrich Wilhelm, *Beyond Good and Evil* tr. Helen Zimmern (1907)

—— *The Birth of Tragedy* tr. Wm. A. Haussmann (1909)

O'Keeffe, Paul, *Some Sort of Genius: A Life of Wyndham Lewis* (2000)

Olney, James (ed.), *T. S. Eliot: Essays from the Southern Review* (1988)

Oser, Lee, *T. S. Eliot and American Poetry* (1998)

The Oxford Book of English Verse ed. A. T. Quiller-Couch (1900)

The Oxford Companion to Classical Literature ed. Paul Harvey, rev. M. C. Howatson (1989)

The Oxford Companion to Music, ed. Percy A. Scholes (9th ed., 1955)

The Oxford Companion to Ships and the Sea ed. Peter Kemp (1976, rev. 1979)

The Oxford Companion to the Year ed. Bonnie Blackburn and Leofranc Holford-Strevens (1999)

The Oxford Dictionary of English Proverbs (1935; 3rd ed., rev. F. P. Wilson, 1970)

The Oxford Dictionary of Nursery Rhymes ed. Iona and Peter Opie (1951)

The Oxford English Dictionary ed. James Murray et al. (1884–present). See below, "Where Every Word is at Home".

The Oxford Nursery Rhyme Book ed. Iona and Peter Opie (1955)

Partridge, Eric, *A Dictionary of Slang and Unconventional English* (1937, 6th ed. 1967). TSE: "Mr. Eric Partridge is pompous, tedious, learned and fond of irrelevant footnotes and references into which no one will ever enquire; he is a young man who will probably succeed in life and I feel that he ought to be encouraged", *Robert Eyres Landor: Selections* ed. Eric Partridge, reader's report (1927).

Pascal, Blaise, *Pascal's Pensées* tr. W. F. Trotter, with Introduction by TSE (1931)

Pater, Walter H., *Studies in the History of the Renaissance* (1873); TSE's copy, with his notes on the text, King's. TSE: "The notes in pencil on the margin of the *Conclusion* were made by me, comparing the text with the later edition. T. S. Eliot" and "This volume was bought for me by my mother at a sale of surplus books of the Mercantile Library, St. Louis U.S.A. for 10 cents. T. S. Eliot". (Pater changed the title of the book in 1877 to *The Renaissance: Studies in Art and Poetry.*)

—— *Marius the Epicurean* (1885)

Patmore, Derek (ed.), *My Friends When Young: The Memoirs of Brigit Patmore* (1968)

Paul the Apostle, Epistle of to the Romans. Authorized Version and Revised Version. Ed. Alfred E. Garvie (Century Bible, 1901). TSE's copy, autographed "T. S. Eliot | Cambridge" and with annotation to the Introduction, Houghton.

Peake, Charles, *"Sweeney Erect" and the Emersonian Hero* in *Neophilologus* Jan 1960, repr. in *Roby ed.*

Pearce, T. S., *T. S. Eliot* (1967)

Perry, Edward Delavan, *A Sanskrit Primer* [1901]; TSE's copy, with a Sanskrit exercise by TSE, Magdalene.

Peter, John, *A New Interpretation of "The Waste Land"* in *EinC* July 1952; repr., with a Postscript, *EinC* Apr 1969.

Petronius, *Saturae et Liber Priapeorum* ed. F. Bücheler (1904); TSE's annotated copy of the *Satyricon*, King's.

Philippe, Charles-Louis, *Bubu de Montparnasse* (1901). TSE wrote a Preface to Laurence Vail's English translation (Paris, 1932).

—— *Marie Donadieu* (1904)

—— *La Mère et l'Enfant* [1911]; TSE's copy, dated "Paris September 1911", Houghton.

Plotinus, *Enneades* ed. Richard Volkmann (2 vols., 1883); TSE's annotated copy, King's.

Poe, Edgar Allan, *The Poems of Edgar Allan Poe, with an essay on his poetry by Andrew Lang* (2nd ed., 1906); TSE's copy, Houghton.

Poètes d'aujourd'hui ed. Adolphe van Bever et Paul Léautaud (1900; 2nd ed., 2 vols., 1908)

Pope, Alexander, *The Poetical Works* (A. L. Burt, publisher, NY); TSE's inscribed copy, listed among books of his at Milton Academy in the 1930s.

Pope, John C., *Prufrock and Raskolnikov* in *American Literature* Nov 1945

Pound, Ezra, *The Spirit of Romance* [1910]; TSE's copy, King's.

——*Selected Poems* ed. T. S. Eliot (1928)

——*A Draft of XXX Cantos* [1933]; TSE's copy of the US ed., dated "Eliot House, March 1933", Houghton.

——*The Letters of Ezra Pound*, ed. D. D. Paige (1951)

——*Literary Essays* ed. T. S. Eliot (1954)

——Interview in *The Paris Review* Summer–Fall 1962

——*EP to LU: Nine Letters written to Louis Untermeyer* ed. J. A. Robbins (1963)

——*Pound/Joyce: The Letters of Ezra Pound to James Joyce with Pound's Essays on Joyce* ed. Forrest Reid (1968)

——*Pound/Lewis: The Letters of Ezra Pound and Wyndham Lewis* ed. Timothy Materer (1985)

——*Pound/The Little Review: The Letters of Ezra Pound to Margaret Anderson* ed. Thomas L. Scott and Melvin Friedman with the assistance of Jackson R. Bryer (1989)

——*Selected Letters to John Quinn, 1915–1924* ed. Timothy Materer (1991)

——*The Letters of Ezra Pound to Alice Corbin Henderson* ed. Ira B. Nadel (1993)

——*Pound, Thayer, Watson, & The Dial: A Story in Letters* ed. Walter Sutton (1994)

——*Ezra Pound to His Parents: Letters 1895–1929* ed. Mary de Rachewiltz, A. David Moody and Joanna Moody (2010)

Powel, Harford, *T. S. Eliot: A Schoolboy Poet* in *The Independent School Bulletin* Jan 1957

Praz, Mario, *T. S. Eliot and Dante* in *Southern Review* Winter 1937, collected in *The Flaming Heart* (1958) and *Unger ed.*

Preston, Priscilla, *A Note on T. S. Eliot and Sherlock Holmes* in *MLR* July 1959

Preston, Raymond, *"Four Quartets" Rehearsed* (1946). The preface thanks TSE for reading a draft and "adding some interesting notes".

Propertius, *Propertius* tr. J. S. Phillimore (1906); TSE's copy, Houghton.

Proust, Marcel, *À la recherche du temps perdu* (1913–27, 8 vols.); tr. C. K. Scott Moncrieff (11 vols., 1922–30) and Stephen Hudson (Vol. 12, 1931). Uniform ed. 1941.

Purohit Swami, Shri, *The Geeta: The Gospel of the Lord Shri Krishna*, tr. Shri Purohit Swami, preface by Sayaji Rao Gaekwar (Faber, 1935)

——and W. B. Yeats, *The Ten Principal Upanishads* (Faber, 1937)

Pusey, E. B., *Private Prayers* ed. H. P. Liddon (1883)

Raffel, Burton, *T. S. Eliot* (1982)

Rainey, Lawrence, *Revisiting The Waste Land* (2005, 2nd ed. 2006)

——(ed.), *The Annotated Waste Land* (2005)

Rajan, B. (ed.), *T.S. Eliot: A Study of his Writings by Several Hands* (1947)

Rawson, C. J., *The Nightmares of Strephon: Nymphs of the City in the Poems of Swift, Baudelaire, Eliot* in *English Literature in the Age of Disguise* ed. Maximillian E. Novak (1977)

Read, Herbert, *T. S. E.—A Memoir* (1966), collected in *Tate ed.*

Rees, Thomas R., *The Technique of T. S. Eliot* (1974)

Reid, B. L., *The Man from New York: John Quinn and His Friends* (1968)

Richards, I. A., *Principles of Literary Criticism* (1925); TSE's annotated copy, Magdalene.

——*Selected Letters* ed. John Constable, with an Introduction by Richard Luckett (1990)

Ricks, Christopher, *T. S. Eliot and Prejudice* (1988)

——*A Note on "Little Gidding"* in *EinC* Jan 1975

——*The Force of Poetry* (1984)

——*To Keep the Ball Rolling* in *TLS* 6 June 1992

——*Gautier and Eliot's Openings* in *TLS* 11 June 1993

——*Eliot's Sources and "a cumulative plausibility"* (*Austin Dobson, John Ford, Kipling, Norman Cameron*) in *ANQ* Summer 1998

——*A Note on "The Hollow Men" and Stevenson's "The Ebb-Tide"* in *EinC* Jan 2001

——*Decisions and Revisions in T. S. Eliot* (2003)

——*True Friendship: Geoffrey Hill, Anthony Hecht and Robert Lowell under the Sign of Eliot and Pound* (2010)

Ridler, Anne, *Working for T. S. Eliot* (2000): expanded from *Poetry Review*, Mar 1983

——Interview with Kieron Winn, Oxford, 9 Feb 2000 (cassette recording)

Rigolot, Carol (ed.), *Lettres atlantiques: Saint-John Perse, T. S. Eliot, Allen Tate 1926–1970* (2006)

Rimbaud, Arthur, *Rimbaud* tr. Oliver Bernard (1962)

Rivers, W. H. R. (ed.), *Essays on the Depopulation of Melanesia* (1922)

Roberts, Michael (ed.), *The Faber Book of Modern Verse* (1935). Of the selection of *Sweeney Among the Nightingales*, *The Waste Land*, *Journey of the Magi*, *Ash-Wednesday* I & II, *Marina*, *Triumphal March* and *Difficulties of a Statesman*, TSE wrote to Roberts, 17 May 1935: "you have chosen poems all of which are favourites of mine".

Roby, Kinley E. (ed.), *Critical Essays on T. S. Eliot: The Sweeney Motif* (1985)

Roper, Derek, *T. S. Eliot's "La Figlia Che Piange": A Picture without a Frame* in *EinC* July 2002

——*Eliot's "Portrait of a Lady" Restored* in *EinC* Jan 2007

Rossetti, Dante Gabriel, *The Early Italian Poets* (1861). (The revised and rearranged *Dante and His Circle*, 1874, has different pagination.)

Royce, Josiah; see Costello, Harry T.

Russell, Bertrand, *The Autobiography of Bertrand Russell* (3 vols., 1967–69)

——and A. N. Whitehead, *Principia Mathematica* (1910); TSE's copy, Vol. 1 only, Valerie Eliot collection.

Sackton, Alexander, *The T. S. Eliot Collection of The University of Texas at Austin* (1975)

Scarfe, Francis, *Eliot and Nineteenth-century French Poetry* in *Martin ed.*

Schmidt, A. V. C., *Eliot, Swinburne and Dante: A Note on "The Waste Land" lines 215–248* in *N&Q* Jan 1976; collected with Schmidt's subsequent notes in *Passion and Precision* (2015).

——*T. S. Eliot and the English Language* in *English Studies in Africa* June 1982 (a)

——*T. S. Eliot and William Cowper: A New "Waste Land" Source* in *N&Q* Aug 1982 (b)

——*Whirling World, Dancing Words: Further Echoes of Sir John Davies in T. S. Eliot* in *N&Q* June 2007

Schneider, Elisabeth, *T. S. Eliot: The Pattern in the Carpet* (1975)

Schofield, William Henry, *English Literature from the Norman Conquest to Chaucer* (1906); TSE's copy, Magdalene.

Schuchard, Ronald, *Eliot's Dark Angel* (1999); incorporating *RES* May & Aug 1974, on TSE's Extension lectures, 1917–18.

Sencourt, Robert, *T. S. Eliot: A Memoir*, ed. Donald Adamson (1971). Robert Sencourt was the nom de plume of Robert Gordon George.

Seneca, *Tragedies* tr. Frank Justus Miller (2 vols., Loeb, 1917); TSE's copy, Magdalene.

Servotte, Herman, and Ethel Grene, *Annotations to T. S. Eliot's "Four Quartets"* (2010)

Sewell, Elizabeth, *Lewis Carroll and T. S. Eliot as Nonsense Poets* in *Braybrooke ed.*

Seymour-Jones, Carole, *Painted Shadow: A Life of Vivienne Eliot* (2001)

Shackleton, Sir Ernest, *South: The Story of Shackleton's Last Expedition 1914–1917* (1919)

Shakespeare, William, The Temple Shakespeare (38 vols., 1901–29); TSE's copies, Magdalene.

The Shakespeare Apocrypha ed. C. F. Tucker Brooke (1908)

Shelley, Percy Bysshe, *The Poetical Works* ed. Edward Dowden (A. L. Burt, NY); TSE's inscribed copy, listed among books of his at Milton Academy in the 1930s.

Sidnell, M. J., *Dances of Death: The Group Theatre of London in the Thirties* (1984)

Sloane, Patricia, *T. S. Eliot's Bleistein Poems: Uses of Literary Allusion in "Burbank with a Baedeker: Bleistein with a Cigar" and "Dirge"* (2000)

Smart, John D., *Tarantula's Web: John Hayward, T. S. Eliot and Their Circle* (2013)

Smidt, Kristian, *Poetry and Belief in the Work of T. S. Eliot* (1961). TSE to Herbert Read, 3 Nov 1961: "obviously he has taken a world of trouble and read practically every scrap of my writing, that he could get hold of".

—— *The Importance of Recognition: Six Chapters on T. S. Eliot* (Tromsø, 1973)

Smith, Carol H., *T. S. Eliot's Dramatic Theory and Practice* (1963)

——*Sweeney in the Jazz Age* (1985) in *Roby ed.*

Smith, Grover, *T. S. Eliot's Poetry and Plays: A Study in Sources and Meaning* (1956)

—— *T. S. Eliot's Lady of the Rocks* in *N&Q* 19 Mar 1949

—— *Tourneur and "Little Gidding"; Corbière and "East Coker"* in *MLN* June 1950

—— *The Making of "The Waste Land"* in *Mosaic* Fall 1972; a revision was incorporated into the 2nd ed of *T. S. Eliot's Poetry and Plays* (1975)

—— *The Waste Land* (1983)

—— *T. S. Eliot and the Use of Memory* (1996)

—— *T. S. Eliot and the Fragmented Selves: From "Suppressed Complex" to "Sweeney Agonistes"* in *Philological Quarterly* Fall 1998

Smith, James, *A Note on the Text of "The Waste Land"* in *Transactions of the Cambridge Bibliographical Society* 6 (1973)

Smith Academy yearbooks 1898–99 to 1904–05 (bound volume, Washington U.)

Soldo, John J., *The Tempering of T. S. Eliot* (1983)

Southam, B. C., *A Student's Guide to the Selected Poems of T. S. Eliot* (1968, 6th ed. 1994)

Spender, Stephen, *Eliot* (1975)

Spingarn, J. E., *A History of Literary Criticism in the Renaissance* (2nd ed., 1908); TSE's annotated copy, Houghton.

Spinoza, Benedicti, *Opera*, ed. J. van Vloten and J. P. N. Land (2 vols., 1895); TSE's copy of Vol. 1 only, unopened (uncut), King's.

Spoo, Robert, *Without Copyrights: Piracy, Publishing, and the Public Domain* (2013)

Spurr, Barry, *Anglo-Catholic in Religion: T. S. Eliot and Christianity* (2010)

Sri, P. S., *Upanishadic Perceptions in T. S. Eliot's Poetry and Drama* in *Rocky Mountain Review* Fall 2008

Stayer, Jayme, *T. S. Eliot as a Schoolboy* in *Twentieth-Century Literature* Winter 2013

Stead, C. K., *Pound, Yeats, Eliot and the Modernist Movement* (1986)

Stead, William Force, *Some Personal Impressions of T. S. Eliot* in *Trinity College* Winter 1965. (The ts, headed "Some Personal Recollections of T. S. Eliot", is annotated by TSE; Donald Adamson collection.)

Stevenson, E. M., *T. S. Eliot and the Lay Reader* (1944); TSE, in a copy of the 2nd ed., 1946: "Inscribed for Ethel Stephenson in gratitude for this thoughtful and thorough analysis."

Stillman, Anne, *Sweeney Among the Marionettes* in *EinC* Apr 2009

Stormon, E. J., *Virgil and the Modern Poet* in *Meanjin* Autumn 1947

Sullivan, J. W. N., *Beethoven: His Spiritual Development* (1927, 1936)

Svarny, Erik, *The Men of 1914: T. S. Eliot and Early Modernism* (1988)

Sweeney, James Johnson, *"East Coker": A Reading* in *Southern Review* Spring 1941; repr. in *Unger ed.* TSE to Theodore Spencer, 21 July 1941: "an admirable piece of detective research".

Symons, Arthur, *The Symbolist Movement in Literature* (1899, 2nd ed. rev. 1908); TSE's lightly annotated copy, Houghton

—— *Knave of Hearts. 1894–1908* (1913)

Tailhade, Laurent, *Poèmes aristophanesques* (1904, new ed. 1915); TSE's copy, McCue collection.

Tambimuttu, M. J. (ed.), *Poetry in Wartime* (1942)

Tate, Allen (ed.), *T. S. Eliot: The Man and His Work* (1966)

Taupin, René, *L'influence du symbolisme français sur la poésie américaine, 1910–1920* (1929). TSE sent a copy to F. S. Flint (Berg; see Patricia Clements, *N&Q* June 1980).

Tennyson, Alfred, *The Poems 1830–1863* [introduction by Ernest Rhys]; TSE's copy, [1906], Houghton.

—— *The Poems of Tennyson* ed. Christopher Ricks (1969, 2nd ed. 1987)

Thormählen, Marianne, *The Waste Land: A Fragmentary Wholeness* (1978)

Tilby, Michael, *T. S. Eliot's Unpublished Marginalia on Gide's Translation of "Little Gidding"* in *Revue de littérature comparée* Apr–June 1986

Tippett, Michael, *Those Twentieth Century Blues* (1991)

Tomlin, E. W. F., *T. S. Eliot: A Friendship* (1988)

Traversi, Derek, *T. S. Eliot: The Longer Poems* (1976)

Underhill, Evelyn, *Mysticism: A Study in the Nature and Development of Man's Spiritual Consciousness* (1911); TSE's copy (12th ed., 1930), with corner of 237 turned down, Magdalene.

Unger, Leonard, *The Man in the Name* (1956)

—— *T. S. Eliot* (1961)

—— (ed.), *T. S. Eliot: A Selected Critique* (1948)

Upanishads, The Twenty-Eight. Vasudev Laxman Shastri Phansikar (Bombay, 1906); TSE's copy (given to him by C. R. Lanman, 6 May 1912), King's.

—— see also Deussen, Paul, and Purohit Swami, Shri

Vickery, John B., *The Literary Impact of "The Golden Bough"* (1973)

Virgil, *Ecologues, Georgics, Aeneid, Minor Poems*, tr. H. Rushton Fairclough (Loeb, 1916)

Warren, Henry Clarke, *Buddhism in Translations* (1896)

Watkins, Floyd C., *T. S. Eliot's Painter of the Umbrian School* in *American Literature* Mar 1964, repr. in *Roby ed.*

Watson, George, *Quest for a Frenchman* in *Sewanee Review* Summer 1976

Webster, John, *Complete Works* ed. F. L. Lucas (4 vols., 1927); TSE's copy, Magdalene.

Webster, Noah, *An American Dictionary of the English Language* (1828)

Weston, Jessie L., *From Ritual to Romance* (1920); TSE's copy, Houghton.

Whistler, Theresa, *The Life of Walter de la Mare* (1993)

Whitman, Walt, *The Complete Poems* ed. Francis Murphy (1975, new ed. 2004)

Whitworth, John (ed.), *The Faber Book of Blue Verse* (1990)

Whitworth, Michael, *"Sweet Thames" and The Waste Land's Allusions* in *EinC* Jan 1998

Williams, Ellen, *Harriet Monroe and the Poetry Renaissance: The First Ten Years of "Poetry", 1912–22* (1977)

Williamson, George, *A Reader's Guide to T. S. Eliot: A Poem-by-Poem Analysis* (1953, 2nd ed. 1967). TSE, 14 May 1953: "I must confess that the subject of the book is one in which I can hardly say that I am deeply interested since I never read the works of T. S. Eliot if I can help it. The labours of proof reading usually terminate my interest in my own writings. However, I shall read this book not because of the subject, but because you are the author."

Williamson, Hugh Ross, *The Poetry of T. S. Eliot* (1932). TSE, 3 May 1932: "You are a rash man to want to do a book on me. For one thing my experience is that books about living men of letters · · · sell very badly. However, if you persist in the attempt I shall be very glad to give a hand."

Willis, Kirk, *"This Place is Hell": Bertrand Russell at Harvard, 1914* in *New England Quarterly* Mar 1989

Wilson, Edmund, *Axel's Castle* (1936), reprinting, with revisions, *T. S. Eliot* from *New Republic* 13 Nov 1929

Wimsatt, W. K., *Prufrock and "Maud": From Plot to Symbol* in *Yale French Studies* 9 (1952), repr. in *Hateful Contraries* (1965)

Wood, Rev. J. G. *The Illustrated Natural History* (2 vols., 1859–63, often repr.)

—— *The Boy's Own Book of Natural History* [1893]

Woodward, Daniel H., *Notes on the Publishing History and Text of "The Waste Land"* in *Papers of the Bibliographical Society of America* 58 (1964); repr. in *Cox & Hinchcliffe eds.*

Woolf, Virginia, *The Letters of Virginia Woolf* ed. Nigel Nicolson and Joanne Trautmann (6 vols., 1975–80)

—— *The Diary of Virginia Woolf* ed. Anne Olivier Bell and Andrew McNeillie (5 vols., 1977–84)

Worthen, John, *T. S. Eliot: A Short Biography* (2009)

Worthington, Jane, *The Epigraphs to the Poetry of T. S. Eliot* in *American Literature* Mar 1949; repr. in *Roby ed.*

Wright, Joseph (ed.), *The English Dialect Dictionary* (6 vols., 1898–1905)

"Where Every Word is at Home"

"The evidence that Shakespeare read with the most prodigious memory for words that has ever existed is almost indisputable, and is consonant with everything that we do know of Shakespeare". *Shakespeare and Montaigne* (1925)

Transit of Venus: Poems by Harry Crosby, Preface (1931): "Crosby was right, very right, in looking for a set of symbols which should relate each of his poems to the others, to himself, rather than using in each poem symbols which should merely relate it to other poems by other people · · · To find the word and give it the utmost meaning, in its place; to mean as many things as possible, to make it both exact and comprehensive, and really to *unite* the disparate and remote, to give them a fusion and a pattern with the word, surely this is the mastery at which the poet aims; and the poet is distinguished by making the word do more *work* than it does for other writers. Of course one can 'go too far' and except in directions in which we can go too far there is no interest in going at all; and only those who will risk going too far can possibly find out just how far one can go."

Turnbull Lecture II (1933): "the word is not merely the sound with a meaning; the word becomes interesting for its meaning elsewhere as well as for its meaning in the context; for its own meaning as well as what the writer means to mean by it". Also: "it is often a useful exercise to take a figure of speech to pieces: if it can be put together again it is all right", *The Varieties of Metaphysical Poetry* 272–73, 269.

To Derek Phit Clifford, 16 Mar 1934: "I do feel that you must get a much greater respect for the individual souls, so to speak, of the various words in the English language. There are a good many words in the language. I am not sure that there are not too many. I hope that you have access to, and occasionally browse in a book which is most valuable for any one who wants to write poetry, I mean the complete Oxford English Dictionary. The numbers of meanings which one word may have, as given in that dictionary, should help to impress on anyone the great care and respect with which words should be used. Also it is a good thing sometimes to examine microscopically the way in which Shakespeare uses words. You will find again and again that this use of a word will be perfectly proper according to previous usage, but that it will bring in a further meaning not previously used, and that often a word will have also a meaning in a particular context, which while true to the general meaning of the word will exist in that place alone. I think that this sort of consideration helps to throw light on the extraordinary vigour of Shakespeare's language." 6 Apr 1934: "one should continue to respect the Oxford Dictionary because one is not entitled to use a word in a new way until one is fully aware of all the ways in which it has been used previously. ¶ I think that just as the ear takes precedence over the eye and reason in poetry so the [*three or four word lacuna in the typed letter*]. This, however, does not absolve one from the duty of using exactly the right word."

The Writer as Artist (1940): "The dictionary is the most important, the most inexhaustible book to a writer. Incidentally, I find it the best reading in the world when I am recovering from influenza, or any other temporary illness, except that one needs a bookrest for it across the bed. You want a big dictionary, because definitions are not enough by themselves: you want the quotations showing how a word has been used ever since it was first used. Of course, even the best dictionary can tell you only half the story; it can only trace the history of a word from author to author—it can never tell you of the contribution made by all the anonymous people who may have used that word in talking, and helped to change or amplify its meaning. The dictionary is a work of art in which, as you say, the whole people—for thirty-odd generations—has contributed: and every time we pass a few words with a friend, we are contributing to some future edition of it. Some, of course, contribute more than others. If you look for all the uses of words—new uses for existing words, I mean, more than new words—which Shakespeare has contributed, you will find how often he discovered new meanings in old words—meanings already latent which only genius could discover. And there are some words, the history of which is almost the history of England."

To Ronald Duncan, 19 Oct 1942: "All the thought about what the poem is to say should take place some time before the poem is started. Once begun, it becomes an exercise in form. And the other thing is to keep a big dictionary and look up the words one uses."

To Robert Waller, 19 Oct 1942 (taking up the retort of Mallarmé to Degas that poems are not made with ideas but with words): "Poetry is made with words not with ideas, though it exploits ideas just as a poet exploits his private experiences and emotions. It isn't that he wants to tell the world about what he feels, but that what he feels is the only thing he has to tell it: he wants to write a poem, and so he uses whatever material he has. A poem is primarily FORM and making words come alive . . . my mind ticks rather slowly, so that I can spend a year or more, off and on, over the same poem and perhaps get it finished before I have outgrown it."

Poetical and Prosaic Use of Words (1943): "Poetry is founded upon conversation, and cannot afford to depart too far from the way people actually talk at the time when it is written. One sometimes has the word which is exactly right, both for sound and meaning, but which cannot be used because it is likely to suggest something irrelevant or absurd to some, if not to all readers. On the other hand, we must distinguish between cognate meanings of a word the awareness of which breaks it up and weakens its force, from those which reinforce it and give it more scope. This reinforcement can be obtained, not merely from the several meanings which a word may have in different contexts for the same generation of readers, but in the various layers of meaning which constitute its history. I find, in trying to write poetry still more than in writing prose, that I constantly refer to the largest English dictionary available: and still more for words, if they are key words, the current use of which I fully understand, than for words of the meaning of which I am not sure; and the reason for using the biggest dictionary, is to study the examples of the meanings of the word, the ways in which it has been used, by English authors since it was first coined. The more of these meanings that can be suggested in one's own use of the word, the better. Of course, the dictionary is not enough, for the biggest can only give a scanty selection of meanings: it cannot include all the uses of that word as a symbol, that is to say, not only the meanings it has had, but the emotions it has aroused."

American Literature and the American Language (1953), "script used" for the address at Washington U. (King's): "The champions of a radical simplification of spelling—who are zealous and vocal in England—overlook the fact that in attempting to base spelling on pronunciation, they are endeavouring to fix the pronunciation . . .

I also hold that a word is something more than the noise it makes: that is to say, it represents its own history, the story of the way in which one meaning has altered, expanded, split up into related meanings, as a consequence of the work it has been called upon to do by successive generations; and therefore it should not disown its origins or disguise its ancestry."

Robert Burchfield (then Editor of the OED): "Mrs. Valerie Eliot confirmed (in a conversation on 7 November 1988) that her husband possessed a copy of the *Shorter Oxford* but not of the OED itself", *Unlocking the English Language* (Faber 1989) 79. In the fourth of these T. S. Eliot Memorial Lectures, Burchfield pointed out that the definition of "definition" placed on the title-page of *Notes towards the Definition of Culture* is not, as it purports to be, from OED, but from the *Shorter Oxford Dictionary.* For TSE and recourse to the dictionary see note to *Gerontion* 52–53, and for evidence of his using OED in 1927, see Commentary to *Montpelier Row*, Author's Notes, 9. In one version of Gerald Kelly's portrait of 1962, a set of OED is visible behind TSE.

OED AND THE PRESENT EDITION

When this edition was begun, the current editions of OED were the print version of the second edition and a CD-ROM, which was several times updated. References to OED in the Commentary are to these manifestations, although a subsequent programme of revision has changed the Dictionary substantially for its presentation online. It continues to be updated every three months.

There have been changes to the order of senses and the definitions, and quotations have been both added and removed. The changes are sometimes substantial:

"JAZZ, *n.* orig. *U.S. slang.*" has become part of "JAZZ, *n.* and *adj.*", and

> 1. A kind of ragtime dance (see quot. 1919[2]); hence, the kind of music to which this is danced; (the usual sense) a type of music originating among American Negroes, characterized by its use of improvisation, syncopated phrasing, a regular or forceful rhythm, often in common time, and a "swinging" quality (see quots.); loosely, syncopated dance-music
>
> Connection with Amer. Eng. *jasm* "energy, enthusiasm" (see Mathews *Dict. Amer.* s.v.) cannot be demonstrated.

has become

> 3. A. A type of popular music originating (esp. in ragtime and blues) among African Americans in the southern United States, typically performed by ensembles and broadly characterized by regular forceful rhythms, syncopated phrasing, modifications to traditional instrumental tone and pitch (such as the use of blue notes), and improvisatory soloing. [OED Online, June 2014.]

The first eleven of the supporting quotations, beginning with 1909 (now thought erroneous) and 1913, have all been replaced, with the new series beginning in 1915.

Our notes on TSE's vocabulary range from those on technical or specialized words ("concitation", "hebetude") to those on common words with uncommonly precise or elaborate significance for TSE ("experience", "prevents"). Often a particular sense is quoted not because it alone is relevant, but because more current or more apparent senses might lead to its being overlooked.

Index of Identifying Titles
for Prose by T. S. Eliot

The purposes of this index are (i) to enable the use of standard Identifying Titles throughout the present edition and beyond, (ii) to enable readers to distinguish between items with similar or identical titles (or none) and (iii) to enable readers to find any prose writing by TSE referred to in the present edition, other than unpublished letters, as readily as possible.

In his 1962 Preface to *Elizabethan Dramatists*, TSE wrote: "The date of each essay is given in the Table of Contents. This is a practice I like to observe in printing any collection of essays; but it is peculiarly important where the critical judgments may depend on the conclusions of current scholarship." In order to keep dates before the reader's eye without repeating publication details on each occasion, references to TSE's prose writings use Identifying Titles consisting of the item's title in italics, followed by the year of first publication by TSE given in brackets in roman: *Ben Jonson* (1919). In the case of posthumous publication, the date of composition (or sometimes that of delivery of a lecture) is given. This index details first publication, and first appearance (if any) in a collection by TSE. Appearances in the final edition of *Selected Essays* (1951) are also listed. The titles of TSE's prose books are also indexed here.

The Identifying Title of an item published by TSE under more than one title is that of the final appearance, although the date remains that of the first publication. The use of other titles is explained in each entry. When an item appeared in two or more parts, the numerals "I ", "II " etc. are adopted as part of the titles before the date—"*Eeldrop and Appleplex* II (1917)"—distinguishing them from section numbers of books, which appear after the date: "*Dante* (1929) II". The alphabetical order of titles is as in Gallup (i.e. definite and indefinite articles are ignored; abbreviations such as "St." and "Mr." are taken as though spelt out; "H. F." precedes "Harvard", "Son of" precedes "Song"). "Separately" indicates that an item was issued independently, though it may also have appeared in a periodical, collection or anthology. Items listed as appearing within *Selected Essays* appear in all editions of that collection unless otherwise specified. Later printings of essays in *Selected Essays* or TSE's other collections are not noted. In the case of items published in TSE's lifetime, the date attached to the title is that of first appearance in print, so that, for instance, *Leadership and Letters* is dated "(1949)" although the address was delivered in 1948. This ensures that the date will be that under which each item is first listed in *Gallup*; it is used even in cases where content or title were later changed (so that although a later text may be standard, the date remains that of the first printing).

Numerous additions to *Gallup* have been made. Some published items identified since the second edition of Gallup's bibliography in 1969 are included, such as those identified by David Bradshaw in *N&Q* June 1995, by Elizabeth R. Eames and Alan M. Cohn in *Some Early Reviews by T. S. Eliot* in *Papers of the Bibliographical Society of America* July 1976 and by Arthur Sherbo in *Studies in Bibliography* 50 (1997). Also listed are many unpublished items: identifying titles have been assigned also to some other documents referred to in the Commentary, such as TSE's *Notes in French on Bergson's*

Lectures (1910–11), made at the Sorbonne, the inventory *TSE's books: Bodleian list* (1934) and Henry Eliot's record of TSE's year in America, *Excerpts from Lectures 1932–1933*. Writings by "F. M.", "Fanny Marlow" and "Feiron Morris" published in the *Criterion* 1924–25 are also included, because the drafts (in the Bodleian Library, with stray leaves at the University of Maryland) show that TSE helped his wife Vivien with the writing of most if not all of them (see *McCue 2016*). (*Mrs. Pilkington* by "Felix Morrison", in *Criterion* Oct 1924, was written by TSE's secretary, Irene Fassett, with editorial advice from Vivien Eliot, and is not included.) The use of "F. M." for more than one persona may have been a gesture towards William Sharp (1855–1905), who wrote also as "Fiona MacLeod" (*Grover Smith 1983* 102). Whether the pieces are signed with initials or one of the names, the Commentary refers always to "F. M." Drafts by "F. M." and Vivien Eliot's manuscripts are in the Bodleian except where specified.

The Identifying Titles of book reviews are the last to be used by TSE when reprinting them, or, in the case of unreprinted reviews, the given titles, though these are often editorial. In some cases an Identifying Title has been taken (following *Gallup*) from the contents list or the wrapper of a periodical. Book reviews that were untitled, jacket material by TSE and reader's reports by him (usually about books submitted to Faber for publication) give the authorial title in italics and within quotation marks. Unless otherwise stated, reader's reports are in the Faber archive. Not all are listed here individually.

Publishers are not generally noted, except when TSE's relation to them is important. Place of publication is noted only if outside Britain or America.

TSE to Bruce Richmond, 6 July 1931: "As for myself, my 'column' reviewing for you has always been deliberately impersonal; I cannot say, without going through it carefully, how much I might not have written differently had I been writing over my signature. It seems to me perfectly legitimate and proper that a man should write differently when he signs and when he writes anonymously; and I cannot help thinking that most of my reviews would have been only the worse, if I had written them with an eye to their future inclusion in a 'bibliography'. Nay, I should be deterred from ever reviewing another book for you, if I thought it was sure to be unearthed later by some industrious bibliographer. As for Leaders, for myself I don't want these included in bibliographies until I have included them in books. They can wait till then. When an author signs or initials anything, he is surely legitimate prey for the bibliographer. But not in anonymity. That is merely one writer's opinion—but I do feel strongly—and I should be surprised to find that any large number of reputable writers thought otherwise."

Contributions to the *TLS* were routinely anonymous during TSE's lifetime (signed reviews becoming the norm only in 1975), and his only signed piece for the paper was *Bruce Lyttelton Richmond* (1961), in which he praised the practice of anonymous reviewing.

Index to the Editorial Material

TSE's correspondents, the authors of quotations used illustratively, and place names are included only selectively. Other than those who were close to TSE, scholars of his work are not listed. Titles appear under their authors, or under "anonymous works" or "anthologies". When citing Volume II, the page reference (or run of references ending with a semi-colon) is prefixed by II. TSE's own prose writings are listed in the Index of Identifying Titles.

Index of Titles and First Lines